SEVEN GENERATIONS

of the descendants of

AQUILA

and

THOMAS CHASE

Compiled by

John Carroll Chase
and
George Walter Chamberlain

PICTON PRESS
CAMDEN, MAINE

"The Chase book is one of the outstanding
American genealogies in every respect"

Walter Goodwin Davis, writing in the introduction to his *The Ancestry of Annis
Spear 1775-1858 of Litchfield Maine* (Portland 1945)

Picton Press is proud to present *Seven Generations of the Descendants of
Aquila and Thomas Chase* with a new *selective additions and corrections*
(beginning on page 625). This book was first published in a single edition
in Derry, New Hampshire in 1928. It was manufactured at that time by
the Record Publishing Company of Haverhill, Massachusetts. This 1993
second printing includes the entire text and the full set of illustrations from
the first edition.

This second printing was done with the cooperation and
support of Dr. Felix Vann who also contributed selective
additions and corrections to the book.

First printing 1983
Second printing December 1993

Available from:
Picton Press
PO Box 1111
Camden, ME 04843-1111
Visa/MasterCard (207) 236-6565

Manufactured in the United States of America
Printed on 60# acid-free paper

ii

Dedicated

to

Lucy Chase Chapman Denny

CHASE HOUSES AND GRAVESTONES IN WEST NEWBURY
1   THE MOSES[4] CHASE HOUSE, BUILT BEFORE 1736
2   THE JOSEPH[3] CHASE HOUSE, BUILT IN 1755
3   THE SAMUEL[3] CHASE HOHSE, BUILT IN 1743

SEVEN GENERATIONS

OF THE DESCENDANTS OF

AQUILA and THOMAS CHASE

COMPILED BY

JOHN CARROLL CHASE

AND

GEORGE WALTER CHAMBERLAIN

DERRY, NEW HAMPSHIRE
1928

RECORD PUBLISHING COMPANY
HAVERHILL, MASS.

To the memory of

BENJAMIN CHASE,

JOHN BOWEN CHACE, M. D.,

AND

GEORGE BIGELOW CHASE, A. M.,

pioneers in the work of collecting and preserving material for the family history, this book is most gratefully dedicated.

"A gift of gifts, this lineage old,
  More precious far than gifts of gold;
    .   .   .   .   .
A precious gift, these links that bind
The lives before with lives behind."

—Mrs. Ira A. Eastman.

INTRODUCTION

About the year 1846 there was a widely circulated story about a large fortune in England belonging to the Chase heirs in America which led to an immediate effort to establish family lines for the purpose of securing this prospective windfall.

Among those who became interested in the matter was Mr. Benjamin[7] Chase of Auburn, N. H., the author of the History of Old Chester, N. H., who began the collection of data relating to his own family and gradually extended his research until he had collected a large amount of material. It is proper to note, however, that he never had any faith in the myth, or in the practicability of securing and equitably distributing the "fortune," if it was actually in existence, and numerous letters in the newspapers of the period attest his strong convictions in regard to the subject.

In 1870, a new generation having come upon the stage, the old story was revived with a renewed effort to secure the "fortune," which naturally resulted in the collection of much additional genealogical data.

John B. Chace, M.D., a practicing physician of Taunton, and a descendant of a William Chace who appeared in Roxbury, in 1630, had accumulated a large amount of material relating to his immigrant ancestor and, incidentally, of the immigrants Aquila and Thomas, who appeared in Hampton, N. H., in 1640. He became imbued with the idea of printing the genealogy of the descendants of these three immigrants, and the material that had been collected by Mr. Benjamin Chase was turned over to him. He labored zealously for several years to accomplish his object but with failing health, due to advancing years, and the lack of means he was forced to abandon the project.

Mr. George Bigelow Chase of Boston, a descendant of Aquila[1] through Aquila,[2] Jr., also had been interested for several years in the subject, and had printed in the Heraldic Journal in 1868 a lengthy article relating to the Chases in England. He took up the work of bringing out a genealogy of the Aquila line and purchased of Dr. Chace the result of his long continued labors, but he never carried on the work to any great extent and a few years later deposited all of the material he possessed with the New England Historic Genealogical Society to become its property after his decease, which took place in 1902.

The genealogical material collected by the late William E. Gould of Brookline and Boston, and the late Joseph Warren Brown of Chicago, Ill., have also aided greatly in bringing this book to a very gratifying degree of completeness. Their collections are also in possession of the above-mentioned Society, and to its courtesy we are indebted for the use of this large quantity of material relating to the Chase family.

Mr. Gould was a native of Portland, Me., the son of Althea[7] (Chase) Gould, daughter of Deacon Asa[6] Chase, (Dr. William,[5] Lt. Wells,[4] Moses,[3] Moses[2]). He was the founder and for many years editor of *The Chase Chronicle,* the official publication of The Chase-Chace Family Association.

Mr. Brown was a native of West Newbury, the grandson of Samuel and Elizabeth[6] (Chase) Carr, daughter of Lt. Moses[5] Chase, (Moses,[4] Moses,[3] Moses[2]).

While the name of Chase has occasional mention as early as the 13th century it was, apparently, never a numerous family and at the present time the name is as rare in England as it is common in this country.

Although the Chesham Chases were entitled to bear arms after 1584, as evidenced by the report of a Herald's Visitation, this *right* does not inure to American descendants unless their line of descent is established, which we have been unable to do, as will be seen in the pages treating of *The Chases of Chesham.* However, in these later days the *right* to use a crest or coat of arms has little influence over those who have the desire to make such use, but know or care nothing about the proprieties governing the right.

On account of the great service rendered the descendants of Aquila and Thomas by Dr. Chace, it is deemed most fitting that a biography and his portrait should appear in this volume.

Inasmuch as the "fortune myth," during the thirty years in which it was rampant, was largely responsible for the collection and preservation of much valuable genealogical material that otherwise would have been lost, it seems proper to give for the benefit of those not familiar with its history, and for future reference, some account of the activities in relation to the matter and the final determination of the utter and total lack of authority for the origin of a story which led to the collection of a large amount of money from credulous and ignorant people, many of whom, probably, could not well afford their contributions.

At the annual reunion of the Chase-Chace Family Association held in West Newbury, June 27, 1907, Hon. Frederic H. Chase, of Boston, then a judge of the Superior Court of Massachusetts, delivered an interesting and instructive address on "The Chase Claim to English Millions," in which he set forth the different statements and claims that had been made from time to time with reference to the "Lawrence-Townley" estate and the Chase interests therein, and traced to their source these statements and claims in order to show what the truth was concerning them.

Although the inheritance had been mentioned as early as 1790 the story was not widely circulated until 1846. In that year a largely attended meeting, with some fifteen hundred persons present, was held in Newburyport, and a large sum of money raised to defray the expense of a committee chosen to prosecute the matter, but history is silent as to the result of this movement. In 1872 the story was revived "in some obscure town in Maine," and a meeting was held and an investigating committee chosen to report at a future meeting to be held in Boston. Apparently the committee did not function and at a meeting held 9 Oct. 1872 a new committee was chosen and authorized to raise funds to meet necessary expenses. The inducement was held out that those who subscribed might have the worth of their money by being given an engraving of the Chase Coat of Arms, a souvenir of doubtful value so far as the Chases in America are concerned. No evidence of the existence of the "fortune" was presented beyond what had already appeared in the form of newspaper articles, letters, speeches made at the meeting held in 1846, and some broad assertions. Following this appeal one of the signers was delegated to visit England to investigate.

The following from the Manchester, N. H., Daily Union of May 16, 1873, would indicate that a discordant note had been struck although enthusiasm ran high and money, while not plentiful, seemed to be forthcoming when needed.

"One of the Chases of Boston, who has been the chief confidant of the Chase heirs, has succeeded in raising sufficient money to insure a trip to England, and sailed on Monday of last week. He will undoubtedly visit the continent, attend the Vienna exposition, have a good time, write home that it will require a little more money to successfully prosecute the claim, and will continue to draw upon their eager expectations until they will suspect that their portion of the immense estate is safely deposited in his breeches pocket. We say to these enthusiasts who have joined their future bliss to this English humbug, 'Be of good cheer, life is short at best.'"

Apparently expectant kinsmen waited in vain for any report of their representative's doings and it is safe to say that he returned with less cash than he took with him.

In 1879 the movement received a new impetus and Mr. James Usher, of New York City, a lawyer of standing, was employed by the Lawrence and Townley families to undertake the work of establishing the claim. He went into the matter with great thoroughness and a full exhaustive account of his efforts and the results attained were given in book form in 1883. Reduced to the lowest terms, there was nothing in it.

At a later date the Hon. Edward J. Phelps, U. S. Minister to England, denounced the scheme as an outrageous fraud.

A later investigation by Mr. Frank Alden Hill, a Boston lawyer, brought out the meagre facts upon which the search of years had been based, a full account of his labors appearing in book form in 1885. "The marriage of a Chase to a woman bearing a name allied to wealth; a small unclaimed annuity; and a family squabble in court."

And yet we hear frequently from those who have an abiding faith in what has been proven beyond doubt to be a "myth" of the most pronounced type.

New material available after the earlier pages of the book had been printed, with some corrections will be found under Additions and Corrections.

Continued research in England has failed to add anything of material value to what has appeared in *The Chases of Chesham.*

The simplicity of the arrangement of the book would seem to make any explanation unnecessary.

JOHN CARROLL CHASE.

Derry, N. H., October, 1928.

CONTENTS

ILLUSTRATIONS

THE CHASES OF CHESHAM,
CO. BUCKS., ENGLAND

The general claim has been made that the brothers, Aquila and Thomas Chase, were descendants of the Chesham family of Chases in England. Mr. George Bigelow Chase of Boston assumed it to be true in the most elaborate contribution to Chase literature that had appeared in printed form, which he published in 1869. This connection has been given in practically every publication relating to Chase families that has later appeared, but our investigations fail to confirm it.

It was assumed, or claimed, that the brothers Aquila and Thomas Chase were sons of the Aquila Chase who was baptized in Chesham, 7 Aug. 1580. The name and dates are entirely consistent with the supposition, but the facts studied at close range show that the assumption is not correct.

Extensive research shows that the above named Aquila Chase went from Chesham to London, there married, was the father of six children, was a merchant tailor, lived in Knight Rider's street, attended the two Established Churches in that street and, with his wife and five of his children, was there buried.

The parish registers fail to show that he had a son Thomas but they do show that he had a son Aquila who was baptized in the parish of St. Nicholas, Cole Abbey. The parish register further shows that Aquila Chase, the tailor, and Aquila his son, there baptized, were also buried there. As there was only one Chase family living in Knight Rider's street, 1606 to 1660, we feel justified in assuming that Aquila and Thomas Chase, the Hampton brothers, could *not* be the sons of Aquila Chase of Chesham, England. *They may be descended from the Chesham family but our researches fail to show such a connection.*

The use of the comparatively infrequent name of Aquila in both Chesham and New England is, however, very suggestive of a connection between the two families.

For the benefit of future investigators who may be interested in the origin of these early settlers of New England, we give the documentary records obtained with our interpretation of the evidence they afford.

In this connection it may be noted that the usual "three brothers" tradition about the early immigrations of families does not apply to

9

the Chases. No evidence has been found to support the claim, which has appeared in print innumerable times, that William Chace was a brother of Aquila and Thomas. In one instance it was stated that this relationship was proven by Aquila's will making a bequest to his niece, "daughter of his brother William." This will, as will be seen, makes no such bequest.

From whence and how William came has not been established, notwithstanding the various statements that have appeared in print. It can be credibly assumed that he was the first of the name to appear in New England, coming, it is supposed, in Governor Winthrop's fleet, although his name does not appear in any of the more or less incomplete lists of passengers. On the records of the First Church of Roxbury, Massachusetts, in the handwriting of the Rev. John Eliot, "Apostle to the Indians," we find the following entry, "William Chase, he came wth the first company, 1630," which would indicate that he first settled in that place.

The Rev. Thomas Chase, a clergyman of the Church of England, appears in Maryland in 1737 and was appointed rector of St. Paul's church in Baltimore in 1743, but we have been unable to establish any English connection. His son, Samuel, was prominent in civic affairs, signed the Declaration of Independence and was assocciate justice of the Supreme Court of the United States from 1796 to his death in 1811, at the age of seventy.

His former residence in Annapolis, Maryland, a three-story brick house, built in 1770, is a very fine specimen of Colonial architecture, particularly the interior, and is an object of great interest to those who visit that historic city.

It was inherited many years ago by the Episcopal Diocese of the state and is now a Home for Old Ladies.

A John Chase came from the Barbadoes and settled in Providence, R. I., in 1720, but, as in the case of the Rev. Thomas, little is known about his descendants.

There are also other lines claiming English ancestry which we have been unable to verify.

While the name of Chase has occasional mention in England as early as the 13th century, it was, apparently, never a numerous family and at the present time the name is as rare there as it is common in this country.

CHASE WILLS.

WILLIAM CHASE, 1581/2.

William Chase of St. Peters by Pauls Wharf, London, made his will, 23 Mar. 1581/2. He mentions the poor of St. Sepulchres in Co. of Cambridge; his brothers Jeremy and Thomas; his cousin William Chase of Hisson; and his sister Rebecca. Proved 30 June 1582.

JOHN CHASE, 1599.

In the name of God the XVIII of Aprill Anno 1599 I John Chase of Hundrich in the parish of Great Chesham and the county of Bucks sicke in bodye but whole in the health of my soule I prayse and thanke my Lord God therefore doe make and ordayne this my last will and testament in manner and forme followinge.

First my soule wch is the most precious thing that I give I comend into the hands of Almighti God my heavenly and most mercifull father through Christe of whom I received y^t my bodye to the earth from whence it was taken in sure and certayne hope and expectiation to have the same raysed up agayne at the last daye by the virtue and power of my Lord and Saviour Jesus Christe whoe dyed for my sinns and rose agayne for my Righteousness that my fayth in him and the worke of his most holy spirite I might not only be quickned from the death of sinns to the lyfe of Right-eousnes but also by the joyning together agayne of my soule wth my bodye I may enjoye and be put into the possession of everlasting lyfe and salva-tion in glorye by th only mercye of God his and my father his meritts and p'fect obedience and the powerfull sanctification of the most holy spirite so be yt.

First for my temperall and worldly goods and substance I will them to be desposed after this sorte.

First I will and bequeath to William Chase myne eldest sonne ten pownds.

Item to Ralphe my sonne V £ to be payd to him at his age of XXIII years.

Item to Samuel X £ and Steven X £ to eyther of them to be payd at the lyke age.

Item I will give and bequeath to Elizabeth, Martha and Anne my daughters and to each of them XXX lb. a pecce to be payd to every of them at th age of XXth years and yt it shalbe the will of God that any of my sayd three sonnes or any of my sayd three daughters shall departe out of this p'sent lyfe before he or shee shall come to th age to have and enjoye their portion or legacye as is before mentioned then my will is that the porcon or legacye of such a one so departed shalbe and remayne to be equaly divided amongst the survivors.

Item I give to the poore people of Chesham aforesayd XX^s in monye.

Item I give to my brother Richard Chase X^{ls} in money.

Item my will is that whatsoever bargaynes I have made and conveyed of land or meadowe of this my ferme of Hundrich wher in I nowe dwell whether the same be by wrighting or by promise made and conveyed that myne executors shall them to be truly performed and accomplished ac-cording to my faythfull meanings.

Item I give and bequeath to my daughter Mary Aldrige X^{ls}.

Item to my sister Chritaian Atkins X^s.

Item to Henry the sonne of my brother William Chase X^s.

All the rest of my goods not given nor bequeathed my debts payd legacys performed and funerall in the comly and christian burill of my body discharged, I will give and bequeath to Alia my wife and to Mathew Chase her and my sonne whome I constitute and ordayne to be the execu-tors of this my last will and testament with thes conditions following.

First my will is that Alice my wife shall not marrye during the tearme of years in my lease of Hundrich farme wherein I dwell conteyned with out the device, consent, approbation & good lyking of the overseers of this my last will and testament or the most parte or number of them whose names shalbe hereafterwards expressed but if she shall refuse so to doe and willbe marryed without the advice, consent approbation and good lyking of them or the moste parte or number of them then my will and mynde is that she shall have only XL £ to be payd to her in moneye by myne other executor and so to departe without having any further to doe wth any parte of my goods or said lease, also I will that myne execu-tors aforesayd shall be severally bownden to myne hereafter named over-seers joyntly and severally in such a competent summe of money as by them shalbe thought meete and convenyent first for the dewe and honest education and bringing up or profitable putting forthe of my children

untill such tyme as they shall come to their severall ages before sett downe
in this my last will and testament and at the wch tyme they shall have
and enjoye the legacys by me to them severally given and granted, severally in lyke manner to be bound to my overseers for the due true and
sure payment of the legacys before given to my sayd children at such
tyme as they shalbe dewe, eyther of myne executors to performe according to the moyeti of them and as they whole shalbe fully payd.

And for myne overseers of this my last will and testament I name
thes following: my loving & faythfull friends my cosen Robert Aldridge
of Beconsfield of this parishe, William Groves, Thomas Breeden and my
brother Richard Chase morover I hartely desire and require my very good
loving and faythfull friend Mr. Richard Bowles that he will please to
help ayde and assist my executors with his good advice and cownsell as in
lyke manner to further in that he may both my sayd executors and overseers for the better execution and performance of this my last will and
testament in all things according to my true purpose and meanynge.

Item I will that yf any matter shall faule out wch may seeme to be
doubtfull and wherof any question maye arise in this my last will and
testment that the same shalbe compounded ended and determyned by my
forenamed friends or the more parte of them.

In witness of the truth hereof I have sette these presents the letters
of my name my selfe and delivered the same to be my deed as my last will
& testament the daye and yeare first before written in the presence of the
undernamed Richard Bowles, Henry Atkins, Humfrey Greenway, Wm.
Sawnders.

Memorandu that before the sealing and delivering herof by the
testator the sume of X£ for Samuel Chase was increased to LX£ and
the sumes of Elizabeth, Martha and Anne which was before XX£ a
peece was increased to XXX£ apeece. Proved 2 August 1599.

JAMES BYRCH, 1618.

18 April 1618, James Byrch of Great Chesham, yeoman, made his will
as follows: to his son James he gave his place called Blackwell at the
water's side when 21; to his son Henry his place called Chequers purchased of John Byrch my uncle; son William, daughter Susan, nephew
William and brother Richard mentioned; brother-in-law Nathaniel Reading and *cousin Henry Chase* mentioned. Sir Francis Cheyney to be overseer. Witnessed by Henry Chase. Proved Oct. 22, 1618.

MARGARET CHASE, 1619.

In the name of God Amen I Margarett Chase of Greate Chesham
in the countie of Bucks widowe beinge sicke in bodie but of good and
perfecte memory thanckes be given to Allmightie God doe make and ordain this my laste will and testament in manner and forme followinge.

Firste I comitt my soule into the handes of Allmightie God hopinge
through his death and passion to have everlastinge life, and my bodie to
be buried in such decent sorte as shall seeme fitt to my executor heare-
after named.

Whereas Katharine Givin deceased my mother did by her last will
and testament in wrightinge give and bequeath unto me the some of fortie
pounds as by the saide will more at large appeareth nowe my will and
minde is and I doe heare by give lymitt and appointe unto my daughter
Katherine Chase the some of thirtie poundes, parcell of the saide legacie
of fortie pounds to be paide unto my saide daughter Katharine when she
shall accomplish the age of one and twentie yeares or at the daie of her
marriage wch shall first happen.

Item I doe give lymit and appointe unto my sonne Henry Chase the
some of tenn pounds, residue of the said legacie of fortie pounds to be

paide unto him when he shall accomplish and be of the age of one & twentie yeares.

Item my will desire & request is that all my husbandes goodes, his debtes beinge firste discharged and myne, and my funerall discharged shall be sold and the money devided equally betweene my said sonne and daughter and I doe make and appointe my well beloved kinsman Mathew Chase, gent. sole executor of this my last will and testament intreatinge his best care hearin.

In witness where of I the saide Margaret Chase have unto this my last will and testament put to my hande and seale this XXVIIth daie of March anno domi 1619. Reade sealed and published and published in the presence of Thomas Stile, Joane Baldwine and John Ball. Proved April 22, 1619 by the executor. (Archdeaconry of Bucks 1618/9 folio 192).

Margret, relict of Henry Chase of Chesham Magna, Co. of Bucks, deceased, adm. granted 11 Feb. 1618/19 (Adm. Acts P.C.C.).*

SAMUEL CHASE, 1627.

Samuel Chase of Dublin, Ireland, gent. made his will 23 July 1627. He mentions his sisters Elizabeth, Martha, and Hannah; his mother Alice Chase and appoints his brother Stephen Chase executor. Proved Jan. 16, 1635/36. (P.C.C.)

MERCY CHASE, 1629.

Mercy Chase of London, widow of Jeremy Chase, later Alderman of Cambridge, made her will 27 July 1629. She mentions her son Jeremy and John; brother Thomas Chase merchant, daughter Mercy Savage, daughter Anne Cole wife of George Cole to be executor; the wife and daughter of Thomas Chase aforesaid; witnessed by Dorothy Chase. Proved 11 Sept. 1629.

THOMAS CHASE, 1631.

Thomas Chase, citizen and grocer of London, made his will 30 Oct. 1631. He mentions his wife Dorothy to be executrix and also two children. Proved 14 Nov. 1631. (P.C.C.)

HUGH CHACE

Commission issued to Susan Jepson, next of kin of Hugh Chace, late of the parish of St. Bartholomew, next the Royal Exchange, London, who died intestate to administer the goods of the said deceased, 12 Nov. 1634. (Consistory Court of London, Vicar General's Book, 1627-37, f. 188d.)

Commission issued to Anne Preston, mother of Hugh Chase, late of the parish of St. Bartholomew's next the Royal Exchange, London, deceased, intestate (as it is said) to administer the goods of the said deceased, 23 Feb. 1636/7. (Ibid. f. 232.)

MATTHEW CHASE

Administration on the estate of Mathew Chase, late of Stone Co. Kent, granted to his widow Elizabeth Chase, 19 Nov. 1638. (P.C.C. Ad. Book, 224.)

EDWARD CHACE

Will of Edward Chace servant to the Hon. English East India Company, in their factory at Bantam, in Java Major, dated 1 Nov. 1638.

I bequeath to my mother Mrs. Dorothy Chase, widow, living in St. Mary Axe, London, 15 pounds.

To my sister Dorothy five pounds.

To Mr. Francis Cleare formerly servant to my father Mr. Thomas Chace two pounds.

*P.C.C. stands for Prerogative Court of Canterbury.

To Mr. Aaron Baker three pounds.

To Mr. Thomas Leninge a book of sermons by Mr. Hyron.

To Mr. Thomas Wilson 20 s.

To Mr. Richard Davies 20 s.

Executors: my mother and sister aforesaid

Supervisors: Mr. Aaron Baker & Mrs. Thomas Wilson.

Witnesses: Stephen Porter & Robert Fuller.

Proved, 29 Aug. 1639 by Dorothy Chase alias Rhoades sister of deceased, Dorothy Chase the mother being dead. (P.C.C., Harvey 138.)

RICHARD CHASE

Commission issued to Rebecca Kitchen, creditor of Richard Chase, *late in parts beyond the sea,* deceased intestate to administer the goods of the said deceased, 2 Aug. 1643. (Commissary Court of London, Ad. Act Book 1639-47, f. 108 d.)

WILLIAM CHASE

Commission issued to Wilfred Chase, brother of William Chase, late of St. Nicholas, Cole Abbey, London, deceased intestate to administer the goods of the said deceased, 13 Feb. 1643/4. (Commissary Court of London, Adm. Act Bood 1639-47, f. 132.)

RALPH CHASE, 1643.

Ralph Chase of Great Marlow, Co. of Bucks, gent. made his will 18 Nov. 1643. He mentions his wife Elizabeth, son Stephen and Stephen's son Stephen, John son of his brother Stephen deceased and his daughters Martha and Hannah. Proved 10 Jan. 1644/45.

STEPHEN CHASE

Administration on the estate of Stephen Chase, late of St. Martins-in-the Field, Co. Middlesex, decd. granted to Anne Chase his widow, 4 June 1646. (P.C.C. Act. Book 65.)

Administration of the same granted to Stephen and Anne Chase children of deceased, the same left unadministered by his relict Anne Chase, 16 Nov. 1654. (Ibid. 136.)

ELIZABETH CHASE, 1651.

Elizabeth Chase made her will, 9 Jan. 1651. She bequeathed to the poor of Great Marlow, Bucks, and mentions her godsons Stephen and Robert Chase. Her nephew Stephen Chase to be executor. Proved 4 Mar. 1651. [Widow of Ralph Chase.]

ELIZABETH CHASE, 1650/51.

Elizabeth Chase of Stone, County of Kent, widow, made her will 24 Jan. 1650/51. Her property in Chesham, Co. of Bucks, she gave to her son Richard her eldest son. She mentions her sons Matthew, John, Ralph and William. She gave a legacy to her son John, *"if he return home, as he has not been heard from for a number of years."* Proved 8 May 1651. [Widow of Matthew Chase of Chesham, 1576-1618, and of Stone, Co. Kent.]

ANNE CHASE, 1652.

Anne Chase of Covent Garden in the parish of St. Martin-in-the-Field, County of Middlesex, late wife of Stephen Chase, apothecary, made her will 12 Oct. 1652. She mentions Richard Chase of Chesham, Co. of Bucks, clerk; her sons Stephen and John Chase; James the son of her son John Chase and her daughters Anne and Mary Chase. Proved 25 June 1653. [This would indicate that the family had removed from Chesham to London.]

Administration of the estate of Jane Chase, late of St. Martin-in-the-Field, Co. Middlesex, dec'd. granted to her husband Thomas Chase, 30 Sept. 1653. (P.C.C. Act Book 7:37.)

JOHN CHASE, 1658.

John Chase of St. Sepulchre, County of Midlesex, collar-maker made a nuncupative will, 9 Mar. 1658. He desired his wife Rebecca to be executrix. Proved 31 Mar. 1658.

THOMAS CHASE, 1658.

Thomas Chase of Stone, Co. of Kent, gent. made a nuncopative will, 8 May 1658. He speaks of his wife and desires his brother Ralph Chase to be executor. Witness Matthew Chase and others.
Proved 25 May 1658.

ANNE CHASE, 1661.

Anne Chase of London, widow, made her will 13 Mar. 1661/2. She wished to be buried in the church of Stone, Co. of Kent, near her late husband Thomas Chase. To her mother Lucy Aleworth 10 pounds; to her brother John Aleworth 5 pounds; to her sister Isabelle Harwood 5 pounds and a pair of sheets and pillow bears marked A.A.; to her aunt Carter her wedding ring; to her uncle Thomas Tracy her round silver pot; to Mr. Ginkins 20/ to buy him a ring to wear in remembrance of me. Residue to my brother John Clarke whom she appoints executor. She speaks of a marriage settlement made of lands in Stone, Co. of Kent, called Little Brooks farm, now in possession of John Chase, citizen and apothecary of London valued at 60 pounds per annum. Proved 16 July 1662. (P.C.C. Land, 81.) [She was Anne Aylesworth and married Thomas Chase of Stone, in Kent, in the parish of St. Bennet and St. Paul, Paul's Wharf, London, 17 Mar. 1656/7.]

MATTHEW CHASE

Will of Mathew Chase of Chesham, Co. Bucks, tanner, dated: 6 May 1663.

I bequeath to my eldest son Mathew the house I now live in with the tanyard & tearns, ne close of pasture called Meadlotts, at his age of 21, he paying my wife 6 pounds a year, as long as she shall live.

To my son Ezeckiell, the house John Payn now lives in called Red Lion, & two tenements adjoining with orchards, and garden, a piece of ground in Town Fell, at the age of 21, he paying my wife ten pounds a year, as long as she shall live.

To my son Richard the freehold I bought of Nathaniel Carter & a close of pasture ground called Pullfele, at his age of 21, he to pay my wife 5 pounds a year.

To my son Robert, the house John Chase now lives in & a close of arable land that John Porter rents to me, at his age of 21.

To my daughter Alice, 200 pounds when she attains the age of 21.

To my youngest son John Chase wood & ground called Godetts alias Goretts in the parish of Wendover, at the age of 21.

To my Kinsman John Chase my goods in the house he now lives in after the death of my mother he paying the widow Chase 40 s.

Residuary legatee and executrix my wife. Signed Mathew Chase. Witnesses: John Grover, John Blacke. Proved 12 Dec. 1663 by Alice Chase widow, relict of deceased. (Archdeaconry Court of Bucks, 1663.)

MATTHEW CHASE, 1666.

Matthew Chase of Stone, Co. of Kent, gent. made his will 4 Apr. 1666. To his brother Mr. Richard Chase and Richard's wife each 20/s. To Richard Chase son of his brother Richard 20/ & to the wife of this

Richard 20/ and to each of his children 1/. To John son of the last Richard 20 pounds. To the poor of Stone 40/; to Robert son of his brother Richard, the annuity of Milton Abbot in Devonshire during Richard Andelayes life and appoints him executor and residuary legatee. Proved 30 Apr. 1666.

ALICE CHASE

Will of Alice Chase of [torn away] dated 11 Apr. 1668.

I bequeath to my eldest son Mathew Chase, a jack, porringers, pewter, furniture and two of my best silver spoons.

To my son Richard 5 pounds

To my ----------[torn away] [daughter Alice Chase].

To my son Ezekiell Chase 40 pounds.

To my son Richard Chase a brass pan & a silver spoon marked 1643.

To my son Robert Chase a bedstead & half dozen silver spoons marked A.L. & 20 pounds.

To my son John Chase furniture & 20 pounds.

To my friend Thomas Moncke 40 s. to distribute among the poor.

Executors: My brother Mr. William [torn away] Richard Biscoe and my Kinsman John Chase.

(Signed) Alice Chase

Witnesse: William Childs, William Hawkins.

[Probate Act torn away.] (Archdeaconry of Bucks, 1668.)

RICHARD CHASE, 1686.

Richard Chase of London, of the Company of Haberdashers, in the parish of St. James-in-the-Field, Co. of Middlesex, made his will 15 July 1686. He mentions his brother John and his wife Frances; his grandchildren Elizabeth and Thomas Hinton and his son Jonathan's wife.

"And whereas I have given unto my children and especially unto my sone John their portions formerly, I doe notwithstanding (for some reasons to my griefe too well knowne yet I doe thinke herein not proper to declare the same) give and devise unto my sonne John the summe of twenty pounds and noe more &c &c".

He speaks of his houses and lands and tenements in the parishes of Ealing, St. Giles Cripplegate, St. Martins-in-the-Fields, St. James-in-the-Fields and church in the Co. of Middlesex & city of London. His son Jonathan to be executor. Proved 10 Aug. 1686.

JOHN CHASE, 1686.

John Chase of the parish of St. Helen in London, gent. made his will 2 Sept. 1686. To be buried in the church of St. Bennet Finks, London. Wife Frances. All his houses in the precinct of St. Katharines, London. He mentions his sister Elizabeth Chase, his eldest son William and his wife Phillip; his second son John; his six youngest children, viz. Elizabeth, John, Mary, Rachel, Richard and Hannah. His cousin Miller who is [illegible]. Wife executrix. Proved 20 Dec. 1686.

PARISH REGISTER OF CHESHAM,
1538-1636.

BAPTISMS.

John sonne of Thomas Chaase baptized the XXXth Dec. 1540.

Rychard sonne of Thomas Chaase baptized the XXIIIth Aug. 1542.

Elyzabeth daughter of Thomas Chaase baptized the XXIIIth Maye 1547.

Agnes daughter of Thomas Chaase baptized the IXth March 1551/2.

William sonne of John Chase baptized the XXVth March 1565.

Robert sonne of Richard Chaase baptized the second Sept. 1565.

Mary daughter of John Chaase baptized the XVII Nov. 1566.
Henry sonne of Richard Chaase baptized the X Aug. 1567.
Henry sonne of William & Isbell Chaase baptized the VI Sept. 1573.
Thomas sonne of John Chaase baptized the thirde Aug. 1572.
Lidia daughter of Rychard & Joan Chaase baptized the IIIth Oct. 1573.
Dina daughter of John & Alice Chaase baptized the XXXI Oct. 1574.
Ezechiel sonne of Rychard & Joan Chaase baptized the XXIIIth April 1576.
Mathew sonne of John & Alice Chaase baptized the VIth Jan. 1576/77.
Dorcas daughter of Rychard & Joan Chaase baptized the second Mar. 1577/78.
Raufe sonne of John & Alice Chaase baptized the XVth Feb. 1578/79.
Aquila sonne of Richard & Joane Chaase baptized the VIIth Aug. 1580.
Samuel sonne of John & Alice Chaase baptized the XVIII Sept. 1581.
Jason sonne of Rychard & Joan Chaase baptized the XX Jan. 1582/3.
Elyzabeth daughter of John & Alice Chaase baptized the second Feb. 1583/4.
Thomas sonne of Richard & Joan Chaase baptized the XVIII July 1585.
John sonne of John & Alice Chaase baptized the VI Mar. 1585/6.
Stephen sonne of John & Alice Chaase baptized the XXI May 1587.
Abigail daughter of Richard & Joan Chaase baptized the XII Jan. 1588/89.
Daniel sonne of John & Alice Chaase baptized the XV July 1590.
Mordechai sonne of Rychard & Joane Chaase baptized the XXX July 1591.
Martha daughter of John & Alice Chaase baptized the XXVIII Mar. 1593.
Anne daughter of John & Alice Chaase baptized the XXIIII Aug. 1596.
Mary daughter of Henry & Mary Chaase baptized the first May 1597.
John sonne of Henry & Marie Chaase baptized XXVI Mar. 1600.
Francis sonne of Mathew & Elizabeth Chaase baptized the XXth Sept. 1601.
Thomas sonne of Robert tanner & Joan Chaase baptized the XII Nov. 1601.
John sonne of Mr. Mathew & Elyzabeth Chase bapt. the IIII Dec. 1603.
Benajah sonne of Robert & Joan Chaase bapt. the XXIXth Maye 1604.
Martha daughter of Henry & Mary Chaase bapt. the XIII June 1604.
Marie daughter of Mr. Matthew & Elizabeth Chaase bapt. the XII Dec. 1605.
Stephen sonne of Henry & Marie Chase bapt. the VII Sept. 1606.
Matthew sonne of Mr. Matthew & Elizabeth Chase bapt. the XXIX May 1608.
Thomas sonne of Mr. Matthew & Elizabeth Chase, bapt. the XXth Feb. 1610/11.
Bridgett daughter of Mr. Matthew & Elizabeth Chase bapt. the first Jan. 1614/15.
Ralph sonn of Mr. Matthew & Elizabeth Chase bapt. the IIII Sept. 1616.
William sonn of Mr. Matthew & Elizabeth Chase bapt. the IIII Jan. 1617/18.
Matthew sonn of Ezekiel & Elizabeth Chase bapt. the VI June 1619.
Thomas sonne of Thomas & Martha Chase bapt. 8th Dec. 1631.
William sonne of Thomas & Martha Chase bapt. 30 Oct. 1636.

MARRIAGES.

Rychard Chaase & Joan Byshoppe married the XVI Maye 1564.
Thomas Welch of Wendover & Agnes Chaase married the XII Nov. 1571.
William Chaase & Isbell Sam of Agmondesham m. the XIII Jan. 1572.
Stephen Grover & Elyzabeth Chaase m. the XVII Nov. 1566.

John Chaase & Alice daughter of Richard Harding of Slowland m. XXVIII Sept. 1573.

Henry Atkins & Xptian [Christian] daughter of Thomas Chaase m. XIIII June 1576.

George Hawkes & Margarite Flinte s[ervant] to Thomas Chaase m. the XVI Nov. 1579.

Rychard Butcher servante to Thomas Chaase and Agnes Patridge servante to Mr. Thomas Ashfielde m. the XXVIII Feb. 1581/2.

{ Henry Gouldson scolem[aste]r & Anne Wynch s[ervan]t to Jo and William Chaase m. XIIII Oct. 1588.

William Aldrige servant to the same & Mary daughter to John Chaase m. XIIII Oct. 1588.

George Lyttelpage & Joan daughter of Widoe Saale and servante to John & William Chaase m. the IXth Feb. 1589/90.

Thomas Payne & Marie Norwood s[ervan]te to Mr. Chase m. xij Nov. 1607.

Henry Chase & Alice Bachilor m. the VIIII Oct. 1612.

William Cheas and Elizabeth Turner m. 22 Sept. 1664.

Thomas Cheas and Susannah Edwards widow m. 14 Sept. 1671.

William Birch and Martha Cheas m. 26 Oct. 1671.

Samuel Cheas and Elizabeth Davey m. 12 Oct. 1676.

John son of Thomas Birtch of Haseldon farm and Mary Chase m. 26 Jan. 1681/2.

William Chase Jr. and Love Peine m. 19 Oct. 1691.

Joseph Gate and Elizabeth Chase m. 22 Oct. 1694.

BURIALS.

Rychard Payne servante to Thomas Chaase bur. the IX Feb. 1562/3.

Thomas sonne of Thomas Chaase bur. the third Aug. 1569.

Elyzabeth wife of Thomas Chaase bur. the second Oct. 1569.

Joan the wyfe of John Chaase, bur. the XVII Aug. 1572.

Thomas sonne of John Chaase bur. the XXVII Oct. 1572.

Dina daughter of John & Alice Chaase bur. the XXIII Aprill 1576.

John sonne of John & Alice Chaase bur. the XVII Mar. 1585/6.

Old father Thomas Chaase of Hundriche bur. the XXVII June 1586.

Daniel sonne of John & Alice Chaase bur. the XXI Mar. 1594/5.

Joan wyfe of Richard Chaase bur. the IIII May 1597.

John Chaase of Hundrich bur. the XXII Apr. 1599.

William sonne of Thomas Dell of Chartridge and servante to Robert Chaase tannr bur. the VIII July 1601.

Martha daughter of Henry & Mary Chaase bur. XXII June 1604.

Jason sonne of Richard Chase bur. IIII June 1606.

Richard Chase senex bur. XXXII Jan. 1610/11.

Marie wife of Henry Chase of Waters bur. the VI Mar. 1611/12.

Mr. Henry Chase bur. the X Dec. 1618.

Mris Margaret Chase widow of Henry Chase bur. the VI Apr. 1519.

——— Marshall servant to Mr. Chase bur. the first Dec. 1616.

Marie daughter of Mr. Matthew Chase bur. 17 Feb. 1630/31.

Alice Chase widow bur. from Agmundesham 17 June 1634.

FROM LONDON PARISH RECORDS

St. Thomas-the-Apostle was united with St. Mary Aldermary. Registers of both are published.

St. Nicholas, Cole Abbey, was united with Nicholas St. Olive. Records are not published.

St. Thomas-the-Apostle and St. Nicholas, Cole Abbey, were originally located in Knight Rider's street (later called Old Fish Street).

Examined the Baptisms of St. Nicholas, Cole Abbey, 1611 to 1627, and the Burials 1611 to 1660 for *Chase items.*

PARISH OF ST. THOMAS-the-APOSTLE, 1558-1754.

Aquila Chaste & Martha Jelliman, m. 22 June 1606.
Anne, daughter of Aquila Chaste, christened 26 Feb. 1607/8.

BURIALS.

Geffry son of John Jelliman bur. 4 Sept. 1603.
—— dau. of John Jelliman bur. 10 Nov. 1603.
Anne daughter of Aquila Chast buried, 19 July 1609.
Martha daughter of Aquila Chaste buried, 11 Mar. 1610/11.
John Gelliman bur. 7 May 1620.
Margerie Jeliman widow, bur. 18 Aug. 1621.

BAPTISMS.

Margaret dau. of John Jelliman bp. 9 Nov. 1588.
Anne dau. of John Jelliman bp. 3 Feb. 1593/4.
Sarah dau. of John Jelliman bp. 18 July 1596.
Geoffrey son of John Jelliman bp. 20 May 1599.
Judith dau. of John Jelliman bp. 10 Jan. 1601/2.

UNITED PARISHES OF ST. MARY WOOLNOTH AND ST. MARY WOOLCHURCH HAW, 1538-1670.

Elinor daughter of Edward Chace, merchant taylor, bp. 2 Sept. 1621.

ST. NICHOLAS ACONS, 1539-1670.

1650 John Chace of Sepulchre & Rebecca Androws of the same m. 29 Dec. 1650.

ST. MARTIN-in-the-FIELDS, 1550-1650.

Anna Chase baptized 7 Oct. 1597.
Isaac Estove & Martha Chasse m. 2 Nov. 1613.
Thomas Chasse buried, 21 Dec. 1613.

PARISH OF ST. PAUL, COVENT GARDEN, 1653-1753.

Thomas Chace of the Parish of Stone, Co. of Kent, gent. & Mrs. Anne Ayleworth of this parish, singlewoman, published three severall Lord's days in the Church at the close of the morning exercises according to the Act [of the Commonwealth] Mar. 1, 8, 15, 1656.

Thomas Chace gent. & Ann Ayleworth, spinster, married by Edward

Roberts, Esq. one of the Justices of the Peace for County of Middlesex, city and liberty of Westminster in presence of Tho. Leigh, Esq. and John Chace, 17 Mar. 1656.

By Act of Parliament the clergy were not permitted to marry at this time.

PARISH OF ST. BENET AND ST. PAUL,
PAUL'S WHARF, 1619-1657.

Thomas Chase & Anne Ayleworth m. 17 Mar. 1656/7.

PARISH OF ST. BOTOLPH BISHOPSGATE,
1558-1753.

Thomas Chase, merchant, & Dorothy Smith mar. by licence, 28 Apr. 1608.

REGISTER OF ST. NICHOLAS, COLE-ABBEY,

BAPTISMS.*

Sara Chace ye daughter of Aquila Chace marchant tayler was baptized ye IXth of .ffebruary 1611 [1611/12].

Elizabeth Chace ye daughter of Aquila Chace marchant tayler was baptized ye XIIIIth of May 1615.

Jone Chase ye daughter of Aquila Chace marchant tayler was baptized ye XXXth day of March 1623.

Aquilla Chase ye sonne of Aquilla Chase was baptized Aprill ye 9th 1626.

BURIALS 1611-1670.

Sara Chace ye daughter of Aquila Chace taylor was buryed in ye Cloyster by ye Church wall hard by ye east Cloyster May ye 2nd 1624.

Joane Chace ye daughter of Aquila Chace tayler was burryed the 17th day of August in ye churchyard 1624.

Martha Chase the wife of Aquilla Chase was buried in the Cloyster the 15th day of August, 1643.

Aquilla Chase Taler was buried upon the ninth day of ffebruary att the feet of Widdowe Maie, 1643 [1643/4].

Aquila Chase was buried in ye Cloyster before Mr. Parkers wyndow the same day [Xth of January] 1659/60.

CHAUNCERY PROCEEDINGS, CHARLES I.

Complaint of Mathew Chase of Stoke Poges, Co. Bucks, gentleman, executor of the will of Richard Bowle late of Great Chesham, Co. Bucks, Esq. dec'd, against Sir Francis Stanton, 3 Feb. 1626/7. Answer of defendant, 14 Feb. 1626/7. (C.105/51-C.2.)

THE MERCHANT TAYLORS' COMPANY OF LONDON.
(Apprentice Books, 1583 to 1669 searched).

Francis Chase son of Matthew Chase of Chesham Magna, Co. Bucks, gentleman, apprenticed to Thomas Browne, merchant adventurer to Spain & Barbary for nine years, 8 Dec. 1617.

Richard Chase, son of Richard Chase of Denham, Co. Bucks, clerk, apprnticed to John Wallis of Foster Lane for seven years, 29 May 1650.

ADDENDA.

3 Feb. 1627. Warrant for issuing letters of marque to Thomas Chase, Richard Slany and others [not named] owners of the John and Francis of London, 140 tons, Thomas Weatherly master.

*Baptisms fully recorded for this period.

3 Mar. 1627. Warrant for issuing letters of marque to Richard Slaney and Thomas Chase owners of the ship John and Francis of London, 140 tons, Thomas Witherly master. (Calendar of Domestic State Papers, 1628-1629, pp. 292, 293.)

16 May 1627. Petition of Thomas Wetherly, captain of the John and Francis of London concerning persons who have stolen away from Gravesend in the night-time since the last stay of ships. Prays that, notwithstanding the stay, his ship may proceed on her voyage under a letter of marque. (Calendar of Domestic State Papers, 1627-1628 p. 179.)

3 Aug. 1643, Commission issued to Rebecca Kitchen, creditor to Richard Chase, late of parts beyond the sea, deceased intestate, to administer the goods of said deceased. (Commissary Court of London.)

CALENDAR OF STATE PAPERS, DOMESTIC, 1634-1635.

18 July 1634. Robert Calvert to his cousin Owen. When the writer met Owen and Mr. Lilly at Islington, on Monday last, he forgot to acquaint them of the following business. Has made searches for the coat armour of *Chase* alias *Chause*, in Suffolk, a branch of which family came into Bucks in Henry VII. [1485-1509] and there have remained since. Matthew Chase of Chesham, county of Bucks, is the elder brother of this family, and a brother to Samuel Chase. Sends the coat and has the pedigree. Prays Owen to use Matthew Chase with respect, and that he may have a confirmation of this coat, unto which he has a just claim. In the writer's visitation in Essex he intends to wait upon Owen. P. S. Prays to be commended to Mr. Lilly. Ralph Chase of Great Marlow, is a *younger brother of Matthew Chase.*

1634. Brief for Matthew Chase against Nathan Garrett in a cause in the Court of Arches relating to the tithes of Stonyfield in the parish of Chesham Woburn, co. of Buckingham.

CHASES IN BUCKINGHAMSHIRE IN THE SUBSIDIES.

1596. Matthew Chase of Chesham assessed for goods.
1624. Matthew Chase of Stoke Poges assessed for goods (4:1563).
1624. Matthew Chase of Wryardesburg assessed for goods (Reg. 1734).
1624. Ralph Chase of Great Marlow assessed for goods (3:1592).
1606. Samuel Chase of Kimbal Magna assessed for goods (Reg. 1701).
1606. Henry Chase of Marks Risborough assessed for goods.
1628. Zachiell Chase of Wyrardisburg assessed for goods (Reg. 1734).
1640. Ezekiel Chase of Fulmer assessed for goods (5:1688).

Richard Chase, A.M., was rector of Chesilhurst, county of Kent, in 1636 and of Stone, county of Kent, 1650 and was sequestered (Somerby Papers, 2:504).

GENEALOGY

Based upon the foregoing documentary evidence the following genealogy is constructed.

1

THOMAS[1] CHAASE, the patriarch from whom the Chesham Chases descend, must have been born about 1520, as "Old father Thomas Chaase of Hundricke" in the parish of Chesham, was buried 27 June 1586. He married before 1541, probably ELIZABETH ———— who was his wife when she was buried in Chesham, 2 Oct. 1569. He and his family were living in Chesham from 1540 to the time of his death in 1586. His servant Richard Payne was buried in Chesham, 9 Feb. 1562/3.

Children, born and baptized in Chesham:

2. JOHN,[2] bp. 30 Dec. 1540.
3. RICHARD, bp. 23 Aug. 1542.
    ELIZABETH, bp. 23 May 1547; m. 17 Nov. 1566, Stephen Grover.
    AGNES, bp. 9 Mar. 1551/2; m. 12 Nov. 1571, Thomas Welch of Wendover.
4. WILLIAM, m. in Chesham, 13 Jan. 1572, Isabell Sam of Agmondesham.
    CHRISTIAN, "called daughter of Thomas Chaase," m. 11 June 1576, Henry Atkins; alive 18 Apr. 1599.

2

JOHN[2] CHAASE (Thomas[1]) was baptized in Chesham, 30 Dec. 1540; buried in Hundrick in the parish of Chesham, 22 Apr. 1599. He married (1) as early as 1564, JOAN ————, who was buried in Chesham, 17 Aug. 1572. He married (2) in Chesham, 28 Sept. 1573, ALICE HARDING, daughter of Richard Harding of Slowland. As his widow, she was buried from Agmondesham, 17 June 1634. He made his will in Hundrich in the parish of Great Chesham, 18 Apr. 1599 which was proved 2 Aug. 1599.

Children, born and baptized in Chesham:

5. WILLIAM,[3] bp. 25 Mar. 1565; new year's day.
    MARY, bp. 17 Nov. 1566; m. 14 Oct. 1588, William Aldridge, servant to Henry Gouldson, school master of Chesham.
    THOMAS, bp. 3 Aug. 1572; bur. 27 Oct. 1572.

Children by second wife, born and baptized in Chesham:

    DINA, bp. 31 Oct. 1574; bur. 23 Apr. 1576.
6. MATTHEW, bp. 6 Jan. 1576/7.
7. RALPH, bp. 15 Feb. 1578/9; alive 18 Apr. 1599.
8. SAMUEL, bp. 18 Sept. 1581.
    ELIZABETH. bp. 2 Feb. 1583/4; alive 18 Apr. 1599.
    JOHN, bp. 6 Mar. 1585/6; bur. 17 Mar. 1585/6.
9. STEPHEN, bp. 21 May 1587.
    DANIEL, bp. 15 July 1590; bur. 21 Mar. 1594/5.
    MARTHA, bp. 28 Mar. 1593; alive 18 Apr. 1599.
    ANNE, bp. 24 Aug. 1596; alive 18 Apr. 1599.

3

RICHARD[2] CHAASE (Thomas[1]) was baptized in Chesham, 23 Aug. 1542; buried there, 31 Jan. 1610/11. He married in Chesham, 16 May 1564, JOAN BISHOP. She was buried there, as Joan the wife of Richard Chaase, 4 May 1597. Like his father he had a servant, Richard Butcher, in 1581.

Children, born and baptized in Chesham:

10. ROBERT,[3] bp. 2 Sept. 1565.
11. HENRY, bp. 10 Aug. 1567.
    LYDIA, bp. 4 Oct. 1573.
12. EZEKIEL, bp. 23 Apr. 1576.
    DORCAS, bp. 2 Mar. 1577/8.
13. AQUILA, bp. 7 Aug. 1580.
    JASON, bp. 20 Jan. 1582/3; bur. 4 June 1606.
14. THOMAS, bp. 18 July 1585.
    ABIGAIL, bp. 12 Jan. 1588/9.
15. MORDECAI, bp. 30 July 1591; untraced.

4

WILLIAM[2] CHAASE (Thomas[1]) was born as early as 1545. He married in Chesham, 13 Jan. 1572, ISABELL SAM of Agmondesham. In his will dated 18 Apr. 1599, John Chase of Chesham gave "to Henry the sonne of my brother William Chase" ten shillings. No later mention of William and Isabell has been found.

Child, born and baptized in Chesham:

16. HENRY,[3] bp. 6 Sept. 1573.

5

WILLIAM[3] CHAASE (John,[2] Thomas[1]) was baptized in Chesham, 25 Mar. 1565, which was new year's day as time was then reckoned. On 18 Apr. 1599 his father calls him "myne eldest sonne" and gives him ten pounds. The parish register of Chesham does not mention him after his baptism prior to 1636.

He was admitted to King's College, University of Cambridge, 24 Aug. 1583, at the age of 18. He was born at Great Chesham, Bucks, and received the degree B.A. 1587-8; M.A. 1591; M.D. 1601; Fellow, 1586-1603; died in College, 1603. (Alumni Cantabrigienses, I :326). He was living in 1599, as he was mentioned in his father's will of that year.

6

MATTHEW[3] CHAASE (John,[2] Thomas[1]) was baptized in Chesham, 6 Jan. 1576/7. He was residuary legatee and executor of his father's will, 18 Apr. 1599. He married about 1598, ELIZABETH ———, called in Philipot's Visitation of Buckingham made in the year 1634, "daughter of Richard Bold." On 3 Feb. 1626/7, Matthew Chase of Stoke Poges, county of Bucks, gentleman, executor of the will of Richard Bowle, late of Great Chesham, Esq. deceased, entered in Chauncery a complaint against Sir Francis Stanton.

He was living in Chesham in 1634. He died in Stone, county of Kent, and his widow Elizabeth administered upon his estate, 19 Nov. 1638. She made her will in Stone, 24 Jan. 1650/51 which was proved 8 May 1651. Therein she mentions her sons Richard, the

eldest, to have the estate in Chesham, county of Bucks, and her other
sons Matthew, John, "if he return as he has not been heard from for
a number of years," Ralph and William.

Matthew[5] Chase of Chesham had granted to him, about 1634,
"Gules, three crosses patonce argent on a canton or, a lion passant
azure." (Philipot's The Visitation of the County of Buckingham,
1634, p 24).

Children, born and baptized in Chesham except the eldest:

17. RICHARD,[3] b. before 1601.
18. FRANCIS, bp. 20 Sept. 1601.
19. JOHN, bp. 4 Dec. 1603.
     MARIE, bp. 11 Dec. 1605; bur. 17 Feb. 1630/31.
20. MATTHEW, bp. 29 May 1608.
21. THOMAS, bp. 20 Feb. 1610/11.
     BRIDGET, bp. 1 Jan. 1614/15.
22. RALPH, bp. 4 Sept. 1616.
23. WILLIAM, bp. 4 Jan. 1617/18.

7

RALPH[3] CHAASE (John,[2] Thomas[1]) was baptized in Chesham,
15 Feb. 1578/9. He received a legacy from his father 18 Apr. 1599
which he was to come into possession of at the age of 23.

He is the Ralph Chase of Great Marlow, county of Bucks, who
made his will 18 Nov. 1643, which was proved 10 Jan. 1644/5. He
mentions his wife ELIZABETH ———, his son Stephen and Stephen's
son Stephen, John, son of his brother Stephen deceased, and his
daughters Martha and Hannah.

His widow Elizabeth Chase made her will 9 Jan. 1651 which was
proved 4 Mar. 1651. She mentions a gift to the poor of Great Marlow and her nephew Stephen Chase.

Children:

24. STEPHEN.[4]
     MARTHA.
     HANNAH.

8

SAMUEL[3] CHAASE (John,[2] Thomas[1]) was baptized in Chesham,
18 Sept. 1581. He is not mentioned in the parish register prior to
1637. He was to receive ten pounds from his father's estate at the
age of 23. Hence he was alive 18 Apr. 1599. He removed to Dublin, Ireland, and there made his will 23 July 1627 which was proved
16 Jan. 1635/6. He mentions his mother Alice Chase, his sisters
Elizabeth, Martha and Hannah (another form of Anne) and his
brother Stephen Chase to be executor. It is evident from this will
that he had neither a wife nor children.

The registers of ten of the parishes of Dublin have been printed
in full and they do not contain the name of Chase.

9

STEPHEN[3] CHAASE (John,[2] Thomas[1]) was baptized in Chesham,
21 May 1587. He received a legacy of ten pounds by the terms of
his father's will, 18 April 1599, "to come into his possession at 23."
On 23 July 1627, his brother Samuel Chase, then of Dublin, Ireland,

appointed him executor of his estate. On 18 Nov. 1643, his brother Ralph Chase, then of Great Marlow, county of Bucks made a bequest to "John, son of my brother Stephen Chase, deceased."

Apparently he removed to St. Martin-in-the-Field, county of Middlesex where his widow ANNE ————, was granted power to administer, 4 June 1646. His widow made her will in the same parish 12 Oct. 1652 which was proved, 25 June 1653. She styles herself widow of Stephen Chase, apothecary of St. Martin-in-the-Field. She mentions Richard Chase of Chesham, county of Bucks, clerk, and her sons Stephen and John (who had a son James) and her daughters Anne and Mary.

Children:

24a. STEPHEN,[4] alive 12 Oct. 1652.
25. JOHN, mar. and had son James, 1652.
   ANNE, alive 16 Nov. 1654.
   MARY, alive 12 Oct. 1652.

10

ROBERT[3] CHAASE (Richard,[2] Thomas[1]) was baptized in Chesham, 2 Sept. 1565. He was a tanner by trade and lived in Chesham, 1601 to 1604. He married about 1600, JOAN TOKEFIELD, who was the mother of his children baptized in Chesham. The parish register calls him a tanner. His servant William Dell, son of Thomas Dell of Chartridge, was buried in Chesham, 8 July 1601.

Children, born and baptized in Chesham:

26. THOMAS,[4] bp. 12 Nov. 1601; alive 1641.
27. BENAJAH, bp. 29 May 1604; alive 1641.

11

HENRY[3] CHAASE (Richard,[2] Thomas[1]) was baptized in Chesham, 10 Aug. 1567. On 18 Apr. 1618, James Birch of Great Chesham in his will of that day mentions "my cousin Henry Chase" who also appears as a witness to the will. He died in Chesham between 18 Apr. 1618 and 11 Feb. 1618/19. The register of Chesham shows that Mr. Henry Chase was buried there, 10 Dec. 1618. His widow Margaret, administered upon his estate 11 Feb. 1618/19. She made her will in Great Chesham, 27 Mar. 1619 which was proved 22 Apr. 1619. She was buried in Chesham, 6 Apr. 1619.

Margaret Chase, in her will, mentions the estate which came to her from her mother Katherine Givin deceased, and her children, Katharine Chase and Henry Chase, both under 21 years of age. Her kinsman Matthew Chase, named as executor.

Children, born in Chesham:

28. HENRY,[4] alive and under 21, 27 Mar. 1619.
   KATHARINE, alive and under 21, on same day.

12

EZEKIEL[3] CHAASE (Richard,[2] Thomas[1]) was baptized in Chesham, 23 Apr. 1576. He married ELIZABETH ————, before 1619 and was living in Chesham that year. She was a widow and living 6 May 1663.

Child, born and baptized in Chesham:

29. MATTHEW,[4] bp. 7 June 1619.

13

AQUILA[3] CHAASE (Richard,[2] Thomas[1]) son of Richard and Joan (Bishop) Chase, was baptized in Chesham, Co. Bucks., 7 Aug. 1580. It is assumed that he is identical with Aquila Chaste who married in the parish of St. Thomas-the-Apostle, London, 22 June 1606.

The church of St. Thomas-the-Apostle was located on Knight Rider's Street (which later was called Old Fish Street) and on the same street in London was located the church of St. Nicholas, Cole Abbey.

Aquila Chaste married in the parish of St. Thomas-the-Apostle, 22 June 1606, MARTHA JELLIMAN, probably daughter of John and Margerie Jelliman. John Gilliman was buried in that parish, 7 May 1620, and Margerie Jelliman, widow, was buried there, 18 Aug. 1621.

Aquila Chaste lived in the parish from 1606 to 1611 and then he appears as a merchant-tailor and lived in the parish of St. Nicholas, Cole Abbey, 1611 to 1644. Two children were baptized and buried in St. Thomas-the-Apostle and four children were baptized in the parish of St. Nicholas, Cole Abbey. Martha the wife of Aquila Chase was buried in the cloyster of the church of St. Nicholas, Cole Abbey, 15 Aug. 1643, and Aquila Chase, tailor, was buried in the same parish, 9 Feb. 1643/4. The parish register styles him six times merchant-tailor. An examination of the apprentice books of the Merchant Taylor's Company of London from 1583 to 1669 fails to show that he was apprenticed to any one in London.

Children, born in Knight Rider's Street, London:

ANNE,[4] bp. 26 Feb. 1607/8; bur. 19 July 1609.
MARTHA, bur. 11 Mar. 1610/11; both in St. Thomas-the-Apostle.
SARA, bp. 9 Feb. 1611/12; bur. 2 May 1624.
ELIZABETH, bp. 14 May 1615.
JOANE, bp. 30 Mar. 1623; bur. 17 Aug. 1624.
AQUILA, bp. 9 Apr. 1626; bur. 10 Jan. 1659/60.
The last four in the parish of St. Nicholas, Cole Abbey.

14

THOMAS[3] CHAASE (Richard,[2] Thomas[1]) was baptized in Chesham, 18 July 1585. His wife was MARTHA ———— and they lived in Chesham, 1631 to 1636. As the burials were not published after 1636, it is not known when they died.

Children, born and baptized in Chesham:

THOMAS,[4] bp. 8 Dec. 1631.
WALLIAM, bp. 30 Oct. 1636.

16

HENRY[3] CHAASE (William,[2] Thomas[1]) was baptized in Chesham, 6 Sept. 1573. He married (1) MARIE ———— who was the mother of his children. She was buried in Chesham, 6 Mar. 1611/12. He then lived in Waters in the parish of Chesham. He married (2) in Chesham, 8 Oct. 1612, ALICE BACHILOR, daughter of Thomas Bachilor, baptized in Chesham, 10 Nov. 1572. (Katherine, wife of

Thomas Bachelor of Chesham was buried, 7 June 1573). Their burials are not recorded in Chesham prior to 1660.

Children by first wife, born and baptized in Chesham:

MARY,[4] bp. 1 May 1597.
30. JOHN, bp. 26 Mar. 1600.
MARTHA, bp. 13 June 1604; bur. 22 June 1604.
31. STEPHEN, bp. 7 Sept. 1606.

17

RICHARD[4] CHAASE (Matthew,[3] John,[2] Thomas[1]) was born before 1601. His baptism is not recorded in the parish register of Chesham. According to Philpot's Visitation of 1634, he was the eldest son, then married to MARY ROBERTS of Willsden, county of Middlesex. In 1634 he was living in Chiselhurst, county of Kent. On 24 Jan. 1650/51, his mother made her will in Stone, county of Kent, and called him her eldest son and gave him her estate in Chesham, county of Bucks.

This must be considered evidence that Matthew Chase of Stone and his widow Elizabeth removed from Chesham to Stone in their old age and that their son Richard was alive in 1651.

Richard[4] Chase was admitted a pensioner at Sidney College, University of Cambridge, 7 May 1614; son of Matthew Chase of Chesham, Bucks; received the degree B.A. 1617/8; M.A. 1621; B.D. 1628; ordained deacon at Peterborough, 22 Sept. 1622; ordained priest 23 Sept. 1622; resided at Chislehurst, Kent, till 1641; resided at Stone, Kent, about 1637. Minister of Chesham Bois, Bucks., 1662. Chaplain to his uncle John Bowle, Bishop of Rochester. (Alumni Cantabrigienses, 1:326).

Children:

RICHARD,[5] b. before 1634.
ROBERT, alive 4 Apr. 1666.

18

FRANCIS[4] CHAASE (Matthew,[3] John,[2] Thomas[1]) was baptized in Chesham, 20 Sept. 1601. According to the records of the Merchant Taylor's Company of London, "Francis Chase, son of Matthew Chase of Chesham Magna, county of Bucks, gentleman," was apprenticed 8 Dec. 1617, for nine years to Thomas Browne, merchant adventurer, to Spain and Barbary. Francis was then 16 years of age.

19

JOHN[4] CHAASE (Matthew,[3] John,[2] Thomas[1]) born and baptized at Chesham, 4 Dec. 1603; admitted a sizar at Sidney College, University of Cambridge, 5 July 1621, at age of 16; son of Matthew Chase, gentleman; born at Chesham, Bucks; received the degree B.A. 1624/5; M.A. 1628. He was a brother of Thomas (1628) and of Richard (1614). (Alumni Cantabrigienses, 1:326).

20

MATTHEW[4] CHAASE (Matthew,[3] John,[2] Thomas[1]) was born in Chesham, 29 May 1608; died in Stone, county of Kent, between 4 Apr. and 30 Apr. 1666. He made his will 4 Apr. 1666 which was proved 30 Apr. following.   No wife or children mentioned but his brother Richard Chase and Richard's wife and their children Richard and Robert are named.

21

THOMAS[4] CHAASE (Matthew,[3] John,[2] Thomas[1]) born and baptized in Chesham, 20 Feb. 1610/11; admitted a pensioner at Sidney College, University of Cambridge, 3 July 1628, at the age of 16; son of Matthew Chase, Esq.; born at Chesham, Bucks; did not take his degree. (Alumni Cantabrigienses, 1:326).

29

MATTHEW[4] CHASE (Ezekiel,[3] Richard,[2] Thomas[1]) was baptized in Chesham, 6 June 1619; died there between 6 May and 12 Dec. 1663.   He was a tanner by trade and married ALICE ——— who died in 1668.   They lived in Chesham.

Children, alive 6 May 1663:

> MATTHEW,[5] under 21 on 6 May 1663; eldest son 11 Apr. 1668.
> EZEKIEL, under 21 in 1663; alive 1668.
> RICHARD, under 21 in 1663; alive 1668.
> ROBERT, under 21 in 1663; alive 1668.
> ALICE, under 21 in 1663; alive 1668.
> JOHN, youngest in 1663; alive 1668.

THOMAS CHASE, a London merchant, married in the parish of St. Botolph Bishopsgate, London, 28 Apr. 1608, DOROTHY SMITH. He was probably a brother of Jeremy Chase, alderman of Cambridge and of William Chase of St. Peter's by Paul's Wharf, London, who made his will 23 Mar. 1581/2.

Apparently he is the Thomas Chase who made his will 30 Oct. 1631, which was proved in London, 14 Nov. 1631.   In this will he styled himself "citizen and grocer" and mentioned his wife Dorothy and two children without giving their names.   Presumably Edward Chace who styled himself "servant to the Hon. English East India Company in their factory at Bantam in Java Major," 1 Nov. 1638, in his will which was proved in London, 29 Aug. 1639, was his son. In his will Edward Chace refers to his mother Mrs. Dorothy Chase, widow, living in St. Mary Axe Street, London, and his sister Dorothy.   The probate of the will, 29 Aug. 1639, shows that his mother died between the date of execution and probate and that his sister was then married and known as Dorothy Rhoades.

The above-named Thomas Chase is believed to be the Thomas Chase who was part owner of the ship *John and Francis* of London, 140 tons, to which letters of marque were issued 3 Feb. and 3 Mar. 1627, whereof Thomas Witherly was master.

Children, born in London:

> EDWARD, d. unm. in Bantam, Java, between 1 Nov. 1638 and 29 Aug. 1639.
> DOROTHY, m. before 29 Aug. 1639, ——— Rhoades.

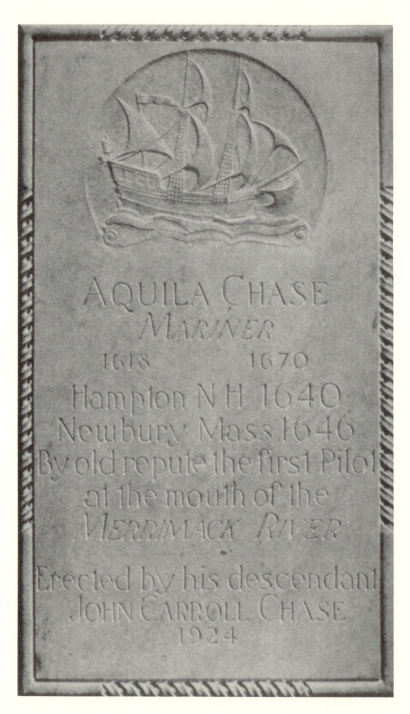

AQUILA CHASE
MARINER
1618   1670
Hampton N H 1640
Newbury Mass 1646
By old repute the first Pilot
at the mouth of the
MERRIMACK RIVER

Erected by his descendant
JOHN CARROLL CHASE
1924

TABLET OF CAEN STONE, THIRTY-TWO INCHES IN HEIGHT
IN THE ENTRANCE CORRIDOR OF THE
NEW ENGLAND HISTORIC GENEALOGICAL SOCIETY'S BUILDING,
9 ASHBURTON PLACE, BOSTON, MASS.

AQUILA CHASE AND HIS DESCENDANTS

AQUILA[1] CHASE appears first at Hampton, N. H. A company under the leadership of Rev. Stephen Bachiler is supposed to have commenced the settlement on 14 Oct. 1638. (Dow's History of Hampton, 10-11). Early in the year 1639 a new band of settlers came with Mr. Timothy Dalton, who became associate pastor of the Hampton church. The town was incorporated by the General Court of the Massachusetts Bay Colony 22 May 1639. It is probable that Aquila and Thomas Chase came with the second company as it appears that emigration was greatly diminished by the year 1640.

Various traditions are extant about the date and manner of their arrival in this country, but they are only traditions with little likelihood of ever being anything else, due to the lack of preservation, or later loss, of the shipping lists of that period.

The first town meeting of Hampton, of which there is a record, was held 31 Oct. 1639, and 24 Dec. of the same year land was allotted to fifteen grantees, the first grants being small house lots. In June 1640 other persons became grantees, among them being Aquila Chase and Thomas Chase.

The Hampton records show that in 1640 there was granted to Aquila Chase six acres for a house lot. In 1644 an additional grant was recorded of six acres of "upland meadow and swamp," which he sold to his "brother Thomas" on his removal to Newbury.*

The home lot of Aquila Chase was a part of what has long been known as the Perkins homestead. Here undoubtedly he erected a log house which he occupied until the summer in 1646. The homestead was located south of Meeting House Green, near the marshes on the road to the ancient Tide Mill.

The town made an agreement with Richard Knight 4 Aug. 1640, that he should build and keep a mill at the Landing about half a mile south of the "Green." It is likely that this was called "The Landing" on account of being the place where the first settlers brought their shallop to shore.

The common lands were granted to the proprietors of house lots

---

*All places mentioned in this genealogy are situated within the present limits of the State of Massachusetts, unless another State or region is indicated in the text, or may be readily inferred from the context.

in Hampton, 23 Feb. 1645/6, Thomas Chase receiving two shares
and his brother Aquila one share. (Dow's History of Hampton, 32-
33). Thomas Chase had at this date a wife and two children while
Aquila had probably only a wife.

He was one of the Hampton petitioners, 7 Mar. 1643/4, for a
modification of the law regulating military drill which had been in
force for three years previously. The petition was presented to the
Governor, Deputy Governor, Council and Deputies of the Massachusetts Bay Colony. (N. H. Provincial Papers, 1: 165). It contains the names of twenty-nine of the Hampton settlers but the
name of Thomas Chase does not appear.

In 1646 he was induced to remove to Newbury, as evidenced
by the following extract from the Newbury records of that year.

"Granted to Aquila Chase, Anno 1646, fower acres of land at the
new towne for a house lott and six acres of upland for a planting lott,
where it can be had, and six acres of marsh where it can be had, also
on condition that he doe goe to sea and do service in the towne with a
boate for four years."

The inducement to remove to Newbury would indicate that he
was a mariner or fisherman and Joshua Coffin in his History of
Newbury states that it is a Chase family tradition that Aquila was the
first person to pilot a vessel across the bar at the mouth of the Merrimack river.

Before he removed to Newbury he was seen gathering pease
on the first day of the week and at the Quarterly Court held at Ipswich, 29 Sept. 1646, he and his wife, and David Wheeler, his
brother-in law, all "of Hampton," were presented for gathering pease
on the Sabbath. The witnesses were William Sanborn and William
Fifield, both inhabitants of Hampton. (Records and Files of the
Quarterly Courts of Essex County, 1: 110). At the next session
of the Court held at Ipswich, 30 Mar. 1646/7, they were presented
again for the same offence and the constable reported that the summons had been sent to Hampton and that the parties were not there
but "were gone to Newbury." (Ibid, 1: 113). On 28 Mar. 1647/48,
they were admonished and their fines were remitted. (Ibid, 139).

The removal must have been soon after the pea-picking episode
as he was not to be found in Hampton when the Court summons
of 29 Sept. 1646, reached there.

The "fower acres of land at the new towne for a house lott' was
in what is now Newburyport, on the northeasterly corner of Chandler's Lane, now Federal Street, and the "way by the Merrimac river,"
now Water Street, as evidenced by the sale of the lot several years
later.

On May eleventh, 1667, Aquila Chase of Newbury acknowledged that he sold unto his *brother* Thomas Chase of Hampton, all
his land in Hampton excepting a dwelling and one acre and a half
of land which had been sold about twenty years before the date of
these presents. (Old Norfolk County Deeds, 2: 122).

This acknowledgment is signed by Aquila Chase and his wife
Ann Chase, and establishes the relationship between Aquila and
Thomas.

A deposition presented at the Quarterly Court held in Ipswich, 25 Sept. 1666, mentions "Accquilla Chas, aged about forty-eight years," which would make 1618 the year of his birth. (Ibid. 3: 347).

He was one of the free-holders and had an interest in all commons belonging to the town of Newbury, 10 Jan. 1653.

He was one of fifty-eight Newbury men who petitioned the General Court of the Massachusetts Bay, 14 May 1654, that the fine imposed upon Lt. Robert Pike of Salisbury be remitted.

Sometime before 1659, or early in that year, he sold his homestead to Robert Rogers of Newbury, who in turn sold it for £40 to William Moody of Newbury, 4 Apr. 1659. (Ipswich Deeds, 2: 206). The western portion of the adjoining lot, at first owned by his brother-in-law, David Wheeler, was sold to Caleb Moody with the house thereon, 16 Jan. 1667. (Currier's Ould Newbury, 1896, p. 149).

Robert Rogers of Newbury and Susanna his wife, for £40 sell to William Moody of the same town:

"all my now dwelling house and all my land lately purchased of Aquilla Chase containing about four acres be it more or less, being bounded with the land of Henry Fay, lately deceased, on the south, the land of William Morse and David Wheeler on the west, the way next Merrimack river on the north and the lane on the east," signed by Robert Rogers and Susanna Rogers, 4 Apr. 1659. Susanna Rogers did consent to the sale of the house and land and did relinquish her thirds, 12 Apr. 1664, before Symon Bradstreet. (Ipswich Deeds, 2: 206).

The foregoing would indicate that Aquila Chase had previously sold to Rogers but there is no deed to that effect on record.

After this sale it can be assumed that he took up his residence on the "six acres of upland for a planting lott," which we are able to locate on the north side of Sawyer's lane, now North Atkinson street, about five hundred feet from its intersection with Low street.

Here he lived until his death, 27 Dec. 1670. The place of his burial is unknown but it was probably in the grave yard at Oldtown as the yard at Sawyer's hill was not in use until some thirty years later.

In 1668 Daniel Merrill bought of John Godfrey eighteen acres with the "housing" near the Great Pine Swamp, which tract was bounded on one side and end by land belonging to Aquila Chase. The Great Pine Swamp lies a few rods west of Low street, and is a positive and permanent identification of location. Daniel Merrill's will, dated 1717, gives his homestead in Newbury to his oldest son, Daniel, who married Esther Chase, daughter of Aquila,[2] Jr.

Daniel, Jr., died about 1725, and the division of the estate is recorded in the probate records. His son Peter had half of the house and probably bought the other half, and lived there. His will was proved in 1778, and gave to his son Jacob all of his real estate. The house stood at the intersection of North Atkinson and Low streets, and was known until its demolition as the Jacob Merrill house.

The will of Aquila[1] Chase, dated 10 Dec. 1670, gives the homestead to his oldest son, Aquila,[2] who made a will (now in the possession of one of his descendants), but died before signing it, and the estate was divided by the heirs in 1723. Daniel Merrill and wife Esther had ten acres of the northwest end, which was bounded by their homestead, and Joseph, the only surviving son, who had settled in what is now West Newbury, had the other seven, which he sold to Daniel Merrill, the deed describing it as "bounding on Sawyer's Lane."

Enoch P.[6] Chase born in 1789, lived in the "Lane" and remembered the Merrill houses, which he located for Mr. Benjamin[7] Chase of Auburn, N. H., who many years later, showed the cellar of the Daniel Merrill house to his son, Benjamin,[8] who, in turn, identified the spot to the writer, John Carroll[9] Chase, and a slight depression may still be seen which marks the place where Aquila[1] Chase lived and died.

AQUILA CHASE'S WILL

"Witness by these presents that I, Aquilla Chase of Newbury in the Countye of Essex in New England being but weake in body, yett of sound and perfect memory, for divers causes and considderrations me therunto moveing, doe make this my last will and testament, And doe dispose of my lands, goods, and chattells, as followeth: First I bequeath my soule into the hands of my blessed Saviour & redeemer Jesus Christ in an asured hope of a resurrection, and my body be buryed when it shall please the Lord to call me hence.

To my well beloved wife Ann I give and bequeath, my house barne and orchard and all my lands both Eareable pasture and marsh meadow ground, lyeing and being in yᵉ bounds of the Towne of Newbury aforesayd together with all my goods and chattels, both within dores and without.

All the sayde house and land before mentioned I give unto Ann my well beloved wife dureing the time of her widdowhood, paying unto my daughter Ann Chase five pounds, in corne or neate cattle, and five pounds more to pay, unto my daughter Prissilla Chase, to be payd within twelve months, after the day of their marriages.

Also I will that my wife give unto my sonn Thomas Chase at the age of one and twenty Tenn pounds in corne or neate cattle, provided the sayd Thomas doe abyde and serve with his mother to the sd age, And if his mother and hee the sd Thomas see cause, that hee should serve for a trade with any other man soe that hee have ye benifitt of a trade, then his mother my well beloved wife, is to pay unto the sayd Thomas but six pounds in the like pay before mentioned, for the rest of my children my will and testament is, that Ann my wife shall give unto them all shee sees good acording to her abillitye, And at the end of her naturall life, I give and bequeath all my house, housing & lands before mentioned unto Aquilla Chase my Eldest sonn, or if Ann my wife marry, my sonne is to possess all my houseing and lands, paying unto his mother three pounds per annum as long as she liveth or three score pounds which shee pleaseth, Furthermore my will is, that Aquilla my sonn shall pay to his brother John Chase the Summ of tenn pounds in corne or neate cattle

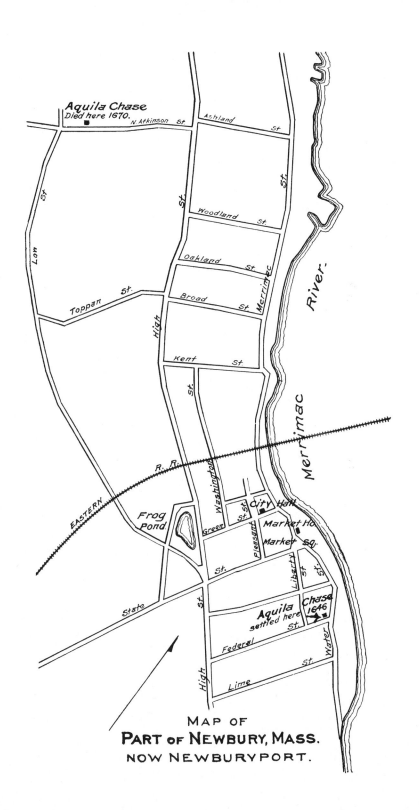

MAP OF
PART of NEWBURY, MASS.
NOW NEWBURYPORT.

And tenn pounds more the sd Aquilla, is to pay unto his Brother Daniell in ye like pay viz. corne, or neate cattle.

Furthermore my will is y^t my sonne-in-law Charles [Annis] shall have my boate loade of grass or sedge of the lower end of Penny Island as long as he liveth, and nobody to molest him till he hath a boateloade, Furthermore my will is that my sonn, Aquilla pay unto his Brother Moses Chase Tenn pounds in corne & cattle.

Also my will is that Aquilla pay unto my daughter Sarah three pounds within two years after her mothers decease and to pay unto my daughter Mary Twenty shillings.

And further my will is that Aquilla my sonne pay unto his sister Elizabeth Chase foure pounds in the like pay.

Also my will is, that Aquilla pay foure pounds in the like paye to his sister Ruth.

All of which summs are to be payd in two yeares after the decease of Ann my well beloved wife. And I doe apoynt Ann my well beloved wife, to be sole executrix of this my last will and testament, & further & doe appoynt Ensigne Stephen Greenleafe and William Chandler to be the overseers of this my last will & testament. Further my will is that Aquilla my sonne shall pay to his Brother Thomas Chase before mentioned the sum of tenn pounds in the like pay with the rest of my children and if any of my younger children be not of age within two years after the decease of my wife, then they are to stay for their portiond till they be of age.

In witness whereof I have heerunto sett my hand and seals this 10th day of December in ye yeare of our Lord 1670.

Witness: The mark of
William Chandler   Aquilla (A.) Chase (Seal)
Steven Greenlefe
    The mark of
James (I. O.) Ordway.

William Chandler & Ens. Stephen Greenleaf testified upon oath in Court held at Ipswich the 28 of March 1671 that this is the last will and testament of Aquilla Chase & that he was of a disposing mind as
Attest.
Robert Lord cleric
(Ipswich County Court, 1666-1682, p. 134-5).

The foregoing is an exact copy of the will as it appears on the record book in the Salem Registry. The original will is not to be found but there are reputed copies varying somewhat from the above, as regards spelling and the use of superior letters. It is possible that they were copied from the original will instead of the record book.

Inventory of the estate of Aquilla Chase of Nubury lately deceased as it was apprissed by those whose names are under written
January the 21st 1670 [1670/71].
Aquilla Chase deceased December the 21st 1670.*

Imp°: House, barne & orchard with twenty foure
acres of Land adjoyning to it	-	-	-	£100:	0:	0
Twenty acres of marsh meadow ground or ther about	60:	0:	0
One horse & one mare	-	-	-	-	12:
Two oven and two steeres	-	-	-	-	18:
Four cowes	-	-	-	-	-	-	-	16:

*27 Dec. is the date given in the published vital records of Newbury. The date given above is from the original probate record of the inventory.

Eleven swine - - - - - -	7:		
Twenty sheepe - - - - - -	13:		
Two heifers & three two yeare old beasts -	12:		
One steere & three calves - - - -	6:		
One feather bed with boulster & pillows, Rugg, blankett & curtaines - - - - -	8:		
Two remnants of cotton cloth - - -	1:	16:	
A remnant of searg - - - - -	0:	16:	3
Wearing apparrell - - - - -	4:	10	
Two shirts - - - - - - -	0:	16	
A peice of new cotton - - - - -	0:	18	
A table cloth, two pillo cases, 4 napkins - -	1:	4:	
A piece of home made cloth - - - -	1:	4	
One new curtaine - - - - -	0:	12	
Six paire of sheetes - - - - -	3:	0	
Linen yarne - - - - - - -	1:	7:	6
20 lb. of woollen yarne - - - -	2:	10:	
One bed & blankett & furniture to it - -	4:	10:	
70 bushells of Indian corne - - - -	10:	10:	
6 bushells of Barley - - - - -	1:	4	
Wheate, Rye & pease - - - - -	1:	16	
Old bacon 10s., a saw 10s., a pillion 10s. -	1:	10	
Two wheels 8s. a muskett & swort, & rest and pike - - - - - - - -	1:	11	
A saddle & bridle - - - - - -	0:	14	
Three Iron potts, hookes & tramells - -	2:	12	
Spitt, fire pann, tonges, peele, fryeing pann, greediron & two skilletts - - - -	1:	2	
Carpenters tooles - - - - -	1:	14	
4 axes 14s. 6d, beetle & wedges 5s. 6d -	1:	0	
Pewter platters, bason, pott & spoones - -	1:	12:	6
A box Iron & heaters 4s, earthenware 2s 6d -		6:	6
Bookes 8s. two chests & a box 9s. bagg 5s -	1:	2:	0
Meale 9s, Meate £12, garden stuff 10s - -	12:	19:	
Hogg lard 12s. butter 10s. Iron geare & grinding stone £1: 2: 6 - - - - -	4:	4:	6
The cart, dung pott & plow - - - -	2:		
Yoakes & chaines - - - - - -	0:	16	
Old Lumber - - - - - -	1:	0	
A hay boate - - - - - - -	15:	0	
	£336:	14:	3

Edmund Woodman & John Bayley.

(Ipswich Quarterly Court, 5: 135).

Children, born in Newbury, except the eldest:

SARAH,[2] b. in Hampton, N. H., about 1645; m. 15 May 1666, Charles Annis, alias Curmac Annis, of Newbury.

ANNE, b. 6 July 1647; m. 27 Apr. 1671, Thomas Barber of Newbury.

PRISCILLA, b. 14 Mar. 1648/9; m. 10 Feb. 1670/1, Abel Merrill of Newbury.

MARY, b. 3 Feb. 1650/51; m. 9 Mar. 1669/70, John Stevens of Newbury and Haverhill.

2. AQUILA, b. 26 Sept. 1652.
3. THOMAS, b. 25 July 1654.
4. JOHN, b. 2 Nov. 1655.

ELIZABETH, b. 13 Sept. 1657; m. (1) 27 June 1678, Zachariah
    Ayer; m. (2) Daniel Favor; living in Newbury, 1696.
RUTH, b. 18 Mar. 1659/60; d. 30 May 1676, aged 16.
5. DANIEL, b. 15 Nov. or 9 Dec. 1661.
6. MOSES, b. 24 Dec. 1663.

SECOND GENERATION

2

SERGT. AQUILA[2] CHASE (Aquila[1]) was born in Newbury (now
Newburyport), 26 Sept. 1652; died there 29 July 1720, in the 68th
year of his age. He married about 1673, ESTHER BOND, daughter of
John and Esther (Blakeley) Bond of Newbury, Rowley and Haverhill. She was born in Newbury, 25 Sept. 1655 and survived her
husband.

He was a husbandman and inherited his father's homestead on
North Atkinson street in what is now Newburyport. He was chosen
a fence viewer at the upper end of Newbury 18 Mar. 1683/4. (Currier's History of Newbury, 1902, p. 116). Aquila Chase, aged 26,
was among those who took the oath of allegiance at Newbury 1678.
(Ibid. 181).

His inventory for taxation in Aug. 1688 included one head, one
house, ten acres of plow land, ten acres of pasture, one horse, two
oxen, four cows, one two-year-old, one year-old, fifteen sheep and
two hogs. (Ibid. 206). He was a member of the town committee
"to stint as to herbage," 12 Dec. 1702. (Ibid. 214). He agreed with
the town to care for one Evan Morris at ten shillings per week, 21
June 1689. (Ibid. 216). He was one of the soldiers under the command of Capt. Thomas Noyes at a training in 1688. He was sergeant of the company and was one of the men who went to Amesbury. (Ibid. 659, 660). He made a will but neglected to sign it and
his estate was divided by agreement of his heirs, 16 Jan. 1722/3.
Daniel Merrill and his wife Esther had ten acres at the northwest
end, Joseph[3] Chase, the only surviving son, had seven acres and the
buildings which he sold to Daniel Merrill, excepting his mother
Esther Chase's dower, 18 Mar. 1722/3. (Essex Co. Deeds, 49: 87).

Esther Chase widow, and Joseph[3] Chase son of Aquila[2] Chase
of Newbury dec'd, were appointed administrators of the estate of
Aquila[2] Chase of Newbury dec'd, 5 Sept. 1720. Sureties Joseph
Bond and John Rogers. Account rendered Feb. 1721/2 mentions
paid Joseph Chase, £13: 1: 4; to Thomas Chase, constable, £2; to
Mary Freize [Freese], widow, 2/3. etc.

Inventory of Aquila[2] Chase, late of Newbury, who deceased 29 July
1720. Item to one Dwelling house and barn and orchard together with
other lands of the homestead in all about 17 acres £250. Item to about
18 acres of salt marsh and flats upon an Island known by the name
Chase's Island £95. It. about 6 acres of mowing land joying upon Artichoke River £85; total £685.

Heirs Joseph, Anne, Hannah, Esther, Priscilla, Jemima, Rebecca and
Abigail. Joseph[3] Chase, Daniel Merrill,. Peter Ordway, Robert Savory,
Esther Merrill, Jemima Ordway, Rebecca Savory, Esther Chase as guard-

ian for Elizabeth Robinson son and sons-in-law and Daughters of Aquila[2] Chase, late of Newbury dec'd, who dyed intestate have made this a full and final settlement of ye estate of our father (and also of ye estate of our brother Benjamin[3] Chase, late of Newbury dec'd, who died intestate) among ourselves. Joseph[3] Chase to have for himself and for his sisters Ann Foulsham, Priscilla Hills and Hannah Hoit whose rights in the estate were purchased about 15 acres of salt marsh lying in Plumb Island River known by the name Chase his Island which is the whole of the Island except 3 acres on the northeasterly end of sd. Island and 2 acres of pasture land joying to ye Fourth parish so called and about 6 acres of medow lying in a place known by the name Rasons Meadow joying to Artichoake River and 14 acres of pasture lying in Planting Hill pasture so called and 3¾ acres being a part of ye lot of land & the [housing?] Daniel Merrill to have all the homestead both housing and adjoyning being about 17 acres which land lyeth near Sawyer's lane, so called, which is in full of his part in behalf of Esther his wife. Peter Ordway to have ½ of a piece of meadow lying in Birchen meadow about 10 acres & ½ in the whole runn & one half of the pasture land lying in Ordway's pasture so called, about 3¾ acres & all the wood lot in Newbury which doth belong to ye Estate of ye Des[t] which is in full for his part in behalf of Jemima his wife. Robert Savory to have 3 acres of salt marsh & flats on northeasterly end of an Island lying in Plumb Island River known by the name of Chase his Island, ½ of piece of meadow in Birchen Meadow about 5¼ acres & one half of pasture lying in Ord-way's pasture so called about 4 acres in full of his in behalf of Rebecca his wife. Jemima and Elizabeth Robinson to have 10¼ acres of pasture in fourth pasture by their guardians. Confirmed 16 Jan. 1722/23.

Daniel Merrill & his wife Esther have the homestead that is they have 10 acres of the northwesterly end of the homestead only and the remainder of the homestead belong to Joseph[3] Chase. (Essex Probate, 5090).*

Children, born in Newbury (now Newburyport):

ESTHER[3], b. 18 Nov. 1674; m. about 1693, Daniel Merrill of New-
bury. She d. in 1751. Eleven children.
7.   JOSEPH, b. 25 Mar. 1677.
ANNE, b. 4 June 1679; m. 27 Oct. 1703, Abraham Folsom of
Exeter, N. H.
PRISCILLA, b. 15 Oct. 1681; m. int. 26 Feb. 1703/4, Joseph Hills.
She d. in Newbury, 14 July 1750, in her 68th year; bur. in
Walnut Hill Cemetery, W. Newbury.
REBECCA, b. about 1694; m. 5 Dec. 1716, Jonathan Moulton. He d.
26 Jan. 1717. She m. (2) 13 Dec. 1722, Robert Savory of Brad-
ford. She d. 24 Oct. 1763, in her 69th year.
JEMIMA, m. 3 Nov. 1721, Peter Ordway of Newbury.
HANNAH, b. in 1689; m. 22 Dec. 1707, Joseph Hoyt of Newbury
and Stratham, N. H.
ABIGAIL, m. — Oct. 1710, Joseph Robinson of Exeter, N. H.

*In his "Old Families of Salisbury and Amesbury," p. 93, Hoyt says that Widow Esther and son Jonathan were appointed to administer upon the estate of Aquila[2] Chase in Sept. 1720. He then lists Jonathan as one of ten children and says he was living in 1720. An examination of the probate records of Essex County shows that this statement, so far as it mentions Jonathan Chase, is entirely incorrect. Administration was granted to Aquila[2] Chase's widow Esther Chase and to his son Joseph[3] Chase 5 Sept. 1720 and the inventory of the estate was presented to the Judge of Probate by Joseph[3] Chase one of the administrators, 5 Dec. 1720. (Essex Co. Probate, 313: 189, 218). Hence it would appear that Aquila[2] had no son named Jonathan.

BENJAMIN, a weaver, m. 20 May 1718, Sarah Bailey. He d. in
Newbury, in July 1718 and his widow Sarah m. (2) there, 13
June 1720, Richard Carr Jr. of Salisbury. No children.

3

THOMAS[2] CHASE (Aquila[1]) was born in Newbury (now Newburyport) 25 July 1654; died in Newbury, 25 Feb. 1733. He married (1) in Newbury, 22 Nov. 1677, REBECCA FOLLANSBEE, daughter
of Thomas Follansbee Sr. of Portsmouth, N. H. and Newbury and
his first wife Mary ———. She was born about 1660, probably in
England, and died in Newbury, 27 Dec. 1711. He married (2) in
Newbury 2 Aug. 1714, ELIZABETH MOORES, who was, probably, the
widow of Jonathan Moores of Newbury and the daughter of William and Mary Woodhead, born in Chelmsford, 28 Dec. 1674.

Thomas[2] Chase learned the carpenter's trade. He was in the
military service in King Philip's War on 27 Aug. 1675 in Capt. Samuel Appleton's Company and was credited £3: 18s. for his service
10 Dec. 1675. (Bodge's Soldiers in King Philip's War, 154). He
was in the Narraganset campaign and in Jan. 1701/2 petitioned for
a grant of land for his services in 1675 and 1676. (Currier's History
of Newbury, 1902, p. 511). In 1678 at the age of 24 he was one of
the male inhabitants of Newbury to take the oath of allegiance. In
1679 his family was under the inspection of Abraham Merrill, tith-
ingman. (Ibid. 117). In 1688 he paid a tax on one head, one house,
eight acres of plow-land, one acre of meadow, one horse, three cows,
two two-year-olds, one yearling, eight sheep and three hogs. (Ibid.
206).

He settled near Amesbury Ferry about thirty rods north of the
intersection of the Ferry road with the road leading by the old cemetery at Sawyer's hill at Curzon's tide mill on the Artichoke river.
His first purchase was fourteen acres from Nicholas Woodman
"bounded with the country highway to Amesbury Ferry," 2 June
1677. His homestead was in what is now Newburyport. It passed
to his son, Nathan,[3] and then to his sons, Edmund[4] and Jonathan[4]
Chase, who sold it in 1798 to Mr. Jackman and removed to Minot,
Me. The old house was taken down in 1875. The land is now a
part of the present estate of F. S. Moseley.

Thomas Follansbee of Newbury, joiner, for £56, sells his
homestead in Newbury "upon ye plaine" to his son-in-law Thomas[2]
Chase 2 Nov. 1711 and Thomas[2] Chase, house carpenter, "for love"
sells the same property to his son Aquila[3] Chase, 2 Apr. 1713. (Essex
Co. Deeds, 26: 281 and Old Norfolk Co. Deeds, 4: 152).

Thomas Chase of Newbury made his will Aug. 3 1732, which
was proved Feb. 25, 1733. All we find is the will.

WILL OF THOMAS[2] CHASE

In the name of God amen, I Thomas Chase of Newbury in the county
of Essex in his majesties Province of the Massachusetts Bay in New England being sensible of my Frailty and mortality, but as yet of perfect mind
and memory Thanks be to God, do make and ordain this my last will and
testament, First of all I commend my soul to God etc, and as touching

ye worldly Goods wherewith it has pleased God to bless me in this Life, I give demise and dispose of in the following manner and form

1 I give and bequeath unto my loving and well beloved wife Elizabeth Chase ye use and improvement of one third part of my Real Estate during her natural Life, and one third Part of my personal estate forever to be at her dispose except my utensils of husbandry Carpenter's Tools & wearing Apparel & I give my horse to my said wife during her remaining my widow, and at her marriage or Decease, I give my said Horse to my son Nathan Chase.

2 I give to my son Thomas Chase his heirs and assigns forever four acres of my Island of salt meadow at the end next the Gut so called, having paid him his Portion already.

3 I give and bequeath to my son Jonathan Chase ten Pounds in Bills of Credit or in other species equivalent to Bills to be paid by my Executor within one year after my decease and one quarter part of my wearing apparel besides what I have given him already

4 I give and bequeath unto my son James Chase ten Pounds in Bills of Credit or other species equivalent to Bills of Credit (beside what I have already given to him) to be paid by my Executor within two years after my deceese & I give my son one Quarter Part of my wearing apparel

5 I give to my Grandson Edward Chase ten Pounds in Bills of Credit or in other species equivelet to Bills of Credit to be paid by my Executor when my said grandson shall arrive to the age of twenty one years

6 I give and bequeath unto my Daughter Ruth Miller fifteen Pounds In Bills of credit or in other Species equivalent to Bills of Credit to be paid by my Executor within four years after my Deceese

7 I give to my Daughter Mary Horton five Pounds in Bills of Credit or in other species equivalent to Bills of Credit to be paid by my Executor within five years after my Decease

8 I give and bequeath unto my Daughter Rebecca Moulton five Pounds in Bills of Credit or in other species equivalent to Bills of Credit to be paid by my executor within six years after my Decease

9 I give & bequeath unto my Daughter Judith Horton five Pounds in Bills of Credit or other species equivalent to Bills of Credit to be paid by my executor within seven years after my decease

10 I give and bequeath unto my Daughter Lizza Chase thirty Pounds in Bills of Credit or in other species equivalent to Bills of Credit within one year after my deceese to be paid by my Executor and I give to my said Daughter Lizza two thirds of my Household Goods, and one Cow & my great Bible after my wife decease and will is that If my Daughter Lizza depart this Life and leave no child, then what is here in given to her shall be paid to my four Daughters above named in equal shares viz in case my said Daughters depart this Life before she receive her Portion herein given to her and leave no child then her sisters shall receive etc & I give to my daughter Lizza one half of my sheep & what I leave at my desease I give to my wife & daughter Lizza. I give and bequeath unto my Son Nathan Chase and to his heirs and assigns forever all my real estate consisting in Housings and Lands, meadows ect, whatsoever and wheresoever it may be and also all my personal estate not before disposed of in this my will, and I do constitute and appoint my son Nathan Chase to be executor to this my will to receive all my Debts and to pay all my Just Debts, Legacies and funeral Charges and my will is that all my Legacies shall be paid in Newbury; and I do revoke and make void all former wills by me made and ratifie and Confirm this to be my last will

and testament. In witness whereof I set to my Hand & seal this third day of August Anno Domini 1732

his
Thomas   T   Chase
mark

Signed sealed and published & declared by the above named Thomas Chase to be his last will and testament in presence of us

(*Essex Probate* 21:28).

Joshua Coffin
Wm. Goodridge
Nath¹ Coffin

Children by first wife, born in Newbury (now Newburyport):

8.   THOMAS,³ b. 15 Sept. 1680.
9.   JONATHAN, b. 13 Jan. 1682/3.
10.   JAMES, b. 15 Sept. 1685.
11.   AQUILA, b. 15 July 1688.
     RUTH, b. 28 Feb. 1690/1; m. 29 May 1716, Nathaniel Miller of Rehoboth.
     MARY, b. 15 Jan. 1694/5; m. about 1619 John Horton of Rehoboth; she was alive 3 Aug. 1732.
12.   JOSIAH, b. 15 July 1697.
     REBECCA, b. 26 Apr. 1700; m. 14 Dec. 1721, Stephen Moulton.
13.   NATHAN, b. 1702.
     JUDITH, entered her intention of marriage, 20 Oct. 1722, with David Horton of Rehoboth; she was alive 3 Aug. 1732.

Child by second wife, born in Newbury (now Newburyport):

     ELIZABETH, b. 9 July 1715; m. 17 Aug. 1732. Benjamin Rogers of Newbury.

4

JOHN² CHASE (Aquila¹) was born in Newbury (now Newburyport), 2 Nov. 1655; died there 26 Feb. 1739/40, aged 84y. 4m. He married (1) in Newbury, 23 May 1677, ELIZABETH BINGLEY, daughter of William and Elizabeth (Preston) Bingley, born in Salisbury, 24 June 1660; died about 1685. He married (2) in Salisbury, 21 Dec. 1687, LYDIA CHALLIS, daughter of Philip and Mary (Sargent) Challis. She was born in Salisbury, 31 May 1665; living 22 Oct. 1730.

He was a soldier in King Philip's War under Capt. William Turner and was in the "Falls Fight" (at Turner's Falls) 19 May 1676 and was one to help bury the brave commander there as he himself certified. (Bodge's Soldiers in King Philip's War, 251). In Jan. 1701/2 he petitioned for a grant of land for this service. (Currier, History of Newbury, 1902, p. 511). At the age of 23 in 1678, he took the oath of allegiance in Newbury. He was a cooper by trade and in 1688 paid a tax on one head, two horses, and one cow.

He settled at first near the bank of the Merrimack river above the "chain-bridge." On 24 Dec. 1698, he purchased "upland in the upper woods," at the "Training Field" in the west end of the town (now in West Newbury). The house which he is supposed to have erected about 1699 is still standing and is the third east of the present Town House.

John Chase of Newbury made his will 22 Oct. 1730, which was proved 17 Nov. 1739. Inventory taken 24 Nov. 1740 by Sam'l March,

John Carr & Joshua Bayley, mentions an old Bible and personal estate amounting to $65.36. (Essex Probate, 5132).

WILL OF JOHN CHASE

In the name of God Amen The twenty second day of Octob[r] One Thousand seven hundred & thirty and in ye fourth year of ye Reign of our sovereign Lord George ye second King of Great Britain &c I John Chase of Newbury In ye County of Essex and in ye Province of the Massach[tts] Bay In New England Husbandman Being at this Time weak of Body And Calling to Mind my Mortallity and knowing that It is appointed for man once to Die Do make, ordain & constitute this my Last will & testament whilst my understanding & memory Is continued To me, as by Gods Goodness It is at this time (blessed be God for it) and First of all Recommend my soul Into ye hands of God That gave it and my body I Recommend to ye earth to be buried in Decent Christian Buryal at the Descretion of my executor and as Touching such worldly estate as it hath pleased God To bless me with in this Life, I do Demise & Dispose of in ye following order or Form

Imprimis I give and Demise unto Lydia my Dearly beloved wife the one third of all my Real Estate During her Natural Life and all my Moveable Estate of what name or Nature soever to her and her Dispose forever.

Item I give unto my son Philip Chase the sum of five shillings to be paid by my Exec[r] out of my estate after my Decease (the Reason why I give this my son no more Is because he hath Received His Portion already

Item I give unto my son Charles Chase five shillings to be paid to him by my executor out of my estate after my decease. The reason why I give this my son no more is because he hath received his portion already.

Item I give to my son Jacob Chase ye sum of five shillings to be paid to him by my exec[r] out of my estate after my decease (the Reason why I give this my son no more is because he bath Received his Portion already

Item I give unto my son Abraham Chase five shillings to be Paid to him by my exec[r] after my Decease out of my estate The Reason why I give this my son no more is because He bath received his Portion Already

Item I give unto my Daughter Phebee Tucker ye sum of six pounds to be paid to her by my executor out of my estate after my decease (Besides what she hath already had

Item I give unto unto my Daughter Mary Safford ye sum of five Shillings to be paid to her by my exec[r] out of my estate after my Decease (the reason why I give her no more is because she hath had her Portion already

Item I give unto Daughter Lydia five shillings to be paid by my exec[r] after my Decease out of my estate (the Reason why I give her no more is because she hath had her Portion already

Item I give unto my grandson John Chase of Hampton the son of my son John Chase the sum of Twenty shillings, to be paid to him by my exec[r] out of my estate which Twenty shillings is all that I should have given to my said son had he been living*

Item I give unto my Daughter Elizabeth the sum of Twenty shillings to be paid to her by my exec[r] out of my estate Provided she come to Newbury for it

*The phraseology of this will settles beyond question the paternity of the John[3] Chase, grandson of Aquila,[1] who married Abigail[3] Chase, granddaughter of Thomas[1] Chase of Hampton, N. H., notwithstanding the numerous conflicting statements that have been published regarding it.

Item   I give and Bequeath unto my Grandson Jonathan Chase the son of my son Charles Chase the sum of Ten Pounds to be paid to him by my exec[r] out of my estate when he shall come to ye age of twenty & one years.

Item   I give and bequeath unto my son David Chase and to his Heirs & Assigns forever all my estate both Real & personal of what name or nature soever that is not otherwise Disposed of in this my Last will & Testament, especially my House & Barn with all my out housing where I now Dwell with my homestead living where I now Dwell Provided this my son execute this my last will & Testament & pay all my Just Debts & Legacies & funeral expences; and I do Constitute & appoint my son David Chase to be my sole exec[r] of this my Last will & Testament and Do give this my son all ye Debts Due to me and I do hereby revoke & Disallow all other wills executors by me made; Rattifying & Confirming this and this only to be my last will & Testament   John Chase

Signed sealed published pronounced & Declared to be ye last will & Testament of John Chase in presence of us witnesses ye Day & year before mentioned.

Sam'l March
Steph[n] Bayley
Joshua Bayley   (Essex Probate 24:89, 185)

Children by first wife, born in Newbury:

WILLIAM,[3] b. 20 Jan. 1678/9; d. unm. before 22 Oct. 1730.
14.   JOHN, b. about 1680.

Children by second wife, born in Newbury:

15.   PHILIP, b. 23 Sept. 1688.
16.   CHARLES, b. 12 Jan. 1689/90.
17.   JACOB.
18.   ABRAHAM.
      PHEBE, m. 25 Aug. 1726, Nathaniel Tucker; living in 1730.
      MARY, m. 30 July 1728, Joseph Safford of Ipswich; living in 1730.
      LYDIA, m. 5 Nov. 1724, William Blay of Haverhill; alive 1730.
      ELIZABETH, alive 22 Oct. 1730, but not in Newbury.
19.   DAVID, b. 20 Oct. 1710.

5

DANIEL[2] CHASE (Aquila[1]) born in Newbury (now Newbury-port) 15 Nov. or 9 Dec. 1661; died there, 8 Feb. 1707. He married in Newbury, 25 Aug. 1683, MARTHA KIMBALL, daughter of Henry and Mary (Wyatt) Kimball. She was born in Wenham, 18 Aug. 1664. She married (2) int. at Newbury, 9 May 1713, Josiah Heath of Haverhill and died before 27 Dec. 1728.

He was a wheelwright and lived in the part of Newbury (now West Newbury) in the house which stands next east of the present Town House. He was 16 when he took the oath of allegiance at Newbury in 1678. (Currier's Hist. of Newbury, 181). He was a snowshoe man in Capt. Hugh March's Co. about 1705 and was a soldier under command of Capt. Thomas Noyes, training in 1688. (Currier, Hist. 1902, p. 660).

His house was 1240 feet east of the east side of Ferry lane, now Bridge street, in what is now West Newbury. The homestead passed into possession of John Carr who married Elizabeth[3] Chase, daughter of Ens. Moses[2] Chase and was occupied by John Carr, his son Daniel and his son Moses Carr, who sold it in 1811 and removed to Hopkinton, N. H.

Children, born in Newbury:

    MARTHA[3], b. 18 Aug. 1684; m. 3 Aug. 1716, David Lawson of Newbury.

    SARAH, b. 18 July 1686; m. 17 Nov. 1714, Francis Danforth of Arundel, Me. (see Danforth Gen., 371).

    DOROTHY, b. 24 Jan. 1688/9; alive in 1713.

20. ISAAC, b. 19 Jan. 1690/91.

    LYDIA, b. 19 Jan. 1692/3; m. 30 Jan. 1715/16, William Evans.

    MEHITABLE, b. 19 Jan. 1694/5; m. 29 Nov. 1715, Timothy Osgood, of Salisbury.

    JUDITH, b. 19 Feb. 1696/7; m. 21 Jan. 1713/14, John Tuttle, of of Lebanon, Conn.

21. ABNER, b. 15 Oct. 1699.

22. DANIEL, b. 15 Oct. 1702.

23. ENOCH.

6

"ENSIGN" MOSES[2] CHASE (Aquila[1]) born in Newbury (now Newburyport) 24 Dec. 1663; died in Newbury (now West Newbury), 6 Sept. 1743, in his 80th year. He married (1) in Newbury, 10 Nov. 1684, ANNE FOLLANSBEE, daughter of Thomas Follansbee Sr. and his first wife Mary of Portsmouth, N. H. and Newbury. She was born probably in Portsmouth, N. H., in 1668; died in Newbury, 18 Apr. 1708, soon after the birth of her youngest son Benoni,[3] aged 40 years. Her gravestone now standing (1927) in the Plains Cemetery in Newburyport is the oldest that has been found of the family. He married (2) 13 Dec. 1713, SARAH JACOBS, daughter of Thomas and Sarah (Brown) Jacobs, born in Ipswich, 26 Sept. 1674; died in Newbury (now West Newbury), 13 Mar. 1739, in the 63d year of her age. She and her husband were buried in the old Ferry Lane (now Bridge street) cemetery in West Newbury where their tombstones may be seen although several rods apart. In addition to the headstone of Ensign Moses may be seen three others bearing the name of Moses of successive generations.

HERE LIES BURIED	HERE LYES BURIED
THE BODY OF	Y[e] BODY OF ANN
INSIGN MOSES CHASE	CHASE Y[e] WIFE OF
WHO DIED SEP 6th	ENSIGN MOSES CHASE
1743 in Y[e] 80th YEAR	AGED 40 YEARS DIED
OF HIS AGE	APRIL Y[e] 18 1708
	BEING Y[e] LORDS DAY

He was the first Chase to settle, in 1689, in the "Upper Woods" as the territory above the Artichoke river was then called. He acquired a farm of one hundred acres, fronting one hundred and six rods on the "Bradford Road" and extending back to the Merrimack river.

He was styled weaver and ensign and the latter title appears upon his tombstone and that of his first wife. He and his wife were admitted to membership in the Second Church in 1713, and he signed

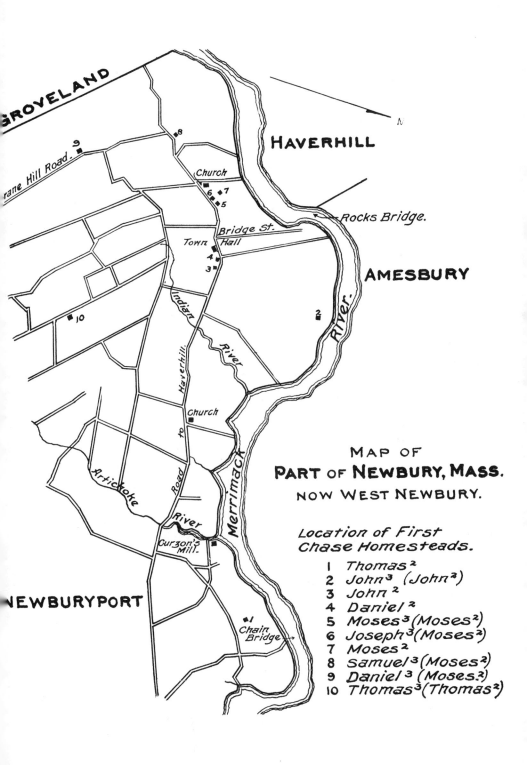

GROVELAND

HAVERHILL

Crane Hill Road. 9

Church

6 7
5

Rocks Bridge.

Bridge St.

Town Hall

AMESBURY

4
3

River.

Indian

River

10

2

Haverhill

to

Church

Road

Artickoke

Curzon's
Mill.

Merrimack

River

MAP OF
PART OF **NEWBURY, MASS.**

NOW WEST NEWBURY.

Location of First
Chase Homesteads.

NEWBURYPORT

Chain
Bridge

1   Thomas²
2   John³ (John²)
3   John²
4   Daniel²
5   Moses³ (Moses²)
6   Joseph³ (Moses²)
7   Moses²
8   Samuel³ (Moses²)
9   Daniel³ (Moses²)
10 Thomas³ (Thomas²)

the covenant and helped form the Fourth Church in 1731. It was "granted to Moses Chase to set in the fore seat by the pulpit" 20 Sept. 1700.

In Aug. 1688, he was taxed on one head, one house, two acres of plow land, one horse, two cows, one two-year-old, one yearling, and seven sheep. (Currier's Newbury, 1902, p. 206). On 13 May 1718, he and several others were granted liberty to use the flats near Holt's rocks on condition that they give one salmon per year to Rev. Christopher Toppan, pastor of the First Church and one to Rev. John Tufts, pastor of the Second Church of Newbury, "if they catch them." (Ibid. 283). He appears on the muster roll of Lt. Caleb Moody in his Company in Her Majesty's service in the woods between Amesbury and "Jamaco" (now Merrimac) in August 1708. (Ibid 536). This service began on 11 Aug. 1708 and he was one of thirty-four soldiers who received powder and bullets under command of Lt. Moody prior to 17 Aug. 1708. (Ibid. 538). He next appears as Ensign of Capt Hugh March's Company of snow-shoe men. This company belonged to the North Regiment in Essex County and was in the service between 1704 and 1710. (Ibid. 540-543).

There are many deeds of land which he bought and sold in Essex County; also deeds recorded in Suffolk County of lands which he bought and sold in Sutton before Worcester County was organized.

The house which he erected stood about 25 rods back from the Haverhill road in the rear of the house which his son Joseph built in 1755 (which house with several additions is still standing in 1927). Here he dwelt from 1689 until his death in 1743.

He made his will 3 July 1740, which was probated 19 Sept. 1743.

WILL OF ENS. MOSES[2] CHASE

In the name of God Amen I Moses Chase of Newbury in the county of Essex in the Province of the Massachusetts Bay in New England being sensible of my own mortality and that it is necessary for me to settle my estate for the Peace of my Children and being at present through the goodness of god to me of good memory & disposing mind Do make & establish these presents to be my last will & Testament First committing my soul to God who gave it & my body to the earth whence its original was taken, by a decent burial with a good hope thro the merits of Christ of having a happy & a glorious resurrection And as to the good things of this world which it hath pleased God of his great goodness to make me the owner of I dispose of them in the manner following viz.

Imprimis To my son Daniel his Heirs or Assigns I give & Bequeath forty pounds money or in good Bills of Credit to be paid by my executors, one half thereof within one year after my Decease and the other half within two years after my Decease: that is to say my son Moses whom I have hereafter appointed one of my executors, to pay my said son Daniel ten pounds within one year after my Decease & ten pounds more within two years after my Decease so as to make the sum of twenty pounds and my son Joseph whom I have hereafter appointed one of my executors to pay to my said son Daniel the sum of ten pounds within one year after my Decease & ten pounds more within two years after my Decease so as to make the sum of twenty pounds. The other part of my said son Daniel's Portion being secured to him by Deed.

Item To my son Samuel his heirs or Assigns I give & Bequeath twenty shillings as money to be paid in equal proportion by my executors the other part of his Portion being secured to him by Deed which I do hereby ratifie and confirm unto him & his heirs & assigns forever: on the considerations mentioned in the Deed thereof, he my said son Samuel or his heirs or Assigns paying to my son Stephen or his heirs or Assigns twenty pounds money or in good Bills of Credit within one year after my decease.

Item To my son Stephen his Heirs & Assigns I give & Bequeath twenty pounds in good Bills of Credit to be paid equally by my executor within one year after my Decease: and the twenty pounds to be paid him by my son Samuel as above expressed. The other part of his portion being secured to him by Deed.

Item To my son Benoni his Heirs & Assigns, I give & Bequeath five shillings in or as money to be paid equally by my executor. The other part of his Portion given him in Lands at Sutton as by the Deeds thereof will appear

Item To my Daughter Elizabeth her Heirs & Assigns for ever I give and Bequeath all my Land & right in the fourth General Pasture (so called) in Newbury and one half of my Household Goods and fifty pounds money or in good passible Bills of Credit to be paid her, her heirs or assigns, by my son Joseph or by his heirs or assigns, within two years after my decease; besides what I have already given her.

Item To my Daughter Hannah Her Heirs & assigns I give & Bequeath one half of my Houshold Goods and fifty pounds money or in good Bills of Credit to be paid to her or to her Heirs or Assigns by my son Moses or by his Heirs or assigns within two years after my decease: besides what I have already given her

Item To my grandson Seth Chase & to his Heirs & to assigns for ever I give & Bequeath one hundred & thirty acres of land which I purchased of Deacon Passafull Hall in the Township of Sutton as by the Deed thereof will appear which Tract of Land I give to my said grandson Seth as a reward for the faithfull service Done for me in my age

Item To my son Moses & to his Heirs & Assigns for ever I give & Bequeath the one half part of my Land in my Homestead with that I have already confirmed to him thereof by Deed on the easterly side of said Homestead with the Buildings thereof said half part being fifty one rods in breadth at the southerly end next the Country Road & forty two rods broad at the lower end near the River, as it is now staked out and my four acres of land at Richardsons Hill (so called) be it more or less and the half of my meadow or marsh Land and the half of my other Lands and of my Comon Rights in Newbury aforesaid, not herein nor before disposed of which Premises are to be & remain to him & his Heirs and Assigns for ever, upon his due & faithfull performing the trust of an executor herein comitted unto him on his part and the one half of my personal estate not herein disposed of otherwise

Item To my son Joseph & to his Heirs & assigns I give & Bequeath one half part of my Land in my Homestead on the westerly side with what I have already confirmed to him thereof by Deed with ths buildings theron; Said half part being fifty five rods broad at the southerly end next the Country Road, and forty six rods broad at the Lower end near the river, as it is now staked out and the money which I had for my Rate Lott at the Boggs (so called) and the half of my meadow or marsh Land and the one half of my other Lands & of my comon Rights in said Town of Newbury, not herein, nor before dispose of: and the other half of my Personal Estate not herein otherwise disposed of: which Premises are to be & remain to him my said son Joseph & to his Heirs & assigns for ever upon his faithfully performing the Trust of an executor on his part as herein is comitted unto him

And I give all my Apparel at my Decease to all my then surviving sons to be equally divided among them

And I do hereby appoint & make my Son Moses & my son Joseph to be executors to this my last will & Testament: and I do order them to pay all my just Debts & my Funeral expences & to pay the several Legacies according to time & manner as is herein expressed, and to receive whatsoever is or shall be due to me at the time of my Decease. And I do hereby disannull & make utterly void all other Wills by me made or caused to be made and I do hereby establish & confirm these Presents only to be my last will & Testament.

In confirmation where of I have hereunto affixed my hand & seal, on the third Day of July, Anno Domini one thousand seven hundred & forty, and in the fourteenth year of the reign of George the second of England

Signed sealed published and Declared
by Ensign Moses Chase of Newbury afore-   his
said to be his last will & Testament in the   Moses C Chase
presence of us whom he desired to be wit-   mark
nesses there to
William Johnson Jr.
Moses Chase 3d
Phineas Hardy

(Essex Probate 5,133)

Inventory of the estate was taken by Joshua Bayley, Edward Woodman and Timothy Morse. The real estate consisted of 35 acres of land valued at £275; salt marsh £20; buildings £25.

Children, born in Newbury (now West Newbury):

Moses,[3] b. 20 Sept. 1685; d. young.
24. DANIEL (twin), b. 20 Sept. 1685.
25. MOSES, b. 20 Jan. 1687/8.
26. SAMUEL, b. 13 May 1690.
ELIZABETH, b. 25 Sept. 1693; m. 14 Dec. 1708, John Carr. She d. in Newbury, 4 Apr. 1764, in her 71st year.
27. STEPHEN, b. 29 Aug. 1696.
HANNAH, b. 13 Sept. 1699; m. int. — Apr. 1719, Green Whittier.
28. JOSEPH, b. 9 Sept. 1705.
29. BENONI, b. 5 Apr. 1708.

THIRD GENERATION

7

JOSEPH³ CHASE (Aquila²), born in Newbury (now Newbury-port), 25 Mar. 1677; died in Littleton, 1763. He married in New-bury, 8 Nov. 1699, ABIGAIL THURSTON, daughter of Daniel and Anne (Pell) Thurston, born in Newbury, 17 Mar. 1677/78.

He removed from what is now West Newbury to Littleton in 1726. His first child was born in Salisbury, others in Newbury. No administration of his estate appears on Middlesex County records.

Children, born in Newbury, except the eldest born in Salisbury:

  30. NATHAN,⁴ b. 2 Aug. 1700.
  31. GEORGE, b. 17 Feb. 1702.
  32. STEPHEN, b. 26 Oct. 1705.
       ANNE, b. 11 Feb. 1707; m. about 1730, Joseph Webster.
       ABIGAIL, b. 27 Mar. 1709; m. about 1727, Simon Tuttle Jr.
       HANNAH, b. 25 Feb. 1711.
       REBECCA, b. 16 Nov. 1714; m. 6 Mar. 1734/5, Thomas Warren.
  33. BENJAMIN, b. 21 June 1717.
  34. JOSEPH, b. 8 Dec. 1719.

8

DEA. THOMAS³ CHASE (Thomas²), born in Newbury (now Newburyport), 15 Sept. 1680; died in Newbury (now West New-bury), 10 Feb. 1756, in his 76th year; buried in Walnut Hill ceme-tery. He married about 1699, SARAH STEVENS, daughter of Dea. Thomas and Martha (Bartlett) Stevens of Amesbury. She died in Newbury (now West Newbury) 25 Oct. 1760, in her 81st year and was buried in the Walnut Hill cemetery.

He had a deed of 34 acres in "the Upper Woods" from his father 5 June 1700, and settled on lot No. 145, which, with additions, is now owned by his descendants, the Thurlows, proprietors of the widely known Cherry Hill Nurseries.

He and his wife were admitted to the Second Church of New-bury, 16 Sept. 1705, and he was chosen a deacon 21 Jan. 1725/26. The Fourth Parish was organized 5 Sept. 1731 and he was one of the original signers of the covenant. He then became a deacon of the Fourth Parish Church. This was in what is now West Newbury.

In his will dated 10 Dec. 1748, proved 1 Mar. 1756, he mentions his widow, his sons Abel, Roger, Ezekiel and Josiah, his daughter Abigail Emery and his granddaughters Martha and Sarah Bartlett. His son Thomas⁴ was to be executor and residuary legatee. He referred to his carpenter's tools, his weaver's tools and to "his clock which is now in the house, made by David Blasdell of Amesbury."

Children, born in Newbury (now West Newbury):

  35. THOMAS,⁴ b. 20 Nov. 1700.
  36. ABEL, b. 25 Feb. 1701.
  37. ROGER, b. 3 June 1704.
       SARAH, b. 29 Jan. 1706; m. 5 Dec. 1723, Richard Bartlett 4th.

38. EZEKIEL, b. 20 Nov. 1709.
39. JOSIAH, b. 30 Nov. 1713.
     ABIGAIL, b. 26 Apr. 1716; m. 27 Jan. 1731/2, David Emery.
     MARTHA, b. 6 Dec. 1718; m. 21 July 1738, Stephen Gerrish of.
     Canterbury, N. H.

9

ENS. JONATHAN[3] CHASE (Thomas[2]), born in Newbury (now Newburyport), 13 Jan. 1682/3; died in Stratham, N. H., 3 May 1749. He entered his intention of marriage at Newbury, 11 July 1702, with JOANNA PALMER of Bradford (probably daughter of Joseph and Sarah Palmer), born in Bradford, 14 Sept. 1680; died in Stratham, N. H., 17 Mar. 1756.

He settled in what is now West Newbury and on 7 Dec. 1716, sold his homestead of 40 acres to William Johnson Jr., a shipwright, and in the same year purchased of Benjamin Hoag of Stratham, N. H., a dwelling house and lands in Stratham. He and his wife were admitted to the Second Church of Newbury in 1715 and later dismissed to the church at Exeter, N. H. He was a large land owner and was called Ensign in his death record. His estate was valued at £7,261.

Jonathan[3] Chase of Stratham made his will 28 Apr. 1749, which was proved 22 May 1749. He mentions his wife Joanna, his sons William, James, and Thomas, his daughters Joanna Norris, Mercy Robinson wife of Jonathan Robinson, his grandchildren Chase Taylor, Jonathan Taylor, Hannah Mason and Ann Taylor, children of his daughter Anne Taylor deceased, his grandson Jonathan Chase of Stratham son of his late son Jonathan Chase, his grandsons Thomas Chase and Moses Chase, his granddaughters Sarah Thurston and Joanna Chase, his grandson James Chase, son of James Chase. His son-in-law Jonathan Robinson named as executor. (N. H. Colonial Wills, 17: 413).

Children, first six born in Newbury, others in Stratham, N. H.:

     JONATHAN,[4] b. 19 May 1703; d. young.
     ANNE, b. 27 Apr. 1706; m. Nathan Taylor. She d. before 1749; they lived in Stratham, N. H.
40. JONATHAN, b. — Sept. 1707.
41. WILLIAM, b. 24 Jan. 1709.
     JOANNA, b. 24 May 1712.
     MERCY, b. 5 Dec. 1715; m. Jonathan Robinson of Stratham, N. H.
42. JAMES, b. 2 Aug. 1718.
43. THOMAS, b. 26 June 1720.

10

JAMES[3] CHASE (Thomas[2]) born in Newbury (now Newburyport), 15 Sept. 1685; died between 8 June and 23 July 1753. He married (1) about 1706, LYDIA JOHNSON, daughter of John and Lydia (Clement) Johnson, born in Haverhill, 7 Dec. 1684. Her father in his will dated 1 Aug. 1732, refers to his daughter Lydia Chase deceased, and bequeaths to his grandson John Chase. She died in Newbury, 2 Aug. 1707. He married (2) in Newbury, 17 Dec. 1707, MARTHA ROLFE, daughter of Ezra and Abigail (Bond) Rolfe of Haverhill. She was born in Haverhill, 23 Mar. 1687/88, and died before 1739. He married (3) in Newbury, 21 May 1739, ELIZABETH PETERSON, who was alive on 8 June 1753.

He was a husbandman and lived in what is now West Newbury near the Meeting House of 1729. He was admitted to the Second Parish Church, 14 May 1700.

In his will dated 8 June 1753 and proved 23 July 1753, he mentions his wife Elizabeth, his sons Nathaniel, Aquila, Ezra and John (deceased and his only son Johnson), his daughters Rebecca Nichols and Mary Mace. His sons James and Ebenezer were to have the homestead.

Child by first wife, born in Newbury (now West Newbury):

44. JOHN,[4] b. 15 July, 1707.

Children by second wife, born in Newbury (now West Newbury):

45. JAMES, b. 14 Aug. 1709.
46. NATHANIEL, b. 10 May 1711.
     REBECCA, b. 14 Feb. 1712; m. 1 Feb. 1732/33, Joseph Nichols of Amesbury.
     AQUILA, b. 14 Apr. 1714; d. young.
47. AQUILA, b. 10 May 1715.
     MARY, b. 19 July 1717; m. 20 Sept. 1739, Reuben Mace.
48. EZRA, b. 25 May 1720.
49. EBENEZER, b. 15 June 1721.

11

AQUILA[3] CHASE (Thomas[2]), born in Newbury (now Newburyport) 15 July 1688; died in Ipswich, 17 Mar. 1713/14. He entered his intention of marriage at Newbury, 31 May 1712, with MARY SMITH of Ipswich and she was appointed administratrix of his estate, 8 May 1714, with Thomas Smith and John Rogers, both of Ipswich, sureties.

The inventory shows a small old house and about three acres of Land £39: 17s. 6d. Her account on 10 May 1715, charges expenses for "ye child which lived about twelve months" and for funeral expenses, viz. by 8 gallons of wine £1: 16s.; by mourning weeds £2: 9s.; by coffin 10s.; by "graf" (grave) 5s.; by mourning "cllouse" (clothes), £2: 6d.; by "hude" (hood) and "saip" (scarf) £2: 10s.; by "glloufs" (gloves) 19 pars, £1: 18s.

Child, born and baptized in Ipswich:

MARY,[4] bp. 25 Apr. 1714; d. there 10 Mar. 1714/15, aged 1y. 10m.

12

JOSIAH[3] CHASE (Thomas[2]), born in Newbury (now Newburyport), 15 July 1697; died in Boston, before 30 July 1723. He married in Boston, 15 May 1718, SARAH PORTER. She was baptized as an adult and joined the New North Church, 10 May 1719. She married (2) in Boston, 30 July 1723, ROBERT FETHERGILL. Administration granted to Sarah Chase, widow, with Matthew Porter and Robert Fethergill, victuallers, all of Boston, sureties, 30 July 1723. Mr. Chase was a tailor by trade.

Child, born in Boston:

50. EDWARD,[4] b. 27 May 1719.

13

Nathan³ Chase (Thomas²), born in Newbury (now New-buryport) about 1702; died between 4 Aug. 1784 and 3 Jan. 1785. He married (1) in Newbury, 29 Nov. 1723, Judith Sawyer, daughter of John and Mary (Merrill) Sawyer, born in Newbury, 16 Oct. 1701. She died there, 20 Feb. 1740, aged 38. He married (2) in Newbury, 30 Dec. 1740, Joanna (Pike) Cheney, widow of John Cheney and daughter of Joseph and Joanna (Head) Pike, born in Newbury, 9 Nov. 1711. Joanna Head was the widow of Henry Head. He married (3) in Newbury, 22 June 1763, Ruth Davis, who died 19 July 1790.

He was a weaver and lived on the north side of the old Ferry Road about three-fourths of a mile east of Curzon's Tide Mill on the Artichoke River (since 1819 the dividing line between New-buryport and West Newbury) and about the same distance from the Chain Bridge. The farm extended from the Ferry Road to the Merrimack River and is included in the large estate of Frederick S. Moseley.

His sons, Edmund and Jonathan, sold the homestead in 1798 and removed to Minot, Me. The old house was taken down about 1875.

Children by first wife, born in Newbury:

51. Nathan,⁴ b. 28 June 1725.
    Mary, b. 1 Nov. 1727; m. 4 Aug. 1749, William Emery of Con-tocook, N. H.
    Moses, b. 31 Mar. 1729; d. young.
52. John, b. 27 July 1731.
    Judith, b. 1 Apr. 1734; m. 9 June 1768, Enoch Roby of Deer-field, N. H.
53. Josiah, b. Sept. 1735.

Children by second wife, born in Newbury:

54. Moses, b. 21 Sept. 1741.
    Lydia, b. 15 Sept. 1742; m. 31 Mar. 1761, William Johnson Jr.
55. Parker, b. 28 Feb. 1745.
56. Edmund, b. 21 June 1748.
57. Stephen, b. 16 July 1750.
58. Jonathan, b. 5 Dec. 1751.

14

John³ Chase (John²) was born in Newbury, about 1680; died before 1710. He married about 1697, Abigail³ Chase, daughter of James² (Thomas¹) and Elizabeth (Green) Chase of Hampton, N. H. She was born a granddaughter of Thomas¹ Chase, the elder brother of Aquila¹ Chase by his wife Elizabeth (Philbrick) Chase. She was born in Hampton, N. H. 27 Aug. 1681. They resided in Hampton, in what is now Seabrook, N. H.

His sons Jonathan, Elihu and John Chase made an agreement about his estate 29 Nov. 1727, viz., that Elihu was to have the home-stead in Hampton and the lands were to be equally divided among the brothers and their sisters are to be paid by each equally. They refer to the "lands that came to us by our Uncle." (N. H. Probate,

2: 324). Thomas² Chase, son of Thomas¹ Chase, the immigrant,
who died unmarried, was their uncle.

Children, born in Hampton, N. H.:

    JAMES,⁴ b. 28 July 1698; d. young.
59. JONATHAN, b. 21 Oct. 1700.
60. ELISABETH, b. 13 Apr. 1703; m. William Russell.
61. ELIHU, b. 7 Sept. 1705.
62. JOHN, b. 18 Sept. 1708.
    HANNAH, b. 10 May 1711; m. 1 Oct. 1730, Thomas Fuller of
    Hampton, N. H.

15

PHILIP³ CHASE (John²), born in Newbury, 23 Sept. 1688; died
in Sutton, 11 July 1764. He married in Newbury, 17 Apr. 1712,
MARY FOLLANSBEE, daughter of Thomas Jr. and Abigail (Rolfe)
Follansbee, born in Newbury or Salisbury, 4 or 24 Apr. 1695; died
in Sutton, 1 Dec. 1786.

He was a blacksmith and removed from Newbury to Sutton
in 1726. He appears as an innholder in Mendon, 15 Sept. 1731. In
his will dated 3 July 1764 and allowed 5 Nov. 1764, he mentions his
wife Mary, his sons Follansbee Chase and Francis Chase and his
daughters Abigail Kenney, Miriam Stockwell, Anna Putnam, Elizabeth Sibley, Lydia Daniels and Judith Carroll. (Worcester Co. Probate, 11365).

He agreed to sweep the Meeting House and to care for ye doors
and windows to open and shut them the present year in Sutton for
three pounds, 29 Mar. 1744.

Children, born in Sutton except the eldest born in Newbury:

    MARY,⁴ b. 31 Dec. 1712; perhaps m. 20 Jan. 1730, Gideon Post.
    ABIGAIL, b. 5 Oct. 1714; m. (1) 18 May 1732, John Gibbs; m.
    (2) 13 Oct. 1763, Theophilus Kenney.
    MIRIAM, b. 31 Aug. 1716; m. Daniel Stockwell.
    ANNE, b. 28 Sept. 1719; m. (1) Nathaniel Stockwell; m. (2)
    3 Nov. 1743, Jonathan Putnam.
    ELISABETH, b. 3 July 1720; m. 14 Mar. 1738/9, James Sibley.
    LYDIA, b. 12 Aug. 1722; m. (1) 3 Mar. 1741/2, Elisha Putnam;
    m. (2) 6 May 1762, John Daniels of Mendon.
63. FOLLANSBEE, b. 29 Sept. 1724.
64. FRANCIS, b. about 1726.
    JUDITH, b. about 1730; m. 12 Nov. 1761, Joseph Carroll.

16

CHARLES³ CHASE (John²), born in Newbury, 12 Jan. 1689/90;
died there, 7 May 1775, aged 85y. 3m. 14d. He married in Newbury, 15 July 1714, HEPZIBAH CARR, daughter of James and Mary
(Sears) Carr of Newbury and Salisbury. She was born in Newbury, 24 Apr. 1692 and died there, 6 July 1765.

He lived in what is now West Newbury near the Rock's Bridge.
He was a constable in 1736. His house stood on the bank of the
Merrimack near Coffin's Lane in 1729.

In his will dated 7 May 1773, proved 29 May 1775, he mentions his daughters Mercy Pressy, Judith Edgerly; his son Jonathan was to have the homestead; his grandchildren Joseph Huse, Carr Huse, Samuel Huse, and Molly Huse, children of his daughter Molly Huse dec'd; his grandchildren Betty Carr, Sarah Carr, and Anna Carr, children of his daughter Betty Carr dec'd; his daughter Hepzibah Saunders; and his grandchildren Carr Chase, Enoch Chase, Samuel Chase, Anna Chase and Joseph Chase. (Essex Probate, 5099). The last named grandchildren were the children of his son Paul Chase who was killed in the French and Indian War.

Children, born in Newbury (now West Newbury):

MERCY,[4] b. 16 Oct. 1715; m. 16 Aug. 1733, John Pressey Jr. of Amesbury.

JUDITH, b. 30 Sept. 1717; m. (1) 19 Feb. 1735/6, William Currier Jr. of Amesbury; m. (2) —— Edgerly.

MOLLY, b. 29 June 1719; m. — Oct. 1737, Joseph Huse. She d. 10 July 1749.

65. PAUL, b. 27 Mar. 1721.

66. JONATHAN, b. 18 Aug. 1723.

ANNE, b. 15 Apr. 1725; d. 10 July 1750.

BETTY, b. 4 Apr. 1727; m. 19 July 1757, Daniel Carr.

CARR, b. 12 Aug. 1729; d. 2 Feb. 1735.

HEPSIBAH, b. 6 Apr. 1731: m. 1 May 1755, Thomas Saunders of Amesbury and Deer Isle, Me. Six children.

CHARLES, b. 28 Feb. 1732; d. 5 Feb. 1735.

17

JACOB[3] CHASE (John[2]), born in Newbury, between 1690 and 1695; died in Haverhill, 11 Sept. 1754. He married in Newbury, 24 Aug. 1716, JOANNA DAVIS of Haverhill, daughter of James Jr. and Sarah (Wiggin) Davis, born in Haverhill, 5 Sept. 1697. The place and date of her death are not known.

He was a cooper and removed from Newbury to Haverhill about 1718. He was taxed in the eastern part of Haverhill, 10 Dec. 1741 and was living in the First Parish there 25 May 1743. He lived later near the Baptist Church in the Rocks Village.

Ezra Chase of Haverhill, gentleman, Ebenezer Chase of the same place, Daniel Noyes of Newbury and Anne his wife, and John Chase of New Hampshire quit claimed unto Enoch Chase of Haverhill, all rights in Haverhill upon which said Enoch Chase's house stands, 11 Oct. 1754. Acknowledged at Plaistow, N. H., 26 Oct. 1754, by Ezra Chase, Ebenezer Chase, John Chase, Daniel Noyes and Anna Noyes. Johannah Chase, widow of Jacob Chase of Haverhill, dec'd acknowledged same at Plaistow, 21 Dec. 1754. (Essex Co. Deeds, 132: 98).

Children, born in Haverhill except the eldest born in Newbury:

67. EZRA,[4] b. 9 July 1717.

68. JOHN, b. 5 Nov. 1719.

PHEBE, b. 17 Nov. 1721.

SARAH, b. 27 Nov. 1722; d. 27 Nov. 1736, a 14, in Haverhill.

ANN, b. 18 Dec. 1724; m. 3 Oct. 1745, Daniel Noyes of Newbury.

69. ENOCH, b. 18 Feb. 1726/7.

70. EBENEZER, b. 27 Mar. 1729.

18

ABRAHAM[3] CHASE (John[2]), born in Newbury, about 1694; died in Plaistow, N. H., shortly before 28 Nov. 1770. He married (1) in Newbury, 16 Nov. 1716, RUTH MORSE, daughter of Benjamin Jr. and Susannah (Merrill) Morse, born in Haverhill, 25 Sept. 1694; died before 1733. He married (2) ABIGAIL ———. He married (3) in Amesbury, 26 Nov. 1746, ELIZABETH (DAVIS) COLBY, the mother of his three youngest children, widow of Elijah Colby and daughter of Joseph and Jemima (Eastman) Davis, born 23 Sept. 1711.

He was living in what is now West Newbury in 1729 near Morse's Lane. He was one of the inhabitants of Haverhill whose estates fell on the north side of the province line in New Hampshire, in 1741. (Chase's History of Haverhill, 311). Apparently he then lived in the First Parish of Haverhill. Plaistow, originally a part of Haverhill, was set off as a separate parish 28 Feb. 1749. His eight eldest children were born in Newbury and his three youngest in Plaistow, N. H.

He made his will 9 Dec. 1761, which was proved 28 Nov. 1770. In it he mentions his grandchildren Ruth Eastman and William Eastman, children of Ruth and William Eastman, and his daughters Ruth Chase and Prudence, and makes his sons Abraham and Ezra Chase executors. Some of his children were baptized in the Second Church of Newbury.

Children by first wife, born in Newbury:

> SUSANNA,[4] b. 1 Sept. 1717; m. in Haverhill 30 Sept. 1735 to Zachariah Johnson.
> RUTH, b. 28 Jan. 1718/9; m. 14 Dec. 1738, William Eastman.
> LYDIA, b. 29 Sept. 1720; m. Jonathan Bartlett.
> PHEBE, bp. 23 Sept. 1722; m. 27 Aug. 1741, Sylvanus Noyes.

71.   EZRA, b. about 1725; co-executor of his father's will, 9 Dec. 1761.
> PRUDENCE, m. Moses Stevens.
> ELIZABETH, m. Jonathan Bartlett.

Child probably by second wife, born in Newbury:

> MARY, b. 21 Oct. 1734; not mentioned in her father's will; probably d. young.

Children by third wife, born in Plaistow, N. H.:

> RUTH, b. 4 Sept. 1748. (Her father calls her Ruth Chase in his will).

72.   ABRAHAM, b. 8 July 1750.
> PARKER, b. 16 Feb. 1754; d. young.

19

DAVID[3] CHASE (John[2]), born in Newbury, 10 Oct. 1710; died there 17 Dec. 1802, aged 92y. 1m. 23d. He married in Newbury, 24 Nov. 1729, SARAH EMERY, daughter of John and Hannah (Morse) Emery, born in Newbury, 5 Dec. 1711; died in Newbury (now West Newbury), 17 Feb. 1783, aged 71y. 3m. Her grave stone in Bridge Street cemetery states that she died 17 Feb. 1782.

Administration on his estate was granted to his son David, the younger, 4 Jan. 1803. He was granted liberty to build a wharf at his own cost at Swett's Ferry, 9 Mar. 1755.

Children, born in Newbury (now West Newbury):

73. DAVID JR.,[4] b. 1 Dec. 1730.
    JOSHUA, b. 21 Oct. 1733; d. 31 May 1752, unm., drowned in Bay of Fundy.
74. ANTHONY, b. 6 Dec. 1735.
75. TRISTRAM, b. 23 Jan. 1737/8.
    SARAH, bp. 1 Apr. 1739; m. 5 Oct. 1768, Moses Brickett.
    LYDIA, bp. 25 Oct. 1741; m. int. 20 Feb. 1771, Dr. William Batchelder of Haverhill.
    HANNAH (twin), bp. 25 Oct. 1741; d. 10 Nov. 1741, a. 2 wks.
    ELIZABETH, bp. 10 Oct. 1742; m. (1) Josiah Burnham.
76. SIMEON, bp. 14 Apr. 1745.
77. EMERY, bp. 7 July 1747.
78. NICHOLAS, b. about 1750.
    MEHITABLE, m. 26 Apr. 1798, Moses Bailey of Dracut.
78a. JOSHUA, b. about 1754.
    HANNAH, m. Zebadiah Austin of Jay, Me., alive 10 June 1805.

20

ISAAC[3] CHASE (Daniel[2]), born in Newbury, 19 Jan. 1690/91; died in Sutton, 27 Feb. 1786. He married (1) in Newbury, 29 Oct. 1710, HANNAH BERRY,* who died in Sutton, 6 or 8 May 1771, aged about 83. "She lived with her husband above 60 years, and hath left of her posterity above 90 children, grandchildren and great grandchildren, of the last about 25." He married (2) in Mendon, 3 Nov. 1772, HANNAH TENNEY of Upton, probably the widow of Moses Tenney of Mendon. Her maiden name was Hannah Whitney of Uxbridge. She was alive 4 Apr. 1787.

He was a wheelwright and husbandman. He removed from Newbury to Sutton about 1722 and lived in that part of the old town which is now Grafton, near the village of Saundersville, a portion of Sutton that was set off to Grafton in 1842.

Children, recorded as born in Sutton:

79. AMBROSE,[4] b. 2 Dec. 1713.
80. DANIEL, b. 5 Mar. 1716.
81. TIMOTHY, b. 12 Jan. 1719.
82. HENRY, b. 2 Mar. 1722.
    ABIGAIL, b. 6 Mar. 1725; m. Daniel Owen.
83. ELISHA, b. about 1728.
    DAUGHTER, m. ———— Tuttle.
    HANNAH, m. James or Joshua Knapp.

21

ABNER[3] CHASE (Daniel[2]) born in Newbury 15 Oct. 1699; died in Amesbury between 29 Mar. and 18 Sept. 1780. He married (1) in Haverhill, 24 Nov. 1721, ELIZABETH WHITTIER, daughter of Joseph and Mary (Peasley) Whittier, born in Haverhill, 19 Sept. 1695. She joined her husband in signing a deed 19 Mar. 1742/3.

*The Vital Records of Newbury give his first wife the name of Berry but it has been printed in The Chase Chronicle as Barry. No Barry family appears in the locality but it was not unusual to call Berry *Barry* in colonial times. She was probably a descendant of the Berry family of Portsmouth, N. H.

(Essex Deeds, 90: 111). He married (2) MARY ——— who survived him.

He was a housewright and lived in the eastern part of Haverhill and in Amesbury. He was received into the Second Church of Amesbury (now Merrimac), 3 Mar. 1727/28. His children were there baptized 1728 to 1738. Mary, widow of Abner Chase, died in Amesbury, 27 Jan. 1828, aged 93.

In his will, made 29 Mar. and proved 18 Sept. 1780, he mentions his wife Mary, and his son-in-law Ebenezer Colby; his daughter Molly Colby to have his homestead; his granddaughter Sarah Sargent to have his first wife's furniture; grandson Chase Sargent to have 100 acres in Hopkinton; granddaughter Mary Webber, grandson Ensign Sargent; daughter Elizabeth Chase to have pasture in Amesbury; negro man Peter; Abner Danforth son of Enoch Danforth to have £50; his friend Francis Chase of Newton, N. H., and wife to be executors. (Essex Probate, 5081).

Children by first wife, born in Haverhill:

  84. ABNER,[4] b. 1 Feb. 1722/3; bp. 17 July 1728.
        REUBEN, b. 20 July 1725; d. 20 Aug. 1725.
        MARY, b. 3 July 1726; m. 15 Mar. 1742, Dea. Ebenezer Colby of Amesbury.
        SARAH, b. 11 Sept. 1727; d. 3 Aug. 1736.
        DANIEL, b. 20 July 1729; d. 28 July 1736.
        ENSIGN, b. 11 Oct. 1731; d. 28 July 1736.
        JOSEPH (twin), b. 24 Feb. 1733/4; d. 13 July 1736.
        JOHN (twin), b. 24 Feb. 1733/4; d. 9 July 1736.
        ELISABETH, b. 26 June 1736; m. 2 Feb. 1754, Ellis (Elias) Sargent of Amesbury.
  85. ENSIGN, b. 13 Mar. 1737/8; bp. 30 Apr. 1738.

22

DANIEL[3] CHASE (Daniel[2]), born in Newbury, 15 Oct. 1702; died in Concord, N. H., shortly before 16 Mar. 1775. He married (1) in Newbury, 22 Jan. 1722/3, MARY CARPENTER, who died about 1725. He married (2), int. in Salisbury, 12 Feb. 1725/26, ELIZABETH COLLINS of Salisbury, probably widow of John Collins of Salisbury.

He was a shipwright and lived in Chandler's Lane (now Federal Street in Newburyport) and removed from Newbury to Concord, N. H., in Mar. 1733. The town was then called Rumford and he was one of the proprietors. He and his family were living in Timothy Walker's Garrison in May 1746. He was chosen surveyor of highways in Rumford, 11 Mar. 1733/34 and again 9 Mar. 1735/36. His will was proved 16 Mar. 1775.

Children by first wife, born in Newbury:

        MARY,[4] b. 22 Mar. 1723; probably died young.
  86. JUDAH, b. 22 Nov. 1724.

Children by second wife, eldest born in Newbury, others in Concord, N. H.:

  87. DANIEL, b. 15 Oct. 1728.
        ALICE, b. 6 Mar. 1731.
  88. JONATHAN, b. 1 Mar. 1732/3.
  88a. ISAAC, b. about 1740; m. Abigail Bradley. He was in the French

and Indian War and was captured in 1758; lived in Warner.

89. ABNER, b. 27 May 1743, O. S.
90. JOHN.
EUNICE, m. Thomas Eastman; d. in Hopkinton, N. H.
MOLLY, m. —— Pearson.

23

ENOCH[3] CHASE (Daniel[2]), born in Newbury; married in Salisbury, 25 Jan. 1726/7, JUDITH COLBY of Amesbury, daughter of Thomas and Frances Colby, born in Amesbury, 22 May 1703. On 22 Apr. 1744, he and his wife Judith were dismissed from the First Church of Amesbury to the Second Church of Amesbury (now included in the town of Merrimac).

Children, born in Amesbury:

JUDITH,[4] b. 30 Oct. 1727.
DOLLY, b. 8 Aug. 1729.
91. HUMPHREY, b. 11 July 1732; lived in No. Yarmouth, Me.
92. ENOCH, b. 1 July 1734.
93. THOMAS, b. 30 Oct. 1736.
SARAH, b. 3 July 1738.
FRANCES, b. 7 Mar. 1739/40.
93a. DANIEL, b. 2 June 1741.
MARTHA, b. 15 Mar. 1742; bp. 20 Mar. 1742/3.
94. DAVID, b. 12 June 1744; not recorded with his brothers and sisters.
95. JOHN, b. 18 Apr. 1745.

24

DANIEL[3] CHASE (Ens. Moses[2]), born in Newbury (now West Newbury), 20 Sept. 1685; died in Sutton (now Millbury) 28 Mar. 1769, aged 84. He married in Newbury, 2 Jan. 1706/7, SARAH MARCH, daughter of George and Mary (Folsom) March, born in Newbury, 6 July 1685; died in Sutton, 7 Dec. 1770; buried in the Armory Cemetery, Millbury.

He lived on what is now Ash Street in West Newbury until 13 April 1726 when he sold his farm and removed to Littleton, where his youngest child was born. Later he removed to that part of Sutton which is now Millbury, where he erected a grist mill on the Blackstone River and became known as "Miller" Chase. The West Newbury house is now owned and occupied by Moses Smith. With his wife, he was admitted to the Second Church of Newbury in July 1715, and in 1726 they were dismissed to the church in Littleton.

Children, born in Newbury except the youngest, born in Littleton:

96. SAMUEL,[4] b. 28 Sept. 1707.
97. DANIEL, b. 18 Sept. 1709.
JOSHUA, b. 19 Nov. 1711; d. 4 Nov. 1740, in Harvard, without issue.
ANNA, b. 13 Nov. 1713; lived in Sutton; m. (1) 25 May, 1736, David Lilley, whose estate was adm. 20 Aug. 1740; m. (2) 25 June 1761, Jonathan Putnam.

SARAH, b. 22 Apr. 1716; d. unm. at age of 20.
NEHEMIAH, b. 27 June 1718; d. unm. 1742.
JUDITH, b. 7 Sept. 1720; m. 30 June 1737, Dea. Thomas Hall of Sutton.
98.   CALEB, b. 29 Nov. 1722.
99.   MOODY, b. 23 Sept. 1723.
100.   MOSES, b. 3 Mar. 1726/7.

25

MOSES³ CHASE' (Ens. Moses²), born in Newbury (now West Newbury) 20 Jan. 1687/8; died there, 17 Sept. 1760, in his 73d year. He married in Amesbury, 12 Oct. 1709, ELIZABETH WELLS, daughter of Rev. Thomas and Mary (Perkins) Wells (Mr. Wells was first pastor of the First Church of Amesbury). She was born in Amesbury, 17 Dec. 1688, died in Newbury, 31 May 1755, in her 67th year. They were buried in the Bridge Street Cemetery in what is now West Newbury.

He lived on the east half of the Ensign Moses Chase homestead in what is now West Newbury. He and his wife were admitted to the Second Church of Newbury in 1715. They were dismissed to the Fourth Church of Newbury, 23 Nov. 1731. He made his will, 24 Nov. 1757 which was proved 6 Oct. 1760. Therein he mentions his sons Wells, Seth, Humphrey, Eleazer, Moses, and Daniel and his daughter Elizabeth Bailey.

Children, born in Newbury (now West Newbury):

101.   WELLS,⁴ b. 4 Oct. 1710.
102.   MOSES, b. 1 July 1713.
103.   SETH, b. 21 Nov. 1715.
104.   HUMPHREY, b. 8 Jan. 1717/8.
        ELISABETH, b. 29 Jan. 1719; m. 4 Sept. 1734, Dea. Joshua Bailey, Jr. He d. 29 Sept. 1786, aged 74y. 5m. 13d.
105.   ELEAZER, b. 25 July 1722.
        ANNA, b. 11 Sept. 1724; d. 29 Nov. 1726, in her 3d year.
106.   DANIEL, b. 31 Dec. 1726.
        ANNA, b. 10 Mar. 1729; d. 27 May 1736, of throat distemper.
        REBECCA, b. 21 July 1731; d. 18 May 1736, in her 5th year.
        ABIGAIL, b. 7 Dec. 1734; d. 15 May 1736 of throat distemper.

26

SAMUEL³ CHASE (Ens. Moses²), born in Newbury (now West Newbury) 13 May 1690; killed by falling from a horse, 24 July 1743. He married in Newbury, 8 Dec. 1713, HANNAH EMERY, daughter of John and Mary (Sawyer) Emery. She married (2), int. in Newbury, 30 Oct. 1762, Dea. James Shute of Rowley. Mrs. Hannah Shute, formerly wife of Samuel Chase, died in Newbury, 6 Oct. 1776, aged 81 years.

He built the brick house now owned by Benjamin Burnham, near the Crane Hill road in the upper part of the village of West Newbury. There is a tradition that the bricks were made on his farm and carried by his wife in her apron to the house. He was a housewright and farmer. He and his wife were admitted to the Second Church of Newbury in 1715.

He made his will 18 Feb. 1741/2 which was proved 1 Aug. 1743. He mentions therein his wife Hannah and his sons John, under 21, Amos, Samuel Jr., Benjamin, under 21, and John; his daughters Hannah, Ann, under 18, and Betty, under 18; his grandson Samuel, son of his son Francis. Francis, the eldest son, was named as executor.

Children, born in Newbury (now West Newbury):

107. FRANCIS,[4] b. 18 Aug. 1715.
108. AMOS, b. 9 Jan. 1718/9.
     HANNAH, b. 23 Mar. 1721; m. 14 Dec. 1738, Abraham Parker Jr. of Bradford.
     MARY, b. 15 Aug. 1724; d. young.
     ANNE, b. 3 Oct. 1727; m. 16 Oct. 1745, Amos Pillsbury.
109. SAMUEL, b. 22 Oct. 1728.
     MARY, b. 24 Dec. 1731; perhaps m. 7 Nov. 1757, Joshua Emerson.
     BETTY, b. 9 Oct. 1734; m. 23 Mar. 1758, Stephen Noyes Jr. of West Newbury. She d. 5 Aug. 1813.
110. BENJAMIN, b. 3 Feb. 1736/7.
111. JOHN, b. 25 Mar. 1740.

27

ENS. STEPHEN[3] CHASE (Ens. Moses[2]) born in Newbury (now West Newbury) 29 Aug. 1696; died in Nottingham West (now Hudson), N. H., 14 June 1756. He married in Newbury, 17 Dec. 1717, SARAH HALE, daughter of Henry and Sarah (Kelley) Hale, born in Newbury, 21 Oct. 1698; died in Hudson, N. H., 26 Dec. 1753; both buried in Blodgett Cemetery in Hudson.

He lived on Crane Neck Hill in what is now West Newbury till about 1748. He sold his homestead there to Ezra Pillsbury 6 Jan. 1747, and removed to Nottingham West (now Hudson), N. H.

He married (2) in his old age Thankful ——— who removed after his death in Westford and there gave a quit claim deed to her husband's estate on 2 Sept. 1756. She was living in Westford in Sept. 1772.

Stephen[3] Chase of Nottingham West made his will, 4 June 1755, which was proved 22 June 1756. He mentions therein his wife Thankful, his sons Henry, Moses, Stephen, Samuel and Joshua, his daughters Jemima Thurston and Sarah Cummings and the heirs of his daughter Thomasine Merrill deceased. (N. H. Colonial Wills, 19: 560).

Children, born in Newbury (now West Newbury):

     BRADFORD,[4] b. 17 Aug. 1719; d. 13 Nov. 1721.
     MINA, b. 17 Nov. 1721; m. 5 Jan. 1740/41, Nathaniel Thurston. She d. 19 Apr. 1815.
     THOMASINE, b. 3 Dec. 1723; m. 1 Nov. 1743, Ens. Daniel Merrill Jr.; lived in Nottingham West; d. at birth of fourth child 30 Jan. 1755.
112. HENRY, b. 25 Feb. 1725/6.
113. STEPHEN, b. 24 Aug. 1728.
     SARAH, b. 13 Mar. 1731; m. Dea. Ebenezer Cummings, and d. 12 Nov. 1772.
113a. BRADFORD, b. 27 Nov. 1733.
114. ENOCH, b. 2 Feb. 1735.
115. MOSES, b. 31 May 1738.

116.   JOSHUA, b. 16 May 1740.
       SAMUEL, b. 2 Aug. 1743; deaf and dumb; lived with Stephen,
       and d. 7 Feb. 1835.

28

LT. JOSEPH[3] CHASE (Ens. Moses[2]), born in Newbury (now
West Newbury) 9 Sept. 1705; died there 27 Nov. 1782, aged 79y.
2m. He married in Newbury, 7 Sept. 1724, MARY MORSE, daughter
of Anthony and Sarah (Pike) Morse, born in Newbury, 18 May
1704; died there 18 Mar. 1787; both buried in Ferry Lane Cemetery,
West Newbury.

He lived on the west half of the Ensign Moses Chase homestead
and about 1755 built the house now (1927) owned and occupied by
John D. Murphy. His wife was admitted to the Second Church of
Newbury 27 Nov. 1726 and he 31 Dec. 1729. He was one of the
organizers of the Fourth Church in 1731.

He made his will, 23 May which was proved 11 Dec. 1782. Therein
he mentions his wife Mary, his surviving sons, Jacob; Moody, Caleb and
Joseph Jr., and his daughters Mary, Anna, Sarah, Elizabeth and Hannah.

Children, born in Newbury (now West Newbury):

       MARY.[4] b. 31 May 1726; m. 27 Oct. 1743, Josiah Morse of
       Chester, N. H., son of Capt. Abel Morse; d. in Chester, N. H.,
       18 July 1815.
117.   JACOB, b. 25 Dec. 1727.
       SARAH, b. 19 June 1730; m. 7 Jan. 1752, Stevens Merrill of
       Plaistow and Warren, N. H. She d. 30 Apr. 1794.
118.   JOSEPH, b. 11 Apr. 1732.
       ANNA, b. 17 Jan. 1733/4; m. 9 Nov. 1752, John Bailey. She d.
       15 Jan. 1803. Eight children.
       SUSANNAH, b. 28 Apr. 1736; d. 11 Feb. 1757, without issue;
       m. 15 June 1756, Stephen Noyes Jr.
       ELISABETH, b. 7 May 1738; m. (1) 13 July 1758, Thomas[5]
       Chase (Thomas,[4] Thomas,[3] Thomas,[2] Aquila[1]).
       AMOS, b. 5 July 1740; d. 30 Oct. 1754, of fever.
       HANNAH, b. 18 June 1742; m. (1) 29 Nov. 1764, Dr. Ebenezer
       Noyes of Dover, N. H.; m. (2) William Hills. She d. 21
       Nov. 1799.
119.   MOODY, b. 7 Oct. 1744.
120.   CALEB, b. 28 July 1746.

29

BENONI[3] CHASE (Ens. Moses[2]), born in Newbury (now West
Newbury) 5 Apr. 1708; died 4 July 1788. He married (1) in Newbury, 4 Sept. 1728, MARY ROGERS, daughter of Thomas Jr. and Hannah (Long) Rogers, born in Newbury, 23 June 1708; died 29 Feb.
1788.

He removed from Newbury to Sutton where he lived for many
years near what is now Wilkinsville. He and his wife were dismissed to the church in Douglas in Oct. 1768. On 22 May 1783, he sold
the land in Douglas "where I now dwell" to his son David Chase.
The son soon removed to Whitingham, Vt. and it is not known

where Benoni and his wife Mary died. It is reported that they had thirteen children but only ten are accounted for.

Children, born in Sutton:

121. THOMAS,[4] b. 3 Apr. 1732.
122. ROGERS, b. 20 June 1734.
123. STEPHEN, b. 29 Mar. 1736.
124. MOSES, b. 5 Oct. 1737.
     MARY, b. 5 Sept. 1739; d. 8 Oct. 1745.
125. BENJAMIN, bp. 25 July 1742.
     HANNAH, b. 5 Sept. 1744.
     ELIJAH, b. 18 Feb. 1747/8; d. 1 Dec. 1748.
     MARY, b. 13 Dec. 1749; m. 28 Jan. 1768, Ward Nye of Rochester.
126. DAVID, b. 17 Apr. 1752.

FOURTH GENERATION

30

NATHAN[4] CHASE (Joseph,[3] Aquila[2]), born in Salisbury, 2 Aug. 1700; died in Littleton, 29 Apr. 1781, aged 80y. 8m. He married about 1727, RUTH, perhaps twin daughter of Robert and Alice Peaslee, born in Amesbury, 7 Dec. 1706. She died in Littleton, 12 Mar. 1788 "in the 85th year of her age." (Littleton Town Records, 339).

Robert Peaslee of Haverhill made his will 26 Dec. 1741, bequeathing to his daughters Abigail and Ruth £200 apiece in full of their portion "of what they have already received." The will shows that Abigail had already married a Collins and the inference is that Ruth had married Nathan Chase. Ruth, the widow of Nathan Chase, late of Littleton, renounced administration 17 July 1781 in favor of her daughter Ellen Wright. Ellen Wright was appointed administratrix with Ezekiel Wright and Peter Wright, all of Littleton, sureties. (Middlesex Probate, 4305). They lived in Littleton.

Children, born in Littleton:

RUTH,[5] b. 25 Aug. 1728; d. young.
OLIVER, b. 20 Sept. 1730; d. at 12 yrs. of age.
ELLEN, b. 21 Dec. 1732; m. 1 Apr. 1755, Peter Wright of Littleton. Five children.
EZEKIEL, b. 11 Feb. 1735/6; d. young.
ELIJAH, b. 11 Oct. 1738; d. young.
RUTH, b. 15 Feb. 1740.
OLIVER, b. 23 Aug. 1743; prob. d. young.
EZEKIEL, b. 9 Aug. 174—; prob. d. young.

31

GEORGE[4] CHASE (Joseph,[3] Aquila[2]), born in Newbury, 17 Feb. 1702; died in Shirley, 4 or 5 Apr. 1784. He married (1) ELIZBETH DAYTON who died about 1736. He married (2) in 1737, LUCY WOOD, daughter of Jeremiah and Dorothy (Bennett) Wood, born in Stow, 16 Mar. 1715; buried in Shirley, 14 Mar. 1787.

He early removed to Littleton and about 1760 removed to Shirley where he remained the rest of his life. He lived on the Centre road in Shirley in what is known now as the Adams house. His will mentions his widow Lucy Chase, Abel Chase, Phebe Chase, Lucy Gates and Elisha Gates. The administrator paid Joshua Chase, Abel Chase, Phebe Chase, Fanny Chase and Abigail Chase, Charles Phips, Hannah Phips and Elizabeth Cummings, 1784. (Middlesex Probate, 4,297).

Child by first wife, born in Littleton:

FRANCES[5], b. 15 Oct. 1734.

Children by second wife, born in Littleton:

LUCY, b. 29 July 1739; m. (1) 30 Jan. 1760, Elisha Gates of Stow; m. (2) Thomas Banister.
ABIGAIL, b. 9 Sept. 1741; unm. 1784.
127. JOSHUA, b. 31 Aug. 1743.
ELISABETH, b. 30 Mar. 1745; m. before 1784, ——— Cummings; d. 9 Nov. 1820.
CHARLES, b. 8 Aug. 1747; died in Lunenburg, from the explosion of a lamp while drawing alcohol; bur. 25 July 1770, unm.
SARAH, b. 14 July 1749.
HANNAH, b. 5 Aug. 1751; m. int. 13 Jan. 1774, Charles Phips of Groton.
128. ABEL, b. 13 June 1754.
ABRAHAM, b. 24 June 1756; d. 10 Apr. 1764.
PHEBE, reported to have gone to Chesterfield, N. H.; unm. 1784.

32

REV. STEPHEN[4] CHASE (Joseph,[3] Aquila[2]), born in Newbury, 26 Oct. 1705; died in New Castle, N. H., 1 Jan. 1778, aged 73. He married in Hampton, N. H., 5 Oct. 1732, JANE WINGATE, daughter of Col. Joshua and Mary (Lunt) Wingate. She was born in Hampton, 12 July 1712.

He graduated from Harvard College 1728 and was ordained minister over the Second Church of Lynn (now Lynnfield), 24 Nov. 1731. He resigned in 1748 and removed to New Castle, where he became minister of the church there, 5 Dec. 1750. He was a man of scholastic attainments.

Children, born in Lynn (now Lynnfield):

ABRAHAM,[5] b. 25 Mar. 1734; d. 25 Mar. 1734.
STEPHEN, b. 22 Feb. 1734/5; d. 4 Dec. 1739.
129. JOSHUA, b. 17 Mar. 1738.
JANE, b. 7 Jan. 1740; m. Samuel Wallace.
130. STEPHEN, b. 22 Jan. 1742.
MARY, b. 19 Oct. 1744; d. 15 Sept. 1749.
131. JOHN WINGATE, b. 14 Aug. 1749.

33

DR. BENJAMIN[4] CHASE (Joseph,[3] Aquila[2]), born in Newbury, 21 June 1717; died of smallpox in Kent, Conn., 14 Apr. 1778. He married (1) in Littleton, 17 June 1740, RACHEL HARTWELL, widow of Ebenezer Hartwell of Groton. They were divorced 12 Feb. 1765. He married (2) in Amenia, Dutchess Co., N. Y., 15 May 1766, MARY DAY (or DAYTON) of New Milford, Conn.

He removed to Littleton before 1740 and settled in Groton,

before 8 Feb. 1743, and about 1765 he removed to Kent, Conn. He
was a surgeon in the army of the Revolutionary War.

Children by first wife, born in Groton:

132. BENJAMIN,⁵ b. 1 Oct. 1741.
133. SOLOMON, b. 8 Sept. 1743.
134. EBENEZER, b. 4 June 1745.
      JOHN, b. 4 Sept. 1747; d. 1 Oct. 1749.
135. JOHN, b. 12 Feb. 1749/50.

Children by second wife, born in Kent, Conn.:

      NATHAN, b. 24 Apr. 1767; d. 12 Nov. 1769.
136. STEPHEN, b. 26 Mar. 1769.

34

JOSEPH⁴ CHASE (Joseph,³ Aquila²), born in Newbury, 8 Dec.
1719; died in Groton, 20 Dec. 1779, in his 61st year. He married in
Littleton, 13 Oct. 1743, SARAH WOOD, daughter of Jeremiah and
Dorothy (Bennett) Wood, born in Littleton, 7 Feb. 1724. She was
admitted to the First Church of Groton, 28 Aug. 1774.

He removed from Newbury to Littleton before 1743. The inventory of his estate was returned 14 May 1785.

Administration of his estate, in Groton, 1780. (Middlesex Probate,
4,302). Joseph Chase of Groton, Moses Chase of Lancaster, Dorothy
Cummings of Lancaster, widow, John Daverson of Stow and Molly his
wife, Sarah Chase of Groton, singlewoman, David Bennett of Groton
and Abigail his wife, and Lucy Brown of Groton for £120 sell Thomas
Wood of Littleton land in southerly part of Groton—60 acres—with a
house and barn thereon, 23 Apr. 1785. (Middlesex Deeds, 106: 484).

Children, born in Littleton:

      JOSEPH,⁵ b. 13 Sept. 1744; d. 10 July 1745.
137. BENJAMIN, b. 9 Aug. 1745.
138. SARAH, b. 7 Oct. 1746.
      DOLLY, b. 8 May 1748; m. 7 Sept. 1778, Thomas Cummings of
      Lancaster.
139. JOSEPH, b. 8 Mar. 1750.
      MOLLY, b. 7 Mar. 1752; m. John Daverson of Stow.
      LUCY, b. 19 Feb. 1753; m. 16 Mar. 1775, John Campbell Brown
      of Groton; schoolmaster there 1775; living there 1785.
140. JONATHAN, b. 7 June 1755.
141. JONAS, b. 27 Feb. 1757.
      LYDIA, b. 22 Apr. 1758.
142. MOSES, b. 15 Sept. 1760.
      ABIGAIL, b. 2 Oct. 1762; m. 4 Dec. 1783, David Bennett of
      Groton and Lancaster.
142a. THOMAS, b. as is assumed about 1765.

35

THOMAS⁴ CHASE (Dea. Thomas,³ Thomas²), born in Newbury,
20 Nov. 1700; died in what is now West Newbury, 14 Oct. 1765 in
his 65th year. He married (1) in Newbury, 3 Sept. 1724, MARY
MOOERS who died there 12 Oct. 1725, aged 21. He married (2) in
Newbury, 24 Nov. 1726, EMMA KENT, daughter of John and Rebecca (Somerby) Kent, born in Newbury, 28 Feb. 1700/1701; died
there 24 Mar. 1784 aged 83. All buried in Walnut Hill Cemetery,

West Newbury. He was called Thomas Chase 3d and resided on
the Dea. Thomas[3] Chase homestead in West Newbury.

```
HERE      LIES      BURIED
THE       BODY        OF
MARY      THE        WIFE
OF        MR       THOMAS
CHASE     THE       THURD
DIED     OCTOBER      12
1725   AGED   21   YEARˢ
THE  FIRST  BURIED  HERE.
```

He and his first wife were admitted to the Second Church of
Newbury 28 Aug. 1725, and his second wife 22 Nov. 1727. He and
his wife Emma were dismissed and united with the Fourth Church
in Dec. 1731.

He made his will 7 Oct. which was proved 24 Oct. 1765. He
mentions his wife Emma, his daughters Sarah Morse, and Emma
Carr, his sons Josiah[5] Chase, Thomas[5] Chase, his father Thomas
Chase,[3] deceased, and his son Abel[5] Chase, who continued on the
homestead.

Child by first wife, born in Newbury:

> SARAH,[5] b. 10 June 1725; m. 15 Sept. 1743, Moses Morse Jr. He
> was b. 25 Nov. 1702; d. 24 Mar. 1783.

Children by second wife, born in Newbury:

> MARY, b. 25 June 1728; d. 1 Dec. 1729.
> ABEL, b. 3 July 1730; d. 23 Aug. 1736.
> THOMAS, b. 1 Sept. 1732; d. 21 Aug. 1736.
> SOMERBY, b. 4 Dec. 1734; d. 10 Aug. 1736.

143.   THOMAS, b. 11 Apr. 1737.
144.   ABEL, b. 15 Apr. 1739.
145.   JOSIAH, b. 15 Sept. 1741.

> EMMA, b. 8 May 1744; m. 23 Dec. 1762, Samuel Carr.
> MARY, b. 19 June 1747; m. 24 Oct. 1771, Ebenezer Sibley of
> Sutton.

36

DEA. ABEL[4] CHASE (Dea. Thomas,[3] Thomas[2]), born in Newbury, 25 Feb. 1701/2; died in Sutton, — Jan. 1778. He married (1)
in Newbury, 14 May 1728, SARAH BRICKETT, probably daughter of
James and Mary Brickett, born in Newbury, 2 Apr. 1707. He married (2) in Newbury, 23 Mar. 1730/31, SARAH HOLMAN, daughter
of Solomon and Mary (Barton) Holman, born in Newbury, — Oct.
1707. He married (3) PERSIS KENDALL, perhaps daughter of Jacob
and Alice (Temple) Kendall, born 23 Aug. 1715.

Dea. Chase and his first wife were admitted to the Church of
Sutton 15 Feb. 1730 and he was assigned a seat in the fifth pew in
1731. His second wife was admitted to the same church, 11 Feb.
1731/2. He was chosen deacon of the Second Church of Sutton
(now Millbury) in Nov. 1767. His son Abel and his widow Persis
administered upon his estate, 7 Apr. 1778. He was a cooper by trade.

Children by second wife, born in Sutton (now Millbury):

146.   ABEL,[5] b. 11 Sept. 1732; m. 3 Jan. 1754, Judith Gale.

> SARAH, b. 15 June 1735; d. 7 Aug. 1761.
> EMMA, b. 11 Oct. 1737; d. 10 Sept. 1761.

MARTHA, b. 7 Nov. 1739; m. 11 Sept. 1760, Francis Stone.
MARY, b. 15 Mar. 1742; m. 21 Apr. 1763, Francis Kidder.
BETTY, b. 4 June 1744; m. 6 July 1780, David Bancroft of Ward.
147. THOMAS, b. 13 Mar. 1746.
148. DAVID, b. 28 Sept. 1748.
RUTH, b. 9 Apr. 1751; m. 23 June 1774, Anthony Sigourney.
JONATHAN, b. 25 Aug. 1753; d. 11 Sept. 1761.
149. MOSES, b. 24 Oct. 1755.

37

DEA. ROGER[4] CHASE (Dea. Thomas,[3] Thomas[2]), born in New-bury, 3 June 1704; died in Clinton, Me., between 27 July and 4 Dec. 1782. He married in Newbury, 16 Mar. 1725/26, ABIGAIL MOR-RISON, daughter of Daniel and Mary (Folsom*) Morrison, of Row-ley, born about 1708. She died in Fairfield, Me., about 1807. Her father gave her a deed of land in Nottingham West (now Hudson), N. H., 3 Mar. 1734 and they removed from Newbury to Hudson about 1735 and were assessed there as late as 1761. He owned the Hill's Garrison house on the Merrimack about one-half mile south of Litchfield, N. H. town line. He was a selectman 1755 and 1758. Later he removed to Maine and lived about ten miles above Fort Halifax on the Kennebec River. He first settled in Maine in old Pownalborough before 13 June 1765. He was captured by the In-dians while hunting on the Dead River and carried to Canada, but escaped and returned home.

He made his will, 27 July 1782, which was proved 4 Dec. 1782. He mentions his son-in-law Asa Pratt, "he paying to his children the heirs of my daughter Sarah dec'd, viz. James, David, Sarah and Elizabeth at 21, certain sums; his wife Abigail, his son Matthew, his daughters, Mary Powers, and Tamar Noble, his sons Ezekiel and Matthew and his grand-children Vernum and Abigail Chase..

Children, first three born in Newbury, others in Nottingham West, N. H.:

150. EZEKIEL,[5] b. 24 May 1728.
151. ROGER, b. 30 June 1731.
152. STEPHEN, b. 1 May 1735.
SALLY, b. 14 Mar. 1738; m. (1) Asa Pratt; m. (2) Joseph Spearing. She d. in Clinton, Me.
153. MATTHEW, b. 20 Oct. 1739.
ABIGAIL, b. 1 June 1742; d. unm. at 18 yrs.
POLLY, b. 20 Mar. 1747/8; m. Levi Powers. She d. in Bloom-field, Me.
TAMAR, b. about 1752; m. in Dresden about 1770, John Noble. She d. in Glenburn, Me., 20 Mar. 1844.

38

DR. EZEKIEL[4] CHASE (Dea. Thomas,[3] Thomas[2]), born in New-bury, 20 Nov. 1709; married (1) in Newbury, 20 May 1729, PRIS-CILLA MERRILL, daughter of Dea. Abel and Abigail (Stevens) Mer-rill, born in Newbury, 1 Mar. 1709/10. She died in Nottingham

*Possibly Daniel Morrison had a second wife between 1700 and 1706 who was the mother of Abigail.

West (now Hudson), N. H., "22 Feb. 1768, in the 59th year of her age."

Dr. Chase removed from Newbury to Groton before 1729 and about 1735 removed to Bradford. About 1740 he removed to Nottingham West (now Hudson), where he became the first resident physician.

He was town clerk of Nottingham West in 1748; assessed there 1741 to 1780; selectman 1744 to 1768; moderator of town meetings 1752 to 1776. He married (2) ELIZABETH ———, who was his wife, 9 Aug. 1773. They lived in Nottingham West 1741 to 1780 when it is supposed that they removed from town.

Children, first two born in Groton, third and fourth in Bradford, others in Nottingham West:

154. EZEKIEL,⁵ b. 28 Aug. 1730.
     ABIGAIL, b. 26 Sept. 1732.
     ———, son, still b. 12 Mar. 1735.
     NATHANIEL, b. 27 Mar. 1736; bp. 4 Apr. 1736; d. 25 Dec. 1736.
     SARAH, b. 14 Mar. 1737/8; bp. 18 Mar. 1739.
     MARTHA, b. 16 Mar. 1743/4; m. Thomas Hamblett; d. 2 July 1767, in her 23d year.
     PRISCILLA, b. 28 Sept. 1749; d. 5 Oct. 1749.

39

REV. JOSIAH⁴ CHASE (Dea. Thomas,³ Thomas²), born in Newbury, 30 Nov. 1713; drowned by missing his path and falling into Spruce Creek in a violent snow storm on his way home from attending a wedding, 26 Dec. 1778. Parson Hasey's Diary states that he died in the snow storm, 26 Dec. 1778.

He graduated from Harvard College in 1738 and was ordained minister of the Spruce Creek Parish of Kittery, Me., 14 Sept. 1750. He married in Newbury, 5 Apr. 1743, SARAH TUFTS, daughter of John and Sarah (Bradstreet) Tufts, born in Newbury, 21 Apr. 1725; died in Kittery, Me., 23 Oct. 1799. She was a descendant of Gov. Simon Bradstreet.

Children, born in Kittery, Me., except the eldest born in Newbury:

155. BRADSTREET,⁵ b. 19 Jan. 1743/4.
156. JOSIAH, b. 15 Apr. 1746.
157. THOMAS, b. 14 Aug. 1747.
158. JOHN, b. 15 June 1749.
     COTTON, b. 21 Feb. 1750/51; d. in infancy.
159. SIMON, b. 8 Jan. 1754.
     SALLY, b. 31 May 1757; m. Stephen Carlisle of York, Me. She d. in Boston, 1850.

40

JONATHAN⁴ CHASE JR. (Ens. Jonathan,³ Thomas²), born in Newbury, — Sept. 1707; died in Stratham, N. H., 18 Aug. 1744. The Stratham Deaths (Register, 30: 427) state that "Jonathan Chase's Junr. child died" 17 Sept. 1742 and another 18 Sept. 1742 and that Jonathan Chase Junʳ died 18 Aug. 1744. Another child died in Stratham 2 Feb. 1762.

He married about 1727, LYDIA ROLLINS, perhaps daughter of Moses and Esther Rollins, born in Stratham, 4 Oct. 1705. His widow Lydia administered upon his estate, in Sept. 1744. She died in Stratham, 2 Jan. 1769.

Children, born in Stratham, N. H.:

    SARAH,[5] b. 6 Jan. 1728; m. Samuel Thurston of Epping, N. H.
160. JONATHAN, b. 1 May 1730.
161. MOSES.
    JOANNA, m. Thomas Perkins of Wakefield, N. H.
    THOMAS, d. on his way home from Halifax, N. S., Aug. 1757.

41

WILLIAM[4] CHASE (Ens. Jonathan,[3] Thomas[2]), born in Newbury, 24 Jan. 1709; died in Stratham, N. H., 10 Apr. 1772. (Register, 48: 341). He married about 1732, PHEBE ROLLINS, daughter of Lt. Thomas Rollins of Stratham. They lost by death four children, whose names were not given in Stratham deaths as follows: 22 Aug.; 26 Aug.; 2 Sept. and 10 Sept. 1742. He deeded land in Stratham to William[5] Chase Jr. Nov. 1769.

Children, born in Stratham, N. H.:

    PHEBE,[5] moved to Wolfboro, N. H.; m. John Taylor.
162. WILLIAM, b. 13 June 1742.
163. JOSIAH, b. about 1744.

42

JAMES[4] CHASE (Ens. Jonathan,[3] Thomas[2]), born in Stratham, N. H., 2 Aug. 1718; died about 1797. He married (1) ANNA GOODRIDGE, perhaps daughter of Edmund and Hannah (Dole) Goodridge, born in Newbury, 10 June 1716. She died about 1740. He married (2) MARY DEARBORN, probably daughter of Lt. Ebenezer and Abigail (Sanborn) Dearborn of North Hampton and Chester. She was born in Hampton, 11 June 1723.

He was living in Stratham in 1737; in Chester in 1740, and in Epping, 1741 to 1790. His will was dated 1 Dec. 1793, and proved 19 July 1797. He was living in Epping in 1790 and his family consisted of one male over 16 years, none under 16, and four females.

Child by his first wife, born in Stratham:

164. JAMES,[5] b. 24 Apr. 1737.

Children by second wife, born in Epping:

    MARY, b. 12 Oct. 1741; m. Eliphalet Dearborn.
    ANNA, b. 29 Nov. 1743; m. 18 Mar. 1779, Josiah Norris.
165. JONATHAN, b. 29 Mar. 1746.
166. JOSIAH, b. 11 July 1751.
    LYDIA, b. 21 Sept. 1755; m. 2 Aug. 1781, Josiah Norris, son of Josiah Norris, who m. Anna[5] above, by his first wife.
    SARAH, b. 10 Aug. 1757; m. and settled in Epping; her husband was a farmer; had three daughters.
    JOANNA, b. 26 Sept. 1760; int. 20 Mar. 1779, Thomas Elliott.
    ABIGAIL, b. 23 Nov. 1763.

43

THOMAS[4] CHASE (Ens. Jonathan,[3] Thomas[2]), born in Stratham, N. H., 26 June 1720; died in Stratham 15 Jan. 1757. He married about 1740, LOVE LEAVITT, daughter of Moses Leavitt of Stratham. They lived in Stratham, and several children, unmarried, died there as follows: 18 Aug. 1742; 8 Dec. 1743; 3 Mar. 1749. Widow Love Chase died in Stratham, 27 Nov. 1802, nearly 85.

Thomas Chase was shot by his son Jonathan in Stratham, 15 Jan. 1757, which was accidental as his son was then but nine years old.

Children, born in Stratham, N. H.:

      SARAH,[5] b. 26 Sept. 1744.
      MARY, b. 18 Dec. 1746; d. young.
167. JONATHAN, b. 22 Feb. 1748/9.
168. DUDLEY LEAVITT, b. 4 June 1751.
      MARY, b. 14 July 1753; m. Josiah Dudley of Brentwood, N. H.
      ANNA, b. 26 Aug. 1756.

44

JOHN[4] CHASE (James,[3] Thomas[2]), born in Newbury, 15 July 1707; died before 11 Feb. 1732, when administration was granted upon his estate. He married in Newbury. 30 July 1728, HANNAH HOYT, daughter of Robert and Martha (Stevens) Hoyt, born in Amesbury, 29 Dec. 1702. Her mother was killed by the Indians, 4 July 1706, and there is a tradition that her daughter Hannah was knocked on the head by the Indians and left for dead but recovered. Their son John was born after the death of his father.

Hannah Chase, widow of John, late of Amesbury, petitioned to have Thomas Stevens administer, 16 Feb. 1732/33. She stated that he left one infant about two years of age. The inventory mentions his bookes and apparel £14: 10; weaver's looms and geer £1: 10; his armes £1: 05; taken 17 Feb. 1732/33. (Essex Probate, 5,131).

Children, born in Newbury:

169. JOHNSON,[5] b. 24 Oct. 1730.
      JOHN, b. 25 June 1733; d. 5 Oct. 1750.

45

CAPT. JAMES[4] CHASE (James,[3] Thomas[2]), born in Newbury, 14 Aug. 1709; died in Haverhill between 27 July 1801 and 6 May 1802. He married (1) in Newbury, 18 Sept. 1739, HANNAH BARTLETT, who died 1745. He married (2) in Newbury, 25 Mar. 1746, ABIGAIL BAILEY, daughter of John and Sarah Bailey, born in Newbury, 14 Jan. 1724. She died in Haverhill, 1 Apr. 1785. He married (3) in Haverhill, 23 Aug. 1785, MEHITABLE EMERSON, widow of Joseph Emerson of Haverhill, who was a daughter of Samuel and Mary (Johnson) Haseltine, born 28 Feb. 1721/22. He was baptized at what is now the First Church of West Newbury, 21 Apr. 1717.

He sold his half of his father's homestead in Newbury (now West Newbury) to Willet Peterson, 6 Jan. 1755, and removed to the

West Parish of Haverhill. The town records of Haverhill call him Captain in 1785.

He made his will 27 July 1801 which was proved 6 May 1802, in which he mentions his wife Mehitable, his sons Edmund and James; Betsey Chase and Relief Chase, daughters of his late son Daniel Chase under 18; Edward Little Chase, son of his late son William under 21; Hannah Burroughs and Mary Bass, children of his daughter Elizabeth; his daughter Abigail, wife of Ephraim Stephens; his grandsons Obadiah Horton Jr. (son of his daughter Elizabeth), and Phineas Chase, son of his son Edmund, to be executors; presented for Probate by Obadiah Horton, trader, of Newburyport. (Essex Probate, 5,127).

Child by first wife, born in Newbury (now West Newbury):

ELISABETH,[6] b. 1 Sept. 1740; m. 15 Nov. 1759, Obadiah Horton Jr.

Children by second wife, born in Newbury (now West Newbury):

170. EDMUND, b. 19 Sept. 1748.
171. JAMES, b. 6 Mar. 1751.
     ABIGAIL, b. 22 Aug. 1756; m. 13 Oct. 1785, Ephraim Stevens.
172. DANIEL, b. 7 Nov. 1761.
173. WILLIAM, d. before 27 July 1801.

46

NATHANIEL[4] CHASE (James,[3] Thomas[2]), born in Newbury, 10 May 1711; died in 1757. He married (1) in Newbury, 15 June 1732, SARAH BARTON, daughter of Ebenezer and Esther (Flood) Barton, born in Newbury, 9 June 1714. He married (2) RUTH PEASLEE, daughter of Joseph and Elizabeth (Hastings) Peaslee, born in Haverhill, 22 June 1710; died shortly before 31 Mar. 1758.

Nathaniel Chase was a cooper and lived in the West Parish of Haverhill from 1743 to 1754. He also lived in Methuen.

Administration on his estate was granted to his son James in 1757.

William Sanders & Esther his wife, Oliver Sanders and Jerusha his wife, Samuel Sanders and Sarah his wife, all of Salem, N. H., and Nathaniel Chase of Methuen and Ruth his wife for £1152 sell Daniel Peasley of Salem all rights in the estate of our father Joseph Peaslee, late of Salem, N. H., 15 Apr. 1756. (Colonial Deeds of N. H., 49: 487).

Children probably by wife Sarah, born in Haverhill:

174. JAMES,[6] b. 25 Dec. 1735.
     MARTHA TAPLEY, b. 22 Mar. 1743/44.
175. ABEL, b. — Aug. 1746; bp. July 1747.
     (CHILD), bp. Aug. 1751 in West Parish.

Child by second wife, born in Haverhill:

ABIGAIL, b. 29 Nov. 1754; m. 26 Jan. 1773, John Marble Jr. He d. in Haverhill, 20 Dec. 1775. She m. (2) 15 Feb. 1781, Joseph Harriman of Haverhill. She d. there 20 June 1834.

47

AQUILA[4] CHASE (James,[3] Thomas[2]), born in Newbury 10 May 1715; died there 1789, aged 75. He married (1) intention in Newbury, 12 Mar. 1736, HANNAH DAVIS of Haverhill. He married (2) in Newbury, 13 Feb. 1738/9, MARY BOWLEY, daughter of John and Hannah Bowley, born in Newbury, 13 Dec. 1719. They lived in Newbury (now Newburyport) and he was buried in the Plains Cemetery.

Children, born in Newbury (now Newburyport):

	MARY,[6] b. 5 Dec. 1739; m. 18 Aug. 1761, Stephen Richardson.
	HANNAH, b. 24 Aug. 1741; m. 27 Nov. 1765, Joseph Connor.
176.	EDMUND, b. 23 May 1743.
177.	MOSES, b. 13 Feb. 1744.
	ELISABETH, b. 21 Jan. 1746; m. 14 Apr. 1762, Enoch Thurston.
178.	SAMUEL, b. 21 Jan. 1747/8.
179.	JOSEPH, b. 13 Apr. 1752.
180.	NATHAN, b. 9 Dec. 1755.
181.	AQUILA, b. 26 Sept. 1757.
	EUNICE, b. 24 Jan. 1760; m. 12 Oct. 1781, Abbe Severance.
182.	JOSIAH, b. 2 Aug. 1762.

48

EZRA[4] CHASE (James,[3] Thomas[2]), born in Newbury, 25 May 1720; died in Leominster 16 Feb. 1799. He married in Newbury, 13 Oct. 1743, ABIGAIL LOWE, perhaps daughter of David and Mary (Lamb) Lowe of Ipswich. She was born 20 May 1723, and died 5 Mar. 1810. (Coffin Papers, 30). They lived in Newbury and Leominster.

Children, first four born in Newbury (now West Newbury):

	ABIGAIL,[6] b. 13 Oct. 1744; m. 26 Nov. 1767, Asa Bailey; d. 1826.
183.	SOMERBY, b. 26 Feb. 1745/6.
	LOIS, b. 20 Apr. 1748; m. 30 Nov. 1768, Edmund Rogers; d. 1 Feb. 1788.
184.	DANIEL, b. 31 May 1750.
185.	NATHANIEL LOWE, b. 31 Aug. 1752.
	REBECCA, b. 13 Mar. 1755; m. 8 Aug. 1779, Joseph Holland (?); She d. 2 Jan. 1790.
186.	JOHN, b. 31 Jan. 1757.
	EUNICE, b. 30 June 1759; m. 12 Aug. 1779, Samuel Jacques Jr. She d. 6 June 1843.
187.	METAPHOR, b. 24 May 1761.
188.	JEREMIAH, b. 13 Apr. 1764.

49

EBENEZER[4] CHASE (James,[3] Thomas[2]), born in Newbury, 15 June 1721; died in Brentwood, N. H., 1 Oct. 1807, aged 86. He married in Newbury, 18 May 1741, DOROTHY FOOT, daughter of Samuel and Dorothy (Colby) Foot, baptized in Amesbury, 11 Sept. 1726.

He and his wife united with the Fourth Church of Newbury (now West Newbury), 2 July 1743. He sold his part of his father's homestead to Willet Peterson, 7 Feb. 1757, and later removed to Brentwood. Perhaps he is the Ebenezer Chase who married the widow Mary Sleeper of Brentwood, in Kingston, N. H., 25 Feb. 1790.

Children, born in Newbury:

MARTHA,[5] bp. 31 July 1743; d. 29 Dec. 1752.
189. ENOCH, bp. 4 Sept. 1743.
SARAH, b. 29 Aug. 1745; m. David Pettingill.
BETSEY, b. 31 Aug. 174-; m. (1) —— Wise; m. (2) ——
Perry.
190. JAMES, b. 9 July 1749.
191. NATHANIEL, b. 15 Jan. 1750; bp. 2 Feb. 1751/2.
STEPHEN, b. 15 Jan. 1754; bp. 27 Jan. 1754; lived in Londonderry, N. H. He left no children.
REBECCA, b. 6 May 1756; m. —— Gordon of New Hampton, N. H.
ANNA, bp. 6 June 1756; m. Gideon George.
192. JOSHUA, bp. 7 May 1758; d. in Revolutionary War.
193. SIMON, b. 31 Jan. 1762; bp. 7 Feb. 1762.
SUSANNAH, b. 22 Mar. 1764; bp. 31 Mar. 1765; m. 1801, John Gordon.
DOROTHY, b. 22 Feb. 1766; bp. 1 Mar. 1767; m. 2 Feb. 1801, Thomas Webster of Waterbury.

50

EDWARD[4] CHASE (Josiah,[3] Thomas[2]), born in Boston, 27 May 1719; baptized at the New North Church of Boston, 31 May 1719. He married in Boston, 26 Aug. 1740, SUSANNA YOUNGMAN who "owned the covenant" and was admitted to the New Brick Church of Boston, 10 May 1741.

Children, baptized at the New Brick Church in Boston:

194. EDWARD,[5] bp. 17 May 1741.
195. JOSIAH, bp. 26 Sept. 1742.
196. EBENEZER, bp. 18 Nov. 1744.

51

NATHAN[4] CHASE (Nathan,[3] Thomas[2]), born in Newbury, 28 June 1725; died in Haverhill, 21 May 1791. He married in Newbury, 24 Nov. 1747, LYDIA MOULTON, daughter of Batt and Hannah (Libby) Moulton, born in Amesbury and baptized in Newbury, 1 Nov. 1724; died in Haverhill, 30 Aug. 1797.

He was a shoemaker and a farmer and removed from Newbury to the East Parish of Haverhill in 1762. Their children were all baptized in the Second Church (now First Church of West Newbury).

Children, born in Newbury:

ELIPHALET,[5] b. 5 Jan. 1749; d. 11 Apr. 1749.
LYDIA, b. 30 Mar. 1750; d. 12 June 1759, of measles.
ABIGAIL, b. 22 June 1752; m. Daniel Currier of Warner, N. H. She d. 25 Dec. 1846, a. 94.
JUDITH, b. 22 Oct. 1754; m. 31 Dec. 1778, James Ayer of Haverhill; she d. 27 Jan. 1789.
197. JOSIAH, b. 18 Apr. 1757.
RUTH, b. 9 Jan. 1760; d. 12 Oct. 1762.
RUTH, b. 5 July 1763; m. 16 Jan. 1783, Enoch Caldwell of Haverhill. She d. 1801.

52

JOHN[4] CHASE (Nathan,[3] Thomas[2]), born in Newbury, 27 July 1731; died there 11 Jan. 1804. He married in Newbury, 27 Nov. 1753, HANNAH PLUMMER, daughter of Samuel and Hannah (Woodman) Plummer, born in Newbury, 25 Oct. 1725; died, a widow, in Newbury, 25 Oct. 1807, a. 82. He lived in Newbury near Brown Spring and Artichoke River and his will was proved 6 Feb. 1804.

Children, born in Newbury:

198. SAMUEL,[5] b. 26 Aug. 1754.
      ABIGAIL, b. 25 Mar. 1756; m. 11 Nov. 1773, Jeremiah Dole.
199. JOHN, b. 19 Apr. 1759.
      NATHAN, b. 23 May 1761; d. 21 July 1803, aged 42y. 2m. 2d.
      HANNAH, b. 2 June 1763; m. (1) 14 Sept. 1786, George Newell; m. (2) 10 June 1834, Henry Merrill; d. 30 Dec. 1836.
200. AMOS, b. 25 Feb. 1766.

53

JOSIAH[4] CHASE (Nathan,[3] Thomas[2]), born in Newbury, — Sept. 1735; died in Deerfield, N. H., 1782. He married (1) 3 Oct. 1764, MARGARET GILL. He married (2) HANNAH SANBORN, daughter of William and Betsey (Dearborn) Sanborn of Exeter, N. H., born 30 Mar. 1740; died 22 Aug. 1831, aged 92.

He served in the French and Indian War and was taken prisoner at Otsego, N. Y., 1 Aug. 1756 and remained in captivity eleven years. He resided in Deerfield, and his will was probated 4 July 1783. There is a tradition that he married first an Indian squaw and that she died soon after his return from captivity. He was selectman of Deerfield 1777 and 1778 and lived there many years.

Child by first wife, born in Deerfield, N. H.:

JOSIAH,[5] b. 3 Aug. 1769; d. age of 19, in Charleston, S. C., in 1787.

Children by second wife, born in Deerfield, N. H.:

201. WILLIAM, b. 9 June 1774.
202. NATHAN, b. 28 May 1777.
203. JONATHAN, b. 24 Dec. 1779.
204. EDMUND, b. 13 Sept. 1781.

54

MOSES[4] CHASE (Nathan,[3] Thomas[2]), born in Newbury, 21 Sept. 1741; died probably in Deerfield, N. H. He married in Newbury, 17 June 1760, SUSANNAH KELLEY. They lived in Deerfield, and he was a tythingman in 1767 and selectman in 1769, 1780 and 1781. In 1790 Moses Chase Sr. was head of a family in Deerfield consisting of two males over 16 years of age, none under 16 and four females.

Children, born probably in Deerfield, N. H.:

205. MOSES,[5] b. 10 May 1761; bp. 19 July 1761.
206. JOSEPH, b. 8 June 1763.
207. PARKER, b. 22 Aug. 1765.
      SUSAN, m. in Epsom, 2 Mar. 1796, Elliott Blaisdell.
      MARY, m. about 1800, Elijah Rollins of Sanbornton, N. H. She d. 25 Oct. 1822.

JOHN, b. 13 Sept. 1769; d. young.
208. JOHN, b. 25 Apr. 1772.

55

PARKER[4] CHASE (Nathan,[3] Thomas[2]), born in Newbury, 28 Feb. 1745. He enlisted from Newbury 2 May 1775 and was in the service 13 weeks in Capt. Ezra Lunt's Co. of Col. Moses Little's Regiment. The company's return made in Oct. 1775 gives his age as 31 years. This age indicates that this soldier was the son of Nathan[3] Chase and not the son of Joseph[4] Chase who was seven years younger. Parker,[4] or another man of the same name, was in the service from 14 Oct. to 22 Nov. 1779. His father made his will 4 Aug. 1784 in which he refers to his son Parker Chase as having already received his portion, implying that he was then alive. Several of his brothers settled in Deerfield, N. H. and it has been stated that he also settled there. However, he is not the Parker Chase who enlisted from Deerfield as that man was a pensioner and furnished a full record of himself and family in his application for a pension.

He married in Newburyport, 5 Jan. 1766, ELIZABETH TURNER. They attended the First Presbyterian Church of Newburyport and their children were there baptized.

Children, born in Newburyport:
208a. ROBERT,[5] bp. 23 Mar. 1766.
LYDIA, bp. 3 May 1767.
ELIZABETH, bp. 8 Sept. 1773.
ESTHER, bp. 8 Sept. 1773.

56

EDMUND[4] CHASE (Nathan,[3] Thomas[2]), born in Newbury, 21 June 1748; died about 1822. He married in Newbury, 30 Nov. 1769, ESTHER MERRILL, daughter of Peter and Priscilla (Annis) Merrill, born in Newbury, 17 Mar. 1748/49.

He sold the Thomas[2] Chase homestead in Newbury in 1798 and removed to Minot, Me.

Children, born in Newbury:
JOANNA,[5] b. 5 Nov. 1770; m. (1) 25 Nov. 1789, Joseph Thurlow; m. (2) 25 May 1796, Samuel Rogers.
209. STEPHEN, b. 19 Jan. 1772.
210. MERRILL, b. 17 Oct. 1773.
PRISCILLA, b. 2 Jan. 1776; m. 15 Jan. 1795, Anthony Whitmore.
RUTH, b. 3 Sept. 1777; d. — Jan. 1788.
SALLY, b. 5 Sept. 1779; m. 22 Sept. 1803, Paul Tenney.
ABIGAIL, b. 17 Apr. 1781; m. Thomas Millet.
211. NATHAN, b. 16 May 1783.
212. EDMUND, b. 9 Dec. 1785.
POLLY, b. 23 Sept. 1787; m. Charles Bradbury. She d. 9 Feb. 1864.
213. CHARLES, b. 6 Apr. 1791.
214. ABNER, b. 1 Apr. 1793.

57

STEPHEN[4] CHASE (Nathan,[3] Thomas[2]), born in Newbury, 16 July 1750; entered his intention at Newbury, 22 May 1773, with MARY SANBORN, daughter of William and Betsey (Dearborn) Sanborn of Exeter, N. H. She was born 19 Sept. 1745. They lived in Deerfield, N. H., but their deaths are not recorded.

Children, born in Deerfield, N. H.

215. WILLIAM SANBORN,[5] b. 12 Feb. 1778.
      ANNA, b. 30 May 1780; b. 25 Nov. 1804, Simeon Sanborn.
216. HENRY DEARBORN, b. 8 Apr. 1783.
      MARY, b. 24 Feb. 1786; unm. d. — June 1870.
      HANNAH, b. 27 June 1788; m. John Sanborn of Sanbornton, N. H. She d. 7 Mar. 1826.

58

JONATHAN[4] CHASE (Nathan[3], Thomas[2]), born in Newbury, 5 Dec. 1751; died in Danville (now South Auburn), Me., 13 Apr. 1825. He married in Newbury, 22 Apr. 1773, HANNAH MERRILL, daughter of John and Anne (Ordway) Merrill, born in Newbury, 13 Dec. 1751; died about 1844. He removed from Newbury to Danville (now South Auburn) in 1798.

Children, born in Newbury:

217. JOHN MERRILL,[5] b. 1 Mar. 1774.
      LYDIA, b. 8 Oct. 1775; m. 15 Oct. 1801, Samuel H. Haskell; lived Wapsie, Iowa.
      MOLLY, b. 12 Aug. 1777; m. 10 Sept. 1807, Moses Smith.
      ANNA, b. 21 June 1779; m. (1) Mar. 1800, John Tyler; m. (2) 7 Oct. 1811, Sullivan Tyler.
218. PETER, b. 23 Jan. 1781.
      JONATHAN, b. 26 Jan. 1783; d. 23 Jan. 1788.
      HANNAH, b. 29 Jan. 1785; m. (1) 18 Mar. 1802, James Stickney; m. (2) — Apr. 1824, Reuben Merrow of Auburn, Me.
      REBECCA, b. 21 Feb. 1787; d. 25 Jan. 1788.
      REBECCA, b. 18 Nov. 1788; m. 23 Jan. 1812, Jacob Royal. She d. 20 Dec. 1829. He was son of William and Susan Royal of Danville, Me.
219. JONATHAN, b. 25 Dec. 1790.
      CHARLOTTE, b. 28 Mar. 1793; m. 4 July 1816, Richworth Jordan; alive in Wapsie, Iowa, in 1871.
220. MOSES, b. 4 July 1795.

59

JONATHAN[4] CHASE (John[3], John[2]), born in Hampton, N. H., 21 Oct. 1700; died in Seabrook, N. H., between 27 June and 30 Aug. 1780. He married in Hampton Falls, N. H., 18 Dec. 1723, PATIENCE HEATH, daughter of Nehemiah and Mary (Goss) Heath, born in Hampton, N. H., 6 Mar. 1706/7. He made his will 27 June, which was proved 30 Aug. 1780, in which he mentions Jonathan, Nehemiah, and Nathaniel. They lived on the John[3] Chase homestead in Seabrook.

Children, born in Seabrook, N. H.

MARY,[5] b. 14 Mar. 1726; m. 2 June 1747, James Lowell of Salisbury, N. H.

ABIGAIL, b. 6 July 1728; m. 6 Sept. 1749, Stephen Fogg.
PATIENCE, b. 4 Nov. 1730; d. young.
JOSEPH, b. 10 Mar. 1732/3; d. unm. 1775.
SARAH, b. 8 May 1737; m. Thomas Brown of Seabrook, N. H.
PATIENCE, b. 3 May 1739; m. 7 June 1759, Simon Clough of Gilmanton, N. H.
221.   JONATHAN, b. 10 Sept. 1741.
222.   NEHEMIAH, b. 29 Feb. 1744.
223.   NATHANIEL, b. 5 Apr. 1746.
A daughter unnamed was bp. at Hampton Falls, 31 Oct. 1735.

60

ELIZABETH[4] CHASE (John,[3] John[2]), born in Hampton, N. H., 13 Apr. 1703. She was the mother of Daniel Chase alias Green, born in Hampton about 1720. His father was probably Abraham Green, but he took his mother's name and his descendants have borne the name of Chase. She married William Russell.
Child, born in Hampton, N. H.:
224.   DANIEL,[5] b. about 1720.

61

ELIHU[4] CHASE (John[3], John[2]), born in Hampton, N. H., 7 Sept. 1705; died in Kensington, N. H., 30 Nov. 1794. He married in Hampton Falls, N. H., 9 Dec. 1730, MARY SWAIN who died 29 May 1790. Their three eldest children were baptized at the Hampton Falls Church. They removed from Hampton Falls to Kensington about 1737.

He made his will 18 Apr. 1777, which was proved 1 Apr. 1795, in which he mentions his wife Mary, sons John, William, Thomas, Elihu and Stephen and his daughters Elizabeth Purington, Mary Purington, Patience Hodgdon, and Content Chase.

Children, born in Kensington (eldest born in Hampton Falls):
225.   JOHN,[5] b. 26 Nov. 1731.
ELISABETH, b. 2 Mar. 1734; m. 31 Mar. 1756, Jonathan Purington.
226.   WILLIAM, b. 5 June 1736.
227.   THOMAS, b. 25 Jan. 1739.
MARY, b. 25 May 1741; m. 1768, Amos Purington.
228.   ELIHU, b. 18 May 1743.
RACHEL, b. 19 July 1745; d. 18 Dec. 1745.
LYDIA, b. 31 Oct. 1746; d. 24 Sept. 1748.
CONTENT, b. 21 Jan. 1748; m. (1) ———— Reynolds of Eliot, Me.; m. (2) Stephen Jenkins.
LYDIA, b. 1755; not mentioned in her father's will.
PATIENCE, b. 26 June 1750; m. 9 July 1772, Peter Hodgdon.
229.   STEPHEN, b. 18 Jan. 1758.

62

JOHN[4] CHASE (John,[3] John[2]), born in Hampton, N. H., 18 Sept. 1708; died between 19 June and 25 Sept. 1776. He married in Hampton, 27 Mar. 1729, ANNA RUNDLETT, perhaps daughter of Owen Rundlett.

He made his will 19 June, which was proved 25 Sept. 1776. They lived in Hampton Falls and Seabrook, N. H.

Children, born in Hampton Falls, N. H. :

230. JAMES,[5] b. 30 Jan. 1730.
231. THOMAS, b. 23 July 1731.
232. JOHN, b. 3 Mar. 1733.
       CHARLES, b. 4 Mar. 1734; d. young.
233. JACOB, b. 9 Feb. 1740; alive 1776.
234. DANIEL, b. 17 Apr. 1741.
235. CHARLES, b. 4 Mar. 1743/4.

63

FOLLANSBEE[4] CHASE (Philip,[3] John[2]), born in Sutton, 29 Sept. 1724; died there 14 Mar. 1799. He married (1) in Sutton, 2 Jan. 1749/50 HANNAH MARSH, daughter of Benjamin and Mehitable (King) Marsh, born in Sutton, 9 Oct. 1729. She died in Sutton, 21 Sept. 1769. He married (2) in Mendon, 13 Apr. 1773, DEBORAH TAFT, probably widow of Robert Taft of Mendon, whose maiden name was Deborah Lovett. He was an innholder in Sutton in 1764 and they lived there.

Children by first wife, born in Sutton:

FOLLANSBEE,[5] b. 28 Feb. 1750/1; d. young.
HANNAH, b. 12 Apr. 1752; m. 11 May 1775, Lazarus LeBaron; d. 1776.
MARY, b. 22 Dec. 1754; m. 29 Feb. 1778, Lazarus LeBaron.
236   REUBEN, b. 24 Feb. 1757.
THOMAS, b. 7 Mar. 1759; d. young.
237. THOMAS FOLLANSBEE, b. 16 Feb. 1760.

64

LT. FRANCIS[4] CHASE (Philip,[3] John[2]), born in Sutton as early as 1730; died in Royalston, 16 Jan. 1791. He married in Sutton, 12 June 1760, MARY PERKINS, daughter of William and Elizabeth Perkins, born in Sutton, 20 Mar. 1741. The Vital Statistics of Sutton give the marriage on 12 June 1760 of Mary Perkins and *Thomas Chase*. The History of Sutton, p. 625, gives the same marriage to Francis Chase. The first three children of Francis Chase are recorded also to his wife *Mary* on the records of Sutton, and Mrs. Mary Chase married in Royalston, 5 Apr. 1792, Capt. Peter Woodbury. She died in Royalston, 15 Apr. 1819. He removed from Sutton to Royalston before Sept. 1777.

From 1769 to 1787 he held each year one of a half-dozen different town offices, constable for four years and selectman for five years being the most important. He was also a soldier in the Revolutionary war.

Children, first three recorded in Sutton, fourth to eighth bapt. in Royalston, 14 Sept. 1777:

238. DAVID,[5] b. 10 Mar. 1761.
       ELISABETH, b. 28 Sept. 1762; m. 28 Oct. 1784, Eliphalet Richardson.
       MARY, b. 23 Feb. 1764; m. 16 Sept. 1788, Caleb Felch.
239. WILLIAM, b. 1765.

SARAH, b. 21 Apr. 1768; m. int. 7 Mar. 1791, Abraham Eddy.
240. ARCHIBALD C., b. 18 May 1770.
241. CHARLES, b. 7 Jan. 1772.
REBECCA, b. 6 Mar. 1774; m. 15 Sept. 1794, Abiel Richardson.
She d. in Waterford, Vt., 17 May 1853.
HANNAH, b. 1 Mar. 1776; m. 14 Feb. 1796, Daniel Brown of
Littleton, Vt.
242. FRANCIS, b. 22 Oct. 1777.
243. DANIEL, b. 22 July 1783.

65

PAUL[4] CHASE (Charles,[3] John[2]), born in Newbury (now West
Newbury), 27 Mar. 1721, and was killed in the French and Indian
War in 1756. He married, in Salisbury, 27 Mar. 1746, SARAH
PIKE, daughter of Joseph and Jemima (Morrill) Pike, born in Sal-
isbury, 16 Feb. 1725. Administration was granted to his widow
Sarah, and she charged in July 1757 for the board of Samuel, aged
7, and Anna and Joseph. He resided in Amesbury and Sandown,
N. H.
Children, first two born in Amesbury:
244. CARR,[5] b. 25 Nov. 1746.
245. ENOCH, b. 8 Oct. 1748.
SAMUEL, b. 1750; no children; killed by the Indians.
246. JOSEPH, b. 26 Apr. 1753.
ANNA, b. about 1755; m. Maj. —— Darling of Hopkinton,
N. H.

66

JONATHAN[4] CHASE (Charles,[3] John[2]), born in Newbury (now
West Newbury), 18 Aug. 1723; died there 6 Oct. 1799. He mar-
ried in Newbury, 24 Jan. 1744/45, JOANNA MORSE, daughter of
Anthony and Judith (Moody) Morse, born in Newbury, 22 Aug.
1726; died there 15 Jan. 1807. They lived in Newbury (now West
Newbury).
Jonathan Chase of Newbury, gentleman, made his will 1 Apr. 1793
which was proved 4 Nov. 1799. He mentions therein his wife Joanna; the
three children of his son Jonathan deceased; the three children of his son
Stephen deceased; his daughters Anna, Abigail and Hepzibah and his son
Joshua to have land and buildings. (Essex Co. Probate, 5,140).
Children, born in Newbury:
247. JONATHAN,[5] b. 23 Oct. 1745.
248. STEPHEN, b. 7 Dec. 1747.
ELIPHALET, b. 12 July 1750; d. young.
ANNA, b. 5 Nov. 1754; m. 1776, John Newcomb. She d. in East-
port, Me., 1814; nine children.
ABIGAIL, b. 28 Dec. 1757; m. 21 Dec. 1780, Benjamin Pettingill.
249. ELIPHALET, b. 9 Mar. 1760.
HEPSIBAH, b. 31 Aug. 1762; m. 14 May 1789, Samuel Stocker.
MOLLY, b. 31 Dec. 1764; m. —— Moody.
250. JOSHUA, b. 12 Jan. 1767.
HANNAH, m. —— Newhall.

*Jonathan[4] Chase (66) did not have a son Abraham as Dr. John B. Chace
stated under Jonathan in his manuscript. Abraham[4] Chase (72) had a son
Abraham[5]. He is 263 in this volume.

67

Dea. Ezra[4] Chase (Jacob,[3] John[2]), born in Newbury, 9 July 1717; died in Haverhill, 3 Mar. 1793, aged 75; buried in Greenwood Cemetery. He married in Haverhill, 2 Dec. 1740, Judith Davis, daughter of William and Mary (Kelley) Davis, born in Haverhill, 12 Mar. 1721/22. She died in Haverhill, 28 Feb. 1808, aged 86. They resided in Haverhill and he was a Deacon.

He made his will 3 Dec. 1792 which was proved 25 Mar. 1793. He mentions his wife Judith to have estate given them by their father William Davis of Haverhill, lately deceased; son Amos Chase to have 24 acres with the buildings in Amesbury which was purchased of Francis Davis; daughter Anna wife of Enoch Nichols; daughter Judith Webster deceased and her daughter Judith Webster; daughter Elizabeth Chase, then unmarried; son William Chase. (Essex Probate, 62: 159, 192).

Administration on the estate of Judith widow of Dea. Ezra Chase was granted to her son William Chase, 11 Mar. 1808. The heirs were Anna Nichols, William Chase, Elizabeth Chase, Judith Webster deceased, her daughter Judith Hoyt and Amos Chase. (Ibid. 76: 98, 218, 206 and 77: 18, 139, 141 and 78: 240).

Children, born in Haverhill:

251. Amos,[5] b. 9 Sept. 1741.
     Mary, b. 27 Aug. 1743; d. 16 Nov. 1747.
     Anna, b. 29 July 1745; m. 18 Aug. 1763, Enoch Nichols of Amesbury.
     William, b. 14 Feb. 1746/7; d. 14 Nov. 1753.
     Mary, b. 16 Apr. 1749; not mentioned in her father's will; prob. d. young.
     Judith, b. 29 Dec. 1751; m. 19 May 1774, Jonathan Webster 3d.
     Elisabeth, b. 21 Apr. 1754; called Elizabeth Chase in her father's will; d. in Haverhill, unm., 19 Apr. 1810, aged 56.
252. William, b. 12 Apr. 1756.

68

John[4] Chase (Jacob,[3] John[2]), born in Haverhill, 5 Nov. 1719; died in Londonderry, N. H., 1790. He married in Haverhill, 27 Oct. 1741, Hannah Ela, daughter of Samuel and Hannah (Clark) Ela, born in Haverhill, 13 Mar. 1721/22. They lived in the East Parish of Haverhill, 1741; removed to Plaistow, N. H., and later to Londonderry.

Children, born and baptized in Haverhill:

     Sarah,[5] b. 25 July 1742; m. Richard Dustin.
253. Jacob, b. 4 Mar. 1743/4.
     Rachel, b. 18 Sept. 1747; m. —— Jacques.
254. John, bp. 11 July 1756.
255. Samuel, b. Dec. 1752; bp. 3 Mar. 1754.
256. Enoch, bp. 17 Oct. 1762.

69

Enoch[4] Chase (Jacob,[3] John[2]), born in Haverhill, 18 Feb. 1726/7. He married in Haverhill, 5 Nov. 1747, Mary Sanders, daughter of Nathaniel and Mary (Bixby) Sanders, born in Haverhill, 3 July, 1728. They lived in Haverhill on the Jacob[3] Chase homestead.

Children, born in Haverhill:

257. NATHANIEL,⁶ b. 30 Oct. 1748.
258. JESSE, b. 17 Nov. 1751.
259. WILLIAM, b. 8 July 1754.

70

EBENEZER⁴ CHASE (Jacob,³ John²), born in Haverhill, 27 Mar. 1729; married 29 Aug. 1751 HEPZIBAH SARGENT, daughter of Charles and Hepzibah (Heath) Sargent, born in Amesbury, 20 Feb. 1728/9. (William Sargent Genealogy, 30). They lived in Haverhill, 1751-1764.

Children, born in Haverhill:

SARAH,⁶ b. about 1753; d. 17 Sept. 1754.
260. JACOB, b. 4 Aug. 1754.
SARAH, b. 17 Sept. 1756; m. about 1788, John Little of Goffstown, N. H. She d. 3 Jan. 1847. Five children.
261. JOSHUA, b. 11 Nov. 1758.
262. CALEB, b. Apr. 1761.
JOANNA, b. 11 May 1764; m. Enos Challis.

71

EZRA⁴ CHASE (Abraham,³ John²), born probably in Newbury, about 1725; one of the co-executors of his father's estate 28 Nov. 1770, Plaistow, N. H. He does not appear as the head of a family in Plaistow in 1790, nor in Atkinson, nor was he an inhabitant of Plaistow in 1764.

72

ABRAHAM⁴ CHASE (Abraham,³ John²), born in Plaistow, N. H., 8 July 1750; married about 1770 MARGARET CHALLIS. In 1790 he was head of a family consisting of two males over 16 years of age, three males under 16 and four females, living in Weare, N. H. This record is consistent with the Chase Manuscripts which state that he had four sons and three daughters. He was taxed in Weare 1788 to 1793 inclusive. He was living in Weare, 2 Feb. 1818, when he administered upon the estate of his son George W. He lived in Plaistow, Deering and Weare.

Abraham Chase of Weare sells John Clement and Moses Merrill of Haverhill land in Hampstead, N. H., formerly owned by Parker Chase, 28 Feb. 1810. (Rockingham Co. Deeds, 196: 317).

Children, first two born in Plaistow, N. H.:

HANNAH,⁶ b. 19 Dec. 1771; m. William Stevens of Plaistow.
263. ABRAHAM, b. 29 Aug. 1773.
264. JOSEPH.
MARGARET, m. Winthrop Clough.
265. WILLIAM, b. 15 Sept. 1783.
266. AMOS, b. about 1788.
BETSEY, m. in Henniker, 8 Apr. 1805, Robert Putney.
GEORGE W., d. unm. shortly before 2 Feb. 1818, a soldier.
SALLY, d. unm.
DOLLY, m. in Weare 18 Feb. 1806, Samuel Scribner.
There is some doubt about the above family. Hannah, Abraham,

Dolly and George are probably correct. Some of the others may belong to Abraham (5), who m. Abigail Cogswell, 22 Feb. 1795, in Haverhill.

72a

PARKER[4] CHASE (Abraham,[3] John[2]), born in Plaistow, N. H., 16 Feb. 1754; inherited one half of his father's lands, 9 Dec. 1761. On 28 Feb. 1810, his brother Abraham Chase, then of Weare, N. H., sold land in Hampstead which was "formerly owned by Parker Chase." (Rockingtam Co. Deeds, 196:317).

It is apparent that this Parker Chase was living in Plaistow in 1790 and that he had a family consisting of one male over 16 years of age, no males under 16 and two females. Nothing further has been found.

73

DAVID[4] CHASE (David,[3] John[2]), born in Newbury (now West Newbury), 1 Dec. 1730; died there 11 Feb. 1805, aged 74. He married in Newbury, 20 Mar. 1755, SARAH JOHNSON, daughter of Rev. William and Betsey (Bradstreet) Johnson, born in Newbury, 19 Mar. 1735; died in Newbury, 5 Oct. 1804, in her 70th year; buried in Bridge Street Cemetery, West Newbury.

He lived on the west bank of the Merrimack in what is now West Newbury and kept Swett's Ferry, the site of the present "Rocks" bridge. They were members of the Fourth Church of Newbury and their children were there baptized. He was called David Chase, the younger, and made a nuncupative will which was presented to Probate, 4 Mar. 1805. His heirs were Benjamin Chase, Daniel Chase, Sarah Woodman, Nicholas Chase guardian of his daughter Hannah, and Stephen Bailey, guardian of Amos, Simeon and William, children of his son Simeon Chase Jr., deceased. (Essex Probate, 372:387).

Children, born in Newbury (now West Newbury):

267. BENJAMIN,[•] bp. 28 July 1776.
268. NICHOLAS.
      SARAH, m. 28 Feb. 1780, Mark Woodman.
      HANNAH, non compos mentis; lived with Nicholas her guardian; never married.
269. DANIEL, bp. 10 Apr. 1774.
270. SIMEON JR,
      DAVID, bp. 28 July 1776; d. — Sept. 1777, age 14m.

74

ANTHONY[4] CHASE (David,[3] John[2]), born in Newbury (now West Newbury), 6 Dec. 1735; died in Haverhill, 5 Nov. 1814. He married (1) in Newbury, 29 June 1758, ABIGAIL WOODMAN, daughter of John and Anna (Adams) Woodman, born in Newbury, 9 Feb. 1737; died 5 Dec. 1780. He married (2) in Haverhill, 7 May 1782, SARAH SWETT who died there as widow of Anthony, — Oct. 1823. They lived in Haverhill.

Children, born in Haverhill:

ROBERT,[•] b. 31 May 1759; d. 17 Apr. 1762 in his 3d y.
SARAH, b. 1 Jan. 1761; m. 6 Apr. 1781, Samuel Ayer, Jr.

271. ROBERT, b. 10 Feb. 1763.
272. WOODMAN, b. 20 Apr. 1765.
273. STEPHEN, b. 24 Apr. 1767.
274. JOSEPH, b. 13 July 1769.
    ABIGAIL, b. 31 Aug. 1771; m. 22 May 1796, Oliver Morse.
275. JOHN, b. 20 Nov. 1773.
    MARY, m. 26 Nov. 1797, William Little.
    HANNAH, m. 18 Dec. 1798, Joseph Tyler.
    NANCY, m. 21 Dec. 1804, Gideon George.

75

TRISTRAM[4] CHASE (David,[3] John[2]), born in Newbury (now
West Newbury), 23 Jan. 1737/8; died there 6 Feb. 1813, aged 76.
He married in Newbury, 9 Dec. 1762, PRISCILLA WOODMAN, daughter of John and Anna (Adams) Woodman, born in Newbury, 20
July 1740; died in West Newbury, 25 Dec. 1825, aged 85. They
lived in West Newbury.
    Children, born in Newbury:
        ABIGAIL,[5] b. 6 Nov. 1763; d. 13 Feb. 1839 (?).
        PRISCILLA, b. 25 May 1766; m. 2 June 1808, Nehemiah Follans-
            bee.
        RUTH, b. 24 Mar. 1768; m. (1) Enoch Smith; m. (2) 1838,
            James Bricket of Hampstead, N. H.
276.   CHARLES, b. 15 Feb. 1770.
        BETHIA, b. 14 Feb. 1772; m. 19 Jan. 1793, Samuel Hopson of
            Rowley.
277.   TRISTRAM, b. 21 Aug. 1774.
        ANNA, b. 9 Nov. 1777; m. 15 Nov. 1800, Moses Little, Jr.
        JUDITH, b. 29 Jan. 1780; m. 21 Jan. 1802, William Hills, Jr.
278.   ENOCH, b. 28 Jan. 1782.
        SARAH, b. 3 Mar. 1785.

76

SIMEON[4] CHASE (David,[3] John[2]), born in Newbury (now West
Newbury) and baptized in the Second Church of Newbury (now the
First Church of West Newbury) 14 Apr. 1745; died in West Newbury, 13 Sept. 1829, aged 84. He married in Newbury, 9 Sept.
1772, HANNAH JOHNSON, daughter of Rev. William and Betty
(Bradstreet) Johnson of Newbury. She died in West Newbury, 7
Mar. 1831, aged 76.
    He was a graduate of Harvard College, 1767, and was a noted
school-teacher in Newbury for more than fifty years. Many stories
are told about his eccentricities. He made his will 18 May 1824,
which was proved 29 Sept. 1829. He gave everything to his wife,
Hannah, with no mention of his children. The account mentions
Charles Chase, Samuel Chase and Abel Chase. (Essex Probate,
5177).
    Children, born in Newbury but not recorded.
279. EZRA.[5]
280. SETH.
    SARAH.
281. DAVID.
    ELMIRA, b. about 1791; d. 13 Sept. 1822, aged 31y.

77

EMERY[4] CHASE (David,[3] John[2]), born in what is now West Newbury and baptized at the Second Church of Newbury (now the First Church of West Newbury), 7 July 1747; died in Andover, and was buried there, 19 Aug. 1788, aged 41. He married in Andover, 25 July 1768, MEHITABLE MOORE [MOOAR], daughter of Benjamin and Abiah Moore, born in Andover, 1 Nov. 1749. She married (2) in Andover, 21 Sept. 1789, Aaron Blanchard. Mr. Chase was a housewright and lived in Andover. His widow administered upon his estate, 2 Feb. 1789, and later it was declared insolvent.

Children, born in Andover:

> MEHITABLE,[5] b. 12 Dec. 1768.
> SALLY, bp. 9 Nov. 1788; alive 2 July 1805.
> CHILD, bur. 24 Jan. 1776, a. 8m.
> CHILD, bur. 5 Sept. 1783, a. 4m.

78

NICHOLAS[4] CHASE (David,[3] John[2]), born in what is now West Newbury about 1750. He married about 1775, RUTH ——— and removed to Wentworth, N. H., before 1790. In that year he was the head of a family consisting of one male over 16 years, three males under 16 and two females living in Wentworth.

Child:

> MARY CADY,[5] b. 21 Nov. 1776.
> Other children whose names have not been learned.

78a

DR. JOSHUA[4] CHASE (David,[3] John[2]), born in Newbury (now West Newbury) about 1754; died there — Dec. 1802, aged 48. He was a physician and entered his intention of marriage at Newbury, 7 Sept. 1780, with MARY SHACKFORD of Portsmouth, N. H. She was daughter of Capt. John and Deborah (Seward) Shackford, born 15 Sept. 1759, grand-daughter of Paul Shackford of Newburyport. She died before her father's estate was settled in 1787.

Joshua Chase, a minor, of Portsmouth owned in common with the representatives of John Shackford of Portsmouth one-third of a parcel of land in Newburyport, it being a part of the estate of Paul Shackford. William Plaisted of Portsmouth was guardian to Joshua and was authorized to sell said estate, at York 4th Tuesday of June 1792. (Essex Co. Probate, 62:91).

Child:

> 282.   JOSHUA,[5] b. about 1782; living in Portsmouth 1792.

79

AMBROSE[4] CHASE (Isaac,[3] Daniel[2]), born in Sutton, 2 Dec. 1713; died there 4 Aug. 1799. He married there 25 July 1734, THANKFUL ROBBINS of Hasnomischo (Grafton). She was daughter of Thomas and Lydia (Adams) Robbins, born in Grafton, 21 Apr. 1714; died in Townsend, Vt. They lived in Sutton (now Millbury), occupying the Isaac[3] Chase homestead.

Children, first six born in Grafton, others in Sutton:

MARY,[5] b. 3 June 1735; m. Nathan Rawson of Uxbridge.
THANKFUL, b. 8 May 1738.
283. ISAAC, b. 11 Feb. 1740/41.
LYDIA, b. 13 Apr. 1743; m. 1764, Jonathan Goldthwaite.
284. SOLOMON, bp. 17 June 1744.
HANNAH, b. 13 June 1748; m. 11 May 1769, Simon[5] Chase. (Family 287)
285. ABEL, b. 9 Aug. 1750.
EDITH, b. 29 Aug. 1753; m. (1) Apr. 1772, James Knapp; m. int. (2) 2 Mar. 1778, Humphrey Holt. Two children by first and six by second union.

80

DANIEL[4] CHASE (Isaac,[3] Daniel[2]), born in Sutton, 5 Mar. 1716; died in Greenwich, about 1790. He married in Grafton, 17 Feb. 1742, MARGARET SAMPSON (called Lawson on the Church Records and Samson and Lamson in the Vital Rcords). A David Lawson and his wife Penelope were living in Grafton in 1744. According to the probate records a Daniel Chase of Sutton died about 1793. He had a deed from his father, 9 Mar. 1738, of 40 acres in Sutton. (Worcester Co. Deeds, 11:256). He purchased land in Petersham of Joseph Chamberlain, 18 Mar. 1745, and about 1750 removed to Greenwich.

Children, two eldest born in Petersham, others in Greenwich:

286. MARK,[5] a hunter and lived in the woods.
287. SIMON, b. 18 May 1746.
EDITH, probably d. young.
288. JOEL.
SARAH, m. in Orange, 17 Oct. 1771, Jonathan Elliott.
289. AARON, b. 3 Jan. 1761.
290. JONAS.
291. PAUL,
FREEDOM, m. John Christian Miller, of Warwick; b. in Greenwich.
LUCY, m. Michael Malcolm.
JUDITH, m. Cromwell Luther.
PATTY, m. Samuel Smith.

81

TIMOTHY[4] CHASE (Isaac,[3] Daniel[2]), born in Sutton, 12 Jan. 1719; died in Royalston, about 1809. He married about 1740, LEAH ROBBINS, daughter of Thomas and Lydia (Adams) Robbins, born in Grafton, 25 Apr. 1718. They resided in Grafton, 1740 to 1746; in Templeton, and in Royalston, 1790. The census of 1790 in Royalston gives him as the head of a family consisting of one male over 16 years, four males under 16 and two females.

Children, first three baptized in Grafton and younger children in Templeton:

292. THOMAS,[5] bp. 18 July 1742.
293. ABNER (twin), bp. 18 July 1742.
294. HENRY, bp. 4 Jan. 1746.

ABIGAIL, m. (1) 4 Mar. 1764, Solomon Chase (Ambrose,[4] Isaac,[3] Daniel,[2] Aquila[1]) (family 284); m. (2) —— Barber.
295.   MOSES, bp. 14 Aug. 1757.
296.   JOHN SARGENT, b. as early as 1750.
297.   TIMOTHY, b. about 1760; bp. 13 July 1774.
298.   NATHANIEL, b. about 1748; bp. 8 Feb. 1756.
299.   JACOB, bp. 8 Feb. 1756.
       NEHEMIAH, d. unm.

82

HENRY[4] CHASE (Isaac,[3] Daniel[2]), born in Sutton, 2 Mar. 1722; died in Petersham shortly before 5 Apr. 1778. He married in Petersham, 29 Dec. 1746, ABIGAIL STRATTON of "Pequioge" (Indian name of Athol). She was daughter of James and Deborah (Rand) Stratton who settled in Athol in 1736. In James Stratton's will made 6 Nov. 1775, he calls her his daughter Abigail Chase. (A Book of the Strattons 1:190, 191). The inventory of her estate was taken 15 Oct. 1793, showing that she died shortly before that date. They lived in Petersham, 1746 to 1777, and his deed calls him a clothier in 1746. In his marriage intention at Hardwick he is described as "of Whitstown," N. Y.

Children, born in Petersham:
300.   HENRY,[5] b. 4 Nov. 1748.
301.   JAMES, b. 26 Feb. 1750.
       HANNAH BEARY, b. 14 Mar. 1752; m. Jacob Ellison, son of John.
302.   CALEB, b. 15 Nov. 1753.
       DEBORAH, b. 1 Sept. 1755; m. int. 23 Mar. 1776, Seth Rider of Athol.
       DORCAS, b. 27 Apr. 1757; m. int. 23 Jan. 1779, Abel Grant of Templeton.
303.   ELISHA, b. 16 Jan. 1759.
       PHEBE, b. 3 Apr. 1761; m. 18 Dec. 1780, John Mahon [Mahan].
       MOLLY, b. 9 Feb. 1763; m. int. 23 Nov. 1779, William Dorral (Dorrell) of Warwick.
       BETTY, b. 8 Dec. 1764; m. 16 Apr. 1789, David Horsley of Hancock, N. H. She d. in Hancock, 11 May 1805.
       STEPHEN, b. 25 Aug. 1766; m. Betsey Skinner. He d. 13 June 1824; she d. 21 June 1851. No children.
       PETER, b. 12 Aug. 1768; d. young.
304.   PETER, b. 24 Feb. 1770.
       LOIS, b. 27 Aug. 1771; m. 22 Apr. 1791, Samuel Stone.

83

ELISHA[4] CHASE (Isaac,[3] Daniel[2]), born in Sutton about 1728; died at "Half Moon" in Waterford, Saratoga Co., N. Y., on his way home from the French and Indian War, 1757. Elisha Chase appears in Capt. Joseph Ingersoll's Co. of Col. Jonathan Bagley's Regt. in an expedition against Crown Point in a return dated at Fort William Henry, 12 Oct. 1756. He was then reported as sick. He served in this company from 18 Feb. to 28 Oct. 1756 and in the report dated at Boston, 14 Feb. 1757, was reported as dead. (Mass. Archives 94:464 and 95:189). His age is given as 27, on 10 Aug. 1756, at Fort William Henry. (Ibid 94;389). Elisha Chase and MARY

WHEELER, both of New Salem, married in Petersham, 8 Apr. 1748. It is assumed that they lived in New Salem, 1747 to 1756 and that their children were born there. The New Salem town records were burned in 1855 or 1856.

Children, born and baptized in New Salem:

305. EBENEZER,[5] bp. 4 June 1749.
306. EZEKIEL, bp. 23 Sept. 1750.
      PRUDENCE, bp. 14 Oct. 1752 or 1753; d. young.
      ISAAC, bp. 12 Oct. 1755; fell into the fire when a child and was a cripple for life.
      ELIZABETH, b. about 1756; m. ——— Owen.

84

ABNER[4] CHASE (Abner,[3] Daniel[2]), born in Haverhill, 1 Feb. 1722/3; baptized with his sisters, Mary and Sarah, at the Second Church of Amesbury (now Merrimac), 7 July 1728. He is not the Abner Chase of Salem, glazier, who lived there in 1764-1784, as that man was born about 1740. He is not mentioned in his father's will dated 29 Mar. 1780.

One Abner Chase witnessed the will of William Stevens of Pauling Precinct, Dutchess Co., N. Y., 22 Mar. 1783. (N. Y. Wills, 12:103). He was head of a family in Pauling in 1790, consisting of one male over 16 years (himself), one male under 16, and three females. If anything further is learned, it will be found under his number in the Appendix.

85

ENSIGN[4] CHASE (Abner,[3] Daniel[2]), born in Haverhill, 13 Mar. 1737/8. He is not a grantor or grantee of Essex County. If anything further is learned about him it will be given in the Appendix. No Ensign Chase was listed as head of a family in 1790.

86

JUDAH[4] CHASE (Daniel,[3] Daniel[2]), born in Newbury, 22 Nov. 1724; died in 1804. He married in Brunswick, Me., 8 Apr. 1752, MARGARET WOODSIDE, eldest daughter of William and Ann (Vincent) Woodside of Brunswick, grand-daughter of Rev. James Woodside who came from England and returned, leaving his son here. She was mentioned in her father's will as his "daughter Chase." Judah Chase settled in the west end of Brunswick (now South Freeport) in 1752, near Flying Point on Maquoit Bay. He served in Capt. William Burns's Co. over 16 weeks in 1746 and again in Capt. John Getchell's Co. in 1757. In 1790 his family consisted of five males over 16 years of age, one male under 16 years, and five females.

Children, born in ancient Brunswick:

ANNE,[5] b. 3 Mar. 1753.
JAMES, b. 23 Mar. 1755.
MARY, b. 5 Aug. 1757.
ISAAC, b. 27 Aug. 1759.
WILLIAM VINCENT, b. 2 Nov. 1761; m. int. in Freeport, Me., 23 Oct. 1790, to Alice Anderson.

ANTHONY, b. 2 Oct. 1763; m. int in Freeport, Me., 17 Nov. 1792, to Anne Anderson.
307. JUDAH, b. 16 Nov. 1765.
  MARGARET, b. 7 Nov. 1767.
308. NATHANIEL, b. 17 Jan. 1770.
  JEAN, b. 18 Apr. 1772.

87

DANIEL[4] CHASE (Daniel,[3] Daniel[2]), born in Newbury, 15 Oct. 1728; died in Concord, N. H., 31 July 1789. He married (1) about 1747, MARY PRATT, born 12 Apr. 1728, and died in Concord, 26 July 1779. He married (2) 22 Nov. 1779, widow ELIZABETH PELL.

Daniel[4] Chase Jr., with his family was ordered to Timothy Walker's garrison in Rumford, 15 May 1746. He was a signer of the Association Test at Concord in 1776. It is said that he served in the French and Indian War. They lived in Concord.

Children, born in Concord, N. H.:

  JONATHAN,[5] b. 3 Apr. 1749; d. 7 June 1771 in Concord.
  MOLLY, b. 20 Mar. 1750; m. Daniel Carter.
309. DANIEL, b. 12 Nov. 1751.
310. PRATT, b. 1 Apr. 1753.
  DOLLY, b. 1 Feb. 1755; d. young.
311. ROBERT, b. 27 Feb. 1757.
312. BENJAMIN, b. 27 Sept. 1758.
  ISAAC, b. 12 Sept. 1760; d. young.
  HANNAH, b. 11 Apr. 1762; m. (1) Moses Kimball; m. (2) Philip Emerson; d. 22 Jan. 1833 in Dexter, Me.
313. JAMES E., b. 1 Mar. 1764.
314. ISAAC, b. 30 Dec. 1766.
315. EBENEZER, b. 23 Sept. 1768.
  DOLLY, b. 29 June 1771.

88

CAPT. JONATHAN[4] CHASE (Daniel,[3] Daniel[2]), born in Newbury, 1 Mar. 1732/3; died in Hopkinton, N. H., 6 Feb. 1815, aged 83. He married 7 June 1760, SARAH STICKNEY, daughter of Col. Jeremiah and Elizabeth (Carleton) Stickney of Concord. She was born in Rumford (now Concord), 14 Oct. 1737, and died in Hopkinton, 10 Mar. 1812, aged 74.

  Capt. Jonathan was at the battle of Bennington and the taking of Burgoyne. In 1755 he belonged to Col. Rogers's Rangers in the French War. In an action with the Indians near Lake George, he noticed a large stump, through a hole in which shots were being fired. He supposed the person behind the stump would naturally wish to know the result of his shot, so after a short interval after a shot he aimed his musket at the hole and discharged it and a huge savage leaped into the air and fell dead. The Indians soon retreated and as Mr. Chase passed the stump he snatched a large wooden hominey spoon which hung to the Indian's side. The spoon was carried home and is preserved as a family relic. It is now in possession of Dr. Leonard Chase of Springfield, Vt. It is a curious specimen of savage workmanship having the figure of an Indian carved on the handle with a projection as a pedestal. He was in a sitting posture and holding to his mouth a water bottle.

The Gen. Assembly of N. H. 25 Jan. 1772, granted to Jonathan Chase, Beech Island in Conn. river between Cornish and Windsor. He commanded a Regiment at the surrender of Burgoyne and was active throughout the War of the Revolution. (N. H. Hist. Coll. Vol. VII, pg. 72, 219, 223, 254, 263 and Adj. Gen. Rep. Col. II, 1866, pps. 306, 309, 330, 331).

Children, born in Concord, N. H.:

316. SAMUEL,* b. 10 Mar. 1761.
317. MOSES, b. 30 Oct. 1763.
318. AARON, b. 27 Oct. 1766.
319. JEREMIAH STICKNEY, b. 27 May 1768.
320. CHARLES, b. 9 July 1770.
321. DANIEL, b. 13 Apr. 1772.
      SARAH, b. 10 July 1774; m. John Sleeper of Kingston, N. H. Children: (1) Jonathan Chase⁶ Sleeper, (2) Sarah Sleeper,* (3) Mary Sleeper, and (4) Elizabeth Sleeper.

88a

ISAAC⁴ CHASE (Daniel,³ Daniel²), born about 1740; died after 28 Mar. 1786. He served in the French and Indian War in 1758 and was captured (Harriman's Hist. of Warner). He and his brothers Daniel and Abner Chase agreed to become settlers in Warner, 9 Aug. 1763. He married ABIGAIL BRADLEY, daughter of Lt. Timothy and Abiah (Stevens) Bradley of Concord, N. H. She was born 2 Sept. 1740. He was one of the leading men in Warner serving as moderator of town meetings 1772-1786 when he resigned the office 28 Mar. 1786. He was living in Warner in 1790.

Child, born probably in Warner:

321a. ISAAC JR.,⁵ b. about 1764.

89

ABNER⁴ CHASE (Daniel,³ Daniel²), born in Concord, N. H., 27 May 1743. O. S.; died in Sunapee, N. H., 3 May 1834, aged 93. He married about 1764, BETSEY BRADLEY, daughter of Timothy and Abiah (Stevens) Bradley. She died in Sunapee, 20 June 1835, aged 93. They lived in Warner, N. H., and joined the Congregational Church there, 5 Feb. 1772. He enlisted as sergeant from Warner, 20 July 1777, and was in the battle of Bennington. He was a pensioner 24 Jan. 1833. They removed from Warner to Wendell (since 1850 Sunapee) where they died.

Children, born in Warner:

      ABIAH W.,⁵ b. 1765; m. William Lowell; she d. 11 Jan. 1849.
      PERMILLA, b. 9 Apr. 1766; m. 28 Oct. 1794, Francis Pingree. She d. 12 Sept. 1843 without issue.
      MARTHA, b. 30 Mar. 1767; m. int. 8 May 1785, James Otterson. She d. 9 Feb. 1845.
322. ABNER, went to Canada and died there.
323. PHILIP, supposed to have been drowned at sea.
      BETSEY, b. 1772; m. Rufus Stowell; d. 25 Nov. 1829. Four children.
      EUNICE, b. 1778; m. John Bickford; she d. Nov. 1808.
324. TIMOTHY BRADLEY, b. 25 Oct. 1781.

90

JOHN[4] CHASE (Daniel,[3] Daniel[2]), born in Concord, N. H., about 1745; died in Conway, N. H., 26 July 1824. He married, 20 Oct. 1763, PHEBE CARR, daughter of Francis Carr of Bow. They lived in Concord, and removed to Conway about 1778. John Chase was the head of a family in Conway in 1790, consisting of two males over 16 years, three males under 16 and five females. She died in Conway, 15 Sept. 1834, aged 96.

John[4] Chase of Conway, gentleman, being weak in body, made his will, 29 June 1824, which was proved 29 July 1824. He mentions wife Phebe, sons Francis, Isaac, Daniel, Oliver and Gilbert T. Chase; the heirs of his son John Jr.; his daughters Mary Rosebrook, Elizabeth Doloff, Sarah Mead and Matilda Weeks. John Chase son of Gilbert T. Chase, and Sarah Chase daughter of Isaac Chase. (Strafford Co. Probate, 32:30).

Phebe Chase of Conway, widow, made her will, 28 Mar. 1834, which was proved 24 Sept. 1834. She mentions her daughters Polly Smith, Sarah Mead, Betsey Dolloff, and Matilda Stanley; her grandson Samuel Chase, son of Gilbert T. Chase; daughter-in-law Phebe Chase and sons Gilbert T., Daniel and Oliver Chase. (Ibid. 48:329).

Children, first two born in Bow, third and fourth in Concord, last five in Conway:

325. JOHN,[5] b. 14 Aug. 1764.
326. FRANCIS, b. 22 May 1766.
    SARAH, b. 20 Mar. 1768; d. young.
    MOLLY, b. 23 May 1770; d. young.
327. ISAAC, b. 18 Sept. 1772.
    MOLLY, b. 14 Mar. 1775; m. (1) James Rosebrook; no children. m. (2) ——— Smith.
    SARAH, b. 9 May 1777; m. James Meade of Eaton, N. H.
    ELISABETH, b. 29 June 1779; m. William Dolloff of Bartlett, N. H.
328. DANIEL, b. 24 Dec. 1782.
329. OLIVER, b. 27 Feb. 1785.
    MATILDA, b. 23 May 1786; m. (1) John Stanley; m. (2) John Weeks. She d. in Somersworth, N. H., about 1864.
330. GILBERT TENANT, b. 1 Jan. 1790.

91

HUMPHREY[4] CHASE (Enoch,[3] Daniel[2]), born in Amesbury, 11 July 1732; died in North Yarmouth, Me., 27 Aug. 1818. He married ELIZABETH LORING, daughter of Rev. Nicholas and Mary (Richmond) Loring. She was born 22 Feb. 1746 and died in North Yarmouth, 16 Sept. 1820. They united with the First Church of North Yarmouth, 16 June 1771. He was a housewright and a farmer and lived near the old meeting house in North Yarmouth. (Old Times in North Yarmouth, 881).

Children, born in North Yarmouth, Me.:

331. THOMAS,[5] bp. 11 Aug. 1776.
    MARY, bp. 17 May 1778; m. Isaiah Booker; d. Jan. 1815, aged 37; four children.
    LUCRETIA, bp. 25 July 1779; alive in 1880.
332. JEREMIAH, bp. 26 Nov. 1780.

ELIZABETH, bp. 23 Feb. 1783; d. young.
SARAH, bp. 4 July 1784; m. Dea. Asa⁶ Chase. (Family 1053)
JANE, bp. 13 Aug. 1786; m. Samuel Hatch; she d. 14 Nov. 1813;
    one child d. young.
333. CHARLES, bp. 16 Sept. 1787.
REUBEN, bp. 3 May 1789; d. young.
334. LEVI, bp. 23 May 1790.

92

CAPT. ENOCH⁴ CHASE (Enoch,³ Daniel²), born in Amesbury,
1 July 1734; living in Salisbury, N. H. in 1791.   He married in
Amesbury, 13 Feb. 1755, MARY DAVIS.   He and his wife Mary renewed their baptismal covenant with the Second Church of Amesbury
(now Merrimac) 20 July 1755.   Perhaps Mary was daughter of
Ephraim and Mary (Page) Davis, born in Amesbury, 3 June 1735.
She probably died before 1759.   He married (2) in Amesbury, 29
Mar. 1759, GERTRUDE HARVEY.   Dr. John B. Chace called her Gertrude Challis but upon what authority is not known.   They removed
from Amesbury to East Kingston, N. H. about 1760 and about 1775
removed to Salisbury, N. H.   In 1790 he was head of a family in
Salisbury consisting of two males over 16 years of age, no males under 16 and four females.
    Child by first wife, born in Amesbury:
335. THOMAS,⁵ b. 1 May 1755; bp. 20 July 1755.
    Child by second wife, born in East Kingston:
336. WILLIAM, b. 2 Oct. 1761.

93

THOMAS⁴ CHASE (Enoch,³ Daniel²), born in Amesbury, 30 Oct.
1736; baptized at the Second Church of Amesbury (now Merrimac),
23 Jan. 1736/7.   He married PHEBE HILL (?).   Nothing has been
found to confirm this marriage or the birth of a son John, as given
in Dr. Chace's records.
    Child:
337. JOHN,⁵ b. 12 May 1767.

93a

DANIEL⁴ CHASE (Enoch,³ Daniel²), born in Amesbury, 2 June
1741.   His birth is recorded in the Vital Records of Amesbury as
son of Enoch and Judith Chase, but Dr. Chace does not give his
name in the family of Enoch and Judith Chase.   If any thing further
is learned it will appear in the Appendix.

94

DAVID⁴ CHASE (Enoch,³ Daniel²), born in Amesbury, 12 June
1744.   Nothing further has been found relating to him.

95

JOHN⁴ CHASE (Enoch,³ Daniel²), born in Amesbury, 18 Apr.
1745; died about 1783.   He married MARY DANFORTH who died in
Apr. 1828.   They lived in Brunswick, Me.   He was rated in Ames-

bury for the year 1763, and removed to Brunswick about 1764. (Old Times in North Yarmouth, 504). He was listed as head of a family in Brunswick in 1790, consisting of one male over 16 years of age, three males under 16, and three females. (Me. Census, 12).
Children:

338. ENOCH,[5] b. 1776.
339. JOHN, lived in Topsham, Me.
     SARAH, m. William Wilson of Topsham, Me.
     HANNAH, m. Joseph Kimball of Lisbon, Me.
     RUTH.
     MARIAN, m. William Kilgore of Brunswick, Me.
340. JAMES.
     MARY, m. James Means of Topsham, Me.
     BETSEY.
341. NATHANIEL, drowned in Brunswick, Me.

96

JUDGE SAMUEL[4] CHASE (Daniel,[3] Ens. Moses[2]), born in Newbury (now West Newbury), 28 Sept. 1707; died in Cornish, N. H., 12 Aug. 1800, aged about 93. He married in May 1728, MARY DUDLEY, daughter of Samuel Dudley Esq. of Sutton. Her mother was Abigail King of Concord. She was born 11 Feb. 1711, and died in Cornish, 12 Feb. 1789. He married (2) ESTHER ———— who survived him.

He lived in Sutton until 1764 when he removed to the new township of Cornish. Here he became the first justice of the peace, the first moderator and the first selectman. Although about seventy years of age he was active in the Revolutionary War and went with his son Col. Jonathan Chase with the Regiment to Saratoga and Bennington in 1777. His name appears in connection with nearly all public meetings and documentary transactions of the Revolutionary War period. He was one of the early Judges of the Superior Court of Cheshire County, then including what is now Sullivan County. His portrait was painted by Gilbert Stuart in 1790 and is now in possession of Mrs. Eldred of Roseville, Ill. Through her kindness a reproduction was made for *The Chase Chronicle* which appears in this volume.

Children, born in Sutton:

342. SAMUEL,[5] b. 28 Nov. 1728.
343. DUDLEY, b. 29 Aug. 1730.
344. JONATHAN, b. 6 Dec. 1732.
     ELISABETH, b. 23 Nov. 1735; m. 7 Nov. 1751, James Richardson of Leicester.
345. MARCH, b. 21 June 1738.
     MARY, b. 2 July 1740; d. ——— Jan. 1742.
     SARAH (twin), b. 2 July 1740; m. 9 Mar. 1758, Ebenezer Rawson; d. 14 Nov. 1814.
346. SOLOMON, b. 1 Sept. 1742.
     MARY, b. 25 Feb. 1743/4; d. Aug. 1745.
     REBECCA.
     ABIGAIL, b. 15 July 1753; d. Nov. 1756.
     ANNA, bp. 27 Apr. 1746; m. 25 June 1761, Daniel Putnam; d. 28 Oct. 1820.

97

DANIEL⁴ CHASE (Daniel,³ Ens. Moses²), born in Newbury, 18
Sept. 1709; died in Sutton, 1788. He married (1) about 1729,
HANNAH TUTTLE of Littleton. She died in Sutton, 18 Feb. 1781,
aged about 80. He married (2) in Sutton, 24 Jan. 1782, MARTHA
FLETCHER of Grafton, probably a widow. They lived in Sutton and
the inventory of his estate was taken, 30 May 1793, with the administration. The church records of Sutton report the death of the
"wife of Daniel Chase," 18 Feb. 1781, aged about 80, and the same
records again report the death of "Hannah, the widow of Daniel
Chase," 15 Dec. 1771, aged about 88. This second record can not
refer to the death of the mother of the following children as this
woman must have been born about 1683 and was about 57 years of
age when the twins were born in 1741, but Daniel⁴ Chase was living
many years after 1771. She could have been the widow of his father
Daniel³ Chase, but no evidence has been found that the senior Daniel
had a second wife Hannah. It is possible that the original record
reads: the widow of David Chase died 15 Dec. 1771, aged about 88.
This conclusion is likely to be revealed by a critical study of the
original church records of Sutton.

Children by first wife, born in Sutton:

    HANNAH,⁵ b. 15 Oct. 1733; d. 11 Dec. 1733.
347.   PAUL, b. 13 Mar. 1734/5.
    HANNAH, b. 11 Jan. 1736/7; m. 3 July 1759, Eliakim Garfield
      of Leicester.
    LUCY, b. 30 Jan. 1738/9; m. 15 Nov. 1764, Benjamin Garfield
      of Grafton.
    *ANNA (twin), b. 1 May 1741; d. 1 Nov. 1745, a. 4y.
    JUDITH (twin), b. 1 May 1741.
    EUNICE, m. Nathaniel Garfield.

98

Lt. CALEB⁴ CHASE (Daniel,³ Ens. Moses²), born in Newbury,
29 Nov. 1722; died in Sutton, 2 Oct. 1808, aged 86. He married, 11
Apr. 1745, SARAH PRINCE, daughter of David and Phebe (Fuller)
Prince of Danvers and Sutton. She was born in Salem Village
(Danvers), 28 Apr. 1728; died in Sutton, 15 Feb. 1803, in her 76th
year. They lived in Sutton, and were buried in the County Bridge
Cemetery in Millbury.

Children, born in Sutton:

    PHEBE,⁵ b. 7 Apr. 1747; d. in infancy.
    MARY, b. 2 Sept. 1748; m. 17 Oct. 1770, John Woodbury; d. 1
      Apr. 1799.
348.   NEHEMIAH, b. 8 Feb. 1751.
349.   DAVID PRINCE, b. 15 Jan. 1753.
350.   CALEB PRINCE, b. 19 Mar. 1755.
351.   JOSEPH, b. 13 Mar. 1757.
    SARAH, b. 1 May 1759; m. 12 Dec. 1781, Peter Dudley; d. 24
      Feb. 1836.
352.   JOHN, b. 12 Mar. 1761.

    *The tombstone states that Anna, twin, d. 1 Nov. 1745 and the town rec-
ords that Judith, twin, d. 1 Nov. 1745.

353. STEPHEN, b. 26 Apr. 1763.
354. MOSES, b. 1 Nov. 1765.
355. DANIEL, b. 9 Jan. 1768.
356. ISRAEL, b. 21 Mar. 1770.
      RACHEL, b. 18 Oct. 1772; m. 6 Nov. 1791, David Dudley. 3d.
      She d. Aug. 1799.

99

MOODY[4] CHASE (Daniel,[3] Ens. Moses[2]), born in Newbury, 23 Sept. 1723; died in Shirley, 27 Apr. 1815. He married in Sutton, 17 Jan. 1748/9, ELIZABETH HALE, daughter of Jonathan and Susannah (Tuttle) Hale, born in Bradford, 25 Sept. 1730; died in Shirley, 9 Nov. 1820, aged 90. They lived in Groton in 1790, and later in Shirley (now Ayer).

Moody[4] Chase, when about 22 years of age, and Col. William Prescott of Groton, of Revolutionary fame, were at a social party at Worcester when a cup of tea was presented to him which he first declined, never having seen any before, but being told what it was, he drank it. He and Col. Prescott at that party selected their partners for life. Elisabeth and Abigail Hale. Col. Wm. Prescott, b. 20 Feb. 1726; m. 1756 or 7, Abigail Hale of Groton, Mass., b. 1733. He settled in that part of Groton called "The Gore" now in Pepperell, Mass. (Prescott Memorial). Moody was the leader of a party of 20 men who went to Hanover to clear off the forest and prepare the site of Dartmouth College.

Moody[4] Chase of Shirley, gentleman, made his will 19 Aug. 1814 and it was probated 29 May 1815. He mentions therein his wife Elizabeth, his daughters Susannah Gould, Elizabeth Sargent, Mary Chase and Judith Chase; his sons Jacob Chase, March Chase; his grandson Jonathan Chase, son of his son William Chase dec'd; his grandchildren Lydia Chase, Elizabeth Chase, Samuel Chase, Moody Chase and William Prescott Chase, children of his son Samuel Chase dec'd; his grandchildren Elizabeth Chase, Mary Chase, Susan Chase and Celina Chase, children of his son March Chase to have residue. (Middlesex Co. Probate, 4303).

Children, born in Sutton:

      SUSANNA,[5] m. 31 Oct. 1769, John Gould of Lyndeborough, N. H.
      She d. 1826.
      WILLIAM, d. young.
357. JACOB, b. 12 Sept. 1761.
      MARY, b. 1767; d. in Pepperell, a. 76, unm., 24 July 1843.
358. SAMUEL, b. 20 Apr. 1768.
      BETSEY, m. int. 12 Dec. 1802, Timothy Sargent of Orford. N. H.
      JUDITH, bp. 12 Mar. 1771; d. in Pepperell, unm., 30 Dec. 1843.
      age 71.
359. MARCH, b. 1776.
360. WILLIAM, b. 1751.
      Three other children died young.

100

CAPT. MOSES[4] CHASE (Daniel,[3] Ens. Moses[2]), born in Littleton. 3 Mar. 1726/7; died in Cornish, N. H., 18 Oct. 1799, aged 72. He married in Sutton, 15 Apr. 1752, HANNAH BROWN, daughter of Jonas and Hannah Brown, born in Sutton, 15 May 1735; died in

Cornish, 16 Jan. 1812, aged 76y. 8 m. They lived in Sutton till about 1764 when he removed to Cornish.

Moses[4] Chase was one of the first settlers in Cornish, and his 7th child Caleb, b. 11 Sept. 1767, is said to have been the first child born there. Moses was a Captain in Col. Jonathan Chase's Reg. in 1777, and one of the Executive Council of N. H., 1787. The General Assembly of N. H., 25 Jan. 1772, granted to Moses Chase 500 acres of land adjoining Connecticut river.

Children, first six born in Sutton, others in Cornish, N. H.:

361. DANIEL,[5] b. 23 Mar. 1753.
362. JOHN, b. 4 Oct. 1755.
    HANNAH, b. 7 Feb. 1758; m. 4 Dec. 1777, Daniel Kimball of Plainfield, N. H. No children. She d. 16 June 1847. They founded Kimball Union Academy at Meriden, N. H.
363. AMOS, b. 19 May 1760.
364. NAHUM C., b. 9 Oct. 1762.
    JUDITH, b. 26 Nov. 1764; m. Sylvanus Bryant; she d. 2 Oct. 1811.
365. CALEB, b. 11 Sept. 1767.
    SUSANNAH, b. 4 Aug. 1769; d. 26 Oct. 1769, a. 2m.
366. MOODY, b. 10 Oct. 1770.
367. MOSES, b. 29 Nov. 1772.
    SUSAN, b. 4 July 1776; d. 20 Oct. 1777.
368. CLEMENT (twin), b. 4 July 1776.
369. HARVEY, b. 13 Nov. 1778.
    SARAH, b. 9 Oct. 1781; m. 1801, Rev. John W. Lord, son of John of Lyme, Conn.

101

LT. WELLS[4] CHASE (Moses,[3] Ens. Moses[2]), born in Newbury (now West Newbury), 4 Oct. 1710; died in Concord, N. H., 2 Dec. 1785. He married (1) in Newbury, 6 Aug. 1734, MARTHA MORSE, born in Newbury, 14 Feb. 1708. In her father's will, made 18 Aug. daughter of Dea. William and Sarah (Merrill) Morse, born in Newbury, 14 Feb. 1708. In her father's will, made 18 Aug. 1744, she is called "my daughter Martha Chase." They lived in Amesbury (now Merrimac). She died in Amesbury, 19 Oct. 1771. He married (2) in Amesbury, 27 Feb. 1773, MARY CURRIER.

With his second wife he removed from Amesbury to Concord about 1780. Possibly his widow is the Mary Chase who died in Amesbury, 20 Mar. 1797, aged 80. His will, made at Concord, 1 Nov. 1784, and proved at Exeter, N. H., 9 Jan. 1786, mentions his wife Mary and her home in Amesbury, his sons Thomas, William, Moses and Wells, his daughter Martha Davis, the heirs of his late daughter Ann Lowell dec'd, his *five sons,* son Daniel Chase to have his lands in Concord.

Children, born in Amesbury (now Merrimac), baptized at Second Church:

370. THOMAS,[5] b. 14 May 1735.
371. WILLIAM, b. 22 Nov. 1736.
372. MOSES, b. 20 Aug. 1738.
373. WELLS, b. 16 Jan. 1740/41.
    ANNA, b. 30 Mar. 1743; m. 15 Sept. 1767, Isaac Lowell.
374. DANIEL, b. 24 Oct. 1744.

MARTHA, b. 18 Apr. 1747; m. 4 Jan. 1769, Ephraim Davis Jr. of
Hadley's Corner in Amesbury.

TIMOTHY, b. 16 Aug. 1749; bp. 20 Aug. 1749; probably d. young,
as he has not been found elsewhere, and is not mentioned in
his father's will, 1 Nov. 1784.

102

MOSES[4] CHASE (Moses,[3] Ens. Moses[2]), born in Newbury (now
West Newbury), 1 July 1713; died there 9 Oct. 1789, aged 76y. 3m.
9d. He married in Newbury, 9 Dec. 1736, JUDITH BARTLETT,
daughter of Richard and Margaret (Woodman) Bartlett, born in
Newbury, 10 Mar. 1712/13; died there, 18 Feb. 1783, in her 71st
year.

They lived in what is now West Newbury, he inheriting with his
brother John the east half of the Ensign Moses[2] Chase homestead.
He made his will 2 Mar. 1786, which was proved 26 Oct. 1789.
Therein he mentions his sons Wells, Stephen, Enoch and Joshua,
his daughters Rebecca, Elizabeth and Judith then unmarried, his son
John[5] to have the easterly half of his homestead and son Moses[5] to
have the westerly half. Samuel Carr, son of Samuel and Elizabeth[6]
(Chase) Carr, purchased one half of Moses[5] Chase in 1803 and the
other half of John[5] Chase in 1811. This homestead has remained
in the Carr family to the present time, passing on the death of Miss
Caroline Carr, great grand-daughter of Samuel and Elizabeth
(Chase) Carr, to the daughters of her sister, Hattie F., who married
George H. Wormwood.

John[5] Chase, son of Moses[4], made his will 8 May 1802, which
was proved 5 Aug. 1811. He gave his estate to his wife Elizabeth
and after her decease to Elizabeth the wife of Samuel Carr Jr. of
Newbury and to Thomas Gray Chase, son of his brother Joshua[5]
Chase, in equal parts. (Essex Probate, 81 : 60).

Children, born in Newbury (now West Newbury):

375. WELLS,[5] b. 9 Sept. 1737.
    REBECCA, b. 14 June 1739; m. 30 Nov. 1768, Samuel Longfellow
    of Byfield. She d. 25 Feb. 1788.
    ELISABETH, b. 19 Sept. 1741; m. 19 Oct. 1772, Daniel Carr of
    Newbury and Hopkinton, N. H.
    JOHN, b. 25 Sept. 1743; d. 24 June 1811; m. 11 July 1771, Elisa-
    beth Carr, dau. of John and Anna (Moody) Carr; d. 22 Sept.
    1835. No children.
    JUDITH, b. 4 Jan. 1745/6; m. 4 July 1793, Stephen Carleton of
    Bradford. She d. 1825.
    WATERS (twin), b. 4 Jan. 1745/6; d. 4 June 1746.
376. STEPHEN, b. 7 Feb. 1748; d. 6 Oct. 1819; no children; lived in
    Leominster; m. 12 Dec. 1771, Sarah Smith.
377. ENOCH, b. 16 Sept. 1750.
378. JOSHUA, b. 28 Feb. 1752.
379. MOSES, b. 4 July 1756.

103

DEA. SETH[4] CHASE (Moses,[3] Ens. Moses[2]), born in Newbury
(now West Newbury), 21 Nov. 1715; died in Sutton, 24 Sept. 1791,
aged 76. He married (1) in Newbury, 31 May 1738, ELIZABETH

BARTLETT, daughter of Richard and Margaret (Woodman) Bartlett, born in Newbury, 5 Mar. 1714; died in Sutton, 22 May 1787, aged 73. He married (2) in Sutton, 17 Mar. 1788, ABIGAIL MARCH, a widow. His remains and those of his first wife were buried in the Dodge Cemetery in Sutton near Grafton town line. He was a deacon of the First Baptist Church in Sutton 1767-1791, and a comb-maker. His will was probated at Worcester in 1791. (No. 11,383).

Children, born in Sutton:

JOSHUA,[5] b. 22 July 1739. When a lad of 17 or 18 years he was in the provincial service in the war with France and on his return, when at a point near Charlestown or Cornish, N. H., left his comrades to visit Croyden where his brother Seth had settled and was not heard from afterward.

380. BRADFORD, b. 8 Aug. 1741.
381. SETH, b. 8 Jan. 1743/4.
ELISABETH, b. 17 Apr. 1746; d. 28 Aug. 1756, in Sutton.
382. JOSIAH, b. 20 Feb. 1747/8.
REBECCA, b. 17 Apr. 1750; m. 23 Apr. 1772, John Bartlett.
RACHEL, b. 25 May 1752; m. 21 Sept. 1773; Isaac Platts Jr. of Bradford.

104

HUMPHREY[4] CHASE (Moses,[3] Ens. Moses[2]), born in Newbury (now West Newbury), 8 Jan. 1717/18; died in Haverhill, 6 June 1794. He married in Haverhill, 23 Aug. 1744, ABIGAIL ELA, daughter of Samuel and Hannah (Clark) Ela, born in Haverhill, 19 Nov. 1719, died there 20 Mar. 1792; buried in Walnut Street Cemetery. They lived in East Haverhill on Corliss Hill. He was a husbandman and carpenter.

He made his will 10 Mar. which was proved 30 June 1794. He mentions therein his children Abigail Colby, Elizabeth, Anna, Rebecca, Ephraim, Moses and Daniel Chase, Moses to have land and buildings in Plaistow, N. H., where he then lived, Daniel to have one half of the homestead in Haverhill, bounded by the land of Josiah Chase, and Ephraim to have the other half. (Essex Probate, 63:128, 179).

Children, born in Haverhill:

ABIGAIL,[5] b. 9 Dec. 1745; m. 10 July 1769, Anthony Colby.
ELISABETH, b. 9 Aug. 1748; d. unm.; called "Aunt Betty."
EPHRAIM, b. 13 June 1750; d. Nov. 6, 1754.
MOSES, b. 19 Sept. 1752; d. 31 Oct. 1754.
ANNA, b. 16 Dec. 1755; m. 18 Dec. 1777, John Chase 3d of Newbury, son of Johnson[5] Chase. (Family 550)
383. EPHRAIM, b. 20 Jan. 1757.
REBECCA, b. 22 Aug. 1759; m. 29 Dec. 1796, Moses Bartlett of Plaistow, N. H.
384. MOSES, b. —— 1762.
385. DANIEL, bp. 7 Oct. 1764.

105

ELEAZER[4] CHASE (Moses,[3] Ens. Moses[2]), born in Newbury (now West Newbury), 25 July 1722; died in Buckfield, Me., in 1808, aged 86. He married (1) JEANNETTE ELDER of Windham, Me., daughter of Samuel Elder who came from Andmore, county

of Antrim, north of Ireland, and settled in Falmouth, Me., in
1730. After her death he married (2), 24 June 1759, Mrs. MARY
(BOOTHBY (?)) BROWN, widow of Ezra Brown, who was killed by
Indians in Buckfield, 14 May 1756. He removed from Standish,
Me., to Buckfield, Me., in 1782. They resided in Windham, 1751,
Standish and Buckfield. He was a Revolutionary soldier. He was
also a soldier in the French and Indian War under command of
Capt. George Berry from 19 May 1746 to 19 Jan. 1747.

Children by first wife, born in Windham:

NATHANIEL,⁵ b. 14 June 1750; bp. 18 Oct. 1750; d. young.
386.   JOSHUA, bp. 25 Feb. 1753, N. S.
MARY, b. 10 Apr. 1755; m. 1774, Nathaniel Freeman of Gorham.
387.   ISAAC, b. 12 Dec. 1757.

Children by second wife, born in Windham:

388.   NATHANIEL, b. 2 Sept. 1761.
MIRIAM, bp. 10 July 1763.
389.   JOSEPH, bp. —— Oct. 1766.
BETSEY, m. 5 Mar. 1789, Ebenezer Cotton of Gorham. She d.
11 Mar. 1838.

106

DANIEL⁴ CHASE (Moses,³ Ens. Moses²), born in Newbury
(now West Newbury), 31 Dec. 1726; died between 14 June and 1
Dec. 1777. He married in Newbury, 19 Oct. 1748, HANNAH SOM-
ERBY, daughter of Abial and Mary (Noyes) Somerby, born in New-
bury, 7 Feb. 1724/25. They resided in Newbury and removed to the
East Parish of Haverhill in 1761.

He made his will 14 June 1777 which was proved 1 Dec. 1777. He
mentions his wife Hannah, son Somerby Chase to have the silver par-
ringer, the great Bible and half the Divinity books except Flavel's works
in folio; daughters Anne Cheney, Hannah Davis and Molly Chase; son
Leonard Chase to have the homestead of 40 acres and be executor. (Essex
Probate, Vol. 54:9, 22).

Children, born in Newbury (now West Newbury):

390.   LEONARD,⁵ b. 19 Dec. 1749.
391.   SOMERBY, b. 6 Aug. 1751.
ANNA, b. 28 Jan. 1753; bp. 11 Feb. 1753; m. (1) 13 June 1777,
Richard Cheney; m. (2) Samuel Welch.
HANNAH, b. 4 Jan. 1756; m. Benjamin Davis.
MOLLY, b. 3 Sept. 1757.

107

DEA. FRANCIS⁴ CHASE (Samuel,³ Ens. Moses²), born in Newbury (now West Newbury), 18 Aug. 1715; died in Newton, N. H.,
25 Dec. 1806. He married in Amesbury, 29 Sept. 1737, SARAH
PIKE, probably daughter of Robert Pike, baptized in Salisbury, 27
Nov. 1715. Her death at Newton, at the age of 77, was caused by
falling from a horse, 14 Oct. 1794.

They lived in Amesbury (now Newton, N. H.). He owned a
saw and grist mill in Litchfield, N. H. He deeded his lot there to
his sons Samuel, Simeon and Joseph in 1774. He and his wife
Sarah were received into the Second Church of Amesbury (now

Merrimac), 14 May 1738, and later one of the founders of the Baptist Church in Newton. He was a soldier in the French and Indian War in 1755, and was in the expedition to Crown Point and Lake George.

Children, first six born in Amesbury, others born in Newton, N. H.:

HANNAH,[*] b. 22 Sept. 1738; m. about 1761, Col. Joseph Welch of Plaistow, N. H.; thirteen children.
392. SAMUEL, b. 23 Oct. 1739.
393. AMOS, b. 6 July 1741.
394. FRANCIS, b. 15 July 1743.
395. JOSEPH. b. 25 Feb. 1744/5.
396. ABNER, b. 19 Nov. 1746.
397. SIMEON, b. 26 Aug. 1748.
SARAH, b. 24 July 1750; m. Abner Currier; d. in Unity, N. H., 1840.
BETSEY, b. 18 Sept. 1752; d. 28 Nov. 1757.
398. DANIEL, b. 21 May 1755.
BETTY, b. 27 Oct. 1758; m. 4 Dec. 1777, Richard Whittier; d. in Canaan, N. H., 1820.
MOLLY, b. 12 Feb. 1760; m. Jonathan Carleton; d. Canaan, N. H., 1830.
399. MOSES, b. 2 Mar. 1763.
RUTH, b. 25 July 1765; d. 28 Nov. 1769.

108

DEA. AMOS[4] CHASE (Samuel[3] Ens. Moses[2]), born in Newbury (now West Newbury), 9 Jan. 1718/9; died in Saco, Me., 2 Mar. 1818, aged 99y. 1m. 4d. He married (1) in 1740, SARAH COLE, daughter of Samuel Cole of Saco. She died in Saco, 4 Feb. 1781, aged 56y. He married (2) DEBORAH ——— who died in Saco, 29 Dec. 1793, aged 66y. He was deacon of the Congregational Church of Saco, 1763. He removed from Newbury to Pepperellborough (now Saco) about 1753 and lived there the rest of his life. He served on the Committee of Correspondence and Safety for Saco in 1774 and 1776. (Ridlon's Saco Valley Settlements and Families, 106). (Also Folsom's History of Saco and Biddeford, 281). On 17 July 1817, he rode three miles to take the hand of the President of the United States, James Monroe, as he passed through Saco from Portland, Me. His homestead in Saco was at the "Elms" below the city proper, and two miles north of the ferry where he originally settled.

Dea. Chase was a commanding figure, six feet in height, vigorous and erect in old age, eloquent in conversation and pre-eminently so in prayer. He is said to have worn his hair long "down over his shoulders, white as snow, and dressed in old style breeches without suspenders." He was indeed a patriarch. He was admitted to the church in Biddeford, 10 June 1744.

Amos[4] Chase of Saco, gentleman, made his will, 10 Apr. 1809, which was proved 25 Mar. 1818. He mentions his sons Samuel, Amos, Joseph, John, Daniel and Abner Chase; Eliphalet Parker and Abraham Parker children of his daughter Rebecca Parker; daughters Sarah Hardy and Hannah Chase lately deceased; the heirs of his daughter Betsey Robin-

son deceased; the heirs of his daughter Olive Nason deceased; daughter
Mary Jones; Daniel Chase to be executor. (York Co. Probate, 27:257).
Children, first four born in Newbury, others in Saco, Me.:

400.   SAMUEL,[5] b. 25 Mar. 1742; bp. 26 June 1743.
       REBECCA, b. 25 Feb. 1743/4; m. 25 Oct. 1763, Chase Parker.
       HANNAH, bp. 2 Feb. 1745; d. unm. 19 Mar. 1809.
       SARAH, b. 10 Aug. 1747; m. Jacob Bedell.
       BETSEY, b. 23 Mar. 1751; bp. 31 Mar. 1751.
401.   AMOS, b. 25 Nov. 1752; bp. 3 Dec. 1752.
402.   JOSEPH, b. 10 Oct. 1754; bp. 24 Nov. 1754.
       ANNA, bp. 25 July 1756.
403.   JOHN, b. 18 Dec. 1757; bp. 16 Apr. 1758.
       OLIVE, b. 29 Dec. 1759; bp. 3 Feb. 1760.
404.   DANIEL, b. 28 Aug. 1762; bp. 5 Sept. 1762.
       MARY, b. 16 Mar. 1764; m. 6 Mar. 1781, Wigglesworth Tappan.
405.   ABNER, b. 29 Apr. 1768.

109

SAMUEL[4] CHASE (Samuel,[3] Ens. Moses[2]), born in Newbury
(now West Newbury), 22 Oct. 1728; died there, 31 Oct. 1769, in
his 40th year, the result of falling from an apple tree. He entered
his intention of marriage at Newbury, 23 Nov. 1751, with SARAH
STEWART of Amesbury. They were married in Kingston, N. H., 24
Dec. 1751. She was daughter of Robert and Ann (Adams) Stewart,
born in Kingston, N. H., 16 Oct. 1732. She married (2) in Newbury, 9 Dec. 1798, Maj. Thomas Noyes. She died there, 15 Jan.
1813, aged 80. They lived in Newbury (now West Newbury).

He made his will ᶜ Oct. 1769, mentioning his three sons Robert, Benjamin and Samuel and "any son that may be born after my death," and
five daughters, Mary, Anna, Sarah, Betty, Hannah and "any daughter
that may be born after my death" each £20.

Children, born in Newbury (now West Newbury):

       MARY,[5] b. 19 Feb. 1753; m. (1) 17 Feb. 1774, Moody Smith; m.
          (2) Ebenezer Hopkinson, son of Jonathan and Rebecca
          (Hardy) Hopkinson.
       ANNA, b. 7 Aug. 1755; m. 17 Apr. 1778, William Bailey; d. 18
          Mar. 1818.
406.   ROBERT, b. 10 Apr. 1757.
407.   BENJAMIN. bp. 15 July 1759.
       SARAH, b. 10 Jan. 1760; m. 18 Mar. 1780, Joshua Bailey.
       SAMUEL, bp. 6 Oct. 1763; d. 19 Apr. 1782, aged 19y.
       ELIZABETH, b. —— 1764; d. 1 Oct. 1773, aged 9y.
       HANNAH, b. 21 Apr. 1768; m. 17 Dec. 1791, Maj. Samuel[5] Bailey
          of Newbury and the homestead passed to the Baileys who held
          it until early in the present century.
408.   AMOS, b. 15 May 1770.

110

BENJAMIN[4] CHASE (Samuel,[3] Ens. Moses[2]), born in Newbury
(now West Newbury), 3 Feb. 1736/7; died in Brunswick, Me., 9
May 1802. He married in Biddeford, Me. 30 Sept. 1762, CATHA-
RINE CAMPBELL who died 9 Oct. 1815. He was the head of a family
consisting of three males over 16 years, one under 16, and four females, living in Brunswick in 1790.

Children, born in Brunswick, Me. :

JOSEPH,[5] b. 16 Sept. 1763; d. 1791, lost at sea.

ELISABETH, b. 25 1765; d. unm. 24 Mar. 1830 in Brunswick.

HANNAH, b. 27 Jan. 1768; m. (1) 14 Dec. 1786, William Stanwood; seven children. She d. 22 Aug. 1833 in Brunswick,
Me.; m. (2) Jeremiah Hodgdon.

SUSANNA, b. 1 May 1771; d. unm. 28 Dec. 1828.

409. SAMUEL, b. 31 Mar. 1774.

DANIEL, b. 10 June 1777; d. 1803, at sea.

111

JOHN[4] CHASE (Samuel,[3] Ens. Moses[2]), born in Newbury (now
West Newbury), 25 Mar. 1740; died 5 July 1811. He married in
Newbury, 16 Feb. 1762, RUTH HILLS, daughter of Moses and Re-
becca (Hills) Hills. She was born in Chester, N. H., 6 Oct. 1742.
John Chase removed to Haverhill, N. H., and later to Littleton,
N. H., in 1782, and was selectman there in 1787. They lived in
Hampstead, Chester, Haverhill, Littleton and Sunapee. They owned
the church covenant at Hampstead, 20 Nov. 1763. His widow mar-
ried (2) Peter Sargent of New London, N. H., and died in 1817.

Children, first and second born in Hampstead, third to sixth
born in Haverhill, N. H. :

REBECCA.[5] bp. 20 Nov. 1763; m. 28 Nov. 1784, Stephen Ordway;
had a large family.

410. MOSES, bp. 14 Nov. 1764.

411. JOHN, b. 14 Mar. 1766.

POLLY, m. Seth Freeman; lived in Plainfield, N. H.; no children.

412. JOSEPH, b. 12 Mar. 1768.

PRUDENCE, b. 17 Jan. 1775; m. 25 Nov. 1792, Ebenezer Sargent,
son of Peter Sargent of New London. She was mother of
Hon. Jonathan E. Sargent, Chief Justice of the Supreme Court
of New Hampshire, 1873-4. She d. 17 Mar. 1858.

112

HENRY[4] CHASE (Ens. Stephen,[3] Ens. Moses[2]), born in Newbury (now West Newbury), 25 Feb. 1725/6. He married about
1748, REBECCA ———— who died 13 July 1763. He married (2) in
Bradford, 24 Oct. 1765, widow MARCY HARDY, perhaps the widow
of Gideon Hardy of Bradford. Her christian name has also been
given as Mary. They removed to Nottingham West (now Hudson),
N. H., about 1748, and he was living there on 21 Mar. 1799. The
Vital Records of Nottingham West call Enoch, born 18 Aug. 1769,
son of Henry and *Rebecca* Chase. This is probably an error in re-
cording this birth. He was head of a family in Nottingham West in
1790, consistnig of two males over 16 years, no males under 16, and
two females.

Children by first wife, born in Nottingham West:

HENRY,[5] b. 14 July 1749; d. unm. 26 June 1770.

REBECCA, b. 25 Sept. 1751; m. Thomas Marsh.

MOLLY, b. 19 Apr. 1756.

SARAH (twin), b. 19 Apr. 1756; d. 23 Oct. 1757.

ANNA, b. 6 Nov. 1760; m. 26 Nov. 1782, Jonathan Gould.

Children by second wife:

SUSANNA, b. 28 Mar. 1766; m. 1786, Ebenezer Marsh of Hudson.

413.   ENOCH, b. 19 Aug. 1769.

PHEBE, b. 4 Sept. 1771.

414 .   MOSES, b. 12 Oct. 1775.

113

STEPHEN[4] CHASE (Ens. Stephen,[3] Ens. Moses[2]), born in Newbury (now West Newbury), 24 Aug. 1728; married (1) about 1751, KATHERINE LUND; married (2) in Nottingham West, 24 Nov. 1757, PHEBE CHANDLER. He was living in Nottingham West (now Hudson), N. H., as late as 1779. He lived on the Chase homestead about one half mile west of the Lowell road, the first farm south of the Thomas Colburn homestead. The last seven children were of the second union. He died in Nottingham West about 1793. He sold 120 acres in Nottingham West to John Chase for £200, 9 Apr. 1786, and apparently made no will. (Hillsborough Co. Deeds, 32: 529).

Children, born in Nottingham West (now Hudson), N. H.:

ENOCH,[5] b. 4 July 1753; d. 27 Aug. 1753, a. 3m. 6d.

415.   STEPHEN, b. 21 Apr. 1755.

Children by second wife, born in Nottingham West:

EPHRAIM CHANDLER, b. 28 Aug. 1758; m. 2 May 1816, Abigail Blodgett. No children.

416.   MICAJAH (twin), b. 28 Aug. 1758.

410.   JOHN, b. 31 Jan. 1761.

SARAH, b. 30 Apr. 1763; m. 23 Mar. 1786, Joseph Winn.

PHEBE, b. 3 Apr. 1765; d. 24 Mar. 1766.

418.   EZEKIEL, b. 5 May 1768.

419.   DANIEL, b. 12 Aug. 1770.

113a

BRADFORD[4] CHASE (Ens. Stephen,[3] Ens. Moses[2]), born in Newbury (now West Newbury), 27 Nov. 1733. His father removed to Nottingham West (now Hudson), N. H., in 1747, and died there in 1756. What became of the son is not known.

114

ENOCH[4] CHASE (Ens. Stephen,[3] Ens. Moses[2]), born in Newbury (now West Newbury), 2 Feb. 1735/6. If anything further is found relating to him, it will appear in the Appendix.

115

MOSES[4] CHASE (Ens. Stephen,[3] Ens. Moses[2]), born in Newbury (now West Newbury), 31 May 1738; married in Nottingham West (now Hudson), N. H., 1 Mar. 1759, ELIZABETH HAMBLETT, daughter of Joseph and Susanna (Durant) Hamblett, born in Nottingham West, 13 Mar. 1738. They lived in Nottingham West (now Hudson) till 1770, when they removed to Washington, N. H. She married (2) Thomas Barney of Washington, N. H. and (3) ——— Dakin and lived in Washington until her death.

Children, born in Nottingham West (now Hudson), N. H., except youngest born in Washington:

420.   MOSES,[5] b. 10 Sept. 1760
      ELISABETH, b. 30 Mar. 1763; m. Levi Barney of Washington.
      SUSAN, m. Joseph Seavey of Pelham.
421.   JOSEPH, b. 31 Dec. 1767.
      LYDIA, m. 6 Nov. 1794, Abisha Gee, of Marlow, N. H.
422.   BENJAMIN DURANT, b. 13 Apr. 1769.
      SARAH, b. 1 May 1778; m. 19 Jan. 1791 Thomas Metcalf; she
      d. 25 Dec. 1842.

116

DEA. JOSHUA[4] CHASE (Ens. Stephen,[3] Ens. Moses[2]), born in Newbury (now West Newbury), 16 May 1740; died in Nottingham West (now Hudson), N. H., 27 Dec. 1822, aged 82y. 7m. He married in Nottingham West, 22 Nov. 1763, MARY HADLEY, daughter of Parrott and Mary (Heath) Hadley of Nottingham West, N. H. She was born in Amesbury, 20 Feb. 1745/6; died in Hudson, 27 Mar. 1838, aged 92y. 23d. They lived in Nottingham West (since 1830, Hudson). He was a soldier in the Crown Point expedition from 10 Apr. to 31 Oct. 1758. He was also a minute man at the battle of Bunker Hill, 17 June 1775, and also in the Continental service in 1779. He was a Deacon after 1796. His widow Mary applied for a pension, 22 Mar. 1837, stating that her husband served in 1775, 1776 and 1777.

Children, born in Nottingham West (now Hudson), N. H.:

423.   BENJAMIN.[5] b. 17 Aug. 1765.
      BETSEY, b. 25 June 1770; m. 25 Nov. 1802, Barnabus Gibson.
      KEZIAH, b. 10 June 1772; m. 28 Feb. 1803, Amos Hobart.
      POLLY, b. 2 May 1774; m. 5 Oct. 1797, Zaccheus Hobart. Another report says she m. Zaccheus Hale.
      JOSHUA, b. 16 Oct. 1776; d. 22 Oct. 1795, 19y. 6m.
424.   JACOB, b. 30 Nov. 1778.
      SARAH, b. 16 Feb. 1781; d. unm. 4 Apr. 1860, aged 79y.
      PHEBE, b. 24 Apr. 1783; m. 5 Dec. 1805, Simeon Shurtliff; she
      d. in Lanesville, Ohio.
425.   SAMUEL, b. 15 Mar. 1785.
      RUTH, b. 10 Mar. 1787; m. 18 Apr. 1809, James Hale. She d.
      14 July 1839.
      LYDIA, b. 7 May 1789; m. 13 June 1809, James Burns. She d.
      in Stanstead, Can., 30 Jan. 1865.

117

JACOB[4] CHASE (Lt. Joseph,[3] Ens. Moses,[2]) born in Newbury (now West Newbury), 25 Dec. 1727; died in Chester, N. H. 12 Dec. 1803. He married (1) 7 Nov. 1751, PRUDENCE HILLS, daughter of Benjamin and Rebecca (Ordway) Hills, born in Newbury 12 Feb. 1726; died in Chester, N. H. 1 May 1775. He married (2) DOLLY (COLBY) WORTHEN, widow of David Worthen and daughter of Enoch and Abial (Sanborn) Colby. She was born 5 Jan. 1730/31; and died in Chester, N. H. 15 Aug. 1816.

He was a prominent citizen of Chester, very frequently moderator and active during the Revolutionary War period, and was a soldier at the battle of Bennington. One item in the selectmen's account for 1780 is a credit to Jacob Chase, Esq., for a present to the town of £157-10, which appears to have been used in the procuring of recruits for the army. He was in Capt. Stephen Dearborn's Co. which marched from Chester to join the Continental army, enlisting 21 July and being discharged, 18 Sept. 1777.

Children, born in Chester, N. H.:

    SARAH,* b. 28 Nov. 1756; m. 4 June 1778, Moses Richardson, son of Daniel. She d. 10 Dec. 1822.

426. STEPHEN, b. 27 Mar. 1759.

427. JOSIAH, b. 6 Apr. 1767.

118

JOSEPH[4] CHASE (Lt. Joseph,[3] Ens. Moses,[2]) born in Newbury (now West Newbury), 11 Apr. 1732; died there 26 Mar. 1804. He married (1) in Newbury, 27 Aug. 1751, SUSANNAH BANCROFT, daughter of Thomas and Lydia (Deane) Bancroft, born in Reading, 14 Dec. 1733; died in Newbury, 15 Jan. 1788, in her 55th year. They were buried in Bridge Street Cemetery, West Newbury. He married (2) in Newbury, 10 Feb. 1789, LYDIA SAWYER, widow of Samuel Sawyer. She died in Newbury, 3 Nov. 1815. They lived on the Joseph[3] Chase homestead in West Newbury. He was a cooper by trade. Administration on his estate was granted to his widow Lydia, 31 Dec. 1805, and her son Samuel Sawyer was appointed her guardian, 9 July 1809.

Children, born in Newbury (now West Newbury):

428. PARKER,[5] b. 9 Apr. 1752.

    JACOB, b. 24 Sept. 1754; d. 18 Sept. 1774, of fever.

    AMOS, b. 8 Nov. 1756; d. 27 Oct. 1774, of fever.

429. JOSEPH, b. 8 Nov. 1758.

    HANNAH, b. 20 Apr. 1762; d. 9 Oct. 1774, of fever.

    SUSANNAH, b. 22 July 1766; d. 30 Oct. 1774, of fever.

430. CALEB, b. 18 Aug. 1768.

    MARY, b. 25 Apr. 1771; m. 25 Apr. 1793, Amos Hills of Bethel, Me.

431. JONATHAN, b. 9 Mar. 1774.

    SARAH, b. 8 Apr. 1777.

119

MOODY[4] CHASE (Lt. Joseph,[3] Ens. Moses,[2]) born in Newbury (now West Newbury), 7 Oct. 1744; died in Chester, N. H. 27 July 1808. He married in Hampstead, N. H. 26 Oct. 1768, ANNA WEBSTER, daughter of John and Elizabeth (Lunt) Webster of Hampstead, N. H. She was born 6 June 1749 and died in Chester, 4 Dec. 1791. He married (2) 19 Apr. 1792, ABIGAIL (WORTH) ROGERS, who was born 24 Dec. 1748; died in Chester, 9 Dec. 1826, aged 78. They owned the Church covenant in Hampstead, 19 Nov. 1769 and removed to Chester that year. He lived in the part of Chester (now Auburn), in a house that stood near the home of Wells Chase Underhill, and nearly opposite where Wells[5] Chase (Moses[4]) settled in 1771.

Children, born in Chester, N. H., first seven baptized in Hampstead, N. H.:

432. JOHN WEBSTER,[6] b. 26 Aug. 1769.
   MARY, b. 24 Feb. 1771; m. 27 Dec. 1808, Benjamin Pike[6] Chase. (Family 1065)
   INFANT, b. 19 Feb. 1773; d. 27 July 1773.
433. JOSEPH, b. 14 Apr. 1774.
434. JACOB, b. 23 Mar. 1776.
435. MOODY, b. 19 Apr. 1778.
436. SAMUEL, b. 11 Aug. 1780.
437. CALEB, b. 4 Feb. 1783.
   ANNA, b. 11 Apr. 1785; d. 12 Dec. 1806, of consumption.
   ELISABETH, b. 16 June 1787; m. (1) 22 Nov. 1810, Moses[5] Chase (Caleb[4]) (family 442); m. (2) David Edmunds.
438. THOMAS, b. 8 Nov. 1789.
   HANNAH HILLS, b. 23 Nov. 1791; m. 30 Jan. 1817, Reuben Underhill; d. in Lowell, 6 Sept. 1850.

120

CALEB[4] CHASE (Lt. Joseph,[3] Ens. Moses,[2]) born in Newbury (now West Newbury), 28 July 1746; died in Thornton, N. H. 13 Feb. 1810. He graduated from Princeton College in 1766 and married in Gorham, Me. 31 Dec. 1769, JOANNA WHITNEY, daughter of Abel and Mary (Came) Whitney. She was born in York, Me. 10 Oct. 1736; died in Hanover, N. H. about 1832.

He was a school-master in Gorham, Me. 1769 to 1779; Proprietor's clerk there 1776 to 1778; town clerk and treasurer and a member of the committee of safety. He removed from Gorham, to Concord, N. H. in 1779, and opened a public house there. He was town clerk of Concord, 1780 to 1792. He removed to Thornton, about 1796 where he resided the rest of his life.

Children, first five born in Gorham, Me. others in Concord, N. H.:

   MARY,[5] b. 31 Jan. 1771; m. 13 Nov. 1794, Samuel A. Morrill of Canterbury, N. H.; she d. 2 Aug. 1857.
439. JOSEPH, b. 9 Aug. 1772.
   ABIGAIL, b. 12 Aug. 1774; m. 5 Apr. 1794, Samuel Merrill. She d. 3 Aug. 1817.
   WILLIAM HILLS, b. 11 Apr. 1776; d. unm. in Concord, 10 Oct. 1791.
440. JACOB, b. 11 Feb. 1778.
441. AMOS, b. 4 Aug. 1780.
   SUSANNAH, b. 28 May 1782; m. 15 Nov. 1804, John Worth of Thornton. N. H.; d. shortly after marriage.
   JOANNA, b. 8 Apr. 1784; m. 6 Nov. 1804, Charles Worthen of Holderness, N. H.; d. 24 Apr. 1867.
   ELISABETH, b. 24 Dec. 1785; m. 20 Mar. 1806, John H. Foss of Campton. She d. 29 Aug. 1856.
442. MOSES, b. 16 Feb. 1787.
   CHARLOTTE, b. 23 Dec. 1789; m. (1) 28 Feb. 1824, William H. Hall of Hanover; m. (2) Capt. William Hall.
443. WILLIAM, b. 2 Mar. 1791.

121

Dr. Thomas[4] Chase (Benoni,[3] Ens. Moses[2]) born in Sutton, 3 Apr. 1732; married there, 26 Sept. 1751, Mary White, said to be a daughter of Obadiah White. He studied medicine with Dr. Benjamin Morse of Sutton and lived in Westborough for a time. Some time after 1760 he removed to the state of New York. There were three Thomas Chases heads of families in New York in 1790, viz. one in Catskill, Albany Co., another in Hillsdale, Columbia Co. and a third in Frederickstown, (now Kent, Carmel and Paterson in Putnam Co.) Dutchess Co.

He may be the Thomas Chase who lived in Ballston or Greenfield, Saratoga Co. in 1804.

Children, first three born in Westborough, fourth baptized in Sutton:

Mary,[5] b. 22 May 1752.
Eunice, b. 14 Dec. 1754.
Hannah, b. 18 Feb. 1757
Eunice, bp. 29 June 1760 (may be the second above).
Tryphosa, m. Capt. Aaron or Allen Hale of Greenfield, Saratoga Co., N. Y. He d. 1829.
Annar (perhaps Hannah), m. Jonathan Burns of northeastern Penn

122

Rogers[4] Chase (Benoni,[3] Ens. Moses,[2]) born in Sutton, 20 June 1734; died in Royalston, 1 Nov. 1814, in his 81st year. He married (1) in Sutton, 1 Nov. 1753, Sarah Walker, daughter of Lt. Obadiah and Hannah Walker, born in Sutton, 9 May 1735. He married (2) in Royalston, aged 77, 25 Dec. 1810, Miss Susannah Burbank, aged 61. He was a Revolutionary War soldier, according to Caswell's History of Royalston. He removed from Sutton to Royalston, after 1760.

Children, born in Sutton:

Royal,[5] d. 31 Aug. 1777, in Royalston.
Betsey, d. unm. 22 Jan. 1831, aged 60.
444.   Elijah, b. 31 July 1757; d. in the Revolutionary army before he was of age.
445.   Silas, b. 31 Aug. 1760.
Sarah, d. unm. 3 Mar. 1843, aged 76, in Royalston.
446.   Ebenezer, b. 9 Oct. 1774.

123

Stephen[4] Chase (Benoni,[3] Ens. Moses,[2]) born in Sutton, 29 Mar. 1736; died in Rochester, Vt. 30 Mar. 1814. He married in Sutton, 3 Nov. 1757, Lois Hill. They lived in Rochester, Vt.

Children:

Lois,[5] b. ———— 1771; m. 1791, Phineas Pond of Keene, N. H.
Mary, b. 24 July 1774; m. 12 May 1795, Lemuel Richardson of Cornish, N. H. She d. 1854.
447.   Benjamin, b. 1776.
Hannah, m. Samuel Root.
Eunice, m. 5 Sept. 1795, Ebenezer Clark. No children.

124

Moses[4] Chase (Benoni,[3] Ens. Moses,[2]) born in Sutton, 5 Oct. 1737; died in Alstead, N. H. 30 Dec. 1814. He was the head of a family consisting of four males over 16 years, none under 16 and one female, living in Alstead, N. H. in 1790. He married and lived in Alstead, N. H.

Children:

448. Asa,[5] b. about 1765.
449. Simeon, b. about 1770.
     Aaron, d. unm.
450. Abner, b. about 1775.

125

Benjamin[4] Chase (Benoni,[3] Ens. Moses[2]) baptized in Sutton, 25 July 1742. The Church records of Sutton call him "son of Benoni Chase," but he is not given in Benoni Chase's family by Dr. John B. Chace. There is no marriage or death of any Benjamin Chase in Sutton. If anything further is found, it will appear in the Appendix.

126

David[4] Chase (Benoni,[3] Ens. Moses[2]), born in Sutton, 17 Apr. 1752; died in Whitingham, Vt. 20 Oct. 1841, aged 89. He married in Douglas, 19 Nov. 1771, Jemima Humes, daughter of Samuel and Martha Humes, born in Douglas, 31 July 1752; died in Whitingham, 4 Mar. 1830.

He was living in Douglas in 1790 and his family then consisted of two males over 16 years of age, four males under 16 and two females. They removed to Whitingham in Feb. 1815. (Brown's Hist. of Whitingham, 173).

Children, born in Douglas:

451. Abraham,[5] b. 25 Sept. 1772.
452. Isaac, b. 29 Jan. 1775.
     Lucy, b. 5 Oct. 1776; d. 4 Nov. 1776.
453. Jacob, b. 15 Feb. 1780.
454. Samuel, b. 22 Feb. 1783.
455. Benjamin, b. 7 Sept. 1786.

FIFTH GENERATION

127

JOSHUA[5] CHASE (George,[4] Joseph,[3] Aquila[2]), born in Littleton 31 Aug. 1743; died in Massena, St. Lawrence Co. N. Y. 11 Mar. 1810. He married in Shirley, 2 June 1770, SUSANNAH FITCH, daughter of John and Susannah (Gates) Fitch, born in Lunenburg, 18 Feb. 1746/7; died in Massena, 10 July 1827. They lived in Shirley, Chesterfield, N. H. and Massena, N. Y. In 1790 he was the head of a family in Chesterfield, consisting of two males over 16 years of age, two males under 16, and four females. (N. H. Census, 12).

Children, first five born in Shirley, others in Chesterfield:

456.   JACOB,[6] b. 30 June 1771.
        ABIGAIL, b. 25 Apr. 1773; m. John Earl of Chester, Vt.
        WILLIAM P., b. 8 June 1775; d. 1778.
        GEORGE, b. 2 Jan. 1778; d. 1778.
        SUSANNAH, b. 17 Oct. 1780; m. in Chester, Vt., Nathan Church.
437.   WILLIAM P., b. 22 June 1783.
        LUCY, b. 8 Apr. 1786; m. Thomas Banister of Massena, N. Y.
        JOHN, b. 15 Aug. 1788; m. Betsey Tucker of Massena; he d. there about 1856, without issue.

128

ABEL[5] CHASE (George,[4] Joseph,[3] Aquila[2]), born in Littleton, 13 June 1754; married, (intention there 9 Jan. 1779), JOANNA (BARTLETT) WARREN, the widow of Jonathan Warren of Watertown, 1773. They resided in Shirley as late as 1784. He removed to Chesterfield, N. H. in 1787 and disappears from that town about 1800. He may have removed to Massena, N. Y. In 1790 he was the head of a family in Chesterfield, consisting of one male over 16 years of age, three males under 16, and three females. (N. H. Census, 12).

Children, first three born in Shirley, others in Chesterfield:

458.   CALEB,[6] b. 16 June 1779.
        MOLLY, b. 18 Mar. 1781; bp. June 1784.
        LYDIA, b. 26 Apr. 1783; bp. June 1784.
459.   GEORGE, b. 27 July 1787.
460.   CHARLES, b. 6 July 1789.

129

DR. JOSHUA[5] CHASE (Rev. Stephen,[4] Joseph,[3] Aquila[2]), born in Lynn (now Lynnfield) 17 Mar. 1738; died in Hampton Falls, N. H., 1782. He married in Hampton Falls, 30 Oct. 1763, ANNA SWETT who administered upon his estate, 2 Dec. 1782. She was daughter of Benjamin Swett of Hampton Falls. Her marriage return calls her "Anna Swett." They lived in Hampton Falls. She married (2) (int. at Salisbury, 12 May 1787), Col. Jonathan Evans of Salisbury.

Children, born in Hampton Falls, N. H.:

MARY,[6] b. 31 Oct. 1765; m. 18 Mar. 1786, James Janvrin, son of John Janvrin. She d. 12 July 1839; seven children.

DAVID, b. 3 July 1768; d. unm. on board ship coming from West Indies.

JOSHUA, b. 30 Nov. 1770; d. unm. on board ship from West Indies.

DOLLY, b. 10 July 1778; d. unm. age 32.

130

STEPHEN[5] CHASE (Rev. Stephen,[4] Joseph,[3] Aquila[2]), born in Lynn (now Lynnfield) 22 Jan. 1742; married 12 July 1771, MARY FROST, daughter of Joseph and Margaret (Colton) Frost. She was born 29 Jan. 1752 and died in Portsmouth, N. H., 15 Sept. 1819. He died in Portsmouth, 31 Mar. 1805. They lived in New Castle and Portsmouth, N. H., from 1778. He graduated at Harvard College in 1764 and was one of the founders of the Portsmouth Athenaeum.

Children, born in New Castle, last three in Portsmouth:

461. JOSEPH,[6] b. 22 Apr. 1772.

WILLIAM, b. 10 Feb. 1774; m. 11 Oct. 1821, Sarah Blunt of Portsmouth. He d. 30 Aug. 1834; no children.

MARY, b. 15 Nov. 1776; m. 22 June 1799, Edmund Tappan. She d. 2 Dec. 1857, aged 81.

HARRIET, b. 14 Aug. 1778; m. 11 Sept. 1800, Oliver Crosby Esq. of Dover, N. H.

SARAH, b. 23 Oct. 1780; m. 9 Jan. 1806. Jeremiah H. Woodman of Rochester, N. H.

462. THEODORE, b. 16 Mar. 1786.

131

JOHN WINGATE[5] CHASE (Rev. Stephen,[4] Joseph,[3] Aquila[2]), born in Lynn (now Lynnfield) 14 Aug. 1749; died 1795. He married in New Castle, N. H., 27 May 1782, ABIGAIL TAPPAN, daughter of Rev. Benjamin and Elizabeth (Marsh) Tappan. She was born in Manchester, 29 Apr. 1757; died in Portland, Me., 26 Jan. 1838, aged 81. She married (2) 15 Jan. 1797, JOHN BAKER of Portsmouth, N. H. By the second union she had one daughter, Abigail Tappan Baker, born in Effingham, N. H., 4 July 1800. The family removed to Portland, Me., about 1801.

Children, born in Portsmouth:

463. STEPHEN,[6] b. 16 May 1783.

464. BENJAMIN TAPPAN, b. 20 Dec. 1786.

JOHN WINGATE, b. 29 Sept. 1790; d. at sea at age of 29.

465. CHARLES, b. 4 Feb. 1794.

132

BENJAMIN[5] CHASE (Dr. Benjamin,[4] Joseph,[3] Aquila[2]), born in Groton, 1 Oct. 1741; died in Amenia, N. Y., 23 Nov. 1772, aged 31. He married in Amenia, 7 Mar. 1767, MERCY BARLOW, daughter of Nathan Barlow. They lived in Amenia, Dutchess Co., N. Y. He was buried in the Steel Works Burying Ground in Amenia. His widow and her three sons were baptized at Amenia, 8 Sept. 1776.

Children, born in Amenia, N. Y.:

466. NATHAN,[6] b. 10 May 1768.
467. EBENEZER, b. 10 Sept. 1770.
468. BENJAMIN, b. 20 Feb. 1773.
      MERCY, m. Robert Browning.

133

SOLOMON[5] CHASE (Dr. Benjamin,[4] Joseph,[3] Aquila[2]), born in Groton, 8 Sept. 1743; died in Westerloo, Albany Co., N. Y., — June 1828, aged 87. He married (1) in Amenia, N. Y., 24 Jan. 1765, REBECCA CHAMBERLAIN who died in Amenia, 10 Dec. 1777, aged 33. He married (2) in Amenia, 18 Aug. 1779, MERCY OLDRIDGE. They lived in Kent, Conn., and Amenia, N. Y.

Children by first wife:

      RACHEL,[6] bp. 19 Jan. 1766; m. Jacob Dorman of Dutchess Co.
469. SOLOMON, b. 20 Oct. 1767.
      REBECCA, b. 31 Mar. 1769; m. Azariah Darrow. She. d. 13 Aug. 1872.
470. STEPHEN, b. 20 July 1770.
      MEHITABLE, b. 13 Mar. 1772; d. unm. 23 Oct. 1795.
      MARY, b. 1 Mar. 1774; never mar.
471. JOHN,[6] b. 1 July 1775.
472. CHARLES YOUNG, b. 4 Oct. 1777.

Child by second wife:

473. JOSEPH LAPHAM, b. 17 June 1784.

134

EBENEZER[5] CHASE (Dr. Benjamin,[4] Joseph,[3] Aquila[2]), born in Groton, 4 June 1745. One Ebenezer Chase was head of a family in 1790 in Newbergh, Ulster Co., N. Y., consisting of one male over 16 years of age, no males under 16, and one female. There are no deeds to or from him in Middlesex County before 1835.

135

JOHN[5] CHASE (Dr. Benjamin,[4] Joseph,[3] Aquila[2]), born in Groton, 12 Feb. 1749/50; his father removed to Kent, Conn., and two of his brothers lived in Amenia, N. Y. He may have removed to New York state.

136

STEPHEN[5] CHASE (Dr. Benjamin[4] Joseph,[3] Aquila[2]), born in Kent, Conn., 26 Mar. 1769. He does not appear as head of a family in 1790, but he is reported to have been the father of the six children following.

Children:

474. BENJAMIN GRANT,[6] Brooklyn, Susquehanna Co., Pa.
475. WILLIAM, Brooklyn, Susquehanna Co., Pa.
476. ALBERT, Montrose, Susquehanna Co., Pa.
477. SALMON.
478. NATHAN.
479. CHAUNCEY, lived in Waterbury, Conn., but not mentioned in the history of Waterbury.

137

BENJAMIN[5] CHASE (Joseph,[4] Joseph,[3] Aquila[2]), born in Littleton, 9 Aug. 1745. His name is not in the Middlesex Co. Records. One Benjamin Chase of Danvers, weaver, purchased land in Danvers, 20 Sept. 1754, but he could not be the native of Littleton.

138

SARAH[5] CHASE (Joseph,[4] Joseph,[3] Aquila[2]), born in Littleton, 7 Oct. 1746; died in Groton, between 15 May 1 Aug. 1826. In the settlement of her father's estate, 23 Apr. 1785, she is called "Sarah Chase of Groton, singlewoman." With a like title she made her will, 15 May 1826, which was lodged in Probate Court, 1 Aug. 1826. Therein she bequeathed to her son Peter Chase, to his wife Sally and to their children, Mary Ann Chase, William Chase and Walter Chase, her property. (Middlesex Probate, 4309).

Child, born in Groton:

480. PETER WOOD,[6] b. 2 Oct. 1779.

139

JOSEPH[5] CHASE (Joseph,[4] Joseph,[3] Aquila[2]), born in Littleton, 8 Mar. 1750. Joseph[4] Chase of Groton for parental love conveys to his son Joseph[5] of Groton, husbandman, 60 acres in Groton, with one half of the buildings thereon, 27 Mar. 1775; acknowledged by the grantor 27 Nov. 1777. (Middlesex Deeds, 106:483). He joined with his brother Moses and sisters, Dolly Cummings, Molly Daverson, Sarah Chase, Abigail Bennett and Lucy Brown in selling this homestead to Thomas Wood of Littleton, 23 Apr. 1785. He was then living in Groton. (Ibid. 106:484). No mention in three deeds of his on 25 Apr. 1785 of a wife. Thomas Wood of Groton for $600 sells him 60 acres in Groton with westerly half of the house and the easterly half of the old barn (the easterly end of the house being set off to the widow, Mary Woods) 15 Nov. 1798. On 7 Dec. 1798 Joseph Chase of Groton for $600 sells the same property in the southerly part of Groton to Joseph Moars of Groton; acknowledged on same day with no mention of a wife. No other deeds to or from him recorded before 1835. He lived in Groton from 1775 to 1799. (Ibid 130:369, 370). He died in Groton, July 1811, aged 61y. 4m.

A singular thing is that while he apparently lived in Groton in 1790, his name is not given as the head of a family there. It may be that he was a single man and lived with some other family.

140

JONATHAN[5] CHASE (Joseph,[4] Joseph,[3] Aquila[2]), born in Littleton, 7 June 1755. There is no deed to or from him in Middlesex Co. before 1835.

141

JONAS[5] CHASE (Joseph,[4] Joseph,[3] Aquila[2]), born in Littleton, 27 Feb. 1757. There is no deed to or from him registered in Middlesex Co. before 1835; living in Littleton 1810 to 1813.

142

Moses[5] Chase (Joseph,[4] Joseph,[3] Aquila[2]), born in Littleton, 15 Sept. 1760; living in Lancaster, 23 Apr. 1785; married in Lancaster, 2 June 1785, Parna [Parney] Hastings, daughter of Nathaniel and Elizabeth (Goodenow) Hastings of Berlin. He was living in Groton as late as 21 Sept. 1819. He served in the Revolutionary War for seven years and was a pensioner in Groton in 1818. He died in Groton, 28 Nov. 1837.

Children, baptized in Groton:

  Elazabeth Hastings,[6] bp. 27 Oct. 1799.
481. Moses, bp. 27 Oct. 1799.
482. America, bp. 27 Oct. 1799.

142a

Thomas[5] Chase (Joseph,[4] Joseph,[3] Aquila[2]), born as was assumed by the first who commenced on the Chase Genealogy, about 1765; married in Newbury, 20 May 1804, Lydia Battis. He lived in Newbury from 1796 to about 1805. His grandson stated that he went into the western country up to the lakes and never returned.

Children, born in Newbury:

482a. Joseph Hatch,[6] b. 16 Oct. 1797.
482b. James, b. about 1799.
  Eliza B., b. 22 July 1803; m. 30 Aug. 1826, John Harmon. She d. 5 Oct. 1865.
482c. John B., b. 23 Apr. 1805.

143

Thomas[5] Chase (Thomas,[4] Dea. Thomas,[3] Thomas[2]), born in Newbury, 11 Apr. 1737; died in Sandown, N. H. 16 Apr. 1784. He married in Newbury, 13 July 1758, Elizabeth[4] Chase, daughter of Lt. Joseph[3] (Ens. Moses,[2]) and Mary (Morse) Chase. She was born in Newbury, (now West Newbury), 7 May 1738, and married (2) 16 Oct. 1788, William Sanborn. She died in Chester, 18 Dec. 1811 and was buried in the Presbyterian Cemetery in what is now Auburn, N. H. They lived in Newbury and in Sandown, N. H.

Children, born in Newbury:

  Mary,[6] b. 2 Apr. 1759; d. in Canterbury, N. H.; m. 5 Oct. 1775, Joseph Bailey, who d. in Chester, N. H., 27 Nov. 1809. No children.
  Caleb (locally known as "Elder"), b. 9 Apr. 1766; m. (1) Nancy West, b. 3 Sept. 1772; d. 2 Sept. 1838 in Chester, N. H. He m. (2) 21 Mar. 1840, widow Dorothy Poor. He d. in Canterbury, N. H., Apr. 1853. No children.

144

Lt. Abel[5] Chase (Thomas,[4] Dea. Thomas,[3] Thomas[2]), born in Newbury, 15 Apr. 1739; died in West Newbury, 29 Dec. 1828, aged 90. He married in Newbury, 2 Apr. 1761, Hannah (Morse) Campbell, widow of John Campbell of Newbury and probably daughter of Samuel and Abigail (Perley) Morse, born in Newbury, 20 Nov. 1738; died there, 20 Sept. 1810, aged 72. They lived in

Newbury (now West Newbury). He was a Lieutenant in the Revolutionary War.

Children, born in Newbury (now West Newbury):

483. JEREMIAH,[6] b. 10 Mar. 1762.
SUSANNAH, b. 27 Jan. 1764; d. unm. 12 Aug. 1801.
EMMA, b. 7 Feb. 1766; m. 29 Dec. 1785, Joseph[5] Chase (Joseph,[4] Joseph,[3] Moses[2]). (Family 429)
ABIGAIL, b. 15 Feb. 1768; m. 22 Oct. 1795, Moses Harrington of Cornish, N. H.
ELIZABETH, b. 17 Feb. 1770; m. 13 Oct. 1796, Moses[5] Chase (Moses,[4] Moses,[3] Moses,[2] Aquila[1]). (Family 379)
484. THOMAS, b. 21 Mar. 1772.
RUTH, b. 5 June 1774; m. 10 Mar. 1802, Jeremiah Carr of Poplin (Fremont), N. H.
MOLLY, b. 13 Feb. 1778; m. 25 Nov. 1800, Joshua Ordway.
NANCY (Anna), b. 1 Feb. 1781; m. John Carr of Fremont, N. H.; d. 2 Nov. 1859, a. 79.

145

DR. JOSIAH[5] CHASE (Thomas,[4] Dea. Thomas,[3] Thomas[2]), born in Newbury, 15 Sept. 1741; drowned in the Saco River at Conway, N. H., 19 Oct. 1796. He married in Andover, 22 Aug. 1765, MEHITABLE FRYE, daughter of Gen. Joseph and Mehitable (Poore) Frye, born in Andover, 8 Apr. 1741; died 11 Feb. 1818. They lived in Canterbury, N. H., 1765 to 1775, Fryeburg, Me., and Conway, N. H. He was surgeon's mate in Col. John Stark Regt. at the battle of Bunker Hill and removed to Fryeburg about 1782. Administration on his estate was granted 5 Nov. 1796. (Strafford Co. Probate, 19:10).

Children, first five born in Canterbury, N. H., others in Fryeburg, Me.:

485. THOMAS,[6] b. 7 Aug. 1766.
HANNAH, b. 30 Aug. 1768; m. in Conway, 6 June 1788, William Webster. Twelve children.
486. JOSEPH F., b. 19 Sept. 1770.
JOSIAH, b. 12 Feb. 1773; d. 21 Mar. 1776.
487. ENOCH S., b. 4 May 1775.
MEHITABLE, b. 29 July 1778; m. 20 Jan. 1798, Daniel Roberts of Conway, N. H.
488. JOSIAH, b. 12 May 1782.
POLLY, b. 5 Aug. 1785; m. 20 Jan. 1813, Robert Carr, M.D., b. 28 Oct. 1783.
OBED H., b. 5 Apr. 1788; d. 27 Feb. 1789.

146

ABEL[5] CHASE (Dea. Abel,[4] Dea. Thomas,[3] Thomas[2]), born in Sutton (now Millbury), 11 Sept. 1732; killed by falling from the roof of a house 11 or 15 Nov. 1787. He married in Sutton, 3 Jan. 1754, JUDITH GALE, daughter of Isaac, and Judith (Sawyer) Gale, born in Sutton, 12 Apr. 1734; died 10 Feb. 1805. They lived in what is now Millbury.

Children, born in Sutton (now Millbury) :

489. ABEL,[6] b. 29 Oct. 1754.

ISAAC, b. 26 June 1756; d. 8 Sept. 1759.

JUDITH, b. 19 Mar. 1758; d. 28 Sept. 1759.

JUDITH, b. 27 Mar. 1760; m. 27 Nov. 1782, Aaron Parker of Ward.

490. ISAAC, b. 12 Sept. 1761.

SARAH, b. 15 Jan. 1763; m. 24 Nov. 1785, Oliver Bond of Millbury.

EMMA, b. 23 Nov. 1764; d. 10 May 1777.

ANNE, b. 7 Sept. 1766; d. 14 Oct. 1776.

PERSIS, b. 22 Mar. 1768; m. 7 May 1789, Jonathan Richardson.

491. JONATHAN, b. 26 Feb. 1770.

SILENCE, bp. 16 Feb. 1772; d. 18 May 1777.

147

THOMAS[5] CHASE (Dea. Abel,[4] Dea. Thomas,[3] Thomas[2]), born in Sutton (now Millbury), 13 Mar. 1746; died in Warwick, 1 July 1839. He married in Sutton, 20 Feb. 1766 DEBORAH KILLUM, [KILHAM]. She was born 28 Nov. 1747; died in Warwick, 27 Aug. 1827. They lived in Sutton till after 1790, then lived in Warwick.

Children, born in Sutton:

WILLIAM WITT,[6] b. 18 Dec. 1766; d. 28 Oct. 1788, aged 21.

SARAH M. (twin), b. 7 Mar. 1769; m. James Stearns; d. in Windham, Vt., 28 Sept. 1856.

MARY (twin), b. 7 Mar. 1769; m. 23 Jan. 1793, Abel Kidder; d. in Stratton, Vt., 29 July 1818.

ABIGAIL, b. 13 May 1771; m. 1796, Thomas Gould; d. in Warwick, 17 Oct. 1822.

DEBORAH, b. 13 Oct. 1773; d. 30 Oct. 1788.

PERSIS, b. 7 Mar. 1776; d. in Royalston, 13 Oct. 1856; m. 5 Apr. 1825, Capt. Daniel Woodbury. b. 22 Mar. 1761; d. 15 Oct. 1842. No children.

EMMA, b. 4 Feb. 1779; m. Joseph Brintnall. She d. 2 Feb. 1861 in Windham, Vt. No children.

JONATHAN, b. 28 June 1781; d. 26 Nov. 1788.

492. CALVIN, b. 6 Jan. 1784.

PATTY, b. 9 May 1787; m. Joseph Brintnall; d. 11 Feb. 1844, in Windham, Vt.

493. THOMAS, b. 2 May 1790.

WILLIAM, b. 28 June 1792; d. 2 July 1792.

148

SERGT. DAVID[5] CHASE (Dea. Abel[4] Dea. Thomas,[3] Thomas[2]), born in Sutton (now Millbury), 28 Sept. 1748; died there, 28 Feb. 1791. He married in Sutton, 28 Apr. 1774, JUDITH HOLMAN, daughter of Thomas and Deborah (Huntington) Holman, born in Sutton, 11 Sept. 1748 or 1749. She married (2) in Sutton, 29 June 1797, OLIVER CURTIS of Ward; died 18 Mar. 1815. They lived in Sutton.

Children, born in Sutton:

494. DAVID,[6] b. 7 Jan. 1778.

RUTH HOLMAN, b. 31 Jan. 1780; m. 31 Jan. 1804, Elias Sibley.

JUDITH, b. 26 Jan. 1782; m. 29 Nov. 1804, Aaron Holman of
Worcester.
EBER, b. 10 Mar. 1784; d. unm. 22 Mar. 1805.
SALLY, b. 18 Dec. 1786; d. Oct. 1804
POLLY, b. 26 May 1788; m. 2 June 1812, Jesse Gleason.
ABEL, b. 20 June 1790; d. July 1811.

149

MOSES[5] CHASE (Dea. Abel,[4] Dea. Thomas,[3] Thomas[2]), born in
Sutton (since 1813, Millbury), 24 Oct. 1755; died in Sutton, 9 Feb.
1790. He married in Sutton, 24 Nov. 1778, MARY KILHAM, probably a kinswoman of the wife of his brother Thomas Chase. She
administered upon her husband's estate, 25 Feb. 1790, and rendered
an account, 7 Dec. 1790. They resided in Sutton.
Children, born in Sutton:

SALLY GILBERT,[6] b. 5 Dec. 1779.
ABEL, b. 30 Mar. 1782; d. 4 May 1782.
BETSEY, b. 5 June 1784.
495.   BRICKET, b. 26 Oct. 1786.
496.   SILAS, b. 26 July 1788.
MIRINDA, b. 19 Nov. 1789; m. 20 June 1820, Capt. Nathaniel
Sibley.

150

EZEKIEL[5] CHASE (Dea. Roger,[4] Dea. Thomas,[3] Thomas[2]), born
in Newbury, 24 May 1728; died in Fairfield, Me., in 1808 or 1810.
He married in Hallowell, Me., in 1747, ANNA SPAULDING. They
lived in Hallowell, 1760 till after 1790, then removing to Fairfield
where he died.
Children, born in Hallowell:

ELEANOR,[6] b. 1748; m. there 21 Nov. 1771, George FitzGerald.
497.   ROGER, b. 5 Sept. 1749.
JACOB, unm.; went to sea and was never heard from.
498.   EZEKIEL, b. 4 June 1761.
499.   DANIEL, b. 31 Aug. 1762.
JONATHAN, b. July 1767; d. in the battle of Yorktown, 19 Oct.
1781.
500.   ABEL, b. 4 Dec. 1774.

151

ROGER[5] CHASE (Dea. Roger,[4] Dea. Thomas,[3] Thomas[2]), born in
Newbury, 30 June 1731. This man is not mentioned later on Newbury records, nor on Nottingham West records and Mr. Benjamin
Chase inferred that he died young. His uncle, Ezekiel Chase, who
settled in Hallowell, Me., had a son Roger.[6] (Family 497).

152

STEPHEN[5] CHASE (Dea. Roger,[4] Dea. Thomas,[3] Thomas[2]), born
in Newbury, 1 May 1735; while hunting, was accidentally shot by his
partner, a Mr. Davis. He married (1) in Fairfield, Me., ———
Varnham. He married (2) in Dresden, Me., MARY ABBOTT who
married (2) ——— Pratt of Clinton, Me. They lived in Augusta,

Me.   Administration on his estate was granted 13 June 1765 to his
father who was then of Pownalborough, Me.   He was granted lot
No. 13 in Cushnoc (Augusta), Me., 28 Apr. 1763, when his name was
spelled "Stevens" Chase.

Children, born in Augusta, Me.:

501.   VARNHAM,
          ABIGAIL, b. 2 Feb. 1765; m. 25 Dec. 1782, Gen. William Kendall
          of Fairfield, Me.

153

MATTHEW[5] CHASE (Dea. Roger,[4] Dea. Thomas,[3] Thomas[2]),
born in Nottingham West (now Hudson), N. H., 20 Oct. 1739; died
in Clinton, Me., after 1790.   He married POLLY HANKERSON who
died in 1810.   His family in 1790 consisted of two males over 16
years of age, three males under 16 and four females.   (Me. Census,
37).   They were living in Fairfield, Me., in 1790.

Children, born in Fairfield, Me., not in order:

502.   THOMAS,[6] b. about 1770.
503.   ASA.
504.   FRANCIS, b. 27 Apr. 1792.
          POLLY, b. 20 Mar. 1769; m. Ziba Burrill of Dover, Me.; b. 10
          Mar. 1765.   Thirteen children; she d. in Dover, 26 Nov. 1827.
          MARTHA, m. David Pratt.
505.   JOSIAH, lived in Philadelphia, Pa.
506.   MATTHEW.
          BETSEY, b. 1773; m. 1794, James Lowe of Clinton, Me.   She d.
          18 Aug. 1858; eight children.
          ABBY, m. William Corson.
          SALLY, m. 30 Nov. 1801, Nathaniel Varney of Canaan, Me.
          ANNA, m. ——— McIntire.

154

EZEKIEL[5] CHASE (Dr. Ezekiel,[4] Dea. Thomas,[3] Thomas[2]), born
in Groton, 28 Aug. 1730; died in Nottingham West (now Hudson),
N. H., 12 July 1767 in his 37th year.   He married SUSANNAH
HAMBLETT.   Ezekiel Chase of Nottingham West and Susannah
Hamblett entered their intention of marriage at Dracut, 4 Nov. 1757.
They lived in Nottingham West (now Hudson), N. H.

155

BRADSTREET[5] CHASE (Rev. Josiah,[4] Dea. Thomas,[3] Thomas[2]),
born in Newbury, 19 Jan. 1743/4.   He married in New Castle, N.
H., 14 Apr. 1771, MARY SHEAFE of New Castle.   He enlisted in
Capt. John Shapleigh's Co. 10 July 1775 and served till 31 Dec. 1775.
He served in Capt. Esaias Preble's Co. of Col. Jacob Gerrish's Regi-
ment from 1 Apr. to 3 July 1778 as Corporal.   He again served in
Capt. Ebenezer Deering's Co. of New Hampshire Troops from 14
June 1779 to 25 June 1781.   He was a resident of the Third Parish
of Kittery, Me., 20 June 1780.   He is not listed in the Census of
1790.   It is stated that they had children.   He was a silversmith.
He signed a deed with his mother and his wife, 14 Mar. 1782.   (York
Deeds, 46:258).

Child, born in Kittery:

> MARY,[6] her grandfather mentioned her in his will, 7 Mar. 1775.
> (York Co. Probate, 13:135).

156

COL. JOSIAH[5] CHASE (Rev. Josiah,[4] Dea. Thomas,[3] Thomas[2]),
born in Kittery, Me., 15 Apr. 1746; died in York, Me., 21 Sept. 1824.
He married about 1768, HANNAH GROW, daughter of Col. Edward
Grow of York, Me. She was born in 1748 and died in York, 22 May
1823. He served as Quartermaster and Paymaster in the Revolutionary Army in 1780. (Mass. Soldiers and Sailors, 3:359). He
was a clothier and lived in York, Me. He made his will, 30 Dec.
1819, which was proved, 4 Oct. 1824, and mentioned sons Cotton,
Josiah, William, Rufus and Jotham and daughters Olive, Hannah,
Sophia, Lydia, and Hadassah, the last named to have his clock, desk
and large Bible; son-in-law Nathaniel Webber executor. (York Co.
Probate 34:133).

Children, born in York, Me.:

507. COTTON,[6] b. 25 July 1770.
508. JOSIAH, b. 7 Feb. 1772.
  EDWARD, b. 5 Feb. 1774; unm.; killed by fall on the ice, 1792.
  JOTHAM, b. 24 Dec. 1775; d. young.
  OLIVE, b. 29 Jan. 1778; m. 9 June 1801, Samuel Messenger of
    Holliston.
  WILLIAM, b. 7 Aug. 1780; m. 2 Jan. 1814, Lydia Littlefield of
    Wells, Me. No children; lived in West Medway.
  HANNAH, b. 25 Feb. 1782; m. (int. 28 Dec. 1804), Amos[6] Chase
    of Limington, Me. (Family 1145) She d. 17 Apr. 1859.
509. RUFUS, b. 2 May 1784.
  HADASSAH, b. 19 Mar. 1786; m. 23 Feb. 1815, Nathaniel Webber
    of York, Me; d. 1 Oct. 1853.
  SOPHIA, b. 12 Mar. 1788; int. 8 June 1812, David Bradbury of
    Bloomfield, N. J.
510. JOTHAM SEWALL, b. 26 June 1790.
  LYDIA, b. 23 June 1793; m. 7 Nov. 1814, John Wilson of Spring-
    field.

157

THOMAS[5] CHASE (Rev. Josiah,[4] Dea. Thomas,[3] Thomas[2]), born
in Kittery, 14 Aug. 1747; died there 8 Apr. 1817. He married in
Kittery, Me., 7 Jan. 1778, SARAH DENNETT, daughter of John and
Mary (Tetherly) Dennett. She was born 8 June 1751 and died
22 Dec. 1828. They lived in Kittery, Me.

Children, born in Kittery, Me.:

511. JOSHUA T.,[6] b. 6 July 1778.
  PATTY, b. 11 Apr. 1779; m. 13 Aug. 1810, Thomas Jackson of
    Portsmouth, N. H.
  SALLY T., b. 27 Jan. 1781; m. 4 Sept. 1802, Daniel Parker Jr.
512. THOMAS, b. 13 Sept. 1788.
  NANCY, b. 16 Mar. 1792; m. 24 Aug. 1820, James Edgecomb of
    Bath, Me.
  RUTH, b. 27 Oct. 1796; m. 17 Apr. 1824, Dennis Shapleigh.

158

John[5] Chase (Rev. Josiah,[4] Dea. Thomas,[3] Thomas[2]), born in Kittery, Me., 15 June 1749; died in North Berwick, Me., 11 Dec. 1826. He married in Kittery, 17 Aug. 1775, Hannah Dennett, daughter of John and Mary (Tetherly) Dennett, born 13 Aug. 1756. (Old Eliot, 4:65).

They lived in Berwick (now North Berwick), Me. He made his will, 28 Feb. 1822, which was proved 18 July 1826. He mentions his daughter Sally Folsom, his grandsons John and William Reed, heirs of his daughter Betsey Reed deceased, his sons Thomas, Josiah, Simon, Mark and John. (York Probate, 36:333).

Children, first two born in Kittery, Me., others in Berwick, Me.:

	Sally,[6] b. 7 Dec. 1775; m. 28 Oct. 1811, Asa Folsom.
	Betsey, b. 6 Nov. 1777; m. Samuel Reed; d. 2 Nov. 1806.
513.	Thomas, b. 10 Mar. 1779.
514.	John, b. 7 Aug. 1781.
515.	Josiah, b. 11 June 1784.
516.	Simon, b. 30 Sept. 1786.
517.	Mark, b. 1 Oct. 1789.
	Abraham, b. 28 Mar. 1792; d. unm. 17 Dec. 1833.

159

Simon[5] Chase (Rev. Josiah,[4] Dea. Thomas,[3] Thomas[2]), born in Kittery, Me., 8 Jan. 1754. He enlisted as a fifer in Capt. Noah Littlefield's Co. of minutemen who marched 19 Apr. 1775. He also served in Capt. Samuel Sawyer's Co. of Col. James Scammon's Regt. from 3 May 1775 to 17 Aug. 1775. His order for a bounty coat was dated at Cambridge 3 Nov. 1775. He is reported to have died in the army in 1776.

Remick's History of Kittery Soldiers, Revolutionary War, p. 70, states that he probably lived in Wells, Me. He left no probated will in York County.

160

Jonathan[5] Chase (Jonathan,[4] Ens. Jonathan,[3] Thomas[2]), born in Stratham, N. H., 1 May 1730; died in Loudon, N. H., 18 Sept. 1808. He married about 1749, Anna Taylor who was born 7 Feb. 1733.

He was the head of a family in Loudon in 1790, consisting of two males over 16 years old, one male under 16, and three females. They moved from Stratham, N. H., to Loudon, N. H., 20 Feb. 1778.

Children, born in Stratham, N. H.:

	Anna,[6] b. 10 June 1750; m. 20 Dec. 1770, Benjamin Hoit of Epping; d. 29 Dec. 1786.
518.	Jonathan, b. 8 Jan. 1752.
519.	Edward, b. 24 Nov. 1754.
	Sarah, b. 17 Mar. 1757; m. 16 Mar. 1779, Thomas Cawley [Calley] of Hampton; d. 15 July 1817.
	Thomas, b. 23 Mar. 1759; d. 9 Feb. 1762.
520.	Levi, b. 5 July 1762.
	Lydia, b. 23 Oct. 1765; m. 15 June 1788, Ebenezer Parker.
	Mercy, b. 28 Mar. 1767; d. young.

MARY, b. 21 Aug. 1769; m. 9 Dec. 1784, Noah Smith, and d. 3
Apr. 1850.
BETSEY, b. 9 July 1772; d. unm. 10 Oct. 1786, in Loudon, N. H.
HANNAH, b. 10 Aug. 1774; m. Jesse Ingalls.

161

MOSES[5] CHASE (Jonathan,[4] Ens. Jonathan,[3] Thomas[2]), born in
Stratham about 1733; died there, 20 May 1798. He married (1)
LUCY MOULTON; married (2) ANNA ROLLINS, daughter of Joshua
and Mary (Clark) Rollins of Stratham. She was born 13 Aug. 1749
and died in Stratham, 25 Jan. 1821, aged 72. They lived in Stratham, N. H.

Children, born in Stratham, N. H.:

    MOSES,[6] d. unm.
    LUCY, m. Joshua Hill of Stratham.
    NANCY, b. in 1772; d. unm. 24 Apr. 1860.
521.   THOMAS, b. 5 June 1775.
522.   ELISHA, b. in 1777.
523.   JONATHAN, b. 2 Oct. 1779.
524.   NICHOLAS, b. 7 Oct. 1782.

162

DEA. WILLIAM[5] CHASE (William,[4] Ens. Jonathan,[3] Thomas[2]),
born in Stratham, N. H. 13 June 1742; died in Sanbornton, N. H.,
25 Aug. 1806. He married about 1761, PHEBE PIPER, daughter of
Thomas and Tabitha (Rollins) Piper, born in Stratham, in 1745.
She died in Sanbornton, N. H., in Jan. 1835, aged 90. The first nine
children were born in Stratham, as they removed from Stratham to
Sanbornton about 1778. He made his will, 24 Mar. 1804, which
was proved 1 Sept. 1806. Therein he mentions his wife Phebe, his
sons James, William, David, Ebenezer, Daniel, and John and daughters Betsey, Nancy, and Jane; Phebe, Polly and Comfort, then
single. (Strafford Co. Probate, 10:308).

Children, eldest nine or ten born in Stratham, others in Sanbornton, N. H.:

525.   JONATHAN,[6] b. 6 Mar. 1762.
526.   WILLIAM, b. 1764.
527.   DAVID, b. 19 June 1766.
528.   EBENEZER, b. 9 Dec. 1767.
    JOHN, d. young.
529.   DANIEL, b. 17 Nov. 1770.
    BETSEY, b. 4 June 1772; m. Mark Taylor of Sanbornton, N. H.;
      d. 8 July 1823.
    NANCY, b. 4 Oct. 1773; m. 10 Aug. 1791, Dea. Nathaniel Norris
      of Hardwick, Vt.
    JANE, b. 3 Apr. 1775; m. Walter Sanborn of New Hampton,
      N. H. Seven children.
530.   JAMES, b. 8 Apr. 1777.
    PHEBE, b. about 1780; m. about 1812, Nathaniel Sanborn of New
      Hampton, N. H.
531.   JOHN, b. 7 May 1782.
    POLLY, b. 25 July 1785; m. Benjamin Sanborn of Meredith, N. H.
      She d. 1848.

COMFORT, m. 19 Aug. 1806, John Dickinson of New Chester (Hill), N. H.

163

JOSIAH[5] CHASE (William,[4] Ens. Jonathan,[3] Thomas[2]), born in Stratham, N. H., about 1744. He married, about 1770, DEBORAH ROLLINS, daughter of John Rollins of Bradford and Damariscotta, Me. He was the head of a family in Stratham in 1790, consisting of three males over 16 years of age, one male under 16 and four females. They lived in Exeter, N. H., and Tuftonboro, N. H. She died about 1794.

Children, born in New Hampshire:

532. MARK,[6] b. in Exeter, N. H., 10 May 1772.
533. JOSIAH.
534. NATHANIEL.
535. THOMAS, b. about 1765.
       SARAH, m. James Lucas of Wolfboro, N. H.
       MARTHA, m. 21 Oct. 1794, James Conner of Wolfboro, N. H.
       DEBORAH, m. Andrew Jewett.
       NANCY, m. Dudley Swan.
       MARY, m. ———— Buell of Sanbornton, N. H.

164

JAMES[5] CHASE (James,[4] Ens. Jonathan,[3] Thomas[2]), born in Stratham, N. H., 24 Apr. 1737, and was living in Gilmanton, (later Gilford), in 1790. He was the head of a family in 1790, consisting of two males over 16 years, one male under 16 and two females. (N. H. Census, 90).

Administration on his estate was granted to his widow Nancy, 21 Aug. 1812, with Nicholas Gilman of Gilford and Jonathan Ladd of Meredith sureties. (Strafford Co. Probate 20:153). Daniel Gale 3d of Gilmanton was guardian to Mark, Nancy and Sally Chase, upwards of 14, "children of James Chase late of Gilford," with John Chase and Daniel Avery, both of Gilmanton, sureties, 18 Apr. 1814. (Ibid. 19:200).

Children, born in Gilmanton:

536. COL. JOHN.[6]
537. THOMAS.
538. MARK, b. 10 Mar. 1776.
539. DUDLEY, b. about 1778.
540. ROBERT.
541. JAMES.
       MARY, m. in Gilmanton, 21 Sept. 1806, Joseph Burnham.
       ANNA, m. in Gilmanton, 11 Aug. 1785, Samuel Avery; lived in Hill, N. H.

165

JONATHAN[5] CHASE (James,[4] Ens. Jonathan,[3] Thomas[2]), born in Epping, N. H., 29 Mar. 1746. There is no will on record in Strafford Co. His wife's name has not been found.

Children, born in Epping, N. H.:

       MARY,[6] m. 29 Apr. 1799, Joseph Hayes of Epping, N. H.
       DAUGHTER, m. ———— Tilton.
       HANNAH E., m. 29 Apr. 1799, Josiah Lawrence of Epping.

166

Josiah[3] Chase (James,[4] Ens. Jonathan,[3] Thomas[2]), born in Epping, N. H., 11 July 1751; died there, 14 Apr. 1814. He married (1) Polly Robinson, perhaps daughter of John and Elizabeth (Folsom) Robinson, born in Exeter, 7 Feb. 1748. He married (2) 12 Oct. 1774, Elizabeth Parsons who died in Epping, N. H., 26 Mar. 1814. Administration on his estate was granted to his son Josiah, 10 Mar. 1814. They lived in Epping.

Children, born in Epping, N. H.:

542. Josiah,[6] b. 5 Feb. 1776.
543. Eliphalet, b. 13 Apr. 1777.
   Polly, b. 1 Apr. 1780; m. 1 Sept. 1801, Elisha Prescott, son of Dea. Ebenezer; lived in Raymond, N. H.
544. Jonathan, b. 2 Mar. 1782.
   Nancy, b. 23 Apr. 1789; m. about 1809, Josiah Folsom, and d. 3 Feb. 1868.
   Rebecca, b. 6 June 1792; m. 24 Dec. 1818, Isaac B. Morrill, and d. 16 Apr. 1857.
545. James, b. 11 May 1794.

167

Jonathan[5] Chase (Thomas,[4] Ens. Jonathan,[3] Thomas[2]), born in Stratham, N. H., 22 Feb. 1748/9, and died in Wolfeborough, N. H., 21 Mar. 1835. He married in 1774, Abigail Wilson. They removed from Stratham to Alton, N. H., after 1795. They settled in the southwesterly corner of Wolfeborough, and perhaps were annexed to Alton. Jonathan Chase of Alton married 18 Dec. 1820, Abigail Meserve of Wolfeborough. He enlisted in Mar. or Apr. 1777 and was in the battle of Stillwater, 7 Oct. 1777. He deposed 11 July 1820 at the age of 71. His second wife was called in his pension papers Abigail Cate. He lived in New Durham Gore (now Alton) at the outbreak of the Revolution and later removed to South Wolfborough. He applied for a pension 25 Apr. 1818 from Alton.

Children:

   Polly,[6] b. about 1775; m. 1794, Isaac Jones; d. 1818.
   John, d. at age of 20 years.
546. Thomas Wilson, b. about 1780.
547. Joshua Wingate, b. 1782.
   Nancy, b. 27 Jan. 1784; m. 22 July 1810, William P. Edgerly. Six children; she d. 26 Jan. 1889, aged 104y. 5m. 28d.
   Sally, b. 1787; m. Winthrop Robertson; had six children.
   Betsey, d. young.
   Lovey, b. 1790; m. 1803, Solomon Giles of New Durham.
   Sophia, b. 1792; m. 4 Feb. 1823, Benjamin Buzzell of Alton.
548. Jonathan, b. 1795.

168

Capt. Dudley Leavitt[5] Chase (Thomas,[4] Ens. Jonathan,[3] Thomas[2]), born in Stratham, N. H., 4 June 1751; died there, 29 Mar. 1816, aged 64. He married in Stratham, 24 Sept. 1780, widow Mary (Ayer) Davis, daughter of Perkins Ayer. She was born in Portsmouth, N. H., 12 Aug. 1754. She was the widow of Samuel

Davis by whom she had a daughter Polly Davis, born 3 May 1772, who married Oliver Chase.

Children, born in Stratham:

NANCY,[6] b. 23 June 1781; m. 1801, Samuel Wiggin of Stratham.
BETTY, b. 8 Jan. 1784, in Exeter, N. H.; m. 28 Feb. 1808, Benjamin Wiggin of Alton, N. H.
549.   ANDREW, b. 10 Mar. 1787.

169

JOHNSON[5] CHASE (John,[4] James,[3] Thomas[2]), born in Newbury, 24 Oct. 1730; died there. He married in Newbury, 19 July 1753, ABIGAIL PIKE, daughter of Thomas and Lois Pike. She was born in Newbury, 30 Dec. 1729; died in Chester, N. H., in 1804.

Children, born in Newbury:

HANNAH,[6] b. 14 Nov. 1754; m. 21 Mar. 1782, John Hazelton, son of Ephraim of Chester, N. H.*
550.   JOHN, b. 17 July 1756.
551.   PERLEY, b. 2 June 1758.
JOHNSON, b. 16 Nov. 1761; d. in Newbury, 2 Mar. 1772.

170

EDMUND[5] CHASE (Capt. James,[4] James,[3] Thomas[2]), born in what is now West Newbury, 19 Sept. 1748; died in Haverhill, 14 June 1815. He married in Haverhill, 25 Nov. 1773, HANNAH PECKER, daughter of James Jr. and Hannah (Cogswell) Pecker, born in Haverhill, 5 Aug. 1751; died there, 6 June 1835, aged 84. They lived in Haverhill.

Children, born in Haverhill:

HANNAH,[6] b. 25 Oct. 1774; m. Isaac Whittier.
SUSANNAH, b. 21 Jan. 1777; m. 13 Dec. 1798, Thomas Boyle.
552.   JAMES, b. 9 Apr. 1779.
PHINEAS NICHOLS, b. 18 Aug. 1781; d. unm. in Medford, 12 Nov. 1805.
SARAH, b. 23 Mar. 1784; m. (1) Samuel Clark; m. (2) ——— Eaton.
553.   WILLIAM, b. 6 July 1786.
ABIGAIL, b. 20 Feb. 1790; d. unm. 12 Nov. 1834.
ELIZABETH, b. 7 Oct. 1791; d. unm. 13 Apr. 1842.
554.   EDMUND, b. 12 Sept. 1794.

171

JAMES[5] CHASE (Capt. James,[4] James,[3] Thomas[2]), born in what is now West Newbury, 6 Mar. 1751; died in Loudon, N. H. He married in Haverhill, 15 Oct. 1772, ELIZABETH HASELTON, daughter of James and Ruth (Ladd) Haselton, born in Haverhill, 1 Dec. 1752.

They lived in Haverhill in 1776 and removed to Loudon, before 1790. He was taxed there in 1801, and was mentioned in his father's will, 27 July 1801.

*John Hazelton was born 9 June 1736. His youngest child, Ruth, born 10 Nov. 1800, married Samuel Clark of Derry, N. H., and died there 1 Oct. 1899. The elapsed time between the birth of the father and the death of the daughter, over 163 years, is unprecedented, as far as the writer has been able to ascertain.

Children, first three born in Haverhill, others in Loudon, N. H.:

ELISABETH,[6] b. 19 May 1773; m. 28 Nov. 1799, Joshua Fletcher.
555.   JAMES BAILEY, b. 10 Mar. 1774.
556.   ISAIAH, b. 5 Dec. 1776.
ABIGAIL, b. 6 Apr. 1783.
557.   WILLIAM, b. 6 May 1785.
558.   AMOS, b. 29 Oct. 1789.
SARAH, b. 9 June 1790.
LEAVITT, b. 30 Dec. 1791.
RUTH, b. 15 Mar. 1794.
TRYPHENA, b. 2 Sept. 1796.

172

DANIEL[5] CHASE (Capt. James,[4] James,[3] Thomas[2]), born in what is now West Newbury, 7 Nov. 1761; died in Haverhill, 22 Sept. 1791. He married there 13 Nov. 1786, MARY CLEMENTS, daughter of Benjamin and Mary (Bartlett) Clements, born in Haverhill, 15 Sept. 1766; died there 11 June 1793. He was a farmer and lived in Haverhill. His will was proved, 5 Dec. 1791, in which he bequeathed his estate to his wife Molly and after her decease to his daughters Elizabeth and Relief. (Essex Probate 61:242).

Children, born in Haverhill:

ELISABETH,[6] b. 18 Sept. 1787; m. 11 Mar. 1810, James Underhill
of Chester; died there 9 Sept. 1875, age 87y. 11m. 21d.
RELIEF, b. 14 Feb. 1789; d. unm. 29 Dec. 1861 or 1862, in Ohio.

173

WILLIAM[5] CHASE (Capt. James,[4] James,[3] Thomas[2]), born in Haverhill about 1763; died there 9 Dec. 1793. He married (intention 9 July 1791 in Haverhill) ELIZABETH JOHNSON. Administration on his estate was granted to Elias Johnson, upon the request of his widow Elizabeth and his father James Chase, 7 Apr. 1794. (Essex Probate, 5, 190).

They attended the West Parish Congregational Church in Haverhill and there his death was recorded.

Child, born and baptized in the West Parish of Haverhill:

559.   EDWARD LITTLE,[6] bp. 3 Oct. 1793; mentioned in his grandfather's
will, 27 July 1801.

174

JAMES[5] CHASE (Nathaniel,[4] James,[3] Thomas[2]), born in Haverhill, 25 Dec. 1735; died probably in Bath, N. H., between 1790 and 1794. He married ABIGAIL ———. He administered upon his father's estate in 1757. He, or another of the same name, was taxed in Notingham West (now Hudson), N. H. in 1779. They were living in Bath, N. H., on 17 Jan. 1788 when the family was warned to go to Wentworth. The widow lived in Bath from 25 Aug. 1794 to 1 Apr. 1808.

Child, born in Nottingham West (now Hudson), N. H.:

ELIZABETH,[6] b. 6 June 1757.
EDNA, alive 17 Jan. 1788.
560.   JOSEPH, alive same day.
ABIGAIL, living in Bath, 2 Aug. 1806.

175

ABEL[5] CHASE (Nathaniel,[4] James,[3] Thomas[2]), born in Haverhill or Salem, N. H., — Aug. 1746; baptized in the West Parish of Haverhill, July 1747; died in New York. He married HANNAH BEDELL, daughter of John and Judith (Colby) Bedell, born 7 Jan. or July 1747. They removed to Bath, N. H., where they lived. His family consisted of two males over 16 years, three males under 16 and three females in 1790 in Bath. Later they removed to New York State.

Children, born in Bath, N. H.:

561.   JOHN,[6] b. 1768.
562.   ROBERT, b. 1770.
      JUDITH, b. 1772; m. 21 Mar. 1795 in Bath, Peter Minard.
563.   ISAIAH, b. 1774.
      LOIS, b. 1776; m. 25 Nov. 1801, Ephraim Corey.
564.   ABEL, b. 1778; d. in Portland, Me., in 1854.
565.   MOODY, b. 6 June 1780.
566.   MOSES, b. 1783.

176

EDMUND[5] CHASE (Aquila,[4] James,[3] Thomas[2]), born in what is now Newburyport, 23 May 1743; living in Parsonsfield, Me. in 1790. He married about 1768, BETSEY GILMAN of New Market, N. H. He removed to Parsonsfield, Me. and was head of a family there in 1790, consisting of three males over 16 years of age, two males under 16 and three females. (Me. Census, 65). They lived in Parsonsfield from 1775. Administration on his estate was granted to his son, Ira C. Chase of Porter, Me. before 2 May 1845. (York Co. Deeds, 187: 211). He was alive 29 Jan. 1835. His wife Betsey was alive 12 Dec. 1832. (Ibid. 156:152).

Children, born in Parsonsfield, Me.:

567.   NATHANIEL,[6] b. 1 May 1769.
      MARY, m. Jedediah Collins.
      BETSEY, m. Nathaniel Mudgett.
568.   ELIPHALET, b. 26 Mar. 1775.
569.   EDMUND, b. 10 Nov. 1778.
570.   NOAH, m. —— Garland.
571.   IRA C., living in Porter, Me., in 1847.

177

MOSES[5] CHASE (Aquila,[4] James,[3] Thomas,[2]), born in what is now Newburyport, 13 Feb. 1744; married in Newbury, 5 June 1766, ANNE SARGENT. He removed to Parsonsfield, Me., and was head of a family consisting of two males over 16 years, three males under 16 and three females in 1790. (Me. Census, 65). He probably married a second wife as his son John[6] is said to have been a half brother to Moses[6] and David.[6] He sold land in Parsonsfield to David Chase of Parsonsfield, 24 Sept. 1822, with no mention of a wife. (York Co. Deeds, 113:88).

Children, not in order:

572.   SAMUEL SARGENT,[6] b. about 1767.
      DAVID, d. young.

DOLLY, living in Parsonsfield; unm. 16 Mar. 1847, aged 68.
573. MOSES, b. 1769.
    HANNAH.
    NANCY.
574. DAVID, b. 1778; taxed Parsonsfield 1798.
575. JACOB.
576. JOHN.

178

SAMUEL[5] CHASE (Aquila,[4] James,[3] Thomas[2]), born in what is what is now Newburyport, 21 Jan. 1747/8; died about 1821, in Burlington, Vt. He married (1) about 1765, MARY CONNER who died soon after the birth of her son Oliver. He married (2) in Methuen, 6 July 1769, SARAH BOWLEY, daughter of John and Elizabeth Bowley, born in Methuen, 31 May 1746. He was a Revolutionary soldier from Newbury 1775 and 1776 and applied for a pension 24 Apr. 1818. He removed to Colchester, Vt., where, in 1790, he was head of a family, consisting of one male over 16 years of age, three males under 16 and three females. (Vt. Census 24). Later he removed to Burlington, Vt., about 1791 where he died. His wife was living, 5 June 1820, aged 73.

Child by first wife, born in Methuen:

OLIVER,[6] b. 5 Dec. 1768; sea captain; owned five ships; d. unm.; . lived in Boston.

Children by second wife:

SARAH, b. about 1770; m. Daniel Morehouse.
POLLY, b. about 1773; m. ―――― Tomlinson.
577. JOSIAH, b. 23 Mar. 1781.
578. JACOB, b. 9 Jan. 1786.
579. JOHN.

179

JOSEPH[5] CHASE (Aquila,[4] James,[3] Thomas[2]), born in what is now Newburyport, 13 Apr. 1752; married in Newbury, 29 May 1773, HANNAH LAKEMAN. The marriage record calls him Joseph Chase 3d, and in 1790, he was head of a family in Newbury, consisting of two males over 16 years, one male under 16 and five females. There were two Joseph Chases 3d living in Newbury in 1788 and 1789, but the census record gives only one in 1790. They removed to Parsonsfield, Me.

Children, born in Parsonsfield, Me.:

SARAH,[6] b. 8 Apr. 1777.
580. OLIVER, b. 16 Oct. 1782.
581. ELIPHALET, b. 15 Dec. 1787.

180

NATHAN[5] CHASE (Aquila,[4] James,[3] Thomas[2]), born in what is now Newburyport, 9 Dec. 1755; died there, 8 Oct. 1822. He married (1) in Newbury, 1 May 1776, DOROTHY SARGENT. The census of 1790 gives him three sons under 16 years. They lived in Newbury. He married (2) SARAH PEAVEY of Newburyport, the mother of his three youngest children.

Children by first wife, born in Newbury:

WILLIAM,[6] b. 3 Dec. 1778; d. young.

582.   NATHAN, b. 14 June 1780.

Children by second wife, born in Newbury:

583.   WILLIAM, b. 3 Dec. 1788.
584.   JOHN, b. 29 May 1789.
       MEHITABLE, b. 7 Sept. 1791.

181

AQUILA[5] CHASE (Aquila,[4] James,[3] Thomas[2]), born in what is now Newburyport, 26 Sept. 1757; died in Newburyport, 13 Jan. 1835, aged 78.   He married in Newbury 9 July 1780, ANNA MOULTON, daughter of Stephen and Abigail (Williams) Moulton, baptized at what is now the First Church of West Newbury, 3 July 1757.   She died in Newbury, 14 July 1826, aged 70.

They lived in Parsonsfield, Me., in 1781, but soon returned to Newbury where they lived, 1784 to 1826.

Children, first born in Parsonsfield, Me., others in Newbury:

ABIGAIL,[6] b. 7 Aug. 1781; m. 15 July 1802, Caleb Lamson.   She
   d. in Cambridge, 17 May 1848.   Four children.
ANNA, b. 20 Feb. 1783; m. 25 Mar. 1807, John Ordway.

585.   WILLIAM, b. 21 July 1785.
       STEPHEN, b. 14 Oct. 1788; went to Montreal, Can.
586.   JACOB, b. 18 Nov. 1790.
587.   ENOCH, b. 14 May 1793.
       MARY (twin), b. 6 Oct. 1795; went with the Mormons.
       ELISABETH (twin), b. 6 Oct. 1795, went with the Mormons.
588.   NATHANIEL (twin), b. 11 Oct. 1800.
589.   CHARLES (twin), b. 11 Oct. 1800.

182

JOSIAH[5] CHASE (Aquila,[4] James,[3] Thomas[2]), born in Newbury, 2 Aug. 1762; married there 11 Oct. 1781, SUSANNAH THURSTON, daughter of Nathaniel and Mina (Chase) Thurston, born in Newbury, 7 May 1763; died 6 Oct. 1813.   They lived in Newbury.

Children, probably born in Newbury:

590.   MOSES,[6] b. 2 Mar. 1782.
591.   JOSIAH, b. 12 Jan. 1784.
       REBECCA, m. (int. 5 Oct. 1805) Jonas Lewis.
       NATHANIEL, d. unm. in Newbury.
       MARY, m. 25 Sept. 1814, Eliphalet Randall of Newbury.   Five
          children.
       CHARLES AQUILA, d. unm. in Newbury.
       SUSAN, d. unm. in Newbury.
       LYDIA F., d. young in Newbury.
       NANCY, m. 12 May 1818, Richard Hawes of Newbury.
       WILLIAM, never married; d. in Newbury.
       HANNAH SAWYER, m. 11 May 1835, Charles Crockett of Concord, N. H.; lived in Essex.
       LYDIA THURSTON, b. 30 Nov. 1806; m. as his second wife, 10
          Nov. 1832, Job Tapley of Brooksville, Me.
       ELIZABETH, b. 18 Mar. 1808; m. Job Tapley of Brooksville, Me.;
          two children; she d. 16 Dec. 1830.

183

Col. Somerby[5] Chase (Ezra,[4] James,[3] Thomas[2]), born in New-bury (now West Newbury), 26 Feb. 1745/6; died in West Newbury, 16 Mar. 1822.   He married in Newbury, 16 Apr. 1777, Sarah Jaques, daughter of Samuel and Mary (Noyes) Jaques, born in Newbury, 6 Nov. 1751; died in West Newbury, 12 May 1836, aged 84.   Four children died in what is now West Newbury, unnamed, on the following dates: 5 May 1777; 24 Jan. 1778; 17 Dec. 1778 and 19 Nov. 1779.   He was a Colonel as early as 1781.

Children, born in Newbury (now West Newbury):

Eliza Jane,[6] b. 20 June 1781; m. 26 Mar. 1804, Reuben Page of Newburyport; five children.
592.   John, b. 7 Sept. 1783.
Sarah, b. 15 July 1785; m. 6 June 1803, Enoch Noyes Jr.
Mary, b. 16 May 1787; m. 23 Sept. 1814, Dea. Newman Follansbee.
593.   Samuel Dennison, b. 4 June 1789.
594.   James Greenough, b. 13 June 1791.
Nancy, b. 29 Apr. 1793; m. Samuel Bailey.
595.   Thomas Hills, b. 8 Apr. 1795.

184

Daniel[5] Chase (Ezra,[4] James,[3] Thomas[2]), born in Newbury, 30 May 1750; died 5 Sept. 1813.   He married (1) in Newbury, 7 May 1777, Elizabeth (Bailey) England, the widow of Stephen England of Newbury.   She died in Newbury in June 1784.   He married (2) in Newburyport, in 1784, Mary Whittier [Whitcher].   She may have been daughter of Morrill and Mary (Sampson) Whitcher, born in Newbury, 4 Dec. 1750.   The wife of Daniel Chase died in Newburyport, in Oct. 1817.   They lived in Newbury.

Children by first wife, born in Newbury:

Huldah,[6] b. 6 Feb. 1778; m. (1) 15 Oct. 1795, Timothy Ayer; m. (2) Thomas Marshall.
Abigail (twin), b. about 1780; m. 18 Dec. 1803, Nathaniel Colburn of Leominster.
Martha (twin), b. about 1780; m. ——— Bartlett; lived in Wendell (Sunapee), N. H.

Children by second wife, born in Newbury:

William, b. 10 June 1785; d. at sea.
Betsey, b. 1788; d. unm. 22 Mar. 1872.
596.   Jacob, b. 25 May 1789.
Rebecca, b. 1790; m. ——— ———; she d. 21 May 1835.

185

Nathaniel Lowe[5] Chase (Ezra,[4] James,[3] Thomas[2]), born in Newbury, 31 Aug. 1752; married in Newbury, 18 Apr. 1773, Lydia Dustin, daughter of John and Mercy (Morse) Dustin, born in Groton, 21 Feb. 1754.   She died 15 Jan. 1842.   He died in West Newbury, 12 Jan. 1836.   He was a private and a drummer in the Revolutionary army 1777 and was a pensioner.   They lived in what is now West Newbury.   His wife was born 21 Feb. 1754 and is said to have been a granddaughter of Hannah Dustin, the Indian heroine. [How?]

Children, born in Newbury (now West Newbury) :

597.   MOSES,[6] b. 16 May 1774.
598.   JOHN, b. 6 Dec. 1775; d. Mar. 1846; lived in Harrisburg, Pa.
       RUTH, b. 18 Oct. 1777; m. Moses Jameson.
599.   EZRA, b. 25 Oct. 1779.
       HANNAH, b. 28 Nov. 1781; m. 17 Aug. 1804, Francis Brown of
           W. Newbury.
600.   ABEL DUSTIN, b. 25 Dec. 1783; d. 1832.
601.   MOODY, b. 6 Nov. 1785.
       JUDITH, b. 18 Feb. 1788; m. 19 Feb. 1806, George Griffin.
       LYDIA D., b. 18 Nov. 1790; m. Isaac Morse of Bradford.
       LUCY, b. 10 Jan. 1792; m. Uriah Hopkinson of Groveland.
602.   SEWALL, b. 7 July 1795.

186

JOHN[5] CHASE (Ezra,[4] James,[3] Thomas[2]), born (probably in
Newbury) 31 Jan. 1757; married in Leominster, 14 May 1780,
ESTHER COLBURN who died there, 3 Jan. 1830, aged 65. He died in
Leominster, 13 Apr. 1819. She was daughter of Jonathan and Sarah
Colburn, born in Leominster, 6 June 1763. He was a comb-maker
and they lived in Leominster.

Children, born in Leominster :

       CLARISSA,[6] b. 12 Mar. 1781; m. 22 Dec. 1802, Luther Merriman.
603.   SOMERBY, b. 31 Jan. 1783.
       ESTHER, b. 8 Feb. 1785; m. 24 Mar. 1801, Stephen Kendall.
       SALLY, b. 5 Sept. 1787; m. 6 Mar. 1808, Abigail Carter.
       REBECCA, b. 9 Mar. 1790; m. 22 Jan. 1808, David Whitcomb.
604.   FRANCIS, b. 1 Apr. 1792.
605.   ELIJAH, b. 14 Feb. 1794.
       EMMA, b. 20 June 1796; m. 10 Oct. 1819, James Carter.
606.   METAPHOR, b. 21 Apr. 1799.
       NANCY, b. 1 Aug. 1801; m. 18 May 1823, Franklin Carter.

187

MAJ. METAPHOR[5] CHASE (Ezra,[4] James,[3] Thomas[2]), born in
Newbury, 24 May 1761; died in Leominster, 14 Apr. 1806, aged 45.
He married in Leominster, 17 May 1781, MARY LEGATE, daughter of
Thomas and Mary (Morris) Legate, born in Leominster 8 Jan. 1762.
In 1790 his family consisted of two males over 16 years, three males
under 16, and three females living in Leominster.   She died in
Fitchburg, 17 Feb. 1841, aged 79.

Children, born in Leominster :

       DAUGHTER,[6] b. 10 Oct. and d. 24 Oct. 1781.
607.   THOMAS LEGATE, b. 22 Dec. 1782.
       MARIA, b. 31 Mar. 1787.
608.   CEPHAS, b. 5 Dec. 1788.
       CHARLES, b. 26 Mar. 1792; d. — June 1839, in Baltimore, Md.,
           graduate of Harvard College, 1813.
609.   GEORGE, b. 26 Mar. 1795.
       ABIGAIL, b. 24 Mar. 1797: m. 29 Apr. 1819, Dr. Peter S. Snow
           of Fitchburg.
       LOUISA, b. 15 July 1799.

188

Jeremiah[5] Chase (Ezra,[4] James,[3] Thomas[2]), born in Newbury, 13 Apr. 1764. His father and mother died in Leominster. One Jeremiah Chase was head of a family in Newbury in 1790, consisting of one male over 16 years of age, one male under 16 and three females. Another Jeremiah Chase was head of a family in Newbury in 1790, consisting of one male over 16 years of age, no males under 16 and one female. (Mass. Census, 87). The first named Jeremiah[6] Chase was son of Abel[5] Chase and the second man of the name in Newbury in 1790 was probably the son of Ezra[4] Chase. He entered his intention of marriage at Newbury, 22 Mar. 1789, with Anna Emerson of Hampstead, N. H. They were married in Atkinson, N. H., 7 July 1789, at which time he was described as of Newbury. No children were recorded in Newbury, Newburyport or West Newbury. There were no children recorded on the town records of New Hampshire.

189

Capt. Enoch[5] Chase (Ebenezer,[4] James,[3] Thomas[2]), born in Newbury and baptized in West Newbury, 4 Sept. 1743; died in Dover, N. H., 22 Feb. 1812, aged 69. He married in Dover, N. H., 31 Dec. 1767, Joanna Balch, daughter of Nathaniel and Joanna (Dodge) Balch of Beverly and Wakefield, N. H., born Dec. 18, 1744; died in Dover, 29 Nov. 1812. They lived in Dover, N. H., and he was called Captain in 1787. A child of Capt. Enoch Chase died there 23 Apr. 1787. He enlisted from Newbury for the reduction of Canada, in 1760, at the age of 17. (Currier's Hist. of Old Newbury, 496).

Children, born in Dover, N. H.:

Lydia,[6] b. 7 Dec. 1779; m. 2 Dec. 1803, David Ricker of Dover, N. H. She d. in Woodstock, Me., 14 Oct. 1837. Nine children.

Mary, b. 1781; m. 19 May 1808, Charles Groves. No children. She d. 6 Sept. 1843.

610. James, b. 1768.
611. Enoch.
612. Joseph.

Eliza, m. 4 Dec. 1812 in Portsmouth, John McCann. No children.

Hannah, b. 20 Feb. 1792; m. 4 Jan. 1818, James Snow; no children.

Joanna, m. in Dover, 26 Feb. 1809, Nathaniel Hilton of Wells, Me.

Rebecca, d. unm. Sept. 1854.

190

James[5] Chase (Ebenezer,[4] James,[3] Thomas[2]), born in Newbury, 9 July 1749; died in Newburyport, 15 Oct. 1832. He married (1) in Newburyport, 25 Sept. 1770, Abigail Bickford who died in May 1796. He married (2) in Newburyport, 18 Oct. 1796, Mehitable Rowe. She died in Newburyport, 2 Oct. 1840, aged 94. His widow Mehitable represented that he died in Newburyport, 15 Oct. 1832; that she was married in Newburyport to said James Chase in 1796 and that he was a Revolutionary pensioner and that she was entitled to the arrears of his pension and the Probate Court established her claim, (Essex Probate, 5128). They lived in Newburyport and he was a ship-carpenter.

Children, born in Newburyport:

613. JAMES,[6] b. 2 Feb. 1771.
614. EBENEZER, b. 4 July 1773.
      ABIGAIL, b. 27 Feb. 1775; m. 5 Jan. 1792, Joseph Coffin.
615. JOHN, b. 22 Aug. 1777; went to Vermont and died there.
616. JOHN BICKFORD, b. 22 Aug. 1778.
      SARAH, b. 12 Aug. 1780; m. John Teel of Newburyport.
617. STEPHEN, b. 13 June 1784.
      JANE, b. 22 Feb. 1786; m. 21 Dec. 1807, Jeremiah Sawyer.
618. MICHAEL, b. 23 Oct. 1789.
      MEHITABLE, b. 1 July 1793; m. 7 Feb. 1813, Joseph Noyes.
      REBECCA, b. 17 May 1796; m. 16 Dec. 1821, Joseph Bragdon Jr.;
      lived in Newburyport.

191

NATHANIEL[5] CHASE (Ebenezer,[4] James,[3] Thomas[2]), born in Newbury 15 Jan. 1750; baptized at Second Church (now First of West Newbury) 2 Feb. 1751/2; died in Kingston, N. H., — Sept. 1824. He married in 1768, MARGARET DUDLEY, daughter of Davison and Anna (Ladd) Dudley, born in Exeter, N. H. She died 21 Mar. 1828. They lived in Kingston or Brentwood, N. H.

Children:

      ANNIE,[6] b. about 1770; m. John Smith of Exeter, N. H.
619. TRUEWORTHY, b. about 1773.
620. STEPHEN, b. about 1778.
      DOROTHY, b. 6 Oct. 1780; m. 2 Feb. 1801, Thomas Webster of
      Waterborough, Me.
      SHUAH, b. 6 June 1787; m. 20 Feb. 1817, Benjamin Wharf of
      Chester, N. H.
621. NATHANIEL, b. 6 Aug. 1789.
      MARGARET, m. Stephen Emery.
622. SIMON, b. 1 July 1791.

191a

STEPHEN[5] CHASE (Ebenezer,[4] James,[3] Thomas[2]), born in Newbury, 15 Jan. 1754; baptized there 27 Jan. 1754; died in Londonderry, N. H., 16 Sept. 1818, aged 64. He married ESTHER HALL of Hudson, N. H. She died 23 Dec. 1820, aged 66. They lived in Londonderry and left no issue.

192

JOSHUA[5] CHASE (Ebenezer,[4] James,[3] Thomas[2]), born in Newbury and baptized in Second Church of Newbury (now the First Church of West Newbury), 7 May 1758. His father removed to Brentwood, N. H., and there died in 1807. He is reported to have died in the Revolutionary War. Another report says he left home young and was never heard from.

193

Simon[5] Chase (Ebenezer,[4] James,[3] Thomas[2]), born in New-bury, 31 Jan. 1762; baptized at the Second Church (now in West Newbury), 7 Feb. 1762; died in Bradford, Vt., 17 Nov. 1853, aged 91y. 9m. 17d. He married in May 1782, Mary George who died in Bradford, Vt., 17 Mar. 1836, aged 77. They lived in Hawke (now Danville), N. H., till 1792, when they removed to Bradford, Vt. In 1790 he was head of a family in Hawke consisting of one male over 16 years of age, none under 16, and five females.

Children, first four born in Hawke, N. H., last in Bradford, Vt.:

> Louisa,[6] b. 16 June 1783; m. 1808, William Clark. She d. 11 May 1849.
> Mary, b. 3 Oct. 1784; m. 1814, Timothy Heath. No children.
> Susannah, b. 13 Dec. 1785; m. 1803, James Welton; d. in Covington, Pa., 6 May 1853. Eighteen children.
> Sally, b. 9 Mar. 1787; m. 1 Dec. 1835, Moses Heath; d. 19 Apr. 1861.

623. Simon, b. 18 June 1800.

194

Edward[5] Chase (Edward,[4] Josiah,[3] Thomas[2]), born in Boston and baptized there in the New Brick Church, 17 May 1741.

195

Josiah[5] Chase (Edward,[4] Josiah,[3] Thomas[2]), born in Boston and baptized there in the New Brick Church, 26 Sept. 1742. He, or another of the same name, married in Boston, 19 Feb. 1765, Katharine Steele. This marriage was solemnized by Rev. Mather Byles, rector of Christ Church.

196

Ebenezer[5] Chase (Edward,[4] Josiah,[3] Thomas[2]), born in Boston and baptized there in the New Brick Church, 18 Nov. 1744.

197

Josiah[5] Chase (Nathan,[4] Nathan,[3] Thomas[2]), born in Newbury, 18 Apr. 1757; died in Haverhill 15 Mar. 1826, aged 69. He married in Haverhill, 17 Feb. 1780, Ruth Bradley, daughter of Isaac and Rachel (Ayer) Bradley, born in Haverhill, 27 Nov. 1764; died there, 10 Sept. 1829, aged 66. They lived in Haverhill and were buried there in the Walnut Cemetery.

Heirs named in petition to settle his estate were Ruth Chase, David Chase, Nathan Chase, D. F. Holt, Adeline Chase, and Lois Chase, 28 Mar. 1826. Adm. granted to son Samuel Chase with John Chase and Jacob Caldwell sureties—all of Haverhill. Also Judith wife of Dudley Holt, Rachel wife of Joseph Kimball, Nathan Chase, Lydia wife of Ephraim Colby and Ruth wife of David Chase. (Essex Probate, 5147).

Children, born in Haverhill:

> Rachel,[6] b. 28 June 1781; m. 5 Feb. 1801, Joseph Kimball of Newbury.

624. SAMUEL, b. 13 May 1783.
      LYDIA, b. 3 Nov. 1785; m. 24 July 1806, Ephraim Colby of Ha-
        verhill.
      RUTH, b. 7 Oct. 1788; m. 6 Mar. 1808, David Chase of Haverhill.
        (Family 811) She d. 4 July 1857.
625. NATHAN, b. 19 Apr. 1791.
      JOSIAH, b. 28 Dec. 1793; d. 22 Apr. 1796, of canker.
      JUDITH A., b. 12 Aug. 1796; m. 25 Apr. 1822, Dudley F. Holt of
        Haverhill.
      JOSIAH, b. 31 Dec. 1798; d. 10 Sept. 1803, of dysentery.
      CAROLINE, b. 29 Apr. 1801; d. 15 Sept. 1803, of dysentery.
      ADALINE B., b. 7 Apr. 1804; m. 6 July 1830, John K. Woodman
        of Northfield, N. H. She d. 5 Apr. 1842.
      LOIS M., b. 10 Nov. 1808; m. 17 Oct. 1831, Isaac W. Merrill, of
        Haverhill. No children.

198

SAMUEL[5] CHASE (John,[4] Nathan,[3] Thomas[2]), born in Newbury,
26 Aug. 1754; died there, 22 Feb. 1834, aged 79. He married there,
25 Nov. 1779, PRISCILLA MERRILL, daughter of Henry and Priscilla
(Lowell) Merrill, born in Newbury, 22 Jan. 1754; died there, 17
Sept. 1814.
They lived in Newbury on the east side of Artichoke River on
the north side of the road.
      Children, born in Newbury:
      PRISCILLA,[6] b. 16 Mar. 1781; m. 21 Feb. 1805, Moses Bailey Jr.
        of Newbury; d. Mar. 1860.
626. NATHAN, b. 20 June 1783.
627. SAMUEL, b. 11 July 1785.
      MARY, b. 3 May 1788; m. 14 Apr. 1813, Dea. Samuel Merrill Jr.
      JUDITH, b. 25 July 1790; m. 28 Apr. 1836, James Ordway.
628. HENRY, b. 24 Oct. 1793.

199

JOHN[5] CHASE (John,[4] Nathan,[3] Thomas[2]), born in Newbury
19 Apr. 1759; died in Parsons (now West Newbury), 5 June 1819,
"aged 60 years on the 19th of Apr. preceding his death." He married in Newbury, 2 Oct. 1781, MOLLY EMERY, daughter of John and
Abigail (Styles) Emery, born in Newbury 25 Oct. 1759; died in Oct.
1841. He was called John "4th" and they lived in Newbury (now
West Newbury), one fourth of a mile south of Brown Spring. Administration was granted to his son Moses Chase of Parsons upon
the request of John Chase of Barrington, N. H., eldest son of the deceased. The heirs mentioned were his widow Molly, his son John
Chase of Barrington, N. H., and Mary, Sally, Hannah, Anna, Elizabeth and Judith Chase who signed the settlement 26 Dec. 1820.
(Essex Probate, 5135).
      Children, born in Newbury:
      MARY,[6] b. 2 Apr. 1782; d. unm. Oct. 1841.
      SARAH, b. 14 Mar. 1784; d. unm. 30 Apr. 1855, in W. Newbury.
      HANNAH, b. 27 Mar. 1786; d. 25 Oct. 1848.
      JOHN, b. 17 Mar. 1788; d. young.
629. JOHN, b. 9 July 1790.

630. MOSES, b. 14 Apr. 1792.
ANN, b. 25 Mar. 1799; d. unm. 9 Apr. 1869.
JUDITH SAWYER, d. young.
NATHAN, d. young.
ELISABETH, b. 25 June 1802; d. unm. 23 Jan. 1867.
JUDITH SAWYER, b. 17 Oct. 1804; m. 22 Nov. 1828, Joseph G.
Rogers of West Newbury.

200

AMOS[5] CHASE (John,[4] Nathan,[3] Thomas[2]), born in Newbury,
25 Feb. 1766; died in Newburyport, 5 Oct. 1844, aged 79. He married in Newbury, 2 Aug. 1787, EUNICE MERRILL, daughter of Richard and Mary (Pillsbury) Merrill, born in Newbury, 21 Apr. 1763;
died in Newburyport, 22 Mar. 1842, aged 79. They lived in Newbury and Newburyport.

Children, born in Newbury:

631. JOSHUA,[6] b. 27 Jan. 1788.
632. ENOCH P., b. 27 Sept. 1789.
633. AMOS, b. 24 Mar. 1791.
634. PLUMMER, b. 13 Mar. 1794.
635. MERRILL, b. 15 June 1797.
EUNICE, b. 10 Feb. 1801; m. 9 May 1822, Moses Ordway.
HANNAH, b. 21 Jan. 1803; m. 10 June 1824, Henry Merrill.

201

WILLIAM[5] CHASE (Josiah,[4] Nathan,[3] Thomas[2]), born in Deerfield, N. H., 9 June 1774; died in Sandwich, N. H., 3 Aug. 1863,
aged 89. He married 4 Sept. 1795, BETSEY FOGG of Deerfield, N. H.,
daughter of James and Apphia (Collins) Fogg of Deerfield. She
was born 30 Oct. 1775; died in Sandwich, 11 Mar. 1848. He was a
farmer and lived in Sandwich, near Whiteface Mountain.

Children, born in Sandwich:

HANNAH SANBORN,[6] b. 11 July 1796; m. Oliver Kennison of
Tilton, N. H.
APPHIA COLLINS, b. 19 Apr. 1798; m. 13 Mar. 1823, Eliphalet
McGaffey of Sandwich; five children; she d. 2 July 1883.
636. JOSIAH, b. 26 May 1800.
MARY, b. 2 Sept. 1802; m. 2 Sept. 1828, Simon Bennett; four
children.
BETSEY, b. 15 Aug. 1804; d. unm. 7 Dec. 1865.
637. JEREMIAH, b. 6 Dec. 1806.
ABIGAIL, b. 13 July 1811; m. 15 Sept. 1833, Luther Tripp of
Swanville, Me. Eight children.
638. WILLIAM, b. 2 Jan. 1814.
639. LEMUEL, b. 16 Dec. 1817.
640. LEVI, b. 29 Sept. 1822.

202

NATHAN[5] CHASE (Josiah,[4] Nathan,[3] Thomas[2]), born in Deerfield, N. H., 28 May 1777; married (1) about 1799, ABIGAIL TOBEY
who was born 31 Mar. 1778; died 16 July 1812. He married (2)
12 Oct. 1813, MEHITABLE MERRILL, perhaps daughter of Jonathan
and Abiah (Stevens) Merrill of Derryfield, N. H., and Newbury,
N. H. She died 19 May 1830, aged 45. They lived in Deerfield.

Child by first wife:

SARAH SANBORN,[6] b. 16 Apr. 1800; m. 13 Aug. 1822, Joseph M.
Silver of Deerfield. Their son, John W., m. Harriet A. Chase.
(Family 1192)

Children by second wife:

ABIGAIL TOBEY, b. Sept. 1814; m. (1) Greenleaf M. Smith; m.
(2) Emery Currier; m. (3) Thomas Brown.

641. ROBERT MERRILL, b. 10 Feb. 1816.

HANNAH JANE, b. June 1817; m. May 1842, Horace Stone of
Lunenburg, Vt.

MARTHA (twin), b. 10 Apr. 1820; m. John Gale of Landaff, N. H.

MARY (twin), b. 10 Apr. 1820; d. 6 Nov. 1824.

EMELINE M. (twin), b. 23 July 1824; m. 20 Feb. 1849, James
S. Whidden.

CATHARINE M. (twin), b. 23 July 1824; m. (1) Samuel P.
Chase, her cousin, (family 642) 16 May 1844; m. (2) William Goodenough; m. (3) Amos Davis.

203

JONATHAN[5] CHASE (Josiah,[4] Nathan,[3] Thomas[2]), born in Deerfield, N. H., 24 Dec. 1779; died in Epsom, N. H., 18 Feb. 1845. He
married (1) in Deerfield, 24 Feb. 1800, MARY PRESCOTT, daughter
of Samuel Prescott of Deerfield. She was born 6 Oct. 1782, and
died 27 Mar. 1827. He married (2) HANNAH PULSIFER. He was
a farmer and a shoemaker and lived in Epsom. There is in Deerfield
the record of the marriage of a Jonathan Chase and Hannah Bean,
8 Feb. 1830. This may be the second marriage of the aforesaid Jonathan.

Children:

JOSIAH,[6] b. 21 June 1800; d. unm. 10 Jan. 1842.

642. SAMUEL PRESCOTT, b. 24 May 1808.

HANNAH WEARE, b. 7 Aug. 1824; m. 11 May 1848, George G.
Fife of Chichester, N. H. He b. 24 Oct. 1825.

204

EDMUND[5] CHASE (Josiah,[4] Nathan,[3] Thomas[2]), born in Deerfield, N. H., 13 Sept. 1781; died there, 19 Dec. 1850. He married in
Deerfield 18 Mar. 1807, LUCY FOGG, daughter of Enoch Fogg of
Kensington, N. H., and Deerfield. She was born 3 Feb. 1778, and
died in Deerfield, 26 Aug. 1854. They lived in Deerfield.

Children, born in Deerfield:

643. CHARLES,[6] b. 5 Jan. 1808.

644. HENRY, b. 16 Dec. 1809.

645. EDMUND PIKE, b. 30 Oct. 1813.

RUFUS, b. 27 June 1816; d. in California, 10 Aug. 1845. No
surviving issue. He m. Susan James.

205

MOSES[5] CHASE, JR. (Moses,[4] Nathan,[3] Thomas[2]), born in New-
bury, 10 May 1761; baptized in what is now the First Church of
West Newbury, 19 July 1761; died in Deerfield, N. H., 18 Nov. 1840.
He married (1) about 1781, THEODATE SANBORN, daughter of Dan-

iel and Elizabeth (Sanborn) Sanborn of Brentwood and Tamworth, N. H. She was born 23 Feb. 1762 and died in Deerfield, 23 Mar. 1824. They lived in Deerfield. He married (2) in Deerfield, 2 June 1830, MRS. MEHITABLE BEAN of Gilmanton, widow of Loammi Bean of Brentwood. Her maiden name was Mehitable Smith. She was living in Kingston, N. H., with her daughter, Betsey Bartlett, 5 Apr. 1855, aged 95. He was a Revolutionary soldier.

Children, born in Deerfield:

> JOANNA,[6] b. 16 June 1783; m. John M. Steele of Sanbornton, N. H.
> SARAH, b. 14 Feb. 1786; m. Nathan Steele.
> ABIGAIL, b. 4 June 1790; m. Jacob Libby of Epsom, N. H.
> SUSAN, b. 29 July 1792; m. 21 Feb. 1821, John M. Steele.
> 646. DAVID, b. 3 Feb. 1794.
> POLLY, b. 22 Feb. 1797; m. Joseph Philbrick.
> THEODATE, b. 9 Apr. 1800; unm.
> ELIZA, b. 22 Apr. 1802; unm.
> LYDIA, b. 28 Feb. 1806; m. 18 Aug. 1825, Joel Bean.

206

JOSEPH[5] CHASE (Moses,[4] Nathan,[3] Thomas[2]), born in Deerfield, N. H., 8 June 1763; died there, 21 Jan. 1840. He married 25 Jan. 1785, ELIZABETH SANBORN, daughter of Daniel and Elizabeth (Sanborn) Sanborn of Brentwood and Tamworth, N. H. She was born 10 Dec. 1762; and died in Deerfield, 20 Oct. 1839. They lived in Deerfield, and his family in 1790, consisted of one male over 16 years, two males under 16, and two females.

Children, born in Deerfield, N. H.

> 647. DANIEL,[6] b. 14 May 1786.
> ELISABETH, b. 27 Dec. 1787; m. 11 Nov. 1811, Josiah Rollins of Deerfield.
> LO-RUHAMAH, b. 25 Oct. 1789; d. 19 Nov. 1789.
> HANNAH, b. 30 Oct. 1792; d. unm. 29 Nov. 1877, aged 85.
> 648. JOSEPH, b. 18 Oct. 1795.
> 649. ABRAHAM, b. 2 Aug. 1797.
> 650. JOSIAH, b. 20 Aug. 1799.
> 651. WILLIAM, b. 27 July 1801.
> ISAAC, b. 30 June 1803; d. young.
> JACOB (twin), b. 30 June 1803; d. young.
> 652. NATHAN, b. 9 Dec. 1805.

207

PARKER[5] CHASE (Moses,[4] Nathan,[3] Thomas[2]), born in Newbury, 22 Aug. 1765; died in Campton, N. H., 22 July 1851. He married (1) about 1783, SARAH EVANS, daughter of William Evans. She died in Deerfield, N. H., 14 Jan. 1800. He married (2) 11 Mar. 1800, MARY [POLLY] HAYES of Allenstown, N. H., born 27 Aug. 1778; alive 3 May 1855. They lived in Deerfield. Later he went to Campton. In 1790 he was head of a family in Deerfield. He was a Revolutionary soldier enlisting from Deerfield, July 1780. He removed from Campton to Illinois and returned to Campton in 1840. Polly Chase deposed, that she was his widow 13 Aug. 1853, at age of 76.

Children by first wife, born in Deerfield:

653. PARKER,[6] b. 31 Dec. 1784.
654. MOSES, b. 24 May 1786.
655. WILLIAM, b. 25 Nov. 1787.
      LYDIA, b. 27 July 1789; m. 14 Jan. 1815, Jacob Nute of North-
        wood, N. H.; lived in Derry, N. H.
      MARY, b. 17 May 1791; m. 1811, Anthony Hunt; lived in Weare,
        N. H.
      WALDRON, b. 26 Apr. 1793; d. 17 Aug. 1793.

Children by second wife, born in Deerfield:

      JEMIMA, b. 7 Dec. 1800; d. 5 Nov. 1804.
656. AARON, b. 20 Feb. 1803.
      SALLY, b. 20 Oct. 1804; d. young.
657. JAMES, b. 26 May 1806.
      SALLY, b. 26 Sept. 1809; m. (1) Baker Whitten; m. (2) Timo-
        thy Glover; she living in Thornton, N. H. 1874.
      NANCY, b. 3 Aug. 1811; m. 19 July 1835, Asa Drew; lived in
        Ashland, N. H., 1874.
658. HAZEN, b. 12 Mar. 1808; went West.
      ROWENA, b. 3 Sept. 1813; m. Seavey Dodge.
659. SETH FOGG, b. 22 Dec. 1815.

208

JOHN[5] CHASE (Moses,[4] Nathan,[3] Thomas[2]), born in Deerfield,
N. H., 25 Apr. 1772; died in Bangor, Me., Apr. 1853. He married
in Kingston, N. H., 17 Dec. 1794, HANNAH SANBORN, daughter of
Daniel and Elizabeth (Sanborn) Sanborn of Brentwood and Tamworth, N. H. She was born, 22 Aug. 1773; died 15 Dec. 1817. He
was a millwright and lived in Wakefield and Tamworth, N. H.

Children, born in Wakefield:

660. DEARBORN.[6]
      MARY, b. Oct. 1803; m. in Tamworth, 27 Feb. 1823, William
        Buzzell.
      ELIZA, b. 18 Nov. 1806; m. 25 May 1831, Nathan Chase. son
        of Joseph, a cousin. (See 652.)
661. HENRY, b. 29 Nov. 1808.

208a

ROBERT[5] CHASE (Parker,[4] Nathan,[3] Thomas[2]), born in Newburyport and baptized there, 23 Mar. 1766. He enlisted from Deerfield, N. H., in the Continental Army 8 Mar. 1781 and was described
in the muster roll as 16 years of age and 5 feet in height, Samuel Folsom, muster master. (N. H. Revolutionary War Rolls, 3 :242). In
his deposition he stated that he was three times wounded. He calls
himself 59 on 20 June 1820. On 1 June 1840 he called himself 79—
statements which are not exact. He married on Squam Island, near
Georgetown, Me., 12 June 1797, ABIGAIL POORE who called herself
52 in 1820 and 84 in 1843. She died in Georgetown, 2 Mar. 1850
and he died there 16 Feb. 1841. (Pension Papers).

Children, born in Georgetown, Me.:

662. PARKER,[6] b. about 1800; aged 20 in 1820.
663. WILLIAM G., b. about 1802; aged 49 in 1849.

664. ZACHARIAH, b. about 1804; alive 20 June 1820.
      ELIZABETH, b. about 1806; alive 1820.
665. ROBERT, b. about 1810; under guardian 21 Aug. 1855. (Pension
      Papers).

209

REV. STEPHEN[5] CHASE (Edmund,[4] Nathan,[3] Thomas[2]), born in
Newbury, 19 Jan. 1772; died in Lincoln, Me., 14 July 1843. He
married 4 Dec. 1798, RUTH H. TYLER of New Gloucester, Me., born
12 Mar. 1778, who died 9 Oct. 1857.

They lived in Lewiston and in Plantation No. 3 (now Woodstock), Me., from 1802. He was the first town clerk and first representative from Woodstock; deacon and preacher in the Baptist
Church in Paris Hill, Me. About 1825 they removed to Lincoln,
Me., where they lived until their death.

Children, born in Maine:

CLARISSA,[6] b. 22 Sept. 1799; m. Daniel Curtis of Woodstock, Me.
RUHAMAH CUTTER, b. 28 June 1801; m. Benjamin Davis.
RUTH TYLER, b. 6 July 1803; m. Simeon [Simon] Fickett.
BETSEY LITTLE, b. 28 Dec. 1804; m. Solon Gates of Lincoln; d.
   in Lincoln, Me., 5 Sept. 1871.
666. THOMAS HERRICK, b. 22 Dec. 1806.
667. PETER MERRILL, b. 25 Dec. 1808.
668. CYRUS HAMLIN, b. 30 Nov. 1810.
STEPHEN SULLIVAN, b. 29 May 1813; d. unm. July 1872.
NOAH CURTIS, b. 29 Oct. 1815; unm.
669. DUDLEY PIKE, b. 14 Feb. 1817.
670. ABNER BEARSE, b. 12 Dec. 1819.

210

MERRILL[5] CHASE (Edmund,[4] Nathan,[3] Thomas[2]), born in Newbury, 17 Oct. 1773; died in Paris, Me., 15 Jan. 1859, also given
9 Jan. 1860. He married (1) 3 Mar. 1796, SALLY TUCKER. He
married (2) 2 Nov. 1814, LUCY (SPOFFORD) FELT. She was the
widow of Joshua Felt of Rumford, Me., and Woodstock, Me., and
the daughter of Eldad and Lucy (Spaulding) Spofford of Temple,
N. H. She was born 8 Apr. 1777. They lived in Woodstock, Me.,
from 1802, having removed from Minot, Me., where he first settled.

Children by first wife, born in Maine:

SALLY,[6] b. 20 Feb. 1797; m. Lemuel Perham; went to Ill.
671. MERRILL, b. 20 Mar. 1799.
ALFRED, b. 2 Nov. 1801; m. 9 Apr. 1831, Elvira Perham. No
   children; lived at Bryant's Pond, Me.
MARY ANN, b. 5 Aug. 1803; m. 23 Mar. 1826, Edmund Bowker
   of Woodstock.
ESTHER MERRILL, b. 26 May 1806; m. 1 Jan. 1837, Galen Gates
   of Carroll, Me.; she d. 1 Mar. 1867.
672. EDMUND, b. 20 Sept. 1808.
LYDIA ATKINSON, b. 13 Oct. 1810; m. 25 Apr. 1829, Mahalon
   Bryant.
ELIZA, b. 21 Dec. 1812; m. Zephaniah Benson Whitman of
   Woodstock.

Children by second wife, born in Woodstock:

LUCINDA, b. 9 Feb. 1816; m. 3 Nov. 1833, Gibbs Benson of Paris, Me.

673. ALDEN, b. 5 June 1819.

211

NATHAN[5] CHASE (Edmund,[4] Nathan,[3] Thomas[2]), born in Newbury, 16 May 1783; died in Newburyport, 17 Dec. 1867. He married (intention at Newbury, 29 Mar. 1807), JUDITH ROGERS, daughter of Nathan and Hannah (Kimball) Rogers, born in Newbury, 20 Oct. 1785; died there 19 June 1872.

He was a carriage maker and lived in the upper part of the present city of Newburyport, locally known as Belleville, being the fifth parish of Newbury.

Children, born in Newbury:

674. JOSEPH RORERS,[6] b. 1 Apr. 1811.
SARAH ROGERS, b. 27 Dec. 1814; d. young.
SARAH ROGERS, b. 5 July 1817; m. 27 Nov. 1839, George W. Whitmore.

675. LUTHER R., b. 6 Mar. 1820.
SUSAN ORDWAY, b. 31 Dec. 1822; m. 3 July 1842, James P. L. Wescott. He was a hotel-keeper in Newburyport and for several years the City Marshal. They were the parents of Katherine Tingley, noted Theosophist and founder of the Theosophical University at Point Loma, Calif., where she resides.
ESTHER MERRILL, b. 25 June 1826; m. Apr. 1855, Levi B. Webster of Kingston, N. H.

676. GEORGE W., b. 3 Aug. 1828.

212

EDMUND[5] CHASE (Edmund,[4] Nathan,[3] Thomas[2]), born in Newbury, 9 Dec. 1785; died in Minot, Me., 1878. Married 17 Dec. 1812, ABIGAIL WOODMAN of Minot. She was born 14 Sept. 1788. He was a carpenter, a Baptist, and lived in Minot. He was a Free Mason for seventy years and was reported to be one of the oldest in the United States at his death.

Children:

677. JOSEPH W.,[6] b. 28 July 1813.
678. JABEZ W., b. 15 Jan. 1816.
BETSEY W., b. 15 May 1819; m. Apr. 1839, John L. Swift of Brunswick, Me. Four children.
ANNA R., b. 5 Nov. 1823; d. 1847.
PHILONA AUGUSTA, b. 31 Aug. 1825; m. 1 Jan. 1855, John N. Noyes of Auburn, Me. Four children.

213

CHARLES[5] CHASE (Edmund,[4] Nathan,[3] Thomas[2]), born in Newbury, 6 Apr. 1791; died in Sumner, Me., 1 Oct. 1836. He married in Oct. 1814, ABIGAIL BRADFORD.

Children:

679. PEABODY BRADFORD,[6] b. 14 Nov. 1815.
SYLVANIA BEARSE, b. 8 Oct. 1817; m. (1) Apr. 1837, Asher Keen; m. (2) Daniel Fletcher.

680. ALONZO FREEMAN, b. 22 Mar. 1821.
SOPHRONIA HERSEY, b. 16 May 1823; m. 24 Oct. 1843, Samuel
G. Cushman.
CHARLES STUART, b. 2 July 1825; d. 24 Oct. 1836.
BENJAMIN FRANKLIN, b. 6 Oct. 1829; m. 22 Mar. 1855, Cynthia
Hannah Bisbee. No children.

214

ABNER[5] CHASE (Edmund,[4] Nathan,[3] Thomas[2]), born in New-
bury, 1 Apr. 1793; died in Turner, Me., 24 June 1875. He married
16 Oct. 1817, ANNA BEARSE. She died in Turner, 10 Feb. 1870.
They lived in Minot, Buckfield and Turner, Me. He was a
Baptist and a school teacher.
Children:
    VALERIA ANN,[6] b. 1 Sept. 1819; m. 17 Mar. 1846, Samuel Stet-
    son, a mechanic, of Auburn, Me.
    JULIETTA WESTON, b. 11 Jan. 1822; m. 6 June 1844, Joseph
    Crooker of Minot.
    ESTHER MERRILL, b. 25 Nov. 1823.
    MARY BRIDGHAM, b. 3 Feb. 1826.
    HORACE BARROWS, b. 8 Aug. 1829; d. 16 Dec. 1831.
    LUCY BEARSE, b. 21 Jan. 1833; m. 31 Dec. 1855; S. T. DeCastor
    of Minot, a painter.
681.   SIMEON LOVELL BEARSE, b. 26 Apr. 1835.

215

WILLIAM SANBORN[5] CHASE (Stephen,[4] Nathan,[3] Thomas[2]),
born in Deerfield, N. H., 12 Feb. 1778; married 28 Nov. 1805, NAN-
CY SANBORN, daughter of John and Anna (Sanborn) Sanborn. She
was born in Hampton, N. H., 7 June 1783. They lived in Deerfield.
Children, born in Deerfield:
682.   STEPHEN,[6] b. 21 Jan. 1807.
    MARY ANN, b. 20 Nov. 1808.
    ELIZA, m. Samuel Long of Deerfield.
    RUTH B., b. 14 July 1817; m. Jan. 1837, Jonathan S. Chase.
    (Family 683)

216

HENRY DEARBORN[5] CHASE (Stephen,[4] Nathan,[3] Thomas[2]), born
in Deerfield, N. H., 8 Apr. 1783; died in Jackson, Me., 25 Nov. 1864.
He married in Sanbornton, 9 Mar. 1809, SALLY SANBORN, daughter
of Jonathan Cram and Judith (Cram) Sanborn of Sanbornton, N. H.
She was born 17 Nov. 1788 and died 1 Mar. 1864, aged 75. They
lived in Deerfield, N. H., and Jackson, Me.
Children:
    JUDITH,[6] b. 2 Nov. 1809; m. Thompson Dyer of Jackson, Me.
    POLLY, b. 20 Apr. 1811; m. Oct. 1833, Alonzo Small.
683.   JONATHAN SANBORN, b. 11 May 1815.

217

JOHN MERRILL[5] CHASE (Jonathan,[4] Nathan,[3] Thomas[2]), born in
Newbury, 1 Mar. 1774; died in Ohio, 27 Oct. 1853. He married 29
Mar. 1797, MIRIAM MURRAY who died in Ohio, 25 Oct. 1851.

They removed from Danville, Me., to Athens Co., Ohio, in 1817. According to Walker's History of Athens Co., Ohio, he resided in the township of Alexander, Athens Co. and died there in 1860.

Children, born in Danville, Me.:

MARY,[6] b. 9 Aug. 1799; d. Aug. 1802.
684.   JOHN M., b. 19 May 1801.
MARY, b. 24 Jan. 1804; d. 13 Mar. 1866; m. (1) 16 Nov. 1823, George Romine; m. (2) 1 Mar. 1838, John Logan. No children.
685.   THOMAS J., b. 6 Jan. 1806.
HANNAH, b. 9 Aug. 1808; m. 11 Oct. 1829, Jeremiah Woodyard.
686.   GARDNER F., b. 11 Sept. 1810.
MIRIAM, b. 1 Mar. 1812; m. 4 Apr. 1833, Jabez Benedict.
ABIGAIL, b. 17 Aug. 1814; m. 4 Apr. 1838, John Bradfield.
LYDIA, b. 23 Jan. 1817; unm.

218

PETER[5] CHASE (Jonathan,[4] Nathan,[3] Thomas[2]), born in Newbury, 23 Jan. 1781; died in Bangor, Me., 20 Apr. 1863. He married 29 Nov. 1808, SUSANNA ROYAL, perhaps daughter of William and Susan Royal of Danville, Me., in 1780. They lived in Danville, and Bangor, Me.

Children, born in Maine:

687.   SYLVANUS,[6] b. 1810.
688.   JONATHAN, b. 16 July 1812.
689.   ALEXANDER HAMILTON, b. 1 Sept. 1814.
690.   WILLIAM, b. 24 Nov. 1817.
JOHN COLBY, d. young.
SUSAN T., b. 5 Aug. 1821; m. Solomon Hopkins.
MATILDA J., b. 28 Feb. 1829; m. James Robinson.
REBECCA.
REBECCA S., b. 15 July 1827; m. James Harriman.
LYDIA A., b. 11 Mar. 1833; m. James Robinson.

219

JONATHAN[5] CHASE (Jonathan,[4] Nathan,[3] Thomas[2]), born in Newbury, 25 Dec. 1790; died in Danville, Me., 23 Dec. 1865. He married (1) 4 Dec. 1817, HANNAH JORDAN, who was born 3 Mar. 1798; died 13 Mar. 1826. He married (2) 18 Feb. 1827, SUSANNA (JORDAN) DRESSER, a widow, born 20 Sept. 1809; died 13 Oct. 1844. He married (3) PHEBE W. (REED) HICKS who was born 21 Feb. 1808. They lived in Danville, Me.

Children by first wife, born in Danville:

CHARLES,[6] d. young.
LYDIA ANN, b. 2 Sept. 1821; m. (1) Wentworth Jordan of Wapsie, Iowa; m. (2) William Cromley.
SARAH, b. 18 Aug. 1823; m. William Sawyer of Danville. She d. 10 Feb. 1864.
691.   CHARLES, b. 16 Aug. 1825.

Children by second wife, born in Danville:

HANNAH, b. 13 Dec. 1828; m. 4 Nov. 1852, Milo Gove of Boston.
MARTHA A., b. 3 May 1830; d. in insane hospital, Augusta, Me.
JONATHAN, b. 8 June 1831; d. 23 Dec. 1850.

692. Moses, b. 20 Sept. 1832; lived in Quincy, Calif.
     James, b. 15 July 1834; d. unm. 3 July 1854.
693. Cyrus, b. 26 July 1836.
     Charlotte, b. 29 Jan. 1839; m. Washington Hale, a cabinet maker, of Gorham, Me.
694. Ira, b. 18 June 1842.
     Children by third wife, born in Danville:
695. George W., b. 28 Nov. 1846; merchant, Auburn, Me.
     Mary E., b. 8 Dec. 1848; d. Dec. 1872.
696. John Henry, b. 30 Oct. 1851; mechanic, Auburn, Me.

220

Moses[5] Chase (Jonathan,[4] Nathan,[3] Thomas[2]), born in Newbury, 4 July 1795; died in Pensaukee, Wis., 23 Dec. 1858. He married 30 Oct. 1817, Lorana Sawtelle who died in Pensaukee, Wis., 5 Sept. 1867. They removed from Maine to Pensaukee, Wis., about 1852.
     Children, born in Maine:
697. John M.,[6] b. 6 Aug. 1819.
     Mary H., b. Feb. 1823; d. 1 Nov. 1841.
698. Jonathan, b. 11 June 1825.
699. Thomas J., b. 30 Mar. 1827.
700. Zachariah, b. 1831.
701. Nehemiah T., b. 1833; lived in Lynn.

221

Jonathan[5] Chase (Jonathan,[4] John,[3] John[2]), born in Hampton Falls, N. H., 10 Sept. 1741. He was one of the early settlers of Pittsfield, N. H., about 1780, but was not the head of a family there in 1790. It is said that he lived near Berry Pond in Pittsfield. He married as early as 1773, Anna Griffith. He may be the Jonathan Chase of Loudon who was the head of a family there consisting of two males over 16 years, one male under 16, and three females in 1790. (N. H. Census, 72).
     Children:
702. Jonathan,[6] b. 18 Mar. 1774.
703. David.
704. William.

222

Nehemiah[5] Chase (Jonathan,[4] John,[3] John[2]), born in Seabrook, N. H., 29 Feb. 1744; died there, 1 Mar. 1782. He married Abigail Marston, daughter of Elisha and Mary (Drake) Marston, born in Hampton, N. H., 25 Nov. 1747. She married (2) Capt. Jeremiah Marston of Orford, N. H., and died 5 Feb. 1803. They lived on the Jonathan Chase farm in Seabrook.
     Children, born in Seabrook:
     Mary.[6]
     Abigail, m. James Brown of Chichester, N. H.
705. Abraham, b. 1767.
     Joseph, b. 1770; unm.
706. Jonathan, b. 28 Nov. 1773.

PATIENCE (twin), b. 28 Nov. 1773; m. Joshua Berry, a farmer, of Pittsfield, N. H.
707.   ELISHA.

223

NATHANIEL[5] CHASE (Jonathan,[4] John,[3] John[2]), born in Seabrook, N. H., 5 Apr. 1746; died in Pittsfield, N. H., Jan. 1834, aged 90y. He married in 1773, SARAH SANBORN, daughter of Reuben and Elizabeth (Ward) Sanborn of Hampton and Epsom, N. H. She was baptized 21 Dec. 1755 and died in Pittsfield, Oct. 1844, aged 89y. 9m. They lived in Pittsfield, he being one of the early settlers there, about 1780.

Children:
708.   SIMON,[6] b. 19 Apr. 1774 or 1775.
       PATIENCE, d. an infant.
       ELIZABETH, m. David Chase of Hampton Falls, N. H. She d. about 1807. (Family 714—1781).
709.   JONATHAN, b. 2 Jan. 1781.
       FREELOVE, m. Gerritt Barry of Portsmouth, N. H. She d. in Moultonborough, 8 Nov. 1865.
       PATIENCE, b. 1786; m. 10 July 1813, Jonathan T. Chase (John[6]). (Family 716—1785)
710.   JOSEPH, b. 1788.
       NEHEMIAH, d. unm.
       MARY, d. unm.
       SALLY, b. 29 Mar. 1794; unm.; blind several years; lived in Pittsfield; alive in 1874.
711.   NATHANIEL, b. 5 Mar. 1797.
       ABIGAIL, b. 10 June 1798; m. 27 Nov. 1823, Jeremiah Clark of Pittsfield; living in 1874, aged 76.

There is great confusion about dates in this family. They have no records and some did not know their own ages.

224

DANIEL[5] CHASE, ALIAS GREEN (Elizabeth,[4] John,[3] John[2]), born in Hampton, N. H., about 1720; married in Hampton Falls, N. H., 17 Apr. 1740, ESTHER SHAW. He was taxed in Hampton Falls in 1747. He was a cordwainer and sold land, "sometime Abraham Green's late of Hampton, dec'd," 19 Mar. 1760. (N. H. Deeds, 66:127). Daniel Chase, alias Green was living in Hampton Falls, 12 Mar. 1770. They lived on Great Hill.

Children, born in Hampton Falls, N. H.:
712.   DUDLEY,[6] lived in Deering, N. H.; d. 1826.
713.   JOHN, lived in Weare, N. H.; d. 1823, aged 72.
714.   DANIEL, lived in Hampton Falls.
       NANCY, m. —— Griffith of Portsmouth, N. H.

225

JOHN[5] CHASE (Elihu,[4] John,[3] John[2]), born probably in Hampton Falls, N. H., 26 Nov. 1731; died in Kensington, N. H., suddenly before 1790. He married 21 Dec. 1752, LYDIA GREEN. They lived in Kensington, and Pittsfield, N. H. He was a farmer. His son

John is recorded as having been born in Pittsfield, 18 Feb. 1760. Administration on his estate was granted, 18 Nov. 1789.

Children, probably born in Kensington:

715. NATHAN GREEN,[6] b. 25 Dec. 1752.
 JUDITH, b. 23 May 1754; m. Levi Greene of Wearè, N. H.
 MARY, b. 25 May 1756; m. Solomon Hanson of Pittsfield.
 ABIEL, m. Simon Greene.
716. JOHN, b. 18 Feb. 1760.
717. DAVID, b. 27 Jan. 1762.
 LYDIA, m. Moses Brown; lived in Monkton, Vt.
 STEPHEN, d. unm. aged 16y.
 PATIENCE, m. 13 Aug. 1791, Joshua Downing of Deering, N. H.
 THEODATE, m. (1) 31 Oct. 1799, Enoch Page; m. (2) Aaron Foster of Unity, N. H.

226

WILLIAM[5] CHASE (Elihu,[4] John,[3] John[2]), born probably in Kensington, N. H., 5 June 1736; died in Gilmanton, N. H., 4 Sept. 1818. He married about 1756, ANNA GREEN who died 10 Jan. 1819. He was a farmer and a Quaker. They lived in Brentwood, Pittsfield, Gilford, and Gilmanton, N. H.

Children, the eighth and perhaps others, born in Brentwood, N. H.:

 LYDIA,[6] m. 13 Feb. 1776, Nathan Shaw.
 RACHEL, b. 3 Dec. 1759; m. Jeremiah Dow of Lincoln, Vt. She d. 9 Apr. 1846.
718. SOLOMON GREEN, b. 24 Feb. 1762.
 ABIAL, b. 1764; m. 10 May 1784, James Lamos of Lincoln, Vt. She d. 3 Apr. 1835.
719. ZACCHEUS, b. 1765.
 HANNAH, m. Joshua Eaton of Rochester, N. Y.
720. THOMAS.
 MIRIAM, b. 11 May 1770; m. John Lamprey.
721. WILLIAM, lived Rochester, N. Y.
 LIZZIE, b. 17 June 1775; m. Ebenezer Odlin; lived in Canaan, Me.
722. ASAHEL, b. in Poplin (now Fremont), N. H.

227

THOMAS[5] CHASE (Elihu,[4] John,[3] John[2]), born in Kensington, N. H., 25 Jan. 1739; died in Fremont, N. H., 19 Mar. 1825. He married (1) in Poplin, (now Fremont), 21 Jan. 1761, N. S., ABIGAIL GREEN, daughter of John Green of Kensington, born 20 Aug. 1740. She died in Poplin, 23 Jan. 1764. He married (2) in Poplin, 17 Apr. 1765, SARAH BEAN, daughter of Joshua and Hannah (Robinson) Bean of Brentwood, N. H. She was born in Brentwood, 17 Oct. 1744; died in Fremont, 5 July 1822, aged 78y 2m. 12d. They lived in Poplin.

Children by first wife, born in Poplin:

723. STEPHEN,[6] b. 7 June 1762.
724. GREEN, b. 13 Jan. 1764.

Children by second wife, born in Poplin:

 DAUGHTER, b. 2 Feb. 1767.

HANNAH, b. 8 Nov. 1768; d. unm. 1845.
725.   LEVI, b. 5 Oct. 1770.
         SARAH, b. 6 July 1776; d. 8 Oct. 1778.
726.   JAMES, b. 6 Oct. 1780.
         DAVID, b. 7 Feb. 1786; d. unm. in Fremont, 22 Aug. 1870, aged 84.

228

ELIHU[5] CHASE JR. (Elihu,[4] John,[3] John[2]), born probably in Kensington, N. H., 18 May 1743; died there, 19 Mar. 1823, aged 79. He married, 14 July 1773, SARAH (GOVE) GREEN, a widow. She died 4 June 1829, aged 82. They lived in Kensington.

Children, born in Kensington:
727.   SAMUEL,[6] b. 2 Jan. 1775.
728.   ASA, b. 14 Feb. 1777.
729.   EZRA, b. 7 Feb. 1779.
730.   HOSEA, b. 30 July 1781.

229

STEPHEN[5] CHASE (Elihu,[4] John,[3] John[2]), born probably in Kensington, N. H., 18 Jan. 1758; died there, 7 July 1823. He married (1) 20 Apr. 1788, ABIGAIL PRESCOTT, daughter of Samuel and Ruth (Smith) Prescott. She was born 14 Sept. 1762, and died in Kensington, 20 June 1790. He married (2) MARY [MOLLY] BROWN. They lived in Kensington.

Child by first wife, born in Kensington:
         RUTH,[6] b. 19 Mar. 1789; m. (1) 5 Aug. 1810, Jonathan Rowe Jr.;
         m. (2) Joseph Merrill.

Children by second wife, born in Kensington:
731.   STEPHEN B., b. 7 July 1795.
732.   JOHN, b. 2 June 1798.
         ABIGAIL, b. 28 Oct. 1799; m. Joseph Pevere.

230

JAMES[5] CHASE (John,[4] John,[3] John[2]), born in Hampton or Seabrook, N. H., 30 Jan. 1730; died in Edgecomb, Me., 15 June 1807. He married in Kensington, N. H., 13 Apr. 1752, ELIZABETH GOVE, daughter of Ebenezer and Elizabeth (Stewart) Gove, born in Kensington, 1 Jan. 1733; died 6 Apr. 1823, aged 91y. 5m.; both buried at "Cross Point." They removed to Sheepscott (now Edgecomb), Me., about 1755. "Four of his sons were Revolutionary soldiers, all lost at sea but one."

Children, most of whom were born in Sheepscott:
         ENOCH,[6] d. young.
733.   JOHN.
734.   MOSES, m. and had Moses;[7] d. at sea with John, 1796.
         BETSEY.
         HANNAH.
735.   EBENEZER, b. 31 Jan. 1767.
         ANNA, b. 7 June 1769, m. 14 Dec. 1736, Thomas Knight of Newbury. Thirteen children.
         LYDIA, b. 1772; m. (1) Thomas Orne; m. (2) Elias Gove.
736.   ENOCH, Rev. Soldier.

231

THOMAS[5] CHASE (John,[4] John,[3] John[2]), born in Seabrook, N. H., 23 July 1731; married (1) 1752, MARY DOW. He married (2) after 10 Mar. 1761, HANNAH (GOVE) BROWN, widow of Jonathan Brown. They lived in Seabrook. He died 19 Sept. 1787. Hannah Gove was the daughter of Lt. Enoch and Sarah (Rowe) Gove, born at Hampton Falls, N. H., 12 Dec. 1739; died 9 Nov. 1821.

Children by first wife, born in Seabrook, N. H.:

737. NATHANIEL,[6] b. 9 Jan. 1753.
738. CHARLES, b. 20 Apr. 1754.
739. AMOS, b. 12 July 1756.
      RACHEL, b. 2 Jan. 1759; m. 22 Nov. 1783, Eliphalet Page of Weare, N. H.
740. WINTHROP, b. 1761.
      DOROTHY. m. 30 Aug. 1790, Elijah Brown of Weare.
      ANNA, b. 3 June 1766; m. Samuel Hanson of Dover and Weare.

Children by second wife, born in Seabrook:

741. THOMAS, b. 1776.
742. DAVID, b. 6 May 1781.
743. EDWARD, a sailor, supposed lost at sea.

232

JOHN[5] CHASE (John,[4] John,[3] John[2]), born in Hampton Falls, N. H., 3 Mar. 1733; married in Hampton Falls, 5 Dec. 1751, RACHEL GOVE, daughter of Enoch and Sarah (Rowe) Gove of Hampton, N. H. She was born in 1733. They removed from Hampton Falls to Edgecomb, Me., before the Revolution. They lived in Edgecomb and Newcastle, Me. He died in Newcastle, 5 Oct. 1787 and his widow Rachel died, 13 July 1808, aged 75.

Children:

744. ENOCH.[6]
      ABIGAIL.
      SARAH.
      RACHEL.
745. CHARLES, bp. at Hampton Falls, 2 Dec. 1753.

233

JACOB[5] CHASE (John,[4] John,[3] John[2]), born in Hampton Falls, N. H., 9 Feb. 1740; was alive in 1776; married in Pownalborough, Me., 14 Oct 1769, MARY RUNDLET. No *Jacob Chase* was the head of a family in the Maine Census 1790. He was living in Wiscasset, Me., in 1776. It may be his widow who was the Mary Chase who married in Pownalborough, 23 July 1784, John Irving of Whitehaven in Great Britain.

234

DANIEL[5] CHASE (John,[4] John,[3] John[2]), born in Hampton Falls, N. H., 17 Apr. 1741; married JANE RUNDLET.

Daniel Chase was head of a family in Seabrook, N. H., in 1790, consisting of one male over 16 years of age, three males under 16 and one female. They lived in Seabrook.

Children, born in Seabrook:

746. JACOB,[6] b. 15 May 1769.
747. CHARLES, b. 1771.
748. DANIEL.
749. JOHN.
      NATHANIEL, d. unm.
750. LEVI.
      JANE, m. Richard Gove of Seabrook.
      ANNE, m. 7 June 1786, Samuel George.
      LYDIA, m. Daniel Dow.
      MARY, m. 15 Sept. 1802, Henry Silsbee of Lynn.

235

CHARLES[5] CHASE (John,[4] John,[3] John[2]), born in Hampton Falls, N. H., 4 Mar. 1743/44; living in Hampton Falls in 1790. He married 1758, SALLY GRIFFITH. He was a blacksmith and lived in Hampton Falls. In 1790 his family contained one male over 16 years of age, none under 16 and one female.

Children, born in Hampton Falls:

> MARY,[6] b. 19 Apr. 1760; m. about 1780, Levi Gove of Seabrook, N. H.; d. about 1832.

751. CHRISTOPHER TAPPAN (twin), b. — July 1764.
752. WILLIAM S. (twin), b. — July 1764.

236

REUBEN[5] CHASE (Follansbee,[4] Philip,[3] John[2]), born in Sutton, 24 Feb. 1757; died there, 27 Aug. 1787, aged 30. He married in Sutton, 27 May 1784, MARY TAFT. She was living as his widow in 1799. In the census of 1790 for Sutton Mary Chase was head of a family consisting of no male over 16 years, one male under 16, and three females.

Children, born in Sutton:

> SUSANNAH,[6] b. 12 Oct. 1784; m. 25 May 1803, Andrew Buxton.

753. REUBEN FOLLANSBEE, b. 10 July 1787.

237

THOMAS FOLLANSBEE[5] CHASE (Follansbee,[4] Philip,[3] John[2]), born in Sutton, 16 Feb. 1760; married in Sutton, 16 Nov. 1781, HULDAH CUMMINGS, daughter of Jacob and Mary (Marble) Cummings, born in Sutton 20 May 1763. They lived in the "Old Sutton Tavern" till after 1800 when they removed to Paris, Me. She died in Paris in 1834. He died 30 Jan. 1839, aged 79.

Children, born in Sutton, except the youngest born in Paris, Me.;

754. GARDNER,[6] b. 1 Apr. 1782.
      POLLY, b. 8 Nov. 1783; m. 1 Jan. 1809, Nathaniel Howe; she d. Aug. 1841.
      HANNAH, b. 10 Apr. 1785; m. 15 Jan. 1809, Simeon Daniels. No children. She d. 13 Apr. 1863.
      DEBORAH, b. 9 June 1790; d. unm. 1854.
      JOHN, b. 2 Mar. 1792; d. unm. 30 June 1815.
      ZIPPORAH, b. 8 Jan. 1795; m. (1) 11 Nov. 1814, Elkanah An-

drews; m. (2) 1 Sept. 1825, John G. W. Coolidge; she d. 16 Mar. 1864.

FREE G., b. 1 May 1798; unm. living in Brookfield, 1872.

MEHITABLE, b. 16 Mar. 1800; m. 23 May 1822, Elliott Parks of North Brookfield; she d. 17 July 1851.

ELIZA A., b. 10 Dec. 1803; d. unm. 27 June 1865.

238

DAVID[5] CHASE (Lt. Francis,[4] Philip,[3] John[2]), born in Sutton, 10 Mar. 1761; died in Royalston, 26 Mar. 1816. He married in Royalston, 29 Nov. 1786, SARAH RAYMOND of Athol. She was the daughter of Edward and Abigail (Patch) Raymond, born in Chelmsford, 26 Sept. 1765; died in Royalston, 4 Nov. 1848. They lived in Royalston.

Children, born in Royalston:

755. CALVIN,[6] b. 15 Sept. 1787.

DAVID, b. 11 May 1789; d. 15 July 1808.

SARAH, b. 1 Mar. 1792; m. 28 May 1812, Eber Clark; d. 18 Jan. 1871.

CHAUNCEY, b. 22 Mar. 1794; d. 28 Oct. 1800.

STEPHEN, b. 8 Sept. 1796; d. 29 Oct. 1800.

POLLY, b. 8 Dec. 1798; d. 30 Oct. 1800.

756. CHAUNCEY, b. 22 May 1801.

POLLY, b. 8 Oct. 1803; m. 8 Apr. 1828, Moses Lovell; she d. 16 May 1830.

NANCY, b. 12 Dec. 1806; m. Hobart Spencer; d. 6 Feb. 1830.

ABIGAIL, b. 22 Jan. 1810; m. 29 Nov. 1832, Artemas Raymond.

239

WILLIAM[5] CHASE (Lt. Francis,[4] Philip,[3] John[2]), born in 1765; baptized in Royalston, 14 Sept. 1777; died in Royalston, 1 July 1835, aged 70. He married in Royalston, 19 Feb. 1794, BETSEY WORKS, daughter of James and Martha Works, born in Royalston, 8 Sept. 1775; died there, 18 May 1834, aged 59. They lived in Royalston.

Children, born in Royalston:

BETSEY,[6] b. 4 Oct. 1794; m. 24 Apr. 1817, Reuben Stockwell. He d. 16 Aug. 1850.

757. WILLIAM, b. 12 Mar. 1796.

FOLLANSBEE, b. 14 Dec. 1797; d. 19 Aug. 1798.

RACHEL, b. 24 Feb. 1799; d. 8 Oct. 1800.

SUSAN, b. 3 Dec. 1800; m. (1) 5 Feb. 1824, Levi Hawks of Deerfield; m. (2) 10 Dec. 1835, Frederick Boyden; m. (3) 26 July 1846, Daniel Boyden.

HULDAH, b. 29 May 1802; m. Feb. 1854. Joseph Howard (2d mar.). No children. He d. 30 Nov. 1866; she d. 3 Dec. 1873.

CHARLOTTE, b. 29 Apr. 1804; m. 16 Oct. 1826, Joseph Howard of Holden; no children. She d. 3 Sept. 1853.

MARTHA, b. 27 May 1805; d. unm. 20 May 1834.

758. THOMAS FOLLANSBEE, b. 22 Mar. 1807.

HANNAH A., b. 2 Jan. 1809; m. 19 June 1831, Gibbs W. Eddy.

759. GEORGE, b. 1 Nov. 1810.

860. FRANCIS, b. 2 Apr. 1812.

SARAH, b. 20 Jan. 1814; m. Kenney Gresham.

JAMES, b. 1 Jan. 1816; m. int. 18 Dec. 1841, Lucy Flagg of Fitzwilliam, N. H.; no children.

240

ARCHIBALD C.[5] CHASE (Lt. Francis,[4] Philip,[3] John[2]), born 18 May 1770; baptized in Royalston, 14 Sept. 1777; married (1) in Royalston, 15 Apr. 1790, SUSANNA PIERCE, daughter of Gad and Mary Pierce, born in Royalston, 5 Mar. 1774. Her death is not recorded in Roylaston. He married (2) in Royalston, 24 Aug. 1806, MRS. MARY MARGARET NICHOLS, daughter of William and Abigail Nichols, born in Royalston, 4 May 1781.

They lived in Royalston till about 1806 when the family removed to West Concord, Vt.

Children by first wife, born in Royalston:

761.   ELIPHALET,[6] b. 28 July 1790.
    POLLY, b. 17 Aug. 1792; m. John Pierce; she d. 12 July 1864.
    SUSANNAH, b. 4 Sept. 1794; m. Nathaniel Foster; she d. 5 Jan. 1865.
    DELIGHT, b. 22 Nov. 1796; m. (1) Levi Ball; m. (2) Curtis Parks; lived in Winchendon.
762.   LORING, b. 31 Aug. 1798.
    BETSEY, b. 23 Feb. 1801; m. Timothy Reed Bacon of Putney, Vt. She d. 1 May 1870 in Haverhill, N. H.
763.   ARCHIBALD, b. 4 Mar. 1803.

Children by second wife, born in Concord, Vt.:

764.   ELMORE, b. 7 Apr. 1807; lived in Concord, Vt.
765.   GEORGE, b. 20 July 1808; married; lived in Royalston and Concord, Vt., 1874.
    ELVIRA, b. 19 June 1810; m. 7 June 1835, Thomas Crosby.
    MARY ANN, b. 25 Dec. 1811; d. 12 Oct. 1835. in Boston.
766.   WILLARD, b. 4 Feb. 1814.
    LOUISA, b. 22 Jan. 1816; m. 18 Mar. 1835, Russell Powers; lived in Lunenburg, Vt.
    SOPHIA, b. 11 Feb. 1818, d. unm. 16 Mar. 1833, in Concord.
767.   CHARLES, b. 19 Nov. 1819; lived in West Concord, 1874.
    SALLY, b. 4 June 1822; m. Ira Weatherby; lived in W. Concord.
    HANNAH, b. 24 Jan. 1824; m. (1) ——— Matthews; m. (2) Dyer Hill.
    HARRIET ELISABETH, b. 22 July 1826; m. 2 Feb. 1864, William Talcott Ramsay of Walpole, N. H. Three children.

241

CHARLES[5] CHASE (Lt. Francis,[4] Philip,[3] John[2]), born 7 Jan. 1772; baptized in Royalston, 14 Sept. 1777; died in Jaffrey, N. H., 22 Mar. 1830. He married in Winchendon, 8 June 1794, HANNAH STEWART, daughter of Jeremiah and Hannah Stewart, born in Winchendon, 4 Nov. 1774. She died 12 Apr. 1857. They lived in Winchendon from 1794 to 1809, then removed to Jaffrey, N. H., where he died.

Children, the five eldest born in Winchendon:

768.   SILAS,[6] b. 27 Nov. 1794.
    LUCY, b. 12 May 1798; m. 13 Aug. 1820, Cyrus Brackett. Had son Myron Brackett.
    HANNAH, b. 23 June 1800; m. 4 June 1822, Joseph Blodgett.
769.   CHARLES, b. 11 Jan. 1806.

> MARY, b. 26 Mar. 1809; m. 8 Jan. 1832, John Nichols of Jaffrey,
> N. H. He d. in Aurora, Ill., 21 Dec. 1863.
> PHEBE, b. 14 Dec. 1811; m. 25 Dec. 1847, Samuel Pierce. Had
> child, b. 17 June 1857; never married.

770. DANIEL, b. 16 July 1814.

242

FRANCIS[5] CHASE JR. (Lt. Francis,[4] Philip,[3] John[2]), born in
Royalston, 22 Oct. 1777; died in Salem, Vt., 21 Apr. 1840. He married in Waterford, Vt., 27 Apr. 1797, SALLY PIKE, daughter of Daniel and Lois Pike, born in Royalston, 24 Sept. 1778; died in Charleston, Vt., 29 Nov. 1846. Francis Chase lived in Charleston, Vt., in
1828 and at other times in Salem, Sutton, and Concord, Vt.

Children:

> POLLY,[6] b. 28 Aug. 1798; m. in Morgan, Vt., 12 Oct. 1817, Thad-
> deus Curtis; lived in Sutton, Vt. Nine children.
> LOIS, b. 9 Sept. 1800; m. 16 June 1822, Asaph Caswell. Three
> children.

771. DANIEL, b. 22 Dec. 1802.

> NELLIE, b. 23 Dec. 1804; m. 4 Feb. 1824, Brigham Caswell; six
> children.
> SALLY, b. 20 Dec. 1806; m. 10 Feb. 1828, Samuel Abbott.

772. FRANCIS, b. 30 Nov. 1808.

> BETSEY, b. 10 Aug. 1811; m. 23 Mar. 1841, Samuel Price; four
> children.

773. NATHAN, b. 19 Mar. 1814.
774. GEORGE W., b. 27 Sept. 1816.

> LYDIA L., b. 22 Sept. 1818; d. unm. 16 Mar. 1843.
> CHESTER W., b. 9 Oct. 1821; d. unm.; lost at sea about 1845.

243

DANIEL[5] CHASE (Lt. Francis,[4] Philip,[3] John[2]), born in Royalston, 22 July 1783. Daniel[6] Chase, son of Francis[5] Chase, wrote from
Compton, Province of Quebec, 9 Jan. 1873, as follows: "My Uncle
Daniel had six sons and two daughters. He settled in Bedford, Cuyahoga Co., Ohio, and died there some years ago. His son Daniel[6]
lives in Bedford, Ohio, now" (1873). He was living in Bedford in
1830.

The following estates were probated in Cuyahoga Co.: Rowland
B. Chase before 1851, Paul Chase, 1854. Eliza Chase 1885. Daniel
A. Chase, 1888-1896.

Children:

775. DANIEL,[6] living in Bedford, Ohio, in 1873.

> Other children not reported.

244

CARR[5] CHASE (Paul,[4] Charles,[3] John[2]), born in Amesbury, 25
Nov. 1746; died in Campton, N. H., 23 Dec. 1809, aged 65y. 28d.
He married in Newburyport, 15 Apr. 1779, SARAH (REMICK) ROWE.
His father died when he was ten years old and his grandfather had
him apprenticed to an anchor-smith. He removed to Campton in
1771, where the family resided. In 1790 his family consisted of one
male over 16 years, there males under 16 and five females.

Children, born in Campton, N. H.:

SARAH CARR,[6] b. 10 Sept. 1779; d. unm.
RACHEL, b. 27 Feb. 1781; d. unm. about 1845.
ANNA, b. 8 Jan. 1783; d. unm. about 1850.
776. PAUL, b. 8 Apr. 1785.
777. TIMOTHY, b. 12 Apr. 1787.
RHODA, b. 25 Feb. 1789; d. unm. 30 June 1867, a. 77y. 11m. 26d.
778. CHARLES, b. 14 Apr. 1791.
779. CARR, b. 5 Aug. 1794.

245

ENOCH[5] CHASE (Paul,[4] Charles,[3] John[2]), born in Amesbury, 8 Oct. 1748.

246

JOSEPH[5] CHASE (Paul,[4] Charles,[3] John[2]), born 25 Apr. 1753, (probably in Sandown, N. H.); died in Pulaski, Oswego Co., N. Y., 17 June 1844. He married (1) 24 Nov. 1772, JUDITH COOPER who died 3 Mar. or 5 July 1782. He married (2) in Peekskill, N. Y., 29 Mar. 1785, SARAH DOOLITTLE, daughter of Reuben Doolittle. She died 5 July 1810. He married (3) 10 Nov. 1812, MARY WHITMAN who died 15 Feb. 1838. He served in the Revolutionary War and applied for a pension 13 May 1818. He removed from South Hampton, N. H., to Oswego Co., N. Y., before 1807. He lived in Richmond, Oswego Co.; in Junius, Seneca Co., 1818; in Mexico, Oswego Co., 1820, aged 67 with his wife Mary aged 47. It is stated that he also lived in Gorham, Ontario Co., N. Y.

Children by the first wife, born in South Hampton, N. H.:

780. SILAS WILLIAM COOPER,[6] b. 11 Apr. 1773.
NANCY, b. 29 Oct. 1774; m. 14 May 1794, Benjamin Bryant of Eastport, Me.
HANNAH, b. 2 Apr. 1780; m. Willoughby Colby.
781. PAUL, b. 3 Mar. 1782.

Children by the second wife:

782. CHARLES CARR, b. 13 June 1786.
ADELIA, m. Benjamin Blodgett.
DANIEL, d. about 5 yrs. old.
SAMUEL, d. about 5 yrs. old.
783. STEPHEN, b. about 1795.
PAMELIA, b. 29 June 1797; m. 23 Mar. 1814, Levi Whitney of Lake Zurich, Ill. He d. 5 Oct. 1855. She lived in Lake Zurich, Ill., 1873.
REBECCA, m. (1) Henry Wolcott; m. (2) Henry Webb.

Children by third wife:

DIANDARASSA, m. ——— Swan; no children.
CALPHURNIA, b. 6 Feb. 1817; m. 13 June 1838, P. S. Bennett of Appleton, Wis.

247

JONATHAN[5] CHASE (Jonathan,[4] Charles,[3] John[2]), born in Newbury, 23 Oct. 1745; died in Newburyport shortly before 24 Apr. 1790. He married (intention in Newbury and Newburyport, 12 and 25 July

1767), HANNAH ROLLINS, daughter of John and Mary (Carr) Rollins, born in Newbury, 16 July 1745; died in Newburyport, 8 Feb. 1829, aged 84. They lived in Newburyport. Widow Hannah was appointed guardian to their son Eliphalet, aged 14, 26 Mar. 1792. He was a housewright by trade. His widow Hannah was appointed administratrix, 24 Apr. 1790.

Children, born in Newburyport:

784. STEPHEN,[6] b. 2 Apr. 1769.
785. WILLIAM, b. 29 Sept. 1770; d. before 9 Apr. 1805.
SARAH, b. 15 Dec. 1768; m. 2 Feb. 1793, David Little of Kennebunk, Me.
786. ELIPHALET, b. 25 Mar. 1778; d. 20 Nov. 1817.

248

STEPHEN[5] CHASE (Jonathan,[4] Charles,[3] John[2]), born in Newbury, 7 Dec. 1747; married there, 29 Aug. 1769, PRUDENCE MORSE, daughter of Joshua and Prudence (Ordway) Morse, born in Newbury, 9 Feb. 1752. They were living in Newburyport in 1773. He died in 1785.

Child, born in Newburyport:

787. JOHN,[6] b. 3 Apr. 1773.
787a. STEPHEN, alive 13 June 1794.

249

ELIPHALET[5] CHASE (Jonathan,[4] Charles,[3] John[2]), born in Newbury, 9 Mar. 1760. He enlisted from the town of Newbury, 23 Aug. 1777, for three years and joined Capt. Samuel Carr's Co. of Col. James Wesson's Regiment. He was on the payroll from 11 Mar. to 20 Oct. 1777. He is reported to have died, 20 Oct. 1777. (Mass. Soldiers and Sailors in the Revolution, 3:348). He was not mentioned in his father's will dated, 1 Apr. 1793.

250

REV. JOSHUA[5] CHASE (Jonathan,[4] Charles,[3] John[2]), born in Newbury, 12 Jan. 1767; died in South Berwick, Me., 6 Feb. 1825. He married in Amesbury, 23 Oct. 1785, MARY STOCKER of Amesbury. She was the daughter of Samuel Stocker, born 9 Oct. 1766 and baptized at the First Church of Newburyport, 6 Sept. 1772; died in South Berwick, Me., 8 Sept. 1861. He was a Baptist minister and lived in South Berwick, 1807 to 1825. He made his will 5 Feb. which was proved 1 Mar. 1825. He mentions his wife Mary, his eldest daughter Mary Morse, daughters Joanna Frost, Sally Thurrell, Sophia Chase, Anna Shorey and sons, Stephen, Jonathan, Benjamin, Joshua and James Chase. Son James and Nehemiah Shorey executors. (York Co. Probate, 34:296).

Children:

MARY,[6] b. 24 Mar. 1787; m. 24 July 1807, Daniel Morse; d. in Cumberland, Me., 24 May 1853. Nine children.
788. STEPHEN, b. 3 Feb. 1788.
789. JONATHAN, b. 4 Feb. 1790.

JOANNA MORSE, b. 23 Jan. 1792; m. Simon Frost of North Berwick, Me.
790.   BENJAMIN PETTINGILL, b. 3 Jan. 1794.
SALLY, b. 3 June 1796; d. 7 Oct. 1848; m. (1) Samuel Thurrell; m. (2) Rufus Lord; m. (3) Peter Knight.
791.   JOSHUA, b. 14 July 1798.
ANNA STOCKER, b. 7 Apr. 1800; m. Nehemiah B. Shorey.
JOHN BRICKETT, b. 23 Mar. 1803; d. 11 Sept. 1821.
792.   JAMES, b. 1 Mar. 1805.
SOPHIA, b. 12 Jan. 1808; m. Aaron Jellison of South Berwick.

251

AMOS[5] CHASE (Dea. Ezra,[4] Jacob,[3] John[2]), born in Haverhill, 9 Sept. 1741; died in Amesbury, 23 Jan. 1824; married there, 17 Mar. 1768, MEHITABLE KELLEY, daughter of Joseph and Elizabeth (Hastings) Kelley; born in Haverhill, 25 Mar. 1746; died in Amesbury, 1821. They lived in Amesbury.

Children, born in Amesbury:

JUDITH,[6] b. 13 Feb. 1769; never married.
EZRA, b. 27 Aug. 1771; m. 25 Sept. 1800, Judith Webster of Haverhill; no children. He d. 29 Aug. 1805. She m. (2) 30 Oct. 1808, Joseph Hoyt Jr. of Newburyport.
793.   JOSEPH, b. 15 Aug. 1774.
ELISABETH, b. 10 June 1778; m. 21 Mar. 1805, Levi Williams of Amesbury. Seven children.
MEHITABLE, b. 4 Oct. 1780; never married.

252

DEA. WILLIAM[5] CHASE (Dea. Ezra,[4] Jacob,[3] John[2]), born in Haverhill, 12 Apr. 1756; died there 8 or 9 Dec. 1838, aged 82. He married, in Kensington, 1 Oct. 1783, ABIGAIL GOVE of Kensington, N. H. She was daughter of Capt. Nathaniel and Susanna (Stickney) Gove, born in Hampton Falls, N. H., 23 Sept. 1761; died in Haverhill, 29 Nov. 1844, aged 83. The return of her death states that she was born in Kensington. He was a deacon of the church. They lived in East Haverhill.

Children, born in Haverhill:

POLLY,[6] b. 15 Aug. 1784; m. 28 Nov. 1805, Samuel Ayer of Plaistow, N. H.; went West. She d. Aug. 1854 in Kenosha. Wis.
SUSAN, b. 9 Dec. 1785; d. unm. 31 May 1868.
ABIGAIL, b. 2 May 1789; m. 1 Jan. 1809, Isaac Webster of Kingston, N. H. She d. Apr. 1859.
794.   WILLIAM DAVIS STICKNEY, b. 18 Mar. 1792.

253

JACOB[5] CHASE (John,[4] Jacob,[3] John[2]), born in Haverhill, 4 Mar. 1743/4; died in Londonderry, N. H., about 1815. He married MARY HARDY of Bradford. She died about 1825. They lived in the northwest corner of Londonderry, N. H. He signed the Association Test there, 29 June 1776.

Children, born in Londonderry (not in order):

795.   JOHN.[6]
MARY, d. at the age of 18y.

796. JONAS.
797. JACOB, b. 22 May 1768.
> HANNAH, m. 9 June 1799, John Weston of Stoddard, N. H.;
> lived in Westport, Essex Co., N. Y.
> SALLY, m. Ebenezer[7] Chase of Bedford and Warner, N. H., and
> of Tisbury. (Family 733)
798. SAMUEL, b. 22 June 1780.
799. THOMAS, b. 15 Dec. 1783.
800. DANIEL.
> MARY, b. 21 Apr. 1792; m. 1 May 1819, James Young of Man-
> chester, N. H.; alive 1874.

254

JOHN[5] CHASE (John,[4] Jacob,[3] John[2]), born in Haverhill and baptized there, 11 July 1756; married about 1786, HANNAH MORRILL of Londonderry, N. H. They lived in Londonderry (now Derry), near Salem, N. H.

Children, born in Londonderry:

> NANCY,[6] b. 16 Sept. 1787; m. 3 Dec. 1812, Hugh Gault of Lon-
> donderry.
801. JOHN, b. 11 Mar. 1791.
801a. SALLY, b. 4 Feb. 1794; had two children, viz. Christopher, born
> May 1818, and Isaac Chase, b. 28 Feb. 1822.
802. FRANCIS MARDEN, b. 15 Apr. 1796.
803. ROBERT TELLER, b. 4 June 1799.
804. MOODY M., b. 1 Sept. 1802.
805. PEASLEY M., b. 30 Nov. 1806.
> BETSEY E., b. 1 Jan. 1810; m. in Derry, N. H., 17 Apr. 1834,
> Isaiah W. Newell of Derry.
806. WILLIAM B. M., b. 1813.

255

SAMUEL[5] CHASE (John,[4] Jacob,[3] John[2]) born in Haverhill, — Dec. 1752; baptized there, 3 Mar. 1754; died 23 Jan. 1847, aged 84y. 1m. He married about 1776, BETSEY MORRILL. They lived in Salem, N. H. He was vigorous at the age of 80, and could reap as much as young men.

Children, born in Salem:

> SARAH,[6] b. 19 Nov. 1777; m. 10 May 1814, Jeremiah Jameson.
807. EZRA, b. 1 Feb. 1780.
808. SIMEON MORRILL, b. 26 June 1782.
> HANNAH ELY, b. 25 Feb. 1785; m. her cousin Daniel[6] Chase
> (Family 800).
> JOHN, d. young.
809. DANIEL CLARK, b. Feb. 12, 1790.
810. ABRAHAM, b. 12 Aug. 1796.

256

ENOCH[5] CHASE (John,[4] Jacob,[3] John[2]), born in Haverhill and there baptized, 17 Oct. 1762; died before 1850. He married (1) in Goffstown, 11 Sept. 1788, SUSANNAH RICHARDS. He married (2) in Plaistow, 27 Mar. 1817, HANNAH BLY who died in Plaistow, N. H., in Mar. 1850. They lived in Hopkinton and Plaistow, N. H.

In 1788 he was living on the Society Land (now Bennington), N. H.
He is supposed to be the Enoch Chase, head of a family in Litchfield,
N. H., in 1790 consisting of one male over 16 years of age, one male
under 16 and one female.

Children by first wife:

811.   DAVID,[6] b. about 1789.
812.   JOHN, lived in Haverhill.

Children by second wife:

ANNA, b. 1 June 1818.
BETSEY, b. 3 Feb. 1820.

257

NATHANIEL[5] CHASE (Enoch,[4] Jacob,[3] John[2]), born in Haverhill,
30 Oct. 1748.   A Nathaniel Chase enlisted in a Suffolk Co. Company
and was on the rolls from 25 Mar. to 25 Dec. 1777.   He did not join
his company but died in a hospital in Boston, 23 Sept. 1779.

258

JESSE[5] CHASE (Enoch,[4] Jacob,[3] John[2]), born in Haverhill, 17
Nov. 1751; died before 1790.   He married before 1777, CHARITY
FOWLER who married (2) in Haverhill, 21 Oct. 1796, David Flanders
of Plaistow, N. H.   Charity Chase was head of a family in Haverhill in 1790, consisting of no males and three females.

Child, born in Haverhill:

813.   WILLIAM,[6] b. 15 Feb. 1777.

259

CAPT. WILLIAM[5] CHASE (Enoch,[4] Jacob,[3] John[2]), born in Haverhill, 8 July 1754; died in Newburyport, 28 Nov. 1804.   He married (1) in Newburyport, 9 Feb. 1794, SARAH COUCH, perhaps
daughter of Joseph and Sarah Couch, born in Newburyport, 29 Oct.
1773.   She died there, 20 Aug. 1802.   He married (2) HANNAH
———— who was granted power to administer upon his estate, 7 Dec.
1804.   She was also appointed guardian of his daughters, Hannah
aged about 10, and Elizabeth aged about 8, on 8 Apr. 1805.   (Essex
Co. Probate 72:118, 221; 73:146 and 78:22).   He was a sea-captain
and lived in Newburyport.

Children by wife Sarah, born in Newburyport:

HANNAH,[6] b. 4 May 1795; alive 8 Apr. 1805.
ELIZABETH RUSSELL, b. 17 Dec. 1796.

Child by wife Hannah, born in Newburyport:

NANCY, b. 1 Mar. 1803; d. 10 Sept. 1804.

260

JACOB[5] CHASE (Ebenezer,[4] Jacob,[3] John[2]), born in Haverhill,
4 Aug. 1754; died about 1818.   He married 21 Dec. 1777, CON-
STANCE SAUNDERS.   They removed to New York state early but he
was not head of a family there in 1790.   He was probably the Revolutionary War soldier of Kingston, N. H., who enlisted at the age of
21 years in Capt. Henry Dearborn's Co. under command of Col. Ben-

edict Arnold, 23 Apr. 1775. It seems as if he was overlooked in enumerating the census of 1790. He certainly was living with his family at that time.

Children:

NANCY ANN,[6] b. 4 May 1778; m. 15 Aug. 1802, Job Saunders.
814. BENJAMIN, b. 2 July 1782.
MARY, b. 14 July 1784; m. — Jan. 1812, George Whaley. She d. 27 Jan. 1871. Four children. (Family 815).
815. JAMES, b. 28 Nov. 1786.
SARAH, b. 7 July 1790; m. Jan. 1807, Edward Whaley.
JOANNA, b. 24 June 1795; m. 22 Mar. 1818, Matthew Burn Jr. She d. in Sheldon, N. Y., 19 May 1838. Five children.

261

JOSHUA[5] CHASE (Ebenezer,[4] Jacob,[3] John[2]), born in Haverhill, 11 Nov. 1758; died in Fairfield, N. Y., 2 Apr. 1819. He married, 15 Dec. 1796, ANNA SAUNDERS. She was born 11 Feb. 1763, and died 1 Mar. 1831. They removed to Fairfield, Herkimer Co., N. Y.

Children:

NANCY ANN,[6] b. 17 Mar. 1798; m. 8 Feb. 1818, Collins Wood; living in Rodman, N. Y., in 1870.
ELMINA, b. 24 Mar. 1800; m. 24 Mar. 1817, Joel Harkness, M.D. They lived in Cherry Flats, Tioga Co., Pa. Ten children. She d. 16 Apr. 1880.

262

CALEB[5] CHASE (Ebenezer,[4] Jacob,[3] John[2]), born in Haverhill, — Apr. 1761; died in 1835. He married (1) ———— CHALLIS; married (2) in Fishersfield, N. H., 16 Aug. 1818, MRS. JOANNA BABB; married (3) MARY STRAW. They lived in Fishersfield (now Newbury), N. H.

Children not in order, probably by the first wife:

816. EBENEZER,[6] b. 29 Mar. 1791.
JOHN, left no children.
PHEBE, b. 26 Nov. 1783; m. 17 Sept. 1805, Israel Gillingham.
MARY, m. Sept. 1810, Richard Thistle of Newbury.
SARAH, m. 21 Feb. 1805, Moses Bailey.
HEPSIBATH, m. William Atwood.
LYDIA, b. 27 Feb. 1794; m. 26 Feb. 1824, Daniel Gillingham.
SUSANNA, m. 22 Oct. 1818, Samuel Quimby.

263

ABRAHAM[5] CHASE (Abraham,[4] Abraham,[3] John[2]), born in Plaistow, N. H., 29 Aug. 1773; married in Haverhill, 22 Feb. 1795, ABIGAIL REDFORD COGSWELL of Haverhill. They lived in Atkinson, N. H.

Children, born in Atkinson, N. H.:

817. DANIEL.[6]
818. STEPHEN, removed to Wisconsin.
819. JAMES.
820. PARKER.
821. DAVID DENNIS, b. 27 Oct. 1802.

ABIGAIL, m. Dominicus Travale.
ELIZA, m. Gad Wythe.
CLARISSA, m. Benjamin Gould.

264

JOSEPH[5] CHASE (Abraham,[4] Abraham,[3] John[2]), married in
Weare, N. H., 26 Dec. 1799, HANNAH KIMBALL, probably daughter
of Jonathan and Hannah (Kimball) Kimball of Haverhill and
Weare, N. H. She was born 24 June 1772. They lived in Pro-
tectworth (now Springfield), N. H.
   Children, born in Springfield, N. H.:
      PATTY,[6] m. —— Gardner; lived in Hopkinton, N. H.
      HANNAH, b. 1802; m. 2 May 1822, Jonathan Kimball of Weare,
         where she d. 3 Feb. 1860. Nine children; lived in Weare,
         Springfield and Wellsboro, Pa.
822. JOSEPH C., b. 1807; d. in Springfield, 30 Oct. 1867, aged 60y. 22d.
         His death certificate states that he was "b. in Springfield; s. of
         Joseph and Hannah; mar."

265

WILLIAM[5] CHASE (Abraham,[4] Abraham,[3] John[2]), born 15 Sept.
1783; died in Grantham, N. H., 18 Apr. 1853. He married (1) in
Boscawen, N. H., 13 Nov. 1806, POLLY THOMPSON, daughter of
William and Mary (Prescott) Thompson of Sanbornton, N. H. She
was born 30 May 1785; died in Grantham, 20 Nov. 1839. He married (2) — Nov. 1840, PHEBE MUZZY who died 1 May 1866. Upon
marriage they removed from Boscawen to Weare, N. H., and about
1814 to Grantham.
   Children, first four born in Weare; last three in Grantham:
      ALMIRA,[6] b. 8 Oct. 1807; m. John Hastings; went West.
      CELINDA, b. 9 Feb. 1809; m. Benjamin B. Jones of Hanover,
         N. H.; d. 4 July 1854.
823. WILLIAM THOMPSON, b. 25 Jan. 1811.
      SALLY, b. 4 Nov. 1813; m. 8 Aug. 1841, George H. Green.
      MARY, b. 2 July 1816; m. Josiah Peters; went West.
      RACHEL S., b. 2 July 1820; m. May 1838, Samuel S. Currier;
         d. 29 July 1846.
   Child by second wife:
      JOHN M., b. 10 Nov. 1842; enlisted from Unity, N. H.; d. 4 Sept.
         1863, in the army.

266

CAPT. AMOS[5] CHASE (Abraham,[4] Abraham,[3] John[2]), born about
1788; died in 1870, aged 82. He married (1) in 1811, NANCY TUT-
TLE, daughter of Simon and Relief (Jones) Tuttle of Weare, N. H.,
who died about 1845. Later he married two other wives whose
names have not been discovered. He witnessed a marriage with
other Quakers at Weare, 10 Sept. 1794. He was a member of the
Universalist Church in Weare in 1853; Captain of militia 1837; carriage maker, 1836-1844; cabinet maker 1836. His shop was burned
in North Weare, 29 Nov. 1844. They lived in North Weare, N. H.

Children, born in Weare:

LAVINA,[6] b. about 1812; d. at age of 18 years.

LUCY, m. Moses Crommet.

SUSAN, m. 18 Apr. 1837, Stephen Fippens of New Boston, N. H.

BETSEY PUTNEY, b. 31 Mar. 1819; m. 11 Sept. 1846, Harris Felch of Weare, N. H.

267

BENJAMIN[5] CHASE (David,[4] David,[3] John[2]), born in Newbury about 1756; baptized there 28 July 1776, and died there 11 Feb. 1815. He married in Haverhill, 13 May 1781, PHEBE BUCK, daughter of Jacob and Hannah (Ames) Buck, born in Haverhill, 11 Sept. 1760. They lived in the North Parish of Haverhill. In 1826 Phebe Chase, widow of the above, proved her heirship to Eliphalet and Johnson Chase in order to obtain certain land bounties. (Essex Probate, 397:523).

Children, born in Haverhill:

824. BENJAMIN,[6] b. 21 Sept. 1781.

ELIPHALET, b. 15 Sept. 1783; unm.; killed at Burlington, Vt. in War of 1812; no children.

825. JOHN, b. 21 Apr. 1785.

ANNA, b. 2 Jan. 1787; m. 14 Oct. 1807, Joseph Gunnison of Newburyport.

SOPHIA, b. 2 Feb. 1790; m. (1) 2 Oct. 1808, Richard S. Dunlap; m. (2) 18 Sept. 1812, Sherburn Straw; m. (3) 29 Jan. 1821, Moses Myrick of Methuen.

SARAH, b. 20 Apr. 1793; d. unm. young.

JOHNSON, b. 5 Nov. 1795; unm.; killed at Burlington, Vt. in War of 1812.

ALEXANDER, b. 2 June 1798; d. 19 Nov. 1802.

PHEBE, b. 22 June 1800; m. 6 Aug. 1823, Samuel Wood of Newburyport.

268

NICHOLAS[5] CHASE (David,[4] David,[3] John[2]), born in Newbury (now West Newbury) about 1758; married HANNAH CHALLIS, 28 June 1781, in the Second Church of Amesbury (now Merrimac). In 1790 he was the head of a family in Wentworth, N. H., consisting of one male over 16, three males under 16, and two females.

Children:

LYDIA,[6] living in 1873.

826. JOSEPH, b. 1798, in Grafton Co., Vt. His son Wallace[7] was living at Chase's Mills, Pa., 20 Mar. 1873.

827. BENJAMIN.

828. MOSES.

269

DANIEL[5] CHASE (David,[4] David,[3] John[2]), born in Newbury and baptized there, 10 Apr. 1774; entered his intention of marriage in Haverhill, 16 Feb. 1793, with ABIGAIL CURRIER, probably daughter of Asa and Rebecca (Plummer) Currier, born in Haverhill, 9 July 1769. No children recorded in Newbury. He died in West Newbury, 14 May 1841, and was buried in Ferry Lane cemetery.

270

SIMEON[5] CHASE JR. (David,[4] David,[3] John[2]), born in Newbury
(now West Newbury) as early as 1760; died shortly before 4 Mar.
1803. He was a mariner and married in Newbury, 15 Apr. 1787,
EUNICE BAILEY, daughter of Stephen and Sarah (Pillsbury) Bailey,
born in Newbury, 28 Oct. 1762. Mrs. Eunice Chase died in Newburyport, 22 Mar. 1842, aged 79.

Stephen Bailey was appointed guardian unto Amos Chase, aged
16, Simeon Chase, aged 13, and William Chase, aged 10, children of
Simeon Chase Jr., late of Newbury, mariner, supposed deceased,
4 Mar. 1803. (Essex Probate, 5,084).

The Probate Court ordered, 5 June 1805, a parcel of real estate
to be sold to David Bailey, "it being the marsh that David Chase, the
younger, late of Newbury, deceased, bought of Nathaniel Rolfe."
(Essex Co. Deeds, 176:160).

Children, born in Newbury, but not recorded there:

829.   AMOS B.,[6] b. 4 Jan. 1788.
830.   SIMEON, b. 31 Aug. 1789.
831.   WILLIAM J., b. 27 Jan. 1792.

271

ROBERT[5] CHASE (Anthony,[4] David,[3] John[2]), born in Haverhill,
10 Feb. 1763; married there, 16 Jan. 1783, BETSEY MCKENZIE. She
died in Skowhegan, Me., Jan. 1848, aged 87. He died in Skowhegan,
29 Aug. 1837, aged 77. (Hanson's Hist. of Norridgewock and
Canaan, Skowhegan, etc., 363). He was the head of a family in
Haverhill in 1790, consisting of two males over 16 years of age, two
males under 16 and three females. They lived in Haverhill and
Skowhegan. There were no children recorded as born in Haverhill.

272

WOODMAN[5] CHASE (Anthony,[4] David,[3] John[2]), born in Haverhill, 20 Apr. 1765; died there, 17 Dec. 1823, aged 58. He married
(intention in Haverhill, 24 Oct. 1788) LYDIA GOODRIDGE, daughter
of John and Lydia (Morrison) Goodridge, born in Haverhill, 27 Aug.
1765; died there, 5 Nov. 1845, aged 80. They lived in Haverhill.

Children, born in Haverhill:

LYDIA,[6] b. 11 Nov. 1789; m. 30 Nov. 1809, Africa Hamlen of
Harvard.

GEORGE WASHINGTON, d. 27 Feb. 1816, aged 7y.

832.   ANTHONY, b. 1800.

HARRIET, d. 9 Aug. 1872, aged 80, unm.

273

STEPHEN[5] CHASE (Anthony,[4] David,[3] John[2]), born in Haverhill,
24 Apr. 1767; died in Northfield, N. H., 21 Apr. 1817. He married
about 1793, ABIGAIL (GILMAN) AMBROSE, widow of Benjamin Ambrose of Amesbury. She died in Northfield, 13 Nov. 1833, aged 70.
They lived in Northfield, where Mr. Chase erected a fulling mill in

1798 and kept a tavern which was standing in 1905. He was a representative, 1803-4 and 1808-9.

Children, born in Northfield:

MEHITABLE AMBROSE,[6] b. 7 Apr. 1795; m. 1 May 1817, Joseph C. Clough of Canterbury, N. H.

PRISCILLA GILMAN, b. 6 Aug. 1796; m. (1) 9 Sept. 1819, Archibald S. Clark. She d. 11 May 1871.

833. BENJAMIN AMBROSE, b. 3 Apr. 1798.

ABIGAIL WOODMAN, m. 5 Dec. 1799; m. 30 Dec. 1823, Dea. Alvah McQuestien of Plymouth, N. H., and d. 15 May 1863.

MYRA, b. 14 Dec. 1801; m. Dea. Greenough McQuestien.

834. JOHN LANGDON, b. 29 Dec. 1803.

274

JOSEPH[5] CHASE (Anthony,[4] David,[3] John[2]), born in Haverhill, 13 July 1769; died there, 17 Feb. 1845. He married in Haverhill, 10 Sept. 1792, DEBORAH WILLIAMS of Amesbury, born 1763, died in Haverhill, 14 May 1847, aged 84. She was the daughter of William and Lydia Williams of Amesbury. They lived in Haverhill.

Children, born in Haverhill:

NANCY,[6] b. 31 July 1793.

TAPPAN, b. 22 May 1795; d. 6 Mar. 1796.

MARY, b. 14 Aug. 1797.

835. TAPPAN, b. 15 Jan. 1800.

WILLIAM, b. 10 Mar. 1802; d. 14 Oct. 1831.

275

JOHN[5] CHASE (Anthony,[4] David,[3] John[2]), born in Haverhill, 20 Nov. 1773; died there, June 1837. He married (1) in Haverhill, 28 June 1798, BETSEY KELLEY who died in Haverhill, 1 June 1817, aged 35. She was the daughter of Joseph and Elizabeth (Colby) Kelley, born in Haverhill, 1 Oct. 1782. He married (2) in Haverhill, 25 June 1818, ANNA AYER who died in Haverhill, 29 July 1843, aged 57. She was the daughter of James and Polly (Brickett) Ayer, born in Haverhill, 19 July 1786. They lived in Haverhill. He made his will, 26 Oct. 1829, which was proved, 13 June 1837. His heirs petitioned for a settlement, 7 Apr. 1868. (Essex Probate, 5137).

Children by first wife, born in Haverhill:

836. JOHN ADAMS,[6] b. 30 Oct. 1799.

837. FREDERICK, b. 10 Dec. 1800.

838. ROBERT, b. 4 Dec. 1802.

MARY, b. 16 Feb. 1808; m. (1) 26 Aug. 1828, Lucius Steele of Ipswich; m. (2) 26 Apr. 1838, Moses Gile.

Children by second wife, born in Haverhill:

ELISABETH, b. 3 Aug. 1820; m. 26 Dec. 1839, Charles Coffin.

LAVINA BRICKETT, b. 13 Oct. 1821; m. 11 June 1846, John B. Nichols, son of David and Betsey Nichols of Haverhill.

276

CHARLES[5] CHASE (Tristram,[4] David,[3] John[2]), born in Newbury, 15 Feb. 1770; married there, 3 Nov. 1796, HANNAH BARTLETT,

daughter of Joseph and Sarah (Morse) Bartlett, born in Newbury,
7 May 1765. He died in Newburyport, 6 Dec. 1845, and she died
there 14 Sept. 1843, aged 78. They lived in Newburyport.

Children, born in Newbury (Newburyport):

SOPHRONIA,[6] bp. 27 May 1798, in Second Church of West New-
bury; d. 8 May 1806, aged 8y.
JOB, d. in Newburyport, 15 Nov. 1818, aged 19y.
HANNAH, b. 18 Sept. 1804; d. 24 Dec. 1805.
SOPHRONIA, b. 18 Oct., d. 20 Oct. 1806.
CHARLES, b. and d. 8 Sept. 1807.

277

TRISTRAM[5] CHASE (Tristram,[4] David,[3] John[2]), born in Newbury, 21 Aug. 1774; died there, 2 Aug. 1857. He married in Newbury (now West Newbury) 24 Sept. 1796, SUSANNAH[5] CHASE,
daughter of Parker[4] and Ruth (Kelley) Chase, born in Newbury,
14 Oct. 1777. They lived in Newbury and Newburyport, moving to
the latter place in 1811. (Family 428)

Children, first five born in Newbury, others in Newburyport:

GEORGE WASHINGTON,[6] b. 6 Apr. 1799; d. 9 Aug. 1852, at sea.
WALTER, b. 2 May 1803; d. unm. 14 Feb. 1828.
SARAH E., b. 26 Aug. 1805; m. 2 Nov. 1823, Peter Le Breton of
Newbury.
839.   LUTHER, b. 10 Nov. 1807.
ANN LITTLE, b. 1 Mar. 1810; unm.; lived in Newburyport.
ARTHUR, b. 22 July 1812; d. 28 Sept. 1838.
SUSANNA, b. 20 July 1814; d. 28 Apr. 1828.
HARRIET NEWELL, b. 14 July 1816; d. 16 Sept. 1838.
ABIGAIL, b. 24 Dec. 1818; unm.

278

ENOCH[5] CHASE (Tristram,[4] David,[3] John[2]), born in Newbury,
28 Jan 1782; married in Newbury, 12 June 1806, MARY[6] CARR,
daughter of Samuel and Emma[5] (Chase) Carr. She was born
17 Oct. 1786; died 4 Apr. 1845. They lived in Haverhill, N. H.

Child, born in Newbury:

840.   WARREN EDSON,[6] b. 12 Oct. 1806.

279

EZRA[5] CHASE (Simeon,[4] David,[3] John[2]), born in Newbury, 1774.
His father spent his whole life there and in West Newbury but no
record of this son has been found. Whether he married or died
single is not known.

280

SETH[5] CHASE (Simeon,[4] David,[3] John[2]), born in Newbury (now
West Newbury) during the Revolutionary War. Like his brother
nothing but his name is now known.

281

DAVID[5] CHASE (Simeon,[4] David,[3] John[2]), born in Newbury
(now West Newbury) about 1780. Nothing but his name is known
at this time.

282

JOSHUA[5] CHASE (Dr. Joshua,[4] David,[3] John[2]), born about 1782. He was a minor living in Portsmouth, N. H., in June 1792, and William Plaisted of Portsmouth was his guardian then and in 1793. No children found recorded on the Town Records of New Hampshire.

283

ISAAC[5] CHASE (Ambrose,[4] Isaac,[3] Daniel[2]), born in Grafton, 11 Feb. 1740/41; married in Sutton, 1 Oct. 1772, ELIZABETH YATES. They lived in Sutton and removed to New Salem, after 1776, and later to Pittsford, Vt. His wife died in Pittsford in June 1800.

Children, eldest born in Sutton:

    JOHN,[6] d. young.

    EUNICE, b. 16 Mar. 1776; m. in Pittsford, 6 Dec. 1798, Eli Hudson. She d. 26 Feb. 1844.

    NATHANIEL, d. at age of 19y.

    NAOMI, d. at age of 14y.

    RUTH, b. 1785; m. Thomas Piper; she d. 23 July 1850.

841. BENJAMIN, b. 2 Sept. 1787.

    CYRUS, b. 12 May 1790; unm. living at Pittsford, 1870.

    CYNTHIA, b. 1 Oct. 1792; m. (1) John Smith; m. (2) 28 Feb. 1831, Thomas Clark.

842. SYLVESTER, b. Apr. 1798.

284

SOLOMON[5] CHASE (Ambrose,[4] Isaac,[3] Daniel[2]), born in Sutton, 30 Nov. 1744; married in Uxbridge, 4 Mar. 1764, ABIGAIL CHASE (Timothy,[4] Isaac,[3] Daniel[2]) daughter of Timothy and Leah (Robbins) Chase of Townsend, Vt. He removed to Townsend in 1788. He died there and she married (2) —— BARBER of Springfield, Vt., where she died.

Children:

    HULDAH,[6] b. 29 Jan. 1765; m. 29 Jan. 1783, James Rice of New Salem; d. 1 Mar. 1840.

843. AMARIAH, b. 14 May 1766.

844. SOLOMON, b. 20 Nov. 1767.

    DELIVERANCE, b. 25 Sept. 1769; m. Thomas Holbrook.

845. JOSIAH, b. 10 June 1771.

    ABIGAIL, b. 5 Dec. 1774; m. Enoch Sargent; she d. in Pittsfield.

    LEAH, b. 1 Sept. 1777; m. Josiah Holden; d. 22 Oct. 1866, in Grand Rapids, Mich.

    RACHEL, b. 5 Sept. 1779; m. Nathan Holden; d. in Mich.

    SALLY, b. 8 Oct. 1782; m. Michael Martin (or Morton); d. in Pa.

846. NEHEMIAH, b. 5 Nov. 1784.

285

ABEL[5] CHASE (Ambrose,[4] Isaac,[3] Daniel[2]), born in Sutton, 9 Aug. 1750; died in Croydon, N. H., Jan. 1806. He married in Sutton, 30 Nov. 1768, ELIZABETH ELLIOTT. They lived in Sutton until 1800 and then removed to Croydon, N. H. His widow returned to Sutton and died there, 2 Dec. 1818.

Children, born in Sutton:

LYDIA,[6] b. 29 May 1770; m. 20 Oct. 1791, John Rawson of Uxbridge.

HANNAH, b. 2 Jan. 1772; m. 7 Apr. 1791, Fisher Hill.

847. ABEL, b. 2 Nov. 1773.
848. JAMES, b. 24 July 1776.
849. AMBROSE, b. 18 July 1778.
850. THADDEUS ELLIOTT, b. 12 July 1781.
851. BRADFORD, b. 21 July 1783.
852. ISAAC, b. 3 July 1785.
853. JONATHAN, b. 10 July 1787.

MEHITABLE, b. 27 Oct. 1789; unm.

THANKFUL, b. 12 Dec. 1791; unm.

854. MANCHESTER, b. 2 July 1798.

286

MARK[5] CHASE (Daniel,[4] Isaac,[3] Daniel[2]), born probably in Petersham about 1744; married in New Salem, 4 Oct. 1770, KEZIAH CORY, perhaps daughter of Francis Cory of New Salem. He was a hunter and lived in the woods. They lived in New Salem in 1782, as he bought and sold land in that town that year. He does not appear as head of a family in any state in 1790.

Children, perhaps born in New Salem:

855. BENJAMIN.[6]
856. LUKE.
857. SAMUEL.

LUCY.

KEZIAH.

287

SIMON[5] CHASE (Daniel,[4] Isaac,[3] Daniel[2]), born in Petersham, 18 May 1746; died in Woodbury, Vt., 9 Sept. 1839, aged 93y. 4m. He married (1) 11 May 1769, HANNAH[5] CHASE (Ambrose,[4] Isaac,[3] Daniel[2]), born in Grafton, 13 June 1748. She died about 1785. He married (2) SARAH (LAWSON) TOWN, widow of Moses Town and daughter of David and Martha[3] (Chase) Lawson. (Family 5) They lived in Greenwich, New Salem, and Woodbury, Vt.

Children by first wife, first two born in Northbridge, others in New Salem:

EDITH,[6] b. 16 Jan. 1769; m. —— Blake.

858. JOHN, b. 22 Aug. 1774.
859. SILAS, b. 27 Nov. 1776, in Greenwich.
860. DANIEL, b. 15 Feb. 1781.
861. NATHAN, b. 3 July 1783.

Children by second wife, born in New Salem:

SARAH, b. 15 Apr. 1787; m. 3 Nov. 1813, Jonathan Wheelock of Woodbury.

862. EZRA, b. 8 Jan. 1789.
863. SETH, b. 28 Feb. 1794.
864. DAVID, b. 30 Mar. 1800.

Possibly James, Samuel and Prudence may have been children of this family.

288

JOEL[5] CHASE (Daniel,[4] Isaac,[3] Daniel[2]), born, probably in Sutton, about 1750; not mentioned among the Chase estates of Worcester Co. He probably was the Joel Chase of Greenwich who enlisted in Capt. Job Cushing's Co., 28 Apr. 1775, serving three months and eleven days. He may also be the Joel Chase of Shrewsbury who was in the Continental Army 1777 to 1780. His name does not appear as head of a family in the census of 1790.

289

AARON[5] CHASE (Daniel,[4] Isaac,[3] Daniel[2]), born in Greenwich, 3 Jan. 1761; died in Swanton, Vt., 3 Oct. 1828. He married about 1788, PRISCILLA HARRINGTON, perhaps daughter of Jason and Abigail (Leadbeater) Harrington, who was born 12 May 1760. Apparently Jason Harrington was living in Athol in 1779. Perhaps they were married in Orange. They lived in Orange, Kingsbury, N. Y., Athol, and Swanton, Vt.

Children, first two born in Orange, others in Kingsbury:

    DANIEL,[6] b. 30 July 1789; m. Esther (Crawford) Smith. No children.

865. AARON, b. 27 Sept. 1791.

    ABIGAIL, b. 17 June 1794; m. (1) 1810 Henry Hall; m. (2) 1828 Eli Carroll. She was alive in 1873.

    NANCY, b. 25 July 1795; m. 26 Aug. 1813, George Lincoln of Boston.

290

JONAS[5] CHASE (Daniel,[4] Isaac,[3] Daniel[2]), born about 1755; a Jonas Chase's estate of Millbury was settled in 1824. (Worcester Probate, 11300). He was taxed in Millbury in 1813. He joined the Congregational Church of Millbury, 8 June 1806. This last item may refer to Jonas Chase, son of Abel[6] Chase of Sutton. He is probably the Jonas Chase who enlisted from Deerfield, 27 Mar. 1781 for three years in the Continental Army. He was described as 16 years of age, stature five feet four inches, complexion and hair light. It is supposed that he never married.

291

PAUL[5] CHASE (Daniel,[4] Isaac,[3] Daniel[2]), born probably in Worcester Co. about 1760. Probably never married as no mention of him has been found.

292

THOMAS[5] CHASE (Timothy,[4] Isaac,[3] Daniel[2]), baptized in Grafton, 18 July 1742; married in Uxbridge, 15 Jan. 1766, HANNAH[5] KNAPP, daughter of Joshua and Hannah[4] (Chase) Knapp. She was a member of the church in Uxbridge and was born there, 3 Aug. 1740. They lived in Sutton, 1767 to 1788. In 1790 he was the head of a family in Sutton consisting of one male over 16 years of age, four males under 16 and eight females. (Mass. Census, 239).

Children, two eldest born in Sutton:
866.   LEMUEL,[6] b. 12 Feb. 1766.
867.   JOSHUA KNAPP, b. 20 Dec. 1767; bp. 24 July 1768.
        JOHN, d. 3 Feb. 1770.
868.   NATHANIEL.
        SON, d. 27 Nov. 1788, aged about 8y.

293

ABNER[5] CHASE (Timothy,[4] Isaac,[3] Daniel[2]), baptized in Grafton, 18 July 1742; died about 1812. He married in Petersham, 30 Dec. 1762, HANNAH LAWSON who died in Apr. 1819. They lived in Petersham and New Salem. At the time of his marriage he was described as of Greenwich. His widow married (2) Asa Curtis.

Children, born probably in New Salem:
        LOIS,[6] b. — Oct. 1765; m. Charles Squire.
869.   ABNER, b. 16 July 1767.
870.   DAVID, b. 25 Oct. 1769, in Petersham.
871.   MOSES.
872.   ENOCH, b. 28 May 1773.
        HANNAH, b. ——— Osgood.
        RHODA, m. Ebenezer Gay.
        EUNICE.

294

LT. HENRY[5] CHASE (Timothy,[4] Isaac,[3] Daniel[2]), baptized in Grafton, 4 Jan. 1746; died in Townshend, Vt., 12 Dec. 1831. He married about 1765, HEPSIBAH WALKER, daughter of Obadiah and Hepsibah (Shumway) Walker of Douglas and Royalston. They lived in Townshend, from 1776. He was a Revolutionary War soldier.

Children, three youngest born in Townshend:
        ABIGAIL,[6] b. 18 July 1766; d. 15 Oct. 1853; m. (1) 27 Nov. 1789,
            Amasa Wheelock; m. (2) her cousin Enoch[6] Chase. (872)
873.   HENRY, b. 24 Oct. 1767.
        EDITH, b. 15 July 1770; d. Aug. 1848; m. about 1785, Charles
            Kimball.
874.   ELIAS, b. about 1772.
875.   BEZALEEL, b. 17 June 1775.
        HEPSIBAH, b. about 1780; m. 3 May 1801, Ebenezer Johnson.
            She d. 6 July 1867, a. 86.
        ELECTA, b. about 1784; m. William Fisher. She d. 9 Aug. 1867,
            a. 83.
876.   SARDIS RILEY, b. 18 May 1788.

295

MOSES[5] CHASE (Timothy,[4] Isaac,[3] Daniel[2]), born and baptized in Templeton, 14 Aug. 1757. There was a Moses Chase head of a family in Sutton in 1790 consisting of one male over 16 years of age, no males under 16 and one female.

296

JOHN SARGENT[5] CHASE (Timothy,[4] Isaac,[3] Daniel[2]), born as early as 1750; married in Templeton, 27 Mar. 1770, ANN HORTON, daughter of Joseph and Alice (Knight) Horton, born in Milton, 21 July 1752. No head of a family named Chase was living in Templeton in 1790.

Child, born in Templeton:

> ANN,[6] b. 3 Nov. 1771; m. in Templeton, 3 Jan. 1793, Asa Woolson Jr. She d. in Springfield, Vt., 29 Nov. 1857. Her picture was reproduced in the *Woolson-Fenno Ancestry*, 1907.

297

TIMOTHY[5] CHASE (Timothy,[4] Isaac,[3] Daniel[2]), baptized 13 July 1774, at Northbridge, according to the church records of Sutton. He married in Southborough, 2 Mar. 1780, SARAH NEWTON of Southborough, They lived in Belchertown and Townshend, Vt. In 1790 his family consisted of one male over 16 years of age, three males under 16 and five females living in Townshend. She united with the Congregational Church in Belchertown in 1807.

Children, eldest born in Southborough:

877. ENOS,[6] b. 5 Dec. 1780.
878. ABNER, rated in Belchertown, 1 May 1810.
879. ASAHEL, rated there same day.
880. MARTIN, rated there same day.

298

LT. NATHANIEL[5] CHASE (Timothy,[4] Isaac,[3] Daniel[2]), born about 1748; baptized in Templeton, 8 Feb. 1756; died in Cattaraugus, N. Y., 18 Dec. 1826, aged 78. He married (1) 6 July 1772, RACHEL PIERCE who died 21 Oct. 1784. He married about 1784 (2) NAOMI KELLEY who died 18 May 1833, aged 66. They lived in Middlebury, Vt., and Townshend, Vt. In 1804 he removed to Franklin County, N. Y., and in 1816 to Cattaraugus, N. Y. He was a lieutenant in the Revolutionary War.

Children by first wife:

881. REUBEN,[6] b. 5 May 1773.
882. NATHANIEL P., b. 30 June 1775.
883. JOHN, b. 18 Aug. 1776; reported to have lived in Gill.
   MOLLY, b. 1778; m. Jesse Cauley [Cawley].
   SALLY, b. 18 May 1780; d. young.

Children by second wife:

884. MOSES, b. 14 Feb. 1786.
   ABIGAIL, b. about 1789; m. 10 Sept. 1808, Charles Welch.
   LUCINDA, m. (1) 1792, William Stimpson, who d. 1830; m. (2) Enoch[6] Chase, of Plattsburg, N. Y. (Family 872)
885. ROBERT.
886. JACOB R., b. 13 Sept. 1794.
   NAOMI, b. 22 Mar. 1798; m. 1 Jan. 1816, William Baxter.
   HIRAM, d. young.
   EUNICE, b. 30 June 1802; m. 25 Dec. 1822, Isaac Thomas.
   IRA, b. 8 May 1804; m. 25 Jan. 1836, Diadamia Purvis; no children; lived in Watseka, Ill., in 1873.
887. MARTIN L., b. 12 Jan. 1811.
   Three other children d. young.

299

JACOB[5] CHASE (Timothy,[4] Isaac,[3] Daniel[2]), born in Templeton, 8 Nov. 1751 and baptized there 8 Feb. 1756; married (1) in Sutton, 17 Mar. 1774, MARY INGERSON [INGERSOLL]. He married (2) ———— HART, a widow. He died in Lee, Oneida Co., N. Y., 25 Oct. 1836. In 1790 he was living in Townshend, Vt., and his family consisted of one male over 16 years, three males under 16 and four females. They lived in Townshend, and Lee, Oneida Co., N. Y.

Children by first wife, younger ones born in Townshend:

    PRUDENCE,[6] d. at about the age of 80.
888. JONATHAN, b. in 1779.
889. MOSES, b. about 1782; m. and had a son.
890. AMOS, b. 21 Mar. 1784.
    JUDITH, b. 22 May 1785; m. 20 May 1801, David Graves. She was living in Lagrangeville, N. Y., in 1873. Fourteen children.
891. JACOB, b. 26 Aug. 1796.

300

HENRY[5] CHASE (Henry,[4] Isaac,[3] Daniel[2]), born in Petersham, 4 Nov. 1748; died in Hartland, Vt., 1855. He married (1) (intention in Petersham, 15 June 1771) RACHEL LINCOLN of New Braintree. They were married in New Braintree, 11 July 1771. She died about 1781. He married (2) in Petersham, 12 Sept. 1782, SUSANNAH SHATTUCK, daughter of Silas and Sarah (Jackson) Shattuck of Templeton and Petersham and of Hartland, Vt. She was born 16 Dec. 1759 and died in 1838. They lived in Hartland, Vt., in 1790, also at some time in Washington Co., N. Y.

Children by first wife, not in order:

892. HENRY,[6] b. 12 Mar. 1776.
    SAVIAH, m. Ezekiel Rann and lived in Townshend, Vt.
    RACHEL, m. Samuel Park; lived in Lyndon, Vt.
    ABIGAIL, m. ———— Perry and lived in Coventry, Vt.

Children by second wife, not in order:

    MARTHA, m. David Elmer; lived in Hartford, Vt.
    LUCY, m. Squire Elmer; lived in Underhill, Vt.
    SARAH, m. ———— Morse of Hartford, Vt.
893. STEPHEN, lived in Hartland, Vt.
894. ASA, had a son James.[7]
895. INCREASE.

301

JAMES[5] CHASE (Henry,[4] Isaac,[3] Daniel[2]), born in Petersham, 26 Feb. 1750; also given as 6 Mar. 1749/50; according to the old style and new style of keeping time. He is supposed to be identical with James Chase who married about 1770 OLIVE FARNHAM who was born, 2 Dec. 1752. They lived in Floyd, Oneida Co., N. Y., settling there shortly after 1790. He is supposed to be the James Chase, head of a family in Pittstown, Albany Co., N. Y., in 1790, consisting of two males over 16 years of age, two males under 16, and five females.

Children:

MARGARET,[7] b. 21 Nov. 1771; m. Willard Morse.
EUNICE, b. 21 Sept. 1773; never married.
OLIVE, b. 11 July 1775; never married.
DORCAS, b. 9 Apr. 1777; m. William Allen.
OLIVIA, b. 23 Mar. 1789.
896. JAMES, b. 4 Oct. 1781.
STEPHEN, b. 11 July 1783; never married.
897. ELLERY R., b. 31 Jan. 1786.
SARAH, b. 6 Sept. 1789; m. Robert Potter.
FANNY, b. 26 Jan. 1792; m. Dr. Ira Cross.

302

CALEB[5] CHASE (Henry,[4] Isaac,[3] Daniel[2]), born in Petersham, 15 Nov. 1753; died in Fort Ann, Washington Co., N. Y., 17 Mar. 1831. He married HANNAH ELLISON, who was born 14 July 1749, and died in Fort Ann, 28 Mar. 1833. They lived in Fort Ann.

Children:

898. LEVI,[6] b. 5 May 1777.
JERUSHA, b. 27 Nov. 1778; m. Benjamin Burgess.
899. JOHN, b. 5 May 1780.
900. OLIVER, b. 29 Sept. 1781.
901. STEPHEN F., b. 3 Aug. 1783.
HANNAH, b. 5 Mar. 1785; m. Norman Phelps.
SARAH, b. 16 May 1787; m. William Johnson.
902. ELLISON, b. 28 Mar. 1789.
THANKFUL, b. 11 Feb. 1791; m. Norman Phelps. No children.
PATIENCE (twin), b. 11 Feb. 1791; m. 6 Nov. 1816, Joseph Burgess; lived in Oakland, Mich. She was alive 10 July 1874, aged 83.
WILLIAM, b. 26 Feb. 1794; m. Charlotte Munsell; no children. He d. in Geneseo, Ill., 6 June 1858.

303

ELISHA[5] CHASE (Henry,[4] Isaac,[3] Daniel[2]), born in Petersham, 16 Jan. 1759; died in Jamaica, Vt., 20 Nov. 1828. He married in Petersham, 4 Jan. 1782, PRUDENCE CURTIS, daughter of David and Sarah Curtis, born in Petersham, 2 Feb. 1765; died in Jamaica, 12 Feb. 1790. He married (2) SALLY BOLTON who was born 15 Apr. 1777; died 26 Jan. 1850. They lived in Jamaica, Vt.

Elisha Chase appears as a private in Capt. Peter Woodbury's Co. of Col. Job Cushing's Regt. in the Revolutionary War and marched from Petersham to Bennington 28 July 1777, serving till 29 Aug. 1777. He also served in Capt. Jotham Houghton's Co. from 24 Oct. to 1 Dec. 1779 at Claverack, N. Y. (Mass. Soldiers and Sailors in the Revolution, 3:349).

Children by first wife, born in Jamaica, Vt.:

LYDIA,[6] b. 8 Aug. 1783; m. June 1814, Phineas Pratt of Sunderland, Vt.; d. in Jamaica, 29 May 1851.
LUCINDA, b. 29 Apr. 1785; m. 17 Sept. 1807, James Prentice of Shaftsbury, Vt., and Eagle, N. Y. She d. 6 Sept. 1848. Ten children.
LOIS, b. 9 Mar. 1787; m. 8 Dec. 1808, James Davidson.

Children by second wife, born in Jamaica:

903.   ASA, b. 18 June 1792.
       FANNY, b. 4 Feb. 1799; m. Stephen H. Horsley.

304

PETER[5] CHASE (Henry,[4] Isaac,[3] Daniel[2]), born in Petersham, 24 Feb. 1770; died in Jamaica, Vt., 16 Aug. 1851.   He married (1) in Petersham, 15 Mar. 1798, MARY HOLT of New Salem, daughter of Jonathan and Maria (Wheeler) Holt, born in New Salem, 18 Sept. 1774; died in Jamaica, 13 May 1829.   He married (2) 20 June 1832, SALLY LAWTON, who died 28 July 1844.   They lived in Jamaica, Vt., removing there in Aug. 1802.

Children by first wife, first three born in Petersham, others in Jamaica:

904.   SEWALL,[6] b. 27 July 1798.
       FANNY, b. 23 Jan. 1800; m. 20 Mar. 1824, Ziba Chapin.   She d. in Jamaica, 3 Feb. 1834.
       MARIA, b. 6 Jan. 1802; m. 2 Feb. 1826, Daniel Stocker; d. 25 Dec. 1843.
       ABIGAIL, b. 3 Jan. 1804; m. 12 May 1825, William Howard; d. 14 Apr. 1860.
905.   DANIEL, b. 28 Sept. 1805; lived in Stratton, Vt.
       HENRY P., b. 21 July 1808; d. 7 Aug. 1831.
       SALLY, b. 24 Sept. 1810; m. 26 June 1834, Marshall Stocker: d. 8 Nov. 1868.
       POLLY, b. 3 May 1812; m. 24 Oct. 1833, George Parsons.
       MARTIN, b. 3 Aug. 1813; d. 15 Oct. 1814.
906.   MARTIN, b. 9 May 1815.
       LUCINA, b. 29 Apr. 1821; d. unm. 6 Sept. 1862.

305

EBENEZER[5] CHASE (Elisha,[4] Isaac,[3] Daniel[2]), born probably in New Salem, — May 1748; died in Hoosic, N. Y., 22 Mar. 1813.   He married in Roxbury about 1775, MARY DRAPER, who died in Hoosic, 20 Dec. 1820.   They lived in Roxbury till 1778 when they removed to Uxbridge and later to Hoosic, N. Y.   He is reported as a Revolutionary War soldier at Bunker Hill and at Saratoga under Gen. Gates.   They lived in Roxbury, Uxbridge, Smithfield, R. I., and Hoosic, N. Y.

Children, first three born in Roxbury, last in Uxbridge:

       PRUDENCE,[6] d. at age of 8 years.
907.   ELISHA D.
       MARY ANN, d. at age of 8 years.
       POLLY, b. 23 Feb. 1779; m. in Pittston, N. Y., 28 Aug. 1799, Daniel Houghton.   She d. in Jacksonville, Ill., 6 Nov. 1838.

306

EZEKIEL[5] CHASE (Elisha,[4] Isaac,[3] Daniel[2]), born probably in New Salem in July 1753; died in Columbus, Ohio, 26 May or 25 July 1813.   He married in 1783, SARAH RISLEY of Gill.   They lived in Hinsdale, N. H., and Guilford, Vt.   In 1790 he was head of a family in Hinsdale, consisting of one male over 16, none under 16 and four females.   They removed to Ohio in 1812.

Children, first four born in Hinsdale, last four in Guilford, Vt.:

FANNY,[6] b. 2 May 1784; m. 1811, Edward Allen of Adams, N. Y.
LUCY, b. 21 Mar. 1786; m. 1806, Potter Edwards. No children.
ELISHA, b. 27 May 1788; d. before 1 June 1790.
SARAH C., b. 2 Aug. 1790; m. 1816, William Sprague in Ohio.
908. ABISHAI C., b. 27 Apr. 1792.
909. ASHER, b. 23 Mar. 1794.
RUTH, b. 27 Feb. 1796.
910. ABEL, b. 16 May 1798.
CLARISSA, b. 11 Apr. 1801; m. 1824, William Connell.

307

JUDAH[5] CHASE (Judah,[4] Daniel,[3] Daniel[2]), born in Brunswick, Me., 16 Nov. 1765. He married in Mount Desert, Me., 9 Feb. 1796, LUCY BARTLETT, probably a granddaughter of Christopher Bartlett (1732-   ) who settled in Mount Desert, in 1785. It is supposed that they lived in Brunswick or vicinity. No family has been reported.

308

NATHANIEL[5] CHASE (Judah,[4] Daniel,[3] Daniel[2]), born in Brunswick, Me., 17 Jan. 1770; died in Litchfield, Me., 3 June 1860, aged 90. The name of his wife has not been found.

Children, born in Brunswick:

911. WILLIAM,[6] b. 1807.
912. ISAAC, b. Wales, Me., 1818; d. 24 Apr. 1886, a. 68.
913. DANIEL, m. Lucy Heath of Brookline. (See History of Litchfield, Me., 77.)

309

DANIEL[5] CHASE (Daniel,[4] Daniel,[3] Daniel[2]), born in Concord, N. H., 12 Nov. 1751; died there 7 Aug. 1793. He married in Haverhill, 3 Sept. 1771, SUSANNAH WILSON, daughter of Ezekiel and Ruth (Jaques) Wilson, born in Haverhill, 23 June 1750. She married (2) in Plymouth, N. H., 3 Sept. 1809, Col. David Webster and died in Plymouth, 6 Apr. 1821. They lived in Haverhill, Amesbury and after 1782 in Concord, N. H.

Children, first born in Haverhill, second in Amesbury, others in Concord:

RUTH,[6] b. 20 Feb. 1772; m. in Concord, 3 Aug. 1791, John Haseltine.
POLLY, b. 12 June 1774; perhaps m. in Concord, 13 Nov. 1794, Samuel Morrill.
914. EZEKIEL, b. 15 Aug. 1783.
MARTHA, b. 29 Nov. 1785; m. John ———.
915. JOHN, b. 9 June 1791.

310

PRATT[5] CHASE (Daniel,[4] Daniel,[3] Daniel[2]), born in Concord, N. H., 1 Apr. 1753. He was the head of a family in Londonderry, Vt., in 1790, consisting of one male over 16 years, one male under 16 and four females. He also lived in Andover, Vt. He enlisted first, 30 Apr. 1775 in Capt. Gordon Hutchins's Co. He enlisted later in the Continental Army at Canterbury, N. H., 4 July 1777, for three years. Another record states that he enlisted 10 May 1777. In 1775 the military roll states that he was 21, his place of abode Hopkinton and his occupation a husbandman. (N. H. Revolutionary War Rolls, 4:3).

311

ROBERT[5] CHASE (Daniel,[4] Daniel,[3] Daniel[2]), born in Concord, N. H., 27 Feb. 1757. No further trace of this man has been found.

312

BENJAMIN[5] CHASE (Daniel,[4] Daniel,[3] Daniel[2]), born in Concord, N. H., 27 Sept. 1758; married and settled in Clinton, Me. He was living in Clinton in 1790 with a family consisting of one male over 16, none under 16 and five females. He erected the first saw mill in Clinton at the "Point" about 1815.

He enlisted 1 Jan. 1776, as a corporal and applied for a pension from Clinton, 4 Apr. 1818, aged 59, and was dropped from the pension rolls under the Act of Congress of 1 May 1820. Dr. John B. Chace's manuscript states that he removed from Maine to Illinois and that he died there.

313

JAMES E.[5] CHASE (Daniel,[4] Daniel,[3] Daniel[2]), born in Concord, N. H., 1 Mar. 1764; died in Corinna, Me., in 1850. He married in Waterville, Me., LUCY LEWIS who was born in Annapolis, N. S., and died in Dexter, Me., in 1843. They lived in Dexter, Waterville and Corinna.

Children, youngest born in Waterville:

916. SANFORD,[6] lived in Corinna, Me.
917. ROBERT.
918. STEPHEN.
919. ELIPHAZ, b. 4 Oct. 1804.
920. JEFFERSON, lived in Dexter.
921. MOSES, lived in Waterville.
922. ELIHU, lived in Waterville.
        BETSEY.
        RHODA.
        HANNAH.
        POLLY.
        ELIZABETH E., b. 5 Nov. 1783; m. Capt. William Pullen. Ten children. They lived in Waterville, Me. She d. 22 Feb. 1872 in Exeter, Me.

314

CAPT. ISAAC[5] CHASE (Daniel,[4] Daniel,[3] Daniel[2]), born in Concord, N. H., 30 Dec. 1766; died — Jan. 1858. He married in Winslow, Me., 24 Apr. 1786, BRIDGET DELANO of Fairhaven who was born 10 Apr. 1764, and died — May 1858. He was living in Concord, N. H., in 1790, but removed to Sidney, Me., before 1800, and

to Fairfield, Me., in 1805. He commanded a company of artillery in
1812.
Children:

    SARAH,[6] b. 22 Nov. 1787; m. 4 July 1806, William N. Kendall of
        Fairfield.
923. GEORGE W., b. 29 May 1790.
    FANNY, b. 28 Mar. 1792; m. 10 Sept. 1810, Samuel G. Bodfish of
        Fairfield and Harmony, Me.
924. ARTHUR L., b. 24 Jan. 1794.
    ASENATH, b. 1 Apr. 1796; m. Capt. Joshua Ellis of Fairfield.
925. DANIEL, b. 5 April 1798.
926. ISAAC, b. 15 May 1800.
927. CHARLES, b. 28 May 1802.
    EMILY, b. 25 Oct. 1804; m. Capt. Caleb Emery of Fairfield.
928. JONAS, b. 29 July 1806.
    AMY, b. 29 July 1810; m. Reuben Buck.

315

EBENEZER[5] CHASE (Daniel,[4] Daniel,[3] Daniel[2]), born in Concord,
N. H., 23 Sept. 1768; drowned in Sebec Pond, Me., and buried 31
Dec. 1828. He married HANNAH EMERSON who died about 1840.
One Ebenezer Chase was head of a family in Vassalborough in 1790,
consisting of one male over 16 years, two males under 16 and one fe-
male. They lived in Townshend, Vt., and removed to Sebec, Me., as
early as 1810.
Children:

929. EBENEZER,[6] b. 1 Apr. 1786.
930. DANIEL, b. 29 Oct. 1787.
    HANNAH, d. unm.
    REBECCA, m. about 1823, John Gray of Sebec.
931. JAMES P., b. 1799.
    ABIGAIL, b. 13 May 1801; m. 26 Feb. 1817, James Smith of
        Sebec.
932. PHILIP E.
    SARAH B., b. 15 Sept. 1804; m. (1) 1820, Philip Badger; m. (2)
        James Cross; m. (3) —————— ——————.
    CATHARINE, m. about 1821, Moses Badger; d. in Ripley, Me.
    POLLY, b. 2 Feb. 1809; m. (1) 25 Jan. 1825, Eliphaz[6] Chase
        (919); m. (2) Mar. 1860, Jonathan Pulsifer of Sumner, Me.

316

SAMUEL[5] CHASE (Capt. Jonathan,[4] Daniel,[3] Daniel[2]), born in
Concord, N. H., 10 Mar. 1761; died in Unity, N. H., 3 Feb. 1819.
He married (1) LUCY STANLEY, a native of Hopkinton and daughter
of Matthew Stanley, who died in her 29th year. He married (2), in
Unity, MARY STANLEY, born in Hopkinton 27 June 1771; died in
Unity, 7 Oct. 1861. She was the daughter of Samuel and Ruth
Stanley. They lived in Unity. He was a Revolutionary soldier and
his widow applied for a pension, 21 Apr. 1840, aged 69. She was
living in Hopkinton, 16 Apr. 1855, aged 84. He kept a Journal dur-
ing the Revolution—a copy of which is in possession of the New
Hampshire Historical Society.

Children, born in Unity:

933.   HORACE,[6] b. 14 Dec. 1788.
       LUCY, b. 16 Jan. 1794; m. 17 Sept. 1815, Wise Bartlett of Lowell;
           d. 14 Aug. 1878.
       VIRGIL, b. 23 June 1796; d. at Goshen, 16 Aug. 1867; m. — Mar.
           1819, Eliza Gilman. No children.
       MATILDA, b. 13 Apr. 1798; m. Oct. 1816, Nathan Brown; d. 27
           Jan. 1824.
934.   OVID, b. 2 June 1800.
       RUTH, b. 2 Sept. 1803; m. 12 Jan. 1831, Ezra Jones Glidden of
           Unity. She d. 24 Dec. 1887.
935.   HOMER, b. 17 Nov. 1805; d. 17 July 1872.

317

MOSES[5] CHASE (Capt. Jonathan,[4] Daniel,[3] Daniel[2]), born in Concord, N. H., 30 Oct. 1763; died in Springfield, Vt., 14 May 1835. He married 8 Jan. 1789, MARY STRAW of Hopkinton, N. H., who was born 23 June 1769, and died in Springfield, Vt., 25 June 1855. They lived in Springfield in 1794, removing from Unity, N. H. He enlisted from Hopkinton, N. H., in 1780 and applied for a pension from Springfield, 17 Sept. 1832. His widow Polly Chase deposed 2 Oct. 1838, that she was his widow; that they were married in Hopkinton 8 Jan. 1789 and that he died in Springfield, 14 May 1835. She was alive 29 Mar. 1855, aged 86 years.

Children, first three born in Unity, last four in Springfield, Vt.:

936.   JONATHAN,[6] b. 13 Oct. 1789.
       WILLIAM, b. 17 Aug. 1791; d. 6 June 1793.
       WILLIAM, b. 8 Oct. 1793; d. 20 Apr. 1794.
       SALLY, b. 18 Mar. 1795; d. 23 Jan. 1797.
937.   LEONARD, b. 11 July 1797.
       POLLY, b. 1 Sept. 1799; m. 6 Nov. 1821, Joel Griswold; d. 1870.
       INFANT, b. 6 June 1808.

318

AARON[5] CHASE (Capt. Jonathan,[4] Daniel,[3] Daniel[2]), born in Concord, N. H., 27 Oct. 1766; died in Lempster, N. H., 12 May 1812. He married (1) 25 Dec. 1790, DOROTHY STEVENS who was born 24 Aug. 1763; died in Sutton, N. H., 17 Nov. 1841. She married (2) 13 Jan. 1814, PHINEAS STEVENS of Sutton. They lived in Lempster

Children, born in Lempster:

938.   JOSEPH PHILBRICK,[6] b. 5 Nov. 1791.
       LYDIA, b. 11 Aug. 1793; m. 26 Dec. 1815, John Stevens.
939.   BARUCH, b. 1 Dec. 1796.
940.   DANIEL, b. 24 May 1799.
941.   MARINER, b. 8 Dec. 1801; taxpayer 1820-1830.
       NANCY S., b. 8 Mar. 1804; m. 24 Mar. 1825, Gilman Currier of
           Bristol, N. H. Seven children.
       MARY, b. 6 Sept. 1807; m. (1) John Smith of Bradford, N. H.;
           m. (2) ——— Burrill from Me.

319

JEREMIAH STICKNEY[5] CHASE (Capt. Jonathan,[4] Daniel,[3] Daniel[2]), born in Hopkinton, N. H., 27 May 1768; died in Goshen, N. H.,

30 Sept. 1858. He married in Concord, N. H., 26 Aug. 1792, ES-
THER MARTIN of Concord, who died in Unity, N. H., 13 Nov. 1845,
aged 75. They lived in Unity.

Children, born in Unity:

> MEHITABLE,[6] b. 23 Aug. 1795; m. about 1814, William Huntoon
> of Unity. She d. 8 Mar. 1867. Eight children (Hunton
> Gen. 60).
>
> ZORAYDA, b. 31 July 1800; d. 16 Aug. 1803.

942. JOHN, b. 2 Apr. 1802.

> ZOROYDA, b. 25 July 1804; m. Jonas Packer of Goshen, N. H.

943. MARTIN, b. 11 July 1806.

> CHROMATA, b. 13 Aug. 1809; m. Isaac Quimby of Newport,
> N. H. She d. 7 Oct. 1844.
>
> SARAH STICKNEY, b. 9 Apr. 1813; m. in Washington, N. H. 3
> Oct. 1845, Isaac Quimby, and d. 20 June 1853.

320

CHARLES[5] CHASE (Capt. Jonathan,[4] Daniel,[3] Daniel[2]), born in
Concord, N. H., 9 July 1770; died in Hopkinton, N. H., 6 Oct. 1848.
He married (1) in Henniker, N. H., 21 Nov. 1793, SARAH CURRIER,
daughter of Dea. John and Sarah (Clark) Currier, born in Hopkin-
ton, 16 Aug. 1770; died there, 29 July 1834. He married (2) in
Concord, 17 Mar. 1835, MARY (EVANS) ADAMS, widow of Samuel R.
Adams. The marriage record as returned calls her Mary Evans.
She was born in 1802; died July 1874. They lived in Hopkinton.

Children by first wife, born in Hopkinton:

944. CARLETON, b. 20 Feb. 1794.

> CYRUS, b. 23 Mar. 1796; m. Harriet Jones of Hopkinton; three
> children d. young; he d. in Boston, 7 June 1854.
>
> SARAH, b. 24 Nov. 1800; m. (1) 3 Mar. 1817, Oliver Martin;
> m. (2) 8 Mar. 1825, Samuel Evans who d. 25 June 1868.

321

DANIEL[5] CHASE (Capt.. Jonathan,[4] Daniel,[3] Daniel[2]), born in
Concord, N. H., 13 Apr. 1772; died in Hopkinton, N. H., 10 July
1852, aged 80. He married in Hopkinton, 7 Apr. 1807, Miss SARAH
TUCKER FERREN who died 31 Aug. 1861, aged 82y. 7m. in Hopkinton.
She was daughter of Francis and Betsey (Buswell) Ferren. They
lived in Hopkinton.

Children, born in Hopkinton:

> POLLY PEARSON,[6] d. 10 Jan. 1811, a. 11m.
>
> HEBER (M. D.), University of Pennsylvania, 1836; d. in Con-
> cord, N. H., 17 Sept. 1850; no issue.
>
> BETSEY F., m. in Hopkinton 14 Sept. 1830, William Restieaux.

321a

ISAAC[5] CHASE (Isaac,[4] Daniel,[3] Daniel[2]), born about 1764; died
in 1840. He married in Warner, N. H., 21 Oct. 1790, MARY HUNT.
In his marriage record he was described as of Kearsarge Gore (Wilmot), adjoining to Warner. They resided on the back road to Wilmot Flat.

Children, births probably not recorded in order:

945. NATHAN.[6]
946. ISAAC.
      ESTHER, perhaps m. in Sutton, N. H., 19 Sept. 1819, Richard
        Palmer.
947. HENRY.
948. JABEZ.
      REBECCA, perhaps m. in New London, N. H., 27 Apr. 1826, Dan-
        iel Emery Jr.
949. JOHN.
950. BENJAMIN.
951. JOSEPH.

322

ABNER[5] CHASE (Abner,[4] Daniel,[3] Daniel,[2]), born about 1770.
His father lived in Warner and Sunapee, N. H. He removed to
Canada and died there. Nothing further has been learned about him.

323

PHILIP[5] CHASE (Abner,[4] Daniel,[3] Daniel[2]), born about 1771;
reported to have been drowned at sea. He married and there were
two sons.

Children:

952. TIMOTHY,[6] living in the West in 1880.
953. PHILIP, also living in the West.

324

TIMOTHY BRADLEY[5] CHASE (Abner,[4] Daniel,[3] Daniel[2]), born in
Warner, N. H., 25 Oct. 1781; died in Danbury, N. H., 21 Nov. 1834.
He was a soldier from Warner in the War of 1812. He married (1)
in Bradford, 19 May 1805, SALLY COLBY who was born in Amesbury, 29 Aug. 1786; died in Warner, 1 Apr. 1823. He married (2)
about 1825, FANNY RUSSELL who was born in Wilmot, N. H., 14
Feb. 1804 and died in Danbury in 1877. They lived in Warner, Sutton and Danbury:

Children by first wife, born in Warner:

       MARY C.,[6] b. 20 Oct. 1805; m. Hiram Philbrick; seven children.
         She d. 4 Dec. 1863.
953a. ABNER, b. 21 Feb. 1808.
954.   HEZEKIAH C., b. 16 Jan. 1811.
       SALLY, b. 10 Nov. 1814; m. (1) Nehemiah Muzzy; m. (2)
         Thaddeus S. Lathrop; two children by each husband; d. in
         Canaan, N. H., 20 Oct. 1868.
       HENRY BRADLEY, b. 23 Apr. 1819; d. 31 Jan. 1823.
       HANNAH, b. and d. 1 Apr. 1823.

Children by second wife, born in Danbury:

       HENRY BRADLEY, b. 11 Jan. 1826; m. Hannah Robinson; no chil-
         dren.
       PAMELIA, b. 4 Mar. 1828; m. James A. Westcott; seven children;
         she d. 1878.
955.   FRANCIS, b. 1 Nov. 1830.
       FANNY, b. 16 July 1833; d. 24 Feb. 1848.

325

John[5] Chase (John,[4] Daniel,[3] Daniel[2]), born in Concord, N. H., 14 Aug. 1764; died in Portsmouth, N. H., — Oct. 1814. He married in Conway, N. H., 17 Dec. 1786, Hannah (Gammit) Washburn, widow of Oliver Washburn. They lived in Burton (now Albany), N. H. He was a soldier in the War of 1812.

Children:
> Mary.[6]
> Hannah, m. Oliver[6] Chase (962).
> Phebe, m. Joseph Moulton of Albany, N. H.

326

Francis[5] Chase (John,[4] Daniel,[3] Daniel[2]), born in Bow, N. H., 22 May 1766. His father removed from Concord, N. H., to Conway, N. H., about 1778. "He was a wanderer, was absent several years, returned on a short visit, went off again and was never heard from. He had a family but nothing is known of them." One Francis Chase was head of a family in Portland, Me., in 1790, consisting of one male over 16 years of age, one male under 16, and four females. He was alive, 29 June 1824, when his father made his will as he was referred to therein.

327

Isaac[5] Chase (John,[4] Daniel,[3] Daniel[2]), born in Concord, N. H., 18 Sept. 1772; died in Effingham, N. H., in 1830. He married in Sanford, Me., Anna Allen who was born in Sanford in 1775 and died in Effingham in 1833. They lived in Conway, N. H., and Effingham.

Children:
> Sarah,[6] b. 1800; m. (1) ———— Leavitt; m .(2) ———— Grant.
> Her first marriage is not on the town records of New Hampshire.
956. Daniel, b. 5 July 1805.
> Maria, b. 1808; m. John Titcomb; three children.
957. John, b. 1812.
> Phebe, b. 1814.

328

Daniel[5] Chase (John,[4] Daniel,[3] Daniel[2]), born in Conway, N. H., 24 Dec. 1782; died about 1865. He married in Conway, 12 Feb. 1807 Nancy (Mason) Horn. They lived in Bartlett, N. H. Nancy, the mother, was born in Porter, Me.

Children:
958. Gilbert M.,[6] b. about 1809.
959. William R., b. about 1811.
> Ursula, b. about 1813.
960. Mark, b. about 1815.

329

Oliver[5] Chase (John,[4] Daniel,[3] Daniel[2]), born in Conway, N. H., 27 Feb. 1785; married 20 Mar. 1806, Abigail Kennett, daughter of John Kennett of Eaton, N. H. They lived in Conway, and Eaton (now Madison), N. H. He was alive as late as, 28 Mar. 1834.

Children, first six born in Conway, seventh in Burton (now Albany,) N. H., and last two in Eaton, N. H.:

POLLY,[6] b. 24 Feb. 1807; m. Samuel Littlefield; lived in Albany. Seven children.
961.   GEORGE, b. 17 Apr. 1809.
962.   OLIVER, b. 7 Oct. 1811.
ABIGAIL, b. 7 Dec. 1814; m. —— Garland; lived in Jackson, N. H. Six children.
LETTICE, b. 12 Mar. 1817; m. David Woodis of Jackson; three children.
963.   CHRISTOPHER C., b. 30 Mar. 1819.
LOIS, b. 9 June 1821; m. George Mack of Sandwich, N. H.; nine children.
964.   JOHN, b. 30 Aug. 1823.
965.   RUFUS, b. 31 Aug. 1825.

330

GILBERT TENANT[5] CHASE (John,[4] Daniel,[3] Daniel[2]), born in Conway, N. H., 1 Jan. 1790; died in Paris, Me., 19 Feb. 1868. He married about 1815, PHEBE JACKSON of Eaton, N. H., who was born, 6 Mar. 1790, and died 31 May 1867. They lived in Conway; removed to Albany, N. H., 1823. He, his wife Phebe and their son Samuel were mentioned in the will of his mother dated 28 Mar. 1834. (Strafford Co. Probate, 48:329).

Children, born in Conway:

966.   JOHN,[6] b. 7 Dec. 1817.
SAMUEL, b. 20 Mar. 1823; m. 21 Mar. 1847, Betsey Carter, b. 20 Mar. 1827; no children; Sandwich, N. H., 1876.

331

DEA. THOMAS[5] CHASE (Humphrey,[4] Enoch,[3] Daniel[2]), born and baptized in North Yarmouth, Me., 11 Aug. 1776; died 3 June 1859, aged 83. He married (1) MARY E. NOYES who died in North Yarmouth, 9 Apr. 1835, aged 55. He married (2) SARAH (HODGKINS) BAKER, widow of John Baker. She died 13 Apr. 1874. He was deacon of the First Church of North Yarmouth.

Children, born in North Yarmouth:

HOSEA J.,[6] m. 23 Jan. 1848, Julia Helen Seabury; she b. 14 Jan. 1830; d. 23 June 1849. He died in North Yarmouth, 20 Oct. 1848, aged 32. (Old Times in North Yarmouth, 302.)
SUSANNA, m. Asa Cutler; lived in Portland, Me., in 1872.
There were other children whose names have not been learned.

332

JEREMIAH[5] CHASE (Humphrey,[4] Enoch,[3] Daniel[2]), baptized in North Yarmouth, Me., 26 Nov. 1780; married twice; lived in Eastport, Me.; left descendants. (Old Times in North Yarmouth, 988). His son was living in 1880. He was a sergeant in Abijah Gregory's

Guards at Eastport, from 21 July to 1 Sept. 1812. (Mass. Militia in War of 1812-14, p. 311).

333

CHARLES[5] CHASE (Humphrey,[4] Enoch,[3] Daniel[2]), baptized in North Yarmouth, Me., 16 Sept. 1787. (Old Times in North Yarmouth, 988). A daughter died in North Yarmouth in Aug. 1834. He died in North Yarmouth, 19 July 1853. He married (1) MARY GARDNER who died 7 June 1827, aged 35. He married (2) MARY HILL who was living in 1880. They lived in North Yarmouth.

Children, born and baptized in North Yarmouth:

968. WILLIAM HENRY,[6] bp. 5 May 1822; lived in Portland, Me., 1872.
OLIVE DRINKWATER, bp. 5 May 1822.
JANE, bp. 5 May 1822.
MARY, bp. 22 Sept. 1822.
MARY GARDNER, bp. 21 Sept. 1828. (Old Times in North Yarmouth, 1061.)

334

LEVI[5] CHASE (Humphrey,[4] Enoch,[3] Daniel[2]), born in North Yarmouth, Me., and baptized there 23 May 1790. He married and had two sons. (Old Times in North Yarmouth, 930). The names of his wife and sons were not reported.

335

THOMAS[5] CHASE (Capt. Enoch,[4] Enoch,[3] Daniel[2]), born in Amesbury, 1 May 1755; baptized in the Second Church of Amesbury (now Merrimac) 20 July 1755. His father removed to Salisbury, N. H., about 1775. No children are recorded to this man on the Town Records of New Hampshire. Perhaps he died young as no record has been found of him.

336

WILLIAM[5] CHASE (Capt. Enoch,[4] Enoch,[3] Daniel[2]), born in East Kingston, N. H., 2 Oct. 1761; died in Salisbury, N. H., 27 Dec. 1845, aged 84. He married in South Hampton, N. H., 11 Feb. 1783, BETSEY FIFIELD who died in 1848, aged 91. They moved to Salisbury, and he built a log-house there about 1783.

Children, born in Salisbury:

969. THOMAS,[6] b. 8 Mar. 1784.
POLLY, b. 25 Apr. 1786; d. unm. 29 Mar. 1837.
NANCY, b. 26 Mar. 1790; never married.

337

JOHN[5] CHASE (Thomas,[4] Enoch,[3] Daniel[2]), born 12 May 1767; married MARY DRINKWATER of Northport, Me. He removed from Concord, N. H., to Lincolnville, Me., about 1790, and died in Charleston, Me., 3 Jan. or 25 Jan. 1842. She died 28 Aug. 1845, aged 78.

Children, born in Lincolnville:

ELIZABETH,[6] b. 1792; m. Robert McGilvery of Stockton, Me.;
d. in July 1852.

MARY, b. 7 Oct. 1794; m. 9 Apr. 1826, Nathan Packard of Searsmont, Me.; living there in 1875.

RHODA, b. 26 Nov. 1796; m. 27 Feb. 1813, Jotham Freathy of
Brooklin, Me.

SARAH, b. 1798; m. 1818, William Frohock of Searsmont, Me.

970. DANIEL, b. 5 June 1801.

PHEBE, b. 1803; m. about 1834, Jonathan Clay; she d. in Dec.
1869.

NANCY, b. 1806; m. 1838, George Gustin of Holden, Me.; she d.
about 1861.

ESTHER, b. 26 Mar. 1811; m. 8 June 1835, Luke Mills of Waterborough, Me.; living in Levant, Me., 1875; eight children.

NATHANIEL, b. about 1813; d. unm. about 1862.

338

ENOCH[5] CHASE (John,[4] Enoch,[3] Daniel[2]), born in 1776; died in
Dixfield, Me., in July 1840. He married (1) LYDIA BABB, who died
in May 1806. He married (2) BETSEY TATE, who was living at the
age of 94 in 1873. They removed from Brunswick, Me., to Dixfield,
Me., where they lived many years.

Child by first wife:

971. SEWALL C.,[6] b. Feb. 1806.

Children by second wife:

LOUISA, b. Jan. 1808; m. Estes H. Newton of Dixfield, Me.

AURILLA P., m. John A. French of Norway, Me.

HANNAH M., m. George H. Kent of Boston.

MARIA J., b. Feb. 1824; m. (1) Elbridge Tucker; m. (2) ———
Clark; lived in Dixfield, Me.

Four other children not named.

339

JOHN[5] CHASE (John,[4] Enoch,[3] Daniel[2]), born in the vicinity of
Brunswick, Me., about 1778; married SARAH DOE; lived in Topsham, Me. His family has not been reported.

340

JAMES[5] CHASE (John[4], Enoch[3], Daniel[2]), born in Me. about
1780; died 4 Mar. 1817. He married ——— ———. They lived in
Brunswick, Me.

Children:

MARY,[6] m. ——— Corson.

JANE, m. ——— Smith.

972. NATHANIEL.

BETSEY, b. 18 Oct. 1812; m. Joel Ward.

341

NATHANIEL[5] CHASE (John[4] Enoch,[3] Daniel[2]), born probably
in Brunswick, Me; drowned there. His family, if he had one, has
not been traced.

342

SAMUEL[5] CHASE (Judge Samuel,[4] Daniel,[3] Ens. Moses[2]), born in Sutton, 28 Nov. 1728; died in Cornish, N. H., 10 July 1790. He married in Grafton, 29 May 1751, SILENCE STOWE who was born in 1727 and died in Cornish, 19 Nov. 1794, aged 67. They removed to Cornish, in 1769.

Children, born and baptized in Grafton:

973. SAMUEL,[6] bp. 3 May 1752.
   RUTH, bp. 24 Dec. 1754; m. 9 Nov. 1773, Nicholas Cady, and d. 6 July 1788; three children.
974. PETER, bp. 26 Oct. 1756.
975. JOSHUA, b. 30 Oct. 1758.
   MARTHA, b. 6 Sept. 1760; m. 23 Apr. 1778, Joseph Spaulding.
   ELIZABETH, bp. 19 June 1763; m. 6 July 1780, Abel Spaulding, and d. 25 May 1801, aged 39.
   SARAH, bp. 6 Apr. 1766; m. 26 Feb. 1793, Abel Johnson, and d. 5 Mar. 1819.

343

DEA. DUDLEY[5] CHASE (Judge Samuel,[4] Daniel,[3] Ens. Moses[2]), born in Sutton, 29 Aug. 1730; died in Cornish, N. H., 13 Apr. 1814, aged 81. He married in Mendon, 23 Aug. 1753, ALICE CORBETT, daughter of Daniel and Sarah (Jones) Corbett of Mendon, born 23 Feb. 1733. She died in Cornish, 13 Sept. 1813, aged 81. He was one of the first settlers of Cornish in 1765. His ninth child Alice, being the first white child born in the new town. He was in Col. Jonathan Chase's Regiment with the Cornish men who marched for Ticonderoga, 27 June 1777. He was Quarter-master of Gen. Enoch Poor's Brigade in 1778; selectman in 1767; representative 1786; one of the founders of the First Church of Cornish, 29 Sept. 1768; vestryman in the Episcopal Church there in 1795; explored the west branch of the White River Valley in Vermont and purchased large tracts in Bethel and Gilead.

Children, first eight born in Sutton, others in Cornish, N. H.:

   JOHN,[6] b. 30 Apr. 1754; d. in July 1754, aged 11 weeks.
   MERCY, b. 6 Apr. 1755; m. 7 Sept. 1778, Stephen Child.
   LOIS, b. 16 Aug. 1756; m. 9 Dec. 1779, Benjamin Smith of Bethel, Vt.
976. SIMEON, b. 14 June 1758.
   ABIGAIL, b. 9 Nov. 1759; m. 4 Jan. 1779, John Morse, and d. 17 July 1792, a. 32y. 8m.
977. SALMON, b. 14 July 1761.
978. ITHAMAR, bp. 27 Sept. 1762.
979. BARUCH, b. 27 Mar. 1764.
   ALICE, b. 17 Oct. 1765; m. 5 Apr. 1789, Biby Lake Cotton of Bethel, Vt.; d. 29 Nov. 1844.
   SARAH, b. 14 Sept. 1767; m. Jireh Durkee. She d. in Burlington, Vt., 2 July 1825.
   DANIEL CORBETT, b. 13 Jan. 1769; d. unm. in Philadelphia, 14 Aug. 1798.
   HEBER, b. 2 Sept. 1770; d. unm. in Demarara, S. A., 14 Sept. 1798. Graduated at Dartmouth College, 1791; physician.

980. DUDLEY, b. 30 Dec. 1771.
      RACHEL, b. 10 Jan. 1774; m. 9 June 1802, Dr. Joseph Adams
      Denison, and d. 23 Aug. 1858.
981. PHILANDER, b. 14 Dec. 1775.

344

GEN. JONATHAN[5] CHASE (Judge Samuel,[4] Daniel,[3] Ens. Moses[2]), born in Sutton, 6 Dec. 1732; died in Cornish, N. H., 14 Jan. 1800. He married (1) in Grafton, 28 Nov. 1759, THANKFUL SHERMAN, daughter of Ephriam and Thankful (Temple) Sherman, born in Grafton, 21 July 1739; died 25 Nov. 1768, aged 29. He married (2) in Hollis, N. H., 22 Oct. 1770, SARAH HALL, daughter of Rev. David and Elizabeth (Prescott) Hall, born in Sutton, 15 Dec. 1742; died in Cornish, 13 Oct. 1806.

Gen. Chase moved from Sutton to Cornish, N. H., and became a recognized leader in the community. He was a farmer, a surveyor, a store keeper and a miller in the new township. When the Revolutionary War came on he mustered a company and was chosen Captain; later he became Colonel of a New Hampshire Regiment and by orders of Maj. Gen. Horatio Gates marched with his regiment from Cheshire County to reinforce the army at Ticonderoga in Oct. 1776. He again marched to reinforce the northern Continental army at Saratoga in 1777. The service was so well rendered that Jonathan Chase was subsequently made General of the State Militia of New Hampshire. The History of Cornish (1:65) reproduced a picture of his homestead as it appeared in 1870. It was used for a time as a station for collecting supplies for the Revolutionary army.

Children by first wife:

> PRUDENCE,[6] b. 5 Aug. 1760; m. 1 Mar. 1778, Nathan Hall, and d. 3 Apr. 1808, a. 48.
> ELISABETH, b. 1765; d. 14 Apr. 1793; m. 16 Jan. 1791, Dr. Nathan Smith of Hanover.
> MARY, m. Ebenezer Brewer; d. 26 Feb. 1795, a. 29.

Children by second wife:

982. JONATHAN, b. 21 Nov. 1771.
      DAVID HALL, b. 1773; graduated at Dartmouth College,, 1793;
      d. unm. 18 Aug. 1794.
      SARAH HALL, b. 1775; m. 18 Sept. 1794, Nathan R. Smith, M.D.,
      Prof. in Dartmouth Medical School.
983. LEBBEUS HALL, b. 21 Jan. 1779.
      PAMELIA, b. 8 Nov. 1780; m. 12 Nov. 1802, Samuel Paine of
      Randolph, Vt.
      GRATIA, b. 1782; m. in 1805, Dr. Erastus Torrey of Windsor, Vt.

345

CAPT. MARCH[5] CHASE (Judge Samuel,[4] Daniel,[3] Ens. Moses[2]), born in Sutton, 21 June 1738; died 26 Sept. 1822. He married (1) in Sutton, 10 Oct. 1759, BEULAH COYE who died 7 May 1795. He married (2) in Sutton, 30 May 1816, MARY DODGE. They lived in Sutton, and were buried in the County Bridge Cemetery. No children. He was commissioned First Lieutenant in Capt. Abraham Batchelder's Co. 4 Apr. 1776; marched from Sutton to Saratoga to

GEN. JONATHAN CHASE HOUSE

reinforce the Northern army 26 Sept. 1777, and served to 26 Oct. 1777. He also served in Col. Nathan Sparhawk's Reg't from 12 Sept. to 12 Dec. 1778, at Dorchester. (Mass. Soldiers and Sailors in the Revolutionary War, 3:360).

346

DR. SOLOMON[5] CHASE (Judge Samuel,[4] Daniel,[3] Ens. Moses[2]), born in Sutton, 1 Sept. 1742; died in Cornish, N. H., 21 Nov. 1828. He was married, in Cornish, by his father, 15 June 1767, to SARAH MARCH, sister of Simeon Chase's wife. She was born in Newbury, 18 May 1744 and died in Cornish 6 Oct. 1840. Dr. Chase was a Captain in the Revolutionary Army and a physician. He first settled in Walpole, N. H., and removed to Cornish in 1774. He served as a physician in the Revolutionary War and his widow Sarah applied for a pension 7 Apr. 1837, aged 93. She died in Cornish, 6 Oct. 1840, leaving Solomon H. Chase of Lunenburg, Vt., only surviving son.

SOLOMON[5] CHASE appears as a private from Sutton in Capt. Ebenezer Cox's Company from 29 Mar. to 13 Nov. 1762—a period of eight months, six days. (Mass. Archives, 99:213).

Children, first two born in Walpole, others in Cornish:

984. SOLOMON HUSE,[6] b. 7 Mar. 1768.
985. SAMUEL MARCH, b. 13 Nov. 1772.
    DANIEL PRINCE, b. 9 Oct. 1775; unm.
    JACOB, b. 12 Sept. 1776; d. 8 Sept. 1780.
    MARY, b. 5 June 1782; d. 20 Apr. 1809, age 27 years.
986. BELA TAPPAN, b. 30 Mar. 1784.
    SARAH, b. 25 Apr. 1787; became a nun; lived with the Catholics in Charlestown, 1829, and later went to Montreal, Can.
987. JOHN, b. 20 Apr. 1789.

347

PAUL[5] CHASE (Daniel,[4] Daniel,[3] Ens. Moses[2]), born in Sutton, 13 Mar. 1734/5; died there 18 Nov. 1789 in his 55th year. He married in Sutton, 17 Aug. 1759, LUCY RICHARDSON of Worcester, born in Worcester, 6 Nov. 1740, daughter of Thomas and Margaret Richardson. She married (2) in Sutton, 13 Feb. 1799, Dea. Benjamin Goddard of Shrewsbury. Mr. Chase lived in Sutton.

Children, born in Sutton:

988. JOSHUA,[6] b. 26 Nov. 1760.
989. THADDEUS, b. 10 Feb. 1763.
    LUCY, b. 18 May 1766; m. 16 Apr. 1788, Daniel Greenwood of Sutton.

348

NEHEMIAH[5] CHASE (Lt. Caleb,[4] Daniel,[3] Ens. Moses[2]), born in Sutton, 8 Feb. 1751; died there, 5 Oct. 1808. He married in Sutton, 17 Dec. 1778, VASHTI BATCHELLER, daughter of Capt. Abraham and Sarah (Newton) Batcheller, born in Sutton, 31 Jan. 1757; died there, 28 Aug. 1825 ,aged 68. He was a Revolutionary soldier, and lived in Sutton.

Children, born in Sutton:

SARAH,[6] b. 9 Jan. 1780; m. 7 Oct. 1799, Simeon Woodbury.
LAVINA, b. 1781; m. 15 Aug. 1801, Capt. Nathaniel Sibley.
ABNER, b. 1783; m. 4 June 1809, Susan Marble. No children.
He d. in Sutton, 25 June 1825.
990. CALEB, b. 23 Sept. 1786.
991. ABRAHAM, b. 27 Sept. 1789.
VASHTI, b. 14 Apr. 1793; m. 16 Nov. 1814, Jeremiah Stone.
992. NEHEMIAH, b. 26 Mar. 1797.

349

DAVID PRINCE[5] CHASE (Lt. Caleb,[4] Daniel,[3] Ens. Moses[2]), born
in Sutton, 15 Jan. 1753; died 22 Mar. 1828. He married (1) in Sutton, 2 Dec. 1777, SARAH GREENWOOD, daughter of Daniel and Jerusha (Eaton) Greenwood, born in Sutton, 11 Apr. 1755; died there,
22 Mar. 1799, aged 43. He married (2) JUDITH BROWN who married (2) ———— Roberts, Esq. He was a harness maker and lived in
Sutton.

Children by first wife, born in Sutton:

993. DAVID,[6] b. 10 Oct. 1778.
994. SILAS, b. 10 Dec. 1783.
995. JOHN, b. 13 July 1788.

Child by second wife, born in Sutton:

SARAH P., b. 11 Aug. 1803; m. 1821, Charles Preston of Charlton.

350

CALEB PRINCE[5] CHASE (Lt. Caleb,[4] Daniel,[3] Ens. Moses[2]), born
in Sutton, 19 Mar. 1755; died in Cornish, N. H., 12 Jan. 1843. He
married in Sutton, 11 Oct. 1774, TABITHA BEMIS of Grafton. She
died in Cornish, 25 Feb. 1831, aged 76. They lived in Brookfield till
1780, then removed to Cornish.

Children, first three born in Brookfield, others in Cornish:

PERSIS,[6] b. 18 Apr. 1775; she d. 22 July 1793, without issue, in
Windsor, Vt. She m. Cyrus Freeman.
996. HENRY BRIGHT, b. 27 Jan. 1777.
MARY, b. 19 Jan. 1779; m. 15 Feb. 1798, Silas Cady of Wind-
sor, Vt. She d. Nov. 1848; nine children.
PHEBE, b. 28 Mar. 1781; m. 26 June 1804, John Parmelee. She
d. 30 Sept. 1838; nine children; lived in Newport, N. H.
997. CALEB SEWALL, b. 18 May 1783.
JUDITH, b. 25 July 1785; m. 1 Jan. 1805, Abel Gates; d. in Plain-
field, N. H., Oct. 1842.
CATHERINE, b. 27 July 1788; m. (1) James Clements; m. (2)
Capt. Simeon Woodbury of Sutton; no children.
DANIEL, b. 6 Aug. 1790; d. unm.; belonged to the army and
lived in Portland, Me.
SARAH PRINCE, b. 27 Mar. 1796; m. 1818, Joseph Parker Jr.
She d. 24 Apr. 1821.
NEHEMIAH, b. 8 Sept. 1798; d. 5 Apr. 1813.

351

JOSEPH[5] CHASE (Lt. Caleb,[4] Daniel,[3] Ens. Moses[2]), born in Sutton, 13 Mar. 1757; died in Cornish, N. H., 20 Feb. 1834, aged 77. He married in Cornish, 16 Oct. 1784, POLLY GERALD [JEROLD], daughter of Dea. Reuben and Joanna (Spaulding) Gerald, born 22 Sept. 1761, in Plainfield, Conn.: died in Cornish, 28 July 1845, aged 84. They lived in Cornish. He enlisted from Sutton in 1775 as a substitute for his brother, David Chase, and he and his brother David were in Capt. Andrew Elliot's Co. four months in 1777. He removed to Cornish, in 1779 and applied for a pension 17 Oct. 1832, aged 75. His widow, Polly Chase, deposed 5 Feb. 1840, aged 78. Her claim was allowed 11 Apr. 1843, at the age of 82 years.

Children, born in Cornish:

SOPHIA,[6] b. 22 Aug. 1785; m. 26 Mar. 1809, Daniel Jackson. She d. 12 Feb. 1836, without issue.

998. JOSEPH, b. 8 Oct. 1787.

POLLY, b. 16 Nov. 1789; m. 21 Mar. 1815, Jesse Kimball. She d. Apr. 1878.

REUBEN, b. 4 Feb. 1792; d. 16 Nov. 1796.

999. THEODORE, b. 16 Feb. 1794.

JOANNA, b. 10 May 1796; m. 8 Dec. 1817, Seth Johnson. She d. 10 Sept. 1849.

1000. JACOB, b. 20 Mar. 1799.

CYRUS, b. 5 Oct. 1801; d. 31 July 1803.

URSULA, b. 26 Nov. 1803; m. 25 Dec. 1826, John Tyler Freeman. She d. 22 May 1849.

CALEB, b. 10 May 1806; d. 10 Mar. 1808.

352

DEA. JOHN[5] CHASE (Lt. Caleb,[4] Daniel,[3] Ens. Moses[2]), born in Sutton, 12 Mar. 1761; died in Quechee, Vt., 21 Apr. 1842. He married (1) in Grafton, 8 Feb. 1795, POLLY DRURY who died in Weathersfield, Vt., 29 May 1798, aged 32. He married (2) in Claremont, N. H., 29 Sept. 1799, ELIZABETH PARKER who was born 28 Dec. 1777; died in Springfield, Vt., 1 Oct. 1861. They lived in Weathersfield, Vt., and were buried in the Ascutneyville Cemetery in Weathersfield.

Children by first wife, born in Weathersfield:

1001. JOHN,[6] b. 7 Dec. 1795.

POLLY DRURY, b. 11 May 1798; m. 9 Feb. 1825, Ralph Ainsworth.

Children by second wife, born in Weathersfield:

LUCIA, b. 14 Nov. 1800; d. 6 May 1865; m. 4 July 1827, Daniel Taylor of Waterloo, Canada.

ELISABETH, b. 6 Apr. 1802; m. 15 Mar. 1821, John Tolles Jr., of Springfield, Vt.

ALMIRA, b. 25 July 1804; m. 24 Aug. 1830, Franklin Haskell of Weathersfield, Vt.; removed to Lawrence, Kans.

1002. AUSTIN PARKER, b. 6 Mar. 1809.

LARKIN PRINCE, b. 29 Sept. 1818; d. 24 Nov. 1819.

353

CAPT. STEPHEN[5] CHASE (Lt. Caleb,[4] Daniel,[3] Ens. Moses[2]), born in Sutton, 26 Apr. 1763; died in Keene, N. H., 6 Apr. 1830. He married in Keene, 28 Nov. 1787, BETSEY BATCHELLER, daughter of Breed and Ruth (Davis) Batcheller, who was born in Nelson, N. H., 24 Aug. 1763, and died in Keene, 11 Aug. 1850, aged 83. Betsey Batcheller was described at her marriage as "of Packersfield," (now) Nelson, N. H.

Children, born in Keene:

CALEB,[6] b. 29 Jan. 1789; d. 7 Apr. 1815.

STEPHEN, b. 19 Mar. 1791; d. 8 June 1797.

BETSEY, b. 2 Apr. 1793; m. 24 Dec. 1815, Reuel Blake.

BELA, b. 2 Dec. 1795; m. (1) 10 Sept. 1821, in Surry, N. H., Eliza Abbott; m. (2) 21 June 1849, Mrs. Edith White of Chesterfield, N. H. He d. 31 Jan. 1868. Edith, his wife, d. 2 Jan. 1873, aged 85. No children.

1003.   STEPHEN, b. 18 July 1798.

ZIBA, b. 12 July 1800; d. unm. 7 July 1850.

1004.   CHARLES, b. 17 July 1803.

1005.   HOSEA, b. 23 Apr. 1805.

REBECCA, b. 23 Jan. 1808; m. (1) 4 Nov. 1828, Joel Kendall; m. (2) 20 Nov. 1860, Lemuel H. Alexander; lived in Winchester, N. H.

1006.   ALBE, b. 13 July 1812.

354

MOSES[5] CHASE (Lt. Caleb,[4] Daniel,[3] Ens. Moses[2]), born in Sutton, 1 Nov. 1765; died 11 Feb. 1827. He married in Sutton, 8 Oct. 1789, BETSEY BROWN of Millbury who died 1 Oct. 1844. They lived in Sutton and Claremont, N. H.

Children, born in Sutton:

1007.   SANFORD,[6] b. 31 Jan. 1791.

1008.   LEONARD, b. 17 Jan. 1796.

BETSEY, b. 23 July 1802; m. 6 Oct. 1830, James O Newton of Weathersfield, Vt.; lived in W. Randolph, Vt., 1872.

355

DANIEL[5] CHASE (Lt. Caleb,[4] Daniel,[3] Ens. Moses[2]), born in Sutton 9 Jan. 1768; died in Claremont, N. H., 2 Dec. 1840. He married (1) in Cornish, N. H., 28 Feb. 1796, POLLY FITCH who was born, 6 Oct. 1778 and died 3 June 1802. He married (2) in Sutton, 9 Sept. 1804, MEHITABLE WOODBURY, daughter of Jonathan and Hannah Woodbury, born in Sutton, 2 Nov. 1774; died in Claremont, 14 Apr. 1807. He married (3) in Claremont, 1 Nov. 1807, NANCY STROBRIDGE who was born in Claremont, 9 July 1786 and died 10 Nov. 1871. They lived in Claremont, where he kept Chase's Tavern from 1794 to 1840.

Children by first wife, born in Claremont:

MARY,[6] b. 11 Jan. 1797; m. 27 Oct. 1817, Austin Corbin of Newport, N. H., and New York City; nationally known banker and railroad magnate. She d. 7 Nov. 1869.

1009. DANIEL PRINCE, b. 22 Jan. 1799.
       SARAH, b. 11 Nov. 1801; d. 29 Nov. 1818.
    Child by second wife, born in Claremont:
1010. WILLARD WOODBURY, b. 10 Nov. 1805.
    Children by third wife, born in Claremont:
       MEHITABLE WOODBURY, b. 3 Feb. 1811; m. 11 Feb. 1834, Amos
          A. Watson. She d. 8 Apr. 1881, in Claremont.
       EMILY, b. 30 Aug. 1815; m. 5 Oct. 1840, Amos Bailey Currier.
       SARAH, b. 4 Nov. 1821; m. 25 Dec. 1843, Christopher F. Nor-
          ton, son of James of Fredonia, N. Y. She d. 13 Feb. 1870.
       NANCY, b. 7 Nov. 1823; m. 25 Dec. 1843, Luther Farwell of
          Claremont; d. 5 Feb. 1907. He was born 11 Aug. 1810 and
          died in Boston, where they lived, 12 Nov. 1896. Their dau.,
          Mary Chase,[8] b. 7 June 1855, m. 1 June 1885, Hosea Starr
          Ballou of Brookline, where they reside. Two sons, Luther
          Farwell and Hosea Starr Ballou, Jr.
1011. JAMES HIRAM, b. 14 Mar. 1830.
       Three children died in infancy.

356

ISRAEL[5] CHASE (Lt. Caleb,[4] Daniel,[3] Ens. Moses[2]), born in Sutton, 21 Mar. 1770; died in Cornish, N. H., 10 Sept. 1824. He married (1) in Cornish 5 June 1798, PRUDENCE HALL, daughter of Nathaniel and Prudence[6] (Chase) Hall, born in Cornish, 2 July 1781;
died 19 Aug. 1811. He married (2) in Plainfield, N. H., 12 Mar.
1813, SARAH CHAPMAN, daughter of Joseph and Martha (Girald)
Chapman, born in Cornish, 14 July 1789; died 12 Sept. 1881, aged 92.
They lived in Cornish till 1817 and removed to Claremont, N. H., late
in life.,
    Children by first wife, born in Cornish:
       MARY B.,[6] b. 1 Apr. 1799; m. 17 May 1827, Israel Hall of Cor-
          nish. She d. 15 Dec. 1834; no children.
1012. GEORGE HALL, b. 12 Apr. 1801; d. in South America.
1013. LEBBEUS, b. 6 Apr. 1804.
       SARAH P., b. 18 Apr. 1806; m. 10 Sept. 1835, Israel Hall;
          she d. 4 Aug. 1838, aged 33.
1014. HENRY HALL, b. 10 May 1809.
    Children by second wife, born in Cornish:
       JOSEPH, b. 10 Dec. 1813; d. 13 Feb. 1814.
       PRUDENCE JANE, b. 28 Jan. 1815; d. 13 Dec. 1860, unm.
       MARTHA J., b. 9 May 1817; d. 28 Jan. 1853, unm.

357

LT. JACOB[5] CHASE (Moody,[4] Daniel,[3] Ens. Moses[2]), born in Sut-
ton, 12 Sept. 1761; died in Pepperell, 5 Dec. 1848. He married in
Groton, 2 May 1786, ABIGAIL HUBBARD, probably daughter of Na-
than and Mary (Patterson) Hubbard, born in Groton, 23 Apr. 1765.
She died in 1790. He married (2), in Groton, 5 Jan. 1797, SALLY
PARK, widow of William Park. She died in 1811. He married
(3) in 1815, ELIZABETH FAIRBANKS, widow of John Fairbanks of
Harvard. She died 21 Dec. 1851, aged 79, without Chase issue.

They lived in Groton and Pepperell. He made his will 23 Aug. 1845 which was proved 13 Feb. 1849. Therein he mentions his wife Elizabeth, his daughter Abigail Priest, his sons Moody, William and Jacob Chase, and the four daughters of his late son Amos Chase, decd., and his son Harvey Chase (Middlesex Probate, 29103).

Children by first wife, born in Groton:

1015.   MOODY,[6] b. 27 Feb. 1786; alive 23 Aug. 1845.
1016.   WILLIAM, b. 14 Aug. 1787.
    CHILD, b. 20 July 1790; d. in infancy.

Children by second wife, born in Pepperell except Abigail born in Groton:

    ABIGAIL, b. 8 Nov. 1797; m. Zimri Priest of Harvard.
1017.   HARVEY, b. 18 Jan. 1800.
1018.   JACOB, b. 21 Jan. 1802.
    SALLIE, b. 29 Feb. 1804; d. 26 Mar. 1812.
1019.   AMOS, b. 9 Mar. 1806.
    MARY ANN, b. 30 Apr. 1808; d. 8 Sept. 1813, in Pepperell.
    JOHN, b. 21 May 1810; d. 8 Dec. 1839, in Pepperell.

358

SAMUEL[5] CHASE (Moody,[4] Daniel,[3] Ens. Moses[2]), born in Sutton, 20 Apr. 1768; died in Pepperell, 6 Nov. 1808, aged 40. He married in Groton, 30 Apr. 1795, ANNA LANGLEY [LONGLEY] of Shirley, daughter of Joshua and Bridget Longley, born in Shirley, 20 Aug. 1776; died in Brookline, N. H., 6 June 1866. They lived in Groton, Shirley and Pepperell. At his decease his homestead was situated in the easterly part of Pepperell on the road leading from Pepperell Meeting House to the Lawrence Mills, so called.

Children, first born in Groton, second to fourth in Shirley, youngest in Pepperell:

    LYDIA LONGLEY,[6] b. 16 Jan. 1796; unm.
    BETSEY, b. 23 Oct. 1798; m. 19 Oct. 1818, Joseph Tucker of Pepperell.
    SAMUEL, b. 22 Feb. 1801; d. unm. in Pepperell, 1 Aug. 1876.
    MOODY, b. 7 Mar. 1803; d. unm. 8 Jan. 1828.
1020.   WILLIAM PRESCOTT, b. 22 Feb. 1808.

359

MARCH[5] CHASE (Moody,[4] Daniel,[3] Ens. Moses[2]), born in Sutton 1776; died in Bolton, 17 June 1827, aged 51. He married in Shirley, 19 Dec. 1805, HEPZIBAH GLEASON, daughter of Jesse and Hepzibah (Jones) Gleason, who was born in Princeton, 6 Jan. 1778, and died in Bolton, 12 July 1823. They lived in Shirley and Bolton.

Children, first four born in Shirley, youngest in Bolton:

    ELISABETH HALE,[6] b. 16 Oct. 1806; d. in Bolton, 10 June 1824.
    MARY, b. 19 Aug. 1809; m. (1) Josiah Brown; m. (2) Charles Wait.
    SUSAN MILDRED, b. 4 Oct. 1811; d. in Shirley, 4 Oct. 1815.
    SELINA, b. 17 Oct. 1813; d. in Shirley, 28 Mar. 1815.
1021.   WILLIAM MOODY, b. 1 Dec. 1817.

360

Lt. William[5] Chase (Moody,[4] Daniel,[3] Ens. Moses[2]), born about 1751; died between 9 Sept. 1779 and 4 Nov. 1783. He married in Sutton, 14 Oct. 1773, Molly Elliott who survived him. He purchased a farm in Groton, 25 May, 1779, which he sold 29 July 1779. In both deeds he is described as William Chase of Sutton and he acknowledged the second deed in Worcester County, 9 Sept. 1779. (Middlesex Deeds, 81:61, 62). Administration on his estate was granted to Joseph Elliott of Sutton, gentleman, with Noah Brooks Kimball and Zadock Putnam, both of Grafton, sureties, 4 Nov. 1782, and he was described as "William Chase, late of Groton, a Continental soldier deceased." The Judge of Probate ordered the distribution of his estate paid to "the widow and *her child.*" 13 Nov. 1783. (Middlesex Probate, 4310). The will of Moody Chase of Groton shows that his son William deceased had a son Jonathan Chase, alive and a legatee, 19 Aug. 1814. Ibid. 4303).

He is the Lt. William Chase of Capt. March Chase's Co. of Col. Jonathan Holman's Regt. who marched from Sutton to Saratoga, 26 Sept. 1777, to reinforce the Northern army for sixteen days and who again enlisted 19 May 1781, for three years in Capt. Fisher's Co. of Col. Cushing's Regt. The description gives his age as 30; his stature five feet, eight inches; complexion dark; occupation a farmer and residence Westborough. (Mass. Soldier and Sailors in the Revolutionary War, 3:369).

His widow is the Molly Chase who married in Grafton, 12 Dec. 1782, Noah Brooks Kimball of Grafton. Molly (Chase) Kimball died in Grafton, 8 Aug. 1806, in her 51st year. In 1776 William and Molly Chase were living in the North Parish of Sutton (now Millbury) and there their oldest children died and were buried in the County Bridge Cemetery.

Children by first husband, born in Sutton:

    Moody,[6] b. 1774; d. 31 July 1776, aged 2y. lacking 2d.

    Susannah, b. 1 Aug. 1776; d. 2 Aug. 1776, aged 18 hours.

1022. Jonathan Hale, b. 1778.

Child by second husband, born in Grafton:

    Anna (Kimball), b. 30 July 1789.

361

Daniel[5] Chase (Capt. Moses,[4] Daniel,[3] Ens. Moses[2]), born in Sutton, 23 Mar. 1753; died in Cornish, N. H., 13 Aug. 1841. He married (1) in Cornish, 5 Sept. 1776, Mehitable Kimball, daughter of Benjamin and Hannah (Richards) Kimball of Plainfield, N. H. She was born in Preston, Conn., 12 Mar. 1757, and died in Cornish, 2 May 1813. He married (2) Mary (Estabrook) Hall, widow of Moody Hall. She was born 9 Feb. 1769 and died in Cornish, 21 May 1824, aged 55. He married (3) 5 Jan. 1825, Mary May of Bradford, Vt. She died in Cornish, 16 Jan. 1831, aged 61. He married (4) 9 Oct. 1833, Mary C. (Kimball) Daniels, widow of John Daniels and daughter of Joseph and Hannah (Morgan) Kimball. She was born — Nov. 1767, and died 27 Jan. 1855. They lived in Cornish.

Children by first wife, born in Cornish:

CLEMENTINA,[6] b. 29 Sept. 1777; d. 22 Oct. 1777.
GERARD, b. 16 Jan. 1779; d. 14 July 1780.
DANIEL, b. 5 Dec. 1780; d. 17 July 1782.
AMOS, d. young.
HANNAH, b. 14 June 1783; m. 15 Feb. 1803, Rev. Joseph Rowell of Cornish.
AMOS, b. 12 July 1785; d. unm. 8 July 1814.
SALLY, b. 11 June 1787; d. 2 May 1790.
MEHITABLE, b. 14 Jan. 1790; d. 30 Apr. 1790.
REBECCA HART, b. 2 May 1791; m. 23 Feb. 1814, David Dana of Pomfret, Vt.
1023.   BENJAMIN KIMBALL, b. 5 Apr. 1798.

362

DEA. JOHN[5] CHASE (Capt. Moses,[4] Daniel,[3] Ens. Moses[2]), born in Sutton, 4 Oct. 1755; died in Cornish, N. H., 14 Dec. 1844. He married (1) in Pomfret, Conn., about 1782, MARTHA COTTON who died in Cornish, 21 Mar. 1789. He married (2) 25 Dec. 1790, LOVISA JOSLYN who died 15 June 1849, aged 84. They lived in Cornish. He enlisted in Capt. Solomon[5] Chase's Co. 15 Aug. 1776 and was a pensioner from 17 Oct. 1832. His widow Lovisa deposed 7 Mar. 1846 in her 81st year that she was his widow and married him 25 Dec. 1790, that her maiden name was Lovisa Joslin and that there were eleven children, and that her husband died 14 Dec. 1844.

Children by first wife, born in Cornish:

1024.   COTTON,[6] b. 8 Aug. 1783.
JOHN, b. 25 May 1785; d. Sept. 1785.
JUDITH, b. 6 Feb. 1787; m. Rev. ——— Williams. She d. about 1810.

Children by second wife, born in Cornish:

MARTHA JOSLYN, b. 4 Dec. 1791; m. 21 Oct. 1816, Moody March Hall. She d. 7 Dec. 1869.
MELISSA, b. 13 Feb. 1793; m. (1) 3 July 1817, Paul Davidson; m. (2) 31 Jan. 1826, Jonathan Wyman. She d. 2 Mar. 1886.
1025.   JOHN, b. 25 Sept. 1794.
LOVISA, b. 25 May 1796; m. 8 Oct. 1822, Joseph K. Johnson of Plainfield, N. H.
SUSAN, b. 20 Jan. 1798; m. 29 Oct. 1821, William Lovatt Sweet. She d. 14 Mar. 1879.
1026.   MOSES, b. 28 Dec. 1799.
1027.   TAYLOR GILMAN, b. 4 Nov. 1801.
HANNAH B., b. 22 Apr. 1803; m. 4 Nov. 1841, Abel Jackson.
SARAH MATTHEWS, b. 5 Feb. 1805; m. 22 Feb. 1830, Sumner Joslyn of Hardwick, Vt.
MARY DRESSER, b. 22 Dec. 1807; m. (1) John Sheldon. She d. 13 May 1882, without issue.
DANIEL MATTHEWS, b. 24 Feb. 1809; d. 10 Aug. 1810.

363

REV. AMOS[5] CHASE (Capt. Moses,[4] Daniel,[3] Ens. Moses[2]), born in Sutton, 19 May 1760; died in Centerville, Pa., 25 Dec. 1849. He graduated from Dartmouth College in 1780 and was ordained Pastor

of the Second Congregational Church of Litchfield, Conn., 27 June
1787. He was dismissed in 1814 and removed to Centerville, Pa.,
where he lived the remainder of his life. He married (1) 30 Nov.
1788, REBECCA HART, daughter of Rev. Levi and Rebecca (Bell-
amy) Hart of Preston (now Griswold), Conn. She died without issue 25 July 1791, in her 26th year. He married (2) 27 June
1792, JOANNA LANMAN, daughter of Peter and Sarah Lanman of
Norwich, Conn. She died in Centerville, Pa., 19 Aug. 1848, aged 81.
Children, born in Litchfield, Conn.:

> REBECCA HART,⁶ b. 17 Apr. 1793; d. 8 Dec. 1871; m. 14 Nov.
> 1850, Jonathan Titus; no children.
> SARAH L., b. 2 Nov. 1794; m. Dec. 1808, Andrew Bloomfield;
> d. 20 Aug. 1842; seven children.
> JOANNA LANMAN, b. 29 June 1796; m. 22 Sept. 1816, Thomas
> H. Sill.
> ELIZABETH BIRD, b. 18 Dec. 1797; m. 29 June 1820, Capt. Wil-
> liam Sheffield; d. 4 Aug. 1877.
> 1028. JOSEPH LANMAN, b. 18 July 1799.
> DANIEL, b. 10 June 1801; d. unm. 2 July 1877.
> 1029. CHARLES, b. 12 May 1803.
> 1030. JAMES LANMAN, b. 10 Feb. 1805.
> 1031. EDWARD HUNTINGTON, b. 18 July 1807.
> MARY H., b. 10 June 1809; d. in Norwich, Conn., 2 Feb. 1823.
> 1032. JULIUS DEMING, b. 6 Nov. 1811.

364

CAPT. NAHUM C.⁵ CHASE (Capt. Moses,⁴ Daniel,³ Ens. Moses²),
born in Sutton, 9 Oct. 1762; died in Cornish, N. H., 27 June 1827.
He married 23 Sept. 1784, DEBORAH FREEMAN, daughter of Daniel
and Mary (Gates) Freeman of Plainfield, N. H. She was born 2
Nov. 1764 and died in Cornish, 30 Mar. 1837, aged 72. They lived
in Cornish.
Children, born in Cornish:

> SUSAN,⁶ b. 10 Sept. 1785; d. 17 Apr. 1788.
> 1033. FREEMAN, b. 27 Jan. 1787.
> DEBORAH, b. 24 Dec. 1789; d. 11 June 1839; m. 29 Apr. 1828,
> Rev. Lathrop Thompson.
> 1034. MOSES, b. 1 Sept. 1795.

365

CAPT. CALEB⁵ CHASE (Capt. Moses,⁴ Daniel,³ Ens. Moses²),
born in Cornish, N. H., 11 Sept. 1767; died in Williamstown, Vt., 1
Sept. 1856, aged 89. He married 21 Jan. 1789, ELIZABETH DEMING,
daughter of Ebenezer and Elizabeth (Dana) Deming of Cornish.
She was born 13 Aug. 1763, and died 20 Sept. 1840. They lived in
Cornish, N. H. He was called Caleb Chase 2d.
Children, born in Cornish:

> BETSEY,⁶ b. 19 Aug. 1789; m. 14 Aug. 1815, Capt. Cotton⁶ Chase.
> (Family 1024).
> MARY, b. 26 Dec. 1790; m. 13 Dec. 1809, Freeman⁶ Chase (Na-
> hum C.⁵ (Family 1033).
> HANNAH BROWN, b. 24 Dec. 1792; d. 5 Feb. 1807.

PERSIS, b. 25 Oct. 1794; m. 9 Apr. 1823, Horace Ware. She d.
1 Dec. 1858.

1035.   CALEB, b. 3 Sept. 1796.

LUCY, b. 13 July 1798; d. 9 Apr. 1834.

HANNAH BROWN, b. 19 Sept. 1806; d. 27 Jan. 1824.

1036.   DANIEL KIMBALL, b. 16 Oct. 1804.

NAHUM, b. 3 Aug. 1800; d. 3 Aug. 1803.

366

MOODY[5] CHASE (Capt. Moses,[4] Daniel,[3] Ens. Moses[2]), born in
Cornish, N.H., 10 Oct. 1770; died there, 11 Apr. 1845. He married
(1) 28 Jan. 1793, REBECCA CHAPMAN, daughter of Capt. Benjamin
and Jemima (Gates) Chapman. She died in Cornish 10 June 1794
aged 23. He married (2) 28 Jan. 1795, RHODA COOK of Claremont,
N. H. She died in Cornish, 21 Feb. 1796, aged 27. He married (3)
LUCY FARNHAM, the mother of his ten younger children. They lived
in Cornish.

Children by first wife, born in Cornish:

1037.   BENJAMIN CHAPMAN,[6] b. 8 Sept. 1793.

INFANT, d. 8 Jan. or June 1794.

Child by second wife, born in Cornish:

RHODA COOK, b. 15 Feb. 1796; m. 9 Feb. 1815, Jesse Vose of
Claremont, N. H., and d. 6 July 1837.

Children by third wife, born in Cornish:

1038.   HARVEY FARNHAM, b. 5 Mar. 1797.

REBECCA CHAPMAN, b. 4 July 1798; d. unm.

1039.   JAMES MORRIS, b. 4 Apr. 1800.

1040.   MOODY, b. 25 Feb. 1802.

LUCY MARIA, b. 3 Mar. 1804; d. unm. 31 Mar. 1825.

HANNAH BROWN, b. 5 Oct. 1806; m. William Withrow of Mal-
comb, Ill.

HARRIET ELIZA, b. 8 Dec. 1808; m. William Withrow. She d.
3 Aug. 1843.

1041.   GEORGE CLEMENT, b. 16 Sept. 1811.

NEWTON WHITTLESEY, b. 13 Nov. 1813; d. 17 Sept. 1839.

1042.   ALBERT, b. 25 Apr. 1817.

367

MOSES[5] CHASE (Capt. Moses,[4] Daniel,[3] Ens. Moses[2]), born in
Cornish, N. H., 29 Nov. 1772; died in Lyndon,Vt., 27 Aug. 1861.
He graduated at Dartmouth College, in 1797; read law and practiced
in Calais, Me., and Bradford, Vt. He married, 20 Jan. 1800, DEB-
ORAH BULL who was born in Hartford, Conn., 9 Sept. 1777, and died
17 Aug. 1837. They lived in Bradford, Vt., and in St. Johnsbury,
Vt.

Children, born in Vermont:

1043.   EPAPHRAS BULL,[6] b. 27 Oct. 1800.

HENRIETTA, b. 20 Jan. 1802; m. (1) ——— Wilson; m. (2) G.
B. Mobley; she d. in Gainsville, Ala., 2 Apr. 1873.

1044.   WILLIAM COLEMAN, b. 19 Dec. 1803.

1045.   GEORGE MONROE, b. 16 Mar. 1806.

MARY ANN, b. 29 Apr. 1808; m. 29 Apr. 1835, Ephraim Chamberlain of St. Johnsbury,, Vt.

HARRIET WADSWORTH, b. 21 Apr. 1812; m. George Alward; she d. in Calif.

DANIEL KIMBALL, b. 23 Feb. 1815; m. 19 Oct. 1839, Elisabeth Rosina Dalrymple; no children.

JANE, b. 21 May 1817; d. 18 Jan. 1818.

JOHN BRYANT, b. 8 Mar. 1821; d. unm. 8 Nov. 1847, in Boston.

368

DEA. CLEMENT[5] CHASE (Capt. Moses,[4] Daniel,[3] Ens. Moses[2]), born in Cornish, 4 July 1776 and died in Cornish, 6 June 1867. He married (1) 10 Sept. 1797, LUCY MURRAY of Litchfield, Conn. She was born 21 Nov. 1778 and died in Cornish, 18 Aug. 1814. He married (2) 23 Mar. 1815, OLIVE SPAULDING, daughter of Dea. Champion Spaulding of Plainfield, N. H. She was born 29 Feb. 1790 and died in Cornish, 11 May 1823. He married (3) 5 Feb. 1824, PRUDENCE SPOFFORD ANDREWS of Bradford, Vt., who was born 31 Aug. 1789 and died in Cornish, 18 July 1863. They lived in Cornish.

Children by first wife, born in Cornish:

PHILEMON MURRAY,[6] b. 28 Mar. 1799; d. unm. in Bath, N. Y., Aug. 1820.

SUSAN, b. 30 Apr. 1801; d. 14 May 1839.

FREEMAN OR TRUMAN, b. 14 Sept. 1803; m. 29 May 1834, Amanda Tisdale of Hanover. He d. 29 Nov. 1835; no children.

GEORGE CLEMENT, b. 1 May 1806; d. 24 Jan. 1807.

LUCY MURRAY, b. 17 Dec. 1807; m. 28 Sept. 1826, Horace Bushnell of Westbrook, Conn. She d. 30 Sept. 1889.

ESTHER ROBBINS, b. 18 Jan. 1813; d. 12 Mar. 1813.

ESTHER ROBBINS 2d, b. 13 Aug. 1814; m. 18 May 1843, William Silloway of Plainfield, N. H., and Racine, Wis.

Children by second wife, born in Cornish:

OLIVE SPAULDING, b. 6 Mar. 1816; m. 19 Jan. 1839, Dr. John B. Judson; she d. in Livingstone Mills, N. Y., 31 Aug. 1866.

EUNICE DANA, b. 13 Sept. 1817; d. 30 Dec. 1832.

1046. CHAMPION SPAULDING, b. 20 Mar. 1820.

PHILEMON MURRAY, b. 12 July 1822; d. 12 July 1823.

Children by third wife, born in Cornish:

INFANT, b. Nov. 1824; d. Nov. 1824.

INFANT (dau), b. 14 Sept. 1825; d. 14 Sept. 1826.

RUTH MARIA, b. 7 Mar. 1827; d. 2 Apr. 1827.

SARAH JULIA, b. 23 Nov. 1829; m. 8 Apr. 1850, Robert H. Lay of Chicago, Ill.; living in Milwaukee, Wis., in 1873.

1047. GEORGE MURRAY, b. 26 Mar. 1833.

369

HARVEY[5] CHASE (Capt. Moses,[4] Daniel,[3] Ens. Moses[2]), born in Cornish, 13 Nov. 1778; died in Cornish, N. H., or Windsor, Vt., 18 Feb. 1857. He married about 1810, EUNICE DANA, daughter of John W. Dana, Esq. She was born 29 May 1783, and died in Cornish, 8 Jan. 1823. They lived in Cornish and Windsor, Vt. He was a lawyer by profession.

Children, first two born in Cornish:

> ALFRED,[6] b. 16 Oct. 1811; d. 28 Sept. 1826.
> ISRAEL PUTNAM, b. 28 May 1815; d. 17 Jan. 1816.
> POLLY DANA, b. 18 Feb. 1818; d. unm. — June 1837.
> CATHARINE, b. 1819; d. unm. 13 June 1896.
> SARAH.

370

THOMAS[5] CHASE (Lt. Wells,[4] Moses,[3] Ens. Moses[2]), born in Amesbury (now Merrimac) 14 May 1735; died in Salisbury, N. H., 14 Jan. 1807. He married in Chester, N. H., about 1757, MARY HALL, daughter of Henry and Joanna (Sargent) Hall of Chester. She was born 14 Nov. 1735.

He was an early schoolmaster in Salisbury, removing there before 1768. He removed to Cornish, N. H., about 1761, but returned to Salisbury, where he died. From 1757 to 1760 or later he lived in Hampstead, N. H.

Children, first two born in Chester, others in Cornish.

> TIMOTHY,[6] b. 22 Jan. 1758; d. 15 July 1770.
> 1048. MOSES, b. 23 Mar. 1759.
> ELISABETH, b. 10 Dec. 1760; m. (1) 24 Aug. 1780, Job Stevens of Plainfield, N. H.; nine children; m. (2) Josiah Stone. She d. 31 Mar. 1850.
> 1049. WILLIAM, b. 19 Oct. 1762.
> JOANNA, b. 11 July 1764; m. John Hobbs; she d. 17 Apr. 1836.
> MARTHA, b. 11 May 1766; m. James Spaudling.
> MARY, b. 10 Apr. 1768; m. 14 Mar. 1793, Joshua[6] Chase. No children. (Family 975).
> HANNAH, b. 24 Dec. 1769; m. about 1790, Abel Spaulding of Waitsfield, Vt. She d. in Deleware, Ohio.
> EMMA, b. 29 Sept. 1772; d. at 18.
> 1050. THOMAS, b. 3 Sept. 1774.
> 1051. WELLS, b. 2 Feb. 1778.

371

DR. WILLIAM[5] CHASE (Lt. Wells,[4] Moses,[3] Ens. Moses[2]), born in Amesbury (now Merrimac), 22 Nov. 1736; died in Falmouth, Me., 22 July 1798. He married (1) Dec. 1763, MARY BUXTON, daughter of William and Lydia (Jones) Buxton, who was born 15 Mar. 1739 and died, 25 June 1777, aged 38. He married (2) 11 Dec. 1777, MIRIAM COLE of Harpswell, Me., who was born, 25 Feb. 1740, and died 16 Aug. 1808. They lived in North Yarmouth, Me., and later in Falmouth, and he was the head of a family in 1790. He joined the church there, 13 Sept. 1778.

Children by first wife, born in Falmouth:

> 1052. WILLIAM,[6] b. 6 Oct. 1764.
> 1053. ASA, b. 22 Dec. 1765.
> MARY, b. 1 Jan. 1768; m. ——— Kilpatrick [Patrick]; she d. 13 Nov. 1809.
> ANNA, b. 19 Nov. 1770; m. ——— Myrick; she d. 2 Dec. 1812.

LUCRETIA, b. 17 Dec. 1774; m. George Knight; three children; she d. 28 Dec. 1837.

STEPHEN, unm.; lived in the Provinces.

Children by second wife, born in Falmouth:

HANNAH, b. 26 Oct. 1781; m. 20 May 1806, Dea. Salathiel Sweetser; she d. 13 Feb. 1830.

1054.   TIMOTHY, b. 27 Sept. 1783.

372

REV. MOSES[5] CHASE (Lt. Wells,[4] Moses,[3] Ens. Moses[2]), born in Amesbury (now Merrimac), 20 Aug. 1738; died there, 5 Feb. 1797, in his 58th year.   He married in Haverhill, 4 Mar. 1762, ELIZABETH WHITTIER, perhaps daughter of Thomas and Susanna (Warner) Whittier, born in Haverhill, 20 July 1744.   She died in Amesbury, 10 Nov. 1801, aged 59, as her stone indicates which is now standing in the Union Cemetery.   He was a hatter and a Baptist minister and was called "Elder" Moses.   He was ordained 2 Dec. 1789 and was the first pastor of the First Baptist Church in Salisbury and Amesbury.   They lived in Amesbury.

Children, born in Amesbury:

SARAH,[6] b. 7 Mar. 1763; m. Aug. 1781, David Currier of Salisbury.

1055.   BAILEY, b. 20 Sept. 1766.

RUTH, b. 7 June 1771; m. 28 Apr. 1793, Joseph Rutherford of Newburyport.

1056.   JAMES, b. 10 Dec. 1774.

1057.   MOSES JAMES, b. 19 Apr. 1782.

373

WELLS[5] CHASE (Lt. Wells,[4] Moses,[3] Ens. Moses[2]), born in Amesbury (now Merrimac), 16 Jan. 1740/41; died in 1788.   He married (1) in Haverhill, 4 Mar. 1762, RUTH MORSE, daughter of William and Judith (Hale) Morse, born in Haverhill, 4 Sept. 1743; died 7 Feb. 1783.   He married (2) 25 May 1783, LYDIA WHEELER of Concord, N. H., who died without issue, 7 Aug. 1783.   He married (3) 24 Nov. 1783, LYDIA GOULD of Henniker, N. H.   They lived in Amesbury, Concord and Salisbury, N. H.

Wells[5] Chase, son of Wells[4] Chase, enlisted in Col. Joseph Gerrish's Co. and served from 6 Apr. 1759 to 9 Dec. 1760.   He was of Amesbury, age 18 and was in the service at Louisburgh. (Mass. Archives, 97:107).

Children by first wife, first and second born in Amesbury:

MARY,[6] b. 9 Sept. 1763; d. 25 Nov. 1763.

ANNA, b. 7 Apr. 1765; d. 20 Oct. 1784.

POLLY, b. 13 July 1767; d. probably before her father.

TIMOTHY, b. 15 Jan. 1770; d. 25 Apr. 1773.

MARTHA, b. 18 Feb. 1772.

1058.   SETH, b. 16 Nov. 1774.

WILLIS, b. 30 Oct. 1776; d. 19 Jan. 1791.

SARAH, b. 3 June 1779.

RUTH, b. 30 May 1782; d. 13 Jan. 1784.

Children by third wife:

> TIMOTHY, b. 17 Nov. 1784; d. 16 Oct. 1787.
> 1059. JAMES, b. 25 Dec. 1786.

374

DANIEL[5] CHASE (Lt. Wells,[4] Moses,[3] Ens. Moses[2]), born in Amesbury (now Merrimac), 24 Oct. 1744; married in Amesbury, 21 or 23 Nov. 1765, MARY DOWNS.   He renewed his baptismal covenant with the Second Church of Amesbury (now Merrimac) in 1766 and his son Ambrose was baptized there, 5 Oct. 1766.   His son Enoch was there baptized, 7 Jan. 1776.   They removed from Amesbury to Concord, N. H., after 1775.   His estate was administered upon by his son Enoch, 16 Feb. 1802.

Children, born in Amesbury:

> 1060. AMBROSE,[6] b. 24 July 1766.
> FRANCES, b. 12 Mar. 1769; m. (1) John Favor; m. (2) Nathaniel Worthen; m. (3) Jonathan Morse.
> 1061. THOMAS, b. 8 July 1771; settled in North Yarmouth, Me.
> 1062. JACOB, b. 2 Nov. 1773; settled in North Yarmouth.
> 1063. ENOCH, b. 10 Nov. 1775.
> 1064. ISAAC, birth not on town records.
> 1064a. DANIEL, b. in Hopkinton, N. H., 16 June 1784, perhaps a child of the above Daniel and Molly.

375

WELLS[5] CHASE (Moses,[4] Moses,[3] Ens. Moses[2]), born in Newbury (now West Newbury), 9 Sept. 1737; died in Chester, N. H., 28 Dec. 1824.   He married in Newbury, 21 Feb. 1760, SARAH HOVEY, daughter of Samuel and Mary (Ilsley) Hovey.   She was born in Rowley, 8 Sept. 1737; died in Chester, 5 Oct. 1814.   He lived in what is now West Newbury till 1771, then removed to Chester (now Auburn), N. H.   The place remained in the family about 130 years and the house he built when he first settled there, afterwards enlarged, is still standing, nearly opposite the home of Edwin T. Underhill, on the "Bunker Hill" road in Auburn.

THE NEW HAMPSHIRE SENTINEL of 4 Mar. 1825, stated that Wells Chase was in the expedition under Gov. William Shirley and went up the Kennebec River against the Indians in 1754 and was in the battle of Ticonderago in 1758.   He also signed the "Association Test" in 1776.

Wells[5] Chase of Newbury appears in Capt. Enoch Bayley's Co. from 26 June to 11 Sept. 1754, for the defence of the Eastern frontiers. (Mass Archives, 93:143).

Children, born in Newbury (now West Newbury):

> 1065. BENJAMIN PIKE,[6] b. 28 June 1762.
> HANNAH, b. 23 Aug. 1766; d. 30 Aug. 1766.

376

STEPHEN[5] CHASE (Moses,[4] Moses,[3] Ens. Moses[2]), born in what is now West Newbury, 7 Feb. 1748; died in Leominster, 7 Oct. 1819, aged 71.   He married in Newbury, 12 Dec. 1771, SARAH

SMITH. She died in Leominster, 14 Oct. 1830, aged 80y. 6m. No children recorded as born to them in Newbury or Leominster. He was the head of a family in Leominster in 1790, consisting of one male over 16 years of age, one male under 16 and one female.

The church records of Leominster show that Joshua Chase, nephew of Stephen Chase, was baptized there, 2 Dec. 1792. He was son of Joshua[5] Chase. Stephen Chase left a will probated at Worcester, 11389. They died childless.

377

ENOCH[5] CHASE (Moses,[4] Moses,[3] Ens. Moses[2]), born in Newbury (now West Newbury), 16 Sept. 1750; died in Leominster, 7 Oct. 1819. He married 6 Apr. 1772, SARAH SAWYER, daughter of Jacob and Elizabeth (Savery) Sawyer, born in Newbury, 1 Oct. 1752; died in Leominster, 14 Oct. 1830, aged 80y. 6m. They lived in Leominster, Andover and Billerica, 1787 to 1796.

Children, first born in Newbury, second to sixth in Leominster, last two in Billerica:

SARAH,[6] b. 7 July 1773; m. 9 Jan. 1794, John Carleton of Billerica.
JACOB, b. 9 Oct. 1775; d. young.
SETH, b. 27 Jan. 1778; d. young.
REBECCA, b. 14 Feb. 1780; m. (1) 22 Dec. 1799, Stephen Bailey; m. (2) 10 Oct. 1804, Parker Noyes.
ELISABETH SAWYER, b. 5 July 1782; m. 6 Nov. 1804, Stephen Chandler Moore of Andover.
1066. JOHN, b. 1 May 1785.
1067. JOSHUA, b. 6 Dec. 1787; lived in Boston, 1831-1837.
EUNICE SAWYER, b. 25 Aug. 1792; m. 30 Sept. 1813, Henry Cochran of Andover.

378

JOSHUA[5] CHASE (Moses,[4] Moses,[3] Ens. Moses[2]), born in Newbury (now West Newbury), 26 Feb. 1752; died in the West Indies, 15 Feb. 1787. He married in Boston, 24 Feb. 1777, SARAH GRAY. He was a cooper and they lived in Boston. His son, Thomas Gray,[6] received a part of the Moses[4] Chase homestead in West Newbury from Joshua's brother John[5] Chase who died without children, 8 Aug. 1802.

Children, born in Boston:

1068. THOMAS GRAY,[6] b. about 1780.
JOSHUA, b. 29 Aug. 1784; d. 4 July 1815, childless. He lived with his uncle Stephen Chase in Leominster.

379

LT. MOSES[5] CHASE (Moses,[4] Moses,[3] Ens. Moses[2]), born in Newbury (now West Newbury) 4 July 1756; died in West Newbury, 8 Nov. 1826, aged 70. He married (1) in Newbury, 14 Aug. 1777, MARY ORDWAY, daughter of Stephen and Abigail (Hadlock) Ordway, born in Newbury, 13 Feb. 1756; died there, 17 June 1783 in her 28th year. He married (2) in Newbury, 9 Mar. 1784, MARY HALE, widow, perhaps of John Hale, and daughter of Nathaniel and Me-

hitable (Nichols) Willet, born in Newbury, 22 Jan. 1755. She died
in Newbury, 16 Mar. 1794. He married (3) 13 Oct. 1796, ELIZA-
BETH[6] CHASE, daughter of Abel[5] and Hannah (Morse) Chase, born
in Newbury, 17 Feb. 1770; died in West Newbury, 21 Nov. 1852,
aged 85. (Family 144).

He was a Revolutionary soldier and a pensioner in 1818, and
lived on the old Moses[2] Chase homestead in West Newbury. He removed to Newburyport, and then to Chester, N. H., where he lived
from 1812 to 1820, then returned to West Newbury. He was a
cooper by trade.

In July 1794 he went with a berrying party of eight others to a
spot on the opposite side of the Merrimack river. On their return
a sudden squall capsized the boat and all were drowned excepting
Mr. Chase, his three children, Polly, Rebecca and Joshua, being
among the lost.

He was appointed guardian of his two children, viz. Jacob and
Sally on 25 Jan. 1796, they having received a portion of the estate of
Abigail Hale. (Essex Probate, 64:138 and 70:183).

Children by first wife, born in Newbury (now West Newbury):

    ELISABETH,[6] b. 29 May 1778; m. 29 June 1797, Samuel Carr,
      son of Samuel and Emma (Chase) Carr; she d. 23 Oct. 1854.
1069. MOSES, b. 17 Oct. 1779.
    MARY [Polly], b. 5 Oct. 1781; drowned 19 July 1794.

Children by second wife, born in Newbury (now West Newbury):

    JACOB, b. 23 Oct. 1784; lost at sea.
    REBECCA, b. 9 May 1787; drowned 19 July 1794.
    JOSHUA, b. 23 July 1789; drowned 19 July 1794.
    SARAH, bp. 14 Aug. 1791; m. 25 Aug. 1812, Joshua Bailey.

Children by third wife, first three born in Newbury (now West
Newbury) and last two in Newburyport:

    MARY, b. 8 Dec. 1797; m. Oliver Brown of W. Newbury and
      Haverhill.
    REBECCA, b. 8 May 1799; d. 7 Sept. 1819, in Chester, N. H.
    MEHITABLE B., m. 3 Dec. 1818, Charles Hills of Georgetown.
    HANNAH MORSE, b. 28 Sept. 1805; m. (1) —— Goodrich;
      m. (2) Joseph Moody.
    SUSAN ANN, b. 12 Dec. 1808; m. 26 Aug. 1841, George Chase
      of W. Newbury.

380

BRADFORD[5] CHASE (Dea. Seth,[4] Moses,[3] Ens. Moses[2]), born in
Sutton, 8 Aug. 1741; died there, 12 July 1783. He married in Sut-
ton, 21 June 1763, ABIGAIL SIBLEY, daughter of Capt. Samuel and
Abigail (Park) Sibley, born in Sutton, 30 May 1745; died 3 Feb.
1824. She married (2) in Sutton, 31 Oct. 1790, NATHANIEL COOPER
JR. of Northbridge who died in Northbridge, 16 July 1821.

They lived in Sutton on the Dea. Seth Chase homestead.

Children, born in Sutton:

1070. NATHAN,[6] b. 18 Apr. 1764.
    ELISABETH, b. 29 Jan. 1766; m. 28 Nov. 1784, Amariah[6] Chase.
      (Family 843).

ELIAS, b. 16 Feb. 1768; d. 26 Oct. 1815; m. 7 Apr. 1797, Priscilla Batcheller of Sutton. No children.

ABIGAIL, b. 21 Mar. 1770; m. 31 Dec. 1794, Elias Partridge of Franklin. She d. 22 Sept. 1838.

HULDAH, b. 31 Jan. 1773; d. 30 Sept. 1776.

SAMUEL SIBLEY, bp. 21 May 1775; d. 7 Oct. 1777.

1071.   PETER, b. 17 Dec. 1776.
1072.   SAMUEL, b. 28 Oct. 1778.
1073.   LUKE, b. 15 May 1782.

381

SETH[5] CHASE (Dea. Seth,[4] Moses,[3] Ens. Moses[2]), born in Sutton, 8 Jan. 1743/4; died in Randolph, Vt., 18 Mar. 1826. He married (1) about 1760, CATHARINE STAFFORD. He moved to Croydon, N. H., 10 June 1766 and was the first settler of that town. He married (2) MARY KENNEY who died 22 Apr. 1827, aged 83. From Croyden, N. H., the family removed to Bethel, Vt., and thence to West Randolph, Vt. There were fifteen children, only eight of whom have been identified.

Children:

RACHEL,[6] m. (1) Silas Trask; m. (2) William Ford; m. (3) Hope Bradley. Two children by first union; no children by second or third marriage. She d. 1 Jan. 1834.

CALEB, b. 1764; lost in the woods when about six years of age and never found.

1074.   JOSHUA, b. 29 Oct. 1767.
1075.   THOMAS, b. 4 Apr. 1768.
1076.   SETH, b. 27 Aug. 1774.
1077.   CALEB, b. 10 Mar. 1779.

LUCY, b. 1781; m. Apr. 1798, Samuel B. Ryder; d. 17 June 1811.

1078.   TIMOTHY, b. 28 Jan. 1784.

382

JOSIAH[5] CHASE (Dea. Seth,[4] Moses,[3] Ens. Moses[2]), born in Sutton, 20 Feb. 1747/8; died in Cherry Valley, N. Y., 2 Aug. 1813, aged 65. He married (1) in 1770, SARAH ALLEN, daughter of Elijah Allen of Sutton. She died in Sutton, 28 Dec. 1770, aged about 21. He married (2) in Grafton, 28 May 1772, HANNAH GODDARD, daughter of Benjamin and Mary (Kidder) Goddard, born in Grafton, 25 Aug. 1749; died in Worcester, N. Y., 5 Dec. 1801. He married (3) SARAH (SHAW) BODWELL who died 23 Mar. 1849, aged 90y. 7m.

They lived in Sutton till 1784, in Princeton 1785-1790 and removed to Worcester (now Maryland), Otsego Co., N. Y., in 1791.

Children, first six born in Sutton, seventh to ninth in Princeton:

SARAH,[6] b. 22 Mar. 1773; m. 30 Aug. 1823, Daniel Seaver.

1079.   ASA, b. 21 Jan. 1775.
1080.   JOSIAH, b. 30 Jan. 1777.
1081.   JOHN, b. 3 June 1779.
1082.   SETH, b. 1 Apr. 1781.
1083.   BENJAMIN, b. 30 May 1783 or 1784.

HANNAH, b. 9 Aug. 1785; m. Thomas Manly Barrett of Concord, N. Y.

1084.   REUBEN, b. 19 Jan. 1788.
       REBECCA, b. 19 June 1790; m. 7 July 1811, Philor Benedict.
       POLLY, b. 18 Mar. 1793; m. 12 Dec. 1813, Barnabas Fuller.
       BETSEY, b. 29 Dec. 1795; m. John Moore of Worcester, N. Y.

383

EPHRAIM[5] CHASE (Humphrey,[4] Moses,[3] Ens. Moses[2]), born in Haverhill, 20 Jan. 1757; died there, 5 Apr. 1836, aged 79. He married (int. 1 Oct. 1790), ABIGAIL SMITH of Plaistow, N. H. She died in Haverhill as his widow, 30 Apr. 1842, aged 75. They lived in Haverhill and were buried in the Walnut Cemetery.

    Children, born in Haverhill:

       ELISABETH,[6] b. 14 Aug. 1791; d. 14 Jan. 1792.
       HUMPHREY, b. 11 Feb. 1793; d. unm. 3 Sept. 1865, 72y.
       ELISABETH, b. 19 Apr. 1795; d. unm. 6 Nov. 1873, aged 78y. 6m.
1085.   AARON, b. 13 Mar. 1804.
       MOSES, b. 20 Sept. 1806; d. unm. 21 Dec. 1830, aged 24y.
1086.   EPHRAIM, b. 7 July 1809.
       SMITH, d. young.

384

MOSES[5] CHASE (Humphrey,[4] Moses,[3] Ens. Moses[2]), born in Haverhill, 1762; died about 1837. He married about 1783, SARAH FLANDERS of Plaistow, N. H. She died 16 Oct. 1831. They lived in Plaistow.

    Children, born in Plaistow:

       JAMES,[6] b. 15 Nov. 1784; unm.
       DANIEL, b. 26 May 1786; unm.; was drowned at the capture of
         the U. S. Ship "Essex," 28 Mar. 1814.
1087.   MOSES, b. 16 Oct. 1789.
       ABIGAIL, b. 26 Mar. 1793; d. young.
1088.   JOSEPH, b. 26 Nov. 1795.
       ANNA, b. 16 Feb. 1800; d. young.
       POLLY WHITE, b. 21 Mar. 1802; d. young.
       ELISABETH, b. 1806/7; m. Hezekiah Kelley of Haverhill. They
         lived in Haverhill. No children.

385

DANIEL[5] CHASE (Humphrey,[4] Moses,[3] Ens. Moses[2]), born in Haverhill, 7 Oct. 1764; died in Londonderry, N. H., 18 Feb. 1845. He married in Plaistow, N. H., 31 Oct. 1793, SARAH BARTLETT of Plaistow, who was born in Plaistow, 22 May 1773 and died in Londonderry, 3 Apr. 1840, aged 68. They lived in Haverhill and Londonderry.

    Children:

       ABIGAIL,[6] b. 5 Apr. 1795; m. about 1820, Joseph Eaton of Lon-
         donderry; d. Nov. 1871.
1089.   DANIEL, b. 14 Nov. 1797.
       SARAH, b. 5 Apr. 1807; m. Oct. 1831, George Wood of Auburn,
         N. H.; d. 26 Nov. 1874.
1090.   ISAAC, b. 21 Aug. 1809.
       MARY W., b. 4 Jan. 1813; d. unm. 6 Sept. 1891, a. 78y. 8m.

386

JOSHUA[5] CHASE (Eleazer,[4] Moses,[3] Ens. Moses[2]), born and baptized in Windham, Me., 25 Feb. 1754, N. S. No Joshua Chase listed as head of a family in Maine in 1790.

387

ISAAC[5] CHASE (Eleazer,[4] Moses,[3] Ens. Moses[2]), born in Windham, Me., 13 Dec. 1757; died in Standish, Me. He was a Revolutionary soldier from Gorham, Me., in 1779 and was granted a pension, 24 Dec. 1833, at the age of 77. He married in Gorham, 13 Sept. 1783, LOIS SMITH. His intention describes him as of Pearsontown (now Standish). He was a pensioner living with his son Isaac in Standish, 1 June 1840, aged 82 years.

Children, born in Standish, Me.:

1091.   GIDEON,[6] b. 16 May 1784.
1092.   ELEAZER, b. 27 May 1786.
        ABIGAIL, b. 1 Dec. 1788; d. unm.; lived more than 80 years.
1093.   ISAAC, b. 20 Mar. 1791.
1094.   DAVID, b. 15 Apr. 1793.
        JANE, b. 28 Oct. 1795; m. Eben Harmon.
        MARY F., b. 18 Nov. 1797; m. Thomas Eames. No children.
        JAMES, b. 20 Feb. 1800; unm.
        ZENAS S., b. 15 Aug. 1802; d. unm. 25 Nov. 1829.

388

REV. NATHANIEL[5] CHASE (Eleazer,[4] Moses,[3] Ens. Moses[2]), born in Windham, Me., 2 Sept. 1761; died in Buckfield, Me., 20 Apr. 1853. He married (1) 28 Sept. 1783, RHODA ELLIOTT of Windham. She died in Buckfield, 22 Apr. 1789. He married (2) in Turner, Me., 3 Sept. 1791, JEMIMA HASKELL of New Gloucester, Me., who died in Buckfield, 14 Dec. 1831, aged 61. He married (3) 20 Feb. 1833, JOANNA (BERRY) BRIGGS, daughter of Dea. William and Joanna (Doane) Berry, born in Buckfield, 11 Mar. 1781; died 27 Dec. 1864. He was a pioneer settler of Buckfield in 1781. He was ordained as a Baptist minister in 1800, and preached in Buckfield, Harrison, Woodstock and Paris, Me.

Children by first wife, born in Buckfield:

        TWINS,[6] d. young.
1095.   DANIEL BOND, b. 18 Mar. 1785.
        DOLLY, b. 12 Mar. 1787; m. 1807, William Tuttle.
        JAIBEL, d. in infancy.

Children by second wife, born in Buckfield:

        MERCY, b. 4 Sept. 1792; m. 1818, William Walker of Peru, Me.
        BETSEY, b. 2 Jan. 1794; m. 1815, Adam Knight of Peru.
        EUNICE, b. 30 Mar. 1796; m. 1822, Isaac[6] Chase of Turner. (Family 1093).
        PRISCILLA, b. 4 May 1798; m. 1823, John Ellis of Canton, Me.
1096.   NATHANIEL, b. 29 June 1800.
        SALOME, b. 13 Apr. 1802; d. 15 Jan. 1806.
        MIRIAM, b. 1 Apr. 1804; m. 1831, Nathan Merrill.
1097.   JOB, b. 29 June 1806.

1098. THOMAS, b. 6 June 1808.
1099. WILLIAM, b. 25 Jan. 1811.
1100. ISAAC, b. 6 Apr. 1815.

389

JOSEPH[5] CHASE (Eleazer,[4] Moses,[3] Ens. Moses[2]), born in Windham, Me., Oct. 1766; died in Buckfield, Me., in 1814, aged 45. He married (1) in Windham, 3 Jan. 1790, HANNAH ELLIOTT of Windham, who died in Buckfield, in 1795. He married (2) in Turner, Me., 16 Sept. 1795, ANNA LEGROW. He removed from Windham to Buckfield in 1782 and lived there until his death. At the time of his first marriage he was described as of Buxton.

Children by first wife, born in Buckfield:

> RHODA,[6] b. 8 Nov. 1790; m. 16 July 1815, Barnard Pompelly of Turner, Me. and Amelia, Ohio. She d. 15 Feb. 1861.
> HANNAH, b. 20 Mar. 1795; m. Daniel Tuttle Jr. of Turner. She d. in Buckfield, 1851. Eleven children.

Children by second wife, born in Buckfield:

1101. JOSEPH, b. 30 Mar. 1797.
1102. ELEAZER, b. 12 Aug. 1798.
> MARY, b. 11 Aug. 1800; m. Amos Shaw. She d. 25 Nov. 1883. Four children.
> NANCY, b. 20 Sept. 1802; m. Alvah Gilbert of Buckfield. Two children.

390

LEONARD[5] CHASE (Daniel,[4] Moses,[3] Ens. Moses[2]), born in Newbury (now West Newbury), 19 Dec. 1749. He married in Haverhill, 24 Nov. 1772, MARY COLBY, daughter of Theophilus and Elizabeth (Hastings) Colby. She was born in Haverhill, 28 Apr. 1752. Her mother made a will, 11 June 1800, in which she mentions her daughter Mary Chase and her grandson Theophilus[6] Chase. They lived in Haverhill and Derry, N. H.

Children, born in Haverhill:

1103. THEOPHILUS,[6] b. 20 Aug. 1773.
1104. DANIEL, b. 25 June 1777.
> MOLLY, b. 21 May 1782.
1105. JACOB, b. about 1787.
1106. JOHN, b. 5 May 1793.

391

SOMERBY[5] CHASE (Daniel,[4] Moses,[3] Ens. Moses[2]), born in Newbury (now West Newbury), 6 Aug. 1751; died in Newburyport, 12 Mar. 1801. He married (1) about 1775, SARAH ———, who died in Newburyport, 10 Nov. 1791, aged 41. He married (2) in Newburyport, 13 June 1793, ABIGAIL TITCOMB, daughter of Joseph and Hannah Titcomb, born in Newburyport, 22 Feb. 1768; died there, 16 Mar. 1836, aged 67.

Children by first wife, born in Newburyport:

> SARAH,[6] bp. 18 Feb. 1776; d. Aug. 1777, aged 18m.
1107. WILLIAM, b. 14 Nov. 1777.

HANNAH, bp. 20 Dec. 1778; m. 10 June 1799, William Howe.
SARAH, bp. 13 Feb. 1780; m. 30 Jan. 1801, Jabez Carr.
PAUL, bp. 25 Feb. 1781; d. at sea on a voyage to Havana, Aug. 1799, aged 18y.
DAVID, bp. 25 Aug. 1782; d. — Nov. 1783.
1109.   TIMOTHY PALMER, b. 19 Apr. 1784.
ELIZABETH, bp. 26 Aug. 1787.
MARGARET, b. —— 1790; alive 25 Sept. 1804.

Children by second wife, born in Newburyport:

1110.   DANIEL, b. 10 Oct. 1793.
1111.   JOSEPH TITCOMB, b. 4 Mar. 1795.

392

COL. SAMUEL[5] CHASE (Dea. Francis,[4] Samuel,[3] Ens. Moses[2]), born in Amesbury, 23 Oct. 1739; died in Litchfield, N. H., 17 May 1816.   He married — Nov. 1760, MARY STEWART, daughter of Robert and Ann (Adams) Stewart, born in Kingston, N. H., 11 Mar. 1739; died in Litchfield, 27 Apr. 1816.   He was an officer in the Revolutionary Army.   They lived in Litchfield.   Administration on his estate was granted to Joseph Chase Jr. of Litchfield, 1 July 1817 who stated that Samuel left no widow but several children.   (Hillsborough Co. Probate, 19:407).

Children, born in Litchfield:

1112.   SAMUEL,[6] b. 17 Nov. 1761.
1113.   EBENEZER, b. 22 Feb. 1764.
1114.   DANIEL, b. 26 July 1766.
1115.   ROBERT, b. 3 Dec. 1768.
POLLY, b. 13 Mar. 1771; d. 5 Aug. 1775.
FRANCIS, b. 18 May 1773; d. 2 Aug. 1775.
1116.   FRANCIS, b. 30 Sept. 1775.
POLLY, b. 9 Nov. 1777; m. James Lund of Litchfield.
1117.   SIMEON, b. 12 Feb. 1780.
CHILD, b. 24 May 1782; d. 2 June 1782.
ANNA, b. 4 Dec. 1783; m. 12 Apr. 1808, Joseph[6] Chase. (1127).

393

LT. AMOS[5] CHASE (Dea. Francis,[4] Samuel,[3] Ens. Moses[2]), born in Amesbury, 6 July 1741; died as the result of falling from a building, 15 May 1815.   He married 21 Oct. 1762, HANNAH CARLETON who was born in Plaistow, N. H., 21 June 1743 and died 26 Aug. 1824   They lived in Litchfield, N. H., and moved to Unity, N. H., 5 Dec. 1771.

Children, first four born in Litchfield and last nine born in Unity:

SUSANNAH,[6] b. 18 Oct. 1763; m. 29 Mar. 1781, Capt. John Huntoon. She d. 20 Sept. 1856.
SARAH, b. 17 July 1765; m. Ephraim Cram, a farmer. She d. 6 May 1854.
PHEBE, b. 28 Feb. 1767; m. 25 Jan. 1785, Daniel Batchelder.
HANNAH, b. 17 June 1769; m. 29 Nov. 1799, Jacob Perkins, son of Joseph and Anna Perkins. She d. 27 Sept. 1831.
1118.   AMOS, b. 23 Mar. 1772.
1119.   JONATHAN CARLETON, b. 22 Feb. 1774.

MOLLY, b. 29 Jan. 1776; d. 22 Dec. 1776.

MARY, b. 21 Nov. 1777; m. Apr. 1797, Jacob Bartlett; d. 7 Dec. 1865. (Family 1164)

1120.   FRANCIS PIKE, b. 12 June 1780.

ELISABETH, b. 24 July 1782; m. Nathan Glidden. She d. in Marlow, N. H., 12 Apr. 1867.

1121.   SIMEON BARTLETT, b. 7 Apr. 1784.

RUTH, b. 5 Aug. 1786; m. 17 Dec. 1809, John Moody. She d. 31 July 1839.

JOSEPH A., b. 18 July 1788; d. 30 Oct. 1869, in Wisconsin; m. 22 Dec. 1852,, Cynthia Jones. No children.

394

FRANCIS[5] CHASE (Dea. Francis,[4] Samuel,[3] Ens. Moses[2]), born in Amesbury, 15 July 1743; died in Newton, N. H., 25 Sept. 1825, aged 82.   He married about 1769, SARAH HUBBARD of Kingston, N. H., who was born, 27 Feb. 1751, and died, 20 Oct. 1843, aged 93. They lived in Newton.   They were published, 23 Nov. 1769.

Children, born in Newton:

ABIGAIL,[6] b. 3 Nov. 1770; m. 1790, Joseph Bartlett of Newton.

JAMES, b. 7 Nov. 1772; d. 2 Sept. 1776,, 3 years old.

1122.   JAMES, b. 24 Aug. 1777.

1123.   RICHARD, b. 27 Nov. 1780.

1124.   FRANCIS, b. 15 Oct. 1784.

MARY, b. 18 Oct. 1788; m. 1 Nov. 1808, Caleb Peaslee.

SARAH (twin), b. 18 Oct. 1788; d. 28 Feb. 1814, of spotted fever.

395

JOSEPH[5] CHASE (Dea. Francis,[4] Samuel,[3] Ens. Moses[2]), born in Amesbury, 25 Feb. 1744/45; died in Litchfield, N. H., 13 June 1829.   He married, 14 Feb. 1767, ELIZABETH DARRAH (DARROW). She was born 13 Apr. 1745 and died 27 Feb. 1837.   They lived in Litchfield.   He made his will 29 Mar. 1823; proved 5 Dec. 1832, mentioning wife Elizabeth, sons Joseph, Francis, John and Robert and daughters Jane Kidder, Elizabeth Bixby, Sally Hills, Polly Dodge and Dolly Gage.   (Hillsborough Probate, 39:466).

Children, six younger children born in Litchfield:

1125.   FRANCIS,[6] b. 27 Feb. 1768.

JANE, b. 25 Mar. 1769; m. 25 Nov. 1790, Sampson Kidder; d. 7 Oct. 1840.

JOSEPH, b. 11 May 1770; d. 3 Sept. 1778.

1126.   JOHN, b. 24 Nov. 1771.

ROBERT, b. 14 Sept. 1773; d. 20 Nov. 1777.

JAMES, b. 3 Apr. 1775; d. 26 Aug. 1778.

ABNER, b. 26 Sept. 1776; d. 21 May 1802, drowned in Saco River, Me.

ELISABETH, b. 20 Aug. 1778; m. (1) Hugh Nabor; m. (2) William Bixby.

1127.   JOSEPH, b. 17 May 1780.

SARAH, b. 27 Nov. 1781; m. 1810, Moody Hills.

POLLY, b. 18 June 1783; m. ——— Dodge.

1128.   ROBERT, b. 24 Apr. 1785.

DOROTHY, b. 14 May 1787; m. 6 Jan. 1807; Solomon Gage of
Bedford, N. H.
JAMES, b. 9 Dec. 1788; d. 5 Apr. 1804.

396

DEA. ABNER[5] CHASE (Dea. Francis,[4] Samuel,[3] Ens. Moses[2]),
born in Amesbury, 19 Nov. 1746; died in Unity, N. H., 6 Mar. 1838,
aged 91y. 3m. 19d. He married 16 Oct. 1771, JOANNA MOODY who
was born in Exeter, N. H., 21 Oct. 1752; died in Unity, 22 Mar. 1806.
He was deacon of the Baptist Church of Unity, where he resided; a
farmer and hotel keeper.
Children, born in Unity:

FRANCIS,[6] b. 2 July 1772; m. 1 Dec. 1793, Eunice Glidden, b. 3
Mar. 1776. She d. 13 Apr. 1863, without issue. He d. 6 Nov.
1850.
SALLY, b. 3 Mar. 1774; m. 4 Sept. 1794, Daniel Bingham. Six
children; she d. 10 Aug. 1861. (Family 1131)
JOSIAH, b. 24 Jan. 1778; d. 2 Mar. 1778.
MELINDA, b. 20 Nov. 1779; m. 19 Nov. 1801, Aaron Sleeper of
Unity. She d. 15 Apr. 1856; six children.
JOANNA. b. 1 Mar. 1782; m. Jeremiah Glidden. She d. in Pan-
ama, N. Y.,, about 1860. Seven children.
1129. ABNER, b. 16 July 1787.

397

SIMEON[5] CHASE (Dea. Francis,[4] Samuel,[3] Ens. Moses[2]), born
(perhaps in Newton, N. H.), 26 Aug. 1748; died in Litchfield, N. H.,
21 July 1832. He married (1) 1 Dec. 1774, DOROTHY PARKER,
daughter of Dea. —— Parker of Litchfield. She was born 1 Dec.
1752 and died in Litchfield, 3 Dec. 1779. He married (2) 16 Feb.
1786, MARY BARTLETT of Newton, N. H. She was born 12 Jan.
1759 and died 11 Apr. 1803. He married (3) 31 Dec. 1807, HAN-
NAH LUND of Merrimac who was born 3 Feb. 1767, and died 19 Oct.
1815. He received from his father a deed of land and one third of a
sawmill and gristmill in Litchfield, 28 Oct. 1774 and lived in that
town.
Children by first wife, born in Litchfield:

DOROTHY,[6] b. 8 Sept. 1775; d. 29 Aug. 1778.
SIMEON, b. 18 Mar. 1777; d. 1 Sept. 1778.

Children by second wife, born in Litchfield:

MARY, b. 28 Nov. 1786; m. 30 Sept. 1806, Simeon Bixby of
Litchfield.
1130. BENJAMIN, b. 20 Nov. 1789.
SIMEON, b. 28 Feb. 1791; d. unm. 10 Aug. 1822, in La. He
was graduated from Yale, 1821. Preceptor in Kingston,
N. H., and New Orleans.
PAINE WINGATE. b. 28 Oct. 1793; d. unm. 8 Nov. 1826, at
Hampton, N. H. Preceptor of Hampton Academy, 1826.
Graduate at Yale, 1821.
1131. MOSES, b. 2 Mar. 1796.
DOROTHY, b. 11 Sept. 1798; m. James Lund Jr.
ELISABETH W., b. 14 Sept. 1801; m. July 1829, Henry A. Mc-
Questen.

398

DANIEL[5] CHASE (Dea. Francis,[4] Samuel,[3] Ens. Moses[2]), born in Newton, N. H., 21 May 1755; died in Newton, 1 Aug. 1803. He married about 1790, HANNAH EATON who died in Newton, 1 Aug. 1804. They lived in Newton.

Children, born in Newton:

1132.   DANIEL,[6] b. 10 Oct. 1792.
ABIGAIL, b. 22 Dec. 1793; m. (1) Dec. 1813, James Peaslee Esq. of Newton; m. (2) Apr. 1830, Johnson Tucker of Amesbury.
SARAH OR LETTA, b. 24 May 1795.
HANNAH, b. 4 Mar. 1797; d. 18 June 1819, aged 22y.
BETTY, b. 8 Oct. 1798; m. Daniel Hoyt of Haverhill.
POLLY, b. 24 Sept. 1800.
1133.   MOSES, b. 13 Feb. 1803.

399

MOSES[5] CHASE (Dea. Francis,[4] Samuel,[3] Ens. Moses[2]), born in Newton, N. H., 2 Mar. 1763; died in Plaistow, N. H., 5 Nov. 1819. He married 17 Apr. 1788, MARY NOYES, daughter of Stephen and Betsey[4] (Chase) Noyes. She was born 23 Mar. 1767; died in West Newbury, 15 Feb. 1853, aged 85y. 10m. She lived in West Newbury in 1847. They lived in Plaistow, and kept a public house there for many years. (Family 26).

Children, born in Plaistow:

1134.   STEPHEN,[6] b. 16 Nov. 1790.
BETSEY, b. 22 Feb. 1794; m. 31 Dec. 1818, True Kimball of Plaistow.
THOMAS NOYES, b. 27 Jan. 1796; m. (1) 27 Apr. 1827, Harriet Dustin, b. 1 Mar. 1802; d .27 Dec. 1841; m. (2) 10 Dec. 1846, Martha L. Webster, b. 21 July 1816. No children.
MARY, b. 19 Feb. 1801; m. 25 Feb. 1829, John Kelley of Atkinson, N. H. She d. 7 Feb. 1869.
SAMUEL SEWALL, b. 25 Oct. 1803; d. 4 Feb. 1805.
1135.   SAMUEL SEWALL, b. 17 Feb. 1805.
WILLIAM NEWTON, b. 13 Feb. 1811; d. 7 Mar. 1815.

400

SAMUEL[5] CHASE (Dea. Amos,[4] Samuel,[3] Ens. Moses[2]), born in Newbury, 25 Mar. 1742; died in Saco, Me., 24 May 1810. He married in Biddeford, 10 May 1764, HANNAH WINGATE who was appointed administratrix of her husband's estate, 12 May 1811. She was daughter of Simon and Lydia (Hill) Wingate.

The division of his estate mentions the following heirs: Sons Samuel and Benjamin Chase to pay Rebecca Warner a daughter; Elisha Hight [Hoyt] and Lydia his wife a daughter; William S. Johnson and Adah his wife a daughter; Donald Cummings in right of his wife Susanna a daughter; Amos Chase deceased a son; Daniel Smith in right of Sally his wife a daughter; William Chase a son; Julian Chase a representative of the late Simon Chase a son. The division was signed by Elisha Hight, William Chase, Daniel Smith, William Waterhouse, Donald Cummings,

Rebecca Warner, William S. Johnson and Seth Storer Jr. guardian of Julian Chase, 30 Oct. 1811. (York Co. Probate, 23:313.)

The family lived in Saco, Me.

Children, born in Saco:

1135a. AMOS,[6] b. 12 Mar. 1765; d. 5 June 1794.
1136. SAMUEL, b. 14 July 1766; alive 30 Oct. 1811.
   SUSANNA, b. 12 Mar. 1768; m. 23 Feb. 1786, Donald Cummings.
1137. SIMON WINGATE, b. 18 Dec. 1769.
   LYDIA, b. 26 Aug. 1771; m. 6 July 1788, Elisha Hight [Hoyt].
1138. BENJAMIN, b. 3 May 1773.
1139. WILLIAM, b. 2 Oct. 1775.
   REBECCA, b. 29 May 1777; m. 1800, Philemon Warner; alive 30 Oct. 1811.
   SARAH, b. 28 Feb. 1782; m. 1811, Daniel Smith.
   HANNAH, b. 31 Jan. 1784; d. 11 May 1790.
   ADAH, b. 30 Apr. 1788; m. 30 Nov. 1808, William S. Johnson of Saco.

401

DEA. AMOS[5] CHASE (Dea. Amos,[4] Samuel,[3] Ens. Moses[2]), born in Saco, Me., 25 Nov. 1752; married (1) in Buxton, Me., 28 Apr. 1774, EMMA ELDEN, daughter of Capt. John and Ruth (Sands) Elden of Buxton. She was born in Biddeford, Me., 9 July 1756. They lived in Limington, Me., in 1773 and Standish, Me., later. One of the founders of the Congregational Church in Limington, 11 Oct. 1789 and deacon from 1795 to 1805. With forty others he joined the Baptist Church. He died in South Limington. He and his wife Emma were admitted to the Church in Buxton, 16 June 1776. He married (2) OLIVE ———— who died in Limington, Me., 31 Mar. 1825. He died there 22 Mar. 1825. He was the first settler in Limington in 1773, settling at Chase's Mills.

Children, born in Limington, Me.:

1140. JOHN ELDEN,[6] b. 31 Aug. 1775.
   ABNER, d. young.
1141. AMOS, bp. 25 May 1777.
1142. ABNER, b. 12 Nov. 1784.
   EMMA ELDEN, b. July 1787; m. 17 Oct. 1804, James E. Libby.
   DEBORAH, b. 10 May 1789; m. 3 Mar. 1808, Josiah[6] Chase of Berwick, Me. (Family 515).
1143. OLIVER SAWYER, b. 16 Sept. 1792.
1144. MOSES, b. 14 Apr. 1796.

402

JOSEPH[5] CHASE (Dea. Amos,[4] Samuel,[3] Ens. Moses[2]), born in Saco, Me., 10 Oct. 1754; died in Bangor, Me., 1797. He married in Buxton, Me., 5 Sept. 1776, OLIVE WOODMAN, daughter of Nathan and Olive (Gray) Woodman of Newbury and Buxton. She was baptized in Newbury, 1 Feb. 1756, and married (2) JOSIAH BLACK of Limington, Me. She died in Limington, Apr. 1841. They lived in Standish, Me. He and his wife Olive were received into the Buxton Church, 28 Dec. 1777. They early lived in Little Ossipee (now Limington), Me. Some of their children were baptized in Scarborough, Me.

Children, born in Standish:

MARY,[6] b. Apr. 1777; bp. at Buxton, 28 Dec. 1777; m. 1795, Benjamin Small of Limington; d. Nov. 1861.

DANIEL, b. June 1779; d. unm. at sea.

1145. AMOS, b. — Jan. 1781.

1146. NATHAN W., b. Aug. 1783.

OLIVE G., b. 27 Apr. 1786; m. Jan. 1802, Abner Libby of Limington; d. 30 Jan. 1851, in Limerick, Me.

1147. JOSEPH, b. 23 Dec. 1788.

1148. JOHN, b. 25 May 1790.

SARAH C., b. 31 Aug. 1793; m. 6 Aug. 1812, Stephen Libby of Limington.

403

JOHN[5] CHASE (Dea. Amos,[4] Samuel,[3] Ens. Moses[2]), born in Saco, Me., 18 Dec. 1757; died there, 5 Nov. 1833, aged 76. His widow died in Saco, 18 Jan. 1835. He made his will, 29 May 1828, which was proved 3 Mar. 1834. Therein he mentions his wife Jerusha; his brother Abner Chase; Amos Chase, son of his brother Daniel Chase deceased; his kinswoman Abigail Smith, wife of Joseph Smith; his niece Martha Jones; John Chase Jordan; his brother Abner Chase to be executor. (York Co. Probate, 44:15). It is apparent that there were no surviving children. They lived in Saco. He married in Saco, 9 Dec. 1779, JERUSHA TARBOX of Biddeford.

404

DANIEL[5] CHASE (Dea. Amos,[4] Samuel,[3] Ens. Moses[2]), born in Saco, Me., 28 Aug. 1762; died in Saco, Me., 1 Sept. 1827. He married, 18 Dec. 1788, ELIZABETH TAPPAN, daughter of Rev. Benjamin and Elizabeth (Marsh) Tappan, born in Manchester, 22 June 1764. (Tappan Genealogy, 24). The inventory of his estate was taken, 20 June 1828, (York Co. Probate, 39:171) and Amos Chase was appointed administrator. His widow died in Saco, 26 June 1834, aged 71.

Children, born in Saco:

1149. BENJAMIN TAPPAN,[6] b. 10 June 1791.

SARAH, b. 6 May 1793.

1150. DANIEL, b. 3 Oct. 1795.

1151. AMOS, b. 14 Jan. 1799.

1152. DAVID TAPPAN, b. 13 Feb. 1802.

ELIZABETH, b. 13 Oct. 1804.

MARY, b. 23 Jan. 1812.

405

ABNER[5] CHASE (Dea. Amos,[4] Samuel,[3] Ens. Moses[2]), born in Saco, Me., 9 Apr. 1768; baptized 10 Apr. 1768. Abner Chase of Little Falls (now Limington) Me. and widow Elizabeth (Hight) Chase of Pepperellborough (now Saco), were married in Saco, 15 Jan. 1798. She was the widow of Amos[6] Chase (1135a) and daughter of George and Eunice (Hill) Hoyt [Hight] of Berwick, Me., born about 1768 (Hoyt Genealogy). They lived in Limington, Me. He made his will, 14 June 1838, which was proved, 4 Oct. 1847. He mentions therein his wife Betsey, his son Amos Hill Chase to have the southerly part of his homestead and his son James Madison Chase the northerly part of the same; his daughters Sally Goodwin, Polly Parker and Lydia Ann Stockin each to have $50; his sons above-named each to have three twenty-fourths of his saw-mill, (York Co. Probate, 60:321).

Children, born in Limington:

SARAH COLE,[6] b. 25 Aug. 1798; m. John Goodwin; d. 11 July 1840.

MARY, b. 1803; entered her intention at Standish, Me., 8 Sept. 1823, with Joshua Parker; d. 1868.

LYDIA ANN, m. ———— Stocking; alive 14 June 1838.

HARRIET, d. unm. before 14 June 1838.

1153. AMOS HILL, alive 14 June 1838.

1154. JAMES MADISON, alive same day.

406

ROBERT[5] CHASE (Samuel,[4] Samuel,[3] Ens. Moses[2]), born in Newbury (now West Newbury) 10 Apr. 1757; froze to death on his own mill pond in Hampstead, N. H., in 1827. He married in Methuen, 7 Dec. 1780, LYDIA BODWELL, daughter of Daniel and Abigail (Ladd) Bodwell, born in Methuen, 15 Mar. 1757. They lived in Sandown, N. H., till 1795, then moved to Hampstead. They joined the church in Hampstead by letter from Sandown, 1 May 1801. His widow died about 1832.

Robert was a soldier at Bennington and on Long Island in the Revolution.

Children, first three born in Sandown, others in Hampstead:

MOLLY,[6] b. 21 Nov. 1782; m. Samuel Plummer; she d. at 35.

RUTH, b. 2 Nov. 1786; d. unm. age 35 .

1155. ROBERT, b. 24 Mar. 1794.

1156. DANIEL BODWELL, b. 6 Aug. 1795.

ALPHEUS, b. 28 May 1798; d. unm. aged 30.

407

BENJAMIN[5] CHASE (Samuel,[4] Samuel,[3] Ens. Moses[2]), baptized in Newbury (now West Newbury) 15 July 1759; died in Sandown, N. H., 31 Dec. 1826. He married (intention at Newbury, 17 Oct. 1781), ALICE BARTLETT, daughter of Daniel and Sarah (Tewksbury) Bartlett, born in Newbury, 19 Sept. 1761; died about 1849. He was a Revolutionary War pensioner in 1818, aged 59.

They lived in Sandown. Alice Chase of Haverhill represents that Benjamin Chase, late of Sandown, was a Revolutionary pensioner and that he died, 31 Dec. 1826; that she is his widow and prays that the probate court will establish her claim, 11 Oct. 1838. Samuel Chase of Haverhill made oath to the truth of her statements. (Essex Probate, 5098).

Children, born in Sandown:

SARAH,[6] m. Samuel Sawyer of Portsmouth, N. H.

ABIGAIL, m. in Portsmouth, 17 Jan. 1824, Nathan Godfrey.

ALICE, b. 15 Feb. 1786; m. J——— Walker.

1157.   SAMUEL, b. 7 Feb. 1788.
       MARY, d. unm.
       NANCY, m. (1) Jeremiah Poor; m. (2) Thomas B. Parsons.
1158.   BENJAMIN, b. 4 June 1794.
       RHODA, d. unm.

408

DEA. AMOS[5] CHASE (Samuel,[4] Samuel,[3] Ens. Moses[2]), born in Newbury (now West Newbury) 15 May 1770; died in Haverhill, 22 Feb. 1852. He married in Newbury, 24 Sept. 1794, JUDITH LITTLE, daughter of Joseph and Mary (Johnson) Little, born in Newbury (now West Newbury), 19 June 1776; died 14 Sept. 1860, aged 84. They lived in Haverhill where he was a shoe manufacturer.

Children, born in Haverhill except the first born in Newbury:

       MARY LITTLE,[6] b. 14 Oct. 1795; m. 2 June 1817, Paul Dole; nine children; she d. 11 Oct. 1830.
1159.   WILLIAM, b. 6 Apr. 1797.
       ELISABETH BARTLETT, b. 3 Jan. 1799; m. Dec. 1820, Joshua Webster of Malden.
1160.   AMOS, b. 18 June 1803.
1161.   HEZEKIAH SMITH, b. 7 Aug. 1805.
       SALOME, b. 23 Apr. 1807; m. (1) 2 Dec. 1830, Noyes Griffin Pearson; m. (2) Sept. 1841, Philip Moppen Schuyler of Boonville, N. Y.
       SAMUEL, b. 8 Apr. 1809; d. 17 Feb. 1830; one of the founders of Baptist Church of Dover, N. H.
       ANNA BRADLEY, b. 19 Apr. 1811; m. 27 Nov. 1834, James Spear Loring of Boston. She d. 27 Oct. 1872.
       EMILY, b. 15 Apr. 1816; d. unm. 11 Aug. 1836.
       BENJAMIN LITTLE, b. 23 Jan. 1821; m. 6 Dec. 1860, Lavina Cram; no children. He was for over 30 years a book seller in Boston.

409

SAMUEL[5] CHASE (Benjamin,[4] Samuel,[3] Ens. Moses[2]), born 31 Mar. 1774; married 20 Dec. 1804, MARY STANWOOD, daughter of William and Mary (Orr) Stanwood, born in Brunswick, Me., 13 June 1781. They lived in Brunswick, Me. He died in Brunswick, 24 Mar. 1830.

Children, born in Brunswick:

       CATHARINE CAMPBELL,[6] b. 13 Oct. 1805; m. 24 Oct. 1832, Capt. William Woodside; living in Brunswick in 1872.
       DANIEL, b. 9 May 1807; d. 26 Jan. 1845, in Portland, Me.
       WILLIAM HENRY, b. 22 Dec. 1808; d. 3 Oct. 1828, at sea.
       MARY ELISABETH, b. 8 Mar. 1811; lived in Brunswick.
       HANNAH MARIA, b. 11 Dec. 1812; m. 10 Feb. 1840, Jacob Pennell of Brunswick.
       JULIA, b. 29 Aug. 1815; m. 17 Dec. 1835, James Pennell of Brunswick.
       SUSAN ORR, b. 12 Jan. 1818.
       ELEANOR STUART, b. 1 Jan. 1826; m. 4 Jan. 1847, Charles Starbird; lived in Boston.

410

MOSES[5] CHASE (John,[4] Samuel,[3] Ens. Moses[2]), born in Hampstead, N. H., 14 Nov. 1764 and baptized there; died in Concord, Vt., 21 Dec. 1856, aged 92. He married 1 Oct 1788, EUNICE MORSE, daughter of Joseph and Jemima (Wheat) Morse, born in Athol, 20 May 1772; died in Concord, 12 Oct. 1835, aged 63. They lived in Lisbon, N. H., and settled in Concord, Vt., before 2 Mar. 1795. They were charter members of the Freewill Baptist Church organized in Concord, 10 Oct. 1821.

Children, two eldest born in Lisbon, third in St. Johnsbury and others in Concord:

SUSAN,[6] b. 14 Nov. 1790; d. 16 Mar. or Nov. 1828; m. Joshua (Brown ?).

ANNA M., b. 28 Nov. 1791; m. (1) 5 Sept. 1813, Henry Howe, who d. 8 Sept. 1822; m. (2) Jail Harvey; she d. 14 May 1849.

REBECCA, b. 5 June 1794; m. Joshua Brown; d. 21 Aug. 1869, aged 72.

1162.   JOSEPH, b. 20 Nov. 1796.

LUCRETIA, b. 9 Aug. 1798; m. (1) Silas Harvey; m. (2) Richard Goss; she d. 20 Aug. 1880, aged 82.

PHEBE, b. 27 Aug. 1803; m. William Reed of Concord. She d. without issue, 6 June 1882, aged 79.

1163.   JOHN DENNISON, b. 23 Sept. 1806.

BETSEY HILLS, b. 9 June 1811; m. Isaac Lewis of Waterford, Vt. She d. 18 Dec. 1864.

411

JOHN[5] CHASE (John,[4] Samuel,[3] Ens. Moses[2]), born — Mar. 1766; died in Sunapee, N. H., 2 Apr. 1851. He married in 1792, ELIZABETH ROGERS, daughter of Richard Carr Rogers. She died in Sunapee, N. H., 13 Mar. 1851, aged 80, born in Hopkinton, N. H. They lived in Sunapee. The house he erected there in 1794 was occupied by his daughter Sarah in 1873.

Children, born in Sunapee:

BETSEY,[6] b. 4 June 1795; d. unm. 311 Oct. 1813, aged 19.

1164.   RICHARD CARR ROGERS, b. 19 Dec. 1798.

1165.   HILLS H., b. 2 July 1800.

ABIGAIL, b. 1 June 1802; m. 30 Sept. 1829, Samuel Bailey; d. 20 Jan. 1879.

SARAH, b. 30 Sept. 1803; m. (1) Charles Gage; m. (2) 26 Dec. 1856, Henry Remington; m. (3) William C. Stowe.

ALVAN, b. 14 Aug. 1806; d. 7 June 1834, age 27.

ALMIRA, b. 14 May 1808; m. (1) Alanson Fletcher; m. (2) Joseph Tucker; lived in Blackstone.

FRANCIS, b. May 1810; d. 19 Feb. 1812.

ELISABETH, b. 18 Oct. 1813; m. 1 June 1843, Dennis G. Knowlton of Sunapee. She d. 10 Aug. 1894.

412

JOSEPH[5] CHASE (John,[4] Samuel,[3] Ens. Moses[2]), born in Chester, N. H., 12 Mar. 1768; died in Painesville, Ohio, 3 Dec. 1859, aged 92. He married in Sunapee, N. H., 7 May 1791, RUTH PIKE who was born in New Rowley (Georgetown). They removed from Wendell (now Sunapee) to Painesville, Ohio, about 1822.

Children, born in Wendell:

SARAH,⁶ b. 29 Aug. 1792; m. Abiathar Young; lived in Painesville, Ohio, in 1874.

PHEBE, b. 30 Mar. 1794; m. in 1817, Richmond Clapp.

1166.   JOSEPH PIKE, b. 1 Mar. 1798.

1167.   JOHN LANGDON, b. 7 Feb. 1805.

JAMES SULLIVAN, b. 13 Apr. 1809; d. 24 Aug. 1829.

GEORGE CLINTON, b. 12 June 1812; d. 6 June 1816.

413

ENOCH⁵ CHASE (Henry,⁴ Stephen,³ Ens. Moses²), born in Nottingham West (now Hudson), N. H., 19 Aug. 1769.

414

MOSES⁵ CHASE (Henry,⁴ Stephen,³ Ens. Moses²), born, probably, in Nottingham West (now Hudson) 12 Oct. 1775.

415

STEPHEN⁵ CHASE (Stephen,⁴ Ens. Stephen,³ Ens. Moses²), born
in Nottingham West (now Hudson), N. H., 21 Apr. 1755; married
LUCINDA CARPENTER, daughter of Benjamin and Annie (Carpenter)
Carpenter of Guilford, Vt. She was born 6 Mar. 1751 and married
(2) ———— Wheeler, of Brattleborough, Vt. He died between
12 July and 3 Oct. 1793. In 1790 he was the head of a family
in Guilford consisting of two males over 16 years of age, three males
under 16, and four females. Her father was Lieut. Governor of
Vermont. They lived in Guilford.

Children:

1168.   CYRUS.⁶

ELISABETH, m. (1) Eliakim Jones.

1169.   ASAPH, b. 18 Apr. 1777.

1170.   ALLEN, b. 7 Feb. 1780.

1171.   STEPHEN, b. Guilford, Vt., 28 Sept. 1782.

LUCINDA, m. 5 Sept. 1805, Eliakim Jones, after the death of
her sister Elizabeth.

AMY, b. May 1787; m. Daniel Fowle of Geneva, N. Y.

LYDIA, m. Samuel Jenks.

416

MICAJAH⁵ CHASE (Stephen,⁴ Ens. Stephen,³ Ens. Moses²), born
in Nottingham West (now Hudson), N. H., 28 Aug. 1758; died between 25 May and 29 June 1789. He married about 1785, ELIZA-
BETH BLODGETT. He made his will 25 May 1789, which was proved
29 June 1789. He mentions therein his wife Elizabeth, his son
Amos, and his brother John⁵ Chase was to be the executor. Witnesses Joshua Chase, Isaac Colburn and Isaac Merrill (Hillsborough
Probate 4:97). Ashael Blodgett of Nottingham West was appointed
guardian to his son Amos, under 14, 19 Oct. 1790. (Ibid. 4:351).
They lived in Nottingham West (now Hudson). Elizabeth Chase,
probably his widow, died in Hudson, 10 Nov. 1819, aged 53.

Child, born in Hudson:

1172.   AMOS B.,⁶ b. 19 July 1787.

417

ENS. JOHN⁵ CHASE (Stephen,⁴ Ens. Stephen,³ Ens. Moses²), born in Nottingham West (now Hudson), N. H., 31 Jan. 1761; died in Hudson, 10 Feb. 1837, aged 76.   He married in Nottingham West, 16 Feb. 1786, ELIZABETH GIBSON, daughter of Dea. Barnabas Gibson of Pelham, N. H.   She was born 6 Apr. 1766 and died in Hudson, 10 Nov. 1819, aged 53y.   They lived in Hudson.
Children, born in what is now Hudson:

> PHEBE,⁶ b. 10 May 1786; d. unm. 12 Dec. 1830.
> JOHN, b. 14 Mar. 1789; d. 21 Apr. 1790.
> ELISABETH, b. 6 Dec. 1791; m. 3 Mar. 1829, Jabez Town of Londonderry, N. H.   She d. 8 Sept. 1838; three children.
> SARAH, b. 14 Mar. 1795; m. William Bailey of Nashua, N. H. No children.

1173.   SOLOMON, b. 12 June 1797.
1174.   JOHN, b. 5 Mar. 1801.

418

EZEKIEL⁵ CHASE (Stephen,⁴ Ens. Stephen,³ Ens. Moses²), born in Nottingham West (now Hudson), N. H., 5 May 1768.

419

DANIEL⁵ CHASE (Stephen,⁴ Ens. Stephen,³ Ens. Moses²), born in Nottingham West (now Hudson), N. H., 12 Aug. 1770; died in Hudson, 28 Dec. 1832.   He married ELIZABETH CALDWELL who died in Hudson, 13 Nov. 1854, aged 77.   They lived on Chase's Hill in Hudson.
Children, born in Nottingham West (now Hudson):

1175.   CHANDLER.⁶
> ANNA, lived in Hudson.

420

MOSES⁵ CHASE (Moses,⁴ Stephen,³ Ens. Moses²), born in Nottingham West (now Hudson), N. H., 10 Sept. 1760; died in Alstead, N. H., 8 July 1812.   He married in Wrentham, 26 Nov. 1789, LOIS (WOOD) MANN who was born 6 Sept. 1760 and died in Alstead, 27 Apr. 1812.   They lived in Alstead.   His inventory was taken in Sept. 1813.
Children, born in Alstead:

> HANNAH,⁶ b. 21 Aug. 1790; d. unm. before 1873 in Windhall, Vt.
> THOMAS M., b. 7 July 1792; d. unm. before 1873 in Argyle, N. Y.
> ALVAH, b. 26 Apr. 1794; d. unm. before 1873 in Windhall.

1176.   IRA, b. 19 Sept. 1795.
1177.   AARON, b. 3 May 1797.
1178.   JACOB, b. 17 Feb. 1799.
1179.   JUSTUS, b. 14 Sept. 1801.

421

Joseph[5] Chase (Moses,[4] Stephen,[3] Ens. Moses[2]), born in Nottingham West (now Hudson), N. H., 31 Dec. 1767; died — Nov. 1806.   He married in Pelham, N. H., 4 Nov. 1790, Mary Hardy of Pelham, who died — July 1814.   They lived in Pelham.

Children, born in Pelham:

1180. Benjamin D.,[6] b. 7 Mar. 1791.
1181. Richard, b. 9 May 1793.
        Mary, d. aged 17 years.
        Mary, d. young.
1182. James, b. 31 Dec. 1802.

422

Benjamin Durant[5] Chase (Moses,[4] Stephen,[3] Ens. Moses[2]), born in Nottingham West (now Hudson), N. H., 13 Apr. 1769; married in Haverhill, 3 Nov. 1792, Polly (Buck) Flanders.   It is said that her maiden name was Buck and that she had three husbands all drowned.   Polly Buck married in Haverhill, 8 June 1786, Winthrop Flanders of Salisbury.   He died in Boston, 2 June 1790.   They lived in Merrimack, N. H.

Children:

1183. Benjamin,[6] b. about 1793.
1184. Moses, b. about 1795.
        Nancy, m. Pelatiah Clark; lived on the homestead.
        Samuel B., d. young.
        Sally, d. young.
1185. Andrew, m. ——— Clark.

423

Benjamin[5] Chase (Joshua,[4] Stephen,[3] Ens. Moses[2]), born in Nottingham West (now Hudson), N. H., 17 Aug. 1765; died there, 17 Sept. 1816.   He married 8 Apr. 1788, Dorothy Barker of Pelham, N. H.   She was born 20 Sept. 1764 and died in Hudson, 28 Nov. 1844.   They lived in Nottingham West (now Hudson) and Pelham.   Their tombstones are in the Gumpus Cemetery in Pelham.   Their son Benjamin occupied the homestead in Pelham and the estate was unsettled at the time of his death.   See Benjamin.[6] (1186).

Children, born in Nottingham West (now Hudson):

        David,[6] b. 16 Nov. 1788; d. 5 Apr. 1794.
        Polly, b. 11 July 1790; d. unm. 28 Jan. 1807.
1186. Benjamin, b. 29 Dec. 1791; d. 14 Dec. 1836.
        Dolly, b. 5 Apr. 1793; m. 23 Dec. 1824, Daniel Ordway of
           Pelham.
        Betsey, b. 24 Oct. 1795; d. 19 Sept. 1797.
        Hannah, b. 18 Feb. 1797; m. 16 Oct. 1821, Dea. Jonathan
           Hills Jr. of Litchfield, N. H.
1187. Joshua, b. 5 Sept. 1798.
1188. Moody, b. 19 Mar. 1800.
        Julia, b. 17 Oct. 1801; m. (1) in Pelham, 11 Nov. 1824, David
           A. Marshall of Hudson; m. (2) Ethan Willoughby of Hollis,
           Me.; m. (3) Joseph Parker of Hudson.
        Ebenezer Barker, b. 8 Mar. 1804; d. 17 June 1813.

SARAH, b. 29 Oct. 1805; m. 1 May 1827, Timothy A. Holt of
Mason. N. H.
1189. SOLOMON D., 6 Oct. 1807.
1190. SAMUEL, b. 11 Dec. 1810.
MARY, b. 16 July 1813; m. 22 Oct. 1840, Warren Hills of Hudson.

424

JACOB[5] CHASE (Joshua,[4] Stephen,[3] Ens. Moses[2]), born in Nottingham West (now Hudson), N. H., 30 Nov. 1778; died in Hudson,
31 Dec. 1863, aged 85. He married in Pelham, N. H., 29 Jan. 1807,
REBECCA BARNETT, daughter of John Barnett of Londonderry, N. H.
She was born 9 Aug. 1783, and died in Hudson, 16 Apr. 1881, aged
97y. 8m. 7d. They lived in Hudson.
Children, born in Hudson:

1191. BENJAMIN FRANKLIN,[6] b. 28 Dec. 1807.
CHARLES, b. 11 Nov. 1810; d. unm. 7 Aug. 1832.
MARY T., b. 14 Jan. 1816; m. 5 Apr. 1837, Cummings Gould of
Tyngsborough.
REBECCA T., b. 6 Apr. 1818; m. 17 Oct. 1856, Horace Sprague.
WILLIAM D., b. 31 Mar. 1821; m. June 1850, Sarah Ellen
Clough of N. Y. City. No children.

425

SAMUEL[5] CHASE (Joshua,[4] Stephen,[3] Ens. Moses[2]), born in
Nottingham West (now Hudson). N. H., 15 Mar. 1785; married in
Strafford, Vt., 6 June 1811, ELIZABETH GOVE, daughter of Nathaniel
and Elizabeth (Sanborn) Gove of Deering, N. H., and Strafford, Vt.
She was born in Strafford, Vt., 5 May 1793 and died about 1890. He
was living in Rochester, N. Y., 1873. They lived in Milford, N. H.,
and Rochester, N. Y.
Children, first and second born in Strafford, Vt., youngest born
in Berkskhire, Vt.:

SAMUEL,[6] b. 30 Oct. 1812; d. 20 Nov. 1812.
MIRANDA GOVE, b. 14 Oct. 1813; m. — Nov. 1832, Abijah
Pierce; living in Grand Rapids, Wis., 1873.
LUCINDA, b. 6 Apr. 1816; m. 10 Oct. 1838, Isaac Chenery
Pierce of West Boylston; lived in Rochester, N. Y.

426

STEPHEN[5] CHASE (Jacob,[4] Lt. Joseph,[3] Ens. Moses[2]), born in
Chester, N. H., 27 Mar. 1759; died there 18 Feb. 1919. He married
3 or 28 Jan. 1787, RHODA[6] BLAKE of Hampton, N. H., daughter of
Henry[5] Blake of Hampton, N. H. (Joshua,[4] Philemon,[3] Philemon,[2]
Jasper[1]). She was born in Hampton, N. H., 27 Mar. 1768; died in
Chester, N. H., 16 Aug. 1845. He was a prominent man in the
town, a noted land surveyor and made a remarkably accurate survey
and plan of Chester for Carrigan's map, authorized by the state. He
wrote a very large proportion of the deeds and wills, administered on
many estates, as a Justice heard many cases in litigation and held the
office of selectman for many years. He had much mechanical ability,
making plows, carts and other tools which were in use for many years

after his death. A diary that he kept from 1784 until near his death with its record of births, marriages, deaths and other events was of great service when the History of Old Chester was in preparation. He lived on the farm where his father, Jacob[4] settled.

Children, born in Chester, N. H.:

    SUSANNA,[6] b. 22 Nov. 1787; d. 26 May 1854; m. 28 Mar. 1811, John Sanborn, who d. in Chester (now Auburn), N. H., 1 Dec. 1838, aged 49.

1192. JOSEPH, b. 2 Aug. 1789.

    STEPHEN, b. 23 May 1791; d. unm. 18 May 1819.

    POLLY, b. 9 Oct. 1793; d. 9 Dec. 1807.

1193. JACOB, b. 26 Feb. 1797.

    DOLLY, b. 12 Jan. 1799; m. 6 Nov. 1821, Robert Crawford of Sandown, and d. 31 Dec. 1864.

    RHODA, b. 2 Apr. 1802; m. Nov. 1829, Ira James of Hampton, N. H. She d. 1 Jan. 1844.

    SALLY, b. 9 June 1804; d. 20 Dec. 1804.

    SALLY, b. 30 Oct. 1805; d. 13 Feb. 1848; m. 1 Apr. 1840, Richard Dearborn. No children.

1194. HENRY FRANKLIN, b. 30 Aug. 1808.

427

JOSIAH[5] CHASE (Jacob,[4] Lt. Joseph,[3] Ens. Moses[2]), born in Chester, N. H., 6 Apr. 1767; died in Grantham, N. H., 27 June 1846, aged 79. He married in Chester, 16 Nov. 1791, LYDIA BLAISDELL, daughter of Isaac and Mary (Currier) Blaisdell, born in Chester, 5 July 1773; died in Grantham, N .H., 1 Apr. 1857. They lived in Chester on a farm adjoining that of his brother, Stephen,[5] until 1817, when they removed to Boscawen, N. H., and in 1819 to Grantham.

Children, born in Chester, N. H.:

    MOSES,[6] b. 14 Nov. 1792; m. Sarah Jenney; d. of small pox, June 27, 1854; no children; lived in Grantham.

1195. WILLIAM. b. 21 July 1796.

    MARY, b. 20 June 1798; m. in Boscawen, 27 Dec. 1821, Isaac Rolfe of Lowell.

    PRUDENCE, b. 29 May 1800; d. unm. 18 Sept. 1842.

    ABIGAIL, b. 26 Mar. 1804; m. in Grantham, 19 July 1849, Darius M. Bean of Grantham.

1196. HIRAM, b. 4 Jan. 1806.

1197. AMOS JOSIAH, b. 4 July 1809.

    ELISABETH, b. 1 June 1813; m. in Grantham, 23 Feb. 1834, William T. Chase of Weare, N. H. (Family 823).

428

PARKER[5] CHASE (Joseph,[4] Lt. Joseph,[3] Ens. Moses[2]), born in Newbury (now West Newbury), 9 Apr. 1752; died there 14 Nov. 1815. He married in Newbury, 28 Dec. 1774, RUTH KELLEY, daughter of John and Hannah (Hale) Kelley, born in Newbury, 22 Nov. 1751; died in Chester, N. H., 17 May 1842, aged 90y. 5m. He was the head of a family in 1790 in Newbury, consisting of one male over 16 years of age, one male under 16 and two females. He was a cooper and administration on his estate was granted to his widow Ruth, 25 June 1816. The heirs mentioned were Jacob, Susanna and Amos. Tristram Chase, merchant, of Newburyport was one of the sureties on the widow's bond (Essex Probate, 5164). They lived in what is now West Newbury.

Children, born in Newbury (now West Newbury) :

ELIZABETH,[6] b. about 1775; m. (1) John Chandler; m. (2) Jeremiah Prescott of Brentwood, N. H. Three children. She d. 6 Feb. 1835.

LYDIA, b. about 1776; m. 18 July 1795, John Burrell. She d. 10 Mar. 1862, aged 86, without issue.

SUSANNAH, b. 14 Oct. 1777; m. in Newburyport, 29 Sept. 1796, Tristram[5] Chase. (Family 277).

1198. THOMAS, b. — Mar. 1779.

SARAH, b. 1781; m. 6 Nov. 1801, Jacob Burrell; she d. 12 Dec. 1802; one daughter.

1199. JACOB, b. 23 June 1782.

HANNAH, m. in Deerfield, N. H., 15 Apr. 1821, Hezekiah Smith, and d. 1856.

1200. AMOS, b. 4 Mar. 1794.

429

JOSEPH[5] CHASE (Joseph,[4] Lt. Joseph,[3] Ens. Moses[2]), born in Newbury (now West Newbury), 8 Nov. 1758; died in Hampstead, N. H., 21 Apr. 1836. He married in Newbury, 29 Dec. 1785, EMMA[6] CHASE, daughter of Lt. Abel[5] and Hannah (Morse-Campbell) Chase. She was born in Newbury, 7 Feb. 1766; died in Hampstead, 11 May 1831, aged 65y. 3m. They lived in what is now West Newbury till 1804 when they removed to Hampstead. Mrs. Chase was admitted to the Congregational Church of Hampstead, 21 Mar. 1819. (Family 143).

Children, born in Newbury (now West Newbury:

HANNAH,[6] b. 23 Dec. 1786; m. 15 Nov. 1804, Moses Jaques of West Newbury.

SUSANNAH, b. 4 Mar. 1788; m. in Hampstead, 10 Dec. 1818, Joshua Eastman of Hampstead.

MARY, b. 8 Nov. 1789; m. 26 Dec. 1815, Thorndike Putnam of Hampstead.

ELISABETH SANBORN, b. 27 Feb. 1792; m. 19 Jan. 1819, John Ordway of Hampstead.

JONATHAN, b. 27 Feb. 1795; a farmer; lived in Sandown, N. H.; d. Oct. 1856; m. 13 Oct. 1841, Hannah C. Harrington, dau. of Abigail[6] Chase and Moses Harrington. (144). No children.

EMMA, b. 21 Feb. 1797; m. 24 Jan. 1826, Dea. William Tenney; removed to Me.

1201. JOSEPH, b. 22 Dec. 1801.

430

CALEB[5] CHASE (Joseph,[4] Lt. Joseph,[3] Ens. Moses[2]), born in Newbury, 18 Aug. 1768; died in Newport, N. H. He married in Newbury, 5 Nov. 1800, HANNAH CARR, daughter of Daniel and Elizabeth[5] (Chase) Carr, born in Newbury, 20 Aug. 1779; baptized at the Fourth Church (now Second Church of West Newbury) 15 Sept. 1782.

They removed from Newbury to Hopkinton, N. H., about 1810 and later to Newport, N. H.

Children, first three born in Newbury, last born in Hopkinton, N. H.:

        BETSEY CARR,[6] b. 12 July 1804; m. 19 Apr. 1832, Seth J. Allen.
1202. JOSEPH TOWNE, b. 12 Apr. 1806.
        JULIA GRANBY, b. 25 Oct. 1808.
1203. ETHAN SMITH, b. 15 Aug. 1811.

431

JONATHAN[5] CHASE (Joseph,[4] Lt. Joseph,[3] Ens. Moses[2]), born in Newbury (now West Newbury), 9 Mar. 1774; died in West Newbury, 29 Mar. 1828, aged 54. He married in Newbury, 30 Nov. 1797, HANNAH BROWN. She died in West Newbury, 19 Aug. 1849, aged 77 or 78. They lived in West Newbury and he was a carpenter by trade.

Hannah Chase, widow, was administratrix of estate of Jonathan Chase, late of West Newbury. Staniford Chase, combmaker, and Jonathan Chase, housewright, sureties, 30 Sept. 1828. Heirs not named but three children were under 21. (Essex Probate, 5141).

Children, born in what is now West Newbury:

1204. INCREASE SUMNER, b. 29 Oct. 1798.
        BETSEY CARR, b. 20 June 1800.
1205. STANIFORD, b. about 1802.
        JOHN, d. young.
        BETSEY B., d. unm. 7 May 1835, aged 24.
1206. HANNIBAL, lived in Baltimore, Md.
        OSGOOD, d. 19 May 1830, aged 23.
1207. HORACE LUMMUS, b. 1815.
1208. JEHU, b. 1814.

432

JOHN WEBSTER[5] CHASE (Moody,[4] Lt. Joseph,[3] Ens. Moses[2]), born in Chester, N. H., 26 Aug. 1769; baptized at Hampstead, N. H., 19 Nov. 1769; died in Chester, 22 Feb. 1863. He married 14 Apr. 1796, PRUDENCE STARK. She was born 12 Sept. 1776; died 29 Sept. 1852. They lived in Lyme, N. H., Hanover, N. H., and Piermont, N. H.

Children, some born in Lyme, N. H.:

1209. WILLIAM STARK,[6] b. 22 Feb. 1797.
        ANNA, b. 23 June 1798; d. Dec. 1823.
        MARY, b. 12 Dec. 1799; d. 26 May 1871; m. (1) Asa Barns,
          who d. 6 May 1854; m. (2) 1860, Newell Barry.
1210. MOODY, b. 28 Sept. 1804.
1211. CALEB C., b. 26 Dec. 1810.
        JOHN, b. 10 Sept. 1813; d. Sept. 1822.

433

JOSEPH[5] CHASE (Moody,[4] Lt. Joseph,[3] Ens. Moses[2]), born in Chester, N. H., 14 Apr. 1774; died in Chester, 6 Sept. 1820, aged 46. He married in Candia, 11 Oct. 1798, NANCY EATON, (called Anna in her marriage record), daughter of Maj. Jesse and Sarah

(Worthen) Eaton of Candia. She was born 30 Sept. 1775; died 19 Jan. 1857. He lived on a part of the homestead in Chester and removed to Canaan, N. H., in 1816. His death is reported from Chester.

Children, born in Chester:

1212. MOODY,[6] b. 5 Mar. 1800.
1213. JESSE EATON, b. 2 Sept. 1801.
     SALLY E., b. 6 Sept. 1803; m. 23 Nov. 1825, Uriah F. Lary of Canaan, N. H.
1214. DAVID E., b. 23 Mar. 1805.
     ASA, b. 10 Feb. 1807; m. Dorothy Currier of Enfield, N. H. Lived at East Hanover and Lebanon. No children. Adopted a child named Mary.
1215. HORACE, b. 18 Mar. 1809.
     NANCY (twin), b. 22 Sept. 1811; m. (1) 22 June 1837, Sylvanus Barnard Currier; m. (2) Moody Chase.[6] (Family 1210).
1216. JOSEPH (twin), b. 22 Sept. 1811.
     EBENEZER, b. 27 May 1814; m. Emily Shaddock; d. in Nashua, N. H., 6 June 1843. No children.

434

JACOB[5] CHASE (Moody,[4] Lt. Joseph,[3] Ens. Moses[2]), born in Chester, N. H., 23 Mar. 1776; baptized in Hampstead, N. H., 25 May 1776; died in Hopkinton, N. H., 13 Feb. 1855. He married 20 Feb. 1806 (intention at Newbury, 30 Dec. 1805) HANNAH BARKER, daughter of Thomas and Hannah (Whittemore) Barker, born in Methuen, 31 Dec. 1777; died in Hopkinton, N. H., 29 Jan. 1854. They lived in West Newbury and removed to Hopkinton in 1811.

Children, first four born in Newbury, others in Hopkinton:

     ALBERT MOODY,[6] b. 21 Jan. 1807; m. 27 May 1834, Mary Putnam Upton; no children reported; d. in Canton, Jan. 1883.
     ANN ELIZA, b. 13 Apr. 1808; m. 22 Dec. 1831, William Palmer Jr.
1217. OTIS NELSON, b. 8 Oct. 1809.
     CARLOS COOLEDGE, b. 15 Apr. 1811; d. 31 Mar. 1812.
     HANNAH WHITTEMORE, b. 12 Dec. 1812; d. unm. 20 Apr. 1857, in Canton.
     JANE MORSE, b. 30 Sept. 1814; d. 15 Mar. 1815.
     SARAH HILL, b. 11 Mar. 1816; d. unm. 29 Apr. 1857, in West Newton.
1218. CYRUS, b. 16 Feb. 1818.
     MARY WEEKS, b. 2 July 1822; m. 6 Apr. 1843, Daniel D. Sargent.
1219. LEONARD WOODS, b. 6 Jan. 1826.

435

MOODY[5] CHASE (Moody,[4] Lt. Joseph,[3] Ens. Moses[2]), born in Chester, N. H., 19 Apr. 1778; baptized in Hampstead, N. H., 31 May 1778; died in Haverhill, 26 Aug. 1833, aged 55. He married in Haverhill, 26 Dec. 1802, ELIZABETH BRADLEY, daughter of Nathaniel and Elizabeth (Ordway) Bradley, born in Haverhill, 4 Nov. 1763; died there, 6 Oct. 1840, aged 77. They lived in Haverhill and kept a public house there, on the site of the present Hotel Webster on Washington Street.

Child, born in Haverhill:

1220.   STEPHEN BRADLEY,[6] b. 20 May 1806.

436

SAMUEL[5] CHASE (Moody,[4] Lt. Joseph,[3] Ens. Moses[2]), born in Chester, N. H., 11 Aug. 1780; died in Portland, Me., 26 July 1867. He married (1) 27 Nov. 1803, SALLY HAYNES, who was born 3 Dec. 1782 and died in Portland, 22 Apr. 1806. He married (2) in Haverhill, 1 Feb. 1807, ABIGAIL BRADLEY. She was born 22 Dec. 1785 and died in Portland, 18 May 1821. He married (3) 23 Nov. 1823, DERORAH ROGERS, daughter of Maj. William Rogers. She was born 23 Apr. 1780; died 29 Oct. 1860. They lived in Portland, 1800-1867. He was a cooper, fish inspector and an alderman.

Children by first wife, born in Portland:

> SOPHIA,[6] b .9 Aug. 1804; m. 3 Feb. 1825, Arthur M. Davis.
> SARAH, b. 3 Apr. 1806; m. 11 Sept. 1832, Stephen Bradley[6] Chase. (Family 1220).

Children by second wife, born in Portland:

> NAOMI, b. 16 Jan. 1808; m. 5 Nov. 1832, Hazen Buttrick, who d. 24 Mar. 1834; lived in Haverhill and Portland, Me. No children.
> MARY, b. 5 Dec. 1809; d. 7 Mar. 1829.

1221.   JOHN DAVENPORT, b. 17 Dec. 1811.

> ELISABETH, b. 14 Mar. 1814; d. 28 Apr. 1814.

1222.   SAMUEL, b. 10 Nov. 1817.

437

CALEB[5] CHASE (Moody,[4] Lt. Joseph,[3] Ens. Moses[2]), born in Chester, N. H., 4 Feb. 1783; died in Portland, Me., 20 Sept. 1850. He graduated at Dartmouth College in 1811; studied theology and was a teacher. He married in Haverhill, 3 Dec. 1816, SUSANNA BURRILL, daughter of Joseph and Susanna (Mulliken) Burrill, born in Haverhill, 14 Apr. 1794; died in Portland, 8 Sept. 1856. They lived in Portsmouth till 1819, then in Portland, Me., where he was a teacher and master of the Central School in Portland, 1821.

Children, born in Portland, except first born in Portsmouth, N. H.

1223.   DANIEL POOR,[6] b. 22 Feb. 1818; was a printer; d. 21 Nov. 1852.

> SUSAN REBECCA, b. 19 May 1820; m. (1) 4 Aug. 1839, Josiah Walker Smith of Bangor, Me.; m. (2) 1 Aug. 1858, Samuel Pierce Osgood; she d. in New York,, N. Y., 27 Sept. 1900. Five children.
> ELIZA ANN, b. 7 Aug. 1822; m. 19 Aug. 1846, James Norris Davis; she d. 26 Sept. 1895; lived in Deering, Me.
> CHARLES COFFIN ADAMS, b. 8 May 1824; d. unm. 5 Aug. 1865.
> OWEN MURDOCK, b. 13 Feb. 1826; d. 6 Oct. 1838.
> MARY CAROLINE, b. 10 Oct. 1828; m. 25 Sept. 1854, Henry H. Haselton; lived in Brooklyn, N. Y.
> INFANT DAU., b. 13 Feb. 1831; d. 23 Feb. 1831.

1224.   WILLIAM DWIGHT, b. 24 June 1832.

> SARAH MOULTON, b. 21 Nov. 1835; unm.; lived in Portland.

438

Thomas[5] Chase (Moody,[4] Lt. Joseph,[3] Ens. Moses[2]), born in Chester, N. H., 8 Nov. 1789; died in Haverhill, 10 May 1852. He married in Chester, 4 Oct. 1817, Sarah Shannon, daughter of Samuel Shannon of Chester. She was born in Raymond, N. H., 16 Jan. 1799.

Children, eldest born in Watertown, second in Candia, N. H., others in Haverhill:

1225. George Washington,[6] b. 8 July 1818.
1226. Sylvester, b. 6 June 1822.
      Sarah Ann, b. 25 Aug. 1825; d. 9 May 1868, in Bradford, Vt.
      Mary Jane, b. 8 Oct. 1827.

439

Joseph[5] Chase (Caleb,[4] Lt. Joseph,[3] Ens. Moses[2]), born in Gorham, Me., 9 Aug. 1772; died in Hanover, N. H., 1 Nov. 1836. He married about 1794, Abigail Eaton, born 1770. They lived in Lebanon, N. H., and in Hanover, N. H., on the old Eaton place near Mill Village.

Children, some born in Hanover:

      Polly,[6] m. in Hanover, 24 Feb. 1830, Asa Wright of Hanover.
      Sarah Curtis, b. 16 Aug. 1806; m. (1) 13 Aug. 1829, John Bridgeman; m. (2) 4 Apr. 1833, Asa Worth of Hanover.
1227. Harvey Herman, lived on the homestead in Hanover.
      Almira, m. in Hanover, 26 Aug. 1827, Joseph Hatch of Burlington, Vt.
1228. Henry, lived in Lowell.
1229. Joseph.

440

Jacob[5] Chase (Caleb,[4] Lt. Joseph,[3] Ens. Moses[2]), born in Gorham, Me., 11 Feb. 1778; died in Derby, Vt., 23 Dec. 1858. He married in Thornton, N. H., 5 Mar. 1801, Hannah Colby, daughter of Enoch and Lydia (Worthen) Colby, born in Thornton, 17 Jan. 1784. (Her father was a Revolutionary War soldier and a member of the Governor's Council of New Hampshire in 1815). They lived in Derby, Vt.

Children, born in Derby:

1230. Gardner,[6] b. 17 Dec. 1801.
      Gilman, b. 27 Jan. 1803; d. unm.
      Betsey B., b. 19 Apr. 1805; m. —— (Howard ?).
1231. Jacob, b. 13 Nov. 1806.
1232. Enoch, b. 16 Jan. 1809.
1233. Horace, b. 25 Dec. 1810.
      Laura, b. 10 Dec. 1812; m. Paul B. Lathrop.
      Lydia I., b. 9 May 1815; m. —— Daggett.
1234. Lucien Bonaparte, b. 5 Dec. 1817.
      Hannah W., b. 25 Dec. 1820; m. Dr. Joseph Chase Rutherford of Newport, Vt. He was b. in Schenectady, N. Y., 1 Oct. 1818, son of Alexander Rutherford.

441

Amos[5] Chase (Caleb,[4] Lt. Joseph,[3] Ens. Moses[2]), born in Concord, N. H., 4 Aug. 1780; died in Campton, N. H., 26 Feb. 1859. He married 1 Jan. 1806, Polly Chandler of Hanover, N. H., daughter of Daniel and Mary (Galusha) Chandler, born in Hanover, 28 June 1788; died 29 Aug. 1857. He was an ironsmith. They lived in Thornton, N. H., and Campton.

Children, eldest born in Thornton:

1235.   Silas C.[6]
      Phebe, b. 11 Jan. 1808; m. in Lowell, 23 Dec. 1832, Daniel Cross, son of Rev. David and Abigail (Case) Cross, b. in Wilmot, N. H., 20 Sept. 1806; lived in Sutton, Vt.
1236.   John, lived in Port Jervis, N. Y.
      Susan, m. ——— ———.
      Polly, m. David Cross of Sutton, Vt.
      Laura J., m. 12 Sept. 1839, Jacob M. Cook; two children. (Chandler Gen., 1883, p. 540.)

442

Moses[5] Chase (Caleb,[4] Lt. Joseph,[3] Ens. Moses[2]), born in Concord, N. H., 16 Feb. 1787; died near Buffalo, N. Y., 24 Sept. 1834. He married 22 Nov. 1810, Elizabeth[5] Chase, daughter of Moody[4] and Anna (Webster) Chase, born in Chester, N. H., 16 June 1787; died 18 May 1858. (Family 119). She married (2) David Edmunds of Fitchville, Ohio. They lived in Concord, and Thornton, N. H., Derby, Vt., and in New York State near Buffalo.

Children:

      Mary Ann,[6] b. 22 Nov. 1811; d. unm. 30 July 1835.
1237.   Caleb Moody, b. 23 Apr. 1815.
      Hannah Elisabeth, b. 16 June 1818; m. Philotus French; lived in Guilford, Mich.
      Charlotta Joanna, b. 28 Mar. 1821; d. 17 Aug. 1833.
1238.   David L., b. 30 Mar. 1826.

443

William[5] Chase (Caleb,[4] Lt. Joseph,[3] Ens. Moses[2]), born in Concord, N. H., 2 Mar. 1791; died in Campton, N. H., 24 Jan. 1838. He married in Sandwich, N. H., 16 Dec. 1817, Lydia Prescott of Sandwich, who died 19 Nov. 1857. They lived in Campton.

Children:

1239.   Benjamin H. P.,[6] b. 4 Oct. 1818.
1240.   William Sylvester, b. 11 Apr. 1825.
1241.   Edmund H., b. 7 Dec. 1826.
      Mary Ann, b. 25 June 1834; m. Allen Royce of Berlin, Vt.

444

Elijah[5] Chase (Rogers,[4] Benoni,[3] Ens. Moses[2]), born in Sutton, 31 July 1757; died in service in the Revolutionary War, 4 Oct. 1776. He enlisted in 1775 in Capt. Gleason's Co. of Col. Thomas Nixon's Regiment and was in the service at the camp at Mt. Washington and at North Castle from which his death was reported. (Mass. Soldiers and Sailors, 3:348).

445

SILAS[5] CHASE (Rogers,[4] Benoni,[3] Ens. Moses[2]), born in Sutton, 31 Aug. 1760; married in Royalston, 11 Feb. 1788, DIADEMIA GAR-FIELD of Warwick, born 14 June 1763 and died in Royalston, 9 June 1838, in her 75th year. She was daughter of Moses and Sarah ( ) Garfield of Charlton. He died in Royalston, 29 Nov. 1836, aged 76. They lived in Royalston, and he was a Revolutionary war soldier.

Children, born in Royalston:

DIADEMIA,[6] b. 12 Jan. 1789; never mar.; d. 8 Aug. 1862.
1242. SILAS, b. 30 Sept. 1790.
PAULINA, b. 7 July 1792; m. 11 Aug. 1814, Benjamin Leath Jr.; d. 2 Oct. 1840; seven children.
JOSEPH WRIFORD, b. 15 July 1794; d. 21 Dec. 1798.
1243. JOSEPH WRIFORD, b. 5 Oct. 1799.
1244. JOHN ROYAL, b. 11 Mar. 1803.

446

EBENEZER[5] CHASE (Rogers,[4] Benoni,[3] Ens. Moses[2]), born in Royalston, 9 Oct. 1774; married there, 20 Feb. 1800, BARSYLVIA PECK, daughter of Solomon and Anna (Wheeler) Peck, born in Royalston, 17 Feb. 1775. Her birth record calls her "Silvia Peck." She died 22 May 1862. He died 26 July 1858. They lived in Athol from 17 May 1800 to the time of their decease.

Children, born in Athol:

CLARISSA,[6] b. 22 Apr. 1801; d. 3 Mar. 1804.
BARNEY, b. 9 Feb. 1803; d. 25 May or Aug. 1825.
1245. ELIJAH, b. 17 Dec. 1804.
CLARISSA, b. 28 Nov. 1806; m. int. 24 Oct. 1829, Lysander F. Townsend; d. 13 Jan. 1838.
SARAH, b. 13 Nov. 1808; m. 18 Feb. 1841, Addison A. Warner. They were living in Mechanicsville, Vt., in 1873. Three children.
SYLVIA, b. 7 Oct. 1810; m. 8 Apr. 1840, David Cole of Mt. Holly, Vt.; lived in Orange.
BETSEY, b. 16 Nov. 1812; m. William Sawyer of Athol.
1246. AMBROSE PECK, b. 5 Mar. 1815.

447

BENJAMIN[5] CHASE (Stephen,[4] Benoni,[3] Ens. Moses[2]), born about 1776; died about 1814. He married BETSEY LOWRY. They lived in New York state. His children Erastus, Matilda and Eunice lived in Keene, N. H.

Children, born in New York state:

BETSEY.[6]
POLLY.
CAROLINE.
1247. ERASTUS, b. 9 Mar. 1801.
MATILDA, m. 6 Apr. 1826, Daniel Goodnow; lived in Keene, N. H.
1248. HIRAM.
EUNICE, b. 5 Aug. 1808; perhaps m. 16 Apr. 1840, Major White of Winchester; d. in Keene, 28 Mar. 1868.

448

Asa[5] CHASE (Moses,[4] Benoni,[3] Ens. Moses[2]), born probably in Sutton, about 1765; died in Douglas, 9 Oct. 1847, aged 82. He married in Douglas, 19 Apr. 1789, OLIVE DUDLEY, daughter of William and Anna (Shephard) Dudley, born in Douglas, 15 Dec. 1771. They lived in Douglas.

Children, born in Douglas:

POLLY,[6] b. 22 Jan. 1790; m. 12 Apr. 1809, Elkanah McIntire of Charlton.

ANNA, b. 2 Apr. 1792; m. 19 Mar. 1820, Rufus Mixer of Charlton.

1249. DAVID, b. 5 Jan. 1795.

OLIVE, b. 8 Mar. 1797.

449

SIMEON[5] CHASE (Moses,[4] Benoni,[3] Ens. Moses[2]), born in Sutton about 1770. He married JEMIMA HOLDEN. They lived in Royalston till 1803 when they removed to Stockbridge, Vt., and later to Brandon, Vt. He died "in Feb. 1850, aged 79 or 80."

Children, first four born in Royalston, fifth and sixth in Stockbridge, others in Brandon:

1250. JAMES,[6] b. 2 Sept. 1794.

OLIVER, m. (1) Feb. 1819, Susan Chamberlain; m. (2) Milla Chamberlain. No children. He d. in Malone, N. Y., 1855.

1251. ORRIN, b. 21 Mar. 1798.

LUCY, b. 18 May 1802; d. unm. Mar. 1822.

SALLY, b. 20 Dec. 1804; m. 1822, Horace Burby (?) of Stockbridge.

1252. IRA, b. 18 June 1807.

1253. AARON, b. 15 June 1809.

ALMIRA, b. 10 July 1811; m. 1824, Lorenzo Abbott.

HANNAH, b. 19 July 1814; m. Warren Clark of Malone, N. Y.

JULIANA, b. 5 May 1817; m. 1835, Chester Blanchard of Brandon, Vt.

450

ABNER[5] CHASE (Moses,[4] Benoni,[3] Ens. Moses[2]), born about 1775. He married (1) HANNAH SLADE, daughter of John and Mary (Mack) Slade of Alstead, N. H. She was born in Alstead, 18 Mar. 1785, and died in Ohio. He married (2) her sister SUSAN (Slade) THAYER, who was born in Alstead, 9 Aug. 1787, and died in Rochester, Vt. They lived in Brookfield, Vt. and Rochester, Vt., where he died.

Children by first wife:

LAVINA,[6] m. Oliver Smith; d. in Rochester.

JOEL, d. in infancy.

JOEL 2d, d. in infancy.

Children by second wife:

MARY, m. Hiram Thurston; d. in Palatine, Ill.

1254. MOSES, b. 30 Apr. 1821.

FANNY, m. Lester Gay; lived in Oregon.

LYMAN, d. at age of 16.

451

Abraham[5] Chase (David,[4] Benoni,[3] Ens. Moses[2]), born in Douglas, 25 Sept. 1772; died in Whitingham, Vt., 11 May 1854, aged 81. He married in Douglas, 5 Oct. 1796, Elizabeth Rich of Sutton, probably daughter of Samuel and Ruth (Putnam) Rich, born in Sutton, 23 Jan. 1772. They removed to Whitingham, Vt., 16 Feb. 1797, and lived in that part of the town called "Sadawga."

Children, born in Whitingham, except the first:

1255. David,[6] b. 12 Dec. 1796.
1256. Samuel, b. 5 Mar. 1799.
1257. Jacob, b. 8 Feb. 1804.
1258. Ellis F. (twin), b. 31 July 1812.
1259. Elliott F. (twin), b. 31 July 1812.

452

Isaac[5] Chase (David,[4] Benoni,[3] Ens. Moses[2]), born in Douglas, 29 Jan. 1775; died in Whitingham, Vt., 30 Mar. 1825. He married in Douglas, 15 Aug. 1799, Susannah Fuller of Douglas. They removed to Whitingham, Vt., 3 Feb. 1800, and lived there. He was a thrifty farmer.

Children, born in Whitingham:

1260. Moses,[6] b. 2 Mar. 1800.
1261. Aaron, b. 2 Nov. 1801.
Susanna (twin), b. 14 Sept. 1804; m. 15 Apr. 1830, Baxter Adams of North Adams.
Isaac (twin), b. 14 Sept. 1804; d. 10 Oct. 1806.
1262. Isaac, b. 19 June 1808.
1263. Hiram, b. 9 Oct. 1812.
Lucy, b. 5 Oct. 1816; d. 29 Dec. 1829.

453

Jacob[5] Chase (David,[4] Benoni,[3] Ens. Moses[2]), born in Douglas, 15 Feb. 1780; died in Whitingham, Vt., 9 Aug. 1858, aged 78. He married (intention in Douglas, 28 Nov. 1804) Anna Morse, daughter of Levi and Lydia Morse, born in Douglas, 18 Mar. 1784. They removed to Whitingham, Vt., 31 Jan. 1806 and lived in the south part of the town. They were members of the Baptist Church.

Children, eldest born in Douglas, the others in Whitingham:

1264. Warren,[6] b. 30 Nov. 1805.
Lydia, b. 13 Jan. 1808; m. Emory Hull; d. 4 Apr. 1871.
1265. Levi, b. 26 Aug. 1810.
Lucy, b. 6 Dec. 1813; d. 6 June 1815.
1266. Jacob, b. 21 May 1815.
1267. Minor, b. 2 Sept. 1817.
Lucy A., b. 9 Nov. 1819; d. 31 Jan. 1838.
Willard, b. 5 Dec. 1823; d. 21 Nov. 1825.

454

Samuel[5] Chase (David,[4] Benoni,[3] Ens. Moses[2]), born in Douglas, 22 Feb. 1783; died in Wilmington, Vt., 7 Nov. 1854. He married (intention in Douglas, 11 June 1805) Mabel Balcom, daughter of Bezaleel and Jemima Balcom, born in Douglas, 15 Aug. 1787.

They removed to Whitingham, Vt., in Feb. 1815, and about 1842 removed to Wilmington, Vt. She died in Wilmington, 21 Mar. 1851.
Children, first three born in Douglas, others in Whitingham:

1268.   RUFUS,[6] b. 11 Oct. 1805.
         DAVID, b. 6 July 1807; d. 10 Aug. 1807.
1269.   DAVID, b. 15 Apr. 1809.
         FANNY, b. 21 Feb. 1818; d. 13 Apr. 1831.
         PAULINA, b. 21 Oct. 1822; m. (1) 2 Mar. 1843, Asahel Rice;
         m. (2) Charles Bowker; m. (3) Newman Carley.

455

BENJAMIN[5] CHASE (David,[4] Benoni,[3] Ens. Moses[2]), born in Douglas, 7 Sept. 1786; died in Whitingham, Vt., 27 Apr. 1863. He married in Douglas, 23 Sept. 1806, SARAH SPRAGUE, who was born 5 Nov. 1785 or 1786 and died 5 Apr. 1869. They removed from Douglas to Whitingham, Vt., 15 Feb. 1815, and resided there until death.
Children, first three born in Douglas, others in Whitingham:

         SUMNER,[6] b. 21 Apr. 1807; m. 16 Mar. 1851, Roxana Faulkner.
         He d. 2 Feb. 1885 in Sadawga, Vt. No children.
         JEMIMA, b. 11 Dec. 1809; m. 5 Dec. 1830, Prentice B. Putnam.
1270.   MERRICK, b. 13 Dec. 1811.
         ABRAHAM, b. 20 Apr. 1816; d. 16 Apr. 1818.
1271.   ABRAHAM, b. 5 Jan. 1820.
         LUCINA, b. 21 Feb. 1821; d. unm. 3 Sept. 1854, aged 33.
1272.   ROYAL, b. 3 Aug. 1827.

SIXTH GENERATION

456

JACOB[6] CHASE (Joshua,[5] George,[4] Joshua,[3] Aquila[2]), born in Shirley, 30 Jan. 1771; died in Lake Mills, Wis., 6 Aug. or Oct., 1847. He married (1) Apr. 1791, OLIVE WILSON, who was born 23 Aug. 1773; died 9 Mar. 1799. He married (2) 25 Apr. 1800, JENNIE NEEDHAM NEWTON, born 1 Jan. 1785; died 24 Feb. 1835. They lived in Massena, St. Lawrence Co., N. Y.

Children by first wife. born in Chester, Vt.:

1273.   ALDEN,[7] b. 12 May 1792; m. 1 Mar. 1820, Phebe W. Stearns. Lived in Lake Mills.

1274.   AZUBAH.

1275.   ALEXANDER, m. twice. Had dau. Emily.

Children by second wife:

1276.   ALVAH, b. 26 Dec. 1802; m. 31 Aug. 1829, Minerva Thompson.

1277.   HIRAM, b. 28 Jan. 1805; m. 1831, Lydia Spaulding. He was living in Messena, N. Y., in 1876.

      OLIVE, b. 6 Nov. 1807; m. Clark Spaulding; lived in Mason. Ingham Co., Mich.; d. 1862.

      ASENATH, b. 24 Jan. 1810; m. 21 June, 1835, Thomas Rea. No children.

      MARY JANE, b. 12 Sept. 1812; m. 14 July 1835, Leonard Northrup.

1278.   JOHN, b. 28 July 1814; d. 28 Sept. 1840.

1279.   CHARLES C., b. 29 Mar. 1816; m. Alice Bailey. No children. He d. in Warsaw, N. Y., 1871.

      AUGUSTUS, b. 25 June 1823; d. young.

457

WILLIAM P.[6] CHASE (Joshua,[5] George,[4] Joshua,[3] Aquila[2]), born in Chesterfield, N. H., 22 June 1783; died 20 July 1855. He married about 1806, MARY SPAULDING of Chester, Vt. She was born 30 Mar. 1788 and died in Massena, N. Y., 1 Mar. 1869. They lived in Massena, St. Lawrence Co., N. Y.

Children:

      SUSAN,[7] b. in Chester, Vt.; m. George Wilson.

      DEBORAH, m. 1833 James Whitman.

      ELISABETH, b. 20 Dec. 1825; m. (1) 26 Nov. 1851, Dr. A. S. Purdy; m. (2) William E. Kelley. She d. abt. 1867.

      PHILENA, d. unm. in Massena.

      ALBINA, d. unm.

      PARK, d. unm. in Massena.

      GEORGE, never married.

1280.   JOSHUA, b. 28 Oct. 1816; m. (1) 15 Oct. 1842, Mary Brownfield; m. (2) 16 Dec. 1851, Susan M. Joyce; m. (3) 15 Mar. 1853, Elisabeth O. Simpson; lived in Hammonsville, Ky.

458

CALEB[6] CHASE (Abel,[5] George,[4] Joseph,[3] Aquila[2]), born in Shirley, 16 June 1779; living with his parents in Chesterfield, N. H., in 1790, under 16. He may be the Caleb Chase who married in Swanzey, N. H., 26 Apr. 1802, SARAH FRARY. No children appear on the town records of New Hampshire as born of this union. Perhaps he removed from Chesterfield to New York state.

459

GEORGE[6] CHASE (Abel,[5] George,[4] Joseph,[3] Aquila[2]), born in Chesterfield, N. H., 27 July 1787. He probably removed with his father's family westward about 1800.

460

CHARLES[6] CHASE (Abel,[5] George,[4] Joseph,[3] Aquila[2]), born in Chesterfield, N. H., 6 July 1789; killed in Second War with Great Britain, 1814. He married in Chesterfield, 23 Feb. 1812, SABRINA REED.

Child, born in Chesterfield:

1281.   CHARLES,[7] b. 28 Aug. 1812; d. in Keene, N. H., 18 July 1901; m. 2 Apr. 1844, Thurza E. Symonds, b. in Hinsdale, N. H., 24 Dec. 1826; d. in Keene, 24 Oct. 1907. Nine children including *Orlando*,[8] b. in Chesterfield, 9 Nov. 1845; m. 16 Apr. 1873, Mary Whitwell, b. in Waterford, N. Y., 17 June 1854. Their children are: Sarah E.,[9] b. 31 Jan. 1875; m. Charles E. Rogers; Lucy W.,[9] b. 31 Aug. 1876; m. Frank O. Van Der Kar; Charles Orlando,[9] b. 26 Nov. 1878; m. 1 June 1904, Mary E. Lane, b. in Albany, N. Y., 12 Dec. 1880. Their children are: *William O.*,[10] b. 28 Jan. 1906; *Richard Lane*,[10] b. 10 Aug. 1907; *Mary Lane*,[10] b. 23 May 1915. Emma A.,[9] b. 19 June 1880; George F.,[9] b. 12 May 1883; m. Edith Merrett; Edith M.,[9] b. 16 Oct. 1887; m. Walter Abbott; Susie J.,[9] b. 19 Jan. 1889; m. Rev. Earl B. Robinson and has three children.

461

CAPT. JOSEPH[6] CHASE (Stephen,[5] Rev. Stephen,[4] Joseph,[3] Aqulia[2]), born in New Castle, N. H., 22 Apr. 1772; lost at sea on the U. S. privateer *Portsmouth* in 1814. He married in Durham, N. H., 21 Nov. 1796, MARGARET CHESLEY, daughter of Ens. Joseph and Comfort (Smith) Chesley. They lived in Portsmouth, N. H.

Children, born in Portsmouth:

MARY,[7] b. 1798; m. 31 Aug. 1819, John Taylor of Waterborough, Me.

ANN MARGARET, b. 1800; d. unm. in Portsmouth.

STEPHEN, b. 1 Aug. 1802; unm.; lost at sea.

Joseph, b. 1804; unm.; lost at sea.

THEODORE, b. 21 July 1807; d. 21 July 1815.

CAROLINE A., b. 1809; m. 7 Sept. 1840, Rev. Timothy Morgan.

ADELINE SMITH, b. about 1811; m. Dr. J. Lawrence Page.

1282.   WILLIAM A. L., b. 1814; went to Texas and was never heard from.

George B Chase

462

THEODORE[6] CHASE (Stephen,[5] Rev. Stephen,[4] Joseph,[3] Aquila[2]), born in Portsmouth, N. H., 16 Mar. 1786; died in Boston, 13 Mar. 1859. He married, 26 Apr. 1831, CLARISSA ANDREWS BIGELOW, daughter of Hon. Tyler and Clarissa (Bigelow) Bigelow, born in Watertown, 1 Nov. 1807; died 16 Feb. 1884. He was a large shipowner and removed from Portsmouth to Boston in 1831.

Children, born in Boston:

1283. THEODORE,[7] b. 4 Feb. 1832; graduated at Harvard College 1853; m. 17 Nov. 1868, Alice Bowdoin Bradlee, dau. of James Bowdoin Bradlee, Esq., of Boston. He died in 1894. No children.

1284. GEORGE BIGELOW, b. 1 Oct. 1835; m. 10 Jan. 1860, Anne Lowndes, dau. of Maj. Rawlins and Gertrude Laura (Livingston) Lowndes of South Carolina.

He was educated at the Chauncy Hall School, at the Boston Latin School, 1848-1851 and graduated from Harvard University in 1856, in the class with Hon. Charles Francis Adams, James Bradstreet Greenough, Gov. George Dexter Robinson, Stephen Salisbury and other distinguished men.

In 1859 the management of his father's shipping business and the care of his mother devolved upon him. During the Civil War he disposed of his ships and became interested in the development of railroads. He became a director of the Rutland Railroad and transfer agent and assumed its liabilities of nearly a million dollars by personally endorsing its notes in 1871. This resulted in the restoration of the securities of the company. He also subscribed liberally to the securities of the Burlington and Missouri Railroad and became a director of the Merrimack Manufacturing Company and its President 1888-1892.

He was treasurer of the Somerset Club 1861-1865, and of the Union Club 1868-1870, and was a member of the Committee on the Treasurer's Accounts of Harvard College 1871-1894, and a trustee of the Boston Public Library 1877-1885.

He became a life member of the New England Historic Genealogical Society in 1870 and a member of the Massachusetts Historical Society in 1876.

He was deeply interested in American History and genealogy and prepared a paper on the Chases of Chesham, England, from data furnished by Horatio Gates Somerby, which appeared in the Heraldic Journal for Oct. 1868, and also prepared and published an historical genealogy of the Lowndes family of South Carolina. He also prepared a memoir of his uncle, George Tyler Bigelow, Chief Justice of the Superior Court, which appeared in the Proceedings of the Massachusetts Historical Society. He purchased from Dr. John B. Chace his large collection of Chase records, which were given to the New England Historic Genealogical Society and have been of inestimable aid in the preparation of this book.

He spent his summers in the British Isles and Europe from 1870 to 1896 and his acquaintance with the English people developed in him "a true appreciation of the mother country, a strong affection for her, and, above all, a deep and abiding conviction of the inestimable importance to civilization of the mutual sympathy and understanding of the two branches of the Anglo-Saxon race."

He was a member of the Episcopal Church and at the time of his death junior warden of St. Paul's Church of Dedham. He died in Dedham, 2 June 1902. Mrs. Chase died 7 May 1906.

Children (1) *Stephen*,[8] b. 30 Jan. 1863; m. 10 Dec. 1908, Mary L. C. Taylor of New York City; d. in Boston 1 Nov. 1927. He graduated at Harvard University in 1886. Children, Theodore[9] and Kathleen, twins, b. 11 Sept. 1909. (2) *Gertrude Lowndes*, b. 23 Oct. 1868; m. 18 April 1891, Harcourt Amory, son of James Singleton and Mary Copley (Green) Amory. He was born in Brookline 10 Feb. 1855, graduated at Harvard University in 1876 and died in Boston, 26 Nov. 1925. Children, Gertrude Livingston, Harcourt and John Singleton Amory.

CHARLES HENRY, b. 5 Mar. 1841; d. 27 Feb. 1849.

463

STEPHEN[6] CHASE (John Wingate,[5] Rev. Stephen,[4] Joseph,[3] Aquila[2]), born in Portsmouth, N. H., 16 May 1783; removed to Portland and married and had several children.

464

BENJAMIN TAPPAN[6] CHASE (John Wingate,[5] Rev. Stephen,[4] Joseph,[3] Aquila[2]), born in Portsmouth, N. H., 20 Dec. 1786; lived in Portland, Me.

465

CHARLES[6] CHASE (John Wingate,[5] Rev. Stephen,[4] Joseph,[3] Aquila[2]), born in Portsmouth, N. H., 2 Feb. 1794; died in Camanche, Iowa, 27 Jan. 1864. He married 19 Aug. 1819, NANCY POORE, daughter of Samuel and Lucy (Thomas) Poore, born in Portland, Me., 31 Oct. 1798; died in Winchester, Va., 1 Jan 1879. He was a master mariner and they lived in Portland, Me.

Children, born in Portland, Me.:

ELLEN,[7] b. 7 Aug. 1820; d. 8 Oct.. 1820.

ELLEN EDGEWORTH, b. 21 June 1823; m. 26 Aug. 1849, Thomas Wm. Jefferson of Camanche, Iowa.

AURELIA TAPPAN, b. 9 July 1825; lived in Camanche, unm.

JULIA POORE, b. 8 June, 1827; unm.

MARY BAKER, b. 26 Apr. 1830; m. 14 Dec. 1854, George Frederick Miller of Winchester, Va.

1285.   GEORGE WILLIAM FROST, b. 26 June 1833; m. 5 Dec. 1855, Elisabeth Agnes Ridenour.

466

NATHAN[6] CHASE (Benjamin,[5] Dr. Benjamin,[4] Joseph,[3] Aquila[2]), born in Amenia, N. Y., 10 May 1766; died in Manlius, Onondaga Co., N. Y. He married in 1796, MARY CATHARINE CROWNHART, who was born in 1772 and died in 1856. They lived in the village of Fayetteville, in Manlius, N. Y.

Children:
1286. BENJAMIN,[7] b. 1800; m. 1820, Elisabeth Eaton.
     NATHAN, b. 1802; unm.; lived Sheboygan, Wis.
     MERCY, b. 1804; m. 1822, Robert Knox.
     SAMUEL, b. 1806; d. unm. 1836.
     CATHARINE, b. 1808; d. 1849; m. 1827, Peter Krisman [Crisman].
1287. BARNWELL, b. 1810; m. 1858, Margaret Heavener, b. 1812.

467

EBENEZER[6] CHASE (Benjamin,[5] Dr. Benjamin,[4] Joseph,[3] Aquila[2]), born in Amenia, N. Y., 10 Sept. 1770; married SUSAN GENUNG. They lived in Schenectady, N. Y.
Children:
1288. ANSON.[7]
1289. NELSON, m. Eliza Jumal; lived in Brooklyn, N. Y.
1290. HIRAM.

468

BENJAMIN[6] CHASE (Benjamin,[5] Dr. Benjamin,[4] Joseph,[3] Aquila[2]), born in Amenia, N. Y., 20 Feb. 1773; married ELIZA LATHROP. He was baptized in Amenia after the death of his father and he probably lived in the state of New York.

469

SOLOMON[6] CHASE (Solomon,[5] Dr. Benjamin,[4] Joseph,[3] Aquila[2]), born 20 Oct. 1767; died 2 July 1808. He married 9 May 1790, ESTHER EVERETT, who was born 31 July 1775, and died 9 May 1824. He was the head of a family on 1 June 1790, in Frederickstown (now Carmel, Patterson and Kent in Putnam Co.) Dutchess Co., N. Y., consisting of one male over 16, one male under 16 and one female.
Children:
1291. ABRAHAM,[7] b. 22 July 1792; m. 8 Dec. 1819, Sylvia Dutcher. He d. 12 Nov. 1828.
     CHLOE, b. 11 June 1794; m. (1) 17 July 1810, Orange L. Orton; m. (2) 28 Dec. 1817, Livius B. Winegar; m. (3) 10 July 1832, John E. Steward.

470

STEPHEN[6] CHASE (Solomon,[5] Dr. Benjamin,[4] Joseph,[3] Aquila[2]), born in Dutchess Co., N. Y., 20 July 1770; married about 1800 ANNA BURCH of Stevenstown, N. Y., born 18 Mar. 1782. Perhaps she was a daughter of Joshua and Ann (Champlin) Burch of Beekman's Precinct, Dutchess Co., N. Y. There were thirteen or fourteen children only ten of whom have been reported. They lived in Dutchess Co. till 1797; then in Rensselaer Co. a few years; then removed to Canada West, near Paris, where they lived 49 years; then removed to Port Huron, Mich. His wife died in Port Huron, in 1854. He died in Green Bay, Wis., about 1869.
Children:
1292. HENRY,[7] b. 18 July 1802; d. 13 Sept. 1887; m. Persis Averill, b. 11 Dec. 1808. Six children, including *Maria*,[8] b. 9 Apr.

1843; m. in Appleton, Wis., 5 July 1865, Robert Doak, b. in Goderich, Canada, 4 Dec. 1836. Their dau. Jane⁹ Doak, b. in De Pere, Wis., 30 July 1877; m. in St. Paul, Minn., 26 June 1901, Isaac Black, b. in Milwaukee, 28 Feb. 1878. They live in New Britain, Conn. Mrs. Black is author of *Mythology for Young People* and *The Children's Cross Word Puzzle Book*.

Lucy, b. 27 Sept. 1804; m. C—— Harrison.

1293. CHARLES.

Rebecca, m. F—— Green.

1294. NATHAN B. b. 15 Feb. 1811; living in De Pere, Wis., in 1873.

Mary, b. 18 Jan. 1813; m. Stephen Wells.

Harriet, b. 6 Feb. 1817; m. J—— Gilnow (?).

Eliza, b. 23 Feb. 1819; m. J—— Clark.

1295. WILLIAM, b. 4 Sept. 1821.

1296. JOSEPH, b. 18 Aug. 1826.

471

JOHN⁶ CHASE (Solomon,⁵ Dr. Benjamin,⁴ Joseph,³ Aquila²), born in Amenia, N. Y., 1 July 1775; died in Warehouse Point, Conn., 26 Dec. 1852, aged 77. He married JANE ABBE of Enfield, Conn., who was born in Enfield, 6 Jan. 1778, daughter of Obadiah and Jane Abbe. He, or another of the same name, was chosen "tything man" in Enfield, 6 Nov. 1837.

Children:

1297. CHARLES,⁷ b. about 1807; m. Lucinda Abbe who d. 25 Sept. 1827, aged 22y. She was dau. of Capt. Richard Abbe.

1298. JOHN, b. 15 Dec. 1809; m. Elizabeth Bates.

Betsey, b. about 1800; m. 25 June 1820, Elisha Kingsbury of Coventry, Conn.

472

REV. CHARLES YOUNG⁶ CHASE (Solomon,⁵ Dr. Benjamin,⁴ Joseph,³ Aquila²), born 4 Oct. 1777; died in Corinth, Vt., 14 Aug. 1840. He married in Sharon, Conn., 27 Mar. 1808, BETSEY PATCHEN, who was born 31 Oct. 1778 and died in Sharon, 10 Dec. 1853. He was an adopted son of Benjamin and Mehitable Young of Sharon, and was there baptized 18 Apr. 1784. He was ordained pastor of the Congregational Church in Corinth, Vt., 25 Jan. 1821, and remained there till death.

Children by adoption only, first born in Bridport, Vt., second in Salisbury, Vt.:

Mary M.,⁷ b. 20 Feb. 1811; m. 7 Feb. 1832, Zenas Reynolds.

1299. GEORGE HENRY, b. 15 July 1815; m. 10 Feb. 1847, Julia A. Hawley.

473

JOSEPH LAPHAM⁶ CHASE (Solomon,⁵ Dr. Benjamin,⁴ Joseph,³ Aquila²), born in Kent, Conn., 17 June 1784; died in Durham, Can., 28 May 1852. He married about 1814, MARY CONVERSE, who was born in Kent, 24 Aug. 1798; died in Farmersburg, Iowa, 22 July 1859 or 1860. They lived in Kent and Washington, Conn., till 1828 when they removed to Durham, Canada.

Children, born first two in Kent, third and fourth in Washington, fifth and sixth in Durham, Canada:

1300. DORMAN,[7] b. 11 Mar. 1817; m. 8 Dec. 1838, Emily Williams.
1301. ELIJAH, b. 7 Sept. 1818; m. (1) 6 Aug. 1851, Charity Snell; m. (2) 23 Mar. 1856, Elisabeth A. Spragg.
1302. JOHN, b. 14 Apr. 1821; m. 26 Apr. 1842, Susanna Crawford. Clergyman; living in Iowa, 1873.
        CAROLINE M., b. 25 Dec. 1822; m. 25 Dec. 1835, James Jackson.
        TAMSON, b. 29 Aug. 1829; m. 4 Jan. 1844, John Crawford.
        MARY ETTE, b. 4 July 1831; m. 1 Jan. 1850, Nathan Snell.

474

BENJAMIN GRANT[6] CHASE (Stephen,[5] Dr. Benjamin,[4] Joseph,[3] Aquila[2]) lived in Brooklyn, Susquehanna Co., Penn.

475

WILLIAM[6] CHASE (Stephen,[5] Dr. Benjamin,[4] Joseph,[3] Aquila[2]) lived in Brooklyn, Susquehanna Co., Penn.

476

ALBERT[6] CHASE (Stephen,[5] Dr. Benjamin,[4] Joseph,[3] Aquila[2]) lived in Brooklyn, Susquehanna Co., Penn.

477

SALMON[6] CHASE (Stephen,[5] Dr. Benjamin,[4] Joseph,[3] Aquila[2]) may have moved West about 1800.

478

NATHAN[6] CHASE (Stephen,[5] Dr. Benjamin,[4] Joseph,[3] Aquila[2]) probably lived in New York state.

479

CHAUNCEY[6] CHASE (Stephen,[5] Dr. Benjamin,[4] Joseph,[3] Aquila[2]) reported to have lived in Waterbury, but not mentioned in the history of Waterbury, Conn. He may have lived in some other Waterbury.

480

PETER[6] CHASE (Sarah,[5] Joseph,[4] Joseph,[3] Aquila[2]), born in Groton, 2 Oct. 1779; died there 9 Mar. 1865. He married in Groton, 29 June 1802, SALLY STONE, daughter of Levi and Lydia (Ward) Stone, born in Groton, 24 Dec. 1776; died there, 22 Nov. 1857. The Church Records of Groton state that Peter Wood, son of Sarah Chase, was baptized 25 Apr. 1779. [1780?]

Children, born in Groton:

1303. WALTER,[7] b. 2 Oct. 1802.
        CLARISSA, b. 3 Aug. 1804.
1304. WILLIAM, b. 28 Sept. 1806.
        MARY ANN, b. 5 Nov. 1814.
1305. WILLIAM AUGUSTUS, b. 29 July 1819.

481

Moses[6] Chase (Moses,[5] Joseph,[4] Joseph,[3] Aquila[2]), born and baptized in Groton, 27 Oct. 1799; died in Fitchburg, 28 July 1849, aged 55, of the small pox. He married in Lancaster, 16 May 1816, Ruth Sargent, who died in Fitchburg, of the small pox, as his widow, 30 July 1849, aged 49. She was born in Lancaster in 1800. Administration on his estate in Worcester Co. in 1849, files 11,342.

Children, born in Lancaster:

Moses,[7] b. 2 Dec. 1817.
Ruth, b. 17 Nov. 1819.
Mary, b. 11 Jan. 1822.

482

America[6] Chase (Moses,[5] Joseph,[4] Joseph,[3] Aquila[2]) was baptized in Groton, 27 Oct. 1799. This baptism is recorded in the records of the First Church of Groton. There is no further record of him in the Vital Records of Groton, nor is his estate mentioned in Middlesex County.

482a

Joseph Hatch[6] Chase (Thomas,[5] Joseph,[4] Joseph,[3] Aquila[2]), born in Newbury, 16 Oct. 1797; died 14 May 1858. He married in Newbury, 11 Dec. 1817, Nancy Brown. They lived in Newbury.

Children, born in Newbury:

Joseph,[7] b. 21 June 1819; drowned at sea, Sept. 1839.
Jacob Brown, b. 27 Aug. 1820; m. 3 July 1844, Hannah J. Thurlow; living in Newburyport in 1871.
James, b. 5 Jan. 1822; d. 22 Mar. 1822.
Eliza, b. 24 Feb. 1823; d. 8 May 1856, in Kansas.
Lydia Ann (twin), b. 24 Feb. 1823; d. 26 Oct. 1823.
Emily B., b. 16 Oct. 1824; d. 9 Feb. 1844.
John, b. 25 July 1826; d. 4 Aug. 1829.
Sarah H., b. 6 May 1828; d. 10 July 1830.
Sarah H., b. 4 Nov. 1832; d. 13 Sept. 1850.

482b

James[6] Chase (Thomas,[5] Joseph,[4] Joseph,[3] Aquila[2]), born about 1798; married in Salem, 14 Sept. 1823, Betsey Teague. He died in Salem, 31 July 1840, aged 41, a grandson of Joseph of Newbury.

Children:

John.[7]
Francis Augustus, bp. 2 Oct. 1836.
Abby Anna, bp. 7 June 1840.
Elizabeth, m. Henry Lunt; d. 9 Oct. 1865.

482c

John B.[6] Chase (Thomas,[5] Joseph,[4] Joseph,[3] Aquila[2]), born in Newbury, 23 Apr. 1805; married in Newbury, 16 Oct. 1824, Susan S. Downs.

483

JEREMIAH[6] CHASE (Lt. Abel,[5] Thomas,[4] Dea. Thomas,[3] Thomas[2]), born in what is now West Newbury, 10 Mar. 1762; died in West Newbury, 30 Oct. 1823, aged 62. He married 2 Feb. 1786, HANNAH PILLSBURY, who died in West Newbury, 10 Nov. 1846, aged 83. She was daughter of William and Mary (Hardy) Pillsbury, born in Newbury, 8 July 1763. They lived in Newbury (now West Newbury) and in Nottingham West (now Hudson), N. H.

Children, born in Newbury:

HANNAH MORSE,[7] b. 16 Oct. 1786; m. 2 Dec. 1813, Stephen Poor. She d. 10 Nov. 1846.

FANNY, b. 24 Nov. 1788; m. 30 Nov. 1809, Robert Howell. She d. 23 July, 1810, aged 22.

ELIZABETH, b. 2 Apr. 1791; m. 21 May 1812, Jonathan Eastman.

SARAH, b. 18 Oct. 1796; m. 7 Sept. 1815, Moses Brown, Jr.

ABIGAIL PERLEY, b. 10 June 1798; m. 19 June, 1832, George W. Wilder.

1306. ABEL, b. 15 Oct. 1800; m. 23 Oct. 1823, Elisabeth D. Wadleigh.

ANNA, b. 4 Feb. 1803; m. 20 Dec. 1830, David B. Marston; he d. Nov. 1843.

1307. WILLIAM, b. 1 Aug. 1805; m. 9 Jan. 1827, Sarah C. Wadleigh.

EMILY, b. 1 Aug. 1810; m. 24 or 29 Aug. 1830, Thomas W. Coleman of Chester (now Auburn), N. H., d. 3 June 1867.

484

CAPT. THOMAS[6] CHASE (Lt. Abel,[5] Thomas,[4] Dea. Thomas,[3] Thomas[2]), born in what is now West Newbury, 21 Mar. 1772; died there, 3 Aug. 1849, aged 77 y. 4 m. He married in Newbury, 12 June 1800, LOIS ORDWAY, daughter of David and Lois (Patten) Ordway, born in Newbury, 30 Jan. 1772; died 3 May 1857, aged 85 y. 2 m. 4 d. They lived in West Newbury.

Child, born in Newbury (now West Newbury):

SUSAN,[7] b. 23 June 1805; m. 16 June 1830 George Thurlow; d. 3 Dec. 1887. He d. 15 June 1879. Three children.

Their son, *Thomas Chase Thurlow*, b. 30 Dec. 1832; m. 15 Oct. 1879, his cousin, Mrs. Sarah (Kimball) Deane, b. in Medford, 1 July 1845; d. in West Newbury, 12 July 1927. He d. 21 July 1909. Four children, George C., Edward K., Winthrop H. and Susan C. Thurlow.

He was associated with his father in a nursery business established about the time he was born, which is now carried on by his sons and nationally known as the Cherry Hill Nurseries. He lived, and a portion of the nursery is on the land that was originally owned by his ancestor, Thomas[2] Chase.

485

THOMAS[6] CHASE (Dr. Josiah,[5] Thomas,[4] Thomas,[3] Thomas[2]), born in Canterbury, N. H., 7 Aug. 1766; died in Fryeburg, Me., 6 Oct. 1855. He married 19 Aug. 1789, MARY SPRING, daughter of Jedediah Spring. She was born in Conway, N. H., 30 Aug. 1768 and died in Fryeburg, 15 Mar. 1816. They lived in Conway in 1790.

Children:

BETSEY S.,[7] b. 21 Mar. 1790; m. 9 Mar. 1817, William Shirley, s. of Edward of Dunbarton, N. H. She d. 5 Jan. 1860. Two children.

1308. HALL, b. 7 Apr. 1792; m. Hannah Spring, dau. of Capt. Seth Spring. He d. in Waterville, Me., 20 July 1851. Four children.

1309. SETH S., b. 2 Apr. 1794; m. June 1819, Elisabeth Shirley, dau. of Edward. He d. 20 Sept. 1828. Six children.

1310. JOSIAH, b. 4 Apr. 1797; drowned at sea Jan. 1824.

1311. JOHN S., b. 5 June 1799; m. S—— Fitch, dau. of Richard. Four children.

LYDIA B., b. 10 July 1801; m. 5 July, 1827, Stephen Gordon. She d. 22 Dec. 1864. Six children.

HANNAH, b. 31 Dec. 1803; m. James Stackpole. No children.

1312. SAMUEL F., d. 17 Dec. 1805; m. Elisabeth Pearson of Biddeford, Me. He d. 18 Feb. 1859. Eight children.

JAMES S., b 21 Oct. 1807; d. 2 Feb. 1810.

WILLIAM R., b. 30 Oct. 1810; d. 20 Apr. 1813.

1313. RICHARD R., b. 18 Aug. 1814; d. 9 Mar. 1840.

486

JOSEPH F.[6] CHASE (Dr. Josiah,[5] Thomas,[4] Thomas,[3] Thomas[2]), born in Canterbury, N. H., 19 Sept. 1770; died 29 Jan. 1823. He married (1) in Conway, N. H., 24 July 1791, MEHITABLE DAY; married (2) 1799, JOANNA DAY, sister to Mehitable; Joanna was born 23 Aug. 1771 in Conway. He married (3) about 1803, SARAH EATON. She died 2 Oct. 1856, aged 86y. 2m. They lived in Conway.

Children by the first wife, born in Conway:

MEHITABLE F.,[7] b. 31 May 1793; m. May 1812, Caleb Abbott of Fryeburg, Me.

1314. ENOCH S., b. 20 Apr. 1795; m. Hannah Witherell; lived in North Adams.

1315. THOMAS, b. 16 Mar. 1797; m. (1) 8 Sept. 1822, Melinda Dresser of Fryeburg, Me.; m. (2) 6 Oct. 1833, Polly Andrews.

Child by second wife:

JOANNA D., b. 14 Mar. 1800; m. 14 May 1834, John Tripp of Hebron, Me. She d. 28 June 1874.

Children by the third wife, born in Conway:

ANNA S., b. 23 Mar. 1804; m. 29 Oct. 1847, Solomon Eastman of Stowe and Chatham, N. H. One son.

ELISABETH B., b. 2 Mar. 1806; m. Ansel Page of Conway.

1316. JOSEPH F., b 10 July 1808; m. 9 Feb. 1831, Lydia R. Lord, of Lowell, Me.

1317. WILLIAM E., b. 15 Feb. 1812; m. 17 June 1838, Emily W. Eastman; lived in Conway. Four children.

SARAH E., b. 9 June 1814; m. James F. Eaton. She d. 7 Sept. 1842; one child.

487

ENOCH S.[6] CHASE (Dr. Josiah,[5] Thomas,[4] Thomas,[3] Thomas[2]), born in Canterbury, N. H., 4 May 1775; died 17 May 1817. He married, —— VANCE of Calais, Me. Children, two daughters, names unknown.

488

JOSIAH[6] CHASE (Dr. Josiah,[5] Thomas,[4] Thomas,[3] Thomas[2]), born 12 May 1782; died 2 Oct. 1856. He married Jan. 1805, HANNAH BUCK who was born, 19 Aug. 1788; died 25 Apr. 1837. It is supposed they lived in Conway, N. H.

Children:

SALLY,[7] b. 1 Jan. 1806; d. 10 Apr. 1806.
EMMA C., b. 8 Oct. 1807; m. 12 Mar. 1840, Charles Osgood.
1318. ASA B., b. 23 Nov. 1809; d. 14 Feb. 1810.
1319. SIMEON C., b. 1 Mar. 1811; m. in Nashua, 15 Mar. 1848, Mrs. Frances H. Weed. No children. They lived in Lowell.
HANNAH, b. 8 June 1813; d. 14 Jan. 1814.
HANNAH B., b. 13 May, 1815; d. 30 Jan. 1816.
MARY S., b. 30 July 1817; m. in Conway, N. H., 15 Sept. 1841, Mason Wiley of Fryeburg, Me. She d. 23 Feb. 1851, without issue.
SAMUEL B., b. 25 July 1820; d. 20 Sept. 1825.
ABBY B., b. 1 May 1824; m. — June 1847, Jacob Kelley.
SUSAN P., b. 17 Jan. 1827; m. Mar. 1855; Oliver Brackett.
1320. JAMES W., b. 19 June, 1829; d. 8 Sept. 1857.

489

LT. ABEL[6] CHASE (Abel,[5] Dea. Abel,[4] Dea. Thomas,[3] Thomas[2]), born in what is now Millbury, 29 Oct. 1754; died in Millbury, 16 Oct. 1833, aged 79. He married in Sutton, 24 Sept. 1779, HANNAH BOND, daughter of Jonas and Hannah (Hicks) Bond, born in Sutton, 13 Mar. 1757; died in Millbury, 11 Mar. 1842, aged 85. They were buried in the West Millbury Cemetery. They lived in Sutton and he was a Revolutionary soldier.

Children, born in Sutton:

HANNAH,[7] b. 9 July 1780; m. 1 July 1802, Joseph Richardson of Auburn.
JONAS, b. 2 Jan. 1782; d. young.
1321. JONAS, b. 20 Aug. 1783; m. Lavina Boyden; lived in Millbury.
SILENCE, b. 8 Dec. 1785; m. 1 May 1806, William Young.
MEHITABLE, b. 15 Sept. 1788; m. 11 Jan. 1809, Kendall Bancroft of Auburn.
ABEL, b. 6 Aug. 1791; d. young.
POLLY, b. 4 July 1793; d. young.

490

ISAAC[6] CHASE (Abel,[5] Dea. Abel,[4] Dea. Thomas,[3] Thomas[2]), born in what is now Millbury, 12 Sept. 1761; died in Westford, Vt., 9 Jan. 1833. He married in Sutton, 8 Jan. 1789, SARAH BOND, daughter of Josiah and Sarah (Melody) Bond, born in Sutton, 21 Sept. 1769; died 7 July 1841. He was a Revolutionary soldier. They lived in Stratton, Vt., and Westford, Vt., from 1797 to 1833.

Children, born in Stratton, last three born in Westford:

1322. TRUMAN,[7] b. 17 Jan. 1790; m. 2 Jan. 1816, Laura Ballard of Georgia, Vt.; he d. 28 Apr. 1871.
1323. IRAH, b. 5 Oct. 1793; m. (1) 15 Mar. 1821, Harriet Savage, dau. of Timothy Savage, at Wilmington, N. C.; m. (2) 13 Oct. 1835, Martha Raymond.

He fitted for college and graduated from Middlebury College in 1814 and from Andover Theological Seminary in 1817; ordained as a Baptist minister at Danvers 17 Sept. 1817; associated with Dr. William Staughton in establishing the first Baptist Theological School in this country in Philadelphia; in 1822 it was removed to Washington and made a part of Columbian College with Dr. Chase as professor of biblical literature, 1822 to 1825; removed to Massachusetts and took part in establishing the Newton Theological Institution of which he was the first professor of Biblical Theology till 1836; and of Ecclesiastical History, 1836 to 1845. He published *Remarks on the Book of Daniel,* 1844; *Life of John Bunyan; The Design of Baptism,* 1851; *The Work claiming to be the Constitution of the Holy Apostles,* and *Infant Baptism an Invention of Man.* He d. in Newton, 1 Nov. 1864.

Among the children by his first wife was *Henry Savage,*[8] b. 17 June 1825; m. 25 Dec. 1857, Sarah Grano Leverett. Their daughter Ellen,[9] b. in Brookline, 26 Mar. 1863; member of many civic and patriotic societies; author of *The Beginnings of the American Revolution,* in three volumes, 1911; lives in Brookline.

1324.   PETER, b. 2 May, 1796; m. 28 Aug. 1821, Martha Stewart; clergyman; he d. at Enosburg, Vt., 10 May 1866.

1325.   ISAAC, b. 3 Nov. 1798; m. Elitha Naranda Ballard. Five children.

SARAH, b. 5 Aug. 1810; m. 7 Sep. 1828, John Morse; she d. in Elgin, Ill., 13 Sept. 1871.

491

JONATHAN[6] CHASE (Abel,[5] Dea. Abel,[4] Dea. Thomas,[3] Thomas[2]), born in what is now Millbury, 26 Feb. 1770; died in Westford, Vt., 5 June 1825. He married in Oxford, 22 Jan. 1797, MEHITABLE JENNISON of Charlton. She was born 11 Feb. 1773; died 6 or 17 Aug. 1859. They lived in Westford from 1797.

Children, born in Westford:

1326.   ABEL,[7] b. 12 Dec. 1797; m. 27 Dec. 1821, Sally Buck; d. 12 Aug. 1865.

JUDITH, b. 20 Jan. 1799; m. (1) Gardner Jennison; m. (2) ——— Beeman.

POLLY, b. 3 or 23 June 1800; m. 3 May 1825, Almon Griffin; lived in Alba, Minn.; d. 1865.

1327.   LUTHER, b. 10 Sept. 1801; m. (1) 15 Mar., 1827 Olive Griffin; m. (2) 2 Mar. 1840, Sarah M. Barrett of Westford. He d. d. 8 May 1863.

1328.   TYLER, b. 28 Jan. 1804; m. 23 Sept. 1827, Sarah Hobart of Hollis, N. H.; living in Westford in 1872.

1329.   Calvin, b. 18 May 1805; m. (1) 8 Nov. 1833, Huldah Lacy; m. (2) Amanda F. McLane; lived in Chesaning, Mich, 1873.

492

CALVIN[6] CHASE (Thomas,[5] Dea. Abel,[4] Thomas,[3] Thomas[2]), born in Sutton, 6 Jan. 1784; died in Miramichi, N. B., 28 July 1817. He married 10 Nov. 1810, REBECCA TOBEY, daughter of John and Mary (West) Tobey, born in Union, Me., 17 Jan. 1793. She married (2) Thomas Chase, brother of Calvin.

Children:

> MARY WEST,[7] b. 27 Sept. 1811; m. 14 Nov. 1837, Nathan P.
> Martin of Union, Me.
> WILLIAM WITT, b. 22 Aug. 1813; d. 30 Oct. 1839.
> ALMEDA, b. 19 Mar. 1815; d. 11 Sept. 1817, in Miramichi, N. B.

493

THOMAS[6] CHASE (Thomas,[5] Dea. Abel,[4] Thomas,[3] Thomas[2])
born in Sutton, 2 May 1790; died in Warwick, 4 Oct. 1870, aged 80.
He married 20 June 1822, REBECCA (TOBEY) CHASE, his brother's
widow, and daughter of John and Mary (West) Tobey, born in Union, Me., 17 Jan. 1793; died in Warwick, 22 Dec. 1864, aged 72.
They lived in Warwick.

Children, born in Warwick:

> EMILY ALMEDA,[7] b. 14 Apr. 1823; m. 27 Mar. 1849, Enoch
> Davis Sprague; d. 30 Sept. 1865, in Richmond, N. H.
> CAROLINE REBECCA, b. 16 Oct. 1824; m. 10 Apr. 1850, Chester
> W. Deloy of Warwick.
> ALMIRA GREENWOOD, b. 25 Dec. 1826; m. 4 July 1849, George
> Woodbury.
1330.
> EDWARD CALVIN, b. 27 Mar. 1829; m. 16 Sept. 1855, Mary Jane
> Goddard; lived in Warwick.
> MARTHA BRINTNALL, b. 10 Oct. 1833; d. 5 Aug. 1856.

494

DAVID[6] CHASE (Sergt. David,[5] Dea. Abel,[4] Dea. Thomas,[3]
Thomas[2]), born in Sutton, 7 Jan. 1778; died 2 Feb. 1850. He mar-
ried in Acton, 24 Feb. 1805, ANNA WOODS, daughter of Moses and
Kezia (——) Woods, born in Acton, 2 Mar. 1780. He was living in
Newton at the time of his marriage. They lived in Littleton. She
was living in Dec. 1870.

Children:

1331.
> EBEN CURTIS,[7] b. 11 Oct. 1806; m. 30 June 1845, Mary Estep of
> Buffalo, N. Y.
1332.
> DAVID WOODS, b. 18 Jan. 1809; m. Apr. 1835, Hannah Dickin-
> son.
1333.
> ABEL HOLMAN, b. 30 Jan. 1811; m. Dec. 1842, Lucretia F. Wood
> of Preston.
> EPHRAIM CROGHAN, b. 19 July 1817; unm.
1334.
> ELIPHALET CONDO, b. 15 May 1819; d. 22 May 1862.
> HELEN MAR, b. 16 Aug. 1826; m. 31 May 1855, William C.
> Bliven.

495

BRICKETT[6] CHASE (Moses,[5] Dea. Roger,[4] Dea. Thomas,[3] Thomas[2]), born in Sutton, 26 Oct. 1786. He was four years old when his
father died and there is no later record of him in Sutton. His estate
is not mentioned in Worcester County.

496

SILAS[6] CHASE (Moses,[5] Dea. Roger,[4] Dea. Thomas,[3] Thomas[2]),
born in Sutton, 26 July 1788. No later record relating to him has
been found by the compiler.

497

ROGER[6] CHASE (Ezekiel,[5] Dea. Roger,[4] Dea. Thomas,[3] Thomas[2]), born in Hallowell, Me., 5 Sept. 1749; died in Concord, Me., 25 Nov. 1819; married (1) widow MARY (SMITH) SPEAR; married (2) widow RACHEL (BROWN) MOORE. They lived in Caratunk Plantation (now Concord), Me., in 1790. He was captured in the French and Indian War and carried to Quebec by the Indians who sold him as a prisoner of war; he escaped and came near starvation on his journey home.

Children by first wife; first three born in Clinton, Me., last four in Concord, Me.:

WILLIAM,[7] d. unm. Sept. 1852, in St. Davids, N. B.

1335. STEPHEN, b. 1773; m. Polly Moore; d. 23 June 1828 in Concord, Me.

1336. ROGER, b. 24 Dec. 1779; m. 4 Mar. 1801, Polly Benjamin of Bingham, Me.; d. 21 Apr. 1844 in Concord, Me.

1337. JOEL, b. 22 Oct. 1791; m. 22 Oct. 1813, Abigail Tucker of Rochester, N. H. Six children; d. 21 Nov. 1826 in Bingham, Me.

TAMAR, m. John Heard of Harmony, Me. One son.

ELEANOR, m. Edward Howes of Bingham, Me. Six children.

ANNA, d. a child.

498

DR. EZEKIEL[6] CHASE (Ezekiel,[5] Roger,[4] Thomas,[3] Thomas[2]), born 4 June 1761, probably in Hallowell, Me.; died 14 Sept. 1843, aged 82. He married about 1782, BETSEY GOODWIN of Fairfield, Me., who died 1 Feb. 1849, aged 82. He enlisted from Hallowell, 18 May 1778, at the age of 16 and served till 1781. In 1790 he was living in Caratunk Plantation, and later they lived in Sebec, Me., where he was a physician. He was a Revolutionary War pensioner living in Sebec, age 77, on 1 June 1840.

Children, not in order, first six born in Fairfield, Me., seventh and eighth in Bingham, Me., last two in Sebec:

1338. FRANCIS,[7] b. 17 Dec. 1784; m. 1817, Mary Carter of Atkinson, Me., who d. about 1867. He d. 27 Feb. 1865.

1339. JONATHAN, b. June 1786; m. Rebecca Smart of Sebec; d. 19 June 1840.

1340. DANIEL, b. 2 Oct. 1789; m. 16 Feb. 1812, Sarah Carter of Atkinson; m. (2) ——— Leavitt. He d. 16 Apr. 1821. By the second wife his son was Cyrus,[8] who m. Mary Stevens Wise. Their son was Christopher,[9] b. 1833; d. in Oakland, Calif., 1912; m. 1861, Emily Chase Gilman, b. 16 Feb. 1843, d. 1924. Their son Clarence Augustine,[10] b. in Sebec, 17 Apr. 1862; m. (1) 1882, Clara Laura Lowell (1864-1895); m. (2) 1900, Nellie Dora Stevens. Their son Harold Clarence,[11] b. 7 Sept. 1885; m. 3 Oct. 1908, Ina L. Bailey and have Louise Lowell,[12] Harold Clarence[12] and Barbara Bailey.[12]

SARAH, b. Apr. 1792; m. 1814, John Currier of Atkinson. She d. 11 Apr. 1842.

MARY, b. May 1801; m. William Hamlin of Milo, Me.. She d. 29 May 1827.

ABIGAIL, b. Sept. 1796; d. unm.

1341. EZEKIEL, b. 6 Mar. 1799; m. 11 May 1823, Mercy Livermore of Milo.

1342. CALEB, b. 7 Mar. 1800; m. 27 June 1833, Hannah Burrill; he d. 1864.

1343. CHARLES V., b. 15 July 1804; m. Mary Brown, of Sebec; he d. 23 May 1841.

1344. OWEN G., b 18 Sept. 1810; m. 11 Feb. 1835, Lucinda Burrill of Atkinson; lived in Sebec.

499

DANIEL⁶ CHASE (Ezekiel,⁵ Dea. Roger,⁴ Dea. Thomas,³ Thomas²), born 31 Aug. 1762 (probably in Hallowell, Me.); died in Sebec, Me., 6 June 1824. He married (1) about 1790, BETSEY BODFISH of Fairfield, Me. He married (2) about 1801, ANNA LEAVITT of Clinton, Me. They lived in Fairfield, Me., and in Sebec, Me. Their three eldest children were baptized at Fairfield, 28 July 1796. (Me. Coll. His. Soc. 4:315.).

Children by the first wife, born in Fairfield:

1345. DANIEL,⁷ b. 5 Aug. 1793; m. (1) 13 Dec. 1818, Sarah Noyes Gregory; m. (2) 23 Aug. 1839, Mehitable Wheeler. He was state senator, 1831, 1832, 1838. He was a Colonel and d. in Atkinson, Me., 8 Mar. 1854.

1346. JOSEPH, b. 26 Feb. 1795; m. (1) 20 Mar. 1818, Comfort Livermore; m. (2) 26 Oct. 1865, Rebecca Comfort nee Manter. He lived in Sebec and Newport, Me.

MERCY, b. 28 July 1796; m. Alvardius Shaw.

1347. ABIJAH, b. 3 Feb. 1797; m. Electa Whidden; d. in Australia, 1853.

BETSEY (twin), b. 3 Feb. 1797; m. Lemuel Shipley; she d. 1 Dec. 1882.

CHALLIS, b. 4 Nov. 1799; d. in St. Petersburg, Russia, unm.

Children by the second wife:

ALONZO, b. 6 Jan. 1802; d. unm. in Rutland, Ohio, 24 Oct. 1862, a. 40y. 10m. 25d.

1348. CYRUS, b. 1 Sept. 1805; m. 24 Nov. 1818, Mary Wise.

1349. DAVID, m. Sarah Roberts. He d. 16 Oct. 1843.

1350. GEORGE, b. 30 Sept. 1809; m. Hannah Roberts.

MARY ANN, m. William Rand.

LOUISA or ELIZA, m. David Holbrook of Sebec.

SOPHRONIA, b. 1817; m. James McGuire. She d. in Sebec, 2 Feb. 1857, aged 40.

500

ABEL⁶ CHASE (Ezekiel,⁵ Dea. Roger,⁴ Thomas,³ Thomas²), born in Hallowell, Me., 4 Dec. 1774; died in Rutland, Ohio, 10 July 1852. He married 20 Oct. 1797, ABIGAIL NELSON, who was born in Gilmanton, N. H., 14 Jan. 1778; died in Rutland, Ohio, 4 Nov. 1849. They lived in Fairfield, Me., 1805-1814, Sebec, Me. 1814 to 1817; and in Rutland, Meigs Co., Ohio, from 1817 to 1852.

Children, fifth to ninth born in Fairfield, last two in Sebec:

1351. CHARLES C.,⁷ b. 20 July 1798; m. 23 Aug. 1822, Mary Triphena Holt; he d. 25 Jan. 1858.

1352. ABEL, b. 23 Dec. 1799; m. 1 Mar. 1828, Esther Noble. Five children. He d. in Rutland, Ohio, 15 Aug. 1848.

1353. ARCHIBALD, b. 24 Aug. 1801; m. 21 Mar. 1824, Elisabeth Price. He d. on Red River, 1840.

HARRIET, b. 20 Dec. 1803; m. 25 July 1822, George Downing; living in Ohio 1872: she d. 17 July 1878.

1354.   JOHN HENRY, b. 14 Jan. 1806; m. 3 Apr. 1829, Olive Skinner. He d. in Rutland, 27 Apr. 1832.

1355.   HIRAM, b. 9 Jan. 1808; m. (1) 14 Feb. 1832, Edna Skinner. Living in Ohio, 1872: d. 18 Aug. 1876.

1356.   FRANCIS, b. 30 June 1810; m. 3 Aug. 1834, Louisa Knight; he d. in Rutland, 15 Dec. 1871.

ELECTA (twin), b. 30 June, 1810; d. 17 July, 1822.

ELIZA, b. 2 Feb. 1813; d. Jan. 1818.

ABIGAIL, b. 16 Apr. 1815; d. 17 July 1822, in Rutland.

1357.   ELIJAH, b. 18 Jan. 1817; m. Elizabeth Bowman. He lived in Olympia, Wash.; d. 18 May 1866.

501

VARNHAM[6] CHASE (Stephen,[5] Roger,[4] Thomas,[3] Thomas[2]), died in Canaan, Me., in 1829; buried in Fairfield, Me. He married ABIGAIL WHITTEN of Canaan. They lived in Canaan, where he was taxed 1781.

Children, born in Canaan:

WILLIAM,[7] d. unm. at sea.

1358.   STEPHEN, m. Susan Wing of Clinton, Me.

1359.   TIMOTHY, m. ———— Eaton.

ABIGAIL, b. 1788; m. 1811, David Kendall; she d. in Canaan, 3 Oct. 1842. Eight children.

FRANCES, m. Parrin Reed; had one son and one daughter. She d. in Canaan, 3 Oct. 1855.

502

THOMAS[6] CHASE (Matthew,[5] Dea. Roger,[4] Thomas,[3] Thomas[2]), born about 1770; died about 1844 at the age of 74. He married (1) about 1790, DOLLY JACKENS of Fairfield, Me., who died about 1857. He married (2) ABIGAIL JUDKINS. They lived in Fairfield or Clinton, Me.

Children by first wife:

1360.   ALGER,[7] m. Patty Burrell, dau. of Ziba and Polly[6] (Chase) Burrell of Dover, Me.

NANCY, b. about 1791; m. 1804 (married at 13), Capt. David Pishon of Fairfield, Me. She d. 7 June 1858.

BETSEY, b. 22 July 1795; m. 1 May 1814, Alexander P. Thompson.

SARAH, b. 12 May 1796; m. Apr. 1813, George Nye of Fairfield.

BLOOMY, m. Joseph Noble of Fairfield.

1361.   EZEKIEL, b. 29 June 1802; m. 28 Feb. 1826, Jerusha Stevens, b. in Greene, Me., 13 Aug. 1806. He d. 1 June 1831. Four children.

MARIA, m. Samuel Thomas.

ELECTA, d. aged 14 or 15 yrs.

THOMAS, d. unm. Feb. 1832.

JEFFERSON, d. in childhood.

DOLLY, b. 28 Nov. 1807; m. (1) 19 Aug. 1824, Amos[6] Chase; m. (2) 25 Nov. 1837, Elias Humphrey. (Family 1142)

Children by second wife:

MATTHEW, drowned unm.

1362.   DAVID, lived Kendall's Mills, Fairfield.
        ELEANOR, m. abt. 1847, George Butterfield; she d. soon after
            marriage.
        ELIZA, m. in 1848, George Butterfield.
1363.   HARRISON, alive in 1871.
        HANKERSON, d. in childhood.
        WILLIAM, d. in childhood.

503

ASA[6] CHASE (Matthew,[5] Roger,[4] Thomas,[3] Thomas[2]), married
MARGARET BODFISH. They lived in Bangor, Me.
    Children:
1364.   HENRY,[7] m. and had children.
        MAHALA.
1365.   RANDOLPH.
        STATIRA.
        HARRIET.
1366.   FRANKLIN, lived in Bangor, Me.
        ANGELINE.
        MARTHA.

504

FRANCIS[6] CHASE (Matthew,[5] Dea. Roger,[4] Dea. Thomas,[3]
Thomas[2]), born in Fairfield, Me., 27 Apr. 1792; died in Blanchard,
Me., 1 Mar. 1855. He married 13 Oct. 1814, BETSEY SPEARING, who
was born in Clinton, Me., 27 July 1794 and died in Waterville, Me.,
27 Jan. 1869. She married (2) Isaac Gage of Waterville, Me. They
lived in Blanchard, Me.
    Children, eldest two born in Clinton, five youngest in Blanchard:
        JOSIAH,[7] b. 21 July 1815; d. unm. 22 Oct. 1848, in Blanchard.
        SARAH ANN, b. 21 July 1817; m. Matthew Pratt; living in
            Clinton, 1872.
1367.   WILLIAM S., b. 24 June 1819; m. Betsey Lewis.
        LAVINA L., b. 25 Sept. 1821; m. 30 June 1852, Cyrus Wade.
1368.   RANDALL, b. 26 June 1823; m. Dorcas Ames; d. at Petersburg,
            in the Civil War.
1369.   FRANCIS, b. 20 Mar. 1826; m. Phebe A. Anderson.
        BETSEY, b. 10 July 1829; m. Daniel Cain of Clinton.
1370.   JOSEPH, b. 7 July 1834; m. Phebe Packard. He d. in Clear
            Water, Minn.

505

JOSIAH[6] CHASE (Matthew,[5] Dea. Roger,[4] Dea. Thomas,[3] Thomas[2]) was born probably in Fairfield, Me. There is a report that he
lived in Philadelphia, Pa.

506

MATTHEW[6] CHASE JR. (Matthew,[5] Dea. Roger,[4] Dea. Thomas,[3]
Thomas[2]) was probably born in Fairfield, Me.

507

COTTON[6] CHASE (Col. Josiah,[5] Rev. Josiah,[4] Dea. Thomas,[3]
Thomas[2]), born in York, Me., 25 July 1770; died there 9 May 1842.

He married 20 Sept. 1798, MIRIAM LEIGHTON, daughter of William and Miriam (Fernald) Leighton of Kittery, Me., born 30 Dec. 1778. Thy lived in York, Me.

Children, born in York, Me.:

1371. JOSIAH,[7] b. 3 Nov. 1799; m. 1826, Mary Bean of Kittery, Me.; d. 24 July 1853. He built a woolen factory on the mill privilege which he inherited from his father Cotton and his grandfather Col. Josiah Chase, clothiers. The Chases manufactured woolen goods from 1768 to 1845. He gave the factory to his sons *Charles E.*[8] and *John L.*[8] *Chase* in 1853. The mill was located near the outlet of Chase's Lake in York.

1372. WILLIAM, b. 17 Nov. 1802; m. Harriet Perkins; lived in Rochester, N. H.; he d. 12 Sept. 1844.

      MIRIAM LEIGHTON, b. 22 Nov. 1807; d. unm. 12 Sept. 1838.

1373. COTTON, b. 10 May 1809; m. 1830, Deborah Stuart of Wells, Me.; lived in York, Me.; d. 14 Feb. 1874.

      CHARLES, b. 3 June 1811; d. 19 Aug. 1814.

1374. EDWARD, b. 15 Jan. 1814; m. Louisa Bragdon of York; lived in Alfred, Me.; d. 14 Aug. 1864.

1375. CHARLES, b. 22 May 1819; m. Martha Plaisted of York; lived first in California; later on home farm in York.

      SARAH JANE, b. 23 Dec. 1821; d. 20 Sept. 1823.

508

JOSIAH[6] CHASE (Col. Josiah,[5] Rev. Josiah,[4] Dea. Thomas,[3] Thomas[2]), born in York, Me., 17 Feb. 1772; died in Caratunk Plantation, Me., 8 Apr. 1846. He married, 12 Aug. 1793, ALICE BENNETT of Sanford, Me., who was born 3 Sept. 1771. They lived in Woolwich, Me., Limington, Me., Concord, Me., and Lexington, Me. He died in Carratunk, Me., while on a visit to Joseph Spaulding.

Children, born in Woolwich, Me.:

1376. EDWARD,[7] b. 29 Aug. 1794; lived in Lexington, Me.

1377. RUFUS, b. 21 Apr. 1796; m. 13 Nov. 1828, Susan Crosby. Seven children living in Lexington, Me., in 1872.

1378. GEORGE, b. 24 May 1798; d. in 1846; m. Livenia Bosworth. Son *Abial Hathaway*,[8] b. in Solon, Me., in 1832; d. in Concord, 21 Aug. 1924, aged 92. He m. (1) Margaret A. Conley, dau. of William Conley. She was b. in Buffalo, N. Y., and d. in Concord, 2 Nov. 1867, aged 28. Their dau. Nellie E.[9] d. there 2 Sept. 1866, aged 1 y. 15 d. He m. (2) in Concord, 13 Sept. 1869, Martha Frances Simpson, dau. of William Simpson. Their son Frederic Hathaway,[9] b. in Concord, 27 July 1870; graduate of Harvard Univ., 1892; Harvard Law School, 1894; m. 17 Aug. 1898, Theodora Kyle of Plattsburg, N. Y., dau. Osceola Hardy and Fannie (Kellogg) Kyle, b. in Vergennes, Vt., and graduated from Wellesley College in 1891. Their children are *Martha*,[10] *Frederick Hathaway Jr.*[10] and *Theodore*.[10] He was Assistant District Attorney of Suffolk Co., 1903-6; justice of Superior Court of Massachusetts, 1911-20; member of the law firm of Stewart and Chase, 1920 to date. Author of *Life of Lemuel Shaw, Chief Justice,* 1918.

      SOPHIA, b. 23 Aug. 1800; m. (1) Joseph Spaulding; she d. 5 Apr. 1833; four children.

      IRENA, b. 18 Dec. 1802.

JUDGE FREDERICK HATHAWAY CHASE

1379.   JOSIAH JR., b. 7 July 1805.
1380.   ABIAL, b. 9 Dec. 1810.
          ELVIRA, b. 30 Oct. 1812; m. 1 June 1835 (his second wife),
          Joseph Spaulding; d. 4 Sept. 1881, at Richmond, Me. Nine
          children.

509

REV. RUFUS[6] CHASE (Col. Josiah,[5] Rev. Josiah,[4] Dea. Thomas,[3]
Thomas[2]), born in York, Me., 2 May 1784; died in Wells, Me., 9
Sept. 1871. He married 29 Sept. 1807, SALLY LITTLEFIELD, born 10
Apr. 1785. They lived in Alfred, Me., Hallowell, Me., and Wells,
Me. He was a Baptist clergyman.
  Children:
          HANNAH,[7] b. 7 Jan. 1809; m. Luther Gibbs of Bridgeton, Me.
          HADASSAH, b. 9 Oct. 1810; d. 1 Mar. 1816.
          SARAH MAXWELL, b. 13 Sept. 1812; m. (1) Dr. O. W. Austin
          of Portland, Me.; m. (2) Dr. John R. Butler, of Hallo-
          well, Me.
1381.   RUFUS MESSENGER, b. 1 Oct. 1814; physician; m. (1) Ann E.
          Pope; (2) Abby Rollins.
          CLARISSA, b. 11 Oct. 1816; m. (1) Benjamin Hewes of Bridge-
          ton, Me.; m. (2) Rev. Daniel Jackson of Pike, N. Y.
          HADASSAH, b. 15 Sept. 1818; m. 19 May 1846, Capt. George
          Goodwin of Wells, Me.
1382.   LYMAN, b. 27 Mar. 1821; clergyman; m. 12 May 1846, Pamela
          L. Soule; lived in Methuen.
          JULIA ANN, b. 1 Aug. 1823; m. Rev. John A. Lowell of Law-
          rence, Mass.
1383.   WILLIAM, b. 4 Oct. 1825; m. 1 Aug. 1853, Sarah Littlefield of
          Kennebunk, Me.

510

JOTHAM SEWALL[6] CHASE (Col. Josiah,[5] Rev. Josiah,[4] Dea.
Thomas,[3] Thomas[2]), born in York, Me., 26 June 1790; died in Bos-
ton, 28 Aug. 1833, aged 93y. 2m. 3d. He married (1) about 1812,
MARY GOULD, daughter of Dea. Moriah Gould of Norridgewock, Me.
She was born 4 Jan. 1792, and died in Saco, Me., 1 Oct. 1853. He
married (2) 19 Oct. 1856, MARIA (CARLISLE) AMES, a widow,
daughter of Stephen and Sarah Carlisle. They lived in 1858 at 6
Bulfinch Place, Boston.
  Children by first wife:
          MARIA,[7] b. 23 Dec. 1814; m. 3 Sept. 1840, William Gray, M.D.;
          d. in Saco, Me., 22 Oct. 1851.
1384.   JOTHAM GOULD, b. 30 Mar. 1816; m. (1) Sarah C. S. G. Thorn-
          ton; d. 10 Mar. 1847; m. (2) 28 May 1850, Cornelia S. Sav-
          age; lived in Springfield. One son.
          FRANCIS ASBURY, b. 23 Mar. 1818; d. 25 Sept. 1819.
          MARY ANN, b. 14 Nov. 1819; m. 26 Dec. 1839, Alonzo Hamilton
          of Boston.
          HANNAH, b. 5 July 1821; m. Henry Whelen of Iowa.
          ELIZA, b. 21 May 1823; m. Thomas Marshall of Iowa.
          LUCY, b. 21 Sept. 1824; m. Frederic W. Taylor, M.D.; she d.
          Sept. 1851.

1385.   RUFUS, b. 27 May 1826; m. Julia E. Ritter. Six children.
   HARRIET, b. 12 Aug. 1830; m. S. J. Wetherell of Ware.
1386.   FRANCIS ASBURY, b. 22 July 1832; lived in Washington, D. C.;
   m. —— Pepper.

511

JOSHUA T.[6] CHASE (Thomas,[5] Rev. Josiah,[4] Dea. Thomas,[3] Thomas[2]), born in Kittery, Me., 6 July 1778; married in Kittery, 28 July 1792, NANCY LITCHFIELD, daughter of Rev. Joseph and Hannah (Salisbury) Litchfield, born in Providence, R. I., 10 Apr. 1774. They lived in Kittery, Me. He was a selectman from 1814 to 1824; representative to General Court 1814 to 1819 and to Maine legislature 1820 to 1829. He had many land transfers between 3 Sept. 1796 and 24 Nov. 1847. He was a member of the convention which adopted the State Constitution in Portland in 1819.
   Children, born in Kittery, Me.:

1387.   CHARLES,[7] m. 10 March 1822, Ann Maria Rice. Surgeon in
   U. S. Navy.
1388.   PAUL, m. 6 May 1828, Edith Deering.
   DAUGHTER, m. Joseph Dame.

512

THOMAS[6] CHASE (Thomas,[5] Rev. Josiah,[4] Dea. Thomas,[3] Thomas[2]), born in Kittery, Me., 13 Sept. 1788; married 22 Jan. 1829, JOANNA WEEKS. They lived in Kittery until 1828 and then removed to Gloucester. He died 15 Feb. 1832, and his widow Joanna, then of Kittery, petitioned for administration (York Co. Probate, 43:413).
   Children:

1389.   THOMAS,[7] under 14, on 4 Feb. 1833; d. in Boston, 23 Dec. 1851,
   a. 23 y.
1390.   JOSHUA, under 14, on same day.

513

THOMAS[6] CHASE (John,[5] Rev. Josiah,[4] Dea. Thomas,[3] Thomas[2]), born in Berwick, Me., 10 Mar. 1779; married 30 Nov. 1804, SARAH LIBBEY, daughter of Daniel and Lucy (Chadbourne) Libbey of North Berwick, Me. She was born 6 July 1785; died 20 Jan. 1865. He died 4 Mar. 1853. They lived in what is now North Berwick, Me., and attended church in Lebanon, Me. He made his will 19 Sept. 1850, in which he mentions his wife Sarah, sons Edward, John D., Simon, and Mark W. and his daughters Betsey Horn, wife of Nicholas P. Horn, Lucinda Furbush, wife of Joseph Furbush, Phebe Furbush, wife of Richard Furbush, Mary Jane Hayes, wife of Mark Hayes, Louise Chase single, and Cyrena Edgerly, wife of Nathaniel Edgerly (York Co. Probate, 10:12).
   Children, born in North Berwick, Me.:

1391.   EDWARD,[7] b. 30 July 1805; lived in Palmyra, Me.; d. 1880.
   BETSEY, b. 13 Oct. 1807; m. and lived in Wilton, Me.; d. 1886.
   CYRENA, b. 19 Oct. 1809; m. (1) 13 Nov. 1828, David Lord of
   Berwick; m. (2) Nathaniel Edgerly.
   LUCINDA, b. 2 Nov. 1811; m. 25 May 1833, Joseph Furbush 2d
   of Lebanon, Me. She d. 1885.

DANIEL, b. 5 Jan. 1814; d. young.

PHEBE, b. 18 June 1815; m. 4 Oct. 1832, Richard Furbush of Lebanon.

1392. JOHN DENNETT, b. 13 Apr. 1817; m. (1) 6 Apr. 1843, Eliza Langley; m. (2) 28 Jan. 1857, Lois Annis Moore; d. 15 Feb. 1885.

1393. SIMON C., b. 1 Nov. 1819; d. Feb. 1880.

MARY JANE, b. 7 June 1822; m. Mark Hayes; lived in Newfields, N. H.

LOUISA, b. 15 June 1825; m. —— Littlefield; lived in Dover, N. H.

1394. MARK W., b. 10 Feb. 1828; lived in Berwick, Me.; m. 26 Jan. 1853, Mary A. Fowler.

514

JOHN[6] CHASE (John,[5] Rev. Josiah,[4] Dea. Thomas,[3] Thomas[2]), born in Berwick, Me., 7 Aug. 1781; died in North Berwick, Me., 27 Feb. 1857. He married (intention in Lebanon, Me., 13 Dec. 1806) MARGARET BROCK of Lebanon. She was born 22 Nov. 1781; died 17 Mar. 1862. They lived in North Berwick. He made his will 7 Feb. 1857, which was proved 5 May 1857. He mentions therein his wife Margaret, his daughters Hannah Brackett wife of Jacob Brackett, Susan Ross wife of Hugh Ross, Sarah Remick wife of Washington Remick, Jane Clark wife of Daniel G. Clark, Harriet Chase and Martha Chase, his sons Andrew and Charles, his grandson Charles C. Doe, his grandchildren John Chase 2d, Andrew Chase, Thomas Chase and Harriet Chase, children of William Chase deceased and his pew in the Predestination Baptist Meeting House in North Berwick. (York Co. Probate, 77:492).

Children:

HANNAH,[7] b. 12 Oct. 1807; m. 22 Feb. 1827, Jacob Brackett of Berwick.

1395. WILLIAM, b. 21 May 1809; m. —— Roberts; d. 9 Jan. 1852, in Berwick.

1396. CHARLES, b. 10 Nov. 1811. He was a machinist and lived in Auburn, Me.

SUSAN, b. 2 Dec. 1813; m. Hugh Ross.

JOANNA, b. 31 Aug. 1815; d. 11 July 1839.

SARAH, b. 16 June 1818; m. Washington Remick of Kittery, Me.

1397. ANDREW, b. 29 Aug. 1820; lived in Lebanon, Me.

HARRIET N., b. 25 June 1822; lived in Somersworth, N. H.; unm. 1872.

MARTHA A., b. 8 Apr. 1824; never married.

FRANCES JANE, b. 17 Dec. 1829; m. Daniel G. Clark of Sanford, Me.

515

JOSIAH[6] CHASE (John,[5] Rev. Josiah,[4] Dea. Thomas,[3] Thomas[2]), born in Berwick, Me., 11 June 1784; died in Limington. Me., 1 June 1850. He married 3 Mar 1808, DEBORAH[6] CHASE, daughter of Amos and Emma (Elden) Chase of Standish and Limington, Me. She was born 10 May 1789 and died in Limington, 6 June 1838. They lived in East Limington. (Family 401).

Children, born in Limington, Me.:

JOSIAH,[7] b. 1 Feb. 1809.
AMOS, b. 17 Aug. 1810.
Josiah and Amos burned to death with their father's dwelling house, 27 Feb. 1814.

1398. COL. JOHN, b. 17 Mar. 1812; lived E. Limington; m. (1) 19 Aug. 1832, Catharine Waterhouse; m. (2) 11 Sept. 1837, Harriet B. Neal; m. (3) 17 Aug. 1854, Mrs. Harriet M. Elder.

HANNAH ELIZA, b. 2 Dec. 1814; m. 15 July 1832, Dominicus Harmon. She d. in Hiram, Me., 30 Oct. 1844.
SARAH, b. 7 Jan. 1818; second wife of William C. Brown. No children.

1399. JOSIAH E., b. 25 May 1819; m. Julia E. Brown; lived E. Limington. Sea captain.

HARRIET N., b. 29 Dec. 1821; first wife of William C. Brown. She d. Mar. 1855.

1400. AMOS A., b. 25 Oct. 1828; m. 2 Aug. 1860, Louise D. Brown.
EMMA A., b. 9 May 1830; m. Henry C. Small of Portland, Me.

516

SIMON[6] CHASE (John,[5] Rev. Josiah,[4] Dea. Thomas,[3] Thomas[2]), born in Berwick, Me., 30 Sept. 1786; died in Rochester, N. H., 21 Jan. 1878. He married 28 Oct. 1813, SARAH WINGATE, daughter of Enoch Wingate of Milton, N. H. She died in Rochester 14 June 1870. He lived in Milton, N. H., 1810 to 1822 and in Rochester the remainder of his life. He made his will 27 Nov. 1877 which was proved in Mar. 1878. He mentions his daughter Betsey Hanson, his grandson Charles C. A. Hanson, his son Enoch W., his grandson Fred Chase, his granddaughter Helen Chase, his daughter Harriet L. Farrington, his granddaughters Nellie and Jessie Farrington; his daughter Mary Y. Drew, his granddaughters Hattie Drew, Jessie Drew and Clara Drew; his son Charles K. Chase, his grandsons Charles S., Harry, Charles A., William H., John D. and Francis M. Chase; his granddaughters Grace and Harriet L. Chase, his daughter Sarah F. Chase and Martha wife of his son Enoch W. Chase. (Strafford Co. Probate 89: 293).

Children, born in Milton, N. H., last four in Rochester, N. H.:

BETSEY SHANNON,[7] b. 4 Aug. 1814; m. 19 Sept. 1839, Dominicus Hanson of Rochester.

1401. ENOCH WINGATE, b. 20 Apr. 1817; m. July 1839, Martha Jane Roberts.

1402. GEORGE W.

1403. (DR.) JOHN DENNETT, b. 6 Mar. 1821; m. 1844, Catherine Ward of Middletown Ct.; lived in Washington, Ga.

MARY YEATON, b. 25 June 1823; m. 1843, Dr. Stephen W. Drew.
HARRIET LOUISE, b. 25 Nov. 1827; m. 27 Feb. 1851, Dr. James Farrington of Rochester.

1404. CHARLES KITTREDGE, b. 17 Mar. 1830; lived in Rochester; m. Apr. 1855, Ella M. Burleigh of Sandwich, N. H.

SARAH FRANCES, b. 2 Oct. 1834; unm.
JOSEPHINE, d. abt. 12 yrs. old.

517

MARK[6] CHASE (John,[5] Rev. Josiah,[4] Dea. Thomas,[3] Thomas[2]), born in Berwick, Me., 1 Oct. 1789; died in Newfield, Me., 3 Feb. 1878. He married 12 Jan. 1823, HULDAH NEAL. She died in June 1887. They lived in Newfield. He made his will 12 Dec. 1860, mentioning his wife Huldah, his daughters Susan F. Tozier, Almira H. Mitchell, Harriet N. Ricker, and Sarah J. Chase, and son William N. Chase. (York Co. Probate, 150:34).

Children, born in Newfield, Me.:

SUSAN F.,[7] b. 22 Jan. 1825; m. 10 May 1848, Oliver Tozier.
HARRIET NEWELL, b. 28 Mar. 1827; m. 2 Dec. 1847, Prof. George Hodgdon Ricker. She d. in Melrose, 9 Mar. 1911.
ALMIRA H., b. 5 Oct. 1829; m. 20 Oct. 1850, Dr. Joseph D. Mitchell; lived in Jacksonville, Fla.
SARAH J., b. 9 Oct. 1831; unm.
HANNAH H., b. 13 Aug. 1834; d. 29 Aug. 1842.
1405. WILLIAM N., b. 22 June 1838; unm.; living in Newfield in 1872.
MARY A., b. 29 Aug. 1843; d. 12 Sept. 1849.

518

JONATHAN[6] CHASE (Jonathan,[5] Jonathan,[4] Ens. Jonathan,[3] Thomas[2]), born in Stratham, N. H., 8 Jan 1752; died in Sanbornton, N. H., 26 Sept. 1828. He married about 1774, MARY CREIGHTON of Exeter, probably daughter of George Creighton of Exeter. She was born 7 June 1745 and died in Sanbornton 1 Jan. 1835, aged 89. He was a Revolutionary soldier in 1777 and 1780. They lived in Stratham and removed to Sanbornton, 20 Feb. 1778.

Children, first two born in Stratham, others in Sanbornton:

MARK,[7] b. 5 Aug. 1775; m. ——— Hoyt of Exeter, N. H., who d. without issue.
ANNA, b. 10 Oct. 1777; d. 2 July 1779.
POLLY, b. 28 Dec. 1779; m. 30 July 1798, Samuel Marston; d. 29 Jan. 1805.
JOANNA, b. 18 Apr. 1782; m. 26 Nov. 1807, Mark Hoyt of Epping, N. H.
BETSEY, b. 2 Sept. 1784; m. 19 July 1807, David H. Clark; she d. 12 June 1819; three children.
NANCY, b. 10 July 1787; m. 26 Oct. 1807, Jacob Rundlett; d. 10 Sept. 1828.

519

EDWARD[6] CHASE (Jonathan,[5] Jonathan,[4] Ens. Jonathan,[3] Thomas[2]), born in Stratham, N. H., 24 Nov. 1754; died in Canterbury, N. H., 19 June 1814, aged 59. He married in Hampton, N. H., 3 Sept. 1780, MARY MOORE, daughter of Thomas Moore Jr. of Stratham. She was born 14 Dec. 1760; died in 1826. They lived in Canterbury, N. H.

Children, born in Canterbury:

1406. LEVI,[7] b. 8 Apr. 1782; m. 3 July 1808, Sally Page of New Sharon, Me. He d. 12 Apr. 1854. Four children, including *Levi Badger*,[8] b. 24 Oct. 1833; author of the *Genealogy and Historical Notices of the Family of Plympton, The History* of *Sturbridge, The History of Southbridge* and *Early Indian Trails Through Nipnet and the Bay Path*; living in Sturbridge in his 95th year (1928).

AARON, b. 10 Sept. 1801; d. unm. Feb. 1830.

520

LEVI[6] CHASE (Jonathan,[5] Jonathan,[4] Ens. Jonathan,[3] Thomas[2]), born in Stratham, N. H., 5 July 1762; died in Loudon, N. H., 12 Nov. 1840. He married in Loudon, Dec. 1803, SUSAN CLOUGH of Salem. She was born in 1779 and died in Loudon, 19 Jan. 1846. They lived on the Jonathan[5] Chase homestead in Loudon.

Children, born in Loudon: :

1407.   JONATHAN,[7] b. Jan. 1805; m. (1) Feb. 1837, Phebe Page of Danville, Vt.; m. (2) Lydia Hand or Ham; m. (3) Clarissa Carr. He d. in Loudon, 25 Sept. 1855.

      SUSAN, b. May 1806; m. Dec. 1821, John Mooney of Loudon. She d. in Northfield, N. H., Apr. 1865.

      EUNICE, b. 1 Nov. 1808; d. unm.

521

THOMAS[6] CHASE (Moses,[5] Jonathan,[4] Ens. Jonathan,[3] Thomas[2]), born in Stratham, N. H., 5 June 1775; married about 1798, ABIGAIL WIGGIN, daughter of Capt. Jonathan and Mehitable (Thurston) Wiggin, born 22 Mar. 1775. They lived in Meredith, N. H.

Children:

1408.   THOMAS,[7] b. 17 Dec. 1799; m. (1) 1826, Mehitable Lovejoy; m. (2) Wdw. Lucinda (Page) Gibbs, Feb. 28, 1862.

      SARAH, b. 15 Mar. 1801; m. Jacob Thompson.

1409.   MOSES, b. 13 Mar. 1803; m. Sarah S. Blood.

      NANCY, b. 5 Jan. 1805; m. James Roberts.

      CLARISSA, b. 27 Feb. 1807; m. (1) Daniel Fox; m. (2) Gipson A. Poore.

1410.   JAMES MADISON, b. 1 Aug. 1809; m. Nancy Roberts, b. 27 Aug. 1813; eleven children.

      AUGUSTA, b. 20 Nov. 1811; m. Charles Bickford.

      BELINDA, b. 12 Mar. 1815; m. David R. Lovejoy.

      ABIGAIL, b. 8 Jan. 1817; m. Smith Hawkins.

522

ELISHA[6] CHASE (Moses,[5] Jonathan,[4] Ens. Jonathan,[3] Thomas[2]), born in Stratham, N. H., in 1777; married (1) in 1799, ELIZARETH EASTMAN, who died in Stratham 29 Aug. 1808 aged 33. He married (2) about 1809, ELIZABETH MERRILL, who died 15 Oct. 1857, aged 79. He died in Stratham, 21 Mar. 1866, aged 89y. 9m. They lived in Stratham.

Children by first wife, born in Stratham:

      NANCY,[7] b. 30 Aug. 1800; m. 14 Dec. 1820, Theophilus Smith Jr.

      STEPHEN, b. 12 May 1806; unm.; lived on the homestead, 1870.

      ELISHA E., b. 25 Aug. 1808; d. in infancy.

Children by second wife, born in Stratham:

1411.   ELISHA, b. 2 Apr. 1812; m. 1835, Sarah W. Jewell, b. 3 Feb. 1813. Ten children.

ELISABETH, b. 11 Feb. 1814; unm.; lived on the homestead, 1870.

1412. MOSES, b. 22 Nov. 1815; m. 1837, Mary Pendergast.

One child by second wife died 21 June 1810, aged 5 d.

523

JONATHAN[6] CHASE (Moses,[5] Jonathan,[4] Ens. Jonathan,[3] Thomas[2]), born in Stratham, N. H., 2 Oct. 1779; died in Meredith, N. H., 10 Aug. 1861, aged 81. He married 10 May 1805, MARY TILTON, who died 1 Dec. 1861, aged 77. They removed from Stratham to Meredith, N. H., about 1809.

Children, first born in Stratham, others in Meredith:

ELMIRA,[7] b. 10 May 1807; m. 5 May 1826, Joshua Wiggin of Meredith.

1413. JOHN, b. 19 Apr. 1810; m. 19 May 1839, Mary Perkins; d. in Meredith, 17 July 1862; five children.

HANNAH M., b. 26 Oct. 1812; d. 23 Sept. 1861, a. 48 y.

MARY A., b. 26 Oct. 1818; m. 18 Sept. 1850, Benjamin G. Young; lived in Meredith, 1870.

CYNTHIA, b. 4 Dec. 1820; m. June 1867, Oliver R. Yeaton of Laconia, N. H.

524

NICHOLAS[6] CHASE (Moses,[5] Jonathan,[4] Ens. Jonathan,[3] Thomas[2]), born in Stratham, N. H., 7 Oct. 1782; died 21 Sept. 1861. He married 3 Aug. 1805, MARY WIGGIN, daughter of Nathan and Mehitable (Norris) Wiggin, born in Stratham, 25 Sept. 1788; died 24 July 1866. They lived in Stratham.

Children, born in Stratham:

HIRAM,[7] b. 7 Nov. 1806; supposed lost at sea; unm.

1414. PHINEAS M., b. 3 Feb. 1808; m. (1) Ann Arnold; m. (2) Linda Pike; seven children.

NATHAN, b. 12 Dec. 1809; d. 12 June 1813.

1415. GEORGE W., b. 24 Dec. 1812; m. (1) Ann Mathes; m. (2) Wdw. Sabina Piper; lived in Newfield, Me.

1416. NATHAN W. (twin), b. 24 Dec. 1812; m. (1) Abigail Marsh; m. (2) ———— Swasey; lived in Augusta, Me.; m. (3) ————————.

MARY ANN, b. 18 Sept. 1815; m. Gideon C. Pitman of Barnstead, N. H.

1417. JAMES N., b. 6 Sept. 1818; m. Susan Sinclair of Stratham.

SOPHIA W., b. 27 Aug. 1820; m. 10 Jan. 1847, William J. Dolloff of Exeter, N. H.

SARAH JANE, b. 15 Aug. 1823; m. John H. Whidden of Newington, N. H.

MELINDA S., b. 28 Dec. 1825; m. John Wiggin of Exeter.

MEHITABLE W., b. 17 June 1831.

525

JONATHAN[6] CHASE (Dea. William,[5] William,[4] Ens. Jonathan,[3] Thomas[2]), born in Stratham, N. H., 6 Mar. 1762; died in Sanbornton, N. H., 17 Apr. 1795, in his 33d year. He married in Sanbornton, 23 Feb. 1782, LUCY PRESCOTT, daughter of William and Susanna (Sanborn) Prescott of Hampton Falls, N. H., and Sanbornton. She was born in Hampton Falls, 24 Dec. 1764; died in Alexandria, N. H., 9 Feb. 1838 ,aged 73y. 2 m. He was a Revolutionary soldier. They lived in Sanbornton. Administration was granted to his widow Lucy, 5 Sept. 1797. (Strafford Co. Probate, 5 :227).

Children, born in Sanbornton:

1418.   LEVI,[7] b. 14 May 1782; m. 12 Nov. 1807, Hannah Buswell; d. in Alexandria, 4 Dec. 1856.

   SUSAN, b. 8 June 1784; m. 8 Oct. 1812, Nathan S. Morrison, b. 8 Oct. 1789. She d. 7 July 1842.

1419.   WILLIAM, b. 20 Feb. 1786; m. 9 May 1813, Dorothy Higgins; d. in Shaftsbury, Vt.; d. 16 Jan. 1850 or 1860.

1420.   JAMES, b. 27 Sept. 1787; m. 3 Mar. 1808, Hannah Kimball. Children *Elvira*,[8] b. 7 May 1809 and *De Witt Clinton*,[8] b. 18 Mar. 1813. (Essex Antiquarian, 1 :16)

   SARAH, b. 22 Aug. 1789; d. unm. 28 July 1848 in her 59th y.

1421.   JOHN, b. 5 Oct. 1791; d. in Manchester, N. H., 5 Jan. 1845; m. (2) 29 Dec. 1823, Mary Ann Danforth.

   PHEBE, b. 26 Aug. 1793; m. 27 July 1816, James Dearborn Wadleigh, b. 18 Feb. 1793. She d. 30 Nov. 1865.

1422.   DAVID, b. 25 Mar. 1795; m. 15 Mar. 1821, Dorothy Blake, dau. of James Blake.

1423.   JONATHAN (twin), b. 25 Mar. 1795; m. 28 Feb. 1822, Sarah Gale, b. 11 Dec. 1806, dau. of Tudor Gale. He lived Fall River, Columbia Co., Wisconsin. They had 3 sons and 4 daus.

   MARY.

   COMFORT.

526

WILLIAM[6] CHASE (Dea. William,[5] William,[4] Ens. Jonathan,[3] Thomas[2]), born in Stratham, N. H., 1764; died in Meredith, N. H., between 17 June 1815 and 17 June 1816. He married ABIGAIL PIPER, daughter of Gideon and Rachel (Sanborn) Piper, born in Pembroke, N. H., 28 Oct. 1762. He was head of a family in Meredith in 1790, consisting of one male over 16 years of age, two males under 16 and one female.

William Chase of Meredith, N. H., husbandman, made his will, 17 June 1815 ,which was proved 17 June 1816. He mentions therein his wife Abigail, his three sons John, William and Nathaniel, who have already received their portions, his daughter Rachel, his sons Abel, Gideon and James to have the residue. (Strafford Co. Probate, 18 :50).

Children:

1424.   JOHN,[7] lived in Meredith.

1425.   WILLIAM.

1426.   NATHANIEL, alive 17 June 1815.

   RACHEL, m. 8 Apr. 1816, Thomas Comer in New Hampton.

1427.   ABEL; m. 28 July 1819, Miss Susan Russell of Meredith.

1428.   GIDEON, lived in New Hampton; m. in New Hampton 6 Aug. 1832, Matilda Jane Sanborn.

1429.   JAMES, perhaps m. 25 Nov. 1834, Eliza Davis of New Hampton.

527

DAVID[6] CHASE (Dea. William,[4] William,[5] Ens. Jonathan,[3] Thomas[2]), born in Stratham, N. H., 19 June 1766; died in Bristol, N. H., 19 Dec. 1835, aged 69y. 6m. He married in Sanbornton, N. H., 18 Sept. 1786, ANNA TAYLOR, daughter of Jonathan and Rachel (Moore) Taylor of Stratham and Sanbornton. She was born in Stratham, N. H., 9 May 1770 ;died in Bristol, N. H., 12 Apr. 1853, in her 83d year. They lived in Sanbornton, New Hampton, N. H., and Bristol.

Children, first four born in Sanbornton, others in New Hampton:

RACHEL,[7] b. 26 Dec. 1787; d. 31 Mar. 1857, a. 70.

1430. MARK, b. 21 Nov. 1789; m. 10 Aug. 1810, Martha Danforth.
1431. DAVID, b. 31 Mar. 1792; m. 7 Feb. 1816, Anna Bussell or Russell.
1432. JONATHAN TAYLOR, b. 27 Oct. 1794; m. Fanny M. Bean of Gilford, N. H.
1433. WILLIAM, b. 16 Jan. 1797; m. 30 July 1826, Virtue Emerson.

PHEBE, b. 23 June 1799; m. Caleb Whittemore. No children. She d. 6 Oct. 1859.

EDE TAYLOR, b. 25 Dec. 1802; d. 29 Jan. 1803.

NANCY, b. 12 Mar. 1809; lived in Boston, unm.

528

EBENEZER[6] CHASE (Dea. William,[5] William,[4] Ens. Jonathan,[3] Thomas[2]), born in Stratham, N. H., 9 Dec. 1767; died in Sanbornton, N. H., 4 Dec. 1854, aged 87. He married 12 June 1786, REBECCA CHENEY, daughter of John and Sarah (Colby) Cheney, born in Haverhill, 21 June 1769; died 27 Oct. 1850, aged 81y. 6m. They lived in Sanbornton.

Children, born in Sanbornton:

REBECCA,[7] b. 20 Oct. 1787; m. 21 Nov. 1811, David Henderson; d. in Hardwick, Vt., 21 Oct. 1860. Four children.

1434. WILLIAM, b. 20 June 1789; m. 10 June 1810, Mary Johnson; d. 20 Oct. 1876. Seven children.
1435. THOMAS, b. 10 Feb. 1792; went to sea in 1811; never returned.

SARAH CHENEY, b. 13 Aug. 1794; m. (1) 2 Dec. 1819, Jacob W. Fifield.

MARIA CROCKETT, b. 12 Dec. 1798; m. 13 Jan. 1828 Darius Dockham; d. 19 Jan. 1877. Two children.

1436. EBENEZER, b. 15 Apr. 1800; m. Aug. 1821, Mary Demerit.

LUCY PIPER, b. 18 Oct. 1805; m. 5 June 1823, Alba Gilman.

BETSEY C., b. 19 Feb. 1807; m. 10 Apr. 1832, Gould D. Ladd.

1437. DANIEL PIPER, b. 25 Aug. 1811; m. Jan. 1834, Dorothy Rundlett; clergyman in N. Danville, N. H. Three children.

529

REV. DANIEL[6] CHASE (William,[5] William,[4] Ens. Jonathan,[3] Thomas[2]), born in Stratham, N. H., 17 Nov. 1770; died in Mount Pleasant, Susquehanna Co., Penn., 2 Mar. 1850, aged 79. He married (1) 1791, CATHARINE PHILBROOK. She was born 19 Nov. 1771 and died in Jan. 1824. He married (2) RHODA BARTHOLOMEW. They moved to Hardwick, Vt., in 1794, and Jackson, Penn., in 1816. He was a Free Will Baptist clergyman.

Children by first wife, last five born in Hardwick:

JUDITH,[7] b. 12 Sept. 1792; m. about 1813, Salmon T. Warren. She d. 18 May 1815. No children.

1438.   JOHN, b. 19 Oct. 1794; m. 11 Nov. 1814, Clarissa Kingsley. Nine children. He d. 13 Mar. 1841.

JANE, b. 11 Jan. 1797; m. 9 Nov. 1818, Billings Whitney. She living in Hartford, Pa., in 1873.

1439.   DANIEL, b. 22 Nov. 1799; m. (1) 8 Jan. 1824, Delia Vail; m. (2) 27 Sept. 1846, Mary A. Vail. He d. 11 Aug. 1860.

1440.   DAVID, b. 9 May 1803; m. Mar. 1827, ———. He d. 13 Nov. 1828, in Penn.

1441.   AMASA, b. 26 Oct. 1805; m. 27 July 1827, Sarah Guile; living in Great Bend (now Hallstead), Pa., in 1873. Their son *Simeon Brewster*,[8] b. 18 Apr. 1828; m. 1 May 1851, Fanny Du Bois, b. 24 Nov. 1828. Their son George Amasa,[9] b. 29 Mar. 1862; d. 29 Dec. 1926; m. 1886, Anna La Barre, b. in Aug. 1867 in Mauch Chunk, Pa.; d. 1905. Children: *Fanny Du Bois*,[10] b. 9 May 1888; *George Amasa*,[10] b. 5 Sept. 1891; *Elwood La Barre*,[10] b. 3 Dec. 1893.

CATHARINE, b. 12 Sept. 1812; m. Jan. 1831, Silas B. Guile. She d. 22 Oct. 1848.

530

JAMES[6] CHASE (Dea. William,[5] William,[4] Ens. Jonathan,[3] Thomas[2]), born (probably in Stratham, N. H.,) 8 Apr. 1777; died in Wheelock, Vt., 4 May 1869, aged 92. He married (1) in Sanbornton, N. H., 17 May 1801, BETSEY COLBY, daughter of Anthony Colby of Haverhill. She died in Sanbornton, 27 Feb. 1807. He married (2) in Sanbornton, 13 Oct. 1807, MARY NORRIS, daughter of Joseph and Comfort (Piper) Norris, born in Stratham, 11 Nov. 1784; died in Wheelock, Vt., 11 Feb. 1866. They lived in Wheelock from 1808 to 1869.

Children by first wife, born in Sanbornton:

SOPHIA,[7] b. 4 Nov. 1801; unm.; lived in Sutton, Vt.

ABIGAIL, b. 1 June 1804; m. 23 June 1832, Demeritt Davis; d. 23 Feb. 1859.

Children by second wife, born in Wheelock:

BETSEY. b. 5 Aug. 1808; m. 25 Mar. 1836, Joshua Elkins; d. in Wheelock, Vt., 3 May 1853.

1442.   JOSEPH N., b. 19 Mar. 1810; m. 16 Aug. 1840, Mary J. Snelling; d. 7 Jan. 1867. Eleven children.

MARTHA, b. 4 Dec. 1811; m. 1 Jan. 1834, Benjamin Eaton of Stanstead, Can.; d. 18 Sept. 1848.

MARY ANN, b. 4 July 1814; m. 21 May 1835, Richard Waldo.

1443.   CHARLES, b. 13 Apr. 1815; m. (1) 5 May 1842, at Sheffield, Vt., Mary Ann Bradley; m. (2) 30 Dec. 1868, Helen Somers.

1444.   JOHN, b. 19 Jan. 1817; m. 6 Apr. 1845, Mary Miles; d. 28 Mar. 1851.

COMFORT N., b. 9 Jan. 1819; m. 12 Feb. 1844, Pelatiah Daniels of Strafford, Vt.

EMELINE, b. 10 Oct. 1820; m. William McLaren of Burke, Vt.; d. 17 Aug. 1847.

LUCIA, b. 13 Feb. 1828; d. 20 Aug. 1828.

531

John[6] Chase (William,[5] William,[4] Ens. Jonathan,[3] Thomas[2]), born in Sanbornton, N. H., 7 May 1782; died in Wheelock, Vt., 22 Mar. 1850, in his 68th year. He married in Boscawan, N. H., 2 Mar. 1806, Betsey Carter of Boscawen. She died 24 June 1864. They removed to Wheelock, Vt., in Mar. 1806.

Children, born in Wheelock:

    Eliza,[7] b. 8 Jan. 1807; m. 14 Mar. 1827, Sewall Bradley. She d. 28 May 1844.

1445. Calvin, b. 4 Mar. 1809; m. 4 Jan. 1831, Belinda F. Hoyt of Lyndon, Vt.

1446. William, b. 29 Aug. 1812; m. 12 June 1838, Fanny H. Randall of Lyndon. He d. 4 Apr. 1871.

    Mary C., b. 7 Aug. 1814; m. 4 May 1836, Joseph Dow. She d. 3 Feb. 1876.

    Julia A., b. 29 Nov. 1824; m. 29 Oct. 1849, Dudley N. Hodgdon of Lancaster, N. H.

532

Mark[6] Chase (Josiah,[5] William,[4] Ens. Jonathan,[3] Thomas[2]), born in Exeter, N. H., 10 May 1772; died in Canada, 15 Apr. 1855, aged about 80. He married about 1795, Ann Thomas, who was born about 1771 and died 12 May 1863. Her son James wrote in 1874 that she was born in Virginia. They lived in the vicinity of Harwich, Kent Co., Canada, from 1800.

Children, eight younger born in London, Upper Canada:

1447. James,[7] b. 17 Jan. 1796; m. Mary Strawn. He was living in Tipton, Iowa, in 1874.

1448. John, b. 2 July 1797; m. (1) 15 Mar. 1821, Nancy Wilcox; m. (2) 5 Jan. 1837, Sarah J. White. He d. 1843.

1449. Nathaniel, b. 29 July 1800; m. 16 June 1822, Catharine Carlisle; lived in Brownstown, N. Y., 1872.

    Deborah, b. 1 Oct. 1801; m. 1816, John Woodford.

1450. Josiah, b. 7 Dec. 1803; m. in Michigan, 1828, Lettie Kneeland.

1451. Jonathan, b. 15 May 1805; m. (1) 5 Apr. 1832, Eleanor McDonald; she d. 18 Feb. 1833; m. (2) 28 Aug. 1834, Margaret Buchanan; living in Harwich, Can., 1872.

1452. Mark, b. 5 Sept. 1806; m. (1) Priscilla Nevil; m. (2) 4 July 1859, Sarah Hawkins.

    Elisabeth, b. 22 Mar. 1808; m. 17 Mar. 1827, Walter Galbraith.

1453. Matthias, b. 19 Oct. 1810; m. Rachel Sigler; d. Sept. 1869.

    Martha, b. 8 May 1812; m. John Nevil.

    Anna, b. 10 May 1815; m. James Burwell.

    Ellen, b. 13 Feb. 1817; m. Moses Cowell; she d. 11 May 1867.

1454. Thomas, b. 6 July 1819; m. Feb. 1845, Ellen Burns.

    Mary, b. 6 Mar. 1824; m. 6 Sept. 1843, George Smith.

533

Josiah[6] Chase (Josiah,[5] William,[4] Ens. Jonathan,[3] Thomas[2]), born about 1775; married Mary Smith. They lived in Portsmouth, N. H.

Child, born in Portsmouth, N. H.:

1455.   JOSIAH,[7] b. 8 Mar. 1790; m. in Lynn, 11 June 1813, Sarah Newman, dau. of Eli and Nancy Newman, b. in Lynn, 17 Dec.
1793; resided in Leesville, Carroll Co., Ohio, in 1874. Eight
children, first three born in Lynn.

534

NATHANIEL[6] CHASE (Josiah,[5] William,[4] Ens. Jonathan,[3] Thomas[2]), died in Alton, N. H., 4 May 1861. He married 7 Feb. 1807,
SUSANNAH RUST, daughter of Richard and Susannah (Connor)
Rust, born (probably in Wolfeborough, N. H.,) 21 Jan. 1787. She
died 12 Nov. 1856. They lived in Alton.

Children, born in Alton:

ABIGAIL,[7] b. 11 Mar. 1807; m. 4 Apr. 1827, Josiah W.[7] Chase.
(Family 535)   She d. 8 Jan. 1874.
SUSAN, b. 11 Oct. 1808; m. 1825, Isaac Jones.
SALLY, b. 11 Jan. 1810; d. 1 Mar. 1814.
1456.   RICHARD, b. 30 Oct. 1812; m .Lucy Shortridge.
CAROLINE, b. 20 Sept. 1814; d. 7 Apr. 1815.
1457.   MARK, b. 17 Nov. 1816; m. Nancy Prentice; d. 16 Nov. 1870.
MARTHA, b. 29 Aug. 1818.
MARY, b. 3 Jan. 1820; m. W——— Pinkham of Milton, N. H.;
d. 7 July 1853.
NANCY, b. 19 Jan. 1821; m. Amos Johnson of New Durham,
N. H.
1458.   NATHANIEL, b. 24 Aug. 1822; m. 16 Nov. 1843, Deborah J.
McDuffee.
ELEANOR, b. 26 Oct. 1824; d. 3 Sept. 1849.
GEORGE, b. 11 Nov. 1825; d. 10 May 1831.
1459.   HENRY RUST, b. 8 Mar. 1827; m. Jane Rollins of Walpole,
N. H.; d. 3 Feb. 1858, in Boston.

535

DEA. THOMAS[6] CHASE (Josiah,[5] William,[4] Ens. Jonathan,[3]
Thomas[2]), born about 1765; died in Canaan, Vt., 26 Mar. 1853, aged
90.   He married about 1790, TABITHA PIPER, daughter of Dea
Stephen and Abigail Church (Wiggin) Piper of Stratham, N. H.
She was born in Stratham, 24 Apr. 1773; died in Stewartstown, N.
H., in 1835.   He was a privateer in the Revolution and was a pen-
sioner living in Stewartstown on 1 June 1840, at the age of 75 in the
family of George Chase. They lived in Wolfeborough, N. H., and
Stewartstown.   He and his wife united with the Freewill Baptist
Church in Wolfeborough, 19 Oct. 1792 and he was chosen Deacon.

Children, born in Wolfeborough:

ABIGAIL,[7] d. at age of 16 yrs.
1460.   NATHANIEL P., b. 18 Oct. 1794; m. 5 Dec. 1816, Martha Piper.
He d. 17 Apr. 1840; five children.
NANCY, b. 30 May 1799; m. (1) abt. 1823, Alfred W. Ingraham
of Canaan; m. (2) 16 Aug. 1835, Nathan Beecher.
THOMAS, b. abt. 1802; m. Emily Moses. No children; he d. in
Stewartstown, 1836.
1461.   JOSIAH W., b. 17 Aug. 1803; m. 4 Apr. 1827, Abigail[7] Chase.
(Family 534)   They lived in South Wolfboro, 1876.

Susan P., b. 13 May 1808; m. 10 June 1827, Oliver B. Capen of Colebrook, N. H. She d. Aug. 1870.

Hannah, b. 7 Mar. 1810; m. 25 Mar. 1837, James Heath of Clarksville, N. H.; three children.

536

Col. John[6] Chase (James,[5] James,[4] Ens. Jonathan,[3] Thomas[2]), born in Gilmanton, N. H., lived on the Chase homestead there; married and had three daughters. John Chase of Gilmanton, gentleman, with Daniel Gale 3d of Gilmanton and Daniel Avery of Gilford, N. H., as sureties was appointed guardian unto Sally Chase, a minor over 14, daughter of James Chase, late of Gilford, 18 Apr. 1814. (StraffordCo. Probate, 19:200). The town records of Gilmanton give no births, marriages or deaths of this family. One John Chase and Lydia Norris were married in Gilmanton by Rev. Isaac Smith, 26 Oct. 1778. It is doubtful if this marriage was that of Col. John Chase. He is more likely to be the John Chase who married in Pittsfield, N. H., 20 Nov. 1828, Betsey Knowlton.

537

Thomas[6] Chase (James,[5] James,[4] Ens. Jonathan,[3] Thomas[2]), born about 1779; died in Northfield, N. H., 25 June 1849, aged 70. He married in Canterbury, N. H., 17 Aug. 1797, Elizabeth Blanchard, daughter of Capt. Edward and Azuba (Kezar) Blanchard of Northfield. She died there, 11 May 1871, aged 90 years. They lived in Northfield.

Children, not in order, born in Northfield:

1462.   John B.,[7] b. 1799; m. 21 Feb. 1830, Mary Jane Ayers of Canterbury. Two children; d. 10 Apr. 1844.

1463.   Edward, b. 1796; m. (1) Clarissa Brown; m. (2) Hannah Blake; m. (3) Mary Piper of Sanbornton, N. H.

1464.   Thomas, b. 10 Sept. 1810; m. Mary Butler Brown; d. 3 Mar. 1881.

Almira, b. 1801; m. Richard Kent Smith of Hopkinton, N. H.

Harriet, b. 6 July 1807; m. 1835, Harrison Brown of Northfield.

Azubah, b. 1804; m. 1825, Asa Burleigh of Boscawen, N. H.; ten children.

Ann, b. 1813; m. (1) 1835, Jesse Hancock; m. (2) 1843, Jonathan Scribner; alive 1874; five children.

538

Mark[6] Chase (James,[5] James,[4] Ens. Jonathan,[3] Thomas[2]), born in Gilmanton, N. H., 10 Mar. 1776; married (1) in Plymouth, N. H., 25 Nov. 1802, Miriam Reed. He married (2) in Plymouth, 17 Mar. 1831, Harriet Clark, daughter of John and Mehitable (Hutchins) Clark, born 26 Nov. 1808. Miriam Reed was daughter of Joseph and Martha (Fletcher) Reed of Plymouth, born 6 June 1782. At the time of his first marriage Mark Chase lived in Sandwich but before his second marriage he removed to Plymouth; he died in Laconia, N. H. There were six children, three by each wife.

Children by first wife:
NAMES,[7] not reported.
Children by the second wife, born in Plymouth:
CLARA JANE.
1465.   JOHN CLARK, killed in a railroad accident at Plymouth, 3 Oct.
1883.   Two daughters.
1466.   GEORGE.

539

DUDLEY[6] CHASE (James,[5] James,[4] Ens. Jonathan,[3] Thomas[2]),
born about 1778; married (1) SARAH TYLER. They went to Maine.
He married (2) MARY ANN ———; married (3) in Loudon, N. H.,
21 Feb. 1799, SUSAN BACHELDER. There is much doubt about these
three marriages.
Children:
WILLIAM TULLOCK,[7] b. 1810; m. 14 Nov. 1847, Amelia Philips,
dau. of John, of Saco, Me. No children.
1467.   JOHN.
A DAUGHTER, m. ——— Simmons.
1468.   CHARLES, went to S. Carolina.
LOUISA, lived in Providence, R. I.
FRANCES, m. Rev. ——— ———.
1469.   GEORGE, lived in Fall River.
There was a George Tyler of Charlestown, Bunker Hill Street, who
is connected with this family.

540

ROBERT[6] CHASE (James,[5] James,[4] Ens. Jonathan,[3] Thomas[2]),
born probably in Gilmanton, N. H., married in Canterbury, N. H.,
13 Sept. 1810, POLLY CROSS. They are said to have lived in Canterbury and Laconia, N. H. There were seven children.
Children, born in Gilmanton:
1470.   JAMES,[7] b. 1813; d. in Canterbury, 20 Jan. 1892, aged 78y. 4m.
2d. He m. 10 Dec. 1843, Abigail Glines, dau. of Isaac and
Abigail (McDaniel) Glines, who d. 24 Jan. 1892.
Other children not reported.

541

JAMES[6] CHASE (James,[5] James,[4] Ens. Jonathan,[3] Thomas[2]),
born about 1772; married in Deerfield, N. H., 20 Sept. 1794, NANCY
AVERY. They lived in Laconia, N. H.; six children. They are also
said to have lived in Conway, N. H. No births of their children on
the Town Records of New Hampshire.

542

JOSIAH[6] CHASE (Josiah,[5] James,[4] Ens. Jonathan,[3] Thomas[2]),
born in Epping, N. H., 5 Feb. 1776. He married (1) 21 June 1803,
RACHEL PRESCOTT, daughter of Capt. John and Lucy (Clifford)
Prescott, born in Epping, 8 Sept. 1784; died there, 23 May 1818. He
married (2) in Epping, 20 Apr. 1820, ABIGAIL BARTLETT. They
lived in Epping.

Children by first wife, born in Epping:

MARY REBECCA,[7] b. 10 Mar. 1805; m. 19 Feb. 1829, Stephen Dow. She d. 13 Nov. 1840.

1471. JOHN PRESCOTT, b. 9 Nov. 1809; m. 27 Jan. 1842, Betsey Sanborn.

ELISABETH P., b. 19 Feb. 1816; m. 23 Feb. 1835, William Thompson.

Children by second wife, born in Epping:

SARAH P., b. 13 Feb. 1822; d. 19 July 1825.

1472. JOSIAH B., b. 29 July 1826; m. 6 Jan. 1859, Hannah P. Bartlett. Four children.

543

COL. ELIPHALET[6] CHASE (Josiah,[5] James,[4] Ens. Jonathan,[3] Thomas[2]), born in Epping, N. H., 13 Apr. 1777; died in Epping, 17 Jan. 1856. He married in Epping 9 Oct. 1805, REBECCA PRESCOTT, daughter of Capt. John and Lucy (Clifford) Prescott, born in Epping, 4 Dec. 1786. They lived in Epping.

Child, born in Epping:

LYDIA N.,[7] b. 29 Dec. 1806; m. 9 June 1823, Benjamin B. Brown, who d. 12 Sept. 1839, a. 38 y 8 m.

544

JONATHAN[6] CHASE (Josiah,[5] James,[4] Ens. Jonathan,[3] Thomas[2]), born in Epping, N. H., 2 Mar. 1782; died there, 12 May 1861, aged 79y. 2m. 10d. He married in Epping 12 Sept. 1811, HONORA PRESCOTT, daughter of Capt. John and Lucy (Clifford) Prescott, born in Epping, 28 July 1793; died there, 26 Feb. 1875, aged 83. They lived in Epping.

Children, born in Epping:

1473. PRESCOTT,[7] b. 18 Jan. 1812; m. 21 June 1838, Sarah Sanborn.

1474. JOSIAH P., b. 24 Mar. 1817; m. 13 Apr. 1838, Shuah B. Brown, b. 5 May 1820; living in Dwight, Ill., in 1870. Twelve children.

545

JAMES[6] CHASE (Josiah,[5] James,[4] Ens. Jonathan,[3] Thomas[2]), born in Epping, N. H., 11 May 1794; died 16 June 1853. He married 14 Mar. 1820, JOANNA B. FLANDERS. She is probably the Joanna B. Chase who died in Exeter, N. H., 2 June 1867, aged 66. Probably they lived in Exeter.

Children:

HANNAH E.,[7] b. 8 Dec. 1821; m. 7 Mar. 1853, Joseph W. Pearson.

ELIPHALET, b. 15 Aug. 1824; d. 25 Jan. 1843, at Exeter, aged 18 y.

546

THOMAS WILSON[6] CHASE (Jonathan,[5] Thomas,[4] Ens. Jonathan,[3] Thomas[2]), born in Stratham or Wolfeborough, N. H., about 1780; died in 1866. He married in Wolfeborough, 25 Jan. 1804. His marriage intention published in the History of Wolfeborough, p. 358, calls his intended NANCY CHASE but the marriage as returned to the State in Concord calls her NANCY THURSTON. He is there desribed as "of Alton." One Nancy Chase died in Wolfeborough, 24 Apr. 1859. The Thurston Genealogy gives no light on this subject. They probably lived in Alton, N. H.

Children:

DUDLEY,[7] d. young.
1475. JOHN, m. Mary J. ———.
ABIGAIL, m. ——— Perkins.
MARTHA, d. young.
BETSEY, m. ——— Caswell.
EMELINE, m. Albert Sayles.
HARRIET N., m. in New Durham, 4 Feb. 1849, Charles N. Darling.
1476. CHARLES SUMNER.
1477. THOMAS, d. in Wolfeborough, 9 Dec. 1888, aged 69 y. 8 m. 17 d.
1478. WILSON, killed in the Civil War.
NANCY JANE, m. Augustus Wilkinson.

547

JOSHUA WINGATE[6] CHASE (Jonathan,[5] Thomas,[4] Ens. Jonathan,[3] Thomas[2]), born in 1782; married in Wolfeborough, N. H., 9 Nov. 1809, RUTH[6] HORNE of Wolfeborough, daughter of Benjamin[5] and ——— (Edmunds) Horne of Wolfeborough. She was of age in 1812. Possibly she may be the Ruth G. Chase, widow, who died in Tuftonborough, N. H., 22 Nov. 1882, aged 88y. 4m. 9d.

Children, born in Wolfeborough:

SOPHRONIA,[7] m. in Wolfborough, 16 May 1830, William Fernald.
MARY H., m. in Wolfborough, 13 May 1833, John D. Horn.

548

JONATHAN[6] CHASE (Jonathan,[5] Thomas,[4] Ens. Jonathan,[3] Thomas[2]), born in 1795; married in Mar. 1811, FANNY LOVEJOY. They removed to New Orleans, La.

Children:

1479. GEORGE WENTWORTH.[7]
SON.
SON.
DAUGHTER.
DAUGHTER.

549

ANDREW[6] CHASE (Capt. Dudley Leavitt,[5] Thomas,[4] Ens. Jonathan,[3] Thomas[2]), born in Stratham, N. H., 10 Mar. 1787; living there in 1873. He married in Stratham, 19 Aug. 1806, SARAH CLARK, who was born 13 Feb. 1786, and died in Stratham, 26 Mar. 1856, aged 70. Dr. John B. Chace called her Sarah Ayer but the Vital Records of Stratham call her Sarah Clark. He married (2) ——— DEARBORN of Stratham.

Children by first wife, born in Stratham:

    SARAH ANN,[7] b. 7 Aug. 1807; m. Abner Littlefield of Lebanon, a farmer.

    DUDLEY LEAVITT, b. 17 Nov. 1808; d. unm. 1827.

1480.   ANDREW, b. 30 Sept. 1810; a carpenter; lived in Exeter, N. H.; m. Mary Curtis, of Durham, N. H., and d. in Exeter 27 June 1872, aged 63.

    MARY ELISABETH, b. 13 July 1812; m. Horace Littlefield of Waldo and Prospect, Me.

1481.   SAMUEL S., b. 17 Nov. 1817; m. in Roxbury, 4 June 1840, Elizabeth Curtis; d. in Stratham in Oct. 1898. Their son *Ashur Moore*,[8] b. in Roxbury, b. 24 Mar. 1841; d. in Jan. 1875; m. Jane M. Weston of Warren, Me., who is now (1928) living at the age of 87. Their son Charles E. B.,[9] is a member of the Board of Dental Examiners, State House, Boston.

1482.   BENJAMIN, b. 19 Mar. 1819; lived in Stratham, N. H.; m. Adeline Mason of Stratham, N. H.; lived in Boston.

1483.   JAMES, b. 1821; a farmer; m. Martha Clark of Stratham.

1484.   LEVI, b. June 1823; m. Priscilla Breed of Lynn.

1485.   JOHN W., b. 1825; m. 17 Sept. 1847, Sarah P. Marston of Stratham; a carpenter and captain of police in Boston.

550

DEA. JOHN[6] CHASE (Johnson,[5] John,[4] James,[3] Thomas[2]), born in Newbury, 17 July 1756; died in Hampstead, N. H., 28 Apr. 1826. He married in Haverhill, 18 Dec. 1777, ANNA[5] CHASE, daughter of Humphrey[4] and Abigail (Ela) Chase, born in Haverhill, 16 Dec. 1755. Her line is Humphrey,[4] Moses,[3] Ens. Moses.[2] She died in Hampstead, 5 Oct. 1832. They lived in Plaistow, N. H., and Hampstead.

Children, first six born in Plaistow, N. H., others in Hampstead:

1486.   HUMPHREY,[7] b. Mar. 1779; m. 19 Nov. 1799, Rebecca Nichols.

    ABIGAIL, b. 1781; m. 12 Nov. 1809, Sewall Hill of Boston. She d. 10 July 1818.

    JOHNSON, b. 11 Nov. 1783; d. unm. 16 or 19 May 1850; clergyman.

    ANNA, b. 27 May 1786; d. 22 Apr. 1788.

    ANNA, b. 24 June 1789; m. 25 July 1808, Noah Hill of Boston; d. 18 June 1818.

1487.   HEZEKIAH, b. 2 Dec. 1791; m. 26 May 1817, Sarah Hoyt; lived in Lynn; d. 26 Mar. 1865.

    SARAH, b. 31 May 1794; m. (1) 18 July 1812, Noah Hill of Boston; m. (2) Nehemiah Berry of Lynn; d. 4 June 1832.

    MOSES, b. 6 Sept. 1797; d. unm. 3 Sept. 1839.

1488.   ISAAC, b. 6 Nov. 1803; m. Mary A. Shambler; d. 22 Dec. 1850. He was American Consul at the Cape of Good Hope.

551

PERLEY[6] CHASE (Johnson,[5] John,[4] James,[3] Thomas[2]), born in Newbury 2 June 1758; died in Chester, N. H., 3 Apr. 1833, aged 74. He married (1) MARY INGALLS, daughter of Nathaniel and Abigail (Huse) Ingalls of Sandown, N. H. She died in Chester, 15 Sept. 1791. He married (2) the widow ACHSAH MUDGET, who died in Chester, 20 Oct. 1832, aged 70. They lived in Chester. He was a

Revolutionary War soldier and a pensioner in 1819, and in June 1832, called himself 74.

Children by first wife, born in Chester:

> NANCY,[7] m. in Chester, 31 Mar. 1829, William O. Ryan.

1489. JOSIAH, b. 21 Oct. 1791; m. (1) 27 Aug. 1816, Abigail Shaw, who d. 20 June 1824, aged 27; m. (2) 26 Apr. 1826, Adaline Ayer, who d. 23 Feb. 1884, aged 83. He d. 25 Apr. 1829.

Children by second wife, born in Chester:

> JOHN, b. 11 Mar. 1801; d. unm. of consumption.
> MARY JANE, b. 20 June 1803; d. unm. of consumption.
> LOUISA, b. 5 May 1805; d. unm. of consumption.

All died within 15 months.

552

JAMES[6] CHASE (Edmund,[5] Capt. James,[4] James,[3] Thomas[2]), born in Haverhill, 9 Apr. 1779; died in Amesbury 31 Dec. 1849. He married (1) 15 Sept. 1805, MARY COLBY who died in 1810; married (2) 22 Oct. 1811, OLIVE (CALDWELL) LUCAS, a widow. She died in Amesbury, 19 Feb. 1853. They lived in West Amesbury (now Merrimac).

Children by first wife, born in Amesbury:

> SOPHIA,[7] b. 25 Aug. 1806; m. 17 Dec. 1835, John Lancaster; d. 4 Nov. 1882.
> ANNA C., b. 1 Nov. 1808; m. 18 May 1855, Daniel D. Haynes; no children; d. 21 June 1888.
> JAMES, b. 17 Jan. 1810; d. 16 Oct. 1824.

Children by second wife, born in Amesbury:

> MARY, b. 6 Nov. 1813; m. 4 Dec. 1834, Samuel S. Tuckwell; she d. 25 Dec. 1874.
> OLIVE, b. 11 July 1815; m. 17 Dec. 1835, Erastus Hutchins; she d. 14 Mar. 1881.

1490. WILLIAM, b. 23 Mar. 1817; m. 29 Nov. 1839, Susan F. Morrill; lived in Amesbury.

> PHINEAS, b. 5 Apr. 1820; m. 1 Jan. 1849, Ann Maria Sargent. No children.

553

WILLIAM[6] CHASE (Edmund,[5] Capt. James,[4] James,[3] Thomas[2]), born in Haverhill, 6 July 1786; died 22 Dec. 1860. He married (1) in Somersworth, N. H., 10 Apr. 1814, ABIGAIL VARNEY, who died 25 Apr. 1819. He married (2) SARAH VARNEY.

Children by first wife, not in order::

> ABIGAIL,[7] b. 2 Apr. 1818; m. Thomas Rines.

1491. PHINEAS.

> MARY H., b. 6 June 1816; d. 16 July 1832.

Children by second wife:

> SARAH E., b. 20 May 1821; d. unm. 16 May 1846.
> WILLIAM P., b. 12 Aug 1825; d. 21 Aug. 1832.
> JAMES E., b. 20 Oct. 1827; d. 20 Aug. 1832.
> WILLIAM J., b. 1 Dec. 1831; d. 13 Apr. 1848.

554

EDMUND[6] CHASE (Edmund,[5] Capt. James,[4] James,[3] Thomas[2]), born in Haverhill, 12 Sept. 1794; died there 28 Jan. 1828. He married in Haverhill, 24 Mar. 1820, CYNTHIA MERRILL, who died in Haverhill, 18 Oct. 1839, aged 39. They lived in Haverhill.

Children, born in Haverhill::

EDMUND EUSTIS,[7] b. 4 May 1821; d. 8 Jan. 1828.
CYNTHIA, b. 8 Oct. 1824.
ELISABETH, b. 22 Dec. 1828; d. 8 Jan. 1855.
1492. EDMUND EUSTIS, b. 9 Mar. 1834.
SARAH A., b. 1 Oct. 1837.

555

JAMES BAILEY[6] CHASE (James,[5] Capt. James,[4] James,[3] Thomas[2]), born in Haverhill, 10 Mar. 1774; died in Loudon, N. H., 25 Sept. 1795. No marriage or children have been found of this man and the inference is that he died single.

556

ISAIAH[6] CHASE (James,[5] Capt. James,[4] James,[3] Thomas[2]), born in Haverhill, 5 Dec. 1776; died in Loudon, N. H., 17 Oct. 1858, aged 82y. 10m. 22d. He married in Loudon, 5 Dec. 1799, ABIGAIL BACHELDER, who died in Loudon, 10 Oct. 1859. They lived in Loudon.

Children, born in Loudon:

HARRIET R.,[7] b. 24 June 1800; m. in Canterbury, 10 June 1829, Alfred Haines.
1493. IRA A., b. 22 Jan. 1804; m. in London, 10 Jan. 1827, Hannah Cate.
NEWELL (twin), b. 21 June 1802; d. Dec. 1802.
PERLEY (twin), b. 21 June 1802; d. 10 Dec. 1803.
1494. WILLIAM FRIEND, b. 8 Mar. 1806; m. in Canterbury, 29 June 1829, Mary H. Currier.
1495. ALBERT M., b. 27 Feb. 1811; m. in Moultonborough, N. H., 29 Apr. 1836, Sarah Jane Green.
EMERSON HARRIS, b. 23 Jan 1815; d. 7 Mar. 1815.
1496. JAMES HASELTON, b. 19 June 1816; m. 4 June 1847, Belinda Palmer who d. 7 Aug. 1859. He was shot in the Civil War and d. 8 Aug. 1863. Four children, including *Ira Batchelder*,[8] b. 18 Aug. 1853; d. 11 July 1891; m. 24 Apr. 1873, Catherine Josephine O'Donnell, b. 27 Aug. 1849. Their son Albert Benedict,[9] b. 16 Aug. 1874, a widower with no children; manufacturer's forwarding agent, New York City. Their daughter Tressa Aquila,[9] unmarried, living in Brooklyn, N. Y.

557

WILLIAM[6] CHASE (James,[5] Capt. James,[4] James,[3] Thomas[2]), born in Loudon, N. H., 6 May 1785; died 23 Nov. 1850. He married (1) in Canterbury, N. H., 1 Dec. 1808, POLLY RING, who was born 18 July 1785; died 12 Mar. 1836. He married (2) 15 Aug. 1837, MERCY DANFORTH, who was born 27 July 1812. They probably lived in Loudon.

Children by second wife, probably born in Loudon:

WILLIAM WESLEY,[7] b. 17 July 1838; d. unm. 17 May 1862, at
Washington, D. C.

1497. SAMUEL PARKER, b. 15 Aug. 1840; m. 4 Mar. 1863, Louisa A.
Farnham.

SARAH ELIZA, b. 18 Nov. 1842; m. 27 Nov. 1859, Alfred I.
Capen.

1498. JAMES SULLIVAN, b. 3 July 1845; m. 23 Dec. 1869, Abbie A.
Brown. They lived in Colebrook, N. H.

558

AMOS[6] CHASE (James,[5] Capt. James,[4] James,[3] Thomas[2]), born
in Loudon, N. H., 29 Oct. 1789. Beyond his birth he has not been
traced.

559

EDWARD LITTLE[6] CHASE (William,[5] Capt. James,[4] James,[3]
Thomas[2]), born and baptized in Haverhill, 3 Oct. 1793; married
there, 12 June 1817, LEVINA STEVENS. He is probably the Edward
L. Chase who died in Plaistow, N. H., 22 Jan. 1858, aged 64 years.

Child, born in Haverhill:

1499. WILLIAM STEVENS,[7] b. 10 Feb. 1822; d. in Plaistow, 31 Mar.
1853.

560

JOSEPH[6] CHASE (James,[5] Nathaniel,[4] James,[3] Thomas[2]), was under age and living in Bath, N. H., 17 Jan. 1788 in his father's family.
He may be the Joseph Chase who died in Orford, N. H., in Feb. 1847,
aged 67y. No family of this man has been found.

561

JOHN[6] CHASE (Abel,[5] Nathaniel,[4] James,[3] Thomas[2]), born in
1768. He may be the John Chase who married in Orford, N. H., 2
Sept. 1799, SALLY NILES. There is great uncertainty about this family. One John and Sarah Chase had the following children recorded
as born in Orford. It does not seem consistent to assume that six children were born to them after they had been married sixteen years:

Children, born in Orford:

JOHN,[7] b. 6 Jan. 1816; d. in Orford, 11 Mar. 1829, a. 13 y.
LUCINDA, b. 30 Jan. 1819.

1500. MOSES, b. 5 June 1821.

1501. WILLARD T., b. 16 May 1823.
HANNAH H., b. 10 Sept. 1825.

1502. GEORGE H., b. 2 Apr. 1828.

562

ROBERT[6] CHASE (Abel,[5] Nathaniel,[4] James,[3] Thomas[2]), born in
Bath, N. H., about 1770; died there, 26 Feb. 1853, aged 87y. He
married (1) in Bath, 16 Mar. 1791, MARY DEXTER. He married (2)
in Bath, 5 Jan. 1810, PEGGY WATERS

Children by first wife, born in Bath:

1503. EBENEZER SIMPSON,[7] b. about 1800; m. 3 July 1822, Lemira
Corey, dau. of Ephraim and Lois[6] (Chase) Corey; he d. in
1851; she d. in Lisbon, N. H., 5 June 1892, aged 89 y. 7 m.
13 d. Children: *Royal Albert*, b. in Bath, 20 July 1842; living in Concord, N. H., in 1927. *Jonathan*, b. in Bath, 13
Mar. 1833.
There were other children whose names have not been found.

1504. ROBERT of Bath, 1832, perhaps a son.

Children by second wife, born in Bath:

SENNA, b. 22 Aug. 1816.

1505. MOSES, b. 1825; d. in Haverhill, 8 Feb. 1884, a. 58 y. 10 m. 2 d.

563

ISAIAH[6] CHASE (Abel,[5] Nathaniel,[4] James,[3] Thomas[2]), born in
Bath, N. H., 1774; married in Bath, 5 Jan. 1795, ESTHER BEDELL.
No children recorded as born in any town in New Hampshire.

564

ABEL[6] CHASE (Abel,[5] Nathaniel,[4] James,[3] Thomas[2]), born in
Bath, N. H., 1778; died in Portland, Me., 1854. He married and had
a large family. There was one Abel Chase who married in Westbrook, Me., 4 July 1824, LYDIA PALMER. This may be a second marriage of the above named Abel, or, perhaps, of his son.

Children:

1506. JOHN,[7] living in Portland, Me., 1872.

1507. ABEL, b. in Westbrook, 22 June 1809; d. 9 June 1881.

565

MOODY[6] CHASE (Abel,[5] Nathaniel,[4] James,[3] Thomas[2]), born in
Bath, N. H., 6 June 1780; died in Goffstown, N. H., 22 Sept. 1859;
married in 1800, SUSAN LOCKE, daughter of Stephen and Sally
(Hopkins) Locke, born in Deering, N. H., 17 July 1785; died in
Grafton, 26 July 1848. They lived in Deering, N. H.

Children, born in Deering, except the first born in Bath:

1508. STEPHEN,[7] b. 9 Nov. 1801; m. (1) 27 Mar. 1823, Nancy Kelley,
b. 4 May 1804; m. (2) in Deering, 25 July 1827, Mehitable
Goodale, b. 8 Feb. 1795; d. in Carmel, Me., 3 Jan. 1881; m.
(3) 18 Dec. 1881, Eliza R. Gustin, a widow; he d. in Princeton, Me., 6 Apr. 1890, aged 88 y. 5 m. They lived in Loudon,
N. H. and removed to Carmel, Me., in 1843. Two children
by the first wife and six by the second, including *James
Harvey*,[8] b. 20 June 1831; m. 15 Nov. 1855, Harriet W. Stover
of Bangor, Me.; crossed the Isthmus of Panama on foot in
1849 and finally reached California; was professor of elocu-
tion in St. Louis; practiced law in Ironton, Mo.; later settled
in the territory of Washington, where he became a Judge;
now (1928) living in Cashmere, Wash., in his 97th year. He
sold the first daily papers which were sent by train from Boston to Manchester, N. H., in 1842. Children: Cora Wilson,[9]
m. Charles Henry Charlton of Clinton, Mo., and Alice B.,[9]
m. Edward Nugent of Cashmere. Their dau. *Mehitable Jane*,[8]
b. 14 Mar. 1838; m. 17 Mar. 1867, Lt. William H. Young, a

soldier of the Civil War who d. 28 Aug. 1898. She now lives with her son in Stoneham, in her 91st year.

RODNEY, b. 13 Mar. 1803; d. 6 Sept. 1805.

RHODA, b. 13 Sept. 1805; m. 18 Feb. 1824, Samuel Palmer, who d. in Grafton, 14 Oct. 1857.

1509. HEROD, b. 16 Sept. 1806; m. (1) Hannah Gove; m. (2) Mrs. Caroline Gove; m. (3) Mrs. Hannah E. Varney; d. in Deering, 22 Apr. 1889, aged 83.

1510. HIRAM (twin), m. 16 Sept. 1806; m. in 1827, Hannah Wood of Deering who d. in 1885; Methodist minister in Me.; d. in Charleston, Me., in 1883, aged 76.

1511. CYRUS, b. 14 Sept. 1808; m. 10 Feb. 1830, Delia Wood, and d. in Stanton, Kan., 25 Sept. 1857.

SARAH, b. 2 Sept. 1811; m. Dea. George Day of Weare, N. H.

1512. DAVID, b. 14 Nov. 1812; m. (1) 1839, Sylvia Call of Weare; m. (2) in 1863, Jane Fairbanks of Westborough.

MARIA LOUISA, b. 13 July 1815; m. (1) 25 Dec. 1839, Freeman Nelson of Shrewsbury; m. (2) Alfred Dunham; she d. 13 Oct. 1867.

LEVI, b. 17 July 1817; d. 27 July 1817.

CALISTA, b. 12 July 1818; m. 1841, Leonard Nelson; she d. 13 Feb. 1859.

JUDITH, b. 28 Dec. 1820; m. Levi Moore Harrington; she d. in Northborough, 22 Feb. 1894.

1513. ROBERT DEXTER, b. 12 Mar. 1823; m. (1) 15 June 1848, Elizabeth Ann Kimball of Hopkinton; m. (2) 4 Aug. 1853, Cecilia B. Lovell; he d. 15 Feb. 1888.

LAVINA CURRIER, b. 18 Oct. 1825; m. 5 Dec. 1844, Jeremiah Whitcomb of Grafton.

Twelve of these fourteen children with their husbands or wives met at the home of their youngest brother Robert Dexter in Grafton in 1854.

566

MOSES[6] CHASE (Abel,[5] Nathaniel,[4] James,[3] Thomas[2]), born in Bath, N. H., 1783; married (1) in Deering, N. H., 23 June 1806, HANNAH STEVENS; married (2) in Deering, 12 Jan. 1848, LUCY HOAG, by whom there was no issue. He died in Deering, 22 June 1871, aged 86y. 7m. 13d. "born in Bath, son of Abel and Hannah."

Children by first wife:

1514. RODNEY,[7] b. 31 Aug. 1806.

CYNTHIA, b. 9 Dec. 1808; m. Hiram Kempfield of Deering.

1515. ABNER H., b. 9 Nov. 1814; m. Pearl Washington.

ABIGAIL, b. 26 May 1816.

MARY ANN, b. 14 Sept. 1819; m. Charles Kempfield of Deering.

567

NATHANIEL[6] CHASE (Edmund,[4] Aquila,[5] James,[3] Thomas[2]), born in Parsonsfield, Me., 1 May 1769; died in Prospect, Me., 13 Feb. 1850. He married about 1795, MARY HAINES, who was born in York, Me., 22 Nov. 1771 and died in Prospect, 13 July 1859. They lived in Swanville and Prospect. They removed from Parsonsfield to North Harwich, Hancock Co., Me., before 26 Jan. 1802. (York Deeds, 68:211).

Children, first five born in Swanville, others in Prospect:

MARY,[7] b. 17 Apr. 1796.
1516. NATHANIEL, b. 11 Feb. 1798; d. 27 Sept. 1854, at Rockport, Me.
SARAH, b. 23 Feb. 1800; d. 28 Dec. 1857, at Waldo, Me.
1517. HENRY, b. 17 May 1802; living in Bucksport, Me., in 1873.
LAVINA, b. 10 Apr. 1804.
HARRIET, b. 27 Mar. 1807.
1518. JOHN, b. 2 Jan. 1809.
ABIGAIL N., b. 9 Jan. 1813.
1519. EDMUND, b. 9 Sept. 1815.
1520. ALFRED B., b. 4 June 1818; m. 2 Feb. 1844, Martha Cook.

568

ELIPHALET[6] CHASE (Edmund,[4] Aquila,[5] James,[3] Thomas[2]), born in Parsonsfield, Me., 26 Mar. 1775; married 1 May 1794, SUSAN MUDGETT, who was born 10 July 1776. They lived in Dixmont, Hancock Co., Me., and removed to Delaware, Ohio, about 1818. He died in Delaware, Ohio, 28 Oct. 1821, aged 46. He sold his land in Parsonsfield to Joseph Grandvill, 23 Apr. 1798, and acknowledged the same, 7 Feb. 1799. (York Deeds, 64:77).

Children, most of whom were born in Dixmont:

SARAH,[7] b. 8 Feb. 1795; m. (1) abt. 1815, Charles Crosby; m. (2) Jonathan Johnson.
1521. ELIPHALET, b. 13 Sept. 1797; m. Catherine Duel; d. in Indiana.
MARY, b. 16 Sept. 1799; m. (1) Mark Twitchel; (2) ——— Hawley.
EDMUND, b. 12 Aug. 1802; d. young.
1522. JOHN M., b. 7 Aug. 1804; m. Eliza Carney; d. in Indiana.
1523. EBENEZER B., b. 12 Apr. 1806; m. Catharine Rosecranz; d. in Porter, Ohio.
CATHARINE, b. 25 Mar. 1808; d. young.
1524. IRA, b. 12 Apr. 1809; m. 11 June 1835, Jane Wilcox; lived in Delaware, Ohio, 1873.
1525. CYRUS, b. 5 Mar. 1811; m. Lucinda Beggs; d. in Porter, Ohio.
1526. SILAS H., b. 18 Aug. 1813; m. Mary E. Munsell; d. in Washington, D. C.

569

EDMUND[6] CHASE (Edmund,[5] Aquila,[4] James,[3] Thomas[2]), born in Parsonsfield, Me., 10 Nov. 1778. He married (1) LOVEY CORSON of Shapleigh, Me. He married (2) BETSEY DAY who was alive 12 Dec. 1832. He purchased a farm of William Parsons, 6 Sept. 1815 and sold the same to Samuel L. Ricker, 12 Dec. 1832, his wife Betsey joining with him in the deed. Administration on his estate was granted to Ira C. Chase of Porter, Me. Edmund Chase of Parsonsfield mortgaged to Ira C. Chase and Joseph F. Heard, both of Porter, "the farm whereon I now live," excepting the burying yard, 12 Mar. 1841 and Ira C. Chase as administrator sold this homestead of 90 acres in Parsonsfield, 2 May 1845. (York Co. Deeds, 187:211).

Child by first wife, born in Parsonsfield:

1527. IRA C.,[7] b. 10 June 1810; m. Betsey Heard (Hurd) of Limington, Me. They were living in Porter, Me., from 1841 to 1849 and probably for a longer time.

Children by second wife, born in Parsonsfield:

> ELIZABETH, b. 15 June 1822; m. 15 Dec. 1849, Irving Piper;
> she d. in Poland, Me., 3 Sept. 1882; he d. in Parsonsfield,
> 14 May 1881.

1528. EDWIN, under 14, had Betsey Chase of Parsonfield for his
      guardian, 1 Jan. 1849. (York Probate, 62:556) Possibly
      there were other children.

570

NOAH[6] CHASE (Edmund,[5] Aquila,[4] James,[3] Thomas[2]), born in
Parsonsfield, Me., about 1780. He married RACHEL GARLAND,
daughter James Garland of Parsonsfield, Me., and of Effingham, N.
H. There were eight children and they lived in Monroe, Me. (Garland Genealogy, 42).

Children:

> JOSEPH,[7] m. ――― Felker and had seven children.
> SYLVESTER.
> NOAH JR., m. ――― Nutter.
> SAMUEL, m. ――― Chase.
> EDMUND, m. ――― Cook.
> OLIVER.
> ELMIRA.
> JULIA.

571

IRA C. CHASE listed as 571 under Family 176 was the son of Edmund[6] Chase Jr. and not a son of Edmund[5] Chase Sr. (See 1527.)

572

SAMUEL SARGENT[6] CHASE (Moses,[5] Aquila,[4] James,[3] Thomas[2]),
born about 1767; died in Lyman, N. H., June 1843. He married in
Bath, N. H., 13 Nov. 1800, BETSEY HADLOCK of Bath. She was born
in 1780 and died in 1832. They lived in Bath. He was a soldier in
the War of 1812 and was a pensioner.

Children not in order, born in Bath:

> RHODA,[7] b. 1804; m. in Jay, Vt., 1826, Stephen Tracy of Enos-
> burg, Vt.

1529. JONATHAN, b. 16 Apr. 1806; m. (1) 18 Feb. 1826, Sally Tracy;
      m. (2) 20 Oct. 1837, Amanda Tracy; lived in North Troy,
      Vt. Twenty-one children.

> CATHARINE, b. 1808; m. 1825, Aaron Tracy of Enosburg, Vt.

1530. JOSEPH, b. 1809; m. (1) Priscilla Williams; m. (2) Betsey
      Clough; lived in Penn.

1531. MOSES, b. 4 Apr. 1810; m. 15 Dec. 1835, Dorothy Sanborn of
      Lyman, N. H.; lived in Necedah, Wis., 1878.

1532. HEZEKIAH, b. 14 May 1812; m. 12 May 1836, Jane E. Hunt of
      Bath, N. H.

> DOROTHY ANN, b. 1814; m. 1838, Henry Dearborn Hadlock of
> Jay, Vt., and Russell, Kans., 1873.

1533. CHRISTOPHER COLUMBUS, b. 22 Oct. 1816; m. 14 Jan. 1840,
      Susan Sanborn of Bath, N. H.; lived in Monroe, N. H., 1873.

> ADALINE.
> MARY.

Betsey.
Anna.

573

Moses[6] Chase (Moses,[5] Aquila,[4] James,[3] Thomas[2]), born in 1769; married 6 Oct. 1805, Polly Blanchard. They lived in Parsonsfield, Me. Thomas Parsons of Parsonsfield for £60 sells Moses Chase of the same town lot No. 4 in the Tenth Range in Parsonsfield, 21 Nov. 1789. (York Co. Deeds, 67:4). Taylor Page of the same town sells Moses Chase Jr. land in Parsonsfield, 2 Oct. 1801. (Ibid. 68:90). Samuel Dalton sells him land and buildings in Parsonsfield, 14 Oct. 1801. (Ibid. 68:90). No probate in York Co.

Children, born in Parsonsfield:

1534. Moses,[7] b. 31 July 1800.
  Polly, b. 17 Sept. 1808.
  Susanna Pearson, b. 9 Dec. 1810.
1535. Hiram, b. 19 May 1813.
  Rebecca Blanchard, b. 31 Aug. 1814; m. 29 Mar. 1832, Samuel Coffin Jr.
  Emily, b. 19 Oct. 1817.
  Lydia Davis, b. 8 Mar. 1818.

574

David[6] Chase (Moses,[5] Aquila,[4] James,[3] Thomas[2]), born in 1778; taxed in Parsonsfield, Me., in 1798; married ———— ————. They lived in North Parsonsfield, Me. He died there about 1857. He was a soldier in the War of 1812. He deposed, aged 70, in Parsonsfield, 29 Sept. 1849. (York Co. Probate Files 21,376). He purchased his father's homestead 24 Sept. 1822. (York Co. Deeds, 113:88).

Children, born in Parsonsfield:

1536. Samuel,[7] lived in Bath, N. H.
1537. Edmund, lived in Parsonsfield.
1538. David W. C., lived there also.
  Betsey. (History of Parsonsfield, Me., 458)
1539. William Wells, lived in Parsonsfield.
  Dorothy, lived in Parsonsfield.

575

Jacob[6] Chase (Moses,[5] Aquila,[4] James,[3] Thomas[2]), was born in Parsonsfield, Me., and died there before 28 Oct. 1822. His wife's name is unknown to the compilers of this volume. David Chase of Parsonsfield was chosen guardian unto James Chase of Parsonsfield, above 14, son of Jacob Chase, late of Parsonsfield, 28 Oct. 1822. (York Co. Probate, 31:43).

Child:

1540. James,[7] b. before 1808.
  There may have been other children.

576

John[6] Chase (Moses,[5] Aquila,[4] James,[3] Thomas[2]), lived in Parsonsfield, Me. Married in Effingham, N. H., 25 Nov. 1803,

ABIGAIL GLIDDEN, daughter of Nicholas and Mary (Libby) Glidden of Effingham. She joined with her brothers and sisters in a quit claim deed to her father's estate, 22 Feb. 1817. (Glidden Genealogy, 134).

David[6] Chase of Parsonsfield, aged 70, deposed that he was well acquainted with Jesse M.[7] Chase, late of Parsonsfield, who died 31 Jan. 1849; that he was a soldier in the War with Mexico; that he was the son of my brother John[6] Chase and his wife Abigail, now Abigail Morrison; that John[6] Chase went West more than 30 years ago; that he went to the Black River and did not return. It has long been believed that he is dead as he has never been heard from. His wife, or widow, married 23 years ago WILLIAM MORRISON and now lives in Effingham, N. H. Jesse M.[7] Chase was a single man to the day of his death. Sworn to 29 Sept. 1849. (York Co. Probate Files, 21,376).

Children, born in Parsonsfield, Me.:

1541.   JOSEPH.[7]
1542.   JOHN.
1543.   LEVI.
        BETSEY.
        MARY.
        JESSE M. served in Mexican War and d. unm. 31 Jan. 1849.

577

JOSIAH[6] CHASE (Samuel,[5] Aquila,[4] James,[3] Thomas[2]), born 23 Mar. 1781; died in Newbury, Ohio, 16 Nov. 1868. He married in Colchester, Vt., about 1805, AMY MOREHOUSE, who died in Lancaster, Ohio, 3 Mar. 1866. They removed to Ohio many years before 1870. In 1816 they were living in Colchester, Vt.

Children, born in Colchester, Chittenden Co.:

        LAURA,[7] b. 4 July 1806; m. 17 Feb. 1826, Selden Smith; lived in Bedford, Ohio, 1876.
        ALMEDA, b. 13 May 1809; m. James Alford. They lived in Lancaster, Ohio.
1544.   ALVIN, b. 20 July 1811; m. Sally Wilcox; he d. 10 Oct. 1872. He d. in Cleveland, Ohio.
1545.   DANIEL A., b. 6 Sept. 1814; m. (1) his cousin Mary M.[7] Chase (Family 578); lived in Cleveland, Ohio; m. (2) Ellen Sebert [Lewort].
1546.   HIRAM JOSIAH, b. 11 Apr. 1816; m. 22 Nov. 1837, Rhoda Scofield, b. in Lyme, N. Y. They lived in Grand Rapids, Mich.
        FANNY, b. 21 July 1823; m. Henry Dando; lived in New London, Ohio.
        WARREN W., b. 20 Dec. 1828; unm. Went to the Mexican War and did not return.

578

JACOB[6] CHASE (Samuel,[5] Aquila,[4] James,[3] Thomas[2]), born 9 Jan. 1786; died in Grand Isle, Vt., 9 Jan. 1831, aged 45. He married BETSEY CONVERSE, who was born in Newburyport 1789; died 15 Apr. 1842, aged 53. They lived in Grand Isle, Vt.

Children, younger born in Grand Isle, Vt.:

CAROLINE,[7] m. Walter Grant, and lived at Rouse's Point, N. Y.; d. 1842.

1547. ASA CONVERSE, b. 12 Mar. 1812; m. 9 July 1842, Diana Fitchet. Lived in Dresden, Ontario, 1872.

MARY M., m. Daniel A.[7] Chase, son Josiah[6] (Family 577); lived in Cleveland, Ohio. No children.

1548. GEORGE J., m. Sarah Davenport. Lived in Essex Junction, Vt., 1872.

ELIZA O., b. 21 Dec. 1819; m. 20 Feb. 1842, Theodore Cady of North Williston, Vt.

1549. JOHN ,b. 17 May 1821; m. 1 Apr. 1850, Mary Harrington; living in St. Albans, Vt., in 1872.

SARAH M., b. 1823; m. John Ackerson of West Chazy, N. Y. She was living in Plattsburg, N. Y., in 1875.

579

JOHN[6] CHASE (Samuel,[5] Aquila,[4] James,[3] Thomas[2]), born about 1790; died in Apr. 1872. He married SARAH MOREHOUSE. They lived in Colchester, Vt where he died.

Children:

MARTIN,[7] d. unm.

SEYMOUR, d. unm.

EMILY, m. about 1838.

1550. CASSIUS M., b. 1 Jan. 1820; m. 1840, Aurora L. Tomlinson, b. 6 May, 1817, dau. of Mary Chase and ———— Tomlinson of Richmond, Vt. He d. 1862, at Pensacola, Fla.

580

OLIVER[6] CHASE (Joseph,[5] Aquila,[4] James,[3] Thomas[2]), born in Newbury, 16 Oct. 1782. In the deed of Nathaniel[6] Chase to his brother Eliphalet[6] Chase of land in Parsonsfield, Me., they refer to 40 acres which had been sold to Oliver Chase, before 26 Jan. 1802. (York Co. Deeds, 64:77 and 68:211). No further information has been learned about this man. He was probably living in Parsonsfield, Me., in 1802.

581

ELIPHALET[6] CHASE (Joseph,[5] Aquila,[4] James,[3] Thomas[2]), born in Parsonsfield, Me., 15 Dec. 1787. No later record of this man has been found.

582

NATHAN[6] CHASE (Nathan,[5] Aquila,[4] James,[3] Thomas[2]), born in Newbury, 14 June 1780; married in Newbury, 18 Feb. 1800, MARY NEAL of Newburyport. Perhaps she is the Mary, widow of Nathan Chase, who died in Newbury, 27 May 1823. They lived in Newbury. He died in Newburyport, 1 Jan. 1822, aged 42.

Children, born in Newbury:

1551. EDMUND,[7] b. 29 June 1800.

HANNAH, b. 19 Mar. 1802.

MARY, b. 18 Dec. 1803.

1552. WILLIAM NEAL, b. 5 June 1806; m. 1829, Olive Parker Stickney.

583

WILLIAM[6] CHASE (Nathan,[5] Aquila,[4] James,[3] Thomas[2]), born in
Newbury 3 Dec. 1788; may be the William Chase who died in Newburyport, 31 Oct. 1828. No family identified.

584

JOHN[6] CHASE (Nathan,[5] Aquila,[4] James,[3] Thomas[2]), born in
Newbury, 29 May 1789.

585

WILLIAM[6] CHASE (Aquila,[5] Aquila,[4] James,[3] Thomas[2]), born in
Newbury, 21 July 1785; died there 7 July 1864. He married in Newbury, 5 May 1811, ELIZABETH REED, daughter of William and Patience (Lurvey) Reed, born in Newburyport, 26 Oct. 1786; died 15
Aug. 1866. They lived in Newbury.
Children, born in Newbury:
> ELISABETH SANBORN,[7] b. 2 Nov. 1811; m. 21 Nov. 1830, John
> Henry Ordway.
> WILLIAM, b. 10 Nov. 1813; d. 6 Aug. 1814.
> WILLIAM, b. 18 May 1816; d. 29 Sept. 1816.
1553. ENOCH SAWYER, b. 7 Mar. 1819; m. (1) 12 Oct. 1842, Mary
> Jane Currier; d. 26 Feb. 1844; m. (2) 16 Oct. 1844, E. S.
> Currier; lived in Amesbury. Six children.
> Four more children d. young.

586

JACOB[6] CHASE (Aquila,[5] Aquila,[4] James,[3] Thomas[2]), born in
Newbury, 18 Nov. 1790; died 12 Feb. 1856. He married about 1810,
ELIZABETH SPRAGUE, who died 23 Oct. 1857, aged 68. They lived in
Newburyport.
Children:
1554. SPRAGUE,[7] b. 6 Jan. 1812; m. (1) 8 Nov. 1832, Susanna D. Ord-
> way, who d. 11 Feb. 1863; m. (2) 2 July 1863, Harriet N.
> Remick.
1554. JACOB, m. 13 June 1833, Eleanor A. Hunt.
> MARY, d. young.
> ELISABETH, d. young.
> MARY, m. 21 Nov. 1839, George Janvrin.
> ELISABETH, m. 24 Oct. 1842, John Janvrin.
> SOPHRONIA B., m. 22 Sept. 1844, John Athorn.
> ELEANOR P., m. 8 Dec. 1847, John C. Stevens of Newburyport.
> JANE, m. Ezekiel Dyer.

587

ENOCH[6] CHASE (Aquila,[5] Aquila,[3] James,[4] Thomas[2]), born in
Newbury, 14 May 1793; married (1) SOPHRONIA BAKER, who died
without issue. The name of his second wife has not been discovered
and his place of abode is uncertain.

Children by the second wife:
1556. AQUILA.[7]
       THEODOCIA.
       SOPHRONIA.
       MARY.
       ELISABETH.

588

NATHANIEL[6] CHASE (Aquila,[5] Aquila,[4] James,[3] Thomas[2]), born in Newbury, 11 Oct. 1800; died 8 Mar. 1871. He married (1) in Newbury, 18 Apr. 1822, HARRIET MARIA DOYLE, who died 31 Oct. 1834. He married (2) in Newbury, 22 Feb. 1835, SALLY (GRAVES) MERRILL. Harriet Maria Doyle was daughter of Charles and Elizabeth (Coffin) Doyle, born in Newbury, 7 July 1803. They lived in Newbury.

Children by first wife, born in Newbury:
    HARRIET ANN,[7] b. 16 Aug. 1822; m. 9 Dec. 1847, Ezra Trumbull of Newburyport.
1557. ENOCH M., b. 29 Aug. 1824; m. 26 Dec. 1846, Mary Jane Dunlap; one of the founders of Topeka, Kan., 1854; d. 24 Apr. 1888. Two children.
    MARY, b. 27 Feb. 1828; m. 21 Sept. 1847, William D. Coffin of Newburyport; a shipwright.
1558. CHARLES D., b. 10 June 1830; m. Hannah Donaldson.

589

CHARLES[6] CHASE (Aquila,[5] Aquila,[4] James,[3] Thomas[2]), born in Newbury, 11 Oct. 1800. He married (1) (intention at Newbury, 27 June 1823) MARY JANE COFFIN, who died in Newbury, 11 Feb. 1826, aged 20. He married (2) in Marblehead, 9 Dec. 1828, HANNAH FROST. They lived in Newburyport and Marblehead.

Children by first wife:
    INFANT,[7] d. young.
    MARY ANN, m. in Lynn, 1 May 1842, Benjamin Tutt of Lynn.

Children by second wife:
    INFANT, d. young.
1559. CHARLES HENRY.
    ELISABETH.
    HANNAH.
1560. JOHN ALBERT.
    HARRIET.
1561. BENJAMIN.
    SARAH.

590

MOSES[6] CHASE (Josiah,[5] Aquila,[4] James,[3] Thomas[2]), born (probably in Newbury) 2 Mar. 1782; died 29 Aug. 1852. He married 29 Feb. 1820, SALLY LEWIS, who was born 3 Apr. 1781; died 30 Apr. 1851.

Children:
    NATHAN P.,[7] b. 2 Oct. 1820; d. 15 Apr. 1821.

REBECCA P., b. 10 Feb. 1822; m. James Dunn.
1562.   HORACE, b. 23 July 1826; m. Sarah L. Bailey.

591

JOSIAH[6] CHASE (Josiah,[5] Aquila,[4] James,[3] Thomas[2]), born (probably in Newbury), 12 Jan. 1784; died 3 Aug. 1835. He married (1),
in Newbury, 25 Nov. 1809, SARAH L. WOODWARD, who died without
issue. He married (2), in Newbury, 5 Feb. 1817, ESTHER STILLMAN
FERNALD of Rockport, who was born 8 Mar. 1798 and died — Oct.
1855.
Children by second wife:

SARAH L.,[7] b. 26 Feb. 1818; m. 19 Oct. 1837, Eben Tucker of
Rockport.
ANNA M., b. 23 Mar. 1820; d. 1823.
SUSAN G., b. 12 Apr. 1822; m. 1 June 1842, Stephen A. Bartlett
of Northwood, N. H.
1563.   THURSTON S., b. 23 May 1824; d. 6 June 1861; m. 7 Sept. 1841,
Sarah L. Goodwin, b. 18 Jan. 1827; d. 5 July 1862. Three
children, including *Edward Thurston,*[8] b. in Newburyport,
29 Nov. 1849; m. 29 Nov. 1874, Elizabeth Holmes Waterman;
lives in Philadelphia; member of the J. E. Caldwell Co., jew-
ellers.
    Children: Augusta Elizabeth,[9] b. 24 July 1876; Thurston
Waterman[9] (1877-1890); Eleanor Haupt,[9] b. 14 Feb. 1884;
m. 11 June 1912, George Henry Woodroffe. Children: *Elizabeth Chase*[10] *Woodroffe* and *Eleanor Thurston Chase*[10] *Woodroffe.*
MARGARET C., b. 25 Dec. 1826; m. 14 Nov. 1849, Moses P. L.[7]
Chase. (Family 632) Nine children; she d. 29 Mar. 1870.
LYDIA E., b. 20 Dec. 1828; d. Aug. 1839.
MARY JANE, b. 1830; m. (1) 12 Dec. 1848, James Davis of
Newburyport; lived in Everett; m. (2) Maj. John Fowler.
ELISABETH T., b. 28 Jan. 1832; m. John B. Hunt of Newbury-
port, 1873.

592

JOHN[6] CHASE (Col. Somerby,[5] Ezra,[4] James,[3] Thomas[2]), born
in what is now West Newbury, 7 Sept. 1783; died in West Newbury
8 Jan. 1865. He married in Newbury 16 Mar. 1803, BETSEY CARLE-
TON, daughter of Amos and Sarah (Dole) Carleton, born in Newbury, 18 Feb. 1785; died 12 June 1858. They lived in West Newbury.
    Administration on his estate was granted to Thomas M.[7] Chase with
Harrison Gray Otis[7] Chase and N. F. Emery sureties, 7 Apr. 1865. The
heirs mentioned were Betsey, wife of Joseph W. Stanwood of Newbury
and Caroline H. Lowe of West Newbury, daughters; Harrison Gray Otis[7]
Chase, a son; Roena, wife of Horace L.[6] Chase, a daughter; Thomas
Meady[7] Chase, Jehu[8] Chase, Horace L.[8] Chase and Otis Gray[8] Chase,
grandsons, Ann Maria Merrill of Lawrence and Sarah Elizabeth, wife of
Francis D.[7] Chase of West Newbury, granddaughters. (Essex Probate,
35,018).
    Children, born in West Newbury:

BETSEY DOLE,[7] b. 1804; m. 23 Oct. 1823, Joseph W. Stanwood
Jr. of Newbury; alive 7 Apr. 1865.

SARAH DOLE, b. 1806; m. (1) Staniford[6] Chase, (Family 1205); m. (2) Moses Merrill.

CAROLINE HOUGHTON, b. 1808; m. (1) Jehu[6] Chase, (Family 1208); m. (2) Gen. Solomon Lowe; she d. 11 Dec. 1897.

1564. HARRISON GRAY OTIS, b. 12 Nov. 1811; m. Eliza Jones; he d. in West Newbury, 4 May 1896, aged 84 y. 5. m. 22 d. Was a comb-maker in West Newbury.

ELVIRA MELVINA, b. 1816; m. 1 Oct. 1835, Horace Lummus Chase, (Family 1207); she d. 1 Oct. 1846, aged 30.

1565. THOMAS MEADY, b. 8 Oct. 1820; m. 8 Feb. 1844, Mary Tasker; d. 25 Jan. 1895.

ROWENA ROXANA, b. 1825; m. Horace Lummus[6] Chase, (Family 1207); d. in 1867; ag. 42.

593

SAMUEL DENISON[6] CHASE (Col. Somerby,[5] Ezra,[4] James,[3] Thomas[2]), born in what is now West Newbury, 4 June 1789; married in 1816, REBECCA R. LUDLOW. He died 1 Feb. 1862. They had a large family and lived in Brooklyn, N. Y.

Children:

CECELIA D.,[7] living in Brooklyn, N. Y., 1873.

SARAH J., living in Brooklyn, N. Y., 1873.

1566. JOHN L.

594

JAMES GREENOUGH[6] CHASE (Col. Somerby,[5] Ezra,[4] James,[3] Thomas[2]), born in what is now West Newbury, 13 June 1791; married in West Newbury, 30 May 1824, JUDITH PILLSBURY, daughter of Silas and Abigail (Cutter) Pillsbury, born in Newbury, 19 Dec. 1798; died 20 Sept. 1871. He died 11 July 1864. They lived in West Newbury.

Children, born in West Newbury:

1567. JAMES ALBERT,[7] b. 26 Sept. 1826; m. Rosamonda Carleton, b. 1823; lived in West Newbury; a comb-maker.

1568. ALFRED.

595

THOMAS HILLS[6] CHASE (Col. Somerby,[5] Ezra,[4] James,[3] Thomas[2]), born in what is now West Newbury, 8 Apr. 1795; died 13 Jan. 1866. He married in Haverhill, 4 Feb. 1823, ANN LADD, daughter of Nathaniel and Sarah (Noyes) Ladd, born in Haverhill, 4 Nov. 1800; died in June 1889. They lived in that part of Bradford (now Groveland).

Children, born in what is now Groveland:

CHARLES MOODY,[7] d. 30 Oct. 1838, aged 20 y. 7 m.

CYNTHIA, b. 1830; d. 6 Sept. 1850, aged 20 y. 7 m.

1569. THOMAS P., b. 9 June 1833; d. 21 Oct. 1867.

596

JACOB[6] CHASE (Daniel,[5] Ezra,[4] James,[3] Thomas[2]), born in Newbury, 25 May 1789; died in Salisbury, Vt., 8 May 1872. He married (1) in Deering, N. H., 19 June 1806, SALLY HALL, born 8 Apr. 1786.

They lived in Deering, and Salisbury, Vt. He married (2) NANCY ——, who was living as his widow in Clayburg, N. Y., in 1874.
Children, the younger born in Salisbury, Vt.:

NANCY,[7] b. 12 May 1807; m. Russell Estes; she d. Aug. 1846.
1570.   WILLIAM FRANCIS, b. 31 Dec. 1809; m. 27 Apr. 1829, Calista Damon; living in Salisbury, Vt., in 1873.
1571.   SIMEON, b. 8 July 1811; m. and living in Bristol, Vt., 1874.
ADELINE, b. 29 Nov. 1813; m. 17 June 1840, Isaac Dow of Clayburg, N. Y.
SIMMONS, b. 17 Nov. 1815; d. 17 Feb. 1819.
1572.   OTIS, b. 13 July 1817; m. and lived in Bristol.
1573.   DANIEL, b. 8 Nov. 1819; m. (1) 1 Jan. 1840, Zilpha Preston; she d. 8 Jan. 1841; he m. (2) 9 June 1842, Laura Williams of Shefford, Canada; lived in Bedford, N. Y.
LORAINE, b. 19 Feb. 1823; m. 18 Sept. 1846, Horace P. Jennings of Bristol.
URSULA, b. 27 Dec. 1824; m. 22 Sept. 1841, Leonard Lamphier of Hyde Park, Vt.

Child by second wife:

MARY, b. 20 May 1830; m. 10 Feb. 1853, Quincy Shattuck of Bristol.

597

MOSES[6] CHASE (Nathaniel Lowe,[5] Ezra,[4] James,[3] Thomas[2]), born in what is now West Newbury, 16 May 1774; died in Bradford, 2 Feb. 1823. He married in Newbury, 10 July 1800, ABIGAIL LITTLE of Amesbury, daughter of William Coffin and Mary (Rowell) Little, born 30 Aug. 1777; died in Sept. 1859. He was a cooper by trade, and lived in West Newbury.
Children, born in what is now West Newbury:

MARY LITTLE,[7] b. 30 Mar. 1801; m. about 1823, Josiah Brown.
1574.   WILLIAM LITTLE, b. 1 Apr. 1804; m. 29 Oct. 1829, Sally Minot; d. 1875.
LYDIA DUSTIN, b. 15 May 1807; m. Timothy Flanders of Haverhill.
1575.   METAPHOR INGERSOL, b. 21 Oct. 1808; m. 27 1836, Mary George.
ABIGAIL JANE, b. 11 Mar. 1811; m. Isaac Morse of Bradford.
ANN MARIA, b. 18 Feb. 1813; m. Edward P. Offutt of Manchester, N. H.
HANNAH B., b. 20 Apr. 1816; m. James Cate of Tilton, N. H. or Gilmanton, N. H.

598

JOHN[6] CHASE (Nathaniel Lowe,[5] Ezra,[4] James,[3] Thomas[2]), born in what is now West Newbury, 6 Dec. 1775; died in Mar. 1846. He married and lived in Harrisburg, Pa.

599

EZRA[6] CHASE (Nathaniel Lowe,[5] Ezra,[4] James,[3] Thomas[2]), born in what is now West Newbury, 25 Oct. 1779. He married in Newburyport, 14 Sept. 1800, ELIZABETH PIDGEON, daughter of William and Deborah (Hodgskins) Pidgeon, baptized in Newburyport, 9 Aug.

1778; died Oct. 1853. They lived in Newburyport, Charlestown, West Chester and Philadelphia, Pa. He died in Philadelphia in 1859. Children:

1576. WILLIAM FREDERIC,[7] b. 18 Aug. 1801; m. 14 May 1822, Anna W. Wiley. He d. 6 Sept. 1831. She m. (2) 1835, Joshua Coffin, Historian of Old Newbury, and d. 28 Mar. 1877. Four children, including *Edwin Theodore,*[8] b. 30 Oct. 1823; m. 14 June 1841, Lucia Tappan Coffin, dau. of Joshua and Clarissa Harlow (Dutch) Coffin, b. 6 Sept. 1820; d. 21 Sept. 1878. Their son Joshua Coffin,[9] b. 23 Sept. 1858; m. (1) 24 Feb. 1892, Sarah Jane Whitner who d. 26 Mar. 1894; m. (2) 24 May 1904, Mary (Justice) Lee. Children: *Franklin Whitner*[10] (1892-1895); *Joshua Coffin*[10] (1894-1907); *Cecilia Justice,*[10] b. 6 Aug. 1905. Their son Charles Frederick,[9] b. 9 Sept. 1862; m. Helen Edith Fowler, dau. of Ezekiel and Helen Agnes (Miles) Fowler, lives at Jackson Heights, N. Y. Children: *Charles Adamson,*[10] b. 13 Mar. 1898; *Walter Fowler,*[10] b. 3 May 1902; m. 18 Sept. 1926, Ruth Ethel Halsted.

1577. JOSEPH WARREN, b. 16 Mar. 1804; m. Hannah Cattel.
1578. HORATIO GATES, b. 28 July 1806; m. Caroline Gallagher.
1579. EZRA, b. 15 Sept. 1808; m. in Lebanon, Penn.
1580. ALFRED D., b. 15 Dec. 1810; m. (1) 7 Nov. 1836, Cynthia (Dunham) Allen; m. (2) 18 Apr. 1866, Phebe C. Short of Pawtucket, R. I.; d. 3 June 1893.
1581. WINFIELD SCOTT, b. 30 Aug. 1818; m. (1) 14 Oct. 1839, Mary C. Stewart; m. (2) 3 May 1847, Amy A. Sabin; m. (3) Emma Chase, dau. of Abel Chase.

BENJAMIN FRANKLIN, b. 7 Sept. 1820; never married.
ELIZABETH P., b. 30 Sept. 1823; m. in San Francisco, Cal., Samuel L. Halliday or Hollowell.

600

ABEL DUSTIN[6] CHASE (Nathaniel Lowe,[5] Ezra,[4] James,[3] Thomas[2]), born in what is now West Newbury, 25 Dec. 1783; died in 1832. He married EMMA HARRISON of Baltimore, Md.

601

MOODY[6] CHASE (Nathaniel Lowe,[5] Ezra,[4] James,[3] Thomas[2]), born in what is now West Newbury, 6 Nov. 1785.

602

SEWALL[6] CHASE (Nathaniel Lowe,[5] Ezra,[4] James,[3] Thomas[2]), born in what is now West Newbury, 7 July 1795.

603

SOMERBY[6] CHASE (John,[5] Ezra,[4] James,[3] Thomas[2]), born in Leominster, 31 Jan. 1783; died there, 6 Oct. 1824, aged 41. He married in Leominster, 5 June 1808, ABIGAIL FULLAM, daughter of Jacob and Elizabeth (Houghton) Fullam, born in Leominster, 22 Aug. 1782; living a widow, 13 June 1829. They lived in Leominster. Children, born in Leominster:

MARY ANN,[7] b. 22 Mar. 1809.
MARTHA, b. 19 Oct. 1810.

1582.   LUKE, b. 4 Feb. 1812; m. 1 Oct. 1840, Sophia Cutler.
   THIRZA, b. 10 Apr. 1814; d. 13 June 1829, a. 15 y. 2 m. 3 d.
   SARAH, b. 25 Feb. 1816; m. 16 Apr. 1840, Charles A. Cutting.
1583.   HENRY, b. 16 Apr. 1818.
1584.   RUFUS HOUGHTON, b. 11 Aug. 1820.
1585.   GEORGE SUMNER, b. 15 Aug. 1822.
   ABIGAIL ADALINE, b. 10 Oct. 1824; d. 3 Apr. 1844, a. 19.

604

FRANCIS[6] CHASE (John,[5] Ezra,[4] James,[3] Thomas[2]), born in
Leominster, 1 Apr. 1792; married (1) in Leominster, 23 Sept. 1811,
BETSEY MERRIAM who died there, 22 July 1847, aged 53. She was
daughter of Amos and Susan ( ) Merriam, born in Leominster,
13 Nov. 1793. He married (2) in Leominster, 2 Aug. 1849, ALMIRA
F. FESSENDEN of Townsend. They lived in Leominster.
Children, by first wife, born in Leominster:
   BETSEY M.,[7] b. 13 Nov. 1814.
   SUSAN C., b. 16 Mar. 1816.
   ISABELLA, b. 26 Feb. 1817; m. 4 Dec. 1845, Benjamin F. Ken-
    dall of South Groton.
   CAROLINE ANN, b. 5 Sept. 1819; m. Gilbert Derby.
   EMMA CARTER, b. 25 Oct. 1822.
1586.   FRANCIS CHRISTOPHER, b. 1 Jan. 1825; m. 2 June 1847, Amelia
   A. Willard.
   SOPHRONIA JANE, b. 3 Dec. 1827; d. 14 July 1830, a. 2 y. 6 m.

605

ELIJAH[6] CHASE (John,[5] Ezra,[4] James,[3] Thomas[2]), born in
Leominster, 14 Feb. 1794. No further information has been found
relating to this man.

606

METAPHOR[6] CHASE (John,[5] Ezra,[4] James,[3] Thomas[2]), born in
Leominster, 21 Apr. 1799; married in Haverhill, 1 Apr. 1819, NANCY
CARR, who died in Leominster, 27 Nov. 1843, aged 45. One Meta-
phor Chase, perhaps this man, lived in Exeter, N. H., in 1820. There
is no adminstration on his estate in Worcester Co.
Child, born in Exeter:
   SON,[7] b. 9 Oct. 1824.

607

THOMAS LEGATE[6] CHASE (Maj. Metaphor,[5] Ezra,[4] James,[3]
Thomas[2]), born in Leominster, 22 Dec. 1782; married there, 5 Jan.
1817, ELIZA KENDALL. No further record in Leominster, nor probate of his estate in Worcester County. The inference is that they
left Leominster.

608

CEPHAS[6] CHASE (Maj. Metaphor,[5] Ezra,[4] James,[3] Thomas[2]),
born in Leominster, 5 Dec. 1788; married in Leominster, 13 June
1813, SALLY CASS. They lived in Leominster but the birth of their
fourth child was recorded in both Leominster and Richmond, N. H.

Children, born in Leominster:

1587. WILLIAM HENRY,[7] b. 24 June 1814.
1588. CHAUNCEY METAPHOR, b. 8 Aug. 1816.
      MARIA CAROLINE, b. 9 June 1819.
      ANNE SOPHIA, b. 17 Nov. 1821.
1589. GEORGE LABAN, b. 24 Nov. 1825.
1590. JOSEPH HASKELL, b. 19 Aug. 1828.
      SOPHRONIA ANN, b. 24 Dec. 1830.

609

GEORGE[6] CHASE (Maj. Metaphor,[5] Ezra,[4] James,[3] Thomas[2]), born in Leominster, 26 Mar. 1795; married (1) in Leominster, 18 Sept. 1815, SOPHRONIA BARNARD, who died suddenly in Lancaster at the house of Thomas Houghton, 27 Dec. 1838, aged 46. He died in Leominster, 9 Aug. 1841, aged 46. He married (2) in Leominster, 20 Feb. 1840, MRS. MARGARETTA P. MURDOCK, who married (2) 23 July 1841, STILLMAN BROOKS. They lived in Millbury till 1818 and then in Leominster.

Children by first wife, first two born in Millbury, others in Leominster:

      MARY SMITH,[7] b. 20 July 1816; m. David Howe 2d.
      JULIA ANN, b. 3 Dec. 1817; m. Thomas C. Stearns.
1591. GEORGE METAPHOR, b. 10 Dec. 1819; d. in Penn Yan, N. Y., 2 Sept. 1849.
      THOMAS ADAMS, b. 21 Jan. 1821; d. 24 Sept. 1827.
1592. CHARLES ADOLPHUS, b. 1 Jan. 1823; m. Frances E. Carter.
1593. ABEL CONANT, b. 1 Feb. 1824; m. Dorothy Farnsworth.
      SOPHRONIA LOUISA, b. 5 Nov. 1828; d. 15 Nov. 1831.
      ABBY LOUISA, b. 22 June 1836.

610

JAMES[6] CHASE (Capt. Enoch,[5] Ebenezer,[4] James,[3] Thomas[2]), born in Dover, N. H., 1768; died shortly before 10 Apr. 1801. He married ELIZABETH GAGE, who married (2) in Dover, 14 Dec. 1807, CAPT. JEREMIAH BANKS, who died at sea.

Administration on the estate of James Chase, late of Dover, deceased, trader, granted to his widow Elizabeth, 10 Apr. 1801. Her account was presented to Probate 27 Nov. 1807. (Strafford Co. Probate, 7:370). Moses Gage of Wakefield and Jonathan Gage of Dover were her sureties, 6 Mar. 1804. (Ibid. 8:441).

Children, born in Dover:

1594. JOHN GAGE,[7] b. about 1796.
      ABIGAIL GAGE, b. about 1798.
1595. JAMES, b. about 1800.

611

ENOCH[6] CHASE (Capt. Enoch,[5] Ebenezer,[4] James,[3] Thomas[2]), born in Dover, N. H., about 1770; married in Berwick (now South Berwick), Me., 8 Feb. 1791, PRUDENCE CLARK. On 12 Jan. 1797, Enoch Chase of Berwick, shipwright, for $500 sells Jonathan Hamilton Jr. of Berwick land and buildings there. His wife Prudence signs with him. (York Co. Deeds, 60:116). In another deed he was styled a merchant of South Berwick, 16 Sept. 1816. (Ibid. 95:184).

Child, born in what is now South Berwick:

1596.   ENOCH,[7] b. 4 Dec. 1792; d. in Rollinsford, N. H., 19 June 1858; m. in Durham, N. H., 30 June 1822, Maria Lord of Somersworth. He lived in Boston, 1822 to 1835; six children.

612

JOSEPH[6] CHASE (Capt. Enoch,[5] Ebenezer,[4] James,[3] Thomas[2]), born in Dover, N. H., about 1772; married in Portsmouth, N. H., 10 May 1806, MARY WINKLEY. No children recorded as born to them on the town records of New Hampshire.

613

JAMES[6] CHASE (James,[5] Ebenezer,[4] James,[3] Thomas[2]), born in Newburyport, 2 Feb. 1771; died in Frankfort, Me., 10 Dec. 1868. He married in Newburyport, 26 Dec. 1793, ALICE CURRIER, who was born 24 July 1771 and died 22 Mar. 1844. They lived in Newburyport till 1814 and in 1816 removed to Frankfort.

Children, born in Newburyport:

REBECCA NOYES,[7] b. 31 July 1794; d. 3 Mar. 1795.
HANNAH, b. 24 Dec. 1795; m. June 1817, William Creasy.
JAMES, b. 7 Oct. 1798; d. 16 Sept. 1801.
REBECCA P., b. 17 Jan. 1801; d. 6 Oct. 1801.
JAMES, b. 18 Sept. 1802; lost at sea, 18 Jan. 1829.
MEHITABLE, b. 11 Mar. 1805; m. 1823, Joseph Keniston of Rockland, Me.
ABIGAIL, b. 21 Dec. 1807; m. 20 Sept. 1829, Seth Averill of Frankfort, Me. Ten children.
ALICE, b. 1 Apr. 1810; m. 1830, Charles H. Danielson; d. Mar. 1846.
SAMUEL CURRIER, b. 16 Aug. 1813; d. Nov. 1831.

614

EBENEZER[6] CHASE (James,[5] Ebenezer,[4] James,[3] Thomas[2]), born in Newburyport, 4 July 1773; died in Kingston, N. H. He married in Newburyport, 16 Sept. 1805, SARAH CURTIS. They lived in Newburyport, Deerfield, N. H., and Concord, N. H.

Child, born in Newburyport:

1597.   EBENEZER,[7] b. 22 Oct. 1806.

615

JOHN[6] CHASE (James,[5] Ebenezer,[4] James,[3] Thomas[2]), born in Newburyport, 22 Aug. 1777. He went to Vermont and died there.

616

JOHN BICKFORD[6] CHASE (James,[5] Ebenezer,[4] James,[3] Thomas[2]), born in Newburyport, 22 Aug. 1778. Possibly John[6] and John Bickford[6] may be one and the same.

617

STEPHEN[6] CHASE (James,[5] Ebenezer,[4] James,[3] Thomas[2]), born
in Newburyport, 13 June 1784; died in Concord, N, H., 18 Oct. 1851.
He married 16 Apr. 1807, ESTHER EASTMAN, daughter of Jacob and
Abigail (Kimball) Eastman, born 27 Oct. 1786; died 12 June 1870.
Children, born in Concord:

1598. JAMES,[7] b. 7 Oct. 1807; mar. and lived in Concord.
1599. JACOB E., b. 25 Sept. 1809; m. Jane Merrill; lived in North Conway, N. H.
ROBERT (twin), b. 1 Oct. 1811; d. young.
1600. JONATHAN EASTMAN (twin), b. 1 Oct. 1811; m. 20 May 1839, Irene Eastman; lived in North Conway; d. in Conway, 21 Mar. 1870.
1601. CHANDLER E., b. 28 Aug. 1813; m. 12 May 1836; Lydia Eastman, b. 1 May 1816. Lived North Conway.
1602. SAMUEL W. L., b. 21 Jan. 1821; physician; m. (1) ———;
m. (2) 20 Oct. 1870, Augusta A. Pease; lived Exeter, Me.
ABIGAIL, b. 21 Apr. 1823; m. Cornelius Stilphen; lived in Bartlett, N. H.

618

MICHAEL[6] CHASE (James,[5] Ebenezer,[4] James,[3] Thomas[2]), born
in Newburyport, 23 Oct. 1789; died in Brooks, Me. He married SARAH SAWYER of Exeter, N. H. They lived in Brooks.
Child:

1603. MICHAEL,[7] lived in Brooks.

619

TRUEWORTHY[6] CHASE (Nathaniel,[5] Ebenezer,[4] James,[3] Thomas[2]), born about 1773; married (1) ANNA WEBSTER of Waterborough, Me.; married (2) LUCY EMERY. They lived in Londonderry,
N. H. He died 27 Nov. 1858 and his second wife died 1863.
Children by first wife, born in Londonderry:

POLLY,[7] d. unm. 1855.
1604. NATHANIEL, d. 1860; m. Mary Blodgett.
JOANNA, m. Andrew Robinson of Londonderry.
PHEBE, m. James Trask of Francestown, N. H.

Children by second wife, born in Londonderry:

ABIGAIL, m. Henry March of Londonderry.
1605. JOHN, m. ——— Bachelder.
1606. GEORGE FERNALD, m. and lived in Lowell; physician.
JANE, m. John Burbank; lived in Nashua, N. H.

620

STEPHEN[6] CHASE (Nathaniel,[5] Ebenezer,[4] James,[3] Thomas[2]),
born in Kingston or Brentwood, N. H., about 1780; married ANNIE
WEBSTER. They lived in Waterborough, Me.

621

NATHANIEL[6] CHASE (Nathaniel,[5] Ebenezer,[4] James,[3] Thomas[2]),
born in Brentwood, N. H., 6 Aug. 1789; married in Londonderry, N.
H., 20 Aug. 1810, LYDIA (CROOKER) MOTT, who was born 7 May

1783; died in Hudson, N. H., 9 Jan. 1872, aged 89. They lived in Londonderry. He died in Hudson, 21 Nov. 1879, aged 84. The Vital Records of Londonderry give the wife's name as Lydia Mott but the death returns of her children call her Lydia Crooker. Perhaps she was a widow Mott at marriage.

Children, born in Londonderry:

> ADALINE,[7] b. 6 Oct. 1812; m. 11 Feb. 1836, Daniel S. Jones; lived in Suncook, N. H.

1607. STEPHEN, b. 1814; m. int. 18 Apr. 1840, Sophronia Foster of Pembroke, N. H.; she d. 4 Apr. 1872.

> ESTHER, b. 18 Feb. 1816; m. Nov. 5, 1838, Edwin Follansbee, and d. 30 July 1863.

1608. NATHANIEL, b. Mar. 1818; m. Almira Shedd; d. in Nashua, 31 July 1884, aged 66 y. 4 m. 9 d.

> ANN, b. 8 Jan. 1820; d. unm. 11 July 1883.
>
> MARGARET, b. 9 Jan. 1822; m. 3 Oct. 1844, Addison Knight of Londonderry.

1609. ABEL, b. 1 Jan. 1824; m. Mary A. Badger; lived in Lowell.

622

SIMON[6] CHASE (Nathaniel,[5] Ebenzer,[4] James,[3] Thomas[2]), born 1 July 1791; died 17 Dec. 1864, aged 73, in Londonderry, N. H. He married 23 Jan. 1813, HULDAH EMERY, daughter of Jacob and Huldah (Thompson) Emery of Waterborough, Me. She was born in Westbrook, Me., 21 Oct. 1791; died 11 Apr. 1878, aged 86y. 5m. 21d. They lived in Brentwood, N. H., Londonderry, N. H., and Waterborough, Me.

Children recorded in Londonderry, N. H.:

> MARY ANN,[7] b. 16 Oct. 1813; m. Nov. 1841, Charles Clark.
>
> JOHN, b. — Aug. 1815; d. 17 Sept. 1821.

1610. ELIJAH GORDON, b. 22 Mar. 1819; m. Sept. 1841, Phebe Hale of Merrimac. He d. 23 June 1877. No children.

> HULDAH, b. 14 Oct. 1823; m. (1) William H. Adams, who d. 1852; no children; m. (2) Charles H. Smith.

1611. SIMON, b. 21 Mar. 1824; m. (1) 2 July 1846, Emily Young; m. (2) ————. He d. 2 Apr. 1851.

1612. JOHN MORRISON, b. 9 June 1826; m. (1) 1850, Ann Maria Howe; m. (2) in 1852, Hannah Clark, b. 30 Apr. 1833; d. 30 Mar. 1890. He d. 6 Aug. 1915. By the second wife their son Elijah G.,[8] b. 29 Sept. 1858; d. 10 Oct. 1917; m. 9 Jan. 1889, Lottie F. Corning, b. 21 Aug. 1867, dau. of William and Hannah Corning. Their son Curtis Corning,[9] b. 27 Dec. 1893; m. 21 Aug. 1917, Marian Perkins, b. 9 May 1894. Their children are *David Gordon*,[10] b. 25 Oct. 1920; *Curtis Corning Jr.*,[10] b. 3 Oct. 1922; *Carolyn*,[10] b. 2 July 1924.

1613. TRUEWORTHY D., b. 11 Sept. 1828; m. 19 May 1853, Nancy M. Pettingill.

1614. AMASA K., b. 8 Apr. 1833; m. (1) 1856, Elizabeth Howe; m. (2) 1868, Sophronia Howe; m. (3) 8 Nov. 1871, Lottie Bothwell.

623

SIMON[6] CHASE (Simon,[5] Ebenezer,[4] James,[3] Thomas[2]), born in Bradford, Vt., 18 June 1800; married 4 Dec. 1823, MARY BELKNAP. They lived in Bradford, he being alive in 1873.

Children:

1615. AMOS B.,[7] b. 24 Nov. 1825; m. 4 July 1848, Emma Corliss.
1616. ALONZO J., b. 21 May 1828; m. 30 June 1851, Emma Little.
1617. HORATIO B., b. 1 July 1830; m. 30 Mar. 1856, Augusta Flanders.
    MARY, b. 1 Sept. 1832; m. 11 May 1852, Solomon Butterfield.
    SARAH, b. 9 Feb. 1835; m. 1 July 1855, Silas Kennedy.
    HARRIET, b. 27 Nov. 1836; m. 9 Feb. 1867, Daniel Flanders.
1618. SIMEON LANGDON, b. 19 Aug. 1839; m. 29 Nov. 1866, Eliza Kelley.
1619. ALBERT J., b. 7 June 1841; m. 28 May 1872, Clara Lowell.

624

SAMUEL[6] CHASE (Josiah,[5] Nathan,[4] Nathan,[3] Thomas[2]), born in Haverhill, 13 May 1783; died there 24 Sept. 1848, aged 65. He married (intention in Haverhill, 2 Sept. 1813), 11 Nov. 1813, SARAH ADAMS GILE of Hopkinton, N. H., granddaughter of Ezekiel Gile of Plaistow, N. H. She died 28 Oct. 1858, aged 66. They lived in Haverhill.

Children, born in Haverhill:

1620. LORENZO,[7] b. 5 Apr. 1815; m. (1) Pamelia Colby; d. 30 Nov. 1844; m. (2) Betsey D. Gove.
1621. CHARLES CHAUNCEY, b. 19 Jan. 1818; m. 30 Nov. 1841, Martha Smith Cowles of Peacham, Vt. He graduated from Dartmouth College in 1839; was master of the Grammar School, Peacham, Vt., 1839-1845; principal of the High School, Lowell, 1845-1900; d. in Lowell, 15 May 1900. Their son *Frederick Arthur,*[8] b. in Lowell, 21 Apr. 1858; m. 26 June 1899, Helen Louise Conant, b. 3 Jan. 1879. Children: (1) Richard,[9] b. 25 Apr. 1902; (2) Alice Louise,[9] b. 21 June 1905. Mr. Chase received the honorary degree A. M. from Dartmouth College in 1892 and is librarian of the City Library of Lowell.
1622. ELBRIDGE WALTER, b. 23 Feb. 1820; m. 24 Aug. 1842, Sarah Ayer Clement, b. 11 June 1820; d. 23 Feb. 1900. He d. 12 June 1883. Their son *Charles Walter,*[8] b. 29 May 1853; m. 15 Nov. 1876, Sarah Agnes Scott who d. 13 Oct. 1911. Their son Walter Scott,[9] b. 2 Aug. 1878; m. 30 June 1904, Cora Marie Bohn, dau. of Gebhard and Lena (Nockin) Bohn, native of Immeshausen, Germany, b. 7 July 1879. Their children are *Sarah Caroline,*[10] b. 9 Mar. 1905; *Gebhard Charles,*[10] b. 9 Mar. 1905; *Walter Bohn,*[10] b. 26 Nov. 1909.
    CELESTIA, b. 9 Jan. 1822; d. 29 Dec. 1823, of throat disease.
    SAMUEL L., b. 8 Mar. 1825; d. 8 Apr. 1825.
1623. SAMUEL AYER, b. 9 May 1826; m. Sarah Hills Esterbrook. He was principal of a public school in Lowell.
    SARAH A., b. 28 June 1828; m. Rev. John Parsons of Lebanon and Limington, Me.; founder of Parsons Library in Alfred, Me.
1624. LEVERETT MILTON, b. 18 July 1832; m. 13 June 1862, Anna Malinda Marion. He graduated from Dartmouth College in

1856; read law and was principal of the Adams Grammar School of Dorchester, 1857 to 1864; principal of the Davis Grammar School of Newton, 1864. He d. in Boston, 19 May 1901.

MARY WHITE, b. 25 Jan. 1835; m. John Bradley of Plaistow, N. H.

ELIZABETH GILE, b. 27 May 1837; m. C. Herbert Bradley of Plaistow.

625

NATHAN[6] CHASE (Josiah,[5] Nathan,[4] Nathan,[3] Thomas[2]), born in Haverhill, 19 Apr. 1791; died in Lynn. He married (1) in Haverhill, 10 Jan. 1823, HANNAH[7] CHASE, daughter of Richard[6] and Martha (Davis) Chase, (Family 1123), born in Haverhill, 2 June 1805. He married (2) in Haverhill, — June 1835, FANNY BATCHELDER.
Children, born probably in Haverhill:

MARTHA JANE,[7] d. at age of 4 yrs.

CLARISSA K., b. 1825; m. 6 Nov. 1848, Samuel W. Kent; lived in Lynn.

MARTHA JANE, b. 1827; m. 23 Aug. 1846, John L. Frisbie.

EMELINE E., m. Warren Langham of Haverhill.

626

NATHAN[6] CHASE (Samuel,[5] John,[4] Nathan,[3] Thomas[2]), born in Newbury, 20 June 1783; died there 21 Apr. 1856. He married in Newbury, 20 Jan. 1806, BETSEY WARNER of Ipswich, who was born 7 Aug. 1786 (or 1 Aug. 1785). She died 13 Mar. 1873, aged 97y. 7m. 12d. They lived at the "Plains" in Newbury, now Newburyport.
Children, born in Newbury:

1625. WILLIAM WARNER,[7] b. 1 Feb. 1806; m. (1) 22 Oct. 1829, Ann Simpson; m. (2) 9 Mar. 1865, Sarah K. Wilder of Bernardston; d. West Indies, Nov. 1880.

HARRIET LOWELL, b. 29 Aug. 1807; m. 6 Sept. 1832, Amaziah Bailey of West Newbury; she d. 16 Apr. 1881. Lived in the Samuel[3] Chase house.

SARAH MERRILL, b. 19 June 1809; m. 1834, Moses Ordway of Concord, N. H.

MARY ANN, b. 25 June 1812; m. Dec. 3, 1835, Joseph Bailey of Amesbury; d. 3 Feb. 1842.

1626. JOHN TILTON, b. 19 Aug. 1814; m. (1) 18 May 1837, Judith Bailey Follansbee; m. (2) 12 Aug. 1847, Abby Poor of West Newbury.

MARTHA ANN, b. 12 Aug. 1817; m. 24 Sept. 1835, Fordyce Hills Noyes of West Newbury.

1627. STANIFORD TAPPAN, b. 17 Sept. 1819; m. 19 Dec. 1844, Salome Bean of Bangor, Me. He d. in Bangor, 13 July 1881.

ELIZABETH MARGARET, b. 13 Oct. 1821; m. 29 Sept. 1844, George Rowe of Concord, N. H.

1628. FRANCIS DEAN, b. 10 Nov. 1824; m. 10 Oct. 1852, Sarah Elizabeth[7] Chase. (Family 1205)

MALVINA LUCASTA, b. 28 Aug. 1829; m. 1848, Leonard Stowe of Newburyport.

627

SAMUEL⁶ CHASE (Samuel,⁵ John,⁴ Nathan,³ Thomas²), born in Newbury, 11 July 1785; died in Methuen, 11 Oct. 1852. He married (1) (intention at Newbury, 30 Jan. 1808) SARAH MERRILL, daughter of Nathan and Sarah (Merrill) Merrill, born in Newbury, 15 Oct. 1790; died in Wentworth, N. H., 5 Oct. 1808. He married (2) (intention in Newbury, 2 Sept. 1810) MARY DOE of Rumney, N. H. She was the daughter of Capt. John and Mary (Sanborn) Doe, born in Rumney, N. H., 13 Feb. 1789; died in Hardwick, Vt., 15 Feb. 1869. They lived in Newbury, Methuen and Derry, and Rumney, N. H.

Children, first two born in Wentworth, others in Newbury, last three in Rumney:

SARAH JANE,⁷ b. 3 Oct. 1811; d. 10 Apr. 1815.

MARY DOE, b. 22 Oct. 1815; d. unm. 1 Jan. 1841, in Rumney.

1629. SAMUEL BEAN, b. 13 May 1817; m. 7 May 1840, Hannah Page, of Lunenburg, b. 2 Feb. 1817.

1630. ALBE BARNEY, b. 14 Jan. 1819; m. 5 May 1844, Nancy Worcester Cram, b. 11 Feb. 1821; lived in Hardwick, Vt.

LUMEN PLUMMER, b. 6 June 1824; d. unm. 24 Aug. 1848, in Rumney.

CAROLINE JUDITH, b. 10 Feb. 1826; d. unm. 11 June 1844, in Rumney.

628

HENRY⁶ CHASE (Samuel,⁵ John,⁴ Nathan,³ Thomas²), born in Newbury, 24 Oct. 1793; married (intention at Newbury 16 Feb. 1821) BETSEY B. WARNER of Londonderry, N. H., born 9 June 1800; died 22 Oct. 1826. He married (2) MARIANNA PAGE who was born, 21 May 1792, and died, 27 Nov. 1857. He died 29 June 1852. They were buried in Forest Hill Cemetery, East Derry.

Child by first wife:

HENRY M.,⁷ b. 1 Aug. 1826; d. 5 Jan. 1863.

Children by second wife:

LIZZIE, b. 22 Feb. 1828; d. 11 June 1870.

1631. NATHANIEL, b. 29 Nov. 1832; lived in Kingston, N. H.

629

JOHN⁶ CHASE (John,⁵ John,⁴ Nathan,³ Thomas²), born Newbury, 9 July 1790; died 8 Jan. 1865. He was living in Barrington, N. H., in 1819. He married (intention in Newbury 8 Mar. 1817) OLIVE DAME of Barrington. His intention in Newbury calls him John 3d.

Child:

1632. DARIUS,⁷ lived in East Haverhill.

630

MOSES⁶ CHASE (John,⁵ John,⁴ Nathan,³ Thomas²), born in Newbury, 14 Apr. 1792; died 25 Oct. 1869. He married in Newbury, 7 Nov. 1814, SARAH DAVIS, perhaps daughter of Stephen and Betty

(Sawyer) Davis, born in Newbury, 19 June 1791. They lived in what is now West Newbury.

Children, born in West Newbury:

1633.   EMERY,[7] b. 26 Sept. 1826.
1634.   EDWARD, b. 3 May 1832; m. 8 Oct. 1855, Mary Elizabeth Ordway.

631

COL. JOSHUA[6] CHASE (Amos,[5] John,[4] Nathan,[3] Thomas[2]), born in Newbury, 27 Jan. 1788; married in Salem, 16 Nov. 1812, ABIGAIL LAMBERT, daughter of Joseph and Abigail (Ober) Lambert, born in Salem, 20 Jan. 1792; she was alive 16 Sept. 1831. He was a hatter and they lived in Salem from 1808. He died in Salem, 9 Nov. 1838, aged 50.

Children, born in Salem:

1635.   JOSEPH LAMBERT,[7] b. 19 May 1813; m. 1840, Esther Laskey of Salem; d. 3 Apr. 1851.
        JAMES LEAVITT, b. 19 May 1815; d. unm. 29 Dec. 1834, on board the barque Eliza on her voyage from Antwerp to Zanzibar.
        MARY LAMBERT, b. 26 Apr. 1817; m. 1839, James Ward, a sea captain of Eastport, Me.
        ABIGAIL EMELINE, b. 23 Jan. 1820; m. 14 Dec. 1836, John W. Goodridge, a sea captain of Salem.
1636.   JOSHUA PLUMMER, b. 16 Jan. 1823; m. 11 Dec. 1851, Martha A. Merrill, dau. of Dea. Samuel and Mary (Chase) Merrill. They lived in Newburyport.
        GEORGE EVERETT, b. 26 Jan. 1825; d. unm., a mariner.
        CAROLINE LOUISA, b. 17 Oct. 1827; m. 1848, John Franklin Reed of Salem.
        ELIZABETH LAMBERT, b. 19 Aug. 1832; d. 13 Dec. 1847.

632

ENOCH PILLSBURY[6] CHASE (Amos,[5] John,[4] Nathan,[3] Thomas[2]), born in Newbury, 27 Sept. 1789; died 16 Oct. 1872. He married in Newbury, 4 Dec. 1817, LAURA MARIA BAILEY, daughter of Moses Little and Elizabeth (Dennis) Bailey of Newbury, Vt. She was born 17 Oct. 1794 and died 29 Mar. 1872. They lived in Newburyport. He had Pillsbury for a second Christian name by legal enactment 24 Mar. 1843. (Mass. Change of Names, 99).

Children, first three born in Newbury:

        ELIZABETH M. LITTLE,[7] b. 23 Nov. 1818; m. 23 Oct. 1839, John Alexander Hill of Newburyport. She d. 31 Dec. 1853.
1637.   MOSES PARSONS LITTLE, b. 22 Nov. 1820; m. 14 Nov. 1849, Margaret Curson Chase. (Family 591) She d. 29 Mar. 1870.
1638.   WILLIAM EDWIN PLUMMER, b. 5 June 1822; m. 28 Apr. 1845, Eliza Page.
1639.   FREDERIC DENNIS, b. 2 Sept. 1824; m. 1 Jan. 1851, Helen Maria Short, b. 28 Apr. 1828.
        ANNA MAY, b. 16 Mar. 1826; m. 28 Jan. 1850, Joseph Henry Westcott.
        LAURA ALICE, b. 25 Oct. 1828; m. 18 Sept. 1854, Rev. Henry Baker.

ABIGAIL LITTLE, b. 19 Mar. 1832; unm.
ALMIRA BROWN, b. 2 May 1834; unm.
EDWARD PAYSON, b. 2 July 1837; d. 20 Feb. 1839.

633

AMOS[6] CHASE (Amos,[5] John,[4] Nathan,[3] Thomas[2]), born in Newbury, 24 Mar. 1791; died 3 June 1872. He married (intention at Newbury 19 Oct. 1816) LYDIA DREW of Peeling (Woodstock), N. H. They lived in West Newbury.

Children, first two born in Newbury:

HANNAH ADELINE,[7] b. 9 Dec. 1817; m. Samuel Bailey.
1640. LEONARD GARDNER, b. 13 Apr. 1820.
ANNE.
1641. PLUMMER.
1642. WILLIAM.

634

REV. PLUMMER[6] CHASE (Amos,[5] John,[4] Nathan,[3] Thomas[2]), born in Newbury, 13 Mar. 1794; died in Newbury, 17 Sept. 1837, aged 43. He graduated at Bowdoin College 1821 and Andover Theological Seminary 1824. He preached in New Gloucester, Me., and was pastor at Carver 1828 to 1835. He married (1) LOUISA LEONARD. He married (2) (intention at Carver, 17 Jan. 1829) LOUISA LEONARD STETSON of West Bridgewater, daughter of John and Lois (Leonard) Stetson, born in Bridgewater, 10 Apr. 1799.

Child, by first wife:

LOUISA,[7] m. —— Freeman of Bridgewater.

Child by second wife, born in Carver:

1643. EDWARD PAYSON, b. 27 June 1832.

635

MERRILL[6] CHASE (Amos,[5] John,[4] Nathan,[3] Thomas[2]), born in Newbury, 15 June 1797; died 8 Sept. 1872. He married in Newbury, 29 Apr. 1819, MARY MIRIAM CALDWELL, daughter of Alexander and [Mary?] Caldwell, born in Newbury, 19 May 1800. She died 8 Aug. 1870. They lived on High street, Newburyport.

Children, four recorded in Newbury:

FREDERIC,[7] b. 24 Sept. 1820; d. at age of 7 m. 15 d.
MARGARET (twin), b. 24 Sept. 1820; d. young.
PHEBE ANN, b. 5 May 1824; m. 9 Dec. 1841, Enoch Goodwin.
HANNAH M., b. 12 June 1822; d. young.
LEWIS M., b. — Aug. 1825; d. young.
1644. BENJAMIN M., b. 4 Aug. 1828; m. 31 Oct. 1850, Frances C. Fox.
MARGARET LEONARD, bp. 27 Dec. 1829; m. 27 June 1847, Luther Hatch of Newburyport.
MARY OLIVE, b. 6 Sept. 1832; m. 8 Aug. 1850, James H. Delano.
1645. JAMES M., b. 8 Aug. 1834; m. 23 June 1859, Julia M. Knapp of Newburyport.

636

Josiah[6] Chase (William,[5] Josiah,[4] Nathan,[3] Thomas[2]), born in Deerfield, N. H., 26 May 1800; died in Searsport, Me., 29 July 1867. He married 6 Nov. 1832, Eliza Marden of Searsport. They lived in Searsport from 1832 till death.

Children, born in Searsport:

1646.   Edmund H.,[7] b. 9 Aug. 1833; m. 27 Oct. 1866, Weltha M.
Seavey; one son Eugene,[8] b. 27 Jan. 1868.
Margaret J. B., b. 1 Jan. 1835.
Mary Ann B., b. 8 Mar. 1838; d. 6 Jan. 1839.
Mary Eliza, b. 9 May 1840; m. George W. Curtis of Searsport; d. about 1905; three children.
Nancy B., b. 8 Feb. 1842; d. 20 July 1844.
Dean Clement, b. 17 Oct. 1843; d. 21 July 1844.
Freeman C., b. 27 July 1846; d. 28 July 1850.

637

Jeremiah[6] Chase (William,[5] Josiah,[4] Nathan,[3] Thomas,[2]), born in Sandwich, N. H., 6 Dec. 1806; married (1) Sept. 1828, Mercy Littlefield, who died 6 June 1868. He married (2) 19 Dec. 1870. Mrs. Mary Thompson of Swanville. They moved to Swanville, Waldo Co., Me., in June 1835.

Children, last ten born in Swanville:

1647.   James L.,[7] b. 25 Feb. 1829.
1648.   John B., b. 18 Nov. 1830; drowned 26 Dec. 1866, in Goose Pond, Swanville.
Eliza A., b. 6 Dec. 1832.
Priscilla J., b. 7 Dec. 1834.
Charles A., b. 7 Oct. 1836; d. 14 Oct. 1864, of consumption.
Julia M., b. 6 Oct. 1838; drowned 14 Aug. 1852.
Jeremiah, b. 28 Oct. 1840; d. 21 Feb. 1862.
David A., b. 22 Sept. 1842; d. Oct. 1864, in the army, near Spottsylvania.
Henry D., b. 6 May 1845; d. May 1846.
1649.   Henry, b. 19 Mar. 1847.
Betsey A., b. 6 Feb. 1849.
Esther M., b. 6 Feb. 1851.
Sarah E., b. 25 Mar. 1853.
Huldah A., b. 25 Oct. 1857; d. 21 Feb. 1862.

638

William[6] Chase (William,[5] Josiah,[4] Nathan,[3] Thomas[2]), born in Sandwich, N. H., 2 Jan. 1814; married (1) in Searsport, Me., Oct. 1835, Sylvinia Munsey, who died 30 Sept. 1860, daughter of Nathaniel and Margaret (Cochran) Munsey, born in Prospect, Me., 17 Feb. 1806. He married (2) Martha J. Staples of Munroe, Me. They lived in Searsport, Me., where he died 28 May 1884.

Children by first wife, born in Searsport:

1650.   William,[7] b. 14 Jan. 1837; m. Nov. 1860, Mary Matthews; d. in the army, 13 May 1863. Two children.
1651.   Charles G.,[7] b. 13 Mar. 1838; m. 1 Jan. 1862, Charlotte W. Pendleton; d. 18 June 1876. Their son Charles Nathan,[8] b. in Thomaston, Me., 31 Oct. 1871; m. 15 June 1904, Frances

Adeline[9] Mosman of Stoughton, a descendant of James[1] Mosman. He is treasurer of the Congregational Church of
Stoughton; four children, viz. Charlotte Adeline,[9] b. 18 Apr.
1905; Herbert Charles,[9] b. 20 June 1906; Abbie Carver,[9] b.
5 Mar. 1914; Ruth Beless,[9] b. Feb. 1916; d. 1918. Their
daughter *Abbie Carver,*[8] b. in Thomaston, 27 May 1875, is a
teacher in the Lincoln Normal School for colored students,
Marion, Ala.

LAVINIA, b. 27 July 1839; m. 26 Nov. 1866, Capt. Amasa D.
Field; d. 17 Nov. 1903; three children.

NATHAN, b. 9 Sept. 1841; d. unm. 21 July 1863, from wounds
at the battle of Gettysburg. He served in the 4th Regiment,
Maine, Vols.

NATHANIEL M., b. — Feb. 1843; d. — Nov. 1843.

1652. NELSON, b. 20 July 1845; m. 1 Jan. 1867, Charlotte B. Eaton;
two children.

HANNAH J., b. 23 Jan. 1847; m. (1) 30 May 1866, Albert
Mason; m. (2) William West of Searsport.

MARY A., b. 24 Aug. 1849; m. Atwood G. Robinson and lived
in Warren, Me.

Children by second wife, born in Searsport:

ANNA M., b. 30 Mar. 1864; unm.

GEORGE W., b. 11 Jan. 1867; married.

ROSCOE, d. unm.

ISRAEL, carpenter, lives in Somerville; unm.

639

LEMUEL[6] CHASE (William,[5] Josiah,[4] Nathan,[3] Thomas[2]), born
in Sandwich, N. H., 16 Dec. 1817; married 7 June 1840, BELINDA S.
HALE, who was born 31 Mar. 1819. They lived in Sandwich.
Children:

JAMES E.,[7] b. 5 Sept. 1842; m. Kate Atwood. No children. He
was in the army of the Potomac; lived in Nebraska.

ELIZABETH E., b. 8 Aug. 1844; m. 28 Nov. 1863, True W.
Brown. Two children.

1653. DANIEL H., b. 31 July 1846; lived in Illinois.

1654. ALFRED P., b. 8 Nov. 1848; m. Sept. 1870, Arminia Fogg.

HANNAH K., b. 2 May 1850; lived in Lakeport, N. H.

OLIVER P., b. 1 Apr. 1853; d. 28 Jan. 1863.

NANCY A., b. 6 Oct. 1855; d. 26 Jan. 1863.

MARTHA E., b. 20 Apr. 1857; d. 26 Jan. 1863.

ABBIE B., b. 5 Sept. 1859; d. 29 Jan. 1863.

ABBIE B., b. 20 Jan. 1864; d. 9 Mar. 1869.

640

LEVI[6] CHASE (William,[5] Josiah,[4] Nathan,[3] Thomas[2]), born in
Sandwich, N. H., 29 Sept. 1822; married (1) 11 Aug. 1844, DOLLY
M. ELLIOTT, who died in Sandwich, 12 Sept. 1848, aged 20. He mar-
ried (2) 17 Mar. 1852, NANCY J. BENNETT of Lowell. They lived
in Sandwich, and in 1854 removed to Middleton. Perhaps she is the
Nancy Chase who died in Wolfeborough, 24 Apr. 1859.

Children by first wife, born in Sandwich:

SARAH A.,[7] b. 22 May 1845; m. 9 Feb. 1867, William A. Evans
of Andover, N. H.

MARY E., b. 24 Aug. 1846; m. 29 July 1864, George W. Winslow of Marblehead. Two children.

Children by second wife, first born in Sandwich, last two born
in Middleton:

IDA J., b. 21 Feb. 1853; m. 10 Jan. 1869, John F. Palmer of
Lowell; one son.

1655. FRANK E., b. 6 Apr. 1855.

NELLIE F., b. 10 Sept. 1868; d. 5 Aug. 1869.

641

ROBERT MERRILL[6] CHASE (Nathan,[5] Josiah,[4] Nathan,[3] Thomas[2]), born in Deerfield, N. H., 10 Feb. 1816; married in Deerfield,
30 Dec. 1840, SALOME SMITH of Deerfield. She was born, 29 Nov.
1816; died 21 Jan. 1907, aged 90y. 1m. 22d. They lived in Deerfield,
where he died 19 Jan. 1875, aged 58y. 11m. 9d.

Child:

1656. ALVAH BARTON,[7] b. 13 Mar. 1841; m. 14 June 1870, Sarah F.
Cross.

642

SAMUEL PRESCOTT[6] CHASE (Jonathan,[5] Josiah,[4] Nathan,[3] Thomas[2]), born in New Hampshire, 24 May 1808; died 18 Feb. 1845. He
married in Deerfield, N. H., 16 May 1844, CATHARINE M.[6] CHASE,
daughter of Nathan[5] and Mehitable (Merrill) Chase, (Family 202),
born 23 July 1824. She married (2) in Deerfield, 14 Apr. 1851,
WILLIAM GOODNOUGH of Barnet, Vt., who served in the Civil War
and died at or near Newbern, N. C. She married (3) AMOS DAVIS
of Danville, Vt. At the time of his marriage he lived in Epsom, N. H.

Child by first husband:

MARY ADELAIDE,[7] b. 26 Sept. 1846; m. 1867, John Armstrong
of Danville, Vt.

Children by second husband, who survived their father:

ABBY GOODNOUGH.

1657. FRANK GOODNOUGH. Four children died about 1862.

643

DR. CHARLES[6] CHASE (Edmund,[5] Josiah,[4] Nathan,[3] Thomas[2]),
born in Deerfield, N. H., 5 Jan. 1808; died there 5 June 1864. He
graduated from the Medical School of Bowdoin College, 1832, and
practiced as a physician in Deerfield and Chelsea. He married (1)
17 May 1833, PRISCILLA WORTHEN JAMES, daughter of Enoch James
of Deerfield, N. H. She was born 10 July 1808; died 26 Sept. 1850.
He married (2) 3 Dec. 1850, ELIZABETH THURLOW BURBANK, who
was born 15 June 1823, daughter of Moses T. Burbank of Campton,
N. H.

Children by first wife:

CHILD,[7] d. young.

CHILD, d. young.

1658. CHARLES DUDLEY, b. 1 Feb. 1837; m. 6 Oct. 1865, Ella Erwin
or Irwin, of Springfield, Ill.

Children by second wife:

WILLIAM BURBANK, b. 8 Jan. 1853; d. 6 Oct. 1853.
1659.   EDMUND TAYLOR, b. 6 June 1854.
1660.   LLOYD WARFIELD, b. 31 Dec. 1858.
1661.   WALTER CHANNING, b. 21 Dec. 1860.

644

HENRY[6] CHASE (Edmund,[5] Josiah,[4] Nathan,[3] Thomas[2]), born in Deerfield, N. H., 16 Dec. 1809; married (1) 9 June 1833, LUCINDA SHEPHERD, daughter of John and Catherine Shepherd of Deerfield. She was born 16 May 1813; died in Long Island, N. Y., 26 Nov. 1853. He married (2) SARAH BARTON who had no issue. He was a carpenter and they lived in New York and in Somerville.

Children by first wife:

MARY ELIZABETH,[7] b. in Bangor, Me., 6 Oct. 1834; m. 6 Oct. 1864, J. Frank Prescott of Deerfield.
JANE HORATIA, b. 1 Sept. 1837; d. 12 Oct. 1839.
LUCY JANE, b. 16 May 1840; m. Edwin A. Platts of Waltham.
BERTHA KATE, b. 16 Jan. 1842; m. May 1864, George E. Fairbanks.

645

EDMUND PIKE[6] CHASE (Edmund,[5] Josiah,[4] Nathan,[3] Thomas[2]), born in Deerfield, N. H., 30 Oct. 1813; married, 8 Nov. 1836, MARY ELIZABETH JAMES, daughter of Ezekiel James of Deerfield. She was born 6 Oct. 1813. They lived on the Chase homestead in Deerfield. He died in Deerfield, 8 Apr. 1889, aged 75y. 5m. 18d.

Children, born in Deerfield: z

CHARLES ALVAH,[7] b. 26 Aug. 1840; d. young.
1662.   ALBERT BAKER, b. 1 July 1842; m. Nettie Hall of Groton.
1663.   CHARLES EDMUND, b. 25 June 1849.
1664.   OSCAR, b. 18 Aug. 1851.

646

DAVID[6] CHASE (Moses,[5] Moses,[4] Nathan,[3] Thomas[2]), born in Deerfield, N. H., 3 Feb. 1794; died in Wentworth, N. H., 2 June 1870. He married 23 Jan. 1821, POLLY PHILBRICK, daughter of Simeon and Mary (Page) Philbrick, born in Sanbornton, N. H., 2 Sept. 1801; she was living in Deerfield in 1877. They lived in Deerfield and Wentworth, N. H.

Children:

1665.   WILLIAM O.,[7] b. 12 Feb. 1827; m. 8 Dec. 1851, Betsey Huse.
JULIA A., b. 10 Jan. 1828; m. 3 Mar. 1849, Joseph Kimball of Orford, N. H.
1666.   MOSES P., b. 19 Aug. 1831; m. 28 Oct. 1853, Hannah E. Brown.
1667.   SIMEON P., b. 29 Sept. 1837; m. 11 Dec. 1860, Sarah W. Cleasbie (Cleasby).
1668.   JOHN D., b. 16 Nov. 1839; m. 6 June 1868, Frances A. Randall.
1669.   GEORGE C., b. 24 Aug. 1843; m. 14 July 1869, Ann Carey.

647

DANIEL[6] CHASE (Joseph,[5] Moses,[4] Nathan,[3] Thomas[2]), born in Deerfield, N. H., 14 May 1786; married (1) about 1809, NANCY GRAVES. He married (2) in Sanbornton, N. H., 31 Jan. 1815 widow SALLY PAGE of Meredith, N, H. About 1811 they removed to Sandwich, N. H., and later lived in Meredith. He died in Sandwich, about 1864.

Child by first wife:

LOUISA,[7] b. 1 Jan. 1812; d. 12 May 1833.

Children by second wife:

1670.   DANIEL.
1671.   PAGE, lived in Tuftonborough, N. H.

648

JOSEPH[6] CHASE (Joseph,[5] Moses,[4] Nathan,[3] Thomas[2]), born in Deerfield, N. H., 18 Oct. 1795; married in Deerfield, 18 Jan. 1813, BETSEY ROLLINS, daughter of Jeremy and Deborah (Prescott) Rollins of Deerfield, born 1 Mar. 1792. They lived in Deerfield.

Children, born in Deerfield:

LO-RUHAMAH,[7] b. Apr. 1814; m. 4 Oct. 1831, George Lane.
DEBORAH R., b. 3 July 1821; m. 14 June 1847, Stephen H. Locke of Nottingham, N. H.
ELIZABETH, d. unm. 4 Nov. 1863.
HANNAH M., d. unm. 30 Aug. 1849.
LUCINDA, unm.
ANNA D., b. Oct. 1831; m. Nov. 1853, George J.[7] Chase of Ipswich. (Family 650)

649

ABRAHAM[6] CHASE (Joseph,[5] Moses,[4] Nathan,[3] Thomas[2]), born in Deerfield, N. H., 2 Aug. 1797; died there, 28 Dec. 1887. He married in Deerfield, 15 Mar. 1820, DEBORAH ROLLINS, daughter of Jeremy and Deborah (Prescott) Rollins, born in Deerfield, 6 Oct. 1797; died there 13 Dec. 1887, aged 80. They lived in Deerfield.

Children, born in Deerfield:

1672.   STEPHEN P.,[7] b. 25 Feb. 1821; m. 30 Dec. 1849, Abigail A. Burroughs.
        CHARLES E., b. 11 Feb. 1824; d. Apr. 1825.
1673.   ABRAHAM A., b. 25 Feb. 1826; m. 9 June 1857, Harriet A. Grow of Topsham, Vt.
        SUSAN M., b. 10 June 1828; m. 22 Dec. 1856, William F. Walker.
        HARRIET REBECCA, b. 8 Aug. 1830; unm.
1674.   JEREMIAH CLINTON, b. 25 June 1835; m. 12 Mar. 1863, Sarah E. Cowdrey.
1675.   ALDEN B.

650

JOSIAH[6] CHASE (Joseph,[5] Moses,[4] Nathan,[3] Thomas[2]), born in Deerfield, N. H., 20 Aug. 1799; died there 4 Nov. 1861. He married in Deerfield, 23 May 1820, DEBORAH CURRIER, daughter of Benjamin and Jemima (Page) Currier, born in Warner, N. H., 10 Mar. 1800; died 31 May 1875. They lived in Deerfield.

Children:

LORINDA,[7] b. 11 Sept. 1821; m. 26 June 1856, Alonzo Wheeler, b. 23 Aug. 1822, in Canada. She d. in Auburn, N. H. No children.

JUDITH, b. 25 Feb. 1823; d. 20 Apr. 1828.

SARAH ANN, b. 4 June 1825; d. 8 July 1852.

JUDITH, b. 17 Jan. 1830; d. 31 Oct. 1849.

1676.   GEORGE J., b. 8 May 1832; m. Nov. 1853, Ann D.[7] Chase. (Family 648)

651

WILLIAM[6] CHASE (Joseph,[5] Moses,[4] Nathan,[3] Thomas[2]), born in Deerfield, N. H., 27 July 1801; married in Deerfield, 11 Mar. 1830, BELINDA ROLLINS, daughter of Jeremy and Deborah (Prescott) Rollins, born 28 Apr. 1801. The Rollins Genealogy, p. 49, gives her name as Melinda Rollins. They lived in Deerfield.

Child, born in Deerfield, N. H.:

1677.   WILLIAM FRANKLIN,[7] b. 19 Nov. 1837; m. Mary Robinson, dau. of Stephen.

652

NATHAN[6] CHASE (Joseph,[5] Moses,[4] Nathan,[3] Thomas[2]), born in Deerfield, N. H., 9 Dec. 1805; married in Candia, 25 May 1831, ELIZA CHASE, daughter of John and Hannah (Sanborn) Chase, born in Wakefield, N. H., 18 Nov. 1806. (Family 208). They lived on the Chase homestead in Deerfield.

Children, born in Deerfield:

MARY E.,[7] b. 22 Dec. 1832; m. Mar. 1853, John P. Buswell of Pittsfield, N. H.

OLIVE ANN, b. 23 Jan. 1835; m. — May 1864, Alfred C. Richards.

HENRY DEARBORN, b. 17 Jan. 1839; d. 16 Sept. 1859.

EDWIN VAN BUREN, b. 2 June 1841; d. 11 Jan. 1855.

1678.   BENJ. FRANKLIN, b. 20 Aug. 1844.

JOSEPH WOODBURY, b. 28 Sept. 1846; d. 2 Mar. 1863 at Carrolton, La.; a member of Co. D, 15th Regt. N. H. Vols.

1679.   JOHN METCALF, b. 12 Feb. 1850.

653

PARKER[6] CHASE (Parker,[5] Moses,[4] Nathan,[3] Thomas[2]), born in Deerfield, N. H., 31 Dec. 1784; died in Charleston, Vt., 15 Sept. 1860. He married Sept. 1808, SARAH LANGLEY of Gilford, N. H., who died 14 Apr. 1868. They removed to Charleston, Vt., in 1825, and settled on lot No. 24. He appears to have been living in Cabot, Vt., in 1809 perhaps only for a short time.

Children, first three born in Meredith, N. H., others in Cabot, Vt.:

SALLY,[7] b. 22 Dec. 1809; m. 2 Nov. 1853, Carlos Maranville; lived in Brandon, Wis.

SOPHRONIA, b. 10 Oct. 1811; m. 2 May 1848, Hiram Fletcher.

SUSAN, b. 6 Oct. 1817; m. 26 Dec. 1835, John D. Goodwin of
New Market, N. H.
1680.   PARKER L., b. 28 Nov. 1819; m. 8 Dec. 1842, Tryphena M.
Spaulding; living in Charleston, 1841.
MARY, b. 31 July 1822; m. 2 Nov. 1856, Samuel Stebbins.

654

MOSES[6] CHASE (Parker,[5] Moses,[4] Nathan,[3] Thomas[2]), born in
Deerfield, N. H., 24 May 1786; married LYDIA PHILBRICK of Mere-
dith, N. H.
Children:
1681.   JOHN,[7] killed by falling from a tree.
LYDIA, m. ——— Currier; lived at Campton, N. H.
SARAH ANN.
1682.   WILDER.

655

WILLIAM[6] CHASE (Parker,[5] Moses,[4] Nathan,[3] Thomas[2]), born
in Deerfield, N. H., 25 Nov. 1787; married in Gilmanton, N. H.,
5 Feb. 1811, MARY CLARK, who was born in 1782; died in Jan. 1837.
They lived in Gilford, N. H.
Children:
1683.   WILLIAM,[7] b. 20 Aug. 1813; m. Apr. 1834, Betsey Boyer, dau.
of Thomas and Lydia (Webster) Boyer of Woodstock, N. H.
1684.   JOHN B., b. 6 Dec. 1814; m. 20 May 1838, Eliza Corey.
1685.   SAMUEL, b. 20 Aug. 1816; m. Apr. 1840, Thirza Gordon of
Woodstock.

656

AARON[6] CHASE (Parker,[5] Moses,[4] Nathan,[3] Thomas[2]), born in
Deerfield, N. H., 20 Feb. 1803; married 21 Feb. 1821, LUCINDA
MINARD. They lived in Cabot, Vt., Woodbury, Vt., Meredith, N. H.,
and he was living in Melrose, in 1874. Nothing has been learned
about his family.

657

JAMES[6] CHASE (Parker,[5] Moses,[4] Nathan,[3] Thomas[2]), born in
Deerfield, N. H., 26 May 1806; died in Campton, N. H., 5 Apr. 1867.
He married ELVIRA WHITNEY. It is also reported that he married
ELVIRA WHITING, but no original record has been found of this
marriage.

658

HAZEN[6] CHASE (Parker,[5] Moses,[4] Nathan,[3] Thomas[2]), born in
Deerfield, N. H., 12 Mar. 1808. He went West and nothing further
has been learned about him.

659

SETH FOGG[6] CHASE (Parker,[5] Moses,[4] Nathan,[3] Thomas[2]), born
in Deerfield, N. H., 22 Dec. 1815; died in Campton, N. H., in Aug.
1857. He married NANCY MOULTON.

660

DEARBORN[6] CHASE (John,[5] Moses,[4] Nathan,[3] Thomas[2]), born in Wakefield, N. H.,; married in Tamworth, N. H., by Rev. Samuel Hidden, NANCY CLARK.

661

HENRY[6] CHASE (John,[5] Moses,[4] Nathan,[3] Thomas[2]), born in Wakefield, N. H., 29 Nov. 1808. He married in Wolfeborough, N. H., 27 Nov. 1834, RUTH R. L. SANBORN, daughter of John and Deborah R. (Frothingham) Sanborn of Wakefield, born 18 Feb. 1812. He died in Wakefield, 27 Jan. 1890, aged 80y. 1m. 30d.

662

PARKER[6] CHASE (Robert,[5] Parker,[4] Nathan,[3] Thomas[2]), born in Georgetown, Me., about 1800; was living at age of 20 on 20 June 1820.

663

WILLIAM G.[6] CHASE (Robert,[5] Parker,[4] Nathan,[3] Thomas[2]), born in Georgetown, Me., about 1802; was living there in 1849. His father and mother were living with him in Georgetown, 1 June 1840.

664

ZACHARIAH[6] CHASE (Robert,[5] Parker,[4] Nathan,[3] Thomas[2]), born in Georgetown, Me., about 1804; living in his father's family, 20 June 1820.

665

ROBERT[6] CHASE (Robert,[5] Parker,[4] Nathan,[3] Thomas[2]), born about 1810 in Georgetown, Me.,; alive and under guardianship, 21 Aug. 1855.

666

CAPT. THOMAS HERRICK[6] CHASE (Rev. Stephen,[5] Edmund,[4] Nathan,[3] Thomas[2]), born in Me., 22 Dec. 1806; married MARY GATES. They had five children, all dying in infancy, except one daughter. He died in Lincoln, Me., 22 June 1873, aged 67. His wife died there 5 Feb. 1870, aged 63y. 5m. They lived in Lincoln.

Children, born in Lincoln, not in order:

CHILD,[7] b. 1850.
ADELIA, d. 25 Oct. 1841.
SON, d. 26 Mar. 1835.
ALFRED G., b. 6 Nov. 1831; d. 21 Nov. 1831.

667

PETER MERRILL[6] CHASE (Rev. Stephen,[5] Edmund,[4] Nathan,[3] Thomas[2]), born in Me., 25 Dec. 1808; married MARY COLE. Their intention was entered on the records of Lincoln, Me., 12 Dec. 1840.

Children, born in Lincoln:

1686.   WILBUR F.,[7] b. 6 June 1842; m. Eliza Hanscom; served 5 years in the Civil War.
1687.   WILLIAM PENN, b. 17 June 1844; was a prisoner at Andersonville.
1688.   CHARLES EDWIN, b. 14 May 1846.
        RHODA F., b. 16 Oct. 1848.
1689.   JOHN P. H., m. 27 June 1876, Helen S. Sanborn; lived Anoka, Minn.
        MARY.

668

DEA. CYRUS HAMLIN[6] CHASE (Rev. Stephen,[5] Edmund,[4] Nathan,[3] Thomas[2]), born in Me., 30 Nov. 1810; married HARRIET BAILEY. Their intention recorded in Lincoln, Me., 5 Nov. 1836. He died in Lincoln, 12 Jan. 1892. His wife was born 25 May 1811; died 10 Mar. 1896. They lived in Lincoln. He was deacon of the Congregational Church, Lincoln, 1847 to 1892.

Children, born in Lincoln:

1690.   FREEMAN H.,[7] b. 2 Sept. 1838; m. 26 Feb. 1866, Isabella J. Buker of Bangor, Me.; lived Orland, Me. He served 3 years in the Civil War; was a prisoner 11 months in Texas and was a lieutenant when discharged.
1691.   STEPHEN MUNSELL, bp. 28 May 1851.
1692.   LORENZO CYRUS, b. 25 Nov. 1848; bp. 28 May 1851; m. 25 Mar. 1872, Esther J. Lancaster.
        LAURA ANN, b. 18 Feb. 1852; d. 16 Aug. 1854.

669

CAPT. DUDLEY PIKE[6] CHASE (Rev. Stephen,[5] Edmund,[4] Nathan,[3] Thomas[2]), born in Me., 14 Feb. 1817; died in Washington, D. C., 7 May 1863, from wounds received in the battle of Chancellorsville. He married 29 Apr. 1844, OLIVIA CARPENTER of Mattamiscontis, Me.

Dudley Pike Chase moved to Minneapolis in 1860. On the breaking out of the rebellion, he, with other brave sons of his adopted State, raised Company A of Berdan's Sharp Shooters, 2d Reg. Soon was commissioned as Captain and after passing through and participating in more than a dozen battles, he was wounded at the battle of Antietam. As soon as he was able he joined his company and while commanding the skirmish line of Sickles's Division at the battle of Chancellorsville, he had his right arm taken off. He was carried to Washington where he died five days after the battle.

Children:

        JULIA B.[7]
1693.   HENRY.
        REBECCA.
        RUTH C.
1694.   SYLVESTER B.
        CLARISSA.
1695.   LINCOLN.

670

ABNER BEARSE[6] CHASE (Rev. Stephen,[5] Edmund,[4] Nathan,[3] Thomas[2]), born in Woodstock, Me., 12 Dec. 1819; died in Lincoln, Me., 1889. He married (1) in Lincoln, 8 Sept. 1845, HANNAH PRINCE MORTON, born in Buckfield, Me., 17 Aug. 1825, who died in Lincoln, 18 Mar. 1862, aged 36y. 7m. He married (2) 27 Aug. 1866, FRANCES E. BUTTERFIELD, daughter of John and Catherine (Colburn) Butterfield of Paris, Me. She was born 1 Mar. 1830. They lived in Lincoln and Winn, Me., till 1877, when they removed to Norway, Me.

Children by first wife:

DAUGHTER,[7] d. 1 Oct. 1846.
ELIZA HERSEY, b. 30 Apr. 1848; m. Edgar T. Davis of Minot, Me.
GEORGE BATES, b. 28 Feb. 1851; d. 17 Mar. 1876, a. 25 y.
MARY HARRIET, b. 28 Oct. 1856; d. 19 May 1862.

Children by second wife:

      AGNES GERTRUDE, b. 20 Nov. 1867; d. 30 Jan. 1868.
1696. S. HARRY, b. 3 Nov. 1870.
      KATIE B., b. 18 Oct. 1872; d. 31 July 1873.

671

MERRILL[6] CHASE (Merrill,[5] Edmund,[4] Nathan,[3] Thomas[2]), born in Me. 20 Mar. 1799; married 30 Mar. 1820, MERCY SWAN, daughter of Elijah and Eunice (Barton) Swan of Paris, Me. They lived in Woodstock, Sumner and Paris, Me.

Children, born in Woodstock:

      EUNICE B.,[7] b. 29 Dec. 1820; m. Darius Sessions of Milton, Me.
      OLIVE W., b. 14 Nov. 1823; m. Ephraim K. Andrews; lived Milton, Me.
      ELVIRA, b. 4 Mar. 1828; d. at age of 4 y.
1697. MERRILL, b. 5 June 1830; m. 1861, Hannah Barton.
1698. ELIJAH S. (twin), b. 5 June 1830; m. 1856, Augusta Nash; lived North Pittston, Me.
      ELVIRA PERHAM, b. 17 Apr. 1833; m. Lucius W. Hackett of Minot, Me.
      ABBIE C., b. 13 May 1836; m. 19 Mar. 1858, John H. Richardson of Pittston, Me.
1699. THADDEUS R., b. 25 June 1840; lived in Sumner, Me.

672

EDMUND[6] CHASE (Merrill,[5] Edmund,[4] Nathan,[3] Thomas[2]), born in Woodstock, Me., 20 Sept. 1808; married 5 Feb. 1832, ANNA SPOFFORD of Rumford, Me., born 16 May 1808. They lived in Woodstock and Orono, Me., and in 1854, removed to Wisconsin and settled in Omro. He was early a schoolmaster and later town clerk, assessor, and a representative from Woodstock, 1843.

Children, first seven born in Woodstock, others in Omro, Wis.:

1700. EARL SEELEY,[7] b. 10 Nov. 1832; m. 25 July 1858, Sarah J. Cotton; lived in Algoma, Wis.
1701. OTIS FISH, b. 14 July 1834; m. 6 Feb. 1866, Ellen E. Richards; lived in Oshkosh, Wis.

FLORINDA, b. 28 Aug. 1836; m. 24 July 1853, William Robbins;
lived in Omro.

MIRSILVIA NICY, b. 19 Sept. 1838; m. 5 Jan. 1857, Ira J. Beals;
lived in Omro.

1702. LE ROY SUNDERLAND, b. 16 May 1840; m. 18 Dec. 1866, Eliza J.
North; lived in Omro.

ANNA SPOFFORD, b. 24 July 1842; m. 18 Dec. 1866, West B.
Barrett of Oshkosh.

LOANZA, b. 8 Jan. 1846; d. 19 July 1850.

LUCINDA COLE, b. 9 Apr. 1848; a teacher and Principal of Public School, Oshkosh; m. 1877, Albert J. Hotchkiss.

1703. ARTHUR EDMUND, b. 31 May 1853; m. 1 Jan. 1874, Alida Eldora
Little, dau. of Thomas Coats and Mary J. (Blake) Little, b.
in Oshkosh, Wis., 22 Nov. 1854. Their son *Thomas Lynn,*[8]
b. in Oshkosh, 15 Oct. 1886; m. 3 Sept. 1912, Eola Maria
Bunting, dau. of Charles Danforth and Lydia (Palmer)
Bunting, b. 24 Oct. 1887. They live in Burmingham, Ala.;
he is civil engineer. Children: Virginia,[9] b. 9 Aug. 1914.
Thomas Bunting,[9] b. 19 Feb. 1926. Their son *Arthur Morgan,*[8] b. 8 Jan. 1893; m. 24 May 1918, Grace L. Lupient. Children: Eugene Lincoln,[9] Lois,[9] Russell Conwell,[9] John Bell[9] and
Jule[9] Chase.

673

ALDEN[6] CHASE (Merrill,[5] Edmund,[4] Nathan,[3] Thomas[2]), born in
Woodstock, Me., 5 June 1819; died at Bryant's Pond, in Woodstock.
8 Jan. 1905. He married 11 June 1840, LUCY S. COLE, daughter of
Capt. Jonathan and Abigail (Whitman) Cole, born 13 Aug. 1820,
who survived him. Teacher for over twenty years; register of deeds
for Oxford County, representative to the Legislature for three terms,
postmaster, Baptist and Freemason. He collected one of the largest
private libraries in the state.

Children, born in Woodstock:

LUCY MERRILL,[7] b. 10 May 1841; d. 11 Oct. 1846.

1704. ALDEN FITZROY, b. 26 Oct. 1842; m. 6 Dec. 1869, Loisa F.
Allen. President Me. Wesleyan Seminary; d. at Kent's Hill,
Me., 22 Oct. 1898.

ESTELLE OPHELIA, b. 1 Sept. 1846; m. 5 Feb. 1872, Rev. Albert
A. Ford of Yarmouth, Me.

1705. AQUILA MONTROSE, b. 22 June 1854; m. 29 Sept. 1878, Anna S.
Faulkner.

674

JOSEPH ROGERS[6] CHASE (Nathan,[5] Edmund,[4] Nathan,[3] Thomas[2]) born in Newbury, 1 Apr. 1811; married in Newbury, 20 Oct.
1832, JANE MELVIN HOYT of Haverhill, born 13 Apr. 1815. They
lived in Newburyport.

Children, born in Newburyport:

1706. CHARLES M.,[7] b. 17 Aug. 1834.

1707. JOSEPH N., b. 7 Apr. 1841.

DANIEL PIKE, b. 7 Nov. 1745; d. 10 Sept. 1746, a. 10 m.

1708. IRA W., b. 1 Jan. 1850.

1709. SETH H., b. 2 Sept. 1852.

MARY J., b. 13 Sept. 1855.

675

LUTHER R.⁶ CHASE (Nathan,⁵ Edmund,⁴ Nathan,³ Thomas²),
born in Newbury, 6 Mar. 1820; married 24 Feb. 1839, LUCY D. FOL-
LANSBEE, who died 28 Mar. 1869. He was a carriage painter and
they lived in Somerville.
Children:

LUCY ANN,⁷ b. 8 May 1844; m. 25 Nov. 1858, William H.
Bailey.
1710. LUTHER WESTON, b. 8 May 1848; m. 14 Nov. 1867, Augusta
Knowles of Cambridge.
EMMA CARR, b. 19 June 1852; m. 14 Nov. 1868, Edward A.
Fowle.

676

GEORGE W.⁶ CHASE (Nathan,⁵ Edmund,⁴ Nathan,³ Thomas²),
born (probably in Newbury), 3 Aug. 1828; died in Newburyport, 10
Apr. 1859. He married about 1854, HARRIET GEORGIANA STOVER of
Newburyport. She was born 1 June 1833.
Children:

LIZZIE B.,⁷ b. 4 July 1855.
1711. GEORGE W., b. 6 July 1859.

677

JOSEPH W.⁶ CHASE (Edmund,⁵ Edmund,⁴ Nathan,³ Thomas²),
born in Minot, Me., 28 July 1813; married (1) 3 Dec. 1840, MARY
A. BUMPUS, who was born 29 May 1818; died 6 Sept. 1868. He married (2) 13 May 1869, ABBIE BICKNELL of Hebron, Me., who was
born 19 Oct. 1833. He was a carpenter and they lived in Minot.
Children by first wife, born in Minot:

1712. MELVILLE W.,⁷ b. 18 Feb. 1842; m. 18 Nov. 1867, Olive C.
Poland of Auburn, Me.; professor of music in Hillsdale
College, Mich.
1713. HERBERT J., b. 29 Dec. 1847; lived in Lewiston, Me.
HATTIE A., b. 4 Aug. 1854.
1714. ALBION S., b. 15 Dec. 1856.
1715. EDWARD P., b. 4 Mar. 1859.

678

JABEZ W.⁶ CHASE (Edmund,⁵ Edmund,⁴ Nathan,³ Thomas²),
born in Minot, Me., 15 Jan. 1816; married in 1842, OLIVE TAYLOR
who was born 18 May 1818. They lived in Auburn, Me.
Children, born in Auburn:

ELLA M.,⁷ b. Mar. 1844; m. 1865, Wallace Rice of Hallowell,
Me.
GEORGIE A., b. 15 May 1846.
MARIETTA E., b. June 1848; m. Dec. 1868, Nathan P. Wood-
man of Auburn.
EMERY, b. 1849; d. young.
1716. FRANK W., b. July 1851.
BELLE B., b. Oct. 1858.
VESTA O., b. Oct. 1863.

679

PEABODY BRADFORD[6] CHASE (Charles,[5] Edmund,[4] Nathan,[3] Thomas[2]), born 14 Nov. 1815; married 8 Mar. 1842, CATHARINE CARY, daughter of Ephraim and Anna (Hill) Cary, born in 1822. They lived in Auburn, Me.

Children:

FRANCES JANE,[7] b. 22 July 1844; unm.
1717.   CHARLES STUART, b. 22 Nov. 1846; m. 20 Sept. 1868, Georgia A. Monroe.
FRANK MILTON, b. 30 Mar. 1855; d. 2 Feb. 1859.

680

ALONZO FREEMAN[6] CHASE (Charles,[5] Edmund,[4] Nathan,[3] Thomas[2]), born 22 Mar. 1821; married in Abington, 29 June 1845, LYDIA ANN CONANT, daughter of John Conant of Abington, born about 1827. They lived in Abington. He died there 1889. She died in Wakefield, 16 Dec. 1918, nearly 92.

Child:

MATILDA M.,[7] m. —— Fiske of Wakefield.

681

REV. SIMEON LOVELL BEARSE[6] CHASE (Abner,[5] Edmund,[4] Nathan,[3] Thomas[2]), born in Minot, Me., 26 Apr. 1835; died in Buckfield, Me., 11 Sept. 1889, aged 54. He married 24 June 1866, JULIA O. WHITE of Buckfield. He graduated at Colby College, 1863 and from the Newton Theological Seminary 1866; Baptist clergyman; pastor Second Baptist Church of Bangor, Me., 1666-72; Rockland, Me., 1872-78; Bath, Me., 1878-79; Freehold, N. J., 1881-83; Methuen, 1833-87.

Child, born in Bangor:

ALBERT WHITE,[7] b. 2 Feb. 1870; d. 22 Dec. 1870.

682

STEPHEN[6] CHASE (William Sanborn,[5] Stephen,[4] Nathan,[3] Thomas[2]), born in Deerfield, N. H., 21 Jan 1807; married in Deerfield, 15 Sept. 1829, SALLY PHILBRICK.

Children:

ELIZABETH,[7] m. —— Langford of Sanbornton; they lived in Deerfield.
1718.   NATHAN.
1719.   STEPHEN, m. —— Patten.

683

JONATHAN SANBORN[6] CHASE (Henry Dearborn,[5] Stephen,[4] Nathan,[3] Thomas[2]), born (probably in Deerfield, N. H.) 11 May 1815; married Jan. 1837, RUTH B.[6] CHASE, daughter of William Sanborn and Nancy (Sanborn) Chase, born in Deerfield, 14 July 1817. (Family 215). They lived on the Chase homestead in Jackson, Me.

Children, born in Jackson, Me.:

1720. WILLIAM HENRY,[7] b. 31 Dec. 1837.
1721. LUCIEN, b. 26 July 1839; m. Sept. 1867, Ellen J. Dalton of
      Lowell.
      ANNE E., b. 18 June 1841.
1722. EDWARD P., b. 21 Apr. 1843.
1723. STEPHEN H., b. 15 June 1845; d. 3 July 1864, at Fortress Mon-
      roe, Va.
1724. OSCAR A., b. 18 Dec. 1846.
      SARAH A., b. 2 July 1851.
      MARY A., b. 17 June 1859.
1725. HERBERT E., b. 25 Sept. 1862.

684

JOHN M.[6] CHASE (John Merrill,[5] Jonathan,[4] Nathan,[3] Thomas[2]),
born in Danville, Me., 19 May 1801; died 11 Sept. 1827. He married
18 Dec. 1823, ALICE YOUNG. He probably removed to Alexander,
Ohio, in 1817, with his parents.

Children, born in Ohio:

1726. WILLIAM,[7] b. 3 Sept. 1824; m. 22 Apr. 1849, Elvira Winn.
      CATHARINE, b. 5 Mar. 1826; m. —— Amory; no children.
      She d. 1865.
1727. JOHN N., b. — May 1827.

685

THOMAS J.[6] CHASE (John Merrill,[5] Jonathan,[4] Nathan,[3] Thomas[2]), born in Danville, Me., 6 Jan. 1806; married (1) 29 Jan. 1826,
REBECCA ROMINE who died 26 Dec. 1853. He married (2) 25 Mar.
1854, CATHARINE HUGGENS. They probably lived in Ohio.

Children by first wife:

1728. EMERIC F.,[7] b. 8 Sept. 1826; m. 13 Aug. 1848, Nancy Winn.
      SAMANTHA, b. 6 Oct. 1827; m. 4 Dec. 1845, William Davis.
1729. GEORGE W., b. 25 Feb. 1830; m. 24 Mar. 1850, Mary A. Brad-
      shaw.
1730. JOHN M., b. 4 Sept. 1831; m. 31 Oct. 1852, Esther Winn.
1731. MOSES, b. 2 Mar. 1836; m. 1859, Sarah Barnes.
      LUCETTA, b. 11 Mar. 1841; d. 11 Oct. 1848.
      MIRIAM A., b. 27 Dec. 1844; m. Melvin Dutton.

Children by second wife:

      SAMARIA, b. 18 July 1855.
1732. JESSE A., b. 1 Oct. 1857.
1733. THOMAS J., b. 2 July 1860.
      ELVIRA, b. 10 Dec. 1863.
1734. MARTIN, b. 13 Apr. 1866.
1735. HOWARD, b. 23 Dec. 1867.

686

GARDNER F.[6] CHASE (John Merrill,[5] Jonathan,[4] Nathan,[3] Thomas[2]), born in Danville, Me., 11 Sept. 1810; living in Alexander, Athens Co., Ohio, in 1869. He married in Ohio, 25 Oct. 1829, ANNA M.
WOODYARD. They lived on the original Chase homestead in Alexander.

Children, born in Alexander:

SUSAN,[7] b. 24 July 1830; m. 17 Mar. 1849, William Robinson.
MARY, b. 18 Apr. 1832; m. 18 Jan. 1859, John F. Martin.
1736.   HOSMER, b. 2 Oct. 1834; m. 11 Feb. 1859, Nancy Reeves.
EMILY, b. 21 Oct. 1836; m. 11 Jan. 1854, Elijah Robinson.
1737.   JOHN M., b. 1 Aug. 1840; m. 29 June 1861, Amanda Williams.
JAMES P., b. 26 Oct. 1844; d. 26 Oct. 1863.

687

SYLVANUS[6] CHASE (Peter,[5] Jonathan,[4] Nathan,[3] Thomas[2]), born
in Me., 1810; married MARTHA CAREY.

688

JONATHAN[6] CHASE (Peter,[5] Jonathan,[4] Nathan,[3] Thomas[2]),
born in Danville, Me., 16 July 1812; died in Bangor, Me., since Jan.
1911. He married (1) in 1844, EMILY HAM; married (2) in 1868
MRS. LUCINDA PHENIX, widow of Rev. Cyrus Phenix of Pittston,
Me. Their intention was entered at Pittston, 20 Oct. 1868. Her first
husband, Rev. Cyrus Phenix died in Pittston, Me., 28 Jan. 1866, aged
47.

Children by first wife, born in Bangor:

1738.   SEAVEY W.[7]
1739.   MELVILLE E., b. about 1852; music teacher Malden, Belfast, Me.
DAUGHTER.

689

ALEXANDER HAMILTON[6] CHASE (Peter,[5] Jonathan,[4] Nathan,[3]
Thomas[2]), born in Danville, Me., 1 Sept. 1814. He married (1)
about 1838, JANE G. FARR. He married (2) LAVINA BOSTON.

Children:

SUSIE J.,[7] b. 10 May 1839.
MARIETTA, b. 25 May 1841.
1740.   ALEXANDER K., b. 27 Nov. 1842.
1741.   EDWARD M., b. 30 Jan. 1848.
ANNIE L., b. 20 Sept. 1850.
1742.   JOHN COLBY, b. 29 Dec. 1856.

690

WILLIAM[6] CHASE (Peter,[5] Jonathan,[4] Nathan,[3] Thomas[2]), born
in Danville, Me., 24 Nov. 1817; married LUCINDA LEAVITT, perhaps
daughter of Joseph and Martha (Merrill) Leavitt of Turner, Me.

691

CHARLES[6] CHASE (Jonathan,[5] Jonathan,[4] Nathan,[3] Thomas[2]),
born in Danville, Me., 16 Aug. 1825; died 12 July 1863. He married
SARAH C. FOSTER.

Child:

ALICE.[7]

692

MOSES[6] CHASE (Jonathan,[5] Jonathan,[4] Nathan,[3] Thomas[2]), born in Danville, Me., 20 Sept. 1832; removed to Quincy, California.

693

CYRUS[6] CHASE (Jonathan,[5] Jonathan,[4] Nathan,[3] Thomas[2]), born in Danville, Me., 26 July 1836; married 28 Jan. 1860, ABBIE H. AT-WOOD. They lived in Westfield, Aroostook Co., Me.
Children:
    MINNETTE.[7]
    KATE.
1743. ELMER.
1744. SELDON.

694

IRA[6] CHASE (Jonathan,[5] Jonathan,[4] Nathan,[3] Thomas[2]), born in Danville, Me., 18 June 1842; married 6 June 1864, EMMA ARVIS [ORVIS?], born 21 Feb. 1848. They lived in Kansas.

695

GEORGE W.[6] CHASE (Jonathan,[5] Jonathan,[4] Nathan,[3] Thomas[2]), born in Danville, Me., 28 Nov. 1846; a merchant in Auburn, Me.

696

JOHN HENRY[6] CHASE (Jonathan,[5] Jonathan,[4] Nathan,[3] Thomas[2]), born in Danville, Me., 30 Oct. 1851; a mechanic in Auburn, Me.

697

JOHN M.[6] CHASE (Moses,[5] Jonathan,[4] Nathan,[3] Thomas[2]), born in Me. 6 Aug. 1819; married (1) 27 Mar. 1842, MINERVA P. GATES of Lowell. She died 5 Oct. 1857. He married (2) 6 Jan. 1859, ANGELINE R. WEAVER. They lived in Lowell, in Poland, Me., and in Brookside, Wis.
Children by first wife, first two born in Lowell:
    MARY C.,[7] b. 18 Feb. 1844; d. 30 Aug. 1844.
    MARY H. S., b. 29 Apr. 1846; m. 19 May 1861, Franklin L. Whiting of Pensaukie, Wis.
1745. NELSON P., b. 2 Sept. 1848, in Poland, Me.

698

JONATHAN[6] CHASE (Moses,[5] Jonathan,[4] Nathan,[3] Thomas[2]), born in Me., 11 June 1825; died 1 June 1875. He married in Newbury, 6 Sept. 1849, ANNA COFFIN THURLOW, daughter of Samuel and Sarah (Ewins) Thurlow, born in Newbury, 8 Aug. 1825. They lived in Newburyport.
Children, born in Newburyport:
    SARAH L.,[7] b. 7 Mar. 1856.
1746. SAMUEL T., b. 23 Feb. 1859.

699

THOMAS J.[6] CHASE (Moses,[5] Jonathan,[4] Nathan,[3] Thomas[2]), born in Danville, Me., 30 Mar. 1827; married 19 Nov. 1852, MARIA E. LARCH. They lived in Cainville, Wis.
Children:
1747. FRANK A.,[7] b. 23 Sept. 1853.
      EMMA A., b. 30 June 1855.
      ALMA S., b. 31 Mar. 1858.
      HATTIE C., b. 10 July 1862.
      HANNAH E., b. 23 Oct. 1867.

700

ZACHARIAH[6] CHASE (Moses,[5] Jonathan,[4] Nathan,[3] Thomas[2]), born in Me. 1831; was living in Cainville, Rock Co., Wis., in 1872.

701

NEHEMIAH T.[6] CHASE (Moses,[5] Jonathan,[4] Nathan,[3] Thomas[2]), born in Me. 1833; lived in Lynn.

702

JONATHAN[6] CHASE (Jonathan,[5] Jonathan,[4] John,[3] John[2]), born in N. H., (probably Seabrook) 18 Mar. 1774; died there, 13 June 1854. He married in Seabrook 15 July 1797, MOLLY GREEN who died 24 May 1835, aged 53y. 5m. They lived in Seabrook.
Children, born in Seabrook:
1748. JONATHAN,[7] b. 14 Dec. 1799; m. 13 May 1827, Lavina Smith, dau. of John and ——— (Morrill) Smith. He d. in Seabrook, 14 May 1869.
      MARY, b. 29 Aug. 1801; m. in Hampton Falls, N. H., 4 June 1822, Abraham Smith.
      WILLIAM,[7] b. 13 Feb. 1803; d. unm. 20 Sept. 1859.
      EDWARD DEARBORN, b. 14 Mar. 1805; d. unm.
      JOHN, b. 25 Dec. 1807; d. unm. 25 Oct. 1847.
      ELIZA, b. 29 Nov. 1810; d. young.
1749. CHEVEY, b. 13 July 1812; m. Adeline Smith, dau. of John Smith. He d. in Seabrook, Oct. 1879, a. 66 y.
1750. STEPHEN NEAL, b. 13 Nov. 1814; m. 1835, Rhoda Walton.
      ELIZA, b. 16 May 1817; m. Benjamin Rowell of Seabrook.
      SARAH, b. 20 Mar. 1823; m. (1) Franklin Griffin of Methuen; m. (2) Parker Wells of Middleton.
      HANNAH G. (twin), b. 20 Mar. 1823; lived on the homestead; d. 9 Mar. 1905, unm.

703

DAVID[6] CHASE (Jonathan,[5] Jonathan,[4] John,[3] John[2]), born in N. H. (probably in Seabrook) about 1776; married in Kensington, N. H., 8 Oct. 1807, HULDAH NASON. Perhaps she is the Huldah Chase who died in Hampton Falls, 26 Nov. 1863.
Children:
1751. CALEB.[7]
1752. DAVID.

704

William[6] Chase (Jonathan,[5] Jonathan,[4] John,[3] John,[2]) born about 1780; married in 20 Dec. 1803, Ruth Lowell of Amesbury, daughter of Ezra and Sarah (Gordon) Lowell, born in Amesbury, 30 Apr. 1783. At the time of his marriage he was of Newburyport. They removed to Eastport, Me., in 1812.

Children:

1753. Lowell.[7]
1754. William.
        Several daughters names not reported.

705

Abraham[6] Chase (Nehemiah,[5] Jonathan,[4] John,[3] John[2]), born in Seabrook, N. H., in 1767; died there in Aug. 1850. He married about 1798, Sarah Gove, daughter of Enoch and Huldah (Green) Gove, born in Seabrook about 1770; died there in Nov. 1850. They lived in Seabrook.

Children, born in Seabrook, N. H.:

        Sally,[7] b. 1799; m. 11 Nov. 1819, Miles Evans of Pittsfield, N. H.
1755.   Abraham, b. 1802; m. Abigail Brown; d. 8 Sept. 1869, a. 63 y. 10 m. 2 d.
        Abigail, b. 12 Dec. 1805; m. (1) 26 May 1825, Tappan[7] (Family 751) Chase; m. (2) True Morrill.
1756.   Enoch, b. 6 Apr. 1808; m. 24 Oct. 1833, Betsey Fogg. He was a farmer; lived in Seabrook.
1757.   Joseph, b. 1 Dec. 1810; m. (1) 1832, Vienna Gove; m. (2) 20 Mar. 1842, Lydia Chase dau. of Chevey Chase.
        Huldah, b. 1813; m. about 1847, Stephen G. Johnson.
        Jane M., b. 1816; m. 1 Sept. 1839, David Fogg, a farmer of Hampton.

706

Jonathan[6] Chase (Nehemiah,[5] Jonathan,[4] John,[3] John[2]), born in Seabrook, N. H., 28 Nov. 1773; married (1) in Lynn, 8 Nov. 1807, Lydia Parrott, daughter of Benjamin and Hepzebeth (Ingalls) Parrott, born in Lynn, 15 Oct. 1791; died there, 2 Oct. 1810. He married (2) in Lynn, 12 Jan. 1812, Sarah Proctor. They lived in Lynn, where he died 14 June 1859, aged 78y.

Children by first wife, born in Lynn:

1758.   Elbridge,[7] b. 20 Sept. 1808.
        Lydia, b. 1 Oct. 1810; m. Samuel Ireland. No children.

Children by second wife, born in Lynn:

1759.   Amos, b. 16 July 1813; lived in California.
1760.   William Kentisber, b. 1 Jan. 1816.
        Abigail, b. 3 Oct. 1818; m. Merrill Gove of Lynn.

707

Elisha[6] Chase (Nehemiah,[5] Jonathan,[4] John,[3] John[2]), born in Seabrook, N. H. Probably he is the Elisha Chase of Seabrook who married in Hampton Falls, N. H., 17 June 1794, Elizabeth Nason. No births of any children recorded in New Hampshire.

708

Lt. Simon[6] Chase (Nathaniel,[5] Jonathan,[4] John,[3] John[2]), born in N. H. (probably in Epsom), 19 Apr. 1774 or 1775; died at the battle of Plattsburgh, N. Y., 11 Sept. 1814. He married about 1794, Huldah Peaslee who was born in Seabrook, N. H., 16 Apr. 1776; died in Salem, 5 Dec. 1854. They lived in Pittsfield, N. H., and later in Lynnfield. He served as Lieutenant in the War of 1812.

Children, born in Pittsfield:

1761.   Elijah,[7] b. 29 Jan. 1795; m. 6 May 1819, Sarah Elliott of Newburyport, b. 2 Sept. 1793; d. 16 June 1870. He lived in Pittsfield.

Elisabeth, b. 11 May 1796; m. 23 Dec. 1818, David Locke of Epson.

1762.   Theophilus, m. Oct. 1823, Elizabeth Carter of Manchester, N. H.

1763.   Joseph, m. Rebecca Barker of Saco, Me. He was "killed while blasting a rock in Wiscasset, Me., 1824, and left a widow and one daughter." (Letter of his brother Nathaniel Chase, dated at Salem, 1 June 1883.)

1764.   Nathaniel, b. 7 Nov. 1801; m. (1) 11 Aug. 1826, Elisabeth Thomas; m. (2) 19 Jan. 1844, Elisabeth[8] Chase (David[7]) (Family 1781).

Mary P., b. 26 Mar. 1806; m. 15 Dec. 1828, Jonathan Stoning of Weare, N. H.

Lucinda, b. 8 [25 ?] 1808 or 9; m. 16 June 1829, Joseph Bursley of Lynn.

Nancy, b. 28 Feb. 1810; m. 1 Nov. 1832, George Stoning, b. 8 Aug. 1808, in Weare, N. H.; living in Orange, Vt., in 1874.

Sarah, b. 10 Feb. 1812; m. Bradford Lord of Lynn.

1765.   Warren, b. 5 Jan. 1813; m. 5 Jan. 1837, Mary P. White of Newport, N. H. He published his autobiography entitled, *Life Line of the Lone One* in Boston, 1861, a book of 310 pages.

709

Jonathan[6] Chase (Nathaniel,[5] Jonathan,[4] John,[3] John[2]), born in Pittsfield, N. H., 2 Jan. 1781; died 5 Dec. 1856, with the Shakers (probably in Canterbury), N. H. He married 25 Feb. 1805, Abiah Hanson, daughter of Solomon and Mary[6] (Chase) Hanson, (Family 225) born 13 Mar. 1788; died 6 Apr. 1840. They lived in Portsmouth, N. H., and Pittsfield.

Children:

Mary,[7] b. 27 Jan. 1806; d. 29 Dec. 1834.

1766.   Nathan H., b. 16 Mar. 1809.

Julina G., b. 16 Apr. 1813; d. unm. 15 May 1844.

Ruhamah, b. 13 Jan. 1816; m. 1843, Edward George of Boston.

Elisabeth, b. 14 Sept. 1818; m. 5 Sept. 1839, Daniel Green.

Lydia M., b. 6 Mar. 1821; m. John Malvern.

1767.   Hanson Michael Servetus, b. in Portsmouth, 8 Apr. 1823; m. in 1850, Mary Ann Brown, b. 10 Nov. 1831. Four children, including *Irving Hanson*,[8] b. 18 Nov. 1858; m. Minnie Elliott, dau. of Ephraim and Lucy Elliott of Thornton, N. H.

Children: Mildred Augusta,[9] b. 30 Apr. 1883; m. 26 July 1907, James Frank Drake of Pittsfield, N. H.; four children; Richard Volney,[9] b. 4 June 1887; m. 15 July 1915; Mary Esther Cheney; three children.

1768. NATHANIEL E., b. 1 May 1825; m. 24 Jan. 1849, Irene P. Gilmore. They lived in Boston.

1769. JOHN R., b. 30 Sept. 1829.

LAVINA ANN, b. 8 Dec. 1833; m. 28 Nov. 1853, John S. Tucker of Laconia, N. H.

1770. JAMES V., b. 10 May 1835.

710

JOSEPH[6] CHASE (Nathaniel,[5] Jonathan,[4] John,[3] John[2]), born in Pittsfield, N. H., 1788; died 1865, aged about 87. He married (1) MARY SHAW; married (2) in 1817, DEBORAH CLARK of Hampton Falls, N. H. She was a sister to Jeremiah Clark who married Abigail[6] Chase, sister of Joseph.[6] They lived in Pittsfield.

Child by first wife, born in Pittsfield:

1771. NEHEMIAH,[7] b. 20 Dec. 1804; m. 27 July 1825, Judith James; lived in Syracuse, N. Y., 1873.

Children by second wife, born in Pittsfield:

JANE, b. 1818; m. 1848, Andrew Jordan of Lawrence.

CHARLES, b. 1820; d. 1837, in Springfield, N. H.

ELIZABETH, b. 1825; m. 1849, Gilbert H. Gilmore; lived in Syracuse, N. Y.

711

NATHANIEL[6] CHASE (Nathaniel,[5] Jonathan,[4] John,[3] John[2]), born in Pittsfield, N. H., 5 Mar 1797; married 14 Oct. 1853, MARY L. J. SMITH, who was born in Plymouth, N. H., 12 Apr. 1832. They lived in Moultonborough, N. H.

Children:

1772. NATHANIEL E.,[7] b. 18 Aug. 1865.

MARY A., b. 8 Apr. 1872.

712

DUDLEY[6] CHASE (Daniel,[5] Elizabeth,[4] John,[3] John[2]), was born in Hampton Falls, N. H., removed to Weare, N. H., where he lived about 20 years, then removed to Deering, N. H. He married about 1769, ALICE ABBOTT, of Berwick, Me., who died after 15 Aug. 1830. He died in Deering in 1826. They lived in Berwick and Deering.

Children, eldest born in Berwick, others in Deering:

1773. NATHANIEL,[7] b. 28 Oct. 1770; m. 1792, Sarah Gove; d. in Alexdria, N. H., 12 Aug. 1847. Three children.

NANCY, b. 2 Nov. 1772; m. 30 Jan. 1793, Dr. Isaac Kelley. She d. 13 July 1826, in Waterborough, Me.

RUTH, b. 13 Oct. 1774; m. 1799, John Hubbard of Hopkinton.

ESTHER, b. 17 Aug. 1776; m. 1799, Dr. Michael Tubbs; she d. 7 Apr. 1832.

1774. DANIEL, b. 24 May 1778; m. (1) Mary Wyman; m. (2) ———— Cobb. He d. 13 Aug. 1839, Clearmont, N. H.

LYDIA, b. 13 Jan. 1780; m. 1805, Eli Tubbs of Marlow, N. H.
        She d. 1842.
1775.   DUDLEY, b. 20 Mar. 1782; m. Mary Peasley; d. 26 Mar. 1852.
1776.   WILLIAM, b. 24 Feb. 1785; m. 10 Jan. 1808, Susan Harvey.
        He d. 13 Sept. 1867; she d. 22 Mar. 1868; lived in Notting-
        ham, N. H.; three children.

713

JOHN[6] CHASE (Daniel,[5] Elizabeth,[4] John,[3] John[2]), son of Daniel
Chase, alias Green, and Esther (Shaw) Chase, was born in Hampton
Falls, N. H. He married (entering his intention at Salisbury, 29 Jan.
1774) SARAH MORRILL of Salisbury. He was then described as "of
Halestown," (now Weare), N. H. He was a famous hunter in the
forests of that locality. He died in 1823, aged 72. His widow died
11 Aug. 1840, aged 84. They resided in Weare. He made his will
13 May 1815, which was proved 3 Sept. 1823. He mentions therein
his wife Sarah, sons Chevey, Charles, David and John Chase and his
daughters, Rhoda Breed, Hannah Gove, Sarah Gove and Susannah
Dow. (Hillsborough Probate 32:379).
        Children, born in Weare:
1777.   CHEVEY,[7] b. 14 Feb. 1775; m. (1) Abigail B. Gove and m. (2)
        Ruth Sawyer; m. (3) Abigail Brown. He d. 16 Mar. 1863.
1778.   CHARLES, b. 11 Mar. 1782; m. (1) about 1808, Fanny Whittle;
        m. (2) Mrs. Nancy (Peaslee) Peterson; lived in Weare.
        He d. 14 Jan. 1861.
1779.   DAVID, b. 12 Sept. 1783; m. Abigail Eaton, who d. 30 Oct. 1842.
1780.   JOHN, b. 12 Mar. 1786; d. in Weare, 9 June 1852; m. 22 Nov.
        1809, Lydia Patterson of Henniker, N. H. She d. 19 Sept.
        1879. Eight children.
        HANNAH, b. 7 Jan. 1779; m. John Gove of Vt. and Salem.
        RHODA, b. 14 Jan. 1777; m. Stephen Breed of Weare; she d.
        23 Oct. 1830.
        SALLY, b. 1788; m. Moses Gove of Weare; she d. 7 Mar. 1862.
        SUSAN, b. 1790; m. 18 Feb. 1808, Winthrop Dow of Kensing-
        ton, N. H.

714

DANIEL[6] CHASE (Daniel,[5] Elizabeth,[4] John,[3] John[2]), was born
in Hampton Falls, N. H., not far from 1750; married HANNAH PER-
KINS. They lived in Hampton Falls.
        Children, born in Hampton Falls:
        SALLY,[7] m. Merrill Currier of Dover, N. H.
1781.   DAVID, b. 7 Oct. 1776; m. (1) in Pittsfield, 14 Oct. 1802, Eliz-
        abeth[6] Chase (Nathaniel[5]) (Family 223); m. (2) in Sea-
        brook, 2 Feb. 1807, Sally Fifield. He d. 2 Mar. 1840; she d.
        14 Sept. 1852; selectman 1824-5; representative 1829-31.
1782.   NATHANIEL, m. 30 Jan. 1803, Sophia Sanborn; lived in Port-
        land, Me., 1803.
        NANCY, m. Dr. ——— Forsaith.
        JOHN, lived in Hampton Falls; d. unm.
1783.   CHEVEY, b. 14 Feb. 1791; m. 24 Mar. 1819, Hannah Fogg of
        Seabrook, N. H.; b. 22 Nov. 1799; lived in Hampton Falls.

715

NATHAN GREENE[6] CHASE (John,[5] Elihu,[4] John,[3] John[2]), born (probably in Kensington, N. H.), 25 Dec. 1752; died in Weare, N. H., 27 Sept. 1847. He married (1) about 1775, PHEBE HOAG of Newton, N. H. She was born 13 Dec. 1751; died in Weare, 1 Jan. 1806. He married (2) ALICE (NEWHALL) BUTMAN, widow of Thomas Butman of Lynn, who died 26 Dec. 1854. He removed to Weare in 1775 and was a prominent member of the Society of Friends.

Children by first wife, born in Weare:

HANNAH,[7] b. 21 Mar. 1776; m. 10 Oct. 1799, Moses Gove of Weare; she d. 15 Sept. 1831, in Lincoln, Vt.

MOLLY, b. 25 Jan. 1778; m. 1795, Daniel Breed, a farmer, son of Zephaniah of Lynn. Lived in Weare. She d. 28 May 1796. No children.

1784. JOHN, b. 20 Aug. 1780; m. 26 Oct. 1804, Betty Dow, dau. of Josiah and Lydia (Gove) Dow.

716

JOHN[6] CHASE (John,[5] Elihu,[4] John,[3] John[2]), born in Kensington, N. H., 18 Feb. 1760; died in Pittsfield, N. H., 6 Apr. 1838. He married 4 Nov. 1783, MARTHA THURSTON who was born 6 Dec. 1760; died in Pittsfield, 26 Sept. 1831. The Pittsfield Town Records state that he married "Mrs. Martha Chase," but the Kensington Town Records call her Martha Thurston. They lived in Pittsfield.

Children, born in Pittsfield:

1785. JONATHAN T.,[7] b. 19 Aug. 1784; m. 10 July 1813, Patience Chase, dau. of Nathaniel.[5] (Family 223)

BETSEY, b. 1 Dec. 1786; m. 1812, Nathan Carr of Loudon.

LYDIA, b. 6 Apr. 1790; m. 24 July 1825, Jacob Dow of Pittsfield.

MARY, b. 24 June 1793; m. 23 Jan. 1818, Caleb Willey of Pittsfield.

MARTHA T., b. 18 Mar. 1795; m. 1 Sept. 1819, Ebenezer Cram Jr. of Pittsfield.

1786. JOHN, b. 24 Sept. 1798.

JUDITH, b. 25 July 1800; m. 29 Nov. 1821, William Clough of Pittsfield.

717

DAVID[6] CHASE (John,[5] Elihu,[4] John,[3] John[2]), born in Kensington, N. H., 27 Jan 1762; died 8 Mar. 1836. He married in Kensington, 1 Mar. 1789, JUDITH JOHNSON who was born 27 Dec. 1769; died 8 May 1844. They lived in Weare, N. H. He made his will, 15 Mar. 1830, which was proved, 5 Apr. 1836. He mentions his wife Judith, his daughter Abial Gove and his sons Peter and Stephen Chase. (Hillsborough Co. Probate, 41:273).

Children probably born in Weare:

PETER J.,[7] b. 13 May 1789; d. unm.

ABIAL, b. 13 Mar. 1791; m. 5 Mar. 1812, Joseph Gove; she d. 18 Oct. 1837.

1787. STEPHEN, b. 8 Mar. 1799; m. June 1820, Lois Morrison of Pittsfield, grand dau. of Solomon and Mary (Chase) Hanson, b. 31 Jan. 1805.

718

SOLOMON GREEN[6] CHASE (William,[5] Elihu,[4] John,[3] John[2]), born in N. H., 24 Feb. 1762; died in Frankfort, Me., 24 Nov. 1840. He married about 1789, ABIGAIL LANE, daughter of Capt. John Lane. She was born 20 Feb. 1764, and died 26 Dec. 1837. They lived in Pittsfield, N. H., till 1806 when they removed to Frankfort (now Winterport) Me., where they both died.

Children, born in Pittsfield:

BETSEY,[7] b. 26 Aug. 1790; m. 1814, Jonathan Norton of Winterport, Me. She d. 1851.

1788.   MARK LANE, b. 19 June 1792; m. 7 Apr. 1813, Sally C. Spearing. He d. 5 Apr. 1850. Nine children.

1789.   JOHN, b. 23 June 1795; m. 26 Apr. 1821, Lydia Whitney of Hampden, Me. Lived in Monroe, Me.

NANCY, b. May 1797; d. unm. Oct. 1815.

SUSAN, b. 1800; m. (1) Joseph Durgin of Dixmont, Me.; m. (2) John Durgin. She d. 1869.

1790.   WILLIAM, b. 7 June 1803; m. 16 Jan. 1833, Betsey Littlefield of Winterport, Me., b. in Frankfort, Me., 8 Mar. 1811. Six children.

719

ZACCHEUS[6] CHASE (William,[5] Elihu,[4] John,[3] John[2]), born in N. H. in 1765; died in Gilmanton (now Belmont), N. H., Nov. 1820, aged 55y. He married in Pittsfield 26 June 1795, HANNAH LAMPREY, probably daughter of John and Miriam[6] (Chase) Lamprey. She died 17 Apr. 1852, aged 83. They lived in that part of Gilmanton which is now Belmont. He made his will 12 Nov. 1820, which was proved 25 Nov. 1820. Therein he mentions his wife Hannah, his daughters Lydia, Polly, Hannah and Mahala Chase, and his sons John, Nathan, and Green Chase. (Strafford Co. Probate, 23:509).

Children, born in what is now Belmont:

LYDIA,[7] b. 22 Apr. 1800; m. Parker P. Nichols; lived in Guilford. No children.

1791.   WILLIAM, b. 12 Mar. 1802; d. 1820.

POLLY, b. 12 Aug. 1804; m. 28 May 1826, Benjamin B. Cate; two children.

HANNAH, b. 3 Nov. 1806; m. 24 Nov. 1830, Jeremiah Sanborn 3d; she d. 1846.

MAHALA, b. 2 Jan. 1808; m. Enoch Moulton; three children.

1792.   JOHN, b. 7 Feb. 1810; m. Eleanor Lamprey; he d. 1866.

1793.   NATHAN, b. 31 Mar. 1812; m. Nancy K. Lamprey; lived in Belmont.

1794.   GREEN, b. 5 June 1814; m. Caroline Tilton.

720

THOMAS[6] CHASE (William,[5] Elihu,[4] John,[3] John[2]), born probably in Brentwood, N. H.; married ——— Tassi; lived in Rochester, N. Y.

Child:

ASAHEL.[7]

721

WILLIAM[6] CHASE (William,[5] Elihu,[4] John,[3] John[2]), born perhaps in Brentwood, N. H.; removed to Rochester, N. Y.

722

REV. ASAHEL[6] CHASE (William,[5] Elihu,[4] John,[3] John[2]), born in Poplin (now Fremont), N. H.; died in Portsmouth, N. H., 5 Apr. 1821. He married Sept. 1794 or May 1795, MARY HODGDON, daughter of Peter and Patience[5] (Chase) Hodgdon, born in Wolfeborough, N. H., 20 Aug. 1778. Her mother Patience[5] Chase was born in Kensington, N. H., 26 June 1750, and married Peter Hodgdon as his second wife, 9 June 1772. (Family 61). He was a Baptist Minister, but his name does not appear in Carter's *Native Ministry of New Hampshire, 1905.*

Children:

> PATIENCE,[7] b. Aug. 1796; d. unm. 28 Feb. 1821.
> MARY, b. Mar. 1799; d. 21 Feb. 1821, age 22 y.
> DAVID, b. June 1801; d. young.
> SARAH, b. 18 Sept. 1803; d. 1820, age 18.
> RUTH, b. 9 Aug. 1805; m. 19 Sept. 1827, Valentine Pickering of Newington, N. H.
> ANNA MARIA, b. 20 Nov. 1808; m. 8 Dec. 1832, John[6] Chase, son of Stephen[5] and Molly Brown of Kensington, N. H. (Family 732)

1795. ASAHEL P., b. 2 Mar. 1811; d. 1860 in California; m. (1) Sophia B. Garland; m. (2) Grace (Peacock ?).

> JOHN PLUMMER, b. 4 Nov. 1813; d. at age of 9 y.
> WILLIAM, b. Sept. 1817; d. unm.
> SARAH, b. 15 Apr. 1821; m. (1) 1845, Caleb Burrill of Nashua, N. H.; m. (2) Otis Parsons.

723

STEPHEN[6] CHASE (Thomas,[5] Elihu,[4] John,[3] John[2]), born in Poplin (now Fremont,) N. H., 7 June 1762; died in Warsaw, N. Y., 28 Feb. 1843. He married 11 Feb. 1784, LOIS ELY, who died in Warsaw, N. Y., 1 Mar. 1838. He settled in Gilmanton, N. H., and in June 1817 removed in a team drawn by four oxen to Warsaw. There he purchased a farm of 400 acres for 87½ cents per acre and engaged in wheat growing.

Children, born probably in Gilmanton:

> ABIAH,[7] b. 9 Nov. 1784; m. John Bean.

1796. THOMAS, b. 3 Aug. 1786; m. 31 Oct. 1808, Rhoda Smith; removed to Warsaw.

1797. DAVID, b. 7 Feb. 1788; m. Deborah Sanborn; d. in Bristol, N. H., 8 Nov. 1856; lived in Gilmanton.

> SARAH, b. 14 Sept. 1789; m. Aug. 1824, John B. Smith. No children.
> HANNAH, b. 3 Feb. 1794; m. Benjamin Bodge.

1798. STEPHEN, b. 6 July 1796; m. (1) 15 July 1821, Elisabeth Hogle; m. (2) 1 Nov. 1841, Wdw. Sarah Price; m. (3) 27 Oct. 1844, Nancy Ingersoll; lived in Warsaw.

> ELISABETH, b. 16 Sept. 1800; m. Almerin Curtis.

724

GREEN[6] CHASE (Thomas,[5] Elihu,[4] John,[3] John[2]), born in Poplin (now Fremont), N. H., 13 Jan. 1764; died in Tuftonborough, N. H., 18 Aug. 1835. He married in Kingston, N. H., 18 Feb. 1790, HANNAH GOVE, daughter of Obadiah and Mary (Dow) Gove, born in Kensington, N. H., 11 Sept. 1768; died in Tuftonborough, 25 Sept. 1858. They lived in Gilford, N. H., Gilmanton, N. H., and Tuftonborough.

Children, eldest born in Gilford:

1799.   JOHN,[7] b. 8 Jan. 1791; m. 30 Mar. 1819, Ruth Burbank.

        PATIENCE, b. 20 Feb. 1794; m. 12 Nov. 1862, Joseph Young of Tuftonborough.

1800.   LEVI B., b. 10 Dec. 1797; m. 24 Nov. 1830, Sarah Nute.

1801.   GREEN, b. 31 July 1801; m. 2 Aug. 1828, Mary P. Patch. He d. 12 Mar. 1876, aged 74, in Tuftonborough, N. H. He probably m. (2) 1862, Hannah E. Sanborn, widow, of Upper Gilmanton.

        MARK, b. 8 Aug. 1804; d. 8 Dec. 1815.

        HANNAH, b. 19 Oct. 1806; d. 30 Dec. 1814.

725

LEVI[6] CHASE (Thomas,[5] Elihu,[4] John,[3] John[2]), born in Poplin (now Fremont), N. H., 5 Oct. 1770; died 12 Apr. 1854, in his 85th year. He married (1) ABIGAIL SLEEPER. He married (2) JUDITH CLIFFORD who died about 1808. He married (3) LYDIA LEATHERS of Salisbury. They lived in Poplin (now Fremont), and Barnstead, N. H.

Child by first wife:

    DAVID,[7] m. in Barnstead, N. H., 11 Sept. 1817, Abigail Adams.

Children by second wife:

    SALLY, b. 1811; d. about 1820.

    JAMES, b. 8 Apr. 1804; m. in Salem, 11 Feb. 1830, Abigail Ann C. Langley; lived in Salem; nine children.

    SAMUEL, b. 1808; m. in Barnstead, 20 June 1835, Abigail (Adams) Chase, widow of his half brother David Chase. They lied in Gilmanton, N. H.; three children.

Child by third wife, born in Barnstead:

    LYDIA JANE, b. 26 Mar. 1820; m. in Pittsfield, N. H., 12 Apr. 1840, John H. Leavitt; lived in Tilton; one daughter.

726

JAMES[6] CHASE (Thomas,[5] Elihu,[4] John,[3] John,[2]), born in Poplin (now Fremont), N. H., 6 Oct. 1780; died in Chichester, N. H., 4 Aug. 1844. He married in Kingston, N. H., 16 Mar. 1804, HARRIET SMITH, daughter of Nathaniel and Judith Smith, born in Amesbury, 4 Nov. 1784; died 19 July 1873, aged 88y. 8m. 15d. They lived in Fremont and Chichester.

Children, born in Fremont:

    JUDITH L.,[7] b. 7 Dec. 1806; d. unm. 1826.

    SARAH DAVIS, b. 4 Oct. 1809; d. 1849.

HARRIET MATILDA, b. 9 May 1813; m. 4 Oct. 1836, Thomas Harrington.
LEONARD S., b. 17 May 1819; d. unm. 11 Aug. 1847.

727

SAMUEL⁶ CHASE (Elihu,⁵ Elihu,⁴ John,³ John²), born in Kensington, N. H., 2 Jan. 1775; died in Deering, N. H., 16 Mar. 1854. He married 7 Feb. 1803, ESTHER MANAHAN, daughter of John and Mary (Nesmith) Manahan of Francestown, N. H. She was born in Feb. 1783; died 7 Feb. 1870. They removed from Kensington to Deering, in 1818 and lived there.

Children, first six born in Kensington, others in Deering:

> MARY M.,⁷ b. in Kensington, 11 May 1804; m. 1 Dec. 1822, in Deering, N. H., David Bailey, son of Thomas and Anna Bailey. He was born 11 Sept. 1794 and died 4 Mar. 1847. They lived in Deering. Their youngest child *Cleora Bailey,*⁸ b. 13 Aug. 1845; m. 20 June 1878, John Cleworth, son of William and Nancy Cleworth. Their son Harold Bailey Cleworth, b. 29 Oct. 1883.

1805. JONATHAN G., b. 12 Mar. 1806; m. 9 Feb. 1840, Clarissa A. Kimball of Kensington; d. 30 Oct. 1870.

1806. EZRA A., b. Sept. 1808; m. Mary Eastman; d. Jan. 1854.

1807. SAMUEL, b. 17 Apr. 1810; m. Lydia Holbrook of Braintree; d. 1869.

1808. WELLS, b. 2 Sept. 1813; m. 8 Sept. 1839, Maria Bailey, dau. of Enoch of Newmarket, N. H.; lived in Boston, 1872.

> SARAH G., b. Dec. 1816; m. Erastus H. Bartlett of Deering.

1809. IRA M., b. in Deering, N. H., 11 May 1821; m. Josephine M. Leland; d. in Lowell, 27 Nov. 1901, aged 80. He served in 1860 on a committee from Dracut to purchase of the proprietors, the Pawtucket Bridge, and was a member of the Historical Association of Lowell. Children: *Cleora F.,*⁸ b. 6 Mar. 1849; m. 4 June 1868, Roscoe W. Turner; she d. 21 June 1872; *Frederic G.,*⁸ b. 18 July 1851; m. 25 Oct. 1877, Loretta Cunningham; d. 20 Dec. 1924; *Laura Jane,*⁸ b. 4 Sept. 1853; *Maria J.,*⁸ b. 1856; d. 30 Dec. 1856; *Edwin E.,* b. 28 Nov. 1857; m. 2 Feb. 1882, Elizabeth Jewett; *Nettie M.,*⁸ 1866-1883; *Roscoe Leland,*⁸ graduate of Massachusetts Institute of Technology, 1884; m. 28 Mar. 1888, Nellie Varnum Colton, b. in Lowell, 26 May 1860, dau. of Dr. John Jay and Czarina Coburn (Varnum) Colton. Their child, Marion Varnum,⁹ b. 28 Dec. 1888; m. Clarence R. Bliss. *Harold Mayson,*⁸ b. in 1872; graduate of the Massachusetts Institute of Technology, 1896; m. in 1924, Margaret Bridgers, dau. of Preston L. Bridgers of Wilmington, N. C., who d. in 1926; superintendent of the Dan River Cotton Mills, Danville, Va.

> BETSEY JANE, b. 5 May 1823; m. Nov. 1852, Theophilus Hilliard Kimball of Kensington.

> OLIVIA [or CLEORA F.], b. 1827; d. unm. 1845.

728

ASA⁶ CHASE (Elihu,⁵ Elihu,⁴ John,³ John²), born in Kensington, N. H., 14 Feb. 1777; died in Springfield, N. H., 18 Nov. 1865. He married 24 Feb. 1799, HULDAH TOWLE, daughter of Jonathan and Miriam (Marston) Towle of Pittsfield, N. H. She was born 26 Jan.

1775 and died in Springfield, 22 Oct. 1858. They lived in Pittsfield till about 1805, then they removed to Springfield.

Children, first three born in Pittsfield, others in Springfield:

1810.   ELIHU,[7] b. 11 Mar. 1800; m. (1) 26 Nov. 1822, Betsey Russell of Francestown, N. H.; m. (2) Jan. 3, 1870, Laura ———. He d. 23 Sept. 1886.

        SARAH, b. 10 Jan. 1802; m. 29 Nov. 1827, Nathan Smith Trow of Springfield. She d. Oct. 1874.

        HANNAH, b. 2 Dec. 1804; d. 11 Jan. 1805.

1811.   JONATHAN, b. 15 Mar. 1806; m. 5 Sept. 1827, Mary Messer of New London, N. H. He d. in Michigan, about 1835.

1812.   ASA, b. 19 Mar. 1812; m. 12 June 1836, Mary Ann Abbott; d. 3 Dec. 1882; she d. 5 Feb. 1886.

        MAHALA, b. 30 July 1817; m. 11 Jan. 1835, Amasa S. Abbott; d. 10 July 1900; he d. 13 May 1898.

729

EZRA[6] CHASE (Elihu,[5] Elihu,[4] John,[3] John[2]), born in Kensington, N. H., 7 Feb. 1779; died there 1860. He married 14 Jan. 1807, JANE WADLEIGH who died in Kensington 11 Apr. 1843, aged 56. They lived in Kensington.

Children, born in Kensington:

        MARY JANE,[7] b. 21 May 1810; m. 11 Mar. 1830, Morris Kimball of Kensington. Her marriage record gives her name as Mary Ann Chase.

1813.   EZRA BAILEY, b. 11 May 1818; m. 18 July 1841, Betsey Clarke, b. 24 Aug. 1816. Four children.

1814.   LORENZO G., b. 18 Feb. 1823; m. 27 Nov. 1845, Judith S. Shaw.

730

HOSEA[6] CHASE (Elihu,[5] Elihu,[4] John,[3] John[2]), born in Kensington, N. H., 30 July 1781; died 7 July 1864. A Mercy Cheney, daughter of Moses and Eunice (Burbank) Cheney was born in Brentwood, N. H., 3 Apr. 1780. Mercy, wife of Hosea Chase, died in 1855. They lived in Weare, N. H., and Candia, N. H.

Children:

1815.   ELIHU,[7] b. 4 Mar. 1804; m. 6 Mar. 1825, Phebe Stockbridge of Stratham, N. H.

        LUCINDA, b. 19 July 1812; m. (1) John A. Cram; no children; m. (2) Carr B. Haynes.

731

STEPHEN B.[6] CHASE (Stephen,[5] Elihu,[4] John,[3] John[2]), born in Kensington, N. H., 7 July 1795; died there. He married (1) 15 Apr. 1825, SUSAN PEVERE of Hampton Falls, N. H., who was born 2 Dec 1803; died in Kensington, 15 Apr. 1851. He married (2) 26 Apr. 1865, MRS. REBECCA (WALTON) JANVRIN. They lived on the Chase homestead in Kensington and Seabrook, N. H.

Children by first wife, born in Kensington:

        WILLIAM P.,[7] b. 2 Aug. 1826; d. unm. 7 Feb. 1850.

        EUNICE P., b. 30 Sept. 1829; m. (1) 2 Apr. 1851, Jefferson

Stevens; m. (2) 21 Mar. 1856, John Chase[8] (David,[7] Family
1781) of Hampton.
MARY JANE, b. 24 Apr. 1832; m. Samuel Dearborn; d. Apr.
1865.

732

JOHN[6] CHASE (Stephen,[5] Elihu,[4] John,[3] John[2]), born in Kensington, N. H., 2 June 1798; died there, 8 Feb. 1889, aged 90y. 8m.
6d. He married in East Kingston, 8 Dec. 1833, ANNA MARIA CHASE,
daughter of Rev. Asahel[6] and Mary (Hodgdon) Chase, born 20 Nov.
1808; alive 16 Feb. 1874. (Family 722). They lived on the Chase
homestead in Kensington.
  Children, born in Kensington:
    MARY ELMER,[7] b. 27 June 1834; d. 14 Aug. 1838.
    MARTHA, b. 13 Sept. 1836; m. Dr. Charles De Chontal.
1816. SILAS MARTIN, b. 6 Jan. 1838; d. 10 Feb. 1866. Was in 14th
    Regt. Mass. Vols. Heavy Artillery; contracted disease in the
    army.
    MARY E., b. 2 Sept. 1841; m. Mark E. Pevere of Lynn.
1817. WARREN HOWE, b. 5 Nov. 1844; d. 8 Feb. 1865, at Winchester,
    Va., of disease; belonged to Troop L, N. H. Cavalry.
1818. EDWARD S., b. 9 Mar. 1846; m. 11 Feb. 1870, Lizzie Heath of
    Manchester, N. H.
    CHARLES O., b. 3 Apr. 1848; unm.

733

JOHN[6] CHASE (James,[5] John,[4] John,[3] John[2]), married 15 Aug.
1778, EDITH HUTCHINS; died at sea in 1796. Administration on his
estate was granted to Solomon Trask of Edgecombe, Me., 6 Nov.
1800. They lived in Edgecombe.
  Children, born in Edgecombe:
    HANNAH,[7] b. 4 June 1779; m. (1) 6 Dec. 1801, Windsor Jones;
    m. (2) Charles Adams.
    JOHN, d. young.
    JONATHAN, was a gunner on board the U. S. Frigate Consti-
    tution; never married.
    EDITH, m. (1) —— Lunt; m. (2) —— Lowell.
    MARY, b. 1782; m. (1) 4 Nov. 1804, Samuel Montgomery; m.
    (2) 7 Apr. 1832, Ichabod Cushman.
1819. ENOCH, b. — Dec. 1781; d. 8 Dec. 1860; m. Mary Smith, b. 9
    Aug. 1784; d. 9 Feb. 1830. Ten children, including Enoch,[8]
    b. in Whitefield, Me., 28 Aug. 1815; d. in Taunton, 18 Jan.
    1895; m. in Dorchester, 2 Sept. 1844, Susan Marshall, b. in
    Milton, 17 Oct. 1822; d. in Taunton, 9 Jan. 1895. Their son
    Charles Francis,[9] b. in Dorchester, 21 May 1852; m. 13 July
    1875, Elizabeth Taylor, dau. of William and Penelope
    (Baker) Taylor. Their only son William Henry,[10] b. in
    Taunton, 1 May 1876; m. 8 July 1915, Clara E. Sherman, dau.
    of Clarence R. and Martha A. (Dunham) Sherman. No chil-
    dren. He is a member of the American Society of Civil En-
    gineers and superintendent of streets in New Bedford for
    several years.
    RHODA, b. 1786; m. 1805, Edward Stuart.

1820.   EBENEZER, m. (1) Sarah[6] [Sally] Chase, dau. of Jacob[5] and
        Mary (Hardy) Chase (Family 253); m. (2) Eliza Patten.
        PHEBE, said to have been a sister to above.

734

MOSES[6] CHASE (James,[5] John,[4] John,[3] John[2]), born in Edgecomb, Me.; died at sea in 1796. He married and left one son.
    Child:
1821.   MOSES.[7]

735

CAPT. EBENEZER[6] CHASE (James,[5] John,[4] John,[3] John[2]), born
31 Jan. 1767; died in Edgecomb, Me., 22 June 1855. He married in
Boothbay, Me., 20 Aug. 1793, JEAN ADAMS, daughter of Samuel and
Sarah (Reed) Adams, born in Boothbay, Me., 19 Mar. 1771; died in
Edgecomb, 14 July 1852. They lived in Edgecomb. He was a pensioner living in Edgecomb, with his son Ebenezer, 1 June 1840, aged
74. He joined the Congregational Church, 30 Aug. 1818; his wife
joined 15 Aug. 1819.
    Children, born in Edgecomb:
        ANDREW,[7] b. 22 Mar. 1794; d. 22 Sept. 1818.
        JANE, b. 22 Jan. 1796; m. Solomon Gove; d. 22 Mar. 1840.
1822.   JOHN, b. 3 Mar. 1797; m. (1) 1818 Sarah Cunningham, who d.
            16 Sept. 1821; m. (2) Nancy Merrill; lived in Edgecomb, Me.
        BETSEY, b. 13 Dec. 1799; m. 9 Dec. 1819, Andrew Clifford.
        SARAH K., b. 10 Sept. 1801; m. (1) 1 May 1823, Isaac Clif-
            ford; m. (2) —— Heal.
1823.   EBENEZER, b. 12 June 1802; m. 3 Mar. 1843, Mary Parsons; d.
            1 Mar. 1892. She d. 5 July 1895. Four children.
        MARY, b. 27 Mar. 1805; m. 3 July 1859, Thomas Parsons. She
            d. 23 July 1859. No children.
        HANNAH, b. 16 May 1807; m. Warren Pinkham; d. Oct. 1851.
1824.   JAMES, b. 7 Mar. 1809; m. 30 Dec. 1832, Betsey Clifford; b.
            13 Dec. 1816; lived Edgecomb, Me.
1825.   JONATHAN, b. 17 Nov. 1811; m. Widow Sarah (Chase) Perry.
            He d. 13 Sept. 1863. They were cousins.
1826.   ENOCH, b. 6 Oct. 1813; m. (1) Sept. 1840, Avis Chase; m.
            (2) Sarah Adams; lived in Edgecomb.
1827.   MOSES, b. 10 Mar. 1815; m. 1841, Susan Clifford.

736

ENOCH[6] CHASE (James,[5] John,[4] John,[3] John[2]), born in Edgecomb, Me. He was a private in Capt. Archibald McAllister's Company of Col. Samuel McCobb's Regiment and served from 11 July to
24 Sept. 1779—a period of two months, thirteen days in the expedition against Major Bagaduce (now Castine), Me. (Mass. Soldiers
and Sailors in the Revolutionary War, 3:349). His family has not
been reported. He does not appear to be the head of a family in
Maine in 1790.

737

NATHANIEL[6] CHASE (Thomas,[5] John,[4] John,[3] John [2]), born in Seabrook, N. H., 9 Jan. 1753; died in Henniker, N. H., 17 Sept. 1847. He married 27 Sept. 1780, MARY BROWN of Hampton, N. H., who died in Henniker, 28 Dec. 1854, aged 92y. 8m. They removed to Henniker in 1780, cleared up a farm and lived there until death.

Children, born in Henniker:

1828. WINTHROP,[7] b. 22 Aug. 1781; m. 25 Oct. 1809, Anna Dow. He d. 1 Dec. 1857.

1829. ABRAHAM, b. 18 May 1783; m. (1) 3 Apr. 1811, Kezia Peaslee; m. (2) Fanny Smith; d. 30 Mar. 1861.

HANNAH (twin), b. 31 Dec. 1785; m. 5 May 1804, Elijah Dow; d. 16 Feb. 1809.

NATHANIEL (twin), b. 31 Dec. 1785; d. 6 Apr. 1796.

1830. JONATHAN, b. 4 Apr. 1788; m. 14 May 1817, Patience Peaslee; d. 20 Oct. 1864.

THOMAS, b. 20 Mar. 1792; never married.

CHARLES, b. 9 Dec. 1793; d. unm. 5 Apr. 1863.

MARY, b. 7 Dec. 1795; never married.

PEACE ANN, b. 26 Nov. 1797; m. 29 Apr. 1828, Samuel[7] Chase, her cousin, son of Charles.[6] (Family 738)

1831. NATHANIEL, b. 20 Mar. 1800; m. 16 Nov. 1825, Elisabeth Leach.

SARAH, b. 17 May 1804; m. 22 Sept. 1830, Estes Purington of Weare, N. H., and d. 16 Oct. 1846.

738

CHARLES[6] CHASE (Thomas,[5] John,[4] John,[3] John[2]), born in Seabrook, N. H., 20 Apr. 1754; died in Kingston, N. H., 1842. He married (1) in Kingston, 19 Oct. 1779, MARY CALEF, daughter of Dea. William Calef of Kingston, who died young. He married (2) 29 Mar. 1783, RHODA Dow of Hampton Falls, N. H. He was a teacher and a Quaker but was disowned for marrying out of the meeting. They lived in Kingston.

Child by first wife, born in Kingston:

CHARLES,[7] b. 26 Jan. 1780; d. young.

Children by second wife, born in Kingston:

1832. CHARLES, b. 26 Jan. 1783; m. 26 May 1828, Mary Dearborn of Kensington, N. H., dau. of Gerald Dearborn.

SARAH, b. 8 July 1785; m. 1 Jan. 1807, Aaron Patten of Kensington.

MARIAN, b. 22 July 1786.

MARY, b. 21 Mar. 1790.

NANCY, b. 3 Apr. 1794; m. 3 Oct. 1844, Moody T. Colby of Kensington.

1833. SAMUEL CALEF, b. 5 Nov. 1796; m. (1) 5 Nov. 1828, Peace Ann[7] Chase (Family 737); m. (2) Nancy A. Judkins.

1834. NATHANIEL, b. 15 Nov. 1798; m. 19 Dec. 1826, Hannah C. Foster.

1835. AMOS, b. 2 Apr. 1801; m. 4 July 1827, Hannah A. Hook of Brentwood, N. H.

Several others d. young.

739

Amos[6] CHASE (Thomas,[5] John,[4] John,[3] John[2]), born in Seabrook, N. H., 12 July 1756; died in Deering, N. H., 8 June 1827. He
married (1) in Amesbury, 22 Apr. 1780, ELIZABETH KIMBALL,
daughter of James and Meribah Kimball of Hopkinton, N. H. She
died 24 June 1794. He married (2) in Amesbury, 22 Apr. 1795,
HULDAH Dow, daughter of Bildad and Eleanor Dow of Seabrook.
She died in Deering, 3 Aug. 1835. He was a Quaker and they lived
in Deering.

Children by first wife:

1836. JOHN,[7] b. 23 Aug. 1782; m. in Weare, N. H., 1 Oct. 1806, Sarah
       Hanson; d. 12 Jan. 1865.
       MARY, b. 6 May 1784; m. (1) in Weare, 22 Oct. 1806, Joseph
       Whittier Jr.; m. (2) ———— Taylor; m. (3) ———— Hanson;
       Biddeford, Me.
1837. EDWARD, b. 15 Jan. 1786; m. in Weare, 15 Mar. 1810, Mary
       Patten; lived in Deering; d. 5 Aug. 1860.
       DOLLY, b. 17 Feb. 1788; m. in Weare, 29 Oct. 1809, Abraham
       Dow of Seabrook.
       RACHEL, b. 7 Feb. 1789; m. in Weare, 29 Dec. 1813, Enoch
       Gove of Weare.
       RHODA, b. 15 Sept. 1791; m. in Hopkinton, 26 Jan. 1812, Sam-
       uel Straw Jr. of Hopkinton.
       ELISABETH, b. 22 Oct. 1794; m. (1) in Weare, 19 Jan. 1815,
       Elisha Frye of Sandwich, N. H.; m. (2) Daniel Buxton;
       living in Lynn, 1872.

740

WINTHROP[6] CHASE (Thomas,[5] John,[4] John,[3] John[2]), born in
Seabrook, N .H., 1761; died in May 1857. He married (1) in Kensington, 17 Mar. 1785, ELIZABETH GREEN; married (2) in Henniker,
N. H., 30 Nov. 1827, ANNA DUDLEY who died in 1856. They lived
in Seabrook in 1790 and later in Henniker.

Children by first wife:

1838. WINTHROP,[7] b. 15 Apr. 1790; m. 14 Feb. 1827, Sarah Hussey;
       d. 11 Jan. 1866; he lived in Weare, N. H.
1839. BRADBURY, m. Alice Dudley, b. Apr. 1799.
       MARY, b. 3 Sept. 1794; m. 16 Nov. 1819, Trueworthy W. Dud-
       ley of Newbury, N. H.
       SARAH, m. Henry Nichols.
       ELISABETH, b. 1802; m. Joel Atkins of Lincoln, Vt.

741

THOMAS[6] CHASE (Thomas,[5] John,[4], John,[3] John[2]), born in Seabrook, N. H., 1776; died at White Haven, N. S., 8 Aug. 1833. He
married about 1799, BETSEY FELCH, daughter of Samuel and Jemima
(Cilley) Felch, born 3 Dec. 1781; died 13 Nov. 1856, aged 74. They
lived in Seabrook. He was a mariner.

Children, born in Seabrook:

       LYDIA,[7] b. 1800; m. Benjamin Rowe of Seabrook.
1840. THOMAS, b. 7 Mar. 1804; d. 14 Aug. 1882, aged 77; captain;
       m. (1) 26 Oct. 1826, Lucinda P. Lake of Seabrook; m. (2)
       20 July 1850, Maria Brown; d. 10 Feb. 1904.

ELIZA, b. 1810; m. 1832, Charles Locke (1811-1883). She d. 1848.

742

DAVID[6] CHASE (Thomas,[5] John,[4] John,[3] John[2]), born in Seabrook, N. H., 6 May 1781; died there, 8 Dec. 1872, aged 90y. 7m. He married 3 Dec. 1807, LYDIA FELCH, daughter of Nicholas and Sarah (Gove) Felch, born Mar. 1788; died in Seabrook 28 Aug. 1859, aged 71 years. He was a master mariner for forty years. They lived in Seabrook.

Children, born in Seabrook:

HANNAH,[7] b. 8 Aug. 1809; d. 2 Dec. 1809.
1841. DAVID, b. 21 Sept. 1810; m. in Hampton Falls, N. H., 3 May 1832, Sarah Janvrin of Seabrook. He d. 12 June 1892, aged 81 y. 4 m.
HANNAH, b. 24 July 1812; m. Capt. William Sanborn of Seabrook.
1842. JOHN, b. 23 Apr. 1814; m. (1) Harriet R. Walton; (m. int. 5 Nov. 1842); m. (2) Miriam S. Jones.
SARAH JANE, b. 1 June 1816; d. 16 Feb. 1820.
SALLY, b. 3 Oct. 1819; m. 31 Jan. 1839, William Walton.
1843. JEREMIAH F., b. 28 Dec. 1824; m. 5 July 1850, Lucinda Felch.
1844. ALBERT, b. 10 Feb. 1827; m. Dec. 1851, Abigail Eaton. He d. 13 May 1859.
LYDIA JANE, b. 12 Nov. 1828; drowned 18 Oct. 1847.

743

EDWARD[6] CHASE (Thomas,[5] John,[4] John,[3] John[2]), born in Seabrook, N. H. He was a sailor and it is supposed that he was lost at sea.

744

ENOCH[6] CHASE (John,[5] John,[4] John,[3] John[2]), born in Edgecomb, Me., in 1781; married MARY SMITH, born in Wiscasset, Me., in 1784, daughter of Abijah and Lydia (Rogers) Smith. They lived in Whitefield, Lincoln Co., Me. Their family consisted of twelve children.

Child, born in Whitefield:

JOHN SMITH,[7] b. 23 Apr. 1827; m. 1 Jan. 1852, Mary Elizabeth Follett, dau. of Robert and Mary R. (Walkup) Follett, b. in Uxbridge, 5 July 1824. He was foreman of the Hopedale Foundry.
Other children not reported.

745

CAPT. CHARLES[6] CHASE (John,[5] John,[4] John,[3] John[2]), baptized in Hampton Falls, N. H., 2 Dec. 1753; died in Newcastle, Me., 1822. He married about 1775, HANNAH STEWART of Alna, Me. She died 21 Feb. 1808. They lived on the Chase homestead in Newcastle. He was captain in the militia.

Children, first born in Edgecomb, Me., others in Newcastle:

JAMES,[7] b. 4 Aug. 1776; d. 22 Dec. 1778.
1845. THOMAS, b. 13 Nov. 1778; m. 25 June 1801, Ann Woodbridge.

POLLY, b. 28 Nov. 1780; m. Cornelius Turner of Wiscasset, Me.
   She d. 12 Mar. 1861.

SARAH, b. 24 Mar. 1783; m. Joseph Leighton of Alna, Me.
1846.   WILLIAM, b. 19 Feb. 1785; m. Alice Keene of Walpole, Me.
   He d. 14 Mar. 1864, aged 79.
1847.   CHARLES, b. 30 Apr. 1787; d. 26 Apr. 1849.
1848.   JOHN, b. 25 July 1789; m. Sophia Jenney of Baltimore, Md.
   Sea captain; lost on a voyage to Tampico, Mex.

SAMUEL, b. 5 Jan. 1792; d. 14 Feb. 1794.

HANNAH, b. 14 Feb. 1794; d. 12 Sept. 1865.

EBENEZER, b. 2 Apr. 1796; d. 11 Jan. 1797.

GEORGE, b. 11 Dec. 1797; d. 14 May 1814.
1849.   FRANKLIN, b. 3 Jan. 1800; m. Ann McLellan, an English lady.

EDWARD, b. 15 Mar. 1803; d. 26 Aug. 1823.

746

JACOB[6] CHASE (Daniel,[5] John,[4] John,[3] John[2]), born in Seabrook,
N. H., 15 May 1769; died 13 Dec. 1844. He married in Salem, 19
Mar. 1795, LUCY BERRY, daughter of John and Rachel Berry of
Lynnfield, born in Lynn, 28 June 1772; died in Lynn, 13 Jan. 1842.
He died in Lynn, 15 Dec. 1844, aged 76, "son of Daniel and Jane of
Seabrook, N. H." They lived in Lynn.

Children, born in Lynn:
1850.   JOHN BERRY,[7] b. 4 Dec. 1795; m. 10 Dec. 1815, Sarah Breed.

JACOB, b. 8 Oct. 1798; d. 12 June 1801 or 6 Dec. 1802.

PHILIP, b. 22 Mar. 1801; d. 16 July 1804.
1851.   JACOB, b. 22 Oct. 1803; m. (1) 4 Oct. 1827, Mary Atwill; m.
   (2) 30 Sept. 1858, Mary Ann Townsend.
1852.   PHILIP, b. 2 Mar. 1806; m. (1) 16 Dec. 1829, Abby Boyce.

LUCY J., b. 22 Apr. 1810; d. 11 May 1811.

SAMUEL GEORGE, b. 25 Aug. 1812; d. 29 July 1821.

LUCY ANN, b. 4 July 1816; m. 22 Aug. 1837, George Webb
   Mudge.

747

CHARLES[6] CHASE (Daniel,[5] John,[4] John,[3] John[2]), born in Seabrook, N. H., 1771; died in Lynn, 23 July 1847, aged 76. He married (intention in Lynn, 5 Aug. 1792) ABIGAIL PHILLIPS. She died
in Lynn, 11 Aug. 1829. He married (2) ELIZABETH SWIFT who died
in Lynn, 21 June 1832. He married a third wife who died in Lynn,
27 July 1835. They lived in Lynn and were Quakers.

Children by first wife, born in Lynn:
1853.   DANIEL,[7] b. 28 Jan. 1793; m. 7 Sept. 1817, Harriet Phillips.
1854.   JOHN, b. 23 Apr. 1796.

PHILLIPS, b. 2 Apr. 1802; d. 26 June 1826.
1855.   JACOB, b. 6 May 1804.
1856.   WILLIAM, b. 15 June 1807; m. 15 Dec. 1829, Susan Ingalls.
1857.   WARREN, b. 9 Oct. 1809; m. Rebecca Dodge.

MARY W., b. 18 Dec. 1814; d. 8 Apr. 1834.

Child by second wife, born in Lynn:

ELISABETH S., b. 7 Apr. 1832; d. 9 Mar. 1833.

748

DANIEL[6] CHASE (Daniel,[5] John,[4] John,[3] John[2]), married in Lynn, 6 Aug. 1797, MARGARET FULLER, daughter of Nathaniel Fuller, baptized in Lynn, 28 July 1776; died there 26 Apr. 1837, aged 61. He died in Lynn in 1807. They lived in Lynn.

Children, born in Lynn:

1858. NATHAN D.,[7] b. 31 May 1800; m. 3 Oct. 1819, Polly Stone.
1859. BLANEY, b. 4 Apr. 1805; m. 15 Mar. 1827, Eliza Doak.
       PEGGY, d. unm.

749

JOHN[6] CHASE (Daniel,[5] John,[4] John,[3] John[2]), born in Seabrook, N. H.; died in Lynn, 19 Jan. 1821. He married (1) in Lynn, 25 Feb. 1798, SARAH BATCHELER. He married (2) in Lynn, 23 Apr. 1815, HANNAH PARROT. They lived in Lynn.

Children, born in Lynn:

1860. CHARLES,[7] b. 28 Aug. 1798; m. Dolly Huntress.
1861. JOHN G., b. 1 June 1800; m. (1) 28 Sept. 1825, Lucy Hawes of Yarmouth; m. (2) Mary Nesbitt.
1862. DANIEL, b. 18 May 1803; m. (1) Sarah Mitchell of Marblehead; m. (2) Dorcas Phinney.
       SARAH, b. 28 May 1805; m. John Phillips.
       GILMAN ROBBINS, b. 1 Sept. 1808; never married.
1863. NELSON OTIS, b. 17 Mar. 1809; m. 23 Jan. 1830, Ann E. Downing. He changed his name to Augustus Otis Chase. His son George Otis,[8] m. Laura Ellen[7] Chase. (Family 966)
       JERUSHA, b. 16 Oct. 1811; d. young.

750

LEVI[6] CHASE (Daniel,[5] John,[4] John,[3] John[2]), married in Lynn, 30 Oct. 1809, SARAH PARROTT, who died in Lynn, 7 July 1826. They lived in Lynn.

Children, born in Lynn:

1864. GEORGE LEVI,[7] b. 28 May, 1813; m. Mary A. Bacon.
       SARAH ANN, b. 15 Feb. 1815; m. 8 Oct. 1834, James Collins.
       ABIGAIL, b. 4 Dec. 1817.
       ABIGAIL, b. 6 May, 1820; m. 30 Oct. 1838, Joseph W. Abbott.

751

CHRISTOPHER TAPPAN[6] CHASE (Charles,[5] John,[4] John,[3] John[2]), born in Hampton Falls, N. H., July 1764; died in 1841. He married 12 Dec. 1786, HANNAH HOOK. They lived in Hampton Falls. He was a blacksmith.

Children, born in Hampton Falls:

       SALLY,[7] b. 23 Sept. 1788; m. (1) May 1805, George Mitchell; m. (2) Currier True; m. (3) Nov. 1821, Winthrop True; m. (4) 5 July 1858, Jonathan Merrill. She d. 15 July 1872.
1865. CHARLES, b. 1789; m. (1) Comfort Philbrick; no children; m. (2) Sally Johnson. He d. 4 Mar. 1844.
       JACOB, b. 1794; m. Susan Harris; d. Jan. 1843; no issue.
       POLLY, b. Oct. 1797; m. 12 Nov. 1826, Jacob Rowe; d. July 1853.

1866.　TAPPAN, b. 21 Sept. 1800; m. 26 May 1825, Abigail[7] Chase of
Seabrook; d. 16 Nov. 1861. She was dau. of Abraham[8]
Chase of Seabrook. (Family 705)

752

WILLIAM S.[6] CHASE (Charles,[5] John,[4] John,[3] John[2]), born in
Hampton Falls, N. H., — July 1764; died in Deering, N. H., 1 July
1859. He married in Kensington, N. H., 26 Sept. 1785, LYDIA GEORGE
of Seabrook, N. H. They removed from Seabrook to Deering in
1789. She died there 5 Feb. 1850.
Children, first born in Seabrook, others in Deering:

MARY,[7] b. — Dec. 1785; m. Dec. 1811, James Whitaker of
Deering; d. 1 Dec. 1865.
SALLY, b. 16 Feb. 1790; m. John Downing, son of Joshua;
no children. He d. 9 Mar. 1868, age 75 y. She d. about 1874.
LYDIA, b. — Aug. 1793; m. John Whitaker of Deering; d. 21
Sept. 1829; no issue survived.
NANCY, b. 17 Mar. 1795; m. Isaac Wilkins of Deering; alive
27 Mar. 1873.
ABIGAIL, b. 16 May 1797; m. James Wilkins; d. 8 Mar. 1818;
he d. 5 Oct. 1852.
BETSEY, b. 1 July 1801; never married; alive in Deering, 1873.

753

REUBEN FOLLANSBEE[6] CHASE (Reuben,[5] Follansbee,[4] Philip,[3]
John[2]), born in Sutton, 10 July 1787; died 18 Dec. 1859. He married
in Sutton, 4 Feb. 1819, SATIRA WALKER, daughter of Asa and Han-
nah (Dudley) Walker, born in Sutton, 25 Sept. 1799. She died in
Sutton, 20 Sept. 1844, aged 44y. 11m. 25d. They lived in Sutton.
Children, born in Sutton:

CATHARINE,[7] b. 15 Feb. 1820.
1867.　JOHN.
MARY ANN.

754

GARDNER[6] CHASE (Thomas Follansbee,[5] Follansbee,[4] Philip,[3]
John[2]), born in Sutton, 1 Apr. 1782; died in Red Hook, N. Y., 1 Jan.
1831. He married in Tivoli, N. Y., 3 Aug. 1815, MARY HATHAWAY
BOURNE who was born 8 Oct. 1788; died 22 Jan. 1863. They lived in
Red Hook, N. Y.
Child:

1868.　THEODORE LIVINGSTONE,[7] b. 23 May 1824; m. 29 Aug. 1864,
Catharine Hughes; lived at 142 South 4th St., Phila.. Pa.

755

CALVIN[6] CHASE (David,[5] Francis,[4] Philip,[3] John[2]), born in Royalston, 15 Sept. 1787; died there 7 Mar. 1827, aged 42. He married
(intention in Royalston, 1 July 1809) in Fitzwilliam, N. H., 10 Jan.
1810, ABIGAIL STONE of Fitzwilliam, daughter of James and Elizabeth (Haven) Stone, born in Fitzwilliam, 25 July 1790. They lived
in Royalston and in Fitzwilliam.

Children, born in Fitzwilliam:

1869. DAVID,[7] b. 30 Apr. 1811; m. Lucy Brigham.
1870. LYMAN, b. 2 Jan. 1813.
    CALVIN, b. 8 Jan. 1815; d. 5 June 1832. Shot by his own. gun.
    JERUSHA, b. 30 Jan. 1817; m. 27 Sept. 1838, Wheaton Wilson.
    HARRIET N., b. 19 Aug. 1819; m. 14 Oct. 1839, Ansell Britton.
1871. ANSELL, b. 24 June 1821.
    ELIZA ANN, b. 31 July 1823; m. 26 Nov. 1845, Edwin Patch.
    ELMIRA, b. 20 Jan. 1826; d. unm. 26 Mar. 1846, in Royalston.

756

CHAUNCEY[6] CHASE (David,[5] Francis,[4] Philip,[3] John[2]), born in Royalston, 22 May 1801; died 26 Feb. 1878. He married in Royalston, 2 Dec. 1830, CAROLINE MORSE, daughter of Russell and Betsey Morse, born in Royalston, 15 Nov. 1808. They lived in Boston and Royalston.

Children, born in Boston:

    CAROLINE AUGUSTA,[7] b. 9 Oct. 1835; m. 1 Nov. 1859, William D. Atkinson.
    ELISABETH WAIT, b. 14 Sept. 1837; unm. 1889.
    ALMIRA ELLIOTT, b. 8 Feb. 1842; d. 16 Sept. 1843.
    HENRIETTA TOWNSEND, b. 13 Jan. 1846; m. 25 Sept. 1866; William Henry Nutting; he d. 23 Nov. 1872.
    ELLA PERKINS, b. 2 Dec. 1849.
    FANNIE RUSSELL, b. 9 Oct. 1853; m. 26 June 1872, Frank W. Adams, M.D.; lived in Fishkill, N. Y.

757

CAPT. WILLIAM[6] CHASE (William,[5] Francis,[4] Philip,[3] John[2]), born in Royalston, 12 Mar. 1796; married in Fitzwilliam, N. H., 19 Mar. 1822, ROXANA BLODGETT, daughter of Timothy and Elizabeth (Stiles) Blodgett, born in Fitzwilliam, 13 Sept. 1801; died in Royalston, 24 Feb. 1837, aged 35. He married (2) in Winchendon, 10 May 1838, MRS. OLIVE A. LANGLEY of Winchendon. He died 10 May 1866. They lived in Royalston.

Children, born in Royalston:

1872. EDWIN STILES,[7] b. 7 Aug. 1824; d. in Boston, 12 Oct. 1896.
    HARRIET, b. 19 May 1826; m. Caleb May, Cedar Falls, Iowa.
    MARTHA AMSDEN, b. 6 Apr. 1828; mar.; five children; Cedar Falls.
1873. WILLIAM MILTON, b. 27 Aug. 1830; lived in Worcester; mar.
    ELLEN ROXANA, b. 12 Dec. 1831; m. Grundy May; five children; Cedar Falls.
1874. JOSEPH, b. 10 Dec. 1832; d. 15 Sept. 1907; m. 23 Apr. 1860, Sarah Jane Overman. Six children, including *William Milton*,[8] b. 24 Oct. 1862; d. 19 Dec. 1920; m. 24 Oct. 1893, Bess Bomboy. Their son Homer Bomboy,[9] b. 15 Aug. 1894; m. 28 Jan. 1928, Helen Peers, b. in Duluth, Minn., 6 Jan. 1900. He is a lawyer in St. Paul, Minn., and lives in Albert Lea, Minn.
1875. FRANCIS NEWELL, b. 9 Mar. 1835.

758

THOMAS FOLLANSBEE[6] CHASE (William,[5] Lt. Francis,[4] Philip,[3] John[2]), born in Royalston, 22 Mar. 1807; married 19 July 1837, ELIZABETH P. GOODRICH. He had a dry goods store at 319 Washington Street, Boston, 1838 to 1840 and later at 368 Washington Street; still later at 2 Oak Place, Boston.

759

GEORGE[6] CHASE (William,[5] Francis,[4] Philip,[3] John[2]), born in Royalston, 1 Nov. 1810; married there, 2 Sept. 1835, ESTHER MORSE, daughter of Russell and Betsey Morse, born in Royalston, 2 Jan. 1813. They lived in Royalston.

Children, born in Royalston:

1876.　GEORGE LYMAN,[7] b. 11 Dec. 1838; m. 28 May 1860, Elvira Tyrrell; wounded and died in battle in the Civil War, 8 June 1864.

CATHARINE ELIZA, b. 16 Apr. 1840; m. 31 Dec. 1865, Josiah Wilder; lived in Petersham.

FREDERICK BOYDEN, b. 7 Feb. 1843; d. 7 Nov. 1867, unm.

HELEN MARIA, b. 23 Nov. 1846; m. Dec. 1868, Forest A. Hicks of Petersham.

HARRIET ELISABETH, b. 14 Jan. 1848; m. 28 Nov. 1872, Luther Stone of Petersham. She d. 22 Oct. 1874.

A son, d. unm.

760

FRANCIS[6] CHASE (William,[5] Francis,[4] Philip,[3] John[2]), born in Royalston, 2 Apr. 1812; married (1) probably in Paxton, 1 Jan. 1840, RUTH SLADE of Paxton, daughter of John and Lucretia Slade, born in Paxton, 17 Jan. 1818. She died in Royalston, 26 June 1846, aged 28y. 5m. He married (2) probably in Paxton, 9 Sept. 1847, LUCRETIA SLADE, sister to his first wife, born in Paxton, 19 Feb. 1822; died in Royalston, 15 Jan. 1864. He was living in Royalston in 1874.

Children by first wife, born in Royalston:

LUCRETIA,[7] b. 13 Mar. 1841; m. (1) 17 Apr. 1861, Charles W. Allard. He d. 15 Sept. 1862; m. (2) 22 Aug. 1863, Edgar J. Allard; lived in South Bend, Ind., 1874.

1877.　WILLIAM HENRY, b. 18 June 1843; lived in Athol, 1874.

JOHN SLADE, b. 25 Aug. 1844; d. 31 Aug. 1864, in Andersonville Prison.

Children by second wife, born in Royalston:

1878.　THOMAS F., b. 11 Aug. 1848; m. 4 July 1873, Anna Alden.

SOPHIA ELIZABETH, b. 20 Sept. 1849; m. 4 Apr. 1871, Allen Harrington.

SARAH M., b. 14 Aug. 1851.

GEORGE W., b. 17 Dec. 1852; d. 13 Feb. 1873.

JOSEPH H., b. 30 Apr. 1854; d. 1 Oct. 1871.

FLORA E., b. 6 June 1856.

1879.　CHARLES F., b. 15 Jan. 1858.

ELLA A., b. 2 Mar. 1860.

FANNIE R., b. 1 Apr. 1862.

761

ELIPHALET[6] CHASE (Archibald C.,[5] Lt. Francis,[4] Philip,[3] John[2]),
born in Royalston, 28 July 1790; married there, 28 July 1813, HAN-
NAH GARFIELD, daughter of Joshua and Abigail Garfield, born in
Royalston, 25 June 1794. He left the country in 1813 and never
was heard from.

762

LORING[6] CHASE (Archibald C,[5] Francis,[4] Philip,[3] John[2]), born
in Royalston, 31 Aug. 1798; died 14 Jan. 1875. He married (1) in
1822, ELIZA BOLTON, daughter of John and Cynthia (Chamberlain)
Bolton, born in Danville, Vt., 20 May 1807. He married (2) widow
CASSANDRA BROWN. They lived in Flanders, Vt., and Royalston.

Children by first wife, born in Flanders, last six born in Royalston:

    EMILY MORRILL,[7] b. 27 Nov. 1828; m. Sylvanus Kendall.
1880. JOHN BOLTON, b. 14 Feb. 1825; m. Kate Chapman.
    CYNTHIA C., b. 14 July 1827.
1881. LORING, b. 5 May 1828.
    MARY BOLTON, b. 7 Sept. 1830; m. John Lamb.
1882. ALVIN BOLTON, b. 7 Feb. 1836.
    ELIZA BOLTON, b. 5 Apr. 1838; d. 26 Jan. 1842.
    ELLEN BOLTON, b. 20 Apr. 1841.
    ELIZA MARIA, b. Dec. 1842.
    ELMORE, b. 6 July 1844; d. 23 Nov. 1844.

763

ARCHIBALD[6] CHASE (Archibald C.,[5] Francis,[4] Philip,[3] John[2]),
born in Royalston, 4 Mar. 1804; married (1) in Royalston, 5 Oct.
1825, LORINDA BARTLETT, daughter of Jonas and Hannah (Bachelor)
Bartlett, born in Royalston, 15 Aug. 1803; died there, 4 July 1837.
He married (2) 5 Dec. 1839, widow LYDIA ANN HASTINGS of Waltham. They lived in Royalston and Winchendon. He was alive, 11
Dec. 1870.

Children by first wife, born in Royalston:

    ROSILLA BARTLETT,[7] b. 7 Apr. 1826; m. 12 Dec. 1845, William
      Crandall of Providence, R. I.
1883. LUKE SWAIN, b. 16 Nov. 1827; m. 20 June 1853, Almira J. Lis-
      comb of Providence, R. I.
1884. IRA PIERCE, b. 5 Sept. 1829; m. in Providence, R. I., 4 July
      1852, Abby Reed, dau. of Augusta of Winchendon.
1885. HARVEY HOLMAN, b. 30 Sept. 1831; m. 22 May 1852, Lucy Ann
      Beal ot Winchendon; lived in Providence, R. I.
1886. HENRY EDDY, b. 17 Dec. 1833; m. 5 May 1861, Margaretta M.
      Lopez. He was killed in the battle of Cedar Run, 19 Oct.
      1864.

Children by second wife:

    ELVIRA LORINDA, b. 28 Jan. 1841; never married.
    GEORGE WALTER, b. 25 Mar. 1842; d. unm. 19 Dec. 1873.

764

ELMORE[6] CHASE (Archibald C.,[5] Lt. Francis,[4] Philip,[3] John[2]),
born 7 Apr. 1807. He married CYNTHIA HILL and lived in Concord,
Vt. He was treasurer of the Universalist Church of Concord in 1835.
Children, not in order:

> ELMORE,[7] was principal of the High School in West Concord
> about 1866.
> CYNTHIA H., m. in 1872, John H. Walbridge of Concord.
> Three children.

765

GEORGE[6] CHASE (Archibald C.,[5] Lt. Francis,[4] Philip,[3] John[2]),
was born 20 July 1808; living in Concord, Vt., in 1874. He married
EUNICE ABBOTT, daughter of Barachias and Anna (Colburn) Abbott
of Landgrove, Vt., born 21 Jan. 1805. (Abbott Genealogical Register, 16). They removed to Concord, in 1842.
Children, eldest born in Landgrove:

1887. ELMORE,[7] living in Jacksonville, Fla., in 1885.
SOPHIA, m. Edwin Guild of Walpole, N. H.
1888. WILLARD, b. in Landgrove, in 1840; m. in 1868, Ann M. Lee,
dau. of David W. Lee; representative 1878; lived in Concord.
SALLY, m. 8 May 1872, Riley D. Pratt of Concord.
MARY A., m. in 1870, John Pratt of Concord.

766

WILLARD[6] CHASE (Archibald C.,[5] Lt. Francis,[4] Philip,[3] John[2]),
born in Concord, Vt., 4 Feb. 1814; died there 1863. He married and
lived in Concord.
Child:

1889. FRANCIS NEWELL,[7] lived in Cedar Falls, Iowa, 1875.

767

CHARLES[6] CHASE (Archibald C.,[5] Lt. Francis,[4] Philip,[3] John[2]),
born in Concord, Vt., 19 Nov. 1819; living in West Concord in 1874.
He was high sheriff of Essex Co., Vt., in 1863 and 1864. He was the
first postmaster at West Concord in 1849. His family has not been
reported.

768

SILAS[6] CHASE, (Charles,[5] Francis,[4] Philip,[3] John[2]), born in
Winchendon, 27 Nov. 1794; died there, 2 Apr. 1876. He married
(intention in Royalston, 19 Apr. 1817) NANCY PRATT, daughter of
Joseph and Sarah (Hunt) Pratt of Fitzwilliam, N. H. She was born,
5 Oct. 1795, and died in Winchendon, 21 May 1873. They lived in
Winchendon but were buried in Fitzwilliam.
Children:

1890. CHARLES,[7] b. about 1822; m. 14 Mar. 1848, Ann S. Thomas.
SARAH, b. about 1827; m. 22 Sept. 1845, John Nolan.
1891. EDWIN, supposed to be a son.

769

CHARLES[6] CHASE (Charles,[5] Francis,[4] Philip,[3] John[2]), born in
Winchendon, 11 Jan. 1806; died there, 18 Mar. 1871. He married,
6 Jan. 1832, PERSIS CALL of Williston, Vt. They lived in Winchendon. No children have been found.

770

DANIEL[6] CHASE (Charles,[5] Francis,[4] Philip,[3] John[2]), born in
Jaffrey, N. H., 16 July 1814; married (intention at Winchendon, 9
July 1837) 16 July 1837, MARY HALE, daughter of Jacob and Betsey
(Brown) Hale, born in Winchendon 20 Nov. 1815. They lived in
Winchendon till about 1854 when they removed to Crystal Lake,
Iowa, where they were living in 1874.

Children, first seven born in Winchendon, others in Fitzwilliam,
N. H.:

> MARY AMANDA,[7] b. 12 June 1838; m. 3 June 1862, S. F.
> Bowker.
> LAURA A., b. 16 Aug. 1840; d. 22 Aug. 1853.
> 1892. DANIEL W., b. 22 Apr. 1843; m. 1 Jan. 1869, Amanda M.
> Derby.
> WILLIAM WALLACE, b. 18 June 1845; d. 23 Oct. 1847.
> HARRIET E., b. 18 June 1849; m. 4 Apr. 1866, Josiah J. Hardie
> of Fitzwilliam, N. H.
> ANDREW J., b. 21 Nov. 1851; never married.
> FLORA A., b. 8 Sept. 1853; d. 7 July 1872.
> 1893. WILLIAM F., b. 16 Mar. 1856.
> 1894. MORRILL D., b. 8 Nov. 1857.
> EMMA A., b. 28 Aug. 1859.
> WARREN E., b. 10 June 1863; d. 4 Feb. 1864.

771

DANIEL[6] CHASE (Francis,[5] Francis,[4] Philip,[3] John[2]), born in
Concord, Vt., 22 Dec. 1802; died 5 Apr. 1874. He married in Holland, Vt., 18 Apr. 1830, ISABEL DICKEY. They lived in Salem, Vt.,
Compton, P. Q., and Boer River, P. Q.

Children, born in Salem, Vt.:

> MARY JANE,[7] b. 21 Dec. 1830; m. 7 June 1865, Mason D. Caswell.
> SARAH A., b. 26 Apr. 1832; m. in Compton, P. Q., 11 Jan. 1860,
> Willard H. Glidden. She d. 3 Apr. 1861. No children.
> 1895. EDGAR, b. 18 Aug. 1837; m. 14 Feb. 1861, Ellen C. Batchelder.
> Five children.

772

FRANCIS[6] CHASE (Francis,[5] Francis,[4] Philip,[3] John[2]), born in
Derby, Vt., 30 Nov. 1808; married (1) 20 Mar. 1835, RHODA PARSONS of Hatley, P. Q. She died 18 May 1842. He married (2) 29
Mar. 1843, MRS. MARY SHATTUCK of Montpelier, Vt. They were
living in West Charleston, Vt., as late as 1870.

Children by first wife, born in Charleston, Vt.;

> AMANDA M.,[7] b. 24 Jan. 1836; m. (1) 4 Dec. 1855, Dennis
> Hamblett; m. (2) 28 Nov. 1860, John Colburn.

PERSIS M., b. 13 Aug. 1838; m. 14 Feb. 1859, Joseph Lyon.
Child by second wife, born in Charleston:
>   MARY MALONA, b. 2 Feb. 1845; m. 12 Sept. 1865, Dr. Abram
>   Prescott Brown.

773

NATHAN[6] CHASE (Francis,[5] Francis,[4] Philip,[3] John[2]), born in
Sutton, Vt., 19 Mar. 1814; married in Charleston, Vt., 20 Mar. 1842,
DELIGHT HUTCHINSON who was born in Concord, Vt., 8 July 1812.
They were living in East Charleston, Vt., as late as 1879.
>   Children, born in Charleston:
>   MARTHA L.,[7] b. 22 June 1843; m. 26 Sept. 1863, Louis Moffat.
>   CHARLES M., b. 15 Nov. 1846; d. 13 Sept. 1855.
>   MARY S., b. 18 Jan. 1848; m. 28 Feb. 1867, William S. Moulton.
>   ELLEN P., b. 30 May 1849; m. 19 May 1870, Carlos Barnes.

774

GEORGE W.[6] CHASE (Francis,[5] Francis,[4] Philip,[3] John[2]), born in
Sutton, 27 Sept. 1816; married in Barnston, Can., 5 Nov. 1843, OR-
ILLA MINER, born in Burke, Vt., 23 June 1822.   They lived in Barn-
ston and Compton, P. Q., and at Moer River, P. Q., in 1873.
>   Children:
>   ELLEN A.,[7] b. 1 Mar. 1846; m. 7 Dec. 1871, Willis B. Hodge.
>   SUSAN AMELIA, b. 11 Nov. 1847.
>   MARTHA MARILLA, b. 10 Feb. 1852; m. 23 Jan. 1873, Austin L.
>   Farnham of Island Pond, Vt.
>   SARAH JANE, b. 30 Oct. 1853.
>   IOLA ELLA, b. 29 Jan. 1856; m. 3 Oct. 1874, John D. Dwyer of
>   Bedford, N. H.

775

DANIEL[6] CHASE (Daniel,[5] Lt. Francis,[4] Philip,[3] John[2]), born
and was living in Bedford, Cuyahoga Co., Ohio, in 1873.   He is supposed to have died there between 1888 and 1896.

776

PAUL[6] CHASE (Carr,[5] Paul,[4] Charles,[3] John[2]), born in Campton,
N. H., 8 Apr. 1785; died 16 Oct. 1865.   He married in Rumney, N.
H., 28 Feb. 1811, BETSEY HAYNES, daughter of James and Betsey
Haynes of Campton.   She died in Lawrence 12 June 1867.   He was a
tanner, shoemaker and trader.   They lived in Franconia, N. H.
>   Children:

1896.   JOSEPH C.,[7] b. 7 Oct. 1812; m. (1) 20 Oct. 1830, Lucretia
>   Demick; she d. 10 July 1847; m. (2) 30 Nov. 1847, Fanny
>   T. Gaylord.   He d. 1859.
>   RHODA, b. 27 May 1814; m. (1) 26 Aug. 1830, Albert Carlton;
>   m. (2) Richard T. Martin; lived in Lawrence.
>   LOUISA, b. 4 Mar. 1816; d. 12 Jan. 1817.
>   BETSEY, b. 1 Oct. 1818; m. 24 July 1833, Lewis Bates Demick.
>   AMANDA, b. 13 Sept. 1820; m. 8 Mar. 1840, Samuel T. Jones;
>   d. Jan. 1866.
1897.   GEORGE W. R., b. 16 Nov. 1822; m. 5 Oct. 1845, Eleanor Steph-
>   ens; lived in Franconia.

1898. JAMES HAYNES, b. 15 Sept. 1824; m. 11 Jan. 1854; Ellen D. Godfrey; lived in Boston.
1899. HARVEY, b. 8 July 1827; m. 3 Aug. 1850, Betsey A. Hall; lived in Cleveland, Ohio.
LUCY A. R., b. 7 Apr. 1830; d. 12 June 1832.
HARRIET M., b. 14 June 1832; m. 23 Apr. 1853, George S. Rollins; lived in Lowell.
LYMAN, b. 20 Sept. 1834; d. unm. 28 July 1849.
PAUL, b. 6 Nov. 1836; worked in New Orleans on a railroad; d. unm.

777

TIMOTHY[6] CHASE (Carr,[5] Paul,[4] Charles,[3] John[2]), born in Campton, N. H., 12 Apr. 1787; died 15 Feb. 1865. He married (1) 4 Nov. 1818, MEHITABLE SMITH, daughter of Nathaniel and Mary (Dalton) Smith, of Sanbornton, N. H. She was born 29 Apr. 1795 and died in Campton, 28 Mar. 1847, in her 52d y. He married (2) SALLY (ROBINSON) HUSE. They lived in Campton.
Children by first wife, born in Campton:
MARY ANN,[7] b. 18 Aug. 1819; m. 1844, Charles H. Smith, son of Capt. Elisha; lived in Campton.
1900. MOSES S., b. 13 Mar. 1821; m. (1) 1846, Lydia B. Smith, dau. of Robert of Campton; m. (2) ——— ———; lived in Chicago, Ill. Six children.
NATHANIEL S., b. 13 Dec. 1822; d. young.
LOUISA A., b. 1 May 1824; m. 1858, David Tilton, a farmer, of Alexandria, N. H.
1901. WALTER, b. 16 Oct. 1825; m. 9 Apr. 1850, Eliza A. Rogers, dau. of John and Abigail (Burbie) Rogers. He was a Baptist clergyman in New Gloucester, Me. Six children.
CHARLES, d. young.
TIMOTHY, d. young.
JONATHAN S., d. young.
1902. JOHN C., b. 12 Oct. 1834; served in the Civil War; lived West Swanzey, N. H.
MARTHA JANE, b. 22 Sept. 1837; m. 1863, Henry Cook of Campton; lived in Minnesota.

778

CHARLES[6] CHASE (Carr,[5] Paul,[4] Charles,[3] John[2]), born in Campton, N. H., 14 Apr. 1791; married (1) in Mar. 1818, MARY CALEF, daughter of Oliver and Elizabeth (Melcher) Calef of Sanbornton, N. H. She died in Campton, 13 Aug. 1823. He married (2) Dec. 1824, widow MARY A. CASS of Hill, N. H. She died 26 Feb. 1853. They lived in Campton.
Children by first wife, born in Campton:
1903. JOHN W.,[7] b. 25 Feb. 1819; m. 23 July 1843, Emily P. Darling, of Campton; lived in Rumney, N. H.
1904. SAMUEL R., b. 11 Jan. 1821; m. 5 Aug. 1852, Clarinda J. Foss.
MARY, b. 17 Aug. 1823; m. 16 Oct. 1862, Peabody Palmer of Campton; lived in Plymouth, N. H.

779

CARR[6] CHASE (Carr,[5] Paul,[4] Charles,[3] John[2]), born in Campton, N. H., 5 Aug. 1794; married in Mar. 1816, ANNA HUSE, daughter of Carr and Sarah (Buell) Huse.

Children:

SARAH ANN,[7] m. Parker Cass; d. before 1870.

1905. SOLOMON ROWE, living in Havana, Ill., in 1872.

780

SILAS WILLIAM COOPER[6] CHASE (Joseph,[5] Paul,[4] Charles,[3] John[2]), born in Newburyport, 11 Apr. 1773; married in Boston, 26 Nov. 1807, MARY SYMONDS of Boston. She died in New York, 21 July, 1836. He died in Savannah, Ga., in Nov. 1818. They lived in Burlington, Vt., and Philadelphia, Pa. He was an officer in the army in 1812.

Children, first born in Newton, N. H., second to fourth in Burlington, Vt., last in Philadelphia, Pa.:

1906. ALGERNON SYDNEY,[7] b. 3 Nov. 1808; m. 31 Dec. 1833, Mary Augusta Tilden; lived in New York City.

1907. AUTUMNUS SIMONDS, b. 30 Aug. 1810; m. 20 Sept. 1832, Mary Ann Peterson of Boston; d. in Nevada, Cal., 1851.

JULIA ANN CASCALINE, b. 15 Feb. 1812; m. Nathaniel Dunbar of Boston; d. in Canton, 19 Oct. 1834.

JOCASTA COLINA, b. 26 Dec. 1813; d. 30 Oct. 1818, in Boston.

ALEXIS SERENO, b. 25 Feb. 1816; d. 28 Feb. 1816, in Philadelphia, Pa.

781

REV. PAUL[6] CHASE (Joseph,[5] Paul,[4] Charles,[3] John[2]), born in South Hampton, N. H., 3 Mar. 1782; married (1) Mar. 1804, MARY CURRIER who died 19 Mar. 1845. He married (2) 3 May 1845, MARY DRAKE. She died 2 Dec. 1859. He married (3) 8 May 1860, DEBORAH (WRIGHT) SHEDD, widow of Benjamin Shedd and daughter of Ephriam and Rebecca (Shedd) Wright. She died 5 Oct. 1870. They lived in Groton, N. H., and in Newport, N. H. He was living there in 1870 in his 88th year.

Children by first wife:

1908. JOHN CURRIER,[7] b. 3 Mar. 1808; m. 8 Feb. 1830, Elisabeth Farmer Currier of Newton, N. H. They lived in Haverhill in 1870.

1909. JOSEPH SIMONDS, b. 2 June 1811; m. 12 July 1839, Hannah Fitz of Chester, N. H.

AURILLA, b. 25 Mar. 1815; m. 13 Nov. 1837, Moses Kelley of Rumney, N. H.

782

CHARLES CARR[6] CHASE (Joseph,[5] Paul,[4] Charles,[3] John[2]), born in Peekskill, N. Y., 13 June 1786; died in Woodhull, Steuben Co., N. Y., 4 Aug. 1861. He married in Palatine, N. Y., 19 Aug. 1810, EVA SCHRAM. They lived in Palatine, St. Johnsville, Manheim and Danube, N. Y. His sister wrote that he died at Painted Post, N. Y.

Children, first two born in Palatine, N. Y.:

1910. ISAAC,[7] b. 1 Nov. 1811.
1911. REUBEN, b. 21 Apr. 1813; m. 15 Jan. 1835, Elisabeth Esterbrooks.
1912. WILLIAM H., b. 18 Nov. 1815, in Manheim, N. Y.
1913. JACOB, b. 28 June 1818, in Danube, N. Y.; lived in Buffalo, N. Y.
SARAH L., b. 2 Feb. 1821, in Manheim.
1914. JOHN C., b. 21 Jan. 1824, in Manheim; lived in Fitchburg, Mich.
1915. CHARLES J., b. 29 Oct. 1832, in Manheim.

783

STEPHEN[6] CHASE (Joseph,[5] Paul,[4] Charles,[3] John[2]), born about 1795; married and lived perhaps in Richmond, Oswego Co., N. Y., for a time.
Children:

1916. NATHANIEL,[7] lived in Bethel, N. Y.
1917. HENRY, b. 29 June 1820; lived at Lake Zurich, Ill.

784

STEPHEN[6] CHASE (Jonathan,[5] Jonathan,[4] Charles,[3] John[2]), born in Newburyport, 2 Apr. 1769; died there, 1789, aged 20 years. Administration upon the estate of Stephen Chase of Newburyport, mariner, was granted to Jonathan Chase, housewright, with Stephen Huse, Esq. and Jonathan Chase, yeoman, sureties, 25 July 1789. (Essex Probate, 57:268).

785

WILLIAM[6] CHASE (Jonathan,[5] Jonathan,[4] Charles,[3] John[2]), born in Newburyport, 29 Sept. 1770; died there 7 Dec. 1804, aged 34. He married in Newburyport, 9 Feb. 1794, SARAH COUCH, daughter of Joseph and Sarah Couch, born in Newburyport, 29 Oct. 1773; died there 20 Aug. 1802, aged 28.
Children, born in Newburyport:

HANNAH,[7] b. 4 May 1795; m. 25 Oct. 1818, Adam McCullock of Kennebunk, Me. Eight children. She d. 19 Oct. 1870, aged 75.
ELIZABETH RUSSELL, b. 17 Dec. 1796; d. 12 Nov. 1849, aged 53; probably m. 17 Nov. 1839, Charles Knight.

786

ELIPHALET[6] CHASE (Jonathan,[5] Jonathan,[4] Charles,[3] John[2]), born in Newburyport, 25 Mar. 1778; died 20 Nov. 1817.

787

JOHN[6] CHASE (Stephen,[5] Jonathan,[4] Charles,[3] John[2]), born in Newburyport, 3 Apr. 1773.

787a

STEPHEN[6] CHASE (Stephen,[5] Jonathan,[4] Charles,[3] John[2]), born probably in Newburyport during the Revolutionary War. Administration was granted on his father's estate 25 July 1785.

Joshua Chase was appointed guardian unto Stephen Chase, son of Stephen Chase, late of Newburyport, with Jonathan Chase and Robert Rogers sureties, 13 June 1794. (Essex Probate, 63:128). His grandfather's estate was divided, 9 Apr. 1805, and no grandson Stephen is mentioned therein. Neither his marriage nor the birth of any son has been found.

Child:

1918.   STEPHEN,[7] alive 13 June 1794.

788

STEPHEN[6] CHASE (Rev. Joshua,[5] Jonathan,[4] Charles,[3] John[2]). born 3 Feb. 1788; married in Berwick, Me., 10 June 1810, ADAH EMERY, daughter of Joshua and Hannah (Goodwin) Emery. She was born in Berwick, Jan. 1789. They lived in South Berwick and Portland, Me. He died in Portland, 28 Aug. 1872.

Children, born in South Berwick, Me.:

1919.   STEPHEN,[7] b. 8 June 1811; m. 14 Mar. 1841, Mary Ann Lane; d. at sea, 1863. Their daughter *Mary Ann,*[8] b. in Brooklyn, N. Y., 5 Dec. 1854; m. 18 Sept. 1879, Frederick Burton Hemingway.

1920.   WILLIAM W.,[7] b. Feb. 1815; d. in Apr. 1890; m. Susan Johnson who d. in Feb. 1891. Their son *Stephen,*[8] b. in Portland, Me., 7 Sept. 1857; m. June 1878, Flora E. Merchant, b. in Isle au Haut, Me., 9 Jan. 1861; d. in Everett, Wash., 30 July 1906. Their daughter Edith,[9] b. in Portland, 14 June 1886, m. 20 Sept. 1911, Chris Frederick Moe, b. 21 Aug. 1886. Children: Chris Frederick Jr.,[10] b. 26 Mar. 1916 and William Chase[10] Moe, b. 25 Nov. 1916, in Seattle, Wash.

789

CAPT. JONATHAN[6] CHASE (Rev. Joshua,[5] Jonathan,[4] Charles,[3] John[2]), born 3 Feb. 1790; died in Westbrook, Me., 23 Mar. 1881, aged 91; married in Berwick, Me., 3 Feb. 1811, TIRZAH EMERY, daughter of Joshua and Hannah (Goodwin) Emery, born in Ber- wick, in June 1791. They lived on Jewell's Island in Casco Bay for over 50 years from 1828 to 1878. On 16 June 1821, Capt. Chase, in command of the sloop *Embargo,* was captured by Spanish pirates, wounded but escaped.

Children:

1921.   JOSHUA[7] (twin).
1922.   BENJAMIN (twin).
1923.   AUGUSTUS.
         TIRZAH.
         ADAH.
         HANNAH.
1924.   JOHN.
1925.   SIMON.
         EMILY.

790

BENJAMIN PETTINGILL[6] CHASE (Rev. Joshua,[5] Jonathan,[4] Charles,[3] John[2]), born 3 Jan. 1794; married HANNAH EMERY, probably daughter of Joshua and Hannah (Goodwin) Emery, born in Berwick, Me., Feb. 1798.

791

JOSHUA[6] CHASE (Rev. Joshua,[5] Jonathan,[4] Charles,[3] John[2]), born 14 July 1798; married 16 Feb. 1819, CLARISSA EMERY, daughter of Joshua and Hannah (Goodwin) Emery, born in Berwick, Me., June 1800.

Children:

1926. JONATHAN.[7]
1927. STEPHEN.
1928. EDWARD.
1929. CHARLES.
        MARY ELIZABETH.
        HANNAH.
1930. JOSHUA.

792

JAMES[6] CHASE (Rev. Joshua,[5] Jonathan,[4] Charles,[3] John[2]), born 1 Mar. 1805; married 9 Mar. 1835, ALMIRA PAINE. They lived in Brooklyn, N. Y.

793

JOSEPH[6] CHASE (Amos,[5] Dea. Ezra,[4] Jacob,[3] John[2]), born in Amesbury, 15 Aug. 1774; died in Amesbury, 4 Aug. 1829, aged 54y. He entered his intention of marriage at Haverhill, 10 Aug. 1794, with ELIZABETH ATWOOD of Atkinson, N. H. There were no children. He was a physician and lived in Amesbury.

794

WILLIAM DAVIS STICKNEY[6] CHASE (Dea. William,[5] Dea. Ezra,[4] Jacob,[3] John[2]), born in Haverhill, 18 Mar. 1792; died 13 Feb. 1867. He married in Haverhill, 3 Dec. 1817, ZELENDA GAGE of Bradford. She was daughter of Uriah and Hannah (Tenney) Gage, born in Bradford, 15 Aug. 1791.

Children, born in Haverhill:

        ZELENDA GAGE,[7] b. 30 Nov. 1818; d. unm. 13 Nov. 1843.
        JULIA ANN, b. 1 May 1820; m. 9 May 1839, John Nichols.
1931. JAMES MUNROE, b. 25 Mar. 1822; m. (1) Mary Elizabeth Jenkins; m. (2) Abbie Maria Cheney.
        ABIGAIL GOVE, b. 9 Feb. 1824; m. 1845, Giles Merrill Kelley.
        MARY FRANCES, b. 20 Aug. 1826; m. 1855, Samuel P. Crocker.
1932. WILLIAM STICKNEY, b. 12 June 1828; m. Lydia Gove; lived in Berlin, Vt. He d. 6 Oct. 1881.

795

JOHN[6] CHASE (Jacob,[5] John,[4] Jacob,[3] John[2]), born in Londonderry, N. H. He married MARY BARRON of Pepperell. They went West to Blackwater, No. Dakota.

796

JONAS[6] CHASE (Jacob,[5] John,[4] Jacob,[3] John[2]), born in Londonderry, N. H.; died in Westford, N. Y., 1 Aug. 1818. He married in Londonderry, about 1799, EUNICE HARDY, daughter of Nathan Hardy of Stoddard, N. H. They removed to Unity, N. H., and to Stoddard, and in Sept. 1810, they removed to Westport, N. Y. She married (2) Edward Phelps of Stoddard.

Children, first five born in Stoddard:

MARGARET,[7] b. 25 Aug. 1800; m. 14 Nov. 1821, Isaac P. Knapp of Westport, N. Y.

1933.   NATHAN H., b. 26 Mar. 1802; m. Sally Felt in Elizabethtown, N. Y.; d. 19 June 1847.

MARY, b. 8 Oct. 1804; m. Lewis W. Daniels of Lawrence, St. Lawrence Co., N. Y.

ANNA, b. about 1806; d. in the summer of 1811.

1934.   HIRAM, b. 11 Oct. 1808; m. 5 Nov. 1835, Almina Fisher, dau. of Abijah Fisher of Chazey, N. Y.; d. Apr. 1852; lived in Piatt Co., Ill.

PERSIS, b. in Westport, Essex Co., N. Y.; d. Mar. 1813.

1935.   HARRISON, b. 26 Feb. 1814; m. 3 Nov. 1838, Lavina Willis. He d. 21 Sept. 1844, in Westport.

1936.   DANIEL, b. Westport; d. 5 Aug. 1853.

797

JACOB[6] CHASE (Jacob,[5] John,[4] Jacob,[3] John[2]), born in Londonderry, N. H., 22 May 1768; died in Unity, N. H., 6 Nov. 1865. He married in Hopkinton, N. H., 28 Mar. 1796, RHODA SARGENT of Hopkinton. They lived in Deering, N. H., and in Unity.

Children, born in Deering:

1937.   JACOB,[7] b. 6 Feb. 1797; m. (1) 6 Jan. 1825, Dorothy Quimby; m. (2) 28 Feb. 1830, Sarah Marshall; d. 6 Nov. 1865.

1938.   CHEVEY, b. 21 July 1798; m. 4 Oct. 1835, Clarissa Gould, dau. of Elias and Sally Gould of Henniker.

SALLY, b. 21 Feb. 1801; d. 14 Jan. 1815.

1939.   STEPHEN SARGENT, b. 27 June 1803; m. Orpha Smith of Claremont, N. H.; lived in Moriah, N. Y.

RHODA, b. 3 July 1806; d. 1 Jan. 1815.

LYDIA, b. 6 Sept. 1808; m. 28 Mar. 1830, Walker Marshall of Lempster; removed to De Soto, Wis.

ELMIRA, b. 9 June 1810; m. 15 Nov. 1832, Thomas Smith; lived in Unity and Moriah, N. Y.

798

SAMUEL[6] CHASE (Jacob,[5] John,[4] Jacob,[3] John[2]), born in Londonderry, N. H., 22 June 1780; died in Essex, Essex Co., N. Y., 13 Oct. 1842. He married Nov. 1808, ELIZABETH McCOY of Goffstown, N. H., who was born in Goffstown, 3 Oct. 1785 and died 23 June 1857. They lived in Bennington, Vt., Hartford, Vt., and Essex, N. Y.

Children, first three born in Bennington, last two in Hartford:

MARY JANE,[7] b. 14 Aug. 1810; d. 29 June 1831.

GILMAN, b. 7 May 1812; d. 8 Feb. 1813.

LOUISA, b. 17 June 1814; d. 22 Feb. 1840.

1940. SAMUEL A., b. 11 July 1816; d. 22 Dec. 1852.
BETSEY M., b. 15 Nov. 1819; m. 8 Aug. 1865, Daniel P. Putnam; lived in Whallonsburg, Essex Co., N. Y., 1875.

799

THOMAS[6] CHASE (Jacob,[5] John,[4] Jacob,[3] John[2]), born in Londonderry, N. H., 15 Dec. 1783; died there 11 Apr. 1859. He married (1) 14 Mar. 1809, MARY PLUMMER, daughter of Nathan and Mary (Palmer) Plummer. She was born 20 Dec. 1783 and died in Londonderry, 15 May 1820. He married (2) 10 Apr. 1821, MARY GILES, daughter of Samuel Giles, who was born 22 Aug. 1794 and died 20 Jan. 1869. They lived in Londonderry.

Children by first wife, born in Londonderry:

> ELISABETH PLUMMER,[7] b. 9 July 1809; d. unm. 1 Jan. 1840.
> EDMUND, b. 12 Dec. 1810; d. 5 July 1823.
> NATHAN PLUMMER, b. 15 June 1812; m. 13 Oct. 1843, Mary Jane Whidden of Londonderry. Lived in Nashua, N. H. No children.
> MARY PLUMMER, b. 19 Mar. 1814; m. 23 Apr. 1840, Lewis A. Watson; she d. abt. 1851; had three children, all dead; lived in Boston.
> INFANT SON, b. 11 July 1816; d. Aug. 1816.
> SARAH A., b. 22 Oct. 1817; m. 1 Dec. 1842, Albert Corning, b. 14 Dec. 1814; lived in Manchester, N. H.
> MARGARET C., b. 12 May 1818; m. 3 Oct. 1843, Albert N. Scott, b. 3 Oct. 1811, in Vermont; lived Boston.
> SUSAN C., b. 12 May 1820; m. 3 Sept. 1839, Harrison Jack of Chester, N. H.

Children by second wife, born in Londonderry:

> SILPHIA G., b. 27 Jan. 1822; d. 9 Feb. 1823.
> ACHSAH P., b. 15 May 1823; m. 4 Sept. 1845, Benjamin Warren Corning; lived in Manchester.
> SALLY M., b. 24 Nov. 1824; d. 9 Dec. 1862; m. 7 Apr. 1852, Samuel L. Corning.

1941. > JAMES GILES, b. 26 Mar. 1826; d. 21 Apr. 1865; lived in Manchester; m. 18 Nov. 1852, Achsah J. Webster.
> JUDITH M., b. 22 Aug. 1828; m. 14 Oct. 1852, John Hatch of Auburn, N. H.
> TRYPHOSA L., b. 29 May 1831; m. 22 Jan. 1867, Ezra B. or George B. McQuestin of Litchfield, N. H.
> HARRIET, b. 26 July 1834; d. 13 Dec. 1834.

800

DANIEL[6] CHASE (Jacob,[5] John,[4] Jacob,[3] John[2]), born in Londonderry, N. H.; married in Mar. 1814, his cousin, HANNAH ELY CHASE. He died in Londonderry, 18 Feb. 1845, aged 79. His wife was daughter of Samuel and Betsey (Morrill) Chase, born 8 Feb. 1784; died Oct. 1839. (Family 255). They lived in Salem, N. H.

Children, born in Salem:

> NANCY,[7] d. unm. 1844.
> BETSEY, d. unm. Mar. 1834.
> DANIEL, d. unm. May 1846.
> JOHN, d. unm. 1848.
> SAMUEL, d. unm. Mar. 1830.

801

JOHN[6] CHASE (John,[5] John,[4] Jacob,[3] John[2]), born in Londonderry, N. H., 11 Mar. 1791; entered his intention at Londonderry in Mar. 1816, POLLY CARTER JONES, daughter of Jesse and Hannah Jones, born in Londonderry, 24 Aug. 1793. They lived in Litchfield. N. H.

Children:

1942. ROBERT R.,[7] m. 22 Dec. 1842, Elizabeth Harvell.
      MARY NANCY, lived in Boston; m. —— Copeland.
      MARTHA, m. —— Nash.
      HANNAH, d. young.

802

FRANCIS MARDEN[6] CHASE (John,[5] John,[4] Jacob,[3] John[2]), born in Londonderry, N. H., 15 Apr. 1796; married there in Mar. 1817, LOVINA JONES, daughter of Jesse and Hannah Jones, born in Londonderry, 6 Nov. 1796; died there 12 Mar. 1856, aged 59. He died 15 Nov. 1869, aged 72. They lived in Londonderry.

Children, born in Londonderry:

1943. ALVIN JONES,[7] b. 30 May 1817; m. 18 Feb. 1847, Lavina Colby.
1944. GEORGE FARRER, b. 3 Sept. 1820; m. 8 Mar. 1843, Roxanna B. Annis.
      SARAH McALLISTER, b. 15 Dec. 1823; m. (1) Rufus Drew; m. (2) 3 Aug. 1846, Davis Vickery.
1945. EDMUND A., b. 19 Dec. 1828; m. Jan. 1853, Lavina Eaton.
      AMANDA, b. 15 May 1833; m. 1 Jan. 1854, George Aiken.
      SOPHRONIA C., b. — Apr. 1835; m. 25 Feb. 1857, Augustus L. Farley of Methuen.
1946. WILLIAM, b. — Oct. 1837; m. Sophia ——; lived in Londonderry.

803

ROBERT TELLER[6] CHASE (John,[5] John,[4] Jacob,[3] John[2]), born in Londonderry, N. H., 4 June 1799; died 19 Dec. 1869. He married in Derry, N. H., June 1827, LUCY M. BURNS, daughter of Lt. John and Elizabeth (Moore) Burns, Bedford, N. H. She died 30 Oct. 1873, aged 67. They lived in Derry ,and were buried in Salem, N. H.

Children:

      HANNAH ELIZABETH,[7] b. — July 1828; d. unm. 21 July 1851.
      ROBERT R., b. 1830; d. unm. 10 Oct. 1852.
      RACHEL ADELINE, b. June 1833; m. Abel Page of Kensington, N. H.

804

MOODY M.[6] CHASE (John,[5] John,[4] Jacob,[3] John[2]), born in Londonderry, N. H., 1 Sept. 1802; died 2 Mar. 1832, aged 30y.; buried in Forest Hill Cemetery, East Derry. He married BETSEY DAVISON. She probably married (2) in Derry, either Lyman Hayes or Israel W. Newell. They lived in Derry, N. H.

Child, born in Derry:

      NATHANIEL,[7] d. 10 Jan. 1849, aged 22 y.

805

PEASLEY M.[6] CHASE (John,[5] John,[4] Jacob,[3] John[2]), born in Londonderry, N. H., 30 Nov. 1806; married (1) in Haverhill, 22 Nov. 1827, MARTHA OSGOOD of Haverhill. He married (2) HANNAH CADY. They lived in Haverhill. It may be that he married (2) 14 May 1838, HANNAH KING in Londonderry. There is a disagreement as to the name of his second wife. Mr. Benjamin Chase gives her name as Hannah Foster of Kingston. He died in Londonderry, 15 Jan. 1854, aged 48.

Child:

1947.   ROBERT,[7]b. 29 Jan. 1840; m. Esther Dustin; lived in Salem, N. H. He d. 28 Jan. 1907. Their daughter *Adaline D.*,[8] b. 9 Mar. 1868; d. 15 July 1869.

806

WILLIAM B. M.[6] CHASE (John,[5] John,[4] Jacob,[3] John[2]), born in Londonderry, N. H., in 1813; married SARAH K. BROWN of Derry, N. H. They lived in Derry. He died 2 Sept. 1857, aged 44y. 8m. She died 18 July 1884, aged 81y. 5.m. 22d.

Children, born in Derry:

EMELINE,[7] m. William Morrill of Salem, N. H.
WILLIAM HENRY, unm.; lived in Salem.
SUSAN, m. Hiram Norris of Danbury, N. H.
JOHN I. O., d. 25 July 1852, a. 4 y. 4 m.
GEORGE F. A., d. 2 Mar. 1848, a. 3 y. 3 m. 18 d.

807

EZRA[6] CHASE (Samuel,[5] John,[4] Jacob,[3] John[2]), born in Salem, N. H., 1 Feb. 1780; died 14 Jan. 1864. He married 30 Dec. 1807, SALLY MARDEN MORRILL, who was born 8 June 1784 and died 17 Mar. 1848. They lived in Canaan, N. H.

Children, born in Canaan:

BETSEY M.,[7] b. 26 Dec. 1808; m. Aug. 1837, Gideon Lowell, b. 26 Oct. 1801; d. 2 Sept. 1863. She d. 21 Nov. 1888; lived in Orange, N. H.
1948.   FRANCIS M., b. 14 Dec. 1812; m. 27 Dec. 1840, Eliza Jane Heath; lived in Canaan; he d. 29 Mar. 1875.
SARAH ANN, b. 11 June 1816; m. 29 Dec. 1836, Aaron Barney of Orange; she d. 8 Jan. 1891.
1949.   SAMUEL BARNES, b. 6 Mar. 1819; m. 3 Nov. 1846, Lucinda Barney, dau. of Otis Barney. He d. 15 Nov. 1893; lived in Canaan.
CHARLES, b. 22 June 1827; m. in Amherst, N. H., 25 Nov. 1849, Lydia George of Rumney, N. H. No children; lived in Manchester, N. H.

808

SIMEON MORRILL[6] CHASE (Samuel,[5] John,[4] Jacob,[3] John[2]), born in Salem, N. H., 26 June 1782; died there 23 Jan. 1870. He married 16 Sept. 1809, MARY MORRILL who was born 26 Mar. 1789; died 2 Aug. 1866. They lived in Salem.

Children, born in Salem:

JOHN,[7] b. 17 Dec. 1809; d. unm. 16 May 1878.
IRA, b. 22 Apr. 1814; d. 6 Apr. 1815.
IRENE, b. 15 Aug. 1817; d. unm. 24 June 1889.
ABIGAIL, b. 21 May 1822; m. 18 Nov. 1847, Christopher Chase, son of Sally[6] Chase, b. 15 May 1818. (Family 254) She d. 21 Sept. 1859.
1950. LUTHER, b. 16 Apr. 1824; m. 23 Jan. 1842, Caroline Matthews. She b. 24 Mar. 1824; d. 23 Dec. 1907; lived in Hampstead.
MARY, b. 1831; d. unm. 3 Aug. 1855, aged 24 y. 8 m.

809

DANIEL CLARK[6] CHASE (Samuel,[5] John,[4] Jacob,[3] John[2]), born in Salem, N. H., 20 Jan. 1788; married 10 Dec. 1822, SALLY CORNING of Manchester, N. H. She was born 25 Feb. 1799. They lived in Derry, N. H., and both died in 1875.

Children, born in Derry:

SALLY,[7] b. 28 Feb. 1824; m. 17 July 1841, Gideon W. Conley of Atkinson, N. H. Twelve children.
1951. DANIEL, b. 10 July 1826; m. 16 July 1850, Belinda Copp, b. 1 Sept. 1832. He d. 8 Aug. 1860. She d. 29 Jan. 1878; lived in Windham, N. H. She m. (2) his brother Amos[7] Chase.
ELIZABETH, b. 10 June 1830; m. Benjamin Smith of Salem; she d. 1847; three children.
HARRIET, b. 29 May 1832; m. James Wilson of Derry, N. H.; lived in Windham.
HANNAH, b. 11 Apr. 1835; m. 6 Jan. 1853, Peter Hicks of Hampstead, N. H. Seven children.
1952. LORENZO, b. 1 May 1840; m. 31 Mar. 1869, Hannah E. (Copp) Goodwin, 1835-1897; lived in Derry.
1953. AMOS, b. 16 Oct. 1843; m. 6 Dec. 1865, Belinda Chase, widow of his brother Daniel;[7] two children.

810

ABRAHAM[6] CHASE (Samuel,[5] John,[4] Jacob,[3] John[2]), born in Salem, N. H., 12 Aug. 1796; married in 1822, MARY WALDRON of Warner, N. H. They lived in Salem.

Children, born in Salem:

1954. ABRAHAM,[7] b. 16 July 1827; m. 26 Aug. 1861, Caroline Matilda Jennings, b. 24 Sept. 1841; d. about 1912. Their son *Ernest Sidney*,[8] b. in Haverhill, 4 Feb. 1879; m. there 5 Aug. 1903, Luella Harvey Young, dau. of John and Frances Adeline (Thurston) Young, b. in Garfield, Me., 12 Feb. 1880. Their children are Grace Mabelle,[9] b. 18 May 1904; Mildred Bassett,[9] b. 9 Oct. 1908; d. 16 Jan. 1916; Melvil William,[9] b. 20 Nov. 1909. Furniture dealer in Concord, N. H.
LYDIA MARIA, d. young.
MARY JANE, m. George Upton of Derry, who d. in the Civil War.
CAROLINE, m. William Webster of Haverhill. He d. in the Civil War.
ALONZO, d. at the age of 16 y.
ABBY (twin), d. at the age of 20 y.
SARAH.

811

DAVID[6] CHASE (Enoch,[5] John,[4] Jacob,[3] John[2]), born about 1785; died in Haverhill, 27 Nov. 1832. He married in Haverhill, 6 Mar. 1808, RUTH[6] CHASE, daughter of Josiah and Ruth (Bradley) Chase, born in Haverhill, 7 Oct. 1788. (Family 197). No children recorded on Haverhill records. There is no will nor administration in Essex County on his estate. His name is only found in his birth, marriage and death.

812

JOHN[6] CHASE (Enoch,[5] John,[4] Jacob,[3] John[2]), born in New Hampshire about 1791; lived in Haverhill. He may be the John Chase who married in Haverhill, 25 June 1818, ANN AYER who died there, a widow, 5 Oct. 1832. He died in Haverhill, 28 Apr. 1826.
Children, born in Haverhill:

> ELIZABETH,[7] b. 3 Aug. 1820; perhaps m. 26 Dec. 1839, Charles Coffin.
> LAVINIA BRACKETT, b. 13 Oct. 1821; m. 11 June 1846, John B. Nichols, son of David and Betsey Nichols, a widower, aged 32.

813

WlLLIAM[6] CHASE (Jesse,[5] Enoch,[4] Jacob,[3] John[2]), born in Haverhill, 15 Feb. 1777; he was not living in his mother's family in Haverhill in 1790, but he may have been living elsewhere.

814

BENJAMIN[6] CHASE (Jacob,[5] Ebenezer,[4] Jacob,[3] John[2]), born 2 July 1782; married 1 Jan. 1809, ABIGAIL MASON who was born, 6 Mar. 1793. They lived in northern New York.
Children:

1955. DANIEL SAUNDERS,[7] b. 10 Feb. 1810; m. (1) Amanda Eddy; m. (2) Betsey (Hicks) Bird; m. (3) Lucy Younglove Hicks. He d. 18 Oct. 1859, in Baltimore, Mich.
MATILDA A., b. 18 Apr. 1811; m. (1) ―――― Call; m. (2) Calvin Norton of Sterling, Ill.; m. (3) ――――.
1956. JACOB M., b. 21 July 1814; d. about 1864 in Sterling, Ill. He m. 9 Apr. 1835, ―――― ――――.
1957. ALVIN W., b. 20 Mar. 1817; m. 22 Apr. 1841, Martha Shutts; lived in Dresden, Ohio; physician.
NANCY E., b. 4 May 1819; lived in Mt. Pleasant, Iowa; d. 18 Apr. 1847.
JOSHUA, b. 27 Nov. 1821; killed by a horse 23 Sept. 1830.
SARAH ANN, b. 25 Mar. 1824; m. James S. Early; lived in Mt. Pleasant, Iowa.
BETSEY A., b. 4 July 1827; d. unm. 8 Oct. 1839.
1958. JAMES S., b. 25 Dec. 1829; lived in Howard Co., Kans.; clergyman.
1959. BENJAMIN P., b. 8 Oct. 1832; d. 8 Feb. 1854.
MALVINA ABIGAIL, b. 26 Sept. 1836; m. 12 Apr. 1857, Andrew J. Wanzer.

815

JAMES[6] CHASE (Jacob,[5] Ebenezer,[4] Jacob,[3] John[2]), born 28 Nov.
1786; married Jan. 1809, MIRIAM CHALLIS.   Perhaps they lived in
Vermont or New York State.
  Children:

> JULIA ANN,[7] b. 11 Aug. 1809; m. about 1840, James Kimball;
> lived in Holland Village, N. Y.
> POLLY, b. 12 Sept. 1820; m. about 1842, Perry Whaley, son of
> George and Mary[6] (Chase) Whaley (Family 260).   They
> lived in Holland, N. Y.

816

CAPT. EBENEZER[6] CHASE (Caleb,[5] Ebenezer,[4] Jacob,[3] John[2]),
born 29 Mar. 1791; died in Ticonderoga, N. Y., 16 Jan. 1831.   He
married in Newbury, N. H., 8 May 1815, MRS. SARAH CHENEY of
Fisherfield (now Newbury), N. H.   She is not identified in the
Cheney Genealogy.   They lived in Newbury and Ticonderoga, N. Y.
  Children, born in Fisherfield (now Newbury):

1960.   DANIEL CHENEY,[7] b. 28 Feb. 1816; m. Jan. 1840, Malinda Bis-
       sell of Newcomb, N. Y.; living in Newcomb in 1870; eight
       children.
       ALMINA S., b. 13 Feb. 1819; m. 20 Sept. 1836, Valorous Hall.
       MARIA, b. 18 Nov. 1820; m. Dec. 1839, Harvey Holt; lived in
       Keene, N. Y. [N. H.?]
1961.   JOHN W., b. 7 Sept. 1822; m. 1845, Mary Jane Smith; captain
       in Civil War; living in Burlington, Vt., in 1871.
       MARIAN W., b. 4 July 1827; m. 7 May 1844, Smith Beede;
       lived in Keene, N. Y. [N. H.?]
1962.   CALEB JUDSON, b. 2 Mar. 1830; m. 23 Jan. 1853, Thankful
       Preston of Long Lake; six children; lived in Newcomb,
       N. Y., 1871.

817

DANIEL[6] CHASE (Abraham,[5] Abraham,[4] Abraham,[3] John[2]), born
in Atkinson, N. H., about 1774.

818

STEPHEN[6] CHASE (Abraham,[5] Abraham,[4] Abraham,[3] John[2]),
born in Atkinson, N. H., about 1776; removed to Wisconsin.

819

JAMES[6] CHASE (Abraham,[5] Abraham,[4] Abraham,[3] John[2]), born
in Atkinson, N. H., about 1780.

820

PARKER[6] CHASE (Abraham,[5] Abraham,[4] Abraham,[3] John[2]), born
in Atkinson, N. H.; removed to Le Ray, Jefferson Co., N. Y.; was
one of the trustees of the First Methodist Church organized in that
town, 20 Nov. 1824.   Family not reported.

821

DAVID DENNIS[6] CHASE (Abraham,[5] Abraham,[4] Abraham,[3] John[2]), born in Atkinson, N. H., 27 Oct. 1802; married (1) about 1825, TRYPHENA LEWIS; married (2) about 1845, PATIENCE R. SMITH. They lived in Jefferson Co., N. Y., till 1856, then they removed to Hancock Co., Ill.

Children by first wife, first five born in Jefferson Co., N. Y., others in Hancock Co., Ill.

1963.   HORACE L.,[7] b. 25 July 1827; m. Martha Lunt.
1964.   ORLEN A., b. 27 July 1830; lived in Jefferson Co., N. Y.
        CLARA E., b. 28 Dec. 1834; m. Stillman Armstrong.
1965.   HARVEY G., b. 5 Oct. 1838; m. 25 Dec. 1865, Nancy J. Laport; lived in Hancock Co., Ill.

Children by second wife, fifth and sixth born in Jefferson Co., N. Y.:

        AMBROSE D., b. 16 Mar. 1849; never married; lived in Adams Co., Ill., and in Stillwater in 1876.
        SUSANNA S., b. 6 Nov. 1855; m. 29 Dec. 1870, George Howard; lived in Hancock Co., Ill.
1966.   JOHN H., b. 12 May 1859; lived in Hancock Co.

822

JOSEPH C.[6] CHASE (Joseph,[5] Abraham,[4] Abraham,[3] John[2]), born in Springfield, N. H., 1807; died there, 30 Oct. 1867, aged 60 y. 22 d. He married in Bethlehem, N. H., 20 Oct. 1830, LUCRETIA DIMOCK of Lisbon, N. H. No births of children recorded in the town records of New Hampshire.

823

WILLIAM THOMPSON[6] CHASE (William,[5] Abraham,[4] Abraham,[3] John[2]), born in Weare, N. H., 25 Jan. 1811; married 23 Feb. 1834, ELIZABETH[6] CHASE, daughter of Josiah[5] and Lydia (Blaisdell) Chase. She was born in Chester, N. H., 1 June 1813. (Family 427). They lived in North Grantham, N. H.

Children, born in Grantham:

        GEORGE W.,[7] b. 3 July 1836; never married.
        CAROLINE E., b. 26 Nov. 1846; never married.

824

BENJAMIN[6] CHASE (Benjamin,[5] David,[4] David,[3] John[2]), born in Haverhill, 21 Sept. 1781; married in Haverhill, 2 Feb. 1802, BETSEY LADD, daughter of Lt. Nathaniel and Sally (Noyes) Ladd, born in Haverhill, 24 Sept. 1784; died there 25 Feb. 1841. They lived in Haverhill.

Children, born in Haverhill:

        MARY JANE,[7] b. 23 Nov. 1802; m. 10 Sept. 1822, Ebenezer Fullington of Amesbury. He b. 10 Mar. 1800. No children.
        ELIZA L., b. 29 June 1810; m. 10 Sept. 1830, Daniel H. Hall.
1967.   JOHN JOHNSON, b. 27 Mar. 1813; m. 10 Sept. 1839, Charlotte M. Cooper of Amesbury.
1968.   EUSTIS, b. 18 Sept. 1823; m. Mary Nichols.
        BENJAMIN, b. 1828; d. 5 Mar. 1833.

825

CAPT. JOHN[6] CHASE (Benjamin,[5] David,[4] David,[3] John[2]), born in Haverhill, 21 Apr. 1785; married LOUISA SPINNEY. He was a sea-captain and they lived in Eastport, Me.; he died about 1809.
Children, born in Eastport:

1969.   JAMES,[7] lived in the eastern part of Maine; mar. and had children.
1970.   JOHN, b. 12 Sept. 1807; m. Caroline E. Sims of Portsmouth, N. H.; three children; he d. 25 Aug. 1869.

826

JOSEPH[6] CHASE (Nicholas,[5] David,[4] David,[3] John[2]), born in Grafton Co., N. H., 1798; married.
Child:

1970a.   WALLACE,[7] living at Chase's Mills, Pa., 20 Mar. 1873.

827

BENJAMIN[6] CHASE (Nicholas,[5] David,[4] David,[3] John[2]), born, probably in northern New Hampshire.

828

MOSES[6] CHASE (Nicholas,[5] David,[4] David,[3] John[2]), born, it is supposed, in northern New Hampshire.

829

AMOS BAILEY[6] CHASE (Simeon,[5] David,[4] David,[3] John[2]), born in Newbury, 24 Mar. 1791; died 28 Nov. 1852. He married in Haverhill, 6 Feb. 1812, MARY COLBY. They lived near the "Rocks Village" in Haverhill. He died in Haverhill, 28 Nov. 1852, aged 63 y. 11 m. 6 d. (Mass. Vital Statistics, 66:121).
Children, born in Newbury (now West Newbury):

EUNICE BAILEY,[7] b. 2 Jan. 1814; m. 16 Apr. 1833, John Marden of West Newbury.
1971.   RUFUS L., b. 25 Oct. 1818; m. 20 Nov. 1845, Jane P. Wells of Amesbury.

830

SIMEON[6] CHASE (Simeon,[5] David,[4] David,[3] John[2]), born in Newbury 31 Aug. 1789; married (1) 11 May 1814, ANNA WOODWARD who died in Haverhill, — July 1831. He married (2) in Haverhill, 16 May 1832, SARAH BROWN. He married (3) in Haverhill, 10 May 1844, BETSEY C. BAILEY, daughter of Stephen and Nancy Bailey, born about 1791. They lived at the "Rocks Village" in Haverhill.
Children by first wife, born in Haverhill:

1972.   SAMUEL W.,[7] b. 16 Dec. 1814; m. Nov. 1833, Lydia Bailey of Derry, N. H.; he was lost at sea in 1856. No children.
ANNA B., b. 30 Aug. 1817; m. William Harrison Bailey of Barre, Vt.
ELIZA JANE, b. 10 Nov. 1820; m. Thomas W. Bailey.

1973. Rufus Knowles, b. 20 Sept. 1823; m. 3 July 1851, Sophronia Jaques of Haverhill. She d. Feb. 1863.

1974. Augustus S., b. 1825; m. 1 Nov. 1849, Maria Jarvis Tremaine of Halifax, N. S.; d. Apr. 1870.

1975. Abram W., b. 4 Sept. 1828; m. (1) 6 Oct. 1851, Mary E. Ham; m. (2) Sarah Brown.

Child by second wife, born in Haverhill:

Mary Catharine, m. 5 Mar. 1857, William Bohannan. No children.

831

William J.[6] Chase (Simeon,[5] David,[4] David,[3] John[2]), born in Newbury, 27 Jan. 1792; married 6 Oct. 1822, Miner Carleton of Plaistow, N. H. She was born 16 Sept. 1788; died 28 Dec. 1865. They lived at Newton Junction, N. H.

Children, born in Plaistow:

1976. John S.,[7] b. 21 July 1821; m. 19 Mar. 1859, Caroline H. Gilman.

Sarah P., b. 19 Aug. 1825; m. 16 Nov. 1844, John F. Hall.

Hannah C., b. 2 Jan. 1828; m. 10 June 1863, Wellman Stevens.

1977. Benjamin, b. 7 Jan. 1830; m. 14 July 1860, Charlotte A. Peaslee.

832

Anthony[6] Chase (Woodman,[5] Anthony,[4] David,[3] John[2]), born in Haverhill 1800; died there 23 Sept. 1851, aged 51. He married in Haverhill, 1 Jan. 1827, Sarah Tompkins, daughter of Rev. Isaac and Mary (Alden) Tompkins, born in Haverhill 7 Dec. 1799; died there, 11 Feb. 1842, aged 42. They lived in Haverhill:

Children, born and died in Haverhill:

Isaac Tompkins,[7] b. 1828; d. 12 Dec. 1841, a. 13 y.

Abby T., d. 27 Sept. 1845, a. 6 y.

833

Benjamin Ambrose[6] Chase (Stephen,[5] Anthony,[4] David,[3] John[2]), born in Northfield, N. H., 3 Apr. 1798; died in Lowell, 1 Sept. 1846. He married in Northfield, 21 June 1820, Hannah Clough Hall, a native of Canterbury, N. H. She died 8 June 1859. He was a manufacturer and lived in Northfield, N. H., till 1840 when he removed to Lowell. He was representative from Northfield in 1831 and 1832.

Children, born in Northfield:

Stephen,[7] b. 30 Mar. 1821; d. 2 Apr. 1821.

Priscilla Clark, b. 14 Jan. 1825; m. 19 Feb. 1851, Benjamin F. Cofran of Northfield.

1978. Charles Greenough, b. 5 July 1827; m. 17 Dec. 1853, Relief Judith McQusten of Plymouth, N. H., b. 17 June 1827; d. 6 May 1901; they lived in Brookline; he d. 8 Nov. 1894. She was dau. of Alvah and Abigail Woodman[6] (Chase) McQuesten (Family 273). Their son *Walter Greenough*,[8] b. in Boston, 30 May 1859; graduate of Harvard University, 1882; M. D. 1901; d. 27 Jan. 1919; m. 20 Oct. 1906, Fannie Scott Hubbard; b. in Liverpool, England, 10 Feb. 1875 (while her parents of Wiscasset, Me., were on a visit). Their son

Charles Greenough,[9] b. 3 June 1908; Harvard 1930; Judith Thaxter,[9] b. 7 July 1910; Winsor School, Boston, 1928. The widow and children live at 279 Marlborough St., Boston.

834

JOHN LANGDON[6] CHASE (Stephen,[5] Anthony,[4] David,[3] John[2]), born in Northfield, N. H., 29 Dec. 1803; died in Illinois, 22 June 1856. He married 11 Sept. 1828, MARILDA D. HALSTEAD who was born 1 Nov. 1805; died 10 Jan. 1850. They removed to Scioto Co., Ohio, and later to Illinois.

Children:

ABIGAIL,[7] b. 18 May 1829; m. 7 Dec. 1848, Daniel Clark; lived in Mason City, Ill., 1874.

ALPHEUS, b. 25 Mar. 1831; d. 19 July 1832.

JOHN, b. 28 Aug. 1833; d. 20 Aug. 1834.

ELIZABETH, b. 20 May 1835; m. Jan. 1866, Alfred Hill.

ORILLA, b. 17 Nov. 1836; d. unm. 29 Sept. 1857.

EMMA W., b. 20 Aug. 1841; m. Jan. 1859, Alonzo E. Currier; lived in Ft. Scott, Kans.

HARRIET, b. 20 Aug. 1843; m. Oct. 1866, S. T. Hickman; lived in New Lancaster, Kans.

STEPHEN A., b. 31 Dec. 1844; never married.

MARY A., b. 1 Dec. 1849; d. 3 Dec. 1850.

835

DEA. TAPPAN[6] CHASE (Joseph,[5] Anthony,[4] David,[3] John[2]), born in Haverhill, 15 Jan. 1800; died there, 27 Apr. 1857. He married in Haverhill, 14 Sept. 1825, HANNAH JOHNSON, daughter of Col. John and Hannah (Bradley) Johnson, born in Haverhill, 8 July 1803. He lived in Haverhill and was a shoe manufacturer.

Children, born in Haverhill:

1979.   GEORGE WINGATE,[7] b. 19 June 1826; m. 30 Dec. 1849, FRANCES A. DYER, dau. of Christopher and Susan (Gordon) Dyer of New Sharon, Me., who was b. 9 June 1830 and d. in Boston. Six children: Frances A., Abby Matilda, George Tappan, George Wingate, Charles Dyer, and Sarah Ann Chase.

Mr. Chase was an exceedingly versatile man and in the course of a rather brief life was identified with many activities, teacher of music, organist, manufacturer, librarian, editor and publisher being the most prominent ones. He compiled and published a *History of Haverhill*, his native town, which has a high rank among books of the kind. Other publications which he edited are *The Musical Journal* which later became *The Masonic Journal, Webb's Pocket Monitor,* and a *Digest of Masonic Laws,* a book of 568 pages, containing over 4000 references.

He was Eminent Commander of the Commandery of Knights Templar in Haverhill, 1863 to 1867, and issued in 1865 his *Tactics for Knights Templar,* also a *Burial Service for Master Masons and Knights Templar.*

He was representative to the General Court in 1859 and 1861 and was later employed in the office of the Secretary of the Commonwealth. He also served on the Publishing Committee of the New England Historic Genealogical Society.

He went west on account of ill health and a few months later died in Stockton, Minn., 13 Aug. 1867, and was buried in Linwood Cemetery in Haverhill.

ABIGAIL JOHNSON, b. 23 Apr. 1828; d. unm. 1 July 1847.

MATILDA, b. 7 Jan. 1830; d. 7 May 1834.

1980. WILLIAM, b. 27 Dec. 1835.

SARAH, b. 14 Feb. 1832; d. unm. 4 Aug. 1848.

MATILDA, b. 7 Feb. 1834; d. unm. 27 Aug. 1852.

1981. CHARLES TAPPAN, b. 28 Aug. 1837; m. 8 Oct. 1857, Charlotte Elizabeth Burr, b. 22 May 1837.

836

JOHN ADAMS[6] CHASE (John,[5] Anthony,[4] David,[3] John[2]), born in Haverhill, 30 Oct. 1799; married (intention in Haverhill, 25 Aug. 1821), 23 Sept. 1821, NANCY JANE RUNDLETT, born in Exeter, N. H., 10 Oct. 1806. They lived in Salem.

Children:

1982. GEORGE A.,[7] b. 4 June 1822; m. 6 Aug. 1849, Josephine Breckinridge. Principal of an Academy, Louisville, Ky.; d. 29 July 1850.

1983. HENRY, b. 5 Apr. 1826; m. 15 Feb. 1847, Susan Courtright [Cartwright]; d. 29 July 1850; no issue.

1984. ROBERT, b. 11 Sept. 1829; m. 12 June 1855, Mary George of Berwick, Me.; lived in Salem.

837

FREDERICK[6] CHASE (John,[5] Anthony,[4] David,[3] John[2]), born in Haverhill, 10 Dec. 1800; married 23 Dec. 1823, MARY P. STETSON. They lived in Bradford and in the East Parish of Haverhill after 1838.

Children, third to fifth born in Bradford:

1985. CHARLES F.,[7] b. 7 Nov. 1824; m. 29 May 1849, Sarah C. Works.

1986. JOHN, b. 3 June 1826; m. June 1849, Martha T. Fowler; d. 12 Aug. 1853.

1987. LUCIEN STEELE, b. 13 Apr. 1833; m. Rebecca Fellows; d. 25 Mar. 1859.

ELIZABETH, b. 14 Aug. 1835; d. unm. 13 Apr. 1918, in Topsfield.

SARAH P., b. 17 May 1837; m. 6 Nov. 1855, George Coffin; d. May 1868.

1988. ARTHUR W., b. 3 Sept. 1841; m. 1 May 1865, Fanny T. Parker.

838

ROBERT[6] CHASE (John,[5] Anthony,[4] David,[3] John[2]), born in Haverhill, 4 Dec. 1802; married in Feb. 1827, ELIZA JEWELL. They lived in Haverhill and Derry, N. H.

Children:

1989. ROBERT,[7] b. 19 Aug. 1830; m. July 1854, Susan A. H. Davis; a manufacturer in Northumberland, N. H.

JOSEPH, b. 5 Nov. 1832; d. unm.

839

LUTHER[6] CHASE (Tristram,[5] Tristram,[4] David,[3] John[2]), born in Newbury, 10 Nov. 1807; died 4 Oct. 1854. He married in Nov. 1838, ROSINA DUNN of Little Rock, Ark. She died 14 June 1857.

Their family consisted of eight children but in 1870, only two survived.

Children surviving:

1990. ARTHUR,[7] lived in Philadelphia, Pa.
       FANNIE, m. Rev. Abel Clokey of Aledo, Ill., Presbyterian clergyman.

840

WARREN EDSON[6] CHASE (Enoch,[5] Tristram,[4] David,[3] John[2]), born (probably in Haverhill, N. H.) 12 Oct. 1806; married 6 Aug. 1834, ELLEN MARIA PETTINGILL, daughter of Thomas Hale and Alphia (Morse) Pettingill, born in Salisbury, N. H., 9 Jan. 1814; died in Portland, Me., 6 May 1879. He died 21 Jan. 1852 or 5 Mar. 1855. He was a physician and they lived in Boscawen, N. H., and Portland, Me.

Children, first two born in Boscawen, N. H., last two in Portland, Me.:

1991. WARREN PETTINGILL,[7] b. 30 Nov. 1835; m. 11 July 1865, Ellen Orianna Chapman. dau. of Gilbert Chapman of Bethel, Me.; lived in Portland, Me.
1992. THOMAS HALE, b. 20 Feb. 1837; lived in Portland, Me.
1993. CHARLES HENRY, b. 26 Sept. 1848; lived in Portland, Me.

841

BENJAMIN[6] CHASE (Isaac,[5] Ambrose,[4] Isaac,[3] Daniel[2]), born 2 Sept. 1787; married 1815, SALLY PARKER.

842

SYLVESTER[6] CHASE (Isaac,[5] Ambrose,[4] Isaac,[3] Daniel[2]), born Apr. 1798; married EUNICE HASKINS.

843

AMARIAH[6] CHASE (Solomon,[5] Ambrose,[4] Isaac,[3] Daniel[2]), born 14 May 1766; died 17 Nov. 1849, aged 83. He married (1) in Grafton, 28 Nov. 1784, ELIZABETH[6] CHASE, daughter of Bradford[5] and Abigail (Sibley) Chase, born in Sutton, 29 Jan. 1766. (Family 380). With his father, Solomon Chase he removed to Townshend, Vt., in 1788 and became a proprietor and land owner there. (Hemenway's Vermont Gazetteer, 5, Pt. 2:537). In 1790 he was head of a family in Townshend consisting of one male over 16 years of age, no males under 16 and one female. (Vt. Census, 55). Next to him was listed his father's name. He married (2) in Orford, N. H., 22 May 1794, ABIAH CORLISS, who died 11 Mar. 1851. Amariah Chase of Sutton enlisted in Capt. March Chase's Co. in 1778 and 1779. He was described as 16 years of age, 5 feet 4 inches in stature and ruddy complexion. He enlisted 10 July 1779 and to the end of the Revolutionary War. (Mass. Soldiers and Sailors in the Revoluetion, 3:343).

They lived in Townshend, Vt., Orford and Stratford, N. H. Apparently there were no children by the first wife. It has been claimed that his second wife was the widow Harden but their marriage record gives no hint of that fact.

Children, the eldest born in Orford:

1994. AMARIAH,[7] b. 19 Apr. 1795; m. Sophia Holden.
1995. DAVID K., b. 5 June 1797; m. Bathsheba Leonard.
1996. SOLOMON, b. 22 July 1799; m. 8 Apr. 1821, Mary Purvis of Seneca Lake, N. Y.; lived in West Liberty, Iowa.
ABIAH, b. 5 June 1801; m. 22 May 1826, Peter Winn, who was b. 5 May 1785; she was living in Spring Dale, Iowa, in 1873.
ASENATH, b. 4 Mar. 1804; m. William Atkins.
ABIGAIL, b. 25 Feb. 1806; m. Isaac Stevens.
ANN, b. — Feb. 1808; m. John McGown.
EMILY, b. 9 May 1810; m. Henry Daniels.

844

SOLOMON[6] CHASE (Solomon,[5] Ambrose,[4] Isaac,[3] Daniel[2]), born 20 Nov. 1767; died in Bath, N. Y., 1839, aged 72. He married in 1790, ALICE SARGENT. They removed to Bath.
Children:

LUCINDA,[7] m. Josiah Holt.
ANNIS, m. Benjamin Emerson.
1997. WILLARD, m. Harriet Hudson.
1998. JAMES, m. Harriet Collins.
CELINDA, m. Chester Perkins.
1999. LUCIUS, m. (1) Deborah Leonard; m. (2) Emily Margison.
2000. SOLOMON, m. Tryphena Hudson; lived in Bath.
DIANTHA, m. Stowell Covel.

845

JOSIAH[6] CHASE (Solomon,[5] Ambrose,[4] Isaac,[3] Daniel[2]), born 10 June 1771; died in Springfield, Vt., 4 Mar. 1813, killed by the falling of a tree. He married 17 Mar. 1804, MELINDA TEMPLE who was born 2 Oct. 1779, and died in Sherburne, Vt., 25 Apr. 1851. They lived in Springfield.
Children, born in Springfield:

LUCENIA, b. 3 June 1805; m. 5 Jan. 1822, Fernando Sargent; lived in Mendon, Vt.
MELINDA, b. 27 Feb. 1807; m. 16 Mar. 1828, Charles Dain.
BETSEY, b. 2 Jan. 1810; m. 29 Nov. 1835, Harry Shedd; lived in Mendon, Vt.
HANNAH, b. 28 Apr. 1812; d. 16 Aug. 1847.
THANKFUL, b. 7 Sept. 1814; d. 26 Nov. 1816.

846

NEHEMIAH[6] CHASE (Solomon,[5] Ambrose,[4] Isaac,[3] Daniel[2]), born 5 Nov. 1784; married LUCINDA GLYNN. They lived in Haverhill, N. H.

847

ABEL[6] CHASE (Abel,[5] Ambrose,[4] Isaac,[3] Daniel[2]), born in Sutton, 2 Nov. 1773; died in Lyon, Oakland Co., Mich., 16 Aug. 1843. He married in Sutton, 23 Jan. 1793, LYDIA ALDRICH, daughter of Timothy and Thankful Aldrich, born in June 1770; died in Farmington, N. Y., 20 Mar. 1820. They removed from New Hampshire to Palmyra, N. Y., about 1818.

Children, born in Croydon, N. H., last two born in Cornish, N. H.:

LUCINA,[7] b. 26 July 1794; m. 18 Feb. 1816, David Elliott, b. 4 Dec. 1786. She d. 25 Mar. 1859.

2001.   ALVAH, b. 16 Apr. 1796; m. 19 May 1818, Sandalana Boynton; lived in Vt.; d. about 1846.

2002.   ICHABOD, b. 21 Jan. 1798; lived in Fletcher, Vt.

2003.   PETER, b. 10 Mar. 1800; m. 11 Oct. 1827, Elizabeth Cramer; d. in Josco, Mich., 31 Aug. 1844. Their son *Ichabod*,[8] b. in Novi, Mich., 29 Nov. 1829; d. in Puyallup, Wash., 20 Aug. 1894; m. 21 Oct. 1848, Margaret B. Gillam. Their daughter Lucena,[9] b. in Elsie, Mich., 30 Aug. 1865; m. 18 May 1882, John Thomas Axtell, M. D. Their dau. *Lillian*[10] *Axtell*, b. 14 June 1883; m. 27 June 1906, John L. Gove, M. D., proprietors of the Axtell Clinic of Newton, Kans. Children John Axtell[11] and William Edward[11] Gove.

2004.   BELA,[7] b. 7 Mar. 1802; d. 9 Mar. 1859. He m. (1) Aurilla Whipple; m. (2) ——— Buck; m. (3) Minerva Shute. Ten children, including *Abel*,[8] b. in Macedon, N. Y., 4 May 1825; d. in Alpine, Kent Co., Mich., 29 Apr. 1898; m. 30 Oct. 1851, Rebecca Jane Herrick, b. in Salem, Mich., 11 Feb. 1834; d. in Alpine, 22 Aug. 1897. Their son Charles Herrick,[9] b. in Alpine, 21 Apr. 1874; m. 28 Apr. 1898, Mary Ann Schindler, b. 7 Aug. 1876. Children, *Carroll Edward*[10] and *Charles Herrick Jr.*[10] They live in Comstock, Mich.

THANKFUL, b. 11 Jan. 1804.

PAMELIA, b. 7 Feb. 1806; m. Thomas Durfee; d. 18 June 1834.

LYDIA B., b. 9 Mar. 1808; m. ——— Thomas. She d. 28 Aug. 1836.

2005.   ABEL EDSON, b. 2 June 1810; d. 30 Apr. 1843; one child.

HIRAM LEUORUDO, b. 4 Apr. 1812; d. 6 July 1828.

848

JAMES[6] CHASE (Abel,[5] Ambrose,[4] Isaac,[3] Daniel[2]), born in Sutton, 24 July 1776; died in Fletcher, Vt., 7 Nov. 1833. He married in Northridge, 1 Sept. 1796, ABIGAIL ALDRICH, daughter of Alexander and Abigail Aldrich, born in Mendon, 9 Nov. 1770; died in Fletcher, Vt., 3 May 1840. They removed from Sutton to Croydon, N. H., in 1800 and to Fletcher in 1821.

Children, first two or three born in Sutton, others in Croydon:

ELIZABETH,[7] b. 8 Jan. 1797; m. Mar. 1816, Jesse Carpenter of Croydon, N. H. She d. 2 Dec. 1870.

2006.   ALDEN, b. 2 Apr. 1799; m. 3 Oct. 1823, Abigail Brown; lived in Fletcher.

2007.   SAMUEL, b. 26 July 1800; m. Oct. 1818, Sarah Metcalf.

LAVINA, b. 15 Apr. 1801; m. 30 Oct. 1822, Jacob Leach.

2008.   LYMAN, b. 9 Nov. 1803; m. 9 Nov. 1828, Betsey Kingsley.

2009.   JEFFERSON, b. 4 Dec. 1804.

HANNAH, b. 17 Nov. 1805; m. 10 Jan. 1828, James D. Hill.

2010.   ELIAS, b. 17 June 1808; m. 21 Mar. 1831, Rachel Taylor; drowned in 1850.

LYDIA, b. 8 July 1810; m. 14 Feb. 1831, Giles G. Taylor of Fletcher. Five children.

2011.   JAMES, b. 29 Oct. 1811; m. 30 Dec. 1830, Milla Ellsworth.

JUDITH, b. 29 May 1813; m. Arnold Darling.

849

CAPT. AMBROSE[6] CHASE (Abel,[5] Ambrose,[4] Isaac,[3] Daniel[2]), born in Sutton, 18 July 1778; died in Fletcher, Vt., 9 Oct. 1834. He married in Westborough, 13 Mar. 1798, SARAH SHERMAN of Grafton. She was the daughter of Aaron and Sarah (Kimball) Sherman, born in Grafton, 14 Dec. 1774. They removed from Sutton to Fletcher in 1828.

Children, born in Sutton:

    CHARLOTTE,[7] b. 27 Dec. 1798; m. 1 Jan. 1818, Ephraim Wheeler.
2012. AMBROSE, b. 28 Mar. 1801; m. 7 May 1822, Lydia Woodbury.
2013. ISAAC T., b. 12 Feb. 1803; m. 26 Feb. 1829, Fidelia Vernon Wetherbee; lived in Fletcher; d. 28 Mar. 1863. Nine children. He d. 1 Oct. 1881. Their son *Manchester*[8] Chase of Georgia, Vt., collected a large amount of material relating to the descendants of Abel[5] Chase.

850

THADDEUS ELLIOTT[6] CHASE (Abel,[5] Ambrose,[4] Isaac,[3] Daniel[2]), born in Sutton, 12 July 1781; died in Fletcher, Vt., 3 Dec. 1835 or 1836. He married (intention in Sutton, 24 Aug. 1806) PRUDENCE SIBLEY, daughter of Abel and Abigail (Nickols) Sibley, born in Sutton, 27 June 1780; died 3 June 1856 in Fletcher, where they had lived since 1812.

Child:

    PRUDENCE,[7] b. 25 Jan. 1807; m. (1) 25 Oct. 1832, Jonathan Wells of St. Albans, Vt.; m. (2) 7 Sept. 1848, Luther Wells, brother to Jonathan; lived in Fletcher.

851

BRADFORD[6] CHASE (Abel,[5] Ambrose,[4] Isaac,[3] Daniel[2]), born in Sutton, 21 July 1783; died in Fletcher, Vt., 29 June 1853. He married, 18 Feb. 1805, POLLY DRURY of Walpole, N. H. She died in Fletcher, 7 Feb. 1854. They lived in Walpole, and Claremont, N. H., and in 1829 removed to Fletcher, where they remained until death.

Children, three born in Walpole, others in Claremont:

    LOREN,[7] b. 10 June 1806; d. 21 July 1806.
2014. OREN, b. 17 July 1807; m. Feb. 1837, Marcia Garland of Eden, Vt.
2015. STILLMAN, b. 14 Aug. 1809; m. 21 Sept. 1841, Rebecca Burdick.
    HANNAH A., b. 14 Feb. 1814; m. 1841, Lyman Walker.
    BRADFORD, b. 20 Sept. 1816; d. 17 Oct. 1841.
    EDNA, b. 26 Sept. 1818; d. 20 Nov. 1836.
2016. GARDNER W., b. 12 May 1825; m. 15 Mar. 1843, Maria A. Wetherell; d. in Civil War at Washington, D. C., 21 Jan. 1863.

852

CAPT. ISAAC[6] CHASE (Abel,[5] Ambrose,[4] Isaac,[3] Daniel[2]), born in Sutton, 3 July 1785; died in Fletcher, Vt., 29 Mar. 1821. He married in Oct. 1808, HANNAH BOYNTON, daughter of Abiel and Lois

(Raymond) Boynton. She was born 12 Nov. 1790 and married (2) Samuel Church. They lived in Fletcher from 1818.

Children, last two born in Fletcher:

ORRIN,[7] b. June 1811; d. at the age of 18 y.

ELIZA E., b. July 1814; m. Franklin Hunt of Fairfax, Vt.

SANDALANA, b. — May 1818; m. Thaddeus E. Lathe of Salem, N. Y.

2017. AMBROSE, b. — Sept. 1820; m. 25 Oct. 1840, Sarah A. Walker of Fairfax, Vt. He was living in Waterville, Vt., in 1873. Six children.

853

JONATHAN[6] CHASE (Abel,[5] Ambrose,[4] Isaac,[3] Daniel[2]), born in Sutton, 10 July 1787; died in Jay, Vt., 30 July 1860. He married in Croydon, N. H., 21 Mar. 1805, HOPESTILL M. GOLDTHWAIT, daughter of Jonathan and Lydia (Chase) Goldthwait, born 17 Feb. 1778 and died in Jay, 11 Aug. 1865. They lived in Croydon, N. H., until 1823 and then in Fletcher and Jay.

Children, born in Croydon:

2018. NEWTON,[7] b. 5 Mar. 1807; m. in Fairfax, Vt., 13 Oct. 1831, Rosina Burdick of Fairfax.

CHESTER, b. 14 Mar. 1811; d. in Croydon, N. H., 11 Nov. 1821.

ROWENA A., b. 24 Sept. 1812; never married.

LOVISA, b. 7 Sept. 1814; d. 27 June 1832, in Fletcher.

ABEL, b. 5 May 1818; d. 4 Mar. 1826.

854

MANCHESTER[6] CHASE (Abel,[5] Ambrose,[4] Isaac,[3] Daniel[2]), born in Sutton, 2 July 1798; died in Fletcher, Vt., 6 Sept. 1864. He married 5 Jan. 1823, SALLY FRENCH, daughter of Isaac and Lucy (Farrer) French, born in Winchendon, 6 Dec. 1803; died 24 Dec. 1866 in Fletcher, where they lived.

Child, born in Cambridge, Vt.:

PRUDENCE,[7] b. 22 Jan. 1827; m. 10 Oct. 1848, Chauncey W. Scott; lived in Fletcher.

855

BENJAMIN[6] CHASE (Mark,[5] Daniel,[4] Isaac,[3] Daniel[2]), born, perhaps, in New Salem.

856

LUKE[6] CHASE (Mark,[5] Daniel,[4] Isaac,[3] Daniel[2]), born in New Salem, probably.

857

SAMUEL[6] CHASE (Mark,[5] Daniel,[4] Isaac,[3] Daniel[2]), born, perhaps, in New Salem.

858

JOHN CHASE (Simon,[5] Daniel,[4] Isaac,[3] Daniel[2]), born in Northbridge, 22 Aug. 1774; married and had seven children. Where they lived is uncertain.

Children:
>JULIA B.[7]
2019. HENRY.
>REBECCA P.
>RUTH C.
2020. SYLVESTER B.
>CLARISSA.
2021. LINCOLN.

859

SILAS[6] CHASE (Simon,[5] Daniel,[4] Isaac,[3] Daniel[2]), born in Greenwich, 27 Nov. 1776; married 6 Jan. 1801, SALLY LAWSON of New Salem. She was born 3 Aug. 1783 and died 11 Jan. 1871. He died in Woodbury, Vt., 4 Mar. 1865. They removed from New Salem to Montpelier, Vt., in 1808 and to Woodbury, Vt., in 1814.

Children, first two born in New Salem, third and fourth in Montpelier, others in Woodbury:

>TAMAR,[7] b. 15 Oct. 1802; m. 18 Web. 1838, Edo [Edmond] Scribner of Wolcott, Vt.
>PRUDENCE, b. 16 July 1805; m. Cyrus Wheelock; d. 28 Mar. 1835.
2022. LYMAN, b. 15 Apr. 1809; m. (1) 6 Jan. 1836, Lydia Dailey; m. (2) 3 Apr. 1856, Hannah L.[7] Chase, dau. of Simeon B.[6] and Susannah (Ladd) Chase of Unity, N. H.; lived in Berlin, Vt., 1870. (Family 1121)
>BETHANA, b. 30 Sept. 1811; m. Nov. 1836, Columbus Hackett of Woodbury, Vt.
2023. ALMON, b. 26 Sept. 1815; m. 17 Oct. 1838, Emily P. Carr; lived in Middlesex, Vt.
2024. CHESTER, b. 3 Aug. 1818; m. Almira Cilley of Woodbury, Vt.; lived in Woodbury, Vt.; seven children.

860

DANIEL[6] CHASE (Simon,[5] Daniel,[4] Isaac,[3] Daniel[2]), born 15 Feb. 1781; died in Colchester, Vt., Dec. 1863. He married in New Salem, 6 Jan. 1801, SALLY ANN SAUNDERS who died in Richmond, Vt., Dec. 1872. They lived in Woodbury, Burlington, Shelburne, and Colchester, Vt. Sally Ann Saunders had a daughter Almeda by a former husband, who married Heman Washburn.

Children:

2025. DANIEL WALDO,[7] m. Hannah Manchester; d. in Colchester, 1871.
>ELLEN CLIMENA, m. 17 Oct. 1827, Peter Hofman; one daughter only, Emma E. Hofman.
>MARY AUGUSTA, m. Amasa Alford.
>MARILLA, m. Cyrus Mills.
2026. HORATIO NELSON, m. Lucy Sherman of Richmond.
2027. AUGUSTUS WILLARD, m. 10 Feb. 1839, Almeda E. Hare of Colchester.
>ALMIRA, m. William Green of Colchester. She d. 29 Jan. 1864.
>LOUISA ANN, m. (1) Asa Alexander; m. (2) —— Trowbridge; m. (3) A. R. Bateman; she was a widow in Rutland, Vt., 1886.
>PHILANDER, d. young.
>ORREN, d. young.

861

NATHAN[6] CHASE (Simon,[5] Daniel,[4] Isaac,[3] Daniel[2]), born in New Salem, 3 July 1783: No further record of him.

862

EZRA[6] CHASE (Simon,[5] Daniel,[4] Isaac,[3] Daniel[2]), born 8 Jan. 1789; married in 1814, LUCINDA THAYER who died in Woodbury, Vt., 29 May 1843. They lived in Woodbury.
Child, born in Woodbury:

> SABRINA,[7] b. 7 Nov. 1822; m. (1) Samuel G. Goodrich, b. in Nottingham, N. H., 21 Mar. 1808; d. 19 Apr. 1838. She m. (2) 13 Apr. 1843, David D. Witham. She was living in Montpelier, Vt., 12 July 1874.

863

SETH[6] CHASE (Simon,[5] Daniel,[4] Isaac,[3] Daniel[2]), born 28 Feb. 1794; married and was the father of nine children. They probably lived in Vermont.
Children:

2029. EARL S.,[7] b. 10 Nov. 1832; m. 25 July 1858, Sarah J. Cotton.
2030. OTIS F., b. 14 July 1834; m. 6 Feb. 1866, Ellen E. Richards.
    FLORINDA, b. 28 Aug. 1836; m. 24 July 1853, William Robbins.
    MIRISILVIA N., b. 19 Sept. 1838; m. 5 Jan. 1857, Ira J. Beals.
2031. LE ROY S., b. 16 May 1840; m. 18 Dec. 1866, Eliza J. North.
    ANNA S., b. 24 July 1842; m. 18 Dec. 1866, West B. Barrett.
    LOANZA, b. 8 Jan. 1846; d. 19 July 1850.
    LUCINDA, b. 9 Apr. 1848.
2032. ARTHUR E., b. 31 May 1853.

864

DAVID[6] CHASE (Simon,[5] Daniel,[4] Isaac,[3] Daniel[2]), born 30 Mar. 1800; married in 1840, SARAH ———. They lived in Woodbury, Vt.
Children, born in Woodbury:

    LUCY MERRILL,[7] b. 10 May 1841.
2033. ALDEN FITZROY, b. 26 Oct. 1842; m. 6 Dec. 1869, Loisa F. Allen.
    ESTELLE OPHELIA, b. 1 Sept. 1846.
2034. AQUILA MONTROSE, b. 22 June 1854.

864a

DANIEL[6] CHASE (Aaron,[5] Daniel,[4] Isaac,[3] Daniel[2]), born in Orange, 30 July 1789; married widow ESTHER (CRAWFORD) SMITH. They lived in Canaan [Can.?] and died about 1868.
Child:

> ELIZABETH, d. young.

865

AARON[6] CHASE (Aaron,[5] Daniel,[4] Isaac,[3] Daniel[2]), born 27 Sept. 1791; died in 1874. He married in Swanton, Vt., 19 Mar. 1822, MERCY HARRIS who was born 12 Oct. 1798, and died 9 Apr. 1861, in Clinton Co., N. Y. He was living in Waterville, Vt., 9 Mar. 1873, aged 82.

Children, born in Franklin Co., Vt.:

2035. MARK,[7] b. 10 Mar. 1823; m. Jane S. Lovering; d. 15 Sept. 1870.
       JAMES DUDLEY, b. 23 May 1824; d. unm. 22 Feb. 1847.
       AMBROSE, b. 9 Oct. 1826; d. 2 Nov. 1833.
       NANCY, b. 6 Jan. 1829; m. Rev. Elam Marsh.
2036. AARON, b. 27 Mar. 1831; m. (1) 22 Aug. 1857, Eveline A.
       Glover; m. (2) 5 Feb. 1871, Mary Jane Marsh; lived in West
       Chazy, Clinton Co., N. Y.
       SARAH ANN, b. 12 May 1833; m. Christopher C. Prouty of
       Jay, Vt.
       STEPHEN HARRISON, b. 13 Aug. 1836; d. unm. 3 Apr. 1862.
       AMELIA, b. 11 Feb. 1839; m. 4 Feb. 1858, Charles McKinney of
       Glenbulah, Wis., 1877.
       ABIGAIL P., b. 6 Oct. 1841; m. Waldo E. Austin of Holden.
2037. ALBERT BENJAMIN, b. 25 Feb. 1844; m. Marcia M. Weston.

866

LEMUEL[6] CHASE (Thomas,[5] Timothy,[4] Isaac,[3] Daniel[2]), born in
Sutton, 12 Feb. 1786; married (1) SARAH HEATON; married (2)
SARAH ———. One Lemuel Chase, a Friend, lived in Pawlet, Vt.
His wife lived to the age of 87, dying before 1882.

Children by first wife:

2038. JAMES.[7]
       SON, d. unm.
       SON, d. unm.
2039. DANIEL.
       Children by second wife:
       ORIANA, m. Reuben Drury.
2040. WILLARD L., m. Betsey Eldridge.
2041. HIRAM, m. (1) Amy Shaw.
       LUCINDA, m. Henry Smith.

867

JOSHUA KNAPP[6] CHASE (Thomas,[5] Timothy,[4] Isaac,[3] Daniel[2]),
born in Sutton 20 Dec. 1767; baptized there 24 July 1768. No later
record of him.

868

NATHANIEL[6] CHASE (Thomas,[5] Timothy,[4] Isaac,[3] Daniel[2]), born
in Sutton about 1775. No record of his birth or baptism has
been found in Sutton. About 1870 it was reported to Dr. John B.
Chace that Thomas and Hannah (Knapp) Chase of Sutton had a son
Nathaniel There was a Nathaniel Chase in Sutton in 1790, whose
family consisted of one male over 16 years of age, four males under
16 years and two females.

A Nathaniel Chase was head of a family in Townshend, Vt., in
1790, consisting of one male over 16 years of age, three males under
16 and four females, and it is assumed that this Nathaniel is No. 298.

If Nathaniel[6] Chase, son of Thomas,[5] was born about 1775, he
would not be old enough to be the head of a family of seven in 1790.
There are no births recorded to any Nathaniel Chase in Sutton and
yet one Nathaniel Chase was head of a family of seven in that town
in 1790.

869

ABNER[6] CHASE (Abner,[5] Timothy,[4] Isaac,[3] Daniel[2]), born 16 July 1767; died in Concord, Erie Co., N. Y., 19 Sept. 1827. He married, in Ludlow Sept. 1789, CATHARINE FISHER who was born 21 Feb. 1772; died 20 Nov. 1841. They lived in New Salem till the Fall of 1815, when they removed to Colden, Erie Co., N. Y., where they lived later.

Children, born in New Salem:

EUNICE,[7] b. 18 Aug. 1790; m. 9 Apr. 1815, Ira McNeal; d. 24 Feb. 1864, in Linn Co., Iowa.

2042.   ABNER, b. 5 Sept. 1800; m. 5 Feb. 1824, Abigail Bell; d. in Concord, N. Y., 26 Sept. 1862.

NAOMI, b. 30 Oct. 1802; m. 11 Oct. 1821, Comfort Knapp; she d. 20 Mar. 1845, in Colden.

MELINDA, b. 21 May 1805; m. Henry Thomas; d. 15 May 1831.

2043.   WINSOR, b. 4 June 1808; m. (1) 1829, Clarissa Price; m. (2) 6 Mar. 1849, Mary Ann Clark; lived in St. Catherines, Ontario, 1834-1873.

2044.   ARZA, b. 27 Mar. 1811 or 1812; m. 22 May 1831, Elizabeth Alger; lived in Colden. Ten children.

LODEMA, b. 3 Mar. 1815; m. 19 Aug. 1832, Ransom Irish; living in Pine Island, Minn., 1873.

870

DAVID[6] CHASE (Abner,[5] Timothy,[4] Isaac,[3] Daniel[2]), born in Petersham, 25 Oct. 1769; died in Little Valley, N. Y., 20 July 1841. He married in New Salem, 29 Apr. 1793, LUCY GAY, daughter of Nathaniel and Lucy (Richards) Gay, baptized at Dedham, 23 May 1773, She died 24 Oct. 1850. They lived in New Salem and Little Falls, N. Y.

Children, born in New Salem:

PARNEY,[7] b. 7 Feb. 1794; m. 1 Apr. 1811, Jonathan Foster of New Salem.

2045.   ALVAN, b. 27 Oct. 1797; m. in Concord, N. Y., Jolly Phillips; he was living in Little Valley, N. Y., 22 Dec. 1872.

LEAFY (RELIEF), b. 30 July 1799; m. in Little Valley, N. Y., Gaius Wheaton.

SALLY, b. 3 Mar. 1804; m. 1826, Nathaniel Bryant; he d. in Minn., 5 Sept. 1860.

2046.   STILLMAN, b. 8 May 1806; m. 14 Nov. 1832, Wealthy Alzina Kelsey, b. 30 Jan. 1812; d. in Little Valley, N. Y., 6 Dec. 1874. He was a physician and d. in Rochester, Minn., 5 Sept. 1860. Their son Kelsey David,[8] b. in Little Valley, 1 Dec. 1841; m. in Homer, N. Y., 18 Feb. 1868, Isabella Electa Gardner, b. in Amber, N. Y., 13 Oct. 1843; d. in Faribault, Minn., 30 Jan. 1913. Their son Kelsey Stillman,[9] b. 15 Apr. 1878, in Crookson, Minn.; m. in Minneapolis, Minn., 22 June 1904, Ruth Law Cole, b. in Worthington, Minn., 25 Nov. 1881. Children: Kelsey D.,[10] b. 17 July 1905; Helen Ruth,[10] b. 31 Dec. 1906; Stephen Cole,[10] b. 29 July 1910; Cynthia Isabella,[10] b. 5 Nov. 1915.

2047.   DAVID, b. 17 Sept. 1808; m. 16 Sept. 1834, Mary Ann Clarke; lived in Rochester, Minn., 1873.

CYRENE, b. 27 Nov. 1817; m. in Little Valley, N. Y., Hiram Davis.

871

Moses[6] Chase (Abner,[5] Timothy,[4] Isaac,[3] Daniel[2]), born in New Salem, 25 Aug. 1771; died in Athol, 13 Sept. 1863. He married in Athol, 6 June 1797, Miriam Twitchell, daughter of Enos and Relief (Fairbanks) Twitchell, born in Athol, 29 Mar. 1777; died there 20 Oct. 1838. He was a blacksmith and lived in Athol.

Children, born in Athol:

Stillman,[7] b. 17 July 1789; d. 8 Sept. 1804.
Royal, b. 20 May 1800; d. 25 Sept. 1801.
Clark, b. 25 Sept. 1802; d. 6 Sept. 1804.
Freeman, b. 9 Jan. 1805; d. 9 Aug. 1808.
Hannah, b. 8 Feb. 1807; m. 7 June 1832, Charles[6] Chase of Keene, N. H. (Family 1004)
2048. Freeman, b. 18 Apr. 1809; m. 6 June 1833, Adeline Pierce; lived in Athol in 1873.
Dulcenia, b. 7 May 1811; m. 6 Oct. 1835, Daniel Ellingwood of Athol; d. 6 Aug. 1864; eight children.
Ephraim Fairbanks, b. 9 Jan. 1814; d. 18 Oct. 1832.
Miriam, b. 1 Sept. 1820; m. 13 Nov. 1838, Albe[6] Chase of Springfield, Vt. (Family 1006)

872

Enoch[6] Chase (Abner,[5] Timothy,[4] Isaac,[3] Daniel[2]), born 28 May 1773; died in Little Valley, N. Y., 28 May 1825. He married (1) in 1793, Abigail[6] (Chase) Wheelock, widow of Amasa Wheelock and daughter of Lt. Henry[5] and Hepsibah (Walker) Chase, born 18 July 1766; died in Lee, Iowa, 15 Oct. 1853. (Family 294). He married (2) Lucinda[7] (Chase) Stimson. (Family 298). They removed to the Holland Purchase, N. Y.

Children by first wife:

2049. Lyman,[7] b. 28 Feb. 1800; m. (1) 1824, Jerusha Doolittle, who d. 25 Mar. 1836; m. (2) 31 July 1837, Sarah O. Smead; lived in Clarida, Iowa.
2050. Kimball, b. 26 Mar. 1806; m. 29 Aug. 1826, Emily Gay; living in Middletown, Iowa, 1872.
2051. Johnson (twin), b. 26 Mar. 1806; m. about 1824, Susan Phillips; lived in Machias, Cattaraugus Co., N. Y.

873

Henry[6] Chase (Lt. Henry,[5] Henry,[4] Isaac,[3] Daniel[2]), born 12 Mar. 1776; died in Dresden, N. Y., 5 May 1835. He married (1) in 1807, Polly Lampson who died in May 1816. He married (2) 6 Oct. 1816, Sybil J. Brewster. They lived in Dresden, Washington Co., N. Y.

Children by first wife, born in Dresden:

2052. Stephen,[7] b. 18 Oct. 1809; m. Patty Barber; d. 22 Oct. 1837. One child Nancy[8], b. 18 Nov. 1834; lived in Dresden.
2053. George W., b. 8 June 1812; m. 20 May 1840, Anna Barber; he d. 9 May 1854.
2054. Jonas L., b. 17 Aug. 1814; m. (1) Patty Chase, widow of his brother Stephen; m. (2) Clarissa Maria Wilson; lived in Dresden.

Children by second wife, born in Dresden:

POLLY, b. 29 June 1817; m. Daniel Turner; d. Nov. 1866.
CLARISSA, b. 19 June 1819; d. 25 Dec. 1819.
BETSEY, b. 30 Dec. 1820; m. 9 Feb. 1843, Orson Wilsey of Dresden.
HENRY L., b. 21 Aug. 1823; d. 12 Apr. 1833.
NATHANIEL B., b. 25 Aug. 1825; never married.
LYDIA K., b. 27 Jan. 1828; m. 30 Jan. 1845, John Wilsey of Dresden.
ESTHER, b. 29 Mar. 1830; d. 26 Feb. 1833.

874

ELIAS[6] CHASE (Lt. Henry,[5] Timothy,[4] Isaac,[3] Daniel[2]), born about 1772; married (1) PHEBE GOULD. Perhaps they lived in New York state.
Children:

2055. WILLIAM HENRY,[7] b. 31 Dec. 1837.
2056. LUCIEN, b. 26 July 1839; m. Sept. 1867, Ellen J. Dalton.
ANN E., b. 18 June 1841.
2057. EDWARD P., b. 21 Apr. 1843.
STEPHEN H., b. 15 June 1845; d. 3 July 1864, at Fortress Monroe, Va.
2058. OSCAR A., b. 18 Dec. 1846.
SARAH A., b. 2 July 1859.
2059. HERBERT E., b. 25 Sept. 1862.

875

BEZALEEL[6] CHASE (Lt. Henry,[5] Timothy,[4] Isaac[3] Daniel[2]), born 17 June 1775; married 13 May 1801, SUSANNAH TAFT. They lived in Jamaica, Vt.
Children, born probably in Jamaica:

2060. HIBBERT T.,[7] living in Fayetteville, Vt., in 1872.
2061. BAYLIES, m. Sarah Howard; living in Simonsville, Vt., in 1872; first lived in Chester, Vt.
2062. ALANSON B., living in Fayetteville, 1872.
2063. SARDIS RILEY, d. in West Townshend, Vt., before 1872.
WINIFRED, m. Henry Whitman of Jamaica.
WEALTHY, m. Amos Howard of Jamaica. She d. before 1872.
2064. ELLIOTT C., d. in Jamaica, before 1872.

876

SARDIS RILEY[6] CHASE (Lt. Henry,[5] Timothy,[4] Isaac,[3] Daniel[2]), born in Townshend, Vt., 18 May 1788; married PERSIS PAINE. He removed to Washington, Ind., and died there.
Child:

LUCINDA,[7] m. ———— Cosgrove, and was living in Washington, Ind., in 1872.

877

ENOS[6] CHASE (Timothy,[5] Timothy,[4] Isaac,[3] Daniel[2]), born in Southborough, 5 Dec. 1780; married SUSAN MOODY, daughter of Joseph Moody of South Hadley. They lived in the south end of

Belchertown, 1 May 1810. He joined the Congregational Church there in 1810 and his wife joined in 1813.

Child, born in Belchertown:

2065. DEXTER,[7] joined the Congregational Church there in 1826.

878

ABNER[6] CHASE (Timothy,[5] Timothy,[4] Isaac,[3] Daniel[2]), born about 1782; taxed in the lower end of Belchertown, 1 May 1810. A search of the town records there will probably give more information.

879

ASAHEL[6] CHASE (Timothy,[5] Timothy,[4] Isaac,[3] Daniel[2]), born about 1785. He was living in Belchertown and was taxed in the lower end of the town 1 May 1810.

880

MARTIN[6] CHASE (Timothy,[5] Timothy,[4] Isaac,[3] Daniel[2]), born about 1787; taxed on a poll in Belchertown, 1 May 1810, then living in the lower end of the town.

881

REUBEN[6] CHASE (Lt. Nathaniel,[5] Timothy,[4] Isaac,[3] Daniel[2]), born 5 May 1773; married about 1800, HANNAH (MERRIFIELD) ESTY. He died about 1856. They lived in the vicinity of Orleans, N. Y.

Children, born in Vermont:

2066. ORRIN,[7] b. 5 Aug. 1802; m. (1) Sophia Dillingham; m. (2) Pamelia Root; living in Orleans, N. Y., in 1873.
2067. LYMAN, m. Martha ———; she was living in Walworth, Wayne Co., N. Y., 1873.

882

NATHANIEL PIERCE[6] CHASE (Lt. Nathaniel,[5] Timothy,[4] Isaac,[3] Daniel[2]), born 30 June 1775; died 4 July 1817. He married in Wrentham, 2 July 1806, NANCY FALES of Walpole, daughter of Moses and Rebecca (Savel) Fales, born in Walpole, 6 Feb. 1786; died 1 Apr. 1864. They lived in Walpole.

Children, born in Walpole:

2068. CURTIS ALONZO,[7] b. 20 Aug. 1807.
        MARY ANN, b. 13 Mar. 1809; m. 20 Dec. 1830, Washington F. Fisher; they lived in Worcester in 1875. Two sons.
        NANCY MARIA, b. 15 Sept. 1816; m. 23 Aug. 1832, Nahum Keene; lived in South Hanson.

883

JOHN[6] CHASE (Lt. Nathaniel,[5] Timothy,[4] Isaac,[3] Daniel[2]), born 18 Aug. 1776; visited his brother, Nathaniel Pierce Chase in Walpole. He married before 1812 and had two children. He lived in the town of Gill and died after 1828.

Children, probably born in Gill:

2069. ORRIN.[7]
       HARRIET.

884

MOSES[6] CHASE (Lt. Nathaniel,[5] Timothy,[4] Isaac,[3] Daniel[2]), born 14 Feb. 1786; died 14 Feb. 1849. He married in Constable, Franklin Co., N. Y., about 1806, AURILLA ELLSWORTH who died in 1848. They lived in Constable.

Children, born in Constable:

2070. HIRAM,[7] b. 13 Aug. 1808.
       SUSANNAH, b. 28 Aug. 1810; m. 12 Feb. 1828, Jonathan Fellows; lived in West Salamanca, N. Y.; d. 1873.
2071. NATHANIEL, b. 25 July 1812; m. (1) Abigail Phillips, who d. Nov. 1846; m. (2) 6 Jan. 1848, Sophronia Whitcomb; d. 1873.
2072. PORTER, b. about 1815; m. Lucy Collins.
       FOSTER, b. about 1817; d. at the age of 18.
2073. DAVID, b. 1821; m. Elizabeth Rider. He d. 13 Oct. 1870.
       HENRIETTA, b. 29 Jan. 1822; m. 10 Nov. 1837, John Kidder.
       AURILLA, b. Mar. 1824; m. (1) Mar. 1843, William Brown; m. (2) Horatio Gardner.

885

ROBERT[6] CHASE (Lt. Nathaniel,[5] Timothy,[4] Isaac,[3] Daniel[2]), married SALLY ESTY. They lived in Franklinville, Cattaraugus Co., N. Y. Children not reported.

886

JACOB R.[6] CHASE (Lt. Nathaniel,[5] Timothy,[4] Isaac,[3] Daniel[2]), born 3 Sept. 1794; died in Marion, Olmstead Co., Minn., 17 Oct. 1861. He married (1) AMY HUBBARD. He married (2) 14 Dec. 1823, RACHEL M. FULLER, born 22 May 1810. He married (3) 16 Jan. 1835, LYDIA A. BUNCE, daughter of Jacob and Laura (Wilcox) Bunce, born 6 Mar. 1815. They lived in Little Valley, N. Y., in Crawford Co., Ohio, in Fulton Co., Ohio, and Olmstead Co., Minn., and Laporte Co., Ind.

Children by the first wife:

       JULIA ANN.[7]
2074. WILLIAM, b. 10 Dec. 1820; m. (1) June 1850, Mary L. Akers; m. (2) 15 Oct. 1859, Abby S. Packard.

Children by second wife:

       ELIZA, b. 10 Nov. 1824; d. at age of 6 y.
       HIRAM V., b. 5 Mar. 1826; killed in battle of Gettysburg.
2075. IRA G. W., b. 17 Nov. 1827; m. 13 Aug. 1848, Sylvia Goodwin; clergyman; living in Elk Point, Dak. Ter., 1874.
       LUCY, b. 14 Nov. 1829.

Children by third wife, seventh to eleventh born in Crawford Co., Ohio:

       ESADORE F., b. 29 July 1836; m. 6 Oct. 1859, Catharine E. Pixley; lived in Sauk, Minn.
       LAURA M., b. 24 Jan. 1838; m. 10 Feb. 1857, John Uptagraff.

ELIZA ANNA, b. 9 Sept. 1840; m. 8 May 1859, Martin Webster.
HARLEY B., b. 10 Aug. 1842; never married.
MARTIN L., b. 17 Dec. 1843; d. Jan. 1845.
WILLIAM HENRY, b. 30 Aug. 1846; d. 1865; killed by Indians.
NANCY JANE, b. 13 Feb. 1848; m. 1870, George Williamson.
2076. ROBERT POMEROY, b. 3 Sept. 1850; m. 20 Mar. 1873, Mary McNelly.
CHARLOTTE, b. 5 Mar. 1853; d. 1854.
2077. RANSOM T., b. 21 Nov. 1854.

886a

IRA[6] CHASE (Lt. Nathaniel,[5] Timothy,[4] Isaac,[3] Daniel[2]), born 8 May 1804; married 25 Jan. 1836, DIADAMIA PURVIS. He was living in Watseka, Iroquois Co., Ill., in 1873.
Child:
SON,[7] b. 17 Nov. 1836; d. 24 Oct. 1854, aged 17 y. 11 m. 23 d.

887

MARTIN L.[6] CHASE (Lt. Nathaniel,[5] Timothy,[4] Isaac,[3] Daniel[2]), born 12 Jan. 1811; living in 1872 in Emmetsburg, Palo Alto Co., Calif. Family not reported.

888

JONATHAN[6] CHASE (Jacob,[5] Timothy,[4] Isaac,[3] Daniel[2]), born in 1779; died in Deerfield, Oneida Co., N. Y., July 1812. He married about 1801, CATHARINE CURRY. Mr. Chase was killed at a barn raising in Deerfield, in July 1812, aged 33 y.
Children, born in Deerfield:
2078. JOHN C.,[7] b. 10 Aug. 1802; m. 1825, Achsah Tyrrell of Lanesborough.
2079. LEVI P., b. 22 Aug. 1804; m. 1831, Laura Stevens of Lanesborough. He d. in Apr. 1843.
MARIA H., b. 18 Mar. 1809; m. 27 Dec. 1828, Thomas J. Peabody of Genoa, N. Y.
SOPHIA C., b. 14 Apr. 1811; m. 19 Oct. 1830, Samuel Partridge of Pittsfield.

889

MOSES[6] CHASE (Jacob,[5] Timothy,[4] Isaac,[3] Daniel[2]), born about 1782; died in Little Falls, N. Y., about 1868. He married but the name of his wife is not known.
Child:
2080. SYLVESTER,[7] lived in Albany, N. Y., in 1873.

890

AMOS[6] CHASE (Jacob,[5] Timothy,[4] Isaac,[3] Daniel[2]), born 21 Mar. 1784; died in Knoxville, N. Y., 14 Sept. 1864. He married in 1809, ISABEL CHURCH, born in N. H., 9 May 1788. They lived in Whitney, Vt., Deerfield, Oneida Co., N. Y., and Augusta, N. Y.
Children, first two born in Whitney, others born in Deerfield:
SQUIRE,[7] b. 6 Apr. 1810; never married; living in Knoxville in 1875.

ACHSAH, b. 2 Apr. 1811; m. 28 Feb. 1833, Hiram E. Bartholmew.

LAVINA, b. 8 May 1815; never married.

MARY, b. 7 Feb. 1824; m. 30 Sept. 1851, Charles Collins.

2081.   GEORGE W., b. 3 Jan. 1826; m. 27 Sept. 1848, Liva Porter; lived in Knoxville.

LUCY, b. 21 Mar. 1829; d. unm. 13 Oct. 1846.

ISABELLA, b. 18 Mar. 1831; never married.

891

REV. JACOB[6] CHASE (Jacob,[5] Timothy,[4] Isaac,[3] Daniel[2]), born in Townshend, Vt., 26 Aug. 1796. The name of his first wife has not been reported. He married (2) 4 Apr. 1832, MARY ROYS. They were living in Fairport, Monroe Co., N. Y., in 1873.

Children by his first wife:

2082.   WILLIAM PENDLETON,[7] b. 7 Sept. 1817; m. 8 Jan. 1849, Matilda Niel.

CLARISSA ALMIRA, b. 14 Sept. 1823; went to California.

2083.   JONATHAN INGERSOLL, b. 10 Sept. 1825; m. 12 June 1850, Julia Kellogg; d. 1 Jan. 1860.

892

HENRY[6] CHASE (Lt. Henry,[5] Timothy,[4] Isaac,[3] Daniel[2]), born in Conway, 24 Oct. 1767; married 1 Jan. 1788, IRENE WHEELOCK, daughter of Caleb and Rachel (Green) Wheelock, born in Mendon, 5 Apr. 1770. They lived in Townshend, Vt., and perhaps elsewhere.

Children, born in Townshend:

2084.   ABNER,[7] b. 25 Oct. 1789; m. 26 Mar. 1815, Mary Cox (1789-1863); living in Little Valley, N. Y., in 1873.

2085.   LUTHER, m. Mar. 1815, ———— ————; d. in Ohio about 1870.

HIRAM, went to Canada 1815; d. there 1820.

MELINDA, m. Simeon Smead, b. 10 June 1800; no issue.

2086.   WHEELOCK, b. 2 Aug. 1800; m. 24 Mar. 1824, Teressa Lyon. He d. 1844.

2087.   CONVERSE, m. Nancy Wheeler.

893

STEPHEN[6] CHASE (Lt. Henry,[5] Henry,[4] Isaac,[3] Daniel[2]), lived in Hartland, Vt.; married a woman whose name has not been reported.

Child, born, probably, in Hartland:

2088.   PERRIN.[7]

894

ASA[6] CHASE (Henry,[5] Henry,[4] Isaac,[3] Daniel[2]), born in Vermont, perhaps at Hartland; married and lived there and in Washington Co., N. Y.

Child:

JAMES.[7]

895

INCREASE[6] CHASE (Henry,[5] Henry,[4] Isaac,[3] Daniel[2]), born in Vermont, probably at Hartland and lived there.

896

JAMES[6] CHASE (James,[5] Henry,[4] Isaac,[3] Daniel[2]), born 4 Oct. 1781; married CLARISSA CORNWELL [Cornell] who was born at Watertown, N. Y., 11 Aug. 1785. There were ten children whose names have not been reported.

897

ELLERY R.[6] CHASE (James,[5] Henry,[4] Isaac,[3] Daniel[2]), born in New Canaan, Conn., 31 Jan. 1786; married MARY POTTER. They had a child or children.

898

LEVI[6] CHASE (Caleb,[5] Henry,[4] Isaac,[3] Daniel[2]), born 5 May 1777; died 15 Aug. 1855. He married ABIGAIL BURGESS.

Children, not in order:

2089. STEPHEN.[7]
2090. CALEB, m. 20 Sept. 1838, Elizabeth McKibben; lived in Pleasant Hill, Salina Co., Nebr.
      MARY ANN.
      SARAH, b. 2 Oct. 1807; m. 19 Aug. 1830, Jeremiah Smith. Four children.

899

JOHN[6] CHASE (Caleb,[5] Henry,[4] Isaac,[3] Daniel[2]), born 5 May 1780; died in Milledgeville, Carroll Co., Ill., 2 June 1862. He married (1) 7 Nov. 1802, MARY BIGELOW, born 13 Nov. 1782; died at Fort Washington, N. Y., 2 Sept. 1822. He married (2) 27 Nov. 1823, MEHITABLE STREETER who died in Howard, Steuben Co. N,. Y., 8 Nov. 1842.

Children by first wife:

PAULINA,[7] b. 27 Nov. 1803; d. 10 Sept. 1822.
THALMA, b. 25 Oct. 1805; m. 22 Oct. 1827, Gurdin Munsell of Fort Ann, N. Y.
MIRANDA, b. 2 May 1811; m. 1 Oct. 1843, James S. McKibben; lived in Sterling, Ill. No issue.
ARZA B., b. 2 Jan. 1814; m. (1) 4 Feb. 1836, Paulina Shaw, who d. in Milledgeville, 1 July 1863; m. (2) 4 Dec. 1864, Adaline Holly.
LE ROY E. F., b. 10 Dec. 1821; d. 6 Sept. 1822.

Child by second wife:

ALZADA, b. 6 Dec. 1824; m. (1) 11 Jan. 1853, James J. Buss; lived in Chicago, Ill., 1873.

900

OLIVER[6] CHASE (Caleb,[5] Henry,[4] Isaac,[3] Daniel[2]), born 29 Sept. 1781; married (1) ELIZABETH BAILEY. He married (2) but the name has not been reported. They probably lived in Fort Anne, Washington Co., N. Y.

Children:

2091. NATHAN.[7]
2092. ELLERY.

           MARY, d. young.
2093.   ALVIN.
2094.   OLIVER, lived in Fort Anne, N. Y.
           BETSEY.
           NELLIE.
           FANNY.
           HANNAH.
           MARY.
           ANN.

901

STEPHEN F.[6] CHASE (Caleb,[5] Henry,[4] Isaac,[3] Daniel[2]), born 3 Aug. 1783; died in Fort Anne, N. Y., 5 Nov. 1864. He married about 1808, ABIGAIL STANLEY who died 25 Aug. 1872. They lived in Fort Anne, Washington Co., N. Y.

     Children, born in Fort Anne:

2095.   DOTY,[7] b. 23 Feb. 1809; m. (1) 14 Oct. 1830, Sarah Brown, who d. 6 Apr. 1852; m. (2) 27 Sept. 1854, Mrs. Lydia Elizabeth Lane; living in Fair Haven, N. Y., 13 Feb. 1873. Seventeen children born in Wolcott, N. Y.
           HARRIET, b. 26 Mar. 1811; m. 1834, Jacob Sanborn.
2096.   GEORGE B., b. 13 Feb. 1813; m. Ruth H. ———, who was b. 5 Dec. 1805. Five children.
2097.   HENRY P., b. 8 May 1815; m. Sophia ———.
           JANE, b. 24 Aug. 1817; m. 1 Jan. 1837, Jacob Clapper.
           ELIZA A., b. 29 July 1819; m. (1) 22 Aug. 1855, Cephas Perkins; m. (2) 22 Aug. 1865, Silas Dutcher.
           ROZILLA, b. 7 Aug. 1821; m. John Quimby.
           BETSEY, b. 12 Nov. 1823; m. John Grandy. She d. Oct. 1870.

902

ELLISON[6] CHASE (Caleb,[5] Henry,[4] Isaac,[3] Daniel[2]), born 28 Mar. 1789; married LUCY MUNSELL. They probably lived in New York state.

     Children, born probably in New York state:

2098.   ALONZO.[7]
2099.   ELLISON.
2100.   ALANSON.
           MELISSA.

903

ASA[6] CHASE (Elisha,[5] Henry,[4] Isaac,[3] Daniel[2]), born in Jamaica, Vt., 18 June 1792; married MRS. POLLY S. SIBLEY. They lived in the western part of New York state.

     Children:

           ACHSAH.[7]
2101.   GALUSHA.
           ZILPHA.
2102.   GILBERT, m. Lucy Forbes of Fort Anne, N. Y.; lived in Fort Ann. Their son George H.,[8] b. 3 Apr. 1820; d. 1896; m. 20 July 1865, Charlotte H. Milho.
           LUCINDA.

904

SEWALL[6] CHASE (Peter,[5] Henry,[4] Isaac,[3] Daniel[2]), born in Petersham, 27 July 1798; died Jamaica 26 Feb. 1847, aged 49: He married 20 Nov. 1842, SOPHIA M. ALLEN of Newfane, Vt. They lived in Jamaica, Vt.

Children, born in Jamaica:

POLLY SOPHIA,[7] b. 1 Mar. 1844.
2103. PETER SEWALL, b. 25 Mar. 1845; lived in Brattleboro, Vt., 1874.
SUSANNA MARIA, b. 25 Nov. 1846.

905

DANIEL[6] CHASE (Peter,[5] Henry,[4] Isaac,[3] Daniel[2]), born in Jamaica, Vt., 28 Sept. 1805, lived in Stratton, Vt.; died in 1888. He married MARY JANE ———, born in 1816, and died in 1902. They were buried in Jamaica.

Children:

2104. FRANKLIN D.,[7] alive in 1902; lived in Somerset, Vt., 1880.
GEORGE S., b. 1843; d. 21 Jan. 1864, in Co. H. 9th Vt. Regt. Civil War.

906

MARTIN[6] CHASE (Peter,[5] Henry,[4] Isaac,[3] Daniel[2]), born in Jamaica, Vt., 9 May 1815; married 18 Dec. 1839, BETSEY BUTTERFIELD who was born 18 Mar. 1821. He died 19 Apr. 1862. His widow was living in Keene, N. H., in 1874.

Children, born in Jamaica, Vt.:

2105. MARTIN WESLEY,[7] b. 23 Nov. 1840.
2106. GEORGE THOMAS, b. 23 May 1842; d. 7 Jan. 1866.
2107. HENRY PETER, b. 27 June 1844; lived in Londonderry, Vt.
BETSEY VIORNIA, b. 17 Mar. 1847; d. Oct. 1849.
MARY LUCINA, b. 26 Feb. 1850.
DANIEL EZRA, b. 29 May 1852; d. 21 July 1852.
2108. JAMES FRANKLIN, b. 5 Dec. 1856; d. in Malden, 30 Mar. 1923; m. (1) Cora J. Lawton of Chester, Vt., who d. in Malden, 30 Oct. 1919; m. (2) 5 Apr. 1921, Mrs. Edna T. Allen of Brockton. Mr. Chase was for a long time the efficient secretary-treasurer of The Chase-Chace Family Association.
SARAH DIANTHA, b. 7 Mar. 1859.

907

ELISHA D.[6] CHASE (Ebenezer,[5] Elisha,[4] Isaac,[3] Daniel[2]), married in Canada and lived in Queenstown, Ontario, Can.

Child:

2109. NICHOLAS W.[7]

908

ABISHAI C.[6] CHASE (Ezekiel,[5] Elisha,[4] Isaac,[3] Daniel[2]), born 27 Apr. 1792; died in Carr Co., Ind., 19 June 1839. He married 26 Mar. 1816, LETITIA CHIPPIE who was born 11 Apr. 1794; died 28 Nov. 1864. They removed to Carr Co., Ind.

Children:

HANNAH,[7] b. 11 Apr. 1817; m. Benjamin Perry and d. in 1850.
2110. ABEL SIMPSON, b. 27 Feb. 1819; m. (1) 3 Apr. 1856, Barbara
White; m. (2) 26 Mar. 1865, Mary J. Harron.
SARAH ANN, b. 11 Apr. 1821; m. Oct. 1850, Benjamin Perry.
CELIA, b. 1 May 1823; m. (1) Samuel Shires; m. (2) Christian
Hipsher.
CLARISSA, b. 1824; d. at age of 6 m.
WILLIAM CLINTON, d. in infancy.
ELMIRA, b. 1827; d. 1840, age 13.
LUCY, b. 22 Feb. 1829; m. 13 Oct. 1855, Robert Benson.
MARY, b. 17 Apr. 1833; d. 13 Sept. 1855.
BENJAMIN, b. 28 Aug. 1837; d. 23 Nov. 1850.

909

ASHER[6] CHASE (Ezekiel,[5] Elisha,[4] Isaac,[3] Daniel[2]), born in
Guilford, Vt., 29 Mar. 1793; married (1) 22 Mar. 1820, NANCY
RICHARDSON who was born 4 Oct. 1797; died 25 July 1847. He mar-
ried (2) 20 May 1848, IRENA AXTELL who was born 13 July 1813.
They lived in Madison Co., Ill., and were living in Villisca, Mont-
gomery Co., Iowa, in 1874.

Children by first wife:

HIRAM,[7] b. 22 Dec. 1820; d. in infancy.
MARY ANN, b. 26 July 1822; m. John Parker.
LUCINDA, b. 9 Feb. 1824; d. in infancy.
2111. GAMALIEL, b. 14 Oct. 1825; m. Cynthia Bradbury.
PAUL, b. 28 Sept. 1827; d. in infancy.
MARIA, b. 31 Dec. 1829; d. at age of 15 y.
ELIZA, b. 26 Sept. 1831; d. in infancy.
2112. SILAS, b. 17 May 1833; m. Ruth Reed.
2113. SIDNEY, b. 12 July 1835; m. Martha Cleveland.
2114. WILLIAM, b. 21 Aug. 1837; m. Catharine Jerred [Gerard].
2115. ASHER, b. 25 July 1842; m. Hannah Morrow.

Children by second wife:

COLUMBUS, b. 5 Mar. 1849; d. same year.
MARIA ELIZABETH, b. 10 Aug. 1850; m. John Drace.
2116. NATHAN A., b. 3 Aug. 1852; m. Mary Beavers.
ELVIRA, b. 26 Apr. 1854; never married.

910

ABEL[6] CHASE (Ezekiel,[5] Elisha,[4] Isaac,[3] Daniel[2]), born in Guilford, Vt., 16 May 1798; married 4 July 1826, POLLY BRADBURY,
daughter of Moses and Agnes (Hunt) Bradbury, born in 1808; died
6 Aug. 1839. They lived in Brown County and Clairmont County,
Ohio.

Children, first born in Brown Co., second born in Clairmont Co.:

CLARISSA,[7] b. 10 Mar. 1827; m. 18 June 1852, D. N. Graham;
living in Abington, Ill., in 1874.
2117. ALBERT G., b. 19 Sept. 1832; m. 28 Aug. 1859, Eliza C. Drace.
Their other children died without issue.

911

DEA. WILLIAM[6] CHASE (Nathaniel,[5] Judah,[4] Daniel,[3] Daniel[2]),
born in Brunswick, Me., 1807; died in Litchfield, Me., 29 Dec. 1893.
He married (1) about 1834, MARY JANE ALEXANDER, daughter of
James and Sally (Lydston) Alexander of Litchfield. She was born
6 Aug. 1812. He married (2) MRS. ELIZABETH MAXWELL. They
lived at the Plains in Litchfield.
Children, born in Litchfield:

2118. ALONZO M.,[7] b. 8 Mar. 1835; m. Caroline S. Lincoln; he d.
       5 Mar. 1867.
       SARAH A., b. 11 Sept. 1837; m. Josiah L. Merrill of Man-
       chester, Me.
2119. WILLIAM E., b. 5 Feb. 1839; m. Sarah J. Whitney of Auburn,
       Me.
       NANCY J., b. 24 Sept. 1840; m. Robert S. Whitney.
2120. JAMES ALEXANDER, b. 11 June 1842; m. (1) Lizzie J. Parsons;
       m. (2) Mary A. Small; lived at the "Plains."
2121. LLEWELLYN, b. 11 July 1844; m. Mary K. King; lived in Mon-
       mouth, Me.
       HANNAH OLIVIA, b. 9 July 1847; m. Charles Whitney.

912

ISAAC[6] CHASE (Nathaniel,[5] Judah,[4] Daniel,[3] Daniel[2]), born in
Wales, Me., in 1818; died in Litchfield, Me., 24 Apr. 1886, aged 68.
He married about 1841, MARY P. STINSON, daughter of Rev. Robert
and Fanny (Patten) Stinson, born 10 May 1822. His portrait is in
the History of Litchfield, Me., p. 76.
Children, born in Litchfield:

2122. ROBERT F.,[7] b. 21 Jan. 1843; m. Sarah Jack; lived in Gardiner,
       Me., and later in North Carolina.
2123. CHARLES EDWIN, b. 1 Mar. 1844; m. (1) Laura Lord; m. (2)
       Julia Gage; m. (3) Clara Gage; m. (4) Flora Roberts.
       ISAAC N., b. 21 Feb. 1847; d. 14 Nov. 1869.
       MARY FRANCES, b. 4 Sept. 1851; m. John A. Hutchinson.

913

DANIEL[6] CHASE (Nathaniel,[5] Judah,[4] Daniel,[3] Daniel[2]), born in
Monmouth or Litchfield, Me.; married LUCY HEATH, daughter of
Samuel Heath of Lisbon, Me. They lived in Brunswick, Me.
Children:

       ELIZABETH ANN,[7] d. unm.
       NANCY DENISON, d. young.
       REBECCA JANE, d. young.
       MARY FRANCIS, unm.; living in Malden (1928).
       HARRIET ELLEN, m. George William Jenkins, a native of Nan-
       tucket; living in Malden.
       ALICE MARIA, m. George Edward Bowker of Brunswick; she
       is deceased.

914

EZEKIEL[6] CHASE (Daniel,[5] Daniel,[4] Daniel,[3] Daniel[2]), born in
Concord, N. H., 15 Aug. 1783; died 9 May 1859. He married in
Groton, N. H., 11 May 1805, MISS SARAH BUSWELL. They removed

from Concord to Watertown, N. Y., before 1817. At the time of his marriage he was living in Holderness, N. H.

Children, the four youngest born in Watertown, N. Y.:

PARTHENIA,[7] b. 6 Feb. 1806.

2124. DANIEL, b. 10 Oct. 1808; m. (1) Lucina Earl; m. (2) Angie ————; lived in Port Huron, Mich., in 1875.

2125. DAVID WEBSTER, b. 29 Aug. 1811; d. in Watertown, about 1872.

2126. JOHN SULLIVAN, b. 29 Sept. 1814.

2127. SAMUEL BROWN, b. 5 May 1816; m. 1 June 1841, Catharine M. Fellows; lived in Rochester, N. Y.; d. in 1845.

2128. JAMES AIKEN, b. 6 Nov. 1818.

2129. WILLIAM EDWIN, b. 29 Feb. 1820.

2130. MOSES JUDSON, b. 21 Apr. 1823.

915

DEA. JOHN[6] CHASE (Daniel,[5] Daniel,[4] Daniel,[3] Daniel[2]), born in Concord, N. H., 9 June 1791; died 20 Apr. 1841, aged 49. He married in Windsor, Vt., 31 Mar. 1816, THEODOCIA BANNISTER, daughter of Silas and Thankful Bannister, born in Windsor, Vt., 9 Mar. 1796; died 6 Mar. 1852 in Carthage, N. Y. They lived in Carthage, Jefferson Co., N. Y. He was Deacon of the Baptist Church at Carthage.

Children, born in Carthage:

2131. ROBERT DAVID,[7] b. 6 Mar. 1817; m. (1) 26 Apr. 1848, Harriet L. Chapin; m. (2) 9 Mar. 1854, Adeline Rose; living in Dover, N. J., in 1876; d. 9 Nov. 1885. No issue.

FANNY SUSAN, b. 9 Aug. 1818; m. 1842, David Andros Northrup; she d. 23 Sept. 1868.

MARY ANN, b. 30 July 1820; m. 29 Jan. 1843, George B. Griffin of Chicago, Ill.

JULIET DOUGLAS, b. 28 July 1822; m. 15 Jan. 1843, Harvey B. Farrington of Buffalo, N. Y. She d. 17 Apr. 1891.

EMILY CLARK, b. 16 Feb. 1825; d. 21 Apr. 1826.

ELIZA VERPLANCK, b. 8 Aug. 1828; m. 1856, Capt. James E. Bennett of Riceville, Iowa.

2132. JOHN J., b. 3 Sept. 1831; m. 17 July 1865, Sophia P. Cook; living in Chicago, Ill., in 1876; d. there 16 Apr. 1895.

DORMA MARIA, b. 12 Nov. 1833; m. Aug. 1851, Capt. James E. Bennett; she d. Nov. 1852, in Honolulu, Sandwich Islands.

916

SANFORD[6] CHASE (James E.,[5] Daniel,[4] Daniel,[3] Daniel[2]), born in Me.; married MARTHA THURSTON of Otisfield, Me.; they lived in Corinna, Me. Their family has not been reported.

917

ROBERT[6] CHASE (James E.,[5] Daniel,[4] Daniel,[3] Daniel[2]), born in Maine.

918

STEPHEN[6] CHASE (James E.,[5] Daniel,[4] Daniel,[3] Daniel[2]), born in Maine.

919

ELIPHAZ[6] CHASE (James E.,[5] Daniel,[4] Daniel,[3] Daniel[2]), born in Me. 4 Oct. 1804; m. 25 Jan. 1825, POLLY[6] CHASE, daughter of Ebenezer[5] and Hannah (Emerson) Chase, b. in Townshend, Vt., 2 Feb. 1809. She married (2) in Mar. 1860, Jonathan Pulcifer of West Sumner, Me., and was living there, 24 Sept. 1872. They lived in Sebec, Me. Mr. Chase went to sea and the last letter his wife received from him was dated at Indian Key, Fla., 16 July 1841.

Children, first born in Waterville, Me., others in Sebec:

CHLOE,[7] b. 27 Aug. 1827; d. in infancy.

ELIPHAZ AUGUSTUS, b. 22 Feb. 1829; went to sea in 1850; never heard from later than 1851.

2133. STEPHEN PHILIP, b. 15 Apr. 1831; m. in Saco, Me., 9 Mar. 1852, Caroline Bowie; lived in Wakefield.

FRANCES M., b. 12 Aug. 1833; m. 15 Apr. 1849, Daniel A. Tower of Waterville, 1872.

MARY A., b. 18 Dec. 1835; m. 28 May 1850, John Ross of Lyman and Lewiston, Me.

920

JEFFERSON[6] CHASE (James E.,[5] Daniel,[4] Daniel,[3] Daniel[2]), born in Maine; married CHLOE LANDER; they lived in Dexter, Me.

921

MOSES[6] CHASE (James E,,[5] Daniel,[4] Daniel,[3] Daniel[2]), born in Maine; married BETSEY SOULE; they lived in Waterville, Me.

922

ELIHU[6] CHASE (James E.,[5] Daniel,[4] Daniel,[3] Daniel[2]), born in Maine; married BETHIAH SOULE; lived in Waterville, Me., and died there.

923

GEORGE W.[6] CHASE (Capt. Isaac,[5] Daniel,[4] Daniel,[3] Daniel[2]), born in Concord, N. H., 29 May 1790; married LYDIA DYER, daughter of James Dyer of Calais, Me.

924

ARTHUR L.[6] CHASE (Capt. Isaac,[5] Daniel,[4] Daniel,[3] Daniel[2]), born in Sidney, Me., 24 Jan. 1794; married SALLY BUCK of Fairfield, Me.

925

COL. DANIEL[6] CHASE (Capt. Isaac,[5] Daniel,[4] Daniel,[3] Daniel[2]), born in Fairfield, Me., 5 Apr. 1798; married in Palmyra, Me., 15 Feb. 1831, MARY S. WHITE of Palmyra, Me., who was born 26 June 1810. They lived in Fairfield. He and his sons served in the Civil War from Fairfield, and he was living there in 1875.

Children, born in Fairfield:

ADELINE M.,[7] b. 29 May 1832.

ANNA E., b. 22 Oct. 1833.

MARIA L., b. 29 May 1835; m. 29 May 1853, Charles A. Chase. (Stephen,[7] family 565.)

2134. JOHN W., b. 22 Nov. 1837; killed at Port Hudson, 28 May 1863.
2135. DANIEL, b. 16 June 1839.

SAMUEL, b. 29 May 1841; d. Oct. 1842.

ELLEN, b. 20 June 1842; d. 14 Apr. 1868.

2136. HENRY C., b. 28 July 1844; wounded at Pleasant Hill, Red River and died in service at St. Louis, Mo.

AMY, b. 10 Mar. 1845; d. 24 Apr. 1845.

2137. AQUILA, b. 27 Jan. 1847.

926

ISAAC[6] CHASE (Capt. Isaac,[5] Daniel,[4] Daniel,[3] Daniel[2]), born in Sidney, Me., 15 May 1800; married 1 Dec. 1825, RACHEL EMERY of Fairfield, Me., daughter of David and Abigail (Goodwin) Emery, born in Fairfield in 1800; died 15 Mar. 1887. They lived in Fairfield.

Children, born in Fairfield:

ORRA ANN,[7] b. 17 Sept. 1826; m. Benjamin Hatch of Fairfield. Three children; d. Dec. 1862.

2138. ALBERT B., b. 11 Feb. 1828; m. Frances Noble; lived in Sidney, Nebr. Seven children.

EMILY EMERY, b. 21 May 1830; m. 13 Sept. 1849, George B. Cain of Fairfield. Two children.

2139. BENJAMIN F., b. 27 Apr. 1832; went to California; m. (1) Mary Ann Leavitt; m. (2) Lucinda W. Noyes.

SARAH S., b. 17 Feb. 1835; m. 23 Feb. 1863, Levi F. Emery of Harmony, Me.

2140. JOHN WESLEY, b. 6 May 1837; m. 22 Nov. 1860, Margaret C. Nolan; Methodist clergyman; d. 27 Dec. 1876. Five children.

927

CHARLES[6] CHASE (Capt. Isaac,[5] Daniel,[4] Daniel,[3] Daniel[2]), born in Sidney, Me., 28 May 1802; living in Illinois in 1872. He married CELIA PITTS of Fairfield, Me.

928

JONAS[6] CHASE (Capt. Isaac,[5] Daniel,[4] Daniel,[3] Daniel[2]), born in Fairfield, Me., 29 July 1806, living in Fairfield, or Clinton, Me., in 1872. He married MARY HUNT of Fairfield. Their family has not been reported. One Jonas Chase was living in Clinton, Me., about 1890, and on his farm was an old town cemetery.

929

DR. EBENEZER[6] CHASE (Ebenezer,[5] Daniel,[4] Daniel,[3] Daniel[2]), born 1 Apr. 1786; married in Cambridge, N. Y., 11 Oct. 1804, BESSEY TIRRELL who died in Bridgewater, Vt., 12 Aug. 1846. He died in Chester, Vt., 13 Apr. 1866. They lived in Londonderry, Townshend, and Athens, Vt. Both were physicians.

Children, first born in Townshend, second in Westminster, Vt., others in Athens:

2141. EBENEZER,[7] b. 15 Aug. 1806; m. 21 Oct. 1827, Louisa (Nelson) Chase; he d. 6 Aug. 1846, in Rockingham, Vt.

2142. DANIEL, b. 30 May 1808; m. Parthena Hadley of Sherburn, Vt. He d. 31 May 1830 in Athens, Vt.
2143. ISAAC T., b. 21 May 1810; m. Phebe Edson; he d. 25 June 1844.
PETER T., b. — Apr. 1812; d. 21 Feb. 1821.
BETSEY, b. — Apr. 1814; d. in infancy, 9 weeks old.
MARIA, b. 1 June 1816; m. Hiram Rice; she d. 14 Aug. 1858, in Somerset, Vt.
ELVIRA, b. — Apr. 1818; d. at 9 m.
ALMIRA SOPHRONIA, b. 2 Feb. 1819; m. (1) Reuben Lippenwell; m. (2) Josiah Rugg.
ELMINA EUSEBIA, b. 14 Apr. 1821; m. (1) 4 Sept. 1838, C. V. Rensalaer Chilson; m. (2) 30 Nov. 1850, James C. Ryder; she was a botanic physician in Randolph, Vt., 1873.
ELZINA A., b. 29 July 1823; m. Leonard Cummings. She d. 21 Dec. 1847.
2144. PHILIP E. O., b. 12 Sept. 1825; m. 20 Sept. 1846, Hannah P. Hubbard; he d. 12 Sept. 1865; Bridgewater.
2145. WILLIAM V., b. 6 Mar. 1827; m. 7 May 1843, Mary Haggett.

930

DANIEL[6] CHASE (Ebenezer,[5] Daniel,[4] Daniel,[3] Daniel[2]), born 29 Oct. 1787; died in Sebec, Me., 7 Dec. 1861. He married about 1813, EUSEBIA DEPUTREN of Sidney, Me. She died 25 July 1869. They lived in Sebec.
Children, born in Sebec:

HANNAH,[7] d. young.
HANNAH, b. 14 Dec. 1814; m. Dec. 1837, Freeman C. Glover. She d. Dec. 1858; eight children.
2146. BENJAMIN, b. 20 June 1817; m. 2 Sept. 1840, Olive Lovell; living in Sebec in 1872. Five children.
REBECCA F., b. 14 June 1819; d. 1826.
OLIVE, b. 23 Nov. 1821; m. about 1843, Charles B. Davis. She d. in 1868. Seven children.
PENELOPE, b. 24 Mar. 1824; m. about 1844, Arnold Sweet. She d. about 1847; two children.
DANIEL OCTAVIUS, b. 8 Aug. 1826; never married.
2147. AARON F., b. 12 Jan. 1829; m. Nancy Trenham; lived in Cambridge or Watertown.
LAURA, b. about 1831.
2148. JOHN T., b. 28 Jan. 1834; m. Abby Herbert of Ornville, Me. Six children.

931

JAMES P.[6] CHASE (Ebenezer,[5] Daniel,[4] Daniel,[3] Daniel[2]), born in 1799; died 19 July 1864, aged 65. He married about 1822, MARY E. BADGER of Waterville, Me., who died at the age of 66, after 1872.
Children:

ABIGAIL B.,[7] b. 5 May 1823; m. in Sebec, Me., 30 Nov. 1843, Timothy Merrill of Bangor, Me. She d. 25 Mar. 1866.
2149. JAMES E., b. 4 Sept. 1824; m. in Canaan, Me., 25 Dec. 1858, Caroline M. Richardson.
2150. PRATT, b. 1 Mar. 1826; m. in Levant, Me., 20 Jan. 1856, Mary A. Austin.
HANNAH E., b. 16 Oct. 1827; m. in Harmon, Me., 1 Mar. 1852, James M. Mayhew.

CATHARINE B., b. 12 May 1829; m. in Foxcroft, Me., 17 Sept. 1848, Abel Towne.

2151.   HENRY G., b. 27 Feb. 1831; m. in Liberty, Me., Mar. 1870, Clara A. Sweet.

MARY E., b. 25 Jan. 1833; m. in Bangor, Me., 19 Nov. 1850, William S. Richardson.

2152.   AARON T., b. 20 Dec. 1834.

SARAH A., b. 28 Sept. 1837; m. 19 Dec. 1858, Benjamin Clark.

LOIS C., b. 26 Apr. 1840; m. in Foxcroft, Me., 26 Apr. 1857, John Terrill.

LUCY S. (twin), b. 26 Apr. 1840; d. 16 Feb. 1843.

BERTHA F., b. 25 Apr. 1842; unm. in 1874.

HUMPHREY F., b. 17 June 1844; d. in Washington, D. C., 22 Dec. 1861.

2153.   WILLIAM W., b. 15 Apr. 1846; m. July 1871, Adaline G. Perham.

2154.   ALBERT A., b. 7 Nov. 1848.

LUCY G., b. 31 May 1853; d. 29 Aug. 1865.

932

PHILIP E.[6] CHASE (Ebenezer,[5] Daniel,[4] Daniel,[3] Daniel[2]), married in Oct. 1825, SALLY L. ANNIS. He died 8 Apr. 1852. They lived in Sebec, Me., and Foxcroft, Me. The widow was living in Foxcroft in 1873.

Children, born in Sebec:

2155.   PHILIP E.,[7] b. 18 Mar. 1826; d. 1854 or 1855.

SARAH, b. 2 June 1827.

2156.   EBENEZER, b. 30 July 1830; lived in Foxcroft in 1873.

2157.   GEORGE W., b. 15 Apr. 1832; d. about 1855.

2158.   RICHARD N., b. 17 May 1835; d. 12 May 1859.

2159.   THOMAS A., b. 8 Mar. 1837; d. about 1863.

MARGARET, b. 7 Aug. 1839.

ALFRED A., b. 10 June 1841; d. 1855.

CHARLES L., b. 2 Oct. 1844; d. 4 July 1854.

933

JUDGE HORACE[6] CHASE (Samuel,[5] Capt. Jonathan,[4] Daniel,[3] Daniel[2]), born in Unity, N. H., 14 Dec. 1788; died in Hopkinton, N. H., 1 Mar. 1875, aged 86 y. 2 m. 14 d. He married (1) 24 Dec. 1818, BETSEY BLANCHARD, daughter of Stephen and Betsey (Estabrook) Blanchard, born 14 Jan. 1789; died in Hopkinton, N. H., 28 June 1843. He married (2) 5 June 1844, LUCY BLANCHARD, sister to his first wife, born 2 Dec. 1797; died in Hopkinton, 22 Dec. 1848. He married (3) 15 Nov. 1849, RUHAMAH (COCHRANE) CLARKE, widow of Daniel W. Clarke of Manchester and daughter of Joseph and Anna (Wilson) Cochrane of New Boston. She was born 25 Feb. 1812; died 16 Feb. 1905. He graduated at Dartmouth College in 1814; read law and practiced in Hopkinton; town clerk 1824-5 and 1829-35; representative 1829; assistant clerk of House of Representatives, 1830-1832; Judge of Probate for Merrimack Co. 1843 to 1855. Author of the *History of Masonry*, 1789 to 1856; Knight Templar.

Horace Chase   *Sincerely Yours, Horace G. Chase*

Children by first wife, born in Hopkinton:

MARY ELIZABETH,[7] b. 16 Aug. 1821; d. 7 June 1843.

2160. SAMUEL BLANCHARD, b. 1 Oct. 1823; m. 1 June 1843, Emma Thompson. Graduated at Dartmouth in 1844.

2161. HORACE GAIR, b. 9 July 1827; m. 14 June 1860, Ellen Marian Sherwin, who d. 18 Apr. 1917. She was dau. of Myron and Ellen (Richards) Sherwin of Chicago. He was educated at Hopkinton Academy and removed to Chicago in 1852 where he was a conveyancer and real estate broker. He died 3 Feb. 1913. Their children were *Samuel Myron*,[8] b. 14 July 1862; m. (1) 12 June 1889, Bertha Delia Ford who d. 12 Aug. 1893; m. (2) 2 Oct. 1901, Etta Elizabeth Ford; *Bessie Louise Blanchard*,[8] m. Louis Moen Grant, who d. 26 Jan. 1921. Their son William Chase[9] Grant, b. 3 May 1896; m. Helen Chism Shriver. *Lucy Blanchard*,[8] m. 24 Apr. 1901, Edward Miffirn Devereux. Their on Edward Chase[9] Devereux, b. 12 Aug. 1910. *Horace Stanley*,[8] b. 19 Aug. 1883; m. 16 Apr. 1913, Gertrude Putnam McMannis. Children: Marian Putnam Chase[9] McMannis and Horace Gair Chase[9] McMannis.

2162. CHARLES CARROLL, b. 18 Sept. 1829; m. 22 Nov. 1858, Julia M. Sawyer.

934

CAPT. OVID[6] CHASE (Samuel,[5] Capt. Jonathan,[4] Daniel,[3] Daniel[2]), born in Unity, N. H., 4 June 1800; married in Wendell (now Sunapee), N. H., 31 Dec. 1833, SARAH W. PIKE. They lived in Canandaigua, N. Y.

Children:

2163. HOMER.[7]
2164. OVID.

935

HOMER[6] CHASE (Samuel,[5] Capt. Jonathan,[4] Daniel,[3] Daniel[2]), born in Unity, N. H., 17 Nov. 1805; married 14 Mar. 1827, LAMIRA GUNNISON who died 17 July 1835. He removed to San José, Calif. There were two daughters whose names have not been reported.

936

JONATHAN[6] CHASE (Moses,[5] Capt. Jonathan,[4] Daniel,[3] Daniel[2]), born in Unity, N. H., 13 Oct. 1789; died in Springfield, Vt., 4 Oct. 1851. He married in Springfield, 18 Mar. 1818, SUSAN FISHER, daughter of Isaac and Elizabeth (Glover) Fisher, born in Lancaster, 1 July 1797. They lived in Springfield.

Children, born in Springfield:

2165. MOSES FISHER,[7] b. 18 Feb. 1819; m. 1 Jan. 1840, Chloe Ann Clement.

MARY ELISABETH, b. 10 Dec. 1821; m. 16 Nov. 1837, Edwin P. Whitmore.

937

DR. LEONARD[6] CHASE (Moses,[5] Capt. Jonathan,[4] Daniel,[3] Daniel[2]), born in Springfield, Vt., 11 July 1797; died in Detroit, Mich., 26 May 1883, in his 86th year. He married in Springfield 12 Sept.

1825, ELIZA WALKER, eldest daughter of Leonard and Betsey (Parker) Walker. She died in 1869. He graduated at Middlebury College in 1821, and practiced medicine in Springfield for half a century.

There was erected in the public square in Springfield in 1913, a beautiful fountain in memory of Charles Sherwin[8] Chase of Detroit, Mich., his father and mother Barton Walker[7] and Sarah (Sherwin) Chase, his brother George Leonard[8] Chase and his grandfather Dr. Leonard[6] Chase, a resident physician from 1823 to about 1870.

Children, born in Springfield:

2166. BARTON WALKER,[7] b. 27 July 1827; m. 2 Apr. 1864, Sarah J. (Sherwin) Barrett. He graduated at Dartmouth in 1847 and received his M.D. degree in 1850. He practised medicine in Vt., in Galena, Ill. and in Eau Claire, Wis., and removed to Detroit, Mich., in 1871. He there engaged in the drug business and in real estate. Their sons were (1) *Charles Sherwin*,[8] b. 8 Jan. 1866; d. in 1912, a benefactor of Springfield, Vt., and also of a hospital in Detroit which he endowed with $100,000; (2) *George Leonard*, b. 12 July 1868; d. in 1912.

2167. CLINTON STRAW, b. 25 May 1831; m. 28 Oct. 1869, Harriet Eliza Sherwin. He graduated at Dartmouth in 1852 and received his M.D. degree in 1855; practised medicine a few years; engaged in the drug business in Eau Claire, Wis., and in Detroit, Mich., until 1879, when he devoted his time to making investments in real estate. Their eldest child died in infancy. The others were: (2) *Alice Sherwin*,[8] b. 6 Jan. 1873; (3) *Alfred Walker*, b. 21 Feb. 1875.

938

JOSEPH PHILBRICK[6] CHASE (Aaron,[5] Capt. Jonathan,[4] Daniel,[3] Daniel[2]), born in Lempster, N. H., 5 Nov. 1791; died in Sutton, N. H., 6 Feb. 1881. He married 29 Sept. 1825, SABRINA MORRILL, daughter of Israel and Rosanna (Parsons) Morrill of Warner, N. H. She died in Sutton, 1 July 1863. They lived in the south village of Sutton.

Children, born in Sutton:

2168. SAMUEL M.,[7] b. 3 May 1826; m. (1) Clarissa Green; m. (2) Sarah P. Getchell; d. 9 Oct. 1858; captain; thirteen children; removed to Lewiston, Me.

2169. FRANK, b. 15 Oct. 1828; m. 6 May 1853, Emily J. Clark of Manchester, N. H.

DOROTHY, b. 19 Mar. 1831; m. (1) 29 Mar. 1855, Samuel Straw; m. (2) 8 May 1879, Nathan B. Bly; Newbury, N. H.

939

BARUCH[6] CHASE (Aaron,[5] Capt. Jonathan,[4] Daniel,[3] Daniel[2]), born in Lempster, N. H., 1 Dec. 1796; died in Claremont, N. H., 9 Feb. 1857, aged 60. No children of his appear on Claremont records. His marriage is not included among the New Hampshire marriages in Concord.

940

DANIEL[6] CHASE (Aaron,[5] Capt. Jonathan,[4] Daniel,[3] Daniel[2]), born in Lempster, N. H., 24 May 1799; died in Sutton, N. H., 13

IN PIOUS MEMORY OF
CARLTON CHASE
FIRST BISHOP OF
NEW HAMPSHIRE
BORN FEB. 20, 1794
CONSECRATED OCT. 20, 1844
DIED JAN. 18, 1870

HE SLEEPS IN JESUS

TOMBSTONES OF BISHOP CARLTON CHASE AND WIFE

Dec. 1835. He married in Sutton, 6 Nov. 1821, MARY C. LITTLE-HALE, daughter of Ezra and Lydia (Richardson) Littlehale, born 29 Apr. 1792; died in Mass. They lived in Sutton.

Children, born in Sutton:

2170. CARLTON.[7]

    JULIA, m. Sanford Stevens; lived in Corinth, Me., and Boston.

    CATHERINE, d. at age of 20.

2171. DANIEL.

941

MARINER[6] CHASE (Aaron,[5] Capt. Jonathan,[4] Daniel,[3] Daniel[2]), born in Lempster, N. H., 8 Dec. 1801; tax-payer in Lempster 1820-1830.

942

JOHN[6] CHASE (Jeremiah Stickney,[5] Capt. Jonathan,[4] Daniel,[3] Daniel[2]), born in Unity, N. H., 2 Apr. 1802; died in Goshen, N. H., 28 Feb. 1870. He married in Weare, N. H., 1 Dec. 1835, HANNAH P. MARSHALL of Weare. They lived in Unity and Goshen. He served as a representative.

Children:

    ZEMIRA,[7] b. 27 June 1838; never married.

    ESTHER, b. 5 Sept. 1843; m. Ira Chandler of Newport, N. H. She d. in May 1870. Two children.

943

HON. MARTIN[6] CHASE (Jeremiah Stickney,[5] Capt. Jonathan,[4] Daniel,[3] Daniel[2]), born in Unity, N. H., 11 July 1806; married in Washington, N .H., 19 June 1832, BETSEY WRIGHT, daughter of Dr. Nathan and Betsey (Lowell) Wright, born in Washington, 8 Oct. 1808. They lived in Washington till 1869, then removed to Marlborough, N. H. He was Judge of the Court of Common Pleas for Sulivan Co. from 1853 till the court was abolished. Served as selectman, town clerk, representative three years, town treasurer, etc. He died in Marlborough, 9 Feb. 1897, aged 90 y. 6 m.

Children, born in Washington:

    HELEN,[7] b. 22 July 1835; never married.

    CAROLINE, b. 27 Oct. 1840; m. 24 Nov. 1863, George L. Fairbanks of Marlborough, N. H. No children.

944

RT. REV. CARLTON[6] CHASE (Charles,[5] Capt. Jonathan,[4] Daniel,[3] Daniel[2]), born in Hopkinton, N. H., 20 Feb. 1794; died in Claremont, N. H., 18 Jan. 1870. He married in Windsor, Vt., 13 Sept. 1820, HARRIET CUTLER, daughter of Dr. Samuel and Janette (Caldwell) Cutler of Bellows Falls, Vt. She was born in Rockingham, Vt., 15 Nov. 1796; died in Claremont, 27 Aug. 1864, aged 68.

CARLTON CHASE was graduated from Dartmouth College in 1817 and studied divinity. He was ordained a deacon of the Protestant Episcopal Church by Bishop Alexander Viets Griswold, D. D., 9 Dec. 1818, and as a priest in 1820. He served as rector of Immanuel Church of Bellows Falls, 1819 to 1844. He was consecrated Bishop of the Diocese of New Hampshire at Christ Church, Philadelphia, Pa., 20 Oct. 1844 by Bishop Philander Chase, his kinsman, and served as rector of Trinity Church of Claremont, 1844 to 1865. He left a successful record of his ministry. The University of Vermont conferred the degree D. D. upon him in 1839. He was Bishop of New Hampshire until his death.

He was in Baltimore when Morse, the inventor, completed the telegraph line between that city and Washington and Samuel F. B. Morse turned to him and asked him to dictate the first message. He replied with these words, now found in all text books of American history, "What hath God wrought!"

Children, born in Bellows Falls, Vt.:

> ELEANOR C.,[7] b. 9 Sept. 1821; m. 6 May 1846, George Mason Morse, M.D., of Clinton; d. 16 Nov. 1861.
>
> FREDERICK CARLTON, b. 28 May 1823; never married; lived in Cleremont.
>
> FRANCIS, b. 7 Jan. 1828; d. 13 Feb. 1829.
>
> ALICE, b. 25 July 1829; d. 19 Mar. 1838.
>
> 2172. FRANCIS, b. 8 Oct. 1831; d. 20 Oct. 1904; graduate of Trinity College, 1852; teacher and rector of St. James Church, Scarsdale, N. Y.; m. 29 June 1869, Mary Catharine Olmstead, b. 10 Aug. 1841. Their dau. *Mary Livingston*,[8] b. 10 Apr. 1871, lives at 601 Madison Ave., New York City.
>
> SARAH JENNETTE, b. 17 Oct. 1833; d. 31 Aug. 1848.
>
> 2173. ARTHUR, b. 21 Oct. 1835; d. 28 Nov. 1888; graduate of Norwich University, 1856; m. 9 Apr. 1863, Garafelia Davis, b. 26 Jan. 1836; d. 9 Mar. 1912. Seven children, including *Charles Francis*,[8] b. 2 Feb. 1864; graduate Dartmouth, 1885; m. (1) 20 June 1894, Elizabeth Hance Parker, who d. 3 June 1912; m. (2) Ruth Stewart Arnold. Children: (1) Eugene Parker,[9] b. 19 Apr. 1895; (2) Helen Carlton,[9] b. 20 May 1897; (3) Charles Francis,[9] b. 1 Apr. 1915; d. 13 May 1917; (3) Margaret,[9] b. 27 July 1918; (5) Alice Arnold,[9] b. 28 Feb. 1920. They live in New Britain, Conn. *Alice Carlton*,[8] b. 12 Nov. 1865; lives in Ware, unm.; *Rev. Arthur*,[8] b. 24 Aug. 1867; m. 18 Oct. 1900, Alice T. Rondthaler, b. 27 July 1868. Children: (1) Eleanor Carlton,[9] b. 20 Dec. 1901; (2) Edward Rondthaler,[9] b. 16 Jan. 1903; d. 4 Jan. 1928; (3) Alice Elizabeth,[9] b. 13 Apr. 1906; (4) Arthur Carleton,[9] b. 2 July 1908; (5) Richard Davis,[9] b. 31 Mar. 1910. They reside in Ware where he is rector. He is author of *History of Ware* (1911).
>
> HARRIET, b. 3 Sept. 1842; m. 23 Oct. 1866, Thomas Jefferson Lasier, editor and printer of Ontonagon, Mich. She d. 11 Feb. 1877. Children: *Eleanor*[8] *Lasier*, b. 22 Oct. 1867, *Harriet Carlton*[8] *Lasier*, b. 3 Jan. 1869; lives in Washington, D. C., and a child b. 17 Dec. 1871.

945

NATHAN[6] CHASE (Isaac,[5] Isaac,[4] Daniel,[3] Daniel[2]), born in Warner or Wilmot about 1791.

946

ISAAC⁶ CHASE (Isaac,⁵ Isaac,⁴ Daniel,³ Daniel²), born in Warner, or Wilmot, N. H.; married in Warner, 23 July 1816, REBECCA FOL-SOM. No births of children appear on the town records of New Hampshire.

947

HENRY⁶ CHASE (Isaac,⁵ Corp. Isaac,⁴ Daniel,³ Daniel²), born in Warner or Wilmot, N. H., about 1795; married in Hopkinton, N. H., 7 Sept. 1828, HANNAH PALMER. The widow, Hannah Chase, daughter of Timothy and Judith (Hardy) Palmer, died in Bristol, N. H., 14 Mar. 1887, aged 80y. 7m. 14d. (New Hampshire Vital Records). One of his sisters married Richard Palmer and another married Daniel Emery.

Child:

DANIEL EMERY,⁷ lived in Medford.

948

JABEZ⁶ CHASE (Isaac,⁵ Isaac,⁴ Daniel,³ Daniel²), born in Wilmot, N. H., about 1800; married in New London, N. H., 25 Dec. 1828, MARY SEWALL said to have been of Northfield, N. H. He removed from Wilmot to New London in 1823.

Children, born in New London:

2174. THOMAS,⁷ m. Lucada Richardson of Springfield, N. H.
2175. ISAAC R., m. Adeline Harvey of Springfield.
    HARRIET, m. Zaccheus Messer of Springfield.
    SARAH, m. John E. Lull of Concord, N. H.
    ANN, m. Henry Lull of Pembroke, N. H.
2176. PHILIP S., m. 19 July 1862, Lavina E. Phelps of New London.
2177. WALTER, m. Rosy L. Fletcher of New London.
    CALEB, d. 12 Aug. 1852, aged 11 y.
    MARY JANE, d. young.

949

JOHN⁶ CHASE (Isaac,⁵ Isaac,⁴ Daniel,³ Daniel²), born in Warner or Wilmot, N. H. He may be the John Chase of Lyme, N. H., who married in Orford, N. H., 1 Feb. 1843, ALMIRA GREENLEAF.

950

BENJAMIN⁶ CHASE (Isaac,⁵ Isaac,⁴ Daniel,³ Daniel²), born probably in Warner, N. H.

951

JOSEPH⁶ CHASE (Isaac,⁵ Isaac,⁴ Daniel,³ Daniel²), born in Warner or Wilmot, N. H.; married in Grafton, N. H., 18 Aug. 1835, NANCY POWELL. His marriage record describes him as "of New London." No birth of children appears on the records of New Hampshire.

952

TIMOTHY[6] CHASE (Philip,[5] Abner,[4] Daniel,[3] Daniel[2]), supposed to be the son of Philip[5] Chase; reported to be living in the West in 1880. Timothy Chase of Wendell (now Sunapee), N. H., and Eliza Davis of Springfield, N. H., were married in Newport, N. H., 22 Aug. 1833, and Timothy Chase and Miss Sally Huse were married in Meredith, N. H., 19 Mar. 1848. It is not known that either marriage was of the above named Timothy.

953

PHILIP[6] CHASE (Philip,[5] Abner,[4] Daniel,[3] Daniel[2]), supposed to be the son of Philip[5] Chase; reported to be living in the West in 1880.

953a

ABNER[6] CHASE (Timothy Bradley,[5] Abner,[4] Daniel,[3] Daniel[2]), born in Sutton, N. H., 21 Feb. 1808; died in Hooksett, N. H., Sept. 1849. He married and lived in the southwestern part of Sutton. Two children,—one a son. His family is not given in the *History of Sutton*.

954

HEZEKIAH C.[6] CHASE (Timothy Bradley,[5] Abner,[4] Daniel,[3] Daniel[2]), born in Warner, N. H., 16 Jan. 1811; married (1) in Danbury, N. H., 6 Jan. 1839, DOROTHY S. GARDNER, daughter of Samuel Walker and Sophia (Greeley) Gardner, born in Sutton, N. H., 24 June 1919; died 26 Jan. 1854. He married (2) in Danbury, 28 Jan. 1855, MARY E. CHADWICK who was born in Albany, N. Y., 5 Mar. 1828. They lived in Danbury and Pembroke, N. H.

Children by first wife, born in Danbury, except second born in Pembroke:

2178. GEORGE WARREN, b. 17 Sept. 1839; m. 11 Mar. 1869, Maria A. Temple; lived in Canaan, N. H. Son *Charles T.*,[8] b. 8 Dec. 1875.
DOROTHY ANN, b. 27 June 1841; d. in Danbury, 4 June 1857.
2179. JOSEPH GREELEY, b. 12 Aug. 1843; m. 8 Mar. 1881, Lizzie West; lived in Concord, N. H.
JOSEPHINE S., b. 28 Aug. 1847; m. 11 July 1872, Rev. Edmund C. Spinney, D.D.; two children; lived in Burlington, Iowa. Dr. Spinney was president of Burlington College.
CARRIE E., b. 4 Dec. 1856; d. 10 June 1857.
CARRIE A., b. 1858; d. Apr. 1859.
2180. FRANK W., b. 16 Sept. 1860; m. 1882, Esther Gero; lived in Manchester, N. H.
BURT H., b. Oct. 1864; at sea in 1882.

955

FRANCIS[6] CHASE (Timothy Bradley,[5] Abner,[4] Daniel,[3] Daniel[2]), born in Danbury, N. H., 1 Nov. 1830; married (1) NANCY A. CURRIER; married (2) ADDIE SHAW. Two children whose names are not given. They lived in Danbury.

956

DANIEL[6] CHASE (Isaac,[5] John,[4] Daniel,[3] Daniel[2]), born in Albany, N. H., 5 July 1805; married in Conway, N. H., 30 Mar. 1829, ABIGAIL H. GARLAND who was born in Conway, 29 Jan. 1811. They removed to and resided in Maple Grove, Hennepin Co., Minn., in 1876.

Children:

MARY ANN,[7] b. 13 Apr. 1830; m. J. D. Burnham of Minneapolis, Minn.
SARAH A. H., b. 25 Aug. 1832; d. 25 Apr. 1844.
EPHRAIM G., b. 28 Aug. 1834; d. 28 Jan. 1835.
MARTHA E., b. 25 Jan. 1836; m. 14 July 1853, Rufus[6] Chase of Bartlett, N. H. (Family 965)
JULIA M., b. 17 May 1837; m. A. Bragdon of Brooklyn, Minn.
2181.   HENRY B., b. 30 Aug. 1839; m. H. A. Jordan of Minneapolis.
ELIZA D., b. 25 Aug. 1841.
WESLEY, b. 10 Apr. 1843; d. 14 Jan. 1862.
ISADORA, b. 2 Oct. 1845; m. C. E. Eddy of Osseo, Minn.
EUGENE, b. 25 Apr. 1847; d. 18 Jan. 1854.
JESSIE F., b. 3 May 1855.
LILLIAN, b. 1 Oct. 1860.

957

JOHN[6] CHASE (Isaac,[5] John,[4] Daniel,[3] Daniel[2]), born in 1812. No report has been given of him.

958

GILBERT M.[6] CHASE (Daniel,[5] John,[4] Daniel,[3] Daniel[2]), born in Bartlett, N. H., about 1809; married in Eaton, N. H., 15 Nov. 1832, as "of Bartlett," MEHITABLE BROWN. His family has not been reported.

959

WILLIAM R.[6] CHASE (Daniel,[5] John,[4] Daniel,[3] Daniel[2]), born in Bartlett, N. H., about 1811; died in Conway, N. H., 24 Aug. 1890, aged 73. He married.

960

MARK[6] CHASE (Daniel,[5] John,[4] Daniel,[3] Daniel[2]), born in Bartlett, N. H., about 1815. He is untraced, not being given in the vital records of New Hampshire.

961

GEORGE[6] CHASE (Oliver,[5] John,[4] Daniel,[3] Daniel[2]), born in Conway, N. H., 17 Apr. 1809; died 9 Jan. 1852. He married a woman whose name has not been reported and they had seven children whose births are not recorded in New Hampshire.

962

OLIVER[6] CHASE JR. (Oliver,[5] John,[4] Daniel,[3] Daniel[2]), born in Conway, N. H., 7 Oct. 1811; m. (1) BELINDA HAM, daughter of Nicholas and Hannah (Chase) Ham of Tamworth, N. H. She was born 9 Mar. 1815.   He married (2) HANNAH[6] CHASE, daughter of John Chase of Albany, N. H.   Perhaps he is the Oliver Chase who died in Hollis, N. H., 2 June 1877.   His family has not been reported.

963

CHRISTOPHER C.[6] CHASE (Oliver,[5] John,[4] Daniel,[3] Daniel[2]), born in Conway, N. H., 30 Mar. 1819; married 9 Sept. 1847, MARY PURINGTON.   They lived in Albany, N. H., Madison, N. H., and Freedom, N. H.

Children, first two born in Albany, other in Madison:
- 2182.   ANDREW J.,[7] b. 3 July 1848.
          CELESTIA, b. 8 Dec. 1849.
- 2183.   GEORGE W., b. 29 Nov. 1851, in Eaton, N. H.
- 2184.   JOHN (twin), b. 29 Nov. 1851, in Eaton.
- 2185.   JAMES O., b. 12 Aug. 1853.
- 2186.   CHRISTOPHER B., b. 30 May 1855, in Tamworth, N. H.
- 2187.   ASHER B., b. 20 July 1857, in Tamworth, N. H.
- 2188.   ODELL R., b. 31 Mar. 1861.

964

JOHN[6] CHASE (Oliver,[5] John,[4] Daniel,[3] Daniel[2]), born 30 Aug. 1823; married in Conway, N. H., 7 Mar. 1852, NANCY R. BERRY who was born in Bridgton, Me., 4 Mar. 1829.   They lived in Conway.

Children, born in Conway:
- JOSEPHINE B.,[7] b. 7 Sept. 1855; m. 12 Dec. 1873, Henry Wilkinson; lived in Portsmouth, N. H.
- 2189.   JOHN F., b. 27 Sept. 1856.
- 2190.   GEORGE B. M., b. 29 June 1863, in Albany, N. H.
- 2191.   HORATIO C., b. 18 Dec. 1869.

965

RUFUS[6] CHASE (Oliver,[5] John,[4] Daniel,[3] Daniel[2]), born 31 Aug. 1825; married 14 July 1853, MARTHA E.[7] CHASE, daughter of Daniel[6] and Abigail H. (Garland) Chase, born in Conway, N. H., 25 Jan. 1836.   (Family 956).   They lived in Bartlett, N. H.

Children, born in Madison, N. H., last born in Bartlett:
- ABBY F.,[7] b. 3 July 1854; m. 12 Mar. 1876, Alpha Hall of Bartlett.
- 2192.   WILLIAM L., b. 29 Apr. 1864.
          MARY E., b. 2 Oct. 1866.
          LYDIA P., b. 8 Sept. 1871.

966

JOHN[6] CHASE (Gilbert Tenant,[5] John,[4] Daniel,[3] Daniel[2]), born in Conway, N. H., 7 Dec. 1817; married in Conway, 3 Sept. 1839, DOLLY S. GILE.   They lived in Paris, Me., after 1842.

Children, first born in Conway, others in Paris:
- HATTIE ATWOOD,[7] b. 24 Feb. 1840; m. 1858, Hezekiah M. Lapham.
- PHEBE, b. 15 Sept. 1844; m. 1872, Aaron Edes of Canton, Me.
- CHARLOTTE ELIZABETH, b. 7 May 1847; m. 1863, Simon R. Ellis.

MARY G., b. 3 Apr. 1849; m. 1874, William Bradbury.
DOLLY JANE, b. 22 May 1851; m. 1873, Henry C. Hammond.
LAURA ELLEN, b. 6 Apr. 1854; m. 1873, George Otis[8] Chase.
(Family 749-1863)
2193.   JOHN, b. 2 May 1858; m. Edna Field.
CLARA ANNA, b. 1862; m. Charles Kimball.

967

HOSEA J.[6] CHASE not brought forward.

968

WILLIAM HENRY[6] CHASE (Charles,[5] Humphrey,[4] Enoch,[3] Daniel[2]), born in North Yarmouth, Me., and baptized there, 5 May 1822. He lived in Portland, Me.

969

THOMAS[6] CHASE (William,[5] Enoch,[4] Enoch,[3] Daniel[2]), born in Salisbury, N. H., 8 May 1784; died there 19 Mar. 1832. He married in Salisbury, 16 Nov. 1815, NANCY JOHNSON who married (2) 29 Feb. 1834, Enoch[7] Chase Jr., son of Enoch[6] Chase of Hopkinton, N. H. They lived in Salisbury. (Family 1063).
Children, born in Salisbury:
2194.   ALBERT G.,[7] b. 24 Nov. 1817; m. 25 Mar. 1841, Clarissa C. Collins of Springfield, b. 8 June 1819. They lived in Eldred, Nebr.
GEORGE W., b. Feb. 1821; d. 23 Aug. 1825.
THOMAS, b. 14 Apr. 1832; never mar.; lived in Eldred, Nebr.

970

DANIEL[6] CHASE (John,[5] Thomas,[4] Enoch,[3] Daniel[2]), born in Lincolnville, Me., 5 June 1801; married 23 Dec. 1824, CATHARINE W. LOWE of Charleston, Me. They were living in Charleston in 1876.
Children, born in Charleston:
JOHN S.,[7] b. 27 Sept. 1825; m. 1 Mar. 1864, Jane Libby; no children; lived in Charleston.
DANIEL B., b. 18 July 1829; unm. 1876.
2195.   CHARLES L., b. 13 May 1832; m. Addie Hatch; lived in San Andreas, Calif., 1876.
MARY E., b. 22 Jan. 1834; m. 16 May 1860, S. P. Marden; no children; lived in Levant, Me.

971

SEWALL C.[6] CHASE (Enoch,[5] John,[4] Enoch,[3] Daniel[2]), born in Feb. 1806; married PRUDENCE NEWTON. They lived in Dixfield, Me.
Children, born in Dixfield:
2196.   HORACE.[7]
HARRIET.
2197.   DENNIS.
2198.   RUTILIUS.
2199.   SEWALL SCOTT, b. 12 Nov. 1833; m. Caroline Melinda Miller.

2200. JOHN.
      MARY.
2201. EMERSON.
      AUGUSTA.
2202. ZENAS.

972

NATHANIEL[6] CHASE (James,[5] John,[4] Enoch,[3] Daniel[2]), born presumably in Brunswick, Me., about 1810. He married ——— ALLEN.

973

SAMUEL[6] CHASE (Samuel,[5] Judge Samuel,[4] Daniel,[3] Ens. Moses[2]), born and baptized in Grafton, 3 May 1752; died in Oct. 1838, aged 84. He married (1) 12 Nov. 1772, ELIZABETH LEET who was born in 1750 and died in Claremont, N. H., 24 Mar. 1781, aged 31. He married (2) 20 Sept. 1781, DAMARIS SABIN who was born in 1749 and died 9 Sept. 1825, aged 76. He was one of the first settlers of Cornish, N. H., and a soldier in the Revolutionary War.

Children by first wife, born in Cornish:

      MARY,[7] b. 16 Aug. 1773; m. 27 Feb. 1791, William Leslie. Three children. She d. 28 June 1797, aged 24.
      SARAH, b. 15 Aug. 1775; m. 10 Nov. 1796, James Balloch, a native of Scotland, who came in 1790. She d. 26 Nov. 1840, a. 65.
      SON, d. 8 Aug. 1777.
2203. SAMUEL, b. 13 Mar. 1779; m. 18 Feb. 1801, Polly Barstow.
      ELIZABETH, b. 4 Mar. 1781; d. 6 Apr. 1803, unm.

Children by the second wife, born in Cornish:

2204. CHARLES, b. 7 May 1783; m. 19 Nov. 1816, Olive Colston; d. 15 Jan. 1865; captain.
      LAVINA, m. Howard Bugbee; second wife.
2205. GEORGE, b. 29 Mar. 1787; m. Mar. 1812, Clarissa Cook, b. 26 Feb. 1787; d. 11 Mar. 1851. He d. in Claremont, N. H., in 1840. Their son *Henry Fiske*,[8] b. in Claremont, 1 Oct. 1826; d. 18 Feb. 1888; m. 27 Jan. 1859, Caroline Sophia Hopkins, dau. of John Burgess and Ruth Hart (Sherman) Hopkins, b. in Plainfield, Conn., 11 Aug. 1832. Their dau. Ida Marion[9] was b. in Malden, 3 Dec. 1862; m. 24 Nov. 1908, George Minot Baker; d. in Concord 18 Dec. 1923. She was a leader among women in the civic, patriotic and charitable organizations of Massachusetts. Her estate of $200,000 was devoted to fifteen charitable and educational institutions.
      LUCINDA, b. 16 Nov. 1789; m. Howard Bugbee; first wife.

974

PETER[6] CHASE (Samuel,[5] Judge Samuel,[4] Daniel,[3] Ens. Moses[2]), born and baptized in Grafton, 26 Oct. 1756; died in Cornish, N. H., 17 July 1792. He married 30 Dec. 1778, SARAH CADY, daughter of Lt. Elijah and Dinah (Spaulding) Cady. She was born 29 Nov. 1757; died 3 May 1826. She married (2) Thomas Young.

Children, born in Cornish:

      SUSANNA,[7] b. 28 Aug. 1781; m. Benjamin Rich; she d. 8 Aug. 1811; aged 30.

ELIZABETH, b. 25 Mar. 1782; d. unm. 4 June 1811.

SARAH, b. 2 Mar. 1783; m. 6 Oct. 1813, Nahum Sturtevant and d. 16 Mar. 1836.

2206.   PETER, b. 6 May 1785; m. 22 Nov. 1810, Martha Stevens. He d. 9 Jan. 1850; lived in Boscawen, N. H.

ZIBA, b. 1788; d. 14 Oct. 1791.

SANFORD, b. Apr. 1791; d. 11 Mar. 1792.

ELIZA.

975

CAPT. JOSHUA⁶ CHASE (Samuel,⁵ Judge Samuel,⁴ Daniel,³ Ens. Moses²), born in Grafton, 30 Oct. 1758; died in Cornish, N. H., 15 Mar. 1812, aged 43. He married in Cornish, 14 Mar. 1793, MARY⁶ CHASE, daughter of Thomas⁵ and Mary (Hall) Chase of Chester, N. H. (Family 370). She was born 10 Apr. 1768, and died 2 June 1793, in her 26th year. No record of any children. The Town Records of Cornish state that "Joshua, son of Samuel and Salome Chase, was born in Cornish, 7 Aug. 1769."

976

SIMEON⁶ CHASE (Dea. Dudley,⁵ Judge Samuel,⁴ Daniel,³ Ens. Moses²), born in Sutton, 14 June 1758; died in Bethel, Vt. 6 Sept. 1847, aged 89. He married 9 Mar. 1789, MARY MARCH who was born May 1759; died in Bethel, 20 July 1847. They lived in Bethel. He enlisted from Cornish, N. H., in the Revolutionary War and applied for a pension from Bethel 25 Jan. 1834, aged 76.

Children, born probably in Bethel:

NANCY,⁷ b. 25 Nov. 1789; m. 19 Feb. 1809, Lebbeus Hall⁶ Chase of Cornish, and d. 15 June 1814. (Family 983)

BETSEY, d. in infancy.

DANIEL CORBETT, d. in infancy.

2208.   SIMEON, b. in 1796; m. 21 Oct. 1821, Olivia Brown; lived in Bethel, and d. May 1827. She was b. in New York state 12 Mar. 1799, and d. 11 Mar. 1865. Three children: Dudley,⁸ Nancy⁸ and George Brown,⁸ who lived in Bethel.

977

SALMON⁶ CHASE (Dea. Dudley,⁵ Judge Samuel,⁴ Daniel,³ Ens. Moses²), born in Sutton, 14 July 1761; died in Portland, Me., 14 Aug. 1806. He married (1) in New Castle, N. H., 27 Nov. 1796, MARY SIMPSON of Portsmouth, N. H. She died in 1801. He married (2) in 1804 in Portland, Mrs. SARAH (TYNG) WALDO, widow of Samuel Waldo, who survived him.

He graduated at Dartmouth College in 1785 and took charge of a school in Portsmouth and studied law with Judge John Sherburne of Portsmouth. On completing his studies he removed to Portland in 1789 and practiced law there until his death. He was a sound, well-read lawyer, with a reputation that gave him the distinction of being called "The Law Book." One of his associates, James Dean Hopkins, said of him: "He was not only an able lawyer, but he was well versed in all the branches of solid learning; in legal science, in mathematical and metaphysical learning, he had few superiors." He had the most extensive practice of any lawyer in Maine, at that time, and confidence in him was unlimited. He was a kind and amiable man, easy and accessible in his manners, and of fine personal appearance.

Child by the first wife, born in Portland:

> GEORGE,[7] b. 29 Sept. 1800; graduated at Harvard College in 1818; studied law and d. unm. in Portland, 11 Nov. 1819.

Child by the second wife, born in Portland:

> ELIZABETH, b. about 1806; m. Dr. —— Howard of Boston, a grandson of Rev. Simeon Howard, minister of the West Church of Boston, 1767-1804.

978

ITHAMAR[6] CHASE (Dea. Dudley,[5] Judge Samuel,[4] Daniel,[3] Ens. Moses[2]), born in Sutton and there baptized, 27 Sept. 1762; died in Keene, N. H., 5 Aug. 1817. He married in Keene, 26 June 1792, JANET RALSTON, daughter of Alexander and Janet Ralston (both parents being natives of Scotland). She was born in Charlestown, 26 July 1773 and removed with her parents to Keene. She died in Hopkinton, N. H., 6 Apr. 1832.

Mr. Chase was a student in Dartmouth College for a time but did not graduate. Soon after his marriage he moved to Cornish, N. H., where he resided until 1810. In Cornish he held at various times most of the town offices, was a justice of the peace, and legal counsellor for the town. In 1810 he removed to Keene to take charge of the Ralston Hotel and to engage in the manufacture of glass. He was a Free Mason and the first Master of Hiram Lodge of Claremont, and a member of the Protestant Episcopal Church. He served as a member of the Governor's Council for New Hampshire from 1811 to 1816.

Children, first eight born in Cornish, last two in Keene:

> HANNAH RALSTON,[7] b. 23 Dec. 1794; m. in Keene, 1 Oct. 1818, John Whipple, Esq., of Dunbarton, N. H.

2210.   ALEXANDER RALSTON, b. 17 Apr. 1797; graduated from Dartmouth College, 1814; engaged in mercantile business in Keene; removed to Ohio; d. at Storrs, near Cincinnati, 23 Mar. 1847, aged 52.

> ABIGAIL CORBETT, b. 26 Mar. 1799; m. in Hopkinton, 3 Aug. 1825, Dr. Isaac Colby, Jr., of Hopkinton.

> DUDLEY HEBER, b. 14 Sept. 1801; d. unm. in Margaretta, South America, in 1821.

> JANET LOGAN, b. 8 Nov. 1803.

> ALICE JANE, b. 29 Oct. 1805; d. unm. in Cincinnati, Ohio, in 1859.

2211.   SALMON PORTLAND, b. 13 Jan. 1808; d. in New York City, 7 May 1873. He m. (1) 4 Mar. 1834, KATHERINE JANE GARNESS, b. in New York City, 21 Aug. 1811; d. in Ohio, 1 Dec. 1835. He m. (2) 26 Sept. 1839, ELIZA ANN SMITH, b. in Cincinnati, 12 Nov. 1821; d. in Ohio, 29 Sept. 1845. He m. (3) 6 Nov. 1846, SARAH BELLE (DUNLAP) LUDLOW, who was b. near Cincinnati, 20 Apr. 1820; d. 13 June 1852.

> Child by first wife, born in Cincinnati: (1) *Katharine*,[8] b. 16 Nov. 1835; d. 6 Feb. 1840. Children by second wife, born in Cincinnati: (2) *Katharine 2d*, b. 13 Aug. 1840; m. 12

Nov. 1863, William Sprague, Governor of Rhode Island; d. 31 July 1899; (3) *Lizzie*, b. 30 May 1842; d. 30 Aug. 1842; (4) *Lizzie 2d*, b. 1 June 1843; d. 24 July 1844. · Children by third wife, born in Cincinnati, (5) *Janet Ralston*, b. 19 Sept. 1847; m. 23 March 1871, William Sprague Hoyt and d. 19 Nov. 1925. He died 20 April 1905. Their children were: Janet Ralston⁹ Hoyt, b. 17 Jan. 1872; Edwin Chase⁹ Hoyt, b. 5 March 1873; Franklin Chase⁹ Hoyt, b. in Pelham, N. Y., 7 Sept. 1876, Presiding Justice of the Children's Court of the City of New York, and Beatrix⁹ Hoyt, b. 5 July 1880. (6) *Josephine Ludlow*,⁸ b. 3 July 1844; d. 28 July 1850; *Sarah Belle Dunlap Ludlow*,⁸ b. and d. the same day, in 1852.

2212.   EDWARD ITHAMAR,⁷ b. 2 Mar. 1810; lawyer in Lockport, N. Y.
2213.   WILLIAM FREDERIC, b. 8 June 1813.
HELEN MARIA, b. 26 Sept. 1815.
One of the daughters of Ithamar Chase is said to have m. Dr. Isaac Rich.

HON. SALMON PORTLAND CHASE, named for his father's brother, Salmon Chase who lived in Portland, Me., until his death two years before our subject was born, graduated from Dartmouth College in 1826 and studied law in Washington, D. C., with Hon. William Wirt, attorney general of the United States in 1817, who was distinguished for his lofty ideals, legal, literary, historic and scientific. While studying law he established and conducted a classical school for boys in Washington, and was admitted to the bar 14 December 1829.

In 1830 he located in Cincinnati, Ohio, and engaged in the practice of law. He did not then ally himself with either of the great political parties but was unalterably opposed to slavery. In 1837 he defended a fugitive slave woman, claimed under the law of 1793, and took the highest ground against the constitutionality of that law. In the same year he defended his friend James G. Birney for harboring a negro slave, and in 1838 he reviewed with great severity a report of the judiciary committee of the Ohio senate, refusing trial by jury to slaves and in a second suit defended Mr. Birney. At the organization of the Liberty party in Ohio in Dec. 1841, he appears as one of its foremost founders.

In those years he acted as counsel for many negroes who were claimed as fugitives from Kentucky and among the most noted whom he defended was John Van Zandt—the original John Van Trompe of *Uncle Tom's Cabin*. This was in the year 1842.

In 1843 the Liberty party held its national convention in Buffalo and nominated James G. Birney for president. Their platform was almost entirely the production of Salmon Portland Chase. In 1844 the Liberty party caused the defeat of Henry Clay for president. Four years later it was superseded by the Free-Soil party whose national convention in Buffalo in 1848 was presided over by Mr. Chase. In 1849 the Democrats and Free-soilers in the Ohio legislature formed a coalition and elected Mr. Chase to the United States Senate, where he served from 1849 to 1855.

In the Senate 26 and 27 Mar. 1850, he made a notable speech against the so-called "compromise measures." When the Democratic party nominated Franklin Pierce for president in 1852 he dissolved his connection with that party. In 1855 he was elected Governor of Ohio by the opponents of Pierce's administration. He was reelected and served as Governor till 1859. He was again elected a Senator to Congress. In the national Republican convention in Chicago, Mr. Chase received 49 votes on the first ballot. On the fifth ballot Mr. Chase's friends gave their votes for Abraham Lincoln. On 4 Mar. 1861, Mr. Lincoln was inaugurated president and selected Mr. Chase as Secretary of the U. S. Treasury.

Horace Greeley said: "When he accepted the office of secretary of the treasury the finances were already in chaos: the current revenue being inadequate, even in the absence of all expenditure or preparation for war, and his predecessor having attempted to borrow $10,000,000 in Oct. 1860 obtained only $7,022,000."

When he went to New York for his first loan, the London Times declared that the Secretary of the Treasury had coerced $50,000,000 from the banks, but would not fare so well at the London Exchange. In his conference with the bankers he said: "If you cannot [loan the government], I shall go back to Washington and issue notes for circulation; for it is certain that the war must go on until the rebellion is put down, if we have to put out paper until it takes a thousand dollars to buy a breakfast." He managed to finance the government during the first three years of the war and received therefor the highest praise.

On 4 Dec. 1864, President Lincoln nominated him as Chief Justice of the United States Supreme Court to fill the vacancy caused by the death of Roger B. Taney, and he was immediately confirmed, and served until his death in 1873.

In the course of his official duties he presided at the impeachment trial of President Andrew Johnson in 1868.

His burial-place, in Spring Grove Cemetery near Cincinnati, is marked by an imposing memorial erected by the Bar Association of Ohio.

For a detailed account of his life and achievements see Schucker's *Life and Public Services of Salmon Portland Chase,* published in New York in 1874.

979

BARUCH[6] CHASE (Dea. Dudley,[5] Judge Samuel,[4] Daniel,[3] Ens. Moses[2]), born in Sutton, 27 Mar. 1764; died in Hopkinton, N. H., 4 Mar. 1841. He graduated at Dartmouth College in 1786. He married in 1792, ELLEN WIGGIN, daughter of Benjamin and Elizabeth (Clement) Wiggin, born in Hopkinton, 25 June 1776. He was a lawyer in Hopkinton; Solicitor of Hillsborough Co. nine years; president of the Merrimack Co. Bank. His widow died, 17 Mar. 1868, aged 92. He enlisted in 1780 in Capt. Solomon Chase's Co. and was a pensioner of Hopkinton, 4 Aug. 1837, aged 73.

Children, born in Hopkinton:

ELMIRA,[7] b. 7 Aug. 1793; d. 1 Sept. 1793.

2214.   BENJAMIN WIGGIN, b. 3 Sept. 1796; m. 1828, Anna Williams. He d. 6 Jan. 1878, in Philadelphia, Pa. She d. 21 Dec. 1889. Four children.

TWO PIONEER BISHOPS

2215. SAMUEL GREENLEAF, b. 23 Oct. 1803; m. in Warner, 24 Mar. 1837, Lydia H. Savory.

980

HON. DUDLEY[6] CHASE (Dea. Dudley,[5] Judge Samuel,[4] Daniel,[3] Ens. Moses[2]), born in Cornish, N. H., 30 Dec. 1771; died in Randolph, Vt., 28 Feb. 1846, aged 74. He married about 1796, OLIVIA BROWN of Norwich, Vt., born 22 Mar. 1779; died in Randolph, 22 Mar. 1846, having completed 67 years.

He graduated at Dartmouth College in 1791, read law with Judge Lot Hall of Westminster, Vt., and was admitted to the Vermont bar in 1794. He removed to Randolph and practiced there throughout his life. He served as a representative in the Vermont Legislature for nine years and was speaker of the House from 1808 to 1812; he was attorney for Orange County, 1803 to 1811; a member of the constitutional conventions of Vermont in 1814 and in 1822; United States senator from Vermont, 1813 to 1817; Chief Justice of the Supreme Court of Vermont, 1817 to 1821; representative and Speaker of the House 1823-1824; again United States senator from Vermont, 1825-1831.

He was a portly, fine looking man, of commanding presence and gentlemanly manners. He and his wife were members of the Protestant Episcopal Church, organized as Grace Church at Randolph Centre. There were no children but he and his good wife educated *twelve*—some being nephews and nieces.

981

RT. REV. PHILANDER[6] CHASE (Dea. Dudley,[5] Judge Samuel,[4] Daniel,[3] Ens. Moses[2]), born in Cornish, N. H., 14 Dec. 1775; died at Robin's Nest, Jubilee, Peoria Co., Ill., 20 Sept. 1852. He married (1) in Bethel, Vt., 29 July 1796, MARY FAY, daughter of Daniel and Mary (Paige) Fay, born in Hardwick, 10 Mar. 1779; died in Worthington, Ohio, 5 May 1818. He married (2) at Zanesville, Ohio, 4 July 1819, SOPHIA MAY INGRAHAM, daughter of Duncan and Susanna Ingraham of Philadelphia, Pa., born in Amsterdam, Holland, 13 Feb. 1783; died 16 Nov. 1864.

PHILANDER CHASE graduated from Dartmouth College in 1796 and studied divinity with Rev. Thomas Ellison of Albany, N. Y. He was ordained a deacon of the Protestant Episcopal Church by the Bishop, Rt. Rev. Samuel Prevost, D. D., in New York City, 10 May 1798 and a presbyter by the same Bishop, 10 Nov. 1799. For several years he was a missionary in the State of New York. He became rector of Christ's Church of Poughkeepsie, N. Y., and remained until 1805. He then went to New Orleans and organized Christ's Church there, 16 Nov. 1805, and was the rector from 1805 to 1811. He was rector of Christ's Church of Hartford, Conn., 1811 to 1817.

In 1817 he removed to Ohio and took charge of three churches and the Academy at Worthington, Ohio. He was elected Bishop of the Diocese of Ohio, 3 June 1818 and consecrated to that office by Rt. Rev. William White, D. D., at Philadelphia, 11 Feb. 1819. Visiting England he obtained there and at home funds to establish Kenyon College at Gambier, Ohio. He thus became the Founder and first President of Kenyon. He also there established Gambier Theological Seminary. He resigned his offices as Bishop and President 9 Sept. 1831, and removed to Michigan where he engaged in missionary work.

The estimation in which he was held by the alumni of Kenyon College is well set forth in the following song:

> "He built the college, built the dam,
> He milked the cow, he smoked the ham;
> He taught the classes, rang the bell
> And spanked the erring freshmen well.
>
> *   *   *   *   *   *   *
>
> "The king, the queen, the lords, and earls,
> They gave their crowns, they gave their pearls,
> Until Philander had enough,
> And hurried homeward with the stuff."

He was elected Bishop of Illinois, 9 Mar. 1835, and again visited England and obtained about $10,000 for educational work in Illinois. His labors culminated in founding Jubilee College at Robin's Nest in the township of Jubilee in 1838. He obtained a charter in 1847, placing the college entirely in the hands of the Episcopal church. He was Bishop of Illinois from 1835 to 1852. He received the degree D. D. from Columbia College in 1819.

He was a man of indomitable perseverance and great strength of will, and was the most energetic and successful pioneer missionary educator of the Episcopal church in the West. He published, *A Plea for the West* in 1826; *The Star of the West,* or *Kenyon College* in 1828; *The Defence of Kenyon College* in 1831, and *Reminiscences, an Autobiography, comprising a History of the Principal Events in the Author's Life* in 1848.

Children by first wife, eldest born in Albany, N. Y.:

2216.   GEORGE,[7] b. 9 Dec. 1797; m. 22 July 1821, Eliza Grover.
2217.   PHILANDER, b. 24 Apr. 1799; m. Rebecca Wells, dau. of Bezaleel Wells of Steubenville, Ohio; clergyman; d. 1 Mar. 1824, in Charleston, S. C., and buried in St. Michael's churchyard.
         EDWIN DUDLEY, b. 24 Apr. 1801; d. 18 Aug. 1801.
2218.   DUDLEY, b. 5 Mar. 1816; m. (1) Oct. 1840, Sarah G. Wells; m. (2) 18 May 1867, Mary O. Stockton; clergyman.
         MARY, b. 25 Apr. 1818; d. 6 Aug. 1818.

Children by second wife:

2219.   HENRY INGRAHAM, b. 7 Oct. 1820; m. 7 Nov. 1841, Susan Greenleaf Ingraham.
         MARY, b. 15 Feb. 1822; m. 14 Apr. 1847, Jacob S. Chamberlain.
2220.   PHILANDER, b. 8 Jan. 1824; m. 14 May 1843, Anna K. Ingraham.

982

JONATHAN[6] CHASE (Gen. Jonathan,[5] Judge Samuel,[4] Daniel,[3] Ens. Moses[2]), born 21 Nov. 1771; died in Cornish, N. H., 5 June 1843. He married in Keene, N. H., 8 June 1796, HANNAH RALSTON, daughter of Alexander and Janette Ralston, born 23 May 1775; died

in Cornish, 17 Feb. 1845.   They resided in Cornish, and occupied the
house which his father erected.
   Children, born in Cornish:
    MARY DUNBAR,[7] b. 11 May 1797; m. 6 Nov. 1832, Rev. George
      Leonard of Windsor, Vt. She d. without issue, 25 Mar. 1864.
    ELIZABETH MALVINA, b. 3 Feb. 1799; d. 10 Mar. 1817.
    JONATHAN, b. 9 Feb. 1801; physician; d. in Lockport, N. Y.,
      without issue, 17 Dec. 1852.
2221.   ALEXANDER RALSTON, b. 24 Sept. 1802; m. 21 Oct. 1834, Emily
      G. Cook of Cornish.   Physician in Lockport.
    DAVID HALL, b. 5 May 1805; d. unm. 26 Aug. 1876, a. 71.
2222.   JAMES BALLOCH, b. 29 May 1807; m. 13 Feb. 1833, Martha M.
      Kniffin; teacher; d. 13 Jan. 1882, in Weeping Water, Nebr.
      Six children.
2223.   GEORGE FRANCIS, b. 22 Nov. 1809; lived in Lockport.
2224.   SAMUEL LOGAN, b. 4 Nov. 1811; m. 14 Oct. 1833, Sarah D.
      French of Chester, N. H.; d. 1 July 1882; physician.
2225.   NATHAN BUCKLEY, b. 1 Aug. 1813; m. 15 Feb. 1844, Sarah
      Elizabeth Branscomb; physician; d. in Holyoke, 28 Aug.
      1888.
2226.   WILLIAM PRESCOTT, b. 13 Apr. 1815; m. 31 Dec. 1843, Mary
      Ann Blanchard; d. 15 Oct. 1860.

983

   COL. LEBBEUS HALL[6] CHASE (Gen. Jonathan,[5] Judge Samuel,[4]
Daniel,[3] Ens. Moses[2]), born in Cornish, N. H., 21 Jan. 1799; died in
Cornish in the house in which he was born, 22 Feb. 1865, aged 86.
He married (1) 19 Feb. 1809, NANCY[7] CHASE, daughter of Simeon[6]
and Mary (March) Chase, born 25 Nov. 1789; died in Cornish, 15
June 1814.   (Family 976).   He married (2) 8 July 1815, NIZAULA
MARCH of Milbury, daughter of Tappan March of Millbury.   Her
christian name is printed *Nizolla* and *Nizaula*.   She was born 7 Apr.
1797 and died in Cornish, N. H., 25 July 1840.   He was Colonel of
the 15th Regiment N. H. Militia.   He owned and occupied the Gen.
Jonathan Chase homestead.
   Children by first wife, born in Cornish:
2227.   SAMUEL ROSCOE,[7] b. 25 Nov. 1809; m. (1) 26 Mar. 1828, Lydia
      Spaulding; m. (2) Mrs. Aurilla Ellis; d. without issue,
      7 Aug. 1889.
    SIMEON MARCH, b. 24 Sept. 1811; d. unm. 28 June 1892.
2228.   SOLON SMITH, b. 13 July 1813; m. Anna Lucinda Putnam.
   Children by second wife, born in Cornish:
    EBENEZER BREWER, b. 30 Nov. 1815; physician; Dartmouth
    NANCY MALVINA, b. 10 Aug. 1817; d. 2 Sept. 1832, unm.
      Medical School, 1838; d. unm. 21 Jan. 1855.
    FRANCIS BARUCH, b. 26 Mar. 1819; graduate of Dartmouth,
      1843; d. unm. 12 Dec. 1844.
    HANNAH WHIPPLE PATCH, b. 15 Sept. 1821; d. unm. 17 Oct.
      1861.
2229.   DUDLEY TAPPAN, b. 2 Apr. 1823; lived in Claremont, N. H.,
      and Windsor, Vt.; Dartmouth, 1848; lawyer; three children
      d. young; m. (1) Adelaide G. Merrifield; m. (2) Sula
      Powers Smith.

2230. CONFUCIUS SULLIVAN, b. 5 July 1827; m. 3 Sept. 1864, Sophia
      I. Mitchell; d. in Pittsburg, Pa., 17 Sept. 1864.
2231. HENRY CLAY, b. 6 June 1830; m. Sophia I. (Mitchell) Chase;
      d. Glasgow, Pa., 20 July 1894.

984

SOLOMON HUSE[6] CHASE (Dr. Solomon,[5] Judge Samuel,[4] Daniel,[3]
Ens. Moses[2]), born in Walpole, N. H., 7 Mar. 1768; married 22 Jan.
1792, MARY HALL, born 19 June 1772. They lived in Langdon, N.
H., and Lunenburg, Vt., in 1803. He died in Lunenburg, 28 Mar.
1845. His widow died, 25 Mar. 1847.
    Children, first four born in Langdon, last in Lunenburg:

> SOPHIA PRESCOTT,[7] b. 13 Feb. 1793; m. 10 May 1818, Daniel
> Rich of Maidstone, Vt. and Northumberland, N. H.
> MARY HALL, b. 31 Jan. 1796; m. 31 Dec. 1821, Jacob Shoff.
> She d. in Lunenburg, 13 Feb. 1826.
> ELIZABETH CAROLINE, b. 2 Aug. 1801; d. 28 Dec. 1817.
> SARAH COLUMBIA (twin), b. 2 Aug. 1801; m. 22 Feb. 1842,
> Curtis Cleveland of Royalton, Vt. and Lunenburg.
> AMANDA BEULAH, b. 1 Oct. 1809; never married.

985

SAMUEL MARCH[6] CHASE (Dr. Solomon,[5] Judge Samuel,[4] Dan-
iel,[3] Ens. Moses[2]), born in Walpole, N. H., 13 Nov. 1772; died in
Langdon, N. H., 19 Feb. 1820. He married 12 Feb. 1803, RUTH
CURTIS CHILD, daughter of Stephen and Mercy[6] (Chase) Child.
(Family 343). She was born in Cornish, 25 Dec. 1780; died at
Robin's Nest, Ill., 11 Mar. 1856. They lived in Langdon.
    Children, born in Langdon:

> PRUDENTIA,[7] b. 19 Dec. 1803; d. in Royalton, Vt., 13 Sept.
> 1823.
> CLARISSA, b. 27 June 1805; d. 11 May 1820 or 1860.

2232.   MARCH, b. 13 Feb. 1807; m. 4 Jan. 1837, Mercy Freeman of
        Plainfield, N. H. Two children; lived in Langdon, 1872.
2233.   SAMUEL, b. 9 Jan. 1809; m. 25 Dec. 1834, Sarah Russell; four-
        teen children; graduate Kenyon Coll., 1829; D.D.
> JONATHAN, b. 27 May 1810; d. unm. 26 Aug. 1836.
> SOLOMON, b. 23 Dec. 1813; d. 18 Jan. 1814.
> DUDLEY, b. 15 Jan. 1816; d. unm. 10 Sept. 1837.
> MARY, b. 29 Dec. 1817; d. unm. 22 Dec. 1847.
> GEORGE, b. 5 June 1820; d. unm. 1 Sept. 1848.

986

BELA TAPPAN[6] CHASE (Dr. Solomon,[5] Judge Samuel,[4] Daniel,[3]
Ens. Moses[2]), born in Cornish, N. H., 30 Mar. 1784; died there 9
Sept. 1841. He married in Cornish, 24 Dec. 1812, ALICE CHILD,
daughter of Stephen and Mercy[6] (Chase) Child, born in Cornish,
2 Apr. 1787; died in Oregon, Ill., 6 May 1857. (Family 343). They
lived in Cornish, on the Chase homestead.
    Children, born in Cornish:

2234.   JOHN FRANKLIN,[7] b. 9 Oct. 1813; m. 21 1833, Mary Elizabeth
        Cummings; he d. Windsor, Vt., 10 Mar. 1849.
2235.   ORAN CORBETT, b. 31 July 1816; m. (1) 10 Nov. 1846, Lucia

Curtis[7] Chase, dau. of Col. Freeman[6] Chase. (Family 1033) She d. 13 Apr. 1858; m. (2) 3 May 1860, Harriet Jane Hadley; removed to Eau Claire, Wis., in 1852.

SARAH JANE, b. 17 May 1819; d. unm. 24 July 1838.

2236. FRANCIS XAVIER, b. 23 June 1824; m. 22 Feb. 1850, Laura E. Harlow. He d. in St. Paul, Minn., 13 Sept. 1866.

MARY URSULA, b. 23 Sept. 1830; d. unm. 26 July 1853, in Windsor, Vt.

987

JOHN[6] CHASE (Dr. Solomon,[5] Judge Samuel,[4] Daniel,[3] Ens. Moses[2]), born in Cornish, N. H., 20 Apr. 1789; died in De Witt, Iowa, 23 Apr. 1870. He married in Claremont, N. H., 14 Oct. 1818, FRIENDLY S. SUMNER who was born in Vt., 9 Mar. 1797. They lived in London, Ontario, near Niagara Falls and in 1830 removed to Yarmouth, Canada West. In Oct. 1869 they removed to De Witt, Iowa.

Children, first born in Claremont, second to fifth in London, Ont., and sixth in Yarmouth, Can. West:

HARRIET,[7] b. 30 June 1819; m. 30 Dec. 1841, William H. B. Morgan; lived in Ridgetown, Ont., 1873.

SARAH MARCH, b. 14 Sept. 1821; m. (1) 9 Nov. 1845, Elbert T. Vary; d. in Keelersville, Mich., 28 Aug. 1873.

MARY URSULA, b. 16 May 1824; m. 30 Aug. 1844, Edward F. Morgan; lived in Union, Ont. No children.

2237. JOHN F., b. 22 June 1826; m. 19 Feb. 1851, Statira Wilson; d. in Delhi, Ont., 6 Feb. 1868.

EMILY, b. 8 Feb. 1829; m. 9 Apr. 1846, Lowell Morton; lived in Cedar Rapids, Iowa.

2238. CHARLES C., b. 3 Dec. 1831; m. 21 July 1853, Sarah Fuller of Galen, N. Y.; lived in Marengo, N. Y., 1873. Four children.

988

LT. JOSHUA[6] CHASE (Paul,[5] Daniel,[4] Daniel,[3] Ens. Moses[2]), born in Sutton, 26 Nov. 1760; died there 6 Jan. 1842. He married in Sutton, 23 Aug. 1787, LYDIA PRENTICE of Grafton who died in Sutton, 14 Mar. 1829, aged 60. They lived in that part of Sutton which is now Millbury and were buried in the County Bridge Cemetery.

Children, born in Sutton (since 1813, Millbury):

NANCY,[7] b. 15 Feb. 1788; m. (1) 27 Oct. 1806, Isaac Stiles; m. (2) 1818, David Blood of Pepperell. She d. Mar. 1858.

2239. PAUL CUSHING, b. 6 Mar. 1790; m. 9 Dec. 1819, Sarah Pierce.

BETSEY, b. 22 Feb. 1792; never married; lived in Millbury.

HANNAH PRENTICE, b. 27 Mar. 1795; m. 4 Dec. 1816, Noah Blood of Pepperell.

2240. PALMER G., b. 13 Dec. 1799; m. 9 Sept. 1821, Sally Burbank; lived in Laconia, N. H.

2241. HENRY PRENTICE, b. 27 Mar. 1807; m. 18 Jan. 1828, Achsah Clement; d. 25 Dec. 1856.

989

THADDEUS[6] CHASE (Paul,[5] Daniel,[4] Daniel,[3] Ens. Moses[2]), born in Sutton, 10 Feb. 1763; married in Sutton, 4 Oct. 1787, PERSIS MARBLE, daughter of Enoch and Abigail (Hollard) Marble. They lived in Sutton (now Millbury). She died as his widow, in Sutton, 29 Mar. 1856, aged 87 y. 4 m. 19 d. She was born in Sutton, daughter of Enoch and Abigail Marble. (Mass. Vital Statistics, 104:207).

Children, born in Sutton (now Millbury) :

CHARLES,[7] d. 10 Feb. 1790, aged 10 m.

POLLY, b. 25 Jan. 1791; m. 7 Jan. 1807, Moses Batcheller.

2242.   CHARLES, b. 17 Sept. 1793; m. 1 May 1814, Mary Putnam. He d. 12 Mar. 1829. His widow m. (2) Dexter Clark.

SALLY, b. 30 June 1799; m. 21 Dec. 1820, Dexter Clark.

990

CALEB[6] CHASE (Nehemiah,[5] Lt. Caleb,[4] Daniel,[3] Ens. Moses[2]), born in Sutton, 23 Sept. 1786; died there 31 Oct. 1848, aged 62. He married (1) in Sutton, 27 Dec. 1806, FANNY HARRIS, daughter of Thomas Harris. She died in Sutton, 1 Nov. 1839, aged 53. He married (2) in Sutton (or Swanzey, N. H.), Sept. 1840, ALMIRA (HARRIS) GROVER of Richmond, N. H. She died 6 Dec. 1857 aged 45. She was widow of Nahum Grover and daughter of Capt. Luke and Asenath (Cole) Harris of Richmond, born 1806.

Children, born in Sutton :

EMILY,[7] b. 21 Feb. 1807; m. (1) 21 Dec. 1825, Nathan Garfield; m. (2) Nahum R. Hapgood.

MELINDA, b. 23 Sept. 1810; m. 2 Sept. 1833, Hymen Barber of Canton.

AMANDA, b. 27 Nov. 1812; m. 12 June 1833, Silas Edwin Chase of Canton; d. 16 Nov. 1844. (Family 994)

SERENA, b. 4 Apr. 1815; m. 19 May 1836, Sumner Pratt of Worcester.

FANNY LAVINA, b. 24 July 1817; m. 2 May 1838, Charles H. Towne.

VASHTI AUGUSTINE, b. 30 Nov. 1819; m. 15 May 1839, Leroy Litchfield; d. 1 Jan. 1841.

ACHSAH ANN, b. 13 Apr. 1822; d. unm. 12 Mar. 1841, a. 18 y. 11 m.

2243.   CALEB HARRIS, b. 26 Mar. 1824.

ABNER HIRAM, b. 25 Nov. 1829; d. 6 Oct. 1832.

991

ENS. ABRAHAM[6] CHASE (Nehemiah,[5] Lt. Caleb,[4] Daniel,[3] Ens. Moses[2]), born in Sutton, 27 Sept. 1789; died in Sutton, 29 Oct. 1857. He married in Sutton, 20 Nov. 1814, MARY DUDLEY, daughter of Jonathan and Lydia (Marble) Dudley, born in Sutton, 10 Aug. 1791; died 28 June 1884. They lived in Sutton.

Children, born in Sutton :

2244.   ABRAHAM DUDLEY,[7] b. 24 Feb. 1817; m. 3 June 1845, Sophia D. Griggs; d. 26 Apr. 1891.

2245.   NEHEMIAH BRADLEY, b. 26 Feb. 1821; m. (1) 26 Feb. 1845, Nancy Samantha Whiting; m. (2) 26 Sept. 1874, Harriet L. S. Harris.

MARY LOUISA, b. 7 Nov. 1823; m. 19 June 1851, Ransom C. Taylor; lived in Worcester.

2246.   LEVI LINCOLN, b. 6 Feb. 1827; m. 20 Dec. 1854, Mary Higgins.

LYDIA SOPHIA, b. 3 Jan. 1832; d. unm. 5 Aug. 1850.

992

NEHEMIAH[6] CHASE (Nehemiah,[5] Lt. Caleb,[4] Daniel,[3] .Ens Moses[2]), born in Sutton, 26 Mar. 1797; married in Sutton,, 1 June 1820, SALLY BOND, daughter of William and Sarah (Waters) Bond, born in Sutton, 7 May 1795. He died in Sutton, 31 Dec. 1833, aged 36. They lived in Sutton.

Child, born in Sutton:

2247. WILLIAM CYRUS,[7] b. 12 June 1826; m. 21 Feb. 1849, Catharine A. White.

993

DAVID[6] CHASE (David Prince,[5] Lt. Caleb,[4] Daniel,[3] Ens. Moses[2]), born in Sutton, 10 Oct. 1778; married in Sutton, 25 May 1800, MEHITABLE GALE, daughter of Nehemiah and Ruth (Marsh) Gale, born in Sutton, 9 Sept. 1782 and called "Hitte." They lived in Monkton, Addison Co., Vt., in Bennington, Vt., and died in Wisconsin.

Children, born in Monkton, Vt., and Bennington, Vt.:

2248. CYRUS PRINCE,[7] b. 10 Jan. 1802; m. 17 Aug. 1822, Sophronia Van Suydam of Hoosic, N. Y.
2249. BENJAMIN FRANKLIN, b. Apr. 1805; m. (1) Mary Fay Robinson; m. (2) Phebe ———.
BETSEY GALE, b. 23 June 1808; m. Daniel R. Allen of Pownal, Vt.; one child.
FANNY DEAN, b. 10 May 1810; m. (1) 1828, Harry Carver; m. (2) Robert Davidson, a native of Scotland.
SARAH GREENWOOD, b. 13 Nov. 1812; d. 10 Mar. 1813.
HARRIET LUCINA, b. 12 Feb. 1816; m. 22 Nov. 1832, William O. Stone; lived in Onondaga, N. Y., 1873.
HENRY AUGUSTUS, b. 15 Mar. 1819; d. 14 Apr. 1820.
MARY SOPHIA, b. 1821; m. ——— Brockway of Ohio.

994

SILAS[6] CHASE (David Prince,[5] Lt. Caleb,[4] Daniel,[3] Ens. Moses[2]), born in Sutton, 10 Dec. 1783; died Feb. 1865. He married (1) (intention in Sutton) 8 Dec. 1809, LUCINA HOLBROOK, daugtehr of Josiah and Anna (Sherman) Holbrook, born in Sutton, 29 May 1788. She died in Sutton, 21 July 1827, aged 39. He married (2) 2 June 1838, BEULAH C. ROBERTS who was born 23 Apr. 1811. They lived in the village of Williamsville [Wilkinsonville?], Worcester Co. in Hubbardston.

Children by first wife:

2250. SILAS EDWIN,[7] b. 3 Mar. 1811; m. (1) Amanda Chase; (Family 990) m. (2) Lurana L. White. He d. 4 Apr. 1872, in Newton.
2251. LAWTON, b. 4 June 1817; teacher in Va., 1861.
LUCINA (twin), b. 4 June 1817; d. 27 Apr. 1840.
2252. DANIEL G., b. 2 May 1819; m. Mar. 1840, Sarah P. Clark.
2253. OLIVER RICE, b. 30 July 1821; m. (1) 1842, Amanda Fletcher; m. (2) Elizabeth Moore; Newton.

Child by second wife:

LUCINA HOLBROOK, b. 7 Oct. 1840; m. Henry Dudley.

995

REV. JOHN[6] CHASE (David Prince,[5] Lt. Caleb,[4] Daniel,[3] Ens. Moses[2]), born in Sutton, 13 July 1788; died in Brookfield, 28 July 1833, aged 45. He married 24 Apr. 1821, POLLY BAYLIES of Southbridge. She was born 17 Apr. 1796 and died in Brookfield, 29 July 1829, aged 33. He was pastor of the First Baptist Church of Brookfield, 1815 to 1830.

Children, born in Brookfield:

> SARAH PRINCE,[7] b. 2 Jan. 1825.
> REBECCA BAYLIES, b. 25 May 1829; m. Elijah Emmons of Brookfield.

996

JUDGE HENRY BRIGHT[6] CHASE (Caleb Prince,[5] Lt. Caleb,[4] Daniel,[3] Ens. Moses[2]), born in Brookfield or Cornish, N. H., 27 Jan. 1777; died in Warner, N. H., 11 Jan. 1854. He married 20 Dec. 1807, DOROTHY BEAN, daughter of Nathaniel Bean of Warner. She was born 11 Sept. 1790 and died 23 Aug. 1843. They lived in Warner. Lawyer and Judge of Probate for Merrimack Co. 1823 to 1840. Speaker of House of Representatives 1817.

Children, born in Warner:

> MARY,[7] b. 24 Sept. 1808; m. 9 Feb. 1831, Francis Grimes; d. 30 Dec. 1849.
> FRANCIS, b. 12 July 1810; d. 3 Mar. 1826.
> 2254. HENRY B., b. 12 May 1812; m. (1) 21 Mar. 1854, Roberta A. Haynes; m. (2) 1858, Emily F. Blossom. He graduated at Dartmouth College in 1835. Captain in Mexican War, 1846; mayor of Clinton, La.
> NEHEMIAH, b. 14 Feb. 1814; d. unm. 17 Mar. 1843, in Burlington, Iowa.
> NANCY, b. 8 June 1817; never married.
> EDWARD WINSLOW, b. 5 Sept. 1819; d. 27 Jan. 1850.
> JOHN PRINCE, b. 29 Apr. 1822; d. unm. 4 Aug. 1842.
> SARAH AUGUSTA, b. 4 Aug. 1824; m. 24 Dec. 1846, Otis Brewer of Roxbury.
> SAMUEL B., b. 3 Jan. 1827; d. unm. 3 Jan. 1866, in Milwaukee, Wis.
> FRANCES BRIGHT, b. 23 Aug. 1829; d. unm. 20 Nov. 1859, in Houston, Texas.

997

CALEB SEWALL[6] CHASE (Caleb Prince,[5] Lt. Caleb,[4] Daniel,[3] Ens. Moses[2]), born in Cornish, N. H., 18 May 1783; died in Portland, Me., Apr. 1831. He married in Sept. 1815, MRS. RUTH (HOMER) BROWN who was born 10 Oct. 1791 and died 29 Oct. 1862. He was a merchant and they lived in Portland.

Children, born in Portland:

> SEWALL HENRY BRIGHT,[7] b. July 1816; d. at sea, unm. 1850.
> CAROLINE ALTHEA, b. 28 Apr. 1818; m. 1 May 1839, Charles Henry Hamlin of Augusta, Me.
> SARAH HOMER, b. 3 July 1826; d. unm. 3 Sept. 1848.
> FRANCES ELLEN, b. 12 Dec. 1827; m. 2 May 1849, S. D. Shepley of Portland, Me.; five children.

998

JOSEPH[6] CHASE (Joseph,[5] Lt. Caleb,[4] Daniel,[3] Ens. Moses[2]), born in Cornish, N. H., 8 Oct. 1787; died in Claremont, N. H., 31 Oct. 1838. He married 7 Mar. 1814, ELIZABETH STEVENS who was born in Plainfield, N. H., 9 Sept. 1792; died 16 Mar. 1884, aged 91. She was the daughter of Job and Elizabeth (Chase) Stevens of Plainfield. (Family 370). They lived in Cornish.

Children, born in Cornish:

> JOB STEVENS,[7] b. 23 and d. 24 Dec. 1814.
> JOSEPH PHILANDER, b. 23 Sept. 1820; d. 12 Dec. 1838, in Claremont, N. H.
> MARY ELIZABETH, b. 1 Mar. 1823; m. 27 Oct. 1844, Thomas Preston Blood; five children. She d. 8 July 1884.

2255.   HENRY STEVENS, b. 8 Aug. 1826; m. 28 Sept 1854. Harriet Columbia Ann Batchelder of Boston; d. 19 Aug. 1874.

> WILLIAM CARLOS, b. 11 Jan. 1829; d. in Boston, 8 Sept. 1853.
> THEODORE JERRALD, b. 30 June 1831; d. 3 Aug. 1834.

999

THEODORE[6] CHASE (Joseph,[5] Lt. Caleb,[4] Daniel,[3] Ens. Moses[2]), born in Cornish, N. H., 16 Feb. 1794; died there 8 June 1876. He married 7 Apr. 1819, JUDITH BRYANT, daughter of Israel and Mehitable (Wyman) Bryant, born 18 Nov. 1793 and died in Cornish, 30 Nov. 1847. They lived in Cornish.

Children, born in Cornish:

> MARTHA,[7] b. 13 Apr. 1820; m. 15 Sept. 1846, Horace Plympton Weld of Cornish.
> MARIA, b. 18 Nov. 1821; m. 9 Apr. 1843, Maj. George Weld, a brother of her sister's husband; d. 9 Sept. 1894; he d. 6 Jan. 1883.

1000

JACOB[6] CHASE (Joseph,[5] Lt. Caleb,[4] Daniel,[3] Ens. Moses[2]), born in Cornish, N. H., 20 Mar. 1799; died there 10 Mar. 1882. He married 27 Oct. 1825, SARAH TINKHAM who was born 25 Sept. 1793 and died in Cornish, 1 Aug. 1872. They lived in Cornish.

Children, born in Cornish:

2256.   FREDERIC J.,[7] b. 30 Sept. 1826; m. 26 Dec. 1854, Hannah P. Kenyon; d. 15 Sept. 1903; she d. 1 Sept. 1877.

2257.   LEWIS T., b. 15 Nov. 1827; m. 25 Dec. 1858, Mary S. Smith.

> LAURA S., b. 10 June 1829; m. 24 Apr. 1877, Rev. John A. Parker; she d. 17 July 1903, without issue.
> MARY J., b. 30 Jan. 1832; m. 29 Aug. 1861, William G. Wyman. No children.
> SARAH A., b. 26 Feb. 1834; d. 7 Sept. 1857, a. 23.

1001

DEA. JOHN[6] CHASE (Dea. John,[5] Lt. Caleb,[4] Daniel,[3] Ens. Moses[2]), born in Weathersfield, Vt., 7 Dec. 1795; died in Springfield, Vt., 27 Apr. 1871. He married in Weathersfield, 13 Apr. 1824, LUCY SHERWIN who was born 2 Nov. 1798; died in Springfield, 14 Feb.

1872. They removed to Springfield in 1851 and lived in "Spencer Hollow."

Child:

2258.   JOHN DRURY,[7] b. 16 Oct. 1825; m. 6 Aug. 1849, Alphleda G. Benson; living in Springfield, in 1873.

1002

AUSTIN PARKER[6] CHASE (Dea. John,[5] Lt. Caleb,[4] Daniel,[3] Ens. Moses[2]), born in Weathersfield, Vt., 6 Mar. 1809; died there 2 Feb. 1845, aged 36. He married (1) in Chester, Vt., 28 June 1836, ACHSAH BULLARD who died in Weathersfield, 6 Feb. 1843, aged 36. He married (2) in Springfield, Vt., 28 Nov. 1843, JULIETTE SELDEN who died in Weathersfield, 1 Feb. 1845, aged 24. They lived in Weathersfield.

Children by first wife, born in Weathersfield:

> SON,[7] b. and d. 10 July 1837.
> ODIN B., b. 15 Dec. 1840; d. 30 June 1841, a. 6 m. 15 d.
> JOHN WILMOT, b. 23 May 1842; d. 7 Apr. 1843.

Child by second wife, born in Weathersfield:

> AUSTIN SELDEN, b. 28 Jan. 1845; d. unm. 1903.

1003

STEPHEN[6] CHASE (Capt. Stephen,[5] Lt. Caleb,[4] Daniel,[3] Ens. Moses[2]), born in Keene, N. H., 18 July 1798; died there 21 Sept. 1881, aged 83. Married there, 22 Feb. 1832, LOUISA DICKINSON who was born in Keene, 15 Jan. 1808, and died 24 Mar. 1895, aged 87. They lived in Keene.

Children, born in Keene:

> EMILY ANN,[7] b. 19 Nov. 1832; d. unm. 15 Dec. 1869.
> SARAH LOUISA, b. 8 Sept. 1834; d. 7 Feb. 1840.
> 2259.   JOSEPH, b. 7 Aug. 1836; d. 12 Mar. 1918; a. 81 y. 7 m.; m. Victoria E. ———, who d. 25 May 1917, a. 66 y. 10 m.
> MARY JANE, b. 15 Sept. 1838; d. 30 Oct. 1860.
> 2260.   ALFRED, b. 15 Oct. 1840; d. 28 Mar. 1905.
> SARAH ELIZABETH, b. 8 Feb. 1843.
> JULIETTE SELDEN, b. 13 Mar. 1845; d. 20 Sept. 1849.
> ELLA AUGUSTA, b. 15 Jan. 1848; d. 27 Sept. 1849.
> EDWARD STEPHEN, b. 16 Feb. 1851; d. 2 June 1860.
> FRANK HENRY, b. 14 Apr. 1854; d. 23 Aug. 1856.

1004

CHARLES[6] CHASE (Capt. Stephen,[5] Lt. Caleb,[4] Daniel,[3] Ens. Moses[2]), born in Keene, N. H., 17 July 1803; died there, 4 Aug. 1866, aged 63 y. He married in Athol, 7 June 1832, HANNAH[7] CHASE, daughter of Moses[6] and Miriam (Twitchell) Chase, born in Athol, 8 Feb. 1807. (Family 871). She died in Keene, 24 Nov. 1884, aged 77 y. 9 m. 16 d. They lived in Keene.

Children, born in Keene:

> HANNAH ABBY,[7] b. 19 Oct. 1833; m. 9 Mar. 1859, George F. Goodnow; living in Chicago, Ill., in 1873.
> DAUGHTER, b. 13 Aug. 1835; d. in infancy.
> CHARLES EPHRAIM, b. 18 Sept. 1837; d. 15 Sept. 1839.

Charles Dwight, b. 24 Sept. 1840; d. in U. S. service in Jackson, Miss., 20 July 1863.

GEORGE MOSES, b. 26 July 1842; d. 20 Dec. 1842.

LUCIA MARIA, b. 16 July 1844; d. 3 Oct. 1859.

CLARA ELIZA, b. 17 Nov. 1847; m. 15 June 1871, J. W. Sturtevant of Keene.

1005

HOSEA⁶ CHASE (Capt. Stephen,⁵ Lt. Caleb,⁴ Daniel,³ Ens. Moses²), born in Keene, N. H., 23 Apr. 1805; died there, 17 Nov. 1874, aged 69. He married in Keene, 4 Nov. 1833, HANNAH DRUSILLA BRITTON, who was born in Westmoreland, N. H., 21 Aug. 1811; died 1896. They lived in Keene.

Children, born in Keene:

MARTHA SKERRY,⁷ b. 10 Nov. 1835; m. 7 Apr. 1858, Edmund J. Perham. She d. in Keene, 13 Feb. 1860; he d. in Knoxville, Md., 26 Oct. 1862.

FRANCES ANN, b. 9 Aug. 1837; d. 26 Sept. 1867, in Keene.

HOSEA BRITTON, b. 21 Aug. 1839; d. 26 Sept. 1839.

ELIZABETH ELLEN, b. 8 Sept. 1841; m. 7 Sept. 1859, Rev. William W. Hayward of Methuen; she d. 21 Aug. 1913.

WILLIAM HUDSON, b. 30 Sept. 1843; d. 23 Sept. 1860.

DANIEL WEBSTER, b. 11 Mar. 1846; d. 23 Aug. 1867, a. 21.

1006

ALBE⁶ CHASE (Capt. Stephen,⁵ Lt. Caleb,⁴ Daniel,³ Ens. Moses²), born in Keene, N. H., 13 July 1812; died in Springfield, Vt., 18 Nov. 1874. He married in Athol, 13 Nov. 1838, MIRIAM⁷ CHASE, daughter of Moses⁶ and Miriam (Twitchell) Chase, born in Athol, 1 Sept. 1820; died in Andover, 7 Mar. 1900. (Family 871). The Vital Records of Keene call this man *Albert* and the marriage record of Athol, *Abba.* They lived in Cornish, N. H., till 1857, when they removed to Springfield, Vt.

Children, born in Cornish, except the youngest born in Springfield:

SARAH M.,⁷ b. 1 May 1841; lived in Claremont, N. H.

CORNELIA A., b. 31 Mar. 1843; m. 8 Feb. 1860, W. H. Haskell of Springfield, Vt.

ELIZABETH ANN, b. 16 Dec. 1844; d. 4 Jan. 1845.

ABBIE E., b. 31 July 1850; m. 15 Jan. 1873, Joseph A. Bowman; d. in Bridgewater, 29 Jan. 1916.

2261. OMAR PASHA, b. 14 Dec. 1853; m. 10 May 1911, Jennie S. Abbott of Andover; killed in an automobile accident at Andover, 28 Nov. 1926; news dealer; one of the founders of the Chase-Chace Family Association; thirteen years secretary-treasurer of same; three years president and long a member of the executive committee; member of many other societies.

2262. HERBERT F., b. 30 June 1859; m. 20 Jan. 1898, M. Leslie Abbott of Andover. One son.

1007

SANFORD⁶ CHASE (Moses,⁵ Lt. Caleb,⁴ Daniel,³ Ens. Moses²), born in Sutton, 31 Jan. 1791; died in Claremont, N. H., 23 Sept. 1816.

He married 12 Feb. 1812, POLLY PARMELEE of Claremont. She died about 1854. They lived in Claremont.

Child, born in Claremont:

2263.   CALEB B.,[7] m. Ann Hoadley; living Felchville, Vt., in 1872. Two children.

1008

LEONARD[6] CHASE (Moses,[5] Lt. Caleb,[4] Daniel,[3] Ens. Moses[2]), born in Sutton, 17 Jan. 1796; married 31 Dec. 1821, POLLY STRAW of Weathersfield, Vt. He died 7 Aug. 1829. They lived in Weathersfield.

Children, born in Weathersfield:

BETSEY,[7] m. Merrill Bryant of Bethel, Vt. She d. 12 May 1852.
SARAH ANN, m. Rev. Joseph C. Aspenwall, who was living in Wis. in 1872. She was not alive then.

1009

DANIEL PRINCE[6] CHASE (Daniel,[5] Lt. Caleb,[4] Daniel,[3] Ens. Moses[2]), born in Claremont, N. H., 22 Jan. 1799; died in Newport, N. H., 31 July 1856. He married in Claremont 17 Oct. 1825, DIANTHA P. DAY, who was born in 1798; died 12 Dec. 1863, aged 66. They lived in Claremont.

Children, born in Claremont:

2264.   DANIEL F.,[7] b. 18 Nov. 1826; m. 1 Sept. 1847, Mehitable Atwood; locomotive engineer, Pacific R. R.
2265.   THOMAS HENRY, b. 20 Dec. 1830; m. Laura Dodge; lived in Newbury, Vt.

1010

WILLARD WOODBURY[6] CHASE (Daniel,[5] Lt. Caleb,[4] Daniel,[3] Ens. Moses[2]), born in Claremont, N. H., 10 Nov. 1805; died there, 9 Aug. 1873. He married in Claremont, 9 Sept. 1833, MARIA DUNLAP, daughter of Samuel and Maria (Clement) Dunlap, born in Washington, N. H., 19 Sept. 1814. They lived in Claremont.

Children, born in Claremont:

2266.   WILLARD DUNLAP[7] (M.D.), b. 4 Dec. 1836; Harvard Medical School, 1866; m. 30 Dec. 1869, Josephine Louisa Clark, b. 4 Feb. 1847, of Wilton, N. H.; d. 1894, Peterborough, N. H. One daughter.
2267.   EDWARD WOODBURY, b. 13 Feb. 1839; m. 17 July 1867, Eliza A. Brown; d. 7 Mar. 1869; one child.
LUTHER AQUILA, b. 2 May 1843; killed in the battle of Fredericksburg, Va., 10 Dec. 1862. Corp 5th N. H. Vol.
AUSTIN CORBIN, b. 11 Feb. 1846; never married.
MEHITABLE MARIA, b. 12 Feb. 1853.

1011

JAMES HIRAM[6] CHASE (Daniel,[5] Lt. Caleb,[4] Daniel,[3] Ens. Moses[2]), born in Claremont, N. H., 14 Mar. 1830; married 25 Dec. 1854, SARAH AUGUSTA LAMPREY who was born in Hampton, N. H., 4 Dec. 1838; died in Concord, N. H., 5 May 1921. He died 1 Aug. 1893.

Children, born in Concord:

James Henry,[7] b. 27 Sept. 1855; d. in Boston, 16 Apr. 1873.

Amy Augusta, b. 30 Sept. 1859; d. 16 Mar. 1907;.m. W. M. Mason. Children: *William Henry*,[8] b. 8 Dec. 1890; m. 4 July 1923, Bernice Cosgrove; *Carol Chase*[8] *Mason*, b. 25 Dec. 1892.

Mabel Norton, b. 9 Mar. 1865; m. 12 Jan. 1887, Benjamin C. White. Children: James Chase[8] White, b. 13 Aug. 1890; d. 24 Oct. 1895; Rose Aldrich[8] White, b. 5 June 1895; m. 17 July 1918, John H. Gregory. She m. (2) 28 June 1926, Kendall Winship.

1012

George Hall[6] Chase (Israel,[5] Lt. Caleb,[4] Daniel,[3] Ens. Moses[2]), born in Cornish, N. H., 12 Apr. 1801; died in South America. No family has been reported.

1013

Lebbeus[6] Chase (Israel,[5] Lt. Caleb,[4] Daniel,[3] Ens. Moses[2]), born in Cornish, N. H., 6 Apr. 1804. He married (1) Amanda Curtis who was born in 1809 and died without issue, 23 Mar. 1837. He married (2) Samantha Stevens.

Children by the second wife:

2268. George Henry.[7]

Amanda.

1014

Capt. Henry Hall[6] Chase (Israel,[5] Lt. Caleb,[4] Daniel,[3] Ens. Moses[2]), born in Cornish, N. H., 10 May 1809; died 13 May 1852. He married in Cornish, 28 Sept. 1841, Lucy C. Powers, daughter of Obed and Cynthia (Comings) Powers, born in Cornish, 10 Feb. 1820. She married (2) Jotham G. Allds of Claremont, N. H. They lived in Cornish.

Child, born in Cornish:

Robert Henry,[7] b. 11 Dec. 1842; sergeant in Co. G. and C. 5th N. H. Regt. Civil War; d. in the army, 25 Aug. 1864.

1015

Moody[6] Chase (Lt. Jacob,[5] Moody,[4] Daniel,[3] Ens. Moses[2]), born in Groton, 27 Feb. 1786; he was mentioned in his father's will dated 23 Aug. 1845, as a legatee.

1016

William[6] Chase (Lt. Jacob,[5] Moody,[4] Daniel,[3] Ens. Moses[2]), born in Groton, 14 Aug. 1787; died in Beardstown, Ill., 7 Nov. 1869. He married (1) 23 Apr. 1815, Hannah Parker who was born in Pepperell, 23 Feb. 1790 and died 7 Mar. 1847. He married (2) in Beardstown, 24 Dec. 1857, Susan Miller who was born in Covington, Ky., in 1815. They lived in Boston 1816-22, New York City 1822-31; Beardstown.

Children by first wife, eldest born in Boston:
2269.   WILLIAM AUGUSTUS,[7] b. 1 Feb. 1816; m. 12 Oct. 1846, Mary M.
        Cook; lived in Pana, Ill., 1872.
        MARIA ANTOINETTE, b. 12 Oct. 1817; m. 20 Nov. 1840, Charles
        Rich.
2270.   EDMUND PARKER, b. 30 May 1821; m. 12 Oct. 1846, Eliza A. D.
        Scripps.
        MARY, b. N. Y. City, 15 Dec. 1831; d. there 24 Dec. 1832.
     Child by second wife, born in Beardstown:
        WILLIAM PRESCOTT, b. 13 Feb. 1839; d. there 11 Jan. 1862.

1017

HARVEY[6] CHASE (Lt. Jacob,[5] Moody,[4] Daniel,[3] Ens. Moses[2]),
born in Pepperell, 18 Jan. 1800; died in Mt. Hope, Ill., in 1844. He
married about 1830, CHARLOTTE VERY who was born in 1798 and
died in Jacksonville, Ill., in 1849. They lived in Richmond, N. Y., in
Jacksonville, Ill., and Mt. Hope, Ill.
     Children, born in Richmond:
        WILLIAM HARVEY,[7] b. 7 Apr. 1831; d. in Jacksonville, 3 July
        1849.
        SARAH ELIZABETH, b. 26 Nov. 1833; m. 11 Mar. 1862, Dr. Solo-
        mon Hasbroock Burhans of Carlisle, N. Y.
        SAMUEL WHIPPLE, b. 13 Feb. 1840; d. in Jacksonville, 4 July
        1856.

1018

JACOB[6] CHASE (Lt. Jacob,[5] Moody,[4] Daniel,[3] Ens. Moses[2]), born
in Pepperell, 21 Jan. 1802; married in Chelmsford, 19 Oct. 1830,
LUCY RICHARDSON, daughter of Oliver and Chloe (Bancroft) Richardson, born in Chelmsford, 27 Jan. 1801. Before his marriage, he
removed to West Richmond, N. Y.
     Child, born in West Richmond:
2271.   CHARLES HENRY,[7] b. Oct. 1835; lived in La Salle Co., Ill.

1019

AMOS[6] CHASE (Lt. Jacob,[5] Moody,[4] Daniel,[3] Ens. Moses[2]), born
in Pepperell, 9 Mar. 1806; died in Springfield, 23 Dec. 1843. He
married (1) 19 Sept. 1833, SARAH WHITNEY STEARNS, daughter of
Eli and Mary (Whitney) Stearns. She was born 13 May 1804 and
died in Groton, 11 Jan. 1837. He married (2) in 1840, MARY BATES
of Springfield who died 16 June 1850. They lived in Groton and
Springfield.
     Children by first wife, born in Groton:
        SARAH AUGUSTA,[7] b. 30 June 1834; m. 3 Apr. 1872, Dr. J. M.
        Stickney of Pepperell.
        MARY CATHARINE, b. 1 July 1835.
     Children by second wife, born in Springfield:
        ELIZABETH ANTOINETTE, b. 28 Mar. 1842.
        MARY STEARNS, b. 31 Jan. 1844.

1020

WILLIAM PRESCOTT[6] CHASE (Samuel,[5] Moody,[4] Daniel,[3] Ens.
Moses[2]), born in Pepperell, 22 Feb. 1808; died in 1869. He married
26 Nov. 1830, EMELINE WHITE who was living in Easton, in 1876.
Children:

2272. WILLIAM LONGLEY,[7] b. 16 Mar. 1832; alive in 1876.
SAMUEL JASON, b. 16 Mar. 1834; d. 15 July 1837.

1021

WILLIAM MOODY[6] CHASE (March,[5] Moody,[4] Daniel,[3] Ens.
Moses[2]), born in Bolton, 1 Dec. 1817; also recorded as born in Shirley; married 17 Apr. 1842, SUSAN PARKER of Boston.

1022

JONATHAN HALE[6] CHASE (Lt. Williams,[5] Moody,[4] Daniel,[3] Ens.
Moses[2]), born in Sutton about 1778; died in Walpole, N. H., 24 Feb.
1865, aged 87. He married in Grafton, 8 Oct. 1801, MARTHA KIM-
BALL, daughter of Aaron and Mary (Goulding) Kimball, born in
Grafton, 18 Aug. 1782; died in Walpole, 19 Oct. 1858. They re-
moved from Grafton to Walpole in 1804. "He was born in Sutton
and left at a tender age by his father who went into the Revolutionary
service, which was the last he knew of him." See Lt. William.[5]
(Family 360).
Children, first born in Grafton, others in Walpole:

2273. CHARLES ELLIOTT,[7] b. 6 Nov. 1802, in Grafton; m. in Walpole,
17 Nov. 1825, Miriam Carpenter, dau .of Davis and Lucy
(Bowker) Carpenter, b. 8 Oct. 1804. Their son *Charles
Elliott*,[8] b. 13 Mar. 1832; .d. 19 Jan. 1908; m. 2 Oct. 1854,
Rhoda Ann Wetherell, b. 24 June 1836; d. in Malden, 11 Mar.
1919. Their son George Elliott,[9] b. 1 Sept. 1864; m. 18 Mar.
1891, Mary Wilder Harvey. Their daughter *Frances Harvey*,[10] b. 5 Jan. 1897; m. 18 May 1922, Charles Arthur Everett
of Lowell. Charles Elliott's[8] youngest daughter, Grace May,[9]
b. 22 Dec. 1874; m. 15 Oct. 1907, Arthur James Plummer, a
graduate of Harvard University, 1894; Harvard Law School,
1901. Their son *Arthur Selwyn*[10] *Plummer*, b. 12 Aug. 1910.
Their daughter *Nancy Carpenter*,[8] b. 1 Aug. 1834; d. 25 Jan.
1925; m. Newton Charles Harris (1833-1903). Children:
Charles Newton[9] Harris, b. 21 Apr. 1863; Edwin Schuyler[9]
Harris, b. 19 June 1867; m. 2 Nov. 1904, Mae McEckron.
Their children are *Mary Nancy*[10] *Harris*, b. 21 June 1905;
Edwin Schuyler[10] *Harris*, b. 16 Mar. 1907; *Elizabeth McEck-
ron*[10] *Harris*, b. 19 Jan. 1909; *James Newton*[10] *Harris*, b. 21
Dec. 1910 and *Jane Ray*[10] *Harris*, b. 22 Mar. 1916. Mabel
Louise[9] Harris, b. 10 Oct. 1868. They live in Schuylerville,
N. Y.

2274. AARON KIMBALL, b. 8 July 1806; m. (1) in Walpole, 3 Dec.
1828, Adeline Clark; m. (2) 26 Apr. 1841, Angeline Ranney
of Westminster, Vt.
MARY KIMBALL, b. 12 Sept. 1812; m. Henry W. Hooper.
Sarah S., b. 30 Apr. 1818; m. Seth B. Cragin.

1023

BENJAMIN KIMBALL[6] CHASE (Daniel,[5] Capt. Moses,[4] Daniel,[3] Ens. Moses[2]), born in Cornish, N. H., 5 Apr. 1798; died there, 16 June 1842. He married in Cornish, 28 Oct. 1835, SARAH ANN P. TAFT of Weathersfield, Vt. She was born 9 June 1815 and died in Cornish 4 Feb. 1888. She married (2) 7 Mar. 1843, Enoch F. Chellis of Plainfield, N. H. They lived in Cornish.

Children, born in Cornish:

2275.   DANIEL,[7] b. 9 July 1836; m. 25 Dec. 1867, Abbie A. Atwood. No children. He d. 21 Nov. 1885.

SARAH JANE, b. 26 Aug. 1838; d. 10 Mar. 1850.

AMOS, b. ———— 1839; d. 8 July 1841.

2276.   BENJAMIN KIMBALL, b. 25 Aug. 1841; m. (1) 3 Jan. 1866, Lucia C. Deming; she d. 30 Oct. 1871; m. (2) Clara E. Allison.

1024

CAPT. COTTON[6] CHASE (Dea. John,[5] Capt. Moses,[4] Daniel,[3] Ens. Moses[2]), born in Cornish, N. H., 8 Aug. 1783; died in Cornish, 1 Oct. 1872. He married in Cornish, 14 Nov. 1815, BETSEY[6] CHASE, daughter of Capt. Caleb[5] and Elizabeth (Deming) Chase, born in Cornish, 19 Aug. 1789; died there 8 July 1868. (Family 365). They lived in Cornish.

Children, born in Cornish:

MARTHA COTTON,[7] b. 21 Sept. 1816; d. unm. 23 May 1881.

2277.   NAHUM, b. 24 July 1818; lived in Albany, N. Y.; d. 18 Nov. 1902.

2278.   CALEB ROWLAND, b. 23 Oct. 1820; d. 11 Jan. 1870.

HANNAH BROWN, b. 16 Aug. 1824; d. 14 Nov. 1827.

CAROLINE HANNAH, b. 18 Dec. 1827; d. unm. 10 Oct. 1860.

1025

JOHN[6] CHASE (Dea. John,[5] Capt. Moses,[4] Daniel,[3] Ens. Moses[2]), born in Cornish, N. H., 25 Sept. 1794; married 13 Sept. 1827, ACHSAH WHITNEY. He died about 1838.

Children:

2279.   GEORGE.[7]

ELIZABETH.

1026

MOSES[6] CHASE (Dea. John,[5] Capt. Moses,[4] Daniel,[3] Ens. Moses[2]), born in Cornish, N. H., 28 Dec. 1799; died there, 16 May 1864. He married 1 May 1832, FIDELIA A. ALDEN, daughter of Dr. Isaac and Hannah (Perry) Alden, born 12 Aug. 1805; died in Cornish, 11 Mar. 1864. They lived in Cornish.

Children, born in Cornish:

HENRY DWIGHT,[7] b. 19 Mar. 1833; d. 19 July 1836.

2280.   JOHN BAXTER, b. 1 Apr. 1834; m. 11 Mar. 1868, Emerette Ayers. No children. He d. 15 Aug. 1871; she d. 22 Apr. 1874.

HARRIET FIDELIA, b. 10 Oct. 1836; d. 18 June 1848.

SARAH ANNABELL, b. 6 Apr. 1839; d. 19 Dec. 1860.

HELEN MARIA, b. 21 Nov. 1841; m. 11 Mar. 1868, Henry Ayers; lived in Ashtabula, Ohio.

ADELINE ESTELLA, b. 25 Apr. 1844; m. 17 Jan. 1871, Darwin B. Kinsman of Plainfield, N. H.

ORMOND ALDEN, b. 15 Apr. 1847; d. 16 Jan. 1865.

2281. GEORGE BYRON, b. 27 Jan. 1850; m. Clara Hart; d. in Rome, Ohio, Feb. 1880.

1027

TAYLOR GILMAN⁶ CHASE (Dea. John,⁵ Capt. Moses,⁴ Daniel,³ Ens. Moses²), born in Cornish, N. H., 4 Nov. 1801; married (1) 1 Oct. 1828, URSULA NEVENS who died without issue. He married (2) in Plainfield, N. H., 26 Sept. 1831, EMILY SPAULDING, daughter of Waterman and Betsey (Stevens) Spaulding, born in Roxbury, Vt., 29 July 1808. His first wife was a daughter of David and Betsey (Pollard) Nevens, born 21 Sept. 1802 and died 19 Nov. 1829. They lived in Cornish till 1838 when they removed to Brighton, Ill.

Children by second wife, first three born in Cornish, others in Brighton, Ill.:

2282. OSCAR ALANSON,⁷ b. 1 July 1832; m. 30 Aug. 1864, Calista Elmira Smith.

DON CARLOS, b. 17 Mar. 1834; d. 30 Oct. 1858, in Brighton.

EMILY SPAULDING, b. 25 Mar. 1836; m. 4 Nov. 1863, George Henry Aylesworth of Brighton.

EGBERT ALONZO, b. 7 Jan. 1843; d. 12 July 1847.

CELIA ADELAIDE, b. 24 Dec. 1844; m. 13 Apr. 1864, George W. Hillyard.

1028

JOSEPH LANMAN⁶ CHASE (Rev. Amos,⁵ Capt. Moses,⁴ Daniel,³ Ens. Moses²), born in Litchfield, Conn., 18 July 1799; married 13 Nov. 1825, SUSAN JANE TITUS, daughter of Jonathan Titus, who was born 26 Aug. 1805; died 17 Dec. 1877. They lived in Titusville, Pa. He died in Titusville, 23 or 30 Apr. 1879, aged 80.

Children, born in Titusville:

MARY LANMAN,⁷ b. 25 July 1826; m. 11 Jan. 1842, Samuel A. Torbett. She d. 12 June 1848; three children.

JOANNA LANMAN, b. 20 Jan. 1828; m. 14 Dec. 1848, Jonathan Watson of Hartford, Conn. She d. 14 Mar. 1858.

2283. JOSEPH TITUS, b. 17 June 1829; d. 26 Feb. 1897; m. 14 Sept. 1853, Elizabeth Adrain, b. 5 Nov. 1832; d. 19 Oct. 1874. Their son *Herbert Adrain*,⁸ b. 27 July 1854, in Meadville, Pa.; m. 7 Sept. 1892, Rose Virginia Shank, b. in Middletown, Pa., 21 May 1865; they live in Titusville, Pa. Children: Margaret,⁹ b. 16 July 1894; m. 6 Sept. 1919, Robert Allison Locke; Herbert Shank,⁹ b. 29 Apr. 1897; m. 19 Aug. 1922, Hazel Noera.

CORNELIUS SUYDAM, b. 27 Dec. 1830; captain; d. from wounds received in the battle of Fair Oaks, at Philadelphia, 17 June 1862.

2284. THOMAS SILL, b. 17 Nov. 1832; m. Sept. 1859, Ida Butterworth; d. 23 June 1865; one child.

2285. WILLIAM WIRT, b. 21 May 1834; m. 11 Nov. 1869, Anna Elizabeth Hurd.

SUSAN EMMA, b. 12 Nov. 1835; d. 14 Oct. 1838.

2286.   EDWARD BISPHAM, b. 21 Jan. 1838.

ADELAIDE P., b. 12 May 1841; m. 24 June 1863, John H. Dalzell of Pittsburgh, Pa.; two children.

2287.   GEORGE AUGUSTUS, b. 6 Dec. 1844.

1029

CHARLES[6] CHASE (Rev. Amos,[5] Capt. Moses,[4] Daniel,[3] Ens. Moses[2]), born in Litchfield, Conn., 12 May 1803; married 13 Oct. 1831, ANN IRWIN. They lived in Painesville, Ohio. He died in Painesville, 22 Dec. 1878, aged 76.

Child:

JANE ADELIA,[7] b. 1 Dec. 1834; m. 18 Mar. 1854, Rev. Abram Smith Dobbs, A.M.

1030

DR. JAMES LANMAN[6] CHASE (Rev. Amos,[5] Capt. Moses,[4] Daniel,[3] Ens. Moses[2]), born in Litchfield, Conn., 10 Feb. 1805; married in 1842, EMMA I. GAGER of Norwich, Conn., who was born 16 July 1810. They lived in Toledo, Ohio. He died in Dec. 1889.

Children:

2288.   GEORGE ALBERT,[7] b. 17 June 1843; served in Civil War; lawyer in Detroit, Mich.; m. Grace Osborn.

HARRIE GAGER, b. 1 Nov. 1844; alive and unm. Jan. 1877.

FRANK M., b. 11 Apr. 1848; d. 16 Aug. 1851.

1031

EDWARD HUNTINGTON[6] CHASE (Rev. Amos,[5] Capt. Moses,[4] Daniel,[3] Ens. Moses[2]), born in Litchfield, Conn., 18 July 1807; married 24 Feb. 1835, SARAH ANN TITUS, daughter of Jonathan Titus, born 18 May 1808; died 3 Mar. 1897. He died 18 June 1878. He served as Associate Judge of Crawford Co. Court, Penn., for ten years.

Children:

EDWARD,[7] b. 1836; d. in infancy.

MARY ANN, b. 24 Oct. 1837; m. 30 Dec. 1856, Reuel Danforth Fletcher, b. in Holland, Vt., 17 Dec. 1831; d. in Titusville, Pa., 31 Aug. 1914. Their daughter *Elizabeth Ellen*[8] *Fletcher*, b. 25 Sept. 1857; graduate of Vassar College; m. 16 Sept. 1885, Dr. Julien E. Hequembourg of Chicago, Ill, who d. 9 Dec. 1910.

ELIZABETH SHEFFIELD, b. 14 July 1840; m. 28 Dec. 1865, Gurdon Sill Berry.

LANMAN, b. 12 Dec. 1847; d. unm. 22 Mar. 1924.

1032

JULIUS DEMING[6] CHASE (Rev. Amos,[5] Capt. Moses,[4] Daniel,[3] Ens. Moses[2]), born in Litchfield, Conn., 6 Nov. 1811; married 31 July 1850, ELIZABETH LOWELL who was born in Ulysses, Tompkins Co., N. Y., 23 June 1818. They were living in Centreville, Pa., as late as 1871.

Children, born in Centreville:

2289. Amos Crosby,[7] b. 29 Aug. 1852; his widow Tillie lives in Ore.
2290. Abraham Lanman, b. 16 Dec. 1855; graduate from Alleghany College, Meadville, Pa., 1886; from the Pacific Theological Seminary, Oakland, Calif., 1888; Congregational clergyman; pastor and mission worker in New Haven, Conn., Brooklyn and New York City, N. Y., Jersey City, N. J., Jacksonville and Tampa, Fla., Boston, Mass., Portland, Ore., and among the lumber men in the camps in Oregon, Washington, Idaho and California; married but has no children.

Georgianna, b. 13 May 1858; teacher in Albuquerque, New Mexico.
2291. Harvey, b. 22 Sept. 1860; teacher; d. in Oakland, Calif.
2292. William Lynn, b. 16 July 1865; living in Oxford, Pa.

1033

Col. Freeman[6] Chase (Capt. Nahum,[5] Capt. Moses,[4] Daniel,[3] Ens. Moses[2]), born in Cornish, N. H., 27 June 1787; married 13 Dec. 1809, Mary[6] Chase, daughter of Capt. Caleb[5] and Elizabeth (Dem-) ing) Chase of Corinsh. (Family 365). She was born there, 26 Dec. 1790. He died in Brownville, Jefferson Co., N. Y., 19 Sept. 1830. His widow removed to Sackets Harbor immediately after his death and was living there 27 Sept. 1830 (letter to her mother).

Children:

Son,[7] b. 1810; d. young.
Polly, b. 1 Nov. 1811.
Clarissa Kimball, b. 21 Sept. 1813; m. in Georgia; lived in Galveston, Texas.
Lucia Curtis, b. 5 Aug. 1816; m. 10 Nov. 1846, Oran Corbett[7] Chase. (Family 986)
2293. Nahum Freeman, b. 26 June 1819; lived in Galveston, Texas.
2294. George Wentworth, b. 8 Aug. 1821; m. Abby ———; lived in Ohio.

1034

Moses[6] Chase (Capt. Nahum,[5] Capt. Moses,[4] Daniel,[3] Ens. Moses[2]), born in Cornish, N. H., 1 Sept. 1795; married 2 Oct. 1825, Julia Anne Hyde, daughter of Elihu and Mary (Hatch) Hyde of Chelsea, Vt. She was born, 21 Apr. 1807; died in Cambridge, 9 Jan. 1900, aged 93. They lived in Cornish until after 1836, then in Chelsea, Vt.

Children, born in Cornish:

2295. Freeman Hatch,[7] b. 28 Aug. 1826; m. Mary Jane Corliss. He d. in Cambridge, 1 Nov. 1906.
Sarah Hyde, b. 10 July 1830; d. 18 May 1842.
Emily Robbins, b. 7 Dec. 1836; d. 3 May 1842.

1035

Caleb[6] Chase (Capt. Caleb,[5] Capt. Moses,[4] Daniel,[3] Ens. Moses[2]), born in Cornish, N. H., 3 Sept. 1796; married (1) Sarah Morgan; married (2) Jane Rayburn. They lived in Boston. Sarah, wife of Caleb Chase, died in Boston, 22 June 1844, aged 37.

1036

DANIEL KIMBALL[6] CHASE (Capt. Caleb,[5] Capt. Moses,[4] Daniel,[3] Ens. Moses[2]), born in Cornish, N. H., 16 Oct. 1804; married in Boston, 2 Dec. 1839, MARIA LOUISA COBB. They lived in Boston.
Children:

2296.   BENJAMIN K.[7]
2297.   DANIEL.

1037

BENJAMIN CHAPMAN[6] CHASE (Moody,[5] Capt. Moses,[4] Daniel,[3] Ens. Moses[2]), born in Cornish, N. H., 8 Sept. 1793; died there 19 Sept. 1829. He married in Cornish, 13 Nov. 1817, ELIZA (STEVENS) ROYCE of Claremont, N. H. She died in Lowell, in Aug. 1846.
Children, born in Cornish, N. H.:

2298.   BENJAMIN CHAPMAN,[7] b. 29 Jan. 1819; graduate of Dartmouth College 1846; clergyman; d. 13 Oct. 1865.
2299.   MURRAY STEVENS, b. 14 Feb. 1821; m. Clara Allen.
        LUTHERA MARIA, b. 16 Jan. 1823; m. Nathan Brown of Boston.
2300.   MAURICE JAMES, b. 4 Mar. 1826; physician; Galesburg, Ill.
2301.   HENRY ALFRED, b. 8 July 1828; m. 7 Feb. 1850, Harriet Ann Pease; living in Lee, 1885.

1038

HARVEY FARNHAM[6] CHASE (Moody,[5] Capt. Moses,[4] Daniel,[3] Ens. Moses[2]), born in Cornish, N. H., 5 Mar. 1797; married 3 Nov. 1836 SARAH D. WOODBURY of New London, N. H. He died in Macomb, Ill., 9 Dec. 1878. They removed from Cornish to Macomb, about 1840. She died 30 Sept. 1857.
Children, eldest born in Cornish:

2302.   JAMES PHINEAS,[7] b. 17 July 1838.
2303.   GEORGE NEWTON.
        SARAH JANE.
        HELEN.

1039

REV. JAMES MORRIS[6] CHASE (Moody,[5] Capt. Moses,[4] Daniel,[3] Ens. Moses[2]), born in Cornish, N. H., 4 Apr. 1800; died in Macomb, Ill., 10 Feb. 1865. He married (1) in 1832, SELINA A. VENABLE, daughter of Judge Venable. She died 30 Sept. 1850. He married (2) in 1854, ANDREA C. LANGE of Quincy, Ill. He graduated from Dartmouth College in 1827 and was a clergyman. They lived in Macomb, Ill.
Children, by first wife:

2304.   HENRY,[7] b. 17 Dec. 1832; graduate Dartmouth College, 1859.
2305.   JOSEPH VENABLE, b. 4 Aug. 1836; graduate Dartmouth, 1861.
2306.   JAMES MORRIS.
2307.   ALBERT MOODY, lived in Liberty, Clay Co., Mo.
2308.   WILLIAM THOMAS.
2309.   GEORGE FRANCIS.
        MARY ALICE.

1040

Rev. Moody[6] Chase (Moody,[5] Capt. Moses,[4] Daniel,[3] Ens. Moses[2]), born in Cornish, N. H., 25 Feb. 1802; died in Parkersburg, Ind., 22 Mar. 1879. He graduated from Dartmouth College in 1829 and from the Andover Theological Seminary in 1832. He was a Presbyterian clergyman. He married (1) 17 Sept. 1832, Sarah Stewart Bailey, daughter of Samuel and Hannah[5] (Chase) Bailey, who was born, 26 Nov. 1804, and died 9 Feb. 1836. He married (2) 7 June 1837, Hannah Jewett.
Child by first wife:
Samuel,[7] d. young.

1041

George Clement[6] Chase (Moody,[5] Capt. Moses,[4] Daniel,[3] Ens. Moses[2]), born in Cornish, N. H., 16 Sept. 1811; died in Downieville, Cal., 20 June 1878. He graduated from Dartmouth College in 1841 and from the Dartmouth Medical School in 1847. Physician in Lyndon, Vt., and Downieville, Cal. He married Maria Field of Lyndon, Vt.
Child:
Abby.[7]

1042

Albert[6] Chase (Moody,[5] Capt. Moses,[4] Daniel,[3] Ens. Moses[2]), born in Cornish, N. H., 25 Apr. 1817; died in San Francisco, Cal., in 1903. He graduated from Dartmouth College, in 1844 and from Dartmouth Medical School in 1847. Physician in Hanover, N. H., and San Francisco, Cal.
Child:
Albert,[7] m. 10 Oct. 1866, Sarah J.[7] Chase. (Family 1239)

1043

Epaphras Bull[6] Chase (Moses,[5] Capt. Moses,[4] Daniel,[3] Ens. Moses[2]), born 27 Oct. 1800; died in Lyndon, Vt., 10 Sept. 1867. He married Louisa Baldwin, daughter of Benjamin Peters and Mehitable (Gardner) Baldwin, born in Bradford, Vt., 1 Sept. 1800. They lived in Lyndon, and both died before 1875.
Children, born in Lyndon:
2310. Henry,[7] b. 10 Oct. 1827; graduate of Yale University, 1850; d. in Calais, Me., 12 Feb. 1904. Five children; lived in Lyndon, Vt.
2311. Charles, living in Lyndon, 1875.
Charlotte, m. Dr. ———— Cahoon; d. in Lyndon before 1875.
Emily, alive in Lyndon. Vt., 1875.
Adaline, alive in Lyndon, Vt., 1875.
Mary, alive in Lyndon, Vt., 1875.
Martha, alive in Lyndon, Vt., 1875.

1044

William Coleman[6] Chase (Moses,[5] Capt. Moses,[4] Daniel,[3] Ens. Moses[2]), born 9 Dec. 1803; died in Central City, Colo., 21 July

1863. He married, 16 Oct. 1828, MARY GILSON who died 1 Sept. 1843. They removed from Bradford, Vt., to the West about 1836. Children, first three born in Bradford:

MARY ANN,[7] b. 31 Aug. 1829; m. 29 Oct. 1848, Jacob B. Hyzer.
WILLIAM MONROE, b. 4 June 1831; d. 30 May 1845.
KIMBALL, b. 29 Oct. 1834; d. 17 Apr. 1836.

2312. GEORGE MILTON, b. 26 May 1837; lived in Cimarron, N. M.
2313. MASON G., b. 17 Apr. 1840; m. 18 Dec. 1869, Ellen Eustace; lived in Helena, Mont.
2314. MANLY M., b. 8 Oct. 1842; m. 21 Oct. 1866, Theresa M. Wade; lived in Cimarron, N. M.

1045

GEORGE MONROE[6] CHASE (Moses,[5] Capt. Moses,[4] Daniel,[3] Ens. Moses[2]), born 16 Mar. 1806; died in Honolulu, Sandwich Islands, 5 Mar. 1855. He married 7 July 1836, HARRIET GREEN NORWOOD of Camden, Me. She was born 23 July 1811. He was U. S. Consul in the Sandwich Islands.

Children:

2315. GEORGE MONROE,[7] b. 18 May 1837; lived in Kansas City, Mo.
HARRIET NORWOOD, b. 4 Jan. 1839; m. Judge Charles B. Rounds of Calais, Me.; living in 1892.
WILLIAM LEDYARD, b. 23 May 1841; d. 14 Mar. 1842.
MINA WINSLOW, b. 15 Nov. 1843; m. ——— Hart of Elizabethtown, N. J.
JOSHUA CLEMENT, b. 12 Sept. 1846; d. 17 Sept. 1848.
JULIA DEBORAH, b. 4 Sept. 1853; d. 15 July 1856.
CHARLES HENRY, b. 10 May 1849; d. 14 Sept. 1849.

1046

HON. CHAMPION SPAULDING[6] CHASE (Dea. Clement,[5] Capt. Moses,[4] Daniel,[3] Ens. Moses[2]), born in Cornish, N. H., 20 Mar. 1820; died in Omaha, Neb., 3 Nov. 1898. He married (1) in Racine, Wis., 1 May 1848, MARY SOPHRONIA BUTTERFIELD of Homer, N. Y. She was born there 6 Jan. 1827; died in Omaha, 3 Jan. 1882. He was educated at Kimball Union Academy and was a teacher in the Academy at Amsterdam, N. Y., in 1841-2; vice-principal of West Hartwick Seminary, N. Y., 1843-4; studied law in Buffalo, N. Y., and was admitted to the bar; went to Racine, Wis., in 1847; member of the Board of Education there 1853-7; delegate to the first National Republican Convention in 1856; state senator of Wisconsin, 1856, 1857; District Attorney, 1859; paymaster of the Union Army with the rank of Major, 1862, serving about four years; honorably discharged Jan. 1866; removed to Omaha, Nebr., and in 1867 became the first Attorney General of that state; regent of the State University, 1869-1875; Mayor of Omaha, 1874, 1875-6, 1879 and 1883; received degree LL. D. in 1883; prominent in Knights Templar Commandery, Grand Army and Sons of the American Revolution.

Child, born in Racine, Wis.:

2316. CHAMPION CLEMENT,[7] b. 25 Feb. 1860; lived in Omaha, Nebr.

1047

GEORGE MURRAY[6] CHASE (Dea. Clement,[5] Capt. Moses,[4] Daniel,[3] Ens. Moses[2]), born in Cornish, N. H., 26 Mar. 1833; died in Eureka, Minn., 3 Mar. 1886. He married (1) 15 Oct. 1854, EMELINE LOUISA CHAPMAN, daughter of Benjamin and Theoda (Colburn) Chapman, born in Cornish, 10 Oct. 1819; died there 7 June 1859. He married (2) 22 Nov. 1860, CYNTHIA A. BUTMAN. They lived in Cornish till Mar. 1865, when they removed to Minn. He served in the Civil War.

Children by first wife, born in Cornish:

2317. HORACE BUSHNELL,[7] b. 25 Oct. 1856; lived in Farmington, Minn.
2318. MURRAY CHAPMAN, b. 25 May 1859; lived in Chicago, Ill.

Children by second wife:

INFANT, b. and d. in Cornish, about 1862.
2319. GEORGE TRUMAN, b. in Minn., 18 Aug. 1869.

1048

MOSES[6] CHASE (Thomas,[5] Lt. Wells,[4] Moses,[3] Ens. Moses[2]), born in Chester, N. H., 23 Mar. 1759; married HANNAH SPAULDING, daughter of Andrew and Abigail (Martin) Spaulding, born 26 Mar. 1760; died in Waitsfield, Vt., 15 Oct. 1807. They lived in Cornish, N. H., till 1793 then in Waitsfield. He married (2) Eunice ———— who died 23 Apr. 1852, aged 92. He died in Waitsfield, 8 Aug. 1831. He was a Revolutionary War soldier, enlisting in 1777. He applied for a pension from Waitsfield, 1 Apr. 1818, and on 29 June 1820, deposed that he was 61 and his wife 58.

Children, first four born in Cornish, others in Waitsfield:

2320. HENRY,[7] b. 27 Apr. 1785.
HANNAH, b. 4 Dec. 1786.
2321. MOSES, b. 11 Jan. 1789; m. 17 Feb. 1820, Temperance Skinner; removed to Antwerp, N. Y., later to Ohio, 1831, and to Illinois.
JUDAH, b. 30 Dec. 1791.
LENAS or ZENAS, b. 14 May 1794.
ANDREW, b. 7 Jan. 1798; d. unm. 29 Nov. 1834.
EMMA, b. 5 May 1800; d. 28 May 1813.
ELIZABETH, b. 7 Oct. 1802; m. 22 Sept. 1822, Sewell W. Thayer.
BENJAMIN, b. 14 Dec. 1804; d. 7 July 1813.

1049

WILLIAM[6] CHASE (Thomas,[5] Lt. Wells,[4] Moses,[3] Ens. Moses[2]), born 19 Oct. 1762; died in Warren, Vt., 1853, aged 91. He married (1) MARTHA TUCKER; married (2) OLIVE MATTHEWS; married (3) CONTENT WOOD who died on the same day as her husband. They removed to Waitsfield, Vt., in 1802 and about 1829 to Granville, N. Y., and in 1832 to Westfield, N. Y. They returned to Waitsfield about 1844 and died in Warren, Vt., in 1853. They had children but no record has been found of them. He was a Revolutionary War soldier.

1050

THOMAS[6] CHASE (Thomas,[5] Lt. Wells,[4] Moses,[3] Ens. Moses[2]), born in Cornish, N. H., 3 Sept. 1774; died there unm. The *History of Cornish* (2:75) and the *History of Waitsfield*, Vt., both state that Thomas Chase went to Waitsfield about 1807 and died there in 1828. The inscription on his tombstone in Waitsfield states that he "died 31 July 1828, in the 60th year of his age." If this inscription is correct, he was born, not in 1774, but in 1768.

Thomas[6] Chase, son of Seth[5] and Catherine (Spofford) Chase, was born 4 Apr. 1768. He married Betsey Hill about 1794 and lived in Stowe, Vt., until 1807, when he removed to Waitsfield. (Family 1075)

1051

WELLS[6] CHASE (Thomas,[5] Lt. Wells,[4] Moses,[3] Ens. Moses[2]), born in Cornish, N. H., 2 Feb. 1778; married RACHEL WORTHEN. The History of Salisbury, N. H., p. 523, states that he resided in Cornish, N. H., and was thrice married. No further information is given in the History of Cornish. "Wells Chase of Salisbury and Miss Rachel Worthen were married in Candia, N. H., 2 Feb. 1803."

1052

WILLIAM[6] CHASE (Dr. William,[5] Lt. Wells,[4] Moses,[3] Ens. Moses[2]), born in Falmouth, Me., 6 Oct. 1764; died at sea, 5 June 1819. He married DEBORAH ———— who survived him. No children have been found. They lived in North Yarmouth, Me.

1053

DEA. ASA[6] CHASE (Dr. William,[5] Lt. Wells,[4] Moses,[3] Ens. Moses[2]), born in North Yarmouth, Me., 22 Dec. 1765; died in Portland, Me., 18 Oct. 1842. He married (1) 1 Jan. 1795, HANNAH MITCHELL, daughter of Seth and Althea (Blanchard) Mitchell, born in North Yarmouth, 7 Oct. 1768; died in Portland, 14 Dec. 1818, aged 50. He married (2) about 1819, SARAH CHASE, daughter of Humphrey and Lydia (Loring) Chase, who died 30 Aug. 1860, aged 77. (Family 91). They lived in North Yarmouth, were members of the Church in Cumberland in 1794 and removed to Portland in 1813. They were members of the Second Parish Church of Portland. He was a representative to the General Court in 1810. The silhouettes of Dea. Chase and his first wife were reproduced in *The Chase Chronicle* for July, 1916 (Vol. 7:27).

Children by first wife, born in North Yarmouth:

> POLLY,[7] b. 26 Nov. 1795; d. 22 Nov. 1813.
> WILLIAM, b. 21 Jan. 1796; d. 22 May 1832.
> SON, b. 8 July; d. 9 July 1800.
> RUFUS ANDERSON, b. 14 Nov. 1802; d. 1 Apr. 1829.
> BARRETT POTTER, b. 12 Jan. 1806; d. 31 Aug. 1810.
> ALTHEA,[7] b. 8 July 1808; d. 6 Feb. 1894; m. 18 June 1834, Dea. Edward Gould, b. in Gorham, Me., 27 Jan. 1805. Seven children, including *William Edward*[8] *Gould*, b. 19 June 1837; d. 15 Apr. 1919; m. 29 Apr. 1859, Emma Maynard Dow, who d.

in Brookline, 22 Feb. 1918. She was a daughter of Gen. Neal Dow, "the father of prohibition" in Maine. Mr. Gould was greatly interested in the history of the Chase family and founded and was for many years editor of *The Chase Chronicle,* published by the Chase-Chace Family Association. He also prepared three typewritten volumes of Chase genealogy, containing numerous kodak prints of portraits, houses, gravestones and autographs relating to the family. These books are now in the library of the New England Historic Genealogical Scoiety in Boston, and have been of great service in compiling this book. Their children were Alice Maynard,[9] Neal Dow,[9] Herbert Chase,[9] Conrad Weiser,[9] and Margaret McLellan[9] Gould.

Their son *John Mead*[8] *Gould,* b. in Portland, 15 Dec. 1839; m. 13 Nov. 1866, Amelia Jenkins Twitchell, dau. of Alphin and Roxanna Atilda Twitchell of Bethel, Me. He served in the Civil War as private, sergt.-major, lieut. and major, and was in many battles. Children: Annie Allender[9] Gould, graduated at Mount Holyoke; missionary in China, 1893; murdered by the "Boxers," 1 July 1900; Oliver Cromwell[9] Gould; m. Grace Brown Chapman; Theodore[9] Gould, graduated at Bowdoin in 1898; m. Susan Frances Hill.

2325. SAMUEL WORCESTER,[7] b. 12 July 1811; d. 20 May 1869; m. Louisa P. Jordan.

Children by second wife, born in Portland:

CHARLES HENRY,[7] b. 27 June 1820; drowned at sea, 1842.
HANNAH MITCHELL, b. 26 Nov. 1821; d. 17 May 1847, unm.
ASA GRENVILLE, b. — May 1823; d. 22 Aug. 1823.
ELIZABETH MARTIN, b. 15 Feb. 1825; d. the same day.

1054

TIMOTHY[6] CHASE (Dr. William,[5] Lt. Wells,[4] · Moses,[3] Ens. Moses[2]), born 27 Sept. 1783; died 15 Feb. 1860. He married (1) 1805 LUCY PORTER, daughter of Nehemiah and Joanna (Barber) Porter, born in North Yarmouth, Me., 21 Sept. 1787; died 15 Feb. 1838. They lived in Paris, Me. He married (2) LUCY PAINE, widow of Otis Paine.

Children:

2326. SEWALL COLE,[7] deacon of High St. Congl. Church, Portland; d. 1874; m. Mary A. Trowbridge.
MARY ANN, m. Marshall Stearns of Paris, Me.; she d. Mar. 1870.
SUSAN M., m. Dea. Lewis Sturtevant of Portland, Me.
HANNAH, m. Alfred Staples of Portland, Me.
2327. EDWARD PAYSON, b. 18 July 1818; d. in Portland, Me., 15 Dec. 1905; m. in Paris, Me., 20 Apr. 1843, Julia Ann Dudley, b. in Woodstock, Me., 20 Mar. 1822. Their son *Albro Elmore,*[8] b. in Paris, Me., 9 Sept. 1844; d. in Portland, 8 Sept. 1921. He graduated from Harvard College 1865, and was principal of the High School in Portland, 1877-1907. He m. in Cambridge, 30 June 1870, Agnes Eliza Nichols, b. in Chelsea, 9 July 1849. Their son Edward Nichols,[9] b. in Portland, 11 Oct. 1874; graduated from Harvard University, 1896, and from Harvard Law School, 1899; m. 1 June 1904, in Pontiac, Mich., Lillian May Hillman, b. in Avon, Mich., 8 May 1872.

Their children born in Concord are: *Margaret Dudley*,[10] b. 3 Nov. 1906, and *Edward Payson*, b. 4 Mar. 1908.

2328. WILLIAM, b. 1 Nov. 1820; lived in Portland and Paris Hill, Me.; d. 12 Mar. 1876; m. Ellen Eaton. Nine children.

2329. GRANVILLE M., b. 2 Dec. 1828; lived in Portland, Me.; d. Dec. 1873; m. Elizabeth Morse.

HANNAH P., m. (1) Daniel Hutchins; m. (2) —— Blake of Chelsea.

1055

CAPT. BAILEY[6] CHASE (Rev. Moses,[5] Lt. Wells,[4] Moses,[3] Ens. Moses[2]), born in Amesbury, 20 Sept. 1766; died in Newburyport, 2 Dec. 1829. He married in Amesbury, 28 Jan. 1790, HANNAH FOLLANSBEE who died in Newburyport, 25 July 1855, aged 87. They were living in Salisbury, N. H., in 1790; removed to Salisbury, Mass., in 1793 and later to Newburyport.

Children, first five born in Salisbury, N. H.:

2330. MOSES BAILEY,[7] b. 13 Jan. 1791; m. 3 Apr. 1824, Sarah Curtis Jaques of Accomack Co., Va. Rector of several Episcopal churches in Va. and N. H.

THOMAS FOLLANSBEE, b. 15 Sept. 1792; d. about 1827.

MARY, b. 23 Apr. 1795; d. 23 Oct. 1796.

2331. BAILEY, b. 27 Mar. 1797; m. 13 Jan. 1823, Mary Stevens Granger. She d. in Newburyport, Oct. 1865.

ROBERT, b. 27 Oct. 1799; d. 27 Dec. 1801.

2332. ROBERT FOLLANSBEE, b. 26 Mar. 1802; m. (1) May 1833, Clarissa G. Leach; m. (2) 16 Oct. 1841, Helen M. Freeman; both lost at sea in the brig *Attention* in Oct. 1842.

MARY JANE, b. 10 Mar. 1804; d. 1 Mar. 1855.

HANNAH ELIZABETH. b. 12 Mar. 1806.

1056

JAMES[6] CHASE (Rev. Moses,[5] Lt. Wells,[4] Moses,[3] Ens. Moses[2]), born in Amesbury, 10 Dec. 1774; married (1) in Salisbury, 14 June 1795, MARY TUCKER, daughter of Ebenezer and Mary (Adams) Tucker, born in Salisbury, 9 Oct. 1775; married (2) in Amesbury, 15 Sept. 1805, POLLY COLBY who died in Amesbury, 14 Feb. 1810, aged 32 y. He married (3) in Amesbury 23 Oct. 1811, OLIVE LUCAS of Charlestown. She was probably Olive Caldwell, the widow of Rufus Lucas of Charlestown. They lived in Amesbury. He was a mariner and died in the West Indies.

Children by second wife, born in Amesbury:

STEPHEN,[7] b. 25 Aug. 1806; d. 1807.

ANNA COLBY, b. 1 Nov. 1808.

JAMES, b. 17 Jan. 1810; d. 16 or 18 Oct. 1824.

Children by third wife, born in Amesbury:

SOPHIA, bp. 9 May 1813.

MARY, b. 6 Nov. 1813.

OLIVE, b. 11 July 1815.

2332a. WILLIAM, b. 23 Mar. 1817.

PHINEAS, b. 5 Apr. 1820; d. 1822.

1057

LT. MOSES JAMES⁶ CHASE (Rev. Moses,⁵ Lt. Wells,⁴ Moses,³ Ens. Moses²), born in Amesbury, 19 Apr. 1782; married in Newburyport, 5 Jan. 1804, ANNA TITCOMB, probably daughter of Enoch and Anna (Jones) Titcomb, born in Newburyport, 26 Oct. 1782, and died there, 4 Oct. 1835, aged 53. He died at Sacketts Harbor, N. Y., about 1816. He changed his name from Moses to Moses James Chase, 29 Feb. 1812. He was a Lieut. in the War of 1812.

Child, born in Newburyport:

2333. MOSES,⁷ b. 4 Jan. 1805.

1058

SETH⁶ CHASE (Wells,⁵ Lt. Wells,⁴ Moses,³ Ens. Moses²), born in Salisbury, N. H., 16 Nov. 1774; died about 1811. He married SARAH HOYT. They lived in Salisbury until 1804 and then removed to Bridgewater, N. H.

Children, first three born in Salisbury, others in Bridgewater:

2334. WILLIS T.,⁷ b. 10 July 1800; m. Mary Palmer; lived in Hopkinton. Three children.
       PHEBE A., b. 8 Mar. 1802; m. Silas Green. Two sons; lived in Utica, N. Y.
2335. MOSES MORSE, b. 11 Sept. 1803; m. (1) Sarah Plummer Adams. Five children. He m. (2) Mrs. —— Winchell; lived in Haverhill.
2336. LORENZO H., b. 17 Mar. 1805; m. Judith Palmer; three children; lived in Haverhill, N. H.
       HANNAH H., b. 5 Dec. 1807; m. Northrop Bouton.

1059

JAMES⁶ CHASE (Wells,⁵ Lt. Wells,⁴ Moses,³ Ens. Moses²), born in Salisbury, 25 Dec. 1786; died in Hillsborough, N. H., 22 Mar. 1884, aged 97 y. 2 m. 28 d. He married in Antrim, N. H., 15 Oct. 1811, LUCINDA ANDREWS, daughter of Issacher and Edith (Goodell) Andrews. She was born in Goffstown, N. H., 19 Apr. 1794. They lived at Hillsborough Bridge, N. H.

Children, born in Hillsborough:

SOPHRONIA,⁷ b. 2 Mar. 1818; m. there 19 Nov. 1840, Isaac Miles Tuttle; d. in Antrim, 1 Apr. 1897. Three children.
SAMANTHA, m. 6 June 1845, Cyrus Hale Sargent of Hillsborough. She d. 11 Apr. 1866. Two children.
ELIZA, perhaps a dau., m. in Hillsborough, 21 July 1844, William B. Walker.

1060

AMBROSE⁶ CHASE (Daniel,⁵ Lt. Wells,⁴ Moses,³ Ens. Moses²), born in Amesbury, 24 July 1766; married in Hopkinton, N. H., 7 May 1788, HANNAH HOYT, daughter of Abner and Hannah (Eastman) Hoyt of Hopkinton, Weare and Chester, N. H. They lived in Hopkinton, till 1797 and then in Canaan. She married (2) —— Howard. He died in Canaan, about 1803.

Children, first four born in Hopkinton, last in Canaan:

2337.   WILLIAM,[7] b. 29 Oct. 1789; m. (1) 7 Jan. 1810, Abigail Richardson; m. (2) Harriet Carey; d. in Pottsdam, N. Y., 5 Dec. 1861.

2338.   JOHN, b. 18 Apr. 1792; m. Sally Hoyt; lived in Craftsbury, Vt.; nine children.

AMBROSE, b. 23 Apr. 1794; m. Phebe Derby; no issue. He d. in California.

2339.   MOSES, b. 14 Mar. 1796; m. Esther Whitcomb; clergyman in Plattsburg, N. Y.; living in Beekmantown, N. Y., 1874.

HANNAH, b. 13 Mar. 1801; m. (1) 1 May 1822, Asa Stark; m. (2) 15 May 1844, James Stickney, b. 10 Jan. 1794. He d. 15 Jan. 1857; lived in Brasher Falls, N. Y., in 1874.

1061

THOMAS[6] CHASE (Daniel,[5] Lt. Wells,[4] Moses,[3] Ens. Moses[2]), born in Amesbury, 8 July 1771; removed to North Yarmouth, Me.

1062

JACOB[6] CHASE (Daniel,[5] Lt. Wells,[4] Moses,[3] Ens. Moses[2]), born in Amesbury, 2 Nov. 1773; married about 1797, LYDIA BACON, daughter of Samuel and Lucy (Lufkin) Bacon, born in North Yarmouth, Me., 19 Dec. 1780; died there 3 Apr. 1838. He died 9 Jan. 1853. They lived in North Yarmouth.

Children, born in North Yarmouth:

MARY D.,[7] b. 1 Dec. 1798.

LUCY BACON, b. 12 Sept. 1800; m. Dr. Amos Osgood; d. 22 Oct. 1861; seven children.

2340.   SAMUEL B., b. Nov. 1803; m. Abigail Dodge; d. 3 Feb. 1857. She d. 20 Feb. 1872; eight children.

ELIZA B., b. 14 Apr. 1809; m. Capt. Samuel Baker; d. 13 Mar. 1837; one son.

LYDIA, b. 27 Jan. 1811; m. 23 Jan. 1835, Edward Gray of Buxton, North Yarmouth and Eastport, Me. Five children.

2341.   JACOB, b. 13 Oct. 1812; d. 21 Feb. 1839.

2342.   RUFUS A., m. Hepzibah Titcomb.

FRANCES BARRY, b. 24 Oct. 1818; m. Capt. Paul Greely Blanchard; d. 27 Apr. 1845.

HENRY B., b. and d. same day. (Bacon Genealogy, 134)

1063

ENOCH[6] CHASE (Daniel,[5] Lt. Wells,[4] Moses,[3] Ens. Moses[2]), born in Amesbury (now Merrimac), 10 Nov. 1775; died in Hopkinton, N. H., 3 Aug. 1851. He married in Mar. 1797, MARY MORSE, perhaps daughter of Caleb and Mary (Woodman) Morse, born in Newbury, 28 Feb. 1772. She died in Hopkinton, 9 Apr. 1860. They lived in Hopkinton, where he was a selectman, 1820-1823.

Children, born in Hopkinton:

CHARLOTTE,[7] b. 30 Dec. 1797; m. Joseph Johnson; she d. 22 Mar. 1867.

2343.   ENOCH JR., b. 25 June 1801; m. (1) 30 Oct. 1823, Sarah Holmes; m. (2) Nancy (Chase) Johnson; he d. 17 Oct. 1879; lived in Hopkinton and Wilmot. (Family 969)

2344. DANIEL D., b. 6 June 1803; m. 1 Sept. 1825, Eliza Sargent; d. 4 Nov. 1831.

2345. THOMAS, b. 12 May 1805; d. in Hopkinton, 14 Aug. 1894, aged 89 y. 3 m. 2 d. He m. 8 Mar. 1831, Mary Lunt Pearson, dau. of Samuel and Hannah (Clough) Pearson, b. in Warner, N. H., 17 Nov. 1810. Six children, including *Salome Pearson*,[8] who m. William Ellis Mudgett, b. in Northfield, Vt., 16 Sept. 1854. Their children born in Contoocook, N. H., were: Nellie May[9] Mudgett, b. 22 Oct. 1877; m. Michael Joseph Ratigan of Saugus, seven children; Lillian Julia[9] Mudgett, m. Arthur M. Lord of Tilton, N. H., and William Chase[9] Mudgett, M.D., b. 8 May 1882; m. 8 June 1910, Edith Cecilia Heizmann, dau. of Albert Aloysius and Sarah Jane (May) Heizmann, b. 22 Nov. 1887. Their children are *Lucille Heizmann*,[10] b. 24 Apr. 1911 and *William Chase*[10] *Mudgett Jr.*, b. 6 July 1917. They live in Southern Pines, N. C.

HANNAH, b. 15 Aug. 1806; m. Joseph Eastman; fifteen children.

ABNER, b. 24 Apr. 1808; d. unm. about 1867 or 1868.

2346. AMBROSE, b. 26 Feb. 1810; m. Joanna L. Gould; lived in Contoocookville, N. H.

2347. JACOB, b. 6 Oct. 1811; m. (1) Eliza (Sargent) Chase; lived in Warner, N. H.; m. (2) Eliza Seavey

2348. ELBRIDGE G., b. 16 July 1813; m. Rhoda Rogers; lived in Andover, N. H.

SALLY J., b. 2 June 1816; m. 27 Aug. 1834, George S. Daniels; lived in Hopkinton, N. H.

1064

ISAAC[6] CHASE (Daniel,[5] Lt. Wells,[4] Moses,[3] Ens. Moses[2]), born in Amesbury, about 1778. No record of his family has been found.

1065

BENJAMIN PIKE[6] CHASE (Wells,[5] Moses,[4] Moses,[3] Ens. Moses[2]), born in Newbury (now West Newbury), 28 June 1762; died in Auburn, N. H., 16 Mar. 1852. He married (1) 6 July 1785, MOLLY HALL, daughter of Caleb and Mary (Bradley) Hall, born in June 1766; died in Chester (now Auburn), 18 Dec. 1790. He married (2) 7 Oct. 1792, ANNA BLASDELL, daughter of Isaac and Mary (Currier) Blasdell, born 13 July 1769; died in Chester (now Auburn), 22 Feb. 1808. He married (3) 27 Dec. 1808, MARY[5] CHASE (Moody,[4] Joseph,[3] Ens. Moses[2]), daughter of Moody and Anne (Webster) Chase, born 24 Feb. 1771; died in Chester (now Auburn), 15 Feb. 1823. They lived in Chester (now Auburn).

Children by first wife, born in Chester (now Auburn):

2349. MOSES,[7] b. 7 Feb. 1786; m. 1 Jan. 1806, Betsey Brown; lived in Chester till 1817, then removed to Baltimore, Md.; d. 18 July 1872.

2350. WELLS, b. 5 Aug. 1788; m. 5 Apr. 1814, Amelia Jameson; lived in Baltimore, Md.; d. 24 July 1869.

Children by second wife, born in Chester (now Auburn):

2351. JOHN, b. 29 Sept. 1793; m. 7 Nov. 1820, Eliza Dawes; lived in Fairfax, Va., where he d. 1 July 1877.

STEPHEN, b. 29 Oct. 1795; d. 4 May 1796.

SARAH, b. 5 Mar. 1797; d. unm. 23 Dec. 1882.

2352. BENJAMIN, b. 7 July 1799; m. 2 Mar. 1826, Hannah Hall, dau. of Moses Kimball and Lucretia (Currier) Hall, b. in Chester, 18 Feb. 1787; d. in Auburn, N. H., 25 Feb. 1876. They lived in Chester (now Auburn) and he d. there 5 May 1889.

His early life was spent on his father's farm, his educational privileges being limited to a few weeks each year in the district school, but before attending any school he had mastered with little aid the common school arithmetic as far as the "Rule of Three," using a piece of chalk and a board in the lack of a slate. His love for mathematics led him to master the higher branches of the science, geometry, trigonometry, surveying, navigation and astronomy, his interest in the lastnamed leading to his calculating the eclipses due for several years to come, his only instruments being "a two foot Gunter's scale and a pair of dividers." Naturally he became the local land surveyor and later prepared a map of the township of "Old Chester," which was of great value in establishing ancient boundaries.

The descendant on his mother's side of two generations of clock-makers, he was a mechanic by inheritance and the building and repairing of sawmills and gristmills in the section of the state in which he lived became his life work.

At the solicitation of Judge Samuel Dana Bell and the Hon. Henry F. French he undertook the compilation and publication of the *History of Old Chester*, a seven hundred page volume, published in 1869, which has been adjudged as being one of the best of the town histories in the state.

The "Chase Fortune" myth, in which he took no stock, led him to take up genealogical research and the result of his extensive labors, now in the possession of the New England Historic Genealogical Society of Boston, has aided greatly in the preparation of this work.

In addition to his mathematical and mechanical tastes his character was well developed in morals. Early in life he adopted the principle of total abstinence from the use of intoxicants and ever afterward drank nothing but water. When the emancipation of the slaves was first advocated he became an ardent supporter of the reform and also of women's rights, and was often a contributor to the *Liberator* and the *Herald of Freedom*.

Notwithstanding a laborious life, the even balance of mental and physical effort conserved his strength and kept his mind clear until near the end, at two months less than ninety years, (For more extended biographies of this branch of the family see the History of Chester, 1926.)

Their children were *Caroline*,[8] b. 14 Sept. 1828; m. Charles Chase (Family 1192); *Louise*,[8] b. 16 Dec. 1829; m. Frank D. Emery, 12 Dec. 1867; d. 18 Mar. 1892, childless; *Benjamin*,[8] b. 18 Aug. 1832; d. 27 Sept. 1912; m. Harriet Davenport Fuller of Dunbarton, N. H., 17 June 1875, who d. 7 Jan. 1912. He was reared on his father's farm, attending the district school and later a select school in Lee, N. H., conducted by a progressive educator, Moses A. Cartland, a cousin of John Greenleaf Whittier, the poet.

He was encouraged in the use of mechanical tools, in which he became exceedingly efficient and was for many years

Your truly Benj Chew

master mechanic in the construction and rebuilding of textile mills.

In 1867 he settled in Derry, N. H., and began the manufacture of certain specialties of wood. The business was incorporated as The Benjamin Chase Co. in 1907, he being the president of the company until his death. He was very ingenious and invented and constructed the intricate machines used in the plant, some of them being in use nowhere else.

He neither sought nor held public office, was a man of quiet ways and always found on the right side of every uplift movement in the community, had the courage of his convictions and hated shams.

Their only child, Harriett Louise,[9] b. 22 Jan. 1881, m. 22 Jan. 1907, Charles Edward Newell, M. D., of Derry, who died there 6 Apr. 1924. Children, first two born in Derry, others in Manchester, N. H.: *Henry Chase,*[10] *Benjamin Chase,*[10] *Edward Chase,*[10] *Louise Thankfull,*[10] *Dorothy Frances,*[10] *Prescott Chase*[10] and *Ruth Lee*[10] *Newell.*

MOLLY, b. 11 Aug. 1801; m. 27 Dec. 1821, John Underhill; d. in Auburn, 5 Feb. 1881. Six children.

2353.   PIKE, b. 8 July 1804; d. 10 Oct. 1898, age 94 y. 3 m. 2 d.; m. 5 May 1833, Hannah S. Lufkin, who d. 26 Feb. 1891; three daughters d. without issue.

DAUGHTER, b. and d. 6 Mar. 1806.

Children by third wife, born in Chester (now Auburn):

ANNA, b. 7 Nov. 1809; m. 8 Feb. 1831, Amherst Coult; she d. 1 July 1852; nine children. (See Coult Family in History of Chester.)

2354.   STEPHEN, b. 30 Aug. 1813; d. in Hanover, N. H., 7 Jan. 1851. He graduated from Dartmouth College in 1832 and was professor of mathematics there from 1838 to 1851. He m. 21 Aug. 1838, Sarah Thompson Goodwin, dau. of Maj. Ichabod and Nancy (Thompson) Goodwin, b. in South Berwick, Me., 8 Dec. 1809. Their son *Frederick,*[8] b. 2 Sept. 1840; d. 19 Jan. 1890; graduated from Dartmouth College in 1860; treasurer of the college, 1875-90; judge of probate for Grafton County, 1876-90; author of *A History of Dartmouth College and the Town of Hanover,* 1890. He m. Mary Fuller Pomeroy who d. 9 Apr. 1925. Seven children including Frederick,[9] b. 9 Apr. 1883; graduate of Dartmouth, 1905; Harvard Law School, 1909; m. Ruth Everett Gallagher. Children: *Hugh Clifford,*[10] b. 27 Nov. 1913; *Robert Hill,*[10] b. 17 Sept. 1916; *Edith Warren,*[10] b. 22 June 1918; *Mary Pomeroy,*[10] Chase, b. 15 Feb. 1922. He is a lawyer in Boston.

Philip Hartley,[9] b. 18 May 1886; graduate of Dartmouth College, 1907; Mass. Institute of Technology, 1909; Harvard Graduate School, 1910; m. 25 Oct. 1913, Theora Hill Williamson, b. 25 July 1885. He is an electrical engineer in Bala, Pa.

1066

JOHN[6] CHASE (Enoch,[5] Moses,[4] Moses,[3] Ens. Moses[2]), born in Leominster, 1 May 1785; died in Andover, 24 Feb. 1843; married in Andover, 28 May 1809, ANNA COCHRAN. They lived in West Andover.

Children, born in Andover:

2355. SETH,[7] b. 28 July 1809; m. (1) Charlotte Saunders; m. (2)
Mary ———.

ELIZA ANN, b. 8 Aug. 1811; m. 4 Sept. 1834, Paul Bailey Follansbee.

SARAH SAWYER, b. 2 Oct. 1813; m. 10 Sept. 1864, Jason E.
Pebbles.

2356. ANDREW JACKSON, b. 9 May 1815; m. Sarah E. W. Ingalls.

2357. JOHN EDWARDS, b. 9 Dec. 1817; m. 29 Nov. 1843, Susan B.
Saunders. Six children.

EUNICE ADAMS, b. 15 May 1820; m. 24 Oct. 1855, William
Smart.

ENOCH BARTLETT, b. 4 Oct. 1822; d. 21 Feb. 1823.

ABIGAIL MEARS, b. 2 May 1824; m. Walter Kendall.

FANNY EVELINA, b. 14 Sept. 1826; m. (2) Hosea Dudley.

CAROLINE AUGUSTA, b. 15 Feb. 1829.

2358. SAMUEL MILTON, b. 30 Apr. 1831; m. 28 May 1862, Abby
Frances Howe; lived in Lowell; d. 17 Dec. 1894.

2359. FRANKLIN NEWTON, b. 3 Sept. 1833; m. (1) 18 June 1862,
Sarah J. Woodruff; m. (2) 14 May 1867, Ellen E. Smith.

1067

JOSHUA[6] CHASE (Enoch,[5] Moses,[4] Moses,[3] Ens. Moses[2]), born
in Billerica, 6 Dec. 1787; living in Boston, 17 July 1832 (Essex Probate, 5115); trader 1831-1833; housewright 1834-1837, lived on Cambridge St. near the Bridge in Boston. He died in Boston, 31 Dec.
1837, aged 50, and was buried in Andover.

1068

THOMAS GRAY[6] CHASE (Joshua,[5] Moses,[4] Moses,[3] Ens. Moses[2]),
born in Boston about 1780. He received a part of the Moses[4] Chase
homestead in West Newbury from his uncle John[5] Chase in 1802.
He died in Sandown, N. H., Nov. 1843. He married (intention
at Newbury, 3 Nov. 1807) PATTY NOYES, daughter of Enoch and
Sarah L. (Emery) Noyes, born in West Newbury. They lived in
West Newbury and Sandown.

Children:

2360. JOHN KIRBY,[7] lived in Lowell.

DAUGHTER.

1069

MOSES[6] CHASE (Lt. Moses,[5] Moses,[4] Moses,[3] Ens. Moses[2]), born
in Newbury (now West Newbury), 17 Oct. 1779; died in Leominster, 4 July 1850. He married (1) about 1800, BETSEY PILLSBURY,
daughter of Daniel and Judith (Bailey) Pillsbury, born and baptized
in Newbury, 15 Sept. 1782; died in Leominster, 21 Sept. 1821. He
married (2) in Leominster, 21 Mar. 1821, LOIS MAY, daughter of
Jacob and Esther (Bowers) May, born in Leominster, 6 Oct. 1797.
They lived in Leominster on his uncle Stephen[5] Chase's farm.

Children by first wife:

SOPHELIA,[7] d. young.

2361. MOSES M., b. 19 Oct. 1808; m. (1) Jane Sawyer; m. (2) June

1844, Sarah F. Holt of Nashua, N. H.; lived in Leominster and Indian Orchard.

SOPHELIA P., b. 10 Oct. 1812; m. 14 Apr. 1836, Emerson Prescott of West Boylston.

Children by second wife, born in Leominster:

2362.   JOHN BROOKS, b. 25 Sept. 1823; teacher, Buxton, Me.
2363.   HENRY LAWRENCE, b. 7 Sept. 1825; m. 25 Nov. 1847, Orissa M. May; teacher in High School, Lynn, 1870.
    MARY JANE, b. 27 May 1827; m. 26 Nov. 1849, Francis Joy.
2364.   ALBERT NEWTON, b. 14 Sept. 1830.
    BETSEY PILLSBURY, b. 30 May 1834; m. Joseph Morse of Lunenburg.
    TWIN SONS, b. and d. 26 Dec. 1836.

1070

NATHAN[6] CHASE (Bradford,[5] Dea. Seth,[4] Moses,[3] Ens. Moses[2]), born in Sutton, 18 Apr. 1764; married in Northbridge, 11 Dec. 1788, MEHITABLE GOLDTHWAITE of Northbridge. They lived in Sutton.

Children, born in Sutton:

    HULDAH,[7] b. 11 Aug. 1790; m. 14 Jan. 1822, Warren Bancroft. She d. in Underhill, Vt., 26 June 1845.
    LOIS, b. 23 Dec. 1792; d. unm. 25 July 1815.
    ABIGAIL, b. 25 Sept. 1794; m. 30 Sept. 1812, Samuel Perry; d. 22 Aug. 1839.
2365.   CHARLES, b. 23 Oct. 1796; m. 17 Sept. 1818, Polly Paine Johnson. He d. in Uxbridge, 28 Sept. 1844. She d. 31 May 1834.
    RUTH, b. 29 Apr. 1801; m. Arad Aldridge. She d. in Princeton.
    LUKE, b. 30 Sept. 1802; d. 23 Apr. 1818.
2366.   ELIAS, b. 13 May 1805; m. 9 Apr. 1829, Adeline Aldrich (1807-1855); living in Northbridge in 1873; d. 1882.

1071

PETER[6] CHASE (Bradford,[5] Dea. Seth,[4] Moses,[3] Ens. Moses[2]), born in Sutton, 17 Dec. 1776; died in Paris, Me., 29 Feb. 1860. He married, 4 Apr. 1802, REBECCA DOBLE who died in Paris, 16 Feb. 1859. She was born 16 Aug. 1779. They lived in Paris, purchasing land there in 1799.

Children, born in Paris:

2367.   SIBLEY,[7] b. 25 Dec. 1803; m. 4 Apr. 1830, Charlotte Heath. Clergyman; d. 10 June 1859.
    ARVILLA, b. 22 Mar. 1805; m. 5 Apr. 1831, Jacob Heath.
2368.   HIRAM, b. 28 Feb. 1806; m. 19 Aug. 1844, E. Ann Thompson; living in North Paris, Me., 1870.
    REBECCA, b. 7 May 1807; m. (1) 9 Oct. 1842, Rev. Addison Abbott; m. (2) 23 Mar. 1856, William H. Drake.
    ELIAS, b. 30 Nov. 1808; d. 22 Apr. 1812.
2369.   LEONARD, b. 11 Mar. 1810; m. 9 Apr. 1835, Abigail G. Hapgood.
    ELIAS 2d, b. 28 Mar. 1812; d. 4 Mar. 1816.
2370.   SOLOMON, b. 20 Sept. 1813; m. (1) 26 Mar. 1837, Nancy H. Stevens; m. (2) 28 Oct. 1845, Harriet Barrett.
    WILLIAM, b. 29 Mar. 1815; d. 24 Feb. 1837.
    ABIGAIL, b. 25 Mar. 1817; m. June 1854, Samuel Holt.
2371.   SETH BRADFORD, b. 30 Nov. 1818; m. 31 Jan. 1847, Mary E. Holmes of Monmouth, Me.; living in Chilmark in 1870.

ELIZA, b. 14 Dec. 1821; m. 1 Feb. 1848, Jonathan Abbott of
    Bethel, Me.
CYNTHIA, b. 10 June 1826; d. 25 Jan. or June 1827 or 1847.

1072

SAMUEL[6] CHASE (Bradford,[5] Dea. Seth,[4] Moses,[3] Ens. Moses[2]),
born in Sutton, 28 Oct. 1778; married in Sutton, 28 Nov. 1799,
MERCY WILMARTH who was born in Attleborough, 28 Feb. 1783.
They removed from Sutton to Westminster, Vt., about 1814.
    Children, last two born in Westminster:
        LYDIA,[7] b. 22 Sept. 1800; m. 27 Jan. 1820, Hiram Rumney of
            Westminster.
        BENONI W., b. 7 Apr. 1803; d. 28 Dec. 1805.
2372.   BENONI W., b. 7 Apr. 1807; m. 29 Oct. 1838, Hannah M. Hoyt
            of Lyndon, Vt.; lived in Salt Lake City, Utah, 1873.
        ASENATH S., b. 19 Aug. 1810; m. 4 Dec. 1829, Russell Hallett
            of Westminster.
        SABRINA S., b. 16 Aug. 1812; d. 24 Sept. 1813.
2373.   LEWIS, b. 20 June 1818; m. 12 Mar. 1839, Deborah Wallace of
            Lyndon, Vt.
        MARIA M., b. 25 Feb. 1822; m. 29 July 1849, James R. Car-
            penter; d. 21 Aug. 1855, in St. Johnsbury, Vt.

1073

LUKE[6] CHASE (Bradford,[5] Dea. Seth,[4] Moses,[3] Ens. Moses[2]),
born in Sutton, 15 May 1782; died in Paris, Me., 25 Sept. 1839 He
married (intention at Sutton, 4 Nov. 1808) 1 Dec. 1808, DORCAS
STEARNS of Lexington, daughter of Phinehas and Mary (Welling-
ton) Stearns, born in Lexington, 8 Aug. 1780; died in Paris, Me.,
6 Aug. 1859. They lived in Benton, Me., till 1816, in Barre 1817 to
1826 and later in Paris.
    Children, first three born in Benton, last two in Barre:
2374.   BRADFORD,[7] b. 14 Sept. 1809; m. 12 Mar. 1835, Mary Kimball;
            lived in Grafton.
2375.   AUSTIN, b. 3 May 1813; m. 21 Sept. 1837, Lucy Batcheller;
            lived in Paris, Me.
2376.   NATHAN, b. 5 Feb. 1815; m. 14 Feb. 1844, Mary Ann H.
            Thayer; lived in Paris, Me.
2377.   ELIAS, b. 19 Apr. 1818; m. (1) 6 May 1840, Laura Clifford;
            m. (2) 18 Oct. 1864, Eunice F. Rawson; lived in Portland,
            Me., 1874.
2378.   LUKE, b. 25 Jan. 1821; m. 27 Nov. 1851, Sarah Smith of Ren-
            frewshire, Scotland, b. 10 May 1831. They lived in Lunen-
            burg; nine children.

1074

JOSHUA[6] CHASE (Seth,[5] Dea. Seth,[4] Moses,[3] Ens. Moses[2]), born
in Croydon, N. H., 29 Oct. 1767; married HANNAH C. EMERY of
Conway, N. H. They lived in Braintree, Vt.
    Children:
        HANNAH.[7]
2379.   SETH, m. in Conway, 23 June 1819, Elizabeth Shirley. She left
            him and gave their two children to the Shakers.

1075

THOMAS[6] CHASE (Seth,[5] Dea. Seth,[4] Moses,[3] Ens. Moses[2]), born 4 Apr. 1768; died in Waitsfield, Vt., 31 July 1828, aged 60. He married BETSEY HILL who died in Waitsfield, 23 Apr. 1852, aged 89. They lived in Stowe, Vt., till 1807 and then removed to Waitsfield where they resided.

Children, born in Stowe:

RACHEL,[7] b. 4 Oct. 1795; m. 10 Mar. 1818, Silas Wheeler of Fayston, Vt.

ELEANOR, b. 14 Dec. 1797; m. 19 Dec. 1824, Jeremiah Thayer of Warren, Vt.

2380. JOSIAH, b. 15 Dec. 1799; m. 12 Aug. 1824, Polly[7] Chase, b. 18 Nov. 1803; d. 25 Jan. 1890. He d. in Waitsfield, 15 Mar. 1879. (Family 1078)

2381. SETH, b. 16 Aug. 1801; m. 1 Jan. 1826, Electa Ellis.

BETSEY, b. 20 Sept. 1803; m. 12 Dec. 1822, Riley Mansfield of Fayston.

1076

SETH[6] CHASE (Seth,[5] Seth,[4] Moses,[3] Ens. Moses[2]), born 27 Aug. 1774; died in Stowe, Vt., Oct. 1830. He married in Braintree, Vt., 5 Dec. 1802, SALLY KENNEY. She was born in Petersham 28 Nov. 1787. She was living in Stowe, with her youngest daughter in her 87th year, 8 Mar. 1875. They lived in Conway, N. H., Bartlett, N. H., and Stowe.

Children, the youngest born in Bartlett, N. H.:

SARAH,[7] b. 7 Feb. 1804; d. 1 Aug. 1804.

SARAH, b. 15 Aug. 1806; m. 1821, Paul Chesley of Stanstead, Quebec; they moved West.

2382. SAMUEL, b. 1808; lived in Underhill, Vt., in 1875.

2383. JONATHAN R., b. 11 Mar. 1811; m. Dolly Chase, dau. of Timothy and Ruth Chase; he was living in Frankfort, Ohio, in 1875. (Family 1078)

MARY K., b. 7 Jan. 1815; m. 22 Nov. 1840, Josiah L. Brown; living in Stowe, Vt., 1875.

1077

CALEB[6] CHASE (Seth,[5] Seth,[4] Moses,[3] Ens. Moses[2]), born 10 Mar. 1779; married 28 Nov. 1805, LUCY BYAM who was born 25 May 1783 and died 28 Nov. 1866. He died in Braintree, Vt., 2 Sept. 1862. They lived in Braintree.

Children:

LUCY,[7] b. 19 Aug. 1806; m. Abel Byam.

OLIVE, b. 11 Aug. 1808; m. (1) Joel Richardson; m. (2) Reuben Wakefield.

ESTHER B., b. 7 Dec. 1810; m. (1) Edmund Kinney; m. (2) Samuel Mann.

BETSEY, b. 7 Jan. 1812; m. 28 Feb. 1839, William L. Harwood.

JAMES M., b. 7 Feb. 1815; d. 7 July 1842.

2384. BENJAMIN B., b. 26 June 1816; m. 14 Mar. 1839, Lydia L. Abbott. Three sons including *Irving Samuel*,[8] b. in Braintree, Vt., 3 Jan. 1843; d. 7 May 1923; m. Martha Hayden Daggett, b. in Randolph, 28 Feb. 1840; d. 28 Apr. 1924. Their

son John Alden,[9] b. 25 June 1877; m. 27 Sept. 1913, Edith
Celestia Cobb. Their children: (1) *John Alden Jr.,*[10] b. 5
Dec. 1914; (2) *Ralph Alden,*[10] b. 3 Mar. 1924. They live at
17 Churchill Terrace, Newtonville.
HARRIET M., b. 10 Apr. 1824; d. 22 Nov. 1827.

1078

TIMOTHY[6] CHASE (Seth,[5] Seth,[4] Moses,[3] Ens. Moses[2]), born in
Randolph, Vt., 29 Jan. 1784; married about 1802, RUTH EMERY,
daughter of Anthony and Naomi (McIntire) Emery. She was born
in 1785 and died 1868. He was living in Waitsfield, Vt., 11 Feb.
1872.
     Children, born in Vermont:
          POLLY,[7] b. 18 Nov. 1803; m. 12 Aug. 1824, Josiah[7] Chase (Fam-
          ily 1075). He d. 15 Mar. 1879; she d. 25 Jan. 1890, in
          Waitsfield.
          NANCY, b. 3 May 1808; m. Luther Corey of Braintree, Vt.;
          eight children.
          LYDIA, b. 28 Jan. 1810; m. Jason Grandy of Waitsfield.
          DOLLY, b. 27 Mar. 1812; m. Jonathan R.[7] Chase (Seth[6]); lived
          in Braintree. (Family 1076)

1079

ASA[6] CHASE (Josiah,[5] Dea. Seth,[4] Moses,[3] Ens. Moses[2]), born in
Sutton, 21 Jan. 1785; married MARY STORRS of Decatur, Otsego Co.,
N. Y.
     Children:
 2385.   JOSIAH,[7] m. Betsey Wiltsey.
 2386.   ORRIN, m. Clarissa Kelsey.
          RHODA, m. ——— Humphrey.
          EMELINE, m. ——— Humphrey.
          MIRANDA, m. ——— Landers.
          MARY, m. Solomon Hillsinger.
          LAURA.

1080

DEA. JOSIAH[6] CHASE (Josiah,[5] Dea. Seth,[4] Moses,[3] Ens. Moses[2]),
born in Sutton, 30 Jan. 1777; died in Otsego, N. Y., 30 May 1859.
He married 17 Feb. 1814, SARAH BARLOW born in Nova Scotia,
6 Apr. 1787; died 8 Nov. 1874. They lived in Otsego, Otsego Co.,
N. Y.
     Children:
          TEMPERANCE,[7] b. 20 Nov. 1814; never married; living in Otsego
          in 1876.
 2387.   GEORGE BARLOW, b. 28 Apr. 1816; m. Jane Hutchinson; he was
          living in Scranton, Pa., in 1876. Their son *Herbert Britton,*[8]
          b. in Scranton, 1 Apr. 1863; m. 24 June 1896, Jennie Louise
          Wakelee of Bridgeport, Conn. They live at 215 Young Ave.,
          Pelham, N. Y. Their children are: Edward Hutchinson,[9] b.
          24 June 1897; m. 26 June 1923, Maude Allen Banks, and
          Grace Jannette,[9] b. 6 Mar. 1899.
 2388.   LUCIUS, b. 25 July 1818; m. Minerva Potter; living in Otsego
          in 1876.

2389.   WHITEFIELD, b. 6 Nov. 1820; living in Camelloupe, B. C., in 1876.

ELVIRA FLUVIA, b. 5 June 1823; never married; living in Louisville, Ky., 1876.

MARY LOUISA, b. 26 Jan. 1826; m. 11 Oct. 1853, James Redfield Smith of Pleasant Valley, Ill.

HARRIET ADELINE, b. 25 Dec. 1828; m. 16 Dec. 1857, Fordyce H. Waterbury of Louisville, Ky.

1081

JOHN[6] CHASE (Josiah,[5] Dea. Seth,[4] Moses,[3] Ens. Moses[2]), born in Sutton, 3 June 1779; died 24 May 1867. He married in Worcester, N. Y., 10 Oct. 1802, ROXANA THOMPSON, daughter of Samuel and Rhoda Thompson. She was born in Swanzey, N. H., 6 Dec. 1782 and died 15 Jan. 1858. They lived in Maryland, and Worcester, Otsego Co., N. Y.

Children, born in Maryland, Otsego Co., N. Y.

2390.   GEORGE WASHINGTON, b. 17 Dec. 1803; m. (1) 22 Feb. 1827, Maria Vanderburgh (b. 12 June 1806; d. 9 June 1833); m. (2) 3 Apr. 1834, Caroline Skeels; living in Quincy, Mich., 1872. Ten children.

2391.   ADONIRAM, b. 7 Dec. 1805; m. (1) about 1831, Delia M. Lacy; m. (2) about 1834, Cornelia White; m. (3) ——— ———; living in Hollisterville, Pa., in 1872. Five children.

2392.   ANSEL, b. 17 Oct. 1807; m. about 1834, Almira Bennett; living in Ridgeway, N. Y., 1872. Seven children.

2393.   BRADFORD, b. 29 Dec. 1809; m. 3 July 1836, Emeline Tappan; living in Baldwinsville, N. Y., 1872. Three children.

2394.   JOHN MANLEY, b. 25 Apr. 1812; m. 12 Sept. 1845, Elvira L. Ludden; living in Ann Arbor, Mich, 1872. Eight children.

ROSETTA, b. 23 May 1814; m. 15 June 1851, Woodbridge L. Barber; living in Yates, N. Y., 1872. No children.

2395.   SAMUEL THOMPSON, b. 19 Feb. 1817; m. — Apr. 1840, Hannah Etta Sperry; living in Schenevus, N. Y., 1872. Five children.

2396.   JOSIAH GODDARD, b. 23 May 1819; m. (1) 9 Oct. 1842, Margaret Bigelow Robertson; m. (2) 18 Mar. 1861, Fanny A. Randall; m. (3) 18 Mar. 1866, Mary E. Randall; living in Quincy, Mich., 1872.

1082

JUDGE SETH[6] CHASE (Josiah,[5] Dea. Seth,[4] Moses,[3] Ens. Moses[2]), born in Sutton, 1 Apr. 1781; died 6 Sept. 1856. He married (1) in 1803, CLARISSA WATERMAN who was born 19 Oct. 1781 and died 1828. He married (2) about 1832, widow ANNA DAVENPORT who died 1857, aged 71. They lived in Worcester, N. Y.

Children by first wife, born probably in Worcester:

RACHEL,[7] b. 6 Mar. 1805; d. 1819, aged 14.

ELVIRA, b. 6 Sept. 1807; d. 1821.

LEVANTIA, b. 13 Oct. 1809; m. Aug. 1830, L. B. Raymond; d. without issue, Aug. 1838.

2397.   WILLIAM HENRY, b. 14 Oct. 1813; colonel in Mexican War.

2398.   LESLIE, b. 31 Mar. 1816; captain; d. Apr. 1849.

1083

BENJAMIN[6] CHASE (Josiah,[5] Dea. Seth,[4] Moses,[3] Ens. Moses[2]), born in Sutton, 30 May 1783 or 1784; moved with his father's family to Worcester, Otsego Co., N. Y., in 1791. He married MEHITABLE RUSSELL, and they had a number of sons and daughters. He died in Delhi, N. Y., about 1824. They had seven children, but the Benjamin who died in Delhi leaving seven children may or may not be identical with the Benjamin who married Mehitable Russell.

Children:

2399. CYRUS,[7] lived in Ill. or Ind.
2400. HENRY, also lived in the same state as Cyrus.

1084

REUBEN[6] CHASE (Josiah,[5] Dea. Seth,[4] Moses,[3] Ens. Moses[2]), born in Princeton, 19 Jan. 1788; married LAURA WATERMAN. Probably they lived in New York state.

1085

AARON[6] CHASE (Ephraim,[5] Humphrey,[4] Moses,[3] Ens. Moses[2]), born in Haverhill, 13 Mar. 1804; married in Dunbarton, N. H., 26 Oct. 1836, PHEBE GILE of Dunbarton who died in Haverhill, 21 Apr. 1848, aged 39. He died there, 8 July 1883, aged 79. They lived in East Haverhill.

Child, born in Haverhill:

2401. MOSES RYLAND,[7] b. 28 Jan. 1838; graduate of Dartmouth College, 1860; m. Love Swain Ellis.

1086

DEA. EPHRAIM[6] CHASE (Ephraim,[5] Humphrey,[4] Moses,[3] Ens. Moses[2]), born in Haverhill, 7 July 1809; died there, 18 May 1874. He married 29 Oct. 1845, SARAH A. GILE, daughter of David and Mary W. Gile of Plaistow, N. H., born 1 Apr. 1813; died 1 July 1906. They lived in East Haverhill.

Children, born in Haverhill:

CHILD,[7] b. and d. young.
2402. DAVID, b. 16 Aug. 1849; m. Cordelia Carr of Derry, N. H.

1087

MOSES[6] CHASE (Moses,[5] Humphrey,[4] Moses,[3] Ens. Moses[2]), born in Plaistow, N. H., 16 Oct. 1789; died in Dexter, Me. He married about 1818, MARY SMITH who died in July 1877. They removed from Haverhill to Dexter, about 1824.

Children:

RUFUS K.,[7] b. 25 May 1819; d. June 1826.
2403. GEORGE G., b. 22 May 1823; m. 30 July 1846, Charlotte A. Fletcher.
2404. SEBA FRENCH, b. 25 May 1829; m. Maria Davenport.
MARY JANE, b. 28 Sept. 1831; m. Albion K. P. Smart.
SARAH CROSBY, b. 1 Apr. 1835; m. Enoch Smart.

1088

JOSEPH[6] CHASE (Moses,[5] Humphrey,[4] Moses,[3] Ens. Moses[2]),
born in Plaistow, N. H., 26 Nov. 1795; died at sea about 1825. He
married in Plaistow, 12 Feb. 1817, RUTH KELLEY who was born in
Plaistow, N. H., 16 May 1797 and died 5 Mar. 1870. She married
(2) James Bartlett of Plaistow, N. H., and had two children by this
union.

Children, born in Plaistow, N. H.:

CLARISSA A.,[7] b. 1818; m. (1) 1836, Thompson Whitehouse;
m. (2) 1848, Zimri Boyden.

2405. JAMES NOYES, b. 31 Dec. 1819; m. (1) 4 Jan. 1847, Julia Ann
Parsons; m. (2) Apphia Webster; Baptist clergyman; d. in
Plaistow, N. H., 1 Sept. 1862.

2406. JOHN KELLEY, b. 22 Apr. 1822; m. 9 Aug. 1842, Mary Stevens
Morse, dau. of Samuel; clergyman, teacher.

2407. SAMUEL CHADWICK, b. 1824; m. (1) 10 Sept. 1848, Nancy
Burrell.

1089

DANIEL[6] CHASE (Daniel,[5] Humphrey,[4] Moses,[3] Ens. Moses[2]),
born 14 Nov. 1797; married about 1819, EDNA EATON who was born
17 Dec. 1801; died in Bradford, 22 Jan. 1844. They lived in Bradford.

Children, born in Bradford:

2408. PRESTON MARSHALL,[7] b. 12 May 1827; Harvard Medical School,
1857; m. 1858, Laurinda Bailey; physician in Danvers.

2409. EDWARD EVERETT, b. 6 Sept. 1829; m. widow Mary Tyler. No
children; lived in Bradford.

1090

ISAAC[6] CHASE (Daniel,[5] Humphrey,[4] Moses,[3] Ens. Moses[2]),
born in Haverhill, 31 Aug. 1809; died in Salem, N. H., 21 Sept. 1869,
aged 60 y. 1 m. 2 d. He married in Londonderry, N. H., 20 Mar.
1843, ELIZABETH PETTINGILL who was born in Londonderry, 20 June
1815. She died in Londonderry, 19 Apr. 1894, aged 78. They lived
in Londonderry.

Children, born in Londonderry:

EPHRAIM,[7] b. 13 Apr. 1844; d. 4 Aug. 1846.

CLARA A., b. 1 May 1845; m. 5 June 1866, James McQuesten of
Litchfield, N. H.

2410. EPHRAIM HUMPHREY, b. 21 Jan. 1848; m. 3 Nov. 1871, Agatha
A. Richardson of Salem, N. H.; lived in Lawrence.

1091

GIDEON[6] CHASE (Isaac,[5] Eleazer,[4] Moses,[3] Ens. Moses[2]), born
in Standish, Me., 16 May 1784; died there 25 Aug. 1856. He married about 1807, SALOME LOMBARD who was born in 1792 and died
25 July 1870. They lived in Hiram, Me., and perhaps elsewhere.

Children, born in Maine:

2411. LEONARD,[7] b. 20 July 1809; m. 20 Sept. 1842, Susan Thompson.

MARTHA, b. 1810; m. Cyrus Davis.

2412. ELEAZER, b. 12 Oct. 1812; m. Mary A. Dearborn.

2413. ISAAC, b. 1814; m. Clara Bennett.
GILBERT, b. 20 Nov. 1817; d. unm.
MARY F., b. 12 Dec. 1818; m. Daniel J. Libbey.
ELIZA J., b. 12 Feb. 1820; m. Warren Harmon.
EUNICE L., b. 12 Dec. 1823; m. (1) Stephen B. March.
MELISSA, b. 19 Sept. 1825; d. unm.
JULIA A., b. — July 1827; m. Joseph F. Adams.

2414. ZENAS S., b. — July 1830; m. (1) Susan J. Storer; m. (2) Rose D. (Newcomb) Rich.

2415. JOHN LOMBARD, b. 18 Mar. 1833; m. (1) Sarah A. Spear; m. (2) ———; m. (3) Susan Jane (Garey) Chase. He d. in Melrose, 30 Nov. 1915, aged 83.

2416. MELVILLE BEVERAGE, b. 19 Oct. 1835; m. 1860, Susan Jane Garey.

1092

ELEAZER[6] CHASE (Isaac,[5] Eleazer,[4] Moses,[3] Ens. Moses[2]), born in Standish, Me., 27 May 1786; married 26 May 1812, SARAH DAVIS who was born in Buxton, Me., 17 Jan. 1790. They lived in Buxton. Their intention was recorded at Standish, 25 Apr. 1813.

Children, born in Buxton:

EUXINE,[7] b. 31 Oct. 1813; m. 24 Dec. 1834, Reuben Harmon; seven children.

2417. SIDNEY B., b. 10 Sept. 1815; m. Betsey V. Quimby of Westbrook, Me.
LOIS SMITH, b. 22 June 1817; m. (1) Stephen M. Libbey; m. (2) Capt. Aaron Bradbury of Limerick, Me.
SARAH PAINE, b. 2 June 1820; m. 1 Aug. 1843, Charles Small of Limington, Me.
ABIGAIL, b. 28 Oct. 1822; d. unm. about 1848.

2418. ALBION K. P., b. 25 Sept. 1824; m. Dorcas A. Plummer; d. in Gorham, Me., June 1868.
MARY HARPER, b. 25 Oct. 1826; m. John Wesley Owen of Buxton.
RENSALAER, b. 30 Mar. 1829; d. 1831.
THADDEUS S., b. 5 Oct. 1831; never married; lawyer.

1093

ISAAC[6] CHASE (Isaac,[5] Eleazer,[4] Moses,[3] Ens. Moses[2]), born in Standish, Me., 20 or 26 Mar. 1791; died in Turner, Me., 17 May 1864. He married (1) in 1822, EUNICE[6] CHASE, daughter of Rev. Nathaniel[5] and Rhoda (Elliott) Chase of Buckfield, Me., born in 1796; died 29 Apr. 1837. (Family 388). He married (2) HANNAH BRIGHAM. They lived in Turner, Me.

Children, born in Turner:

2419. SOLON,[7] b. 14 Jan. 1822; m. Ann J. Phillips; five children; he d. 23 Nov. 1909. He was twice a candidate for Congress from Maine on the currency question, 1876-84. He was a unique, typical New Englander, a Maine farmer and trainer of "them steers." He was called the founder of the Greenback party and editor of *Chase's Chronicle.* He lived at Chase's Mills.

2420. OTHO, b. 16 Aug. 1825; m. (1) Deborah T. Cushing by whom there was no issue; m. (2) Elizabeth Blake Johnson; eleven children; he d. 3 Jan. 1907.

MARIA, b. 1828; m. 1850, Homer Record; d. 30 July 1864 without issue.

MARY, b. 1830; m. 1849, Dr. Henry D. Irish; d. 20 Mar. 1887.

CHARLES CARROLL, b. 1833; d. 1837.

EUXINE, b. 1835; d. 1858.

ANN JUDSON, b. 1837; m. 1860, Ichabod Allen; d. 1864; one child.

1094

DAVID[6] CHASE (Isaac,[5] Eleazer,[4] Moses,[3] Ens. Moses[2]), born in Standish, Me., 15 Apr. 1793; died there 26 Mar. 1866. He married, 14 Mar. 1821, HANNAH MOORE PHINNEY who was born in Gorham, Me., 15 Feb. 1805. He was a house carpenter and lived in Standish.

Children, born in Standish:

ALMA F.,[7] b. 10 Oct. 1822; m. 14 Nov. 1846, Joseph Holmes of Cornish, Me.

MARGARET S., b. 8 June 1824; d. in infancy.

JAMES HANSON, b. 6 Aug. 1826; d. at age of 3 y.

ZENAS ADAMS, b. 8 Sept. 1828; d. in Calif. in 1849.

MARGARET A., d. in infancy.

2421.   CHARLES O. L., b. 30 May 1833; m. (1) 18 May 1859, Eunice Walker; m. (2) 1867, Harriet Sterling; lived in Standish.

HANNAH MARIA, b. 9 June 1836; m. 9 Oct. 1859, Frank Allen of Limerick, Me.; lived in Arlington.

2422.   WILBER, b. 14 June 1838; m. 2 Feb. 1860, Ellen Thorn of Standish.

H. AUGUSTA, b. 14 Aug. 1840; m. 5 Sept. 1867, Oliver H. Dow.

MARGARETTA P., b. 6 Sept. 1842; m. 5 Sept. 1867, Henry A. Higgins of Standish; lived in Washington, D. C.

ISAAC COLEMAN, b. 14 Feb. 1845; d. in New Orleans, La., May 1864.

2423.   JAMES LEWIS, b. 4 Jan. 1848; lived in North Berwick, Me.

INEZ S., b 5 Jan. 1852; m. —— Phinney; lived in Standish.

1095

DANIEL BOND[6] CHASE (Rev. Nathaniel,[5] Eleazer,[4] Moses,[3] Ens. Moses[2]), born in Buckfield, Me., 18 May 1785; died there 8 July 1855. He married (1) 1805, ABIGAIL RECORD who died in Buckfield, 30 Mar. 1844. He married (2) in 1846, DIADAMIA THOMPSON. He was twice elected a representative to the State Legislature. They lived in Buckfield.

Children, born in Buckfield:

2424.   DANIEL,[7] b. 13 Apr. 1807; m. 11 Oct. 1837, Betsey Allen; lived in Buckfield.

DAVID R., b. 26 Dec. 1808; d. unm. in Boston, July 1852.

JACOB ELLISON, b. 8 May 1811; d. unm. in New York, Feb. 1853.

2425.   CHARLES G., b. 5 Sept. 1813; m. Margaret Lamb of New York. He d. Dec. 1853, aged 40.

2426.   STEPHEN DECATUR, b. 1 Aug. 1817; m. 1843, Olive Briggs; lived in Hebron, Me.

2427.   CYRUS G., b. 1 Sept. 1819; m. 1861, Lucy Record; lived in Buckfield.

RHODA A., b. 12 Mar. 1822; d. July 1824.

1096

Col. Nathaniel[6] Chase (Rev. Nathaniel,[5] Eleazer,[4] Moses,[3] Ens. Moses[2]), born in Buckfield, Me., 29 June 1800; died in Readfield, Me., 4 Sept. 1878. He married (1) Mar. 1826, Eunice Wescott, who died 31 Aug. 1842. He married (2) 1843, Mrs. Hannah (Bicknell) Hanaford, who d. in 1850; married (3) 23 Dec. 1850, Abby Gould, who died 27 June 1853, and married (4) 1854, Sabina Gould. They lived in Readfield and Turner, Me.

Children by first wife:

  Amanda,[7] b. 1828; d. 1830.

2428. Lewis, b. 1830; m. 6 Sept. 1854, Elvira G. Dyer of Sidney, Me. Prominent in the nursery business and founder of The Chase Nursery Co., in Rochester, N. Y., where he lived for many years.

2429. Ethan Allen, b. 1832; m. 3 Nov. 1860, Augusta Field; lived in Rochester, N. Y., and later in Riverside, Calif., where he had large interests in orange growing and was prominent in civic affairs.

2430. Martin Van Buren, b. 1835; m. 28 Nov. 1860, Helen A. Waite of Sidney, Me.

1097

Job[6] Chase (Rev. Nathaniel,[5] Eleazer,[4] Moses,[3] Ens. Moses[2]), born in Buckfield, Me., 29 June 1806; married in 1831, Rebecca D. Latham, daughter of Barzillai and Mary (Washburn) Latham, born in Buckfield, 23 Jan. 1805. They lived in Turner, Me., Sangerville, Me., and later in Livermore, Me.

Children, first two born in Sangerville, last in Turner:

  Mary Latham,[7] b. 5 Apr. 1832; m. 3 Feb. 1853, Horace M. Bearce.

2431. George Franklin, b. 24 Nov. 1834; m. 14 Feb. 1860, Ann Maria Strickland.

  Julia Constantia, b. 10 Dec. 1840; m. 8 Mar. 1871, Seth D. Washburn of Livermore.

1098

Hon. Thomas[6] Chase (Rev. Nathaniel,[5] Eleazer,[4] Moses,[3] Ens. Moses[2]), born in Buckfield, Me., 6 June 1808; died there 13 Mar. 1866. He married 14 Jan. 1832, Esther M. Daggett, daughter of Don Delance and Susan (Root) Daggett. She died 13 July 1887. He was representative and in 1865 State Senator. They lived on the Chase homestead in Buckfield.

Children, born in Buckfield:

  Melona R.,[7] b. 17 July 1835; m. 26 Apr. 1854, Dr. Charles D. Bradbury of Woodstock, Me. Four children.

2432. Roscoe G., b. 3 Nov. 1837; m. Nov. 1865, Ellen E. Gerrish.

  Abbie F., b. 23 Oct. 1839; m. 13 Dec. 1865, M. Dana Holbrook of Malden and Braintree; four children.

  Charles, b. 18 July 1841; killed in Battle of Cold Harbor, Va., 3 June 1864, unm.

2433. George H., b. 5 May 1844; m. 24 Sept. 1865, Miranda Morton of Paris, Me.; lived in Malden; was street commissioner; d. there Oct. 1915.

2434. HOWARD AQUILA, b. 15 Oct. 1846; m. 23 Nov. 1871, Mary Elizabeth Gibbs, b. in May 1844; d. in Feb. 1911. He d. in Aug. 1925; lived in Geneva, N. Y., and Philadelphia. Their children are *Howard Gibbs,*[8] *Mary E.,*[8] who m. Harry C. Lockwood, *Charles Thomas,*[8] b. 27 Sept. 1876; lives in Philadelphia and has sons Charles Thomas[9] and Walter Thomas.[9] *Alice E.,*[8] who m. Wendell Phillips Raine and *Anne Arnold.*[8]

LUCY ANN, b. 20 May 1849; d. 22 Nov. 1860.

2435. WILLIAM D., b. 26 Aug. 1852; m. 15 Aug. 1877, Lizzie C. Withington; lived in Auburn, Me., and Lawrence.

2436. HOMER N., b. 30 Sept. 1855; m. Emma F. Emerson, living in Auburn, Me., in 1928.

1099

WILLIAM[6] CHASE (Rev. Nathaniel,[5] Eleazer,[4] Moses,[3] Ens. Moses[2]), born in Buckfield, Me., 25 June 1811; died after 1900. He married in 1835, VESTA FERNALD who died in Buckfield, 14 Feb. 1899. He was County Commissioner. They lived in Buckfield.

Children, born in Buckfield:

PERSIS M.,[7] b. 26 Apr. 1837; m. 28 Dec. 1857, Thomas W. Bowman. She d. 17 Sept. 1869.

WILLIAM W., b. 15 Dec. 1840; d. 15 Feb. 1841.

MARY FRANCES, b. 29 Apr. 1842; m. 4 Mar. 1866, Nathan D. Harlow; she d. 15 Aug. 1868.

ALICE A., b. 16 Mar. 1851; d. 1868.

Another son d. in infancy.

1100

ISAAC[6] CHASE (Rev. Nathaniel,[5] Eleazer,[4] Moses,[3] Ens. Moses[2]), born in Buckfield, Me., 6 Apr. 1815; died in Peru, Me., 2 May 1879. He married (1) 28 Mar. 1837, PHILENA F. SWEET (SWETT?) who died 21 Jan. 1848. He married (2) 11 Apr. 1852, ANGELIA SHACKLEY. They lived in Peru, Me.

Children by first wife:

2437. DE WITT CLINTON,[7] b. 3 Dec. 1837; m. (1) 23 May 1859, Flora Newman of Carthage, Me.; m. (2) 15 May 1864, Clara A. Newman.

LEROY R., b. 20 July 1839; d. 16 Oct. 1844.

2438. LESLIE R., b. 29 Sept. 1843.

2439. LEROY R., 2d, b. 17 Oct. 1845.

2440. ISAAC, b. 29 Nov. 1847.

Children by second wife:

2441. HENRY A., b. 26 Nov. 1853.

CLARENCE M., b. 23 Nov. 1856; d. 1865.

PHILENA F., b. 18 May 1863; d. 1872.

2442. CHARLES CLARENCE, b. 14 May 1875.

1101

JOSEPH[6] CHASE (Joseph,[5] Eleazer,[4] Moses,[3] Ens. Moses[2]), born in Buckfield, Me., 30 Mar. 1797; married about 1815, ALMIRA SHAW. They lived in Buckfield.

Children, born in Buckfield:

ELMIRA JANE,[7] b. 23 Mar. 1816; m. Rasseleus Cole.

MIRIAM, b. 5 Nov. 1818; m. Lucian Philbrick.   Ten children.
SARAH ANN, b. 5 Feb. 1825; d. 1 Apr. 1848.
2443.   LEWIS M., b. 23 June 1830; m. (1) Eunice Cole; m. (2) Eva
Bisbee; lived in Buckfield.   Eight children.

1102

ELEAZER[6] CHASE (Joseph,[5] Eleazer,[4] Moses,[3] Ens. Moses[2]),
born in Buckfield, Me., 12 Aug. 1798; died there 10 Feb. 1885.   He
married ANN KNEELAND.   They lived in Buckfield, Me.   No family
is given in the *History of Buckfield*.

1103

THEOPHILUS[6] CHASE (Leonard,[5] Daniel,[4] Moses,[3] Ens. Moses[2]),
born in Haverhill, 20 Aug. 1773; married in Amesbury, 19 Nov. 1795,
ANNA FARRINGTON, daughter of Samuel and Electa Farrington, born
in Amesbury, 14 Oct. 1775.   They lived in Amesbury.
Children, not in order, born in Amesbury:

MIRIAM F.,[7] b. 1804; m. 5 Oct. 1826, Samuel C. Hovey of Boxford and Groveland, who was b. 16 July 1805, and d. 29 Dec.
1890.   She d. 6 Apr. 1888.   Their youngest son, *Benjamin
L. Hovey*, b. 16 Jan. 1851; m. 31 July 1873, Mae Sophia
Peaslee of Newton, N. H.   Their only child, Lewis Richard[9]
Hovey, b. 17 May 1874; m. Helen Cleveland Smith, 19 Apr.
1899, in Haverhill He is treasurer and manager of The Rec-
ord Publishing Co. of Haverhill, the publishers of this vol-
ume and many histories and genealogies.   Children: *Martin
Richard[10] Hovey, Miriam Bradford[10] Hovey, Laurance Smith[10]
Hovey* and *Carleton B.[10] Hovey*.
HANNAH, d. young.
SOPHIA.
ADRIAN, d. young.
LAVINA.
LEONARD, d. young.
MARY.
ELECTA F., b. 4 Sept. 1811; m. int. 23 Feb. 1832, Jacob S. Full-
ington; living 26 Jan. 1873.
2444.   ANDREW JACKSON, b. 24 Apr. 1814 or 1815; m. (1) 2 Feb.
1840, Ann M. Dyas; m. (2) 17 Apr. 1856, Dorothy C. Pink-
ham.   By second wife son *Waldo Farrington*,[8] b. 12 Feb.
1862; m. 8 Sept. 1897, Susie W. Voigt.   Children: Helen
Frances,[9] b. 2 Feb. 1900; Farrington Wakefield,[9] b. 4 June
1901; m. 20 Apr. 1927, Mary Agnes Weaver.   Andrew Jackson lived in San Diego, Calif., and Waldo Farrington lives
in Los Angeles, Calif.
HANNAH, m. Eben P. Jewett of Groveland.
ELIZA ANN.

1104

DANIEL[6] CHASE (Leonard,[5] Daniel,[4] Moses,[3] Ens. Moses[2]), born
in Haverhill, 25 June 1777.   No further record has been found relating to him.

1105

JACOB[6] CHASE (Leonard,[5] Daniel,[4] Moses,[3] Ens. Moses[2]), born in Haverhill, about 1787. No further record has been found relating to him.

1106

JOHN[6] CHASE (Leonard,[5] Daniel,[4] Moses,[3] Ens. Moses[2]), born 5 May 1793, in Haverhill, but not recorded on the Vital Records there; died at Italy Hill, Yates Co., N. Y., 14 Feb. 1869. He married in Middlebury, Vt., 18 Jan. 1818, ADELINE ROBINSON of Middlebury. They lived in Italy Hill, and perhaps in Middlebury.

Children:

ELIZA A.,[7] b. 11 Mar. 1827; m. 25 Aug. 1849, H. C. Smith of Italy Hill.
2445. ALLEN B., b. 11 July 1834; m. 11 Jan. 1865, Sarah M. Gennings.
AMANDA A., b. 27 July 1839; m. 16 Nov. 1859, John J. Robson.
SARAH J., b. 5 Oct. 1841; m. 16 Apr. 1862, William Brown.
Several children died young, names not reported.

1107

WILLIAM[6] CHASE (Somerby,[5] Daniel,[4] Moses,[3] Ens. Moses[2]), born in Newburyport, 14 Nov. 1777. He may be the child of Somerby that died in Nov. 1783.

1108

PAUL[6] CHASE (Somerby,[5] Daniel,[4] Moses,[3] Ens. Moses[2]), born in Newburyport, and baptized there, 25 Feb. 1781; died at sea on a voyage to Havana, in Aug. 1799. He probably never married.

1109

TIMOTHY PALMER[6] CHASE (Somerby,[5] Daniel,[4] Moses,[3] Ens. Moses[2]), born in Newburyport, 19 Apr. 1784; married before 1808, LUCINDA ——— who was the mother of his children. They lived in Newburyport.

Children, born in Newburyport:

2446. JOSEPH,[7] b. 5 May 1808.
ELIZA GIDDINGS, b. 21 Aug. 1810.
SALLY CURTIS, b. 10 Feb. 1813.

1110

DANIEL[6] CHASE (Somerby,[5] Daniel,[4] Moses,[3] Ens. Moses[2]), born in Newburyport, 10 Oct. 1793; married there, 25 Apr. 1816, MARIA JANE DESMAZES [DESMARES], daughter of John Baptiste and Lucy (Amory) Desmazes, born in Newburyport, 4 Dec. 1795. No children given in the Newburyport records. His wife died in Newburyport, Oct. 1817.

1111

JOSEPH TITCOMB[6] CHASE (Somerby,[5] Daniel,[4] Moses,[3] Ens. Moses[2]), born in Newburyport, 4 Mar. 1795; married there, 28 Oct. 1821, REBECCA MERRILL, perhaps daughter of Daniel and Susannah

Merrill, born in Newburyport, 20 Apr. 1789. They lived in New-buryport.

Children, born in Newburyport:

    ELIZABETH TITCOMB,[7] b. 8 Apr. 1823.
2447. JOSEPH TITCOMB JR., b. 7 Mar. 1826.
    REBECCA ANN, b. 30 Apr. 1828.

1112

SAMUEL[6] CHASE (Col. Samuel,[5] Dea. Francis,[4] Samuel,[3] Ens. Moses[2]), born in Litchfield, N. H., 17 Nov. 1761; died there 14 May 1816, aged 76 y. 7 m. He married ELIZABETH WHITTIER. He was an officer in the militia. They lived in Litchfield.

Children, born in Litchfield:

2448. SAMUEL,[7] m. Betsey Kendall. Four children.
    LUTHER, d. unm.
    THOMAS, d. unm.
2449. SARGEANT.
    SARAH, m. James Howell of Manchester, N. H.
    SHERBURN, unm.; blown up in a powder mill.
    ELIZA, mar. and lived in Georgetown.

1113

EBENEZER[6] CHASE (Col. Samuel,[5] Dea. Francis,[4] Samuel,[3] Ens. Moses[2]), born in Litchfield, N. H., 22 Feb. 1764; died in Dunbarton, N. H., 22 Sept. 1831, aged 68. He married in June 1786, NANCY PARKER, daughter of Capt. John Parker. She was born 22 Oct. 1762; died in Dunbarton, 13 Feb. 1839, aged 76. They lived in Litchfield, and Dunbarton. He was selectman of Dunbarton, 1799 and 1800.

Children, born in Dunbarton:

    NANCY,[7] b. 28 Dec. 1786; m. 1810, Aaron Ray of Hopkinton, N. H.; d. 31 May 1867.
2450. JOHN,[7] b. 19 Aug. 1788; m. 1815, Nancy Stark; dau. of Archibald and Mary (Anderson) Stark and niece of Gen. John Stark (Hist. of Goffstown); civil engineer at Chicopee; d. 11 May 1866, childless. He removed to Meredith Bridge (now Laconia), N. H., in 1813 and resided in Dover, N. H., 1820 to 1829. In 1830 he removed to Chicopee Fall and in 1833 to Cabotville (now Chicopee), where he became agent of the Springfield Canal Co. He was an able projecting engineer for manufacturing establishments. He was a director of the First National Bank of Chicopee and an incorporator of the Massachusetts Institute of Technology and a vice-president of that institution in 1862-3.
    SAMUEL STEWART, b. 4 Apr. 1790; d. 17 July 1791.
    ESTHER, b. 14 May 1792; m. 16 Sept. 1817, Nicholas Dolbear of Epsom. Six children. Dau. *Sabra Dolbear*, m. Jacob P.[7] Chase of Auburn, N. H. (Family 1200)
    POLLY (twin), b. 14 May 1792; m. 20 Apr. 1837, William Anderson; d. without issue, 5 Aug. 1866.
    SABRA, b. 9 Mar. 1794; m. Michael Murray of Chicopee; d. 27 July 1877.
    HANNAH, b. 9 Jan. 1796; m. 8 Mar. 1838, John Lull of Weare, N. H.

2451. SIMEON, b. 18 Oct. 1798; m. 17 Oct. 1820, Elizabeth Bailey; she d. 10 May 1840. He d. in San Francisco, Calif., 10 June 1851. Three children.

SON, b. 11 Oct. 1800; d. 24 Oct. 1800.

2452. CALVIN, b. 7 Feb. 1802; m. 14 Mar. 1825, Eliza B. Ham, b. in Dover, N. H., 29 Aug. 1805. Their eldest son, *Samuel Stewart*,[8] b. in Dover, 29 Dec. 1825; m. 5 Feb. 1852, Charlotte J. Page of Barre. He was a civil engineer and took charge of the construction of the dam and canals at Chicopee Falls and of dam and canals of the water shop of the United States government at Springfield. The property later became the Holyoke Water Power Co., of which he was treasurer. He also gave much time to the construction of the churches and public school buildings of Holyoke. He became a member and a fellow of the American Society of Civil Engineers in 1868 and 1870. He d. in Holyoke, 29 May 1873, aged 48.

1114

DANIEL[6] CHASE (Col. Samuel,[5] Dea. Francis,[4] Samuel,[3] Ens. Moses[2]), born in Litchfield, N. H., 26 July 1766; died in Nashua, N. H., 4 Nov. 1847. He married in Pelham, N. H., 5 Dec. 1793, HANNAH GAGE, born in Pelham, 7 May 1769; died 10 Sept. 1820. They lived in Litchfield.

Children, born in Litchfield:

2453. NATHANIEL GAGE,[7] b. 12 Jan. 1795; m. Lydia Winchester; lived in Andover; one son.

2454. FREDERICK, b. 8 June 1796; m. (1) in Dunbarton, N. H., 24 Nov. 1825, Sally Stinson, who d. 2 Feb. 1829. He m. (2) in Dunbarton, Nov. 1829, Lucretia Stinson. He lived in Nashua and was a captain and lumber dealer.

2455. JOHN TAYLOR GILMAN, b. 15 May 1800; m. 22 Apr. 1827, Lucretia McQueston; d. 9 May 1850; eight children.

MARY, b. 17 July 1804; m. Reuben Hill; lived in Red Wing, Minn.

ELIZABETH UNDERHILL, b. 28 May 1809; m. July 1843, John Tripp of Lowell.

1115

ROBERT[6] CHASE (Col. Samuel,[5] Dea. Francis,[4] Samuel,[3] Ens. Moses[2]), born in Litchfield, N. H., 3 Dec. 1768; died in Nashua, N. H., 6 Nov. 1838. He married about 1792, SALLY HALL of Bradford, born 1 Mar. 1773; died 31 Dec. 1860. They lived in Dunbarton till 1836 and then in Nashua. He was a selectman of Dunbarton 1806 and 1807.

Children, born in Dunbarton:

HANNAH,[7] b. 27 Sept. 1793; d. 21 Nov. 1795.

2456. WILLIAM G., b. 7 Nov. 1795; m. ———— Nichols; lived in Bucksport, Me.; d. 9 May 1861.

2457. THOMAS, b. 16 Mar. 1798; president of a bank in Nashua.

2458. ROBERT, b. 27 Sept. 1800; m. in Bow, N. H., 10 Sept. 1829, Betsey Carr, who d. in Dunbarton in Sept. 1844; he d. 12 May 1862; no children.

HANNAH, b. 15 Oct. 1802; d. 28 Oct. 1802.

WEALTHY, b. 14 Nov. 1803; d. unm. 31 Oct. 1851.

ELIZA, b. 27 Sept. 1805; m. Aaron Wing; lived in Bangor, Me.; d. 24 Mar. 1867.

HENRY, b. 11 Aug. 1807; d. 27 Dec. 1822.

MARY JANE, b. 14 Dec. 1809; m. Solomon D. Emerson of Lowell; d. 29 Jan. 1844.

SARAH, b. 17 Oct. 1812; m. Reuben E. French of Concord, N. H.; d. 1 May 1868.

2459.   CHARLES, b. 30 Sept. 1814; m. Mar. 1862, Eliza A. Flanders of Bedford, N. H.; no children; lived in Manchester, N. H.

MARGARETTA, b. 12 Aug. 1818; d. 5 Dec. 1818.

MARGARETTA ANN, b. 15 May 1820; d. unm. 12 Sept. 1843.

1116

FRANCIS[6] CHASE (Col. Samuel,[5] Dea. Francis,[4] Samuel,[3] Ens. Moses[2]), born in Litchfield, N. H., 30 Sept. 1775; died there 25 Sept. 1853. He married in Londonderry, N. H., 19 Sept. 1813, DOROTHY BIXBY, who was born 16 Oct. 1777; died 9 Oct 1861. She was daughter of Daniel and Lydia (Parker) Bixby of Litchfield. They lived in Litchfield.

Children, born in Litchfield:

LYDIA,[7] b. 4 July 1814; m. Martin N. Horn of Lowell.

2460.   SAMUEL, b. 29 Aug. 1815; m. about 1850, Susan White; lived in Litchfield.

FRANCIS, d. unm. 1826.

MARGARET A., b. 13 July 1819; m. 29 Dec. 1842, Isaac McQueston of Litchfield; representative 1865-6.

1117

LT. SIMEON[6] CHASE (Col. Samuel,[5] Dea. Francis,[4] Samuel,[3] Ens. Moses[2]), born in Litchfield, N. H., 12 Feb. 1780; married in Londonderry, N. H., 20 Dec. 1807, SARAH BIXBY, daughter of William and Sarah (Thompson) Bixby, born (probably in Litchfield), 6 Nov. 1786; died 1 Apr. 1857. They lived in Litchfield.

Children, born in Litchfield:

MARY ANN,[7] b. 22 Apr. 1809; m. 1 May 1861, James P. Robertson; d. without issue in Concord, N. H., 7 Sept. 1898.

SARAH J., b. 10 July 1810; m. 20 Nov. 1834, Isaac N. Center; two children; d. 6 May 1838.

MARGARET, b. 3 Nov. 1813; m. 30 June 1834, James Thompson; d. 3 Dec. 1867. Ten children; (see Bixby Genealogy, 437).

1118

DR. AMOS[6] CHASE (Lt. Amos,[5] Dea. Francis,[4] Samuel,[3] Ens. Moses[2]), born in Unity, N. H., 23 Mar. 1772; died 4 July 1815. He married in Washington, N. H., 3 Sept. 1798, PATTY SAMPSON, daughter of Abner and Lucy (Farnsworth) Sampson, born in Washington, 5 May 1777; died 23 Oct. 1859. They lived in Unity, Cornish and Washington, N. H.

Children, elder born in Cornish, younger in Washington:

AMOS,[7] b. 22 Oct. 1801; d. unm. 9 Mar. 1843.

2461.   ABNER, b. 18 Sept. 1803; m. (1) 28 Sept. 1828, Betsey Parker of Groveland. She was b. 13 Aug. 1797; d. 19 Jan. 1847. He m. (2) 1 Sept. 1847, Susan Hardy. Children by first wife: (1) *Amos P.,*[8] b. 29 Nov. 1829; m. 10 Apr. 1850, Elizabeth Rowe; (2) *George Henry,*[8] b. 31 May 1831; m. 4 Oct. 1825, Patience T. Adams. Their son Charles Merrill,[9] b. 4 Sept. 1858; m. Agnes Woodburn of West Newbury. Their son *Harry Woodburn*[10] Chase LL. D., b. in Groveland, 11 Apr. 1883; graduated at Dartmouth College in 1904; professor at Clark University, 1909-1919; professor at the University of North Carolina, 1914 to 1919, then president to date; m. 26 Dec. 1910, Lucetta Crum of Logansport, Ind.; one daughter; (3) *Hannah P.,*[8] b. 30 July 1832; m. 4 Sept. 1850, Robert W. Adams; (4) *Mosely D.,*[8] b. 28 Feb. 1838; m. 10 Apr. 1859, Mary Stickney; (5) *Emily A.,*[8] b. 29 Mar. 1840; m. Charles Cobden.

1119

Rev. Jonathan Carleton[6] Chase (Lt. Amos,[5] Dea. Francis,[4] Samuel,[3] Ens. Moses[2]), born in Unity, N. H., 22 Feb. 1774; died 11 Nov. 1836. He married about 1802, Nancy Moody of Unity. She was born 22 Jan. 1782; died in Whitefield, N. H., 25 Dec. 1858, aged 77. He was a Methodist clergyman, but his name is not included in Carter's *Native Ministers of New Hampshire,* 1905. They lived in Unity 1802 to 1817 and perhaps longer.

Children, born in Unity:

Aurelia,[7] b. 11 Aug. 1803; m. Baker Dodge; she d. 26 Apr. 1829.

2462. Orrin M., b. 11 Dec. 1807; m. 4 Jan. 1830, Mary Jane Batchelder; d. 17 Apr. 1877. Five children.

Betsey, b. 25 Mar. 1815; d. 6 Apr. 1832.

Amaret, b. 6 July 1817; m. Orlando Jones. She d. 9 Apr. 1844.

1120

Francis Pike[6] Chase (Lt. Amos,[5] Dea. Francis,[4] Samuel,[3] Ens. Moses[2]), born in Unity, N. H., 12 June 1780; died there 25 Dec. 1824. He married in 1803, Hannah Ladd, daughter of James and Margaret (Glidden) Ladd of Unity who died there, 19 Sept. 1834. They lived in Unity.

Children, born in Unity:

Luthera,[7] b. 18 May 1805; d. unm. after 1872.

Samantha, b. 16 Apr. 1807; d. 18 Nov. 1834.

2463. Nahum P., b. 19 Dec. 1808; m. 1840, Emeline Haggerty of Schuylerville, N. Y.; lived in Decorah, Iowa, 1873; two sons.

2464. Alvah Coburn, b. 25 Feb. 1811; m. 1832, Lavina Warren; lived in Decorah, Iowa; two children; he d. 15 Oct. 1851.

Hannah, b. 31 Mar. 1813; m. 26 Feb. 1836, Edward W. Moore of Springfield, Vt.; d. 5 Aug. 1860.

Margaret, b. 25 June 1816; m. 26 May 1843, Eleazer B. Montgomery.

2465. Amos Carlton, b. 24 Apr. 1819; m. 24 Feb. 1841, Susan C. Howard of Schuylerville, N. Y.; lived in Waterbury, Vt.

James Glidden, b. 19 Mar. 1821; d. unm. 12 Feb. 1863.

Sarah F., b. 24 Aug. 1825; m. 8 Nov. 1848, George H. Leet; living in North Charlestown, N. H., 1872.

1121

SIMEON BARTLETT[6] CHASE (Lt. Amos,[5] Dea. Francis,[4] Samuel,[3] Ens. Moses[2]), born in Unity, N. H., 7 Apr. 1784; died 22 Apr. 1861. He married 15 Oct. 1809, SUSANNAH LADD, daughter of Nathaniel and Sally (Marshall) Ladd, born 22 Aug. 1782; died 29 Sept. 1871. They lived in Unity and in Middlesex, Vt.

Children:

2466.   DANIEL,[7] b. 17 May 1810; m. 1 Dec. 1839, Louisa M. Wilson.
       PHEBE G., b. 5 Mar. 1812; d. unm.
2467.   NATHANIEL LADD, b. 30 Oct. 1813; m. (1) 7 May 1846, Charlotte Atherton; m. (2) 5 July 1859, Mrs. Chastine B. Perkins; Methodist clergyman; d. in Manchester, N. H., May 1875.
       HANNAH L., b. 19 Aug. 1815; m. 3 Apr. 1856, Lyman[7] Chase, as his second wife. (Family 859)
2468.   AMOS, b. 8 Feb. 1818; m. 7 Apr. 1842, Olive N. Preston.
2469.   JOSEPH, b. 1 May 1821; m. 1846, Cynthia G. Lawrence.
       MARY (twin), b. 1 May 1821; d. 21 Apr. 1822.
       SALLY L., b. 22 Feb. 1823; m. 5 Nov. 1856, Joseph Chandler, his second wife.
       SIMEON C., b. 5 Feb. 1829; d. 25 Jan. 1830.

1122

JAMES[6] CHASE (Francis,[5] Dea. Francis,[4] Samuel,[3] Ens. Moses[2]), born in Newton, N. H., 24 Aug. 1777; died there 4 or 13 Oct. 1838. He married in Amesbury, 1 Mar. 1808, HANNAH FARRINGTON, born 14 July 1779; died in Newton, 11 Oct. or 21 Nov. 1847. They lived in Newton.

Children, born in Newton:

       ALMIRA,[7] b. 8 Apr. 1809; m. 6 May 1827, John C. Bartlett.
2470.   WILLIAM GRAVES, b. 28 May 1814; m. 31 Dec. 1841, Mary Ann[7] Chase (Stephen[6]). (Family 1134) Nine children.

1123

RICHARD[6] CHASE (Francis,[5] Dea. Francis,[4] Samuel,[3] Ens. Moses[2]), born in Newton, N. H., 27 Nov. 1780; died about 1855. He married (intention at Amesbury, 26 May 1804), 12 Aug. 1804, MARTHA DAVIS. They lived in Haverhill and Newton.

Children, first three born in Haverhill:

       HANNAH,[7] b. 2 June 1805; m. 10 Jan. 1823, Nathan[6] Chase of Haverhill. (Family 625)
2471.   FRANCIS, b. 26 July 1807; m. 31 Oct. 1849, Mary Judith Eaton.
2472.   EPHRAIM DAVIS, b. 12 Dec. 1809; m. (1) Hannah Peaslee; m. (2) Sarah W. (Swain) Eaton.
2473.   RICHARD HUBBARD, b. 2 Feb. 1812; m. 1853, Matilda Ayer.
       SARAH, b. 18 Feb. 1814; d. unm. 26 June 1836.
       SON, b. 23 Apr. 1816; d. young.
       CALEB PEASLEE, b. 23 Apr. 1817; d. 5 June 1837.
       ABIGAIL MARTHA, b. 5 June 1820; d. unm.

1124

FRANCIS[6] CHASE (Francis,[5] Dea. Francis,[4] Samuel,[3] Ens. Moses[2]), born in Newton, N. H., 15 Oct. 1784; died 8 June 1816.

He married about 1811, Lucy Johnson who died 7 Dec. 1841, aged 52.

Children:

2474.   Surena,[7] b. 12 Dec. 1812; m. Betsey Sleeper; d. 28 Aug. 1838; lived in Kingston, N. H.

2475.   Frederick P., b. 3 Aug. 1814; m. Henrietta B. Bassett; physician, New York City.

1125

Francis[6] Chase (Joseph,[5] Dea. Francis,[4] Samuel,[3] Ens. Moses[2]), born in Litchfield, N. H., 27 Feb. 1768; died in Claremont, N. H., 3 Apr. 1828, aged 60. He married in Claremont, 15 Nov. 1792, Mary Weade who was born in Kingston, N. H., 9 Dec. 1771; died in Claremont, 18 May 1840. They lived in Claremont, and were buried in the Old Village Cemetery.

Children, born in Claremont:

Maria,[7] b. 16 May 1793; m. 3 Feb. 1814, James McLaughlin of Claremont; she d. 19 July 1858; lived in Fairfax, Iowa.

2476.   Elijah, b. 3 Oct. 1794; m. 11 July 1829, Delia Turner of St. Johnsbury, Vt.; d. 14 Oct. 1846; she d. 28 Aug. 1866.

Betsey, b. 23 Sept. 1796; m. (1) 12 Jan. 1815, John McCollum; m. (2) 9 Sept. 1845, Jonas Cutting; he d. 8 May 1868.

Polly, b. 23 Sept. 1798; d. 2 Oct. 1799.

Joseph, b. 22 July 1800; d. 23 Oct. 1812.

Sarah, b. 12 Mar. 1803; m. 30 Sept. 1830, Daniel Huntoon; alive 21 Apr. 1873.

Francis, b. 19 Dec. 1805; d. 4 June 1830.

Mary, b. 8 Sept. 1807; d. 31 Jan. 1824.

Sophia W., b. 15 Sept. 1810; d. 31 Dec. 1822.

Susan, b. 22 June 1815; d. 20 Oct. 1817.

1126

John[6] Chase (Joseph,[5] Dea. Francis,[4] Samuel,[3] Ens. Moses[2]), born in Litchfield, N. H., 24 Nov. 1771; died in 1848. He married in Dunbarton, N. H., 19 Jan. 1797, Mary Parker of Litchfield. She was born in 1775 and died in 1832. They lived in Plainfield, Vt., and Schoharie Co., N. Y.

Children, born in Plainfield, Vt.:

2477.   John Parker,[7] b. 1798; m. 1821, Jerusha Willsey; lived in Schoharie Co., N. Y.

2478.   Joseph, b. 1801; m. 1822, Sylvia Willsey; he d. 1830.

2479.   Abner, b. 1805; m. 1831, Sarah Putnam; lived in Washington Co., Vt.

Mary, b. 1808; m. 1834, Isaac Bachellor; lived in Washington Co., Vt.

Amasa, b. 1811; m. 1843, Sarah Hagar; no children. He was living in Fayetteville, N. Y., in 1872.

1127

Dea. Joseph[6] Chase (Joseph,[5] Dea. Francis,[4] Samuel,[3] Ens. Moses[2]), born in Litchfield, N. H., 17 May 1780; died in Windham, N. H., 4 Sept. 1871, in the 92d year of his age. He married 12 Apr. 1808, Anna[6] Chase, daughter of Col. Samuel[5] and Molly (Stuart)

Chase, born 4 Dec. 1783; died in Aug. 1865. (Family 392). They lived in Litchfield and late in life removed to Windham.

Children, born in Litchfield:

JANE,[7] b. 17 Jan. 1809.

JAMES, b. 13 May 1811; d. 24 Apr. 1812.

2480.   EDWIN, b. 17 Mar. 1813; m. (1) 26 Sept. 1836, Mary Kimball, who d. 1 July 1839; m. (2) 5 Nov. 1839, Maria Adams. They lived in Holyoke. Their son by the first wife was *Joseph Edwin*,[8] b. 22 Mar. 1839; m. 22 Mar. 1864, Alma Frances Coffin of Londonderry, N. H. Their son Joseph Theodore,[9] b. in Holyoke, 2 Feb. 1882; a graduate of Dartmouth College, 1906; m. 12 June 1911, Coralie Johnston. Children: *Josie Alma*,[10] b. 3 Oct. 1914; *Chester Everett*,[10] b. 19 June 1916. They live in Roanoke Rapids, N. C. By the second marriage their daughter *Sarah Pratt*,[8] b. in Holyoke; m. Judge ——— Decker and was widely known in connection with Women's Clubs. She d. 17 July 1912.

2481.   HORACE, b. 24 Oct. 1815.

ENOCH PILLSBURY, b. 15 Feb. 1818; d. 17 Mar. 1818.

2482.   ENOCH PILLSBURY, b. 29 Feb. 1820; m. 19 Dec. 1844, Amy Sophia Adams of Hudson, N. H.

ANNA, b. 25 Sept. 1822; d. 16 Aug. 1825.

ANNA, b. 13 Nov. 1826; m. in Londonderry, N. H., 14 Jan. 1850, Charles Pelham.

1128

ROBERT[6] CHASE (Joseph,[5] Dea. Francis,[4] Samuel,[3] Ens. Moses[2]), born in Litchfield, N. H., 24 Apr. 1785; married MARGARET McQUESTEN. His family has not been reported.

1129

ABNER[6] CHASE (Dea. Abner,[5] Dea. Francis,[4] Samuel,[3] Ens. Moses[2]), born 16 July 1787; died 2 Mar. 1845. He married in Claremont, N. H., 9 Sept. 1812, MARY GOSS who was living in 1872. They lived in Lempster, N. H.

Children, born in Lempster:

MARY MATILDA,[7] b. 12 Apr. 1813; d. unm. in Plymouth, N. H., about 1880, aged 66.

2483.   CHARLES HENRY, b. 12 Dec. 1814; m. 6 June 1841, Anna H. Wellman, a Methodist clergyman.

MINERVA EGLANTINE, b. 29 June 1816; m. 25 June 1839, Rev. Lorenzo D. Barrows, D.D., of Tilton, N. H.

FANNY FLORENA, b. 31 Mar. 1818; d. 17 Mar. 1838.

2484.   LUCIUS AQUILA, b. 13 Mar. 1820; m. Harriet Smith, b. in Holliston, 19 Jan. 1824; d. 2 Feb. 1907. He was one of the publishers of the *American Agriculturist* and d. 3 Oct. 1894. Their child *Helen Harriet*,[8] b. 1 May 1843; m. Joseph Holbrook Dyer, b. 2 Nov. 1842; d. Sept. 1879. Their daughter Mary[9] Dyer, b. 5 Apr. 1870; m. (1) 14 June 1894, Henry De Merritt Young, who was lost on the *City of Portland*, 28 Nov. 1898. Their son Dyer[10] Young, b. 22 Mar. 1896; m. 10 Jan. 1920, Harriette Buckhart. Mrs. Young m. (2) 28 Apr. 1906, Dana Pierce of Highland Park, Ill.

LUCIA PRISCILLA (twin), b. 13 Mar. 1820; d. 6 Apr. 1832.

MRS. SARAH PLATT DECKER

CYNTHIA ELIZA, b. 3 May 1825; m. 10 Aug. 1852, Calvin S.
Harrington.
2485. BENJAMIN KIRKE, b. 9 Aug. 1830; m. 13 Jan. 1859, Lucy
Campbell.

1130

REV. BENJAMIN⁶ CHASE (Simeon,⁵ Dea. Francis,⁴ Samuel,³ Ens.
Moses²), born in Litchfield, N. H., 20 Nov. 1789; died in Natchez,
Miss., 11 Oct. 1870. He married (1) 25 July 1814, ROXANA D.
WOODBURY, of New London, N. H., daughter of Lt. Benjamin and
Zillah Woodbury, born 27 Mar. 1790; died without issue in 1818.
He married (2) MARY DUNNING of New Haven, Conn. He mar-
ried (3) in 1828, Mrs. ANNA W. (HENDERSON) SMITH who died in
1845. He graduated at Middlebury College in 1814, and was a Pres-
byterian clergyman in Conn. and in Miss. Washington College, Pa.,
conferred upon him the degree of D. D. in 1857.
Children by second wife:
LUCALAH.⁷
SUSAN.
2486. BENJAMIN, physician.
2487. SIMEON.
2488. WINGATE.

1131

MOSES⁶ CHASE (Simeon,⁵ Dea. Francis,⁴ Samuel,³ Ens. Moses²),
born in Litchfield, N. H., 2 Mar. 1796; married 22 Sept. 1825, ME-
LINDA BINGHAM, daughter of Daniel and Sally⁶ (Chase) Bingham,
born 1796. Her mother was a daughter of Abner⁵ and Joanna
(Moody) Chase. (Family 396). They lived in Litchfield.
Children, born in Litchfield:
GEORGE W.,⁷ b. 4 Oct. 1826; d. 14 Oct. 1832.
2489. SIMEON, b. 4 Apr. 1828; m. Sarah Greenwood; lived in Chica-
go, Ill.
HARRIET DUSTIN, b. 14 Dec. 1829; m. Samuel M. Howell.
INFANT, b. 23 June 1831; d. soon.
INFANT, b. 17 Aug. 1833; d. young.
PAINE WINGATE, b. 11 June 1834; noted preceptor in New Or-
leans, and Kingston, N. H.; d. unm. 12 Sept. 1869.
DAUGHTER, b. 29 Jan. 1836; d. young.
SARAH ANN, b. 9 Jan. 1837; m. Hiram M. Blake of Chicago,
Ill.
2490. HERBERT MOSES, b. 27 Mar. 1839; m. 15 Sept. 1870, Abbie
Spaulding; lived in Litchfield, N. H.
MARY MELINDA, b. 18 Oct. 1840; m. Henry M. Bauscher,
teacher in New Paltz Academy, N. Y.

1132

DANIEL⁶ CHASE (Daniel,⁵ Dea. Francis,⁴ Samuel,³ Ens. Moses²),
born in Newton, N. H., 10 Oct. 1792; married ABIGAIL ROWELL.
They lived in Hopkinton, N. H.
Children:
HANNAH.⁷
2491. WILLIAM.

1133

Rev. Moses[6] Chase (Daniel,[5] Dea. Francis,[4] Samuel,[3] Ens. Moses[2]), born in Newton, N. H., 13 Feb. 1803; died in Burrillville, R. I., 7 Jan. 1866. He married 25 July 1829, Mary Peaslee. He was a Methodist clergyman.

Child, born in Milton, N. H.:

2492. Ira Eaton,[7] b. 1 June 1833; m. 1 Jan. 1856, Josephine Brown of New Bedford; a physician in Haverhill.

1134

Stephen[6] Chase (Moses,[5] Dea. Francis,[4] Samuel,[3] Ens. Moses[2]), born in Plaistow, N. H., 16 Nov. 1790; married 15 Apr. 1819, Sarah Merrill, daughter of Abel Merrill and Anne (Emery) born 13 June 1795. They lived in Haverhill and Plaistow. He was living, 30 Nov. 1870, in Haverhill.

Children, born probably in Plaistow:

Mary Ann,[7] b. 12 Mar. 1820; m. 30 Dec. 1841, William Graves[7] Chase (James[6]) of Newton, N. H.; she d. 26 Feb. 1914. (Family 1122)

Lydia A., b. 19 Feb. 1822; m. Feb. 1847, Capt. John Anderson of Boston.

Alfred, b. 20 Nov. 1823; d. 9 Mar. 1843.

Warren, b. 9 Nov. 1825; d. 14 June 1849.

Flavius, b. 11 Nov. 1827; d. 16 Aug. 1848.

Sarah Melvina, b. 23 Feb. 1830; d. 26 Jan. 1847.

2493. Horace, b. 21 Dec. 1831; m. 13 Sept. 1866, Jeannette H. Floyd; physician in Boston.

2494. Milton, b. 16 Nov. 1833; m. 12 Jan. 1868, Fannie A. Emery; lived in Haverhill.

Charlotte Augusta, b. 17 Nov. 1835; d. 17 Sept. 1848.

1135

Samuel Sewall[6] Chase (Moses,[5] Dea. Francis,[4] Samuel,[3] Ens. Moses[2]), born in Plaistow, N. H., 17 Feb. 1805; died in West Newbury, 23 Jan. 1885, aged 80. He married in West Newbury, 11 Sept. 1834, Eunice Noyes Colby of Epping, N. H. She died in 1886, aged 71. They lived at the Training Field in West Newbury.

Children, born in West Newbury:

Abbie Dow,[7] b. 5 June 1835; m. 11 Sept. 1856, S. W. Sawyer of Andover, N. H.; lived in Plaistow.

2495. Samuel Noyes, b. 21 Aug. 1836; m. May 1861, Ellen Bateman; carriage-maker of Blackwood, N. J.

2496. Thomas Noyes, b. 18 July 1838; graduated at Dartmouth College in 1862; m. 31 July 1862, Mary Maria Tuttle of Acton; professor of Greek and Latin at Atlanta (Ga.) University, 1869 to 1905. Dean 1894-6; d. Bellows Falls, Vt.

Mary Emma, b. 9 Aug. 1840; m. 23 Nov. 1864, Elijah B. Hoyt of Newton, N. H.; d. 23 Apr. 1912.

Ellen L., b. 28 Mar. 1842; d. 29 Dec. 1842.

Elizabeth Ellen, b. 3 Sept. 1843; d. 21 Mar. 1865.

2497. Charles Parker, b. 6 May 1845; graduated at Dartmouth College in 1869; professor Olivet College, 1872 to 1881; professor in Chandler School, 1883-1892; treasurer of Dartmouth College from 1890 to 1916; d. in Hanover, N. H., 10 Aug. 1923.

ANNA F., b. 3 June 1847; d. young.
BENJAMIN NOYES, b. 18 Oct. 1850; d. 4 Feb. 1870.
MOSES, b. 29 Mar. 1852; d. same day.

1135a

AMOS⁶ CHASE (Samuel,⁵ Dea. Amos,⁴ Samuel,³ Ens. Moses²), born in Saco, Me., 12 Mar. 1765; died there, 5 June 1794. He married ELIZABETH HOYT [HIGHT], daughter of George and Eunice (Hill) Hoyt of Berwick, Me. She was born about 1768 and married (2) in Jan. 1798, Abner⁵ Chase of Limington, Me. (Family 405). Amos⁶ Chase was called in the Church Records of Pepperellborough (now Saco) Amos "3d."

Children, born and baptized in what is now Saco:

BETSEY HIGHT⁷ [HOYT], bp. 5 Apr. 1789.
HANNAH, bp. 1 May 1791.

1136

SAMUEL⁶ CHASE (Samuel,⁵ Dea. Amos,⁴ Samuel,³ Ens. Moses²), born in Saco, Me., 14 July 1766. He and his brother Benjamin were to pay the heirs of their father their shares of the estate, 30 Oct. 1811.

1137

SIMON W.⁶ CHASE (Samuel,⁵ Dea. Amos,⁴ Samuel,³ Ens. Moses²), born in Saco, Me., 18 Dec. 1769; died before 30 Oct. 1811. In the division of his father's estate 30 Oct. 1811, his son Julian⁷ Chase was the representative of his share of the estate of Samuel⁵ Chase, late of Saco.

Child:

2498. JULIAN,⁷ under age, 30 Oct. 1811. His guardian was Seth Storer Jr.

1138

BENJAMIN⁶ CHASE (Samuel,⁵ Dea. Amos,⁴ Samuel,³ Ens. Moses²), born in Saco, Me., 3 May 1773. He was assigned a portion of his father's estate, 30 Oct. 1811, and was to pay the other heirs a part of their shares.

1139

CAPT. WILLIAM⁶ CHASE (Samuel,⁵ Dea. Amos,⁴ Samuel,³ Ens. Moses²), born in Saco, Me., 2 Oct. 1775; died there 28 July 1817; married (intention at Saco, 7 July 1804) ALICE SPOFFORD. They lived in Saco. He was a mariner. His widow Alice was appointed administratrix, 17 Nov. 1817. (York Co. Probate, 26:27)

Children, born in Saco:

WILLIAM,⁷ b. 5 June 1806; lost at sea, 27 Aug. 1827.
HARRIET, b. 1 Mar. 1808.
ALMIRA, b. 3 Dec. 1809; m. John Johnson.

1140

JOHN ELDEN[6] CHASE (Dea. Amos,[5] Dea. Amos,[4] Samuel,[3] Ens. Moses[2]), born in Limington, Me., 31 Aug. 1775; baptized in Buxton, Me., 16 June 1776; died 7 May 1810. He married 13 Feb. 1797, ABIGAIL HOOPER, daughter of Robert and Elizabeth (Whitaker) Hooper, who was born, 13 Feb. 1777, and was living in 1872. They lived in Limington. Administration on his estate was granted to his widow Abigail, 18 June 1810 (York Co. Probate, 22:28).

Children, born in Limington:

ELIZABETH,[7] b. 14 Jan. 1799; m. 10 May 1818, Joseph White-house; she d. 4 Dec. 1832. Seven children.

2499. JOHN E., b. 11 Feb. 1801; m. 12 May 1822, Widow Fannie (York) Chase; he d. about 1866; living in Bradford, Me., in 1872, and later in Machias, Me.

2500. ABNER, b. 26 Feb. 1804; m. 24 Apr. 1816, Fannie York.

EMMA, b. 10 Feb. 1807; d. 12 July 1824.

2501. HOOPER, b. 30 June 1809; m. (1) Maria Pease; m. (2) Susan Small; lived in Bangor, Me. He d. Dec. 1899.

1141

ABNER[6] CHASE (Dea. Amos,[5] Dea. Amos,[4] Samuel,[3] Ens. Moses[2]), born in Limington, Me., 12 Nov. 1784; drowned in the Little Ossipee River, 24 Apr. 1816. He married, 21 Dec. 1814, ABIGAIL (HOOPER) CHASE, the widow of his brother John Elden[6] Chase. She died in 1872.

Children, born in Limington:

LEUMON,[7] d. in infancy.

SOPHRONIA, b. 1 Jan. 1817; d. 16 Apr. 1887.

1142

AMOS[6] CHASE (Dea. Amos,[5] Dea. Amos,[4] Samuel,[3] Ens. Moses[2]), was baptized in Limington, Me., 25 May 1777. He is supposed to be the Amos Chase who died in Bangor, Me., 7 Nov. 1831. That Amos married 19 Aug. 1824, DOLLY[7] CHASE, daughter of Thomas[6] and Dolly (Jackens) Chase, born 28 Nov. 1807. (Family 502). They lived in Blanchard, Me. She married (2) 25 Nov. 1837, Elias Humphrey and by him had six children, born in Pittsfield, Me.

Children, born in Blanchard:

ABBIE,[7] b. 14 June 1825; d. 14 May 1826.

ABBIE 2d, b. 1 Apr. 1827; d. 30 July 1848.

AMOS JEFFERSON, b. 12 Dec. 1828; d. at about 19 y.

2502. BENJAMIN FRANKLIN, b. 16 Aug. 1830; m. (1) 4 Aug. 1852, Esther A. Danforth; seven children; m. (2) 5 July 1872, S. J. Howes of Chicago, Ill.

1143

OLIVER SAWYER[6] CHASE (Dea. Amos,[5] Dea. Amos,[4] Samuel,[3] Ens. Moses[2]), born in Limington, Me., 16 Sept. 1792; died there, 5 Mar. 1824. He married 12 Nov. 1821, CATHARINE C. MILLER who was born 20 June 1803; alive 1873. They lived in Limington.

Children, born in Limington:

> EMMA E.,[7] b. 20 Apr. 1822; m. 16 May 1842, Gideon L. Norcross. Five children; she d. 15 Sept. 1857.

2503. STEPHEN SAWYER, b. 4 May 1823; m. 1 Nov. 1857, Eliza Morey. Two children.

1144

MOSES[6] CHASE (Dea. Amos,[5] Dea. Amos,[4] Samuel,[3] Ens. Moses[2]), born in Limington, Me., 14 Apr. 1796; died in Scarborough, Me., 1 Mar. 1842. He married 5 Mar. 1818, MARY LIBBY, daughter of Harvey and Sarah (Small) Libby, born in Limington, 26 Dec. 1796; died in Saco, Me., 1 Mar. 1842.

Children, born probably in Limington:

> MESERVE,[7] b. 12 Apr. 1819; d. 19 May 1819.
>
> MARIA, b. 14 June 1820; m. 25 Dec. 1840, James Andrews; lived in Saco.

2504. SUMNER B., b. 4 Oct. 1821; m. 3 Sept. 1846, Almira B. Cobb; physician; lived in Osage, Iowa. Five children, including *Charles S.*,[8] b. 1 May 1853; m. 23 Aug. 1882, Eulalie Ritner, b. 8 Apr. 1854; physician, in Iowa City, Iowa. Their son Sumner Bereman,[9] b. 6 Apr. 1888; m. Edith Virginia Hoaglin, b. 28 Oct. 1893; physician in Fort Dodge, Iowa. Their daughter *Rosemary*,[10] b. 15 Sept. 1919.

2505. JACOB LIBBY, b. 27 Oct. 1823; m. 25 Nov. 1845, Elizabeth Johnston; lived in Osage, Iowa. Five children.

> EMMA, b. 14 Jan. 1827; m. 30 Oct. 1844, George Parcher; lived in Saco.
>
> SARAH ANN, b. 5 June 1829; m. 18 Dec. 1847, Edward F. Merrill; she d. 19 Oct. 1856.
>
> MARY, b. 9 Aug.; d. 1 Sept. 1831.
>
> ALTHEA, b. 2 June 1833; d. unm. 14 May 1854.
>
> MARY ELLEN, b. 18 Apr. 1835; m. 2 Oct. 1853, James H. Merrill; lived in Maywood, Ill.
>
> JOHN R., b. 1 Nov. 1838; d. 18 Sept. 1840.

1145

AMOS[6] CHASE (Joseph,[5] Dea. Amos,[4] Samuel,[3] Ens. Moses[2]), born in Standish, Me., — Jan. 1781; died in Oct. 1829; married — Feb. 1805, HANNAH[7] CHASE, daughter of Col. Josiah and Hannah (Grow) Chase, born in York, Me., 25 Feb. 1782; died 17 Apr. 1859, aged 77. (Family 156). They lived in Standish, Me., and in N. H.

Children, born in Standish:

> OLIVE C.,[7] b. 18 Nov. 1805; m. 1828, Nathan P. Whitney; alive in 1872, in Holliston; seven children.
>
> HANNAH, m. William N. Brooks of Upton; d. in N. Y.
>
> DAUGHTER, d. young.
>
> SOPHIA, m. ———— Bliss of Vt. No children.
>
> EMILY, m. Aaron Pond of Milford. Six children.
>
> MARY, m. George P. Connor of Central Falls, R. I.
>
> Ten children in this family but the others d. without issue, names unknown.

1146

NATHAN W.[6] CHASE (Joseph,[5] Dea. Amos,[4] Samuel,[3] Ens. Moses[2]), born in Standish, Me., — Aug. 1783; died in Bangor, Me., Oct. 1867. He married in 1807, ANNIS AYER of Standish.

1147

JOSEPH[6] CHASE (Joseph,[5] Dea. Amos,[4] Samuel,[3] Ens. Moses[2]), born in Standish, Me., 23 Dec. 1787; died in Upton, Me., 14 May 1866. He married (1) 1 July 1809, SABRA L. WHEELER who was born in Rowley, 2 Feb. 1791 and died in Poy Sippi, Wis., 29 Aug. 1869. He married (2) AFFIE (BARTLETT) JACKSON. They lived in Bridgton, Me., until 1830 when they removed to Upton.

Children by first wife, born in Bridgton:

2506.   PERLEY G.,[7] b. 22 Sept. 1810; m. 15 Nov. 1837, Caroline Colby of Brownfield, Me.; living in Berlin, Wis., 1872.
ANNIS M. A., b. 29 Mar. 1812; m. about 1828, John Lowell; d. Sept. 1830.
LOUISA A., b. 4 July 1814; m. (1) Thomas P. Martin; m. (2) ——— French.
PAULINA H., b. 12 Nov. 1816; m. 15 Nov. 1836, Robert Ridlon.
2507.   JOSEPH W., b. 16 Feb. 1818; m. 1 Jan. 1843, Martha A. Pratt.
ABBIE O., b. 11 Feb. 1821; m. James Rundlett.
ELLEN M. B., b. 5 Oct. 1824; m. (1) 17 Sept. 1848, John Quincy A. Pratt; m. (2) 12 Apr. 1869, Richard D. Moore of Poy Sippi, Wis.
2508.   NATHAN O., b. 9 or 29 Oct. 1826; m. 9 May 1853, Louisa Hill; lived in Berlin, Wis., in 1873. Seven children.
2509.   WILLIAM W., b. 13 Mar. 1828; m. 19 Feb. 1851, Susan E. Newcomb.
OREN L., b. 13 Oct. 1830; d. Oct. 1832.

Children by second wife, born in Upton, Me.:

2510.   DANIEL, living in Berlin, Wis., in 1873.
ANNIS M., b. 21 Sept. 1839; m. ——— Brown; lived in Cambridge, N. H.
2511.   HORATIO, b. 12 Aug. 1841; lived in Upton, 1873.
2512.   CHARLES, b. 14 Dec. 1843; lived in Upton.
JOHN, d. in Civil War, aged 26.
JAMES H., d. in Civil War, aged 21.

1148

JOHN[6] CHASE (Joseph,[5] Dea. Amos,[4] Samuel,[3] Ens. Moses[2]), born in Standish, Me., 25 May 1790; died at sea, 1814, on a voyage to New Orleans, La. He married in 1814, ——— CLARK. No children have been reported.

1149

BENJAMIN TAPPAN[6] CHASE (Daniel,[5] Dea. Amos,[4] Samuel,[3] Ens Moses[2]), born in Saco, Me., 10 June 1791; married 2 Oct 1815, SUBMIT WOODMAN. They lived in Buxton, Me. He died about 1844.

Children, born in Buxton:

2513.   BENJAMIN FRANKLIN,[7] b. 13 July 1816; m. Jane Harden. Five children.

CAROLINE, b. 15 Aug. 1818; d. 29 Mar. 1900.
ELIZABETH, b. 17 Dec. 1820; d. 27 Jan. 1879.
SUSAN WOODMAN, b. 14 Feb. 1823.
JANE MARIA, b. 21 Sept. 1824; d. 25 Mar. 1825.
2514. WILLIAM AUGUSTUS, b. 14 May 1826; d. 18 June 1911; m. 9 July 1850, Olive Chase. Three children.
HELEN MARIA, b. — June 1833; d. 8 Nov. 1862. (The Chase Chronicle, 4: 52)

1150

DANIEL[6] CHASE (Daniel,[5] Dea. Amos,[4] Samuel,[3] Ens. Moses[2]), born in Saco, Me., 3 Oct. 1796; died in Baltimore, Md., in 1872. He removed to Baltimore about 1820; married and had three daughters. He was a successful merchant in Baltimore.
Children, born in Baltimore:
MARY,[7] m. Hiram Woods of Baltimore.
Two other daughters' names unknown.

1151

AMOS[6] CHASE (Daniel,[5] Dea. Amos,[4] Samuel,[3] Ens. Moses[2]), born in Saco, Me., 14 Jan. 1799; died there, 12 Aug. 1873. He married in Portsmouth, N. H., 12 Dec. 1833, MARY FRANCES AKERMAN who was born 15 Oct. 1817, and died in Kennebunkport, Me., 10 Aug. 1887. They lived in Saco.
Children, born in Saco:
MARY ELIZABETH,[7] b. 22 June 1834; m. 12 Dec. 1855, Bartlett Palmer of Boston; six children.
FRANCES ELLEN, b. 23 Aug. 1843; m. 18 June 1868, Edward Eastman of Saco.

1152

DAVID TAPPAN[6] CHASE (Daniel,[5] Dea. Amos,[4] Samuel,[3] Ens. Moses[2]), born in Saco, Me., 13 Feb. 1802; married 17 Sept. 1830, MARTHA E. HAYNES.
Children:
2515. HENRY,[7] b. 6 Mar. 1832; physician in Baltimore, Md.
CATHARINE AUGUSTA, b. 19 July 1835; d. 22 July 1835.
2516. EDMOND, b. 8 Oct. 1836.
DANIEL, b. 14 June 1841; d. 28 Aug. 1841.
2517. DANIEL 2d, b. 21 Aug. 1843.
2518. GEORGE, b. 29 Dec. 1849; lived in Portland, Me., 1872.

1153

AMOS HILL[6] CHASE (Abner,[5] Dea. Amos,[4] Samuel,[3] Ens. Moses[2]), born in Limington, Me., about 1807; inherited one half of his father's farm by will dated 14 June 1838. He married LYDIA DAVIS.

1154

JAMES MADISON[6] CHASE (Abner,[5] Dea. Amos,[4] Samuel,[3] Ens. Moses[2]), born in Limington, Me., about 1810; he inherited one half of his father's homestead by will dated 14 June 1838 and came into

possession of the property in 1847. He removed to Hiawatha, Brown
Co., Kans.

1155

ROBERT[6] CHASE (Robert,[5] Samuel,[4] Samuel,[3] Ens. Moses[2]), born
in Sandown, N. H., 24 Mar. 1794; died 11 July 1846. He married in
Hampstead, N. H., 23 June 1822, ABIGAIL W. THOMAS who was
born 23 Feb. 1800; died 31 July 1866. They lived in Hampstead.
Children, born in Hampstead:

> IRA STEWART,[7] b. 19 June 1823; d. 24 Nov. 1839.
2519.   WILLIAM MOSES, b. 4 Mar. 1825; m. (1) 6 Mar. 1843, Matilda
>   Caldwell; m. (2) 6 Apr. 1848, Lucy Ann Noyes of Atkin-
>   son, N. H.
2520.   CALEB THOMAS, b. 1 May 1829.
>   SARAH ABIGAIL, b. 3 Dec. 1832; d. 10 Feb. 1857, unm.
>   MARY ELISABETH, b. 12 Feb. 1834; d. 29 Nov. 1857, unm., in
>   Haverhill.
>   HANNAH MARIA, b. 16 July 1839; m. 24 Feb. 1866, ———
>   ———.
>   ANNA AUGUSTA, b. 15 May 1841; d. 31 July 1864, a. 24 y.

1156

DANIEL BODWELL[6] CHASE (Robert,[5] Samuel,[4] Samuel,[3] Ens.
Moses[2]), born in Hampstead, N. H., 6 Aug. 1795; died 25 July 1873.
He married (1) in 1818, HARRIET BROWN, daughter of Benjamin
Brown of Kingston, N. H. She was born in 1795; died 19 Sept. 1823,
aged 30. He married (2) in Poplin (now Fremont), 8 Nov. 1829,
SARAH BROWN, daughter of Elijah and Joanna Brown of Fremont,
born 10 Mar. 1799; died 29 Mar. 1863. They lived in Fremont. He
was a representative to N. H. legislature.
Children by first wife, born in Poplin (now Fremont):

> RUTH H.,[7] b. 14 June 1819; m. Isaiah L. Robinson of Fremont;
>   lived in Nashua.
> MARY PLUMMER, b. 1 Mar. 1821; m. Moses Brown of Bow,
>   N. H.

Children by second wife, born in Poplin:

> SARAH ANN, b. 26 May 1830; d. 24 Feb. 1834.
> DANIEL B., b. 4 May 1832; d. 24 July 1833.
> SARAH A., b. 15 Dec. 1835.
> HATTIE B., b. 10 Mar. 1838; d. 19 Dec. 1856.
> DANIEL B. 2d., b. 20 July 1841; d. 5 Sept. 1842.

1157

DEA. SAMUEL[6] CHASE (Benjamin,[5] Samuel,[4] Samuel,[3] Ens.
Moses[2]), born in Sandown, N. H., 7 Feb. 1788; died in Haverhill,
24 Jan. 1871. He married (1) in Haverhill, 29 Apr. 1811, BETSEY
COGSWELL who died in Haverhill, 1814. He married (2) in Haverhill, 24 Dec. 1818, HANNAH COGSWELL who died in Haverhill, 21
Feb. or 4 Mar. 1824, aged 28 y. He married (3) in Haverhill, 6 May
1825, PRISCILLA COGSWELL. Betsey Cogswell was daughter of John
and Betty (Griffin) Cogswell, born in Haverhill, 28 June 1789. Hannah Cogswell, her sister, was born there 19 Dec. 1797. Priscilla

Cogswell was a cousin, daughter of Thomas and Lydia (Harriman) Cogswell, born in Haverhill, 5 July 1803. They lived in Haverhill on the westerly corner of Lindell and Water streets.

Child by first wife, born in Haverhill:

ELIZA,[7] b. 15 Mar. 1812; m. 27 Dec. 1832, Elias Theodore Ingalls. Their son was Hon. John James Ingalls of Kansas.

Child by second wife, born in Haverhill:

2521. CHARLES WILLIAM, b. 17 Mar. 1822; d. 6 June 1898; m. 25 Oct. 1845, Abigail H. Gardner, b. 12 May 1824; d. 14 Dec. 1913. Six children, including *Harry W.*,[8] b. 23 Dec. 1856; d. 31 Dec. 1919; m. 19 Sept. 1883, Adelia L. Giddings. Children: Charles Alden[9] (1887-1918); Gardner,[9] b. 26 May 1888; Barbara,[9] b. 11 May 1889. *Nellie G.*,[8] b. 2 July 1863; m. 31 May 1917, Ezra W. B. Taylor of Haverhill.

Children by third wife, born in Haverhill:

GEORGE BENJAMIN, b. 15 Mar. 1826; d. 23 Mar. 1826.
CATHARINE COGSWELL, b. 22 Dec. 1827; m. William H. Hill; d. 3 Apr. 1882.
BENJAMIN HENRY, b. 4 Feb. 1830; d. 8 May 1834.

2522. ROBERT STUART,[7] b. Haverhill, 17 Sept. 1831; d. 6 July 1916; m. Ada L. Harvey of Portsmouth, N. H., b. 30 July 1833. Their son *Arthur Taft*,[8] b. in Haverhill, 6 July 1864; graduate Massachusetts Institute of Technology, 1886; m. 26 June 1890, Minnie May Gardner, b. Haverhill, 8 May 1867, dau. of John V. and Etta (Foster) Gardner. Their daughter Priscilla,[9] b. 15 June 1899. They live at 986 Memorial Drive, Cambridge.

2523. EDWARD HENRY, b. 28 Feb. 1835; m. Elizabeth Taylor of Wilkes-Barre, Pa.

ANN MARIA, b. 22 Sept. 1836; m. Charles J. Kitredge, M.D.

2524. GEORGE SAMUEL, b. 17 Feb. 1839; m. Carrie Parker of Derry, N. H.; d. 1919.

FRANCES PRISCILLA, b. 18 Apr. 1843; m. Charles A. Brooks; d. 27 Feb. 1867.

1158

BENJAMIN[6] CHASE (Benjamin,[5] Samuel,[4] Samuel,[3] Ens. Moses[2]), born in Sandown, N. H., 4 June 1794; died in Zanesville, Ohio. He married ELIZA SWAN who died in Ansonville, Clearfield Co., Penn., in 1869. They lived in Broome County, N. Y., and Zanesville, Ohio. One report states that Benjamin Chase removed from Ohio to Broome Co., Penn., in 1825 and died there. His brother Samuel[6] Chase was the grandfather of Hon. John James Ingalls, born in Middleton, Mass., 29 Dec. 1833, and a United States senator from Kansas, 1874-1892.

Children:

JOSEPH A.[7]
BARLOW CLARK, register and recorder of the Orphans Court.
JOHN MITCHELL, b. in Zanesville, 11 Mar. 1820; removed to Broome Co., N. Y., 1825; removed to Knox, Clearfield Co., Penn., in 1833 with his mother, brother and sister; d. in Clearfield, 11 Mar. 1899. He m. 18 Sept. 1845, Tabitha Scott Williams, who d. in Clearfield, Mar. 1901. Their son *John Mitchell*,[8] b. in Clearfield, 9 Feb. 1852; m. 27 July 1871, Jane

Tabitha Phillips; living in Clearfield.   Children: Edmund
Burke,[9] deceased; Charles Ernest;[9] John Wallace;[9] William
Clark,[9] deceased; Deliver Paul,[9] deceased; Austin Roy,[9] b. 2
Apr. 1883; m. 28 Nov. 1911, Nellie May Bushman; he is
President Judge of the Courts of the 46th Judicial District of
Pennsylvania.   Children: *Mildred Gertrude;*[10] *Eleanor Jane;*[10]
Miriam Ann[10] and *Sarah Louise.*[10]   Oscar Ray;[9] Benjamin
Franklin;[9] and James Mitchell,[9] a member of Congress
from Pennsylvania.   *Joseph R.,*[8] b. 14 Aug. 1866, and *Benjamin Franklin,*[8] b. 1 Feb. 1869, are executors of the estate of
John Mitchell[7] Chase Sr.   Benjamin Franklin[8] is also American Consul in Messina, Italy, 1922-24.
RHODA.
ELIZA.

1159

WILLIAM[6] CHASE (Dea. Amos,[5] Samuel,[4] Samuel,[3] Ens.
Moses[2]), born in Haverhill, 6 Apr. 1797; died 10 Mar. 1875.   He
married — Dec. 1827, SYLVIA WASHBURN.
Children:
2525.   WILLIAM.[7]
        ABBY ANN.

1160

AMOS[6] CHASE (Dea. Amos,[5] Samuel,[4] Samuel,[3] Ens. Moses[2]),
born in Haverhill, 18 June 1803; married in Haverhill, 17 Apr. 1832,
SARAH PEARSON.   They lived in Haverhill.
Children, born and died in Haverhill:
        CHILD,[7] d. 5 Apr. 1833.
        LAURA E., d. 22 Feb. 1834, aged 22 months.
        SARAH PEARSON, b. 31 Mar. 1835; m. 16 Feb. 1864, in Charlestown, Harlan Page Conant and d. in Somerville, 18 Nov.
        1926.   Four children.   (See Conant Genealogy.)

1161

HEZEKIAH SMITH[6] CHASE (Dea. Amos,[5] Samuel,[4] Samuel,[3] Ens.
Moses[2]), born in Haverhill, 7 Aug. 1805; married (1) 7 Dec. 1841,
ELISABETH AUGUSTA SCHUYLER, daughter of Capt. Peter Schuyler
of New York.   She died 23 Aug. 1855.   He married (2) 30 Dec.
1858, AMANDA GRIGGS, daughter of Dea. Thomas Griggs.   They
lived in Boston.   Shoe manufacturer 1870 in Boston.
Children by first wife:
        BENJAMIN LITTLE,[7] d. in infancy.
        DAUGHTER, at age of 18, in 1870.
        CHARLES L., d. in Haverhill, 24 Sept. 1852, aged 4 m.
Children by second wife:
2526.   SON, b. 1861.
        DAUGHTER, b. 1868.

1162

JOSEPH[6] CHASE (Moses,[5] John,[4] Samuel,[3] Ens. Moses[2]), born in
Concord, Vt., 20 Nov. 1796; died in St. Johnsbury, Vt., 19 Nov.
1867, in his 71st year.   He married in Littleton, N. H., 25 Dec. 1823,

ELIZABETH EASTMAN, daughter of Jonathan and Phebe (Leach) Eastman, born in Littleton, 22 Apr. 1793; died in St. Johnsbury, 24 July 1870, aged 77.

They lived in Concord till about 1850 and then removed to Wheelock, Vt. In 1853 they removed to St. Johnsbury where they spent their last years.

Children, born in Concord:

> MARTHA,[7] b. 11 Feb. 1823; m. 4 Dec. 1845, Levi Goss of Concord and St. Johnsbury; he d. 17 Jan. 1884; she d. 2 Jan. 1893. Ten children.
>
> LAURISTON, b. 2 June 1828; m. 15 Oct. 1851, Diana Hunter. He disappeared about 1863. She m. (2) Ephraim Fairbanks of Norwark, Vt. She d. 20 Oct. 1875. Four children, including *Martha Ann*,[8] b. 15 June 1862; m. 15 Oct. 1890, Robert Jeremiah Peck, son of Charles and Elizabeth (Munson) Peck of New Haven, Conn. Their dau. Lucille Marguerite,[9] b. in Cocoa, Fla., 3 Mar. 1895; m. 2 June 1917, R. Howard Berg of Hempstead, L.I. Children *Royal Howard*[10] *Berg Jr.*, b. 20 Sept. 1923; *Robert Brewster*[10] *Berg*, b. 23 Nov. 1924; *Bradford*[10] *Berg*, b. 13 Jan. 1928. All reside in Sanford, Fla.

1163

JOHN DENNISON[6] CHASE (Moses,[5] John,[4] Samuel,[3] Ens. Moses[2]), born in Concord, Vt., 23 Sept. 1806; died there, 27 Aug. 1869. He married in St. Johnsbury, Vt., 6 Jan. 1829, SARAH SPAULDING, daughter of Reuben and Sarah (Swett) Spaulding, born in St. Johnsbury, 28 Aug. 1800. They lived in Concord, and Orange, Mass.

Children, born in Concord, Vt.:

2527. DENNISON,[7] b. 13 Apr. 1830; m. 4 Jan. 1855, Clementina Gregory; lived in Orange.

2528. JEFFERSON, b. 24 July 1831; m. 14 Nov. 1854, Caroline M. Adams; lived in Orange.

> PAMELIA, b. 9 Dec. 1834; m. 2 Jan. 1856, Horace Underwood; lived in St. Johnsbury.

1164

RICHARD CARR ROGERS[6] CHASE (John,[5] John,[4] Samuel,[3] Ens. Moses[2]), born in Sunapee, N. H., 19 Dec. 1798; married 22 July 1817, LENITY A. M. BARTLETT, daughter of Jacob and Mary[6] [Polly] (Chase) Bartlett, of Unity, N. H. (Family 393). They lived in Au Sable Forks, Essex Co., N. Y., where he was living, 25 Jan. 1871.

Children:

2529. FRANCIS H.,[7] lived in Philadelphia and Kalamagoo, Mich.

> ELIZABETH, m. Thomas D. Trumbull of Au Sable, N. Y.

2530. RICHARD S., farmer in Elizabethtown, N. Y.

2531. JOHN B., lived in Au Sable Forks.

> MARY, m. and lived in Au Sable Forks.

1165

HILLS H.[6] CHASE (John,[5] John,[4] Samuel,[3] Ens. Moses[2]), born in Sunapee, N. H., 2 July 1800; married in Sunapee 10 Mar. 1823, DOROTHY SARGENT of Sunapee. He was a physician and they lived

in Syracuse, N. Y. Dorothy Sargent was daughter of Moses and Betsey (Sargent) Sargent, born in Sunapee, 14 Apr. 1798.
Children, first two born in Sunapee, N. H.:

> CHLOE DANE,[7] b. 20 Mar. 1825; m. 1842, John Comstock.
> 2532. CHARLES SARGENT (twin), b. 20 Mar. 1825.
> SARAH GAGE.
> 2533. JOHN, lived in Kalamazoo, Mich.
> 2534. HENRY.
> 2535. DUDLEY.
> 2536. VAN BUREN, lived in Syracuse, N. Y.
> 2537. GEORGE.
> ELIZABETH, lived in Oswego, N. Y.
> 2538. THOMAS.
> 2539. JOSEPH, lived in Syracuse, N. Y.
> 2540. HORACE.
> 2541. FRANCIS.
> 2542. RUDO.

1166

JOSEPH PIKE[6] CHASE (Joseph,[5] John,[4] Samuel,[3] Ens. Moses[2]), born in Wendell (now Sunapee), N. H., 1 Mar. 1798; died in Wisconsin, June 1872. He married and had a family which has not been reported.

1167

JOHN LANGDON[6] CHASE (Joseph,[5] John,[4] Samuel,[3] Ens. Moses[2]), born in Wendell (now Sunapee), N. H., 7 Feb. 1805; died in Albany, N. Y., 18 July 1836. He married in Burton, Ohio, 12 Nov. 1828, JULIA BARNES who was born in North Haven, Conn., and was living in Hastings, Minn., on 28 Mar. 1873. They lived in Concord and Painesville, Ohio.
Children, born in Concord, Ohio:

> ROSALIE ELIZABETH,[7] b. 3 Apr. 1830; m. (1) 7 Nov. 1850, Eli T. Booth; m. (2) 26 Dec. 1865, Charles Q. Ball.
> 2543. EDGAR ELIAS, b. 1 Jan. 1832; m. 31 May 1855, Abigail Tucker. Five children.
> ANN ELIZA, b. 16 Feb. 1834; d. 6 June 1834.

1168

CYRUS[6] CHASE (Stephen,[5] Stephen,[4] Ens. Stephen,[3] Ens. Moses[2]), married ABIGAIL CARLETON. There were two children at least.
Children:

> EUNICE,[7] alive 1802; m. 25 Mar. 1810, John Turner.
> ABIGAIL, alive 1802.

1169

ASAPH[6] CHASE (Stephen,[5] Stephen,[4] Ens. Stephen,[3] Ens. Moses[2]), born in Guilford, Vt., 18 Apr. 1777; died 14 Oct. 1844. He married Oct. 1798, TAMAR CLARK who died 31 Oct. 1870, aged 96. They lived in Rutland, Jefferson Co., N. Y.
Children:

> RELIEF,[7] m. John Coates of Rutland.

BETSEY, m. Henry Weston of Hartland, Vt.

NANCY, m. John Boyden of Saranac.

DELIA or DELLA.

2544. CHANDLER C., b. 22 July 1810; m. 27 Dec. 1829, Louisa Kent, b. 6 Aug. 1810. She was of Brattleboro, Vt. They were living in Watertown, N. Y., in 1870.

1170

ALLEN[6] CHASE (Stephen,[5] Stephen,[4] Ens. Stephen,[3] Ens. Moses[2]), born 7 Feb. 1780; died about 1863, at the age of 83. He married (1) 8 Oct. 1801, HANNAH UNDERWOOD; married (2) 4 June 1826, POLLY DUNBAR.

Children by first wife:

ELECTA,[7] b. 25 Apr. 1803; m. (2) John Hine.

AMY, b. 14 Oct. 1807; m. 1831, Leonard Stone.

SARAH, b. 22 June 1809; m. 21 Mar. 1830, Norman Webster.

2545. SAMUEL, b. 8 Feb. 1815.

2546. EDWIN, b. 5 Apr. 1818; d. Sept. 1862.

Children by second wife:

2547. HORACE, b. 1831; m. 1852, Sarah Ann Bentley; lived in Royalton, Vt.

BETSEY.

EMILY.

1171

STEPHEN[6] CHASE (Stephen,[5] Stephen,[4] Ens. Stephen,[3] Ens. Moses[2]), born in Guilford, Vt., 28 Sept. 1782; married 31 Jan. 1800, PERSIS PARKE who died about 1872, over 92. He died 22 Feb. 1853. His mother was a daughter of Benjamin Carpenter, once Lieut. Governor of Vermont. They lived in Penn Yan, Yates Co., N. Y., and in Geneva, N. Y., for a time.

Children:

ELIZA,[7] m. Nathan Reed.

2548. STEPHEN.

EVELINE, m. Samuel M. Warren.

2549. ROBERT P., physician, San Francisco, Cal., 1873.

PERSIS LILLIAN, b. 18 Mar. 1818; m. 10 Mar. 1836, Joseph Lammon Tuttle of Geneva, N. Y.

2550. PORTER, m. Helen Robinson.

MARGARET, m. Henry Bowers.

MARY, m. James Young.

2551. CYRUS, lived in Hortonville, Wis.

Three died in infancy, names not reported.

1172

AMOS B.[6] CHASE (Micajah,[5] Stephen,[4] Stephen,[3] Ens. Moses[2]), born in Nottingham West (now Hudson), N. H., 19 July 1787; died 12 Jan. 1841, aged 52. He married in Nottingham West, 11 Apr. 1820, SARAH CROSS, daughter of Peter and Sarah Cross, born in Nottngham West about 1790; died in Manchester, N. H., 26 July 1875, aged 85 y. 4 m. They lived in Bedford, N. H. Administration on his estate was granted to James Prince of Hudson, 2 Mar. 1841, and an allowance was made to his widow Sarah. (Hillsborough Co. Probate, 46:31).

Children, born in Dunstable:

> SARAH CORDELIA,[7] b. 18 Feb. 1821; d. in Manchester, N. H., unm., 15 Jan. 1894, aged 73 y. 10 m. 27 d.
> LUCY ANN, b. 24 June 1824; d. 7 Feb. 1842.

1173

SOLOMON[6] CHASE (Ens. John,[5] Stephen,[4] Stephen,[3] Ens. Moses[2]), born in Hudson, N. H., 12 June 1797; married 26 June 1829, MIRANDA W. JONES, daughter of Abraham and Hepsibah (Fiske) Jones, born 5 Aug. 1807. They lived in Hudson.

Children, born in Hudson:

> CHARLES EDWARD AUSTIN,[7] b. 19 Mar. 1830; d. 29 Dec. 1833.
> 2552. WILLIAM FRANK, b. 30 Aug. 1831; m. Sarah Frances Greeley, dau. of Samuel Greeley of Hudson.
> SARAH M., b. 6 Apr. 1833; m. 21 May 1856, Frank Davis; lived in Calif.
> MARTHA, b. 28 June 1835; m. 29 Oct. 1854, Preble Pease of Hudson. She d. 3 Apr. 1862.
> 2553. JOHN GIBSON, b. 19 Apr. 1837; m. 9 Dec. 1867, Mira Johnson; lived in Antioch, Calif.
> KATE HOLMAN, b. 14 Mar. 1839; m. 29 Oct. 1860, Joshua Pease; lived in Red Wing, Minn.; no issue.
> HENRY HARRISON, b. 1 Nov. 1840; d. 14 Apr. 1841.
> MARIA HOWE, b. 9 Oct. 1842; d. 2 May 1869.

1174

JOHN[6] CHASE (Ens. John,[5] Stephen,[4] Stephen,[3] Ens. Moses[2]), born in Hudson, N. H., 5 Mar. 1801; married (1) June 1827, LUCY JONES, daughter of Abraham and Hepsibah (Fiske) Jones, born 7 May 1803; died in Hudson 22 Aug. 1853, aged 50. They lived in Hudson, where he died 22 Nov. 1882, aged 81 y. 8 m. He married (2) 5 Dec. 1854, ABIGAIL (JONES) AMBROSE, sister of his first wife. She d. 16 May 1863. He married (3) 28 June 1864, LOIS W. (DAVIS) UNDERWOOD.

Children, born in Hudson:

> ANN ELIZABETH,[7] b. 1828; d. 28 Nov. 1845.
> EDGAR BLODGETT, b. 16 Feb. 1830; d. 11 Jan. 1853, a. 26 y.
> LUCY A., d. 7 Feb. 1842, a. 17 y. 7 m.
> EDWARD A., d. 13 Sept. 1833.
> LAURA A., d. young.
> LUCY ELLEN, b. 4 July 1835; m. Frederick Augustus Buttrick; lived on Chase homestead in Hudson.
> Perhaps they had a second daughter named Lucy A., who d. in Hudson, 12 Oct. 1833.

1175

CHANDLER[6] CHASE (Daniel,[5] Stephen,[4] Stephen,[3] Ens. Moses[2]), born in Hudson or Pelham, N. H., about 1797; died in Pelham, 16 Feb. 1844, aged 47. His wife was ANNIS D. ———— who died in Pelham, 15 Oct. 1877, aged 80 y. 10 m. His estate was divided, 2 Mar. 1852, and those mentioned therein as interested heirs were Mary

Elizabeth Woodbury and William Woodbury her husband, Annis
Chase for herself and as guardian of Harriet Ann Chase, daughter of
said deceased, being all the known heirs. (Hillsborough Probate,
61 :110,314). Annis Chase was appointed guardian to Harriet Ann
Chase, under 14, 6 June 1848. (Ibid 42 :180)

Children, born in Pelham :

    MARY ELIZABETH,[7] b. about 1828; m. William Woodbury; she
        d. 6 July 1856, a. 28 y.

    JOHN C. D., d. 25 Aug. 1832, a. 1 y. 10 m. 15 d.

    HARRIET ANN, under 14, on 6 June 1848; alive 7 Oct. 1851.

1176

IRA[6] CHASE (Moses,[5] Moses,[4] Stephen,[3] Ens. Moses[2]), born
probably in Alstead, N. H., 19 Sept. 1795; married 18 Aug. 1822,
ELIZABETH WILLIAMS, daughter of Elder Abraham Williams. They
lived in Utica, N. Y., settling there in 1821. He died there 8 Jan.
1863.

Children, born in Utica :

        ELIZABETH JANE,[7] b. 10 Mar. 1824; d. 11 Sept. 1842.

2554. HENRY W., b. 9 Mar. 1825.

        HELEN AMELIA, b. 24 Feb. 1827; d. 11 Aug. 1842.

        IRA, b. 5 Mar. 1829; d. 13 Apr. 1829.

2555. IRA 2d, b. 17 Mar. 1830; d. 13 Apr. 1870.

        WILLIAM EUSTIS, b. 12 Mar. 1833; d. 12 Oct. 1834.

1177

AARON[6] CHASE (Moses,[5] Moses,[4] Stephen,[3] Ens. Moses[2]), born
in Alstead, N. H., 3 May 1797; died in Bloomington, Ind., 29 Aug.
1864. He married 9 Jan. 1827, DEBORAH GILSON. They lived in
Cambridge, Washington Co., N. Y., and Bloomington, Ind.

Children, born in Cambridge :

2556. BLOOMFIELD S.,[7] b. 10 Sept. 1827; m. 21 May 1854, Sarah E.
      Rose; lived in Bloomington.

2557. LEROY H., b. 7 June 1829; m. (1) 21 May 1851, Rebecca Green,
      who d. 30 May 1852; m. (2) 10 Apr. 1855, Sarah E. Eg-
      nore (?).

2258. GEORGE MORTIMER, b. 5 Mar. 1836; d. 17 Jan. 1927; m. in Oct.
      1859, Sarah Ann Killion, b. in Martinsville, Ind., 24 Aug.
      1840; d. in Kansas City, Mo., in Nov. 1903. Their son *Clar-*
      ence William,[8] b. in Bloomington, Ind., 29 Nov. 1862; m.
      1 May 1889, Ida May Lysle. Their children: (1) James
      Lysle,[9] b .11 Aug. 1890; (2) May Lysle,[9] b. 7 Mar. 1898; (3)
      Clarence William,[9] b. 23 June 1901; (4) George Mortimer,[9]
      b. 11 May 1904. They live in Leavenworth, Kans.

2559. AARON GLENROY, b. 16 Mar. 1840; m. Sept. 1860, Ellen Pressell.

1178

JACOB[6] CHASE (Moses,[5] Moses,[4] Stephen,[3] Ens. Moses[2]), born in
Alstead ,N. H., 17 Feb. 1799; died in Marcellus, N. Y.

1179

JUSTUS[6] CHASE (Moses,[5] Moses,[4] Stephen,[3] Ens. Moses[2]), born
in Alstead, N. H., 14 Sept. 1801; married about 1827, NANCY ———

who died 2 Oct. 1863. They lived in Watertown, N. Y., where he was alive in 1873.

Children:

ELLEN,[7] b. 3 July 1828; d. 6 Aug. 1846.
2560. ALVAH MANN, b. 22 July 1830.
2561. JUSTUS, b. 27 Feb. 1832; m. 4 July 1855, Harriet Masury.
ELIZABETH, b. 16 June 1834.
2562. MONTROVILLE W., b. 16 June 1837.

1180

BENJAMIN D.[6] CHASE (Joseph,[5] Moses,[4] Stephen,[3] Ens. Moses[2]), born 7 Mar. 1791; married in Pelham, N. H., 1 Dec. 1814, MARY HARDY of Pelham. She was born 24 July 1789 and died — Sept. 1869. She was a daughter of Dudley and Dorcas (Wyman) Hardy of Pelham. They lived in Pelham. He was alive in 1871.

Children, born in Pelham:

JOSEPH,[7] b. 29 Sept. 1815; d. 17 Oct. 1816.
MARY B., b. 8 Jan. 1817; d. unm.
BENJAMIN F., b. 12 Feb. 1820; d. 14 Oct. 1820.
2563. WILLIAM H., b. 29 Sept. 1821; m. 19 May 1846, Abigail K. Ordway of Hooksett, N. H.; lived in Hudson, N. H.; town clerk and representative; no children.
HARRIET G., b. 29 June 1824; d. 18 Sept. 1825.
HARRIET E., b. 13 Apr. 1827; d. 7 Oct. 1830.
BENJAMIN F., b. 1 May 1829; d. 5 Oct. 1830.

1181

RICHARD[6] CHASE (Joseph,[5] Moses,[4] Stephen,[3] Ens. Moses[2]), born in Pelham, N. H., 9 May 1793; died in Dec. 1870. He married (1) MARY JANE GAULT who died about 1830. He married (2) in Antrim, N. H., 12 Apr. 1831, LUCINDA SAWYER, daughter of Enoch and Sarah (Little) Sawyer. They lived in Bedford and Hillsborough, N. H. She was born in Goffstown, N. H., 9 Aug. 1788; died in Hillsborough, 8 June 1852, aged 64.

Children by first wife, born in Bedford:

FANNY,[7] b. 23 Oct. 1817; m. 28 May 1833, Daniel Vose of Bedford. She d. in New Boston, N. H., 24 Feb. 1873.
2564. JOSEPH, d. in Hartford, Conn., 1869.
MARY JANE, m. Gordon B. Wilson of Hillsborough.
2565. JAMES, b. 4 Sept. 1822; m. in Nashua, N. H., 4 June 1846, Sarah J. Heath.
JOHN, d. unm.
ELIZABETH, b. 12 Aug. 1826; m. 22 Dec. 1852, James H. Ray of Hillsborough; she d. 1 July 1906.

Children by the second wife:

ABIGAIL, m. 29 July 1855, Ira C. Connor of Henniker, N. H.
LUCY (twin), m. John Rogers of Warner, N. H.

1182

JAMES[6] CHASE (Joseph,[5] Moses,[4] Stephen,[3] Ens. Moses[2]), born in Pelham, N. H., 31 Dec. 1802; married SARAH FRENCH of Canaan, Vt. They removed to Jackson, Mich.

Children:

CAROLINE.[7]
JAMES MONROE, d. in a Confederate prison in the Civil War.
ANGELINE.
PERSIS.

1183

BENJAMIN[6] CHASE (Benjamin Durant,[5] Moses,[4] Stephen,[3] Ens. Moses[2]), born about 1794. One Benjamin Chase died in Acworth, N. H., 23 Apr. 1865, aged 71. His death report states that he was single. No marriage has been found but it is stated that he had two daughters and a son and that he lived at some period in Alstead, N. H.

Children:

AMANDA M.,[7] m. Horace Richardson of Alstead; removed to Acworth in 1853.
SALLY, possibly, who m. in Hanover, N. H., 3 Aug. 1841, George Huntington Green.
2566. WILLIAM H., lived in Hudson, N. H.

1184

MOSES[6] CHASE (Benjamin Durant,[5] Moses,[4] Stephen,[3] Ens. Moses[2]), born about 1795; probably died in Alstead, N. H., 14 Jan. 1858 ,aged 66. Another Moses Chase, died in Alstead, 9 Jan. 1852, aged 67. The last named man could not have been the son of Benjamin Durant Chase by his wife Polly Flanders. His uncle Moses[5] Chase (Family 420) lived in Alstead, 1789 to 1813. Moses[6] Chase and BETSEY WOODS, both of Acworth, were married in Marlow, N. H., 25 Feb. 1816. She was daughter of William C. and Nancy (Priest) Woods of Acworth. They lived in Acworth.

Children:

2567. ANDROS,[7] m. Huldah Clark; dau. of Ephraim and Huldah (Williams) Clark of Acworth.
NANCY A., m. Peletiah Clark, brother to Huldah.
2558. GEORGE MORTIMER, b. 5 Jan. 1836.

1185

ANDREW[6] CHASE (Benjamin Durant,[5] Moses,[4] Stephen,[3] Ens. Moses[2]), born probably in Merrimack, N. H., about 1800; married ———CLARK. They lived in Alstead, N. H.

1186

BENJAMIN[6] CHASE (Benjamin,[5] Joshua,[4] Stephen,[3] Ens. Moses[2]), born in Nottingham West (now Hudson), N. H., 19 Dec. 1791; died in Pelham, N. H., 14 Dec. 1836. He married in Pelham, 11 Feb. 1823, PHILENA GAGE of Pelham. She was a daughter of Benjamin and Joanna Gage of Pelham, born 20 Sept. 1800; alive in 1871. Mr. Chase and two children were buried in the Gumpus Cemetery in Pelham, where they lived.

Administration on his estate was granted to Samuel M. Richardson of Pelham, 3 Jan. 1837. Her thirds were set off to widow Philena in which the widow Dolly Chase had a life interest. (Hillsborough Probate 37:324 and 41:555). The farm was held in common with Joshua Chase, Solomon D. Chase, Samuel Chase, Mary Chase, widow Julia Marshall, Daniel Ordway and his wife Dolly, Jonathan Hills and his wife Hannah, Timothy A. Holt and his wife Sarah, and Philena Chase was appointed guardian to the minor children of the deceased, David, William Gage and Benjamin Gage, 6 June 1848. (Ibid. 45:15).

Children, born in Pelham:

JOANNA,[7] b. 20 Apr. 1824; d. 26 July 1826.

BENJAMIN G., b. 24 Feb. 1826; d. 24 Mar. 1826.

2568.   DAVID, b. 26 Mar. 1827; m. 30 May 1849, Maria Marsh; b. 29 Mar. 1827; lived in Lowell, 1871.

2569.   WILLIAM GAGE, b. 21 Feb. 1829; m. (1) 11 Dec. 1851, Rhoda J. Marsh, who d. 24 May 1852; m. (2) 4 Dec. 1853, Lydia A. Grant; lived in Lowell.

2570.   BENJAMIN G., b. 8 Feb. 1835; m. 1862, Hannah J. Wyman; in 13th N. H. Vol. Civil War; d. 14 Sept. 1864, aged 29.

1187

JOSHUA[6] CHASE (Benjamin,[5] Joshua,[4] Stephen,[3] Ens. Moses[2]), born in Nottingham West (now Hudson), N. H., 5 Sept. 1798; married 26 Oct. 1834, ANNA HOLT, daughter of Timothy and Anna Holt of Bethel, Me. She was born in Bethel, 21 Dec. 1801. They lived in Hudson till 1840 and then in Bethel.

Children, first born in Hudson:

TIMOTHY HOLT,[7] b. 12 Nov. 1835; never married; d. in Colo.

HENRY ELMORE, b. 24 Sept. 1837; d. 14 June 1840.

2571.   HENRY ELMORE, b. 29 Apr. 1841; d. in the army at Newburn, N. C., 5 July 1863.

2572.   WILLIAM WIRT, b. 13 Aug. 1846; m. 19 Feb. 1879, Sarah Lucinda Holt.

1188

MOODY[6] CHASE (Benjamin,[5] Joshua,[4] Stephen,[3] Ens. Moses[2]), born in Nottingham West (now Hudson), N. H., 19 Mar. 1800; died in Hudson, 5 Feb. 1861. He married 25 Nov. 1827, SUBMIT MARSHALL. She was born 10 June 1810; died in Hudson, 10 Nov. 1863. They lived in Litchfield, Grafton, Orange and Hudson—all in N. H.

Children, first born in Litchfield, second in Grafton, third to fifth in Orange, last two in Hudson:

SARAH,[7] b. 3 Oct. 1829.

2573.   SAMUEL, b. 1 June 1833; m. in Nashua, N. H., 16 Nov. 1862, Harriet Ellen Brown. One child; living in Hudson in 1873.

ELVIRA, b. 3 June 1835; m. 1 Apr. 1862, George Hamlet; lived in Nashua, N. H., 1873.

MARY E., b .6 Nov. 1837; lived unm. in Nashua, 1873.

CAROLINE F., b. 5 Sept. 1839; lived unm. in Nashua, 1873.

2574.   CHARLES, b. 5 June 1841; m. 18 July 1867, Rosa A. Lenaham; lived in Merrimack, N. H., 1873.

2575.   GEORGE HENRY, b. 1 Nov. 1847; d. 29 Sept. 1869.

1189

SOLOMON D.[6] CHASE (Benjamin,[5] Joshua,[4] Stephen,[3] Ens. Moses[2]), born in Nottingham West (now Hudson), N. H., 6 Oct.

1807; married OLIVE RICHARDSON. They lived in Lowell. Administration on his estate was granted 18 Sept. 1849, and his widow Olive had her allowance, 3 Dec. 1850. No mention of his children in his estate. (Middlesex Probate, 29,113). He died in Lowell, 15 Sept. 1849, aged 40 y. 23 d. He was a blacksmith.

Children:

    DAUGHTER.
    DAUGHTER.

1190

SAMUEL[6] CHASE (Benjamin,[5] Joshua,[4] Stephen,[3] Ens. Moses[2]), born in Nottingham West (now Hudson), N. H., 11 Dec. 1810. He married LUCY HUBBARD PARKER, daughter of Josiah and Nancy (Bailey) Parker, born 11 Sept. 1811. They lived in Pelham, N. H., where he died, 25 May 1861, aged 50. She died, 17 Sept. 1895.

Children, born in Pelham:

    EDWARD MILTON,[7] scalded to death in childhood.
    SON, d. in infancy.
    EMMONS W., d. young.
    LUCY ELLEN, b. 18 Aug. 1843; d. 29 Nov. 1865.
    MARY L., b. 17 Dec. 1846; d. 4 Mar. 1885.
2576.   FRANK NORTON, b. 1849.

1191

BENJAMIN FRANKLIN[6] CHASE (Jacob,[5] Joshua,[4] Stephen,[3] Ens. Moses[2]), born in Hudson, N. H., 28 Dec. 1807; married (1) 28 Aug. 1834, SARAH HODGDON, daughter of Reuben and Hannah (Walker) Hodgdon, born 22 Oct. 1806. She died in Hudson, 17 Mar. 1855, aged 48. He married (2) 17 Apr. 1856, MARY M. THOMAS of Lowell, born 26 Jan. 1813. He served in the Civil War in Co. I, 13th N. H. Reg't. They lived in Nashua, N. H.

Children by first wife, born in Hudson:

2577.   GILMAN FRANKLIN,[7] b. 6 June 1835; m. 20 Mar. 1861, Mary C. Hobbs; lived in Nashua.
    CORNELIA, b. 23 June 1846; m. 24 Dec. 1866, William C. Marshall.

1192

CAPT. JOSEPH[6] CHASE (Stephen,[5] Jacob,[4] Lt. Joseph,[3] Ens. Moses[2]), born in Chester, N. H., 17 Aug. 1789; died there, 14 Sept. 1841. He married in Chester, 4 Nov. 1817, MEHITABLE HALL, daughter of Maj. Benjamin and Abigail (Emerson) Hall of Chester, who was born in Chester, 6 Jan. 1794, and died there, 7 June 1882, aged 88. He was selectman of Chester, 1833-35, and representative to the legislature, 1839-40. They lived in Chester.

Children, born in Chester:

2578.   STEPHEN,[7] b. 19 Aug. 1818; m. 17 Aug. 1845, Martha J. Squires. He was a mechanic and d. in Chicopee, 2 Feb. 1855. One daughter who m. Horace W. Eddy.
2579.   CHARLES, b. 17 Dec. 1820; m. (1) 16 Dec. 1847, Caroline[8] Chase, dau. of Benjamin[7] (Family 1185), b. 14 Sept. 1828; d. 10 Aug. 1849; m. (2) 8 Apr. 1852, Amelia Jameson Under-

hill, dau. of John and Molly[7] (Chase) Underhill, b. 17 Apr. 1828; d. 25 Feb. 1859; m. (3) 7 Sept. 1859, Amanda Underhill, sister to his second wife, b. 1 Mar. 1831; d. 12 Jan. 1901. He was selectman of Chester, 1879, 1880, 1882, 1885 and 1886 and d. 17 May 1892.

His eldest son *John Carroll*,[8] b. in Chester, 26 July 1849, was educated at Chester Academy, Pinkerton Academy at Derry, N. H., and Massachusetts Institute of Technology; became a civil engineer and was connected with construction work in Manchester, N. H., Boston, New York City and Wilmington, N. C., being a member of the State Board of Health the last four years of his living there, and in 1895 removed to Derry, N. H., to become associated with his mother's brother, Benjamin[8] Chase, in a manufacturing business, and on the incorporation several years later became the general manager and treasurer, which last-named position he still holds. Trustee Pinkerton Academy since 1890, fellow of the American Public Health Association, member of the American Society of Civil Engineers and many other like organizations. President of the New England Historic Genealogical Society since 1921 and member of numerous family, historical and patriotic societies. Knight Templar and Odd Fellow. Author of *The History of Chester including Auburn*, 1926, *A Supplement to the History of Old Chester*, and compiler of this genealogy. He m. 21 Oct. 1871, Mary Lizzie Durgin, dau. of Samuel and Lydia Ann (Emery) Durgin of West Newbury who was b. 16 May 1852 and d. 7 Dec. 1927. Their daughters Caroline Louise[9] and Alice Durgin[9] are graduates of Pinkerton Academy and Wellesley College, the elder being the wife of Rafraele Lorini, M. D., of Coronado, Calif., and the younger the wife of Prof. Samuel Cate Prescott, Sc. D., head of the Department of Biology and Public Health of the Massachusetts Institute of Technology of which he is a graduate. Three children, *Robert Sedgewick*,[10] *Samuel Chase*[10] and *Eleanor*[10] *Prescott*.

The youngest son, *Charles Burnside*,[8] b. 11 July 1867; m. 2 Sept. 1911, Sarah Russell MacMurphy, dau. of Rev. Jesse Gibson and Mary Lucy (James) MacMurphy, b. 29 Sept. 1871. They reside in Derry. (History of Chester, N. H., 1926.)

2580. GEORGE WASHINGTON, b. 15 May 1823; m. in Auburn, 13 Mar. 1846, Lydia Dickey; lived on the homestead in Chester; d. there 5 Dec. 1891. Twelve children.

2581. BENJAMIN HALL, b. 23 Nov. 1825; m. 28 Nov. 1850, Cynthia H. Sherman; lived in Manchester, N. H.; d. there 30 June 1906. One child d. young.

2582. JOHN, b. 12 Apr. 1828; killed in the battle of Gettysburg, July 1863.

2583. JOSEPH WARREN, b. 2 Dec. 1830; m. 20 Oct. 1853, Mary P. Edwards; lived in Worcester and Chester; d. in Chester, 9 Feb. 1920. Their youngest son, *Edward Curtis*,[8] b. 27 June 1870; living in Chester (1928), unm.

HARRIET A., b. 30 Mar. 1833; m. 5 May 1859, John W. Silver of Deerfield, N. H., and d. there 28 July 1919. Three children d. without issue.

1193

JACOB[6] CHASE (Stephen,[5] Jacob,[4] Lt. Joseph,[3] Ens. Moses[2]), born in Chester, N. H., 26 Feb. 1797; died there 13 Nov. 1861. He married (1) in Exeter, N. H., 21 Mar. 1827, HANNAH C. JAMES of Hampton, N. H. She died in Chester, 9 July 1850, aged 49. He married (2) 18 May 1851, NANCY HAZELTON, daughter of Thomas and Lucretia T. (Hills) Hazelton, born 25 July 1813; died in Chester, 3 Oct. 1874. They lived on the Chase homestead in Chester, where Jacob[4] settled in 1751. He was representative to the legislature in 1859.

Children by first wife, born in Chester:

GEORGE JAMES,[7] b. 25 Dec. 1827; d. unm. 28 Oct. 1861.
MARY AUGUSTA, b. 23 Sept. 1829; d. unm. 24 July 1855.

Children by second wife, born in Chester:

LAURA JANE, b. 24 Oct. 1854; d. 5 Dec. 1861.
ISABEL CRAWFORD, b. 20 Aug. 1857; m. 19 Jan. 1886, George M. Clark of Manchester, N. H. Children: *Leroy F.*,[8] b. 10 Dec. 1886; m. 18 Sept. 1911, Katherine Smith; *Harold*,[8] b. 24 July 1889; m. 10 Sept. 1913, Olive Rowe; *Eugene*,[8] b. 3 June 1891; *Morris Clark*,[8] b. 31 Dec. 1896; m. 5 Sept. 1919, Eloise Marston.

1194

HENRY FRANKLIN[6] CHASE (Stephen,[5] Jacob,[4] Lt. Joseph[3], Ens. Moses[2]), born in Chester, N. H., 30 Aug. 1808; died 20 Mar. 1867. He married in Claremont, 12 Nov 1839, ABIGAIL FOGG MITCHELL, born 9 Dec. 1812; died 12 Oct. 1883. They lived in Chester, N. H., until 1855 when they removed to Westminster, Vt. He was a selectman in 1848-49-50.

Children, born in Chester:

ANNA MARIA,[7] b. 1 June 1843; m. 15 Oct. 1874, Julius N. Morse of Keene, N. H., editor of the *Cheshire Republican*; d. without issue.
ABBY, b. 30 June 1846; m. 9 May 1880, Cyrus M. Cook; she d. without issue 16 Jan. 1919.
STEPHEN, b. 14 July 1849; living in Hinsdale, N. H., unm., 1928.

1195

WILLIAM[6] CHASE (Josiah,[5] Jacob,[4] Lt. Joseph,[3] Ens. Moses[2]), born in Chester ,N. H., 21 July 1796; married (1) in Springfield, N. H., 26 Oct. 1826, LOIS CLEMENT, daughter of David and Thankful (Howe) Clement, born in Grantham, N. H., 7 June 1799; married (2) SOPHIA KNIGHT; married (3) DOROTHY SPRINGER. They lived in Grafton and Grantham.

Child by second wife:

LOUISA SOPHIA,[7] b. 4 Mar. 1836.

Child by the third wife:

2584. WILLIAM HENRY, b. 11 July 1838.

1196

HIRAM[6] CHASE (Josiah,[5] Jacob,[4] Lt. Joseph,[3] Ens. Moses[2]), born in Chester, N. H., 4 Jan. 1806; married 8 Feb. 1838, BETSEY MOR-RILL. They lived in Grantham, Manchester and Derry, N. H. He died in Charlestown, 18 Dec. 1882, which was reported back to Manchester with age given as 76 y. 11 m. 17 d.

Children, born in Grantham:

SARAH JANE,[7] b. 19 Sept. 1838; m. 24 Apr. 1861, Henry M. Sanborn of Concord, N. H. Two children.

ABIGAIL ANN, b. 9 Feb. 1839; m. (1) 7 Jan. 1865, Charles F. Harding of Charlestown; m. (2) Jonathan Homer Edgerly. No children.

HENRY FRANKLIN, b. 12 Sept. 1841; d. 1 Apr. 1859.

HIRAM ORMSBEE, b. 22 Nov. 1843; killed on picket duty at Drury's Bluff, 16 May 1864; Co. A 10th N. H. Regt.

PRUDENCE HILLS, b. 26 Mar. 1845; m. 27 Sept. 1867, Gilman M. Stokes of Boston, and d. 31 Mar. 1915. No children.

2585. CHARLES JOSIAH, b. 11 Dec. 1846; m. 4 Feb. 1868, Mary A. Durgin of Groton, N. H. Two children.

1197

AMOS JOSIAH[6] CHASE (Josiah,[5] Jacob,[4] Lt. Josiah,[3] Ens. Moses[2]), born in Chester, N. H., 4 July 1809; died in Manchester, N. H., 30 Aug. 1880, aged 71 y. 1 m. 26 d. He married in Grantham, N. H., 22 Nov. 1831, LAVINA DUNBAR who was born in Grantham, 14 Oct. 1806, daughter of Calvin and Sarah Dunbar. She died in Manchester, 26 Sept. 1890, aged 83 y. 11 m. 12 d. They lived in Manchester and in Grantham.

Children, born in Grantham:

2586. ORLANDO DARWIN,[7] b. 23 June 1833; m. 17 May 1856, Eunice Orrilla Griggs, b. 27 Sept. 1831; lived in Canada.

LORENZO DOW, b. 3 Aug. 1834; d. 13 Aug. 1834.

2587. FREDERIC DUNBAR, b. 11 July 1837; m. 15 Nov. 1860, Lydia J. B. Barrett, b. 10 Dec. 1836.

LUCINDA LAVINA, b. 20 Nov. 1845; m. Charles W. Temple of Manchester, and d. 25 Sept. 1908. Two sons d. unm.

1198

THOMAS[6] CHASE (Parker,[5] Joseph,[4] Joseph,[3] Ens. Moses[2]), born in Newbury (now West Newbury), — Mar. 1779. He married (1) in Pembroke, N. H., 1 Apr. 1810, MEHITABLE HEAD of Pembroke who died in 1812. He married (2) in Belfast, Me., 13 Apr. 1813, KEZIAH ELLIS of Jackson Plantation, Me. They removed to Monroe, Me., in 1811.

Child by first wife:

ELIZA,[7] d. 1812.

Children by second wife, born in Monroe:

REBECCA, b. — Mar. 1814.

NANCY, b. — Feb. 1816.

2588. THOMAS, b. — June 1818.

MEHITABLE, b. — June 1821.

ELIZABETH, b. — May 1824.

2589.   GEORGE W., b. — July 1826.
      LYDIA, b. — Sept. 1828.
      HANNAH, b. — Nov. 1832.
      KEZIAH J., b. — Mary 1834.
2590.   THOMAS J., b. — Aug. 1836.

1199

JACOB[6] CHASE (Parker,[5] Joseph,[4] Joseph,[3] Ens. Moses[2]), born in Newbury (now West Newbury), 23 June 1782; died in Havana, Cuba, after 20 Oct. 1818. He married in Newburyport, 25 Sept. 1803, ALICE HODGES. They lived in Newbury and in Newburyport.

Children, first born in Newbury, others in Newburyport:

2591.   RUFUS PARKER,[7] b. 1 Apr. 1804.
2592.   JACOB, b. 28 June 1805.
      CAROLINE, b. 4 Jan. 1807.

1200

AMOS[6] CHASE (Parker,[5] Joseph,[4] Joseph,[3] Ens. Moses[2]), born in Newbury (now West Newbury), 4 Mar. 1794; died in Auburn, N. H., 5 June 1882, aged 88 y. 1 m. 1 d. He married in Chester, N. H., 8 July 1817, RUTH KELLEY, daughter of Dr. Ezekiel Hale and Hannah (Hazelton) Kelley, born in Chester, 2 Oct. 1791; died in Auburn 6 June 1871, aged 79. He was a mechanic and lived in that part of Chester which is now Auburn.

Children, born in Chester (now Auburn):

      HANNAH HALE KELLEY,[7] b. 3 Sept. 1817; d. unm. 1898.
2593.   JACOB PARKER, b. 14 Sept. 1823; m. Sabra Dolbear, 21 Oct. 1852; d. 18 Apr. 1883, age 53 y. 9 m. He d. 5 Apr. 1907. (Family 1113)
      ALMENA ANN, b. 16 Mar. 1827; m. Dennis Dunavan; d. 19 Sept. 1892.
      EDWARD CLARK, b. 6 Aug. 1833; d. 7 June 1847.

1201

DEA. JOSEPH[6] CHASE (Joseph,[5] Joseph,[4] Lt. Joseph,[3] Ens. Moses[2]), born in Newbury (now West Newbury), 22 Dec. 1801; died in Hampstead, N. H., 28 Mar. 1872. He married 5 June 1839, ELISABETH MORSE. He was a Deacon of the Congregational Church of Hampstead from 16 Aug. 1859 to the time of his death, having joined the church there 5 May 1839. His wife was the daughter of Dea. Robert Morse and was born in Derry, N. H., 11 June 1812; died in Hampstead, 3 Aug. 1862.

Children, born in Hampstead:

      EMMA ALICE,[7] b. 10 May 1843; d. 15 May 1844.
      MARY ELIZABETH, b. 11 Mar. 1846; m. Silas W. Tenney; she d. 15 Mar. 1875, in Danville, N. Y.
      JOSEPH, b. 15 Nov. 1849; d. 28 Nov. 1869.

1202

JOSEPH TOWNE[6] CHASE (Caleb,[5] Joseph,[4] Lt. Joseph,[3] Ens. Moses[2]), born 12 Apr. 1806; died in Newport, N. H., 5 Jan. 1856, aged 50 y. He married in Newport, 21 Mar. 1832, ELIZABETH D.

ALLEN, daughter of Mark W. and Betsey (Webber) Allen of Hopkinton, N. H., and Newport, who was born 20 Mar. 1812.   They lived in Newport.

Children, born in Newport:

2594.   ARTHUR B.,[7] b. 3 Jan. 1833; m. Ann Richards.
           ARETUS T., b. 30 Oct. 1835; d. 23 June 1854.
2595.   HENRY M., b. 8 Mar. 1841; m. Cornelia Smith; he was a professor in a Conservatory of Music in Minneapolis, Minn.
2596.   GEORGE A., b. 6 May 1843; m. Augusta Eastman.
           HELEN FRANCES, b. 8 May 1848; adopted by Judge Albert S. Waite of Newport and assumed his name; m. Stephen Vosburg of Greenfield; d. in Apr. 1876.
2597.   JOSEPH E., b. 17 June 1852.

1203

ETHAN SMITH[6] CHASE (Caleb,[5] Joseph,[4] Lt. Joseph,[3] Ens. Moses[2]), born in Hopkinton, N. H., 15 Aug. 1811; married (1) MARY DODGE of Lempster, N. H. He married (2) in Newport, N. H., 24 Oct. 1844, SUSAN D. HOYT, daughter of Joseph S. and Judith (Davis) Hoyt, born 7 Oct. 1828. They lived in Newport.

Child by first wife, born in Newport:

           MARION S.,[7] b. 25 Jan. 1840; graduate of Mt. Holyoke Seminary.

Children by second wife, born in Newport:

2598.   ALVAH S., b. 17 Dec. 1846; m. Clara Barnard.
           ADDIE H., b. 31 Dec. 1849; graduated at Kimball Union Academy in 1870.
           LOUISA, b. 19 Aug. 1855; graduate of Kimball Union Academy in 1876.
           NELLIE G., b. 4 Sept. 1862.

1204

INCREASE SUMNER[6] CHASE (Jonathan,[5] Joseph,[4] Lt. Joseph,[3] Ens. Moses[2]), born in what is now West Newbury, 29 Oct. 1798; married in Newbury, 14 May 1818, MARIA NOYES, daughter of John and Elizabeth (Pillsbury) Noyes, born in Newbury, 23 Jan. 1802. They lived in West Newbury.

Children, born in what is now West Newbury:

2599.   MOSES BROWN,[7] b. 1818; m. Elizabeth P. George.
           ANN MARION, b. 1822; m. Osgood Brown of Bethel, Me.
2600.   RUFUS HILLS, b. 1823; b. (1) 11 Aug. 1844, Sarah Hodge Rogers of Byfield.
           ENOCH DOLE, b. about 1825; d. 11 Feb. 1825.
           CAROLINE HOUGHTON, b. 1826; m. Frank Brown Stanwood of Lowell; she d. 13 Dec. 1895. Five children.
2601.   ENOCH DOLE, b. 1829; m. (1) Hannah Jane Carr; m. (2) ——— Sibley.
           BETSEY BROWN, b. 1836; d. unm. 22 July 1896.
           MARIA SUMNER, b. 1841; never married.
2602.   INCREASE SUMNER, b. 7 May 1847; d. 18 Apr. 1865.

1205

STANIFORD[6] CHASE (Jonathan,[5] Joseph,[4] Lt. Joseph,[3] Ens. Moses[2]), born about 1802; married (intention in West Newbury, 1 Apr. 1826) SARAH DOLE[7] CHASE, born 1806, daughter of John[6] and Betsey (Carleton) Chase. (Family 592). She married (2) Moses G. Merrill. They lived in West Newbury. He died in West Newbury, 9 July 1838, aged 36.

Children, born in West Newbury:

CASTINE BARON,[7] b. 22 Jan. 1827; d. 20 Dec. 1846.
AUGUSTUS SULLIVAN, b. 17 July 1828; d. 31 July 1848.
STANIFORD SABINE, b. 29 May 1830; d. 29 June 1838, a. 8 y.
BETSEY CARLETON, b. 20 Aug. 1832; d. 31 Mar. 1838.
STANIFORD SABINE, bp. 2 Sept. 1838; d. 15 Nov. 1838.
SARAH ELIZABETH, b. 10 Jan. 1834; m. 10 Oct. 1852, Francis Dean[7] Chase. (Family 626)
SUSAN BROWN, bp. 5 Mar. 1837; d. 25 Sept. 1838.

1206

HANNIBAL HAMILTON[6] CHASE (Jonathan,[5] Joseph,[4] Lt. Joseph,[3] Ens. Moses[2]), born in what is now West Newbury, 18 Aug. 1810; died in Baltimore, Md., 19 Apr. 1882. He married (1) about 1836, SUSANNAH DISNEY, born 20 Dec. 1816; died 2 Feb. 1850. He married (2) in West Newbury, 20 Dec. 1864, SARAH REBECCA NEWELL, daughter of Moses and Sally (Moody) Newell, born in West Newbury, 4 Dec. 1827; died in Baltimore, 27 Dec. 1914.

Children by first wife, born in Baltimore:

SUSANNAH,[7] b. 21 May 1837; d. 22 Feb. 1915; m. 15 Dec. 1864, Joseph Prout of Anne Arundel Co., Md., who d. 15 Dec. 1903. Three children.
ISABEL, b. 8 Apr. 1843; d. 10 Sept. 1887.
EMMA, b. 2 May 1845; d. 23 Jan. 1887.
2602a. HANNIBAL HAMILTON, b. 1848; d. 23 Mar. 1889; m. in West Newbury, 9 June 1874, Frances E. Newell. Five children.

Children by second wife, born in Baltimore:

SARAH NEWELL, b. 10 Sept. 1866; m. 24 Oct. 1909, James Shriver.
2602b. EDWARD STANIFORD, b. 10 Oct. 1867; m. 12 May 1890, Annie Adams.
REBECCA HANNAH, b. 16 Feb. 1869; m. 27 Dec. 1894, Harry S. Vincent, b. 23 Sept. 1869. Children: *Rebecca Newell*[8] *Vincent*, b. 25 July 1896; *Helen Peyton*[8] *Vincent*, b. 3 Jan. 1899; m. 21 Oct. 1922, E. Milton Lilly of Ridgewood, N. J. Two children.
NEWELL DICKSON, b. 16 Jan. 1871; m. 20 Dec. 1905, Nina Reid; four children.

1206a

OSGOOD[6] CHASE (Jonathan,[5] Joseph,[4] Lt. Joseph,[3] Ens. Moses[2]), born in Newbury (now West Newbury) about 1807; died in West Newbury, 19 May 1830, aged 23. He married ANN TUTTLE. They lived in Boston.

Child, born in Boston:

OSGOOD,[7] b. 25 Nov. 1828; d. 20 May 1909; m. (1) in 1855, Sarah Elizabeth Hanhaford, b. in 1836; d. 1906; m. (2) Lillie Bruce. Their son *Frank*,[8] b. in Somerville, 26 June 1856; m. 4 Dec. 1879, Sue Taylor Mitchell, b. in Lafayette Co., Mo., 16 Dec. 1858. Children: Sue Mitchell,[9] b. 25 Feb. 1881; Frank Mitchell,[9] b. 2 June 1882; Lily Bruce,[9] b. 15 Dec. 1883; Mildred Elizabeth,[9] b. 29 Feb. 1888. They live in San Diego, Calif.

1207

HORACE LUMMUS[6] CHASE (Jonathan,[5] Joseph,[4] Lt. Joseph,[3] Ens. Moses[2]), born in West Newbury in 1815; died there, 13 July 1869. He married (1) in West Newbury, 1 Oct. 1835, ELVIRA MELVINA[7] CHASE, daughter of John[6] and Betsey (Carleton) Chase, (Family 592), born in 1816; died in West Newbury, 2 Oct. 1846, aged 30. He married (2) ROWENA ROXANA CHASE, sister to his first wife. She died in 1867, aged 42. They lived in West Newbury.

Children, born in West Newbury:

2603. HORACE LUMMUS JR.,[7] b. 27 Mar. 1836; lived in Groveland.
    ADELADE CLIFTON, b. 12 Mar. 1838; d. 11 May 1839.
    ADELADE CLIFFORD, d. 23 May 1846, aged 8 y. 2 m. 11 d.
2604. JEHU, b. 23 Jan. 1844.
2605. OTIS GRAY, b. 1 Oct. 1846; adopted by his uncle Harrison Gray Otis[7] Chase; d. in West Newbury, 24 Feb. 1912; m. there, 1 Jan. 1870, Sarah Abby Follansbee, dau. of Somerby Chase and Mary Abby (Whittier) Follansbee, b. in West Newbury, 25 Jan. 1851; d. there, 28 May 1913. Their son, *Harry Gray*,[8] b. in West Newbury, 10 Sept. 1871; Lieutenant Colonel in the Quartermaster's Corps, Massachusetts National Guards; m. 23 Nov. 1897, Mary Franklin Cook, dau. of Col. Benjamin Franklin and Evelina Tuck (Leach) Cook, b. in Gloucester, 24 Mar. 1871. Their children are: Lt. Harrison Gray Otis,[9] b. 4 May 1899; m. 26 Oct. 1924, Ruth Tenney; Evelyn Abby,[9] b. 6 Jan. 1901; m. 6 Mar. 1926, Lt. Vaughan John Weatherby. Other children were *Herbert Somerby*,[8] *Eliza Isabel*,[8] m. John W. Macdonald, and *Edgar Sawyer*[8] *Chase*.

1208

JEHU[6] CHASE (Jonathan,[5] Joseph,[4] Joseph,[3] Ens. Moses[2]), born in what is now West Newbury, 1814; died there 25 Mar. 1854. He married in West Newbury, 10 June 1828, CAROLINE HOUGHTON[7] CHASE, born 1808; died 23 Dec. 1877, aged 68 y. 9 m.; daughter of John[6] and Betsey (Carleton) Chase of West Newbury. (Family 592). She married (2) Gen. Solomon Lowe of Boxford. They lived in West Newbury.

Children, born in West Newbury:

    JULIA DE ROUBIGNE,[7] b. 6 Sept. 1830; d. 19 June 1844.
2606. JOHN HANNIBAL, b. 22 Nov. 1832; d. 17 Jan. 1892.
    HENRY OSGOOD, b. 19 Oct. 1835; d. 31 Jan. 1854.
    CAROLINE M., d. 4 Feb. 1849, a. 6 y. 5 m.
    JULIA DE ROUBIGNE, b. 15 July 1846; d. 13 May 1871, aged 24 y. 10 m.

1209

WILLIAM STARK[6] CHASE (John Webster,[5] Moody,[4] Lt. Joseph,[3] Ens. Moses[2]), born 22 Feb. 1797; married 29 Dec. 1823, LAVINA KENDRICK of Lyme, N. H., who was born 24 Jan. 1793 ,and died 18 Sept. 1873. They lived in Piermont, N. H.

Children, probably born in Piermont:

    JULIA ANN,[7] b. 2 Feb. 1825; m. 16 Sept. 1845, Luther W. Mead of Piermont.

2607. WILLIAM CARLOS, b. 10 Aug. 1827; m. 4 Aug. 1856, Hannah Waldron.

    JOHN STILLMAN, b. 21 Mar. 1829; d. 26 May 1832.

2608. LEWIS KENDRICK, b. 3 Sept. 1831; m. 4 July 1854, Rubie K. Woodward of Piermont.

2609. ASA PERRY, b. 9 Jan. 1837; m. 23 Jan. 1866, Mary J. Cochran of Piermont; two children.

1210

MOODY[6] CHASE (John Webster,[5] Moody,[4] Lt. Joseph,[3] Ens. Moses[2]), born 28 Sept. 1804; married (1) 26 Nov. 1831, ELMIRA KENDRICK who died 14 Dec. 1870. He married (2) NANCY[6] (CHASE) CURRIER, widow of Barnard Currier and daughter of Joseph[5] and Nancy (Eaton) Chase of Canaan, N. H. (Family 433). She was born 22 Sept. 1811. They lived in Piermont, N. H.

Children by first wife, born in Piermont:

    ANNE,[7] b. 23 Dec. 1832; d. 8 Apr. 1842.

    AMANDA C., b. 30 May 1834.

    ADNA K., b. 9 Dec. 1838.

    LORA, b. 26 July 1841.

    TWINS, b. and d. 27 June 1844.

2610. JOHN, b. 14 June 1846.

1211

CALEB C.[6] CHASE (John Webster,[5] Moody,[4] Lt. Joseph,[3] Ens. Moses[2]), born in Lyme, N. H., 26 Dec. 1810; died in Manchester, N. H., 13 Aug. 1853. He married 1 Aug. 1838, LORA GOODELL. She married (2) David Hurlburt. They lived in Lyme and Manchester.

Children, born in Lyme:

    ROYAL STORRS,[7] b. 9 July 1839; d. 22 Apr. 1844.

    ADINO BURTON, b. 9 June 1843; graduated at Dartmouth College in 1866; d. unm. in Crawfordville, Ind., 14 Dec. 1889.

2611. CARLOS MILTON, b. 1 Sept. 1845; living in Buckley, Ill., 1875, then unmarried.

    SON (not named), b. 15 Dec. 1846; d. 16 Dec. 1846.

1212

MOODY[6] CHASE (Joseph,[5] Moody,[4] Lt. Joseph,[3] Ens. Moses[2]), born in Chester, N. H., 5 Mar. 1800; married (1) in Canaan, N. H., 24 Sept. 1829, LUCY H. WALWORTH, daughter of Charles and Marianne (Pillsbury) Walworth, born in Canaan, 9 Apr. 1801 and died 21 Nov. 1861. He married (2) 18 Feb. 1863, ELIZA JANE WALWORTH, sister of his first wife, born in Canaan, 20 Oct. 1810. They lived in Canaan, and then in Williamsfield, Ashtabula Co., Ohio, where he was living in 1870.

Child, born in Canaan:

> OSCAR F.,[7] b. 24 June 1831; never married; living in Williamsfield, Ohio, in 1870.

1213

JESSE EATON[6] CHASE (Joseph,[5] Moody,[4] Lt. Joseph,[3] Ens. Moses[2]), born in Chester, N. H., 2 Sept. 1801; died in Carthage, Ohio, 4 Dec. 1877. He married in Canaan, N. H., 14 Apr. 1822, HANNAH M. JOHNSON of Dorchester, N. H. They removed from Dorchester to Carthage, Athens Co., Ohio, in Sept. 1833.

Children, born in New Hampshire:

2612.   WILLIAM S.,[7] b. 27 Aug. 1822; m. 29 Dec. 1853, Tabitha Tribet, b. in N. J., 6 July 1830; lived in Carthage.

ALVIRA M., b. 2 May 1824; m. 1 Oct. 1846, Caleb Wells; lived in Troy, Ohio.

LYDIA JOHNSON, b. 29 Nov. 1826; d. unm. 29 Dec. 1857.

2613.   JOSEPH, b. 17 Mar. 1828; m. 1 Dec. 1857, Almira Lottridge, b. 1 Mar. 1839; lived in Carthage.

1214

DAVID E.[6] CHASE (Joseph,[5] Moody,[4] Lt. Joseph,[3] Ens. Moses[2]), born in Chester, N. H., 23 Mar. 1805; married 29 July 1837, LOUISA M. BALCOM, daughter of Thaddeus and Mary (Melvin) Balcom, born 1 Sept. 1816. He was a manufacturer and lived in Lowell.

Child:

2614.   GEORGE ALBERT,[7] b. 7 Nov. 1840.

1215

HORACE[6] CHASE (Joseph,[5] Moody,[4] Lt. Joseph,[3] Ens. Moses[2]), born in Chester, N. H., 18 Mar. 1809; married in Canaan, N. H., 24 Dec. 1835, ABIGAIL STANIELS MARTIN, daughter of William Martin of Lebanon. She was born in Pembroke, N. H., 26 June 1817. They lived in Canaan, where he died 3 Jan. 1877, aged 66 y. 10 m.

Children, born in Canaan:

2615.   WILLIAM MARTIN,[7] b. 28 Dec. 1837; graduated from the Chandler School of Dartmouth College in 1858, receiving the degree of B. S.; A. M. in 1879, and in 1898 the honorary degree of LL. D. He studied law and was admitted to the New Hampshire bar 21 Aug. 1862; chairman of the commission to revise the public laws of New Hampshire in 1889; appointed associate justice of the Supreme Court of New Hampshire in 1891 and served until 28 Dec. 1907 being retired on account of the age limit; member of the State Senate 1909-1911; director and president of the First National Bank of Concord; president of Board of Education; trustee of New Hampshire State Library, Plymouth Normal School and Dartmouth College. He m. 18 Mar. 1863, Ellen Sherwood Abbott of Concord. He d. in Concord, 3 Feb. 1918. One son *Arthur Horace*,[8] b. 16 Feb. 1864.

2616.   HENRY MARTIN, b. 27 Aug. 1857.

1216

JOSEPH[6] CHASE (Joseph,[5] Moody,[4] Lt. Joseph,[3] Ens. Moses[2]), born in Chester, N. H., 22 Sept. 1811; married 10 Feb. 1841, LOUISA JONES, daughter of Samuel and Rachel (Wentworth) Jones, who was born in Lebanon, Me., 20 Nov. 1817. They lived in Lowell. where he was a manufacturer.

Children, born in Lowell:

WARREN SEYMOUR,[7] b. 19 Oct. 1843; d. 4 Nov. 1864.

2617.   FREDERICK W., b. 10 Aug. 1850; overseer in a Lowell factory.

1217

OTIS NELSON[6] CHASE (Jacob,[5] Moody,[4] Lt. Joseph,[3] Ens. Moses[2]), born in Newbury, 8 Oct. 1809; married 31 Dec. 1831, JOANNA COLBURN, daughter of Oliver and Mary (Holden) Colburn. She was born in Tyngsborough, — Oct. 1807 and died 4 May 1841. He died 6 Aug. 1841, in Nashua, N. H. At the time of their marriage he lived in Dunstable (now Nashua).

Children, born in Nashua:

2618.   OTIS NELSON,[7] m. Martha Ela; living in Boston in 1874.

2619.   ALBERT BARKER, lived in Pueblo, Col.

LORING AUGUSTUS, unm., living in Chicago, Ill., in 1874.

1218

CYRUS[6] CHASE (Jacob,[5] Moody,[4] Lt. Joseph,[3] Ens. Moses[2]), born in Hopkinton, N. H., 16 Feb. 1818; died in Hookset, N. H., 29 Dec. 1850. He married in Londonderry, Vt., Oct. 1845, LAURA CHAPIN STOWELL, daughter of Col. Josiah and Laura (Chapin) Stowell, born in Derry, N. H., 2 Oct. 1818; died in Chicago, Ill., 16 May 1913, aged 94. They lived in Hookset.

Child, born in Hookset:

2620.   GEORGE HARLAN,[7] b. 26 July 1847; d. in Chicago, 13 May 1882; m. in Monroe, Mich., 26 Oct. 1869, Hattie Grosvenor Winans; five children.

1219

LEONARD WOODS[6] CHASE (Jacob,[5] Moody,[4] Lt. Joseph,[3] Ens. Moses[2]), born in Hopkinton, N. H., 6 Jan. 1826; died in Gorham, N. H., 12 July 1857. He married (1) CLARA DANFORTH who died in about six months. He married (2) SARAH J. MASON; married (3) ELIZA RECORD. They lived in Gorham.

Child by second wife:

2621.   CYRUS LEROY,[7] b. May 1851.

Child by third wife:

LAURA ETTA, b. about 1855.

1220

STEPHEN BRADLEY[6] CHASE (Moody,[5] Moody,[4] Lt. Joseph,[3] Ens. Moses[2]), born in Haverhill, 20 May 1806; died in Portland, Me., 15 May 1874. He married 11 Sept. 1832, SARAH[6] CHASE, daughter of

Samuel[5] and Sally (Haynes) Chase, born in Portland, 3 Apr. 1806. (Family 436). They lived in Haverhill and in Portland.
Children, first two born in Haverhill:

2622.   HAZEN MOODY,[7] b. 29 Jan. 1835; m. 15 May 1862, Fanny L. Hale, dau. of William and Lydia (Ayer) Hale; d. 1 Nov. 1911. Their son Frank H.,[8] is reference librarian in the Boston Public Library.
EMMA ELIZABETH, b. 27 July 1836; d. 12 Mar. 1845.
HOWARD BRADLEY, b. 2 Dec. 1843; never married.

1221

JOHN DAVENPORT[6] CHASE (Samuel,[5] Moody,[4] Lt. Joseph,[3] Ens. Moses[2]), born in Portland, Me., 17 Dec. 1811; married 1 Sept. 1836, LOUISA QUEREAU, daughter of Joshua and Sarah (Voorhees) Quereau. They lived in Brooklyn, N. Y.
Children, probably born in Brooklyn:

2623.   GEORGE FRANCIS,[7] b. 18 Oct. 1837.
MARY LOUISA, b. 6 Sept. 1839; d. 8 May 1841.
2624.   ALBERT QUEREAU, b. 1 Aug. 1842.
SARAH EMMA, b. 6 Jan. 1846; d. 18 Aug. 1846.
MARY BRADLEY, b. 25 Aug. 1848; d. 16 Mar. 1863.
2625.   WILLIAM EDWIN, b. 25 Apr. 1851.
IDA BURROWS, b. 11 Nov. 1855.

1222

SAMUEL[6] CHASE (Samuel,[5] Moody,[4] Lt. Joseph,[3] Ens. Moses[2]), born in Portland, Me., 10 Nov. 1817; married 3 July 1840, MARY P. TODD.
Child:

MARIA LOUISA,[7] b. 14 Mar. 1842; m. 25 Dec. 1861, Augustus B. Forbes, b. 16 Feb. 1842; she d. 7 Mar. 1870.

1223

DANIEL POOR[6] CHASE (Caleb,[5] Moody,[4] Lt. Joseph,[3] Ens. Moses[2]), born in Portsmouth, N. H., 22 Feb. 1818; died 21 Nov. 1852. He was a printer.

1224

WILLIAM DWIGHT[6] CHASE (Caleb,[5] Moody,[4] Lt. Joseph,[3] Ens. Moses[2]), born in Portland, Me., 24 June 1832; married, 8 May 1867, LYDIA ADELAIDE WOODS, daughter of William Woods of Morrisania, N. Y. She was born in New York City, 24 Dec. 1837; died 7 July 1896. He died in Brooklyn, N. Y., 6 Jan. 1913.
Children, born in Brooklyn:

SUSAN BURRILL,[7] b. 28 June 1872; d. 5 Apr. 1916.
2626.   SAMUEL OSGOOD.

1225

GEORGE WASHINGTON[6] CHASE (Thomas,[5] Moody,[4] Lt. Joseph,[3] Ens. Moses[2]), born in Watertown, 8 July 1818; married in Utica, N. Y., 10 May 1842, SUSAN F. VANDERHEYDEN. They lived in Utica, N. Y., and removed to California before 1859.

Children, born probably in Utica, N. Y.:
SARAH ISABELLA,⁷ b. 30 Apr. 1843.
2627. JACOB VANDERHEYDEN, b. 25 Jan. 1845.

1226

SYLVESTER⁶ CHASE (Thomas,⁵ Moody,⁴ Lt. Joseph,³ Ens. Moses²), born in Candia, N. H., 6 June 1822; married in Haverhill, 4 Dec. 1845, MARY ANN SARGENT, daughter of Rufus K. and Hannah (Shaw) Sargent, born in 1826. They lived in Haverhill.
Children, born in Haverhill:
2628. SON,⁷ b. 22 Feb. 1846.
ANNA CLAYTON, b. 15 June 1848.

1227

HARVEY HERMAN⁶ CHASE (Joseph,⁵ Caleb,⁴ Lt. Joseph,³ Ens. Moses²), born, perhaps, in Hanover, N. H. He probably is the Harvey Chase who married (1) in Hanover, 17 Oct. 1819, SYBIL HALL. The same man married (2) in Hanover, 29 Mar. 1821, PERCY HALL, perhaps a sister to Sybil. He lived on the Joseph Chase homestead in Hanover.

1228

HENRY⁶ CHASE (Joseph,⁵ Caleb,⁴ Lt. Joseph,³ Ens. Moses²), born probably in Hanover, N. H. He lived in Lowell.

1229

JOSEPH⁶ CHASE (Joseph,⁵ Caleb,⁴ Lt. Joseph,³ Ens. Moses²), born probably in Hanover, N. H. He married in Manchester, N. H., 21 June 1847, RACHEL W. HARVELL.

1230

GARDNER⁶ CHASE (Jacob,⁵ Caleb,⁴ Lt. Joseph,³ Ens. Moses²), born in Derby, Vt., 17 Dec. 1801; married HANNAH PIERCE.

1231

JACOB⁶ CHASE (Jacob,⁵ Caleb,⁴ Lt. Joseph,³ Ens. Moses²), born in Derby, Vt., 13 Nov. 1806; married MARY MORSE.

1232

ENOCH⁶ CHASE (Jacob,⁵ Caleb,⁴ Lt. Joseph,³ Ens. Moses²), born in Derby, Vt., 16 Jan. 1809; married (1) in Coldwater, Mich., 24 Mar. 1835, JULIA ANN ELLSWORTH who died 5 Jan. 1837. He married (2) in Springville, Ind., 24 Sept. 1837, NANCY M. BROMLEY. He was a physician, graduating from the Medical School of Dartmouth College in 1831. He lived in Milwaukee, Wis., from 1835 to 1892, and died there, 23 Aug. 1892.
Child by the first wife, born in Milwaukee:
JULIA ANN,⁷ b. 24 Dec. 1836; never married; alive in 1873.

Children by the second wife, born in Milwaukee:

2629.   GEORGE H., b. 27 July 1838; m. 1867, Nelly Smith.
        LUCIEN B., b. 15 Aug. 1841; d. 1 Jan. 1863.
        HANNAH, b. 18 Oct. 1843; m. Samuel H. Bunnell.
        LILLIAS, b. 18 Nov. 1846; d. 29 Nov. 1847.
        ANN FOLLANSBEE, b. 29 Sept. 1848; m. George O. Swett (?).
        NELL, b. 12 Jan. 1851; d. 15 Nov. 1851.
        ENOCH, b. 14 Sept. 1852; d. 15 Sept. 1854.
2630.   CLARENCE, b. 3 Apr. 1855.
        HORACE, b. 26 Aug. 1857; d. 20 Mar. 1860.
2631.   CLIFFORD, b. 19 May 1859.

1233

HORACE[6] CHASE (Jacob,[5] Caleb,[4] Lt. Joseph,[3] Ens. Moses[2]), born in Derby, Vt., 25 Dec. 1810; married (1) 3 Oct. 1837, SARAH ANN GRAY; married (2) MARY H. DAVIS. They lived in Chicago, Ill.

1234

HON. LUCIEN BONAPARTE[6] CHASE (Jacob,[5] Caleb,[4] Lt. Joseph,[3] Ens. Moses[2]), born in Derby, Vt., 5 Dec. 1817; died in Clarksville, Tenn., 14 Dec. 1864. He married JULIA A. DE LA PLACE.. He removed to Clarksvville and became interested in political affairs. In 1844 he was elected a representative to the 29th Congress, taking his seat 1 Dec. 1845, and was re-elected to the 30th Congress, serving until 3 Mar. 1849. He was the author of a *History of Mr. Polk's Administration* (1850) and of *English Serfdom and American Slavery* (1854).

1235

SILAS C.[6] CHASE (Amos,[5] Caleb,[4] Lt. Joseph,[3] Ens. Moses[2]), born in Thornton, N. H., about 1808; died in Campton, N. H., 12 Nov. 1879, aged 69. He married, SARAH NUTTER of Campton. There were two children whose names have not been reported.

1236

JOHN[6] CHASE (Amos,[5] Caleb,[4] Lt. Joseph,[3] Ens. Moses[2]), born in Thornton or Campton, N. H., about 1810; lived in Port Jervis, Orange Co., N. Y.

1237

CALEB MOODY[6] CHASE (Moses,[5] Caleb,[4] Lt. Joseph,[3] Ens. Moses[2]), born 23 Apr. 1815; died 6 Feb. 1868. He married (1) 31 Dec. 1841, BETSEY E. DAVIS, born 15 Jan. 1826 and died in Monticello, Iowa, 6 May 1872. He married two other women whose names have not been reported. They lived in Buffalo, N. Y., in 1844; in Huron, Ohio, 1845; in Wattsburg, Pa., in 1848; in Cleveland, Ohio, in 1849.

Children by first wife:

    PHEBE,[7] b. — June 1844; d. 1845 in Huron.
    MARY ANN, b. 5 July 1846; m. 14 Dec. 1865, Dr. William George Hunt of Monticello, Iowa, 1874.

HANNAH ROSETTA, b. — Feb. 1848; d. Aug. 1849.
CHILD, b. — Nov. 1849; d. 7 Jan. 1850.
Child by third wife:
MARY ALICE, b. 7 Mar. 1867.

1238

DAVID L.[6] CHASE (Moses,[5] Caleb,[4] Lt. Joseph,[3] Ens. Moses[2]),
born 30 Mar. 1826; married 10 Dec. 1848, MARY A. DEAN. Their
children are reported not to have lived to grow up.

1239

BENJAMIN H. P.[6] CHASE (William,[5] Caleb,[4] Lt. Joseph,[3] Ens.
Moses[2]), born in New Hampshire, 4 Oct. 1818; died in Middlesex,
Vt., 29 Apr. 1864. He married 2 Dec. 1841, MARY PHILINDA HAR-
RINGTON of Middlesex. They lived in Montpelier, Vt.
Children, born in Montpelier:
HARRIET E.,[7] b. 15 Feb. 1843; m. 1 May 1861, George N. Kent.
She was living in Kewaunee, Wis., in 1873.
SARAH J., b. 20 Dec. 1849; m. 10 Oct. 1866, Albert[7] Chase,
M.D., of Middlesex (Family 1042) and d. 22 Mar. 1869,
without issue.
FLORENCE A., b. 8 Sept. 1862.

1240

WILLIAM SYLVESTER[6] CHASE (William,[5] Caleb,[4] Lt. Joseph,[3]
Ens Moses[2]), born in Campton, N. H., 11 Apr. 1825; died in Oct.
1865. He married in Lebanon, N. H., 26 Mar. 1850, MARY A. PRES-
COTT, calling himself 24 and her 23.
Child, born in Newport, N. H.:
SON,[7] b. 6 July 1853. (Christian name not reported)

1241

EDMUND H.[6] CHASE (William,[5] Caleb,[4] Lt. Joseph,[3] Ens.
Moses[2]), born 7 Dec. 1826; married 13 Aug. 1847, LESTINA GUP-
TILL of Waterbury, Vt. They lived in Middlesex, Vt., till 1856, when
they removed to Montpelier, Vt., where they were living in 1873.
Children, first four born in Middlesex, others in Montpelier:
EMMA,[7] b. 17 Nov. 1849.
ELLEN, b. 9 June 1851.
2632.   WILLIAM, b. 1 June 1853.
2633.   FRANK, b. 14 July 1855.
2634.   FRED, b. 8 Mar. 1857.
2635.   BERTRUM, b. 27 May 1871.

1242

CAPT. SILAS[6] CHASE (Silas,[5] Rogers,[4] Benoni,[3] Ens. Moses[2]),
born in Royalston, 30 Sept. 1790. He married in Dorchester, 13
Apr. 1815, ANNA ATKINS LEEDS, daughter of Samuel and Margaret
Leeds of Dorchester, born there in 1799. He died in Dorchester, 31
Oct. 1820, aged 31. She married (2) in Dorchester, 18 May 1823,
WILLIAM JONES of New Hampshire.

Children, born in Dorchester:

>   LOISA,[7] b. 8 Jan. 1817; m. Elijah P. Balcome of Dorchester.
>   SILAS HENRY, b. 1820; d. Sept. 1822, aged 2 years.

1243

JOSEPH WRIFORD[6] CHASE (Silas,[5] Rogers,[4] Benoni,[3] Ens. Moses[2]), born in Royalston, 5 Oct. 1799; died there 2 June 1871. He married 6 Jan. 1825, MELINDA GALE, daughter of Jonathan and Mary (Bancroft) Gale, born in Warwick, 18 Feb. 1800; died in Royalston, 4 Apr. 1869. They lived in Royalston.
Children, born in Royalston:

>   AURILLA MELINDA,[7] b. 23 Jan. 1827; m. Nov. 1855, Alexander Morse of Sullivan, N. H. She d. 29 Sept. 1861, in Orange.
>   SILAS ROYAL, b. 13 Mar. 1829; d. unm.
>   JOSEPH WRIFORD, b. 9 June 1835; d. unm.
>   MARY JANE, b. 25 Oct. 1838; m. 26 Dec. 1869, John King of Royalston. She d. in Royalston, 24 June 1877. Their daughter Maybel Josephine King, b. in Royalston, 21 Dec. 1872; lives in Cambridge and is secretary-treasurer of the Chase-Chace Family Association and editor of *The Chase Chronicle*.

1244

JOHN ROYAL[6] CHASE (Silas,[5] Rogers,[4] Benoni,[3] Ens. Moses[2]), born in Royalston, 11 Mar. 1803; died in Johnstown, N. Y., 6 Nov. 1828, aged 25. He married RACHEL KIPP. They lived in Johnstown.
Child, born and died in Johnstown:

>   JULIA DIADAMIA,[7] b. 31 Jan. 1829; d. 5 Aug. 1842.

1245

ELIJAH[6] CHASE (Ebenezer,[5] Rogers,[4] Benoni,[3] Ens. Moses[2]), born in Athol, 17 Dec. 1804; married (intention in Royalston, 8 Sept. 1827) TRYPHOSA BLODGETT, probably daughter of Joseph and Thankful (Hawkes) Blodgett of Fitzwilliam, N. H., born in Deerfield, 7 Apr. 1808. He died 5 Apr. 1872. They lived in Keene, N. H., and Mt. Holly, Vt.
Children, first born in Royalston, second in Athol, others in Mt. Holly, Vt.:

>   2635a. JOSEPH E.,[7] m. 29 Nov. 1854, Anna Cheney of Orange; lived in Templeton; one daughter, *Addie M.*[8]
>   2636.   PHILIP ELIJAH, b. 22 Oct. 1832; m. 31 May 1865, Mary E. Barrett; lived in Mt. Holly, Vt.; captain in Civil War. Son *George P.*,[8] attorney.
>   SON, b. 3 July 1834; d. 14 July 1834.
>   2636a. AMBROSE P., b. 16 Sept. 1836; m. Eunice ———; lived in Mt. Holly, Vt.; served in Civil War.
>   SUSAN, b. 1838; d. 1840.
>   SUSAN ANGELINE, b. 18 July 1841; m. H. C. Dickerman, and d. 31 Oct 1871.; three children.
>   ANNA E., b. 8 Jan. 1844; m. 8 Apr. 1874, Martin Dodge, who d. in De Kalb, Ill., 3 Jan. 1902. She lives in De Kalb (1928).
>   EDWIN B., b. 2 May 1846; d. in Civil War; Second Vt. Regt.

2636b. EUGENE R., b. 15 June 1848; m. (1) Amy Hemmenway who d. July 1866; one son *Edwin B.*;[8] m. (2) Fanny Driver; son *Ray E.*[8]

1246

AMBROSE .PECK[6] CHASE (Ebenezer,[5] Rogers,[4] Benoni,[3] Ens Moses[2]), born in Athol, 5 Mar. 1815; married (1) in Hubbardston, 5 Feb. 1839, SALLY NICHOLS who was born 14 Jan. 1813, and died in Athol, 9 Oct. 1865. He married (2) 1 May 1866, POLLY NICHOLS, sister to Sally, who was born 31 Dec. 1812. They lived in Gardner.

Child by first wife:

CLARA E.,[7] b. 8 Oct. 1839; d. 5 Oct. 1840.

1247

ERASTUS[6] CHASE (Benjamin,[5] Stephen,[4] Benoni,[3] Ens. Moses[2]), born in New York state, 9 Mar. 1801; died in Keene, N. H., 2 Apr. 1874, aged 73. He married 16 Feb. 1831, MARY RICHARDSON, daughter of Lemuel and Mary[5] (Chase) Richardson (Family 123), of Rochester, Vt., born 14 June 1809; living in Keene, 14 Aug. 1874. They lived in Keene.

Children:

2637. HENRY LYMAN,[7] b. 5 Apr. 1832; lived in Keene, N. H., 1874. He lived in the Sandwich Islands, 1856 to 1874.
EBENEZER CLARK, b. 18 Apr. 1834; d. 4 Apr. 1858.
LUTHER WHITNEY, b. 22 May 1836; d. 14 Apr. 1858.
2638. IRA ERASTUS, b. 12 July 1838; lived in Keene, N. H., 1874.
WILLIAM HIRAM, b. 9 Sept. 1840; d. 7 Feb. 1868; all d. in Keene.

1248

HIRAM[6] CHASE (Benjamin,[5] Stephen,[4] Benoni,[3] Ens. Moses[2]), born about 1806.

1249

DAVID[6] CHASE (Asa,[5] Moses,[4] Benoni,[3] Ens. Moses[2]), born in Douglas, 5 Jan. 1795 .

1250

JAMES[6] CHASE (Simeon,[5] Moses,[4] Benoni,[3] Ens. Moses[2]), born in Royalston, 2 Sept. 1794; married in Middlebury, Vt., 12 Oct. 1814, SALLY CLAGHORN. They lived in Middlebury, Stockbridge, and Barnard, Vt., Brandon, and Bangor, N. Y. They were living in Belmont, N. Y., in 1870.

Children, first born in Middlebury; second to fifth in Stockbridge; sixth in Barnard; seventh in Brandon; eighth and ninth in Bangor; and tenth in Brandon:

SARAH A.,[7] b. 24 June 1816; m. Dec. 1838, Jonathan Kennison. She d. Iowa, 11 Dec. 1866.
MARY A., b. 5 Apr. 1819; m. (1) Mar. 1839, Chester Blanchard; m. (2) 1858, Curtis A. Sheldon.
2639. JAMES H., b. 26 Dec. 1821; m. May 1850, Lavinia Dolloff; d. in Chautauqua, N. Y., 7 Dec. 1864.

LUCY, b. 31 Mar. 1824; m. May 1852, Stephen Batchelder.
2640.　ASA, b. 25 Dec. 1826; d. in Bangor, 6 Mar. 1849.
EMILY, b. 5 May 1829; m. May 1850, Darius O. Darling.
2641.　HENRY O., b. 24 Apr. 1832; m. Sept. 1854, Angeline Haseltine.
2642.　ORRIN, b. 10 June 1835; m. 13 Apr. 1870, Eliza Reynolds.
2643.　OSCAR F., b. 8 Dec. 1837; m. 1 Jan. 1866, Georgie Bennett.
DAVID S., b. 29 Apr. 1842; d. 11 Nov. 1844.

1251

ORRIN[6] CHASE (Simeon,[5] Moses,[4] Benoni,[3] Ens. Moses[2]), born in Royalston, 21 Mar. 1798; married 3 Aug. 1822, LUCY ABBOTT who was born 30 Oct. 1805, and died 15 Aug. 1866. They lived in Windsor Co., Vt., and Gates Mills, Ohio. He was living there in 1876.

Children, first five born in Windsor Co., Vt., sixth in Newburgh, Ohio; others in Gates Mills:

LAVINIA,[7] b. 27 Mar. 1824; m. 29 Dec. 1842, David Hoag.
ELIZA ANN, b. 22 Apr. 1826; m. 25 Dec. 1843, Philip Hoag.
ALMIRA, b. 5 May 1827; d. 3 Mar. 1843, in Gates Mills.
2644.　AUGUSTUS, b. 12 Oct. 1830; d. 3 Feb. 1843, in Gates Mills.
AUGUSTA (twin), b. 12 Oct. 1830; d. in N. Y.
AMANDA, b. 3 Mar. 1835; m. 9 Oct. 1856, H. J. Humphrey.
SERAPH, b. 15 Apr. 1838; m. Mar. 1864, Charles Dickinson.
2645.　ORRIN, b. 15 June 1840; m. 15 Oct. 1862, Emerean Mapes.
ALONZO, b. 18 Feb. 1841; d. 28 July 1844.
RAPHELLA, b. 18 Sept. 1844; m. 28 Oct. 1868, Isaac Morts.
2646.　HENRY, b. 12 Aug. 1846; m. 26 June 1867, Eliza Bliss.

1252

IRA[6] CHASE (Simeon,[5] Moses,[4] Benoni,[3] Ens. Moses[2]), born in Stockbridge, Vt., 18 June 1807; married (1) in 1828, RHODA BLANCHARD who died in 1839. He married (2) in Brandon, N. Y., about 1840, ELIZABETH EMERY who was born in Plattsburg, N. Y., 23 Feb. 1823. She was the daughter of William and Margaret (Haseltine) Emery of Swanton, Vt., and Schuyler Falls, N. Y. She died in Fort Jackson, N. Y., about 1883. They were living in Hopkinton, N. Y., in 1870.

Children by the second wife, three to eleven born in Belmont, Franklin Co., N. Y.:

2647.　OLIVER J.,[7] b. 12 Apr. 1842; m. Mar. 1866, Alvira Ingram.
JULIANA E., b. 11 July 1844; m. 2 Apr. 1861, George D. Northrop.
ALMIRA M., b. 19 Feb. 1846; m. 11 June 1867, Haskell Blake.
2648.　VOLENTINE H., b. 1 Jan. 1848; m. 1 July 1869, Louisa Fish.
AUGUSTA L., b. 6 Jan. 1850; d. 27 Jan. 1863.
FLORENCE A., b. 25 Feb. 1852.
IDA T., b. 18 Dec. 1853.
ESTELLA R., b. 19 Jan. 1856.
LEONORA E., b. 5 Aug. 1859.
2649.　WILLARD W., b. 12 Jan. 1865.

1253

AARON[6] CHASE (Simeon,[5] Moses,[4] Benoni,[3] Ens. Moses[2]), born in Brandon, Vt., 15 June 1809; married (1) in 1832, MARY ANN WHITCOMB who died about 1853; married (2) in 1854, LYDIA DAVIS.

He died in Brandon, Franklin Co., N. Y., in 1865. His second wife was living in Malone, N. Y., in 1870.
Children by first wife:

ADELINE,[7] m. John Thomas.
AMANDA, m. Allen Davis.
ALMIRA.
CORNELIA, m. Benjamin Potter.
LORENZO, d. in service, Civil War.
LOUISA, m. Harlow Davis.
FANNY.
CORDELIA.
There were three children by his second wife, perhaps included above.

1254

MOSES[6] CHASE (Abner,[5] Moses,[4] Benoni,[3] Ens. Moses[2]), born in Rochester, Vt., 30 Apr. 1821. He married in Lowell, 15 Nov. 1846, ROSINA HILL, daughter of Benjamin and Sarah (Scales) Hill, born in Sharon, Vt., 4 Apr. 1823. They lived in Lowell, Mass., Pomfret, Royalton and Bethel, Vt. He died in Riverdale, Nebr., 16 Apr., 1894
Children, born in Vermont:

2650.   MOSES ROSCOE,[7] b. 10 May 1849; m. Eva Graves.
        FLORA ROSINA, b. 17 July 1850; m. Wallace Keyes; four children; lived in Riverdale, Nebr.
        FANNIE, b. 25 Oct. 1851; m. Harry C. Dunham; lived in Colorado Springs, Colo.
2651.   ROLLO MINER, b. 4 Sept. 1854; m. 18 June 1879, Susan Elizabeth Newell; graduated from Baltimore Medical College, 1890, and from Boston Dental College, 1876; lived in Bethel, Vt.

1255

DAVID[6] CHASE (Abraham,[5] David,[4] Benoni,[3] Ens. Moses[2]), born 12 Dec. 1796; married 12 Feb. 1818, IRENA KINGSBURY, daughter of Joseph and Mary (Merrill) Kingsbury of Fairfax, Vt., born in 1793 and died 21 Jan. 1854, aged 60. He died in Whitingham, Vt., 18 June 1880, aged 83. They lived in Whitingham.
Children, born in Whitingham:

BETSEY,[7] b. 2 Nov. 1818; m. 19 Apr. 1840, George Upton.
2652.   JOSEPH, b. 28 Apr. 1821; m. 15 Aug. 1853, Caroline Beaman.
        CAROLINE, b. 28 Mar. 1824; m. 14 Dec. 1843, Zachariah Wheeler.
        ADELINE, b. 14 May 1826; m. 27 Feb. 1845, Milo Hatch.
2653.   GEORGE A., b. 29 Jan. 1831; m. 15 Oct. 1852, Ruth Stratton.
        The first three lived in Whitingham and last two in Halifax, Vt.

1256

SAMUEL[6] CHASE (Abraham,[5] David,[4] Benoni,[3] Ens. Moses[2]), born in Whitingham, Vt., 5 Mar. 1799; married 25 Feb. 1819, BETSEY CLEMENT, daughter of Moses and Rachel (Perham) Clement, born in Dracut, 30 Sept. 1800. They lived in Bennington, Vt., from 1835 to 1871 or later.

Children, born in Whitingham:

CHARLES,[7] b. 24 Jan. 1820; d. 27 Jan. 1826.
SOPHRONIA, b. 3 Dec. 1821; m. 28 Jan. 1840, Daniel Huling.
2654.   BARBER, b. 7 July 1824; m. 11 Jan. 1847, Susan Stratton.
ABIGAIL, b. 19 Jan. 1828; m. 9 July 1848, Abijah D. Fillmore.
She d. 27 Feb. 1859.
2655.   SAMUEL PERHAM, b. 15 June 1832; m. Huldah Craig; lived in
Marshalltown, Iowa.

1257

JACOB[6] CHASE (Abraham,[5] David,[4] Benoni,[3] Ens. Moses[2]), born
in Whitingham, Vt., 8 Feb. 1804; married 28 Apr. 1826, LUCINDA
BOYD of Wilmington, Vt.   They lived in Wilmington, Vt.

Children, born in Wilmington:

JULIA,[7] b. 18 June 1831; d. 23 Sept. 1833.
2656.   ABRAHAM F., b. 24 May 1835.
SUSAN, b. 18 June 1839.

1258

ELLIS F.[6] CHASE (Abraham,[5] David,[4] Benoni,[3] Ens. Moses[2]),
born in Whitingham, Vt., 31 July 1812; married (1) SALLY BOYD of
Whitingham; married (2) about 1855, LYDIA STANLEY of Halifax,
Vt.   They lived in Whitingham and later removed to Halifax.

Child by first wife:

RHODA C.,[7] b. 6 Dec. 1837; m. Newman Dalrymple.

Children by the second wife:

FREDERICK E., b. 9 July 1857; d. 15 Oct. 1867.
FLORA M., b. 31 Oct. 1859.
2657.   FRANK, b. 21 Dec. 1866.
2658.   FREDERICK E., b. 17 Aug. 1869.

1259

ELLIOTT F.[6] CHASE (Abraham,[5] David,[4] Benoni,[3] Ens. Moses[2]),
born in Whitingham, Vt., 31 July 1812; married (1) HANNAH FOS-
TER of Whitingham; married (2) ELIZA GREENE of Bennington, Vt.
He died in Whitingham, 22 Feb. 1871.   They lived in Whitingham.

Children, born in Whitingham:

CORESSA A.,[7] b. 27 July 1854.
2659.   NORMAN A., b. 5 June 1856.

1260

MOSES[6] CHASE (Isaac,[5] David,[4] Benoni,[3] Ens. Moses[2]), born in
Whitingham, Vt., 2 Mar. 1800; married 7 Oct. 1821, ANNA BRIGGS.
He died in Whitingham, 6 Oct. 1850.   They lived in Whitingham.

Children, born in Whitingham:

WILLIAM C.,[7] b. 14 Aug. 1823; d. 28 July 1845.
2660.   JOSIAH B., b. 10 Apr. 1826; m. 4 Mar. 1852, Elsie P. Warren;
lived on the Moses[6] Chase homestead.
SUSAN, b. 10 Feb. 1829; d. 14 July 1831.
MELINDA L., b. 6 Oct. 1831; m. 10 July 1854, Samuel Newell.
IZANNA E., 2. 23 Mar. 1835; m. 25 Dec. 1856, Charles Tuttle.

2660a. PHILANDER M., b. 19 Dec. 1837; m. 15 Nov. 1862, Augusta
Bliss. He d. 25 July 1866.
PHILINDA A. (twin), b. 19 Dec. 1837; m. 25 Apr. 1856, Charles
Carkins [Caulkins ?].

1261

AARON[6] CHASE (Isaac,[5] David,[4] Benoni,[3] Ens. Moses[2]), born in
Whitingham, Vt., 2 Nov. 1801; married (1) 19 Oct. 1826, LUCY
CAULKINS; married (2) 11 Oct. 1832, ELMIRA SCOTT; married (3)
15 May 1852, ESTHER ALLEN. He died in North Adams, 28 Dec.
1852. They lived in North Adams.
Children by first wife:
ISAAC,[7] b. 23 July 1827; d. 6 Aug. 1828.
2661. MILO, b. 23 Feb. 1832; m. 18 Jan. 1852, Cornelia Gibson. They
lived in North Adams.
Children by second wife:
LUCY, b. 29 July 1833; m. 22 Apr. 1852, Henry Lanfair. She d.
9 May 1861.
MARY K., b. 13 Oct. 1840; m. 16 Sept. 1857, Horace Lanfair of
Stanford, Vt.

1262

ISAAC[6] CHASE (Isaac,[5] David,[4] Benoni,[3] Ens. Moses[2]), born in
Whitingham, Vt., 19 June 1808; died there 22 Jan. 1872. He mar-
ried, 19 June 1833, HARRIET GOODNOW. They lived on the Isaac[5]
Chase homestead in Whitingham.
Children, born in Whitingham:
2662. JOSEPH S.,[7] b. 2 June 1838; m. 11 Mar. 1865, Nancy Kingsbury.
MARINDA H., b. 2 Dec. 1842; m. 18 Feb. 1868, Irvin Brown of
Halifax, Vt.
CHARLES, b. 26 Oct. 1845; d. 23 Sept. 1848.

1263

HIRAM[6] CHASE (Isaac,[5] David,[4] Benoni,[3] Ens. Moses[2]), born in
Whitingham, Vt., 9 Oct. 1812; married 23 Apr. 1835, ANNIS HALL,
daughter of Loten and Rhoda (Nichols) Hall of Halifax, Vt. They
lived in Marlboro, Vt.
Children:
2663. LEROY M.,[7] b. 11 June 1839; m. 10 Aug. 1871, Ada P. Gallup;
lived in Marlboro.
SUSAN R., b. 4 Aug. 1843; d. 8 Feb. 1872.

1264

WARREN[6] CHASE (Jacob,[5] David,[4] Benoni,[3] Ens. Moses[2]), born
in Douglas, 30 Nov. 1805; married about 1830, ANNA FAIRBANKS,
daughter of Asa and Lucy (Saunders) Fairbanks, born in Whitingham, Vt., 2 Feb. 1813; died there 23 Dec. 1858. He died in Whitingham, 4 Apr. 1861, aged 56. They lived in Whitingham.
Children, born in Whitingham:
DIANTHA L.,[7] b. 24 Oct. 1832; d. in Shelburne Falls, 25 July
1867.

2664.   ALBERT W., b. 20 June 1834; d. 4 May 1857, in Whitingham.
        WILBUR F., b. 5 Jan. 1841; m. Frances M. Dickinson. They
        lived on the Warren[6] Chase homestead in Whitingham.

1265

LEVI[6] CHASE (Jacob,[5] David,[4] Benoni,[3] Ens. Moses[2]), born in
Whitingham, Vt., 26 Aug. 1810; died in Heath, 9 Feb. 1851. He
married about 1834, SARAH HARRIS born in Colrain in 1812. She
married (2) JOHN GOODNOW and died 5 Aug. 1866, aged 54 and was
buried in the North Burying Ground in Heath. They lived in Heath.
Children, born in Heath:
        LYMAN FRANCIS, b. 10 July 1835; d. 14 Aug. 1847.
        SARAH ELVIRA, b. 23 Dec. 1836.
2665.   GEORGE LEVI, b. 23 Aug. 1839.

1266

JACOB[6] CHASE (Jacob,[5] David,[4] Benoni,[3] Ens. Moses[2]), born in
Whitingham, Vt., 21 May 1815; married 8 May 1844, CAROLINE
GORE of Monroe, Vt. They removed to Whitingham in 1865 and in
1875 to Jacksonville, Vt.
Children:
        HELENA L.,[7] b. 12 June 1847.
        EMMA A., b. 14 Apr. 1851; m. 20 Aug. 1871, Dr. F. J. Kennedy.

1267

MINOR[6] CHASE (Jacob,[5] David,[4] Benoni,[3] Ens. Moses[2]), born in
Whitingham, Vt., 2 Sept. 1817; married 16 Jan. 1845, LUCINDA C.
TARBELL of Mason, N. H. He died 8 Aug. 1881. They lived on the
Jacob[5] Chase homestead in Whitingham.

1268

RUFUS[6] CHASE (Samuel,[5] David,[4] Benoni,[3] Ens. Moses[2]), born
in Douglas, 11 Oct. 1805; died in Whitingham, Vt., 27 Apr. 1846.
He married about 1829, MARY HALL of Barney [Barnet?]. They
lived in Whitingham.
Children, born in Whitingham:
        GEORGE E.,[7] b. 16 Feb. 1830; d. 25 Apr. 1832.
        CHARLES N., b. 31 Oct. 1831; d. May 1832.
2666.   WILLIAM B., b. 9 Apr. 1833; m. 28 Dec. 1859, Marietta C. Bea-
        mont of Ashfield; physician in Swampscott.
2667.   SAMUEL B., b. 5 Mar. 1836; m. Hattie E. Stafford; lived in
        Whitingham; d. there 1917 a. 81. Four sons, two daughters.
2668.   SIDNEY R., b. 17 Oct. 1838; m. Celia W. Mason; lived in
        Charlestown, and South Acton, 1917.

1269

DAVID[6] CHASE (Samuel,[5] David,[4] Benoni,[3] Ens. Moses[2]), born
in Whitingham, Vt., 15 Apr. 1809; died there 21 Mar. 1837. He
married BETSEY TAINTER who survived her husband many years.
They lived in Whitingham.

Children, born in Whitingham:

MARY M.,[7] b. 16.June 1830; m. Joseph Hicks; lived in Wauconda, Ill.

2669. CHARLES N., b. 27 Aug. 1832; m. Augusta Sweetzer of Troy, N. H.; lived in Winchendon.

2670. GEORGE WASHINGTON, b. 9 Sept. 1835; m. Melissa Green; physician in St. Joseph, Mo.

1270

MERRICK[6] CHASE (Benjamin,[5] David,[4] Benoni,[3] Ens. Moses[2]), born in Douglas, 13 Dec. 1811; married 11 Sept. 1834, SARAH MARIA BRIGHAM who was born in Whitingham, Vt., 12 Aug. 1816. They lived in Whitingham and in Somerset, Vt., after 1846 and were living in Greenwich, N. Y., in 1871.

Children, first four born in Whitingham, last two born in Somerset:

SYLVESTER SUMNER,[7] b. 3 Sept. 1835; m. 15 Apr. 1858, Maria Elizabeth Bray Seaver of Boston. She d. 12 July 1864; m. (2) Sophia Eddy Chittenden.

REBECCA ELVIRA, b. 19 Feb. 1839; m. 3 Apr. 1856, Dr. Daniel Alexander, b. in Athens, Vt., 13 Jan. 1831; lived in Bridgewater, Vt.

2671. JOHN BRIGHAM, b. 6 May 1841; m. 12 May 1864, Ann Hay of Greenwich, N. Y., b. there, 24 Feb. 1844; d. 18 Feb. 1919. He d. 13 Dec. 1923. Their son *George A.*,[8] b. in Valley Junction, Nebr., 28 Aug. 1883; a lawyer in Denver, Colo., m. 1 Dec. 1913, Elizabeth Kenyon; divorced in 1918. Their daughter Margaret Ann,[9] b. 25 Sept. 1915.

2672. CHARLES EMERSON, b. 17 Jan. 1844.

SARAH MARIA, b. 12 Oct. 1847.

2673. ADDISON MARTIN, b. 30 Oct. 1855.

1271

ABRAHAM[6] CHASE (Benjamin,[5] David,[4] Benoni,[3] Ens. Moses[2]), born in Whitingham, Vt., 5 Jan 1820; married 23 Apr. 1844, CATHARINE REED. They lived in Whitingham. He was an independent thinker, a close observer, and was frequently elected to town offices there.

Children, born in Whitingham:

2674. OSCAR R.,[7] b. 12 Sept. 1844; m. 12 Feb. 1866, Rosa A. Atherton.

2675. AUGUSTUS L., b. 9 Mar. 1849; m. 3 Dec. 1873, Mary Louise Mann.

AUGUSTA L. (twin), b. 9 Mar. 1849; m. 15 Dec. 1869, Gilbert A. Boyd.

2676. CHARLES S., b. 13 May 1855.

FRANK L., b. 24 Aug. 1859; d. 3 Aug. 1863.

1272

ROYAL[6] CHASE (Benjamin,[5] David,[4] Benoni,[3] Ens. Moses[2]), born in Whitingham, Vt., 16 Aug. 1827; married 4 July 1851, MARIETTA [also called MARGARET] HOWARD. They lived in Whitingham.

Children, born in Whitingham:

   CARRIE M.,[1] b. 31 Aug. 1852.
   LUANA S., b. 4 Sept. 1855.
2677. GEORGE W., b. 24 Feb. 1858.
   OLIVE M., b. 15 Sept. 1860.
2678. ROYAL B., b. 21 May 1863.
2679. WALTER B., b. 3 June 1869.
   WALLACE D. (twin), b. 3 June 1869; d. 2 Aug. 1870.
   ALMA M., b. 8 Nov. 1871.

ANCIENT CHASE HOMES
1 BIRTHPLACE OF JUDGE SAMUEL[4] CHASE, WEST NEWBURY
2 BIRTHPLACE OF BISHOP CARLTON CHASE, HOPKINTON, N. H.
3 THE DANIEL[2] CHASE HOUSE, WEST NEWBURY
4 THE JOHN[2] CHASE HOUSE, BUILT ABOUT 1699, WEST NEWBURY

THE DESCENDANTS OF

THOMAS CHASE of HAMPTON

NEW HAMPSHIRE

A large proportion of the descendants of Thomas[1] Chase, bearing the name of Chase, appear among the descendants of Aquila[1] (beginning with Family No. 14,) on account of the intermarriage of their grand-children.

Had a complete genealogy of Thomas[1] appeared as a separate volume it would have been about double its present size.

THOMAS CHASE AND HIS
DESCENDANTS

THOMAS[1] CHASE, a brother of Aquila,[1] first appears in New England, at Hampton, N. H., among the second group of settlers there having a grant of land in June 1640. (History of Hampton, 1:18) He married about 1642, ELIZABETH PHILBRICK [PHILBROOK], daughter of Thomas and Elizabeth Philbrick who settled in Watertown as early as 1636 and removed to Hampton in 1645. Her father made his will, 12 Mar. 1663/4, being "very aged" which was probated, 8 Oct. 1667. One clause of the will reads as follows: "and thatt att the Deseace of my Daughter Elizabeth Garland, her son, James Chase shall have one Cow in lew of the Cow which I have Given my daughter Elizabeth." (Probate Records of the Province of New Hampshire, 1635-1717, p. 72)

Thomas[1] Chase died in Hampton shortly before 5 Oct. 1652, upon which day his widow Elizabeth Chase was granted administration upon his estate. She married (2) 26 Oct. 1654, JOHN GARLAND, first of the name in Hampton. He died there, 4 Jan. 1672, aged 50 years and she married (3) in Hampton, 19 Jan. 1673/4, HENRY ROBIE [ROBY] of Hampton, and died there, 11 Feb. 1677.

He and his brother Aquila[1] received grants at the same time. Fourteen persons had received grants on 24 Dec. 1639, and one person on 14 Jan. 1640. These earliest grants were of large tracts for farms but those made in June 1640, to the number of fifty-six were small tracts for house lots.

On 23 Feb. 1645/6, there were granted to sixty proprietors of house lots in Hampton one or more shares in the "Common." Aquila Chase received one share and Thomas Chase two shares while some others received three shares. The common land had been already divided into 147 shares which were given to those who had house lots. (Dow's History of Hampton, 1:33)

Thomas[1] Chase was married about two or three years before his brother was married and he not only had a wife on 23 Feb. 1645/6, but at least two small children. This is why he received two shares of the common lands while his brother had only one.

Dow in his History of Hampton (2:635) states that Thomas was "the elder of the brothers." It is believed that this statement is based upon the fact that Thomas married and was the father of two children before the marriage of Aquila. If the inference is correct Thomas Chase must have been born as early as 1617, or possibly one or two years earlier. This is a reasonable conjecture but must be considered only as approximately true.

No statement of the age of Thomas[1] Chase has been found in any record.

Thomas[1] Chase's homestead was opposite that of his wife's father Thomas Philbrick, and near the Jesse Lamprey house (recently known as the James N. Brown house) a short distance southeast of "The Meeting-House Green."

"Thomas Chase entered his caution about a parcell of meadow & upland with comonage bought of Henry Ambrose, ye 30th of ye 1st mo. [Mar.] 1650." (Old Norfolk Records, 1:8)

"The widdow Chase enters her caution for tenn acres of upland, lying in ye north field wth several parcells of marsh & meadow: all lying in ye bounds of Hampton, wth priviledges belonging to a house lot wth one share of the oxe comon bought of Henry Ambrose 15 of ye 1st mo 1652" [15 Mar. 1652/3]. (Ibid. 1:37)

For confirmation of the deed of Aquila[1] Chase to his brother Thomas Chase made about twenty years before 15 May 1667, see Aquila[1] Chase. (p. 30)

Thomas Chase of Hampton, county of Norfolk, seaman, for £4 sells John Philbrick of Hampton, planter, four acres of upland, meadow and swamp in Hampton, 9 Nov. 1649, in the presence of Thomas Philbrick and James Philbrick. His autograph signature appears on the original deed, as do those of Thomas and James Philbrick (The Chase Chronicle, 10:57). This shows that he and his wife's father were not illiterate.

Edward Colcord of Hampton sells to Thomas[1] Chase of the same town, seaman, three and one-half acres of meadow butting upon a river towards ye west and ye great ox comon towards ye east, also a share of ye great ox comon and half of ye other comonage belonging to Thomas Jones of whom Colcord bought it, 16th 12 mo. 1646 [16 Feb. 1646]. (Ibid 2:233).

Administration on the estate of Thomas[1] Chase of Hampton was granted to his widow Elizabeth Chase, 5 Oct. 1652. The inventory was taken by Robert Page, Abraham Perkins and William Fifield, 2 June 1653. The estate was valued at £111: 18s. 10d. which was attested by Elizabeth Chase the widow.

The Court ordered, 4 Oct. 1653, that the five children of Thomas[1] Chase of Hampton shall have out of their father's estate these amounts: Thomas[2] Chase, the oldest, £16, and Joseph[2] Chase, James[2] Chase, Isaac[2] Chase, and Abraham[2] Chase £8 each, when they are twenty-one years of age. The widow, Elizabeth Chase, gave a bond of £50, with Thomas Philbrick and John Cass as sureties. 3 Oct. 1654, the Court ordered, with the consent of the administratrix, that the children's portions be paid out of the lands. On 10 Oct. 1665, the Court appointed Christopher Hussey, Ens. John Sanborn and Thomas Philbrick, Jr., a committee to divide the estate among the children, with the consent of the administratrix who was to have £4 out of the lands. (Norfolk Co. Court Records in N. H. Probate Records 1 :23-4).

At a Quarterly Court held at Hampton, 26 Sept. 1648, Thomas[1] Chase and Aquila[1] Chase brought a suit against William Howard which was continued to the Salisbury Court. (Records and Files of the Quarterly Courts of Essex County, 1 : 151).

Thomas Philbrook gave a receipt for 20 shillings from Robert Nanny, as a cask boy, "a nadbroy tasecon," dated 30 Nov. 1648. Witness Thomas Chaes. (Ibid 1 :160).

At a Court held at Hampton, 1 Oct. 1650, Thomas[1] Chace brought a suit against Mr. Edward Gilman "for not making good a sufficient boat according to bargain." (Ibid 1 :201).

At the same Court "Mr. Hussie, John Sanborn and Thomas Chase had their bonds released in the cases of Richard Waldern and Edward Colcord. (Ibid 203).

18 Nov. 1650, there was due to William Payne & Co. of Ipswich £20 from Thomas Chase. (Ibid 296).

Thomas[1] Chase by his autograph acknowledged his indebtedness to Edward Gilman for building a vessel, pay to be made in freighting, carrying boards from Exeter to Boston, at 18d. per hundred, 3 May 1651. (Ibid 296).

Thomas[1] Chase in Aug. 1652 was owing Edward Gilman £20 he having delivered some boards to Mr. Davison. (Ibid 298).

Rev. Stephen Bachiler, with the first company, removed to Winnacunnet (Hampton) in Oct. 1638. (Dow's History of Hampton, 1 :11). In the record of a Quarterly Court held at Salisbury, 11 Nov. 1679, is found "A note of the families in Hampton the first summer that Mr. Bacheller came to Hampton," followed by a list "The second Sumer." Among those in the second list are mentioned "Goodman Fillbrek and Thomas[1] Chaes." This is documentary evidence that Thomas[1] Chase was in Hampton in 1640. (Records and Files of the Quarterly Courts of Essex County, 7 :280).

John Farmer, in his classification of the early settlers of Hampton, places Thomas Chase among the "young men that had lots," following the settlers in "the Second Summer" after Mr. Bachiler came. (Provincial Papers of New Hampshire, 1 :151-2).

Inventory of estate of Thomas[1] Chase late of Hampton deceased, 14: 4 mo. 1653. [superscription]
Y[e] 2: of y[e] 4: mo: 1653:
A trew Inventary of y[e] estatt of y[e] latt Desesed housband of y[e] wedow Chase of hampton as ffoloeth:

	li.	s.	d.
ye house and hous lott containing aboutt ten Akeres -	20 :	0 :	0
ten Akeres of Salt marsh att - - - - -	5 :	0 :	0
5 Akeres of Salt marsh att - - - - -	1 :	10 :	0
12 Akeres more of Salt marsh att - - -	3 :	00 :	0
8 Akeres of Fresh medow att - - - -	8 :	00 :	0
34 Akeres of upland att - - - - -	8 :	00 :	0
5 Shares of Commones att - - - - -	6 :	00 :	0
20 Akeres more of upland - - - - -	5 :	00 :	0
5 Akeres more of Fresh medow att - - - -	1 :	10 :	0
2 oxen att - - - - - - - -	12 :	00 :	0

3 Cowes att - - - - - - - -	13:	10:	0
2 young bestes of 2 yeare old - - - - -	6:	00:	0
2 Shottes att - - - - - - - -	1:	00:	0
2 bras Ketteles and an Iron pott att - - - -	3:	00:	0
on[e] Iron pott a warming pan and a bras skillett att -	1:	00:	0
in puter att - - - - - - - -	1:	10:	0
tramills pott hokes friing pan att - - - -	0:	14:	0
ye Dary vesseles att - - - - - - -	1:	00:	0
3 bedes and beding - - - - - - -	10:	00:	0
Cheste tabeles and cheares and other bomber att -	2:	00:	0
	li	s	
The Som is - - - - - - -	108	14	0

his
Robert Pag X mark
Abraham Perkins
William Fifield

More: recovvred by a iudgm^t att Salisbury Court
14th of ye 4th mo: (53) of Willi: Ffurbur - -   3: 4: 10
Five pound more Pa cowe   Som: tot: 111: 18: 10

This was given uppon oath by Elizabeth Chase
to bee a true inventory of hir husbands estate
Tho: Chase late deceased:

Tho: Bradbury rec^d

Inventories: Tho: Chase 1653.

(Essex County Probate Files 5185)

Children, born in Hampton:

2. THOMAS,[2] b. 1643.
3. JOSEPH, b. 1645.
4. JAMES, b. 1649.
5. ISAAC, b. 1 Apr. 1650.
6. ABRAHAM, b. 6 Aug. 1652.
   The last two were recorded as born in Hampton and their births
   are to be found in the Old Norfolk Co. Returns from Hampton.

SECOND GENERATION

2

THOMAS² CHASE (Thomas¹), born in Hampton, N. H., 1643; died there, 23 Oct. 1714. At a Quarterly Court held at Salisbury, 9 Apr. 1667, he was confirmed as guardian of his brother Isaac Chase who had made choice of him for guardian. (Records and Files of the Quarterly Courts of Essex County, 3:407). Thomas² "Chas," aged about twenty-three years, deposed before Samuel Dalton of Hampton, commissioner, 20 June 1667. (Ibid 425). His uncle Thomas Philbrick, aged forty-two years, deposed before the same magistrate at the same time. (Ibid). At a Quarterly Court held at Salisbury, 13 Apr. 1669, he was convicted "for not coming to the public ordinance." (Ibid 4:132). He with others was presented at the Court held at Salisbury, 12 Apr. 1670," for not frequenting the public ordinances of Christ on Lord's days and using reproachful speeches against Mr. Cotton and his doctrine." (Ibid 238). At a Court held at Salisbury, 14 Apr. 1674, he and twelve others were convicted "for breach of the law called Quaker's meeting" and admonished. (Ibid 298). At a Court held at Hampton, 13 Oct. 1674, a warrant was ordered to be issued for court fees due from these same persons upon presentments at the last Salisbury court. (Ibid 409). On 30 May 1676, he was appointed administrator of the estate of Abraham² Chase. (Ibid 6:142).

Ralph Hall of Exeter sells two-thirds of 15 acres of salt marsh in Hampton on the south side of Falls River, with allowance of two acres for creeks and ponds, to Thomas Chase of Hampton, 3 Dec. 1668. (Old Norfolk Deeds, 2:233).

Thomas Sleeper of Hampton quitclaims to Thomas² Chase of Hampton land that Sleeper sold to him above 20 years ago, 5 acres of salt marsh by Birche Island, 3 acres of fresh meadow by the land of Christopher Palmer and 10 acres of upland in ye North Playne, 3 Nov. 1669. (Ibid 2:233).

Samuel Fellows of Salisbury sells Thomas Chase of Hampton, planter, his portion of the division in Hall's Farm in Salisbury, 7 Mar. 1669/70. (Ibid 2:243).

Ralph Hall of Exeter sells Thomas Chase of Hampton, planter, one third of 15 acres of salt marsh in Hampton, 30 Nov. 1670. (Ibid 2:296).

Thomas Chase of Hampton "for ye love and good will that I have and doe beare unto ye people of God (called Quakers) doe give, grant, etc. . . . to John Hussey of Hampton above said, on behalf of ye said People of God . . . a certain piece of land for a burying place containing 60 rods or thereabouts in Hampton to be improved for a burying place or to build a meeting house if they think best," 1 Jan. 1689. (Essex Co. Deeds, 10:88).

Thomas² Chase of Hampton "being aged & weke of body" made his will, 26 Apr. 1712, which was proved, 8 Dec. 1714. He mentions

therein his brothers Joseph[2] Chase, Isaac[2] Chase and Jacob Garland;
Mary[3] Chase, daughter of James[2] Chase; the widow Duglis and her
daughter Mary Duglis; his "cousin" [niece] Abigail[3] Chase, daughter
of his brother James[2] Chase, now widow of John[3] Chase deceased
and her sons Jonathan,[4] Elihu[4] and John[4] Chase under 21; his brother
Isaac[2] Chase's eldest son; Elizabeth[4] and Hannah[4] Chase the two
daughters of Abigail[3] Chase by John[3] Chase her husband; Henry
Williams and Christian and Lydia Haskins their daughter; Sarah
Downer and Ephriam Hoyt; his "cousin" [niece] Abigail[3] Chase
widow of John[3] Chase deceased to be executrix. (New Hampshire
Wills, 1:685-8). He never married and his niece Abigail[3] Chase,
wife of John[3] Chase, grandson of Aquila,[1] cared for him in his old
age and inherited his homestead in Hampton. The estate was valued
at £837:10s.

3

JOSEPH[2] CHASE (Thomas[1]), born in Hampton, N. H., 1645;
died there, 12 Jan. 1717/8. He married in Hampton, 31 Dec. 1671,
RACHEL PARTRIDGE, daughter of William and Ann Partridge, born in
Salisbury, 19 June 1650; died in Hampton, 27 Oct. 1718. They lived
in Hampton near "The Landing" where a few graves of the Chase
and Freese family still remain in 1928.

Thomas Philbrick Jr. of Hampton for £10 sells Joseph Chase
of Hampton, four acres of the east field in Hampton, bounded on ye
south with a highway, 23 Jan. 1666. (Old Norfolk Deeds, 2:234).

John Garland of Hampton sells him one share in the "Cowes
common" and one share in the "oxen common" of Hampton, 30 Jan.
1667. (Ibid 2:235).

Joseph Chase of Hampton for £14 sells David Lamprey of the
same town about four acres of upland in Hampton, "in ye east field
with a common way on ye south going towards ye sea," 24 Mar.
1673/4; acknowledged by him and his wife Rachel, 28 Dec. 1674.
(Ibid 3:30).

Joseph[2] Chase of Hampton, "being Antient," made his will, 14
June 1704, which was proved 12 Feb. 1717/8, with a codicil dated,
19 May 1716. He mentions therein his wife Rachel; his daughter
Anne[3] Sinkeler and her children, the eldest son and the other children
now born—her sons under 24 and her daughters under 18; his
daughter Elizabeth[3] Hilyard and her eldest son or daughters; his
daughter Rachel[3] Freese and her sons and daughters; "Unto ye poore
among the people called Quakers fifty pounds in money;" reserves
"household good for the entertaining of strangers more particularly
Quakers;" his sons-in-law Benjamin Hilyard and Jacob Freese to be
executors with his wife Rachel; codicil mentions his son-in-law Jacob
Freese to have one half of his sloop; Rachel Lock now Rachel Moulton to have £5; Elizabeth Swett, daughter of Moses Swett £5;
Elizabeth[4] Chase, daughter of John[3] Chase deceased, £10 at the
age of 18; Moses Swett £10; James Stanyon and Anne his wife a
debt and £5; Mary Dow, wife of Henry Dow, £5; Lydia Norton,
wife of Samuel Norton, £5. Inventory taken 27 Feb. 1717/8,
amounting to £3430: 11: 9. (N. H. Wills, 1:526-530).

The Rev. Alonzo H. Quint, D. D., in his account of those who were captured at Cochecho, 27 June 1689, gives one as Joseph Chase (Provincial Papers of N. H., 2: 50). In Rev. John Pike's *Journal* the name was "Jo: Chh" which was intended for John Church who escaped from the Indians before they reached Winnepesaukee.

Children, born in Hampton:

HANNAH,[3] b. 5 June 1672; d. 10 June 1674, or 4 Dec. 1674.

ELIZABETH, b. 11 Mar. 1674; d. 8 Sept. 1675.

JONATHAN, b. 14 Mar. 1676; drowned "att Corituck," (1) 1 Feb. 1696.

ANN, b. 9 Jan. 1677/8; m. (1) 25 Aug. 1697, Bradstreet Wiggin; m. (2) John Sinclair of Hampton. Four children by first husband and four by second. (2)

ELIZABETH, b. 14 Feb. 1684/5; m. 3 Apr. or Aug. 1706, Benjamin Hilliard of Hampton, his second wife; m. (2) 17 June 1725, Capt. Joseph Tilton of Hampton.

RACHEL, b. 27 Apr. 1687; m. (1) before 14 June 1704, Lt. Jacob Freese who d. 5 Nov. 1727; m. (2) 4 Jan. 1737, Andrew Wiggin.

4

JAMES[2] CHASE (Thomas[1]), born in Hampton, 1649; died shortly before, 7 Mar. 1703/4. He married in Hampton, 2 Nov. 1675, ELIZABETH GREEN, daughter of Judge Henry and Mary Green of Hampton. She was born in Hampton, 11 June 1656, and married (2) JOSEPH CASS of Hampton.

Rev. John Wheelwright, trustee in trust of the wife and children of Robert Nanny, late of Boston deceased, brought a suit against James Chase 'for not paying [for] 12,000 feet of good merchantable boards due for rent of a part of a saw mill now [1674] standing upon Taylor's river in Hampton, according to an agreement dated, 2 Jan. 1672, at a Court held at Salisbury, 14 Apr. 1674. The verdict was for the plaintiff, and the case was appealed to the Court of Assistants. (Records and Files of the Quarterly Courts of Essex County, 5 :295).

John Severans of Salisbury, victualler, for £6 sells James Chase of Hampton, planter, six acres" in a place called Halls farme" in Salisbury, 23 Apr. 1669. (Old Norfolk Deeds, 2 :207).

John Ilsley of Salisbury for £25 sells James Chase of Hampton, planter, two divisions of upland in Hall's farm in Salisbury, 28 Jan. 1672. The same was deeded back to Ilsley, 5 June 1673. (Ibid 2 :409; 448).

Administration on his estate was granted to John[3] Chase of Hampton, 7 Mar. 1703/4. James[2] Chase was called his father-in-law. An agreement was made and concluded 4 June 1705, between John[3] Chase, John Chapman and Mary[3] Chase, all of Hampton, who set forth that whereas James[2] Chase of Hampton, late deceased, left lands and three daughters, viz. Abigail,[3] Dorothy[3] and Mary[3] Chase, and that administration is granted to John[3] Chase above named, they agree that John Chapman shall have his part in the home lot in right

(1) Corituck probably Caritunk or Carrartoank (Indian for "Falls on the Kennebec." (Me. Hist. Collections, 4 : 105)

(2) She was living as Mrs. Ann Sinkler of Stratham, 19 Apr. 1717. (Essex Co. Deeds, 31 :72, 214)

of his wife Dorothy and that Mary[3] Chase shall have a piece of salt marsh lying near the Great Boars Head and that John[3] Chase shall have one share in the ox-common in right of his wife Abigail, to which they set their hands on the day above written, John[3] Chase, John Chapman and Mary[3] Chase. (N. H. Probate Wills, 1 :522-524).

Children, born in Hampton:

HANNAH,[2] b. 22 Dec. 1677.

ABIGAIL, b. 27 Aug. 1681; m. about 1697, John[3] Chase (John,[2] AQUILA[1]). See *Aquila Chase's Descendants*. (Family 14)

DOROTHY, b. 17 Mar. 1685/6; m. 16 Mar. 1705, John Chapman, who d. 17 Oct. 1705.

MARY, b. 8 Feb. 1688; alive and unmarried 4 June 1705.

5

LT. ISAAC[2] CHASE (Thomas[1]), born in Hampton, 1 Apr. 1650; died in Tisbury, 19 May 1727, aged about 80 years. The Dr. John B. Chace Manuscript states that he was born 1 Apr. 1647. Dow in his History of Hampton gives 1 Apr. 1650. He married (1) in Hampton, 20 Feb. 1673, MARY PERKINS, daughter of Isaac and Susannah Perkins, born in Hampton, 23 July 1658; died about 1674. He married (2) in Tisbury, 5 Dec. 1675, MARY TILTON who died in Tisbury, 14 June 1746, in her 88th year. She was the daughter of William and Susanna Tilton of Lynn. They removed from Hampton to Tisbury in 1674. His estate comprised nearly the whole of the present village of Vineyard Haven. He was a blacksmith.

In naming the heirs of Thomas[1] Chase and of Abraham[2] Chase the above Isaac[2] was named after James[2] and the probabilities are that he was younger than his brother James,[2] notwithstanding that his gravestone calls him "about 80." He was a Quaker and the town records of Tisbury contain the following. "Febbary 5 1674, the townsmen of Tysbury do not give unto isack chace of Hampton liberty to settle in the town   Recorded by ordar of the town."

He made his will, 12 Feb. 1721/2, which was proved 7 July 1727. He mentions therein his wife Mary, his five daughters, viz. Rachel[3] Knight, Mary[3] Weeks, Hannah[3] Pease, Sarah[3] Cobb and Priscilla[3] Folger, his son Abraham[3] Chase, his grandchildren Thomas[4] and Sarah[4] Chase, children of his son Thomas[3] deceased, and his six grandchildren, children of his son Isaac[3] deceased, his sons James,[3] Joseph[3] and Jonathan[3] Chase. (Dukes Co. Probate).

Children by the second wife, born in Tisbury:

7. THOMAS,[3] b. 9 Nov. 1677.

RACHEL, b. 25 Oct. 1679; m. (1) 19 July 1700, Samuel Knight of Charlestown and Sudbury, where he d. about 1721; m. (2) Samuel Munkley.

8. ISAAC, b. 21 Jan. 1681/2.

9. ABRAHAM, b. 10 Jan. 1683/4.

10. JAMES, b. 15 Jan. 1685/6.

MARY, b. 17 Jan. 1687/8; m. 14 Jan. 1704, Benjamin Weeks of Falmouth.

11. JOSEPH, b. 26 Feb. 1689.

12. JONATHAN, b. 28 Dec. 1691.

HANNAH, b. 25 Nov. 1693; m. 30 Oct. 1712, Nathan Pease.

SARAH, b. 15 Oct. 1695; m. 27 June 1716, Samuel Cobb of Tisbury.

PRISCILLA, b. 12 Nov. 1697; m. 18 Nov. 1718, Nathaniel Folger;
d. 30 Dec. 1753; four children.

ELIZABETH, b. 7 Sept. 1703; d. unm. 27 Sept. 1719, aged about
16 y.

6

ABRAHAM² CHASE (Thomas¹), born in Hampton, N. H., 6 Aug.
1652; died being "slain in ye warres" in 1676. He was one of the
Hampton men who was sent for the defense of Marlborough in Mar.
1676. (Dow's History of Hampton, 1:224).

Thomas² Chase was appointed administrator of the estate of
Abraham² Chase by Maj. Pike and Mr. Samuel Dalton on the second
Tuesday in Apr. 1676 and brought in an inventory to the Court held
at Hampton, 30 May 1676. (Records and Files of Essex County
6:142). At the Court held at Salisbury, 14 Nov. 1676, Thomas
Chase,² administrator of the estate of Abraham² Chase, moved the
Court to order that the estate be divided among the surviving breth-
ren, Thomas,² Joseph,² James² and Isaac² Chase. Mr. Samuel Dalton
and Ens. John Sanborn were ordered to take an account of the administrator of what debts he had or should pay upon account of said
estate. (Ibid 214).

Samuel Dalton, one of the commissioners of Hampton to end
small cases made the following record in his private Journal:

"On 29: 3: 1673, Abraham² Chase, making a bold attempt when
the commissioners were seated in the meeting house, by firing off a
pistol in at the window, burning a hole in the collers and breaking
down some of the glass, whereby some of those who stood near were
in danger, was fined." (Ibid 5:235). With others he was convicted
and admonished for breach of the law called "Quaker's meeting," at
the Court held at Salisbury, 14 Apr. 1674 (Ibid 298). At the next
session the Court ordered a warrant to be issued for court fees due
from him. (Ibid 409). He was unmarried and in his twenty-fourth
year at the time of his death.

THIRD GENERATION

7

THOMAS³ CHASE (Lt. Isaac²), born in Tisbury, 9 Nov. 1677; died in Virginia during a coasting voyage in his sloop *Vineyard*, 22 Dec. 1721. He married in Edgartown, 21 Feb. 1704, JANE SMITH, daughter of Benjamin and Jedidah (Mayhew) Smith, born about 1685. She married (2) in Tisbury, 15 May 1724, THOMAS CATHCART, son of Robert and Phebe (Coleman) Cathcart. He was born about 1692 and died childless, 19 Nov. 1730. Mr. Chase was master-mariner and lived at Homes Hole in Tisbury. His estate was divided 15 Oct. 1725. He was master of the sloop *Vineyard* which arrived in Boston from Conn. 24 May 1716.

Children, born in Tisbury:

13. THOMAS,⁴ b. 29 Dec. 1713.
    SARAH, b. 14 Dec. 1717; m. (1) 8 Nov. 1733, Samuel Daggett; m. (2) about 1745, Ebenezer Allen; d. in Tisbury 1 Dec. 1803, in her 86th year. Three children.

8

ISAAC³ CHASE (Lt. Isaac²), born in Tisbury, 21 Jan. 1681/2; died at sea, 13 Oct. 1716. He married in Edgartown, 3 Apr. 1702, MARY PEASE, daughter of James and Elizabeth (Norton) Pease, born about 1680. She married (2) in Chilmark, 9 July 1720, RICHARD CROOKER [CROCKER]. Mr. Chase was a mariner and a blacksmith and lived at "Chickemmoo" (a weir fishing place) in Chilmark. His estate was administered upon by his brother Abraham³ Chase, 25 Feb. 1719/20. Rev. William Homes of Chilmark wrote "13 Oct. 1716, Isaac Chase was lost this day being in a sloop, was cast away." (Register 49:414).

Administration on his estate was granted to his widow Mary Chase, 25 Feb. 1720. (Dukes Co. Probate). Division of his estate, 19 Apr. 1734 names Nathan⁴ the eldest son and Cornelius,⁴ Stephen,⁴ Joseph,⁴ Isaac⁴ and Levi.⁴

Children, born in Chilmark:

14. NATHAN,⁴ b. 16 July 1702.
    CORNELIUS, b. 14 July 1705; d. unm. about 1727.
15. STEPHEN, b. 24 Sept. 1708.
16. ISAAC, b. 15 July 1712.
17. JOSEPH, b. 22 Dec. 1713.
18. LEVI, b. 30 Mar. 1716.

9

ABRAHAM³ CHASE (Lt. Isaac²), born in Tisbury, 10 Jan. 1683/4; died 20 Dec. 1763. He married (1) about 1709, ABIGAIL BARNARD, daughter of Nathaniel and Mary (Barnard) Barnard of Nantucket. William C. Folger of Nantucket in his compilation stated positively that in all probability she was the daughter as above indicated. She was born about 1685 and died in Tisbury, 15 Oct. 1731, aged 46 y. He married (2) 5 Mar. 1732, MERCY NICKERSON of Falmouth, [probably daughter of Nathaniel and Katherine (Stewart) Nickerson of Chatham] who was born in 1710. She married (2) THOMAS WINSTON and died as his widow in Tisbury, 11 Sept. 1786, in her 77th year. Mr. Chase was a ferryman, innholder and trader and lived at "Homes Hole." He made his will, 1 Feb. 1760, which was probated, 5 Mar. 1764.

Children, born in Tisbury:

> MARY,⁴ b. about 1710; m. 23 Sept. 1731, Reuben Bunker; four children; she d. 14 Nov. 1795.
> ELEANOR, b. 8 Oct. 1712; m. 29 Nov. 1734, James Long.
> ABIGAIL, b. 30 Oct. 1714; m. John Wheldon of "Homes Hole;" eight children.
> 19. ABRAHAM, b. 14 Feb. 1716.
> TIMOTHY, b. 23 July 1717; probably d. without issue.
> HANNAH, b. 15 Mar. 1725; m. (1) 21 Sept. 1742, John Ferguson; m. (2) 28 Mar. 1769, Christopher Luce; d. 26 Nov. 1798.

Children by second wife, born in Tisbury:

> 20. VALENTINE, b. 15 June 1735.
> 21. ZACCHEUS, b. 15 June 1737.
> DAVID, b. 4 June 1739; d. 18 Oct. 1739.
> WAITSTILL MERCY, b. 9 Apr. 1741; m. (1) 3 July 1758, John West of Dartmouth; m. (2) Jeremiah Crapo.
> MARGARET, b. 21 May 1750; m. 11 Apr. 1769, Samuel Look; d. 10 Oct. 1815. Twelve children.

10

JAMES³ CHASE (Lt. Isaac²), born in Tisbury, 15 Jan. 1685/6; died in Nantucket in 1728 or 1729. He married about 1708, RACHEL BROWNE, daughter of John and Rachel (Gardner) Browne, born 14 Dec. 1687; died in Nantucket, 24 Sept. 1741. They removed from "Homes Hole" to Newport, R. I., about 1712. She returned to Nantucket before she settled her husband's estate.

Children, first two born in "Homes Hole," others in Newport:

> ANNE,⁴ b. 22 Apr. 1709; m. 5 Dec. 1733, Timothy Folger.
> 22. BENJAMIN, b. 28 Aug. 1710.
> RACHEL, b. 30 Aug. 1712; m. 18 Feb. 1730, Peter Fitch.
> 23. JAMES, b. 31 July 1715.
> BROWNE, b. 13 Mar. 1717/8; d. 26 May 1798.
> ELIZABETH, b. 16 Feb. 1720; m. 18 Jan. 1738/9, George Gardner.
> JEDIDAH, b. 15 Feb. 1723; m. 16 Feb. 1744, Robert Barker.

11

JOSEPH³ CHASE (Lt. Isaac²), born in Tisbury, 26 Feb. 1689; died in Edgartown, 1 May 1749, aged 60 y. 2 m. 20 d. He married in Nantucket, 16 Sept. 1714, LYDIA COFFIN, daughter of Nathaniel and Damaris (Gayer) Coffin, born in Nantucket, 16 May 1697; died in Edgartown, 17 July 1749, aged 52 y. 2 m. 11 d. He was a hatter and lived at "Homes Hole;" removed to Nantucket before 1729 and about 1737 to Edgartown where he and his wife were buried. At Edgartown he owned a lot on the harbor front, south of Main street.

Children:

24. ABEL,⁴ b. 9 Oct. 1719.

> MARY, b. 9 Apr. 1720/1; bp. at Nantucket, 26 Sept. 1731; m.
> 4 Oct. 1748, David Dunham of Edgartown. Three children.
>
> PRISCILLA, b. about 1722; m. 17 Mar. 1740/41, Henry Smith Sr.
> of Nantucket (then called Sherbourn).
>
> DAMARIS, b. 12 May 1724; m. about 1742, Peter Ripley of Edgar-
> town; she d. 6 Dec. 1761. Seven children.
>
> LYDIA, b. 6 June 1725; bp. at Nantucket, 26 Sept. 1731; m. Shu-
> bael Dunham of Edgartown and after 1762 of Tisbury; she d.
> 29 Oct. 1806. Twelve children.
>
> RACHEL, b. 26 Apr. 1730; bp. at Nantucket, 26 Sept. 1731; m. 9
> July 1769, Thomas Gwinn, his third wife.
>
> SARAH, b. 7 Apr. 1735; m. 1 Oct. 1753, Seth Pease; she d. 1 May
> 1799; eight children.
>
> BENJAMIN, b. 14 May 1737; probably d. young.
>
> JOSEPH, bp. 24 Sept. 1738; supposed to have been drowned.

25. THOMAS, b. 10 Apr. 1739; bp. 24 June 1739.

> Eight of the above named children were baptized at Edgartown,
> 24 Sept. 1738.

12

JONATHAN³ CHASE (Lt. Isaac²), born in Tisbury, 28 Dec. 1691;
died in Newport, R. I., 20 July 1742 or 1743. He married about
1710, MEHITABLE ——— about whom nothing is known. He was a
vintner and lived at "Homes Hole" and later removed to Newport,
R. I.

Children:

> ANNE,⁴ b. 1 Nov. 1711; m. (1) Richard Edwards; m. (2) 10 July
> 1740, John Scott.

26. PERKINS, b. 6 Jan. 1713.

> MEHITABLE, b. 4 May 1716; m. 9 July 1738, George Lawrence.

27. JONATHAN, b. 1 Feb. 1718.

> JEDIDAH, b. 4 Sept. 1720; d. 1 Dec. 1729.
>
> PHILANDA, b. about 1722; m. 8 Apr. 1741, Eleazer White.
>
> ABIGAIL, b. 30 Jan. 1724; m. 17 June 1744, John Downs.

28. ANDREW, b. 30 Aug. 1726.

29. HEMAN, b. 6 Apr. 1728.

30. PHILIP, b. 3 Oct. 1730.

FOURTH GENERATION

13

THOMAS[4] CHASE (Thomas,[3] Thomas[2]), born in Tisbury, 29 Dec. 1713; died in Virginia, 7 Jan. 1738/9. He married in Tisbury, 16 Aug. 1733, ELIZABETH ATHEARN, daughter of Jabez and Katherine (Belcher) Athearn, born in Tisbury, 13 Apr. 1715. She married (2) 16 Dec. 1740, CAPT. PETER WEST of Tisbury. She died 2 Sept 1789. Mr. Chase was a mariner and they lived at "Homes Hole."

Children, born in Tisbury:

31. SAMUEL,[5] b. 26 May 1734.
 JEDIDAH, b. 14 Feb. 1736; m. (1) 9 Nov. 1757, Elijah Daggett; m. (2) after 1771, ——— Kimball of Tisbury; seven children.
 SARAH, b. 8 Apr. 1739; m. 15 Nov. 1755, Jonathan Manter of Tisbury, and d. 20 Dec. 1831; eleven children.

14

NATHAN[4] CHASE (Isaac,[3] Lt. Isaac[2]), born in Chilmark, 16 July 1702; died in Tisbury, between 30 Aug. and 20 Nov. 1750. He married in Nantucket, 24 Oct. 1723, PARNELL LONG, daughter of Robert and Sarah (Skiff) Long, who died in Tisbury between 12 Sept. and 4 Oct. 1757. They lived in Nantucket till 1739 when they removed to Tisbury.

Children, born in Nantucket:

32. THOMAS,[5] b. about 1725.
 JONATHAN, d. without issue about 1757.
 BENJAMIN, served in the French and Indian War, 1758; made his will 24 May 1758, which was proved 2 Jan. 1759; no issue. He was in Capt. Josiah Thacher's Co. from 10 Apr. to 30 Oct. 1758 and was reported dead on 30 Oct. 1758. (Mass. Archives, 96: 126, 433)
33. SHUBAEL, alive 24 May 1758.
34. ISAAC.
 MARY, m. 25 Aug. 1748, Thomas Smith of Martha's Vineyard; nine children.
 ANNA, m. Joseph Hovey.

15

STEPHEN[4] CHASE (Isaac,[3] Lt. Isaac[2]), born in Chilmark, 24 Sept. 1708; married (1) in Nantucket, 7 Sept. 1730, PATIENCE MARSHALL, daughter of Joseph and Mary (or Mercy) (Short) Marshall, born in Nantucket, 11 July 1708; died there, 27 Feb. 1740/41. He married (2) in Nantucket, 3 Jan. 1742, DINAH FOLGER, daughter of Jonathan and Margaret (Gardner) Folger, born in Nantucket, 24 June 1720. She died 18 Feb. 1786. He died in Nantucket, 28 Aug. 1787. They lived in Nantucket.

Children, born in Nantucket:

35. CHARLES,[5] b. 31 May 1731.
 RUTH, b. 1 Sept. 1734 (sic); d. young.

CORNELIUS, b. 21 Sept. 1734; d. in 1739.
ABIGAIL, b. 15 Apr. 1737; m. (1) 31 Jan. 1760, Jethro Gardner;
m. (2) 31 Dec. 1767, Henry Dow.
REBECCA, b. 10 July 1739; m. —— Hardy of Hudson, N. Y.
Children by second wife, born in Nantucket:
MARGARET, b. 10 May 1743; m. 8 Dec. 1768, Chrispus Gardner of
L. I. He was son of David and Elizabeth Gardner.
DEBORAH, b. 5 May 1750; m. 9 Jan. 1772, John Morris.
MIRIAM, b. 12 Dec. 1747; m. 30 Oct. 1765, Benjamin Ray, son
of Samuel and Mary (Fullington) Ray; went to Hudson.
MARY, b. 13 Sept. 1756; m. (1) William Bunker; m. (2) William
Slade.
36. JOSEPH, b. 23 Mar. 1752.
37. REUBEN, b. 23 June 1754.
38. ZIMRI, b. 11 Dec. 1758.

16

ISAAC[4] CHASE (Isaac,[3] Lt. Isaac[2]), born in Chilmark, 15 July
1712; married (1) in Nantucket, 24 Feb. 1736/7, MARY COFFIN,
daughter of Joseph and Bethiah (Macy) Coffin, born in Nantucket,
9 Feb. 1720; died 2 Oct. 1765. He married (2) BETHIAH (MAY-
HEW) NORTON, widow of Jacob Norton and daughter of Paine and
Mary (Rankin) Mayhew of Chilmark. She was born 31 Mar. 1712;
died 29 Mar. 1796. He was a carpenter and they lived in Tisbury.
Children by first wife, born in Tisbury:

EUNICE,[5] b. 4 Aug. 1738; m. (1) Valentine [4] Chase; (Family 20)
m. (2) 29 Dec. 1761, David Merry.
RHODA, b. 4 May 1741; m. 3 Nov. 1757, James Winslow.
39. GEORGE, b. 30 Mar. 1744.
ISAAC, b. 8 May 1746; d. — Nov. 1771.
MARY, b. 11 June 1748; m. 10 Dec. 1767, Capt. George West of
Tisbury and after 1790 of Union, Me.; she d. 17 May 1802;
six children.
40. JOSEPH, b. 6 Aug. 1750.
HANNAH, b. 16 Aug. 1756; m. 9 July 1778, Elisha Luce; she d.
7 Feb. 1799; nine children. (Family 44)
41. CORNELIUS, b. 10 June 1759.

17

JOSEPH[4] CHASE (Isaac,[3] Lt. Isaac[2]), born in Chilmark, 22 Dec.
1713; married in Nantucket, 26 Dec. 1737, MIRIAM COFFIN, daughter
of Joseph and Bethiah (Macy) Coffin, born in Nantucket, 2 Dec.
1717. He was a mariner and lived in Nantucket.
Children, born in Nantucket:
42. FRANCIS,[5] b. 10 Sept. 1738.
PAUL, b. 2 Aug. 1741; d. 3 Dec. 1756.

18

LEVI[4] CHASE (Isaac,[3] Lt. Isaac[2]), born in Chilmark, 30 Mar.
1716; died in Sandwich, 24 Mar. 1774, aged 57 y. 11 m. 14 d. He
married (1) in Barnstable, 19 Feb. 1744, MARY PIKE, probably the
Mary who was a daughter of Leonard and Ann (Snow) Pike of

Truro, baptized there 6 Mar. 1725/6. Leonard Pike lived in Truro and there eleven children were baptized between 1725 and 1744, Mary being the eldest daughter. Mr. Chase married (2) in Barnstable, 23 Sept. 1762, HANNAH BLOSSOM of Barnstable. The ceremony was performed by Rev. Oakes Shaw. (The Mayflower Descendant, 19:156). In 1756 he purchased for £20 pew No. 7, in the northwest corner of the lower floor in the new Meeting House in Sandwich. He married (3) in Bridgewater, 20 Mar. 1771, SILENCE FOBES, daughter of John and Abigail Fobes, born in Bridgewater, 1 Mar. 1721/22. The widow Silence Chase was admitted to the Church of Christ in Lee, Berkshire Co., 11 Nov. 1792. She died there, a widow, 31 Aug. 1797, in her 76th year.

Levi Chase of Sandwich being "under decay of body" made his will, 31 Jan. 1774. To his wife Silence he gave an honorable support for life, she to be cared for by his son Levi. He also gave property to his sons Leonard, Levi, Isaac and Nathan Chase and to his daughters Sarah Chase and Tabitha Freeman £13:6:8 each besides other things (Barnstable Co. Probate, 17:188).

Children, born in Sandwich:

43. LEONARD,⁶ b. about 1745.
    TABITHA, m. 14 Mar. 1765, Edmund Freeman, b. in Sandwich, 10 Oct. 1743, son of Thomas and Kezia (Hoxie) Freeman. His widow Tabitha adm. upon his estate 14 Dec. 1778. She made her will 1807; seven children. (Freeman Genealogy, 48:83.)
43a. LEVI, b. 5 Mar. 1750.
    ISAAC, b. in 1752; d. in Sandwich, 14 Sept. 1779, in his 28th year.
    NATHAN, alive 31 Jan. 1774.
    SARAH, b. about 1754; m. after 1774, Timothy Goodspeed; twelve children; she d. 30 July 1836. (Goodspeed Genealogy, 313.)

19

ABRAHAM⁴ CHASE (Abraham,³ Lt. Isaac²), born in Tisbury, 14 Feb. 1716; died shortly before May 1752. He married about 1737, DELIVERANCE NICKERSON, daughter of William Nickerson. She was born in 1712 and died in Tisbury, a widow, 3 Sept. 1788 in her 77th year. He was a trader and they lived at Homes Hole. His property was valued at £183:7s. His widow, Deliverance, was granted letters of administration, 5 May 1752.

Children, born in Tisbury:

ABIGAIL,⁶ b. about 1738; m. (int. 26 Nov. 1758) John Burgess of Rochester. Their son Tristram Burgess, b. in 1770, was a member of Congress and late Chief Justice of Rhode Island.
ELIZABETH, b. about 1740; m. 24 Dec. 1767, Matthew Merry; she d. 2 May 1818; five children.
MERCY, b. 17 Feb. 1743; m. 5 Dec. 1765, Jethro Athearn; she d. 27 July 1820; seven children.
44. TIMOTHY, b. 22 June 1745.
45. BENJAMIN, b. about 1747.
    MARY, b. Jan. 1749; m. (1) 17 Jan. 1769, Nathaniel Ketchum; m. (2) 18 June 1778, Joseph Merry.
    DELIVERANCE, b. about 1751; m. 17 Jan. 1773, Charles Edmundson.

20

VALENTINE[4] CHASE (Abraham,[3] Lt. Isaac[2]), born in Tisbury, 15 June 1735; died before 6 Apr. 1761. He married about 1755, EUNICE[5] CHASE, daughter of Isaac and Mary (Coffin) Chase, born in Tisbury, 4 Aug. 1738. (Family 16). She married (2) in Tisbury, 29 Dec. 1761, DAVID MERRY who removed to New Vineyard, Me., about 1794. She died 6 Aug. 1797. There were two children by her first husband and seven by her second. Mr. Chase lived in Homes Hole.

Children, born in Tisbury:

46. ABRAHAM,[5] b. 9 Dec. 1756.
     EUNICE, b. 18 Mar. 1759.

21

ZACCHEUS[4] CHASE (Abraham,[3] Lt. Isaac[2]), born in Tisbury, 15 June 1737; died at sea in 1778. He married (1) in Tisbury, 22 Feb. 1759, HANNAH BUTLER, daughter of David and Ann (Hatch) Butler, born in Tisbury, 20 June 1736; died there, 10 May 1770. He probably married (2) DELIVERANCE (CAHOON) DAGGETT, widow of Peter Daggett. Mr. Chase was a cooper and mariner and lived at Homes Hole.

Child by first wife, born in Tisbury:

47. NICKERSON,[5] b. about 1773.

22

BENJAMIN[4] CHASE (James,[3] Lt. Isaac[2]), born in Tisbury, 28 Aug. 1710; married in Nantucket, 12 Dec. 1734, MARGARET GARDNER, daughter of Joseph and Ruth (Coffin) Gardner of Nantucket. She died in Nantucket as his widow, 22 May 1796. He is probably the Benjamin Chase who died in Nantucket, 14 Nov. 1767. They lived in Nantucket.

Children:

MARGARET,[5] b. 1752; m. in Nantucket, 21 Mar. 1771, Isaac Ross of Conn.
BROWN, d. of small pox, unm., 23 Dec. 1771.

23

JAMES[4] CHASE (James,[3] Lt. Isaac[2]), born in Newport, R. I., 31 July 1715; married in Nantucket, 15 Dec. 1737, ANNA GARDNER, daughter of Ebenezer and Judith (Coffin) Gardner, born in Nantucket, 16 Jan. 1720/21; died there, 11 July 1791. He died about 1788. He was called the "rigger." They lived in Nantucket.

Child, born in Nantucket:

48. JAMES,[5] b. 10 Nov. 1738.

24

ABEL[4] CHASE (Joseph,[3] Lt. Isaac[2]), born (probably in Tisbury), 9 Oct. 1719; married in Chilmark, 14 Feb. 1744, MERCY MAYHEW, daughter of Zephaniah and Bethiah (Wadsworth) Mayhew, born in

Chilmark, 22 July 1725; died 23 Feb. 1807. He died 25 Jan. 1808. He was a hatter and lived in Edgartown.

Children, born in Edgartown:

49. BENJAMIN,[5] b. 23 Dec. 1745.
50. ZEPHANIAH, b. 14 Mar. 1748.
    HENRY, b. 5 Oct. 1756; d. unm. 8 July 1832.

25

THOMAS[4] CHASE (Joseph,[3] Lt. Isaac[2]), baptized at Edgartown, 24 June 1739; died in Boston, 17 May 1787. He married about 1763, ANNA FIELDS who died 21 Oct. 1769, aged 31. He married (2) in Boston, 10 Oct. 1771, ELIZABETH BAGNALL who entered her intention 20 Nov. 1792, with WILLIAM GREENLEAF. They were married in Bolton, 29 Nov. 1792.

As a young man he removed to Boston and became a distiller in Auchmuty Lane. His distillery was near the famous Liberty Tree, at the junction of Orange, Essex and Newbury streets. John Adams left an account that one of the meetings of the "Sons of Liberty" was held in his office. He is said to have been one of those who suspended the effigies of Bute and Oliver from the Liberty Tree 14 Aug. 1765. He was a volunteer guard on the *Dartmouth* on the night of 29 Nov. 1773; also a member of the "Anti-Stamp Fire Society" and joined St. Andrews Lodge of Freemasons in 1769. He was a member of the Committee of Inspection in 1774. He joined the army and was Deputy Quartermaster General of the Massachusetts Troops in 1779.

The Massachusetts Centinel of 19 May 1787, contains this item: "Died—Last Thursday evening Thomas Chase, late Deputy-Quarter-Master-General for the Northern department, which office he sustained with integrity. He was humane, benevolent, and a sincere friend to his country. His funeral will proceed from the House of Mr. Robert Ruggles, in Newbury-Street, tomorrow afternoon, at six o'clock, which his friends and acquaintance are requested to attend."

Elizabeth Chase of Bolton made an ante-nuptial contract with William Greenleaf, 26 Nov. 1792, and placed in the hands of John Avery Jr. of Boston, to hold in trust, certain property in Boston and part of a house and farm in Bolton then in her occupation. (Suffolk Co. Deeds, 175: 153-5).

Children, born in Boston:

ANNA,[5] b. 20 Nov. 1764; d. young.
ANNA, b. 10 Aug. 1765; m. in Bolton, 22 Nov. 1787, Abel Allyne of Braintree.
51. THOMAS, b. 23 June 1767.
JOSEPH, b. 23 Mar. 1769; d. in infancy.

Children by the second wife, born in Boston:

ABIGAIL, b. 10 June 1772; m. 11 Feb. 1795, Ralph Coffin.
52. JOSEPH WARREN, b. about 1775.
ELIZA WARREN, b. 10 May 1781; m. (1) 1 Feb. 1801, Benjamin Prentice; m. (2) Dea. ——— Churchill.

26

PERKINS[4] CHASE (Jonathan,[3] Lt. Isaac[2]), born (probably in Tisbury) 6 Jan. 1713; married in Newport, R. I, 9 July 1738, ELIZABETH

IRESON. He died in Newport, in 1745. No children have been found in the records.

27

JONATHAN[4] CHASE (Jonathan,[3] Lt. Isaac[2]), born in Tisbury or Newport, R. I., 1 Feb. 1718; married in Newport, R. I., 9 June 1739, ANN KELLEY. The Vital Records of Newport as printed call her ANN SHELLEY. The name Shelley is not found there but the name Kelley is. The printed record is probably a mistake for Kelley.

28

ANDREW[4] CHASE (Jonathan,[3] Lt. Isaac[2]), born 30 Aug. 1726; married ANNA ALDEN. Their family consisted of seven children.

29

HEMAN[4] CHASE (Jonathan,[3] Lt. Isaac[2]), born 6 Apr. 1728; married PAMELIA (BREETER?). There were eight children in this family; names unknown to the compiler.

30

PHILIP[4] CHASE (Jonathan,[3] Lt. Isaac[2]), born 3 Oct. 1730; married ANNA BUDD. There were seven children.

FIFTH GENERATION

31

SAMUEL[5] CHASE (Thomas,[4] Thomas,[3] Lt. Isaac[2]), born in Tisbury, 26 May 1734; died in Livermore, Me., 2 Aug. 1801. He married about 1752, JEDIDAH MAYHEW, daughter of Dr. Thomas and Lydia (Lothrop) Mayhew, born at Chilmark, 3 Mar. 1733; died 23 Feb. 1807. Samuel Chase of Tisbury appears as a private in Capt. Jeremiah Mayhew's Co. and served from 6 Apr. to 1 Nov. 1759 at Annapolis Royal. (Mass. Archives, 97:279). They lived in Tisbury till after 1790 and then removed to Livermore.

Children, born in Tisbury:

SARAH,[6] b. 9 Sept. 1753; m. 27 Oct. 1774, William Merry who removed from Tisbury to Lenox in 1775, and d. 3 Aug. 1826; nine children.
53. THOMAS, b. 30 Sept. 1755.
ELIZABETH, b. about 1757; m. 3 Nov. 1784, Ward Tilton of Chilmark and Livermore. Four children.
54. SAMUEL, b. about 1759.
55. LOTHROP, b. about 1760.
56. SARSON, b. 28 Nov. 1762.
57. TRISTRAM, b. about 1764.
OLIVE, b. 12 Aug. 1766; m. 26 Mar. 1789, James Norton of Chilmark and Livermore; nine children.
LYDIA, b. 4 Feb. 1772; m. 11 Sept. 1794, Moses Hillman of Chilmark, Monmouth, Me., and Livermore, and d. 25 July 1819; ten children.
PAINE, b. about 1774; lost at sea.
PRUDENCE, b. 6 July 1776; m. 19 Feb. 1795, Napoleon Jones.

32

THOMAS[5] CHASE (Nathan,[4] Isaac,[3] Lt. Isaac[2]), born in Nantucket about 1725; died there 7 Mar. 1807. He married (1) ANNA SMITH of Martha's Vineyard. He married (2) in Edgartown, 23 Apr. 1751, SARAH CLAGHORN, daughter of Thomas and Abiah (Smith) Claghorn of Edgartown. She was born about 1727. They were living in Tisbury in 1790 at which time his family consisted of one male over 16 years of age, three males under 16 years, and two females.

Children by first wife:

58. ABRAHAM,[6] d. in the West Indies in June 1800.
59. NATHANIEL.
60. NATHAN.

Children by second wife:

61. JAMES, b. about 1755.
    ANN, b. about 1760; d. unm. 12 Jan. 1837, aged 77, at the Quaise Farm.
    MARY, b. 29 Apr. 1769; m. 4 Apr. 1787, Samuel Lambert of Tisbury; she d. 2 Dec. 1859; eight children.
    LYDIA, m. 21 Aug. 1792, Nathaniel Clapp.

33

SHUBAEL[5] CHASE (Nathan,[4] Isaac,[3] Lt. Isaac[2]), married in Tisbury, 27 July 1758, SARAH MANTER, daughter of George and Katherine (Athearn) Manter of Tisbury, born there 14 Sept. 1734. They lived in Nantucket in 1765. She died 3 Mar. 1797 probably in Nantucket.

Children, born in Nantucket:

PARNELL,[6] b. 14 Nov. 1759; m. there, 21 Mar. 1779, George Brown, son of Francis and Eunice (Coffin) Brown.
62. GEORGE, b. 16 July 1761.

34

ISAAC[5] CHASE (Nathan,[4] Isaac,[3] Lt. Isaac[2]), died 12 Oct. 1763. He married in Nantucket, 23 Nov. 1752, MERCY CHADWICK, daughter of Richard and Deborah (Swain) Chadwick, born in Nantucket, 15 Feb. 1731/2. She married (2) in Nantucket, 2 July 1769, BENJAMIN PITTS; married (3) DANIEL SWAIN. They lived in Nantucket.

Children, born in Nantucket:

63. JONATHAN,[6] b. 28 July 1753.
64. ISAAC, b. 23 Oct. 1754.
65. BENJAMIN, b. 10 Aug. 1760.

35

CHARLES[5] CHASE (Stephen,[4] Isaac,[3] Lt. Isaac[2]), born in Nantucket, 31 May 1731; married in Nantucket, 30 Jan. 1755, JANE [JENNETTE] COLEMAN, daughter of Jonathan and Mehitable (Davis) Coleman, born in Nantucket 23 Oct. 1735; died there, 25 Jan. 1820, as the widow of Charles Chase. He died in Nantucket, 8 Feb. 1815, aged 83 y. 8 m. They lived in Nantucket.

Children, born in Nantucket:

HEPHZIBETH,[6] b. in 1755; m. in Nantucket, 5 July 1774, Ethan Tappan of Long Island, N. Y.

PAUL, perhaps not on order; d. at Plum Island, Feb. 1782.

66.   CHARLES, b. 1763; d. 10 Dec. 1813.
67.   WILLIAM, b. 23 July 1766.
68.   STEPHEN, b. 3 July or Aug. 1773.

ABIGAIL, m. in Nantucket, 29 Aug. 1819, John Sherman 2d of New Bedford.

36

JOSEPH[5] CHASE (Stephen,[4] Isaac,[3] Lt. Isaac[2]), born in Nantucket, 23 Mar. 1752; married there, 15 Feb. 1778, REBECCA FOLGER, daughter of Reuben and Dinah (Hussey) Folger, born in Nantucket, 3 June 1758. They lived in Nantucket. He died there, 10 Aug. 1833. She died there, 1 Aug. 1833.

Children, born in Nantucket:

69.   JOSEPH,[6] b. 9 Sept. 1778.

BETSEY, b. 31 Oct. 1780; m. int. 16 Jan. 1802, Obed[6] Chase, son of Francis[5] Chase. (Family 84)

MARGARET, b. 18 Oct. 1784; m. (1) 5 May 1805, Alfred Coffin; m. (2) 3 Nov. 1839, Henry Riddell of Nantucket.

CHARLOTTE, b. 31 Jan. 1787; m. 20 Nov. 1842, Barzillai Coffin of Nantucket.

70.   GEORGE H., b. 31 Dec. 1792.
71.   CHARLES F., b. 21 Jan. 1795.
72.   WILLIAM F., b. 27 Jan. 1799.
73.   EDWARD, b. 21 Apr. 1801.

MARY, perhaps a daughter.

37

CAPT. REUBEN[5] CHASE (Stephen,[4] Isaac,[3] Lt. Isaac[2]), born in Nantucket, 23 June 1754; married there, 19 June 1783, JUDITH GARDNER, daughter of Peleg and Anna (Ramsdell) Gardner, born in Nantucket, 20 Feb. 1759. He died there, 15 Feb. 1824 and she died there, 15 Mar. 1837, aged 78. They lived in Nantucket.

Children, born in Nantucket:

MARY,[6] b. 2 4Mar. 1784; m. (int. 20 Feb. 1802) before 30 Mar. 1802, Freeman Sherman, son of John and Margaret (Ellis) Sherman; his first wife.

ANNA, b. 31 May 1786; m. 29 May 1804, Nathaniel Rand, son of Ebenezer and Hannah (Waters) Rand.

74.   PETER G., b. 10 May 1788.

SUSAN, b. 13 June 1791; m. (1) 22 Aug. 1811, Obed Alley; m. (2) 28 Apr. 1846, Judge Samuel Mitchell of Nantucket.

75.   REUBEN, b. 21 Dec. 1797.
76.   OBED, b. 20 Mar. 1803.

38

ZIMRI[5] CHASE (Stephen,[4] Isaac,[3] Lt. Isaac[2]), born in Nantucket, 11 Dec. 1758; married DINAH BARNARD, daughter of Tristram Barnard. No birth of children recorded on Nantucket town records. A memorandum note states that he was married in North Carolina. He died in Liberty, Ind., 22 Nov. 1840.

39

GEORGE[5] CHASE (Isaac,[4] Isaac,[3] Lt. Isaac[2]), born in Tisbury, 30 Mar. 1744; died 22 Feb. 1778. He married in Tisbury, 16 Feb. 1769, LUCY NORTON, daughter of Jacob and Bethiah (Mayhew) Norton, born 7 Apr. 1745. She married (2) in Tisbury, 18 Apr. 1782, JOSIAH LUCE of Tisbury. He died 27 July 1786, she surviving; three children by her second husband.

Child:

77.   PETER,[6] went to England; untraced.

40

JOSEPH[5] CHASE (Isaac,[4] Isaac,[3] Lt. Isaac[2]), born in Tisbury, 6 Aug. 1750; married (1) in Chilmark, 26 Nov. 1772, MARTHA HILLMAN, daughter of Benjamin and Love (Cathcart) Hillman, born in Chilmark, 4 Nov. 1748; died 9 Jan. 1788, aged 39 y. 2 m. 5 d.; buried in Tisbury. He married (2) in Tisbury, 14 July 1796, MRS. EUNICE ROATH [ROTCH] who was born about 1768 and died in Tisbury, 7 Sept. 1818 in her 50th year. He died in Tisbury, 3 Nov. 1824, aged 74 y. 2 m. 10 d.

Children by first wife, born in Tisbury:

SON,[6] b. about 1773; d. at sea in the spring of 1794.
LOVE, b. about 1774; m. 7 Nov. 1793, William Downes.
HANNAH, b. 3 Feb. 1776; m. 10 Jan. 1802, Stephen New.
RHODA, b. 14 Sept. 1779; m. Freeman Daggett.
78.   FRANCIS, b. 1 July 1781.
79.   JOSEPH, b. 29 Apr. 1783.
80.   CONSTANT, b. about 1786.

Children by second wife, born in Tisbury:

81.   WILLIAM R., b. 27 Dec. 1800.
82.   GEORGE, b. 5 July 1803; removed to Wiscasset, Me.
    ISAAC, b. 1805; d. 1831, unm. in Nantucket Roads.
    MARY, b. 1807; m. William Howard Davis.
83.   TRISTRAM L., b. 1809.

41

CORNELIUS[5] CHASE (Isaac,[4] Isaac,[3] Lt. Isaac[2]), born in Tisbury, 10 June 1759. No further record has been found of him.

42

FRANCIS[5] CHASE (Joseph,[4] Isaac,[3] Lt. Isaac[2]), born in Nantucket, 10 Sept. 1738; married there, 5 Jan. 1764, NAOMI GARDNER, daughter of Reuben and Theodate (Gorham) (Coffin) Gardner, born in Nantucket, 29 Oct. 1746; died there, 15 Nov. 1827. He died 21 Sept. 1802 in Nantucket. They lived in Nantucket.

Children, born in Nantucket:

LYDIA,[6] b. 4 Nov. 1764; m. 29 Jan. 1784, George Gorham Hussey of Nantucket.
ELIZABETH, b. 22 May 1766; m. 9 Mar. 1784, Capt. Asa Gardner of Nantucket.
NAOMI, b. 23 Mar. 1769; m. 1 Jan. 1795, Seth Hussey.
MIRIAM, b. 15 Sept. 1771; m. (1) 3 Sept. 1789, Timothy Parker; m. (2) 29 Nov. 1792, Charles Coffin of Nantucket.

DAVID, b. 21 Dec. 1773; d. 23 Mar. 1787.

JUDITH, b. 9 Jan. (or June) 1776; m. 4 Apr. 1799, Richard Gardner Swain of Nantucket.

84.   OBED, b. 19 Dec. 1778.

85.   FRANCIS, b. 19 Oct. 1781.

86.   PAUL, b. 19 June 1784.

EUNICE, b. 4 Mar. 1787; m. 20 Oct. 1808, Alexander Swain of Nantucket.

PHEBE, b. 16 Aug. 1789; m. George Mitchell.

43

LEONARD[5] CHASE (Levi,[4] Isaac,[3] Lt. Isaac[2]), born in Sandwich, about 1745; died in West Barnstable or Sandwich in "1815, aged 70." He married in Barnstable, 12 Nov. 1772, HANNAH BODFISH. Hannah, the wife of Leonard Chase was baptized and admitted to the West Church of Barnstable in 1811. In 1790 he was head of a family in Sandwich, consisting of one male over 16 years of age, two males under 16 and four females. He served in the Revolutionary War in Capt. Ebenezer Jenkins's Co. of Col. Freeman's Reg't on the alarm at Falmouth and Dartmouth 6 Sept. 1778 for one week (Mass. Soldiers and Sailors in War of the Revolution, 3 : 249). He inherited one quarter part of his father's real estate and was co-executor, 31 Jan. 1774.

At a town meeting held in the West Meeting House in Barnstable, 20 Oct. 1784: "Voted to remit Leonard Chase's rates in merchants bills upon condition that he produce a certificate from the town of Sandwich that he has paid his taxes there the same year."

At a precinct meeting in Barnstable, 8 Apr. 1804, "Voted that Leonard Chase be sexton of the North Meeting House the present year, he to ring the Bell on Sabbath days and all other public days and take care and wind up the clock and attend and open the doors of the House on all public days and it is agreed by vote of the precinct that he shall have $17 as full compensation the present year." He continued to serve for several years and his compensation was increased. He was to repair the Meeting House in 1811.

There is no record of his will or of the probate of his estate in Barnstable County. The town records of Sandwich do not contain the births of his children. It is conjectured that there were two sons and three daughters born between 1772 and 1790.

Children probably born in Sandwich of this union:

LEONARD,[6] b. about 1779; d. in Barnstable, 22 July 1850, aged 71; m. 30 June 1804, Cynthia Phinney who d. in Barnstable, 29 Mar. 1834, aged 52y. Two children buried in Lothrop's Hill Cemetery in Barnstable.

ENOCH, perhaps a son, m. in Barnstable, 11 Mar. 1792, Thankful Chase.

43a

LEVI[5] CHASE (Levi,[4] Isaac,[3] Lt. Isaac[2]), born in Sandwich, 5 Mar. 1750; married in Barnstable, 13 Oct. 1776, TEMPERANCE CROCKER, born in 1756; died in Pompey, Onondaga Co., N. Y., 8 Jan. 1830. She was admitted to the West Church of Barnstable as "ye wife of Levi Chase" about July 1782. She was admitted to the Church of Christ in Lee, Berkshire Co., 12 Aug. 1792. He was corporal in Capt. Simeon Fish's Co. in Sept. 1778 and in Sept. 1779 on the alarm at Falmouth his muster roll being dated at Sandwich. (Mass. Soldiers & Sailors in the Revolution, 3: 359). In 1790 he was head of a family in Lee, consisting of one male over 16 years of age, three males under 16 and six females, including his wife and stepmother. (Mass. Census, 28). The births of nine children are recorded in Lee but probably four or five were born in Sandwich.

Children, born in Sandwich and Lee:

>POLLY,⁶ b. 5 Dec. 1777; m. in Lee, 3 June 1795, Reuben Pixley Jr. of Lee.
>
>SILENCE, b. 31 July 1779; m. in Lee, 22 Feb. 1793, Levi Fowler of Stockbridge.
>
>86a.   LEVI, b. 25 May 1781.
>
>MERCY, b. 8 Jan. 1782; d. 5 Feb. 1782.
>
>SETH, b. 13 Mar. 1783; d. — May 1783.
>
>THOMAS, b. 1 June 1785.
>
>NABBY, b. 17 Apr. 1788.
>
>BETSEY, b. 2 Dec. 1789.
>
>TABITHA, b. 7 July 1791; d. 27 July 1791.

44

TIMOTHY⁵ CHASE (Abraham,⁴ Abraham,³ Lt. Isaac²), born in Tisbury, 22 June 1745; died there, 28 Nov. 1818, aged 72 y. 10 m. 5 d. He married 23 Nov. 1773, REBECCA BASSETT, daughter of Nathaniel and Hannah (Hall) Bassett, born 23 Oct. 1750; died 28 Oct. 1821.

He was a miller and lived at Homes Hole. He built the windmill formerly located on Main Street in Vineyard Haven, now forming a part of the house of the late Brig. Gen. A. B. Carey.

Children, born in Tisbury:

>ABIGAIL,⁶ b. — Jan. 1775; d. 30 Mar. 1776, aged 14 m. 25 d.
>
>INFANT, b. 9 Mar. 1777; d. 20 Mar. 1777.
>
>87.   BENJAMIN, b. 2 Mar. 1779.
>
>88.   TIMOTHY, b. 28 Nov. 1781.
>
>DELIVERANCE, b. 21 Jan. 1784; m. 4 Nov. 1804, Edmund Crowell of Tisbury.
>
>REBECCA, b. 14 Feb. 1787; m. 24 Jan. 1811, Capt. Tristram Luce, son of Elisha and Hannah⁵ (Chase) Luce of Edgartown. (Family 16)
>
>HANNAH, b. 5 Sept. 1789; m. 14 Oct. 1810, Elisha Luce Jr. of Tisbury.

45

BENJAMIN⁵ CHASE (Abraham,⁴ Abraham,³ Lt. Isaac²), born in Tisbury, about 1747.

46

ABRAHAM⁵ CHASE (Valentine,⁴ Abraham,³ Lt. Isaac²), born in Tisbury, 9 Dec. 1756; died in Cincinnati, Ohio, Nov. 1832. He married 5 Nov. 1778, ELIZABETH BOURNE of Falmouth.

47

NICKERSON[5] CHASE (Zaccheus,[4] Abraham,[3] Lt. Isaac[2]), born in Tisbury about 1773; died there, 7 Nov. 1844, aged 71. He married in Edgartown, 1 Jan .1801, FANNY NORTON, daughter of Obed and Rebecca (Shaw) Norton of Tisbury and Edgartown. He was a lighthouse keeper.

Children:

JAMES S.,[6] d. in Edgartown, 14 Aug. 1810.
SERENA C., d. in Tisbury, 8 July 1816, aged 9 y. 2 d.

48

JAMES[5] CHASE (James,[4] James,[3] Lt. Isaac[2]), born in Nantucket, 10 Nov. 1738; married there, (intention 5 Jan. 1760) MARY FOLGER, daughter of Peter and Christian (Swain) Folger, born in Nantucket, 9 Mar. 1739/40; died there, 15 Aug. 1818, aged 78 y. 5 m. He died 26 Sept. 1819 ,aged 80 y. 10 m.   They lived in Nantucket.

Children, born in Nantucket (not all recorded there):

89. FRANCIS,[6] b. 21 Nov. 1761.
90. PETER, b. 27 June 1764.
      ANNA, b. 1 July 1766; m. 21 June 1792, Latham Hussey.
91. ARIEL, b. 25 May 1770.
      MARY, b. 10 Oct. 1772; m. 6 Mar. 1794, Edward Wyer Jr.
      BROWN (twin), b. 22 Dec. 1774; d. 26 May 1798.
      PHEBE (twin), b. 22 Dec. 1774; m. 20 May 1800, Thaddeus Hussey, son of Obed and Priscilla Hussey.
      RACHEL, b. 26 May 1779; m. 29 Apr. 1800, Reuben R. Bunker.
92. JAMES FRANKLIN, b. 16 May 1784.

49

BENJAMIN[5] CHASE (Abel,[4] Joseph,[3] Lt. Isaac[2]), born in Edgartown, 23 Dec. 1745; married in Nantucket, 27 Feb. 1768, ELIZABETH BROCK, daughter of Thomas and Patience (Gardner) Brock, baptized in Nantucket, 13 Aug. 1747; born in 1745.   She died in Nantucket, 25 Oct. 1801.

50

ZEPHANIAH[5] CHASE (Abel,[4] Joseph,[3] Lt. Isaac[2]), born in Edgartown, 14 Mar. 1748; died in Lexington, N. Y., 30 May 1828; married (1) in Chilmark, 10 Oct. 1773, ABIGAIL SKIFFE, daughter of Joseph and Remember (Gibbs) Skiffe of Chilmark, born there, 4 July 1748; died 27 Mar. 1784. He married (2) in Tisbury, 16 Jan. 1785, LOVE (WEST) SKIFFE, widow of Nathaniel Skiffe, daughter of Peter and Elizabeth (Athearn-Chase) West of Tisbury.   She was born in Tisbury, 5 Oct. 1756; died 8 July 1832.

They removed to Woodstock, Ulster Co., N. Y., before 1790 when he was listed as head of a family consisting of one male over 16 years of age, seven males under 16 and three females.   Later they lived in Lexington, Greene Co. and in Windham, N. Y.

Children by first wife, born in Martha's Vineyard:

93. BENJAMIN[6] (twin), b. 21 Jan. 1774.
    ELIZABETH (twin), b. 21 Jan. 1774; d. at age of 18 d.
94. JOSEPH, b. 2 Dec. 1775.
    THOMAS, b. 18 Oct. 1777; d. unm. 22 Jan. 1821.

Children by second wife, last six born in Woodstock:

95. DAVID, b. 3 Jan. 1786.
    WEST, b. 25 Jan. 1788; d. Sept. 1792.
96. CHARLES, b. 9 Sept. 1790.
    ABIGAIL, b. 28 Oct. 1792; m. 23 May 1811, Jared Johnson who d.
    15 Nov. 1851.
    ELIZABETH, b. 23 Feb. 1795; m. 17 Mar. 1814, Anson Bushnell;
    five children.
97. WEST, b. 30 Mar. 1797.
    PETER (twin), b. 18 Jan. 1799;. d 6 July 1799.
    REBECCA (twin), b. 18 June 1799; m. 5 Nov. 1818, Richard Howk
    (Houk); she d. 15 Apr. 1863; two children.

51

THOMAS[5] CHASE (Thomas,[4] Joseph,[3] Lt. Isaac[2]), born in Boston, 23 June 1767; married 4 Sept. 1791, SARAH GREENLEAF, daughter of Gen. William and Sally (Quincy) Greenleaf, born in Boston, 21 Feb. 1773. They lived in Boston, Putney, Vt., and Philadelphia, Pa. (Greenleaf Genealogy, 306).

Children:

98. THOMAS GREENLEAF,[6] b. 3 Mar. 1793.
    ABEL BARTLETT, b. 19 Mar. 1795; lieut. in the army; d. 11 Oct.
    1814 at Fort Mifflin.
99. WILLIAM HENRY, b. 4 June 1798.
100. GEORGE EDWARD, b. 2 May 1803; d. 1844.

52

JOSEPH WARREN[5] CHASE (Thomas,[4] Joseph,[3] Lt. Isaac[2]), born in Boston, about 1775; married in Columbia, Me., July 1804, SARAH FELLOWS of Plantation No. 22, (now Jonesborough, Washington Co.) Me.

SIXTH GENERATION

53

THOMAS⁶ CHASE (Samuel,⁵ Thomas,⁴ Thomas,³ Lt. Isaac²), born in Tisbury, 30 Sept. 1755; died in Livermore, Me., Apr. 1844. He married in Tisbury, 8 Mar. 1780, DESIRE LUCE, daughter of Joseph and Jedidah (Claghorn) Luce of Tisbury, born there, 22 June 1756; died 14 May 1851. They removed from Tisbury to Livermore in 1791.

He enlisted on a privateer in the American Revolution. On the coast of England the ship's crew were captured by a British man-of-war. After being transferred several times as prisoners of war they were landed at Plymouth, England, and taken before two justices and a clerk and arraigned for treason. They were committed to "Mill Prison" on suspicion of treason against his most Gracious Majesty George III. They were kept for twenty-three months, during which time they underwent great privations and sufferings. At the end of the period they were exchanged for British prisoners, sent to France and landed at a small town ten miles below Nantes. Here Thomas Chase and his associates reenlisted at L'Orient in the squadron that was being fitted out for John Paul Jones, his ship being the Alliance commended by Capt. Landais. Mr. Chase claimed that it was the Alliance—not the Pallas—that disabled the Countess of Scarborough; that it was in consequence of the broadsides from the Alliance that she struck and that the Pallas, coming up, was left in charge of the prize while the Alliance went to the aid of Paul Jones.

He was a man of much mechanical ingenuity and an excellent worker in wood, and being employed under John Paul Jones for several months, as cabin joiner, he saw much of the famous commander.

Children, first four born in Tisbury, others in Livermore:

101. THOMAS,⁷ b. 22 Feb. 1782; m. (1) 1802, Phebe Hathaway; m. (2) 1828, Rachel Bachelor. His grand daughter Elizabeth⁹ Chase (Thomas⁸) b. 9 Oct. 1832, in Strong Me., m. (1) Paul Akers, a noted sculptor, who d. 21 May 1861. She m. (2) in 1865, in New York, E. M. Allen. She achieved distinction as an author and poet, and was the literary editor of the Portland, Me., *Advertiser* for several years. The poem "Rock Me to Sleep, Mother" is a widely known product of her pen.

LURA, b. 11 Mar. 1784; m. (1) 16 Apr. 1801, Samuel Livermore; m. (2) in Feb, 1826, John Fuller.

102. LOTHROP, b. 22 Mar. 1787; m. in 1814, Abigail Lake; physician; Vassalboro, Me.

103. JAMES, b. 16 Nov. 1789; m. 26 Feb. 1819, Anna Pitts of Livermore.

REBECCA, b. 20 Sept. 1792; m. 31 Dec. 1818, Tristram Tilton.

OLIVE (twin), b. 8 Nov. 1795; d. unm.

LYDIA (twin), b. 8 Nov. 1795; m. in Aug. 1817, Asa Barton.

LUCY, b. 14 Sept. 1801; m. (1) 3 Oct. 1821, Charles Benjamin, son of Lt. Samuel and Tabitha (Livermore) Benjamin, b. 2 Aug. 1795; d. in Winthrop, Me., 10 May 1834. She m. (2)

Nov. 1842, Lemuel Stanley and d. in Winthrop, 9 Nov. 1844.
Her daughter *Bettie Livermore*[8] *Benjamin*, b. 9 Mar. 1824; d.
12 Apr. 1898; m. in Winthrop, 2 July 1856, John Milton Benjamin. Three children, including Fannie Russell[9] Benjamin,
b. 4 Jan. 1863, who m. Frank Ware Herrick of Lexington.
Their children: Robert Webster[10] Herrick and Marjory Porter[10] Herrick.

54

SAMUEL[6] CHASE (Samuel,[5] Thomas,[4] Thomas,[3] Lt. Isaac[2]), born
in Tisbury about 1759; married and lived in London, England.

55

LOTHROP[6] CHASE (Samuel,[5] Thomas,[4] Thomas,[3] Lt. Isaac[2]),
born in Tisbury about 1760; went to Virginia and there married.

56

SARSON[6] CHASE (Samuel,[5] Thomas,[4] Thomas,[3] Lt. Isaac[2]), born
in Tisbury, about 1764; married (1) 1 Mar. 1792, JANE BOARDMAN,
daughter of Rev. Andrew and Katherine (Allen) Boardman of Chilmark, born there, 14 Aug. 1767. He married (2) MARY MAYHEW,
daughter of Nathan and Susannah (Athearn) Mayhew of Chilmark,
born there, 10 Mar. 1774. He removed to Livermore, Me., about
1791 and died there.

Children:

    JANE,[7] m. (int. 23 June 1810) Isaac Haskell of New Gloucester,
      Me.
104. MAYHEW, d. in Livermore, Feb. 1874; shoemaker.
105. SARSON, carriage maker, lived in Livermore and in 1874 in
      Charlestown.
    MARY, m. Charles Howard.

57

CAPT. TRISTRAM[6] CHASE (Samuel,[5] Thomas,[4] Thomas,[3] Lt.
Isaac[2]), born about 1762; married MARY MERRY, daughter of Matthew and Elizabeth[5] (Chase) Merry of Tisbury. He was lost at sea
about 1801: His widow married (2) COL. JESSE STONE. He was a
ship master and lived in Livermore, Me., on the west side of Long
Pond.

Children, not in order:

106. CHARLES T.,[7] living in Dixfield, Me., 1874.
    BETSEY, m. Nathaniel Benjamin.
    ABBY, m. Charles Barrell.

58

ABRAHAM[6] CHASE (Thomas,[5] Nathan,[4] Isaac,[3] Lt. Isaac[2]), married in Nantucket, 4 Nov. 1790, JERUSHA HEATH, daughter of Joseph
and Catherine (Matthews) Heath, born in Nantucket, 25 Aug. 1767;
died in Nantucket, 4 Sept. 1843. He died in the West Indies, 7 June
1800. They lived in Nantucket.

Children:

107.   TIMOTHY.[7]
     LYDIA, b. 4 Jan. 1797; m. 27 Mar. 1817, Leonard Fisher.
     MARIA.

59

NATHANIEL[6] CHASE (Thomas,[5] Nathan,[4] Isaac,[3] Lt. Isaac[2]), born in Nantucket. William C. Folger's genealogical records of Nantucket state that he was the son of Thomas and Anna (Smith) Chase. If this is true, he was born before 1751. No other record of him has been found.

60

NATHAN[6] CHASE (Thomas,[5] Nathan,[4] Isaac,[3] Lt. Isaac[2]), born in Nantucket, said by William C. Folger to have been a son of Thomas and Anna (Smith) Chase, but no record of his birth, marriage or death has been found.

61

JAMES[6] CHASE (Thomas,[5] Nathan,[4] Isaac,[3] Lt. Isaac[2]), born about 1755; married in Yarmouth, 14 Aug. 1775, MERCY GODFREY, daughter of Caleb and Mary (Pinkham) Godfrey, born in Barnstable, 20 Jan. 1755. They lived in Nantucket. She died in Nantucket, as his widow, 19 Mar. 1836, aged 82, or 19 Mar. 1837, aged 83 y. 2 m.
    Children, born in Nantucket:

108.   NATHAN,[7] b. 25 Sept. 1777; m. 5 July 1798, Sally Noble, dau. of John and Eunice Noble.
     SARAH, b. 2 Mar. 1780; m. 28 Dec. 1795, Joseph McCleave, son of Robert and Hannah McCleave.
109.   JAMES, b. 10 Sept. 1781; m. 1 Sept. 1803, Mary Long, dau. of Abraham and Mary Long; he d. June 1819.
     FREDERICK, b. 15 Aug. 1783; d. 30 May 1804.
     SUSAN, b. 30 June 1785; m. 3 July 1806, John Bunker, son of George Bunker of Fairhaven.
110.   BENJAMIN, b. 19 Apr. 1789; m. 16 Apr. 1812, Deborah Fitzgerald, dau. of James Fitzgerald.
     SOPHIA, b. 21 May 1791; m. 25 Feb. 1816, John Crosby; m. (2) Timothy Robbins; m. (3) as his second wife, George Barrett.

62

GEORGE[6] CHASE (Shubael,[5] Nathan,[4] Isaac,[3] Lt. Isaac[2]), born in Nantucket, 16 July 1761; married there, 17 July 1788, REBECCA COFFIN, daughter of Barnabas and Abigail (Folger) Coffin, born in Nantucket, 22 Apr. 1764. He married (2) 14 May 1829, PHEBE COFFIN. He died in Nantucket, 16 Dec. 1840. They lived in Nantucket.
    Children, born in Nantucket:

111.   SHUBAEL,[7] b. 23 May 1789; m. 13 June 1811, Hephsibeth Swain, dau. of Timothy and Eunice (Gardner) Swain.
     PARNELL, b. 1 Feb. 1791; m. 25 Oct. 1808, Tristram Swain 2d, son of David and Phebe (Coleman) Swain of Nantucket.
     ELIZABETH, b. 20 Nov. 1793; m. 12 Feb. 1818, Alexander Swain 2d, son of Alexander and Rachel (Starbuck) Swain.

112. PETER F., b. 2 Nov. 1795; m. 20 Mar. 1823, Eliza Bunker, dau. of Moses and Mary (Wyer) Bunker of Nantucket.
113. BENJAMIN COFFIN, b. 24 Nov. 1797; m. 3 July 1820, Eunice Paddock, dau. of Peter and Judith Paddock.
SALLY, b. 20 Mar. 1800.

63

JONATHAN[6] CHASE (Isaac,[5] Nathan,[4] Isaac,[3] Lt. Isaac[2]), born in Nantucket, 28 July 1753; married there, 9 Mar. 1783, MARY SMITH, daughter of Job and Phebe (Baxter) Smith, born in Nantucket, 19 Sept. 1763. No birth of children recorded in Nantucket. He died in Nantucket, 13 Nov. 1821. She died in Nantucket, 9 June 1836, aged 72 y. 9 m. They lived in Nantucket.
Children:

BENJAMIN;[7] never married.
114. REUBEN, m. 25 Dec. 1838, widow Rebecca (Russell) Cleveland.
PHEBE, m. 10 Mar. 1808, Nathan Swain, son of Elisha and Margaret (Gardner) Swain.

64

ISAAC[6] CHASE (Isaac,[5] Nathan,[4] Isaac,[3] Lt. Isaac[2]), born in Nantucket, 23 Oct. 1754; married there, 22 Feb. 1778, EUNICE BROWN, daughter of Francis and Eunice (Coffin) Brown, born in Nantucket, 20 Sept. 1758. He died in Nantucket, 30 July 1814, aged 60 y. 6 m. She died there, 23 Jan. 1831. They lived in Nantucket.
Children, born in Nantucket:

EUNICE,[7] b. 27 Dec. 1780; m. 29 July 1802, Zebulon Coffin, son of John and Susanna (Clark) Coffin of Nantucket.
PRISCILLA, b. 8 Aug. 1782; m. 9 Sept. 1801, William Wilkes Morris, son of Jonathan Morris.
115. GEORGE BROWN, b. 7 Apr. 1786; m. (1) 22 Oct. 1807, Elizabeth Ramsdell; m. (2) Rebecca (Chadwick) Beebe; removed to Auburn, N. Y., 1827.
116. FRANKLIN, b. 8 Sept. 1787; m. 31 Jan. 1816, Nancy Ellis, dau. of Simeon and Deborah (Long) Ellis.
117. ISAAC, b. 6 Aug. 1789; m. 17 June 1817, Sally Ellis, sister of Nancy Ellis.
118. PETER, b. 13 Jan. 1794.
ANN, b. 1 Nov. 1797.

65

BENJAMIN[6] CHASE (Isaac,[5] Nathan,[4] Isaac,[3] Lt. Isaac[2]), born in Nantucket, 10 Aug. 1760.

66

CHARLES[6] CHASE (Charles,[5] Stephen,[4] Isaac,[3] Lt. Isaac[2]), born in Nantucket in 1763; married there, 16 Apr. 1789, EUNICE COFFIN, daughter of Barnabas and Abigail (Folger) Coffin, born in Nantucket, 31 July 1766, and died there, 25 May 1815, aged 48 y. 10 m. He died in Nantucket, 10 Dec. 1813. They lived in Nantucket.

Children, born in Nantucket:

119. CROMWELL,[7] b. 17 May 1791.
120. MOSES, b. 11 July 1793; m. 24 July 1817, Elizabeth W. Joy, dau.
     of Reuben and Mary (Swain) Joy of Nantucket.
     ELIZA, b. 15 Nov. 1795; m. 5 Dec. 1830, Charles Coffin Myrick
     of Nantucket as his second wife.
     NANCY, b. 29 Mar. 1798; m. 4 Dec. 1817, Charles Coffin Myrick,
     son of George Myrick of Nantucket.
121. ALEXANDER, perhaps not in order.
122. ZIMRI, perhaps not in order.
     A son of "cousine" Eunice was b. in Sept. 1796, another son b.
     Jan. 1803, and a child b. in Apr. 1805. This is found in the
     diary of Kezia (Coffin) Fanning and is supposed to refer to
     Eunice (Coffin) Chase and her children.

67

WILLIAM[6] CHASE (Charles,[5] Stephen,[4] Isaac,[3] Lt. Isaac[2]), born
in Nantucket, 23 July 1766; married there, 13 Aug. 1789, MERAB
[MERIBAH] GARDNER, daughter of Joseph and Abigail (Clark)
Gardner, born in Nantucket, 11 July 1769; died there as his widow,
20 Nov. 1820. He died in Nantucket, 4 Mar. 1819, aged 52 y. 8 m.
They lived in Nantucket.

Children, born in Nantucket:

MARY,[7] b. 25 Dec. 1797; m. (int. 27 Apr. 1822) Benjamin Ray,
son of Seth and Eunice (Paddock) Ray of Nantucket.
EMELINE, b. 24 Mar. 1805; m. (1) (int. 7 Dec. 1822) Thomas
Clasby (Clisby); m. (2) William Gayer Macy.
123. CHARLES G., b. 6 Jan. 1809.

68

STEPHEN[6] CHASE (Charles,[5] Stephen,[4] Isaac,[3] Lt. Isaac[2]), born
in Nantucket 3 July or Aug. 1773; married there, 25 June 1793, MAR-
GARET BARNARD, daughter of Robert and Margaret (Whitney) Barnard, born in Nantucket, 11 July 1770; died 26 Mar. 1836 as his
widow, aged 65 y. 8 m. He died in Nantucket, 9 Jan. 1824. They
lived in Nantucket.

Children, born in Nantucket:

124. WILLIAM H.,[7] b. 27 Jan. 1795.
125. PAUL, b. 8 Apr. 1797; m. (int. 23 Sept. 1820) Mary Chase, dau.
     of Job (son of Benjamin and Martha ———) and Ruth
     (Macy) Chase of Nantucket.
126. ROBERT BARNARD, b. 7 Apr. 1799; m. 19 June 1825, Hepsabeth
     Macy, dau. of Job and Deborah (Gardner) Macy.
     SARAH, b. 22 May 1801; m. (int. 10 May 1823) Peleg Ray of
     Nantucket, son of David Ray.
     LOUISA, b. 3 May 1803; m. 26 Mar. 1826, Charles C. Russell of
     Nantucket. He moved to Ohio.
127. CHARLES W., b. 31 Mar. 1805; m. 11 Sept. 1828, Elizabeth
     Brown, dau. of William and Elizabeth (Coffin) Brown.
     CHARLOTTE JANE, b. 18 Nov. 1807; m. 30 May 1830, Peter G.
     Smith of Nantucket, son of Solomon Smith.
128. JOSEPH C., b. 18 Sept. 1810; m. 11 May 1834, Margaret P. Brock,
     dau. of Peter and Waite (Pease) Brock.
129. WILLIAM S., b. 18 July 1812; m. 13 Apr. 1837, Betsey P. Smith,
     dau. of Moses and Susan (Pollard) Smith.

69

JOSEPH[6] CHASE (Joseph,[5] Stephen,[4] Isac,[3] Lt. Isaac[2]), born in
Nantucket, 9 Sept. 1778; married (int. 15 Sept. 1798) POLLY COF-
FIN, daughter of Bartlett and Margaret (Pinkham-Tupper) Coffin,
born in Nantucket, 24 Nov. 1779.   He was lost at sea, 13 Dec. 1807.
They lived in Nantucket.

Children, born in Nantucket:

MARY C.,[7] b. 31 Mar. 1799; m. 28 May 1818, George Harris, son
of David and Miriam Harris of Nantucket.

ANN, b. 20 Sept. 1800; m. 20 Aug. 1818, William Austin, son of
Benjamin and Lydia (Folger) Austin.

BETSEY, b. 18 Feb. 1804; never married.

CHARLOTTE C., b. 15 July 1806; m. 8 Apr. 1830, Timothy W.
Riddell, son of Henry and Hepzibeth (Wyer-Coleman) Riddell of Nantucket.

70

GEORGE H.[6] CHASE (Joseph,[5] Stephen,[4] Isaac,[3] Lt. Isaac[2]), born
in Nantucket, 31 Dec. 1792; married there (1) 27 Apr. 1820, RE-
BECCA COFFIN, daughter of Gideon and Mary Coffin, born in Nan-
tucket, 3 Jan. 1799; died 11 Nov. 1832, aged 33.   He married (2) in
Nantucket, 10 Nov. 1833, JUDITH M. RIDDELL, widow of Samuel
Riddell, formerly widow of Willard Robinson, and daughter of Zac-
cheus and Judith (Starbuck) Macy, born in Nantucket, 26 June 1801.
They lived in Nantucket.

Children by first wife, born in Nantucket:

130.   JOSEPH B.,[7] b. 22 Apr. 1821; m. 7 Aug. 1849, Sarah B. Ray; dau.
of Edward and Lydia Ray of Nantucket.

ROWLAND C., b. 22 Aug. 1832; never married.

71

CHARLES F.[6] CHASE (Joseph,[5] Stephen,[4] Isaac,[3] Lt. Isaac[2]), born
in Nantucket, 21 Jan. 1795; married there, 2 Sept. 1832, DEBORAH
A. (WORTH) RUSSELL, widow of Alexander Russell and daughter of
Barzillai and Mary (Pinkham) Worth, born in Nantucket, 2 June
1801.   She married (1) in Nantucket, 23 Sept. 1824, ALEXANDER
RUSSELL, son of George and Elizabeth (Swain) Russell, born in
Nantucket, 13 Feb. 1801.

Children, born in Nantucket:

131.   ALEXANDER R.,[7] perhaps not in order.

132.   THOMAS W., probably not in order.

72

WILLIAM F.[6] CHASE (Joseph,[5] Stephen,[4] Isaac,[3] Lt. Isaac[2]),
born in Nantucket, 27 Jan. 1799; died 16 Sept. 1888; married there,
4 Dec. 1828, ASENATH W. (HOLMES) ABRAHAMS, widow of William Abrahams, and daughter of Bartlett and Abigail Holmes of
Barnstable.   She was born 14 Nov. 1798; died 27 Sept. 1884.   They
lived in Nantucket.

Children, born in Nantucket:

CHARLOTTE,[7] perhaps not in order.

133.   WILLIAM B., b. 13 Dec. 1832; m. 20 Aug. 1866, Rebecca F.
Bunker, dau. of Samuel and Eunice Bunker; she b. 30 Dec.
1835; d. 12 Mar. 1906. Their dau. Charlotte B., b. 7 Oct.
1872, lives at 43 North St., New Bedford, Mass. Their son
William R., b. 23 June 1867, m. Kate J. Bartlett; three children.

73

EDWARD[6] CHASE (Joseph,[5] Stephen,[4] Isaac,[3] Lt. Isaac[2]), born in
Nantucket, 21 Apr. 1801; married (1) about 1828, ANN MARIA
ROWLAND, born Nov. 1810; died 15 Feb. 1836; married (2) in Nan-
tucket, 21 Dec. 1837, SUSAN U. PARKER, daughter of Joseph and
Anna (Upham) Parker, born in Nantucket, — Mar. 1812. He mar-
ried (3) 15 Jan. 1854, ABBY (HUSSEY) DAYTON who married (1) in
Nantucket, 28 Sept. 1836, William H. Dayton, son of Nehemiah and
Peggy (Sylvia) Dayton. She was daughter of Peter and Sally
(Drew) Hussey, born io Nantucket, 28 Oct. 1813. He died 13 June
1859. His second wife died 8 July 1849. They lived in Nantucket.

Children by first wife, born in Nantucket:

MARY ANN,[7] b. 30 Oct. 1829; m. as second wife, William H.
Lawrence.

ELIZABETH ANN, b. 29 June 1832; m. 30 Nov. 1853, William H.
Lawrence.

REBECCA F., b. 30 Sept. 1834.

Children by second wife, born in Nantucket:

EDWARD P., b. 17 Nov. 1838; never married.

134.   JOHN B., b. 25 July 1840; m. Cornelia Stearns.
135.   GEORGE P., b. 25 Jan. 1842.
SUSAN M., b. 19 or 25 July 1845.
136.   CHARLES WILLIAM, b. 30 Sept. 1847.

74

PETER G.[6] CHASE (Reuben,[5] Stephen,[4] Isaac,[3] Lt. Isaac[2]), born
in Nantucket, 10 May 1788; married there, 29 June 1809, LURANA
WYER, daughter of Hugh and Susan Wyer, born 4 Apr. 1789. She
died 1 Oct. 1829. He died in Nantucket, 22 Feb. 1821. They lived
in Nantucket.

Children, born in Nantucket:

137.   ROWLAND B.,[7] b. 31 Mar. 1810; m. 3 June 1835, Lydia Davis,
dau. of Charles and Hannah (Gardner) Davis.
ELIZABETH W., b. 21 Apr. 1814; m. 19 Oct. 1837, Edmund Macy,
son of Job and Deborah (Gardner) Macy.
138.   CHARLES G., b. 25 Oct. 1815; m. 1841, Charlotte Fulton of Ohio
or N .Y.
139.   PETER G., b. 25 Mar. 1817; m. (int. 7 July 1839) Susan C. Swain,
dau. of Abraham and Anna (Coleman) Swain.
140.   OLIVER C., b. 1818.

75

REUBEN[6] CHASE (Reuben,[5] Stephen,[4] Isaac,[3] Lt. Isaac[2]), born
in Nantucket, 21 Dec. 1797; married in Nantucket, 10 Apr. 1821,

ELIZABETH BISSELL, daughter of William and Abigail (Swain) Bissell, born 13 Oct. 1799. He died 25 June 1870. They lived in Nantucket.

Children, born in Nantucket:

141. WILLIAM E.,[7] b. 26 Jan. 1822; m. 22 June 1851, Charlotte A. Sanford, dau. of George and Rachel Sanford.

ELIZA ABBY, b. — Jan. 1832.

JUDITH G., b. 17 Oct. 1835; m. Lewis C. Eldridge of Dennisport.

MARY JANE, b. 26 Aug. 1839.

142. JOHN R., b. 21 May 1842; d. 14 Oct. 1864.

76

OBED[6] CHASE (Reuben,[5] Stephen,[4] Isaac,[3] Lt. Isaac[2]), born in Nantucket, 20 Mar. 1803; married (1) in Nantucket, 23 June 1825, SUSAN H. BARNARD, daughter of Paul and Mary (Bocot) Barnard, born in Nantucket, 17 May 1806; died there 4 July 1832, aged 26. He married (2) in Nantucket, 28 Oct. 1832, SARAH B. COFFIN, daughter of David and Phebe (Barnard) Coffin, born in Nantucket, 20 Mar. 1802. He was a cooper in Nantucket.

Children by first wife, born in Nantucket:

143. EDWARD B.,[7] b. 17 Apr. 1826.

144. OBED R., b. 15 Apr. 1829; m. Hannah M. (Fitzgerald) Fuller.

SUSAN H., b. 27 July 1830; m. 3 Aug. 1851, Charles H. Robinson.

Children by second wife, born in Nantucket:

ELIZA C., b. 14 Sept. 1833; m. Frederick B. Murphy.

145. REUBEN GARDNER, b. 28 Apr. 1836; m. 8 Aug. 1859, Lucy C. M. Howard of Me.

MARY ANN, b. 17 Nov. 1840; never married.

SARAH JANE, b. 7 Aug. 1843; m. 10 Oct. 1862, Nathaniel B. Macy.

146. DAVID C., b. 16 Aug. 1845.

78

FRANCIS[6] CHASE (Joseph,[5] Isaac,[4] Isaac,[3] Lt. Isaac[2]), born in Tisbury, 1 July 1781; married there, 8 Dec. 1804, PRISCILLA LUCE, daughter of Malachi and Ann (Luce) Luce, born about 1781. She married (2) 21 Oct. 1819, DAVID LUCE, son of Enoch and Thankful (Wheldon) Luce of Tisbury. He died in Tisbury, 25 July 1815, aged 34 y. 1 m. 24 d. No children recorded on Tisbury records.

Children:

147. CHARLES GRANDISON,[7] b. 1806; d. 1854, aged 48.

148. FRANCIS, lived in South Berwick, Me.

149. HERMAN, lived in Kittery, Me.

79

JOSEPH[6] CHASE (Joseph,[5] Isaac,[4] Isaac,[3] Lt. Isaac[2]), born in Tisbury, 29 Apr. 1783; married there, 22 June 1819, HANNAH ROBINSON of Chilmark, daughter of Shadrach and Deborah (Robinson) Robinson, born in Chilmark, 7 Aug. 1795. No children's births recorded on Martha's Vineyard records.

Children:

150.   HENRY,[7] b. 27 Mar. 1823; m. Feb. 1852, Mary B. Hancock; lived in Tisbury.

MARTHA HILLMAN, b. 1824; m. Prof. David P. Butler of Boston.

151.   ISAAC, m. Frances N. Hancock; lived in Boston.

80

CONSTANT[6] CHASE (Joseph,[5] Isaac,[4] Isaac,[3] Lt. Isaac[2]), born in Tisbury, about 1786; married there, 28 May 1812, CHARLOTTE N. LUCE, daughter of Jonathan and Charlotte (Luce) Luce, born in Tisbury about 1795. His Christian name has also been given as Constantine.

Children, probably born in Tisbury:

152.   JOSEPH,[7] b. 3 May 1817; dentist; d. in Vineyard Haven, 9 Jan. 1916, in his 99th year; m. Clara Luce. Three children, including *Col. Constantine[8] Chase*, son of Joseph[7] and Clara (Luce) Chase, who was a distinguished military officer, U. S. A. He enlisted as second lieutenant of the Third Mass. Artillery, 9 Sept. 1863; promoted to first lieutenant 15 Oct. 1864; brivetted captain, 13 Mar. 1865 for faithful and meritorious services during the war; mustered out 18 Sept. 1865; appointed second lieutenant of First Artillery, 11 May 1866; transferred to Third Artillery, 28 Sept. 1866; brevetted first lieutenant, 2 Mar. 1867, for gallant and meritorious services; first lieutenant, 26 Mar. 1868; regimental adjutant from 12 to 22 Apr. 1887; regimental quarter-master, 1 May 1887 to 13 Apr. 1891; captain to assistant quarter-master, 13 Apr. 1891; transferred to Fourth Artillery, 20 Apr. 1892; major of Third Artillery, 15 Dec. 1900; Artillery Corps, 2 Feb. 1901; lieutenant colonel, 11 Sept. 1902; died 20 Sept. 1902.

CHARLOTTE LUCE, b. 17 Sept. 1821; d. 3 Sept. 1822.

153.   HIRAM LUCE, b. 19 May 1825.

MARY ELLEN, b. 25 May 1828; d. 1 Jan. 1833.

81

DEA. WILLIAM R.[6] CHASE (Joseph,[5] Isaac,[4] Isaac,[3] Lt. Isaac[2]), born in Tisbury, 27 Dec. 1800; married there, 26 Sept. 1821, TEMPERANCE GRAY, born about Apr. 1798. She died in Tisbury, 19 May 1873, aged 75 y. 25 d. and Dea William Chase died there, 30 June 1881, aged 81 y. 6 m. 2 d. They were buried in the Middletown Cemetery in West Tisbury.

Children, born in Tisbury:

154.   JOHN GRAY,[7] b. 22 June 1820; m. Ann Maxfield.

155.   GEORGE, b. — Oct. 1823; m. (1) 3 Jan. 1853, Celia P. Skiff; m. (2) Caroline E. Rogers; d. 31 Oct. 1870, aged 47.

MARY GRAY, b. 25 Dec. 1825; m. Otis Tilton.

156.   ALPHEUS, b. — Aug. 1826; m. (1) Isabelle E. Ferguson, who d. 10 Oct. 1854; m. (2) Abigail Chase.

PATIENCE G., b. 1827; m. Rufus N. Smith.

EUNICE ROTCH, b. 24 July 1829; m. Franklin Gray.

REBECCA LUCE, b. 25 Feb. 1831; m. William K. Waggoner.

157.   WILLIAM, b. 29 Dec. 1833; m. Susan G. Rogers, who d. 26 Dec. 1863.

158. JOSEPH, b. — Jan. 1835; m. Marian E. Chapman.
HARRIET NEWELL, b. 24 Sept. 1837; d. 26 June 1862, unm.
ANN JUDSON, b. 11 Sept. 1840; Samuel D. Kidder.

82

CAPT. GEORGE[6] CHASE (Joseph,[5] Isaac,[4] Isaac,[3] Lt. Isaac[2]), born
in Tisbury, 15 July 1803; died St. Helena, Calif., 27 Feb. 1878;
buried in Oakland Cemetery, Yonkers, N. Y. He married in Wiscasset, Me., 7 Oct. 1825, MARY ELMES, daughter of William and
Abigail (Stone) Elmes, born in Wiscasset, 6 July 1807; died at sea,
22 Aug. 1867; buried in Panama, later her remains were removed to
Oakland Cemetery, Yonkers. He was a sea-captain, sailing from
New Bedford. They lived in Boston.

Children, first six born in Boston:

MARY ABIGAIL,[7] b. 6 July 1827; m. 13 Apr. 1847, David McKay;
she d. 24 July 1859, aged 32; two children.

SARAH ESTHER, b. 3 Sept. 1829; m. in Holy Trinity Church of
Brooklyn, N. Y., 25 July 1849, William Bowers Bourn of
Somerset. Children: *Mary Champney[8] Bourn*, b. 11 Feb. 1855;
m. James Ellis Tucker, brother of Bishop Tucker of Rich-
mond, Va.; no children; Mrs. Tucker now lives in San Fran-
cisco. *William Bowers[8] Bourn*, b. 1 June 1857; m. Agnes
Moody, dau. of Horace Moody of Newburyport and Yonkers,
N. Y.; lives at "Filoli," San Mateo, Calif. Their dau. Maud
Chase[9] Bourn, m. Arthur Rose Vincent of Muckross Abbey,
County Kerry, Ireland. Their children are: *Elizabeth Rose[10]
Vincent* and *William Bourn[10] Vincent*. *Zaidee Francis[8] Bourn*,
b. 5 June 1859; m. Horace Moody; she d. 15 Oct. 1898; no
children. *Frank Washington[8] Bourn*, b. 20 June 1861; d. 25
Feb. 1872. *Ida Hoxie[8] Bourn*, b. 2 Apr. 1864; lives in San
Francisco, Calif., unm. *Maud Elouise Chase[8] Bourn*, b. 15
Nov. 1867; m. William Alston Hayne. Their sons are William
Alston Bourn[9] Hayne, m. 24 Jan. 1924, Marion Wallace Gibbs,
dau. of Judge Gibbs of Pasadena, Calif. One child William
Alston[10] Hayne, b. 29 May 1925. Francis Bourn[9] Hayne, grad-
uate of Harvard Univ., 1926.

CHARLOTTE MORTON, b. 11 July 1831; m. 18 Dec. 1854. William
Wells Starr of Yonkers; she d. 11 Apr. 1874. Their son is
George W. Starr, mining engineer, Grass Valley, Calif.

GEORGIANA, b. 24 Mar. 1834; m. 15 Sept. 1860, Henry W. Bashford of Yonkers, N. Y., b. 17 July 1827; d. 25 Feb. 1904, son
of John and Esther Ann (Guion) Bashford. She d. 7 Jan.
1924, in Yonkers. Their children were: *Esther[8] Bashford*, b.
20 Sept. 1861, lives in Yonkers. *Mary Chase[8] Bashford*, b. 8
Feb. 1863; m. 26 July 1919, Robert Parkhill Getty of Yonkers;
live in Waukegan, Ill. *Henry[8] Bashford*, b. 6 July 1864; lives
in Yonkers, unm. *Edward Everett[8] Bashford*, b. 13 Aug. 1868;
m. 6 Oct. 1898, Florence Libby Beames, b. 17 May 1875; one
dau. Damasita Mazenet[9] Bashford, b. 2 Aug. 1899; m. 19 June
1920, John Stryker Piper of Yonkers; she is deceased. *Georgiana[8] Bashford*, b. 26 Aug. 1874; m. 21 Dec. 1898, Lt. Col. Clare
Franklin Beames. Their sons born in Mexico City were: Clare
Franklin[9] Beames, b. 27 July 1900; Walden Chase[9] Beames, b.
9 May 1902, and Thomas Cornell[9] Beames, b. 16 Mar. 1904.
Clare Franklin[9] Beames, m. 23 Sept. 1927, Evelyn West of

Syracuse, N. Y. Walden Franklin Beames, m. 14 Nov. 1924, Alice Hilton. Their dau. Georgiana Alice[10] Beames, b. 11 Sept. 1925.

EMILY FRANCES, b. 29 Feb. 1836; m. Edney Stagg Tibbey, b. in Sydney, New South Wales, 13 Feb. 1835. She d. 12 Mar. 1912.

CAROLINE, b. 29 Sept. 1839; m. 9 Jan. 1862, John Brayton Bowers of Somerset; she d. 24 Mar. 1910. Children: *George[8] Bowers*, now deceased; *Mary Manzanita[8] Bowers*, m. William H. Bray; one son; *Edith Brayton[8] Bowers*, m. Dr. William C. Dawson of San Francisco, Calif.

JOHN H., b. 12 Jan. 1843; d. 25 Nov. 1864.

GEORGE, b. 4 Oct. 1847; d. 1911; lived in California; m. and had children.

83

TRISTRAM L.[6] CHASE (Joseph,[5] Isaac,[4] Isaac,[3] Lt. Isaac[2]), born in Tisbury, 1809; married there (1) Sept. 1835, HEPSIA D. NORTON, who died in West Tisbury, 28 Sept. 1839, aged 21 y. 5 d. He married (2) in Tisbury, 27 Nov. 1841, HANNAH M. ROBINSON. He was a master mariner and they lived at "Homes Hole" in Tisbury.

Children by second wife, born in Tisbury:

AMY DOWNS,[7] b. 22 Dec. 1842; m. Cyrus Manter.

THOMAS GIFFORD ROBINSON, b. 4 July 1847; d. young.

84

OBED[6] CHASE (Francis,[5] Joseph,[4] Isaac,[3] Lt. Isaac[2]), born in Nantucket, 19 Dec. 1778; married (1) (int. 16 Jan. 1802) 20 Mar. 1802, BETSEY[6] CHASE, daughter of Joseph[5] and Rebecca (Folger) Chase, (Family 36), born in Nantucket, 31 Oct. 1780; died 17 July 1802. He married (2) in Nantucket, 17 July 1808, ELIZABETH COFFIN, daughter of Abner and Elizabeth (Gardner) Coffin, born in Nantucket, 9 Sept. 1777; died 10 May 1844, aged 66 y. 6 m. No children by first wife recorded in Nantucket. He died in Nantucket, 25 July 1818, aged 39 y. 6 m.

Child by second wife, born in Nantucket:

159.   OBED G.,[7] b. 25 Apr. 1812; m. 1 Jan. 1845, Ann or Amy W. Sherman, dau. of Nicholas of Chautauqua, N. Y.

85

FRANCIS[6] CHASE (Francis,[5] Joseph,,[4] Isaac,[3] Lt. Isaac[2]), born in Nantucket, 19 Oct. 1781; married there (1) 14 June 1803, ANNA GARDNER, daughter of Micajah and Anna (Glazier) Gardner, born in Nantucket, 12 Sept. 1784. She died in Nantucket, 26 July 1840. He married (2) in Nantucket, 2 Jan. 1845, ABIGAIL (GWINN) GERRISH, aged 58, of Boston, widow of Francis Gerrish of Boston. He died 15 Nov. 1855. His second wife was born 30 July 1788. They lived in Nantucket.

Children, born in Nantucket:

160.   JOHN G.,[7] b. 5 Dec. 1803; m. there, 16 June 1829, Lydia Clark, dau. of Obed and Anna (Coffin) Clark of Nantucket.

SUSAN G., b. 6 Oct. 1805; m. there, 5 July 1824, William Rawson, son of Stephen and Abigail (Heath) Rawson of Nantucket.

161. WILLIAM G., b. 6 Dec. 1807; m. Elizabeth Congdon of Newport, R. I.

ANNA GLAZIER, b. 24 Mar. 1810; m. there, 19 Mar. 1829, Thomas Derrick of the West Indies.

162. NATHANIEL, b. 29 Aug. 1812; m. there, 1839 (int. 8 Sept.), Martha R. Hathaway, dau. of Charles and Lucretia (Remson) Hathaway of Nantucket.

86

PAUL[6] CHASE (Francis,[5] Joseph,[4] Isaac,[3] Lt. Isaac[2]), born in Nantucket, 19 June 1784; married 14 Jan. 1809, ROSE ANNA TYLEE who was born 14 Apr. 1788. He died 11 Jan. 1834 in Nantucket. They lived in Nantucket.

Children:

163. FRANCIS EDWARD,[7] b. 20 May 1810; m. 4 Jan. 1840, Fidelia G. Owen; he d. 25 Dec. 1849; one daughter.

SARAH ELIZABETH, b. 24 Feb. 1813; m. 20 Feb. 1833, Alfred Bentley.

ANNE LOUISA, b. 6 Sept. 1819; m. 17 June 1837, Edward S. Howard of New York.

164. PAUL, date of birth not given.

86a

DEA. LEVI[6] CHASE (Levi,[5] Levi,[4] Isaac,[3] Lt. Isaac[2]), born in Sandwich or Lee, 25 May 1781; died in Lafayette, Medina Co., Ohio. 11 Mar. 1845. He removed to Pompey, Onondaga Co., N. Y., before 1802. He returned and married in Lee, 11 Feb. 1802, SALLY BASSETT, born 13 Apr. 1782; died in Lafayette, Ohio, 28 Apr. 1853. They lived in Pompey Hill, Onondaga Co. from 1802 to 1834. In the fall of 1834, they emigrated West and purchased 531 acres at $4.50 per acre, in La Fayette, Medina Co., Ohio, where they remained till death. There were thirteen children, eleven of whom grew to maturity. Mr. Chase was deacon in the Baptist Church.

Children, born in Pompey, N. Y.:

THOMAS C.[7]

LEVI.

JOHN B., b. 24 Mar. 1811; m. (1) June 1836, Anna Wood, who d. 27 Nov. 1846; m. (2) 3 July 1839, Sophia Gates.

PHILURA.

HARRIET, b. 13 Dec. 1813; m. 5 June 1835, William Fox Moore, b. in England, 18 Mar. 1807; d. 2 Oct. 1890. She d. 24 July 1851. Their son *Richard Avery*[8] *Moore*, b. in La Fayette, 23 Oct. 1850; m. 17 Jan. 1872, Kate Goula Elma Young, b. in London, England, 7 May 1855. Their daughter Myrtelle May[9] Moore, b. in Greenbush, Mich., 24 June 1879; m. 17 May 1905, James Francis Canavan, M. D., b. 11 Mar. 1876; d. 26 July 1907. Mrs. Canavan is a physician and curator of the Warren Museum of the Harvard Medical School; associate professor of neuropathology in the Boston University Medical School and instructor in neuropathology in the University of Vermont Medical School.

POLLY.

SARAH, m. S. E. Kinney of Litchfield, Ohio.

CHARLES.

ORRILLA.
ADA A.
MARSHALL, living in Michigan in 1880.

87

BENJAMIN[6] CHASE (Timothy,[5] Abraham,[4] Abraham[3] Lt. Isaac[2]), born in Tisbury, 2 Mar. 1779; married there, 20 Feb. 1805 or 1806, ALICE FOSSETT SPALDING, daughter of Dr. Rufus and Lydia Spalding, born in Brooklyn, Conn., 28 Feb. 1788. No children's births recorded in Tisbury.

88

TIMOTHY[6] CHASE (Timothy,[5] Abraham,[4] Abraham,[3] Lt. Isaac[2]), born in Tisbury, 28 Nov. 1781; married there, 27 Sept. 1804, CONTENT DUNHAM, daughter of David and Deborah (Luce) Dunham, born in Tisbury, 8 Nov. 1779. She died in the East Parish of Tisbury, 11 Sept. 1809, aged 29 y. 10 m. 3 d. He married (2) in Tisbury, 7 June 1818, SARAH LUCE, born about Aug. 1793. He died in 1852.

Children by first wife, born in Tisbury:

    MARY,[7] b. 28 June 1805.
165. ABRAHAM, b. 2 Oct. 1807.

Children by second wife, born in Tisbury:

    CONTENT, b. 4 Mar. 1819.
    SOPHRONIA, b. 10 Apr. 1821.
166. TIMOTHY, b. 27 Dec. 1822.
    SARAH, b. 4 Dec. 1824.
    MARY, b. 7 Apr. 1827.
    ABIGAIL, b. 14 Aug. 1829.
    BETSEY A., b. 29 Jan. 1831.
167. BENJAMIN, b. 2 Apr. 1833.

89

FRANCIS[6] CHASE (James,[5] James,[4] James,[3] Lt. Isaac[2]), born in Nantucket, 21 Nov. 1761; married 21 Oct. 1784, ELIZABETH LUCAS of Boston.

90

PETER[6] CHASE (James,[5] James,[4] James,[3] Lt. Isaac[2]), born in Nantucket, 27 June 1764; married there, 18 July 1789, ELIZABETH HUSSEY, daughter of Bachelder and Anna (Coffin) Hussey, born in Nantucket, 20 Aug. 1766. He was a master mariner and died in Nantucket, 19 Sept. 1842, aged 78. She died there as his widow, 10 Oct. 1847, aged 81 y. 1 m. 19 d.

Children, born in Nantucket:

168. GEORGE COFFIN,[7] b. 25 May 1790; m. (1) 9 Dec. 1813, Winnifred Swain; m. (2) 15 Mar. 1821, Abigail J. Barney.
169. DANIEL COFFIN, b. 16 July 1792; m. 27 Dec. 1818, Ann Bunker, dau. of Latham and Susanna (Barnard) Bunker.

170. BENJAMIN WHEELWRIGHT, b. 13 Aug. 1794; m. (1) 11 Dec. 1817, Ann Swain, dau. of John and Mary (Gardner) Swain; m. (2) 18 Apr. 1848, Sarah (Folger) Barney, widow of Thomas Barney and dau. of Joseph and Judith (Inott) Folger.
171. DAVID FOLGER, b. 16 Aug. 1796; m. 11 Dec. 1821, Nancy Barnard, dau. of Thomas and Eunice (Gardner) Barnard.
LYDIA HUSSEY, b. 26 Sept. 1798.
172. FREDERICK A., b. 26 Dec. 1800; m. 31 Jan. 1828, Mary Ann Myrick, dau. of Matthew and Abigail Myrick.
MARY ANN, b. 12 Mar. 1803.
ELIZA ANN, b. 18 May 1805; m. 4 Oct. 1826, Edward G. Barney.
173. WILLIAM HENRY, b. 26 Nov. 1808; m. 28 Jan. 1838, Eliza Ann Tuck, dau. of Samuel J. and Judith (Gardner) Tuck.

91

ARIEL[6] CHASE (James,[5] James,[4] James,[3] Lt. Isaac[2]), born in Nantucket, 25 May 1770; married (int. 7 Feb. 1795) JANE TRIPP, daughter of Job and Hannah (Carver) Tripp, born 2 June 1775; died 19 Oct. 1838. He died in Newport, R. I., in May 1813.
Children:

SARAH FOLGER,[7] b. 28 Aug. 1798; m. 20 Dec. 1820, Oliver Slocum of Dartmouth and Chilmark; she d. May 1880.
FRANKLIN BROWN, b. — Sept. 1800; m. 8 May 1823, Sarah Sherman, dau. of Isaac and Elizabeth Sherman.
JOSEPH TRIPP, b. 16 Aug. 1802; m. (1) 4 July 1824, Lucy Ann Howland, dau. of Joseph Howland 3d, b. 1804; d. 12 Oct. 1827; m. (2) 28 Sept. 1834, Hannah Hawes, dau. of Ebenezer and Thankful Hawes, b. 1813; d. 2 Apr. 1867. He d. in New Bedford, 7 Apr. 1853. Their son (by first wife) *Ariel,*[8] b. in New Bedford, 1 Apr. 1825; d. 20 June 1889; m. 27 June 1859, Ann Eliza Davenport, dau. of Richard and Rhoda (Coe) Davenport, b. 20 June 1831; d. 28 Feb. 1903. Their son Richard Davenport,[9] b. in New Bedford, 31 Aug. 1870; m. 26 Oct. 1905, Mary Manson Robinson, b. in Greenland, N. H., 7 Oct. 1869. Their children are *Rhoda Davenport*[10] and *Marianne.*[10]

92

JAMES FRANKLIN[6] CHASE (James,[5] James,[4] James,[3] Lt. Isaac[2]), born in Nantucket, 16 May 1784; married there, 23 June 1809, ELIZA FOLGER, daughter of Joseph and Judith (Inott) Folger, born in Nantucket, 27 Mar. 1784. They lived in Nantucket.
Children, born in Nantucket:

NANCY M.,[7] b. 1 June 1810; m. 19 Aug. 1833, Ebenezer M. Hinckley.
JUDITH F., b. 13 Oct. 1812; m. 4 Nov. 1838, Samuel G. Davis.
ELIZABETH J., b. 29 Nov. 1815; m. 17 Jan. 1837, Reuben B. Gardner.
175. JOSEPH F., b. 20 Dec. 1818; m. 8 July 1855, Maria Louisa Jenkins.
176. JAMES FRANKLIN, b. 6 Apr. 1821; m. 30 Oct. 1853, Ann W. Brock.
177. FRANCIS B., b. 26 Sept. 1823; m. 27 Sept. 1855, Mary Hussey Folger.
PHEBE H., b. 10 Feb. 1826; m. 1 Jan. 1849, Edgar H. Lovell.
MARY JANE, b. 14 Oct. 1829; never married.

93

BENJAMIN[6] CHASE (Zephaniah,[5] Abel,[4] Joseph,[3] Lt. Isaac[2]), born in Chilmark, 21 Jan. 1774; married 4 Aug. 1799, LYDIA SKIFF. They lived in Lexington and Jewett, Green Co., N. Y. He died in Jewett Center, N. Y., 28 Feb. 1862. She died 12 Feb. 1829.

Children, born in Lexington:

ELIZABETH,[7] b. 14 Mar. 1800; m. 17 Sept. 1820, Lumen Whitcomb; ten children, all living in 1872.

LYDIA, b. 22 July 1802; m. 3 Mar. 1822, Orrin Burgess; she d. 16 Feb. 1860; nine children.

178. BENJAMIN, b. 1 Feb. 1804; m. 6 May 1827, Elizabeth Burgess; four children.

ABIGAIL, b. 17 Mar.. 1807; d. 1 Jan. 1821.

179. WILLIAM, b. 17 June 1809; m. (1) 27 Oct. 1836, Pamelia Woolcott; m. (2) 28 Feb. 1850, Elizabeth P. Jump; lived in Fitchville, Huron Co., Ohio; three children by first wife, two by second. He d. 17 June 1888 and his widow Elizabeth d. 28 July 1893.

LUCINDA, b. 26 Mar. 1811; m. 30 Mar. 1830, Matthias Hill Chittenden; five children.

MARY, b. 9 Mar. 1813; m. 9 Sept. 1835, Samuel W. Cook; five children.

SARAH, b. 28 June 1816; m. 30 May 1841, Peleg W. Chamberlain; lived in Lexington and Hopkins, Mich.; eight children.

180. ALBERT, b. 4 Jan. 1819; m. 1 Sept. 1844, Laura Orinda Woodworth; lived in Hensonville, N. Y. He d. there, 13 Oct. 1902. Fire children, including *Emory Albert,*[8] b. in Hensonville, 31 Aug. 1854; d. 25 June 1921; educated at the Fort Edward Collegiate Institute; studied law and was admitted to the bar in 1880; elected Associate Judge of the Supreme Court of New York in 1896 and re-elected for a second term in 1910; then appointed by Governor Dix Associate Judge of the Court of Appeals for the State of New York and served as a member of the higher courts for twenty-four years. He m. in 1885, Mary Elizabeth Churchill, who, with a daughter Mrs. James Lewis Malcolm of Catskill, N. Y., and a son Albert Woodworth[9] Chase of New York City, survive.

181. IRA, b. 3 Oct. 1821; m. 20 May 1850, Esther S.[7] Chase (Family 96); three children.

94

JOSEPH[6] CHASE (Zephaniah,[5] Abel,[4] Joseph,[3] Lt. Isaac[2]), born in Martha's Vineyard, 2 Dec. 1775; died 2 July 1831. He married 10 Nov. 1805, JEMIMA HOWK [HOUK] who died 16 Dec. 1847, aged 60 y. 4 m. 18 d.

Children:

SAMUEL,[7] d. a young man, 5 Feb. 1832, aged 22y. 9m. 6d.

182. JOHN, b. 17 Feb. 1812; m. 10 Oct. 1841, Electa[7] Chase (Rev. Charles[6]); d. 17 Aug. 1854; Methodist clergyman; (Family 96) two children; lived in Irving, Kans.

183. ISAAC, d. 26 Mar. 1835, aged 21y. 5m.

JUDGE EMORY ALBERT CHASE

95

DAVID[6] CHASE (Zephaniah,[5] Abel,[4] Joseph,[3] Lt. Isaac[2]), born in Martha's Vineyard, 3 Jan. 1786; married (1) 13 Oct. 1808, ABIGAIL PRATT, daughter of Zadok Pratt of Saybrook, Conn., born 3 Aug. 1786; died 20 Aug. 1849. He married (2) 13 Feb. 1850, CHARLOTTE JOHNSON who died 22 May 1867. He died in Lexington, N. Y., 27 Aug. 1871. They lived in Jewett Centre, Green Co., N. Y.

Children, born in Jewett:

EUNICE,[7] b. 2 July 1809; m. 15 Sept. 1836, Aaron Pond; she d. 26 Apr. 1837.

EMELINE HARRIET, b. 20 Feb. 1811; m. 1 Nov. 1832, James Harrington, b. 17 Oct. 1810; d. 5 Feb. 1905. She d. 17 Apr. 1878; buried at Jewett, N. Y. Their son *David Chase[8] Harrington*, b. in Lexington, N. Y., 8 Dec. 1834; m. (1) 11 Sept. 1856, Ann Jannette Kemmerrer, dau. of David Kemmerer of Scranton, Pa. She d. 20 Nov. 1904; he m. (2) 18 July 1906, Jeanne Ethleen Smith. He was a lawyer and principal of the School of Law in Scranton. Ten children, including Blandina Jayne[9] Harrington, b. 8 Nov. 1862; m. 4 Mar. 1906, Thomas Jefferson Foster, b. 1 Jan. 1843. Their only child is *Thomas Jefferson[10] Foster Jr.*, b. 4 Oct. 1900; m. 18 Apr. 1927, Elizabeth Catherine Leach, dau. of Andrew K. and Mary Eliza (McCromb) Leach. They live in Wilkes-Barre, Pa.

185. DAVID NOBLE, b. 22 Mar. 1813; m. (1) 22 Feb. 1837, Louisa Rowley; m. (2) 15 Apr. 1859, Amy Curtis; Methodist clergyman, Lexington; three children, including *Rev. Pratt Noble*,[8] b. Oct. 1848; d. at his home in Kingston, N. Y., Nov. 1923. (Chase Chronicle, 14: 16.)

POLLY, b. 29 July 1815; m. 27 Apr. 1836, Rev. Israel B. Whitcomb, Baptist clergyman.

LUCY ANN, b. 12 Nov. 1817; m. 18 Feb. 1838, Aaron Pond.

186. CHARLES PRATT, b. 3 May 1820; m. 23 Feb. 1842, Ruth D. Baldwin; four children.

ABIGAIL, b. 21 Aug. 1822; m. 5 Apr. 1859, Augustus H. Carr.

96

REV. CHARLES[6] CHASE (Zephaniah,[5] Abel,[4] Joseph,[3] Lt. Isaac[2]), born in Woodstock, N. Y., 9 Sept. 1790; died 24 May 1844. He married 30 Nov. 1809, ELEANOR HOWK [HOUK] who was born 3 Oct. 1789; died 10 June 1868. He was a Methodist minister.

Children:

CYNTHIA,[7] b. 22 Sept. 1810; m. 10 May 1837, Rev. Reuben H. Bloomer; d. 3 May 1842.

ELECTA, b. 2 July 1812; m. 11 Oct. 1841, Rev. John[7] Chase (Family 94) (Joseph,[6] Zephaniah[5]). Two children; he d. 17 Aug. 1854.

CHARLES LAMBERT, b. 27 Aug. 1814; d. 5 Oct. 1817.

ALMIRA. b. 30 Dec. 1816; m. Rev. Reuben H. Bloomer.

ALMA LOVISA, b. 25 Mar. 1819; m. 7 Mar. 1850, Charles Enslow.

ESTHER STOWE, b. 24 Dec. 1820; m. 20 May 1850, Ira[7] Chase (Benjamin[6]) (Family 93). Three children.

MANLY, b. 23 Mar. 1823; d. 29 June 1838.

LUCY, b. 3 Apr. 1825; m. 18 Nov. 1844, George D. Wells.

ELIZA, b. 26 June 1827; never married; d. 8 Dec. 1882.

187. CHARLES WESLEY, b. 20 Sept. 1829.
188. DAVID FLETCHER, b. 13 Nov. 1831; m. 12 Oct. 1864, Emily F.
      Taber; no children.
      HORACE W., b. 1 July 1835; never married.

97

WEST[6] CHASE (Zephaniah,[5] Abel,[4] Joseph,[3] Lt. Isaac[2]), born in
Woodstock, N. Y., 30 Mar. 1797; married 30 Sept. 1817, JULIA M.
NEWTON, who was born 5 May 1800; died 29 Nov. 1879. He died
22 May 1860.
    Children:
189. NEWTON,[7] b. 18 Dec. 1818; m. (1) 17 Mar. 1841, Lucina Bald-
      win, d. 30 June 1845; m. (2) 7 Apr. 1847, Almira Whitcomb;
      d. 8 June 1880.
      LAURA, b. 25 Dec. 1820; d. 28 Dec. 1820.
      EUNICE, b. 6 Nov. 1821; m. 22 Feb. 1842, Samuel A. Baldwin.
      LAURA ELIZABETH, b. 22 June 1824; m. (1) 15 Oct. 1845, George
      Delamater; m. (2) 15 May 1871, George Wells, d. 16 Sept.
      1908.
      FIDELIA ANN, b. 24 Sept. 1827; m. 27 Apr. 1864, Luther Rowley.
      CAROLINE L., b. 28 Aug. 1830; m. 14 Nov. 1859, Christopher
      Bascom.
      JANE ESTELLE, b. 8 Jan. 1838; m. 27 Oct. 1857, John Tibbetts.

98

THOMAS GREENLEAF[6] CHASE (Thomas,[5] Thomas,[4] Joseph,[3] Lt.
Isaac[2]), born in Bolton, 3 Mar. 1793; married 19 Feb. 1840, HARRIET
CLARA GOODWIN, daughter of Capt. Gale and Clarissa (Whetmore)
Goodwin, born 7 Feb. 1818.
    Children:
      CLARA ANNIE,[7] b. 12 Nov. 1840.
      THOMAS, b. 11 June 1843.
      ALLYN GARDINER, b. 26 Mar. 1849.
      GEORGE EMMANUEL, b. 8 Mar. 1852.
      EMELINE GOODWIN, b. 27 Mar. 1854; d. 15 Aug. 1856.

99

MAJ. WILLIAM HENRY[6] CHASE (Thomas,[5] Thomas,[4] Joseph,[3]
Lt. Isaac[2]), born 4 June 1798; married ANNA PAUL MATTHEWS. He
graduated at the U. S. military academy in 1815 and was assigned to
the engineer corps and employed in repairing Fort Niagara 1817-8;
assigned to construct defences for New Orleans in 1819 at Forts Pike
and Macomb; first lieutenant, 1819 to 1825; captain 1825 to 1854;
had charge of constructing defences in Pensacola harbor, Fla., of
Fort Morgan, Ala., and Fort Jackson, La.; promoted to Major in
1838 and was in charge of improvements in Mobile Bay and Fort
Taylor, Key West, Fla., till 1856; appointed Superintendent of the
U. S. Military Academy; resigned from the Army 31 Oct. 1856 and
became president of the Alabama and Florida railroad. At the beginning of the Civil War he joined the Confederates and was active in
the seizure of Pensacola navy-yard. He died in Pensacola, Fla., 8
Feb. 1870.

Child:

ANNE PAUL,[7] m. Joel Matthews.

100

GEORGE EDMOND[6] CHASE (Thomas,[5] Thomas,[4] Thomas,[3] Lt. Isaac[2]), born 2 May 1803; died in 1844. He graduated from West Point in 1828 and served in the U. S. army until his death. He married, 13 Apr. 1837, ELIZABETH FLOWER.

Children:

ANNE GREENLEAF,[7] b. 23 Dec. 1839.

190. WILLIAM FLOWER, b. 26 Feb. 1842; two sons.

191. THOMAS BARTLETT, b. 29 Nov. 1843; served in the Confederate Army, 1862-1865; lives in Shreveport, La. He is a Scottish Rite Mason, 33rd degree, and was Grand Commander of Knights Templar in 1899. He is still active in Masonry and business at the age of 84.

OLD GRAVESTONES OF CHASE FAMILY

Plains Cemetery, Newburyport

Here lyes buried ye body of Ann Chase ye wife of Ensign Moses² Chase aged 40 years, died April 18, 1708 being ye Lords Day.

Ferry Lane (Bridge Street) Cemetery, West Newbury

Ann, daughter of Moses³ and Elizabeth Chase, died Nov. 29, 1726, aged 3 years.

Abigail, daughter of Moses³ and Elizabeth Chase, died May 15, 1736, aged 2 years.

Rebakah, daughter of Moses³ and Elizabeth Chass, died May 18, 1736, aged 5 years.

Ann, daughter of Moses³ and Elizabeth Chass, died May 27, 1736, aged 8 years.

Sarah [Jacobs] wife of Ensign Moses² Chase, died March 13, 1739, aged 63.

Here Lies Buried the Body of Ensign Moses² Chase who died Sept. 6, 1743 in ye 80th year of his age.

Samuel³ Chase, died July 24, 1743, aged 54.

Amos, son of Lieut. Joseph³ and Mary Chase, died Oct. 30 1754, aged 15 years.

Mrs. Elizabeth, wife of Moses³ Chase, died May 31, 1755 aged 67.

Moses³ Chase, died Sept. 17, 1760, aged 73.

Walnut Hill Cemetery, West Newbury

Mrs. Mary wife of Thomas⁴ Chase, died Oct. 12, 1725 aged 21 years.

Mary, daughter of Thomas⁴ and Emme Chase, died Dec. 1, 1729, aged 2 years.

Summersbee, son of Thomas⁴ Chase, died Aug. 21, 1736, aged 4 years.

Thomas, son of Thomas⁴ Chase, died Aug. 21, 1736, aged 4 years.

Abel, son of Thomas⁴ Chase, died Aug. 23, 1736, aged 7 years.

Mrs. Martha Gerrish [dau. of Thomas³ Chase] died Oct. 3, 1739, aged 21 years.

Mary, daughter of Thomas⁴ Chase Jr. died Nov. 28, 1748 in her 2d year. [Thomas⁴ Family, 43.]

Dea. Thomas³ Chase died Feb. 10, 1756 in ye 76th year of his age.

Mrs. Sarah wife of Dea. Thomas³ Chase, died Oct. 25, 1760 aged 81 years.

Thomas⁴ Chase, died Oct. 14, 1765, aged 65.

Mrs. Emme, widow of Thomas⁴ Chase, died March 24, 1783, aged 82.

Yours &c
John B. Chace

JOHN BOWEN CHACE, M. D.

JOHN BOWEN[7] CHACE, M. D. (John,[6] Stephen,[5] John,[4] Samuel,[3] William,[2] William[1]), of Taunton, was born in Swansea, June 14, 1816. His father died while still a young man, leaving his only son to the care of his mother, Deborah née Macomber, who afterward married William Wilbur of Little Compton, R. I. During his early years he attended the district school of his native town. When about eleven years of age he was sent to the Friends' school in Providence, R. I. There he spent the next five years, including most of the vacation seasons. He was (to judge from reports of his school life still in existence), diligent and faithful in his school work. He was very fond of the higher mathematics, and in later life thoroughly enjoyed wrestling with hard problems until he conquered them.

At the age of seventeen he began the study of medicine with Dr. Wilbur of Fall River, and in 1838 received the degree of M. D. at the Jefferson Medical College, Philadelphia. In the fall of the same year he began the practice of medicine in Somerset. There he married Rebecca, daughter of Eber and Sybil Chace who belonged to the Society of Friends. Three sons and a daughter died in infancy. Two sons and three daughters grew to manhood and womanhood, sons and daughters for whose lives he thanked God upon his dying bed.

In 1848, in company with others, he went to California as a physician. The voyage was made on the "old Bark Ann," by way of Cape Horn. He was away about two years and his stay in California was not without its hardships.

From California he embarked as surgeon on an East Indian ship, and then lived a short time in Manila. While there an English physician, Dr. Reed, presented him with an elegant and valuable lace handkerchief containing one hundred dollars in gold as an expression of appreciation for professional service rendered to his wife.

On his return from the East Indies, in 1850, he lived in Somerset five years, and then in Westport two years, removing to Taunton in 1857, where he remained until his death, with the exception of a short time spent in the state of New York.

"As a physician he was faithful and successful, but it was in surgery that he had especial pride. Here his clear judgment, perfect anatomical knowledge, and steady hand, combined to give him a high rank." He often remarked, "It is much easier for a surgeon to take off a badly injured limb than it is to save it; but it is far better for the man to have his limb, even if he can make but little use of it."

He despised shams and make-believe sickness, but he had long patience with real sickness. When asked what enabled him to cure so many people of chronic ailments, his reply was short and to the point—"Patience."

He was a member of the Massachusetts Medical Society from 1848 until his death, and of the North District Medical Society, serving on its board of censors. During the Civil War he was assistant examining surgeon for recruits and substitutes for eastern Massachusetts, and for ten years he served as United States Examiner of Pensioners, until his last illness compelled him to resign, a few months before his death.

He was a member of the Christian denomination, to which he was strongly attached, and while there was a church of that name in Taunton, his house was always "ministers' hotel." While in Westport he held pastoral charge of the small church at Brownell's Corners for some months, and in Somerset and other places he assisted smaller churches by occasionally preaching for them.

In his family relations he was a true and faithful husband and father. He trained his children with especial care. Young physicians, troubled fathers and neighbors in their perplexities often sought his aid, glad to avail themselves of the wise counsel of a true friend.

His genealogical researches, which continued while strength lasted, covered a period of more than thirty years. He thoroughly enjoyed the work, to which he devoted a large expenditure of time, money, and persistent effort, and the inability to complete and publish the result of his labor was a great disappointment.

The voluminous amount of material he had collected and acquired has been of incalculable value in the preparation of the volume in which this well-deserved memoir appears.

His last illness was one of intense and prolonged suffering, borne with patience and faith until the end, which came 31 May 1881.

ADDITIONS and CORRECTIONS

1

AQUILA[1] CHASE, the immigrant, married about 1644, ANN WHEELER, daughter of John and Ann (Yeoman) Wheeler. She was probably born between 1620 and 1630, as she was the mother of eleven children, born in Hampton, N. H., and Newbury (now Newburyport) between the years 1644 and 1664. Aquila Chase died in Newbury, 27 Dec. 1670 and "ANNE CHASE SR." and DANIEL MISSILLOWAY [SILLOWAY] were married in Newbury, 14 June 1672. "An, the wife of Daniell Mussiloway,"died there, 21 Apr. 1687.

Her father, John Wheeler, came in the ship *Mary* and *John*, sailing for New England on or about 26 Mar. 1634. In the shipping list of those who took the oath of allegiance his name was written "John Wheyler." (Drake's The Founders of New England, 70).

He came from Salisbury in Wiltshire. In the parish register of St. Edmund in Salisbury is the marriage record of"JOHN WHELYER & AGNES YEOMAN" on 1 Dec. 1611. (Wiltshire Parish Register Marriages, 13 : 43).

At that period the Christian names *Agnes, Annes* and *Ann* were frequently used interchangeably for one and the same person.

The marriage record of Aquila Chase and Ann Wheeler has not been preserved, but the fact has been established by the will of her father.

John Wheeler of Newbury, "considering my old age and my owne weakness," made his will, 28 Mar. 1668. He mentions his children and among them, "my daughter Anne Chase" to have four pounds. He also gave "to my Sonne Edward Wheeler of the Citty of Salisbury in the Realme of England ten pounds of which he is to pay three pounds and ten shillings to the Chamber[lain] of the Citty aforesaid, also I give & bequeath to my Son Adam Wheeler of the said Citty forty shillings." (Wheeler Genealogy, 394).

John Wheeler was the eldest son of Dominick and Mercy (Jelly) Wheeler and was born in Salisbury about 1589. The register of St. Edmund contains the marriage of DOMINICK WHEELER and MERCY JELLYE, 3 June 1588. (Wiltshire Marriages, 13 : 22). The last mentioned man must have been born as early as 1568. He died in Salisbury, England, between 12 Dec. 1615 and 16 Feb. 1615/16, when his will was probated, a portion being as follows :—

"Domny Wheller of the Cittye of newe Sarvm [Salisbury] in the County of Wiltes, Sherma,' beinge by the p'vidence of god stricken Sicke of body but of perfect & good memory thanks be vnto god, I do by this

my laste will & Testament I will & give vnto my wife Mercy Wheller all
& Singular my goodes & Cattell x x x x x x during her naturall life &
after her life ther Endinge that then both thes things afor Specified to
Come vnto John Wheller the Eldeste Sonne of the forsaid Domny Whel-
ler. I will also and give vnto my sone John Wheller a littel Clock & a
plater; moreover I will & give vnto Annes Wheller the wife of John
Wheller five chillings or anything to the value thereof. I will and give
vnto Edward Wheller, my son John Wheller's Eldeste sone, on[e] silver
Spone & to his brother John Wheller one pottinger." (Essex Institute
Historical Collections, 44: 292.)

Therefore, Ann Wheeler, the wife of Aquila Chase, was the
daughter of John and Ann (Yeoman) Wheeler of Salisbury in Wiltshire and Salisbury and Newbury, Mass., and the granddaughter of
Dominick and Mercy (Jelly) Wheeler who lived in the parish of
St. Edmund, Salisbury, 1588 to 1616.

15

PHILIP[3] CHASE (John[2]), born in Newbury, 23 Sept. 1688; removed to Sutton in 1726 and was living there in 1756. He served in
Capt. John Taplin's Co. from 15 Mar. to 12 Oct. 1756, as a volunteer
and was at Fort William Henry. He was reported as sick at Albany,
12 Oct. 1756. The military roll calls him a farmer, residence Sutton
and age 48. No other Philip Chase has been found and although this
age is not his true age yet, probably, the service rendered was by him.

24

DANIEL[3] CHASE (Ens. Moses[2]) lived on the Crane Hill road in
what is now West Newbury and not on Ash street as stated on
page 55.

38

DR. EZEKIEL[4] CHASE married (2) about 1770, ELIZABETH (DU-
RANT) SPAULDING, widow of Leonard Spaulding of Concord. Her
intention of marriage with her first husband was entered on the town
records of Chelmsford 18 Dec. 1737. Her son, Benjamin Spaulding,
removed to Buckfield, Me., and she passed her last days with him and
died in Buckfield, in 1799, aged 80 years. She was the wife of Dr.
Chase on 9 Aug. 1773.

51

The mother of LYDIA MOULTON was Hannah Sibley—not Hannah Libby as stated on page 69.

62

JOHN[4] CHASE of Hampton served in Capt. Samuel Hinckes's
Co. from 4 Dec. 1723 to 16 June 1724—a period of 28 weeks at Fort
Mary [at Winter Harbor on the Kennebec]. (Mass. Archives,
91: 123).

88a

Corp. Isaac⁴ Chase (Daniel,³ Daniel²), born in Concord, N. H., about 1739; served in the French and Indian War at Fort William Henry in 1757 as corporal. He also collected bounties for soldiers in the Revolutionary War. According to the *New Hampshire Patriot* of 23 Dec. 1817, he died in Warner, N. H., 9 Dec. 1817, in his 79th year.
Child:

321a. Isaac Jr.,ᵉ b. about 1764; d. in 1840. He married in Warner, 21 Oct. 1790, Mary Hunt, daughter of Nathan Hunt of Warner (Hunt Genealogy, 18).

96

Judge Samuel⁴ Chase was born on "Crane Hill" road in what is now West Newbury. The house is still (1928) standing and is now the home of Moses Smith, who is a descendant of Samuel³ Chase (Ens. Moses²) through the Baileys.

108

Dea. Amos⁴ Chase's daughter Sarah⁵ married in Pepperellborough (now Saco), Me., 9 Sept. 1766, Abel Hardy. She was living as Sarah Hardy 10 Apr. 1809. She probably did not marry Jacob Bedell, as stated on page 96.
His daughter Betsey⁵ married there, 17 Sept. 1767, Isaac Robinson. She was not alive on 10 Apr. 1809. His daughter Olive,⁵ married there 25 July 1782, Robert Edgecomb Nason and died before 10 Apr. 1809.

110

Benjamin⁴ Chase served in Capt. Samuel Cobb's Co. from 2 Apr. to 18 Nov. 1758 in the expedition to Lake George. He also enlisted from Biddeford at the age of 22, in Col. William Pepperell's Regiment, for the invasion of Canada, 2 Apr. 1759. He next appears as Sergeant in Capt. Joshua Moody's Co. from 2 Nov. 1759 to 18 Apr. 1761. He was at Louisburg on 1 Jan. 1760. He is described as of Biddeford in the military rolls. (Mass. Archives, 97: 58, 109, and 99: 6).

121

Dr. Thomas⁴ Chase was a member of the Westborough, alarm list, 1 Apr. 1757. (Mass. Archives).

132

Benjamin⁵ Chase appears as a private in Capt. John Church's Co. in the expedition to Crown Point, serving from 1 May to 14 Dec. 1759—a period of 32 weeks, 4 days. His "master" was William Baker and his residence was Lancaster. (Mass. Archives, 97: 389).

146

Abel⁵ Chase appears as Corporal in Capt. Solomon Holman's Co. from Sutton and served from 10 Aug. to 18 Aug. 1757—a period of 17 days—marching as far as Sheffield for the relief of Fort William Henry. (Mass. Archives).

147?

A THOMAS CHASE appears in Capt. Selah Barnard's Co. in the French and Indian War. He served from 6 Apr. to 26 May 1759; residence, New Salem; service to the westward. (Mass. Archives, 97:299a). He also appears in Capt. Thomas Cowdin's Co. in the service from 10 May to 17 Nov. 1761; residence New Salem. (Ibid. 99: 113.) He also served in the same company from 1 July to 1 Nov. 1762. The military record states that his father was Thomas Chase.

The above may have been Thomas Chase 147. There is, however, much uncertainty about the identity of the man who rendered this service.

153

MATTHEW[5] CHASE (Dea. Roger,[4] Dea. Thomas,[3] Thomas[2]), early removed from Nottingham West (now Hudson), N. H., to Clinton, Me. Among his children was Polly or Mary,[6] b. in Clinton 20 Mar. 1769; d. in Dover, Me. 26 Nov. 1827. She m. in 1786, Ziba Burrill, b. in Abington, 12 Mar. 1765; d. in Dover, 2 Oct. 1833. Their dau. Miriam[7] Burrill, b. 20 May 1787; d. in Waterville, Me., 16 Oct. 1828. She m. 1804, Asa Faunce, b. in Sandwich, 11 Sept. 1776; d. in Waterville, 10 Dec. 1824. Their dau. *Jane[8] Faunce,* b. in Waterville, 11 Aug. 1807; d. there 8 Jan. 1882. She m. 9 Nov. 1828, Ebenezer Farwell Bacon, b. in Sidney, Me., 2 Sept. 1796; d. in Waterville, 25 Oct. 1841. Their dau. Caroline Frances[9] Bacon, b. in Waterville, 7 Jan. 1830; d. in Cambridge, 1 Oct. 1899. She m. in Waterville, 2 Dec. 1853, Rev. James Monroe Palmer, graduate Colby College, 1847. Among their six children was William Lincoln[10] Palmer, b. in Portland, Me., 19 Sept. 1868; m. (1) 14 Apr. 1892, Jennie Christine Giesler, for whom the Palmer Memorial Hospital of Boston was named; b. in Princeton, Me., 22 July 1873; d. 1 Apr. 1919. Their children are Jennie Carolyn[11] Palmer, b. 22 Nov. 1894; m. 28 June 1920, Sheldon Smith Mayo. Marion Prescott[11] Palmer, b. 29 Sept. 1897; m. 17 June 1918, Walter Lafayette Abbott Jr. William Lincoln[11] Palmer Jr., b. 7 July 1909.

181

ABIGAIL[6] CHASE (Aquila,[5] Aquila,[4] James,[3] Thomas[2]), born 7 Oct. 1781; m. 15 July 1802, Caleb Lamson. She d. in Cambridge, 17 May 1848. Their son Rufus[7] Lamson, b. in Newbury, 2 Oct. 1809; m. Mary Jane Butler, dau. of John and Jane (Brookings) Butler, b. 6 July 1808; d. 21 Apr. 1885. He d. in Cambridge, 13 July 1879. Their son *Rufus William[8] Lamson,* b. 29 Sept. 1833; d. 27 Aug. 1912; m. 23 Feb. 1858, Cyrene Dam Eaton, b. 27 Feb. 1837; d. 14 Jan. 1920. Their son Albert Henry[9] Lamson, b. 21 Oct. 1862; m. (1) Mary Ella Weeks, dau. of Jonathan and Mary (Dame) Weeks, b. 14 Apr. 1849; d. 6 Sept. 1906; m. (2) 23 Nov. 1927, Helen Lee Smith, b. in Antrim, N. H., 27 Jan. 1864. They live in Boston, and New London, N. H.

208

JOHN[5] CHASE married in Kingston, N. H., 17 Dec. 1794, HANNAH SANBORN—not Chase as stated on page 132.

210

ELIZA[6] CHASE (Merrill,[5] Edmund,[4] Nathan,[3] Thomas[2]), born in Paris, Me., 21 Dec. 1812; m. 25 Nov. 1832, ZEPHANIAH BENSON WHITMAN, b. 27 Sept. 1810; d. 24 Nov. 1884. She d. 3 July 1883. They lived in Woodstock, Me. Their daughter, Maria Josephine[7] Whitman, b. 25 June 1848; m. 9 Aug. 1868, Charles Milner Bryant, son of Christopher and Sally (Felt) Bryant, b. in Greenwood, Me., 3 Nov. 1844; lived in Sauk Centre, Minn. Their son, *Charles Montrose*[8] *Bryant*, b. 1 Nov. 1870; m. (1) 18 Feb. 1893, Alice M. Hughes; m. (2) 23 Oct. 1900, Hattie M. Brooks; m. (3) 22 Apr. 1908, Mary Lamont Cunningham; m. (4) 14 Sept. 1914, Kathleen McKenzie. Children: Arlene Helen[9] Bryant, b. 19 Oct. 1894. Charles Montrose[9] Bryant, b. 8 July 1908. William Campbell[9] Bryant, b. 19 Dec. 1915. Alexander Graham[9] Bryant, b. 6 Mar. 1916. Marcus Whitman[9] Bryant, b. 19 Mar. 1919. They own and operate a farm of 1000 acres near St. Johns, Rolette Co., N. Dak.

210

LUCINDA[6] CHASE (Merrill,[5] Edmund,[4] Nathan,[3] Thomas[2]), born in Woodstock, Me., 9 Feb. 1816; married, 3 Nov. 1833, GIBBS BENSON of Paris, Me. He died there, 7 Apr. 1881. She died 14 June 1891. Their daughter, Julia[7] Benson, b. 14 Dec. 1834; living in Los Angeles, Calif., in 1927, at the age of 93. She m. 10 Mar. 1854, Luther Emerson Tubbs, b. 1 May 1834; d. in Ontario, Calif. Their son *Harden Benson*[8] *Tubbs,* b. 6 June 1870; lives in Fond Du Lac, Wis.

254

JOHN[5] CHASE died in Londonderry, 24 Feb. 1835, aged 71; buried in Forest Hill Cemetery, East Derry. His widow HANNAH, died 4 Mar. 1841, aged 73 and is buried there.

287

SIMON[5] CHASE and SARAH TOWN, both of New Salem, were married in Orange, 5 May 1785.

289

AARON[5] CHASE and PRISCILLA HARRINGTON were married in Orange, 22 Mar. 1789.

321a

ISAAC[5] CHASE died in Warner N. H., about 1840. His father, ISAAC[4] CHASE, also of Warner, was active during the American Revolution and collected bounties for soldiers from Warner. It was the elder Isaac who was a corporal at Fort William Henry in 1757 and who served in the expedition in 1760.

355

DANIEL[5] CHASE (Lt. Caleb,[4] Daniel,[3] Ens. Moses[2]), corrected, with additions.

MARY,[6] b. 11 Jan. 1797; d. 7 Nov. 1869; m. 27 Oct. 1817, Austin Corbin Sr. of Newport, N. H. Their son Austin[7] Corbin Jr. was the banker and railroad magnate of New York.

NANCY, b. 7 Nov. 1823; d. in Brookline, 5 Feb. 1907. She m. 25 Dec. 1843, Luther Farwell of Claremont, N. H. They lived in Boston. Their children were: Clara Chase[7] Farwell, b. 17 Dec. 1852; m. 1 Jan. 1878, Albert T. Stahl who d. 16 Mar. 1892. One daughter *Grace Farwell[8] Stahl*. Mary Chase[7] Farwell, b. 7 June 1855; m. 1 June 1885, Hosea Starr Ballou of Brookline, Harvard University, 1881. Their sons are: *Luther Farwell[8] Ballou*, Yale University, 1915, and *Hosea Starr[8] Ballou Jr.*, Harvard, 1915.

363

Children of Rev. Amos[5] and Joanna (Lanman) Chase:

SARAH LANMAN,[6] b. 2 Nov. 1794.

JOANNA BOYLSTON, b. 29 June 1796; m. Thomas H. Sill of Erie, Pa.; she d. 21 June 1899; he was a member of Congress from Penn.

ELIZABETH BIRD, b. 18 Dec. 1797; m. Capt. William Sheffield of Farmington, Conn.; d. 4 Aug. 1877.

1029.   CHARLES LANMAN, b. 12 May 1803.

MARY HUNTINGTON, b. 10 June 1809.

364

CAPT. NAHUM[5] CHASE died in Cornish, 27 June 1827. It was his widow Deborah Chase who married, 29 Apr. 1828, Rev. Lathrop Thompson. His daughter Deborah died 11 June 1839, unmarried. This is the correction of an error found in Child's History of Cornish, 2:78.

366

MOODY[5] CHASE and LUCY FARNUM were married in Litchfield (now Morris), Conn., 6 June 1796.

370

HANNAH[6] CHASE (Thomas,[5] Lt. Wells,[4] Moses,[3] Ens. Moses[2]), b. in Cornish, 24 Dec. 1769; d. in Delaware, Ohio, 2 Mar. 1832. She m. about 1790, Abel Spalding, b. 28 Dec. 1764; d. in Norton, Ohio, 16 June 1845. Their dau. Mary Chase[7] Spalding, b. 23 May 1794; d. 16 Apr. 1875; m. 1 Feb. 1815, Ebenezer Baker who d. 20 Nov. 1852. Their son *Rodney Spalding[8] Baker*, b. 6 June 1830; m. 15 Nov. 1857, Nancy Agnes Wray, b. 6 Aug. 1839; d. 3 Aug. 1924. He d. in Bartley, Nebr., 23 Sept. 1905. Their dau. Cilvina[9] Baker, b. 18 Sept. 1862; m. 5 Oct. 1887, Joseph Creighton Moore, b. 23 Feb. 1856. Their children are: *Thayer Spalding[10] Moore* (1888-1888). *Joseph Wendell[10] Moore*, b. 1892; missionary to Philippine Islands; m. Clara Ethel Nordby. Their daughter is Clara Florence[11] Moore, b. 15 Dec.

1917. *Elsie Florence*[10] *Moore* and *Alice Chase*[10] *Moore* of Lincoln, Nebr.

399

MOSES[5] CHASE married 17 Apr. 1788, MARY NOYES, daughter of Stephen and Betsey (Chase) Noyes, born in Newbury, 23 Mar. 1767.

437

SUSAN REBECCA,[6] b. 19 May 1820; m. (1) in Boston, 4 Aug. 1839, Josiah Walker Smith who was b. in Pownal, Me., 4 May 1818; d. in Portland, Me., 28 Feb. 1857; m. (2) in Boston, 1 Aug. 1858, Samuel Pierce Osgood. She d. in New York, N. Y., 27 Sept. 1900. Her child by first husband was *Annie Augusta*[8] *Smith,* b. in Bangor, 21 Mar. 1845; m. in St. John, N. B., 19 Jan. 1865, Charles Daniel Thomson, b. on Indian Island, Charlotte Co., N. B., 31 Mar. 1840; d .in Moncton, N. B., 26 Oct. 1902. She d. there, 18 Apr. 1881. Their son William Chase[9] Thomson, b. in St. John, 5 Jan. 1866; lives in Montreal, P. Q.

502

THOMAS[6] CHASE (Matthew,[5] Dea. Roger,[4] Thomas,[3] Thomas[2]) married (1) about 1790, DOLLY JACKENS, whose name has caused considerable discussion. There was one James "Jackings" head of a family in Fairfield, Me., in 1790. Frederick "Jackings" appears as head of a family in Hancock (now Clinton) Me., and David "Jacking" was head of a family in Wales in 1790. It is supposed that Thomas[6] Chase's first wife died as early as 1837 and that it was his second wife and widow who died in 1857.

Their son:

1360. ALGER,[7] b. in Fairfield or Clinton, Me., about 1792; m. Patty Burrell, daughter of Ziba and Polly[6] (Chase) Burrell of Dover, Me., b. 12 Feb. 1795. Among their nine children was *Martha,*[8] b. in Blanchard, Me., 6 June 1819; d. in Princeton, Minn., Mar. 1904; m. in 1842, John Rines, b. in Canaan, Me., 4 Apr. 1819; d. in Brunswick, Minn., 16 Apr. 1888. Their daughter Margaret[9] Rines, b. in Battlebrook, Minn., 24 Mar. 1863; m. in Princeton, 24 May 1882, Henry Clay Head, b. in Hooksett, N. H., 8 Jan. 1848, son of Samuel and Rhoda H. (Williams) Head. (His father was first cousin to Natt Head, Governor of New Hampshire, 1879-80.) Their only child is *Natt*[10] *Head,* b. in Princeton, 7 July 1883, who lives in Del Monte, Calif., and is assistant manager of Hotel Del Monte. Henry Clay Head is a lawyer in Sawtelle, Calif.

599

EDWIN THEODORE[8] CHASE (William Frederic,[7] Ezra,[6] Nathaniel Lowe,[5] Ezra,[4] James,[3] Thomas[2]), born 30 Oct. 1823; died in Philadelphia, Pa., 15 May 1886. He married 14 June 1841, LUCIA TAPPAN COFFIN, daughter of Joshua Coffin, the historian and his first wife Clarissa Harlowe (Dutch) Coffin. She was born in Hampton, N. H., 6 Sept. 1820 and died in Germantown, Pa., 21 Sept. 1878. Their twelfth child was Sydney Octavius,[9] born in Germantown, 4

Aug. 1860; m. in Sanford, Fla., 22 Oct. 1895, Laura Du Val Whitner, dau. of Capt. Benjamin Franklin Whitner of Fort Reed, Fla. Their children are *Randall*,[10] *Sydney Octavius*[10] and *Franklin Whitner*[10] *Chase*. They live in Sanford, Fla.

603

1583. HENRY[7] CHASE (Somerby,[6] John,[5] Ezra,[4] James,[3] Thomas[2]), b. in Leominster, 16 Apr. 1818; d. in Hopedale, 1905; m. (1) in 1843, MARY PRUDENCE WILDER who d. about 1862; m. (2) in 1866, LUCY CAROLINE EATON, dau. of William A. and Emily (Johnson) Eaton ,b. in Phillipston, 31 Mar. 1844; now living. Children by first wife: *Albert Birney*,[8] b. 5 Sept. 1844.*Edward Wilder*,[8] b. 1846. *James Lawrence*,[8] b. 1848. *Walter Henry*,[8] b. 1853; d. 1866. *Frederick Washburn*,[8] b. 1856; in Worcester postoffice 55 years. *Alice Emerett*,[8] b. 1859; m. Creaton Entrekin; lives in Columbus, Ohio. By second wife: *William Henry*,[8] b. 1869; lives in Hopedale. *Louis Carleton*,[8] b. 1871; lives in Hyde Park. *Charles Eaton*,[8] b. 1873. *George Clinton*,[8] b. in Worcester, 3 Oct. 1884; m. 26 Mar. 1910, Maude B. Monroe, dau. of Butler J. and Ellen G. Monroe; they live in South Orange, N. J. One son Clinton Monroe[9] Chase.

847

2004. BELA,[7] b. 7 Mar. 1802; d. 9 May 1859; m. (1) Aurilla Whipple; m. (2) ——— Buck; m. (3) Minerva Shute. Ten children by first wife, one by second and two by third. By first they had *Abel*,[8] b. in Mascedon, N. Y., 4 May 1825; d. in Alpine, Kent Co., Mich., 29 Apr. 1898; m. 30 Oct. 1851, Rebecca Jane Herrick, b. Salem, Mich., 11 Feb. 1834; d. in Alpine, 22 Aug. 1897. Their son Charles Herrick,[9] b. in Alpine, 21 Apr. 1874; m. there, 28 Apr. 1898, Mary Ann Schindler, b. in Dorr, Mich., 7 Aug. 1876. Their children born in Alpine: *Carroll Edward*,[10] b. 10 Sept. 1903. *Charles Herrick Jr.*,[10] b. 1 Mar. 1907. They live in Comstock, Mich.

870

DAVID[6] CHASE (Abner,[5] Timothy,[4] Isaac,[3] Daniel[2]) married in New Salem 29 Apr. 1793, LUCY GAY of Dedham. One descendant claimed that she was daughter of Nathaniel and Lucy (Richards) Gay, baptized at Dedham, 23 May 1773. Another descendant claimed that she was daughter of Ebenezer and Mary (Esty) Gay, born in Dedham, 14 Sept. 1771. (Dedham Vital Records, 110). It is impossible to state, without research, which is correct.

Children, with addenda:

> PARNEY,[7] m. (1) Jonathan Foster; m. (2) ——— Furnace; two children by first husband and four by second.
> ALVIN, b. 27 Oct. 1796; m. Mary Phillips who d. in Little Valley, 20 June 1874; he d. there 27 July 1873; nine children.
> RELIEF, m. Gains Wheaton; three children.
> SALLY, m. Nathaniel Bryant; seven children.
> CYRENE, m. (1) Eli Day and (2) Hiram Davis.

874

ELIAS[6] CHASE (Lt. Henry,[5] Timothy,[4] Isaac,[3] Daniel[2]), born about 1772. The family of children which are printed as his belong to Jonathan Sanborn Chase 683. It is supposed that the aforesaid Elias removed in 1776 with his parents to Townsend, Vt. It is stated that he married (1) PHEBE GOULD but further information is lacking.

881

2066. ORRIN[7] CHASE (Reuben,[6] Lt. Nathaniel,[5] Timothy,[4] Isaac,[3] Daniel[2]), born in Vermont, 5 Aug. 1802; living in Olean, N. Y., in 1873. He married (1) SOPHIA DILLINGHAM; married (2) PAMELIA ROOT. There were five children, including *Reuben*,[8] b. in Wayne Co., N. Y., 1831; d. in Olean, 1863; m. in 1859, Agnes Keir of Olean. Their son Augustus Lincoln,[9] b. in Olean, 25 July 1860; m. (1) in Lamotte, Iowa, 8 Oct. 1886, Emma Belknap; m. (2) 18 Oct. 1893, Olive Sawyer. Their children are: *Raymond Albrook*,[10] b. in Salida, Colo., 18 July 1889; m. 8 Sept. 1911, Nona S. Shumway. *Jesse Morris*,[10] b. in Denver, Colo., 17 May 1891; m. there 27 Oct. 1913, Edith Agnes Egger. *Harold Albert*,[10] b. in Denver, 4 Dec. 1897; m. in Pocatello, Idaho, 12 Mar. 1921, Dorothy Emery. Mr. Chase, the father, received the degree Ph. D. and has been field secretary of the University of Denver. He now resides at 501 E. 69th street, Los Angeles, Calif. He m. (3) 1 May 1927 Bertha M. Fisher.

Orrin[7] had two brothers Robert[7] and Lyman.[7]

947

HENRY[6] CHASE (Isaac,[5] Isaac,[4] Daniel,[3] Daniel[2]), born in Warner about 1795; married in Hopkinton, N. H., 7 Sept. 1828, HANNAH PALMER. One of his sisters married Richard Palmer and another married Daniel Emery. The widow Hannah Chase, described as daughter of Timothy and Judith (Hardy) Palmer, died in Bristol, N. H., 14 Mar. 1887, aged 80 y. 7 m. 14 d.

Child:

DANIEL EMERY.[7]

979

2214. BENJAMIN WIGGIN[7] CHASE (Baruch,[6] Dea. Dudley,[5] Judge Samuel,[4] Daniel,[3] Ens. Moses[2]), born in Hopkinton, N. H., 3 Sept. 1796 died in Philadelphia, Pa., 6 Jan. 1878. He married in 1828, ANNA WILLIAMS who died 21 Dec. 1889. Six children, including *Charles Cazenove*,[8] b. 22 Mar. 1830; d. 9 July 1905; m. 29 May 1855, Harriet Weaver, who d. 31 Dec. 1906. Their son Charles Cazenove,[9] b. 2 Apr. 1861; m. 13 Oct. 1891, Anna Powell Long. Children *Dorothy*,[10] b. 4 June 1893; m. Winchester H. Biggar of Montreal, Can. *Charles Cazenove*,[10] b. 20 Dec. 1894; m. Oct. 1922, Elva Van Voorhis of Canton, Ohio. *Samuel Long*,[10] (twin) b. 20 Dec. 1894; d. Oct. 1919. *Morris Reeves*,[10] b. 10 Aug. 1897; m. 30 Apr. 1928, Elizabeth Speed Love of Richmond, Vt. Charles Cazenove[9] lives in Massillon, Ohio.

1061

Thomas[6] Chase (Daniel,[5] Lt. Wells,[4] Moses,[3] Ens. Moses,[2] Aquila[1]), was born in Amesbury, Mass., 8 July 1771 and settled in North Yarmouth, Me. We have nothing more relating to him.

1065

Benjamin[7] Chase (2352), Family 1065, not 1185, as printed on page 449.

1127

2480. Edwin[7] Chase (Dea. Joseph,[6] Joseph,[5] Dea. Francis,[4] Samuel,[3] Ens. Moses[2]), born in Litchfield, N. H., 17 Mar. 1813; died in Holyoke, Oct. 1882. He married (1) in Goffstown, N. H., 27 Sept. 1836, Mary Kimball who died in Nashua, 1 July 1839; married (2) in Nashua, 5 Nov. 1839, Lydia Maria Adams, b. in Nashua, 24 Jan. 1818; d. in Holyoke, 15 Apr. 1895. By the second wife there were eight children, including *Mary Maria,*[8] b. in Nashua, 3 Jan. 1847; d. in Somerville, 13 May 1921; m. in Holyoke, 22 Oct. 1872, Arthur Augustus Shaw, b. in Canton, 22 July 1845; d. in Somerville, 12 Oct. 1920. Their children are: Edwin Adams[9] Shaw, b. in Boston, 8 May 1876; m. 27 Aug. 1906, Ethel H. Sparrow, b. in Wollaston, 28 Jan. 1879. Their children are *Hester Marie,*[10] and *Edmund Chase*[10] *Shaw.* Dr. Shaw graduated at Tufts College in 1898; received the degree of Ph. D. at Harvard University 1918; instructor in Education at Tufts College, 1918-20; professor of Education there since 1927. Charles Augustus[9] Shaw Jr., b. 24 Aug. 1879; m. 24 Apr. 1905, Gertrude Tufts Bacon. Children *Dorothy Gertrude,*[10] *Barbara*[10] and *Ruth Frances*[10] *Shaw.*

1192

John Carroll[8] Chase, married (2) in Vancouver, B. C., 14 July 1928, Florence Anne Buchanan, of Brookline, born in Halifax, N. S., 17 Feb. 1873, daughter of William and Charlotte S. Buchanan.

1230

Gardner[6] Chase (Jacob,[5] Caleb,[4] Lt. Joseph,[3] Ens. Moses[2]), born in Derby, Vt., 17 Dec. 1801; died there 9 Apr. 1858, aged 56 y. He married 27 Dec. 1825, Hannah Pierce, daughter of Moses Pierce, born 7 May 1807; died 30 Aug. 1893.
Children, born in Derby:

> Hortense,[7] m. 25 Sept. 1850, Dr. Chester W. Cowles who d. in Derby, 21 May 1900.
> Enoch B., d. 26 May 1868, aged 35; lieut. Civil War.
> George W., d. 23 Aug. 1863, aged 27; lieut. Civil War.
> Arthur S., b. 10 Nov. 1840; d. in Derby, 29 Apr. 1895.
> Julia F., d. 9 Nov. 1846, aged 19 y. 5 m.
> Mary K., d. 10 Jan. 1847, aged 1 y. 8 m.

1231

JACOB[6] CHASE (Jacob,[5] Caleb,[4] Lt. Joseph,[3] Ens. Moses[2]), born in Derby, Vt., 13 Nov. 1806; died there, 4 or 6 Oct. 1870, aged 64; married MARY MORSE, born in Vermont; died in Derby, 5 Mar. 1855, aged 42.

Children, born in Derby:

ELLEN M.,[7] b. 14 Feb. 1837; m. Almon Roberts; d. 15 Mar. 1904.
LUCIAN B., b. about 1838; m. Mary Jane Buck who d. 31 Jan. 1879, aged 35 y. 8 m. 23 d.
EVELYN L., b. 1840; m. 1861, Joseph W. Steele, son of Solomon Steele.
HENRY C., b. 1842; went West; soldier in Civil War.

UNCONNECTED FAMILIES

PROBABLY DESCENDED FROM AQUILA[1] CHASE

AARON CHASE, born about 1788; m. (1) about 1806, REBECCA MORRIS; married (2) about 1823, SARAH CONKLIN. He died about 1830. They lived in Greenfield, Saratoga Co., N. Y. He was probably of the sixth generation. He is not Aaron Chase, 318, as Dr. John B. Chace stated.

Children by first wife, born in Greenfield:

POLLY MARGARET, b. 28 Feb. 1807; m. John Damp.
SARAH, b. 11 May 1809; d. young.
SARAH, b. 18 July 1811; m. 15 Sept. 1833, Enoch Richardson White of Greenfield.
DIANTHA, b. 6 June 1815; d. unm.
DIANA, b. 18 May 1817; m. 1838, William Rawson of Troy, N. Y.
AARON, b. 21 Mar. 1820; m. 3 Feb. 1866, Maria Ward; lived in Conesus, Livingston Co., N. Y.

Child by second wife:

TIMOTHY, b. 17 Nov. 1824; lived in Oberlin, Ohio, and in Manterville, Minn., in 1873.

AARON CHASE (Aaron), born 21 Mar. 1820, married 3 Feb. 1866, MARIA WARD. They lived in Conesus, Livingston Co., N. Y.

Child, born in Harnellsville, N. Y.:

MINNIE, b. 28 July 1868.

DANIEL CHASE married about 1807, LYDIA LUFKIN, daughter of Nathaniel and Rachel (Butler) Lufkin, baptized in North Yarmouth, Me., 22 Sept. 1791. They lived in Minot and North Yarmouth, Me.

Children born in North Yarmouth, except the first born in Minot:

DANIEL LUFKIN, b. 20 Feb. 1808; d. at sea, 10 Feb. 1829.
AMBROSE, b. 24 Mar. 1810.
JOHN, b. 25 Mar. 1811; m. (1) Clarissa Benson.
MARY, b. 14 Jan. 1814; m. Wadsworth Hayes.
LYDIA STOVER, b. 30 Oct. 1816; d. 28 Apr. 1837.
BETSEY JEWELL (twin), b. 30 Oct. 1816.

LOUISA, b. 22 Mar. 1820; m. Eben Whitney.
ENOCH, b. 4 Apr. 1822; d. same year.
LUCY, b. 15 Mar. 1823.
JANE BUXTON, b. 22 June 1824; d. 27 May 1858.
WILLIAM L., b. 15 Feb. 1829; m. Lovina Gray of Sumner, Me.
(Old Times in Nort Yarmouth, 1079.)

CAPT. DANIEL CHASE of Brunswick, Me., born about 1807; died 26 June 1845, aged 38.   He married in Sanbornton, N. H., 15 Aug. 1837, DOROTHY CECILIA RIVINGSTON DURGIN, daughter of Elijah Durgin, born 16 Oct. 1809.   She married (2) 30 Nov. 1857, Capt. Daniel Smith of Meredith, N. H.   Capt. Daniel Chase resided in Portland, Me.
    Child by first husband, born in Brunswick, Me.:
        MELINDA ELLEN, b. 3 June 1839; d. 7 July 1854, in Sanbornton.

DAVID CHASE (Stephen), born in Nottingham West, about 1777; married in Dunstable, 31 Dec. 1801, SALLY HILDRETH of Nottingham West (now Hudson).   He died about 1842.
    Children:
        WILLIAM.
        ALFRED.
        HANNAH, m. ——— Stevens.   One daughter Mary Stevens.
        MARY.
        JEREMIAH, b. 22 Nov. 1808; m. 19 Dec. 1838, Margaret Fiske,
            b. 1 Feb. 1814; lived in Groton, Vt., in Jay and Dickinson,
            N. Y.
            Children:
            Louisa Jane, b. 25 Dec. 1839; m. 1 Jan. 1872, George L.
                Rosebrook.
            Mary Elizabeth, b. 6 Oct. 1841; m. 29 Nov. 1860, Allen Farr.
            Horatio Merrill, b. 2 Jan. 1844; d. 16 May 1863.
            Nathaniel Perkins, b. 2 Dec. 1845; m. 22 July 1866, Ora Ter-
                rill.
            David, b. 25 Apr. 1849; d. 21 Feb. 1857.
            Eben Fiske, b. 23 Apr. 1851; m. 17 Feb. 1879, Johanna Hazen.
            George Shearer, b. 17 Feb. 1853; m. 17 Oct. 1883, Florence
                M. Geer.
            Phebe Ann, b. 28 July 1855; m. (1) 19 June 1895, James S.
                Guild; m. (2) Harry J. Griswold.
            Emma Maria, b. 29 Mar. 1859; m. in Dickinson, N. Y., 21
                Dec. 1880, Samuel K. Coe.   Their children are Margaret
                Cornelia Coe, b. 21 May 1884; m. 27 Dec. 1905, J. Ralph
                Smith.   Horatio George Coe, b. 27 Sept. 1885; d. 12 Nov.
                1891.

HENRY CHASE, born 12 Mar. 1776; died 5 May 1835.   He married (1) in 1807, POLLY SAMPSON who died in Apr. 1815.   He married (2) 6 Oct. 1816, SIBYL J. BREWSTER.   They lived in Dresden, Washington Co., N. Y.
    Children by first wife:
        STEPHEN, b. 18 Oct. 1809; m. Patty Barber; d. 22 Oct. 1837.
        GEORGE W., b. 8 June 1812; m. 20 May 1840, Anna Barber; d.
            9 May 1854.

JONAS L., b. 17 Aug. 1814; m. (1) Patty Chase, widow of
Stephen; m. (2) Maria Wilson.

Children by second wife:

POLLY, b. 29 June 1817; m. Daniel Turner; she d. Nov. 1866.
CLARISSA, b. 19 June 1819; d. 25 Dec. 1819.
BETSEY, b. 30 Dec. 1820; m. 9 Feb. 1843, Orson Wilsey.
HENRY L., b. 21 Aug. 1823; d. 12 Apr. 1833.
NATHANIEL B., b. 25 Aug. 1825; never married.
LYDIA K., b. 27 Jan. 1828; m. 30 Jan. 1845, John Wilsey; lived
in Prairie Centre, 1872.
ESTHER, b. 29 Mar. 1830; d. 26 Feb. 1833.

JAMES CHASE, b. 18 Aug. 1782; d. 25 Nov. 1852. He m. Mehitable Baker, b. 16 Sept. 1784; d. 23 Mar. 1860. They lived in Bowdoin, Me. She was dau. of Capt. Smith Baker of Litchfield, Me.,
and Elizabeth (Bunker) Baker, b. 6 Sept. 1784.

Children:

BUNKER, b. 28 Mar. 1805; d. 13 June 1863.
JAMES, b. 23 Jan. 1808.
MARY, b. 8 Apr. 1810; m. ——— Dennett.
LUCY A., b. 26 Apr. 1813; m. ——— Ferrin.
ORRIN B., b. 19 July 1817; d. 9 Aug. 1860.
ELIZABETH B., b. 8 Sept. 1822; d. 28 Sept. 1828.
FRANCES A., b. 13 Apr. 1831; m. ——— Johnson.

Judah, Brunswick, head 1790, family 5-1-5.
James, Brunswick, head 1790, family 1-2-3.
Benjamin; Brunswick, head 1790, family 3-1-4; at Flying Point 1774.
John, Brunswick, head 1790, family 1-3-3.
William, Falmouth, head 1790, family 1-3-4.
Humphrey, North Yarmouth, head 1790, family 1-4-6.
William, North Yarmouth, head 1790, family 1-0-1.
Francis, Portland, head 1790, family 1-1-4.
John, Windham, head 1790, family 1-1-3.

ROBERT CHASE, whose parentage is not positively known, born
in Exeter, N. H., in Nov. 1782; died in Camden, Me., 1 May 1852,
aged 70 y. He may be the son of Robert[5] Chase (271) who removed
to Skowhegan, Me. The children of this Robert[5] Chase have not
been identified. He served an apprenticeship as a blasksmith in
Portsmouth, N. H., and removed to Camden in Mar. 1803. He married 26 Jan. 1806, BETSEY HOLT of York, Me. He was selectman of
Camden 1811, 1813-1824 and a representative 1837 and 1838.

Children, born in Camden:

MARY J.,[7] m. James Burd.
SAMUEL, a blacksmith, of Camden, 1859.
ROBERT.
BENJAMIN.
KATHERINE, m. Valentine Mansfield.
ELMIRA, m. William W. Currier.
ELIZABETH, m. Jacob Graffam.
LUCY A., m. Joseph Graffam.
(Robinson's Hist. of Camden and Rockport, 300-1.)

STEPHEN CHASE, whose parentage we have been unable to ascertain, is said to have been born in Hudson, N. H. He enlisted as a private in Capt. William Walker's Co., 6 May 1775 and served three months, three days. He enlisted again as a private in Capt. James Ford's Co. 30 June and served until 5 July 1777. This company marched from Nottingham West (now Hudson) for Ticonderoga. He enlisted again in Capt. Peter Cross's Co. 7 Aug. and served till 18 Aug. 1778 from Hudson. The selectmen of Nottingham West reported that Stephen Chase and Stephen Chase Jr. had taken the Association Test in Hudson, 3 July 1776. He married in Nottingham West, 31 Oct. 1776, HANNAH BLODGETT who deposed at Topsham, Vt., on 30 Mar. 1837 that he died in Topsham, 28 Oct. 1827, that she was 80 years of age and his widow and that he was a Revolutionary soldier and that after the war they removed to Topsham.

Children::

> DAVID, b. near 1777.
> STEPHEN.
> JOSHUA.
> SARAH, m. Aaron Davis.
> MARY ANN, m. Levi Taber.
> BETSEY, b. about 1811; d. 9 Aug. 1822.

THOMAS CHASE, b. in Windham, Me., 7 Sept. 1797; d. in Portland, Me., 6 Sept. 1854; m. in North Yarmouth, 10 Dec. 1821, Elizabeth Delano, daughter of Edmund Chandler Delano. She d. in Portland, 14 Dec. 1877.

Children:

> MARTHA ANN, b. Freeport, 1 Oct. 1822.
> JULIA, b. 8 Mar. 1824; d. in Cumberland, 4 July 1828.
> PHILIP SWEETSER, b. 29 Jan. 1826.
> CHARLES POLAND, b. 13 Jan. 1828.
> EMILY ALLEN, b. 16 Apr. 1830; m. A. Reed of Portland.
> WILLIAM JORDAN, b. 27 Jan. 1833; d. in Otisfield, 25 Aug. 1842.
> EZEKIEL DELANO, b. 26 Feb. 1835.
> FRANCIS HENRY, b. 13 Dec. 1837.
> SAMUEL RAY, b. 27 Dec. 1839.
> ALMENA STEVENS, b. 7 Apr. 1842; d. 26 Aug. 1849.
> (Delano Genealogy, 249.)

Page 430—SARAH PLATT[8] DECKER instead of Sarah Pratt.
Page 499—GEORGE EDMOND[6] CHASE instead of George Edward, No. 100.
Page 517—Ancestry of GEORGE EDMOND[6] CHASE, No. 100, should be Thomas,[5] Thomas,[4] Joseph,[3] Lt. Isaac,[2] Thomas.[1]

INDEX OF ENGLISH FAMILIES

INDEX OF DESCENDANTS OF AQUILA CHASE

Elizabeth Sheffield,⁷ 396.
Elizabeth S.,⁷ 314.
Elizabeth Titcomb,⁷ 424.
Elizabeth T.,⁷ 268.
Elizabeth Underhill,⁷ 425.
Elisabeth Wait,⁷ 317.
Elizabeth,⁸ 300, 307, 427, 471.
Elizabeth Hance,⁸ 368.
Elizabeth Holmes,⁸ 268.
Elizabeth,⁹ 309.
Elizabeth Speed,¹⁰ 529.
Elizabeth, 533, 534.
Elizabeth B., 533.
Ella,⁷ 284.
Ella Augusta,⁷ 388.
Ella A., 318.
Ella M.,⁷ 293.
Ella Perkins,⁷ 317.
Ellen,⁵ 59.
Ellen,⁶ 378.
Ellen Maria,⁶ 340.
Ellen,⁷ 224.
Ellen,⁷ 224, 249, 264, 362, 400, 404, 419, 432, 445, 446, 463.
Ellen A.,⁷ 322.
Ellen Bolton,⁷ 319.
Ellen Climena,⁷ 345.
Ellen C.,⁷ 321.
Ellen D.,⁷ 323.
Ellen Edgeworth,⁷ 224.
Ellen E.,⁷ 291, 346, 410, 420.
Ellen J.,⁷ 295, 350.
Ellen L.,⁷ 432.
Ellen Marian,⁷ 365.
Ellen M.,⁷ 531, 242.
Ellen M. B.,⁷ 436.
Ellen Orianna,⁷ 340.
Ellen P.,⁷ 322.
Ellen Roxana,⁷ 317.
Ellen Sherwood,⁷ 458.
Ellen,⁹ 232.
Ellery R.,⁶ 163, 355.
Ellery,⁷ 355.
Elliott F.,⁹ 219, 468.
Elliott C.,⁷ 350.
Ellis F.,⁶ 219, 468.
Ellison,⁶ 163, 356.
Ellison,⁷ 356.
Elmer,⁶ 297.
Elmina,⁶ 161.
Elmina Eusebia,⁷ 363.
Elmira,⁸ 79.
Elmira,⁶ 457, 469.
Elmira,⁷ 245, 262, 317, 328, 358, 378.
Elmira Jane,⁷ 421.
Elmira, 533.
Elmore,⁶ 144, 320.
Elmore,⁷ 319, 320 320.
Elsie P.,⁷ 468.
Elva Van,¹⁰ 529.

Elvira,⁶ 133, 144, 288.
Elvira,⁷ 239, 291, 295, 318, 358, 363, 415, 448.
Elvira Fluvia,⁷ 415.
Elvira G.,⁷ 420.
Elvira Lorinda,⁷ 319.
Elvira L.,⁷ 415.
Elvina Melvina,⁷ 269, 456.
Elvira Perham,⁷ 291.
Elvira,⁸ 246.
Elwood La Barre,¹⁰ 248.
Elzina A.,⁷ 363.
Emeline,⁶ 393.
Emeline Louisa,⁶ 401.
Emeline M.,⁶ 130.
Emeline,⁷ 248, 254, 331, 414, 415, 427.
Emeline E.,⁷ 278.
Emerette,⁷ 394.
Emerean,⁷ 466.
Emeric F., 295.
Emerson,⁷ 374.
Emerson Harris,⁷ 257.
Emery,⁴ 53, 80.
Emery,⁷ 280, 293.
Emily,⁶ 167, 181, 204, 213, 296, 395.
Emily,⁷ 227, 229, 250, 263, 265, 276, 296, 326, 341, 349, 383, 384, 399, 435, 443, 466.
Emily Almeda,⁷ 233.
Emily Ann,⁷ 388.
Emily B.,⁷ 228.
Emily Clark,⁷ 360.
Emily Emery,⁷ 362.
Emily F.,⁷ 386.
Emily G.,⁷ 381.
Emily J.,⁷ 366.
Emily Morrill,⁷ 319.
Emily P.,⁷ 323, 345.
Emily Robbins,⁷ 397.
Emily Spaulding,⁷ 395.
Emily W.,⁷ 230.
Emily,⁸ 221.
Emily A.,⁸ 427.
Emily Chase,⁹ 234.
Emily Allen, 534.
Emma,⁴ 518.
Emma,⁵ 62, 156, 192, 201, 241.
Emma,⁶ 109, 110, 124, 188, 211, 271, 297.
Emma Elden,⁶ 201.
Emma I.,⁶ 396.
Emma,⁷ 271 277, 365, 401, 434, 435, 455, 463.
Emma Alice,⁷ 453.
Emma A.,⁷ 242, 298, 321, 470.
Emma Carr,⁷ 293.
Emma Carter,⁷ 272.
Emma C.,⁷ 231.
Emma Elizabeth⁷ 460.

Emma E.,⁷ 435.
Emma F.,⁷ 421.
Emma W.,⁷ 338.
Emma,⁹ 529.
Emma A.,⁹ 222.
Emma Maria, 532.
Emmons W.,⁷ 449.
Enoch,³ 42, 55.
Enoch,⁴ 51, 55, 57, 76, 87.
Enoch,⁵ 51, 69, 75, 76, 79, 88, 92, 97, 98, 125, 146, 149, 150, 156, 174, 206.
Enoch,⁶ 109, 122, 125, 140, 141, 160, 161, 190, 191, 215, 266, 273, 310, 313, 349, 406, 461.
Enoch Pillsbury,⁶ 280.
Enoch P.,⁶ 32, 129.
Enoch S.,⁶ 230.
Enoch,⁷ 274, 299, 309, 310, 373, 406, 462.
Enoch Bartlett,⁷ 410.
Enoch B.,⁷ 530.
Enoch Dole,⁷ 454.
Enoch M.,⁷ 267.
Enoch Sawyer,⁷ 266.
Enoch S.,⁷ 230.
Enoch Pillsbury,⁷ 430.
Enoch Wingate,⁷ 242.
Enoch,⁸ 309.
Enoch, 532.
Enos,⁶ 161, 350.
Ensign,⁴ 54, 83.
Eola Maria,⁸ 292.
Epaphras Bull,⁶ 186, 399.
Ephraim,⁵ 93, 194.
Ephraim Chandler,⁵ 98.
Ephraim,⁶ 194, 416.
Ephraim,⁷ 417.
Ephraim Crogham,⁷ 233.
Ephraim Davis,⁷ 428.
Ephraim Fairbanks,⁷ 349.
Ephraim G.,⁷ 371.
Ephraim Humphrey,⁷ 417.
Erastus,⁶ 217, 465.
Ernest Sidney,⁸ 332.
Esadore F.,⁷ 352.
Estelle Ophelia,⁷ 292, 346.
Estella R.,⁷ 466.
Esther,² 31, 32, 35, 36.
Esther,³ 36.
Esther,⁴ 71, 88.
Esther,⁵ 71, 124, 126, 138, 169.
Esther,⁶ 124, 159, 170, 174, 225, 259, 275, 307, 318, 346, 469.
Esther Merrill,⁶ 133, 134, 135.
Esther M.,⁶ 420.
Esther Robbins,⁶ 187.
Esther Stillman,⁶ 268.
Esther,⁷ 235, 276, 280, 295,

Freeman Hatch,[7] 397.
Freeman H.,[7] 290.
Friendly S.,[6] 383.

Galusha,[7] 356.
Gamaliel,[7] 358.
Garafelia,[7] 368.
Gardner,[6] 136, 142, 215, 316, 461, 530.
Gardner F.,[8] 295.
Gardner W.,[7] 343.
Gardner,[9] 439.
Gebhard Charles,[10] 277.
George,[4] 46, 59.
George,[5] 77.
George,[6] 104, 124, 143, 144, 145, 167, 172, 181, 192, 222, 273, 318, 320, 371.
George Clement,[6] 186, 187, 399.
George Clinton,[6] 206.
George Hall,[6] 391.
George Monroe,[6] 186, 400.
George Murray,[6] 187, 401.
George Washington,[6] 154, 156, 215, 460.
George W.,[6] 134, 137, 293. 297, 322, 361.
George,[7] 221, 235, 238, 250, 252, 314, 374, 376, 380, 382, 394, 437, 442.
George Albert,[7] 396, 458.
George Augustus,[7] 396.
George A.,[7] 339, 454, 467.
George Barlow,[7] 414.
George Bates,[7] 291.
George Benjamin,[7] 439.
George Bigelow,[7] 1, 3, 9, 223.
George Byron,[7] 395.
Gorge B.,[7] 356.
George B. M.,[7] 372.
George C.,[7] 285.
George Everett,[7] 280.
George E.,[7] 470.
George Farrer,[7] 330.
George Fernald,[7] 275.
George Francis, 381, 398, 460.
George Franklin,[7] 420.
George F. A.,[7] 331.
George G.,[7] 416.
George Harlan,[7] 459.
George Henry,[7] 226, 391, 448.
George H.,[7] 258, 420, 462.
George James,[7] 451.
George J.,[7] 265, 286, 287.
George Laban,[7] 273.
George Levi,[7] 315. 470.
George Lyman,[7] 318.
George Metaphor,[7] 273.
George Milton,[7] 400.

George Monroe,[7] 400.
George Mortimer,[7] 445.
George Moses,[7] 389.
George Newton,[7] 398.
George Samuel,[7] 439.
George Sumner,[7] 272.
George S.,[7] 357.
George Thomas,[7] 357.
George Truman,[7] 401.
George Walter,[7] 319.
George Warren,[7] 370.
George Washington,[7] 415, 450, 471.
George Wentworth,[7] 254, 397.
George William Frost,[7] 224.
George Wingate,[7] 338.
George W.,[7] 242, 245, 283, 293, 295, 318, 335, 349, 354, 364, 372, 373, 431, 453, 472, 530.
George W. R.,[7] 322.
George,[8] 250.
George A.,[8] 471.
George Brown,[8] 375.
George Clinton,[8] 528.
George Henry,[8] 427.
George H.,[8] 356.
George Leonard,[8] 366.
George Otis,[8] 315, 373.
George P.,[8] 464.
George Tappan,[8] 338.
George Wingate,[8] 338.
George Amasa,[9] 248.
George Elliott,[9] 393.
George F.,[9] 222.
George Mortimer,[9] 445.
George Amasa,[10] 248.
George Shearer, 532.
George W., 532.
Georgia A.,[7] 294.
Georgianna,[7] 397.
Georgie[7] 466.
Georgia A.,[7] 293.
Gerard,[6] 184.
Gertrude Lowndes,[8] 224.
Gertrude Putnam,[8] 365.
Gideon,[6] 195, 417.
Gideon,[7] 246.
Gilbert Tenant,[5] 86, 172.
Gilbert,[6] 171.
Gilbert M.,[6] 371.
Gilbert,[7] 356, 418.
Gilman,[6] 215.
Gilman,[7] 328.
Gilman Franklin,[7] 449.
Gilman Robbins,[7] 315.
Grace,[7] 305, 396.
Grace,[8] 242.
Grace L.,[8] 292.
Grace Jannette,[9] 414.
Grace May,[9] 393.
Grace Maybelle,[9] 332.

Granville M.,[7] 404.
Gratia,[6] 176.
Green,[6] 139, 306.
Green,[7] 304, 306.

H——— A———,[7] 371.
H. Augusta,[7] 419.
Hadassah,[6] 113.
Hadassah,[7] 239.
Hall,[7] 230.
Hankerson,[7] 237.
Hannah,[3] 35, 36, 44, 45, 53, 56, 57.
Hannah,[4] 24, 46, 50, 53, 57, 58, 59, 66, 67, 70, 72, 74, 76, 79, 89, 90, 94, 159, 480.
Hannah,[5] 68, 70, 72, 74, 75, 77, 78, 79, 81, 84, 88, 89, 91, 94, 95, 96, 97, 100, 102, 108, 113, 114, 118, 120, 121, 130, 132, 136, 141, 144, 147, 149, 150, 152, 153, 155, 158, 159, 160, 163, 167, 171, 192, 193, 196, 197, 199, 200, 211, 212, 213, 215, 218, 287, 361, 399, 525.
Hannah Beary,[5] 82.
Hannah,[6] 109, 113, 115, 118, 121, 124, 125, 128, 129, 131, 136, 139, 140, 142, 143, 144, 146, 149, 150, 152, 156, 158, 160, 163, 166, 167, 170, 171, 174, 184, 188, 189, 190, 193, 196, 197, 200, 201, 207, 208, 211, 218, 229, 231, 260, 267, 302, 304, 306, 313, 315, 319, 326, 331, 338, 343, 351, 369, 371, 372, 380, 391, 399, 401, 402, 404, 405, 418, 420, 425, 427, 428, 438, 443, 461, 468, 526, 529, 530, 533.
Hannah Brown,[6] 185, 186.
Hannah B.,[6] 184.
Hannah Clough,[6] 337.
Hannah C.,[6] 412, 451.
Hannah Drusilla,[6] 389.
Hannah Elizabeth,[6] 216.
Hannah Ely,[6] 149, 329.
Hannah E.,[6] 116.
Hannah Jane,[6] 130.
Hannah Maria,[6] 204.
Hannah Moore,[6] 419.
Hannah Morse,[6] 192.
Hannah M.,[6] 458.
Hannah Prince,[6] 291.
Hannah P.,[6] 367.
Hannah Sanborn,[6] 129.
Hannah Sawyer,[6] 122.
Hannah Weare,[6] 130.

ng

Payment | Confirm | Order Complete

nter::

7 Toll Free Phone Support or **Live Chat**
s Train All Rights Reserved.

George M. Bodge

- Soldiers in King Philip's War

E 83.67

INDEX OF DESCENDANTS OF THOMAS CHASE

INDEX OF NAMES OTHER THAN CHASE

MERRILL, continued
Mary, 128, 129, 280, 467.
Mary Ellen, 435.
Mehitable, 129, 284.
Miriam, 195.
Moses, 77, 269.
Moses G., 455.
Nancy, 310.
Nathan, 195, 279.
Peter, 31, 71.
Priscilla, 34, 63, 71, 128.
Rebecca, 423.
Richard, 129.
Ruth, 140.
Sally, 266, 315.
Samuel, 101, 128, 280.
Sarah, 58, 91, 279, 432.
Sarah Ann, 435.
Sarah A., 359.
Sarah Dole, 269, 455.
Susannah, 423.
Stevens, 58.
Thomasine, 57.
Timothy, 363.
MERRIMAN, Clarissa, 124.
Luther, 124.
MERRY, David, 488, 490.
Elizabeth, 489. 501.
Eunice, 488, 490.
Joseph, 489.
Mary, 489, 501.
Matthew, 489, 501.
Sarah, 492.
William, 492.
MESERVE, Abigail, 117.
MESSENGER, Olive, 113.
Samuel, 113.
MESSER, Harriet, 369.
Mary, 308.
Zaccheus, 369.
METCALF, Sarah, 99, 342.
Thomas, 99.
MILES, Helen Agnes, 271.
Mary, 248.
MILHO, Charlotte H., 356.
MILLER, Caroline Melinda, 373.
Catharine C., 434.
Freedom, 81.
George Frederick, 224.
John Christian, 81.
Mary Baker, 224.
Nathaniel, 39.
Ruth, 38, 39.
Susan, 391.
MILLET, Abigail, 71.
Thomas, 71.

MILLS, Cyrus, 345.
Esther, 174.
Luke, 174.
Marilla, 345.
MINARD, Lucinda, 288.
Peter, 120.
MINER, Orilla, 322.
MISSILLOWAY, Anne, 521.
Daniel, 521.
MITCHELL, Abigail Fogg, 451.
Almira H., 243.
Althea, 402.
George, 315, 496.
Hannah, 402.
Joseph D., 243.
Phebe, 496.
Sally, 315.
Samuel, 494.
Sarah, 315.
Seth, 402.
Sophia I., 382.
Sue Taylor, 456.
Susan, 494.
MIXER, Anna, 218.
Rufus, 218.
MOARS, Joseph, 107.
MOE, Charles Chase, 326.
Chris Frederick, 326.
Edith, 326.
MOFFAT, Louis, 322.
Martha L., 322.
MONROE, Butler J., 528.
Ellen G., 528.
Georgia A., 294.
James, 95.
Maude B., 528.
MONTGOMERY, Eleazer B., 427.
Margaret, 427.
Mary, 309.
Samuel, 309.
MOODY, Agnes, 509.
Caleb, 31, 43.
Horace, 509.
Joanna, 199, 431.
John, 198.
Joshua, 523.
Joseph, 350.
Judith, 75.
Nancy, 427.
Ruth, 198.
Sally, 455.
Susan, 350.
William, 31.
Zaidee Francis, 509.
MOONEY, John, 244.
Susan, 244.

MOORE, Alice Chase, 527.
Benjamin, 80.
Betsey, 194.
Chandler, 191.
Cilvina, 526.
Clara Ethel, 526.
Clara Florence, 526.
Edward W., 427.
Ellen, M. B., 436.
Elizabeth, 330, 385.
Elizabeth, Sawyer, 191.
Elsie Florence, 527.
Hannah, 427.
Harriet, 511.
John, 194.
Joseph Creighton, 526.
Joseph Wendell, 526.
Kate Gould Elma, 511.
Lois Annis, 241.
Mary, 243.
Mehitable, 80.
Myrtelle May, 511.
Polly, 234.
Rachel, 234, 247.
Richard Avery, 511.
Richard D., 436.
Thayer Spaulding, 526.
Thomas, 243.
William Fox, 511.
MOORES, Elizabeth, 37.
Mary, 61.
MOREHOUSE, Amy, 264.
Daniel, 121.
Sarah, 121, 265.
MOREY, Eliza, 435.
MORGAN, Caroline A., 222.
Edward F., 383.
Hannah, 183.
Harriet, 383.
Mary Ursula, 383.
Sarah, 397.
Timothy, 222.
William H. B., 383.
MORRILL, ——, 298.
Abigail, 299.
Betsey, 149, 329, 452.
Emeline, 331.
Hannah, 149.
Isaac B., 117.
Israel, 366.
Mary, 101, 331.
Polly, 165.
Rebecca, 117.
Rosanna, 366.
Sabrina, 366.
Sally Marden, 331.
Samuel, 165.
Samuel A., 101.
Sarah, 75, 302.
Simeon, 149.

NESMITH, Mary, 307.
NEVENS, Betsey, 395.
David, 395.
Ursula, 395.
NEVIL, John, 249.
Martha, 249.
Priscilla, 249.
NEW, Hannah, 495.
Stephen, 495.
NEWCOMB, Ann, 75.
John, 75.
Rose D., 418.
Susan E., 436.
NEWELL, Benjamin
Chase, 409.
Betsey, 149, 330.
Charles Edward, 409.
Dorothy Frances, 409.
Edward Chase, 409.
Frances E., 455.
George, 70.
Hannah, 70.
Harriett Louise, 409.
Henry Chase, 409.
Isaiah, 149.
Israel W., 330.
Louise Thankfull, 409.
Melinda L., 468.
Moses, 455.
Prescott Chase, 409.
Ruth Lee, 409.
Sally, 455.
Samuel, 468.
Sarah Rebecca, 455.
Susan Elizabeth, 467.
NEWHALL, ———, 75.
Alice, 303.
Hannah, 75.
NEWMAN, Clara A.,
421.
Eli, 250.
Flora, 421.
Nancy, 250.
Sarah, 250.
NEWTON, Betsey, 180.
Estes H., 174.
James O., 180.
Jennie, 221.
Julia M., 516.
Louisa, 174.
Prudence, 373.
Sarah, 161, 177.
NICHOLS, ———, 425.
Abigail, 144, 343.
Agnes Eliza, 403.
Anna, 76.
Betsey, 155, 333.
David, 155, 333.
Enoch, 76.
Henry, 312.
John, 145, 327.
John B., 155, 333.

NICHOLS, continued
Julia Ann, 327.
Lavina Brickett, 155.
Lavinia Brackett, 333.
Lydia, 304.
Mary, 145, 335.
Mary Margaret, 144.
Mehitable, 192.
Parker P., 304.
Polly, 465.
Rebecca, 48, 255.
Rhoda, 469.
Sally, 465.
Sarah, 312.
William, 144
NICKERSON, Deliver-
ance, 489.
Katherine, 485.
Mercy, 485.
Nathaniel, 485.
William, 489.
NIEL, Matilda, 354.
NILES, Sally, 258.
NIXON, Thomas, 216.
NOBLE, Bloomy, 236.
Esther, 235.
Eunice, 502.
Frances, 362.
John, 63, 502.
Joseph, 236.
Sally, 502.
Tamar, 63.
NOCKIN, Lena, 277.
NOERA, Hazel, 395.
NOLAN, John, 320.
Margaret C., 362.
Sarah, 320.
NORCROSS, Emma E.,
435.
Gideon L., 435.
NORDBY, Clara Ethel,
526.
NORRIS, Comfort, 248.
Hiram, 331.
James, 214.
Joseph, 248.
Mary, 248.
Mehitable, 245.
Susan, 331.
NORTH, Eliza J., 292,
346.
NORTHRUP, David
Andros, 360.
Fanny Susan, 360.
George D., 466.
Juliana, 466.
Leonard, 221.
Mary Jane, 221.
NORTON, Bethiah, 488,
495.
Betsey, 304.

NORTON, continued
Calvin, 333.
Christopher F., 181.
Elizabeth, 484.
Fanny, 498.
Hepsia D., 510.
Jacob, 488, 495.
James, 492.
Jonathan, 304.
Lucy, 495.
Lydia, 480.
Matilda A., 333.
Obed, 498.
Olive, 492.
Rebecca, 498.
Samuel, 480.
Sarah, 181.
NORWOOD, Harriet
Green, 400.
NOYES, Ann, 51.
Betsey, 200, 527.
Betty, 57.
Daniel, 51.
Ebenezer, 58.
Elizabeth, 454.
Enoch, 123, 410.
Fordyce Hills, 278.
Hannah, 58.
John, 454.
John N., 134.
Joseph, 191.
Lucinda W., 362.
Lucy Ann, 438.
Maria, 454.
Martha Ann, 278.
Mary, 94, 123, 200, 527.
Mary E., 172.
Mehitable, 126.
Parker, 191.
Patty, 410.
Philona Augusta, 134.
Rebecca, 191.
Sally, 335.
Sarah, 123, 269.
Sarah L., 410.
Stephen, 57, 58, 200, 527.
Susannah, 58.
Thomas, 35, 41, 96.
NUGENT, Alice B., 259.
Edward, 259.
NUTE, Jacob, 132.
Lydia, 132.
Sarah, 306.
NUTTER, ———, 262.
Sarah, 462.
NUTTING, Henrietta
Townsend, 317.
William Henry, 317.
NYE, George, 236.
Mary, 59.
Sarah, 236.
Ward, 59.

SELECTIVE ADDITIONS AND CORRECTIONS

Submitted by Dr. Felix H. Vann of 67 Forest at Duke Drive, Durham, NC 27705-5639. Dr. Vann encourages correspondence on his own line in the Chase, family given below, and hopes by his own example to encourage other Chase family descendants to add to the body of work on this early American family. The publisher would also like to mention The Chase Newsletter as a source for correspondence (address: The Chase Newsletter, Ray Watson, Jr, 289 Beech Hill Rd, Rockport, ME 04856).

page 202   **404**
DANIEL[5] CHASE (Dea. Amos[4], Samuel[3], Ens. Moses[2]) He m. Elizabeth Tappan (Toppan). They had 7 children, all b. in Saco, Maine

page 436   **1149**
BENJAMIN TAPPAN[6] CHASE (Daniel[5], Dea. Amos[4], Samuel[3], Ens. Moses[2]). b. 10 June 1791, in Saco, ME; m. 2/12 Oct. 1815, to Submit Woodman. They lived in Buxton, ME. He d. 29 Aug., 1846; she d. 27 Jan., 1847.

page 437   **1150**
DANIEL[6] CHASE (Daniel[5], Deac. Amos[4], Samuel[3], Ens. Moses[2]). b. 3 Oct. 1796, in Saco; m. 20 Apr. 1819, in Falmouth or possibly Saco, to Lucy Staples, b. 23 Oct. 1797, in Falmouth, ME, of unk parents. They removed from Saco in 1820, to Baltimore, MD. He d. 1 July 1872, in Baltimore and she d. 23 Mar. 1862 in Baltimore; both are bur. in Greenmount Cemetery in Baltimore. He was a merchant importer and exporter, a partner in Kirkland, Chase and Co., who traded with the West Indies and South America. They had three daughters - 7th Gen.
     i.   Catherine[7] Chase; b. 9 Mar. 1820 in Baltimore, who m. John Guy Rous in 1837 of Baltimore. She d. in 1897 in Baltimore; he d. date unk. They had four children, eighth generation - children of the above
        1.   Lucy Chase[8] Rous b. 1842 in Baltimore; m. John Cassard, 1863 in Baltimore; she d. 1863 in Baltimore.
        2.   Charles Chase[8] Rous; or Charles Augustus Rous; b. and d. dates unk. He m. Fannie Wood, date unk in Baltimore. They had a famous son (Francis) Peyton[9] Rous, MD, graduated from Johns Hopkins Medical School, Baltimore, a scientist who won the Nobel Prize in Medicine and Physiology for work done at the Rockefeller Institute, NYC, in discovering the viral nature of chicken sarcoma. He was b. 5 Oct. 1879 in Baltimore and d. 16 Feb. 1970 in NYC. He won the Nobel prize in 1967 and received many other distinguished awards in his busy scientific career. He had three daughters.
        3.   Daniel Chase[8] Rous; b. date unk, who died young.
        4.   Allen Chapman[8] Rous, b. dat unk, who died young.

ii.   Mary Elizabeth[7] Chase, b. 23 Oct. 1824 in Baltimore; m. Allen Armstrong Chapman of Westbrook, CT, who removed to Baltimore in 1830, on 5 Nov. 1840; she d. on 23 May 1901; he d. on 4 Mar. 1890; both d. in Baltimore and are bur. in Greenmount Cemetery. They had fifteen children, nine of whom lived to adult life.

Eighth generation - children of above:

1.   Daniel Chase[8] Chapman b. 22 June 1842 in Baltimore, MD; d. in infancy, on 7 July 1842.

2.   Daniel Chase[8] Chapman, II b. 8 June 1844 in Baltimore, MD. m. Anna Maria Harris on 23 Nov. 1869 in Baltimore. He died 11 May 1892; she died 15 June 1950, aet 104. He graduated from Yale University in 1866; he was a merchant with Kirkland, Chase & Co., in Baltimore. Both are bur. in Greenmount Cemetery.

3.   Nathan Allen[8] Chapman b. 14 July 1846 in Baltimore. He m. his 3rd cousin (Chapman side), Mary Parkhurst Chapman, of Teaneck, NJ on 28 Dec. 1876 in Englewood, NJ. He d. 24 Sept. 1927 in Tampa, FL. she d. in Englewood, NJ on 13 Oct. 1889. They had four children: a son who d. in infancy in Rutherford, NJ on 11 Nov. 1877; a son Lebbeus[9] Chapman, IV b. on 6 Oct 1878 in Teaneck, NJ; a son, Allen Armstrong[9] Chapman, II, b. on 13 Apr. 1880, in Teaneck, NJ who d. in childhood in 1891/92; and a daughter, Edith Van Buren[9] Chapman b. 5 Sept 1875, in Teaneck, NJ. She was 6 mos of age when her mother d. and was brought up by her father's sister, Edith[8] Chapman, in Baltimore. Her older brother, Lebbeus[8] C. IV, was brought up by her mother's family (his uncle, Dr. Frank C. Chapman, of Englewood, NJ; he was a noted ornithologist at the American Museum of Natural History in NYC)

4.   Helen Chase[8] Chapman b. 13 Feb. 1849 in Baltimore, MD. m. Edwin Edgar Montell on 11 Jan. 1870 in Baltimore; he was a coal merchant in that city. She d. on 18 June 1930 in Baltimore. He d. on 20 June 1923 in Baltimore. Both are bur. in Greenmount Cemetery. They had four children, all born in Baltimore: a son, Allen Chapman[9] Montell b. 7 Feb. 1871, d. in infancy on 4 June 1872. A daughter, Mary[9] Montell b. 29 Mar. 1873 in Baltimore; she never married; she d. on 13 July 1955 in Baltimore where she had been a business woman. A daughter, Elizabeth (Bessie) Chapman[9] Montell, b. 28 Sept. 1875 in Baltimore; she m. James Franklih Turner of that city on 12 July 1912; she d. in Nov 1969; both are bur. in Greenmount Cemetery; a son, Edwen Edgar[9] Montell, Jr. b. 12 June 1879 in Baltimore; he m. twice (1) to Viola Cunion, in NYC, date unk; the name of his 2nd wife and place of marriage are unk. Place of burial unk.

5.   Mary Lucretia[8] Chapman b. 22 Feb. 1851 in Baltimore. She d. in early childhood, date unk; is buried in Baltimore.

6.   Allen Armstrong[8] Chapman, Jr. b. 7 July 1852 in Baltimore; he also died in early childhood; buried in Baltimore.

7.   Mary Elizabeth[8] Chapman II, b. 18 July 1853, Baltimore; she never married. She d. 7 Jan 1940 in Richmond, VA at the home of her sister, Lucy Chase[8] Chapman Denny. She worked as a secretary, was

an avid church worker and a volunteer for many charitable causes in Baltimore. She was described by many members of her family as a "veritable Saint".

8.   "Infy"[8], an infant daughter b. on 2 Sept. 1855 who d. at birth and is buried in Baltimore

9.   Lucy Chase[8] Chapman b. 29 1857 in Baltimore. She m. Collins Denny of Winchester, VA on 5 July 1881. He was Princeton graduate, 1876; a law graduate from the Univ. VA, 1877, practiced law in Baltimore until he became a minister in of the Meth. Epis. Ch. (South), 1879; was Chaplin of the Univ. VA for several years, taught ethics and moral philosophy at Vanderbilt Univ. for about 15 years, was elected Bishop of the M.E.Ch.So. in 1911, moved to Richmond, VA in 1913 where he lived. She d. 31 Aug. 1940 and he d. 12 May 1943. Both are buried at Riverview Cemetery in Richmond. They had six children.

   i.   Margaret Collins[9] Denny b. 10 Apr 1882 in Baltimore, MD. She m. John Wesley Dixon 5 Apr. 1905 in Nashville, TN. He was a Methodist minister. He d. in 1944 in Parksely, Accomac Co., VA. She d. 19 May 1964 in Richmond. Both are buried in Riverview Cemetery. They had five children: Elizabeth Denny[10] Dixon m. to Theodore Marshall Whitfield; John Wesley[10] Dixon, Jr. who died in childhood; Mary Barbour[10] Dixon, m. to Harold Wesley Phillips; John Wesley[10] Dixon, Jr. (II) m. to Vivian Ardelia Slagle; and William Denny[10] Dixon m. to Dorothy Geraldine Taylor.

   ii. Elizabeth Chapman[9] Denny, b. 7 Jan. 1884 at Fincastle, Botetourt Co. VA. She m. Eugene Ellis Vann of Birmingham, AL 20 May 1908 in Nashville, TN. They went as missionaries and teachers to Brazil in 1908 and back to the U.S. in 1914. Both were Vanderbilt Univ. graduates, later earned MA degrees; he taught at Stanford Univ. and Brown Univ. Latin American History and Economics, as well as Portuguese and Spanish; he later became a business executive with the Home Ins. Co. in 1921, NYC, travelling throughout Latin America. She worked for the Censorship office during WWI, when he worked for the U.S. State Dept. They removed to Bergen Co., NJ in 1923 until 1965. He d. 6 Jan. 1965, in Leonia, NJ; she moved to Richmond, VA where she d. 29 Mar. 1977. Both are buried in Richmond's Riverview Cemetery. They had twin sons, b. 9 Jan. 1909, Collins Denny Vann[10] & Felix Huffman Vann[10] in Rio de Janeiro, Brazil; Collins d. 14 Feb. 1909 in Rio.

   iii. William Ritenour[9] Denny b. circa 1888, probably in Charlotteville, Albemarle Co, VA; died in early childhood, circa 1890 Baltimore.

   iv. Edith Allen[9] Denny b. 21 Dec. 1890 in Charlottesville, VA. She m. Roscoe Marvin White, 2 Apr. 1913, at Nashville, TN. They are both deceased and are buried in Riverview Cemetery, Richmond. They had three children: Collins Denny[10] White, a lawyer in Richmond, m. to Martha Virginia Smith; Lucy

Chapman[10] White (deceased) who m. Reeves Westwood Winfree, of Richmond; and Roscoe Marvin[10] White, Jr. a Methodist minister who m. Bette ___.

v. Lucy Chase[9] Denny b. 21 Jan. 1893, in Nashville, TN. She m. twice: (1) Thomas Elbert Wright of Roanoke, VA, a lawyer on 10 Aug. 1921, and d. on 17 Apr. 1924; and (2) Preston William Slosson, a Professor of Modern European History at the Univ. of Mich. on 21 June 1927. Both are deceased & are buried in Riverview Cemetery, Richmond. She had four daughters, two by each husband; Lucy Chase[10] Wright m. to Jim Bob Stevenson, of Kent Ohio; Mary Elizabeth[10] Wright, m. twice (1) David Firestone and (2) George Fearnehough of Ann Arbor, MI; Flora May[10] Slosson, m. Wilhelm Wuellner of Berkely, CA; and Edith Denny[10] Slosson who has been m. twice; her first husband died and she m. (2) Dean E. Tyson of Warren, OH

vi. Collins[9] Denny, Jr. b. 10 June 1899, in Nashville, TN. He grad. from Princeton Univ. in 1921 and received a law degree from the Univ. of VA, in 1924. He m. on 10 Sept. 1932, Rebecca Smith Miller of Culpepper Co., VA. He practiced law for many years in Richmond, VA. He died 14 Jan., 1964 and is buried at Hollywood Cemetery in that city. His wife was born on 19 June 1906, in Richmond. They had two sons: Collins Denny[10] III, b. 5 Dec., 1934 in Richmond and Clifford Miller[10] Denny b. 5 June 1937 in Richmond.

10. Elizabeth Chase[8] Chapman b. 2 Mar. 1861 in Baltimore. she m. William Chapman Lowndes of Baltimore, 17 Nov. 1880; he d. 30 June 1930 and she d. 5 Mar 1936. They lived in Baltimore and are buried in Greenmount Cemetery. They had 3 sons: William Chapman[9] Lowndes, Jr. who m. twice (1) Bessie Hanley, deceased and (2) Elsie Frederick; Andrew Jackson[9] Lowndes II, m. Anna Benson Harris; they had a dau. Betty Maxwell[10] Lowndes; and Lucien Chase[9] Lowndes, m. to Nellie Christopher (her 2nd)

11. Katharine Chase[8] Chapman, b. 2 Mar. 1861 in Baltimore, MD; m. Benjamin Franklin Bond 27 Apr. 1887 in Baltimore; he was a paper manufacturer. She d. 15 Oct. 1907 in Baltimore. He d. 12 Apr. 1921, in Baltimore. Both are buried in Greenmount Cemetery. They had six children.

i. Kathleen Livingston[9] Bond b. 29 1888; single; music teacher and missionary in China prior to WWII; in Macao during WWII; d. 19 Nov. 1977, in Hackettstown, NJ; bur. in Baltimore, MD

ii. Benjamin Franklin[9] Bond, Jr., b. 12 Nov. 1890, in Hagerstown, MD; m. (1) Dora Gertrude Boker on 28 Nov. 1915 in Baltimore; m. (2) name unk. Dora b. 21 Aug. 1906 & d. 24 Sept. 1967. He d. 19 Nov. 1972 in Hackettstown, NJ; bur. in Baltimore. They had two children: Benjamin Franklin[10] Bond III, b. 10 May 1917 in Baltimore; m. Inis Pulliam, 6 Jan. 1939. They have one son, Walden Lee Bond. B. F. Bond Jr also had a dau., Margaret Ann[10] Bond, b. 28 Mar. 1921 in Baltimore, m. to Wm. H.

Patterson, 20 Mar. 1943.

iii. Allen Chapman[9] Bond b. 15 Dec. 1892 in Baltimore; d. in childhood on 21 Aug. 1906; bur. in Baltimore.

iv. Mary Elizabeth[9] Bond, b. 6 Dec. 1894 in Baltimore; single; Public Health Nurse, in NYC, Hackensack, NJ and Boston, MA; d. Oct. 1979 in Hackettstown, NJ; bur. in Baltimore.

v. Chase Chapman[9] Bond b. 16 May 1897 in Baltimore; d. in childhood 10 May 1910 in Baltimore; bur. Baltimore.

vi. Eugene Ayres[9] Bond b. 13 Apr. 1899, in Hagerstown, MD; m. 29 May 1931 to Jessica Hill in Providence, RI; Grad. of Johns Hopkins Univ; in WWI, Paper Business and Chesepeake & Potomac Tel. Co. They retired to Dorset, VT

12. Edith[8] Chapman b. 3 June 1863 in Baltimore; single; d. 4 July 1954 in Baltimore; bur. in Greenmount Cemetery. Business woman, church worker & volunteer in charitable organizations.

13. Grace Allen[8] Chapman b. 14 Dec. 1865 in Baltimore; m. Stephen Williams Orne of Memphis, TN on 12 Oct. 1892 in Baltimore; he d. 10 Jan 1902 in Aiken, SC; they lived in Ridgewood (Bergen Co. NJ) and Hagerstown, MD. She d. on 5 Jan. 1952, in Hagerstown. Both are bur. in Baltimore in Greenmount Cemetery. They had 5 children.

i. Edith Chapman[9] Orne, b. 19 June 1893, Ridgewood, NJ d. in infancy, 25 Aug. 1894 in Ridgewood.

ii. Merrill[9] Orne b. 31 Dec. 1895 in Ridgewood, NJ; d. in infancy, 24 Feb. 1897 in Ridgewood.

iii. Stephen Williams[9] Orne, Jr. b. 31 Oct. 1897 in Ridgewood, NJ; m. twice (1) Theresa Zumdahl, 3 June 1924; (2) Mrs. Margaret Lee ca 1980. He d. ca 1986 in Sun City, AZ. He had one dau. Mary Louise[10] Orne, b. 10 Mar. 1927, in Cleveland, OH, m. Dale E. Harrison on 25 Nov. 1950; the live in Pittsburgh, PA.

iv. Helen Montell[9] Orne b. 14 Apr. 1899 in Ridgewood, NJ; m. on 29 Jan. 1925 to Harold Holt Mercereau, in Baltimore. She attended college at Goucher College (Baltimore) and Case-Western Reserve (Cleveland), thru 1923 and did Social Work at J.H. Hosp in Baltimore, 1924. He was in WWI and grad. at Johns Hopkins in 1920; later a salesman; he d. 20 Dec. 1960 in Hagerstown, MD where he is bur. She d. on 30 Nov. 1989 in Hagerstown, where she is bur. They had one dau. Grace Allen[10] Mercereau b. on 15 May 1928 in Cleveland, OH. She m. Robert Warren Cline on 24 June 1950 in Hagerstown, MD and had four children. She d. in May 1993 in Williamsport, MD

v. Elizabeth Allen[9] Orne b. 19 Apr. 1902 in Hagerstown, MD; m. George L. Krebs on 25 June 1925 in Hagerstown, MD. They ware divorced but had 2 children: a son, Stephen Orne[10] Krebs who m. June Amelia Robbins, 14 June 1947 in Ann Arbor, MI; he was b. 27 June 1924 in Baltimore and d. 25 May 1964 in Plattsburgh, NY; they had 4 children, born in Lansing, MI. E.A.[9] Orne also had a dau., Elizabeth Jean[10] Krebs b. 21 Jan. 1928 in Hagerstown, MD; she m. James Robert Earle on 29 Oct.

1946 in Hagerstown. They have three children.

14.   Allen Armstrong Chapman Jr, II b. 11 Oct. 1869, d. 4 Apr 1871; bur. in Baltimore

15.   Margaret Chapman, b. 22 Apr 1872; d. 13 Aug. 1872 in Baltimore.

iii.   Helen Augusta[7] Chase b. 4 Jan. 1834 in Baltimore, MD; m. Hiram Woods, Jr. of Baltimore on 29 June 1852 (they were first cousins; both Chase and Woods families had moved from Saco, Me. to Baltimore in the 1820s); she d. on 8 Jan. 1883 in Baltimore; he d. on 7 Dec. 1901 in Baltimore. They had twelve children, all born in Baltimore, MD

1.   Edward Payson[8] Woods b. date ? in Baltimore d. in infancy

2.   Daniel Chase[8] Woods b. date ? in Baltimore, d. in infancy

3.   Hiram Woods[8] III, b. 11 Nov. 1853 in Baltimore, MD; m. Laura Hall on 28 Oct. 1886, in Baltimore. He d. on 15 Jan. 1931 in Baltimore & she d. on date ? in Baltimore; both are buried in Greenmount Cemetery. They had three children: Dr. Allan Churchill[9] Woods of Baltimore an ophthalmplogist in Baltimore and Director of the Wilmer Eye Institute of Johns Hopkins Univ. and a distinguished physician, a dau., Laura Alexander[9] Armstrong, a lawyer from Hagerstown, MD and a second dau., Helen[9] m. to Arthur W. Machen, Sr., of Baltimore

4.   Frank Churchill[8] Woods of Baltimore who m. Virginia Lee Hall (possible sister of Laura Hall?)

5.   Helen Chase[8] Woods m. (late in life) Joshua Levering (as his third wife; no known children).

6.   Elizabeth Fuller[8] Woods m. Richard H. Woodward; they lived in Annapolis, MD

7.   Herbert[8] Woods, d. in infancy

8.   Allan Chase[8] Woods, d. in infancy

9.   Bessie Middleton[8] Woods, d. in infancy

10.   Katharine Herbert[8] Woods, m. D. Dorsey Guy.

11.   Lucy Chase[8] Woods; she was badly crippled; never m.; she lived with and was cared for by her sister

12.   Ethel Standish[8] Woods, who never married.

Ninth Generation

Children of Hiram[8] Woods, III, M.D. & Laura Hall (Hiram[7] Woods, II or Jr., & Helen Augusta[7] Chase, Elizabeth[6] Chase & Daniel[6] Chase, Daniel[5] Chase, Dea. Amos[4], Samuel[3], Ens. Moses[2], Aquila[1])

i.   Allan Churchill[9] Woods, M.D. b. in Baltimore; m. Anne Powell Byrd of Richmond (?), VA. He was b. ca 1890 and d. aet 73, ca 1963. He followed in the footsteps of his father, becoming an ophthalmologist after graduating from the John Hopkins Medical School, in 1910. He taught and did research, retiring in 1955 receiving many distinguished honors in the medical profession. He served in the Army Medical Corps, during World War I as a Major. He had three children, a son, Dr. Alan Churchill[10] Woods; two daughters, Mrs. K. Aubrey Gorham and Mrs. George S. Nalle, of Austin, TX and 11 grandchildren.